Housing Statistics
of the United States
Second Edition

Housing Statistics
of the United States

Second Edition

Edited by Patrick A. Simmons

Bernan Press
Washington, DC

ISBN: 0-89059-108-3

ISSN: 1521-5601

Book design and composition by Northeastern Graphic Services, Inc., Hackensack, NJ.

Printed in the United States of America on acid-free paper that meets the American National Standards Institute Z39-48 standard.

99 98   4 3 2 1

Bernan Press
1130 Connecticut Avenue, NW
Suite 675
Washington, DC 20036
email: info@bernan.com

Contents

About the Editor

Patrick A. Simmons is the Director of Housing Demography at the Fannie Mae Foundation. Prior to joining the Foundation, he held several positions in the Office of Housing Research at the Fannie Mae Corporation, including Manager of Housing Policy Research. He has undertaker extensive research in the areas of housing and mortgage market discrimination, homelessness, and urban housing policy. He served as Associate Editor of *Housing Policy Debate* and the *Journal of Housing Research* and has published numerous reports and articles. Currently, he is working on a multi-year research project on the effects of immigration on the U.S. housing markets.

Preface

I had two primary objectives in preparing the second edition of *Housing Statistics of the United States*. The first was to produce comprehensive updates of the book's data tables and accompanying technical notes and source documentation. The second objective was to expand the book's subject and geographic coverage, to which end I have added about 20 new data tables. These new tables extend the book's subject content to include topics such as population estimates and projections, poverty rates, private mortgage insurance, and financial characteristics of Fannie Mae and Freddie Mac. The book's geographic coverage is enhanced by 10 new state-level tables on topics including housing permits, home sales, and homeownership rates. I highlight some of these state-level data in a new introductory article that analyzes regional housing production trends during the last two decades.

Readers of the first edition will be familiar with the structure of the book. The heart of the book continues to be the collection of approximately 250 data tables organized around the topics of demographics and housing demand; housing stock, production, and investment; housing market outcomes; housing finance; and federal housing programs. These data tables are accompanied by two appendices, one that examines the characteristics of the data contained in each table and one that describes housing data sources.

In using the book, please be aware of the following:

- The appendices contain important information on the characteristics of the data. Table footnotes highlight key definitions and comparability issues, but the user is encouraged to refer to the table notes in Appendix A for additional information. Appendix A contains definitions for most of the terms included in the tables and also provides useful information on data limitations and factors that affect comparability across and within data series. It also provides references to publications that contain more detailed discussions of data characteristics. Appendix B offers short descriptions of the major data sources that were used in compiling the tables.

- Most of the data are estimates from sample surveys and therefore are subject to sampling error. When comparing data over time or across regions, states, or population groups, keep in mind that apparent differences may be attributable solely to sampling variability. Many of the publications referenced in Appendix A contain standard errors for the estimates that can be used to assess sampling variability and to conduct appropriate statistical tests. All of the data presented herein are subject to nonsampling variability that may be caused by factors such as inadequate coverage, respondent error, and errors in data collection and processing.

- Although the most current annual data were included in the tables as the book went to press, some of the data will have been updated or revised by the time of publication. This is particularly true for the data that are released on a monthly or quarterly basis. Some of these data are not only released frequently, but are also subject to revision for several months after initial dissemination.

- Every effort has been made to select and assemble the data carefully and to identify and correct any errors that may have been introduced in the compilation process. The responsibility of the editor and publisher of this volume is limited to reasonable care in the reproduction and presentation of data obtained from established sources.

As with the first edition, the current edition of *Housing Statistics* would have been impossible to produce without the assistance of many people. I am very indebted to those in government and the private sector who supported my data collection efforts. I owe special thanks to Eric Belsky of the Joint Center for Housing Studies at Harvard University and John Goodman of the National Multi Housing Council for providing helpful comments on an earlier draft of the introductory article. Eric has been a reviewer for both editions of *Housing Statistics* and his many valuable insights and suggestions have substantially strengthened the book. I also appreciate the support and input received from Bernan Press' editorial and production team, which includes Sean Long, Courtenay Slater, and George Hall. My gratitude also extends to my colleagues at the Fannie Mae Foundation for their support and encouragement. Once again, however, my deepest thanks go to my family and friends and particularly to Ethel and John Simmons, Andy, Andrea, and Reshmi.

Regional Housing Production in the United States, 1980 to 1997

by Patrick Simmons

Introduction

The United States is in the seventh year of the longest housing production expansion of the past three decades. Housing production during this upswing has not been distributed equally across the nation, however. Since 1991, the South and West have generated more than two-thirds of the nation's new housing and have accounted for all of the 10 leading states in per capita housing production. These leading states, which are clustered within the Mountain and South Atlantic divisions, have produced one-third of the nation's new housing in the past 7 years.

The geography of the current housing expansion is similar to that of the housing upturn of the mid-1980s, but it also has several distinguishing characteristics. Although the South and West are still the most prolific housing production regions, they have lost some share of national production in the current expansion as new housing activity in the Midwest has increased substantially. Within the South and West, growth is more heavily concentrated in the Mountain and South Atlantic divisions; therefore, more states in these divisions are among the top housing producers in the current expansion. Finally, per capita production rates have dropped sharply in the current upswing. In fact, only one of the nation's current production leaders—Nevada—would have been among the top 10 states in production per capita during the earlier expansion.

This article describes these and other regional and state housing production patterns. Using data tables that have been newly added to the book, the article first examines regional and state production patterns since 1980. It then compares the geography of the current housing expansion with that of the mid-1980s expansion. Next, it describes geographic variations in the types of housing produced. Finally, it examines the Census Bureau's state population projections to provide some tentative insights into regional housing production prospects in the next decade.

Regional Housing Production Since 1980

The South and West have consistently led the nation in new housing activity since 1980 (see Figure 1). Between 1980 and 1997, the South generated 14.2 million new housing starts and manufactured housing (mobile home) placements, a number roughly equal to the output of the other three regions combined. The West accounted for another quarter of the nation's housing production, or 7.0 million units. Whereas the Midwest experienced a rebound in housing production following the 1991 recession, production levels in the Northeast have yet to recover.

Because regions and states differ considerably in population size, a more refined comparison of housing activity across areas is achieved by examining per capita housing production rates[1]. Per capita production is a good measure of the intensity of housing activity because it distinguishes rapidly growing areas from slow-growth areas that have high production volumes simply because of their large populations.

After adjusting for population size differences, the South still emerges as the nation's top housing production region, leading in the number of new housing units

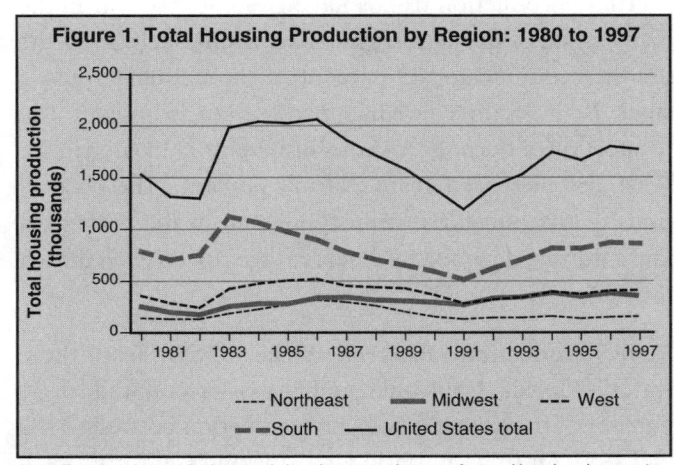

Figure 1. Total Housing Production by Region: 1980 to 1997

Note: Total housing production equals housing starts plus manufactured housing placements.

Source: Tables 2.39 and 2.46.

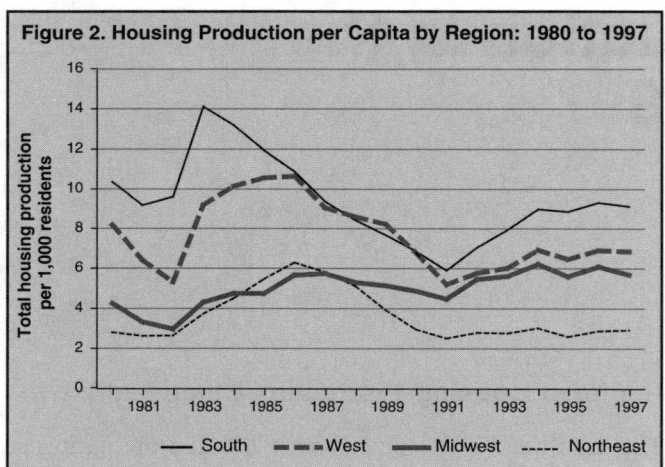

Figure 2. Housing Production per Capita by Region: 1980 to 1997

Note: Total housing production equals housing starts plus manufactured housing placements.
Source: Tables 1.25, 2.39, and 2.46.

produced per capita in every year except 1988 and 1989 (see Figure 2). However, using a per capita measure narrows the production gap between the South and West considerably. In fact, production rates in these regions were almost identical between 1986 and 1991. The South has since regained the lead in housing activity and on a per capita basis currently produces 30 percent more housing than the West, 60 percent more than the Midwest, and over 200 percent more than the Northeast.

An examination of per capita production rates also highlights recent differences in the fortunes of the Midwest and Northeast. Production rates in these regions diverged sharply after tracking closely between 1980 and 1988. The Northeast is the only region that has not experienced a significant increase in its rate of housing production during the current expansion. Conversely, production rates in the Midwest increased steadily between 1991 and 1994 and are currently close to production rates in the West.

These production trends have generated a shift in the distribution of the nation's housing inventory. In 1980, the South accounted for 33 percent of the nation's housing stock. By 1996, this share had increased to 36 percent. The proportion of the nation's housing inventory located in the West also increased, from 19 to 21 percent. The proportions of the housing inventory located in the Northeast and Midwest declined by 2 percentage points each during the period.[2]

State Production Patterns Since 1980. Just three states—Florida, California, and Texas—accounted for 30 percent of the nation's housing production between 1980 and 1997. During this period, Florida and California each added approximately 3 million new housing units.[3] Pro-

duction has been so great in these states that the number of newly built homes in each is greater than the entire housing stock of states as large as Virginia or Massachusetts. Texas added 2.4 million units between 1980 and 1997, a total that is equivalent to the current housing inventory of Missouri.

No other state comes close to the production volumes of Florida, California, and Texas. North Carolina, the fourth ranked state, produced approximately 1.4 million housing units between 1980 and 1997. In fact, the next 10 states combined produced roughly the same number of new housing units as Florida, California, and Texas during the period.

Switching from production volumes to per capita rates produces a substantially different picture of state housing production leaders during the past 20 years. Although Florida ranked third in the nation in average per capita production between 1980 and 1997, neither California nor Texas ranked in the top 10. California had an average production rate slightly below that of the nation and ranked 24th among all states during the period. Nevada and Arizona joined Florida as the leading states in average per capita production between 1980 and 1997.

A Comparison of Two Housing Expansions

Since 1980, the nation has experienced two periods of increasing housing production. In addition to the current expansion, production levels also increased between 1982 and 1986 (see top line of Figure 1).

The housing expansion of the 1980s was considerably more vigorous than the current upswing. Between 1982 and 1986, national housing production averaged 1.9 million units per year and the per capita rate of production averaged 7.7 housing units per 1,000 residents. In the current expansion, total production has averaged only 1.6 million units per year and the production rate has averaged 5.8 units per 1,000 residents.

The South and West led the nation in housing production in both expansions. However, the Midwest's share of total housing production increased by almost 10 percentage points between the two periods, from 13 to 22 percent, thereby decreasing the proportion of total production captured by the South and West. The Midwest was also the only region in which per capita production between 1991 and 1997 exceeded the rate of the 1980s expansion, rising from 4.2 to 5.4 new housing units per 1,000 residents. Production rates in each of the other regions have been about one-third lower in the current expansion.

State Production Leaders During the Two Expansions.
The maps in Figure 3 show that the South Atlantic and Mountain states have been the foci of housing production activity in both of the recent expansions. Seven states from these divisions—four in the South Atlantic and three in the Mountain divisions—were among the top 10 in average production per capita in both periods. In the current upswing, there has been even further geographic consolidation, with these divisions accounting for 9 of the top 10 states.

High housing production rates in the Mountain states and Oregon during the 1990s are related to California's economic recession and resultant out-migration from the state. Between 1990 and 1997, California lost an esti-

mated 2 million persons as a result of domestic migration. Conversely, the six Western states that were among the top per capita housing producers gained almost 1.6 million persons as the result of net domestic migration.[4]

Table 1, which provides production rates for the top and bottom 10 states in each period, reveals a substantial slowdown in housing activity in the leading states. Between 1982 and 1986, the top 10 states averaged 15 new housing units per 1,000 residents. In the current expansion, the average rate for the 10 leading states has fallen to 11 units per 1,000 residents. Only Nevada currently has a production rate that would have qualified for top-10 status in the 1980s expansion.

The strength and duration of Nevada's housing production boom is noteworthy. Not only has Nevada been among the top three states in both of the last two housing expansions, but also in the current upswing its rate of housing production has been almost double that of the next most active state and more than three times the national rate. The state has never ranked lower than seventh in per capita housing production in any year since 1980 and has led the nation in every year since 1987.

Types of Housing Produced in the Current Expansion

Not only does the intensity of housing production vary substantially across regions and states, but also the type of housing produced varies. Traditionally, the South has relied on manufactured housing to a much greater extent than the other regions. In 1990, 11 percent of the South's housing stock was composed of manufactured housing, compared with 8 percent in the West, 5 percent in the Midwest, and 3 percent in the Northeast. The housing stock in the Midwest is characterized by a high proportion of single-family housing, whereas the Northeast and West have higher proportions of multifamily housing (i.e., five or more units per structure) than the nation as a whole. Single-family units accounted for 57 percent of all housing units in the Northeast, compared with 63 to 69 percent in the other regions.

These patterns of structure type are only partially reflected in current production data. Manufactured housing continues to be disproportionately important in the South, accounting for 22 percent of total housing production in that region between 1991 and 1997 versus only 10 to 15 percent in the other regions. Although the Northeast had the lowest proportion of single-family housing in its 1990 housing stock, it has had the highest share of single-family housing in its current production. Since 1991,

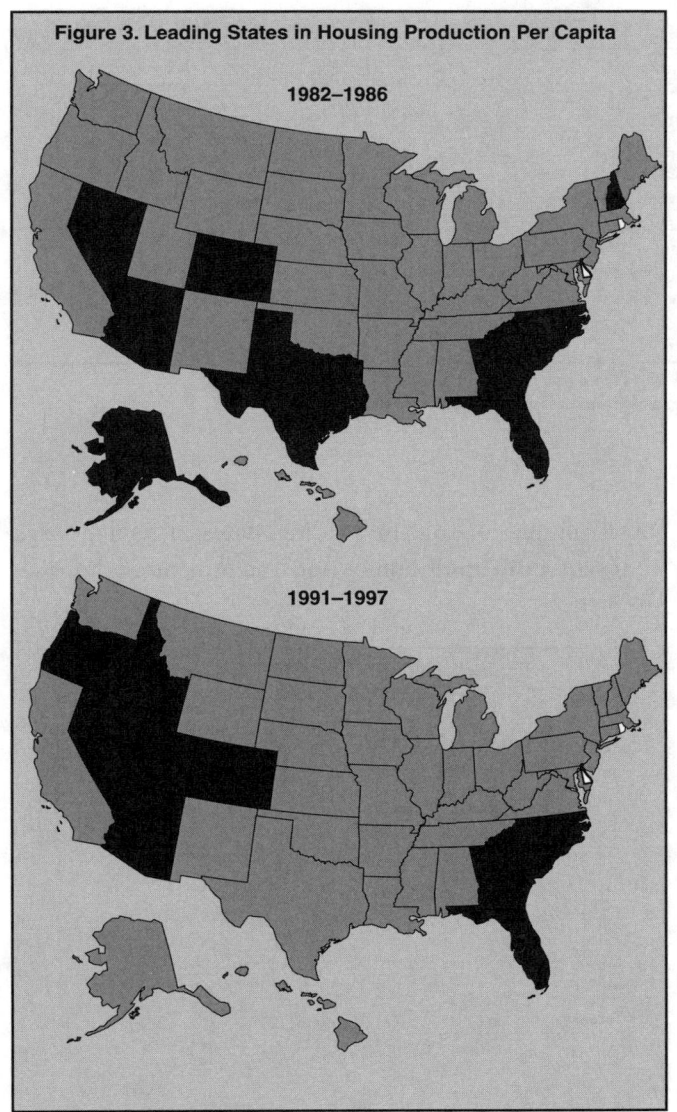

Figure 3. Leading States in Housing Production Per Capita

1982–1986

1991–1997

Note: States with dark shading were in top ten in housing production per capita during period. Housing production per capita is measured as units authorized by permit plus manufactured housing placements divided by estimated resident population.

Source: Tables 1.25, 2.35, and 2.48.

Table 1: TOP AND BOTTOM 10 STATES IN HOUSING PRODUCTION PER CAPITA

Top 10 States

1982 to 1986		1991 to 1997	
State	Production per 1,000 residents	State	Production per 1,000 residents
Arizona	22.1	**Nevada**	20.5
Florida	18.7	**Arizona**	11.8
Nevada	16.3	**North Carolina**	11.7
Georgia	13.8	Idaho	11.0
Alaska	13.8	**Georgia**	10.7
Texas	13.6	**South Carolina**	10.5
New Hampshire	12.9	**Colorado**	9.7
North Carolina	12.9	**Florida**	9.6
Colorado	12.7	Utah	9.5
South Carolina	12.6	Oregon	9.3
Average	14.9	Average	11.4

Bottom 10 States

1982 to 1986		1991 to 1997	
State	Production per 1,000 residents	State	Production per 1,000 residents
Montana	4.3	**Illinois**	4.2
Wisconsin	4.2	Oklahoma	4.0
Michigan	4.0	**Pennsylvania**	3.7
Pennsylvania	3.8	California	3.2
Nebraska	3.7	Alaska	3.2
Ohio	3.3	New Jersey	2.9
Illinois	3.3	Massachusetts	2.8
New York	2.9	Connecticut	2.6
West Virginia	2.9	Rhode Island	2.5
Iowa	2.5	**New York**	2.0
Average	3.5	Average	3.1

Note: States in bold are in top/bottom 10 in both periods. Alaska is the only state that went from the top 10 to the bottom 10.

Housing production per capita is measured as units authorized by permit plus manufactured housing placements divided by estimated resident population.

Excludes the District of Columbia.

Source: Tables 1.25, 2.35, and 2.48.

single-family housing has accounted for 75 percent of current production in the Northeast, but only between 60 and 68 percent in the other regions.

Types of Housing Produced in the Leading States. The type of housing produced also varies considerably across the 10 most active states (see Figure 4). Consistent with the regional patterns just described, manufactured housing accounts for the largest share of production in two Southern states, North and South Carolina. Manufactured housing accounted for over 30 percent of total production in these states between 1991 and 1997, compared with 20 percent or less in the other production leaders.

Site-built single-unit housing has been particularly important in the Mountain states, accounting for over 70 percent of total production in Arizona, Colorado, and Utah. Multifamily production showed no pattern across the leading states and accounted for the greatest shares of total production in Florida, Nevada, and Oregon. Ore-

gon is unique among the leading states in having large shares of both multifamily and manufactured housing production.

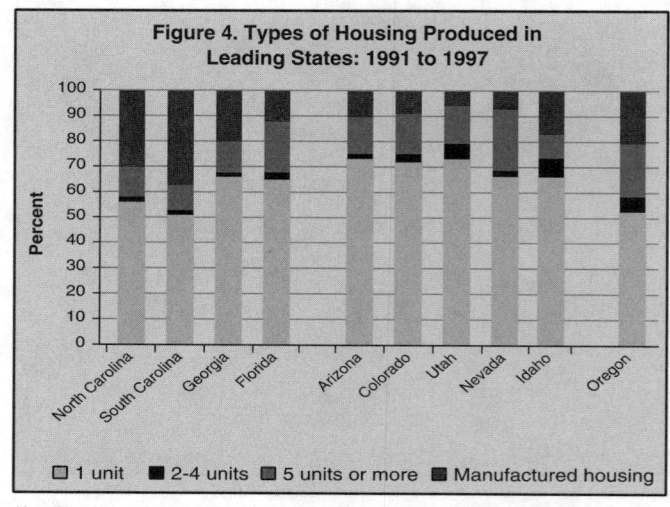

Figure 4. Types of Housing Produced in Leading States: 1991 to 1997

□ 1 unit   ■ 2-4 units   ▨ 5 units or more   ■ Manufactured housing

Note: Housing production is measured by housing units authorized by permit and manufactured housing placements.

Source: Tables 2.35 and 2.48.

As large as these differences are, the leading states do not reflect the full geographic variability in the types of housing produced. For example, manufactured housing accounted for at least a third of production in eight states, but less than 1 percent in another five. In West Virginia, manufactured housing placements accounted for 60 percent of new housing production between 1991 and 1997.

Regional Population Projections and Their Implications for Future Production Patterns

Regional production patterns are affected by numerous factors, including geographic variations in population and employment growth, replacement demand, and demand for second homes. These factors are difficult to predict and might change substantially in the future. However, some tentative insights into future housing production can be gleaned from the Census Bureau's most recent state population projections.[5]

These projections suggest that the South and West will continue to lead the nation in housing production. If the projections are accurate, population in the West and South will grow at annual rates of 1.4 and 1.0 percent, respectively, between 2000 and 2010. In comparison, the Midwest is projected to grow by 0.4 percent per year and the Northeast by 0.3 percent per year in the next decade. Although the Northeast and Midwest are unlikely to experience substantial new production as a result of population growth, their large and aging housing inventories suggest considerable potential replacement demand moving into the next century.

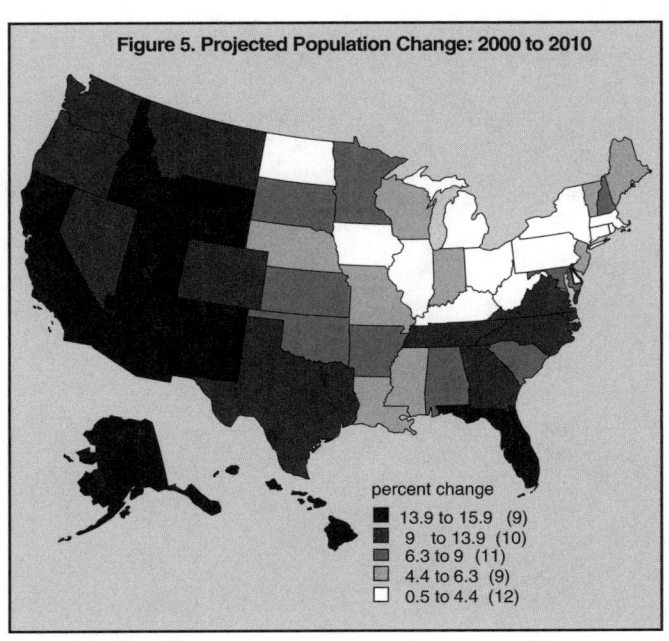

Figure 5. Projected Population Change: 2000 to 2010

percent change
- 13.9 to 15.9 (9)
- 9 to 13.9 (10)
- 6.3 to 9 (11)
- 4.4 to 6.3 (9)
- 0.5 to 4.4 (12)

Source: Table 1.26.

State Population Projections. The state population projections depicted in Figure 5 suggest that the Mountain and South Atlantic divisions will continue to experience strong housing production in the next decade. The Mountain division is projected to experience particularly rapid population growth in the next decade, accounting for five of the six fastest growing states in the nation. Three of these states—Arizona, Idaho, and Utah—are currently among the nation's top housing producers. Nevada, which is currently the most active housing producer, is projected to rank 10th in population growth rate between 2000 and 2010.

All of the leading housing production states in the South Atlantic division are projected to grow faster than the nation between 2000 and 2010. However, the Census Bureau's projections suggest that only Florida will be among the 10 fastest-growing states.

The Census Bureau population projections do not bode well for housing production in the states of the Northeast and Midwest. Combined, these regions are projected to account for 9 of the 10 slowest-growing states between 2000 and 2010.

Summary

The U.S. housing sector has exhibited considerable strength during the current economic expansion. Homeownership rates and home sales reached record levels in 1997 and the net addition of 4 million homeowners between 1994 and 1997 set a 3-year record.[6] Housing production, although falling short of historical highs, has expanded steadily since 1991.

The current housing production cycle, like those before it, is characterized by considerable geographic variation in the intensity of housing production and in the types of new housing produced. The South and West regions, and more specifically the Mountain and South Atlantic divisions, have led the nation in housing activity during the two most recent housing expansions. If recent population projections are any indication, these areas will remain foci of housing production into the new millenium.

Compared with the expansion of the mid-1980s, the current housing upswing is characterized by substantially lower per capita production rates in the most active housing states. In addition, the leading states have become even more geographically concentrated within the Mountain and South Atlantic divisions.

The structural characteristics of new housing also vary geographically. Following historical patterns, the South continues to rely on manufactured housing to a greater extent than other regions. Even within the subset of the nation's most active housing states, there is considerable geographic variability in the structural characteristics of new housing currently being produced.

---

[1]The per capita production rate equals the sum of housing starts and manufactured housing placements in a given calendar year divided by the estimated July 1 resident population in the same year. The Census Bureau is the source of all data used to calculate per capita production rates. The housing starts data are from the Survey of Construction, the manufactured housing placements data are from the Survey of New Mobile Home Placements, and the population estimates are from the Census Bureau's Population Estimates Program.

[2]The 1980 distribution is from the Census of Housing and the 1996 distribution is from the Census Bureau's Household and Housing Unit Estimates Program.

[3]Because the Census Bureau does not publish estimates of housing starts by state, total housing production for states is measured as housing units authorized by building permit plus manufactured housing placements. This is an imperfect measure of new housing production, but there is a close correspondence between housing units authorized by building permits and housing starts. See the notes to Tables 2.34–2.45 in Appendix A for additional discussion of the relationship between housing units authorized by permit and housing starts.

The regional patterns described in the preceding section would not have differed substantially if building permits had been used instead of housing starts. The primary difference is that the South's housing production increases slightly if housing starts are used instead of building permits.

[4]Net domestic migration estimates are from the Census Bureau's Population Estimates Program. See table located at <http://www.census.gov/population/www/estimates/statepop.html>.

[5]Net migration is a better indicator of short-term growth in housing demand than is total population change. However, housing production intensity corresponds relatively well with the overall population growth rate for the leading production states. Of the 10 leading states in per capita housing production between 1991 and 1997, 9 were among the top 12 states in population growth rate for the period. The only state that ranked high in per capita housing production but not in population growth was South Carolina, which was the 22nd fastest-growing state between 1991 and 1997.

Despite the correspondence between population growth rates and housing production intensity, it is important to keep in mind that the Census Bureau's population projections might be subject to considerable forecast error. Interstate and international migration streams are particularly difficult to predict and might change suddenly as a result of changes in state economies or immigration policy.

[6]See the Harvard University Joint Center for Housing Studies' *State of the Nation's Housing 1998* for additional discussion of the current homebuying boom.

PART 1: DEMOGRAPHICS AND HOUSING DEMAND

Median Household Income and Net Worth by Race and Hispanic Origin of Householder: 1993

Source: Tables 1.30 and 1.40.

Hispanic and Black Americans face housing challenges that derive in part from their low economic status. Both groups experience rather severe economic deprivation relative to Whites, whether measured in terms of household income or net worth (see figure). In 1993, the median household income of Hispanic households was only 70 percent of that of White households. Black households fared even worse, with only 60 percent of the income of White households.

As large as these differences are, they pale in comparison to interethnic disparities in household wealth. The median net worth of Black and Hispanic households in 1993 was less than $5,000, barely 10 percent of the median net worth of White households. These disparities in wealth are at least partly attributable to interethnic differences in access to the wealth-generating potential of homeownership. In turn, the low wealth and incomes of Black and Hispanic households make homeownership attainment more difficult for these groups, thereby helping to perpetuate economic inequality.

Household and Family Characteristics

TABLE 1.1. MONTHLY AND ANNUAL HOUSEHOLD ESTIMATES: 1955 TO 1997
(In thousands)

YEAR	January	February	March[1]	April	May	June	July	August	September	October	November	December	Annual[2]
1955	.....	.....	.....	47,788	.....	48,120	.....	47,807	48,223	48,310	48,398	48,529	.....
1956	48,640	48,782	48,684	48,715	48,633	48,743	48,786	48,704	48,982	49,130	49,276	49,178	48,854
1957	49,347	49,409	49,476	49,502	49,718	49,950	50,014	49,836	49,946	.....	50,279	50,079	.....
1958	50,187	49,923	50,402	50,296	50,508	50,853	50,921	50,954	51,042	50,902	50,768	50,955	50,643
1959	51,027	51,328	51,316	51,514	51,796	51,760	51,792	51,829	51,900	51,976	51,916	52,044	51,683
1960	52,071	52,202	52,643	52,652	52,936	53,217	53,219	53,444	53,325	53,479	53,639	53,276	53,009
1961	53,443	53,394	53,391	53,503	53,680	54,152	54,363	54,316	54,469	53,172	54,305	54,459	53,887
1962	54,452	54,674	53,732	53,786	54,639	54,554	54,781	54,678	54,944	54,977	54,916	55,106	54,603
1963	54,994	55,195	54,772	54,906	55,413	55,264	55,374	55,579	55,625	.....	.....	.....	.....
1964	56,062	56,146	55,721	55,979	56,256	56,463	56,694	56,602	56,646	56,800	56,798	57,028	56,433
1965	57,092	56,996	56,900	57,251	57,477	57,648	57,848	57,789	57,903	57,878	57,875	57,798	57,538
1966	57,696	58,053	57,910	58,399	58,710	58,830	59,032	58,821	58,921	58,712	58,703	58,671	58,538
1967	58,728	58,850	58,588	59,010	59,058	59,360	60,045	60,112	60,242	60,180	60,057	60,162	59,533
1968	60,441	60,400	60,526	60,662	60,618	60,938	61,016	61,170	61,402	61,371	61,435	61,462	60,953
1969	61,712	61,688	61,877	62,047	62,133	62,246	62,349	62,411	62,627	62,806	62,826	62,709	62,286
1970	62,784	62,848	63,012	63,355	63,488	63,745	63,922	64,129	64,159	64,355	64,248	64,255	63,692
1971	64,885	64,256	64,500	64,886	64,885	65,124	65,194	65,209	65,538	65,693	65,783	66,034	65,166
1972	66,509	66,690	66,741	66,666	66,821	67,081	67,131	67,256	67,514	67,605	67,712	67,868	67,133
1973	68,128	68,260	68,405	68,257	68,459	68,634	68,924	69,090	69,354	69,465	69,554	69,510	68,837
1974	69,560	69,631	69,952	70,105	70,428	70,573	70,709	70,909	71,074	71,246	71,205	71,305	70,558
1975	71,290	71,050	71,285	71,496	71,547	71,777	72,087	72,087	72,031	72,475	72,621	72,659	71,867
1976	73,021	72,061	73,040	73,072	73,142	73,306	73,515	73,482	73,767	73,836	74,096	74,035	73,364
1977	74,177	74,400	74,318	74,460	74,276	74,454	74,612	74,937	75,237	75,408	75,625	75,524	74,786
1978	75,769	75,805	76,073	76,217	76,318	76,390	76,392	76,642	77,034	77,156	77,320	77,166	76,524
1979	77,223	77,205	77,438	77,754	78,035	78,172	78,126	78,084	78,085	78,404	78,649	78,613	77,982
1980	78,920	79,089	79,320	79,284	79,426	79,582	79,589	79,982	80,109	80,120	80,173	80,053	79,637
1981	80,378	80,685	80,779	80,796	80,867	81,080	80,938	81,225	81,172	81,344	81,520	81,459	81,020
1982[3]	83,569	83,666	83,718	83,603	83,625	83,465	83,465	83,655	83,791	83,912	84,186	84,121	83,731
1983	84,058	84,086	84,146	84,107	84,233	84,249	84,460	84,510	84,821	85,233	85,471	85,407	84,565
1984	85,525	85,617	85,732	85,857	86,125	86,292	86,421	86,626	86,921	87,070	87,050	86,915	86,346
1985	86,828	87,202	87,184	87,485	87,684	87,889	87,997	88,202	88,433	88,534	88,592	88,615	87,887
1986	88,817	88,829	88,805	88,879	88,924	89,025	89,147	89,145	89,293	89,448	89,657	89,771	89,145
1987	89,997	90,123	89,962	90,060	90,331	90,355	90,537	90,533	90,802	90,945	91,175	91,379	90,517
1988	91,601	91,656	91,545	91,713	91,917	92,036	92,188	92,245	92,372	92,270	92,416	92,277	92,020
1989	92,699	93,102	93,322	93,465	93,304	93,223	93,539	93,720	94,029	93,737	93,613	93,489	93,437
1990	93,477	93,733	93,927	94,076	94,063	94,465	94,491	94,705	94,591	94,383	94,371	94,400	94,224
1991	94,863	95,095	94,987	95,102	95,121	95,371	95,288	95,508	95,568	95,347	95,368	95,411	95,252
1992	95,776	95,888	95,984	96,309	96,456	96,586	96,426	96,383	96,469	96,674	96,766	96,665	96,365
1993	97,029	97,069	97,077	97,156	97,219	97,436	97,731	98,206	98,346	98,470	98,572	98,420	97,728
1993[4]	97,001	97,063	97,090	97,142	97,195	97,409	97,703	98,203	98,359	98,472	98,579	98,395	97,718
1994	97,962	98,033	97,950	98,142	98,214	98,446	98,508	98,956	99,316	99,432	99,708	99,640	98,692
1995	99,889	99,652	99,776	99,743	100,013	100,041	99,910	99,910	99,802	100,363	100,308	100,417	99,985
1996	100,415	100,417	100,585	100,826	101,157	101,264	101,153	101,076	101,131	101,230	101,201	101,361	100,985
1997	101,374	101,825	101,905	101,886	102,090	102,162	102,249	102,371	102,680	102,742	102,739	102,392	102,201

Source: U.S. Bureau of the Census, Current Population Survey/Housing Vacancy Survey.

(1) The March estimates in this table differ from household estimates from the Current Population Survey - March Supplement, which are shown in Tables 1.4-1.7. See Appendix A for explanation.
(2) Average of monthly estimates.
(3) In January 1982, the Current Population Survey/Housing Vacancy Survey switched from weights based on the 1970 Census to weights based on the 1980 Census. The change to new weights increased the household estimate by almost 1.7 million.
(4) Revised estimates using weights based on the 1990 Census with adjustment for net undercount. The unrevised 1993 estimates (preceding row in the table) use weights based on the 1980 Census, without adjustment for undercount.

Household and Family Characteristics

TABLE 1.2. CENSUS COUNTS AND INTERCENSAL AND POSTCENSAL ESTIMATES OF HOUSEHOLDS FOR THE U.S., REGIONS, AND STATES: 1980 TO 1996
(In thousands)

AREA	April 1, 1980 (Census)	July 1, 1981	July 1, 1982	July 1, 1983	July 1, 1984	July 1, 1985	July 1, 1986	July 1, 1987	July 1, 1988	July 1, 1989	April 1, 1990 (Census)	July 1, 1991	July 1, 1992	July 1, 1993	July 1, 1994	July 1, 1995	July 1, 1996
United States	80,390	82,130	82,945	83,635	85,202	86,554	87,743	88,855	90,234	91,484	91,947	93,179	94,654	95,358	95,988	97,386	98,751
Northeast	17,471	17,690	17,734	17,805	18,068	18,258	18,420	18,570	18,788	18,916	18,873	18,961	19,093	19,080	19,058	19,180	19,298
Midwest	20,859	21,072	21,055	21,038	21,299	21,493	21,635	21,818	22,085	22,273	22,317	22,534	22,798	22,878	22,928	23,156	23,390
South	26,486	27,335	27,871	28,307	28,977	29,580	30,113	30,556	31,045	31,569	31,822	32,388	32,994	33,363	33,733	34,351	34,949
West	15,574	16,033	16,285	16,486	16,857	17,223	17,574	17,910	18,316	18,726	18,935	19,296	19,769	20,038	20,269	20,699	21,113
Alabama	1,342	1,368	1,378	1,386	1,410	1,431	1,448	1,467	1,484	1,500	1,507	1,532	1,558	1,574	1,582	1,603	1,624
Alaska	131	138	149	163	171	178	181	179	183	187	189	194	202	206	207	210	214
Arizona	957	1,004	1,037	1,067	1,114	1,165	1,220	1,272	1,319	1,354	1,369	1,392	1,432	1,466	1,518	1,624	1,687
Arkansas	816	828	831	838	853	862	870	878	884	890	891	899	910	919	925	938	951
California	8,630	8,851	8,965	9,063	9,252	9,453	9,650	9,844	10,066	10,296	10,381	10,531	10,748	10,812	10,829	10,941	11,101
Colorado	1,061	1,104	1,137	1,163	1,189	1,212	1,230	1,244	1,255	1,271	1,282	1,306	1,348	1,388	1,424	1,466	1,502
Connecticut	1,094	1,116	1,125	1,135	1,157	1,175	1,190	1,205	1,223	1,233	1,230	1,233	1,234	1,227	1,222	1,225	1,231
Delaware	207	210	212	215	220	224	229	234	239	245	247	253	258	262	264	270	276
District of Columbia	253	254	254	254	256	258	260	260	259	256	250	247	246	243	238	233	231
Florida	3,744	3,948	4,059	4,165	4,325	4,473	4,608	4,748	4,886	5,033	5,135	5,237	5,340	5,379	5,451	5,551	5,648
Georgia	1,872	1,931	1,964	1,997	2,061	2,125	2,184	2,242	2,297	2,343	2,367	2,425	2,489	2,533	2,587	2,654	2,723
Hawaii	294	301	307	312	318	324	329	337	344	350	356	365	374	376	380	384	389
Idaho	324	332	334	336	343	347	347	348	351	357	361	373	384	395	405	419	430
Illinois	4,045	4,076	4,065	4,055	4,089	4,110	4,118	4,138	4,171	4,200	4,202	4,239	4,284	4,294	4,295	4,322	4,352
Indiana	1,927	1,942	1,942	1,939	1,966	1,985	1,997	2,016	2,040	2,061	2,065	2,101	2,133	2,149	2,156	2,182	2,209
Iowa	1,053	1,061	1,055	1,049	1,057	1,055	1,048	1,047	1,058	1,064	1,064	1,069	1,083	1,084	1,084	1,093	1,103
Kansas	872	887	892	895	906	913	920	926	938	945	945	948	959	962	965	975	982
Kentucky	1,263	1,283	1,292	1,301	1,316	1,330	1,340	1,350	1,365	1,376	1,380	1,397	1,418	1,430	1,437	1,457	1,478
Louisiana	1,412	1,451	1,477	1,492	1,508	1,521	1,530	1,516	1,507	1,507	1,499	1,514	1,534	1,539	1,543	1,559	1,572
Maine	395	403	406	410	420	427	433	442	453	462	465	470	474	474	473	477	483
Maryland	1,461	1,494	1,506	1,520	1,556	1,588	1,625	1,660	1,703	1,734	1,749	1,778	1,806	1,816	1,830	1,853	1,871
Massachusetts	2,033	2,069	2,076	2,088	2,131	2,163	2,183	2,204	2,236	2,256	2,247	2,249	2,264	2,264	2,269	2,297	2,322
Michigan	3,195	3,205	3,184	3,168	3,212	3,255	3,300	3,344	3,382	3,412	3,419	3,452	3,493	3,494	3,500	3,534	3,576
Minnesota	1,445	1,477	1,487	1,492	1,517	1,541	1,561	1,581	1,617	1,639	1,648	1,667	1,689	1,702	1,716	1,740	1,763
Mississippi	827	844	852	856	869	879	888	895	903	911	911	924	934	941	948	964	979

See notes at end of table.

Household and Family Characteristics

TABLE 1.2. CENSUS COUNTS AND INTERCENSAL AND POSTCENSAL ESTIMATES OF HOUSEHOLDS FOR THE U.S., REGIONS, AND STATES: 1980 TO 1996 - Continued
(In thousands)

AREA	April 1, 1980 (Census)	July 1, 1981	July 1, 1982	July 1, 1983	July 1, 1984	July 1, 1985	July 1, 1986	July 1, 1987	July 1, 1988	July 1, 1989	April 1, 1990 (Census)	July 1, 1991	July 1, 1992	July 1, 1993	July 1, 1994	July 1, 1995	July 1, 1996
Missouri	1,793	1,816	1,816	1,824	1,853	1,875	1,894	1,917	1,941	1,956	1,961	1,976	1,994	2,001	2,009	2,031	2,052
Montana	284	289	293	296	301	303	302	301	303	305	306	309	315	321	326	335	341
Nebraska	571	580	582	582	589	592	591	591	598	602	602	606	614	615	616	624	631
Nevada	304	324	335	342	355	367	380	397	418	444	466	496	517	535	562	591	619
New Hampshire	323	333	337	342	354	365	377	390	402	411	411	413	417	419	423	431	439
New Jersey	2,549	2,592	2,606	2,621	2,666	2,704	2,737	2,762	2,791	2,803	2,795	2,813	2,838	2,839	2,841	2,866	2,889
New Mexico	441	456	467	479	491	503	515	523	530	538	543	554	569	578	592	607	619
New York	6,340	6,386	6,386	6,403	6,479	6,529	6,564	6,587	6,643	6,669	6,639	6,661	6,706	6,702	6,684	6,709	6,737
North Carolina	2,043	2,101	2,133	2,161	2,227	2,287	2,332	2,384	2,439	2,492	2,517	2,568	2,609	2,646	2,680	2,738	2,796
North Dakota	228	233	237	239	243	245	244	243	244	243	241	240	242	242	242	244	247
Ohio	3,834	3,871	3,866	3,861	3,902	3,937	3,964	3,999	4,046	4,081	4,088	4,134	4,178	4,187	4,187	4,223	4,260
Oklahoma	1,119	1,153	1,196	1,218	1,223	1,223	1,221	1,207	1,202	1,206	1,206	1,211	1,230	1,235	1,238	1,250	1,265
Oregon	992	1,009	1,005	998	1,012	1,021	1,031	1,043	1,067	1,088	1,103	1,131	1,157	1,180	1,197	1,223	1,249
Pennsylvania	4,220	4,265	4,269	4,272	4,319	4,343	4,376	4,411	4,459	4,494	4,496	4,528	4,562	4,559	4,552	4,575	4,594
Rhode Island	339	344	345	347	354	360	365	370	375	378	378	380	381	378	376	376	378
South Carolina	1,030	1,065	1,082	1,093	1,121	1,149	1,171	1,194	1,218	1,244	1,258	1,291	1,315	1,328	1,331	1,352	1,376
South Dakota	243	245	246	247	251	254	254	256	259	259	259	260	263	265	267	270	273
Tennessee	1,619	1,650	1,663	1,673	1,705	1,737	1,760	1,791	1,820	1,844	1,854	1,887	1,921	1,941	1,965	2,002	2,041
Texas	4,929	5,139	5,335	5,475	5,606	5,723	5,835	5,868	5,920	6,026	6,071	6,196	6,341	6,458	6,570	6,741	6,894
Utah	449	463	474	481	493	503	511	515	523	532	537	553	571	586	600	621	639
Vermont	178	182	184	186	189	192	195	199	205	209	211	214	217	218	220	223	227
Virginia	1,863	1,919	1,944	1,969	2,024	2,072	2,117	2,168	2,226	2,271	2,292	2,332	2,383	2,414	2,439	2,476	2,511
Washington	1,541	1,589	1,603	1,608	1,640	1,670	1,700	1,736	1,787	1,833	1,872	1,922	1,978	2,019	2,049	2,097	2,139
West Virginia	686	695	695	694	698	699	696	695	692	691	689	695	702	705	705	709	714
Wisconsin	1,652	1,679	1,685	1,687	1,713	1,732	1,744	1,760	1,792	1,812	1,822	1,842	1,868	1,883	1,891	1,917	1,943
Wyoming	166	174	179	178	178	178	177	171	170	170	169	170	174	176	178	181	184

Source: U.S. Bureau of the Census, State Housing Unit and Household Estimates. Data for 1980 and 1990 are from the decennial census.

Components may not add to totals due to rounding.

The methodology used to develop household estimates for the 1991-1996 period is different from that used for the 1981-1989 period. See Appendix A for explanation.

Household and Family Characteristics

TABLE 1.3. TOTAL HOUSEHOLDS AND ONE-PERSON HOUSEHOLDS BY STATE: 1940 TO 1990

AREA	Total households					
	1940	1950	1960	1970	1980	1990
United States	34,854,532	42,826,281	53,023,875	63,449,747	80,389,673	91,947,410
Alabama	673,815	786,839	884,116	1,034,113	1,341,856	1,506,790
Alaska	....	30,329	57,250	79,059	131,463	188,915
Arizona	131,133	210,374	366,630	539,157	957,032	1,368,843
Arkansas	495,825	524,391	523,552	615,424	816,065	891,179
California	2,138,343	3,333,406	4,982,108	6,573,861	8,629,866	10,381,206
Colorado	316,000	391,235	529,419	690,928	1,061,249	1,282,489
Connecticut	448,682	569,638	752,736	933,269	1,093,678	1,230,479
Delaware	70,541	90,390	128,582	164,804	207,081	247,497
District of Columbia	173,445	224,142	252,066	262,538	253,143	249,634
Florida	519,887	821,501	1,550,414	2,284,786	3,744,254	5,134,869
Georgia	752,241	889,269	1,070,325	1,369,225	1,871,652	2,366,615
Hawaii	....	112,290	153,064	203,088	294,052	356,267
Idaho	141,727	169,110	193,839	218,960	324,107	360,723
Illinois	2,192,724	2,582,000	3,084,971	3,502,138	4,045,374	4,202,240
Indiana	961,498	1,168,916	1,387,878	1,609,494	1,927,050	2,065,355
Iowa	701,824	780,167	841,357	896,311	1,053,033	1,064,325
Kansas	511,109	586,650	672,899	727,364	872,239	944,726
Kentucky	698,538	778,754	851,867	983,665	1,263,355	1,379,782
Louisiana	592,528	724,945	892,344	1,052,038	1,411,788	1,499,269
Maine	218,968	254,443	280,355	302,923	395,184	465,312
Maryland	465,683	641,222	863,001	1,175,073	1,460,865	1,748,991
Massachusetts	1,120,694	1,305,194	1,534,985	1,759,692	2,032,717	2,247,110
Michigan	1,396,014	1,790,702	2,239,079	2,653,059	3,195,213	3,419,331
Minnesota	728,359	845,265	991,981	1,153,946	1,445,222	1,647,853
Mississippi	534,956	554,765	568,070	636,724	827,169	911,374
Missouri	1,068,642	1,197,597	1,360,054	1,520,567	1,793,399	1,961,206
Montana	159,963	175,470	202,240	217,304	283,742	306,163
Nebraska	360,744	394,148	433,448	473,721	571,400	602,363
Nevada	33,291	50,241	91,520	160,052	304,327	466,297
New Hampshire	132,936	155,203	180,020	225,378	323,493	411,186
New Jersey	1,100,260	1,373,637	1,806,439	2,218,182	2,548,594	2,794,711
New Mexico	129,475	176,993	251,209	289,389	441,466	542,709
New York	3,662,113	4,325,139	5,248,710	5,913,861	6,340,429	6,639,322
North Carolina	789,659	994,356	1,204,715	1,509,564	2,043,291	2,517,026
North Dakota	152,043	162,105	173,362	181,613	227,664	240,878
Ohio	1,897,796	2,313,990	2,852,557	3,289,432	3,833,828	4,087,546
Oklahoma	610,481	663,203	734,593	850,803	1,118,561	1,206,135
Oregon	337,492	479,047	558,214	691,631	991,593	1,103,313
Pennsylvania	2,515,524	2,915,879	3,350,839	3,705,410	4,219,606	4,495,966
Rhode Island	187,706	225,447	257,335	291,965	338,590	377,977
South Carolina	434,968	514,638	603,551	734,373	1,029,981	1,258,044
South Dakota	165,428	182,978	194,821	200,807	242,523	259,034
Tennessee	714,894	871,474	1,003,301	1,213,187	1,618,505	1,853,725
Texas	1,678,396	2,189,178	2,778,116	3,433,996	4,929,267	6,070,937
Utah	139,487	187,825	241,532	297,934	448,603	537,273
Vermont	92,435	103,496	110,732	132,098	178,325	210,650
Virginia	627,532	845,259	1,072,840	1,390,636	1,863,073	2,291,830
Washington	537,337	735,746	894,168	1,105,587	1,540,510	1,872,431
West Virginia	444,815	518,281	521,142	547,214	686,311	688,557
Wisconsin	827,207	967,448	1,146,342	1,328,804	1,652,261	1,822,118
Wyoming	69,374	84,185	99,187	104,600	165,624	168,839

See notes at end of table.

Household and Family Characteristics

TABLE 1.3. TOTAL HOUSEHOLDS AND ONE-PERSON HOUSEHOLDS BY STATE: 1940 TO 1990 - Continued

AREA	1-person households					
	1940	1950	1960	1970	1980	1990
United States	2,677,281	3,993,399	7,074,971	11,146,184	18,247,536	22,580,420
Alabama	35,213	52,479	84,065	151,108	273,632	358,078
Alaska	....	5,329	9,266	10,839	26,467	41,826
Arizona	15,120	25,710	49,723	88,863	199,699	337,681
Arkansas	31,243	45,566	65,719	105,966	173,842	213,778
California	288,913	466,018	889,633	1,378,643	2,130,878	2,429,867
Colorado	36,189	48,844	81,847	124,444	249,781	340,962
Connecticut	27,124	41,609	87,455	149,429	235,768	297,161
Delaware	5,108	7,679	14,047	25,219	43,210	57,451
District of Columbia	17,211	32,023	68,070	84,239	100,021	103,626
Florida	49,740	90,401	225,568	426,321	885,498	1,309,954
Georgia	42,115	61,252	108,082	197,180	383,806	537,702
Hawaii	....	11,739	18,495	25,901	50,304	68,985
Idaho	14,605	18,437	25,774	36,208	64,540	80,800
Illinois	167,013	252,958	443,874	646,348	970,057	1,081,113
Indiana	72,291	107,490	171,247	265,072	412,992	496,841
Iowa	56,975	79,359	115,947	165,709	245,931	275,466
Kansas	46,722	66,178	94,090	134,179	207,287	245,156
Kentucky	39,886	56,902	90,353	149,531	252,075	321,247
Louisiana	41,766	66,544	109,742	168,389	300,842	356,060
Maine	18,122	24,828	35,210	50,957	84,293	108,474
Maryland	31,768	47,669	87,060	175,126	304,207	394,572
Massachusetts	81,004	115,334	218,107	331,247	495,677	580,774
Michigan	91,065	145,009	260,252	412,505	672,901	809,449
Minnesota	59,617	84,200	135,415	204,600	335,791	413,531
Mississippi	33,449	42,681	60,798	97,832	168,444	212,949
Missouri	88,622	130,367	206,344	293,412	427,373	510,684
Montana	24,113	25,332	33,987	43,037	66,350	80,491
Nebraska	31,252	41,331	61,517	91,537	138,942	159,671
Nevada	5,897	8,061	17,266	31,047	74,843	119,627
New Hampshire	12,164	16,584	23,602	38,238	68,643	90,364
New Jersey	62,195	97,600	203,456	351,545	537,510	646,171
New Mexico	10,832	16,056	26,866	43,136	92,862	124,883
New York	279,996	416,898	811,702	1,194,544	1,649,325	1,806,263
North Carolina	31,905	53,394	99,641	200,840	407,650	596,959
North Dakota	12,042	14,679	20,672	30,933	52,028	63,953
Ohio	138,000	196,419	344,686	547,009	859,331	1,020,450
Oklahoma	44,890	71,031	113,575	162,844	261,764	309,369
Oregon	44,608	61,608	90,272	132,825	232,957	278,716
Pennsylvania	160,227	229,609	400,108	640,571	955,900	1,150,694
Rhode Island	13,842	20,050	35,158	53,075	81,388	99,111
South Carolina	25,051	35,171	56,640	101,385	197,379	281,347
South Dakota	14,498	18,139	24,922	36,428	56,909	68,308
Tennessee	36,627	56,180	96,999	174,781	330,052	442,129
Texas	114,837	194,799	349,591	559,054	1,068,518	1,452,936
Utah	11,084	17,059	28,876	42,764	77,096	101,640
Vermont	7,354	9,758	13,823	22,236	39,283	49,366
Virginia	34,854	55,555	101,271	200,672	382,597	523,770
Washington	80,242	103,607	157,125	216,864	372,269	476,320
West Virginia	22,781	35,450	52,654	87,765	142,031	168,735
Wisconsin	58,242	79,175	140,147	225,001	371,266	443,673
Wyoming	8,867	10,317	14,232	18,786	35,327	41,287

Source: U.S. Bureau of the Census, Census of Housing 1940-1990.

Based on tables prepared by Robert Bonnette.

Alaska and Hawaii are not included in 1950 U.S. total.

Household and Family Characteristics

TABLE 1.4. HOUSEHOLDS BY TYPE: 1947 TO 1997
(In thousands)

YEAR	Total households	Family households				Nonfamily households		
		Total	Married couple	Other Family		Total	Male householder	Female householder
				Male householder	Female householder			
1947	39,107	34,964	30,612	1,129	3,223	4,143	1,388	2,755
1948	40,532	36,629	31,900	1,020	3,709	3,903	1,198	2,705
1949	42,182	38,080	33,257	1,197	3,626	4,102	1,308	2,794
1950	43,554	38,838	34,075	1,169	3,594	4,716	1,668	3,048
1951	44,673	39,502	34,391	1,154	3,957	5,171	1,732	3,439
1952	45,538	40,235	35,164	1,119	3,952	5,303	1,757	3,546
1953	46,385	40,540	35,577	1,206	3,757	5,845	1,902	3,943
1954	46,962	40,998	35,926	1,315	3,757	5,964	1,925	4,039
1955	47,874	41,732	36,251	1,328	4,153	6,142	2,059	4,083
1956	48,902	42,593	37,047	1,408	4,138	6,309	2,058	4,250
1957	49,673	43,262	37,718	1,241	4,304	6,411	2,038	4,374
1958	50,474	43,426	37,911	1,278	4,237	7,047	2,329	4,718
1959	51,435	43,971	38,410	1,285	4,276	7,464	2,449	5,015
1960	52,799	44,905	39,254	1,228	4,422	7,895	2,716	5,179
1961	53,557	45,383	39,620	1,199	4,564	8,174	2,779	5,395
1962	54,764	46,262	40,404	1,268	4,590	8,502	2,932	5,570
1963	55,270	46,872	40,888	1,295	4,689	8,398	2,838	5,560
1964	56,149	47,381	41,341	1,204	4,836	8,768	2,965	5,803
1965	57,436	47,838	41,689	1,167	4,982	9,598	3,277	6,321
1966	58,406	48,399	42,263	1,163	4,973	10,007	3,299	6,708
1967	59,236	49,086	42,743	1,190	5,153	10,150	3,419	6,731
1968	60,813	50,012	43,507	1,195	5,310	10,801	3,658	7,143
1969	62,214	50,729	44,086	1,221	5,422	11,485	3,890	7,595
1970	63,401	51,456	44,728	1,228	5,500	11,945	4,063	7,882
1971	64,778	52,102	44,928	1,254	5,920	12,676	4,403	8,273
1972	66,676	53,163	45,724	1,331	6,108	13,513	4,839	8,674
1973	68,251	54,264	46,297	1,432	6,535	13,986	5,129	8,858
1974	69,859	54,917	46,787	1,421	6,709	14,942	5,654	9,288
1975	71,120	55,563	46,951	1,485	7,127	15,557	5,912	9,645
1976	72,867	56,056	47,297	1,424	7,335	16,811	6,548	10,263
1977	74,142	56,472	47,471	1,461	7,540	17,669	6,971	10,698
1978	76,030	56,958	47,357	1,564	8,037	19,071	7,811	11,261
1979	77,330	57,498	47,662	1,616	8,220	19,831	8,064	11,767
1980	79,108	58,426	48,180	1,706	8,540	20,682	8,594	12,088
1980 [1]	80,776	59,550	49,112	1,733	8,705	21,226	8,807	12,419
1981	82,368	60,309	49,294	1,933	9,082	22,059	9,279	12,780
1982	83,527	61,019	49,630	1,986	9,403	22,508	9,457	13,051
1983	83,918	61,393	49,908	2,016	9,469	22,525	9,514	13,011
1984	85,407	61,997	50,090	2,030	9,878	23,410	9,752	13,658
1985	86,789	62,706	50,350	2,228	10,129	24,082	10,114	13,968
1986	88,458	63,558	50,933	2,414	10,211	24,900	10,648	14,252
1987	89,479	64,491	51,537	2,510	10,445	24,988	10,652	14,336
1988	91,066	65,133	51,809	2,715	10,608	25,933	11,310	14,624
1989	92,830	65,837	52,100	2,847	10,890	26,994	11,874	15,120
1990	93,347	66,090	52,317	2,884	10,890	27,257	11,606	15,651
1991	94,312	66,322	52,147	2,907	11,268	27,990	12,150	15,840
1992	95,669	67,173	52,457	3,025	11,692	28,496	12,428	16,068
1993	96,391	68,144	53,171	3,026	11,947	28,247	12,254	15,993
1993 [2]	96,426	68,216	53,090	3,065	12,061	28,210	12,297	15,914
1994	97,107	68,490	53,171	2,913	12,406	28,617	12,462	16,155
1995	98,990	69,305	53,858	3,226	12,220	29,686	13,190	16,496
1996	99,627	69,594	53,567	3,513	12,514	30,033	13,348	16,685
1997	101,018	70,241	53,604	3,847	12,790	30,777	13,707	17,070

Source: U.S. Bureau of the Census, Current Population Survey - March Supplement.

As of March, except for 1947-1949 and 1951-1955, which are as of April.
(1) Revised using population controls based on the 1980 Census.
(2) Revised using population controls based on the 1990 Census with adjustment for net undercount.

Household and Family Characteristics

TABLE 1.5. AVERAGE POPULATION PER HOUSEHOLD AND FAMILY: 1947 TO 1997
(Totals in thousands)

YEAR	Households				Families [1]			
	Total	Population per household			Total	Population per family		
		All ages	Under 18	18 years and older		All ages	Under 18	18 years and older
1947	39,107	3.56	....	....	35,794	3.67	....	....
1948	40,532	3.49	1.10	2.48	37,237	3.64	1.19	2.44
1949	42,182	3.42	1.09	2.33	38,624	3.58	1.19	2.39
1950	43,554	3.37	1.06	2.31	39,303	3.54	1.17	2.37
1951	44,673	3.34	1.10	2.23	39,929	3.54	1.23	2.31
1952	45,538	3.32	1.12	2.20	40,578	3.54	1.25	2.29
1953	46,385	3.28	1.09	2.19	40,832	3.53	1.24	2.29
1954	46,962	3.34	1.13	2.20	41,202	3.59	1.30	2.29
1955	47,874	3.33	1.14	2.19	41,951	3.59	1.30	2.29
1956	48,902	3.32	1.15	2.17	42,889	3.58	1.31	2.27
1957	49,673	3.33	1.17	2.16	43,497	3.60	1.34	2.27
1958	50,474	3.34	1.19	2.15	43,696	3.64	1.37	2.27
1959	51,435	3.34	1.20	2.14	44,232	3.65	1.39	2.26
1960	52,799	3.33	1.21	2.12	45,111	3.67	1.41	2.26
1961	53,557	3.34	1.22	2.13	45,539	3.70	1.42	2.27
1962	54,764	3.31	1.21	2.10	46,418	3.67	1.42	2.25
1963	55,270	3.33	1.22	2.10	47,059	3.68	1.43	2.25
1964	56,149	3.33	1.23	2.10	47,540	3.70	1.44	2.25
1965	57,436	3.29	1.21	2.09	47,956	3.70	1.44	2.26
1966	58,406	3.27	1.19	2.08	48,509	3.69	1.42	2.27
1967	59,236	3.26	1.17	2.08	49,214	3.67	1.41	2.27
1968	60,813	3.20	1.14	2.06	50,111	3.63	1.38	2.25
1969	62,214	3.16	1.11	2.05	50,823	3.60	1.36	2.24
1970	63,401	3.14	1.09	2.05	51,586	3.58	1.34	2.25
1971	64,778	3.11	1.07	2.04	52,227	3.57	1.32	2.25
1972	66,676	3.06	1.03	2.03	53,296	3.53	1.29	2.25
1973	68,251	3.01	1.00	2.02	54,373	3.48	1.25	2.23
1974	69,859	2.97	0.96	2.00	55,053	3.44	1.21	2.23
1975	71,120	2.94	0.93	2.01	55,712	3.42	1.18	2.23
1976	72,867	2.89	0.89	2.00	56,245	3.39	1.15	2.23
1977	74,142	2.86	0.87	1.99	56,710	3.37	1.13	2.24
1978	76,030	2.81	0.83	1.98	57,215	3.33	1.10	2.23
1979	77,330	2.78	0.81	1.97	57,804	3.31	1.08	2.23
1980 [2]	80,776	2.76	0.79	1.97	59,550	3.29	1.05	2.23
1981	82,368	2.73	0.76	1.96	60,309	3.27	1.03	2.23
1982	83,527	2.72	0.75	1.97	61,019	3.25	1.01	2.24
1983	83,918	2.73	0.74	1.99	61,393	3.26	1.00	2.26
1984	85,407	2.71	0.73	1.98	61,997	3.24	0.99	2.25
1985	86,789	2.69	0.72	1.97	62,706	3.23	0.98	2.24
1986	88,458	2.67	0.71	1.96	63,558	3.21	0.98	2.23
1987	89,479	2.66	0.71	1.96	64,491	3.19	0.96	2.22
1988	91,066	2.64	0.70	1.94	65,133	3.17	0.96	2.21
1989	92,830	2.62	0.69	1.93	65,837	3.16	0.96	2.21
1990	93,347	2.63	0.69	1.94	66,090	3.17	0.96	2.21
1991	94,312	2.63	0.69	1.94	66,322	3.18	0.96	2.22
1992	95,669	2.62	0.69	1.93	67,173	3.17	0.97	2.20
1993	96,391	2.63	0.70	1.94	68,144	3.16	0.96	2.20
1993 [3]	96,426	2.66	0.71	1.95	68,216	3.19	0.99	2.20
1994	97,107	2.67	0.72	1.95	68,490	3.20	0.99	2.21
1995	98,990	2.65	0.71	1.93	69,305	3.19	0.99	2.20
1996	99,627	2.65	0.71	1.94	69,594	3.20	1.00	2.20
1997	101,018	2.64	0.71	1.93	70,241	3.19	0.99	2.20

Source: U.S. Bureau of the Census, Current Population Survey - March Supplement.

As of March, except for 1947-1949 and 1951-1955, which are as of April.

(1) Estimates of families in this table differ from the estimates of family households in Table 1.4 for years before 1980. This is true because unrelated subfamilies were counted as families prior to 1980. See Appendix A for definitions and additional explanation.

(2) Uses population controls based on the 1980 Census.

(3) Revised using population controls based on the 1990 Census with adjustment for net undercount.

Household and Family Characteristics

TABLE 1.6. HOUSEHOLDS BY RACE AND HISPANIC ORIGIN OF HOUSEHOLDER: 1970 TO 1997
(In thousands)

YEAR	Total [1]	White	Black	Hispanic [2]
1970	63,401	56,602	6,223	....
1971	64,374	57,575	6,180	....
1972	66,676	59,463	6,578	....
1973	68,251	60,618	6,809	....
1974	69,859	61,965	7,040	....
1975	71,120	62,945	7,262	....
1976	72,867	64,392	7,486	2,948
1977	74,142	65,353	7,776	3,081
1978	76,030	66,934	7,977	3,304
1979	77,330	68,028	8,066	3,291
1980 [3]	80,776	70,766	8,586	3,684
1981	82,368	71,872	8,847	3,906
1982	83,527	72,845	8,961	3,980
1983	83,918	73,182	8,916	4,085
1984	85,407	74,376	9,236	4,326
1985	86,789	75,328	9,480	4,883
1986	88,458	76,576	9,797	5,213
1987	89,479	77,284	9,922	5,418
1988	91,066	78,469	10,186	5,698
1989	92,830	79,734	10,561	5,910
1990	93,347	80,163	10,486	5,933
1991	94,312	80,968	10,671	6,220
1992	95,669	81,675	11,083	6,379
1993 [4]	96,391	82,083	11,190	6,626
1994	97,107	82,387	11,281	7,362
1995	98,990	83,737	11,655	7,735
1996	99,627	84,511	11,577	7,939
1997	101,018	85,059	12,109	8,225

Source: U.S. Bureau of the Census, Current Population Survey - March Supplement.

As of March.
(1) Includes other races not shown separately.
(2) Persons of Hispanic origin may be of any race.
(3) Uses population controls based on the 1980 Census.
(4) Unrevised. Uses population controls based on the 1980 Census.

Household and Family Characteristics

TABLE 1.7. HOUSEHOLDS BY AGE OF HOUSEHOLDER: 1960 TO 1997
(Thousands of households, except as noted)

| YEAR | All households | Age of householder | | | | | | | | Median age (Years) |
		Under 25	25-29	30-34	35-44	45-54	55-64	65-74	75 and older	
1960	52,799	2,559	4,317	5,407	11,614	10,878	8,599	6,380	3,045	47.3
1961	53,557	2,628	4,341	5,387	11,596	11,047	9,026	6,355	3,179	47.6
1962	54,764	2,909	4,349	5,435	11,802	10,906	9,057	6,960	3,346	47.6
1963	55,270	2,889	4,386	5,314	12,005	11,072	9,103	6,909	3,592	47.7
1964	56,149	3,110	4,546	5,167	12,176	11,192	9,327	6,998	3,630	47.7
1965	57,436	3,413	4,808	5,119	12,009	11,523	9,600	7,173	3,790	47.9
1966	58,406	3,571	4,991	5,086	11,944	11,806	9,745	7,224	4,038	48.1
1967	59,236	3,587	5,288	5,099	11,998	11,892	9,909	7,321	4,143	48.1
1968	60,813	3,852	5,336	5,325	12,003	12,038	10,394	7,536	4,327	48.2
1969	62,214	4,094	5,910	5,447	11,817	12,230	10,622	7,540	4,554	48.1
1970	63,401	4,359	6,101	5,593	11,810	12,216	10,824	7,744	4,756	48.1
1971	64,778	4,737	6,239	5,682	11,813	12,588	11,021	7,793	4,909	48.1
1972	66,676	5,194	6,794	6,009	11,529	12,758	11,138	8,165	5,090	48.0
1973	68,251	5,476	7,116	6,447	11,721	12,805	11,212	8,369	5,104	47.6
1974	69,859	5,857	7,527	6,804	11,703	12,939	11,149	8,716	5,162	47.3
1975	71,120	5,834	7,810	7,137	11,861	12,916	11,301	8,910	5,350	47.3
1976	72,867	5,877	8,298	7,212	12,227	12,820	11,631	9,258	5,544	47.2
1977	74,142	5,991	8,385	7,782	12,482	12,905	11,780	9,210	5,606	46.9
1978	76,030	6,220	8,598	8,233	12,969	12,602	12,183	9,383	5,842	46.6
1979	77,330	6,342	8,679	8,317	13,328	12,585	12,284	9,753	6,042	46.6
1980 [1]	80,776	6,569	9,252	9,252	13,980	12,654	12,525	10,112	6,432	46.1
1981	82,368	6,443	9,514	9,639	14,463	12,694	12,704	10,226	6,685	45.9
1982	83,527	6,109	9,525	9,802	15,326	12,505	12,947	10,379	6,933	45.8
1983	83,918	5,695	9,465	9,639	16,020	12,354	13,074	10,603	7,067	45.9
1984	85,407	5,510	9,848	9,960	16,596	12,471	13,121	10,700	7,201	45.6
1985	86,789	5,438	9,637	10,377	17,481	12,628	13,073	10,851	7,305	45.4
1986	88,458	5,503	9,781	10,629	17,997	13,099	12,852	11,157	7,439	45.2
1987	89,479	5,197	9,652	10,850	18,703	13,211	12,868	11,250	7,748	45.3
1988	91,066	5,228	9,614	10,969	19,323	13,630	12,846	11,410	8,045	45.3
1989	92,830	5,415	9,624	11,300	19,952	14,018	12,805	11,590	8,127	45.1
1990	93,347	5,121	9,423	11,049	20,555	14,514	12,529	11,733	8,423	45.3
1991	94,312	4,882	9,246	11,077	21,304	14,751	12,524	12,001	8,526	45.4
1992	95,669	4,859	8,810	11,197	21,774	15,547	12,559	12,043	8,878	45.7
1993	96,391	5,022	8,614	11,127	21,718	16,576	12,438	11,834	9,061	45.9
1993 [2]	96,426	5,257	8,859	11,198	21,862	16,413	12,154	11,668	9,014	45.6
1994	97,107	5,265	8,472	11,245	22,293	16,837	12,188	11,639	9,168	45.7
1995	98,990	5,444	8,400	11,052	22,914	17,590	12,224	11,803	9,562	45.9
1996	99,627	5,282	8,354	10,871	23,227	18,007	12,401	11,908	9,578	46.0
1997	101,018	5,160	8,647	10,667	23,823	18,843	12,469	11,679	9,729	46.1

Source: U.S. Bureau of the Census, Current Population Survey - March Supplement.

As of March.

(1) Uses population controls based on the 1980 Census.

(2) Revised using population controls based on the 1990 Census with adjustment for net undercount.

Household and Family Characteristics

TABLE 1.8. FAMILIES BY PRESENCE OF OWN CHILDREN UNDER 18: 1950 TO 1997
(In thousands)

YEAR	All families [1]	Families with children under 18				
		Total	Married-couple families	1-parent families		
				Total	Mother only	Father only
1950	39,303	20,324	18,824	1,500	1,272	229
1951	39,944	21,279	19,389	1,890	1,659	231
1952	40,608	21,353	19,606	1,747	1,514	233
1953	40,877	21,718	19,920	1,798	1,521	277
1954	41,263	22,544	20,645	1,899	1,615	283
1955	41,951	23,190	21,064	2,126	1,870	256
1956	42,889	23,743	21,631	2,112	1,814	298
1957	43,497	24,260	22,139	2,121	1,855	265
1958	43,696	24,541	22,426	2,115	1,822	293
1959	44,232	25,069	22,894	2,175	1,943	232
1960	45,111	25,690	23,358	2,332	2,099	232
1961	45,539	25,889	23,514	2,375	2,185	190
1962	46,418	26,271	23,788	2,483	2,229	254
1963	47,059	26,911	24,321	2,590	2,229	361
1964	47,540	27,068	24,439	2,629	2,361	268
1965	47,956	27,140	24,406	2,734	2,485	249
1966	48,509	27,004	24,276	2,728	2,450	278
1967	49,214	27,561	24,646	2,915	2,584	331
1968	50,111	27,964	24,895	3,069	2,772	297
1969	50,823	28,347	25,136	3,211	2,888	323
1970	51,586	28,812	25,541	3,271	2,971	345
1971	52,227	28,786	25,091	3,695	3,365	331
1972	53,296	29,445	25,482	3,963	3,598	365
1973	54,373	29,571	25,387	4,184	3,798	386
1974	55,053	29,750	25,278	4,472	4,081	391
1975	55,712	30,057	25,169	4,888	4,404	484
1976	56,245	30,177	25,110	5,067	4,621	446
1977	56,710	30,145	24,875	5,270	4,784	486
1978	57,215	30,369	24,625	5,744	5,206	539
1979	57,804	30,371	24,514	5,857	5,288	569
1980 [2]	59,550	31,022	24,961	6,061	5,445	616
1981	60,309	31,227	24,927	6,300	5,634	666
1982	61,019	31,012	24,465	6,547	5,868	679
1983	61,393	30,818	24,363	6,455	5,718	737
1984	61,997	31,046	24,340	6,706	5,907	799
1985	62,706	31,112	24,210	6,902	6,006	896
1986	63,558	31,670	24,630	7,040	6,105	935
1987	64,491	31,898	24,646	7,252	6,297	955
1988	65,133	31,920	24,600	7,320	6,273	1,047
1989	65,837	32,322	24,735	7,587	6,519	1,068
1990	66,090	32,289	24,537	7,752	6,599	1,153
1991	66,322	32,401	24,397	8,004	6,823	1,181
1992	67,173	32,746	24,420	8,326	7,043	1,283
1993 [3]	68,144	33,257	24,707	8,550	7,226	1,324
1994	68,490	34,018	25,058	8,961	7,647	1,314
1995	69,305	34,296	25,241	9,055	7,615	1,440
1996	69,594	34,203	24,920	9,284	7,656	1,628
1997	70,241	34,665	25,083	9,583	7,874	1,709

Source: U.S. Bureau of the Census, Current Population Survey - March Supplement.

As of March, except for 1951-1955, which are as of April.

(1) Beginning in 1980, unrelated subfamilies are no longer counted as families. Because of this change, the estimates of families in this table differ from the estimates of family households in Table 1.4 for years before 1980. See Appendix A for definitions and additional explanation.

(2) Uses population controls based on the 1980 Census.

(3) Unrevised. Uses population controls based on the 1980 Census.

Household and Family Characteristics

YEAR	TABLE 1.9. AVERAGE NUMBER OF OWN CHILDREN UNDER 18 PER FAMILY, BY FAMILY TYPE: 1955 TO 1997							
	All families				Families with own children under 18			
	Total	Married-couple families	Female, no husband present	Male, no wife present	Total	Married-couple families	Female, no husband present	Male, no wife present
1955	1.21	1.27	0.96	0.39	2.19	2.20	2.17	1.98
1960	1.33	1.39	1.04	0.35	2.33	2.34	2.24	1.88
1965	1.38	1.43	1.20	0.45	2.44	2.44	2.42	2.13
1970	1.27	1.30	1.20	0.54	2.28	2.29	2.29	1.93
1971	1.28	1.30	1.32	0.53	2.31	2.31	2.33	2.00
1972	1.22	1.24	1.28	0.52	2.22	2.22	2.20	1.93
1973	1.18	1.19	1.26	0.50	2.17	2.18	2.20	1.87
1974	1.15	1.16	1.27	0.52	2.14	2.14	2.12	1.90
1975	1.13	1.12	1.27	0.60	2.09	2.09	2.10	1.85
1976	1.10	1.09	1.26	0.49	2.04	2.05	2.03	1.59
1977	1.07	1.06	1.23	0.54	2.01	2.02	1.99	1.66
1978	1.04	1.03	1.22	0.55	1.96	1.98	1.93	1.63
1979	1.01	1.00	1.16	0.56	1.93	1.95	1.86	1.63
1980 [1]	1.00	0.98	1.17	0.55	1.91	1.93	1.87	1.55
1981	0.97	0.96	1.11	0.55	1.88	1.91	1.79	1.59
1982	0.95	0.93	1.13	0.52	1.87	1.89	1.80	1.53
1983	0.94	0.92	1.09	0.53	1.87	1.89	1.81	1.46
1984	0.93	0.92	1.05	0.59	1.85	1.89	1.76	1.50
1985	0.92	0.90	1.06	0.62	1.85	1.88	1.79	1.53
1986	0.91	0.90	1.06	0.57	1.83	1.86	1.78	1.46
1987	0.90	0.88	1.05	0.58	1.81	1.84	1.74	1.51
1988	0.89	0.88	1.03	0.58	1.81	1.84	1.74	1.51
1989	0.90	0.88	1.04	0.58	1.82	1.86	1.74	1.55
1990	0.89	0.88	1.04	0.60	1.83	1.87	1.72	1.50
1991	0.90	0.88	1.05	0.61	1.84	1.88	1.74	1.50
1992	0.90	0.88	1.08	0.64	1.85	1.88	1.79	1.51
1993 [2]	0.90	0.87	1.07	0.65	1.84	1.88	1.76	1.48
1994	0.91	0.89	1.08	0.67	1.84	1.88	1.75	1.49
1995	0.91	0.89	1.10	0.66	1.84	1.89	1.76	1.49
1996	0.92	0.89	1.11	0.69	1.86	1.90	1.81	1.49
1997	0.91	0.89	1.08	0.69	1.84	1.89	1.75	1.55

Source: U.S. Bureau of the Census, Current Population Survey - March Supplement.

As of March, except for 1955, which is as of April.
(1) Uses population controls based on the 1980 Census.
(2) Unrevised. Uses population controls based on the 1980 Census.

Household and Family Characteristics

TABLE 1.10. PARENT/CHILD SITUATIONS, BY RACE AND HISPANIC ORIGIN OF HOUSEHOLDER OR REFERENCE PERSON, 1970 TO 1997
(In thousands)

YEAR	All family groups					Maintain own household (Family households)				
	Total with own children under 18	2-parent	1-parent			Total with own children under 18	2-parent	1-parent		
			Total	Maintained by				Total	Maintained by	
				Mother	Father				Mother	Father
ALL RACES										
1970	29,631	25,823	3,808	3,415	393	28,731	25,532	3,199	2,858	341
1980 [1]	32,150	25,231	6,920	6,230	690	31,022	24,961	6,061	5,445	616
1981	32,501	25,218	7,283	6,513	770	31,227	24,927	6,300	5,634	666
1982	32,886	24,795	8,091	7,286	805	31,012	24,465	6,547	5,868	679
1983	33,027	24,739	8,288	7,395	893	30,818	24,363	6,455	5,718	737
1984	33,246	24,701	8,544	7,599	945	31,046	24,339	6,706	5,907	799
1985	33,353	24,573	8,779	7,737	1,042	31,112	24,210	6,902	6,006	896
1986	33,939	25,010	8,930	7,842	1,088	31,670	24,630	7,040	6,105	935
1987	34,242	25,005	9,236	8,128	1,107	31,898	24,645	7,252	6,297	955
1988	34,345	24,977	9,368	8,146	1,222	31,920	24,600	7,320	6,273	1,047
1989	34,609	25,096	9,513	8,315	1,199	32,322	24,735	7,587	6,519	1,068
1990	34,670	24,921	9,749	8,398	1,351	32,289	24,537	7,752	6,599	1,153
1991	34,973	24,863	10,110	8,745	1,365	32,401	24,397	8,004	6,823	1,181
1992	35,378	24,879	10,499	9,028	1,472	32,746	24,420	8,326	7,043	1,283
1993 [2]	36,058	25,157	10,901	9,339	1,562	33,257	24,707	8,550	7,226	1,324
1994	37,008	25,598	11,410	9,854	1,556	34,018	25,058	8,961	7,647	1,314
1995	37,168	25,640	11,527	9,833	1,694	34,296	25,241	9,055	7,615	1,440
1996	37,077	25,361	11,717	9,855	1,862	34,203	24,920	9,284	7,656	1,628
1997	37,619	25,577	12,042	10,012	2,030	34,665	25,083	9,583	7,874	1,709
WHITE										
1970	26,115	23,477	2,638	2,330	307	....	....	....	....	....
1980 [1]	27,294	22,628	4,664	4,122	542	26,474	22,415	4,058	3,558	500
1981	27,433	22,512	4,921	4,326	595	26,523	22,296	4,228	3,694	534
1982	27,445	22,021	5,423	4,766	657	26,237	21,744	4,492	3,926	566
1983	27,343	22,011	5,332	4,625	707	26,006	21,701	4,305	3,707	598
1984	27,508	21,978	5,529	4,766	763	26,207	21,701	4,506	3,856	650
1985	27,629	21,873	5,757	4,912	844	26,232	21,565	4,666	3,922	744
1986	28,041	22,076	5,964	5,070	894	26,575	21,756	4,818	4,040	778
1987	28,180	22,076	6,104	5,190	914	26,717	21,787	4,930	4,141	789
1988	28,104	22,013	6,090	5,100	990	26,618	21,699	4,918	4,066	852
1989	56,284	22,106	6,086	5,150	936	26,805	21,809	4,996	4,141	855
1990	28,294	21,905	6,389	5,310	1,079	26,718	21,579	5,138	4,199	939
1991	28,443	21,893	6,550	5,482	1,068	26,793	21,531	5,262	4,337	925
1992	28,847	21,909	6,938	5,753	1,186	27,045	21,517	5,528	4,488	1,040
1993 [2]	29,225	22,058	7,167	5,901	1,265	27,335	21,686	5,650	4,552	1,098
1994	29,645	22,310	7,335	6,144	1,191	27,642	21,884	5,758	4,748	1,010
1995	29,846	22,320	7,525	6,239	1,286	27,951	22,005	5,946	4,841	1,105
1996	29,947	22,178	7,769	6,329	1,440	28,086	21,835	6,251	4,975	1,276
1997	30,242	22,294	7,948	6,396	1,552	28,236	21,914	6,322	4,997	1,325

See notes at end of table.

Household and Family Characteristics

TABLE 1.10. PARENT/CHILD SITUATIONS, BY RACE AND HISPANIC ORIGIN OF HOUSEHOLDER OR REFERENCE PERSON, 1970 TO 1997 - Continued
(In thousands)

YEAR	All family groups — Do not maintain own household									
	Related to householder (Related subfamilies)					Unrelated to householder (Unrelated subfamilies)				
	Total with own children under 18	2-parent	1-parent			Total with own children under 18	2-parent	1-parent		
			Total	Maintained by				Total	Maintained by	
				Mother	Father				Mother	Father
ALL RACES										
1970	819	282	537	489	48	81	9	72	68	4
1980 [1]	825	257	568	512	56	303	13	291	273	18
1981	939	283	656	578	78	335	8	327	301	26
1982	1,568	316	1,252	1,139	113	307	15	292	279	13
1983	1,869	368	1,501	1,355	146	340	8	332	322	10
1984	1,820	344	1,476	1,363	113	380	18	362	329	33
1985	1,857	348	1,508	1,392	116	384	15	369	339	30
1986	1,883	353	1,530	1,399	131	386	27	360	338	22
1987	1,916	342	1,574	1,451	123	428	18	409	380	29
1988	1,998	366	1,632	1,480	152	427	11	416	393	23
1989	1,844	342	1,503	1,398	104	443	19	424	398	26
1990	1,893	361	1,531	1,378	153	488	23	466	421	45
1991	1,984	424	1,560	1,418	142	587	42	545	504	41
1992	2,011	415	1,596	1,462	134	622	44	577	523	55
1993 [2]	2,136	410	1,726	1,556	170	666	40	625	557	68
1994	2,305	505	1,800	1,636	164	684	34	650	571	78
1995	2,241	377	1,864	1,668	195	631	22	609	550	59
1996	2,316	421	1,895	1,706	189	558	21	538	493	45
1997	2,360	465	1,895	1,651	244	594	29	564	487	77
WHITE										
1970	572	200	372	335	36	....	....	....	....	....
1980 [1]	578	205	373	339	34	242	8	233	225	8
1981	632	208	424	381	43	277	8	269	251	18
1982	955	266	689	607	82	253	11	242	233	9
1983	1,070	302	768	665	103	267	8	259	253	6
1984	1,021	265	756	668	88	280	12	267	242	25
1985	1,091	297	794	722	72	306	11	296	268	28
1986	1,166	300	866	771	95	300	20	280	259	21
1987	1,112	271	841	745	96	351	18	333	304	29
1988	1,167	304	863	743	120	319	10	309	291	18
1989	1,068	282	786	725	61	320	15	304	284	20
1990	1,188	304	884	779	105	388	22	366	332	34
1991	1,189	328	861	752	109	460	33	427	393	34
1992	1,296	351	944	851	93	507	41	465	413	52
1993 [2]	1,326	337	989	878	112	563	35	528	472	56
1994	1,443	402	1,041	925	116	561	24	536	470	66
1995	1,371	296	1,075	940	135	524	20	504	458	46
1996	1,413	327	1,086	955	131	448	15	433	400	33
1997	1,509	353	1,156	988	168	497	26	471	411	60

See notes at end of table.

Household and Family Characteristics

TABLE 1.10. PARENT/CHILD SITUATIONS, BY RACE AND HISPANIC ORIGIN OF HOUSEHOLDER OR REFERENCE PERSON, 1970 TO 1997 - Continued
(In thousands)

YEAR	All family groups					Maintain own household (Family households)				
	Total with own children under 18	2-parent	1-parent			Total with own children under 18	2-parent	1-parent		
			Total	Maintained by				Total	Maintained by	
				Mother	Father				Mother	Father
BLACK										
1970	3,219	2,071	1,148	1,063	85	....	....	....	....	....
1980 [1]	4,074	1,961	2,114	1,984	129	3,820	1,927	1,892	1,793	99
1981	4,172	1,981	2,191	2,041	150	3,873	1,938	1,934	1,823	111
1982	4,521	2,029	2,491	2,365	126	3,918	2,003	1,914	1,821	93
1983	4,699	1,946	2,752	2,583	169	3,890	1,901	1,989	1,862	127
1984	4,744	1,934	2,809	2,652	157	3,918	1,876	2,042	1,913	129
1985	4,659	1,856	2,802	2,641	160	3,891	1,822	2,068	1,942	126
1986	4,772	2,022	2,752	2,597	155	4,059	1,997	2,063	1,934	129
1987	4,963	2,059	2,904	2,747	157	4,184	2,023	2,161	2,025	136
1988	5,057	2,055	3,003	2,812	191	4,195	2,016	2,180	2,020	160
1989	5,148	2,005	3,143	2,905	238	4,332	1,969	2,362	2,170	192
1990	5,087	2,006	3,081	2,860	221	4,378	1,972	2,405	2,232	173
1991	5,173	1,933	3,240	3,000	239	4,380	1,884	2,496	2,294	202
1992	5,164	1,948	3,216	2,994	221	4,445	1,926	2,519	2,335	184
1993 [2]	5,364	1,987	3,377	3,135	242	4,560	1,945	2,616	2,434	182
1994	5,614	1,978	3,636	3,350	287	4,793	1,924	2,868	2,630	238
1995	5,491	1,962	3,529	3,197	332	4,682	1,926	2,756	2,489	267
1996	5,434	1,942	3,493	3,171	322	4,583	1,901	2,682	2,404	278
1997	5,679	2,020	3,659	3,268	391	4,886	1,974	2,913	2,594	319
HISPANIC ORIGIN [3]										
1970	....	....	....	....	....	....	....	....	....	....
1980 [1]	2,194	1,626	568	526	42	2,083	1,589	494	458	36
1981	2,396	1,718	678	605	73	2,260	1,671	589	527	62
1982	2,456	1,734	722	666	56	2,272	1,676	596	553	44
1983	2,525	1,758	766	702	64	2,306	1,694	612	559	53
1984	2,674	1,867	807	740	67	2,415	1,791	624	571	53
1985	2,848	1,962	886	802	84	2,602	1,892	710	642	68
1986	3,043	2,057	987	881	106	2,755	1,987	769	684	85
1987	3,165	2,115	1,051	927	124	2,859	2,034	825	729	96
1988	3,321	2,205	1,116	977	139	2,991	2,123	868	754	114
1989	3,382	2,315	1,067	960	107	3,096	2,234	862	766	96
1990	3,429	2,289	1,140	1,003	138	3,051	2,188	863	745	118
1991	3,582	2,395	1,187	1,029	158	3,203	2,273	930	799	131
1992	3,771	2,473	1,298	1,112	186	3,333	2,321	1,012	853	159
1993 [2]	3,838	2,494	1,344	1,157	187	3,345	2,355	990	830	160
1994	4,369	2,786	1,583	1,364	219	3,790	2,609	1,181	1,006	175
1995	4,525	2,879	1,646	1,404	243	3,984	2,743	1,240	1,048	192
1996	4,560	2,858	1,702	1,483	219	4,048	2,731	1,317	1,138	179
1997	4,870	3,115	1,756	1,500	256	4,305	2,962	1,342	1,138	204

See notes at end of table.

Household and Family Characteristics

	All family groups									
	Do not maintain own household									
	Related to householder (Related subfamilies)					Unrelated to householder (Unrelated subfamilies)				
YEAR	Total with own children under 18	2-parent	1-parent			Total with own children under 18	2-parent	1-parent		
			Total	Maintained by				Total	Maintained by	
				Mother	Father				Mother	Father
BLACK										
1970	235	72	163	151	12	....	....	....	....	....
1980 [1]	203	30	174	153	21	51	4	47	38	9
1981	254	43	249	179	70	45	0	45	39	6
1982	560	26	534	505	29	43	0	43	39	4
1983	745	45	700	660	40	64	0	63	61	2
1984	744	56	687	665	22	82	2	80	74	6
1985	703	32	671	639	32	65	2	62	60	2
1986	641	23	619	593	26	72	2	70	70	0
1987	717	35	682	661	21	62	0	61	61	0
1988	766	39	727	701	26	96	0	96	91	5
1989	713	36	677	637	40	103	0	103	97	6
1990	629	33	596	557	39	80	1	80	71	9
1991	689	46	644	614	30	103	3	99	92	7
1992	621	21	600	564	36	98	1	97	96	1
1993 [2]	719	39	680	632	49	84	3	82	69	12
1994	735	52	683	644	40	87	2	84	76	9
1995	729	34	695	642	52	80	2	79	66	13
1996	767	38	729	691	38	84	2	82	76	6
1997	713	46	667	607	60	80	0	80	67	13
HISPANIC ORIGIN [3]										
1970	....	....	....	....	....	....	....	....	....	....
1980 [1]	83	33	50	45	5	28	4	24	23	1
1981	110	46	63	58	5	27	1	26	20	6
1982	153	57	96	87	9	31	1	29	26	3
1983	188	61	127	117	10	32	4	27	26	1
1984	229	73	155	143	12	30	3	27	26	1
1985	215	66	149	134	15	31	4	27	26	1
1986	246	64	182	161	21	42	6	36	36	0
1987	258	68	190	167	23	48	13	36	31	5
1988	291	77	214	193	21	39	5	34	30	4
1989	256	79	177	166	11	31	2	29	28	1
1990	308	86	222	207	16	70	15	55	51	4
1991	304	103	201	178	23	74	19	55	52	3
1992	354	128	226	206	20	85	24	60	53	7
1993 [2]	382	120	262	242	20	110	18	92	85	7
1994	444	154	290	258	32	135	23	112	100	12
1995	448	123	325	277	48	95	13	82	79	3
1996	437	124	312	277	35	74	3	71	67	4
1997	477	137	340	297	43	88	15	72	64	8

TABLE 1.10. PARENT/CHILD SITUATIONS, BY RACE AND HISPANIC ORIGIN OF HOUSEHOLDER OR REFERENCE PERSON, 1970 TO 1997 - Continued (In thousands)

Source: U.S. Bureau of the Census, Current Population Survey - March Supplement.

As of March.
(1) Uses population controls based on the 1980 Census.
(2) Unrevised. Uses population controls based on the 1980 Census.
(3) Persons of Hispanic origin may be of any race.

Household and Family Characteristics

YEAR	TABLE 1.11. UNMARRIED-COUPLE HOUSEHOLDS, BY PRESENCE OF CHILDREN UNDER 15 YEARS OLD: 1977 TO 1997 (In thousands)		
	Total	Without children under 15 years old	With children under 15 years old
1977	957	754	204
1978	1,137	865	272
1979	1,346	985	360
1980	1,589	1,159	431
1981	1,808	1,305	502
1982	1,863	1,387	475
1983	1,891	1,366	525
1984	1,988	1,373	614
1985	1,983	1,380	603
1986	2,220	1,558	662
1987	2,334	1,614	720
1988	2,588	1,786	802
1989	2,764	1,906	858
1990	2,856	1,966	891
1991	3,039	2,077	962
1992	3,308	2,187	1,121
1993	3,510	2,274	1,236
1994	3,661	2,391	1,270
1995	3,668	2,349	1,319
1996	3,958	2,516	1,442
1997	4,130	2,660	1,470

Source: U.S. Bureau of the Census, Current Population Survey - March Supplement.

As of March.

Household and Family Characteristics

TABLE 1.12. YOUNG ADULTS LIVING AT HOME BY AGE AND SEX: 1981 TO 1997
(In thousands)

YEAR	Male				Female			
	18-24 years old		25-34 years old		18-24 years old		25-34 years old	
	Total in age group	Living at home, child of householder	Total in age group	Living at home, child of householder	Total in age group	Living at home, child of householder	Total in age group	Living at home, child of householder
1981	14,367	....	18,625	....	14,848	....	19,203	....
1982	14,368	....	19,090	....	14,815	....	19,614	....
1983	14,344	8,803	19,438	2,664	14,702	7,001	19,903	1,520
1984	14,196	8,764	19,876	2,626	14,482	6,779	20,297	1,548
1985	13,695	8,172	20,184	2,685	14,149	6,758	20,673	1,661
1986	13,324	7,831	20,956	2,981	13,787	6,433	21,097	1,686
1987	13,029	7,981	21,142	3,071	13,433	6,375	21,494	1,655
1988	12,835	7,792	21,320	3,207	13,226	6,398	21,649	1,791
1989	12,574	7,308	21,461	3,130	13,055	6,141	21,777	1,728
1990	12,450	7,232	21,462	3,213	12,860	6,135	21,779	1,774
1991	12,275	7,385	21,319	3,172	12,627	6,163	21,586	1,887
1992	12,083	7,296	21,125	3,225	12,351	5,929	21,368	1,874
1993	12,049	7,145	20,856	3,300	12,260	5,746	21,007	1,844
1994	12,683	7,547	20,873	3,261	12,792	5,924	21,073	1,859
1995	12,545	7,328	20,589	3,166	12,613	5,896	20,800	1,759
1996	12,402	7,327	20,390	3,213	12,441	5,955	20,528	1,810
1997	12,534	7,501	20,039	2,909	12,452	6,006	20,217	1,745

Source: U.S. Bureau of the Census, Current Population Survey - March Supplement.

As of March.
Unmarried college students living in dormitories are counted as living in their parent(s) home.

Household and Family Characteristics

TABLE 1.13. MARITAL STATUS OF THE POPULATION AGE 15 AND OLDER BY SEX AND RACE: 1950 TO 1997
(In thousands)

YEAR AND RACE	Males						Females					
	Total	Married	Unmarried				Total	Married	Unmarried			
			Total	Never married	Widowed	Divorced			Total	Never married	Widowed	Divorced
ALL RACES												
1950 [1]	54,601	36,866	17,735	14,400	2,264	1,071	57,102	37,577	19,525	11,418	6,734	1,373
1960 [1]	60,273	41,781	18,492	15,274	2,112	1,106	64,607	42,583	22,024	12,252	8,064	1,708
1970	70,559	47,109	23,450	19,832	2,051	1,567	77,766	48,148	29,618	17,167	9,734	2,717
1980	81,947	51,813	30,134	24,227	1,977	3,930	89,914	52,965	36,950	20,226	10,758	5,966
1990	91,955	55,833	36,121	27,505	2,333	6,283	99,838	56,797	43,040	22,718	11,477	8,845
1993	94,854	56,833	38,021	28,775	2,468	6,778	102,400	57,768	44,631	23,534	11,214	9,883
1994	96,768	57,068	39,700	30,228	2,222	7,250	104,032	58,185	45,847	24,645	11,073	10,129
1995	97,704	57,750	39,953	30,286	2,284	7,383	105,028	58,984	46,045	24,693	11,082	10,270
1996	98,593	57,656	40,937	30,691	2,478	7,768	106,031	58,905	47,127	25,528	11,078	10,521
1997	100,159	57,923	42,236	31,315	2,690	8,231	107,076	58,829	48,247	26,073	11,058	11,116
WHITE												
1950 [1]	49,302	33,451	15,850	12,892	1,986	972	51,404	34,042	17,362	10,241	5,902	1,219
1960 [1]	54,130	38,042	16,088	13,286	1,816	986	57,860	38,545	19,315	10,796	7,099	1,420
1970	62,868	42,732	20,135	17,080	1,722	1,333	68,888	43,286	25,602	14,703	8,559	2,340
1980	71,887	46,721	25,167	20,174	1,642	3,351	77,882	47,277	30,604	16,318	9,296	4,990
1990	78,908	49,542	29,367	22,078	1,930	5,359	84,508	49,986	34,522	17,438	9,800	7,284
1993	80,755	50,305	30,451	22,738	1,954	5,759	86,045	50,668	35,377	17,660	9,512	8,205
1994	82,026	50,226	31,800	23,704	1,878	6,218	86,765	50,766	36,000	18,235	9,424	8,341
1995	82,566	50,658	31,909	23,667	1,921	6,321	87,484	51,390	36,094	18,250	9,399	8,445
1996	83,463	50,882	32,581	23,894	2,128	6,559	88,134	51,388	36,745	18,691	9,392	8,662
1997	84,540	50,860	33,680	24,471	2,264	6,945	88,756	50,987	37,769	19,139	9,404	9,226
BLACK												
1950 [1]	5,299	3,415	1,885	1,508	278	99	5,698	3,534	2,164	1,178	832	154
1960 [1]	6,143	3,739	2,404	1,988	296	120	6,747	4,038	2,709	1,456	965	288
1970	6,936	3,949	2,987	2,468	307	212	8,108	4,384	3,723	2,248	1,120	355
1980	8,292	4,053	4,239	3,410	308	521	10,108	4,508	5,600	3,401	1,319	880
1990	9,948	4,489	5,459	4,319	338	802	11,966	4,813	7,152	4,416	1,392	1,344
1993	10,442	4,431	6,012	4,750	426	836	12,495	4,820	7,676	4,867	1,401	1,408
1994	10,639	4,486	6,153	5,007	295	851	12,872	4,863	8,009	5,190	1,322	1,497
1995	10,825	4,632	6,193	5,031	310	852	13,097	4,942	8,155	5,250	1,380	1,525
1996	10,922	4,515	6,407	5,115	277	1,015	13,292	4,947	8,345	5,451	1,330	1,564
1997	11,113	4,623	6,491	5,137	340	1,014	13,514	5,058	8,457	5,584	1,307	1,566

Source: U.S. Bureau of the Census, Current Population Survey - March Supplement.

As of March.

(1) 1950 and 1960 data are for the population 14 years old and over. In these years, the category "Black" includes all nonwhites.

Household and Family Characteristics

YEAR	TABLE 1.14. MEDIAN AGE AT FIRST MARRIAGE BY SEX: 1947 TO 1997 (Years)	
	Men	Women
1947	23.7	20.5
1948	23.3	20.4
1949	22.7	20.3
1950	22.8	20.3
1951	22.9	20.4
1952	23.0	20.2
1953	22.8	20.2
1954	23.0	20.3
1955	22.6	20.2
1956	22.5	20.1
1957	22.6	20.3
1958	22.6	20.2
1959	22.5	20.2
1960	22.8	20.3
1961	22.8	20.3
1962	22.7	20.3
1963	22.8	20.5
1964	23.1	20.5
1965	22.8	20.6
1966	22.8	20.5
1967	23.1	20.6
1968	23.1	20.8
1969	23.2	20.8
1970	23.2	20.8
1971	23.1	20.9
1972	23.3	20.9
1973	23.2	21.0
1974	23.1	21.1
1975	23.5	21.1
1976	23.8	21.3
1977	24.0	21.6
1978	24.2	21.8
1979	24.4	22.1
1980	24.7	22.0
1981	24.8	22.3
1982	25.2	22.5
1983	25.4	22.8
1984	25.4	23.0
1985	25.5	23.3
1986	25.7	23.1
1987	25.8	23.6
1988	25.9	23.6
1989	26.2	23.8
1990	26.1	23.9
1991	26.3	24.1
1992	26.5	24.4
1993	26.5	24.5
1994	26.7	24.5
1995	26.9	24.5
1996	27.1	24.8
1997	26.8	25.0

Source: U.S. Bureau of the Census, Current Population Survey - March Supplement.

The median age at first marriage is an approximation derived indirectly from tabulations of marital status and age. See Appendix A definition of "age at first marriage" for additional explanation.

Household and Family Characteristics

TABLE 1.15. LIVING ARRANGEMENTS OF CHILDREN UNDER 18 YEARS OLD: 1968 TO 1997
(In thousands)

YEAR	Total children under 18	Living with 2 parents	Living with 1 parent Total	Mother only Total	Divorced	Married, spouse absent	Widowed	Never married	Father only Total	Divorced	Married, spouse absent	Widowed	Never married	Living with other relatives	Living with non-relatives only
1968	70,326	60,030	8,332	7,556	2,053	3,422	1,616	465	776	178	310	249	39	1,660	304
1969	70,317	59,857	8,509	7,744	2,056	3,700	1,539	441	765	218	277	245	28	1,602	349
1970	70,213	59,694	8,438	7,678	2,338	3,351	1,421	565	760	168	301	262	32	1,599	482
1970 r	69,162	58,939	8,199	7,452	2,296	3,234	1,395	527	748	177	287	254	30	1,547	477
1971	70,255	58,606	9,478	8,714	2,622	3,866	1,449	773	764	158	310	257	37	1,707	464
1972	68,811	57,201	9,634	8,838	2,799	3,901	1,506	632	796	218	304	263	12	1,593	383
1973	67,950	55,807	10,093	9,272	3,103	3,745	1,533	892	821	273	262	252	24	1,629	421
1974	67,047	54,561	10,489	9,647	3,278	3,789	1,614	966	842	313	244	259	20	1,532	465
1975	66,087	53,072	11,243	10,231	3,644	3,857	1,565	1,166	1,014	388	381	212	32	1,409	363
1976	65,129	52,101	11,121	10,310	4,017	3,797	1,357	1,139	811	390	229	174	18	1,500	407
1977	64,062	50,735	11,311	10,419	4,211	3,618	1,255	1,335	892	372	214	272	33	1,626	390
1978	63,206	49,132	11,711	10,725	4,335	3,509	1,250	1,633	985	417	285	211	72	1,940	423
1979	62,389	48,295	11,529	10,531	4,259	3,487	1,241	1,544	997	493	305	136	63	2,142	423
1980	61,744	47,286	12,162	11,131	4,630	3,519	1,260	1,721	1,031	503	281	172	75	1,912	384
1980 r	63,427	48,624	12,466	11,406	4,766	3,610	1,286	1,745	1,060	515	288	183	75	1,949	388
1981	62,918	48,040	12,619	11,416	4,912	3,540	1,158	1,807	1,203	614	296	181	112	1,911	348
1982 [1]	62,407	46,797	13,702	12,512	5,103	3,518	1,123	2,768	1,189	658	273	144	114	1,556	352
1983 [1]	62,281	46,632	14,006	12,739	5,190	3,334	1,004	3,212	1,267	691	306	116	154	1,349	294
1984	62,139	46,555	14,025	12,646	5,167	3,423	925	3,131	1,378	716	289	144	229	1,226	333
1985	62,475	46,149	14,635	13,081	5,280	3,367	939	3,496	1,554	750	383	162	260	1,339	352
1986	62,763	46,384	14,759	13,180	5,350	3,322	902	3,606	1,579	796	321	145	318	1,348	272
1987	62,932	46,009	15,071	13,420	5,325	3,288	821	3,985	1,651	814	432	95	310	1,484	368
1988	63,179	45,942	15,329	13,521	5,010	3,371	838	4,302	1,808	861	443	132	371	1,516	392
1989	63,637	46,549	15,493	13,700	5,227	3,380	803	4,290	1,793	803	307	182	501	1,341	254
1990	64,137	46,503	15,867	13,874	5,118	3,416	975	4,365	1,993	1,004	351	150	488	1,421	346
1991	65,093	46,658	16,624	14,608	5,206	3,583	780	5,040	2,016	916	462	110	528	1,428	383
1992	65,965	46,638	17,578	15,396	5,507	3,790	688	5,410	2,182	932	491	165	594	1,334	415
1993	66,893	47,181	17,872	15,586	5,687	3,739	649	5,511	2,286	950	475	114	747	1,442	398
1994	69,508	48,084	18,590	16,334	5,799	3,838	696	6,000	2,257	1,077	411	113	655	2,150	684
1995	70,254	48,276	18,938	16,477	6,019	3,901	695	5,862	2,461	1,182	447	135	696	2,352	688
1996	70,908	48,224	19,752	16,993	6,039	3,927	662	6,365	2,759	1,276	526	120	837	2,137	795
1997	70,983	48,386	19,799	16,740	5,824	3,751	566	6,598	3,059	1,380	596	127	955	1,983	815

Source: U.S. Bureau of the Census, Current Population Survey - March Supplement.

As of March.
Excludes householders, subfamily reference persons, and their spouses. Also excludes inmates of institutions.
(r) Revised using population controls based on the decennial census for that year.
(1) Introduction of improved data collection and processing procedures that helped to identify parent-child subfamilies.

Household Projections

YEAR AND AGE OF HOUSEHOLDER	Total households	Family households					Nonfamily households		
		Total	Married couples without children under 18 at home	Married couples with children under 18 at home	Lone parents with children under 18 at home	Other family types	Total	Single person	2 or more persons

TABLE 1.16. PROJECTED HOUSEHOLDS BY AGE OF HOUSEHOLDER AND HOUSEHOLD TYPE: 1995 TO 2010

YEAR AND AGE OF HOUSEHOLDER	Total households	Total	Married couples without children under 18 at home	Married couples with children under 18 at home	Lone parents with children under 18 at home	Other family types	Total	Single person	2 or more persons
1995									
15 to 24 years old	4,843,838	2,577,720	613,497	752,694	894,985	316,544	2,266,118	1,145,069	1,121,049
25 to 34	19,027,180	13,705,518	2,715,063	7,329,711	3,149,528	511,216	5,321,662	3,616,601	1,705,061
35 to 44	23,106,397	18,323,412	2,543,290	11,413,653	3,543,748	822,721	4,782,985	3,774,732	1,008,253
45 to 54	17,972,538	13,939,807	6,530,800	4,778,566	1,052,455	1,577,986	4,032,731	3,489,522	543,209
55 to 64	12,605,829	9,104,602	7,116,157	614,561	141,121	1,232,763	3,501,227	3,207,474	293,753
65 to 74	12,068,559	7,369,133	6,138,488	115,695	22,844	1,092,106	4,699,426	4,531,656	167,770
75 or older	9,575,858	4,019,733	3,153,883	3,618	7,637	854,595	5,556,125	5,433,335	122,790
All ages	99,200,199	69,039,925	28,811,178	25,008,498	8,812,318	6,407,931	30,160,274	25,198,389	4,961,885
2000									
15 to 24 years old	4,942,536	2,635,709	627,299	769,627	935,676	303,107	2,306,827	1,164,948	1,141,879
25 to 34	17,434,244	12,555,730	2,486,035	6,717,315	3,013,375	339,005	4,878,514	3,317,390	1,561,124
35 to 44	24,096,670	19,227,942	2,672,684	11,979,008	3,845,588	730,662	4,868,728	3,841,426	1,027,302
45 to 54	21,325,053	16,204,934	7,600,114	5,558,292	1,215,370	1,831,158	5,120,119	4,428,903	691,216
55 to 64	14,483,140	10,122,112	7,915,491	688,304	151,832	1,366,485	4,361,028	3,994,702	366,326
65 to 74	11,713,638	6,962,338	5,799,628	111,397	20,887	1,030,426	4,751,300	4,580,253	171,047
75 or older	10,741,248	4,508,672	3,539,308	4,509	9,017	955,838	6,232,576	6,095,459	137,117
All ages	104,736,529	72,217,437	30,640,559	25,828,452	9,191,745	6,556,681	32,519,092	27,423,081	5,096,011
2005									
15 to 24 years old	5,398,605	2,885,192	686,676	842,476	1,038,669	317,371	2,513,413	1,269,274	1,244,139
25 to 34	16,971,689	12,189,400	2,413,501	6,521,329	2,986,403	268,167	4,782,289	3,251,957	1,530,332
35 to 44	22,802,618	18,254,326	2,537,351	11,372,445	3,742,137	602,393	4,548,292	3,588,602	959,690
45 to 54	23,734,625	17,918,912	8,403,970	6,146,187	1,343,918	2,024,837	5,815,713	5,030,592	785,121
55 to 64	17,998,118	12,301,627	9,619,872	836,511	184,524	1,660,720	5,696,491	5,217,986	478,505
65 to 74	11,951,680	6,942,530	5,783,128	111,080	20,828	1,027,494	5,009,150	4,828,821	180,329
75 or older	11,533,104	4,841,056	3,800,229	4,841	9,682	1,026,304	6,692,048	6,544,823	147,225
All ages	110,390,439	75,333,043	33,244,727	25,834,869	9,326,161	6,927,286	35,057,396	29,732,055	5,325,341
2010									
15 to 24 years old	5,704,505	3,048,545	725,554	890,175	1,097,476	335,340	2,655,960	1,341,260	1,314,700
25 to 34	17,848,206	12,788,475	2,532,118	6,841,834	3,197,119	217,404	5,059,731	3,440,617	1,619,114
35 to 44	20,858,312	16,707,832	2,322,389	10,408,979	3,508,645	467,819	4,150,480	3,274,729	875,751
45 to 54	24,869,562	18,777,104	8,806,461	6,440,547	1,408,283	2,121,813	6,092,458	5,269,976	822,482
55 to 64	21,426,387	14,505,069	11,342,964	986,345	217,576	1,958,184	6,921,318	6,339,927	581,391
65 to 74	13,745,500	7,898,406	6,579,373	126,374	23,695	1,168,964	5,847,094	5,636,599	210,495
75 or older	11,891,448	4,991,472	3,913,314	4,991	9,983	1,063,184	6,899,976	6,748,177	151,799
All ages	116,343,920	78,716,903	36,222,173	25,699,245	9,462,777	7,332,708	37,627,017	32,051,285	5,575,732

Source: Masnick, George S., Nancy McArdle, and William C. Apgar, Jr. "U.S. Household Trends: The 1990s and Beyond." Joint Center for Housing Studies of Harvard University. July 1996.

Household Projections

		Family households				Nonfamily households			Average number of persons	
YEAR AND SERIES	All households	Total	Married couple	Other family		Total	Female householder	Male householder	Per house-hold	Per family
				Female householder	Male householder					

TABLE 1.17. PROJECTED HOUSEHOLDS BY HOUSEHOLD TYPE: 1995 TO 2010

YEAR AND SERIES	All households	Total	Married couple	Female householder	Male householder	Total	Female householder	Male householder	Per house-hold	Per family
SERIES ONE [1]										
1995	97,722,883	68,382,680	53,432,915	11,438,681	3,511,084	29,340,203	16,084,937	13,255,266	2.62	3.15
1996	98,856,603	69,089,808	53,893,439	11,606,809	3,589,560	29,766,795	16,269,403	13,497,392	2.61	3.14
1997	99,965,175	69,760,723	54,319,173	11,773,519	3,668,031	30,204,452	16,463,794	13,740,658	2.61	3.14
1998	101,042,864	70,387,012	54,707,260	11,934,856	3,744,896	30,655,852	16,670,950	13,984,902	2.60	3.13
1999	102,118,600	71,014,836	55,091,779	12,100,606	3,822,451	31,103,764	16,875,311	14,228,453	2.60	3.13
2000	103,245,963	71,668,930	55,495,517	12,272,004	3,901,409	31,577,033	17,094,590	14,482,443	2.59	3.12
2001	104,344,445	72,310,665	55,885,976	12,446,308	3,978,381	32,033,780	17,304,585	14,729,195	2.59	3.11
2002	105,456,124	72,917,696	56,266,221	12,599,164	4,052,311	32,538,428	17,549,113	14,989,315	2.58	3.11
2003	106,566,127	73,511,099	56,626,719	12,757,287	4,127,093	33,055,028	17,801,273	15,253,755	2.58	3.10
2004	107,672,899	74,107,904	56,988,327	12,917,753	4,201,824	33,564,995	18,048,628	15,516,367	2.57	3.09
2005	108,818,659	74,732,880	57,370,994	13,083,981	4,277,905	34,085,779	18,301,408	15,784,371	2.57	3.09
2006	109,981,970	75,361,827	57,755,561	13,251,031	4,355,235	34,620,143	18,561,511	16,058,632	2.56	3.08
2007	111,162,259	75,997,067	58,147,607	13,418,598	4,430,862	35,165,192	18,828,993	16,336,199	2.55	3.07
2008	112,362,848	76,615,834	58,527,251	13,582,132	4,506,451	35,747,014	19,119,565	16,627,449	2.55	3.07
2009	113,567,967	77,241,400	58,908,384	13,751,082	4,581,934	36,326,567	19,405,806	16,920,761	2.54	3.06
2010	114,825,428	77,894,830	59,308,021	13,926,532	4,660,277	36,930,598	19,702,084	17,228,514	2.53	3.05
SERIES TWO [2]										
1995	97,694,760	68,837,033	54,267,416	11,154,518	3,415,099	28,857,727	15,913,381	12,944,346	2.62	3.14
1996	98,801,180	69,642,938	54,926,039	11,248,424	3,468,475	29,158,242	16,053,245	13,104,997	2.62	3.14
1997	99,879,980	70,413,821	55,553,244	11,339,611	3,520,966	29,466,159	16,201,540	13,264,619	2.61	3.13
1998	100,924,490	71,140,587	56,145,060	11,424,475	3,571,052	29,783,903	16,360,945	13,422,958	2.61	3.13
1999	101,965,560	71,870,306	56,736,808	11,512,401	3,621,097	30,095,254	16,516,369	13,578,885	2.60	3.12
2000	103,057,635	72,627,721	57,350,917	11,604,767	3,672,037	30,429,914	16,686,075	13,743,839	2.60	3.12
2001	104,119,045	73,374,380	57,955,355	11,698,670	3,720,355	30,744,665	16,845,060	13,899,605	2.59	3.11
2002	105,189,833	74,089,499	58,553,140	11,771,580	3,764,779	31,100,334	17,035,496	14,064,838	2.59	3.10
2003	106,259,988	74,792,966	59,134,015	11,849,247	3,809,704	31,467,022	17,233,314	14,233,708	2.58	3.10
2004	107,324,286	75,501,804	59,720,229	11,927,775	3,853,800	31,822,482	17,424,375	14,398,107	2.58	3.09
2005	108,425,541	76,240,892	60,331,974	12,010,490	3,898,428	32,184,649	17,619,226	14,565,423	2.57	3.09
2006	109,542,588	76,985,707	60,948,962	12,093,094	3,943,651	32,556,881	17,820,103	14,736,778	2.57	3.08
2007	110,675,857	77,737,669	61,574,606	12,175,879	3,987,184	32,938,188	18,027,943	14,910,245	2.56	3.08
2008	111,833,083	78,471,219	62,183,689	12,255,980	4,031,550	33,361,864	18,262,171	15,099,693	2.56	3.07
2009	112,991,763	79,215,583	62,800,539	12,340,240	4,074,804	33,776,180	18,488,895	15,287,285	2.55	3.07
2010	114,199,622	79,990,044	63,441,719	12,428,486	4,119,839	34,209,578	18,723,493	15,486,085	2.55	3.06
SERIES THREE [3]										
1995	97,574,189	68,872,603	54,064,426	11,336,429	3,471,748	28,701,586	15,799,625	12,901,961	2.62	3.14
1996	98,641,315	69,674,088	54,674,787	11,463,777	3,535,524	28,967,227	15,914,198	13,053,029	2.62	3.14
1997	99,680,030	70,439,696	55,252,827	11,588,373	3,598,496	29,240,334	16,037,537	13,202,797	2.62	3.13
1998	100,683,716	71,161,368	55,795,398	11,706,994	3,658,976	29,522,348	16,171,073	13,351,275	2.61	3.13
1999	101,683,469	71,885,581	56,338,766	11,827,365	3,719,450	29,797,888	16,300,363	13,497,525	2.61	3.12
2000	102,734,349	72,637,651	56,904,364	11,952,311	3,780,976	30,096,698	16,443,281	13,653,417	2.61	3.12
2001	103,754,014	73,378,966	57,461,517	12,077,637	3,839,812	30,375,048	16,574,784	13,800,264	2.60	3.11
2002	104,784,362	74,090,082	58,010,418	12,184,607	3,895,057	30,694,280	16,737,426	13,956,854	2.60	3.11
2003	105,813,805	74,789,113	58,543,186	12,295,128	3,950,799	31,024,692	16,907,152	14,117,540	2.60	3.10
2004	106,835,305	75,493,071	59,080,407	12,406,575	4,006,089	31,342,234	17,069,178	14,273,056	2.59	3.10
2005	107,892,079	76,227,200	59,642,441	12,522,567	4,062,192	31,664,879	17,233,807	14,431,072	2.59	3.09
2006	108,963,276	76,967,698	60,209,569	12,638,983	4,119,146	31,995,578	17,403,252	14,592,326	2.58	3.09
2007	110,051,064	77,716,383	60,784,900	12,756,689	4,174,794	32,334,681	17,579,493	14,755,188	2.58	3.08
2008	111,161,226	78,446,730	61,342,277	12,872,767	4,231,686	32,714,496	17,780,666	14,933,830	2.57	3.07
2009	112,270,638	79,187,519	61,906,394	12,993,258	4,287,867	33,083,119	17,973,497	15,109,622	2.57	3.07
2010	113,425,776	79,957,976	62,494,303	13,117,622	4,346,051	33,467,800	18,172,225	15,295,575	2.56	3.06

Source: Day, Jennifer Cheeseman. 1996. "Projections of the Number of Households and Families in the United States: 1995 to 2010." U.S. Bureau of the Census, Current Population Reports P25-1129.

As of July 1.

(1) Series 1 is the preferred series, based on a time-series model that projects trends by age and sex in the proportions of persons maintaining households of different types. Series 1 also reflects the effects of projected changes in the age/sex structure of the population.

(2) Series 2 reflects the consequences of projected changes in the age/sex structure of the population only, assuming that household formation propensities by age/sex hold constant at 1990 levels.

(3) Series 3 reflects the consequences of projected changes in both the age/sex structure and the racial/Hispanic origin composition of the population. Series 3 assumes that household formation propensities hold constant at 1990 levels by age/sex and race/Hispanic origin.

See Appendix A for additional discussion of the projections.

Household Projections

TABLE 1.18. PROJECTED HOUSEHOLDS BY AGE OF HOUSEHOLDER: 1995 TO 2010

YEAR AND SERIES	All households	Age of householder (Years)							
		Under 25	25-29	30-34	35-44	45-54	55-64	65-74	75 and older
SERIES ONE [1]									
1995	97,722,883	4,826,422	7,954,321	10,828,763	22,756,496	17,722,949	12,330,779	11,849,494	9,453,659
1996	98,856,603	4,712,158	7,957,658	10,570,450	23,183,301	18,449,029	12,464,083	11,796,570	9,723,354
1997	99,965,175	4,699,653	7,889,119	10,270,289	23,516,798	19,179,155	12,735,252	11,681,972	9,992,937
1998	101,042,864	4,757,876	7,768,887	9,976,774	23,766,619	19,727,324	13,236,547	11,587,631	10,221,206
1999	102,118,600	4,853,767	7,593,297	9,742,411	23,915,505	20,433,561	13,658,068	11,475,046	10,446,945
2000	103,245,963	4,966,404	7,411,228	9,633,941	23,913,799	21,209,525	14,001,868	11,446,183	10,663,015
2001	104,344,445	5,091,884	7,203,807	9,639,162	23,777,022	22,056,714	14,318,251	11,421,208	10,836,397
2002	105,456,124	5,189,858	7,168,063	9,559,421	23,487,486	22,407,059	15,239,967	11,398,805	11,005,465
2003	106,566,127	5,289,788	7,228,437	9,418,921	23,150,516	22,916,971	15,949,721	11,424,493	11,187,280
2004	107,672,899	5,354,326	7,371,091	9,212,378	22,846,544	23,420,242	16,642,660	11,502,174	11,323,484
2005	108,818,659	5,398,630	7,550,822	8,995,778	22,560,079	23,923,589	17,330,619	11,597,383	11,461,759
2006	109,981,970	5,449,415	7,752,912	8,747,893	22,283,210	24,395,069	18,022,922	11,755,606	11,574,943
2007	111,162,259	5,489,105	7,927,473	8,707,514	21,870,697	24,775,404	18,720,412	12,037,184	11,634,170
2008	112,362,848	5,546,979	8,092,081	8,783,114	21,398,771	25,062,402	19,256,448	12,541,726	11,681,327
2009	113,567,967	5,638,503	8,189,724	8,952,431	20,925,955	25,249,350	19,941,012	12,953,459	11,717,533
2010	114,825,428	5,724,185	8,258,199	9,167,335	20,580,708	25,282,625	20,693,054	13,298,052	11,821,270
SERIES TWO [2]									
1995	97,694,760	4,839,877	7,947,380	10,825,237	22,756,202	17,656,603	12,304,625	11,885,057	9,479,779
1996	98,801,180	4,730,651	7,949,708	10,564,339	23,172,536	18,352,454	12,431,695	11,843,038	9,756,759
1997	99,879,980	4,723,210	7,880,110	10,261,565	23,495,708	19,050,252	12,696,281	11,738,880	10,033,974
1998	100,924,490	4,786,633	7,758,503	9,965,251	23,734,779	19,564,860	13,189,900	11,654,603	10,269,961
1999	101,965,560	4,887,902	7,581,550	9,728,206	23,873,654	20,234,764	13,603,900	11,551,791	10,503,793
2000	103,057,635	5,006,074	7,398,260	9,616,885	23,862,604	20,971,995	13,940,525	11,533,100	10,728,192
2001	104,119,045	5,137,241	7,189,713	9,618,940	23,717,457	21,777,554	14,249,859	11,518,282	10,909,999
2002	105,189,833	5,240,542	7,151,977	9,535,600	23,418,612	22,089,398	15,160,747	11,505,496	11,087,461
2003	106,259,988	5,345,893	7,210,220	9,391,799	23,073,841	22,558,290	15,860,598	11,541,401	11,277,946
2004	107,324,286	5,415,522	7,350,325	9,182,005	22,762,111	23,018,878	16,543,138	11,629,747	11,422,560
2005	108,425,541	5,464,693	7,527,086	8,962,354	22,467,780	23,478,040	17,220,386	11,735,885	11,569,317
2006	109,542,588	5,520,323	7,725,893	8,711,494	22,182,840	23,904,066	17,901,366	11,905,682	11,690,924
2007	110,675,857	5,564,632	7,896,901	8,667,025	21,762,791	24,239,037	18,586,620	12,200,744	11,758,107
2008	111,833,083	5,627,209	8,057,584	8,737,802	21,283,792	24,481,147	19,111,081	12,721,441	11,813,027
2009	112,991,763	5,723,680	8,151,182	8,901,406	20,803,801	24,624,156	19,782,124	13,148,816	11,856,598
2010	114,199,622	5,813,910	8,215,285	9,109,518	20,450,337	24,615,261	20,519,070	13,508,085	11,968,156
SERIES THREE [3]									
1995	97,574,190	4,827,940	7,914,853	10,796,227	22,737,700	17,650,755	12,301,436	11,869,778	9,475,501
1996	98,641,315	4,714,516	7,911,799	10,524,664	23,145,553	18,345,867	12,426,557	11,822,740	9,749,619
1997	99,680,030	4,704,294	7,835,460	10,210,878	23,459,854	19,042,506	12,689,347	11,714,233	10,023,458
1998	100,683,716	4,766,208	7,706,663	9,906,338	23,688,894	19,556,275	13,179,429	11,625,731	10,254,178
1999	101,683,469	4,864,567	7,524,231	9,661,058	23,817,251	20,225,111	13,590,701	11,518,128	10,482,422
2000	102,734,350	4,979,425	7,335,268	9,543,842	23,794,875	20,961,103	13,924,140	11,495,219	10,700,478
2001	103,754,012	5,106,896	7,121,269	9,541,768	23,638,465	21,766,016	14,229,196	11,475,722	10,874,680
2002	104,784,363	5,205,997	7,079,986	9,454,097	23,327,754	22,078,485	15,135,461	11,458,235	11,044,348
2003	105,813,807	5,306,775	7,136,005	9,305,999	22,972,078	22,545,329	15,831,443	11,489,754	11,226,424
2004	106,835,305	5,371,601	7,271,652	9,093,962	22,648,458	23,003,558	16,511,036	11,573,498	11,361,540
2005	107,892,080	5,416,073	7,443,011	8,871,576	22,344,128	23,458,668	17,185,508	11,674,903	11,498,213
2006	108,963,277	5,467,194	7,635,313	8,617,673	22,051,068	23,879,465	17,864,302	11,839,286	11,608,976
2007	110,051,066	5,506,215	7,799,301	8,570,946	21,622,887	24,209,733	18,546,962	12,129,377	11,665,645
2008	111,161,227	5,563,222	7,951,803	8,639,652	21,137,554	24,446,422	19,069,054	12,644,357	11,709,163
2009	112,270,638	5,653,163	8,037,344	8,799,284	20,652,246	24,583,739	19,738,001	13,065,804	11,741,057
2010	113,425,775	5,735,225	8,093,729	9,002,736	20,294,196	24,568,530	20,472,792	13,418,058	11,840,509

Source: Day, Jennifer Cheeseman. 1996. "Projections of the Number of Households and Families in the United States: 1995 to 2010." U.S. Bureau of the Census, Current Population Reports P25-1129.

As of July 1.

(1) Series 1 is the preferred series, based on a time-series model that projects trends by age and sex in the proportions of persons maintaining households of different types. Series 1 also reflects the effects of projected changes in the age/sex structure of the population.
(2) Series 2 reflects the consequences of projected changes in the age/sex structure of the population only, assuming that household formation propensities by age/sex hold constant at 1990 levels.
(3) Series 3 reflects the consequences of projected changes in both the age/sex structure and the racial/Hispanic origin composition of the population. Series 3 assumes that household formation propensities hold constant at 1990 levels by age/sex and race/Hispanic origin.

See Appendix A for additional discussion of the projections.

Household Projections

TABLE 1.19. PROJECTED FAMILY HOUSEHOLDS BY FAMILY TYPE AND AGE OF HOUSEHOLDER: 1995 TO 2010

YEAR AND SERIES	Total	All family households							
		Age of householder (Years)							
		Under 25	25-29	30-34	35-44	45-54	55-64	65-74	75 and older
SERIES ONE [1]									
1995	68,382,680	2,466,451	5,186,673	8,053,888	17,937,880	14,039,208	9,059,615	7,436,769	4,202,196
1996	69,089,808	2,397,551	5,167,641	7,835,891	18,215,601	14,584,531	9,133,493	7,409,190	4,345,910
1997	69,760,723	2,381,735	5,102,267	7,588,401	18,417,974	15,130,865	9,307,380	7,343,375	4,488,726
1998	70,387,012	2,400,792	5,004,045	7,347,599	18,552,828	15,531,013	9,647,739	7,291,642	4,611,354
1999	71,014,836	2,439,602	4,871,508	7,152,111	18,607,779	16,054,163	9,926,320	7,229,464	4,733,889
2000	71,668,930	2,487,664	4,736,429	7,050,148	18,544,523	16,630,000	10,146,610	7,221,169	4,852,387
2001	72,310,665	2,541,648	4,586,794	7,032,107	18,377,502	17,259,599	10,345,509	7,214,930	4,952,576
2002	72,917,696	2,582,736	4,547,342	6,952,468	18,092,632	17,498,343	10,980,938	7,209,805	5,053,432
2003	73,511,099	2,623,887	4,569,100	6,829,438	17,772,975	17,860,688	11,457,879	7,233,905	5,163,227
2004	74,107,904	2,646,650	4,642,742	6,659,746	17,480,342	18,216,303	11,919,308	7,290,376	5,252,437
2005	74,732,880	2,660,620	4,739,414	6,484,336	17,202,411	18,570,326	12,373,944	7,356,741	5,345,088
2006	75,361,827	2,677,675	4,849,456	6,287,674	16,932,806	18,897,566	12,828,195	7,464,305	5,424,150
2007	75,997,067	2,688,903	4,941,911	6,241,130	16,561,852	19,153,193	13,281,701	7,650,784	5,477,593
2008	76,615,834	2,708,492	5,027,484	6,277,646	16,147,273	19,334,257	13,616,966	7,979,029	5,524,687
2009	77,241,400	2,745,223	5,071,408	6,381,384	15,735,282	19,438,090	14,054,984	8,246,925	5,568,104
2010	77,894,830	2,780,525	5,097,571	6,517,292	15,421,323	19,422,307	14,537,776	8,472,509	5,645,527
SERIES TWO [2]									
1995	68,837,033	2,516,150	5,284,062	8,138,015	18,161,922	14,062,138	9,143,156	7,422,877	4,108,713
1996	69,642,938	2,456,809	5,282,374	7,937,213	18,484,618	14,609,637	9,235,132	7,398,100	4,239,055
1997	70,413,821	2,451,212	5,232,865	7,705,242	18,733,210	15,158,748	9,429,385	7,335,227	4,367,932
1998	71,140,587	2,481,143	5,148,681	7,478,506	18,914,455	15,561,239	9,793,842	7,286,158	4,476,563
1999	71,870,306	2,531,499	5,028,264	7,296,885	19,016,459	16,087,921	10,097,763	7,226,867	4,584,648
2000	72,627,721	2,591,635	4,904,324	7,209,888	18,999,071	16,668,388	10,344,431	7,221,515	4,688,469
2001	73,374,380	2,658,050	4,764,260	7,208,258	18,876,323	17,303,710	10,571,230	7,218,375	4,774,174
2002	74,089,499	2,711,020	4,737,405	7,142,511	18,630,551	17,546,176	11,246,171	7,215,871	4,859,794
2003	74,792,966	2,764,081	4,774,241	7,031,724	18,349,398	17,914,247	11,762,704	7,242,918	4,953,653
2004	75,501,804	2,797,679	4,865,296	6,871,839	18,095,184	18,275,727	12,266,413	7,302,343	5,027,323
2005	76,240,892	2,821,944	4,980,667	6,705,144	17,855,103	18,636,183	12,766,338	7,371,708	5,103,805
2006	76,985,707	2,849,280	5,110,432	6,515,289	17,622,478	18,969,927	13,269,070	7,482,256	5,166,975
2007	77,737,669	2,870,156	5,221,848	6,479,910	17,282,889	19,231,684	13,774,015	7,671,805	5,205,362
2008	78,471,219	2,899,696	5,326,068	6,530,397	16,896,035	19,418,677	14,159,378	8,003,539	5,237,429
2009	79,215,583	2,947,398	5,386,020	6,650,542	16,509,498	19,527,662	14,654,270	8,274,595	5,265,598
2010	79,990,044	2,993,397	5,426,726	6,803,870	16,223,655	19,515,254	15,198,931	8,502,862	5,325,349
SERIES THREE [3]									
1995	68,872,603	2,525,005	5,286,196	8,140,980	18,168,298	14,068,770	9,148,682	7,422,296	4,112,376
1996	69,674,088	2,467,509	5,281,850	7,937,403	18,489,815	14,617,546	9,240,930	7,396,023	4,243,012
1997	70,439,696	2,463,393	5,229,500	7,702,671	18,737,156	15,167,741	9,435,256	7,332,050	4,371,929
1998	71,161,368	2,493,951	5,143,262	7,473,858	18,916,960	15,571,888	9,799,319	7,281,998	4,480,132
1999	71,885,581	2,544,848	5,022,095	7,289,285	19,017,588	16,099,500	10,103,193	7,221,125	4,587,947
2000	72,637,651	2,605,522	4,897,693	7,199,869	18,998,235	16,680,816	10,349,338	7,214,932	4,691,246
2001	73,378,966	2,671,904	4,757,146	7,196,569	18,873,649	17,317,061	10,575,527	7,210,631	4,776,479
2002	74,090,082	2,724,505	4,730,484	7,129,200	18,626,278	17,561,773	11,249,264	7,207,009	4,861,569
2003	74,789,113	2,777,145	4,767,206	7,017,509	18,343,676	17,930,768	11,765,055	7,232,817	4,954,937
2004	75,493,071	2,810,533	4,857,314	6,857,992	18,086,962	18,293,215	12,268,144	7,290,938	5,027,973
2005	76,227,200	2,834,964	4,971,395	6,691,593	17,844,996	18,653,921	12,767,615	7,358,867	5,103,849
2006	76,967,698	2,863,533	5,099,169	6,501,860	17,611,029	18,987,652	13,270,304	7,467,836	5,166,315
2007	77,716,383	2,886,305	5,208,006	6,466,891	17,270,492	19,249,701	13,774,902	7,655,979	5,204,107
2008	78,446,730	2,918,175	5,309,152	6,517,324	16,883,386	19,436,889	14,160,086	7,986,299	5,235,419
2009	79,187,519	2,968,551	5,366,270	6,636,679	16,496,736	19,546,280	14,654,466	8,255,861	5,262,676
2010	79,957,976	3,017,356	5,404,168	6,789,054	16,211,006	19,533,935	15,198,754	8,482,057	5,321,646

See notes at end of table.

Household Projections

TABLE 1.19. PROJECTED FAMILY HOUSEHOLDS BY FAMILY TYPE AND AGE OF HOUSEHOLDER: 1995 TO 2010 - Continued

YEAR AND SERIES	Total	Married couples							
		Age of householder (Years)							
		Under 25	25-29	30-34	35-44	45-54	55-64	65-74	75 and older
SERIES ONE [1]									
1995	53,432,915	1,441,619	3,779,946	6,161,975	13,766,186	11,210,122	7,520,910	6,254,978	3,297,179
1996	53,893,439	1,390,730	3,748,064	5,974,748	13,934,104	11,620,557	7,571,103	6,235,000	3,419,133
1997	54,319,173	1,372,415	3,683,155	5,765,261	14,042,147	12,029,516	7,703,579	6,183,040	3,540,060
1998	54,707,260	1,373,857	3,594,695	5,562,389	14,096,154	12,319,209	7,972,988	6,143,517	3,644,451
1999	55,091,779	1,387,778	3,482,570	5,394,796	14,087,721	12,705,251	8,188,850	6,095,642	3,749,171
2000	55,495,517	1,407,915	3,370,340	5,298,217	13,987,361	13,131,415	8,355,723	6,093,718	3,850,828
2001	55,885,976	1,431,071	3,249,121	5,264,341	13,808,709	13,597,149	8,503,923	6,093,273	3,938,389
2002	56,266,221	1,447,683	3,206,485	5,185,374	13,540,693	13,753,365	9,011,592	6,093,558	4,027,471
2003	56,626,719	1,463,452	3,207,263	5,074,171	13,247,638	14,005,948	9,385,444	6,117,977	4,124,826
2004	56,988,327	1,467,669	3,244,419	4,929,195	12,975,570	14,251,370	9,744,689	6,169,499	4,205,916
2005	57,370,994	1,468,053	3,297,158	4,781,876	12,713,781	14,493,910	10,096,708	6,228,830	4,290,678
2006	57,755,561	1,470,099	3,358,925	4,620,217	12,458,560	14,713,594	10,446,706	6,323,617	4,363,843
2007	58,147,607	1,468,612	3,408,168	4,569,376	12,130,171	14,876,282	10,793,292	6,485,425	4,416,281
2008	58,527,251	1,471,463	3,452,149	4,579,763	11,771,745	14,978,961	11,042,132	6,767,682	4,463,356
2009	58,908,384	1,484,718	3,467,189	4,639,297	11,417,454	15,020,723	11,372,995	6,998,000	4,508,008
2010	59,308,021	1,498,726	3,470,361	4,721,562	11,136,775	14,967,969	11,739,126	7,192,625	4,580,877
SERIES TWO [2]									
1995	54,267,416	1,509,726	3,940,786	6,308,718	14,126,608	11,325,221	7,646,143	6,227,422	3,182,792
1996	54,926,039	1,470,782	3,937,499	6,152,267	14,380,044	11,765,906	7,723,890	6,207,878	3,287,773
1997	55,553,244	1,465,396	3,898,870	5,970,813	14,575,524	12,207,841	7,887,144	6,156,655	3,391,001
1998	56,145,060	1,480,690	3,834,040	5,793,780	14,717,750	12,530,661	8,192,900	6,117,630	3,477,609
1999	56,736,808	1,509,394	3,742,469	5,651,605	14,797,842	12,954,234	8,446,706	6,070,608	3,563,950
2000	57,350,917	1,545,032	3,649,107	5,582,479	14,783,377	13,421,765	8,652,743	6,069,492	3,646,922
2001	57,955,355	1,584,152	3,544,169	5,578,804	14,686,966	13,933,116	8,842,092	6,070,051	3,716,005
2002	58,553,140	1,616,106	3,523,366	5,526,309	14,493,748	14,128,537	9,408,443	6,070,899	3,785,732
2003	59,134,015	1,647,204	3,550,055	5,438,532	14,272,865	14,425,766	9,840,616	6,096,115	3,862,862
2004	59,720,229	1,665,299	3,617,201	5,312,901	14,072,762	14,717,460	10,262,055	6,148,315	3,924,236
2005	60,331,974	1,678,858	3,702,337	5,182,924	13,882,113	15,008,428	10,680,475	6,208,308	3,988,531
2006	60,948,962	1,694,073	3,798,404	5,035,383	13,696,815	15,277,690	11,101,479	6,303,554	4,041,564
2007	61,574,606	1,704,917	3,880,956	5,007,057	13,428,564	15,489,185	11,523,521	6,465,473	4,074,933
2008	62,183,689	1,720,524	3,958,057	5,045,373	13,123,782	15,639,827	11,845,677	6,747,442	4,103,007
2009	62,800,539	1,747,965	4,002,140	5,137,794	12,819,507	15,727,409	12,259,963	6,977,295	4,128,466
2010	63,441,719	1,775,970	4,032,257	5,255,740	12,594,331	15,716,024	12,717,044	7,171,139	4,179,214
SERIES THREE [3]									
1995	54,064,426	1,498,383	3,909,950	6,273,834	14,055,390	11,315,539	7,620,147	6,208,032	3,183,151
1996	54,674,787	1,458,189	3,902,805	6,104,727	14,296,761	11,747,927	7,694,164	6,182,529	3,287,685
1997	55,252,827	1,452,072	3,857,586	5,913,311	14,478,071	12,182,450	7,853,677	6,125,398	3,390,262
1998	55,795,398	1,467,036	3,786,523	5,728,213	14,604,891	12,493,295	8,159,559	6,080,453	3,475,428
1999	56,338,766	1,494,446	3,688,740	5,581,410	14,669,876	12,905,475	8,410,988	6,027,097	3,560,734
2000	56,904,364	1,528,241	3,590,299	5,509,308	14,640,412	13,361,008	8,612,536	6,020,394	3,642,166
2001	57,461,517	1,565,769	3,482,238	5,502,835	14,528,803	13,859,662	8,797,607	6,015,608	3,708,995
2002	58,010,418	1,596,154	3,459,300	5,444,871	14,322,454	14,036,337	9,363,580	6,011,298	3,776,424
2003	58,543,186	1,625,408	3,485,171	5,351,626	14,088,514	14,319,164	9,791,344	6,030,895	3,851,064
2004	59,080,407	1,642,107	3,548,666	5,220,351	13,878,765	14,597,626	10,205,348	6,078,026	3,909,518
2005	59,642,441	1,654,360	3,629,017	5,085,752	13,679,220	14,876,127	10,614,741	6,132,459	3,970,765
2006	60,209,569	1,667,707	3,720,744	4,935,705	13,483,120	15,133,330	11,025,467	6,223,017	4,020,479
2007	60,784,900	1,676,219	3,799,384	4,905,135	13,204,375	15,331,353	11,437,741	6,380,155	4,050,538
2008	61,342,277	1,689,015	3,871,841	4,942,394	12,890,721	15,467,284	11,746,435	6,659,777	4,074,810
2009	61,906,394	1,713,202	3,912,218	5,030,497	12,580,611	15,540,648	12,147,286	6,885,371	4,096,561
2010	62,494,303	1,738,152	3,939,120	5,142,796	12,351,173	15,515,572	12,590,536	7,073,268	4,143,686

See notes at end of table.

Household Projections

YEAR AND SERIES	TABLE 1.19. PROJECTED FAMILY HOUSEHOLDS BY FAMILY TYPE AND AGE OF HOUSEHOLDER: 1995 TO 2010 - Continued								
		Other family, female householder							
	Total	Age of householder (Years)							
		Under 25	25-29	30-34	35-44	45-54	55-64	65-74	75 and older
SERIES ONE [1]									
1995	11,438,681	740,833	1,054,424	1,471,453	3,212,791	2,147,341	1,167,505	921,884	722,450
1996	11,606,809	727,957	1,064,813	1,446,169	3,288,862	2,247,046	1,180,594	913,060	738,308
1997	11,773,519	729,985	1,065,049	1,415,750	3,353,051	2,348,743	1,207,039	899,438	754,464
1998	11,934,856	742,938	1,058,459	1,385,430	3,407,076	2,430,384	1,255,438	887,069	768,062
1999	12,100,606	761,187	1,043,912	1,363,162	3,447,983	2,532,068	1,297,856	873,052	781,386
2000	12,272,004	781,639	1,027,314	1,358,584	3,469,425	2,642,932	1,333,034	865,013	794,063
2001	12,446,308	804,156	1,006,503	1,370,889	3,471,967	2,765,100	1,366,281	857,730	803,682
2002	12,599,164	822,061	1,009,554	1,370,118	3,453,337	2,825,573	1,455,320	850,726	812,475
2003	12,757,287	840,608	1,025,971	1,360,955	3,427,731	2,906,454	1,526,192	847,823	821,553
2004	12,917,753	854,235	1,054,039	1,341,900	3,407,156	2,987,908	1,596,044	849,083	827,388
2005	13,083,981	864,163	1,087,847	1,320,049	3,390,864	3,070,348	1,665,743	852,111	832,856
2006	13,251,031	875,118	1,124,793	1,292,792	3,376,219	3,149,793	1,736,011	859,262	837,043
2007	13,418,598	884,386	1,157,939	1,296,173	3,340,534	3,218,404	1,808,160	875,386	837,616
2008	13,582,132	896,597	1,189,842	1,316,281	3,294,420	3,275,875	1,864,567	907,178	837,372
2009	13,751,082	913,716	1,212,299	1,350,452	3,247,762	3,321,789	1,935,786	933,132	836,146
2010	13,926,532	929,291	1,230,291	1,392,084	3,219,402	3,349,371	2,012,873	954,031	839,189
SERIES TWO [2]									
1995	11,154,518	725,499	1,001,535	1,421,577	3,133,256	2,061,300	1,147,205	934,035	730,111
1996	11,248,424	710,576	1,002,507	1,385,691	3,181,390	2,137,524	1,155,395	927,765	747,576
1997	11,339,611	710,281	994,010	1,345,477	3,217,244	2,214,092	1,176,531	916,563	765,413
1998	11,424,475	720,680	979,333	1,305,887	3,242,428	2,270,182	1,218,719	906,540	780,706
1999	11,512,401	736,158	957,655	1,274,525	3,254,889	2,343,753	1,254,840	894,783	795,798
2000	11,604,767	753,673	934,525	1,260,095	3,248,930	2,424,394	1,283,744	889,119	810,287
2001	11,698,670	773,166	908,033	1,261,493	3,225,585	2,513,878	1,310,589	884,200	821,726
2002	11,771,580	788,092	903,230	1,250,668	3,182,199	2,545,336	1,390,242	879,454	832,359
2003	11,849,247	803,700	910,461	1,232,566	3,133,496	2,594,619	1,452,110	878,952	843,343
2004	11,927,775	814,707	927,859	1,205,831	3,089,919	2,643,276	1,512,419	882,736	851,028
2005	12,010,490	822,151	950,027	1,177,021	3,050,762	2,691,715	1,572,082	888,355	858,377
2006	12,093,094	830,613	974,574	1,143,814	3,013,417	2,736,305	1,631,671	898,274	864,426
2007	12,175,879	837,558	995,480	1,137,976	2,957,737	2,770,392	1,692,388	917,591	866,757
2008	12,255,980	847,340	1,015,000	1,146,757	2,893,516	2,793,909	1,737,804	953,418	868,236
2009	12,340,240	861,674	1,026,264	1,167,534	2,829,566	2,806,936	1,796,386	983,203	868,677
2010	12,428,486	874,378	1,033,535	1,194,242	2,781,907	2,803,622	1,859,559	1,007,703	873,540
SERIES THREE [3]									
1995	11,336,429	741,164	1,022,343	1,448,130	3,195,970	2,073,579	1,173,209	948,525	733,509
1996	11,463,777	728,429	1,023,820	1,419,683	3,252,202	2,157,591	1,184,638	945,726	751,688
1997	11,588,373	729,674	1,018,175	1,384,342	3,297,854	2,240,980	1,208,839	938,361	770,148
1998	11,706,994	740,625	1,006,694	1,348,950	3,333,582	2,308,170	1,250,458	932,305	786,210
1999	11,827,365	757,127	989,735	1,317,881	3,356,321	2,391,671	1,288,413	924,268	801,949
2000	11,952,311	776,129	970,418	1,303,141	3,359,947	2,482,627	1,320,392	922,455	817,202
2001	12,077,637	796,229	945,874	1,305,075	3,346,510	2,583,078	1,350,007	920,889	829,975
2002	12,184,607	811,316	942,849	1,297,346	3,311,359	2,631,699	1,428,693	919,418	841,927
2003	12,295,128	827,230	950,464	1,282,989	3,271,096	2,693,148	1,493,350	922,433	854,418
2004	12,406,575	838,193	969,725	1,261,645	3,231,933	2,753,024	1,559,022	929,234	863,799
2005	12,522,567	845,861	994,343	1,237,105	3,197,403	2,811,244	1,625,496	938,128	872,987
2006	12,638,983	856,044	1,020,081	1,206,027	3,167,156	2,864,911	1,693,276	950,495	880,993
2007	12,756,689	865,582	1,041,191	1,202,348	3,118,714	2,909,558	1,761,442	972,475	885,379
2008	12,872,767	878,707	1,060,983	1,211,772	3,061,214	2,944,484	1,817,462	1,009,006	889,139
2009	12,993,258	896,947	1,071,884	1,235,141	3,001,687	2,968,690	1,886,292	1,040,965	891,652
2010	13,117,622	913,251	1,078,420	1,265,387	2,957,449	2,975,815	1,960,158	1,068,459	898,683

See notes at end of table.

Household Projections

TABLE 1.19. PROJECTED FAMILY HOUSEHOLDS BY FAMILY TYPE AND AGE OF HOUSEHOLDER: 1995 TO 2010 - Continued

YEAR AND SERIES	Total	Other family, male householder							
		Age of householder (Years)							
		Under 25	25-29	30-34	35-44	45-54	55-64	65-74	75 and older
SERIES ONE [1]									
1995	3,511,084	283,999	352,303	420,460	958,903	681,745	371,200	259,907	182,567
1996	3,589,560	278,864	354,764	414,974	992,635	716,928	381,796	261,130	188,469
1997	3,668,031	279,335	354,063	407,390	1,022,776	752,606	396,762	260,897	194,202
1998	3,744,896	283,997	350,891	399,780	1,049,598	781,420	419,313	261,056	198,841
1999	3,822,451	290,637	345,026	394,153	1,072,075	816,844	439,614	260,770	203,332
2000	3,901,409	298,110	338,775	393,347	1,087,737	855,653	457,853	262,438	207,496
2001	3,978,381	306,421	331,170	396,877	1,096,826	897,350	475,305	263,927	210,505
2002	4,052,311	312,992	331,303	396,976	1,098,602	919,405	514,026	265,521	213,486
2003	4,127,093	319,827	335,866	394,312	1,097,606	948,286	546,243	268,105	216,848
2004	4,201,824	324,746	344,284	388,651	1,097,616	977,025	578,575	271,794	219,133
2005	4,277,905	328,404	354,409	382,411	1,097,766	1,006,068	611,493	275,800	221,554
2006	4,355,235	332,458	365,738	374,665	1,098,027	1,034,179	645,478	281,426	223,264
2007	4,430,862	335,905	375,804	375,581	1,091,147	1,058,507	680,249	289,973	223,696
2008	4,506,451	340,432	385,493	381,602	1,081,108	1,079,421	710,267	304,169	223,959
2009	4,581,934	346,789	391,920	391,635	1,070,066	1,095,578	746,203	315,793	223,950
2010	4,660,277	352,508	396,919	403,646	1,065,146	1,104,967	785,777	325,853	225,461
SERIES TWO [2]									
1995	3,415,099	280,925	341,741	407,720	902,058	675,617	349,808	261,420	195,810
1996	3,468,475	275,451	342,368	399,255	923,184	706,207	355,847	262,457	203,706
1997	3,520,966	275,535	339,985	388,952	940,442	736,815	365,710	262,009	211,518
1998	3,571,052	279,773	335,308	378,839	954,277	760,396	382,223	261,988	218,248
1999	3,621,097	285,947	328,140	370,755	963,728	789,934	396,217	261,476	224,900
2000	3,672,037	292,930	320,692	367,314	966,764	822,229	407,944	262,904	231,260
2001	3,720,355	300,732	312,058	367,961	963,772	856,716	418,549	264,124	236,443
2002	3,764,779	306,822	310,809	365,534	954,604	872,303	447,486	265,518	241,703
2003	3,809,704	313,177	313,725	360,626	943,037	893,862	469,978	267,851	247,448
2004	3,853,800	317,673	320,236	353,107	932,503	914,991	491,939	271,292	252,059
2005	3,898,428	320,935	328,303	345,199	922,228	936,040	513,781	275,045	256,897
2006	3,943,651	324,594	337,454	336,092	912,246	955,932	535,920	280,428	260,985
2007	3,987,184	327,681	345,412	334,877	896,588	972,107	558,106	288,741	263,672
2008	4,031,550	331,832	353,011	338,267	878,737	984,941	575,897	302,679	266,186
2009	4,074,804	337,759	357,616	345,214	860,425	993,317	597,921	314,097	268,455
2010	4,119,839	343,049	360,934	353,888	847,417	995,608	622,328	324,020	272,595
SERIES THREE [3]									
1995	3,471,748	285,458	353,903	419,016	916,938	679,652	355,326	265,739	195,716
1996	3,535,524	280,891	355,225	412,993	940,852	712,028	362,128	267,768	203,639
1997	3,598,496	281,647	353,739	405,018	961,231	744,311	372,740	268,291	211,519
1998	3,658,976	286,290	350,045	396,695	978,487	770,423	389,302	269,240	218,494
1999	3,719,450	293,275	343,620	389,994	991,391	802,354	403,792	269,760	225,264
2000	3,780,976	301,152	336,976	387,420	997,876	837,181	416,410	272,083	231,878
2001	3,839,812	309,906	329,034	388,659	998,336	874,321	427,913	274,134	237,509
2002	3,895,057	317,035	328,335	386,983	992,465	893,737	456,991	276,293	243,218
2003	3,950,799	324,507	331,571	382,894	984,066	918,456	480,361	279,489	249,455
2004	4,006,089	330,233	338,923	375,996	976,264	942,565	503,774	283,678	254,656
2005	4,062,192	334,743	348,035	368,736	968,373	966,550	527,378	288,280	260,097
2006	4,119,146	339,782	358,344	360,128	960,753	989,411	551,561	294,324	264,843
2007	4,174,794	344,504	367,431	359,408	947,403	1,008,790	575,719	303,349	268,190
2008	4,231,686	350,453	376,328	363,158	931,451	1,025,121	596,189	317,516	271,470
2009	4,287,867	358,402	382,168	371,041	914,438	1,036,942	620,888	329,525	274,463
2010	4,346,051	365,953	386,628	380,871	902,384	1,042,548	648,060	340,330	279,277

Source: Day, Jennifer Cheeseman. 1996. "Projections of the Number of Households and Families in the United States: 1995 to 2010." U.S. Bureau of the Census, Current Population Reports P25-1129.

As of July 1.

(1) Series 1 is the preferred series, based on a time-series model that projects trends by age and sex in the proportions of persons maintaining households of different types. Series 1 also reflects the effects of projected changes in the age/sex structure of the population.
(2) Series 2 reflects the consequences of projected changes in the age/sex structure of the population only, assuming that household formation propensities by age/sex hold constant at 1990 levels.
(3) Series 3 reflects the consequences of projected changes in both the age/sex structure and the racial/Hispanic origin composition of the population. Series 3 assumes that household formation propensities hold constant at 1990 levels by age/sex and race/Hispanic origin.

See Appendix A for additional discussion of the projections.

Household Projections

TABLE 1.20. PROJECTED NONFAMILY HOUSEHOLDS BY SEX AND AGE OF HOUSEHOLDER: 1995 TO 2010

YEAR AND SERIES	Total	All nonfamily households							
		Age of householder (Years)							
		Under 25	25-29	30-34	35-44	45-54	55-64	65-74	75 and older
SERIES ONE [1]									
1995	29,340,203	2,359,971	2,767,648	2,774,875	4,818,616	3,683,741	3,271,164	4,412,725	5,251,463
1996	29,766,795	2,314,607	2,790,017	2,734,559	4,967,700	3,864,498	3,330,590	4,387,380	5,377,444
1997	30,204,452	2,317,918	2,786,852	2,681,888	5,098,824	4,048,290	3,427,872	4,338,597	5,504,211
1998	30,655,852	2,357,084	2,764,842	2,629,175	5,213,791	4,196,311	3,588,808	4,295,989	5,609,852
1999	31,103,764	2,414,165	2,721,789	2,590,300	5,307,726	4,379,398	3,731,748	4,245,582	5,713,056
2000	31,577,033	2,478,740	2,674,799	2,583,793	5,369,276	4,579,525	3,855,258	4,225,014	5,810,628
2001	32,033,780	2,550,236	2,617,013	2,607,055	5,399,520	4,797,115	3,972,742	4,206,278	5,883,821
2002	32,538,428	2,607,122	2,620,721	2,606,953	5,394,854	4,908,716	4,259,029	4,189,000	5,952,033
2003	33,055,028	2,665,901	2,659,337	2,589,483	5,377,541	5,056,283	4,491,842	4,190,588	6,024,053
2004	33,564,995	2,707,676	2,728,349	2,552,632	5,366,202	5,203,939	4,723,352	4,211,798	6,071,047
2005	34,085,779	2,738,010	2,811,408	2,511,442	5,357,668	5,353,263	4,956,675	4,240,642	6,116,671
2006	34,620,143	2,771,740	2,903,456	2,460,219	5,350,404	5,497,503	5,194,727	4,291,301	6,150,793
2007	35,165,192	2,800,202	2,985,562	2,466,384	5,308,845	5,622,211	5,438,711	4,386,700	6,156,577
2008	35,747,014	2,838,487	3,064,597	2,505,468	5,251,498	5,728,145	5,639,482	4,562,697	6,156,640
2009	36,326,567	2,893,280	3,118,316	2,571,047	5,190,673	5,811,260	5,886,028	4,706,534	6,149,429
2010	36,930,598	2,943,660	3,160,628	2,650,043	5,159,385	5,860,318	6,155,278	4,825,543	6,175,743
SERIES TWO [2]									
1995	28,857,727	2,323,727	2,663,318	2,687,222	4,594,280	3,594,465	3,161,469	4,462,180	5,371,066
1996	29,158,242	2,273,842	2,667,334	2,627,126	4,687,918	3,742,817	3,196,563	4,444,938	5,517,704
1997	29,466,159	2,271,998	2,647,245	2,556,323	4,762,498	3,891,504	3,266,896	4,403,653	5,666,042
1998	29,783,903	2,305,490	2,609,822	2,486,745	4,820,324	4,003,621	3,396,058	4,368,445	5,793,398
1999	30,095,254	2,356,403	2,553,286	2,431,321	4,857,195	4,146,843	3,506,137	4,324,924	5,919,145
2000	30,429,914	2,414,439	2,493,936	2,406,997	4,863,533	4,303,607	3,596,094	4,311,585	6,039,723
2001	30,744,665	2,479,191	2,425,453	2,410,682	4,841,134	4,473,844	3,678,629	4,299,907	6,135,825
2002	31,100,334	2,529,522	2,414,572	2,393,089	4,788,061	4,543,222	3,914,576	4,289,625	6,227,667
2003	31,467,022	2,581,812	2,435,979	2,360,075	4,724,443	4,644,043	4,097,894	4,298,483	6,324,293
2004	31,822,482	2,617,843	2,485,029	2,310,166	4,666,927	4,743,151	4,276,725	4,327,404	6,395,237
2005	32,184,649	2,642,749	2,546,419	2,257,210	4,612,677	4,841,857	4,454,048	4,364,177	6,465,512
2006	32,556,881	2,671,043	2,615,461	2,196,205	4,560,362	4,934,139	4,632,296	4,423,426	6,523,949
2007	32,938,188	2,694,476	2,675,053	2,187,115	4,479,902	5,007,353	4,812,605	4,528,939	6,552,745
2008	33,361,864	2,727,513	2,731,516	2,207,405	4,387,757	5,062,470	4,951,703	4,717,902	6,575,598
2009	33,776,180	2,776,282	2,765,162	2,250,864	4,294,303	5,096,494	5,127,854	4,874,221	6,591,000
2010	34,209,578	2,820,513	2,788,559	2,305,648	4,226,682	5,100,007	5,320,139	5,005,223	6,642,807
SERIES THREE [3]									
1995	28,701,586	2,302,935	2,628,658	2,655,246	4,569,402	3,581,985	3,152,754	4,447,482	5,363,124
1996	28,967,227	2,247,008	2,629,950	2,587,261	4,655,737	3,728,321	3,185,627	4,426,717	5,506,606
1997	29,240,334	2,240,900	2,605,960	2,508,208	4,722,697	3,874,767	3,254,091	4,382,183	5,651,528
1998	29,522,348	2,272,255	2,563,402	2,432,480	4,771,935	3,984,387	3,380,111	4,343,732	5,774,046
1999	29,797,888	2,319,717	2,502,137	2,371,773	4,799,662	4,125,611	3,487,509	4,297,003	5,894,476
2000	30,096,698	2,373,902	2,437,575	2,343,972	4,796,640	4,280,288	3,574,801	4,280,288	6,009,232
2001	30,375,048	2,434,994	2,364,124	2,345,199	4,764,816	4,448,956	3,653,669	4,265,091	6,098,199
2002	30,694,280	2,481,492	2,349,503	2,324,896	4,701,476	4,516,712	3,886,197	4,251,225	6,182,779
2003	31,024,692	2,529,628	2,368,799	2,288,490	4,628,402	4,614,561	4,066,388	4,256,936	6,271,488
2004	31,342,234	2,561,071	2,414,338	2,235,971	4,561,493	4,710,342	4,242,892	4,282,560	6,333,567
2005	31,664,879	2,581,109	2,471,615	2,179,982	4,499,133	4,804,746	4,417,893	4,316,037	6,394,364
2006	31,995,578	2,603,661	2,536,144	2,115,813	4,440,039	4,891,813	4,593,997	4,371,449	6,442,662
2007	32,334,681	2,619,910	2,591,295	2,104,055	4,352,394	4,960,030	4,772,059	4,473,398	6,461,540
2008	32,714,496	2,645,047	2,642,652	2,122,329	4,254,167	5,009,532	4,908,968	4,658,058	6,473,743
2009	33,083,119	2,684,615	2,671,074	2,162,605	4,155,509	5,037,458	5,083,534	4,809,943	6,478,381
2010	33,467,800	2,717,869	2,689,562	2,213,682	4,083,191	5,034,592	5,274,040	4,936,001	6,518,863

See notes at end of table.

Household Projections

TABLE 1.20. PROJECTED NONFAMILY HOUSEHOLDS BY SEX AND AGE OF HOUSEHOLDER: 1995 TO 2010 - Continued

YEAR AND SERIES	Total	Female householder							
		Age of householder (Years)							
		Under 25	25-29	30-34	35-44	45-54	55-64	65-74	75 and older
SERIES ONE [1]									
1995	16,084,937	1,041,997	1,058,230	993,939	1,775,981	1,807,110	1,958,639	3,229,576	4,219,465
1996	16,269,403	1,023,490	1,068,657	976,861	1,818,032	1,891,018	1,980,598	3,198,664	4,312,083
1997	16,463,794	1,026,125	1,068,894	956,313	1,853,516	1,976,602	2,024,962	3,150,942	4,406,440
1998	16,670,950	1,044,521	1,062,279	935,833	1,883,380	2,045,307	2,106,158	3,107,611	4,485,861
1999	16,875,311	1,070,463	1,047,680	920,791	1,905,992	2,130,880	2,177,319	3,058,507	4,563,679
2000	17,094,590	1,099,451	1,031,022	917,698	1,917,846	2,224,179	2,236,335	3,030,344	4,637,715
2001	17,304,585	1,131,362	1,010,136	926,011	1,919,250	2,326,989	2,292,111	3,004,831	4,693,895
2002	17,549,113	1,156,557	1,013,198	925,489	1,908,952	2,377,881	2,441,485	2,980,295	4,745,256
2003	17,801,273	1,182,776	1,029,674	919,300	1,894,797	2,445,947	2,560,383	2,970,123	4,798,273
2004	18,048,628	1,201,981	1,057,843	906,429	1,883,424	2,514,495	2,677,568	2,974,538	4,832,350
2005	18,301,408	1,215,744	1,091,774	891,669	1,874,418	2,583,873	2,794,496	2,985,146	4,864,288
2006	18,561,511	1,231,026	1,128,853	873,257	1,866,323	2,650,731	2,912,381	3,010,196	4,888,744
2007	18,828,993	1,244,073	1,162,118	875,541	1,846,597	2,708,471	3,033,420	3,066,684	4,892,089
2008	19,119,565	1,261,592	1,194,137	889,124	1,821,105	2,756,836	3,128,050	3,178,059	4,890,662
2009	19,405,806	1,286,125	1,216,674	912,205	1,795,314	2,795,476	3,247,528	3,268,983	4,883,501
2010	19,702,084	1,308,378	1,234,731	940,327	1,779,636	2,818,688	3,376,851	3,342,197	4,901,276
SERIES TWO [2]									
1995	15,913,381	1,020,329	1,005,150	960,249	1,732,016	1,734,702	1,924,584	3,272,144	4,264,207
1996	16,053,245	998,923	1,006,125	936,009	1,758,623	1,798,848	1,938,323	3,250,181	4,366,213
1997	16,201,540	998,263	997,598	908,845	1,778,444	1,863,285	1,973,781	3,210,935	4,470,389
1998	16,360,945	1,013,037	982,868	882,103	1,792,365	1,910,488	2,044,557	3,175,824	4,559,703
1999	16,516,369	1,035,046	961,111	860,918	1,799,253	1,972,402	2,105,155	3,134,635	4,647,849
2000	16,686,075	1,059,867	937,898	851,171	1,795,959	2,040,266	2,153,645	3,114,794	4,732,475
2001	16,845,060	1,087,484	911,311	852,115	1,783,055	2,115,572	2,198,681	3,097,561	4,799,281
2002	17,035,496	1,108,456	906,490	844,803	1,759,071	2,142,045	2,332,310	3,080,935	4,861,386
2003	17,233,314	1,130,508	913,747	832,576	1,732,148	2,183,520	2,436,100	3,079,175	4,925,540
2004	17,424,375	1,145,996	931,208	814,516	1,708,061	2,224,467	2,537,276	3,092,431	4,970,420
2005	17,619,226	1,156,237	953,456	795,056	1,686,414	2,265,231	2,637,369	3,112,117	5,013,346
2006	17,820,103	1,167,942	978,092	772,625	1,665,771	2,302,757	2,737,337	3,146,864	5,048,675
2007	18,027,943	1,177,735	999,073	768,682	1,634,992	2,331,444	2,839,197	3,214,536	5,062,284
2008	18,262,171	1,191,805	1,018,663	774,614	1,599,492	2,351,234	2,915,388	3,340,048	5,070,927
2009	18,488,895	1,212,384	1,029,968	788,648	1,564,141	2,362,198	3,013,667	3,444,390	5,073,499
2010	18,723,493	1,230,562	1,037,265	806,689	1,537,796	2,359,409	3,119,649	3,530,220	5,101,903
SERIES THREE [3]									
1995	15,799,625	1,006,850	990,212	945,400	1,714,782	1,722,041	1,912,806	3,252,206	4,255,328
1996	15,914,198	981,696	989,480	917,853	1,737,334	1,783,557	1,924,266	3,225,750	4,354,262
1997	16,037,537	978,232	978,724	887,240	1,753,007	1,845,326	1,957,530	3,182,256	4,455,222
1998	16,171,073	991,334	961,075	857,912	1,762,407	1,889,565	2,025,747	3,142,924	4,540,109
1999	16,300,363	1,011,326	936,362	834,451	1,764,626	1,948,737	2,083,755	3,097,548	4,623,558
2000	16,443,281	1,034,048	909,987	822,935	1,756,657	2,013,760	2,129,326	3,073,733	4,702,835
2001	16,574,784	1,059,636	880,387	822,374	1,739,235	2,086,501	2,170,956	3,052,639	4,763,056
2002	16,737,426	1,078,481	873,167	813,352	1,710,306	2,110,268	2,301,226	3,032,181	4,818,445
2003	16,907,152	1,098,262	878,831	799,012	1,678,865	2,148,588	2,401,505	3,026,781	4,875,308
2004	17,069,178	1,111,266	894,447	778,999	1,650,334	2,186,330	2,499,219	3,036,457	4,912,126
2005	17,233,807	1,118,959	914,637	757,422	1,624,734	2,223,477	2,595,679	3,052,405	4,946,494
2006	17,403,252	1,127,821	937,010	732,910	1,600,544	2,256,981	2,692,009	3,083,230	4,972,747
2007	17,579,493	1,134,053	955,767	727,171	1,566,059	2,281,782	2,790,246	3,146,938	4,977,477
2008	17,780,666	1,144,329	972,818	731,655	1,527,194	2,297,312	2,862,531	3,268,296	4,976,531
2009	17,973,497	1,160,377	981,584	744,006	1,488,779	2,303,959	2,957,173	3,368,019	4,969,600
2010	18,172,225	1,173,131	986,572	760,167	1,459,465	2,296,897	3,059,364	3,448,548	4,988,081

See notes at end of table.

Household Projections

TABLE 1.20. PROJECTED NONFAMILY HOUSEHOLDS BY SEX AND AGE OF HOUSEHOLDER: 1995 TO 2010 - Continued

YEAR AND SERIES	Total	Male householder							
		Age of householder (Years)							
		Under 25	25-29	30-34	35-44	45-54	55-64	65-74	75 and older
SERIES ONE [1]									
1995	13,255,266	1,317,974	1,709,418	1,780,936	3,042,635	1,876,631	1,312,525	1,183,149	1,031,998
1996	13,497,392	1,291,117	1,721,360	1,757,698	3,149,668	1,973,480	1,349,992	1,188,716	1,065,361
1997	13,740,658	1,291,793	1,717,958	1,725,575	3,245,308	2,071,688	1,402,910	1,187,655	1,097,771
1998	13,984,902	1,312,563	1,702,563	1,693,342	3,330,411	2,151,004	1,482,650	1,188,378	1,123,991
1999	14,228,453	1,343,702	1,674,109	1,669,509	3,401,734	2,248,518	1,554,429	1,187,075	1,149,377
2000	14,482,443	1,379,289	1,643,777	1,666,095	3,451,430	2,355,346	1,618,923	1,194,670	1,172,913
2001	14,729,195	1,418,874	1,606,877	1,681,044	3,480,270	2,470,126	1,680,631	1,201,447	1,189,926
2002	14,989,315	1,450,565	1,607,523	1,681,464	3,485,902	2,530,835	1,817,544	1,208,705	1,206,777
2003	15,253,755	1,483,125	1,629,663	1,670,183	3,482,744	2,610,336	1,931,459	1,220,465	1,225,780
2004	15,516,367	1,505,695	1,670,506	1,646,203	3,482,778	2,689,444	2,045,784	1,237,260	1,238,697
2005	15,784,371	1,522,266	1,719,634	1,619,773	3,483,250	2,769,390	2,162,179	1,255,496	1,252,383
2006	16,058,632	1,540,714	1,774,603	1,586,962	3,484,081	2,846,772	2,282,346	1,281,105	1,262,049
2007	16,336,199	1,556,129	1,823,444	1,590,843	3,462,248	2,913,740	2,405,291	1,320,016	1,264,488
2008	16,627,449	1,576,895	1,870,460	1,616,344	3,430,393	2,971,309	2,511,432	1,384,638	1,265,978
2009	16,920,761	1,607,155	1,901,642	1,658,842	3,395,359	3,015,784	2,638,500	1,437,551	1,265,928
2010	17,228,514	1,635,282	1,925,897	1,709,716	3,379,749	3,041,630	2,778,427	1,483,346	1,274,467
SERIES TWO [2]									
1995	12,944,346	1,303,398	1,658,168	1,726,973	2,862,264	1,859,763	1,236,885	1,190,036	1,106,859
1996	13,104,997	1,274,919	1,661,209	1,691,117	2,929,295	1,943,969	1,258,240	1,194,757	1,151,491
1997	13,264,619	1,273,735	1,649,647	1,647,478	2,984,054	2,028,219	1,293,115	1,192,718	1,195,653
1998	13,422,958	1,292,453	1,626,954	1,604,642	3,027,959	2,093,133	1,351,501	1,192,621	1,233,695
1999	13,578,885	1,321,357	1,592,175	1,570,403	3,057,942	2,174,441	1,400,982	1,190,289	1,271,296
2000	13,743,839	1,354,572	1,556,038	1,555,826	3,067,574	2,263,341	1,442,449	1,196,791	1,307,248
2001	13,899,605	1,391,707	1,514,142	1,558,567	3,058,079	2,358,272	1,479,948	1,202,346	1,336,544
2002	14,064,838	1,421,066	1,508,082	1,548,286	3,028,990	2,401,177	1,582,266	1,208,690	1,366,281
2003	14,233,708	1,451,304	1,522,232	1,527,499	2,992,295	2,460,523	1,661,794	1,219,308	1,398,753
2004	14,398,107	1,471,847	1,553,821	1,495,650	2,958,866	2,518,684	1,739,449	1,234,973	1,424,817
2005	14,565,423	1,486,512	1,592,963	1,462,154	2,926,263	2,576,626	1,816,679	1,252,060	1,452,166
2006	14,736,778	1,503,061	1,637,369	1,423,580	2,894,591	2,631,382	1,894,959	1,276,562	1,475,274
2007	14,910,245	1,516,741	1,675,980	1,418,433	2,844,910	2,675,909	1,973,408	1,314,403	1,490,461
2008	15,099,693	1,535,708	1,712,853	1,432,791	2,788,265	2,711,236	2,036,315	1,377,854	1,504,671
2009	15,287,285	1,563,898	1,735,194	1,462,216	2,730,162	2,734,296	2,114,187	1,429,831	1,517,501
2010	15,486,085	1,589,951	1,751,294	1,498,959	2,688,886	2,740,598	2,200,490	1,475,003	1,540,904
SERIES THREE [3]									
1995	12,901,961	1,296,085	1,638,446	1,709,846	2,854,620	1,859,944	1,239,948	1,195,276	1,107,796
1996	13,053,029	1,265,312	1,640,470	1,669,408	2,918,403	1,944,764	1,261,361	1,200,967	1,152,344
1997	13,202,797	1,262,668	1,627,236	1,620,968	2,969,690	2,029,441	1,296,561	1,199,927	1,196,306
1998	13,351,275	1,280,921	1,602,327	1,574,568	3,009,528	2,094,822	1,354,364	1,200,808	1,233,937
1999	13,497,525	1,308,391	1,565,775	1,537,322	3,035,036	2,176,874	1,403,754	1,199,455	1,270,918
2000	13,653,417	1,339,854	1,527,588	1,521,037	3,039,983	2,266,528	1,445,475	1,206,555	1,306,397
2001	13,800,264	1,375,358	1,483,737	1,522,825	3,025,581	2,362,455	1,482,713	1,212,452	1,335,143
2002	13,956,854	1,403,011	1,476,336	1,511,544	2,991,170	2,406,444	1,584,971	1,219,044	1,364,334
2003	14,117,540	1,431,366	1,489,968	1,489,478	2,949,537	2,465,973	1,664,883	1,230,155	1,396,180
2004	14,273,056	1,449,805	1,519,891	1,456,972	2,911,159	2,524,012	1,743,673	1,246,103	1,421,441
2005	14,431,072	1,462,150	1,556,978	1,422,560	2,874,399	2,581,269	1,822,214	1,263,632	1,447,870
2006	14,592,326	1,475,840	1,599,134	1,382,903	2,839,495	2,634,832	1,901,988	1,288,219	1,469,915
2007	14,755,188	1,485,857	1,635,528	1,376,884	2,786,335	2,678,248	1,981,813	1,326,460	1,484,063
2008	14,933,830	1,500,718	1,669,834	1,390,674	2,726,973	2,712,220	2,046,437	1,389,762	1,497,212
2009	15,109,622	1,524,238	1,689,490	1,418,599	2,666,730	2,733,499	2,126,361	1,441,924	1,508,781
2010	15,295,575	1,544,738	1,702,990	1,453,515	2,623,726	2,737,695	2,214,676	1,487,453	1,530,782

Source: Day, Jennifer Cheeseman. 1996. "Projections of the Number of Households and Families in the United States: 1995 to 2010." U.S. Bureau of the Census, Current Population Reports P25-1129.

As of July 1.

(1) Series 1 is the preferred series, based on a time-series model that projects trends by age and sex in the proportions of persons maintaining households of different types. Series 1 also reflects the effects of projected changes in the age/sex structure of the population.
(2) Series 2 reflects the consequences of projected changes in the age/sex structure of the population only, assuming that household formation propensities by age/sex hold constant at 1990 levels.
(3) Series 3 reflects the consequences of projected changes in both the age/sex structure and the racial/Hispanic origin composition of the population. Series 3 assumes that household formation propensities hold constant at 1990 levels by age/sex and race/Hispanic origin.

See Appendix A for additional discussion of the projections.

Household Projections

TABLE 1.21. PROJECTED FAMILIES WITH CHILDREN UNDER 18 BY FAMILY TYPE: 1995 TO 2010

YEAR AND SERIES	All families	Families with children under 18			
		Total	Married couple	Other family	
				Female householder	Male householder
SERIES ONE [1]					
1995	68,382,680	32,585,420	24,606,935	6,434,580	1,543,905
1996	69,089,808	32,805,697	24,720,317	6,507,453	1,577,927
1997	69,760,723	32,950,828	24,770,078	6,571,209	1,609,541
1998	70,387,012	33,001,413	24,739,546	6,624,257	1,637,610
1999	71,014,836	33,057,691	24,713,309	6,678,623	1,665,759
2000	71,668,930	33,116,539	24,685,785	6,737,016	1,693,738
2001	72,310,665	33,174,193	24,655,456	6,798,020	1,720,717
2002	72,917,696	33,036,636	24,468,178	6,829,106	1,739,352
2003	73,511,099	32,915,537	24,291,409	6,865,639	1,758,489
2004	74,107,904	32,799,077	24,118,115	6,903,407	1,777,555
2005	74,732,880	32,699,092	23,957,648	6,944,446	1,796,998
2006	75,361,827	32,589,305	23,788,678	6,984,458	1,816,169
2007	75,997,067	32,477,331	23,615,690	7,027,702	1,833,939
2008	76,615,834	32,360,426	23,434,446	7,074,699	1,851,281
2009	77,241,400	32,258,837	23,263,529	7,126,846	1,868,462
2010	77,894,830	32,203,228	23,126,269	7,189,026	1,887,933
SERIES TWO [2]					
1995	68,837,033	32,927,283	25,211,389	6,230,178	1,485,716
1996	69,642,938	33,215,036	25,457,687	6,251,530	1,505,819
1997	70,413,821	33,427,411	25,640,179	6,263,952	1,523,280
1998	71,140,587	33,543,650	25,740,585	6,265,923	1,537,142
1999	71,870,306	33,665,980	25,845,679	6,269,431	1,550,870
2000	72,627,721	33,791,044	25,949,975	6,276,723	1,564,346
2001	73,374,380	33,914,629	26,051,210	6,286,640	1,576,779
2002	74,089,499	33,837,763	25,988,688	6,267,529	1,581,546
2003	74,792,966	33,777,914	25,936,992	6,254,144	1,586,778
2004	75,501,804	33,721,804	25,888,226	6,241,698	1,591,880
2005	76,240,892	33,681,772	25,852,471	6,232,064	1,597,237
2006	76,985,707	33,630,584	25,806,783	6,221,428	1,602,373
2007	77,737,669	33,574,875	25,754,831	6,213,487	1,606,557
2008	78,471,219	33,512,846	25,693,251	6,208,869	1,610,726
2009	79,215,583	33,465,097	25,641,146	6,209,161	1,614,790
2010	79,990,044	33,464,735	25,626,700	6,217,435	1,620,600
SERIES THREE [3]					
1995	68,872,603	32,951,468	25,093,724	6,344,197	1,513,547
1996	69,674,088	33,236,382	25,313,240	6,384,484	1,538,658
1997	70,439,696	33,445,527	25,468,265	6,416,020	1,561,242
1998	71,161,368	33,558,706	25,540,609	6,437,837	1,580,260
1999	71,885,581	33,677,917	25,620,110	6,458,864	1,598,943
2000	72,637,651	33,799,808	25,700,222	6,482,367	1,617,219
2001	73,378,966	33,919,974	25,778,388	6,507,292	1,634,294
2002	74,090,082	33,840,544	25,690,835	6,505,705	1,644,004
2003	74,789,113	33,778,119	25,616,315	6,507,907	1,653,897
2004	75,493,071	33,719,761	25,545,963	6,510,237	1,663,561
2005	76,227,200	33,677,764	25,489,522	6,514,839	1,673,403
2006	76,967,698	33,624,784	25,423,352	6,518,370	1,683,062
2007	77,716,383	33,567,830	25,350,855	6,525,077	1,691,898
2008	78,446,730	33,504,658	25,269,434	6,534,512	1,700,712
2009	79,187,519	33,455,996	25,197,888	6,548,684	1,709,424
2010	79,957,976	33,454,732	25,164,816	6,570,097	1,719,819

Source: Day, Jennifer Cheeseman. 1996. "Projections of the Number of Households and Families in the United States: 1995 to 2010." U.S. Bureau of the Census, Current Population Reports P25-1129.

As of July 1.

(1) Series 1 is the preferred series, based on a time-series model that projects trends by age and sex in the proportions of persons maintaining households of different types. Series 1 also reflects the effects of projected changes in the age/sex structure of the population.
(2) Series 2 reflects the consequences of projected changes in the age/sex structure of the population only, assuming that household formation propensities by age/sex hold constant at 1990 levels.
(3) Series 3 reflects the consequences of projected changes in both the age/sex structure and the racial/Hispanic origin composition of the population. Series 3 assumes that household formation propensities hold constant at 1990 levels by age/sex and race/Hispanic origin.

See Appendix A for additional discussion of the projections.

Household Projections

TABLE 1.22. PROJECTED PERSONS LIVING ALONE BY AGE AND SEX: 1995 TO 2010

YEAR AND SERIES	Total	All persons living alone							
		Age of householder (Years)							
		Under 25	25-29	30-34	35-44	45-54	55-64	65-74	75 and older
SERIES ONE [1]									
1995	24,304,033	1,181,410	1,835,873	2,074,653	3,850,320	3,098,124	2,964,004	4,201,450	5,098,199
1996	24,685,504	1,157,708	1,850,792	2,044,403	3,968,992	3,249,886	3,016,890	4,176,616	5,220,217
1997	25,066,732	1,158,916	1,848,755	2,004,956	4,073,314	3,404,214	3,104,059	4,129,486	5,343,032
1998	25,453,243	1,177,852	1,834,233	1,965,479	4,164,738	3,528,491	3,248,815	4,088,228	5,445,407
1999	25,832,268	1,206,240	1,805,755	1,936,369	4,239,374	3,682,242	3,377,316	4,039,542	5,545,430
2000	26,230,735	1,238,757	1,774,641	1,931,474	4,288,175	3,850,291	3,488,176	4,019,214	5,640,007
2001	26,610,359	1,274,773	1,736,362	1,948,864	4,311,999	4,033,077	3,593,602	4,000,705	5,710,977
2002	27,038,352	1,303,882	1,738,892	1,948,769	4,307,968	4,126,728	3,851,453	3,983,580	5,777,080
2003	27,470,583	1,333,586	1,764,581	1,935,710	4,293,862	4,250,602	4,060,959	3,984,447	5,846,836
2004	27,897,645	1,354,350	1,810,436	1,908,171	4,284,548	4,374,573	4,269,221	4,004,010	5,892,336
2005	28,336,475	1,369,627	1,865,625	1,877,375	4,277,523	4,499,949	4,479,030	4,030,877	5,936,469
2006	28,785,843	1,386,509	1,926,765	1,839,076	4,271,527	4,621,048	4,692,990	4,078,429	5,969,499
2007	29,245,216	1,400,439	1,981,309	1,843,688	4,238,164	4,725,745	4,912,301	4,168,502	5,975,068
2008	29,735,137	1,419,024	2,033,812	1,872,892	4,192,188	4,814,643	5,092,416	4,335,082	5,975,080
2009	30,218,649	1,446,233	2,069,532	1,921,907	4,143,468	4,884,429	5,313,828	4,471,218	5,968,034
2010	30,727,167	1,471,805	2,097,681	1,980,961	4,118,321	4,925,642	5,555,549	4,583,741	5,993,467
SERIES TWO [2]									
1995	23,960,324	1,162,951	1,766,100	2,009,026	3,672,424	3,021,491	2,866,838	4,248,900	5,212,594
1996	24,246,935	1,136,950	1,768,740	1,963,985	3,746,969	3,145,793	2,898,125	4,231,952	5,354,421
1997	24,530,005	1,135,535	1,755,378	1,910,975	3,806,292	3,270,382	2,961,384	4,192,131	5,497,928
1998	24,814,655	1,151,583	1,730,536	1,858,880	3,852,238	3,364,253	3,077,955	4,158,079	5,621,131
1999	25,089,174	1,176,829	1,693,028	1,817,389	3,881,465	3,484,254	3,177,324	4,116,110	5,742,775
2000	25,381,467	1,206,016	1,653,636	1,799,161	3,886,329	3,615,608	3,258,455	4,102,838	5,859,424
2001	25,651,828	1,238,599	1,608,192	1,801,902	3,868,269	3,758,337	3,332,932	4,091,226	5,952,371
2002	25,964,241	1,264,361	1,600,946	1,788,707	3,825,706	3,816,278	3,546,184	4,080,918	6,041,141
2003	26,280,506	1,290,758	1,615,106	1,764,007	3,774,749	3,900,638	3,711,868	4,088,885	6,134,495
2004	26,587,559	1,308,595	1,647,587	1,726,686	3,728,689	3,983,576	3,873,491	4,115,971	6,202,964
2005	26,902,936	1,321,110	1,688,257	1,687,072	3,685,282	4,066,175	4,033,735	4,150,573	6,270,732
2006	27,225,780	1,335,225	1,733,977	1,641,438	3,643,432	4,143,367	4,194,769	4,206,497	6,327,075
2007	27,557,137	1,346,595	1,773,430	1,634,613	3,579,101	4,204,551	4,357,718	4,306,416	6,354,713
2008	27,924,401	1,362,511	1,810,797	1,649,729	3,505,418	4,250,513	4,483,255	4,485,605	6,376,573
2009	28,278,820	1,386,659	1,833,049	1,682,160	3,430,712	4,278,817	4,642,358	4,633,868	6,391,197
2010	28,653,823	1,409,094	1,848,498	1,723,056	3,376,629	4,281,528	4,815,942	4,758,027	6,441,049
SERIES THREE [3]									
1995	23,841,122	1,152,540	1,743,036	1,984,981	3,652,262	3,010,641	2,858,480	4,234,383	5,204,799
1996	24,100,620	1,123,469	1,743,841	1,934,023	3,720,923	3,133,157	2,887,686	4,213,974	5,343,547
1997	24,356,320	1,119,900	1,727,859	1,874,825	3,774,110	3,255,777	2,949,177	4,170,952	5,483,720
1998	24,611,945	1,134,890	1,699,570	1,818,117	3,813,145	3,347,455	3,062,853	4,133,708	5,602,207
1999	24,857,627	1,158,413	1,658,875	1,772,659	3,835,021	3,465,680	3,159,722	4,088,581	5,718,676
2000	25,120,990	1,185,653	1,615,976	1,751,811	3,832,365	3,595,180	3,238,348	4,072,007	5,829,650
2001	25,361,537	1,216,399	1,567,189	1,752,688	3,806,735	3,736,494	3,309,416	4,056,972	5,915,644
2002	25,643,996	1,240,252	1,557,420	1,737,438	3,755,926	3,792,965	3,519,477	4,043,185	5,997,333
2003	25,930,246	1,264,561	1,570,146	1,710,166	3,697,378	3,874,734	3,682,211	4,048,079	6,082,971
2004	26,206,149	1,280,113	1,600,276	1,670,851	3,643,780	3,954,788	3,841,581	4,071,960	6,142,800
2005	26,489,147	1,290,227	1,638,197	1,628,929	3,593,857	4,033,689	3,999,563	4,103,348	6,201,337
2006	26,778,130	1,301,519	1,680,902	1,580,891	3,546,553	4,106,416	4,158,489	4,155,555	6,247,805
2007	27,075,550	1,309,339	1,717,385	1,572,038	3,476,444	4,163,320	4,319,240	4,252,003	6,265,781
2008	27,407,524	1,321,310	1,751,341	1,585,616	3,397,862	4,204,477	4,442,610	4,427,038	6,277,270
2009	27,725,678	1,340,885	1,770,103	1,615,645	3,318,958	4,227,582	4,600,088	4,571,002	6,281,415
2010	28,062,318	1,357,878	1,782,277	1,653,748	3,261,078	4,224,867	4,771,868	4,690,358	6,320,244

See notes at end of table.

Household Projections

YEAR AND SERIES	Total	TABLE 1.22. PROJECTED PERSONS LIVING ALONE BY AGE AND SEX: 1995 TO 2010 - Continued							
		Women living alone							
		Age of householder (Years)							
		Under 25	25-29	30-34	35-44	45-54	55-64	65-74	75 and older
SERIES ONE [1]									
1995	14,131,130	525,530	730,096	768,954	1,458,546	1,569,666	1,830,110	3,124,124	4,124,104
1996	14,303,740	515,601	737,290	755,741	1,493,081	1,642,548	1,850,628	3,094,221	4,214,630
1997	14,480,066	516,666	737,453	739,845	1,522,222	1,716,888	1,892,081	3,048,057	4,306,854
1998	14,664,328	525,555	732,890	724,000	1,546,748	1,776,565	1,967,949	3,006,141	4,384,480
1999	14,843,547	538,531	722,818	712,363	1,565,319	1,850,894	2,034,440	2,958,641	4,460,541
2000	15,035,436	553,270	711,325	709,971	1,575,053	1,931,934	2,089,583	2,931,397	4,532,903
2001	15,216,490	569,501	696,915	716,401	1,576,207	2,021,236	2,141,699	2,906,717	4,587,814
2002	15,433,063	582,581	699,028	715,998	1,567,749	2,065,441	2,281,271	2,882,983	4,638,012
2003	15,653,609	595,975	710,395	711,210	1,556,125	2,124,564	2,392,366	2,873,143	4,689,831
2004	15,869,964	605,580	729,829	701,252	1,546,785	2,184,104	2,501,862	2,877,413	4,723,139
2005	16,092,545	612,573	753,239	689,833	1,539,388	2,244,366	2,611,117	2,887,675	4,754,354
2006	16,321,294	620,272	778,821	675,589	1,532,740	2,302,440	2,721,265	2,911,908	4,778,259
2007	16,557,368	626,669	801,771	677,356	1,516,539	2,352,593	2,834,362	2,966,551	4,781,527
2008	16,814,311	635,175	823,861	687,864	1,495,604	2,394,603	2,922,782	3,074,289	4,780,133
2009	17,064,942	647,424	839,410	705,721	1,474,423	2,428,166	3,034,420	3,162,244	4,773,134
2010	17,326,905	658,853	851,869	727,477	1,461,547	2,448,328	3,155,257	3,233,068	4,790,506
SERIES TWO [2]									
1995	14,011,383	514,379	693,475	742,890	1,422,438	1,506,771	1,798,290	3,165,303	4,167,837
1996	14,150,750	502,965	694,148	724,137	1,444,290	1,562,490	1,811,127	3,144,056	4,267,537
1997	14,292,462	502,339	688,265	703,121	1,460,568	1,618,460	1,844,258	3,106,092	4,369,359
1998	14,440,537	509,369	678,102	682,432	1,472,001	1,659,461	1,910,389	3,072,128	4,456,655
1999	14,582,459	520,326	663,092	666,043	1,477,658	1,713,239	1,967,011	3,032,283	4,542,807
2000	14,736,571	532,924	647,076	658,502	1,474,952	1,772,186	2,012,319	3,013,090	4,625,522
2001	14,878,507	546,951	628,734	659,233	1,464,355	1,837,597	2,054,400	2,996,420	4,690,817
2002	15,053,206	557,858	625,407	653,576	1,444,658	1,860,593	2,179,260	2,980,336	4,751,518
2003	15,231,901	569,111	630,414	644,116	1,422,547	1,896,618	2,276,239	2,978,634	4,814,222
2004	15,404,684	576,806	642,461	630,145	1,402,765	1,932,185	2,370,776	2,991,457	4,858,089
2005	15,582,314	581,991	657,811	615,089	1,384,987	1,967,592	2,464,301	3,010,500	4,900,043
2006	15,765,036	587,876	674,807	597,736	1,368,034	2,000,188	2,557,708	3,044,113	4,934,574
2007	15,954,749	592,582	689,283	594,685	1,342,757	2,025,106	2,652,884	3,109,575	4,947,877
2008	16,168,677	599,320	702,798	599,274	1,313,601	2,042,295	2,724,076	3,230,989	4,956,324
2009	16,373,329	609,543	710,598	610,132	1,284,570	2,051,818	2,815,905	3,331,924	4,958,839
2010	16,587,410	618,876	715,632	624,089	1,262,933	2,049,396	2,914,932	3,414,951	4,986,601
SERIES THREE [3]									
1995	13,918,696	507,608	683,169	731,402	1,408,285	1,495,774	1,787,285	3,146,015	4,159,158
1996	14,037,314	494,274	682,664	710,091	1,426,806	1,549,207	1,797,992	3,120,423	4,255,857
1997	14,158,364	492,218	675,243	686,407	1,439,678	1,602,860	1,829,074	3,078,349	4,354,535
1998	14,284,500	498,412	663,067	663,717	1,447,398	1,641,287	1,892,814	3,040,302	4,437,503
1999	14,404,334	508,359	646,017	645,567	1,449,220	1,692,683	1,947,015	2,996,407	4,519,066
2000	14,535,723	519,890	627,820	636,658	1,442,675	1,749,163	1,989,597	2,973,369	4,596,551
2001	14,654,100	532,892	607,399	636,224	1,428,367	1,812,347	2,028,495	2,952,964	4,655,412
2002	14,804,932	542,733	602,417	629,244	1,404,609	1,832,991	2,150,216	2,933,174	4,709,548
2003	14,959,363	552,834	606,325	618,150	1,378,788	1,866,275	2,243,914	2,927,951	4,765,126
2004	15,107,104	559,283	617,099	602,667	1,355,357	1,899,058	2,335,217	2,937,311	4,801,112
2005	15,258,654	563,206	631,029	585,974	1,334,332	1,931,325	2,425,347	2,952,738	4,834,703
2006	15,414,308	567,668	646,464	567,011	1,314,466	1,960,426	2,515,355	2,982,556	4,860,362
2007	15,577,033	570,629	659,405	562,571	1,286,144	1,981,969	2,607,146	3,044,184	4,864,985
2008	15,762,683	575,463	671,169	566,039	1,254,226	1,995,458	2,674,687	3,161,579	4,864,062
2009	15,938,606	583,433	677,217	575,595	1,222,677	2,001,231	2,763,118	3,258,047	4,857,288
2010	16,122,429	590,073	680,658	588,098	1,198,603	1,995,098	2,858,603	3,335,946	4,875,350

See notes at end of table.

Household Projections

TABLE 1.22. PROJECTED PERSONS LIVING ALONE BY AGE AND SEX: 1995 TO 2010 - Continued

YEAR AND SERIES	Total	Men living alone Age of householder (Years)							
		Under 25	25-29	30-34	35-44	45-54	55-64	65-74	75 and older
SERIES ONE [1]									
1995	10,172,903	655,880	1,105,777	1,305,699	2,391,774	1,528,458	1,133,894	1,077,326	974,095
1996	10,381,764	642,107	1,113,502	1,288,662	2,475,911	1,607,338	1,166,262	1,082,395	1,005,587
1997	10,586,666	642,250	1,111,302	1,265,111	2,551,092	1,687,326	1,211,978	1,081,429	1,036,178
1998	10,788,915	652,297	1,101,343	1,241,479	2,617,990	1,751,926	1,280,866	1,082,087	1,060,927
1999	10,988,721	667,709	1,082,937	1,224,006	2,674,055	1,831,348	1,342,876	1,080,901	1,084,889
2000	11,195,299	685,487	1,063,316	1,221,503	2,713,122	1,918,357	1,398,593	1,087,817	1,107,104
2001	11,393,869	705,272	1,039,447	1,232,463	2,735,792	2,011,841	1,451,903	1,093,988	1,123,163
2002	11,605,289	721,301	1,039,864	1,232,771	2,740,219	2,061,287	1,570,182	1,100,597	1,139,068
2003	11,816,974	737,611	1,054,186	1,224,500	2,737,737	2,126,038	1,668,593	1,111,304	1,157,005
2004	12,027,681	748,770	1,080,607	1,206,919	2,737,763	2,190,469	1,767,359	1,126,597	1,169,197
2005	12,243,930	757,054	1,112,386	1,187,542	2,738,135	2,255,583	1,867,913	1,143,202	1,182,115
2006	12,464,549	766,237	1,147,944	1,163,487	2,738,787	2,318,608	1,971,725	1,166,521	1,191,240
2007	12,687,848	773,770	1,179,538	1,166,332	2,721,625	2,373,152	2,077,939	1,201,951	1,193,541
2008	12,920,826	783,849	1,209,951	1,185,028	2,696,584	2,420,040	2,169,634	1,260,793	1,194,947
2009	13,153,707	798,809	1,230,122	1,216,186	2,669,045	2,456,263	2,279,408	1,308,974	1,194,900
2010	13,400,262	812,952	1,245,812	1,253,484	2,656,774	2,477,314	2,400,292	1,350,673	1,202,961
SERIES TWO [2]									
1995	9,948,941	648,572	1,072,625	1,266,136	2,249,986	1,514,720	1,068,548	1,083,597	1,044,757
1996	10,096,185	633,985	1,074,592	1,239,848	2,302,679	1,583,303	1,086,998	1,087,896	1,086,884
1997	10,237,543	633,196	1,067,113	1,207,854	2,345,724	1,651,922	1,117,126	1,086,039	1,128,569
1998	10,374,118	642,214	1,052,434	1,176,448	2,380,237	1,704,792	1,167,566	1,085,951	1,164,476
1999	10,506,715	656,503	1,029,936	1,151,346	2,403,807	1,771,015	1,210,313	1,083,827	1,199,968
2000	10,644,896	673,092	1,006,560	1,140,659	2,411,377	1,843,422	1,246,136	1,089,748	1,233,902
2001	10,773,321	691,648	979,458	1,142,669	2,403,914	1,920,740	1,278,532	1,094,806	1,261,554
2002	10,911,035	706,503	975,539	1,135,131	2,381,048	1,955,685	1,366,924	1,100,582	1,289,623
2003	11,048,605	721,647	984,692	1,119,891	2,352,202	2,004,020	1,435,629	1,110,251	1,320,273
2004	11,182,875	731,789	1,005,126	1,096,541	2,325,924	2,051,391	1,502,715	1,124,514	1,344,875
2005	11,320,622	739,119	1,030,446	1,071,983	2,300,295	2,098,583	1,569,434	1,140,073	1,370,689
2006	11,460,744	747,349	1,059,170	1,043,702	2,275,398	2,143,179	1,637,061	1,162,384	1,392,501
2007	11,602,388	754,013	1,084,147	1,039,928	2,236,344	2,179,445	1,704,834	1,196,841	1,406,836
2008	11,755,724	763,191	1,107,999	1,050,455	2,191,817	2,208,218	1,759,179	1,254,616	1,420,249
2009	11,905,491	777,116	1,122,451	1,072,028	2,146,142	2,226,999	1,826,453	1,301,944	1,432,358
2010	12,066,413	790,218	1,132,866	1,098,967	2,113,696	2,232,132	1,901,010	1,343,076	1,454,448
SERIES THREE [3]									
1995	9,922,426	644,932	1,059,867	1,253,579	2,243,977	1,514,867	1,071,195	1,088,368	1,045,641
1996	10,063,306	629,195	1,061,177	1,223,932	2,294,117	1,583,950	1,089,694	1,093,551	1,087,690
1997	10,197,956	627,682	1,052,616	1,188,418	2,334,432	1,652,917	1,120,103	1,092,603	1,129,185
1998	10,327,445	636,478	1,036,503	1,154,400	2,365,747	1,706,168	1,170,039	1,093,406	1,164,704
1999	10,453,293	650,054	1,012,858	1,127,092	2,385,801	1,772,997	1,212,707	1,092,174	1,199,610
2000	10,585,267	665,763	988,156	1,115,153	2,389,690	1,846,017	1,248,751	1,098,638	1,233,099
2001	10,707,437	683,507	959,790	1,116,464	2,378,368	1,924,147	1,280,921	1,104,008	1,260,232
2002	10,839,064	697,519	955,003	1,108,194	2,351,317	1,959,974	1,369,261	1,110,011	1,287,785
2003	10,970,883	711,727	963,821	1,092,016	2,318,590	2,008,459	1,438,297	1,120,128	1,317,845
2004	11,099,045	720,830	983,177	1,068,184	2,288,423	2,055,730	1,506,364	1,134,649	1,341,688
2005	11,230,493	727,021	1,007,168	1,042,955	2,259,525	2,102,364	1,574,216	1,150,610	1,366,634
2006	11,363,822	733,851	1,034,438	1,013,880	2,232,087	2,145,990	1,643,134	1,172,999	1,387,443
2007	11,498,517	738,710	1,057,980	1,009,467	2,190,300	2,181,351	1,712,094	1,207,819	1,400,796
2008	11,644,841	745,847	1,080,172	1,019,577	2,143,636	2,209,019	1,767,923	1,265,459	1,413,208
2009	11,787,072	757,452	1,092,886	1,040,050	2,096,281	2,226,351	1,836,970	1,312,955	1,424,127
2010	11,939,889	767,805	1,101,619	1,065,650	2,062,475	2,229,769	1,913,265	1,354,412	1,444,894

Source: Day, Jennifer Cheeseman. 1996. "Projections of the Number of Households and Families in the United States: 1995 to 2010." U.S. Bureau of the Census, Current Population Reports P25-1129.

As of July 1.

(1) Series 1 is the preferred series, based on a time-series model that projects trends by age and sex in the proportions of persons maintaining households of different types. Series 1 also reflects the effects of projected changes in age/sex structure of the population.

(2) Series 2 reflects the consequences of projected changes in the age/sex structure of the population only, assuming that household formation propensities by age/sex hold constant at 1990 levels.

(3) Series 3 reflects the consequences of projected changes in both the age/sex structure and the racial/Hispanic origin composition of the population. Series 3 assumes that household formation propensities hold constant at 1990 levels by age/sex and race/Hispanic origin.

See Appendix A for additional discussion of the projections.

Household Projections

TABLE 1.23. PROJECTED HOUSEHOLDS BY HOUSEHOLD TYPE, RACE, AND HISPANIC ORIGIN: 1995 TO 2010

YEAR, RACE, AND HISPANIC ORIGIN	All households	Family households				Nonfamily households			Average number of persons	
		Total	Married couple	Other family		Total	Female householder	Male householder	Per household	Per family
				Female householder	Male householder					
TOTAL										
1995	97,574,189	68,872,603	54,064,426	11,336,429	3,471,748	28,701,586	15,799,625	12,901,961	2.62	3.14
1996	98,641,315	69,674,088	54,674,787	11,463,777	3,535,524	28,967,227	15,914,198	13,053,029	2.62	3.14
1997	99,680,030	70,439,696	55,252,827	11,588,373	3,598,496	29,240,334	16,037,537	13,202,797	2.62	3.13
1998	100,683,716	71,161,368	55,795,398	11,706,994	3,658,976	29,522,348	16,171,073	13,351,275	2.61	3.13
1999	101,683,469	71,885,581	56,338,766	11,827,365	3,719,450	29,797,888	16,300,363	13,497,525	2.61	3.12
2000	102,734,349	72,637,651	56,904,364	11,952,311	3,780,976	30,096,698	16,443,281	13,653,417	2.61	3.12
2001	103,754,014	73,378,966	57,461,517	12,077,637	3,839,812	30,375,048	16,574,784	13,800,264	2.60	3.11
2002	104,784,362	74,090,082	58,010,418	12,184,607	3,895,057	30,694,280	16,737,426	13,956,854	2.60	3.11
2003	105,813,805	74,789,113	58,543,186	12,295,128	3,950,799	31,024,692	16,907,152	14,117,540	2.60	3.10
2004	106,835,305	75,493,071	59,080,407	12,406,575	4,006,089	31,342,234	17,069,178	14,273,056	2.59	3.10
2005	107,892,079	76,227,200	59,642,441	12,522,567	4,062,192	31,664,879	17,233,807	14,431,072	2.59	3.09
2006	108,963,276	76,967,698	60,209,569	12,638,983	4,119,146	31,995,578	17,403,252	14,592,326	2.58	3.09
2007	110,051,064	77,716,383	60,784,900	12,756,689	4,174,794	32,334,681	17,579,493	14,755,188	2.58	3.08
2008	111,161,226	78,446,730	61,342,277	12,872,767	4,231,686	32,714,496	17,780,666	14,933,830	2.57	3.07
2009	112,270,638	79,187,519	61,906,394	12,993,258	4,287,867	33,083,119	17,973,497	15,109,622	2.57	3.07
2010	113,425,776	79,957,976	62,494,303	13,117,622	4,346,051	33,467,800	18,172,225	15,295,575	2.56	3.06
WHITE										
1995	83,126,521	58,479,769	48,220,803	7,565,962	2,693,004	24,646,752	13,733,078	10,913,674	2.56	3.07
1996	83,870,268	59,042,942	48,678,983	7,626,463	2,737,496	24,827,326	13,806,829	11,020,497	2.56	3.06
1997	84,586,111	59,573,563	49,108,160	7,684,439	2,780,964	25,012,548	13,887,408	11,125,140	2.55	3.06
1998	85,270,711	60,064,518	49,505,179	7,737,368	2,821,971	25,206,193	13,977,437	11,228,756	2.55	3.05
1999	85,952,036	60,558,865	49,903,203	7,792,563	2,863,099	25,393,171	14,062,807	11,330,364	2.55	3.05
2000	86,675,553	61,076,096	50,320,749	7,850,453	2,904,894	25,599,457	14,159,185	11,440,272	2.54	3.04
2001	87,370,922	61,584,148	50,730,510	7,909,191	2,944,447	25,786,774	14,244,386	11,542,388	2.54	3.04
2002	88,076,002	62,066,424	51,133,853	7,952,171	2,980,400	26,009,578	14,357,115	11,652,463	2.53	3.03
2003	88,782,502	62,540,921	51,524,485	7,999,440	3,016,996	26,241,581	14,474,920	11,766,661	2.53	3.02
2004	89,479,238	63,020,178	51,919,221	8,047,896	3,053,061	26,459,060	14,583,993	11,875,067	2.52	3.02
2005	90,204,246	63,525,190	52,335,592	8,099,845	3,089,753	26,679,056	14,693,713	11,985,343	2.52	3.01
2006	90,941,737	64,035,621	52,756,804	8,151,890	3,126,927	26,906,116	14,807,915	12,098,201	2.51	3.01
2007	91,686,940	64,549,166	53,183,680	8,203,138	3,162,348	27,137,774	14,926,884	12,210,890	2.51	3.00
2008	92,453,446	65,046,441	53,595,232	8,252,703	3,198,506	27,407,005	15,069,543	12,337,462	2.50	2.99
2009	93,211,104	65,548,824	54,010,476	8,304,635	3,233,713	27,662,280	15,202,425	12,459,855	2.50	2.99
2010	94,010,462	66,078,448	54,447,373	8,360,230	3,270,845	27,932,014	15,340,100	12,591,914	2.49	2.98
BLACK										
1995	11,152,480	7,844,987	3,866,625	3,377,296	601,066	3,307,493	1,726,806	1,580,687	2.85	3.43
1996	11,354,230	7,987,265	3,942,263	3,430,891	614,111	3,366,965	1,754,751	1,612,214	2.84	3.42
1997	11,556,106	8,127,533	4,015,991	3,484,223	627,319	3,428,573	1,784,228	1,644,345	2.83	3.40
1998	11,752,819	8,262,713	4,086,011	3,536,278	640,424	3,490,106	1,813,872	1,676,234	2.83	3.39
1999	11,947,894	8,396,721	4,155,791	3,587,600	653,330	3,551,173	1,843,552	1,707,621	2.82	3.39
2000	12,149,243	8,533,897	4,226,890	3,640,548	666,459	3,615,346	1,875,390	1,739,956	2.81	3.38
2001	12,346,142	8,668,890	4,297,086	3,692,709	679,095	3,677,252	1,906,471	1,770,781	2.80	3.37
2002	12,544,860	8,801,250	4,367,069	3,742,600	691,581	3,743,610	1,940,840	1,802,770	2.80	3.36
2003	12,739,981	8,929,032	4,433,789	3,791,446	703,797	3,810,949	1,976,638	1,834,311	2.79	3.35
2004	12,936,105	9,056,607	4,500,717	3,839,909	715,981	3,879,498	2,013,307	1,866,191	2.78	3.34
2005	13,136,816	9,186,541	4,569,036	3,889,260	728,245	3,950,275	2,051,719	1,898,556	2.77	3.34
2006	13,337,353	9,316,038	4,636,652	3,938,739	740,647	4,021,315	2,090,298	1,931,017	2.77	3.33
2007	13,546,255	9,450,472	4,706,742	3,990,304	753,426	4,095,783	2,130,864	1,964,919	2.76	3.32
2008	13,754,037	9,582,154	4,773,951	4,041,802	766,401	4,171,883	2,172,068	1,999,815	2.75	3.31
2009	13,968,615	9,718,463	4,843,645	4,095,257	779,561	4,250,152	2,214,450	2,035,702	2.74	3.31
2010	14,185,450	9,856,032	4,914,444	4,148,909	792,679	4,329,418	2,257,713	2,071,705	2.74	3.30

Projection series 3. See notes at end of table.

Household Projections

TABLE 1.23. PROJECTED HOUSEHOLDS BY HOUSEHOLD TYPE, RACE, AND HISPANIC ORIGIN: 1995 TO 2010 - Continued

YEAR, RACE, AND HISPANIC ORIGIN	All households	Family households				Nonfamily households			Average number of persons	
		Total	Married couple	Other family		Total	Female householder	Male householder	Per household	Per family
				Female householder	Male householder					
AMERICAN INDIAN, ESKIMO, AND										
1995	686,847	513,374	332,015	136,800	44,559	173,473	82,582	90,891	3.17	3.65
1996	700,121	522,746	338,280	138,958	45,508	177,375	84,553	92,822	3.16	3.63
1997	713,397	531,997	344,406	141,130	46,461	181,400	86,608	94,792	3.14	3.62
1998	726,702	541,118	350,355	143,345	47,418	185,584	88,772	96,812	3.13	3.60
1999	740,165	550,353	356,343	145,634	48,376	189,812	90,963	98,849	3.11	3.59
2000	754,180	560,006	362,590	148,044	49,372	194,174	93,202	100,972	3.10	3.57
2001	768,538	569,944	369,012	150,562	50,370	198,594	95,477	103,117	3.08	3.56
2002	782,688	579,597	375,269	152,976	51,352	203,091	97,803	105,288	3.07	3.54
2003	797,248	589,510	381,621	155,529	52,360	207,738	100,220	107,518	3.06	3.53
2004	811,919	599,542	388,047	158,108	53,387	212,377	102,614	109,763	3.04	3.51
2005	827,029	609,936	394,757	160,746	54,433	217,093	105,048	112,045	3.03	3.50
2006	842,551	620,635	401,665	163,454	55,516	221,916	107,507	114,409	3.01	3.48
2007	858,157	631,341	408,547	166,195	56,599	226,816	110,026	116,790	3.00	3.47
2008	874,260	642,354	415,567	169,043	57,744	231,906	112,608	119,298	2.99	3.46
2009	890,053	653,238	422,553	171,835	58,850	236,815	115,101	121,714	2.98	3.44
2010	906,036	664,325	429,667	174,682	59,976	241,711	117,559	124,152	2.96	3.43
ASIAN AND PACIFIC ISLANDER										
1995	2,608,341	2,034,473	1,644,983	256,371	133,119	573,868	257,159	316,709	3.52	3.99
1996	2,716,696	2,121,135	1,715,261	267,465	138,409	595,561	268,065	327,496	3.52	3.99
1997	2,824,416	2,206,603	1,784,270	278,581	143,752	617,813	279,293	338,520	3.51	3.98
1998	2,933,484	2,293,019	1,853,853	290,003	149,163	640,465	290,992	349,473	3.51	3.98
1999	3,043,374	2,379,642	1,923,429	301,568	154,645	663,732	303,041	360,691	3.51	3.98
2000	3,155,373	2,467,652	1,994,135	313,266	160,251	687,721	315,504	372,217	3.50	3.97
2001	3,268,412	2,555,984	2,064,909	325,175	165,900	712,428	328,450	383,978	3.50	3.97
2002	3,380,812	2,642,811	2,134,227	336,860	171,724	738,001	341,668	396,333	3.50	3.97
2003	3,494,074	2,729,650	2,203,291	348,713	177,646	764,424	355,374	409,050	3.49	3.96
2004	3,608,043	2,816,744	2,272,422	360,662	183,660	791,299	369,264	422,035	3.49	3.97
2005	3,723,988	2,905,533	2,343,056	372,716	189,761	818,455	383,327	435,128	3.49	3.96
2006	3,841,635	2,995,404	2,414,448	384,900	196,056	846,231	397,532	448,699	3.49	3.96
2007	3,959,712	3,085,404	2,485,931	397,052	202,421	874,308	411,719	462,589	3.48	3.96
2008	4,079,483	3,175,781	2,557,527	409,219	209,035	903,702	426,447	477,255	3.48	3.96
2009	4,200,866	3,266,994	2,629,720	421,531	215,743	933,872	441,521	492,351	3.48	3.96
2010	4,323,828	3,359,171	2,702,819	433,801	222,551	964,657	456,853	507,804	3.47	3.96

Projection series 3. See notes at end of table.

Household Projections

TABLE 1.23. PROJECTED HOUSEHOLDS BY HOUSEHOLD TYPE, RACE, AND HISPANIC ORIGIN: 1995 TO 2010 - Continued

YEAR, RACE, AND HISPANIC ORIGIN	All households	Family households				Nonfamily households			Average number of persons	
		Total	Married couple	Other family		Total	Female householder	Male householder	Per household	Per family
				Female householder	Male householder					
HISPANIC ORIGIN [1]										
1995	7,368,163	5,884,537	4,067,342	1,295,701	521,494	1,483,626	668,109	815,517	3.58	3.93
1996	7,643,450	6,103,298	4,219,884	1,343,334	540,080	1,540,152	694,478	845,674	3.56	3.91
1997	7,916,601	6,319,716	4,369,654	1,391,126	558,936	1,596,885	720,803	876,082	3.55	3.90
1998	8,194,930	6,538,758	4,520,828	1,439,700	578,230	1,656,172	748,793	907,379	3.53	3.88
1999	8,473,701	6,757,549	4,671,095	1,488,761	597,693	1,716,152	777,252	938,900	3.52	3.87
2000	8,760,637	6,981,640	4,825,118	1,538,882	617,640	1,778,997	807,526	971,471	3.51	3.86
2001	9,050,587	7,207,758	4,980,376	1,589,742	637,640	1,842,829	838,632	1,004,197	3.50	3.85
2002	9,340,520	7,432,166	5,134,594	1,639,805	657,767	1,908,354	870,703	1,037,651	3.49	3.84
2003	9,634,693	7,658,881	5,289,934	1,690,776	678,171	1,975,812	904,060	1,071,752	3.48	3.83
2004	9,931,171	7,886,388	5,445,459	1,742,097	698,832	2,044,783	938,314	1,106,469	3.47	3.82
2005	10,236,089	8,120,035	5,605,445	1,794,674	719,916	2,116,054	973,833	1,142,221	3.46	3.81
2006	10,549,060	8,358,919	5,769,023	1,848,257	741,639	2,190,141	1,010,810	1,179,331	3.45	3.81
2007	10,864,976	8,600,147	5,933,816	1,902,600	763,731	2,264,829	1,047,875	1,216,954	3.44	3.80
2008	11,191,010	8,846,772	6,102,143	1,957,866	786,763	2,344,238	1,087,580	1,256,658	3.43	3.79
2009	11,521,966	9,096,665	6,272,227	2,014,177	810,261	2,425,301	1,128,078	1,297,223	3.42	3.78
2010	11,866,338	9,355,801	6,448,945	2,072,234	834,622	2,510,537	1,170,702	1,339,835	3.41	3.77

Source: Day, Jennifer Cheeseman. 1996. "Projections of the Number of Households and Families in the United States: 1995 to 2010." U.S. Bureau of the Census, Current Population Reports P25-1129.

As of July 1.

(1) Persons of Hispanic origin may be of any race. These data do not include households of Puerto Rico.

Data are from projection series 3, which reflects the consequences of projected changes in both the age/sex structure and the racial/Hispanic origin composition of the population. Series 3 assumes that household formation propensities hold constant at 1990 levels by age/sex and race/Hispanic origin. See Appendix A for additional discussion of the projections.

State Population Estimates and Projections

AREA	\multicolumn{10}{c}{TABLE 1.24. RESIDENT POPULATION OF THE REGIONS AND STATES: 1900 TO 1990}
	1900	1910	1920	1930	1940	1950	1960	1970	1980	1990
United States	76,212,168	92,228,496	106,021,537	123,202,624	132,164,569	151,325,798	179,323,175	203,302,031	226,542,199	248,709,873
Northeast	21,046,695	25,868,573	29,662,053	34,427,091	35,976,777	39,477,986	44,677,819	49,060,514	49,136,816	50,809,229
Midwest	26,333,004	29,888,542	34,019,792	38,594,100	40,143,332	44,460,762	51,619,139	56,590,294	58,866,998	59,668,632
South	24,523,527	29,389,330	33,125,803	37,857,633	41,665,901	47,197,088	54,973,113	62,812,980	75,367,068	85,445,930
West	4,308,942	7,082,051	9,213,889	12,323,800	14,378,559	20,189,962	28,053,104	34,838,243	43,171,317	52,786,082
Alabama	1,828,697	2,138,093	2,348,174	2,646,248	2,832,961	3,061,743	3,266,740	3,444,354	3,894,025	4,040,587
Alaska	63,592	64,356	55,036	59,278	72,524	128,643	226,167	302,853	401,851	550,043
Arizona	122,931	204,354	334,162	435,573	499,261	749,587	1,302,161	1,775,399	2,716,546	3,665,228
Arkansas	1,311,564	1,574,449	1,752,204	1,854,482	1,949,387	1,909,511	1,786,272	1,923,322	2,286,357	2,350,725
California	1,485,053	2,377,549	3,426,861	5,677,251	6,907,387	10,586,223	15,717,204	19,971,069	23,667,764	29,760,021
Colorado	539,700	799,024	939,629	1,035,791	1,123,296	1,325,089	1,753,947	2,209,596	2,889,735	3,294,394
Connecticut	908,420	1,114,756	1,380,631	1,606,903	1,709,242	2,007,280	2,535,234	3,032,217	3,107,564	3,287,116
Delaware	184,735	202,322	223,003	230,380	266,505	318,085	446,292	548,104	594,338	666,168
District of Columbia	278,718	331,069	437,571	486,869	663,091	802,178	763,956	756,668	638,432	606,900
Florida	528,542	752,619	968,470	1,468,211	1,897,414	2,771,305	4,951,560	6,791,418	9,746,961	12,937,926
Georgia	2,216,331	2,609,121	2,895,832	2,908,506	3,123,723	3,444,578	3,943,116	4,587,930	5,462,982	6,478,216
Hawaii	154,001	191,874	255,881	368,300	422,770	499,794	632,772	769,913	964,691	1,108,229
Idaho	161,772	325,594	431,866	445,032	524,873	588,637	667,191	713,015	944,127	1,006,749
Illinois	4,821,550	5,638,591	6,485,280	7,630,654	7,897,241	8,712,176	10,081,158	11,110,285	11,427,409	11,430,602
Indiana	2,516,462	2,700,876	2,930,390	3,238,503	3,427,796	3,934,224	4,662,498	5,195,392	5,490,210	5,544,159
Iowa	2,231,853	2,224,771	2,404,021	2,470,939	2,538,268	2,621,073	2,757,537	2,825,368	2,913,808	2,776,755
Kansas	1,470,495	1,690,949	1,769,257	1,880,999	1,801,028	1,905,299	2,178,611	2,249,071	2,364,236	2,477,574
Kentucky	2,147,174	2,289,905	2,416,630	2,614,589	2,845,627	2,944,806	3,038,156	3,220,711	3,660,324	3,685,296
Louisiana	1,381,625	1,656,388	1,798,509	2,101,593	2,363,880	2,683,516	3,257,022	3,644,637	4,206,116	4,219,973
Maine	694,466	742,371	768,014	797,423	847,226	913,774	969,265	993,722	1,125,043	1,227,928
Maryland	1,188,044	1,295,346	1,449,661	1,631,526	1,821,244	2,343,001	3,100,689	3,923,897	4,216,933	4,781,468
Massachusetts	2,805,346	3,366,416	3,852,356	4,249,614	4,316,721	4,690,514	5,148,578	5,689,170	5,737,093	6,016,425
Michigan	2,420,982	2,810,173	3,668,412	4,842,325	5,256,106	6,371,766	7,823,194	8,881,826	9,262,044	9,295,297
Minnesota	1,751,394	2,075,708	2,387,125	2,563,953	2,792,300	2,982,483	3,413,864	3,806,103	4,075,970	4,375,099
Mississippi	1,551,270	1,797,114	1,790,618	2,009,821	2,183,796	2,178,914	2,178,141	2,216,994	2,520,770	2,573,216
Missouri	3,106,665	3,293,335	3,404,055	3,629,367	3,784,664	3,954,653	4,319,813	4,677,623	4,916,766	5,117,073
Montana	243,329	376,053	548,889	537,606	559,456	591,024	674,767	694,409	786,690	799,065
Nebraska	1,066,300	1,192,214	1,296,372	1,377,963	1,315,834	1,325,510	1,411,330	1,485,333	1,569,825	1,578,385
Nevada	42,335	81,875	77,407	91,058	110,247	160,083	285,278	488,738	800,508	1,201,833
New Hampshire	411,588	430,572	443,083	465,293	491,524	533,242	606,921	737,681	920,610	1,109,252
New Jersey	1,883,669	2,537,167	3,155,900	4,041,334	4,160,165	4,835,329	6,066,782	7,171,112	7,365,011	7,730,188
New Mexico	195,310	327,301	360,350	423,317	531,818	681,187	951,023	1,017,055	1,303,302	1,515,069
New York	7,268,894	9,113,614	10,385,227	12,588,066	13,479,142	14,830,192	16,782,304	18,241,391	17,558,165	17,990,455
North Carolina	1,893,810	2,206,287	2,559,123	3,170,276	3,571,623	4,061,929	4,556,155	5,084,411	5,880,095	6,628,637
North Dakota	319,146	577,056	646,872	680,845	641,935	619,636	632,446	617,792	652,717	638,800
Ohio	4,157,545	4,767,121	5,759,394	6,646,697	6,907,612	7,946,627	9,706,397	10,657,423	10,797,603	10,847,115
Oklahoma	790,391	1,657,155	2,028,283	2,396,040	2,336,434	2,233,351	2,328,284	2,559,463	3,025,487	3,145,585
Oregon	413,536	672,765	783,389	953,786	1,089,684	1,521,341	1,768,687	2,091,533	2,633,156	2,842,321
Pennsylvania	6,302,115	7,665,111	8,720,017	9,631,350	9,900,180	10,498,012	11,319,366	11,800,766	11,864,720	11,881,643
Rhode Island	428,556	542,610	604,397	687,497	713,346	791,896	859,488	949,723	947,154	1,003,464
South Carolina	1,340,316	1,515,400	1,683,724	1,738,765	1,899,804	2,117,027	2,382,594	2,590,713	3,120,729	3,486,703
South Dakota	401,570	583,888	636,547	692,849	642,961	652,740	680,514	666,257	690,768	696,004
Tennessee	2,020,616	2,184,789	2,337,885	2,616,556	2,915,841	3,291,718	3,567,089	3,926,018	4,591,023	4,877,185
Texas	3,048,710	3,896,542	4,663,228	5,824,715	6,414,824	7,711,194	9,579,677	11,198,655	14,225,513	16,986,510
Utah	276,749	373,351	449,396	507,847	550,310	688,862	890,627	1,059,273	1,461,037	1,722,850
Vermont	343,641	355,956	352,428	359,611	359,231	377,747	389,881	444,732	511,456	562,758
Virginia	1,854,184	2,061,612	2,309,187	2,421,851	2,677,773	3,318,680	3,966,949	4,651,448	5,346,797	6,187,358
Washington	518,103	1,141,990	1,356,621	1,563,396	1,736,191	2,378,963	2,853,214	3,413,244	4,132,353	4,866,692
West Virginia	958,800	1,221,119	1,463,701	1,729,205	1,901,974	2,005,552	1,860,421	1,744,237	1,950,186	1,793,477
Wisconsin	2,069,042	2,333,860	2,632,067	2,939,006	3,137,587	3,434,575	3,951,777	4,417,821	4,705,642	4,891,769
Wyoming	92,531	145,965	194,402	225,565	250,742	290,529	330,066	332,416	469,557	453,588

Source: U.S. Bureau of the Census, 1900-1990 Censuses.

State Population Estimates and Projections

AREA	1980	1981	1982	1983	1984	1985	1986	1987	1988	1989
	TABLE 1.25. ESTIMATED RESIDENT POPULATION OF THE REGIONS AND STATES: 1980 TO 1997 (In thousands)									
United States	227,225	229,466	231,664	233,792	235,825	237,924	240,133	242,289	244,499	246,819
Northeast	49,183	49,270	49,334	49,537	49,718	49,869	50,071	50,302	50,584	50,757
Midwest	58,901	58,912	58,784	58,691	58,775	58,820	58,848	59,018	59,254	59,468
South	75,721	76,965	78,302	79,449	80,417	81,409	82,428	83,208	83,891	84,700
West	43,419	44,319	45,244	46,115	46,914	47,827	48,786	49,762	50,770	51,894
Alabama	3,900	3,919	3,925	3,934	3,952	3,973	3,992	4,015	4,024	4,030
Alaska	405	418	450	488	514	532	544	539	542	547
Arizona	2,738	2,810	2,890	2,969	3,067	3,184	3,308	3,437	3,535	3,622
Arkansas	2,289	2,293	2,294	2,306	2,320	2,327	2,332	2,342	2,343	2,346
California	23,801	24,286	24,820	25,360	25,844	26,441	27,102	27,777	28,464	29,218
Colorado	2,909	2,978	3,062	3,134	3,170	3,209	3,237	3,260	3,262	3,276
Connecticut	3,113	3,129	3,139	3,162	3,180	3,201	3,224	3,247	3,272	3,283
Delaware	595	596	599	605	612	618	628	637	648	658
District of Columbia	638	637	634	632	633	635	638	637	630	624
Florida	9,840	10,193	10,471	10,750	11,040	11,351	11,668	11,997	12,306	12,638
Georgia	5,486	5,568	5,650	5,728	5,835	5,963	6,085	6,208	6,316	6,411
Hawaii	968	978	994	1,013	1,028	1,040	1,052	1,068	1,080	1,095
Idaho	948	962	974	982	991	994	990	985	986	994
Illinois	11,435	11,443	11,423	11,409	11,412	11,400	11,387	11,391	11,390	11,410
Indiana	5,491	5,480	5,468	5,450	5,458	5,459	5,454	5,473	5,492	5,524
Iowa	2,914	2,908	2,888	2,871	2,859	2,830	2,792	2,767	2,768	2,771
Kansas	2,369	2,385	2,401	2,416	2,424	2,427	2,433	2,445	2,462	2,473
Kentucky	3,664	3,670	3,683	3,694	3,695	3,695	3,688	3,683	3,680	3,677
Louisiana	4,223	4,283	4,353	4,395	4,400	4,408	4,407	4,344	4,289	4,253
Maine	1,127	1,133	1,137	1,145	1,156	1,163	1,170	1,185	1,204	1,220
Maryland	4,228	4,262	4,283	4,313	4,365	4,413	4,487	4,566	4,658	4,727
Massachusetts	5,746	5,769	5,771	5,799	5,841	5,881	5,903	5,935	5,980	6,015
Michigan	9,256	9,209	9,115	9,048	9,049	9,076	9,128	9,187	9,218	9,253
Minnesota	4,085	4,112	4,131	4,141	4,158	4,184	4,205	4,235	4,296	4,338
Mississippi	2,525	2,539	2,557	2,568	2,578	2,588	2,594	2,589	2,580	2,574
Missouri	4,922	4,932	4,929	4,944	4,975	5,000	5,023	5,057	5,082	5,096
Montana	789	795	804	814	821	822	814	805	800	800
Nebraska	1,572	1,579	1,582	1,584	1,589	1,585	1,574	1,567	1,571	1,575
Nevada	810	848	882	902	925	951	981	1,023	1,075	1,137
New Hampshire	924	937	948	958	977	997	1,025	1,054	1,083	1,105
New Jersey	7,376	7,407	7,431	7,468	7,515	7,566	7,622	7,671	7,712	7,726
New Mexico	1,309	1,333	1,364	1,394	1,417	1,438	1,463	1,479	1,490	1,504
New York	17,567	17,568	17,590	17,687	17,746	17,792	17,833	17,869	17,941	17,983
North Carolina	5,899	5,957	6,019	6,077	6,164	6,254	6,322	6,404	6,481	6,565
North Dakota	654	660	669	677	680	677	670	661	655	646
Ohio	10,801	10,788	10,757	10,738	10,738	10,735	10,730	10,760	10,799	10,829
Oklahoma	3,041	3,096	3,206	3,290	3,286	3,271	3,253	3,210	3,167	3,150
Oregon	2,641	2,668	2,665	2,653	2,667	2,673	2,684	2,701	2,741	2,791
Pennsylvania	11,868	11,859	11,845	11,838	11,815	11,771	11,783	11,811	11,846	11,866
Rhode Island	949	953	954	956	962	969	977	990	996	1,001
South Carolina	3,135	3,179	3,208	3,234	3,272	3,303	3,343	3,381	3,412	3,457
South Dakota	691	690	691	693	697	698	696	696	698	697
Tennessee	4,600	4,628	4,646	4,660	4,687	4,715	4,739	4,783	4,822	4,854
Texas	14,338	14,746	15,331	15,752	16,007	16,273	16,561	16,622	16,667	16,807
Utah	1,473	1,515	1,558	1,595	1,622	1,643	1,663	1,678	1,689	1,706
Vermont	513	516	519	523	527	530	534	540	550	558
Virginia	5,368	5,444	5,493	5,565	5,644	5,715	5,812	5,932	6,037	6,120
Washington	4,155	4,236	4,277	4,300	4,344	4,400	4,453	4,532	4,640	4,746
West Virginia	1,951	1,954	1,950	1,945	1,928	1,907	1,882	1,858	1,830	1,807
Wisconsin	4,712	4,726	4,729	4,721	4,736	4,748	4,756	4,778	4,822	4,857
Wyoming	474	492	506	510	505	500	496	477	465	458

See notes at end of table.

State Population Estimates and Projections

TABLE 1.25. ESTIMATED RESIDENT POPULATION OF THE REGIONS AND STATES:
1980 TO 1997 - Continued
(In thousands)

AREA	1990	1991	1992	1993	1994	1995	1996	1997
United States	249,440	252,124	255,002	257,753	260,292	262,761	265,179	267,636
Northeast	50,873	50,949	51,072	51,242	51,349	51,428	51,502	51,588
Midwest	59,764	60,186	60,648	61,086	61,452	61,838	62,182	62,460
South	85,731	86,899	88,117	89,358	90,607	91,825	93,010	94,187
West	53,071	54,090	55,166	56,068	56,884	57,670	58,486	59,400
Alabama	4,048	4,090	4,138	4,193	4,232	4,262	4,287	4,319
Alaska	553	569	587	597	601	602	605	609
Arizona	3,679	3,763	3,868	3,994	4,149	4,308	4,434	4,555
Arkansas	2,354	2,370	2,394	2,424	2,451	2,481	2,506	2,523
California	29,929	30,413	30,892	31,183	31,369	31,558	31,858	32,268
Colorado	3,304	3,369	3,462	3,563	3,657	3,742	3,816	3,893
Connecticut	3,289	3,288	3,277	3,273	3,270	3,267	3,267	3,270
Delaware	669	680	689	698	706	716	723	732
District of Columbia	604	594	585	577	566	552	539	529
Florida	13,018	13,286	13,501	13,712	13,956	14,181	14,419	14,654
Georgia	6,506	6,622	6,761	6,896	7,049	7,192	7,334	7,486
Hawaii	1,113	1,131	1,150	1,160	1,173	1,179	1,183	1,187
Idaho	1,012	1,039	1,066	1,101	1,135	1,165	1,188	1,210
Illinois	11,446	11,518	11,601	11,675	11,737	11,795	11,845	11,896
Indiana	5,555	5,601	5,648	5,700	5,742	5,788	5,828	5,864
Iowa	2,780	2,791	2,807	2,820	2,829	2,841	2,848	2,852
Kansas	2,481	2,493	2,516	2,535	2,554	2,570	2,579	2,595
Kentucky	3,692	3,715	3,752	3,793	3,824	3,856	3,882	3,908
Louisiana	4,219	4,241	4,271	4,285	4,307	4,329	4,341	4,352
Maine	1,231	1,235	1,235	1,237	1,236	1,234	1,239	1,242
Maryland	4,798	4,857	4,904	4,945	4,989	5,027	5,060	5,094
Massachusetts	6,018	5,996	5,991	6,008	6,029	6,061	6,085	6,118
Michigan	9,310	9,390	9,466	9,524	9,580	9,655	9,731	9,774
Minnesota	4,387	4,428	4,472	4,524	4,567	4,607	4,649	4,686
Mississippi	2,577	2,591	2,610	2,635	2,663	2,691	2,711	2,731
Missouri	5,126	5,158	5,194	5,238	5,281	5,325	5,364	5,402
Montana	800	808	823	840	855	869	877	879
Nebraska	1,581	1,591	1,603	1,613	1,623	1,636	1,649	1,657
Nevada	1,219	1,285	1,333	1,382	1,459	1,530	1,601	1,677
New Hampshire	1,112	1,107	1,113	1,122	1,134	1,146	1,160	1,173
New Jersey	7,757	7,782	7,824	7,869	7,911	7,956	8,002	8,053
New Mexico	1,520	1,548	1,582	1,617	1,656	1,686	1,711	1,730
New York	18,002	18,028	18,080	18,139	18,154	18,146	18,134	18,137
North Carolina	6,657	6,748	6,833	6,948	7,062	7,187	7,309	7,425
North Dakota	637	634	635	637	640	641	643	641
Ohio	10,862	10,929	11,000	11,058	11,095	11,133	11,163	11,186
Oklahoma	3,147	3,166	3,204	3,229	3,248	3,271	3,295	3,317
Oregon	2,859	2,920	2,975	3,036	3,089	3,143	3,196	3,243
Pennsylvania	11,895	11,942	11,981	12,022	12,043	12,046	12,040	12,020
Rhode Island	1,005	1,004	1,001	998	994	990	988	987
South Carolina	3,499	3,555	3,593	3,625	3,654	3,683	3,717	3,760
South Dakota	697	708	715	723	730	735	738	738
Tennessee	4,891	4,946	5,013	5,083	5,158	5,235	5,307	5,368
Texas	17,046	17,358	17,680	18,035	18,385	18,738	19,091	19,439
Utah	1,730	1,771	1,821	1,875	1,929	1,974	2,018	2,059
Vermont	564	567	570	574	579	583	586	589
Virginia	6,214	6,282	6,383	6,465	6,538	6,601	6,666	6,734
Washington	4,901	5,016	5,144	5,250	5,339	5,436	5,520	5,610
West Virginia	1,792	1,798	1,806	1,816	1,819	1,822	1,820	1,816
Wisconsin	4,902	4,946	4,991	5,038	5,075	5,113	5,146	5,170
Wyoming	453	458	464	469	475	479	480	480

Source: U.S. Bureau of the Census, Population Estimates Program.

As of July 1.

State Population Estimates and Projections

TABLE 1.26. PROJECTED RESIDENT POPULATION OF THE REGIONS AND STATES: 1995 TO 2025
(In thousands)

AREA	1995	2000	2005	2010	2015	2020	2025
United States	262,755	274,634	285,981	297,716	310,133	322,742	335,050
Northeast	51,466	52,107	52,767	53,692	54,836	56,103	57,392
Midwest	61,804	63,502	64,825	65,915	67,024	68,114	69,109
South	91,890	97,613	102,788	107,597	112,384	117,060	121,448
West	57,596	61,413	65,603	70,512	75,889	81,465	87,101
Alabama	4,253	4,451	4,631	4,798	4,956	5,100	5,224
Alaska	604	653	700	745	791	838	885
Arizona	4,218	4,798	5,230	5,522	5,808	6,111	6,412
Arkansas	2,484	2,631	2,750	2,840	2,922	2,997	3,055
California	31,589	32,521	34,441	37,644	41,373	45,278	49,285
Colorado	3,747	4,168	4,468	4,658	4,833	5,012	5,188
Connecticut	3,275	3,284	3,317	3,400	3,506	3,621	3,739
Delaware	717	768	800	817	832	847	861
District of Columbia	554	523	529	560	594	625	655
Florida	14,166	15,233	16,279	17,363	18,497	19,634	20,710
Georgia	7,201	7,875	8,413	8,824	9,200	9,552	9,869
Hawaii	1,187	1,257	1,342	1,440	1,553	1,677	1,812
Idaho	1,163	1,347	1,480	1,557	1,622	1,683	1,739
Illinois	11,830	12,051	12,266	12,515	12,808	13,121	13,440
Indiana	5,803	6,045	6,215	6,318	6,404	6,481	6,546
Iowa	2,842	2,900	2,941	2,968	2,994	3,019	3,040
Kansas	2,565	2,668	2,761	2,849	2,939	3,026	3,108
Kentucky	3,860	3,995	4,098	4,170	4,231	4,281	4,314
Louisiana	4,342	4,425	4,535	4,683	4,840	4,991	5,133
Maine	1,241	1,259	1,285	1,323	1,362	1,396	1,423
Maryland	5,042	5,275	5,467	5,657	5,862	6,071	6,274
Massachusetts	6,074	6,199	6,310	6,431	6,574	6,734	6,902
Michigan	9,549	9,679	9,763	9,836	9,917	10,002	10,078
Minnesota	4,610	4,830	5,005	5,147	5,283	5,406	5,510
Mississippi	2,697	2,816	2,908	2,974	3,035	3,093	3,142
Missouri	5,324	5,540	5,718	5,864	6,005	6,137	6,250
Montana	870	950	1,006	1,040	1,069	1,097	1,121
Nebraska	1,637	1,705	1,761	1,806	1,850	1,892	1,930
Nevada	1,530	1,871	2,070	2,131	2,179	2,241	2,312
New Hampshire	1,148	1,224	1,281	1,329	1,372	1,410	1,439
New Jersey	7,945	8,178	8,392	8,638	8,924	9,238	9,558
New Mexico	1,685	1,860	2,016	2,155	2,300	2,454	2,612
New York	18,136	18,146	18,250	18,530	18,916	19,359	19,830
North Carolina	7,195	7,777	8,227	8,552	8,840	9,111	9,349
North Dakota	641	662	677	690	704	717	729
Ohio	11,151	11,319	11,428	11,505	11,588	11,671	11,744
Oklahoma	3,278	3,373	3,491	3,639	3,789	3,930	4,057
Oregon	3,141	3,397	3,613	3,803	3,992	4,177	4,349
Pennsylvania	12,072	12,202	12,281	12,352	12,449	12,567	12,683
Rhode Island	990	998	1,012	1,038	1,070	1,105	1,141
South Carolina	3,673	3,858	4,033	4,205	4,369	4,517	4,645
South Dakota	729	777	810	826	840	853	866
Tennessee	5,256	5,657	5,966	6,180	6,365	6,529	6,665
Texas	18,724	20,119	21,487	22,857	24,280	25,729	27,183
Utah	1,951	2,207	2,411	2,551	2,670	2,781	2,883
Vermont	585	617	638	651	662	671	678
Virginia	6,618	6,997	7,324	7,627	7,921	8,204	8,466
Washington	5,431	5,858	6,258	6,658	7,058	7,446	7,808
West Virginia	1,828	1,841	1,849	1,851	1,851	1,850	1,845
Wisconsin	5,123	5,326	5,479	5,590	5,693	5,788	5,867
Wyoming	480	525	568	607	641	670	694

Source: Campbell, Paul. 1997. "Population Projections: States, 1995-2025." U.S. Bureau of the Census, Current Population Reports P25-1131. May 1997.

Projected resident population as of July 1.

Data are from projection series A, which is a time-series model that uses state-to-state migration observed from 1975-76 through 1993-94. See Appendix A for additional discussion of the projection methodology.

Income and Wealth

YEAR	TABLE 1.27. MEDIAN HOUSEHOLD INCOME FOR THE UNITED STATES AND REGIONS: 1975 TO 1996									
	Current dollars					Constant 1996 CPI-U-X1 adjusted dollars [1]				
	United States	Region				United States	Region			
		Northeast	Midwest	South	West		Northeast	Midwest	South	West
1975	11,800	12,339	12,574	10,539	12,189	32,943	34,448	35,104	29,423	34,029
1976	12,686	13,074	13,683	11,461	13,038	33,509	34,534	36,142	30,273	34,439
1977	13,572	14,232	14,270	12,407	13,980	33,694	35,332	35,427	30,802	34,707
1978	15,064	15,509	15,673	13,655	15,511	35,015	36,050	36,431	31,740	36,054
1979	16,461	16,864	17,307	14,968	17,446	34,902	35,756	36,696	31,736	36,990
1980	17,710	18,192	18,313	16,298	19,009	33,763	34,682	34,913	31,071	36,240
1981	19,074	19,825	19,691	17,341	20,444	33,215	34,523	34,290	30,198	35,601
1982	20,171	20,707	20,820	18,591	21,192	33,105	33,985	34,170	30,512	34,781
1983	20,885	21,818	21,068	19,386	22,217	32,900	34,370	33,188	30,539	34,998
1984	22,415	23,550	22,586	20,623	24,457	33,849	35,563	34,107	31,143	36,933
1985	23,618	25,485	23,551	21,397	25,782	34,439	37,162	34,342	31,201	37,595
1986	24,897	26,494	24,851	22,578	27,001	35,642	37,928	35,576	32,322	38,654
1987	26,061	28,164	25,785	23,968	27,870	35,994	38,899	35,613	33,104	38,493
1988	27,225	30,425	27,540	24,607	28,836	36,108	40,352	36,526	32,636	38,245
1989	28,906	32,643	28,750	25,870	31,086	36,575	41,304	36,378	32,734	39,334
1990	29,943	32,676	29,897	26,942	31,761	35,945	39,226	35,890	32,343	38,128
1991	30,126	33,467	29,927	27,178	32,253	34,705	38,553	34,475	31,309	37,155
1992	30,636	32,999	30,804	27,609	33,324	34,261	36,903	34,449	30,876	37,267
1993 [2]	31,241	33,747	31,400	28,441	33,739	33,922	36,643	34,095	30,882	36,634
1994	32,264	34,926	32,505	30,021	34,452	34,158	36,976	34,413	31,783	36,474
1995	34,076	36,111	35,839	30,942	35,979	35,082	37,177	36,897	31,856	37,041
1996	35,492	37,406	36,579	32,422	37,125	35,492	37,406	36,579	32,422	37,125

Source: U.S. Bureau of the Census, Current Population Survey - March Supplement.

(1) See Appendix B under "Consumer Price Index" (CPI) for a discussion of the use of the CPI as a price deflator.
(2) 1993 data are the first to be collected in a completely computer-assisted survey information collection (CASIC) environment. As a result of this change, data for 1993 are not strictly comparable to earlier years. See Appendix B for additional discussion of recent changes in the Current Population Survey (CPS).

Income and Wealth

	Current dollars					Constant 1996 CPI-U-X1 adjusted dollars [1]				
YEAR	United States	Region				United States	Region			
		Northeast	Midwest	South	West		Northeast	Midwest	South	West
1975	13,779	14,459	14,260	12,662	14,191	38,468	40,367	39,811	35,350	39,619
1976	14,922	15,165	15,726	13,748	15,486	39,415	40,057	41,539	36,314	40,905
1977	16,100	16,680	16,474	15,069	16,627	39,970	41,410	40,898	37,410	41,278
1978	17,730	18,147	18,003	16,652	18,666	41,212	42,182	41,847	38,707	43,388
1979	19,554	20,101	19,997	18,082	20,846	41,460	42,620	42,399	38,339	44,199
1980	21,063	21,449	21,261	19,703	22,667	40,155	40,891	40,533	37,563	43,213
1981	22,787	23,190	22,809	21,603	24,337	39,681	40,383	39,720	37,619	42,380
1982	24,309	24,732	24,161	23,207	25,913	39,896	40,590	39,653	38,088	42,529
1983	25,401	26,279	24,990	24,233	26,966	40,014	41,397	39,367	38,174	42,480
1984	27,464	28,645	26,612	26,203	29,450	41,474	43,257	40,187	39,569	44,473
1985 [2]	29,066	31,146	28,149	27,044	31,475	42,383	45,416	41,046	39,435	45,896
1986	30,759	32,982	29,645	28,846	33,040	44,034	47,216	42,439	41,295	47,299
1987	32,410	34,691	31,272	30,380	34,837	44,763	47,914	43,192	41,960	48,116
1988	34,017	37,458	33,317	31,351	35,824	45,116	49,680	44,188	41,580	47,513
1989	36,520	41,113	35,217	33,230	39,020	46,210	52,021	44,561	42,047	49,373
1990	37,403	40,953	36,387	34,180	40,443	44,901	49,162	43,681	41,032	48,550
1991	37,922	41,647	36,715	34,685	41,091	43,685	47,977	42,295	39,956	47,336
1992	38,840	42,019	37,853	35,624	42,259	43,435	46,991	42,332	39,839	47,259
1993 [2]	41,428	45,319	39,442	38,249	45,284	44,983	49,208	42,827	41,531	49,170
1994	43,133	47,938	41,597	39,987	45,595	45,665	50,752	44,039	42,334	48,272
1995	44,938	48,039	45,344	41,276	47,688	46,265	49,457	46,683	42,495	49,096
1996	47,123	51,555	46,648	43,932	48,874	47,123	51,555	46,648	43,932	48,874

TABLE 1.28. MEAN HOUSEHOLD INCOME FOR THE UNITED STATES AND REGIONS: 1975 TO 1996

Source: U.S. Bureau of the Census, Current Population Survey - March Supplement.

(1) See Appendix B under "Consumer Price Index" (CPI) for a discussion of the use of the CPI as a price deflator.

(2) The upper reportable limit of earnings in the Current Population Survey (CPS) - March Supplement was increased from $99,999 to $299,999 in March 1986 and from $299,999 to $999,999 in March 1994. These changes affected estimates of mean income, the distribution of aggregate income, and the index of income concentration (Gini ratio) in 1985 and 1993. The 1993 data are also the first to be collected in a completely computer-assisted survey information collection (CASIC) environment. As a result of these changes, data for 1985 and 1993 are not strictly comparable to earlier years. See Appendix B for additional discussion of recent changes in the CPS.

Income and Wealth

AREA	1984	1985	1986	1987	1988	1989	1990	1991	1992	1993 [1]	1994	1995	1996
				TABLE 1.29. MEDIAN MONEY INCOME OF HOUSEHOLDS, BY STATE: 1984 TO 1996 (Current dollars)									
United States	22,415	23,618	24,897	25,986	27,225	28,906	29,943	30,126	30,636	31,241	32,264	34,076	35,492
Alabama	17,310	18,333	19,132	19,734	19,948	21,284	23,357	24,346	25,808	25,082	27,196	25,991	30,302
Alaska	32,356	34,782	31,356	33,233	33,103	36,006	39,298	40,612	41,802	42,931	45,367	47,954	52,779
Arizona	21,425	23,877	25,500	26,749	26,435	28,552	29,224	30,737	29,358	30,510	31,293	30,863	31,637
Arkansas	15,674	17,451	18,730	18,827	20,172	21,433	22,786	23,435	23,882	23,039	25,565	25,814	27,123
California	25,287	26,981	29,010	30,146	30,287	33,009	33,290	33,664	34,903	34,073	35,331	37,009	38,812
Colorado	25,801	28,182	27,192	26,476	26,214	26,806	30,733	31,499	32,484	34,488	37,833	40,706	40,950
Connecticut	29,951	31,090	32,721	32,862	36,213	42,321	38,870	42,154	40,841	39,516	41,097	40,243	42,119
Delaware	25,819	22,980	25,626	29,244	30,505	32,068	30,804	32,585	35,678	36,064	35,873	34,928	39,309
District of Columbia	20,408	21,076	24,322	27,455	26,741	26,752	27,392	29,885	30,247	27,304	30,116	30,748	31,966
Florida	19,785	21,343	22,849	24,489	25,406	26,085	26,685	27,252	27,349	28,550	29,294	29,745	30,641
Georgia	19,984	21,049	24,370	26,714	26,566	27,542	27,561	27,212	28,797	31,663	31,467	34,099	32,496
Hawaii	28,877	28,961	29,003	35,022	33,024	35,035	38,921	37,246	42,113	42,662	42,255	42,851	41,772
Idaho	21,092	20,761	20,749	20,755	23,450	24,654	25,305	26,116	27,704	31,010	31,536	32,676	34,709
Illinois	23,752	24,870	26,511	27,084	29,524	31,300	32,542	31,884	31,551	32,857	35,081	38,071	39,554
Indiana	22,770	22,675	22,728	22,519	26,293	25,898	26,928	27,089	28,530	29,475	27,858	33,385	35,147
Iowa	19,863	20,927	22,459	22,190	24,305	26,265	27,288	28,553	28,743	28,663	33,079	35,519	33,209
Kansas	24,629	22,788	23,926	25,583	25,566	26,862	29,917	29,295	30,346	29,770	28,322	30,341	32,585
Kentucky	17,680	17,361	19,874	20,673	19,907	23,283	24,780	23,764	23,485	24,376	26,595	29,810	32,413
Louisiana	18,949	21,179	20,890	21,349	20,497	22,861	22,405	25,299	25,439	26,312	25,676	27,949	30,262
Maine	20,648	20,519	23,424	23,600	26,402	28,221	27,464	27,868	29,617	27,438	30,316	33,858	34,696
Maryland	29,708	30,136	30,604	34,970	36,552	36,016	38,857	36,952	37,203	39,939	39,198	41,041	43,993
Massachusetts	26,959	28,207	30,339	32,241	33,213	36,086	36,247	35,714	36,359	37,064	40,500	38,574	39,494
Michigan	22,965	24,242	26,605	27,702	29,472	30,775	29,937	32,117	32,267	32,662	35,284	36,426	39,225
Minnesota	24,436	23,856	26,443	28,082	29,087	30,185	31,465	29,479	30,981	33,682	33,644	37,933	40,991
Mississippi	15,430	16,413	16,513	18,513	18,166	19,917	20,178	19,475	20,570	22,191	25,400	26,538	26,677
Missouri	20,775	21,939	21,925	23,720	23,443	26,497	27,332	27,926	27,361	28,682	30,190	34,825	34,265
Montana	19,536	20,236	20,328	20,474	22,231	23,692	23,375	24,827	26,525	26,470	27,631	27,757	28,684
Nebraska	21,397	21,799	21,772	23,268	25,159	26,319	27,482	29,549	30,048	31,008	31,794	32,929	34,014
Nevada	25,776	23,274	26,217	26,878	27,983	29,340	32,023	32,937	31,908	35,814	35,871	36,084	38,540
New Hampshire	25,914	26,403	30,548	32,338	34,625	37,532	40,805	36,032	39,436	37,964	35,245	39,171	39,407
New Jersey	27,776	30,980	31,715	34,241	36,287	39,120	38,734	40,049	39,000	40,500	42,280	43,924	47,468
New Mexico	20,630	20,423	19,845	20,758	19,296	22,602	25,039	26,540	25,860	26,758	26,905	25,991	25,086
New York	22,027	23,639	25,025	26,384	28,915	31,496	31,591	31,794	31,051	31,697	31,899	33,028	35,410
North Carolina	20,569	21,451	21,861	22,760	24,415	26,406	26,329	26,853	27,771	28,820	30,114	31,979	35,601
North Dakota	20,771	21,205	21,508	22,576	24,092	25,229	25,264	25,892	26,959	28,118	28,278	29,089	31,470
Ohio	23,123	25,174	25,115	25,773	27,740	29,021	30,013	29,790	31,404	31,285	31,855	34,941	34,070
Oklahoma	21,148	21,205	20,948	21,691	23,667	23,667	24,384	25,462	25,284	26,260	26,991	26,311	27,437
Oregon	21,399	21,894	24,773	25,038	27,748	28,529	29,281	30,190	31,927	33,138	31,456	36,374	35,492
Pennsylvania	20,346	22,877	23,807	25,424	26,742	28,690	29,005	30,367	29,882	30,995	32,066	34,524	34,899
Rhode Island	21,612	24,625	26,540	28,292	29,842	30,124	31,968	30,836	30,432	33,509	31,928	35,359	36,986
South Carolina	20,309	20,036	21,968	25,049	25,533	23,798	28,735	27,463	27,578	26,053	29,846	29,071	34,665
South Dakota	19,409	18,142	19,898	21,151	22,294	24,108	24,571	24,639	26,259	27,737	29,733	29,578	29,526
Tennessee	16,782	17,778	18,256	21,179	20,856	22,611	22,592	24,453	24,318	25,102	28,639	29,015	30,790
Texas	23,024	23,743	24,162	24,721	24,963	25,886	28,228	27,733	27,953	28,727	30,755	32,039	33,072
Utah	23,057	25,238	26,281	26,529	26,313	30,717	30,142	28,016	34,251	35,786	35,716	36,480	37,038
Vermont	22,578	26,000	24,599	25,415	28,988	31,295	31,098	29,155	32,755	31,065	35,802	33,824	32,358
Virginia	26,525	28,429	29,715	29,996	32,648	34,118	35,073	36,137	38,198	36,433	37,647	36,222	39,211
Washington	25,017	24,000	26,881	27,319	32,327	31,961	32,112	33,970	33,900	35,655	33,533	35,568	36,676
West Virginia	16,843	15,983	16,464	17,207	19,353	21,677	22,137	23,147	20,271	22,421	23,564	24,880	25,247
Wisconsin	20,743	23,246	26,430	26,369	29,575	29,123	30,711	31,133	33,308	31,766	35,388	40,955	40,001
Wyoming	23,816	22,081	23,559	27,590	26,419	29,521	29,460	29,050	30,209	29,442	33,140	31,529	30,953

See notes at end of table.

Income and Wealth

TABLE 1.29. MEDIAN MONEY INCOME OF HOUSEHOLDS, BY STATE: 1984 TO 1996 - Continued
(Constant 1996 CPI-U-X1 adjusted dollars)

AREA	1984	1985	1986	1987	1988	1989	1990	1991	1992	1993 [1]	1994	1995	1996
United States	33,849	34,439	35,642	35,891	36,108	36,575	35,945	34,705	34,261	33,922	34,158	35,082	35,492
Alabama	26,140	26,733	27,389	27,256	26,457	26,931	28,039	28,046	28,862	27,234	28,793	26,758	30,302
Alaska	48,861	50,718	44,888	45,900	43,904	45,559	47,176	46,784	46,748	46,615	48,030	49,370	52,779
Arizona	32,354	34,817	36,505	36,945	35,060	36,128	35,082	35,408	32,832	33,128	33,130	31,774	31,637
Arkansas	23,669	25,447	26,813	26,003	26,754	27,120	27,354	26,997	26,708	25,016	27,066	26,576	27,123
California	38,186	39,343	41,530	41,637	40,169	41,767	39,963	38,780	39,033	36,997	37,405	38,102	38,812
Colorado	38,962	41,094	38,927	36,568	34,767	33,918	36,894	36,286	36,327	37,448	40,054	41,908	40,950
Connecticut	45,229	45,335	46,842	45,388	48,029	53,550	46,662	48,561	45,673	42,907	43,510	41,431	42,119
Delaware	38,989	33,509	36,685	40,391	40,458	40,576	36,979	37,537	39,899	39,159	37,979	35,959	39,309
District of Columbia	30,818	30,733	34,819	37,920	35,466	33,850	32,883	34,427	33,826	29,647	31,884	31,656	31,966
Florida	29,877	31,122	32,710	33,823	33,696	33,006	32,034	31,394	30,585	31,000	31,014	30,623	30,641
Georgia	30,178	30,693	34,887	36,896	35,234	34,850	33,086	31,348	32,204	34,380	33,314	35,106	32,496
Hawaii	43,607	42,230	41,520	48,371	43,799	44,331	46,723	42,907	47,096	46,323	44,736	44,116	41,772
Idaho	31,851	30,273	29,704	28,666	31,101	31,195	30,378	30,085	30,982	33,671	33,387	33,641	34,709
Illinois	35,868	36,265	37,952	37,407	39,157	39,605	39,065	36,730	35,284	35,677	37,140	39,195	39,554
Indiana	34,385	33,064	32,537	31,102	34,872	32,769	32,326	31,206	31,906	32,004	29,493	34,371	35,147
Iowa	29,995	30,515	32,152	30,648	32,235	33,234	32,758	32,893	32,144	31,123	35,021	36,568	33,209
Kansas	37,192	33,229	34,252	35,334	33,908	33,989	35,914	33,747	33,936	32,325	29,985	31,237	32,585
Kentucky	26,699	25,315	28,451	28,553	26,402	29,461	29,747	27,376	26,264	26,468	28,156	30,690	32,413
Louisiana	28,615	30,883	29,905	29,486	27,185	28,927	26,896	29,144	28,449	28,570	27,183	28,774	30,262
Maine	31,181	29,920	33,533	32,595	35,017	35,709	32,969	32,103	33,121	29,793	32,096	34,858	34,696
Maryland	44,862	43,944	43,812	48,299	48,479	45,572	46,646	42,568	41,605	43,366	41,499	42,253	43,993
Massachusetts	40,711	41,131	43,432	44,530	44,050	45,660	43,513	41,142	40,661	40,245	42,878	39,713	39,494
Michigan	34,680	35,349	38,087	38,261	39,088	38,940	35,938	36,998	36,085	35,465	37,355	37,502	39,225
Minnesota	36,901	34,786	37,855	38,786	38,578	38,194	37,772	33,959	34,647	36,572	35,619	39,053	40,991
Mississippi	23,301	23,933	23,639	25,569	24,093	25,201	24,223	22,435	23,004	24,095	26,891	27,322	26,677
Missouri	31,372	31,991	31,387	32,761	31,092	33,527	32,811	32,170	30,598	31,143	31,962	35,853	34,265
Montana	29,501	29,508	29,101	28,278	29,485	29,978	28,061	28,600	29,663	28,741	29,253	28,577	28,684
Nebraska	32,312	31,787	31,168	32,137	33,368	33,302	32,991	34,040	33,603	33,669	33,660	33,901	34,014
Nevada	38,924	33,938	37,531	37,123	37,114	37,125	38,442	37,943	35,683	38,887	37,977	37,149	38,540
New Hampshire	39,133	38,500	43,732	44,664	45,923	47,490	48,985	41,508	44,102	41,222	37,314	40,328	39,407
New Jersey	41,945	45,174	45,402	47,292	48,127	49,499	46,499	46,136	43,614	43,975	44,762	45,221	47,468
New Mexico	31,153	29,780	28,409	28,670	25,592	28,599	30,058	30,574	28,920	29,054	28,484	26,758	25,086
New York	33,263	34,470	35,825	36,441	38,350	39,853	37,924	36,626	34,725	34,417	33,772	34,003	35,410
North Carolina	31,061	31,279	31,296	31,435	32,381	33,412	31,607	30,934	31,057	31,293	31,882	32,923	35,601
North Dakota	31,366	30,921	30,790	31,181	31,953	31,923	30,328	29,827	30,149	30,531	29,938	29,948	31,470
Ohio	34,918	36,708	35,954	35,597	36,791	36,721	36,029	34,318	35,120	33,970	33,725	35,973	34,070
Oklahoma	31,936	30,921	29,989	29,959	31,389	29,946	29,272	29,332	28,276	28,513	28,575	27,088	27,437
Oregon	32,315	31,925	35,464	34,582	36,802	36,098	35,151	34,778	35,705	35,982	33,303	37,448	35,492
Pennsylvania	30,725	33,359	34,081	35,115	35,468	36,302	34,819	34,982	33,418	33,655	33,948	35,543	34,899
Rhode Island	32,636	35,908	37,994	39,076	39,579	38,117	38,376	35,523	34,033	36,385	33,802	36,403	36,986
South Carolina	30,669	29,216	31,449	34,597	33,864	30,112	34,495	31,637	30,841	28,289	31,598	29,929	34,665
South Dakota	29,310	26,454	28,485	29,213	29,568	30,504	29,496	28,384	29,366	30,117	31,478	30,451	29,526
Tennessee	25,343	25,923	26,135	29,252	27,661	28,610	27,121	28,169	27,195	27,256	30,320	29,872	30,790
Texas	34,769	34,622	34,590	34,144	33,108	32,754	33,887	31,948	31,260	31,192	32,560	32,985	33,072
Utah	34,819	36,801	37,623	36,641	34,899	38,867	36,184	32,274	38,304	38,857	37,813	37,557	37,038
Vermont	34,095	37,913	35,215	35,102	38,446	39,598	37,332	33,586	36,631	33,731	37,904	34,823	32,358
Virginia	40,056	41,455	42,539	41,429	43,301	43,170	42,104	41,629	42,718	39,559	39,857	37,292	39,211
Washington	37,778	34,996	38,482	37,732	42,875	40,441	38,549	39,133	37,911	38,715	35,502	36,618	36,676
West Virginia	25,435	23,306	23,569	23,766	25,668	27,428	26,575	26,665	22,669	24,345	24,947	25,615	25,247
Wisconsin	31,324	33,897	37,836	36,420	39,225	36,850	36,867	35,865	37,249	34,492	37,465	42,164	40,001
Wyoming	35,965	32,198	33,726	38,106	35,039	37,354	35,366	33,465	33,783	31,969	35,085	32,460	30,953

Source: U.S. Bureau of the Census, Current Population Survey - March Supplement.

(1) 1993 data are the first to be collected in a completely computer-assisted survey information collection (CASIC) environment. As a result of this change, data for 1993 are not strictly comparable to earlier years. See Appendix B for additional discussion of recent changes in the Current Population Survey (CPS).

See Appendix B under "Consumer Price Index" (CPI) for a discussion of the use of the CPI as a price deflator.

Income and Wealth

TABLE 1.30. MEDIAN HOUSEHOLD INCOME BY RACE AND HISPANIC ORIGIN: 1967 TO 1996

| YEAR | Current dollars | | | | | | Constant 1996 CPI-U-X1 adjusted dollars [1] | | | | | |
| | All races | Race and Hispanic origin | | | | | All races | Race and Hispanic origin | | | | |
		White	Black	Asian and Pacific Islander	Hispanic origin [2]	White, not Hispanic		White	Black	Asian and Pacific Islander	Hispanic origin [2]	White, not Hispanic
1967	7,143	7,449	4,325	....	....	....	30,874	32,197	18,694	....	....	....
1968	7,743	8,062	4,754	....	....	....	32,225	33,552	19,785	....	....	....
1969	8,389	8,755	5,292	....	....	....	33,407	34,864	21,074	....	....	....
1970	8,734	9,097	5,537	....	....	....	33,181	34,560	21,035	....	....	....
1971	9,028	9,443	5,578	....	....	....	32,865	34,376	20,306	....	....	....
1972	9,697	10,173	5,938	....	7,677	10,318	34,267	35,949	20,984	....	27,129	36,462
1973	10,512	11,017	6,485	....	8,144	11,114	34,943	36,622	21,557	....	27,072	36,945
1974	11,197	11,710	6,964	....	8,906	11,810	33,850	35,401	21,053	....	26,924	35,703
1975	11,800	12,340	7,408	....	8,865	12,433	32,943	34,451	20,682	....	24,749	34,711
1976	12,686	13,289	7,902	....	9,569	13,560	33,509	35,102	20,872	....	25,276	35,818
1977	13,572	14,272	8,422	....	10,647	14,555	33,694	35,432	20,908	....	26,432	36,134
1978	15,064	15,660	9,411	....	11,803	15,955	35,015	36,401	21,875	....	27,435	37,087
1979	16,461	17,259	10,133	....	13,042	17,502	34,902	36,594	21,485	....	27,653	37,109
1980	17,710	18,684	10,764	....	13,651	19,015	33,763	35,620	20,521	....	26,025	36,251
1981	19,074	20,153	11,309	....	15,300	20,444	33,215	35,094	19,693	....	26,643	35,601
1982	20,171	21,117	11,968	....	15,178	21,471	33,105	34,657	19,642	....	24,910	35,238
1983	20,885	21,902	12,429	....	15,906	....	32,900	34,502	19,579	....	25,057	....
1984	22,415	23,647	13,471	....	16,992	24,138	33,849	35,709	20,343	....	25,660	36,451
1985	23,618	24,908	14,819	....	17,465	25,468	34,439	36,320	21,609	....	25,467	37,137
1986	24,897	26,175	15,080	....	18,352	26,770	35,642	37,471	21,588	....	26,272	38,323
1987	26,061	27,458	15,672	....	19,336	28,213	35,994	37,924	21,646	....	26,706	38,967
1988	27,225	28,781	16,407	32,267	20,359	29,574	36,108	38,172	21,760	42,795	27,002	39,224
1989	28,906	30,406	18,083	36,102	21,921	31,060	36,575	38,473	22,881	45,681	27,737	39,301
1990	29,943	31,231	18,676	38,450	22,330	31,945	35,945	37,492	22,420	46,158	26,806	38,349
1991	30,126	31,569	18,807	36,449	22,691	32,323	34,705	36,367	21,665	41,989	26,140	37,236
1992	30,636	32,209	18,755	37,801	22,597	33,290	34,261	36,020	20,974	42,274	25,271	37,229
1993 [3]	31,241	32,960	19,533	38,347	22,886	34,173	33,922	35,788	21,209	41,638	24,850	37,105
1994	32,264	34,028	21,027	40,482	23,421	35,126	34,158	36,026	22,261	42,858	24,796	37,188
1995	34,076	35,766	22,393	40,614	22,860	37,178	35,082	36,822	23,054	41,813	23,535	38,276
1996	35,492	37,161	23,482	43,276	24,906	38,787	35,492	37,161	23,482	43,276	24,906	38,787

Source: U.S. Bureau of the Census, Current Population Survey - March Supplement.

(1) See Appendix B under "Consumer Price Index" (CPI) for a discussion of the use of the CPI as a price deflator.
(2) Persons of Hispanic origin may be of any race.
(3) 1993 data are the first to be collected in a completely computer-assisted survey information collection (CASIC) environment. As a result of this change, data for 1993 are not strictly comparable to earlier years. See Appendix B for additional discussion of recent changes in the Current Population Survey (CPS).

Income and Wealth

TABLE 1.31. MEAN HOUSEHOLD INCOME BY RACE AND HISPANIC ORIGIN: 1967 TO 1996

YEAR	Current dollars						Constant 1996 CPI-U-X1 adjusted dollars [1]					
	All races	Race and Hispanic origin					All races	Race and Hispanic origin				
		White	Black	Asian and Pacific Islander	Hispanic origin [2]	White, not Hispanic		White	Black	Asian and Pacific Islander	Hispanic origin [2]	White, not Hispanic
1967	7,989	8,281	5,197	....	....	....	34,531	35,793	22,463	....	....	....
1968	8,760	9,075	5,790	....	....	....	36,457	37,768	24,097	....	....	....
1969	9,544	9,898	6,300	....	....	....	38,006	39,416	25,088	....	....	....
1970	10,001	10,351	6,761	....	....	....	37,994	39,324	25,685	....	....	....
1971	10,383	10,759	6,912	....	....	....	37,798	39,167	25,162	....	....	....
1972	11,286	11,725	7,501	....	8,824	11,861	39,882	41,434	26,507	....	31,182	41,914
1973	12,157	12,627	8,053	....	9,462	12,768	40,412	41,974	26,769	....	31,453	42,443
1974	13,094	13,579	8,661	....	10,317	13,732	39,585	41,051	26,183	....	31,190	41,513
1975	13,779	14,288	9,247	....	10,524	14,463	38,468	39,889	25,816	....	29,381	40,378
1976	14,922	15,496	10,096	....	11,308	15,695	39,415	40,931	26,668	....	29,869	41,457
1977	16,100	16,729	10,791	....	12,565	16,936	39,970	41,531	26,790	....	31,194	42,045
1978	17,730	18,387	12,027	....	13,942	18,604	41,212	42,740	27,956	....	32,407	43,244
1979	19,554	20,325	13,002	....	15,780	20,560	41,460	43,094	27,568	....	33,458	43,593
1980	21,063	21,913	13,970	....	16,674	22,201	40,155	41,776	26,633	....	31,788	42,325
1981	22,787	23,742	14,856	....	18,373	24,041	39,681	41,344	25,870	....	31,995	41,865
1982	24,309	25,311	15,747	....	18,732	25,683	39,896	41,541	25,844	....	30,743	42,151
1983	25,401	26,455	16,531	....	19,369	....	40,014	41,675	26,041	....	30,512	....
1984	27,464	28,597	17,966	....	21,129	29,094	41,474	43,185	27,131	....	31,907	43,935
1985 [3]	29,066	30,259	19,335	....	21,823	30,848	42,383	44,123	28,194	....	31,822	44,982
1986	30,759	32,040	20,232	....	23,173	32,676	44,034	45,867	28,964	....	33,174	46,778
1987	32,410	33,795	21,161	....	24,786	34,456	44,763	46,676	29,227	....	34,233	47,589
1988	34,017	35,468	22,477	40,341	25,993	36,192	45,116	47,041	29,811	53,504	34,474	48,001
1989	36,520	38,041	23,995	44,880	27,992	38,803	46,210	48,134	30,361	56,788	35,419	49,098
1990	37,403	38,912	24,814	46,412	27,972	39,774	44,901	46,712	29,788	55,716	33,579	47,747
1991	37,922	39,523	25,043	46,278	28,872	40,371	43,685	45,530	28,849	53,311	33,260	46,507
1992	38,840	40,594	25,450	46,850	28,822	41,625	43,435	45,397	28,461	52,393	32,232	46,550
1993 [3]	41,428	43,285	27,229	50,244	30,291	44,426	44,983	46,999	29,566	54,556	32,890	48,238
1994	43,133	45,034	29,259	52,562	31,582	46,181	45,665	47,678	30,977	55,648	33,436	48,892
1995	44,938	46,729	30,400	55,228	31,201	48,253	46,265	48,109	31,298	56,859	32,122	49,678
1996	47,123	48,994	32,460	56,547	34,005	50,476	47,123	48,994	32,460	56,547	34,005	50,476

Source: U.S. Bureau of the Census, Current Population Survey - March Supplement.

(1) See Appendix B under "Consumer Price Index" (CPI) for a discussion of the use of the CPI as a price deflator.

(2) Persons of Hispanic origin may be of any race.

(3) The upper reportable limit of earnings in the Current Population Survey (CPS) - March Supplement was increased from $99,999 to $299,999 in March 1986 and from $299,999 to $999,999 in March 1994. These changes affected estimates of mean income, the distribution of aggregate income, and the index of income concentration (Gini ratio) in 1985 and 1993. The 1993 data are also the first to be collected in a completely computer-assisted survey information collection (CASIC) environment. As a result of these changes, data for 1985 and 1993 are not strictly comparable to earlier years. See Appendix B for additional discussion of recent changes in the CPS.

Income and Wealth

		Family households				Nonfamily households				
			Type of family				Sex of householder			
							Male		Female	
YEAR	All households	All	Married-couple	Male householder, no wife present	Female householder, no husband present	All	All	Living alone	All	Living alone
CURRENT DOLLARS										
1980	17,710	21,162	23,180	18,775	10,830	9,456	....	11,527	....	6,690
1981	19,074	22,552	25,106	20,542	11,441	10,385	....	12,837	....	7,405
1982	20,171	23,614	26,067	21,216	11,883	11,420	....	13,817	....	8,157
1983	20,885	24,783	27,329	22,882	12,239	12,010	....	14,120	....	9,141
1984	22,415	26,651	29,686	24,551	13,473	12,987	....	15,202	....	9,639
1985	23,618	28,022	31,161	24,354	14,316	13,798	....	16,312	....	9,774
1986	24,897	29,743	32,876	26,302	14,337	14,149	....	16,468	....	9,976
1987	26,061	31,247	34,953	26,705	15,480	14,849	19,924	16,994	11,774	10,718
1988	27,225	32,491	36,436	28,642	16,051	16,148	20,999	18,284	12,877	11,622
1989	28,906	34,633	38,664	30,336	17,383	17,115	22,423	19,617	13,755	12,190
1990	29,943	35,707	39,996	31,552	18,069	17,690	22,489	19,964	14,099	12,548
1991	30,126	36,403	41,075	31,010	17,965	17,778	23,022	20,259	14,327	12,834
1992	30,636	36,991	41,966	30,310	18,366	17,730	23,111	19,979	14,438	12,933
1993 [1]	31,241	37,484	43,129	29,849	18,545	18,880	24,728	21,372	14,883	12,995
1994	32,264	39,390	45,041	30,472	19,872	18,947	24,593	21,216	14,948	13,431
1995	34,076	41,224	47,129	33,534	21,348	19,929	26,023	22,586	15,892	14,331
1996	35,492	43,082	49,858	35,658	21,564	20,973	27,266	24,050	16,398	14,626
CONSTANT 1996 CPI-U-X1 ADJUSTED DOLLARS [2]										
1980	33,763	40,344	44,191	35,793	20,647	18,027	....	21,976	....	12,754
1981	33,215	39,272	43,720	35,772	19,923	18,084	....	22,354	....	12,895
1982	33,105	38,756	42,781	34,820	19,503	18,743	....	22,677	....	13,387
1983	32,900	39,041	43,051	36,046	19,280	18,919	....	22,243	....	14,400
1984	33,849	40,246	44,829	37,075	20,346	19,612	....	22,957	....	14,556
1985	34,439	40,861	45,438	35,512	20,875	20,120	....	23,786	....	14,252
1986	35,642	42,579	47,064	37,653	20,524	20,255	....	23,575	....	14,281
1987	35,994	43,157	48,276	36,884	21,380	20,509	....	23,471	....	14,803
1988	36,108	43,092	48,325	37,988	21,288	21,417	....	24,250	....	15,414
1989	36,575	43,822	48,922	38,385	21,995	21,656	28,372	24,822	17,405	15,424
1990	35,945	42,865	48,014	37,877	21,691	21,236	26,997	23,966	16,925	15,063
1991	34,705	41,936	47,318	35,723	20,695	20,480	26,521	23,338	16,504	14,785
1992	34,261	41,368	46,931	33,896	20,539	19,828	25,845	22,343	16,146	14,463
1993 [1]	33,922	40,701	46,830	32,410	20,136	20,500	26,850	23,206	16,160	14,110
1994	34,158	41,702	47,685	32,261	21,039	20,059	26,037	22,461	15,826	14,219
1995	35,082	42,441	48,521	34,524	21,978	20,517	26,791	23,253	16,361	14,754
1996	35,492	43,082	49,858	35,658	21,564	20,973	27,266	24,050	16,398	14,626

TABLE 1.32. MEDIAN HOUSEHOLD INCOME BY HOUSEHOLD TYPE: 1980 TO 1996

Source: U.S. Bureau of the Census, Current Population Survey - March Supplement.

(1) 1993 data are the first to be collected in a completely computer-assisted survey information collection (CASIC) environment. As a result of this change, data for 1993 are not strictly comparable to earlier years. See Appendix B for additional discussion of recent changes in the Current Population Survey (CPS).
(2) See Appendix B under "Consumer Price Index" (CPI) for a discussion of the use of the CPI as a price deflator.

Income and Wealth

		Family households				Nonfamily households				
			Type of family				Sex of householder			
							Male		Female	
YEAR	All households	All	Married-couple	Male householder, no wife present	Female householder, no husband present	All	All	Living alone	All	Living alone
CURRENT DOLLARS										
1980	21,063	24,118	26,171	21,743	13,480	12,711	....	14,347	....	8,891
1981	22,787	26,004	28,297	23,693	14,389	14,066	....	16,081	....	9,930
1982	24,309	27,563	30,052	23,976	15,208	15,440	....	17,025	....	11,017
1983	25,401	28,844	31,535	26,386	15,703	16,285	....	17,649	....	12,049
1984	27,464	31,285	34,232	28,417	17,265	17,514	....	19,074	....	12,986
1985 [1]	29,066	33,182	36,350	29,096	18,347	18,559	....	20,124	....	13,345
1986	30,759	35,204	38,753	31,040	18,692	19,287	....	20,681	....	13,728
1987	32,410	37,184	40,881	32,728	20,499	20,402	25,276	21,753	16,646	14,754
1988	34,017	38,913	42,875	34,291	21,167	22,077	26,992	23,404	18,218	16,017
1989	36,520	41,918	46,126	37,200	22,952	23,432	29,329	25,816	19,059	16,731
1990	37,403	43,050	47,649	36,798	23,380	24,022	29,522	25,510	19,803	17,392
1991	37,922	43,704	48,589	36,936	23,535	24,292	29,746	25,749	20,074	17,795
1992	38,840	44,693	49,854	37,046	23,917	24,686	30,151	26,578	20,464	17,848
1993 [1]	41,428	47,724	53,603	36,760	25,102	26,358	32,477	27,738	21,638	18,539
1994	43,133	49,866	56,053	37,554	25,847	27,414	33,494	28,772	22,552	19,717
1995	44,938	51,985	58,493	40,527	27,343	28,608	35,363	30,934	23,204	20,127
1996	47,123	54,373	61,345	43,751	28,348	30,576	37,009	32,728	25,411	21,874
CONSTANT 1996 CPI-U-X1 ADJUSTED DOLLARS [2]										
1980	40,155	45,980	49,893	41,452	25,699	24,233	....	27,352	....	16,950
1981	39,681	45,283	49,276	41,259	25,057	24,495	....	28,003	....	17,292
1982	39,896	45,237	49,322	39,350	24,960	25,340	....	27,942	....	18,081
1983	40,014	45,438	49,677	41,566	24,737	25,654	....	27,802	....	18,981
1984	41,474	47,244	51,694	42,913	26,072	26,448	....	28,804	....	19,610
1985 [1]	42,383	48,385	53,005	42,427	26,753	27,062	....	29,344	....	19,459
1986	44,034	50,397	55,478	44,436	26,759	27,611	....	29,606	....	19,653
1987	44,763	51,357	56,463	45,203	28,312	28,178	34,910	30,044	22,991	20,378
1988	45,116	51,610	56,865	45,480	28,074	29,280	35,799	31,040	24,162	21,243
1989	46,210	53,040	58,364	47,070	29,042	29,649	37,111	32,666	24,116	21,170
1990	44,901	51,680	57,201	44,174	28,067	28,837	35,440	30,624	23,773	20,878
1991	43,685	50,346	55,974	42,550	27,112	27,984	34,267	29,662	23,125	20,500
1992	43,435	49,981	55,753	41,429	26,747	27,607	33,718	29,723	22,885	19,960
1993 [1]	44,983	51,819	58,203	39,914	27,256	28,620	35,264	30,118	23,495	20,130
1994	45,665	52,793	59,344	39,759	27,364	29,023	35,460	30,461	23,876	20,874
1995	46,265	53,520	60,220	41,724	28,150	29,453	36,407	31,847	23,889	20,721
1996	47,123	54,373	61,345	43,751	28,348	30,576	37,009	32,728	25,411	21,874

Source: U.S. Bureau of the Census, Current Population Survey - March Supplement.

(1) The upper reportable limit of earnings in the Current Population Survey (CPS) - March Supplement was increased from $99,999 to $299,999 in March 1986 and from $299,999 to $999,999 in March 1994. These changes affected estimates of mean income, the distribution of aggregate income, and the index of income concentration (Gini ratio) in 1985 and 1993. The 1993 data are also the first to be collected in a completely computer-assisted survey information collection (CASIC) environment. As a result of these changes, data for 1985 and 1993 are not strictly comparable to earlier years. See Appendix B for additional discussion of recent changes in the CPS.
(2) See Appendix B under "Consumer Price Index" (CPI) for a discussion of the use of the CPI as a price deflator.

Income and Wealth

YEAR	All house-holders 15 and over [1]	Age of householder (Years)							
		15-24	25-34	35-44	45-54	55-64	65 and older		
							All	65-74	75 and older
CURRENT DOLLARS									
1967	7,181	5,615	8,012	8,996	9,098	6,957	2,760	....	....
1968	7,743	6,028	8,592	9,826	9,772	7,629	3,180	....	....
1969	8,389	6,360	9,326	10,732	10,937	8,267	3,329	....	....
1970	8,734	6,669	9,690	11,131	11,413	8,906	3,498	....	....
1971	9,028	6,581	10,077	11,616	12,016	9,344	3,813	....	....
1972	9,697	7,061	10,877	12,688	13,125	10,034	4,169	....	....
1973	10,512	7,496	11,834	13,963	14,081	10,877	4,583	....	....
1974	11,197	8,112	12,422	14,886	15,373	11,470	5,292	....	....
1975	11,800	8,138	13,127	15,542	16,322	12,485	5,585	....	....
1976	12,686	8,862	13,995	16,721	17,664	13,412	5,962	....	....
1977	13,572	9,571	15,075	18,076	19,377	14,311	6,347	....	....
1978	15,064	11,014	16,502	19,928	21,181	16,028	7,081	....	....
1979	16,461	11,913	18,203	22,096	23,048	17,936	7,879	....	....
1980	17,710	12,711	19,337	23,627	25,121	19,547	8,781	....	....
1981	19,074	13,242	20,513	25,384	27,044	21,041	9,903	....	....
1982	20,171	13,816	21,281	26,370	27,985	22,075	11,041	....	....
1983	20,885	13,402	21,746	27,679	30,352	22,778	11,718	....	....
1984	22,415	14,028	23,735	29,784	31,516	24,094	12,799	....	....
1985	23,618	15,049	25,085	31,066	33,223	25,557	13,254	....	....
1986	24,897	15,310	25,898	32,787	35,660	26,776	13,845	....	....
1987	26,061	16,447	26,966	35,185	37,205	27,560	14,443	17,122	11,288
1988	27,225	17,040	28,408	36,554	38,213	28,903	14,923	17,473	11,806
1989	28,906	18,663	29,823	37,635	41,523	30,819	15,771	18,959	12,101
1990	29,943	18,002	30,359	38,561	41,922	32,365	16,855	20,292	13,150
1991	30,126	18,313	30,842	39,349	43,751	33,304	16,975	20,063	13,933
1992 [2]	30,636	17,663	31,239	39,853	44,436	33,993	17,135	20,371	13,620
1993 [2]	31,241	19,333	31,281	40,862	46,207	33,474	17,751	21,310	14,328
1994	32,264	19,340	33,151	41,667	47,261	35,232	18,095	21,422	14,731
1995	34,076	20,979	34,701	43,465	48,058	38,077	19,096	23,031	15,342
1996	35,492	21,438	35,888	44,420	50,472	39,815	19,448	23,411	15,995

See notes at end of table.

Income and Wealth

YEAR	All householders 15 and over [1]	Age of householder (Years)					65 and older		
		15-24	25-34	35-44	45-54	55-64	All	65-74	75 and older
CONSTANT 1996 CPI-U-X1 ADJUSTED DOLLARS [3]									
1967	31,039	24,270	34,630	38,884	39,324	30,070	11,930	....	....
1968	32,225	25,087	35,758	40,894	40,669	31,750	13,235	....	....
1969	33,407	25,327	37,138	42,737	43,554	32,921	13,257	....	....
1970	33,181	25,336	36,813	42,287	43,358	33,834	13,289	....	....
1971	32,865	23,957	36,684	42,287	43,743	34,016	13,881	....	....
1972	34,267	24,952	38,437	44,837	46,381	35,458	14,732	....	....
1973	34,943	24,918	39,338	46,415	46,807	36,157	15,235	....	....
1974	33,850	24,524	37,553	45,002	46,474	34,675	15,998	....	....
1975	32,943	22,720	36,648	43,390	45,568	34,856	15,592	....	....
1976	33,509	23,408	36,967	44,167	46,658	35,427	15,748	....	....
1977	33,694	23,761	37,425	44,875	48,105	35,528	15,757	....	....
1978	35,015	25,601	38,358	46,322	49,234	37,256	16,459	....	....
1979	34,902	25,259	38,595	46,849	48,868	38,029	16,706	....	....
1980	33,763	24,233	36,865	45,043	47,892	37,265	16,740	....	....
1981	33,215	23,060	35,721	44,204	47,094	36,641	17,245	....	....
1982	33,105	22,675	34,927	43,279	45,929	36,230	18,121	....	....
1983	32,900	21,112	34,256	43,603	47,814	35,882	18,459	....	....
1984	33,849	21,184	35,842	44,977	47,593	36,384	19,328	....	....
1985	34,439	21,944	36,578	45,300	48,445	37,267	19,327	....	....
1986	35,642	21,917	37,075	46,937	51,050	38,332	19,820	....	....
1987	35,994	22,716	37,244	48,596	51,386	38,065	19,948	23,648	15,591
1988	36,108	22,600	37,677	48,481	50,681	38,334	19,792	23,174	15,658
1989	36,575	23,615	37,736	47,620	52,540	38,996	19,955	23,989	15,312
1990	35,945	21,611	36,445	46,291	50,326	38,853	20,234	24,360	15,786
1991	34,705	21,096	35,529	45,329	50,400	38,366	19,555	23,112	16,051
1992	34,261	19,753	34,935	44,568	49,694	38,015	19,162	22,781	15,231
1993 [2]	33,922	20,992	33,965	44,368	50,172	36,347	19,274	23,139	15,558
1994	34,158	20,475	35,097	44,113	50,035	37,300	19,157	22,680	15,596
1995	35,082	21,598	35,726	44,748	49,477	39,201	19,660	23,711	15,795
1996	35,492	21,438	35,888	44,420	50,472	39,815	19,448	23,411	15,995

TABLE 1.34. MEDIAN HOUSEHOLD INCOME BY AGE OF HOUSEHOLDER: 1967 TO 1996 - Continued

Source: U.S. Bureau of the Census, Current Population Survey - March Supplement.

(1) Householders 15 years old and over beginning in March 1980, and householders 14 years old and over for previous years.
(2) 1993 data are the first to be collected in a completely computer-assisted survey information collection (CASIC) environment. As a result of this change, data for 1993 are not strictly comparable to earlier years. See Appendix B for additional discussion of recent changes in the Current Population Survey (CPS).
(3) See Appendix B under "Consumer Price Index" (CPI) for a discussion of the use of the CPI as a price deflator.

Income and Wealth

YEAR	All householders 15 and over [1]	Age of householder (Years)					65 and older		
		15-24	25-34	35-44	45-54	55-64	All	65-74	75 and older
CURRENT DOLLARS									
1967	8,192	5,911	8,547	9,918	10,369	8,336	4,534	....	....
1968	8,760	6,355	9,017	10,627	11,043	9,163	4,849	....	....
1969	9,544	6,686	9,864	11,727	12,182	9,924	5,196	....	....
1970	10,001	7,115	10,313	12,193	12,858	10,573	5,418	....	....
1971	10,383	7,139	10,617	12,827	13,479	11,047	5,762	....	....
1972	11,286	7,716	11,483	14,046	14,719	11,940	6,330	....	....
1973	12,157	8,235	12,522	15,261	15,824	12,833	6,857	....	....
1974	13,094	8,701	13,300	16,244	17,244	13,941	7,634	....	....
1975	13,779	8,989	13,959	17,091	18,233	14,841	8,063	....	....
1976	14,922	9,805	15,012	18,533	19,738	16,115	8,708	....	....
1977	16,100	10,494	16,148	20,101	21,537	17,498	9,309	....	....
1978	17,730	12,161	17,704	22,021	23,698	19,434	10,291	....	....
1979	19,554	13,367	19,546	24,635	26,004	21,741	11,138	....	....
1980	21,063	14,227	20,713	26,052	28,169	23,504	12,628	....	....
1981	22,787	15,073	22,123	28,078	30,090	25,520	14,246	....	....
1982	24,309	15,940	23,433	29,353	31,941	27,249	15,869	....	....
1983	25,401	15,451	24,121	31,442	34,203	27,807	16,386	....	....
1984	27,464	16,644	26,178	33,389	36,003	30,516	18,279	....	....
1985 [2]	29,066	17,708	27,904	35,606	38,316	32,045	18,800	....	....
1986	30,759	18,155	29,304	37,662	41,068	33,708	19,816	....	....
1987	32,410	19,791	30,265	40,056	43,981	35,401	20,438	23,135	16,572
1988	34,017	20,912	32,114	42,091	45,506	36,858	21,454	24,075	17,716
1989	36,520	21,566	33,873	44,109	49,832	40,112	23,452	27,024	18,475
1990	37,403	21,484	34,484	45,076	50,003	41,459	24,586	27,942	19,862
1991	37,922	21,219	35,252	45,253	50,700	42,592	24,424	27,636	20,068
1992	38,840	21,484	36,111	46,365	52,374	42,943	24,790	28,658	19,784
1993 [2]	41,428	23,041	37,510	49,473	57,770	44,814	25,965	29,999	20,844
1994	43,133	23,214	39,338	51,812	58,996	47,762	26,645	30,649	21,704
1995	44,938	25,000	41,421	53,230	59,636	50,349	28,579	33,587	22,352
1996	47,123	26,789	42,897	55,384	63,580	52,065	29,280	34,014	23,598

TABLE 1.35. MEAN HOUSEHOLD INCOME BY AGE OF HOUSEHOLDER: 1967 TO 1996

See notes at end of table.

Income and Wealth

YEAR	All householders 15 and over [1]	Age of householder (Years)					65 and older		
		15-24	25-34	35-44	45-54	55-64	All	65-74	75 and older
TABLE 1.35. MEAN HOUSEHOLD INCOME BY AGE OF HOUSEHOLDER: 1967 TO 1996 - Continued									
CONSTANT 1996 CPI-U-X1 ADJUSTED DOLLARS [3]									
1967	35,408	25,549	36,943	42,869	44,818	36,031	19,597	....	....
1968	36,457	26,448	37,527	44,227	45,959	38,135	20,181	....	....
1969	38,006	26,625	39,281	46,700	48,512	39,520	20,692	....	....
1970	37,994	27,030	39,179	46,322	48,848	40,167	20,583	....	....
1971	37,798	25,989	38,650	46,695	49,069	40,215	20,976	....	....
1972	39,882	27,267	40,578	49,636	52,014	42,193	22,369	....	....
1973	40,412	27,374	41,625	50,730	52,601	42,659	22,794	....	....
1974	39,585	26,304	40,208	49,108	52,131	42,145	23,079	....	....
1975	38,468	25,096	38,971	47,715	50,903	41,433	22,510	....	....
1976	39,415	25,899	39,653	48,953	52,136	42,566	23,001	....	....
1977	39,970	26,052	40,089	49,903	53,468	43,440	23,110	....	....
1978	41,212	28,268	41,152	51,187	55,085	45,173	23,921	....	....
1979	41,460	28,342	41,443	52,233	55,136	46,097	23,616	....	....
1980	40,155	27,123	39,488	49,667	53,703	44,809	24,075	....	....
1981	39,681	26,248	38,525	48,895	52,399	44,440	24,808	....	....
1982	39,896	26,161	38,459	48,175	52,422	44,721	26,044	....	....
1983	40,014	24,340	37,998	49,531	53,880	43,804	25,813	....	....
1984	41,474	25,134	39,532	50,421	54,368	46,082	27,603	....	....
1985 [2]	42,383	25,821	40,689	51,920	55,872	46,727	27,414	....	....
1986	44,034	25,990	41,951	53,916	58,792	48,255	28,368	....	....
1987	44,763	27,335	41,801	55,324	60,745	48,895	28,228	31,953	22,889
1988	45,116	27,735	42,592	55,825	60,354	48,884	28,454	31,930	23,497
1989	46,210	27,288	42,860	55,812	63,054	50,755	29,674	34,194	23,377
1990	44,901	25,791	41,397	54,112	60,027	49,770	29,514	33,543	23,844
1991	43,685	24,444	40,610	52,131	58,405	49,065	28,136	31,836	23,118
1992	43,435	24,026	40,384	51,851	58,571	48,024	27,723	32,049	22,125
1993 [2]	44,983	25,018	40,729	53,718	62,727	48,660	28,193	32,573	22,633
1994	45,665	24,577	41,647	54,854	62,459	50,566	28,209	32,448	22,978
1995	46,265	25,738	42,644	54,802	61,397	51,836	29,423	34,579	23,012
1996	47,123	26,789	42,897	55,384	63,580	52,065	29,280	34,014	23,598

Source: U.S. Bureau of the Census, Current Population Survey - March Supplement.

(1) Householders 15 years old and over beginning in March 1980, and householders 14 years old and over for previous years.

(2) The upper reportable limit of earnings in the Current Population Survey (CPS) - March Supplement was increased from $99,999 to $299,999 in March 1986 and from $299,999 to $999,999 in March 1994. These changes affected estimates of mean income, the distribution of aggregate income, and the index of income concentration (Gini ratio) in 1985 and 1993. The 1993 data are also the first to be collected in a completely computer-assisted survey information collection (CASIC) environment. As a result of these changes, data for 1985 and 1993 are not strictly comparable to earlier years. See Appendix B for additional discusion of recent changes in the CPS.

(3) See Appendix B under "Consumer Price Index" (CPI) for a discussion of the use of the CPI as a price deflator.

Income and Wealth

YEAR	Number of households [1] (Thousands)	Percent distribution of aggregate income					Top 5 percent	Gini ratio
		Lowest fifth	Second fifth	Third fifth	Fourth fifth	Highest fifth		

TABLE 1.36. INCOME INEQUALITY: SHARE OF AGGREGATE INCOME RECEIVED BY EACH FIFTH AND TOP 5 PERCENT OF HOUSEHOLDS, 1967 TO 1996

YEAR	Number of households (Thousands)	Lowest fifth	Second fifth	Third fifth	Fourth fifth	Highest fifth	Top 5 percent	Gini ratio
1967	60,813	4.0	10.8	17.3	24.2	43.8	17.5	0.399
1968	62,214	4.2	11.1	17.5	24.4	42.8	16.6	0.388
1969	63,401	4.1	10.9	17.5	24.5	43.0	16.6	0.391
1970	64,778	4.1	10.8	17.4	24.5	43.3	16.6	0.394
1971	66,676	4.1	10.6	17.3	24.5	43.5	16.7	0.396
1972	68,251	4.1	10.5	17.1	24.5	43.9	17.0	0.401
1973	69,859	4.2	10.5	17.1	24.6	43.6	16.6	0.397
1974	71,163	4.4	10.6	17.1	24.7	43.1	15.9	0.395
1975	72,867	4.4	10.5	17.1	24.8	43.2	15.9	0.397
1976	74,142	4.4	10.4	17.1	24.8	43.3	16.0	0.398
1977	76,030	4.4	10.3	17.0	24.8	43.6	16.1	0.402
1978	77,330	4.3	10.3	16.9	24.8	43.7	16.2	0.402
1979	80,776	4.2	10.3	16.9	24.7	44.0	16.4	0.404
1980	82,368	4.3	10.3	16.9	24.9	43.7	15.8	0.403
1981	83,527	4.2	10.2	16.8	25.0	43.8	15.6	0.406
1982	83,918	4.1	10.1	16.6	24.7	44.5	16.2	0.412
1983	85,290	4.1	10.0	16.5	24.7	44.7	16.4	0.414
1984	86,789	4.1	9.9	16.4	24.7	44.9	16.5	0.415
1985 [2]	88,458	4.0	9.7	16.3	24.6	45.3	17.0	0.419
1986	89,479	3.9	9.7	16.2	24.5	45.7	17.5	0.425
1987	91,124	3.8	9.6	16.1	24.3	46.2	18.2	0.426
1988	92,830	3.8	9.6	16.0	24.3	46.3	18.3	0.427
1989	93,347	3.8	9.5	15.8	24.0	46.8	18.9	0.431
1990	94,312	3.9	9.6	15.9	24.0	46.6	18.6	0.428
1991	95,699	3.8	9.6	15.9	24.2	46.5	18.1	0.428
1992	96,426	3.8	9.4	15.8	24.2	46.9	18.6	0.434
1993 [2]	97,107	3.6	9.0	15.1	23.5	48.9	21.0	0.454
1994	98,990	3.6	8.9	15.0	23.4	49.1	21.2	0.456
1995	99,627	3.7	9.1	15.2	23.3	48.7	21.0	0.450
1996	101,018	3.7	9.0	15.1	23.3	49.0	21.4	0.455

Source: U.S. Bureau of the Census, Current Population Survey - March Supplement.

(1) Households as of March of the following year.

(2) The upper reportable limit of earnings in the Current Population Survey (CPS) - March Supplement was increased from $99,999 to $299,999 in March 1986 and from $299,999 to $999,999 in March 1994. These changes affected estimates of mean income, the distribution of aggregate income, and the index of income concentration (Gini ratio) in 1985 and 1993. The 1993 data are also the first to be collected in a completely computer-assisted survey information collection (CASIC) environment. As a result of these changes, data for 1985 and 1993 are not strictly comparable to earlier years. See Appendix B for additional discussion of recent changes in the CPS.

Income and Wealth

YEAR	Number of families [1] (Thousands)	Percent distribution of aggregate income					Top 5 percent	Gini ratio
		Lowest fifth	Second fifth	Third fifth	Fourth fifth	Highest fifth		

TABLE 1.37. INCOME INEQUALITY: SHARE OF AGGREGATE INCOME RECEIVED BY EACH FIFTH AND TOP 5 PERCENT OF FAMILIES, 1947 TO 1996

YEAR	Number of families [1] (Thousands)	Lowest fifth	Second fifth	Third fifth	Fourth fifth	Highest fifth	Top 5 percent	Gini ratio
1947	37,237	5.0	11.9	17.0	23.1	43.0	17.5	0.376
1948	38,624	4.9	12.1	17.3	23.2	42.4	17.1	0.371
1949	39,303	4.5	11.9	17.3	23.5	42.7	16.9	0.378
1950	39,929	4.5	12.0	17.4	23.4	42.7	17.3	0.379
1951	40,578	5.0	12.4	17.6	23.4	41.6	16.8	0.363
1952	40,832	4.9	12.3	17.4	23.4	41.9	17.4	0.368
1953	41,202	4.7	12.5	18.0	23.9	40.9	15.7	0.359
1954	41,951	4.5	12.1	17.7	23.9	41.8	16.3	0.371
1955	42,889	4.8	12.3	17.8	23.7	41.3	16.4	0.363
1956	43,497	5.0	12.5	17.9	23.7	41.0	16.1	0.358
1957	43,696	5.1	12.7	18.1	23.8	40.4	15.6	0.351
1958	44,232	5.0	12.5	18.0	23.9	40.6	15.4	0.354
1959	45,111	4.9	12.3	17.9	23.8	41.1	15.9	0.361
1960	45,539	4.8	12.2	17.8	24.0	41.3	15.9	0.364
1961	46,418	4.7	11.9	17.5	23.8	42.2	16.6	0.374
1962	47,059	5.0	12.1	17.6	24.0	41.3	15.7	0.362
1963	47,540	5.0	12.1	17.7	24.0	41.2	15.8	0.362
1964	47,956	5.1	12.0	17.7	24.0	41.2	15.9	0.361
1965	48,509	5.2	12.2	17.8	23.9	40.9	15.5	0.356
1966	49,214	5.6	12.4	17.8	23.8	40.5	15.6	0.349
1967	50,111	5.4	12.2	17.5	23.5	41.4	16.4	0.358
1968	50,823	5.6	12.4	17.7	23.7	40.5	15.6	0.348
1969	51,586	5.6	12.4	17.7	23.7	40.6	15.6	0.349
1970	52,227	5.4	12.2	17.6	23.8	40.9	15.6	0.353
1971	53,296	5.5	12.0	17.6	23.8	41.1	15.7	0.355
1972	54,373	5.5	11.9	17.5	23.9	41.4	15.9	0.359
1973	55,053	5.5	11.9	17.5	24.0	41.1	15.5	0.356
1974	55,698	5.7	12.0	17.6	24.1	40.6	14.8	0.355
1975	56,245	5.6	11.9	17.7	24.2	40.7	14.9	0.357
1976	56,710	5.6	11.9	17.7	24.2	40.7	14.9	0.358
1977	57,215	5.5	11.7	17.6	24.3	40.9	14.9	0.363
1978	57,804	5.4	11.7	17.6	24.2	41.1	15.1	0.363
1979	59,550	5.4	11.6	17.5	24.1	41.4	15.3	0.365
1980	60,309	5.3	11.6	17.6	24.4	41.1	14.6	0.365
1981	61,019	5.3	11.4	17.5	24.6	41.2	14.4	0.369
1982	61,393	5.0	11.3	17.2	24.4	42.2	15.3	0.380
1983	61,997	4.9	11.2	17.2	24.5	42.4	15.3	0.382
1984	62,706	4.8	11.1	17.1	24.5	42.5	15.4	0.383
1985 [2]	63,558	4.8	11.0	16.9	24.3	43.1	16.1	0.389
1986	64,491	4.7	10.9	16.9	24.1	43.4	16.5	0.392
1987	65,204	4.6	10.7	16.8	24.0	43.8	17.2	0.393
1988	65,837	4.6	10.7	16.7	24.0	44.0	17.2	0.395
1989	66,090	4.6	10.6	16.5	23.7	44.6	17.9	0.401
1990	66,322	4.6	10.8	16.6	23.8	44.3	17.4	0.396
1991	67,173	4.5	10.7	16.6	24.1	44.2	17.1	0.397
1992	68,216	4.3	10.5	16.5	24.0	44.7	17.6	0.404
1993 [2]	68,506	4.1	9.9	15.7	23.3	47.0	20.3	0.429
1994	69,313	4.2	10.0	15.7	23.3	46.9	20.1	0.426
1995	69,597	4.4	10.1	15.8	23.2	46.5	20.0	0.421
1996	70,241	4.2	10.0	15.8	23.1	46.8	20.3	0.425

Source: U.S. Bureau of the Census, Current Population Survey - March Supplement.

(1) Families as of March of the following year.
(2) The upper reportable limit of earnings in the Current Population Survey (CPS) - March Supplement was increased from $99,999 to $299,999 in March 1986 and from $299,999 to $999,999 in March 1994. These changes affected estimates of mean income, the distribution of aggregate income, and the index of income concentration (Gini ratio) in 1985 and 1993. The 1993 data are also the first to be collected in a completely computer-assisted survey information collection (CASIC) environment. As a result of these changes, data for 1985 and 1993 are not strictly comparable to earlier years. See Appendix B for additional discussion of recent changes in the CPS.

Income and Wealth

TABLE 1.38. MEAN AND MEDIAN FAMILY NET WORTH, BY SELECTED CHARACTERISTICS: 1989, 1992, AND 1995
(Thousands of constant 1995 CPI-U adjusted dollars, except as noted)

FAMILY CHARACTERISTIC [2]	1989			1992			1995 [1]		
	Net worth		Percent of families	Net worth		Percent of families	Net worth		Percent of families
	Median	Mean		Median	Mean		Median	Mean	
ALL FAMILIES	56.5	216.7	100.0	52.8	200.5	100.0	56.4	205.9	100.0
FAMILY INCOME (1995 DOLLARS)									
Less than $10,000	1.6	26.1	15.4	3.3	30.9	15.5	4.8	45.6	16.0
$10,000 to $24,999	25.6	77.9	24.3	28.2	71.2	27.8	30.0	74.6	26.5
$25,000 to $49,999	56.0	121.8	30.3	54.8	124.4	29.5	54.9	119.3	31.1
$50,000 to $99,999	128.1	229.5	22.3	121.2	240.8	20.0	121.1	256.0	20.2
$100,000 and more	474.7	1,372.9	7.7	506.1	1,283.6	7.1	485.9	1,465.2	6.1
AGE OF FAMILY HEAD									
Under 35 years old	9.2	66.3	27.2	10.1	50.3	25.8	11.4	47.2	24.8
35 to 44 years old	69.2	171.3	23.4	46.0	144.3	22.8	48.5	144.5	23.2
45 to 54 years old	114.0	338.9	14.4	83.4	287.8	16.2	90.5	277.8	17.8
55 to 64 years old	110.5	334.4	13.9	122.5	358.6	13.2	110.8	356.2	12.5
65 to 74 years old	88.4	336.8	12.0	105.8	308.3	12.6	104.1	331.6	11.9
75 years old and over	83.2	250.8	9.0	92.8	231.0	9.4	95.0	276.0	9.8
EDUCATION OF FAMILY HEAD									
No high school diploma	28.5	92.1	24.3	21.6	75.8	20.4	26.3	87.2	19.0
High school diploma	43.4	134.4	32.1	41.4	120.6	29.9	50.0	138.2	31.6
Some college	56.4	213.8	15.1	62.6	185.4	17.7	43.2	186.6	19.0
College degree	132.1	416.9	28.5	103.1	363.3	31.9	104.1	361.8	30.5
RACE OR ETHNICITY OF FAMILY HEAD									
White non-Hispanic	84.7	261.4	75.1	71.7	237.8	75.1	73.9	244.0	77.5
Non-White or Hispanic	6.8	82.1	24.9	16.9	87.9	24.9	16.5	74.4	22.5
CURRENT WORK STATUS OF FAMILY HEAD									
Professional, managerial	106.6	262.7	16.9	78.8	248.5	16.8	89.3	252.8	15.9
Technical, sales, clerical	40.9	98.9	13.4	48.0	105.4	14.8	43.3	109.3	14.9
Precision production	58.4	94.2	9.6	38.4	85.5	7.0	43.5	79.3	8.2
Machine operators and laborers	23.1	67.2	10.6	23.5	56.8	10.0	37.3	70.0	13.1
Service occupations	9.3	53.2	6.6	15.7	52.9	6.2	15.8	60.0	6.6
Self-employed	200.7	765.4	11.2	155.6	644.3	10.9	152.9	731.5	9.7
Retired	77.5	199.2	25.0	76.3	201.2	26.0	81.6	218.3	25.0
Other not working	0.7	62.9	6.7	5.5	68.5	8.2	4.5	60.4	6.5
TENURE									
Owner-occupied	119.9	311.7	63.8	106.1	289.6	63.9	102.3	295.4	64.7
Renter-occupied or other	2.4	49.4	36.2	3.6	42.7	36.1	4.5	42.2	35.3

Source: Board of Governors of the Federal Reserve System, Survey of Consumer Finances. See Kennickell, Arthur B., Martha Starr-McCluer, and Annika E. Sunden. "Family Finances in the U.S.: Recent Evidence from the Survey of Consumer Finances." *Federal Reserve Bulletin*, January 1997.

(1) 1995 data are preliminary.
(2) The definition of family used in these tabulations differs from that used by the U.S. Bureau of the Census. See Appendix A.

All dollar amounts are in constant 1995 CPI-U adjusted dollars. See Appendix B under "Consumer Price Index" (CPI) for a discussion of the use of the CPI as a price deflator.

Income and Wealth

	1984			1988		
ASSET TYPE	Percent of households that own asset type	Median value of holdings for asset owners (Constant 1993 CPI-U adjusted dollars)	Distribution of net worth	Percent of households that own asset type	Median value of holdings for asset owners (Constant 1993 CPI-U adjusted dollars)	Distribution of net worth
ALL ASSETS	....	45,411	100.0	....	43,617	100.0
Interest-earning assets at financial institutions	71.8	4,262	14.5	72.9	4,263	14.1
Savings accounts	62.9	....	....	61.6	....	....
Money market deposit accounts	15.7	....	....	15.2	....	....
Certificates of deposit	19.1	....	....	17.7	....	....
Interest-earning checking	24.8	....	....	34.3	....	....
Other interest-earning assets	8.5	13,165	3.2	9.4	13,311	4.2
Money market funds	3.8	....	....	3.6	....	....
Government securities	1.4	....	....	2.2	....	....
Corporate or municipal bonds	2.6	....	....	2.8	....	....
Other interest-earning assets	2.8	....	....	3.3	....	....
Checking accounts	53.9	624	0.6	48.3	594	0.6
Stocks and mutual fund shares	20.0	5,410	6.8	21.8	5,502	6.5
Own home	64.3	56,430	41.3	63.6	52,545	43.0
Rental property	9.8	48,033	9.0	9.0	45,676	7.9
Other real estate	10.0	20,559	4.4	10.5	22,038	4.3
Vehicles	85.8	5,705	5.9	86.3	5,388	5.8
Business or profession	12.9	8,754	10.3	12.5	12,744	8.8
U.S. savings bonds	15.0	417	0.5	17.5	666	0.6
IRA or Keogh accounts	19.5	6,679	2.2	24.2	11,000	4.2
Other financial investments	7.0	17,777	5.0	6.6	19,769	3.0

See notes at end of table.

Income and Wealth

ASSET TYPE	TABLE 1.39. OWNERSHIP RATES, MEDIAN VALUE OF ASSET HOLDINGS, AND THE DISTRIBUTION OF NET WORTH BY ASSET TYPE: 1984 TO 1993 - Continued					
	1991			1993		
	Percent of households that own asset type	Median value of holdings for asset owners (Constant 1993 CPI-U adjusted dollars)	Distribution of net worth	Percent of households that own asset type	Median value of holdings for asset owners (Dollars)	Distribution of net worth
ALL ASSETS	....	38,500	100.0	....	37,587	100.0
Interest-earning assets at financial institutions	73.2	3,709	14.3	71.1	2,999	11.4
Savings accounts	62.4	....	....	60.1	....	....
Money market deposit accounts	14.9	....	....	12.6	....	....
Certificates of deposit	22.0	....	....	16.0	....	....
Interest-earning checking	37.8	....	....	36.9	....	....
Other interest-earning assets	9.0	16,058	5.0	8.6	12,998	4.0
Money market funds	4.2	....	....	3.9	....	....
Government securities	2.2	....	....	2.1	....	....
Corporate or municipal bonds	3.4	....	....	3.1	....	....
Other interest-earning assets	2.2	....	....	2.2	....	....
Checking accounts	46.0	529	0.5	45.9	499	0.5
Stocks and mutual fund shares	20.7	5,490	7.1	20.9	6,960	8.3
Own home	64.7	43,070	42.6	64.3	46,669	44.4
Rental property	9.0	31,270	6.5	8.4	29,300	6.7
Other real estate	10.7	20,140	5.4	9.3	19,415	4.6
Vehicles	86.4	5,555	6.4	85.7	5,140	6.4
Business or profession	11.7	10,203	7.3	10.8	7,000	6.4
U.S. savings bonds	18.1	610	0.6	18.5	775	0.8
IRA or Keogh accounts	22.9	11,886	5.2	23.1	12,985	6.7
Other financial investments	2.8	19,031	3.1	5.2	21,001	3.0

Source: U.S. Bureau of the Census, Survey of Income and Program Participation. See Eller, T. J., and Wallace Fraser. 1995. "Asset Ownership of Households: 1993." U.S. Bureau of the Census. Current Population Reports P70-47.

See Appendix B under "Consumer Price Index" (CPI) for a discussion of the use of the CPI as a price deflator.

Income and Wealth

TABLE 1.40. MEDIAN VALUE OF HOLDINGS FOR ASSET OWNERS, BY SELECTED CHARACTERISTICS: 1993
(In dollars)

CHARACTERISTIC	Net worth	Interest-earning assets at financial institutions	Other interest-earning assets	Regular checking accounts	Stocks and mutual fund shares	Equity in business or profession	Equity in motor vehicles	Equity in own home	Rental property equity	Other real estate equity	U.S. savings bonds	IRA or Keogh accounts	Other assets
TOTAL	37,587	2,999	12,998	499	6,960	7,000	5,140	46,669	29,300	19,415	775	12,985	21,001
RACE AND HISPANIC ORIGIN OF HOUSEHOLDER													
White	45,740	3,199	13,648	499	7,100	7,000	5,472	49,500	29,300	19,415	775	13,999	21,860
Black	4,418	799	3,500	390	3,900	2,500	3,242	28,796	19,000	8,000	450	4,700	....
Hispanic origin [1]	4,656	1,098	....	375	2,365	200	3,333	36,069	13,000	13,000	525	7,000	....
AGE OF HOUSEHOLDER													
Less than 35 years	5,786	999	2,976	395	2,800	3,650	4,135	15,978	11,600	9,000	376	4,450	3,800
35 to 44 years	29,202	1,998	7,363	498	4,700	7,533	5,343	34,968	27,500	17,500	575	9,900	12,000
45 to 54 years	57,755	2,999	9,999	492	5,800	9,500	6,483	49,991	38,000	23,000	825	14,900	19,950
55 to 64 years	91,481	5,748	19,999	499	14,800	9,000	6,493	64,987	46,800	24,000	1,150	19,600	26,000
65 years and over	86,324	9,999	27,500	495	18,200	4,736	4,691	64,467	25,000	29,000	2,250	19,977	29,100
65 to 69 years	92,500	7,999	29,999	495	18,900	4,736	6,275	65,654	34,000	28,000	1,900	21,700	....
70 to 74 years	95,748	10,499	25,000	550	18,900	5,000	5,138	67,000	23,000	29,000	1,950	19,363	29,009
75 years and over	77,654	11,999	24,999	589	16,400	3,000	3,333	62,085	19,500	20,000	2,950	13,688	29,009
EDUCATION OF HOUSEHOLDER													
Less than 12 years	21,877	2,999	14,878	335	4,990	1,980	3,342	39,824	12,000	11,000	950	12,018	....
High school: 4 years	32,619	2,295	12,498	394	4,000	7,947	4,846	44,600	22,000	17,000	700	10,849	18,900
College													
1 to 3 years	32,098	1,999	11,999	498	5,771	6,800	5,343	44,058	29,200	19,000	575	11,500	17,531
4 or more years	75,316	4,970	12,998	732	9,800	9,500	7,238	59,916	45,000	28,000	975	15,963	24,000
TYPE OF HOUSEHOLD BY AGE OF HOUSEHOLDER													
Married-couple households	61,905	3,488	11,599	499	6,960	9,800	6,738	49,991	34,800	19,000	875	14,934	23,700
Less than 35 years	12,941	1,248	2,976	389	2,800	4,800	5,288	16,748	12,473	9,000	475	4,996	....
35 to 54 years	61,874	2,799	8,999	495	4,900	9,800	7,345	44,940	34,526	19,000	700	12,985	18,000
55 to 64 years	127,752	7,050	15,748	640	13,500	9,000	8,400	70,630	49,520	28,000	1,383	22,000	25,000
65 years and over	129,790	11,999	26,800	562	21,600	7,000	6,704	71,230	40,000	34,000	2,700	23,000	39,600
Male householder	13,500	1,999	9,999	498	6,900	4,000	3,450	35,007	18,000	18,000	750	10,136	11,600
Less than 35 years	4,300	999	....	395	2,800	1,500	3,333	16,741	....	....	200	4,500	....
35 to 54 years	18,426	1,999	7,999	498	7,900	3,800	3,666	33,645	29,000	18,000	900	10,136	....
55 to 64 years	44,670	4,400	....	467	16,000	....	3,850	49,264	....	....	....	19,000	....
65 years and over	60,741	11,000	35,800	550	16,000	....	3,348	53,100	10,000	13,000	2,000	19,500	....
Female householder	13,294	2,131	17,000	349	7,520	946	3,348	44,985	10,000	17,000	500	8,900	17,625
Less than 35 years	1,342	699	....	292	2,500	400	3,170	10,810	....	....	175	3,800	....
35 to 54 years	8,405	1,199	8,000	290	4,500	1,500	3,342	30,536	14,666	16,000	475	7,800	....
55 to 64 years	44,762	2,999	24,999	300	20,500	....	3,400	49,864	16,000	8,000	500	14,513	....
65 years and over	57,679	7,999	25,000	471	13,860	....	2,983	57,984	3,800	19,415	1,500	13,000	27,313

See notes at end of table.

Income and Wealth

TABLE 1.40. MEDIAN VALUE OF HOLDINGS FOR ASSET OWNERS, BY SELECTED CHARACTERISTICS: 1993 - Continued

(In dollars)

CHARACTERISTIC	Net worth	Interest-earning assets at financial insti-tutions	Other interest-earning assets	Regular checking accounts	Stocks and mutual fund shares	Equity in business or pro-fession	Equity in motor vehicles	Equity in own home	Rental property equity	Other real estate equity	U.S. savings bonds	IRA or Keogh accounts	Other assets
LABOR FORCE ACTIVITY OF HOUSEHOLDERS UNDER 65 YEARS													
Total	26,739	1,999	9,998	499	4,900	7,000	5,325	39,963	29,300	19,000	575	11,998	15,976
With labor force activity	28,101	1,999	8,249	499	4,900	7,500	5,488	38,544	29,300	19,000	575	11,410	14,758
With job entire period	31,499	1,999	7,999	498	4,900	7,976	5,665	39,004	29,300	19,000	575	11,400	14,758
With job part of period	7,917	1,100	....	315	6,300	-50	3,838	32,782	15,000	18,000	350	10,000	....
No job during period, spent time looking or on layoff	2,500	999	....	329	3,300	....	2,950	26,000	....	....	200	11,900	....
No labor force activity	14,962	2,950	19,999	287	9,500	5,000	3,927	48,517	40,000	22,000	900	15,900	22,500
MONTHLY HOUSEHOLD INCOME													
Lowest quintile	4,249	1,594	9,999	263	3,300	946	1,657	38,940	2,000	8,700	350	10,000	....
Second quintile	20,230	1,999	12,999	299	4,916	1,980	3,348	40,973	13,000	14,000	475	11,000	15,499
Third quintile	30,788	1,998	12,499	445	4,650	4,800	4,625	42,984	27,250	17,000	525	9,500	19,510
Fourth quintile	50,000	2,747	9,999	499	5,900	9,500	6,491	41,850	29,300	19,415	675	11,800	17,600
Highest quintile	118,996	5,999	14,999	780	9,992	17,075	9,898	66,068	47,500	29,000	1,075	16,100	27,375
REGION													
Northeast	46,556	3,499	14,878	484	7,300	4,000	5,683	69,691	22,250	34,000	800	13,971	23,696
Midwest	40,575	2,998	10,199	393	6,400	7,947	5,599	40,154	21,000	19,000	775	13,811	19,000
South	30,549	2,499	14,000	499	5,900	9,800	5,038	36,986	29,000	15,500	700	12,000	19,000
West	39,550	2,999	12,650	499	8,555	7,000	4,725	59,977	46,000	19,000	775	12,669	22,935
TENURE													
Owner	79,410	3,999	14,998	499	7,978	9,800	6,571	46,669	30,000	20,000	990	14,934	23,700
Renter	1,899	1,047	7,499	345	3,825	2,105	3,242	....	22,000	14,000	270	5,700	9,500

Source: U.S. Bureau of the Census, Survey of Income and Program Participation. See Eller, T. J., and Wallace Fraser. 1995. "Asset Ownership of Households: 1993." U.S. Bureau of the Census. Current Population Reports P70-47.

(1) Persons of Hispanic origin may be of any race.

Income and Wealth

AREA	TABLE 1.41. PERCENTAGE OF PERSONS BELOW THE POVERTY LEVEL BY STATE: 1969 TO 1989		
	1969	1979	1989
United States	13.7	12.4	13.1
Northeast	10.1	11.2	10.6
Midwest	10.8	10.5	12.0
South	20.3	15.4	15.7
West	11.7	11.3	12.6
Alabama	25.4	18.9	18.3
Alaska	12.6	10.7	9.0
Arizona	15.3	13.2	15.7
Arkansas	27.8	19.0	19.1
California	11.1	11.4	12.5
Colorado	12.3	10.1	11.7
Connecticut	7.2	8.0	6.8
Delaware	10.9	11.9	8.7
District of Columbia	17.0	18.6	16.9
Florida	16.4	13.5	12.7
Georgia	20.7	16.6	14.7
Hawaii	9.3	9.9	8.3
Idaho	13.2	12.6	13.3
Illinois	10.2	11.0	11.9
Indiana	9.7	9.7	10.7
Iowa	11.6	10.1	11.5
Kansas	12.7	10.1	11.5
Kentucky	22.9	17.6	19.0
Louisiana	26.3	18.6	23.6
Maine	13.6	13.0	10.8
Maryland	10.1	9.8	8.3
Massachusetts	8.6	9.6	8.9
Michigan	9.4	10.4	13.1
Minnesota	10.7	9.5	10.2
Mississippi	35.4	23.9	25.2
Missouri	14.7	12.2	13.3
Montana	13.6	12.3	16.1
Nebraska	13.1	10.7	11.1
Nevada	9.1	8.7	10.2
New Hampshire	9.1	8.5	6.4
New Jersey	8.1	9.5	7.6
New Mexico	22.8	17.6	20.6
New York	11.1	13.4	13.0
North Carolina	20.3	14.8	13.0
North Dakota	15.7	12.6	14.4
Ohio	10.0	10.3	12.5
Oklahoma	18.8	13.4	16.7
Oregon	11.5	10.7	12.4
Pennsylvania	10.6	10.5	11.1
Rhode Island	11.0	10.3	9.6
South Carolina	23.9	16.6	15.4
South Dakota	18.7	16.9	15.9
Tennessee	21.8	16.5	15.7
Texas	18.8	14.7	18.1
Utah	11.4	10.3	11.4
Vermont	12.1	12.1	9.9
Virginia	15.5	11.8	10.2
Washington	10.2	9.8	10.9
West Virginia	22.2	15.0	19.7
Wisconsin	9.8	8.7	10.7
Wyoming	11.7	7.9	11.9

Source: U.S. Bureau of the Census, Census of Population 1970-1990.

Geographic Mobility

TABLE 1.42. HOUSEHOLDERS WHO ARE RECENT MOVERS BY TENURE AND STATE: 1960 TO 1990

AREA	1960						
	Owner-occupied housing units			Renter-occupied housing units			Recent-mover share of all households
	Total	Recent movers [1]		Total	Recent movers [1]		
		Number	Percent		Number	Percent	
United States	32,796,720	4,011,702	12.2	20,227,155	7,774,224	38.4	22.2
Alabama	528,031	68,410	13.0	356,085	146,122	41.0	24.3
Alaska	27,679	7,154	25.8	29,571	19,426	65.7	46.4
Arizona	234,347	56,365	24.1	132,283	77,858	58.9	36.6
Arkansas	321,219	40,979	12.8	202,333	92,347	45.6	25.5
California	2,910,093	505,113	17.4	2,072,015	1,057,790	51.1	31.4
Colorado	337,565	55,138	16.3	191,854	100,227	52.2	29.3
Connecticut	465,672	46,071	9.9	287,064	85,526	29.8	17.5
Delaware	85,971	10,669	12.4	42,611	16,516	38.8	21.1
District of Columbia	75,532	6,862	9.1	176,534	61,700	35.0	27.2
Florida	1,047,217	219,797	21.0	503,197	264,896	52.6	31.3
Georgia	601,631	81,005	13.5	468,694	191,363	40.8	25.4
Hawaii	62,937	8,628	13.7	90,127	38,576	42.8	30.8
Idaho	136,746	21,675	15.9	57,093	31,242	54.7	27.3
Illinois	1,782,127	195,937	11.0	1,302,844	442,910	34.0	20.7
Indiana	986,098	111,341	11.3	401,780	171,177	42.6	20.4
Iowa	581,352	63,332	10.9	260,005	96,396	37.1	19.0
Kansas	463,350	55,246	11.9	209,549	96,945	46.3	22.6
Kentucky	547,750	63,020	11.5	304,117	127,070	41.8	22.3
Louisiana	526,366	66,463	12.6	365,978	140,975	38.5	23.2
Maine	186,379	17,466	9.4	93,976	34,514	36.7	18.5
Maryland	556,391	62,495	11.2	306,610	115,332	37.6	20.6
Massachusetts	857,436	76,397	8.9	677,549	177,384	26.2	16.5
Michigan	1,665,603	172,611	10.4	573,476	248,824	43.4	18.8
Minnesota	714,960	75,393	10.5	277,021	109,967	39.7	18.7
Mississippi	327,894	39,302	12.0	240,176	93,277	38.8	23.3
Missouri	874,532	109,526	12.5	485,522	196,807	40.5	22.5
Montana	129,399	17,687	13.7	72,841	36,083	49.5	26.6
Nebraska	280,867	31,209	11.1	152,581	59,242	38.8	20.9
Nevada	51,491	12,664	24.6	40,029	24,150	60.3	40.2
New Hampshire	117,232	12,184	10.4	62,788	20,354	32.4	18.1
New Jersey	1,107,841	111,670	10.1	698,598	195,904	28.0	17.0
New Mexico	163,926	33,098	20.2	87,283	51,716	59.3	33.8
New York	2,350,265	218,555	9.3	2,898,445	651,574	22.5	16.6
North Carolina	724,631	80,656	11.1	480,084	188,583	39.3	22.3
North Dakota	118,566	12,743	10.7	54,796	21,697	39.6	19.9
Ohio	1,922,686	216,276	11.2	929,871	376,688	40.5	20.8
Oklahoma	492,263	66,494	13.5	242,330	122,124	50.4	25.7
Oregon	386,608	58,559	15.1	171,606	90,252	52.6	26.7
Pennsylvania	2,289,741	178,300	7.8	1,061,098	314,444	29.6	14.7
Rhode Island	140,336	12,150	8.7	116,999	31,211	26.7	16.9
South Carolina	345,756	41,203	11.9	257,795	95,905	37.2	22.7
South Dakota	130,864	15,309	11.7	63,957	24,357	38.1	20.4
Tennessee	639,600	78,386	12.3	363,701	153,468	42.2	23.1
Texas	1,799,477	269,446	15.0	978,639	495,833	50.7	27.5
Utah	173,296	23,324	13.5	68,236	36,176	53.0	24.6
Vermont	73,115	6,804	9.3	37,617	12,754	33.9	17.7
Virginia	658,078	79,367	12.1	414,762	167,798	40.5	23.0
Washington	612,443	84,899	13.9	281,725	147,858	52.5	26.0
West Virginia	335,068	29,586	8.8	186,074	66,930	36.0	18.5
Wisconsin	786,617	73,702	9.4	359,725	133,663	37.2	18.1
Wyoming	61,676	11,036	17.9	37,511	20,293	54.1	31.6

See notes at end of table.

Geographic Mobility

TABLE 1.42. HOUSEHOLDERS WHO ARE RECENT MOVERS BY TENURE AND STATE: 1960 TO 1990 - Continued

AREA	1970						Recent-mover share of all households
	Owner-occupied housing units			Renter-occupied housing units			
	Total	Recent movers [1]		Total	Recent movers [1]		
		Number	Percent		Number	Percent	
United States	39,885,092	4,288,403	10.8	23,559,658	9,372,311	39.8	21.5
Alabama	689,390	77,673	11.3	344,723	139,722	40.5	21.0
Alaska	39,730	9,261	23.3	39,329	24,278	61.7	42.4
Arizona	352,104	68,575	19.5	187,053	104,735	56.0	32.1
Arkansas	410,437	49,915	12.2	204,987	92,675	45.2	23.2
California	3,611,630	454,154	12.6	2,959,875	1,423,712	48.1	28.6
Colorado	438,133	65,838	15.0	252,795	139,989	55.4	29.8
Connecticut	583,410	45,484	7.8	349,640	113,724	32.5	17.1
Delaware	112,050	11,642	10.4	52,754	21,938	41.6	20.4
District of Columbia	74,040	5,449	7.4	188,498	57,726	30.6	24.1
Florida	1,566,948	259,881	16.6	717,834	356,088	49.6	27.0
Georgia	836,511	113,538	13.6	532,714	229,801	43.1	25.1
Hawaii	95,249	12,057	12.7	107,840	48,195	44.7	29.7
Idaho	153,587	21,018	13.7	65,373	36,021	55.1	26.0
Illinois	2,080,907	198,598	9.5	1,419,876	491,413	34.6	19.7
Indiana	1,153,240	121,896	10.6	456,203	205,842	45.1	20.4
Iowa	642,662	62,690	9.8	253,649	107,431	42.4	19.0
Kansas	502,578	51,957	10.3	224,786	112,195	49.9	22.6
Kentucky	657,993	69,239	10.5	325,672	140,110	43.0	21.3
Louisiana	663,833	69,609	10.5	388,262	154,368	39.8	21.3
Maine	212,212	20,307	9.6	90,711	35,726	39.4	18.5
Maryland	690,246	61,833	9.0	484,480	185,693	38.3	21.1
Massachusetts	1,012,000	75,726	7.5	747,557	228,988	30.6	17.3
Michigan	1,974,736	211,246	10.7	678,319	304,067	44.8	19.4
Minnesota	824,595	80,597	9.8	329,351	150,385	45.7	20.0
Mississippi	421,915	50,700	12.0	214,852	84,271	39.2	21.2
Missouri	1,021,168	112,936	11.1	499,399	213,077	42.7	21.4
Montana	142,774	16,969	11.9	74,530	38,330	51.4	25.4
Nebraska	314,315	31,914	10.2	158,992	68,570	43.1	21.2
Nevada	93,682	19,716	21.0	66,370	39,188	59.0	36.8
New Hampshire	153,774	17,245	11.2	71,604	27,872	38.9	20.0
New Jersey	1,350,052	115,895	8.6	868,130	252,063	29.0	16.6
New Mexico	192,235	26,898	14.0	97,154	54,070	55.7	28.0
New York	2,795,566	221,625	7.9	3,118,183	688,211	22.1	15.4
North Carolina	987,063	107,988	10.9	522,501	204,290	39.1	20.7
North Dakota	124,231	11,204	9.0	57,382	26,688	46.5	20.9
Ohio	2,225,854	214,006	9.6	1,063,519	429,315	40.4	19.6
Oklahoma	588,868	73,920	12.6	261,935	143,282	54.7	25.5
Oregon	457,024	62,240	13.6	234,607	129,213	55.1	27.7
Pennsylvania	2,549,001	178,394	7.0	1,156,409	356,125	30.8	14.4
Rhode Island	169,392	12,330	7.3	123,196	37,154	30.2	16.9
South Carolina	485,412	60,803	12.5	248,946	96,140	38.6	21.4
South Dakota	139,687	13,029	9.3	61,120	25,829	42.3	19.4
Tennessee	809,159	89,061	11.0	403,802	173,805	43.0	21.7
Texas	2,222,060	287,036	12.9	1,211,513	639,081	52.8	27.0
Utah	206,655	21,961	10.6	91,279	50,868	55.7	24.4
Vermont	91,285	10,440	11.4	40,813	16,145	39.6	20.1
Virginia	863,071	91,339	10.6	527,564	224,040	42.5	22.7
Washington	738,251	97,624	13.2	367,336	207,922	56.6	27.6
West Virginia	376,785	34,374	9.1	170,429	61,881	36.3	17.6
Wisconsin	918,152	80,790	8.8	410,652	161,633	39.4	18.2
Wyoming	69,440	9,783	14.1	35,160	18,426	52.4	27.0

See notes at end of table.

Geographic Mobility

TABLE 1.42. HOUSEHOLDERS WHO ARE RECENT MOVERS BY TENURE AND STATE: 1960 TO 1990 - Continued

AREA	Owner-occupied housing units			Renter-occupied housing units			Recent-mover share of all households
	Total	Recent movers [1]		Total	Recent movers [1]		
		Number	Percent		Number	Percent	
United States	51,796,395	6,126,736	11.8	28,593,278	12,135,188	42.4	22.7
Alabama	941,237	107,051	11.4	400,619	172,676	43.1	20.8
Alaska	76,659	16,515	21.5	54,804	34,282	62.6	38.6
Arizona	653,825	129,331	19.8	303,207	181,532	59.9	32.5
Arkansas	575,469	74,323	12.9	240,596	114,034	47.4	23.1
California	4,825,384	689,490	14.3	3,804,482	1,725,854	45.4	28.0
Colorado	684,417	127,991	18.7	376,832	222,747	59.1	33.0
Connecticut	699,259	61,216	8.8	394,419	136,666	34.6	18.1
Delaware	143,077	15,367	10.7	64,004	28,272	44.2	21.1
District of Columbia	89,828	8,371	9.3	163,315	42,438	26.0	20.1
Florida	2,557,184	423,699	16.6	1,187,070	580,025	48.9	26.8
Georgia	1,216,432	154,308	12.7	655,220	292,824	44.7	23.9
Hawaii	151,916	19,292	12.7	142,136	59,549	41.9	26.8
Idaho	233,388	37,781	16.2	90,719	55,704	61.4	28.8
Illinois	2,534,762	260,079	10.3	1,510,612	572,902	37.9	20.6
Indiana	1,381,924	150,696	10.9	545,126	253,619	46.5	21.0
Iowa	756,521	80,934	10.7	296,512	135,468	45.7	20.6
Kansas	612,433	75,453	12.3	259,806	133,767	51.5	24.0
Kentucky	884,869	98,999	11.2	378,486	168,278	44.5	21.2
Louisiana	925,168	115,337	12.5	486,620	211,905	43.5	23.2
Maine	280,380	27,092	9.7	114,804	52,453	45.7	20.1
Maryland	905,667	91,633	10.1	555,198	209,233	37.7	20.6
Massachusetts	1,169,807	91,442	7.8	862,910	279,335	32.4	18.2
Michigan	2,321,972	248,609	10.7	873,241	389,023	44.5	20.0
Minnesota	1,035,738	117,894	11.4	409,484	197,806	48.3	21.8
Mississippi	587,712	68,030	11.6	239,457	101,028	42.2	20.4
Missouri	1,248,801	140,088	11.2	544,598	241,132	44.3	21.3
Montana	194,580	29,942	15.4	89,162	48,945	54.9	27.8
Nebraska	390,924	46,139	11.8	180,476	84,788	47.0	22.9
Nevada	181,255	39,347	21.7	123,072	75,462	61.3	37.7
New Hampshire	218,840	25,362	11.6	104,653	45,934	43.9	22.0
New Jersey	1,580,120	132,668	8.4	968,474	293,653	30.3	16.7
New Mexico	300,568	50,431	16.8	140,898	79,732	56.6	29.5
New York	3,083,170	243,174	7.9	3,257,259	838,562	25.7	17.1
North Carolina	1,397,426	153,592	11.0	645,865	267,444	41.4	20.6
North Dakota	156,515	20,431	13.1	71,149	35,560	50.0	24.6
Ohio	2,623,022	258,496	9.9	1,210,806	514,468	42.5	20.2
Oklahoma	790,606	113,301	14.3	327,955	182,397	55.6	26.4
Oregon	645,952	99,789	15.4	345,641	195,490	56.6	29.8
Pennsylvania	2,950,662	227,398	7.7	1,268,944	438,330	34.5	15.8
Rhode Island	199,075	17,518	8.8	139,515	48,893	35.0	19.6
South Carolina	722,559	82,959	11.5	307,422	129,598	42.2	20.6
South Dakota	168,002	21,150	12.6	74,521	35,775	48.0	23.5
Tennessee	1,110,083	126,387	11.4	508,422	229,282	45.1	22.0
Texas	3,169,588	455,887	14.4	1,759,679	978,406	55.6	29.1
Utah	317,207	48,324	15.2	131,396	80,887	61.6	28.8
Vermont	122,560	13,200	10.8	55,765	25,254	45.3	21.6
Virginia	1,221,590	149,503	12.2	641,483	284,982	44.4	23.3
Washington	1,011,322	153,835	15.2	529,188	292,773	55.3	29.0
West Virginia	504,921	51,976	10.3	181,390	71,406	39.4	18.0
Wisconsin	1,127,367	108,967	9.7	524,894	233,846	44.6	20.7
Wyoming	114,652	25,939	22.6	50,972	30,769	60.4	34.2

See notes at end of table.

Geographic Mobility

TABLE 1.42. HOUSEHOLDERS WHO ARE RECENT MOVERS BY TENURE AND STATE: 1960 TO 1990 - Continued

AREA	Owner-occupied housing units			Renter-occupied housing units			Recent-mover share of all households
	1990						
	Total	Recent movers [1]		Total	Recent movers [1]		
		Number	Percent		Number	Percent	
United States	59,031,378	5,524,646	9.4	32,916,032	13,683,377	41.6	20.9
Alabama	1,062,148	94,392	8.9	444,642	193,206	43.5	19.1
Alaska	106,000	14,021	13.2	82,915	48,280	58.2	33.0
Arizona	879,000	111,776	12.7	489,843	281,606	57.5	28.7
Arkansas	620,077	59,099	9.5	271,102	128,116	47.3	21.0
California	5,774,899	692,531	12.0	4,606,307	1,964,992	42.7	25.6
Colorado	798,607	90,439	11.3	483,882	260,341	53.8	27.4
Connecticut	807,559	55,386	6.9	422,920	149,844	35.4	16.7
Delaware	173,874	17,540	10.1	73,623	29,387	39.9	19.0
District of Columbia	97,085	7,955	8.2	152,549	43,588	28.6	20.6
Florida	3,453,022	419,333	12.1	1,681,847	836,565	49.7	24.5
Georgia	1,536,829	161,378	10.5	829,786	403,053	48.6	23.8
Hawaii	191,894	18,553	9.7	164,373	63,987	38.9	23.2
Idaho	252,687	29,644	11.7	108,036	57,500	53.2	24.2
Illinois	2,699,121	240,244	8.9	1,503,119	549,742	36.6	18.8
Indiana	1,450,899	129,867	9.0	614,456	265,117	43.1	19.1
Iowa	745,371	61,632	8.3	318,954	131,440	41.2	18.1
Kansas	641,760	57,934	9.0	302,966	148,580	49.0	21.9
Kentucky	960,508	87,158	9.1	419,274	179,621	42.8	19.3
Louisiana	988,012	74,763	7.6	511,257	226,113	44.2	20.1
Maine	327,928	26,142	8.0	137,384	57,851	42.1	18.1
Maryland	1,137,307	111,628	9.8	611,684	226,687	37.1	19.3
Massachusetts	1,331,533	86,419	6.5	915,577	300,682	32.8	17.2
Michigan	2,427,472	214,631	8.8	991,859	405,540	40.9	18.1
Minnesota	1,183,738	107,678	9.1	464,115	211,542	45.6	19.4
Mississippi	651,612	56,125	8.6	259,762	113,331	43.6	18.6
Missouri	1,348,733	121,707	9.0	612,473	272,166	44.4	20.1
Montana	205,938	20,847	10.1	100,225	48,715	48.6	22.7
Nebraska	400,416	32,282	8.1	201,947	87,641	43.4	19.9
Nevada	255,490	46,877	18.3	210,807	117,526	55.8	35.3
New Hampshire	280,415	23,488	8.4	130,771	56,845	43.5	19.5
New Jersey	1,813,646	130,752	7.2	981,065	294,354	30.0	15.2
New Mexico	365,913	38,883	10.6	176,796	90,472	51.2	23.8
New York	3,466,277	238,588	6.9	3,173,045	752,403	23.7	14.9
North Carolina	1,711,882	157,999	9.2	805,144	351,666	43.7	20.2
North Dakota	157,950	12,609	8.0	82,928	36,142	43.6	20.2
Ohio	2,758,131	220,177	8.0	1,329,415	516,047	38.8	18.0
Oklahoma	821,299	75,988	9.3	384,836	206,586	53.7	23.4
Oregon	695,957	85,284	12.3	407,356	193,778	47.6	25.3
Pennsylvania	3,176,693	206,055	6.5	1,319,273	431,029	32.7	14.2
Rhode Island	224,829	16,095	7.2	153,148	52,451	34.2	18.1
South Carolina	878,824	80,821	9.2	379,220	167,826	44.3	19.8
South Dakota	171,148	15,550	9.1	87,886	36,722	41.8	20.2
Tennessee	1,261,048	121,376	9.6	592,677	271,106	45.7	21.2
Texas	3,695,184	358,900	9.7	2,375,753	1,262,940	53.2	26.7
Utah	366,010	36,759	10.0	171,263	95,568	55.8	24.6
Vermont	145,368	13,692	9.4	65,282	28,165	43.1	19.9
Virginia	1,519,644	158,203	10.4	772,186	342,819	44.4	21.9
Washington	1,171,714	141,715	12.1	700,717	350,308	50.0	26.3
West Virginia	510,058	35,078	6.9	178,499	70,482	39.5	15.3
Wisconsin	1,215,324	96,138	7.9	606,794	243,222	40.1	18.6
Wyoming	114,545	12,515	10.9	54,294	29,687	54.7	25.0

Source: U.S. Bureau of the Census, Census of Housing 1960-1990. Table prepared by Robert Bonnette.

(1) Recent movers are those householders who moved into their unit in the 15 months prior to the census. See Appendix A, Tables 1.43-1.47, for a discussion of the differences among data sources in the definition of a recent mover.

Geographic Mobility

TABLE 1.43. ANNUAL GEOGRAPHICAL MOBILITY BY TYPE OF MOVEMENT: 1947 TO 1997
(In thousands)

MOBILITY PERIOD	Total, 1 year old and over	Same house (non-movers)	Total movers [1]	Different house in the United States					Movers from abroad
				Total	Same county	Different county			
						Total	Same state	Different state	
1947-48	141,698	113,026	28,672	28,210	19,202	9,008	4,638	4,370	462
1948-49	144,101	116,498	27,603	27,127	18,792	8,335	3,992	4,344	476
1949-50	146,864	118,849	28,015	27,526	19,276	8,250	4,360	3,889	491
1950-51	148,400	116,936	31,464	31,158	20,694	10,464	5,276	5,188	306
1951-52	150,494	120,016	30,478	29,840	19,874	9,966	4,854	5,112	638
1952-53	153,038	121,512	31,526	30,786	20,638	10,148	4,626	5,522	740
1953-54	155,679	125,654	30,025	29,207	19,046	9,981	4,947	5,034	998
1954-55	158,609	126,190	32,419	31,492	21,086	10,406	5,511	4,895	927
1955-56	161,497	127,457	34,040	33,098	22,186	10,912	5,859	5,053	942
1956-57	164,371	131,648	32,723	31,834	21,566	10,268	5,192	5,076	889
1957-58	167,604	133,501	34,103	33,263	22,023	11,240	5,656	5,584	840
1958-59	170,658	137,018	33,640	32,804	22,315	10,489	5,419	5,070	836
1959-60	174,451	139,766	34,685	33,811	22,564	11,247	5,724	5,523	874
1960-61	177,354	140,821	36,533	35,535	24,289	11,246	5,493	5,753	998
1961-62	179,663	144,445	35,218	34,364	23,341	11,023	5,461	5,562	854
1962-63	182,541	146,109	36,432	35,411	23,059	12,352	5,712	6,640	1,021
1963-64	185,312	148,125	37,187	36,327	24,089	12,238	6,191	6,047	859
1964-65	187,974	149,128	38,846	37,866	25,122	12,744	6,597	6,147	978
1965-66	190,242	152,656	37,586	36,703	24,165	12,538	6,275	6,263	883
1966-67	192,233	155,710	36,523	35,200	22,339	12,861	6,308	6,553	1,323
1967-68	194,621	156,735	37,886	36,603	22,960	13,643	6,607	7,035	1,283
1968-69	196,642	159,310	37,332	35,933	22,993	12,940	6,316	6,625	1,399
1969-70	198,955	160,860	38,095	36,541	23,225	13,316	6,250	7,066	1,554
1970-71	201,506	163,800	37,705	36,161	23,018	13,143	6,197	6,946	1,544
1975-76	208,069	171,276	36,793	35,645	22,399	13,246	7,106	6,140	1,148
1980-81	221,641	183,442	38,200	36,887	23,097	13,789	7,614	6,175	1,313
1981-82	223,719	185,592	38,127	37,039	23,081	13,959	7,330	6,628	1,088
1982-83	225,874	188,465	37,408	36,430	22,858	13,572	7,403	6,169	978
1983-84	228,232	188,853	39,379	38,300	23,659	14,641	8,198	6,444	1,079
1984-85	230,333	183,863	46,470	45,043	30,126	14,917	7,995	6,921	1,427
1985-86	232,998	189,760	43,237	42,037	26,401	15,636	8,665	6,971	1,200
1986-87	235,089	191,396	43,693	42,551	27,196	15,355	8,762	6,593	1,142
1987-88	237,431	195,258	42,174	40,974	26,201	14,772	7,727	7,046	1,200
1988-89	239,793	197,173	42,620	41,153	26,123	15,030	7,949	7,081	1,467
1989-90	242,208	198,827	43,381	41,821	25,726	16,094	8,061	8,033	1,560
1990-91	244,884	203,345	41,539	40,154	25,151	15,003	7,881	7,122	1,385
1991-92	247,380	204,580	42,800	41,545	26,587	14,957	7,853	7,105	1,255
1992-93	250,210	208,162	42,048	40,743	26,212	14,532	7,735	6,797	1,305
1993-94	255,774	212,939	42,835	41,590	26,638	14,952	8,226	6,726	1,245
1994-95	258,175	215,870	42,306	41,528	27,900	13,627	7,886	5,741	778
1995-96	260,406	217,868	42,538	41,177	26,696	14,481	8,009	6,472	1,361
1996-97	262,976	219,585	43,391	42,088	27,740	14,348	7,960	6,389	1,303

Source: U.S. Bureau of the Census, Current Population Survey - March Supplement. See Faber, Carol S. 1998. "Geographical Mobility: March 1996 to March 1997 (Update)." U.S. Bureau of the Census, Current Population Reports, P20-510.

(1) Movers in the Current Population Survey are persons one year old and over who were living in a different place of residence at the time of the survey than they were one year earlier. See Appendix A for a discussion of the differences among data sources in the definition of a recent mover.

Geographic Mobility

TABLE 1.44. ANNUAL GEOGRAPHICAL MOBILITY RATES BY TYPE OF MOVEMENT: 1947 TO 1997
(Percent)

| MOBILITY PERIOD | Total, 1 year old and over | Same house (non-movers) | Total movers [1] | Different house in the United States | | | | | Movers from abroad |
| | | | | Total | Same county | Different county | | | |
						Total	Same state	Different state	
1947-48	100.0	79.8	20.2	19.9	13.6	6.4	3.3	3.1	0.3
1948-49	100.0	80.8	19.2	18.8	13.0	5.8	2.8	3.0	0.3
1949-50	100.0	80.9	19.1	18.7	13.1	5.6	3.0	2.6	0.3
1950-51	100.0	78.8	21.2	21.0	13.9	7.1	3.6	3.5	0.2
1951-52	100.0	79.7	20.3	19.8	13.2	6.6	3.2	3.4	0.4
1952-53	100.0	79.4	20.6	20.1	13.5	6.6	3.0	3.6	0.5
1953-54	100.0	80.7	19.3	18.8	12.2	6.4	3.2	3.2	0.6
1954-55	100.0	79.6	20.4	19.9	13.3	6.6	3.5	3.1	0.6
1955-56	100.0	78.9	21.1	20.5	13.7	6.8	3.6	3.1	0.6
1956-57	100.0	80.1	19.9	19.4	13.1	6.2	3.2	3.1	0.5
1957-58	100.0	79.7	20.3	19.8	13.1	6.7	3.4	3.3	0.5
1958-59	100.0	80.3	19.7	19.2	13.1	6.1	3.2	3.0	0.5
1959-60	100.0	80.1	19.9	19.4	12.9	6.4	3.3	3.2	0.5
1960-61	100.0	79.4	20.6	20.0	13.7	6.3	3.1	3.2	0.6
1961-62	100.0	80.4	19.6	19.1	13.0	6.1	3.0	3.1	0.5
1962-63	100.0	80.0	20.0	19.4	12.6	6.8	3.1	3.6	0.6
1963-64	100.0	79.9	20.1	19.6	13.0	6.6	3.3	3.3	0.5
1964-65	100.0	79.3	20.7	20.1	13.4	6.8	3.5	3.3	0.5
1965-66	100.0	80.2	19.8	19.3	12.7	6.6	3.3	3.3	0.5
1966-67	100.0	81.0	19.0	18.3	11.6	6.7	3.3	3.4	0.7
1967-68	100.0	80.5	19.5	18.8	11.8	7.0	3.4	3.6	0.7
1968-69	100.0	81.0	19.0	18.3	11.7	6.6	3.2	3.4	0.7
1969-70	100.0	80.9	19.1	18.4	11.7	6.7	3.1	3.6	0.8
1970-71	100.0	81.3	18.7	17.9	11.4	6.5	3.1	3.4	0.8
1975-76	100.0	82.3	17.7	17.1	10.8	6.4	3.4	3.0	0.6
1980-81	100.0	82.8	17.2	16.6	10.4	6.2	3.4	2.8	0.6
1981-82	100.0	83.0	17.0	16.6	10.3	6.2	3.3	3.0	0.5
1982-83	100.0	83.4	16.6	16.1	10.1	6.0	3.3	2.7	0.4
1983-84	100.0	82.7	17.3	16.8	10.4	6.4	3.6	2.8	0.5
1984-85	100.0	79.8	20.2	19.6	13.1	6.5	3.5	3.0	0.6
1985-86	100.0	81.4	18.6	18.0	11.3	6.7	3.7	3.0	0.5
1986-87	100.0	81.4	18.6	18.1	11.6	6.5	3.7	2.8	0.5
1987-88	100.0	82.2	17.8	17.3	11.0	6.2	3.3	3.0	0.5
1988-89	100.0	82.2	17.8	17.2	10.9	6.3	3.3	3.0	0.6
1989-90	100.0	82.1	17.9	17.3	10.6	6.6	3.3	3.3	0.6
1990-91	100.0	83.0	17.0	16.4	10.3	6.1	3.2	2.9	0.6
1991-92	100.0	82.7	17.3	16.8	10.7	6.0	3.2	2.9	0.5
1992-93	100.0	83.2	16.8	16.3	10.5	5.8	3.1	2.7	0.5
1993-94	100.0	83.3	16.7	16.3	10.4	5.8	3.2	2.6	0.5
1994-95	100.0	83.6	16.4	16.1	10.8	5.3	3.1	2.2	0.3
1995-96	100.0	83.7	16.3	15.8	10.3	5.6	3.1	2.5	0.5
1996-97	100.0	83.5	16.5	16.0	10.5	5.5	3.0	2.4	0.5

Source: U.S. Bureau of the Census, Current Population Survey - March Supplement. See Faber, Carol S. 1998. "Geographical Mobility: March 1996 to March 1997 (Update)." U.S. Bureau of the Census, Current Population Reports, P20-510.

(1) Movers in the Current Population Survey are persons one year old and over who were living in a different place of residence at the time of the survey than they were one year earlier. See Appendix A for a discussion of the differences among data sources in the definition of a recent mover.

Geographic Mobility

MOBILITY PERIOD AND TYPE OF MIGRATION	Northeast	Midwest	South	West
TABLE 1.45. ANNUAL INMIGRATION, OUTMIGRATION, NET MIGRATION, AND MOVERS FROM ABROAD BY REGIONS: 1980 TO 1997 (Numbers in thousands)				
1980-81				
Inmigrants	464	650	1,377	871
Outmigrants	706	1,056	890	710
Net internal migration	-242	-406	487	161
Movers from abroad	207	180	412	514
Net migration (Including abroad)	-35	-226	899	675
1981-82				
Inmigrants	473	793	1,482	931
Outmigrants	685	1,163	1,012	819
Net internal migration	-212	-370	470	112
Movers from abroad	229	134	401	324
Net migration (Including abroad)	17	-236	871	436
1982-83				
Inmigrants	439	661	1,211	880
Outmigrants	625	947	973	645
Net internal migration	-186	-286	238	235
Movers from abroad	192	149	323	315
Net migration (Including abroad)	6	-137	561	550
1983-84				
Inmigrants	487	820	1,399	834
Outmigrants	578	1,102	973	887
Net internal migration	-91	-282	426	-53
Movers from abroad	213	141	383	341
Net migration (Including abroad)	122	-141	809	288
1984-85				
Inmigrants	482	842	1,329	994
Outmigrants	691	1,053	1,169	734
Net internal migration	-209	-211	160	260
Movers from abroad	228	168	532	499
Net migration (Including abroad)	19	-43	692	759
1985-86				
Inmigrants	502	1,011	1,355	910
Outmigrants	752	996	1,320	710
Net internal migration	-250	15	35	200
Movers from abroad	198	158	342	502
Net migration (Including abroad)	-52	173	377	702
1986-87				
Inmigrants	398	858	1,374	916
Outmigrants	732	969	1,095	750
Net internal migration	-334	-111	279	166
Movers from abroad	214	193	277	458
Net migration (Including abroad)	-120	82	556	624
1987-88				
Inmigrants	430	715	1,338	613
Outmigrants	671	818	886	721
Net internal migration	-241	-103	452	-108
Movers from abroad	261	146	414	379
Net migration (Including abroad)	20	43	866	271
1988-89				
Inmigrants	370	777	1,318	791
Outmigrants	714	703	1,071	768
Net internal migration	-344	74	247	23
Movers from abroad	292	170	375	629
Net migration (Including abroad)	-52	244	622	652

See notes at end of table.

Geographic Mobility

MOBILITY PERIOD AND TYPE OF MIGRATION	Northeast	Midwest	South	West
TABLE 1.45. ANNUAL INMIGRATION, OUTMIGRATION, NET MIGRATION, AND MOVERS FROM ABROAD BY REGIONS: 1980 TO 1997 - Continued (Numbers in thousands)				
1989-90				
Inmigrants	461	908	1,428	964
Outmigrants	758	1,024	1,198	781
Net internal migration	-297	-116	230	183
Movers from abroad	328	169	500	562
Net migration (Including abroad)	31	53	730	745
1990-91				
Inmigrants	346	782	1,421	835
Outmigrants	932	797	987	668
Net internal migration	-585	-15	433	167
Movers from abroad	209	208	351	617
Net migration (Including abroad)	-376	193	784	784
1991-92				
Inmigrants	409	816	1,305	755
Outmigrants	701	878	1,081	626
Net internal migration	-292	-62	224	129
Movers from abroad	255	175	383	442
Net migration (Including abroad)	-37	113	607	571
1992-93				
Inmigrants	313	841	1,145	769
Outmigrants	647	608	1,044	770
Net internal migration	-334	233	101	-1
Movers from abroad	230	198	513	364
Net migration (Including abroad)	-104	431	614	363
1993-94				
Inmigrants	348	706	1,336	746
Outmigrants	676	737	960	763
Net internal migration	-328	-31	376	-17
Movers from abroad	267	132	451	396
Net migration (Including abroad)	-61	101	827	379
1995-96				
Inmigrants	441	842	1,284	792
Outmigrants	675	775	1,134	775
Net internal migration	-234	68	150	16
Movers from abroad	285	130	470	476
Net migration (Including abroad)	51	198	620	492
1996-97				
Inmigrants	481	661	1,338	688
Outmigrants	600	814	947	806
Net internal migration	-119	-154	391	-118
Movers from abroad	239	169	445	450
Net migration (Including abroad)	120	15	836	332

Source: U.S. Bureau of the Census, Current Population Survey - March Supplement. See Faber, Carol S. 1998. "Geographical Mobility: March 1996 to March 1997 (Update)." U.S. Bureau of the Census, Current Population Reports, P20-510.

Movers in the Current Population Survey are persons one year old and over who were living in a different place of residence at the time of the survey than they were one year earlier. See Appendix A for a discussion of the differences among data sources in the definition of a recent mover.

Geographic Mobility

TABLE 1.46. GEOGRAPHIC MOBILITY BY TENURE: 1986 TO 1997
(In thousands)

MOBILITY PERIOD AND TENURE	Total persons	Same house (non-movers)	Total movers [1]	Different house in the United States						Movers from abroad
				Total	Same county	Different county				
						Total	Same state	Different state		
1986-87										
Total, 1 year and over	235,089	191,396	43,693	42,551	27,196	15,355	8,762	6,593		1,142
In owner-occupied units	159,355	143,141	16,214	15,899	9,836	6,063	3,812	2,251		315
In renter-occupied units	75,734	48,255	27,479	26,652	17,360	9,292	4,950	4,342		827
1987-88										
Total, 1 year and over	237,431	195,258	42,173	40,974	26,201	14,772	7,727	7,046		1,200
In owner-occupied units	160,924	145,685	15,238	14,903	9,155	5,748	3,279	2,469		335
In renter-occupied units	76,508	49,572	26,935	26,071	17,047	9,024	4,448	4,576		864
1988-89										
Total, 1 year and over	239,793	197,173	42,619	41,153	26,123	15,030	7,949	7,081		1,467
In owner-occupied units	162,193	147,081	15,112	14,724	8,611	6,113	3,457	2,656		388
In renter-occupied units	77,599	50,092	27,507	26,429	17,512	8,918	4,493	4,425		1,078
1989-90										
Total, 1 year and over	242,208	198,827	43,381	41,821	25,726	16,094	8,061	8,033		1,560
In owner-occupied units	162,877	147,830	15,047	14,701	8,463	6,238	3,276	2,962		346
In renter-occupied units	79,331	50,997	28,334	27,121	17,263	9,856	4,785	5,072		1,214
1990-91										
Total, 1 year and over	244,884	203,345	41,539	40,154	25,151	15,003	7,881	7,122		1,385
In owner-occupied units	164,173	149,723	14,450	14,171	8,207	5,964	3,155	2,809		279
In renter-occupied units	80,711	53,623	27,088	25,983	16,944	9,039	4,726	4,313		1,105
1991-92										
Total, 1 year and over	247,380	204,580	42,800	41,545	26,587	14,957	7,853	7,105		1,255
In owner-occupied units	165,612	150,824	14,788	14,418	8,546	5,872	3,064	2,808		371
In renter-occupied units	81,768	53,756	28,012	27,127	18,042	9,086	4,789	4,297		884
1992-93										
Total, 1 year and over	250,210	208,162	42,048	40,744	26,212	14,532	7,735	6,797		1,305
In owner-occupied units	168,837	153,520	15,317	15,008	8,973	6,035	3,171	2,863		309
In renter-occupied units	81,373	54,641	26,732	25,736	17,239	8,497	4,563	3,934		996
1993-94										
Total, 1 year and over	255,774	212,939	42,835	41,590	26,638	14,952	8,226	6,726		1,245
In owner-occupied units	171,205	155,950	15,255	14,938	8,936	6,002	3,329	2,673		317
In renter-occupied units	84,569	56,989	27,580	26,652	17,702	8,950	4,897	4,053		928
1995-96										
Total, 1 year and over	260,406	217,868	42,537	41,176	26,696	14,480	8,009	6,471		1,361
In owner-occupied units	176,773	162,230	14,543	14,247	9,102	5,144	3,178	1,966		296
In renter-occupied units	83,633	55,638	27,995	26,930	17,594	9,336	4,831	4,505		1,065
1996-97										
Total, 1 year and over	262,976	219,585	43,391	42,088	27,740	14,348	7,960	6,389		1,303
In owner-occupied units	179,918	164,858	15,061	14,777	9,413	5,363	3,220	2,143		284
In renter-occupied units	83,058	54,727	28,331	27,311	18,327	8,985	4,740	4,245		1,020

Source: U.S. Bureau of the Census, Current Population Survey - March Supplement. See Faber, Carol S. 1998. "Geographical Mobility: March 1996 to March 1997 (Update)." U.S. Bureau of the Census, Current Population Reports, P20-510.

(1) Movers in the Current Population Survey are persons one year old and over who were living in a different place of residence at the time of the survey than they were one year earlier. See Appendix A for a discussion of the differences among data sources in the definition of a recent mover.

Geographic Mobility

TABLE 1.47. GEOGRAPHIC MOBILITY RATES BY TENURE: 1986 TO 1997
(Percent)

MOBILITY PERIOD AND TENURE	Total persons	Same house (non-movers)	Total movers [1]	Different house in the United States						Movers from abroad
				Total	Same county	Different county				
						Total	Same state	Different state		
1986-87										
Total, 1 year and over	100.0	81.4	18.6	18.1	11.6	6.5	3.7	2.8		0.5
In owner-occupied units	100.0	89.8	10.2	10.0	6.2	3.8	2.4	1.4		0.2
In renter-occupied units	100.0	63.7	36.3	35.2	22.9	12.3	6.5	5.7		1.1
1987-88										
Total, 1 year and over	100.0	82.2	17.8	17.3	11.0	6.2	3.3	3.0		0.5
In owner-occupied units	100.0	90.5	9.5	9.3	5.7	3.6	2.0	1.5		0.2
In renter-occupied units	100.0	64.8	35.2	34.1	22.3	11.8	5.8	6.0		1.1
1988-89										
Total, 1 year and over	100.0	82.2	17.8	17.2	10.9	6.3	3.3	3.0		0.6
In owner-occupied units	100.0	90.7	9.3	9.1	5.3	3.8	2.1	1.6		0.2
In renter-occupied units	100.0	64.6	35.4	34.1	22.6	11.5	5.8	5.7		1.4
1989-90										
Total, 1 year and over	100.0	82.1	17.9	17.3	10.6	6.6	3.3	3.3		0.6
In owner-occupied units	100.0	90.8	9.2	9.0	5.2	3.8	2.0	1.8		0.2
In renter-occupied units	100.0	64.3	35.7	34.2	21.8	12.4	6.0	6.4		1.5
1990-91										
Total, 1 year and over	100.0	83.0	17.0	16.4	10.3	6.1	3.2	2.9		0.6
In owner-occupied units	100.0	91.2	8.8	8.6	5.0	3.6	1.9	1.7		0.2
In renter-occupied units	100.0	66.4	33.6	32.2	21.0	11.2	5.9	5.3		1.4
1991-92										
Total, 1 year and over	100.0	82.7	17.3	16.8	10.7	6.0	3.2	2.9		0.5
In owner-occupied units	100.0	91.1	8.9	8.7	5.2	3.5	1.9	1.7		0.2
In renter-occupied units	100.0	65.7	34.3	33.2	22.1	11.1	5.9	5.3		1.1
1992-93										
Total, 1 year and over	100.0	83.2	16.8	16.3	10.5	5.8	3.1	2.7		0.5
In owner-occupied units	100.0	90.9	9.1	8.9	5.3	3.6	1.9	1.7		0.2
In renter-occupied units	100.0	67.1	32.9	31.6	21.2	10.4	5.6	4.8		1.2
1993-94										
Total, 1 year and over	100.0	83.3	16.7	16.3	10.4	5.8	3.2	2.6		0.5
In owner-occupied units	100.0	91.1	8.9	8.7	5.2	3.5	1.9	1.6		0.2
In renter-occupied units	100.0	67.4	32.6	31.5	20.9	10.6	5.8	4.8		1.1
1995-96										
Total, 1 year and over	100.0	83.7	16.3	15.8	10.3	5.6	3.1	2.5		0.5
In owner-occupied units	100.0	91.8	8.2	8.1	5.1	2.9	1.8	1.1		0.2
In renter-occupied units	100.0	66.5	33.5	32.2	21.0	11.2	5.8	5.4		1.3
1996-97										
Total, 1 year and over	100.0	83.5	16.5	16.0	10.5	5.5	3.0	2.4		0.5
In owner-occupied units	100.0	91.6	8.4	8.2	5.2	3.0	1.8	1.2		0.2
In renter-occupied units	100.0	65.9	34.1	32.9	22.1	10.8	5.7	5.1		1.2

Source: U.S. Bureau of the Census, Current Population Survey - March Supplement. See Faber, Carol S. 1998. "Geographical Mobility: March 1996 to March 1997 (Update)." U.S. Bureau of the Census, Current Population Reports, P20-510.

(1) Movers in the Current Population Survey are persons one year old and over who were living in a different place of residence at the time of the survey than they were one year earlier. See Appendix A for a discussion of the differences among data sources in the definition of a recent mover.

Consumer Preferences and Opinions

YEAR AND RESPONSE CATEGORY	TABLE 1.48. OPINIONS ON THE RELATIVE BENEFIT OF OWNING VERSUS RENTING: 1992 TO 1994; 1996 (Percent)		
	All adults	Owners	Renters
1992			
Better off owning	79	86	67
Better off renting	8	3	17
Depends/not sure	13	11	16
1993			
Better off owning	86	90	78
Better off renting	5	3	9
Depends/not sure	9	7	13
1994			
Better off owning	86	87	84
Better off renting	2	1	5
Depends/not sure	12	12	11
1996			
Better off owning	89	94	83
Better off renting	4	1	8
Depends/not sure	7	5	9

Source: Fannie Mae, National Housing Survey.

Data in the table represent responses to the question: "Generally speaking, would you say that people are better off owning a residence or better off renting?" This question was not asked in the 1995 National Housing Survey.

Based on a sample survey of adults in the contiguous United States.

Consumer Preferences and Opinions

HOUSING TYPE AND RATING	TABLE 1.49. PREFERENCES FOR HOUSING TYPE: 1992, 1996, AND 1997 (Percent)								
	1992			1996			1997		
	All adults	Owners	Renters	All adults	Owners	Renters	All adults	Owners	Renters
SINGLE-FAMILY DETACHED HOUSE WITH A YARD ON ALL SIDES									
Ideal	80	82	75	73	74	71	71	74	67
Acceptable with some reservations	12	11	15	19	18	20	20	19	22
Acceptable with major reservations	3	3	3	2	3	2	3	2	3
Not acceptable	4	3	6	5	4	6	5	4	7
Refused/not sure	1	1	1	1	1	1	1	1	1
SINGLE-FAMILY ATTACHED TOWNHOUSE									
Ideal	16	11	26	19	15	26	15	12	21
Acceptable with some reservations	42	40	44	45	44	45	43	43	43
Acceptable with major reservations	13	15	10	8	10	6	11	11	10
Not acceptable	26	31	17	26	29	20	30	33	25
Refused/not sure	3	3	3	2	2	3	1	1	1
LUXURY APARTMENT IN A BUILDING WITH MANY AMENITIES									
Ideal	18	10	31	18	14	26	....	....	....
Acceptable with some reservations	26	24	28	29	29	30	....	....	....
Acceptable with major reservations	15	17	13	12	13	10	....	....	....
Not acceptable	38	46	25	39	42	32	....	....	....
Refused/not sure	3	3	3	2	2	2	....	....	....
TRADITIONAL APARTMENT BUILDING WITH 10 OR MORE UNITS									
Ideal	6	2	13	6	4	10	6	3	11
Acceptable with some reservations	19	12	32	23	17	34	22	15	33
Acceptable with major reservations	22	22	21	17	19	14	15	15	14
Not acceptable	50	61	31	53	59	41	56	66	40
Refused/not sure	3	3	3	1	1	1	1	1	2
TRADITIONAL APARTMENT BUILDING WITH LESS THAN 10 UNITS									
Ideal	8	2	17	9	5	16	6	2	15
Acceptable with some reservations	22	16	31	30	26	38	25	18	37
Acceptable with major reservations	21	21	23	16	17	15	16	18	15
Not acceptable	46	57	27	43	50	30	52	61	33
Refused/not sure	3	4	2	2	2	1	1	1	-
DUPLEX OR 2-FAMILY HOUSE									
Ideal	12	5	25	12	7	20	10	6	18
Acceptable with some reservations	34	31	39	38	37	42	38	33	44
Acceptable with major reservations	20	22	15	14	16	10	14	16	11
Not acceptable	32	39	19	35	39	26	37	44	26
Refused/not sure	2	3	2	1	1	2	1	1	1
APARTMENT IN SOMEONE ELSE'S HOUSE									
Ideal	3	1	8	2	1	5	....	....	....
Acceptable with some reservations	9	7	13	14	12	19	....	....	....
Acceptable with major reservations	16	14	19	14	15	12	....	....	....
Not acceptable	69	75	57	68	71	62	....	....	....
Refused/not sure	3	3	3	2	1	2	....	....	....

Source: Fannie Mae, National Housing Survey.

Respondents were asked to rate each type of housing separately. See Appendix A for wording of the survey question.

Based on a sample survey of adults in the contiguous United States.

- Zero or rounds to zero.

PART 2: HOUSING STOCK, PRODUCTION, AND INVESTMENT

Multifamily Housing Production: 1964 to 1997

Source: Table 2.39.

Total housing starts decreased slightly between 1996 and 1997, but multifamily (i.e., five or more units per structure) housing production increased for the fourth consecutive year (see figure). Since reaching a low of 133,000 starts in 1993, multifamily housing production has increased steadily and reached almost 300,000 units in 1997. During the past 4 years, the multifamily share of total housing starts has also increased substantially, rising from 10 to 20 percent.

Despite this steady improvement, multifamily housing production remains low by historical standards. Multifamily starts in 1997 were well below the annual average of 400,000 starts registered during the past 34 years and paled in comparison to historical peaks. Three times as many multifamily units were started during 1972 and almost twice as many were started in 1985.

The multifamily share of total starts is also low by historical standards. Between 1964 and 1997, the multifamily share averaged 26 percent and peaked at just under 40 percent during the late 1960s and early 1970s.

Evolution of the Housing Stock

TABLE 2.1. ESTIMATES OF THE TOTAL HOUSING INVENTORY BY OCCUPANCY AND TENURE: 1966 TO 1997
(In thousands)

YEAR AND QUARTER	Total housing units	Vacant units											Occupied units		
			Year-round vacant												
								Held off market							
		Total vacant	Total year-round vacant	For rent	For sale only	Rented or sold, awaiting occupancy	Total held off market	For occasional use	URE	For other reasons	Seasonal vacant	Total occupied	Owner-occupied	Renter-occupied
1966	65,212	6,726	4,909	1,778	522	349	2,261	546	434	1,280	1,817	58,486	37,109	21,377
1967	66,014	6,538	4,762	1,566	499	348	2,349	571	460	1,318	1,776	59,476	37,842	21,634
1968	67,171	6,218	4,446	1,392	439	389	2,227	551	438	1,238	1,772	60,952	38,918	22,034
1969	68,479	6,218	4,437	1,296	408	402	2,332	619	454	1,258	1,782	62,261	40,049	22,211
1970	69,778	6,137	4,391	1,299	427	427	2,238	615	429	1,195	1,746	63,640	40,834	22,806
1971	71,320	6,238	4,559	1,353	422	478	2,307	652	416	1,239	1,680	65,081	41,816	23,266
1972	73,313	6,368	4,665	1,421	432	516	2,297	642	419	1,237	1,703	66,945	43,096	23,849
1973	75,407	6,558	4,851	1,521	467	524	2,340	588	433	1,320	1,706	68,849	44,424	24,425
1974	77,462	6,904	5,155	1,661	557	543	2,393	617	452	1,325	1,750	70,558	45,615	24,943
1975	78,821	6,896	5,202	1,647	591	536	2,429	649	470	1,309	1,694	71,925	46,463	25,462
1976	80,189	6,774	5,190	1,546	598	564	2,482	705	467	1,310	1,584	73,415	47,518	25,897
1977	81,645	6,861	5,224	1,472	574	651	2,528	707	438	1,383	1,637	74,784	48,461	26,324
1978	83,496	6,948	5,260	1,433	524	650	2,653	689	467	1,498	1,688	76,548	49,739	26,810
1979	85,061	7,129	5,415	1,431	566	640	2,778	710	541	1,528	1,714	77,932	51,086	26,847
1979 [1]	85,735	7,589	5,893	1,579	607	705	3,003	794	591	1,618	1,696	78,146	50,972	27,174
1980	87,739	8,101	5,996	1,575	734	623	3,064	814	568	1,683	2,106	79,638	52,223	27,415
1981	88,988	7,967	6,034	1,500	746	585	3,203	884	605	1,715	1,934	81,020	53,007	28,013
1981 [2]	90,862	8,070	6,136	1,524	759	595	3,259	909	615	1,735	1,934	82,793	54,084	28,709
1982	91,876	8,145	6,369	1,670	843	554	3,302	959	588	1,754	1,776	83,731	54,237	29,495
1983	93,044	8,479	6,693	1,810	862	633	3,389	926	642	1,821	1,787	84,565	54,671	29,894
1984	95,256	8,910	7,080	1,934	947	664	3,535	992	622	1,921	1,830	86,346	55,671	30,675
1985	97,333	9,446	7,400	2,221	1,006	664	3,510	977	659	1,875	2,046	87,887	56,152	31,736
1986 [3]	99,318	10,173	7,821	2,588	937	683	3,614	991	741	1,883	2,352	89,145	56,844	32,302
1987 [4]	101,811	11,294	8,265	2,752	978	688	3,848	1,066	787	1,996	3,029	90,517	57,915	32,602
1988	103,653	11,633	8,533	2,802	968	678	4,085	1,213	887	1,985	3,100	92,020	58,700	33,320

See notes at end of table.

Evolution of the Housing Stock

TABLE 2.1. ESTIMATES OF THE TOTAL HOUSING INVENTORY BY OCCUPANCY AND TENURE: 1966 TO 1997 - Continued
(In thousands)

YEAR AND QUARTER	Total housing units	Total vacant	Vacant units								Seasonal vacant	Occupied units		
			Year-round vacant									Total occupied	Owner-occupied	Renter-occupied
			Total year-round vacant	For rent	For sale only	Rented or sold, awaiting occupancy	Held off market							
							Total held off market	For occasional use	URE	For other reasons				
1989	104,970	11,481	8,518	2,611	986	661	4,260	1,297	948	2,014	2,963	93,489	59,755	33,734
1989 [5]	105,729	12,240	9,349	2,732	1,082	705	4,830	1,565	1,014	2,251	2,891	93,489	59,755	33,734
1990	106,283	12,059	9,128	2,662	1,064	660	4,742	1,485	1,068	2,189	2,931	94,224	60,248	33,976
1991	107,276	12,023	9,137	2,780	1,070	602	4,686	1,494	1,084	2,107	2,886	95,253	61,010	34,242
1992	108,316	11,926	8,932	2,769	970	628	4,564	1,443	1,011	2,111	2,994	96,391	61,823	34,568
1993	109,716	11,988	8,883	2,791	887	624	4,581	1,510	980	2,091	3,105	97,728	62,998	34,730
1993 [6]	109,611	11,894	8,937	2,809	894	625	4,609	1,508	994	2,108	2,957	97,717	62,533	35,184
1994	110,952	12,257	9,229	2,858	953	772	4,646	1,612	815	2,219	3,028	98,695	63,136	35,558
1995	112,655	12,669	9,570	2,946	1,022	810	4,793	1,667	801	2,325	3,099	99,985	64,739	35,246
1996	114,139	13,155	9,945	3,008	1,082	834	5,022	1,709	852	2,461	3,209	100,984	66,041	34,943
1997	115,621	13,419	10,114	2,978	1,133	867	5,136	1,818	885	2,433	3,305	102,202	67,143	35,059
QUARTERLY DATA														
1995														
First quarter	112,359	12,587	9,401	2,882	1,003	712	4,804	1,643	869	2,292	3,186	99,772	64,050	35,722
Second quarter	112,743	12,811	9,794	2,969	1,046	865	4,914	1,726	837	2,351	3,017	99,932	64,668	35,264
Third quarter	112,530	12,656	9,557	2,966	987	900	4,704	1,630	710	2,364	3,099	99,874	64,885	34,989
Fourth quarter	112,987	12,624	9,529	2,966	1,050	763	4,750	1,671	786	2,293	3,095	100,363	65,355	35,008
1996														
First quarter	113,258	12,786	9,656	3,026	1,066	723	4,841	1,604	853	2,384	3,130	100,472	65,453	35,019
Second quarter	114,207	13,125	9,949	2,975	997	894	5,083	1,678	883	2,522	3,176	101,082	66,147	34,935
Third quarter	114,534	13,414	10,197	3,080	1,119	954	5,044	1,812	796	2,436	3,217	101,120	66,288	34,832
Fourth quarter	114,555	13,291	9,979	2,950	1,146	763	5,120	1,742	877	2,501	3,312	101,264	66,277	34,987
1997														
First quarter	115,064	13,362	10,007	2,886	1,176	807	5,138	1,751	906	2,481	3,355	101,702	66,497	35,205
Second quarter	115,722	13,676	10,356	3,043	1,107	905	5,301	1,920	960	2,421	3,320	102,046	67,094	34,952
Third quarter	115,804	13,371	10,031	3,018	1,062	941	4,992	1,795	880	2,317	3,358	102,433	67,556	34,877
Fourth quarter	115,892	13,268	10,078	2,966	1,187	813	5,112	1,805	793	2,514	3,190	102,624	67,424	35,200

Source: U.S. Bureau of the Census, Current Population Survey/Housing Vacancy Survey.

URE = Temporarily occupied by persons with usual residence elsewhere. See Appendix A for additional explanation.

(1) Revised data reflecting a supplemental sample and refined estimation procedures.
(2) Revised data reflecting revisions in processing procedures.
(3) Beginning in 1986 vacant seasonal mobile homes were included in the count of vacant seasonal units.
(4) Seasonal vacant housing units were underestimated prior to 1987. Estimates of seasonal vacants for 1987 have been adjusted to reflect this.
(5) Revised data reflecting new edit procedures, which allocated cases that would have been classified as "not reported" under previous procedures. Also revised to include year-round vacant mobile homes in the estimate of year-round vacant housing units.
(6) Revised using weights based on the 1990 Census.

Evolution of the Housing Stock

TABLE 2.2. ESTIMATES OF THE TOTAL HOUSING INVENTORY FOR REGIONS BY OCCUPANCY AND TENURE: 1988 TO 1997
(In thousands)

		Northeast												
		Vacant units										Occupied units		
			Year-round vacant											
						Rented or sold, awaiting occupancy	Held off market							
YEAR AND QUARTER	Total housing units	Total vacant	Total year-round vacant	For rent	For sale only		Total held off market	For occasional use	URE	For other reasons	Seasonal vacant	Total occupied	Owner-occupied	Renter-occupied
1988	21,690	2,440	1,436	376	192	144	724	176	180	368	1,004	19,250	11,797	7,453
1989	21,782	2,365	1,445	367	185	124	770	176	172	422	920	19,417	12,044	7,373
1989 [1]	21,783	2,366	1,477	370	189	127	791	184	174	433	889	19,417	12,044	7,373
1990	21,706	2,378	1,466	475	195	105	690	158	166	366	912	19,328	12,094	7,234
1991	21,903	2,406	1,532	546	180	101	704	178	167	359	874	19,498	12,157	7,341
1992	21,997	2,418	1,557	549	163	111	734	182	178	374	861	19,579	12,245	7,334
1993	22,242	2,479	1,594	571	166	105	751	226	161	364	885	19,764	12,328	7,436
1993 [2]	22,108	2,461	1,593	572	165	105	751	226	161	364	868	19,647	12,137	7,510
1994	22,300	2,567	1,712	590	182	142	797	264	133	400	855	19,734	12,127	7,606
1995	22,392	2,629	1,823	586	187	141	909	289	161	459	806	19,763	12,252	7,511
1996	22,541	2,705	1,849	601	201	139	908	282	164	462	856	19,836	12,339	7,497
1997	22,564	2,696	1,822	543	207	149	923	274	201	448	874	19,868	12,398	7,470
QUARTERLY DATA														
1995														
First quarter	22,552	2,761	1,867	599	195	153	920	322	144	454	894	19,791	12,258	7,533
Second quarter	22,378	2,690	1,856	603	184	134	935	289	180	466	834	19,688	12,269	7,419
Third quarter	22,219	2,519	1,762	573	182	147	860	266	153	441	757	19,700	12,247	7,453
Fourth quarter	22,416	2,546	1,807	568	185	131	921	278	167	476	739	19,871	12,234	7,637
1996														
First quarter	22,567	2,632	1,830	574	210	135	911	297	167	447	802	19,935	12,244	7,691
Second quarter	22,437	2,682	1,788	621	172	121	874	259	161	454	894	19,755	12,300	7,455
Third quarter	22,548	2,746	1,883	630	197	150	906	284	150	472	863	19,802	12,436	7,366
Fourth quarter	22,619	2,765	1,898	580	224	151	943	288	179	476	867	19,854	12,377	7,477
1997														
First quarter	22,643	2,740	1,871	504	231	134	1,002	296	194	512	869	19,903	12,266	7,637
Second quarter	22,486	2,664	1,776	537	199	139	901	283	205	413	888	19,822	12,360	7,462
Third quarter	22,583	2,721	1,822	575	192	160	895	261	196	438	899	19,862	12,508	7,354
Fourth quarter	22,540	2,657	1,817	556	205	161	895	255	211	429	840	19,883	12,457	7,426

See notes at end of table.

Evolution of the Housing Stock

TABLE 2.2. ESTIMATES OF THE TOTAL HOUSING INVENTORY FOR REGIONS BY OCCUPANCY AND TENURE: 1988 TO 1997 - Continued
(In thousands)

Midwest

YEAR AND QUARTER	Total housing units	Total vacant	Total year-round vacant	For rent	For sale only	Rented or sold, awaiting occupancy	Total held off market	For occasional use	URE	For other reasons	Seasonal vacant	Total occupied	Owner-occupied	Renter-occupied
1988	24,798	2,280	1,710	548	187	144	831	137	221	474	570	22,518	15,194	7,324
1989	25,226	2,405	1,724	528	202	151	843	140	238	465	681	22,821	15,452	7,369
1989 [1]	25,326	2,505	1,844	547	223	159	914	157	248	510	661	22,821	15,452	7,369
1990	25,407	2,449	1,780	516	203	164	897	147	238	512	669	22,958	15,501	7,456
1991	25,749	2,449	1,796	558	202	148	887	150	239	498	653	23,300	15,658	7,642
1992	25,850	2,414	1,730	558	188	150	834	129	225	480	684	23,435	15,748	7,688
1993	26,034	2,417	1,695	551	173	157	814	136	203	475	722	23,616	15,919	7,697
1993 [2]	25,739	2,335	1,686	546	173	155	812	132	201	479	649	23,403	15,697	7,706
1994	26,106	2,497	1,810	568	176	194	873	159	188	526	687	23,609	15,978	7,630
1995	26,224	2,531	1,871	575	218	196	882	176	164	542	660	23,693	16,387	7,306
1996	26,479	2,664	1,992	609	227	200	956	173	213	570	672	23,815	16,807	7,008
1997	26,709	2,626	1,928	623	213	206	886	190	182	514	698	24,083	16,979	7,104
QUARTERLY DATA														
1995														
First quarter	26,322	2,549	1,882	555	231	172	924	195	184	545	667	23,773	16,151	7,622
Second quarter	26,275	2,573	1,921	579	211	212	919	196	170	553	652	23,702	16,246	7,456
Third quarter	26,105	2,542	1,874	571	206	241	856	158	140	558	668	23,563	16,512	7,051
Fourth quarter	26,196	2,465	1,811	594	224	161	832	156	163	514	654	23,732	16,637	7,094
1996														
First quarter	26,499	2,693	1,998	649	248	167	934	180	196	558	695	23,806	16,754	7,052
Second quarter	26,544	2,621	1,958	556	188	232	982	175	220	587	663	23,923	16,860	7,063
Third quarter	26,371	2,649	2,012	603	239	230	940	172	220	548	637	23,722	16,764	6,958
Fourth quarter	26,497	2,690	1,995	626	233	168	968	165	216	587	695	23,807	16,849	6,958
1997														
First quarter	26,737	2,736	2,038	668	233	208	929	208	191	530	698	24,001	16,944	7,057
Second quarter	26,894	2,743	2,010	650	188	214	958	214	202	542	733	24,151	16,989	7,162
Third quarter	26,681	2,591	1,871	612	202	230	827	164	173	490	720	24,090	17,026	7,064
Fourth quarter	26,540	2,437	1,797	564	230	174	829	175	160	494	640	24,088	16,955	7,133

See notes at end of table.

Evolution of the Housing Stock

TABLE 2.2. ESTIMATES OF THE TOTAL HOUSING INVENTORY FOR REGIONS BY OCCUPANCY AND TENURE: 1988 TO 1997 - Continued
(In thousands)

YEAR AND QUARTER	Total housing units	Total vacant	Total year-round vacant	For rent	For sale only	Rented or sold, awaiting occu-pancy	Total held off market	For occa-sional use	URE	For other reasons	Sea-sonal vacant	Total occu-pied	Owner-occu-pied	Renter-occu-pied
							South						
				Vacant units								Occupied units	
					Year-round vacant			Held off market						
1988	36,269	4,719	3,660	1,228	414	230	1,788	611	332	845	1,059	31,549	20,766	10,784
1989	36,853	4,590	3,665	1,118	443	222	1,882	655	367	861	925	32,263	21,276	10,988
1989 [1]	37,363	5,100	4,185	1,196	490	244	2,255	842	407	1,006	915	32,263	21,276	10,988
1990	37,611	5,032	4,119	1,089	464	240	2,327	812	490	1,026	913	32,578	21,418	11,160
1991	37,770	4,979	4,030	1,101	490	195	2,245	776	487	982	949	32,791	21,665	11,126
1992	38,061	4,831	3,807	1,026	389	220	2,171	758	438	975	1,024	33,231	21,880	11,351
1993	38,700	4,860	3,802	1,008	371	222	2,202	780	458	964	1,058	33,840	22,368	11,472
1993 [2]	38,930	4,861	3,841	1,020	378	223	2,221	776	473	971	1,020	34,069	22,367	11,702
1994	39,423	4,895	3,817	1,045	395	275	2,103	810	321	972	1,078	34,529	22,650	11,879
1995	40,254	5,031	3,879	1,076	399	306	2,098	808	313	977	1,152	35,223	23,487	11,736
1996	40,976	5,227	4,079	1,108	435	336	2,200	832	302	1,066	1,148	35,749	24,119	11,630
1997	41,787	5,469	4,376	1,183	477	344	2,372	940	331	1,101	1,093	36,318	24,686	11,632
QUARTERLY DATA														
1995														
First quarter	39,932	4,919	3,781	1,082	372	251	2,076	747	366	963	1,138	35,013	23,149	11,864
Second quarter	40,353	5,099	4,005	1,066	421	327	2,191	858	333	1,000	1,094	35,254	23,428	11,826
Third quarter	40,402	5,061	3,859	1,069	389	327	2,074	810	268	996	1,202	35,341	23,552	11,789
Fourth quarter	40,331	5,045	3,873	1,087	413	321	2,052	817	286	948	1,172	35,286	23,819	11,467
1996														
First quarter	40,379	4,915	3,814	1,079	385	289	2,061	734	320	1,007	1,101	35,464	23,937	11,527
Second quarter	41,158	5,362	4,242	1,120	461	378	2,283	815	331	1,137	1,120	35,796	24,067	11,729
Third quarter	41,196	5,349	4,166	1,132	449	381	2,204	880	268	1,056	1,183	35,847	24,202	11,645
Fourth quarter	41,174	5,281	4,094	1,100	446	294	2,254	899	289	1,066	1,187	35,893	24,272	11,621
1997														
First quarter	41,343	5,345	4,202	1,115	470	338	2,279	857	347	1,075	1,143	35,998	24,422	11,576
Second quarter	41,614	5,503	4,449	1,207	467	353	2,422	970	346	1,106	1,054	36,111	24,585	11,526
Third quarter	41,867	5,422	4,335	1,180	443	378	2,334	965	345	1,024	1,087	36,445	24,844	11,601
Fourth quarter	42,325	5,607	4,520	1,229	528	310	2,453	969	285	1,199	1,087	36,718	24,894	11,824

See notes at end of table.

Evolution of the Housing Stock

TABLE 2.2. ESTIMATES OF THE TOTAL HOUSING INVENTORY FOR REGIONS BY OCCUPANCY AND TENURE: 1988 TO 1997 - Continued
(In thousands)

West

YEAR AND QUARTER	Total housing units	Total vacant	Total year-round vacant	For rent	For sale only	Rented or sold, awaiting occupancy	Total held off market	For occasional use	URE	For other reasons	Seasonal vacant	Total occupied	Owner-occupied	Renter-occupied
1988	20,896	2,194	1,727	650	176	161	741	289	155	298	467	18,702	10,943	7,759
1989	21,110	2,122	1,684	598	157	165	764	326	171	267	438	18,988	10,983	8,005
1989 [1]	21,258	2,270	1,844	619	180	175	870	382	185	303	426	18,988	10,983	8,005
1990	21,560	2,199	1,763	582	202	152	827	368	174	285	436	19,360	11,235	8,125
1991	21,853	2,190	1,780	575	198	157	850	390	191	268	410	19,664	11,530	8,134
1992	22,409	2,263	1,838	636	230	148	824	374	169	281	425	20,146	11,950	8,196
1993	22,739	2,231	1,792	661	176	141	814	368	158	288	439	20,508	12,384	8,125
1993 [2]	22,834	2,236	1,817	670	178	142	826	373	160	293	419	20,598	12,333	8,266
1994	23,120	2,299	1,890	655	200	161	874	380	174	320	409	20,821	12,376	8,444
1995	23,785	2,478	1,997	709	218	167	903	395	162	346	481	21,307	12,614	8,693
1996	24,141	2,557	2,025	690	219	159	957	422	173	362	532	21,584	12,776	8,808
1997	24,560	2,627	1,986	629	236	167	954	413	170	370	641	21,933	13,080	8,853
QUARTERLY DATA														
1995														
First quarter	23,552	2,358	1,871	646	205	136	884	380	175	329	487	21,194	12,491	8,703
Second quarter	23,738	2,450	2,012	720	230	192	870	383	155	332	438	21,288	12,725	8,563
Third quarter	23,803	2,532	2,061	753	210	186	912	396	148	368	471	21,271	12,575	8,696
Fourth quarter	24,044	2,569	2,040	753	228	150	945	420	169	355	529	21,475	12,664	8,810
1996														
First quarter	23,815	2,548	2,016	725	223	131	937	394	171	372	532	21,267	12,518	8,749
Second quarter	24,065	2,456	1,958	678	176	161	943	428	171	344	498	21,609	12,920	8,689
Third quarter	24,417	2,668	2,133	714	234	192	993	476	157	360	535	21,749	12,886	8,863
Fourth quarter	24,263	2,552	1,989	644	243	149	953	388	193	372	563	21,711	12,780	8,931
1997														
First quarter	24,339	2,540	1,895	599	242	127	927	389	174	364	645	21,799	12,865	8,934
Second quarter	24,729	2,767	2,122	649	253	200	1,020	453	207	360	645	21,962	13,161	8,801
Third quarter	24,668	2,633	1,982	650	225	172	935	405	165	365	651	22,035	13,177	8,858
Fourth quarter	24,505	2,569	1,946	618	225	168	935	405	138	392	623	21,936	13,118	8,858

Source: U.S. Bureau of the Census, Current Population Survey/Housing Vacancy Survey.

URE = Temporarily occupied by persons with usual residence elsewhere. See Appendix A for additional explanation.

(1) Revised data reflecting new edit procedures, which allocated cases that would have been classified as "not reported" under previous procedures. Also revised to include year-round vacant mobile homes in the estimate of year-round vacant housing units.
(2) Revised using weights based on the 1990 Census.

Evolution of the Housing Stock

TABLE 2.3. CENSUS COUNTS AND INTERCENSAL AND POSTCENSAL ESTIMATES OF TOTAL HOUSING UNITS FOR THE NATION, REGIONS, AND STATES: 1980 TO 1996

(In thousands)

AREA	April 1, 1980 (Census)	July 1, 1981	July 1, 1982	July 1, 1983	July 1, 1984	July 1, 1985	July 1, 1986	July 1, 1987	July 1, 1988	July 1, 1989	April 1, 1990 (Census)	July 1, 1991	July 1, 1992	July 1, 1993	July 1, 1994	July 1, 1995	July 1, 1996
United States	88,410	89,979	90,961	91,952	93,478	95,126	96,792	98,468	99,951	101,320	102,264	103,671	104,587	105,632	106,920	108,372	109,800
Northeast	19,087	19,219	19,300	19,383	19,505	19,676	19,900	20,163	20,429	20,665	20,811	20,977	21,071	21,171	21,284	21,427	21,530
Midwest	22,822	23,030	23,118	23,193	23,329	23,490	23,673	23,903	24,130	24,343	24,493	24,749	24,941	25,171	25,436	25,727	26,014
South	29,417	30,173	30,717	31,319	32,230	33,111	33,907	34,605	35,184	35,708	36,065	36,630	37,020	37,479	38,078	38,738	39,416
West	17,083	17,556	17,826	18,057	18,414	18,850	19,313	19,797	20,208	20,604	20,895	21,315	21,555	21,810	22,122	22,479	22,840
Alabama	1,467	1,491	1,504	1,517	1,540	1,564	1,589	1,615	1,637	1,657	1,670	1,690	1,705	1,726	1,753	1,782	1,814
Alaska	163	169	176	187	200	211	218	223	227	230	233	233	234	235	237	240	242
Arizona	1,110	1,171	1,211	1,253	1,318	1,399	1,478	1,547	1,598	1,637	1,659	1,687	1,709	1,737	1,778	1,832	1,890
Arkansas	899	909	916	924	938	953	966	978	987	995	1,001	1,009	1,018	1,028	1,043	1,060	1,077
California	9,279	9,478	9,582	9,661	9,804	10,003	10,246	10,531	10,777	11,013	11,183	11,403	11,501	11,588	11,667	11,746	11,827
Colorado	1,194	1,237	1,266	1,295	1,340	1,383	1,415	1,442	1,460	1,471	1,477	1,490	1,501	1,522	1,555	1,597	1,640
Connecticut	1,159	1,172	1,181	1,190	1,203	1,218	1,239	1,264	1,290	1,310	1,321	1,331	1,336	1,343	1,349	1,359	1,365
Delaware	239	242	245	248	253	258	264	270	278	285	290	296	300	304	309	314	318
District of Columbia	277	279	280	279	279	278	278	278	279	279	278	277	275	273	272	270	268
Florida	4,379	4,601	4,750	4,861	5,047	5,254	5,458	5,648	5,822	5,984	6,100	6,262	6,353	6,424	6,538	6,657	6,771
Georgia	2,028	2,075	2,109	2,152	2,224	2,303	2,383	2,465	2,534	2,599	2,638	2,700	2,743	2,794	2,862	2,940	3,021
Hawaii	334	345	351	356	359	363	368	373	378	384	390	400	407	413	419	426	433
Idaho	375	384	388	391	395	400	403	406	409	411	413	421	427	438	452	467	481
Illinois	4,320	4,338	4,338	4,341	4,354	4,367	4,388	4,421	4,455	4,487	4,506	4,545	4,570	4,603	4,641	4,683	4,724
Indiana	2,092	2,112	2,120	2,126	2,136	2,149	2,166	2,189	2,211	2,231	2,246	2,279	2,308	2,333	2,367	2,404	2,444
Iowa	1,131	1,138	1,139	1,139	1,141	1,142	1,142	1,141	1,141	1,142	1,144	1,151	1,157	1,166	1,175	1,187	1,197
Kansas	955	967	974	981	993	1,006	1,017	1,026	1,034	1,041	1,044	1,054	1,062	1,071	1,083	1,096	1,109
Kentucky	1,369	1,384	1,393	1,402	1,416	1,432	1,449	1,464	1,479	1,495	1,507	1,526	1,541	1,562	1,586	1,612	1,638
Louisiana	1,548	1,580	1,606	1,631	1,667	1,696	1,713	1,719	1,719	1,718	1,716	1,719	1,724	1,733	1,747	1,763	1,780
Maine	501	508	512	517	523	531	541	553	566	579	587	597	603	610	616	624	630
Maryland	1,571	1,596	1,612	1,631	1,668	1,705	1,745	1,785	1,825	1,863	1,892	1,928	1,949	1,977	2,004	2,027	2,049
Massachusetts	2,208	2,229	2,243	2,258	2,277	2,303	2,338	2,380	2,421	2,454	2,473	2,489	2,497	2,507	2,519	2,535	2,547
Michigan	3,590	3,621	3,631	3,636	3,649	3,669	3,700	3,739	3,779	3,818	3,848	3,890	3,917	3,948	3,984	4,025	4,067
Minnesota	1,613	1,640	1,656	1,673	1,696	1,720	1,746	1,775	1,806	1,831	1,848	1,873	1,890	1,912	1,936	1,959	1,981
Mississippi	912	924	931	939	952	967	979	989	997	1,005	1,010	1,019	1,026	1,036	1,049	1,066	1,083
Missouri	1,989	2,007	2,016	2,028	2,047	2,073	2,101	2,133	2,162	2,186	2,199	2,225	2,246	2,273	2,303	2,339	2,374
Montana	328	334	338	341	346	351	354	357	358	360	361	362	363	365	369	373	377
Nebraska	625	632	635	637	640	644	647	651	654	658	661	667	673	678	685	692	699
Nevada	340	360	373	383	399	415	430	447	465	495	519	554	576	595	621	654	691
New Hampshire	386	395	401	407	415	426	443	463	481	496	504	511	514	518	522	527	531

See notes at end of table.

Evolution of the Housing Stock

TABLE 2.3. CENSUS COUNTS AND INTERCENSAL AND POSTCENSAL ESTIMATES OF TOTAL HOUSING UNITS FOR THE NATION, REGIONS, AND STATES: 1980 TO 1996 - Continued

(In thousands)

AREA	April 1, 1980 (Census)	July 1, 1981	July 1, 1982	July 1, 1983	July 1, 1984	July 1, 1985	July 1, 1986	July 1, 1987	July 1, 1988	July 1, 1989	April 1, 1990 (Census)	July 1, 1991	July 1, 1992	July 1, 1993	July 1, 1994	July 1, 1995	July 1, 1996
New Jersey	2,772	2,796	2,809	2,822	2,845	2,879	2,923	2,972	3,017	3,054	3,075	3,101	3,113	3,126	3,144	3,170	3,186
New Mexico	508	523	534	545	559	578	593	607	619	627	632	640	647	656	671	691	711
New York	6,868	6,881	6,891	6,904	6,925	6,959	7,011	7,070	7,132	7,189	7,227	7,271	7,294	7,316	7,338	7,367	7,392
North Carolina	2,274	2,318	2,353	2,389	2,450	2,522	2,601	2,671	2,731	2,782	2,818	2,876	2,919	2,975	3,043	3,120	3,197
North Dakota	259	263	265	267	271	273	274	275	275	276	276	278	279	282	284	288	291
Ohio	4,108	4,145	4,160	4,168	4,187	4,209	4,235	4,271	4,309	4,346	4,372	4,410	4,438	4,473	4,511	4,553	4,594
Oklahoma	1,237	1,263	1,285	1,319	1,361	1,386	1,396	1,402	1,405	1,406	1,406	1,410	1,414	1,421	1,430	1,441	1,453
Oregon	1,083	1,111	1,123	1,129	1,135	1,141	1,149	1,157	1,167	1,179	1,194	1,223	1,242	1,260	1,285	1,313	1,343
Pennsylvania	4,597	4,633	4,652	4,669	4,694	4,726	4,763	4,807	4,856	4,905	4,938	4,985	5,016	5,051	5,089	5,133	5,163
Rhode Island	373	377	379	381	384	388	392	399	405	411	415	418	420	422	423	426	427
South Carolina	1,153	1,180	1,199	1,218	1,251	1,292	1,329	1,359	1,384	1,408	1,424	1,455	1,477	1,503	1,533	1,567	1,604
South Dakota	277	281	282	282	284	287	289	290	291	292	292	296	298	302	306	312	316
Tennessee	1,747	1,772	1,784	1,799	1,826	1,864	1,904	1,942	1,975	2,006	2,026	2,058	2,084	2,115	2,152	2,194	2,240
Texas	5,548	5,742	5,906	6,134	6,431	6,653	6,808	6,906	6,954	6,986	7,009	7,074	7,128	7,206	7,306	7,424	7,556
Utah	490	506	515	523	535	553	569	582	590	595	598	606	615	628	648	670	692
Vermont	223	228	232	236	240	245	250	255	261	267	271	275	278	281	283	287	289
Virginia	2,021	2,063	2,088	2,113	2,160	2,215	2,273	2,339	2,399	2,459	2,496	2,551	2,582	2,620	2,666	2,711	2,752
Washington	1,689	1,743	1,771	1,791	1,818	1,849	1,884	1,919	1,956	1,998	2,032	2,093	2,129	2,168	2,215	2,263	2,304
West Virginia	748	754	758	761	765	768	771	774	777	780	781	781	781	783	786	790	793
Wisconsin	1,864	1,888	1,903	1,915	1,932	1,950	1,969	1,990	2,013	2,036	2,056	2,083	2,103	2,130	2,160	2,190	2,218
Wyoming	188	195	199	202	204	205	206	205	205	204	203	203	203	204	205	207	209

Source: U.S. Bureau of the Census, State Housing Unit and Household Estimates. Data for 1980 and 1990 are from the decennial census.

Components may not add to totals due to rounding.

Evolution of the Housing Stock

TABLE 2.4. UNITS IN STRUCTURE BY STATE: 1940 TO 1990

AREA	1940						
	All housing units	1 unit, detached	1 unit, attached	2-4 units	5 or more units	1-4 units, with business	Other [1]
United States	37,325,470	23,730,637	2,835,176	5,723,658	3,928,298	940,726	166,975
Alabama	708,043	567,373	70,169	53,360	10,951	4,477	1,713
Alaska	....	....	....	....	....	....	....
Arizona	147,079	116,624	9,211	8,229	5,023	2,661	5,331
Arkansas	520,613	450,427	27,120	28,208	6,866	5,304	2,688
California	2,340,373	1,581,673	134,363	240,925	316,157	41,005	26,250
Colorado	354,660	261,068	19,342	31,919	32,234	7,190	2,907
Connecticut	488,543	213,259	30,337	168,257	59,278	15,689	1,723
Delaware	75,567	40,826	19,571	8,601	3,238	2,920	411
District of Columbia	185,128	29,354	54,144	36,487	59,079	5,613	451
Florida	590,451	436,850	27,956	64,822	44,744	10,219	5,860
Georgia	796,715	607,763	73,449	84,023	23,337	6,348	1,795
Hawaii	....	....	....	....	....	....	....
Idaho	152,835	128,459	4,669	9,163	5,283	2,753	2,508
Illinois	2,280,826	1,146,712	69,514	536,736	437,641	82,691	7,532
Indiana	1,005,952	775,217	61,157	103,319	40,235	22,105	3,919
Iowa	726,654	596,927	23,505	63,366	24,507	15,069	3,280
Kansas	545,721	463,587	17,559	38,505	14,474	9,285	2,311
Kentucky	729,206	581,818	37,991	74,522	19,049	14,248	1,578
Louisiana	619,233	444,613	90,183	48,749	22,831	10,678	2,179
Maine	260,659	172,759	22,135	45,317	12,709	6,851	888
Maryland	500,156	240,964	128,738	89,394	21,888	18,095	1,077
Massachusetts	1,221,252	480,115	79,135	479,261	153,061	27,368	2,312
Michigan	1,519,378	1,041,577	47,638	277,802	110,377	34,940	7,044
Minnesota	773,042	552,645	20,613	116,826	60,940	19,083	2,935
Mississippi	557,246	475,048	37,793	35,028	3,841	4,041	1,495
Missouri	1,140,493	764,095	40,492	197,202	107,784	27,136	3,784
Montana	177,443	141,102	5,753	12,238	12,389	3,816	2,145
Nebraska	387,368	323,211	9,127	26,409	19,571	6,961	2,089
Nevada	36,770	29,658	1,962	1,696	1,636	907	911
New Hampshire	158,044	95,018	15,559	32,070	11,157	3,815	425
New Jersey	1,223,887	563,364	124,517	299,170	175,989	57,142	3,705
New Mexico	145,642	115,417	13,845	8,341	3,689	2,813	1,537
New York	4,032,460	1,307,414	192,159	889,721	1,483,526	152,656	6,984
North Carolina	820,888	692,568	45,045	63,979	10,998	6,197	2,101
North Dakota	162,881	135,292	4,311	12,361	5,832	4,333	752
Ohio	1,977,693	1,322,796	116,436	339,127	137,942	54,062	7,330
Oklahoma	647,485	534,552	37,856	39,827	21,736	9,975	3,539
Oregon	369,811	297,977	7,853	18,718	34,581	6,776	3,906
Pennsylvania	2,618,056	1,195,299	767,317	393,769	133,230	120,167	8,274
Rhode Island	203,469	77,797	10,683	91,327	17,102	6,016	544
South Carolina	458,899	369,623	30,459	45,941	8,151	3,793	932
South Dakota	179,744	153,149	4,254	11,596	5,132	4,322	1,291
Tennessee	742,030	586,975	50,842	68,405	25,859	7,927	2,022
Texas	1,804,884	1,437,513	122,636	150,629	58,182	22,643	13,281
Utah	147,291	108,450	9,206	14,468	12,265	1,937	965
Vermont	106,362	70,434	10,382	18,827	3,586	2,873	260
Virginia	659,787	503,586	40,541	82,478	20,735	10,959	1,488
Washington	590,439	464,031	9,439	29,900	72,466	9,970	4,633
West Virginia	459,725	367,313	28,457	40,901	11,482	9,985	1,587
Wisconsin	897,719	607,929	26,825	184,988	42,091	33,057	2,829
Wyoming	76,868	60,416	2,928	6,751	3,444	1,855	1,474

See notes at end of table.

Evolution of the Housing Stock

TABLE 2.4. UNITS IN STRUCTURE BY STATE: 1940 TO 1990 - Continued

AREA	1950					
	All housing units	1 unit, detached	1 unit, attached	2-4 units	5 or more units	Mobile home [2]
United States	45,983,398	29,115,698	2,798,632	8,676,183	5,077,667	315,218
Alabama	843,857	667,469	40,974	106,593	26,717	2,104
Alaska	....	....	....	....	....	....
Arizona	240,750	182,422	15,179	23,181	11,794	8,174
Arkansas	575,163	495,500	15,504	49,538	12,447	2,174
California	3,590,660	2,404,877	194,736	484,200	448,335	58,512
Colorado	436,226	308,154	19,861	57,729	45,200	5,282
Connecticut	611,162	286,644	19,734	221,285	81,800	1,699
Delaware	97,013	51,671	26,627	13,410	4,768	537
District of Columbia	229,738	30,139	65,227	51,730	82,513	129
Florida	952,131	677,693	38,579	133,329	82,938	19,592
Georgia	966,672	724,747	40,263	152,028	46,489	3,145
Hawaii	....	....	....	....	....	....
Idaho	188,328	153,481	4,292	18,195	9,290	3,070
Illinois	2,671,647	1,377,396	54,117	700,958	523,183	15,993
Indiana	1,232,314	921,991	55,807	185,116	56,502	12,898
Iowa	811,912	645,259	17,612	106,644	35,147	7,250
Kansas	625,148	495,086	17,201	81,968	25,541	5,352
Kentucky	820,141	642,141	22,857	121,689	30,333	3,121
Louisiana	777,672	565,944	62,507	110,882	35,794	2,545
Maine	311,441	210,651	12,371	66,751	20,842	826
Maryland	689,116	315,202	165,950	148,592	56,799	2,573
Massachusetts	1,400,185	565,447	49,287	585,877	197,182	2,392
Michigan	1,971,842	1,401,718	48,860	372,733	132,620	15,911
Minnesota	918,434	664,879	16,898	160,173	71,186	5,298
Mississippi	609,329	517,211	17,480	62,588	10,129	1,921
Missouri	1,268,354	854,907	38,406	249,102	120,495	5,444
Montana	194,256	149,268	5,887	22,498	14,358	2,245
Nebraska	417,245	331,621	10,524	47,958	23,789	3,353
Nevada	56,515	41,142	4,142	6,516	2,992	1,723
New Hampshire	190,563	117,068	7,375	49,310	16,498	312
New Jersey	1,501,473	697,941	130,127	448,662	221,557	3,186
New Mexico	199,706	151,892	16,094	19,199	8,223	4,298
New York	4,633,806	1,508,584	244,781	1,191,087	1,681,413	7,941
North Carolina	1,058,367	876,694	31,250	119,826	26,141	4,456
North Dakota	175,769	142,632	2,932	20,605	7,027	2,573
Ohio	2,402,565	1,571,798	107,018	510,439	193,038	20,272
Oklahoma	715,691	594,511	19,595	68,986	28,850	3,749
Oregon	524,003	410,398	15,122	43,080	47,589	7,814
Pennsylvania	3,036,494	1,359,364	853,932	617,136	197,545	8,517
Rhode Island	244,147	97,892	7,270	113,711	24,801	473
South Carolina	557,672	456,018	16,267	70,314	13,378	1,695
South Dakota	194,573	157,286	5,030	21,378	7,119	3,760
Tennessee	921,837	720,018	33,791	124,483	39,312	4,233
Texas	2,393,828	1,883,065	92,639	292,591	103,042	22,491
Utah	200,554	140,667	9,523	31,769	17,183	1,412
Vermont	121,911	80,174	4,250	31,002	6,104	381
Virginia	901,483	639,895	51,582	136,798	68,700	4,508
Washington	809,701	620,806	24,156	70,045	87,305	7,389
West Virginia	544,075	430,215	22,518	71,859	17,683	1,800
Wisconsin	1,055,843	711,526	19,454	267,663	49,446	7,754
Wyoming	92,086	64,594	3,044	14,977	6,530	2,941

See notes at end of table.

Evolution of the Housing Stock

AREA	TABLE 2.4. UNITS IN STRUCTURE BY STATE: 1940 TO 1990 - Continued					
	1960					
	All housing units	1 unit, detached	1 unit, attached	2-4 units	5 or more units	Mobile home [2]
United States	58,314,784	40,103,346	3,655,210	7,551,865	6,237,798	766,565
Alabama	967,498	800,237	53,571	74,773	28,985	9,932
Alaska	67,157	39,466	4,791	5,557	14,304	3,039
Arizona	415,760	320,786	27,036	26,860	17,835	23,243
Arkansas	586,516	514,973	23,641	30,286	12,736	4,880
California	5,464,886	3,769,340	312,103	544,220	737,622	101,601
Colorado	594,408	434,660	32,164	52,494	62,111	12,979
Connecticut	818,428	481,234	30,873	206,910	92,955	6,456
Delaware	143,699	91,612	29,736	11,472	7,310	3,569
District of Columbia	262,639	34,730	70,572	43,527	113,733	77
Florida	1,776,945	1,310,549	85,827	159,326	156,156	65,087
Georgia	1,169,871	915,194	64,009	120,147	57,832	12,689
Hawaii	165,390	108,966	13,808	20,885	21,706	25
Idaho	223,533	184,571	8,455	12,814	10,930	6,763
Illinois	3,274,982	1,926,948	102,457	645,783	567,324	32,470
Indiana	1,503,031	1,208,199	71,289	130,858	64,691	27,994
Iowa	905,271	764,525	23,071	67,701	38,239	11,735
Kansas	740,244	621,574	25,569	57,312	24,006	11,783
Kentucky	925,383	765,083	36,846	78,359	35,019	10,076
Louisiana	978,361	740,691	69,779	113,788	44,658	9,445
Maine	364,603	257,422	12,946	63,363	24,692	6,180
Maryland	934,251	509,406	232,912	103,968	78,444	9,521
Massachusetts	1,690,860	844,042	66,467	554,896	218,689	6,766
Michigan	2,548,373	1,985,855	88,819	288,005	156,294	29,400
Minnesota	1,116,775	864,594	24,317	130,688	86,474	10,702
Mississippi	628,945	545,752	23,284	43,263	10,319	6,327
Missouri	1,491,273	1,096,927	50,622	202,313	124,798	16,613
Montana	233,285	176,453	9,761	22,589	17,405	7,077
Nebraska	472,915	381,677	14,353	39,971	29,799	7,115
Nevada	101,546	65,603	7,507	10,905	9,505	8,026
New Hampshire	224,420	151,683	9,137	45,392	15,312	2,896
New Jersey	1,998,456	1,126,037	146,971	442,517	273,775	9,156
New Mexico	281,892	221,524	21,068	17,993	8,370	12,937
New York	5,693,681	2,216,218	227,780	1,230,438	1,987,939	31,306
North Carolina	1,322,839	1,147,871	50,883	71,453	33,499	19,133
North Dakota	194,597	155,229	4,949	19,576	9,826	5,017
Ohio	3,040,952	2,207,225	155,247	429,039	206,549	42,892
Oklahoma	815,609	705,912	29,611	39,971	32,029	8,086
Oregon	622,726	503,664	21,190	32,785	50,997	14,090
Pennsylvania	3,581,046	1,983,406	931,404	425,833	208,969	31,434
Rhode Island	286,712	143,636	7,381	107,743	26,439	1,513
South Carolina	678,355	583,185	25,376	42,594	16,128	11,072
South Dakota	216,449	178,230	6,176	16,385	8,729	6,929
Tennessee	1,084,322	903,099	53,847	75,241	42,343	9,792
Texas	3,152,953	2,623,673	147,386	208,864	136,152	36,878
Utah	262,582	199,301	10,570	27,435	20,418	4,858
Vermont	136,307	96,742	5,542	24,814	6,874	2,335
Virginia	1,168,641	897,329	76,043	88,125	89,887	17,257
Washington	1,009,484	787,921	35,986	60,018	110,619	14,940
West Virginia	574,354	490,159	27,421	35,641	15,888	5,245
Wisconsin	1,288,499	937,237	39,938	234,216	66,044	11,064
Wyoming	113,080	82,996	4,719	12,759	6,441	6,165

See notes at end of table.

Evolution of the Housing Stock

| AREA | TABLE 2.4. UNITS IN STRUCTURE BY STATE: 1940 TO 1990 - Continued | | | | | |
| | 1970 | | | | | |
	Year-round housing units	1 unit, detached	1 unit, attached	2-4 units	5 or more units	Mobile home [2]
United States	67,699,084	44,800,684	1,989,867	9,006,950	9,828,696	2,072,887
Alabama	1,114,845	909,466	14,961	88,033	50,978	51,407
Alaska	88,555	44,483	967	12,848	20,146	10,111
Arizona	578,771	405,532	16,969	40,414	63,609	52,247
Arkansas	672,967	570,458	3,845	43,374	25,624	29,666
California	6,976,261	4,477,973	197,515	710,416	1,392,999	197,358
Colorado	742,858	519,105	13,934	63,646	115,026	31,147
Connecticut	968,815	564,273	8,013	240,573	146,351	9,605
Delaware	174,990	107,815	24,310	13,901	19,963	9,001
District of Columbia	278,390	37,071	65,266	33,967	141,840	246
Florida	2,490,838	1,692,936	35,623	209,808	380,371	172,100
Georgia	1,466,687	1,082,964	14,848	148,073	144,367	76,435
Hawaii	215,892	135,809	4,187	22,686	53,049	161
Idaho	238,293	190,449	1,140	17,562	13,203	15,939
Illinois	3,692,447	2,142,533	44,646	689,722	741,789	73,757
Indiana	1,711,896	1,317,076	18,018	181,026	127,793	67,983
Iowa	954,975	776,369	4,138	85,886	64,297	24,285
Kansas	787,508	634,965	7,935	70,194	47,724	26,690
Kentucky	1,060,689	839,476	6,494	98,447	72,981	43,291
Louisiana	1,146,105	870,181	23,230	141,308	73,081	38,305
Maine	339,440	228,755	2,158	64,915	27,362	16,250
Maryland	1,234,680	631,128	218,943	128,411	235,855	20,343
Massachusetts	1,839,028	908,120	18,203	591,106	310,671	10,928
Michigan	2,845,448	2,134,080	26,403	339,347	270,606	75,012
Minnesota	1,219,591	886,632	5,250	135,731	162,238	29,740
Mississippi	697,271	592,639	4,129	47,169	22,753	30,581
Missouri	1,665,506	1,211,916	14,731	224,677	163,304	50,878
Montana	240,755	176,967	1,427	25,903	19,523	16,935
Nebraska	511,473	402,653	3,219	43,435	47,328	14,838
Nevada	171,658	101,511	1,638	19,536	28,453	20,520
New Hampshire	248,799	156,434	1,613	53,661	24,470	12,621
New Jersey	2,305,293	1,240,532	93,936	513,780	442,020	15,025
New Mexico	322,294	256,781	5,607	20,789	20,206	18,911
New York	6,159,314	2,344,282	139,436	1,346,207	2,251,829	77,560
North Carolina	1,619,548	1,314,871	18,708	117,552	69,943	98,474
North Dakota	200,465	146,942	1,210	26,884	15,784	9,645
Ohio	3,447,860	2,439,566	35,175	516,860	370,435	85,824
Oklahoma	937,815	790,208	5,823	54,150	60,034	27,600
Oregon	735,631	556,746	8,954	45,709	86,421	37,801
Pennsylvania	3,880,102	2,079,891	736,240	598,319	378,081	87,571
Rhode Island	307,309	157,243	1,481	110,430	35,817	2,338
South Carolina	804,858	662,922	3,768	59,260	28,697	50,211
South Dakota	221,636	176,143	1,123	20,268	12,465	11,637
Tennessee	1,297,000	1,023,895	12,445	116,477	95,765	48,418
Texas	3,809,086	3,010,366	47,127	258,708	398,198	94,687
Utah	311,982	231,227	3,117	39,009	29,440	9,189
Vermont	149,762	98,004	456	31,427	10,511	9,364
Virginia	1,484,952	1,061,247	48,374	131,162	193,748	50,421
Washington	1,204,902	898,165	12,328	79,596	170,835	43,978
West Virginia	592,845	485,269	4,166	51,285	25,002	27,123
Wisconsin	1,416,427	992,158	5,934	271,138	118,723	28,474
Wyoming	114,572	84,457	706	12,165	6,988	10,256

See notes at end of table.

Evolution of the Housing Stock

TABLE 2.4. UNITS IN STRUCTURE BY STATE: 1940 TO 1990 - Continued

AREA	1980						
	Year-round housing units	1 unit, detached	1 unit, attached	2-4 units	5 or more units	Mobile home [2]	Boat, tent, van, etc.
United States	86,758,717	53,595,586	3,587,019	9,681,832	15,478,306	4,401,056	14,918
Alabama	1,450,755	1,073,053	35,534	89,380	132,345	120,190	253
Alaska	154,051	76,635	3,445	23,230	34,046	16,391	304
Arizona	1,071,787	640,407	60,081	63,440	174,797	132,652	410
Arkansas	889,193	685,821	14,906	50,523	64,045	73,651	247
California	9,223,120	5,257,625	500,542	863,199	2,215,995	382,958	2,801
Colorado	1,169,574	726,383	40,915	84,484	249,962	67,692	138
Connecticut	1,144,520	669,829	30,949	233,687	200,863	9,097	95
Delaware	230,301	130,128	30,556	13,784	38,442	17,365	26
District of Columbia	276,857	34,203	63,350	32,959	145,955	375	15
Florida	4,278,634	2,358,193	146,729	339,826	1,012,548	419,689	1,649
Georgia	2,013,839	1,363,860	50,172	163,145	281,686	154,677	299
Hawaii	332,205	158,174	13,562	33,386	126,665	184	234
Idaho	360,031	251,593	7,872	27,913	31,703	40,837	113
Illinois	4,304,425	2,447,539	97,725	687,300	957,845	113,580	436
Indiana	2,065,115	1,506,922	43,126	185,587	223,779	105,542	159
Iowa	1,121,314	855,253	12,499	94,440	114,811	44,172	139
Kansas	950,511	711,696	22,688	73,498	92,063	50,467	99
Kentucky	1,355,434	980,534	19,497	110,365	136,565	108,261	212
Louisiana	1,537,183	1,053,437	52,844	152,809	170,177	107,654	262
Maine	428,245	275,735	6,825	67,843	42,737	35,009	96
Maryland	1,549,680	768,491	286,867	118,940	346,929	28,207	246
Massachusetts	2,141,364	1,075,428	42,468	570,557	438,427	14,399	85
Michigan	3,450,696	2,465,717	85,403	317,952	431,774	149,565	285
Minnesota	1,530,293	1,045,006	28,672	133,009	264,815	58,639	152
Mississippi	904,523	691,869	15,379	51,046	72,040	74,070	119
Missouri	1,962,576	1,390,992	39,392	209,585	222,806	99,493	308
Montana	315,098	204,033	4,640	34,504	31,134	40,727	60
Nebraska	618,833	458,592	11,706	44,027	76,262	28,192	54
Nevada	337,649	169,455	14,892	31,936	78,277	43,011	78
New Hampshire	349,172	213,873	5,069	59,332	50,046	20,795	57
New Jersey	2,690,377	1,431,076	134,252	540,456	562,221	22,188	184
New Mexico	493,489	319,536	14,264	38,406	60,193	61,028	62
New York	6,706,199	2,600,184	187,516	1,398,613	2,398,966	120,288	632
North Carolina	2,224,196	1,617,286	52,652	143,907	188,524	221,573	254
North Dakota	252,749	161,745	4,443	28,486	36,235	21,803	37
Ohio	4,078,064	2,772,888	95,400	495,556	575,099	138,843	278
Oklahoma	1,229,522	942,874	23,111	68,636	123,994	70,782	125
Oregon	1,071,613	711,856	30,939	76,692	162,300	89,315	511
Pennsylvania	4,512,674	2,407,402	815,381	575,254	551,383	162,851	403
Rhode Island	362,918	192,431	5,288	103,055	59,572	2,535	37
South Carolina	1,122,927	814,648	24,995	73,560	93,950	115,532	242
South Dakota	269,644	191,654	2,965	23,079	30,174	21,725	47
Tennessee	1,737,123	1,254,284	40,018	134,917	199,675	107,972	257
Texas	5,485,273	3,712,924	152,009	324,224	1,009,477	285,686	953
Utah	481,066	329,163	13,165	55,640	59,894	23,170	34
Vermont	196,459	126,096	2,387	35,854	18,456	13,631	35
Virginia	2,000,075	1,309,208	128,540	142,506	324,361	95,229	231
Washington	1,651,680	1,112,525	33,414	116,419	284,061	104,477	784
West Virginia	737,033	549,000	9,780	56,177	45,590	76,300	186
Wisconsin	1,756,311	1,189,136	25,363	269,804	216,472	55,380	156
Wyoming	182,347	109,194	2,832	18,905	18,170	33,207	39

See notes at end of table.

Evolution of the Housing Stock

AREA	TABLE 2.4. UNITS IN STRUCTURE BY STATE: 1940 TO 1990 - Continued						
	1990						
	All housing units	1 unit, detached	1 unit, attached	2-4 units	5 or more units	Mobile home [2]	Other [3]
United States	102,263,678	60,383,409	5,378,243	9,876,407	18,104,610	7,399,855	1,121,154
Alabama	1,670,379	1,133,927	31,943	96,104	168,875	224,307	15,223
Alaska	232,608	124,185	15,963	30,358	37,400	20,280	4,422
Arizona	1,659,430	867,884	109,989	88,371	318,319	250,597	24,270
Arkansas	1,000,667	708,751	18,175	60,820	71,478	131,542	9,901
California	11,182,882	6,119,265	811,684	966,355	2,605,638	555,307	124,633
Colorado	1,477,349	884,431	87,437	89,997	313,215	88,683	13,586
Connecticut	1,320,850	748,626	66,681	243,600	230,989	12,118	18,836
Delaware	289,919	156,013	40,161	13,919	42,760	34,944	2,122
District of Columbia	278,489	34,602	71,321	30,699	139,020	82	2,765
Florida	6,100,262	3,032,769	335,798	462,438	1,448,209	762,855	58,193
Georgia	2,638,418	1,638,847	73,412	198,036	400,235	305,055	22,833
Hawaii	389,810	202,990	34,041	24,182	122,496	389	5,712
Idaho	413,327	285,885	9,102	29,151	28,943	56,529	3,717
Illinois	4,506,275	2,557,169	157,771	648,275	953,967	150,733	38,360
Indiana	2,246,046	1,574,160	57,445	170,801	267,554	156,821	19,265
Iowa	1,143,669	852,993	17,735	86,956	117,506	56,857	11,622
Kansas	1,044,112	747,318	34,868	74,100	109,430	71,195	7,201
Kentucky	1,506,845	1,010,860	25,285	109,291	161,842	185,336	14,231
Louisiana	1,716,241	1,083,921	79,002	152,060	183,735	196,236	21,287
Maine	587,045	378,413	11,753	74,077	54,783	54,532	13,487
Maryland	1,891,917	938,514	393,185	104,332	399,894	42,729	13,263
Massachusetts	2,472,711	1,237,786	88,746	597,143	497,917	23,928	27,191
Michigan	3,847,926	2,673,184	130,583	267,767	487,552	246,365	42,475
Minnesota	1,848,445	1,230,561	69,267	115,347	321,665	90,864	20,741
Mississippi	1,010,423	710,298	17,060	56,813	76,997	136,948	12,307
Missouri	2,199,129	1,489,661	57,345	212,483	257,683	164,021	17,936
Montana	361,155	237,533	8,432	29,327	27,307	54,021	4,535
Nebraska	660,621	479,124	15,767	39,656	84,017	37,046	5,011
Nevada	518,858	235,912	26,819	49,889	130,621	69,655	5,962
New Hampshire	503,904	297,777	23,072	68,105	73,007	35,334	6,609
New Jersey	3,075,310	1,637,129	234,829	526,997	599,650	33,551	43,154
New Mexico	632,058	387,830	28,352	38,833	64,673	102,948	9,422
New York	7,226,891	2,929,333	301,794	1,320,073	2,372,932	194,934	107,825
North Carolina	2,818,193	1,830,229	74,318	177,700	281,787	430,440	23,719
North Dakota	276,340	172,938	10,286	21,127	42,373	27,055	2,561
Ohio	4,371,945	2,896,826	147,651	461,286	619,663	205,595	40,924
Oklahoma	1,406,499	1,005,020	32,851	69,010	155,917	129,850	13,851
Oregon	1,193,567	764,258	32,355	86,371	165,439	134,325	10,819
Pennsylvania	4,938,140	2,636,631	909,676	507,488	564,132	254,920	65,293
Rhode Island	414,572	218,776	11,188	109,460	66,304	4,689	4,155
South Carolina	1,424,155	898,161	33,891	91,572	147,156	240,525	12,850
South Dakota	292,436	202,166	5,249	19,166	31,645	31,357	2,853
Tennessee	2,026,067	1,358,124	55,399	145,992	259,108	188,517	18,927
Texas	7,008,999	4,388,813	215,201	390,675	1,383,649	547,911	82,750
Utah	598,388	393,374	23,702	57,715	82,553	34,986	6,058
Vermont	271,214	168,272	9,367	40,864	24,118	22,702	5,891
Virginia	2,496,334	1,531,857	216,199	143,530	422,648	159,352	22,748
Washington	2,032,378	1,272,721	48,086	138,785	365,589	187,533	19,664
West Virginia	781,295	546,165	11,415	46,445	49,102	118,733	9,435
Wisconsin	2,055,774	1,342,230	50,380	277,221	256,616	101,149	28,178
Wyoming	203,411	129,197	6,212	15,645	16,502	33,474	2,381

Source: U.S. Bureau of the Census, Census of Housing 1940-1990. Based on tables prepared by Robert Bonnette.

(1) Includes occupied mobile homes/trailers, tourist cabins, and boats whose occupants have no other usual place of residence.

(2) In 1970 and earlier censuses, mobile homes had to be occupied to be counted as housing units.

(3) Living quarters such as houseboats, railroad cars, campers, vans, and caves. This category was substantially overstated.

Evolution of the Housing Stock

TABLE 2.5. PLUMBING FACILITIES BY STATE: 1940 TO 1990

AREA	1940				1950 [1]				1960			
	Housing units reporting plumbing facilities	Complete plumbing facilities	Lacking complete plumbing facilities		Housing units reporting plumbing facilities	Complete plumbing facilities	Lacking complete plumbing facilities		All housing units	Complete plumbing facilities	Lacking complete plumbing facilities	
			Number	Percent			Number	Percent			Number	Percent
United States	35,026,442	19,174,344	15,852,098	45.3	44,502,192	28,729,475	15,772,717	35.5	58,314,784	48,537,001	9,777,783	16.8
Alabama	667,203	131,528	535,675	80.3	819,380	264,008	555,372	67.8	967,498	595,120	372,378	38.5
Alaska	....	....	....	....	29,410	15,446	13,964	47.5	67,157	47,433	19,724	29.4
Arizona	137,944	64,207	73,737	53.5	232,695	151,695	81,000	34.8	415,760	359,962	55,798	13.4
Arkansas	494,890	81,587	413,303	83.5	558,586	164,801	393,785	70.5	586,516	333,240	253,276	43.2
California	2,187,884	1,825,597	362,287	16.6	3,497,226	3,085,547	411,679	11.8	5,464,886	5,184,180	280,706	5.1
Colorado	331,227	153,340	177,887	53.7	422,287	262,934	159,353	37.7	594,408	510,377	84,031	14.1
Connecticut	454,481	369,232	85,249	18.8	591,246	492,128	99,118	16.8	818,428	758,360	60,068	7.3
Delaware	71,648	42,742	28,906	40.3	93,894	66,169	27,725	29.5	143,699	125,883	17,816	12.4
District of Columbia	172,780	142,177	30,603	17.7	223,675	198,114	25,561	11.4	262,639	242,369	20,270	7.7
Florida	556,826	299,622	257,204	46.2	920,417	561,104	359,313	39.0	1,776,945	1,510,304	266,641	15.0
Georgia	750,687	177,891	572,796	76.3	933,743	341,395	592,348	63.4	1,169,871	776,131	393,740	33.7
Hawaii	....	....	....	....	118,706	72,649	46,057	38.8	165,390	137,574	27,816	16.8
Idaho	144,938	55,691	89,247	61.6	182,705	115,690	67,015	36.7	223,533	190,766	32,767	14.7
Illinois	2,136,878	1,363,094	773,784	36.2	2,583,070	1,765,179	817,891	31.7	3,274,982	2,834,658	440,324	13.4
Indiana	944,657	430,738	513,919	54.4	1,194,361	682,880	511,481	42.8	1,503,031	1,242,682	260,349	17.3
Iowa	689,161	288,220	400,941	58.2	788,895	410,441	378,454	48.0	905,271	725,612	179,659	19.8
Kansas	519,021	207,146	311,875	60.1	605,026	355,632	249,394	41.2	740,244	622,742	117,502	15.9
Kentucky	688,086	180,231	507,855	73.8	796,204	288,872	507,332	63.7	925,383	557,996	367,387	39.7
Louisiana	591,736	193,999	397,737	67.2	754,298	314,223	440,075	58.3	978,361	689,590	288,771	29.5
Maine	247,598	111,473	136,125	55.0	293,734	156,985	136,749	46.6	364,603	253,434	111,169	30.5
Maryland	456,754	276,122	180,632	39.5	666,425	483,103	183,322	27.5	934,251	835,720	98,531	10.5
Massachusetts	1,137,730	941,107	196,623	17.3	1,357,544	1,097,910	259,634	19.1	1,690,860	1,529,037	161,823	9.6
Michigan	1,437,558	897,763	539,795	37.5	1,900,441	1,368,663	531,778	28.0	2,548,373	2,248,976	299,397	11.7
Minnesota	733,373	334,036	399,337	54.5	893,373	477,485	415,888	46.6	1,116,775	870,316	246,459	22.1
Mississippi	526,237	73,780	452,457	86.0	590,303	153,723	436,580	74.0	628,945	328,103	300,842	47.8
Missouri	1,083,262	465,510	617,752	57.0	1,218,176	600,289	617,887	50.7	1,491,273	1,105,195	386,078	25.9
Montana	170,273	62,906	107,367	63.1	187,807	108,687	79,120	42.1	233,285	185,801	47,484	20.4
Nebraska	372,092	157,579	214,513	57.7	401,955	230,297	171,658	42.7	472,915	390,252	82,663	17.5
Nevada	34,129	19,199	14,930	43.7	53,504	41,071	12,433	23.2	101,546	91,615	9,931	9.8
New Hampshire	150,108	91,215	58,893	39.2	181,262	119,314	61,948	34.2	224,420	186,897	37,523	16.7
New Jersey	1,130,911	920,693	210,218	18.6	1,457,868	1,240,418	217,450	14.9	1,998,456	1,868,909	129,547	6.5
New Mexico	136,839	37,301	99,538	72.7	188,995	99,308	89,687	47.5	281,892	224,342	57,550	20.4
New York	3,675,979	3,020,833	655,146	17.8	4,443,617	3,822,868	620,749	14.0	5,693,681	5,240,221	453,460	8.0
North Carolina	774,620	183,644	590,976	76.3	1,027,220	361,161	666,059	64.8	1,322,839	852,121	470,718	35.6
North Dakota	154,961	30,314	124,647	80.4	170,639	58,152	112,487	65.9	194,597	130,272	64,325	33.1
Ohio	1,862,362	1,153,011	709,351	38.1	2,333,889	1,660,123	673,766	28.9	3,040,952	2,650,545	390,407	12.8
Oklahoma	609,716	199,870	409,846	67.2	690,780	365,849	324,931	47.0	815,609	645,707	169,902	20.8
Oregon	349,735	214,160	135,575	38.8	508,836	387,040	121,796	23.9	622,726	561,370	61,356	9.9
Pennsylvania	2,439,368	1,531,167	908,201	37.2	2,948,409	2,153,876	794,533	26.9	3,581,046	3,176,707	404,339	11.3
Rhode Island	196,221	149,455	46,766	23.8	239,162	150,541	88,621	37.1	286,712	247,741	38,971	13.6
South Carolina	435,207	92,195	343,012	78.8	539,814	188,609	351,205	65.1	678,355	417,049	261,306	38.5
South Dakota	171,004	43,362	127,642	74.6	189,263	73,189	116,074	61.3	216,449	150,911	65,538	30.3
Tennessee	705,720	171,910	533,810	75.6	894,288	328,599	565,689	63.3	1,084,322	706,248	378,074	34.9
Texas	1,708,045	647,231	1,060,814	62.1	2,319,411	1,265,429	1,053,982	45.4	3,152,953	2,526,847	626,106	19.9
Utah	139,472	84,665	54,807	39.3	195,093	159,248	35,845	18.4	262,582	246,495	16,087	6.1
Vermont	102,216	59,934	42,282	41.4	117,353	78,520	38,833	33.1	136,307	110,817	25,490	18.7
Virginia	625,417	219,632	405,785	64.9	871,645	439,612	432,033	49.6	1,168,641	848,051	320,590	27.4
Washington	558,070	359,737	198,333	35.5	782,220	633,178	149,042	19.1	1,009,484	910,991	98,493	9.8
West Virginia	431,160	148,316	282,844	65.6	527,660	243,295	284,365	53.9	574,354	388,678	185,676	32.3
Wisconsin	856,593	439,018	417,575	48.7	1,024,777	607,031	417,746	40.8	1,288,499	1,067,474	221,025	17.2
Wyoming	73,665	30,164	43,501	59.1	89,021	55,090	33,931	38.1	113,080	95,180	17,900	15.8

See notes at end of table.

Evolution of the Housing Stock

TABLE 2.5. PLUMBING FACILITIES BY STATE: 1940 TO 1990 - Continued

AREA	1970 Year-round housing units	1970 Complete plumbing facilities	1970 Lacking complete plumbing facilities Number	1970 Lacking complete plumbing facilities Percent	1980 Year-round housing units	1980 Complete plumbing facilities	1980 Lacking complete plumbing facilities Number	1980 Lacking complete plumbing facilities Percent	1990[2] All housing units	1990[2] Complete plumbing facilities	1990[2] Lacking complete plumbing facilities Number	1990[2] Lacking complete plumbing facilities Percent
United States	67,656,566	62,984,221	4,672,345	6.9	86,692,823	84,359,133	2,333,690	2.7	102,263,678	101,161,982	1,101,696	1.1
Alabama	1,114,640	926,277	188,363	16.9	1,450,011	1,375,018	74,993	5.2	1,670,379	1,642,879	27,500	1.6
Alaska	88,343	73,181	15,162	17.2	154,171	135,398	18,773	12.2	232,608	203,584	29,024	12.5
Arizona	578,490	548,294	30,196	5.2	1,066,437	1,039,057	27,380	2.6	1,659,430	1,627,959	31,471	1.9
Arkansas	672,795	549,101	123,694	18.4	888,740	841,975	46,765	5.3	1,000,667	982,261	18,406	1.8
California	6,976,744	6,833,068	143,676	2.1	9,220,421	9,095,286	125,135	1.4	11,182,882	11,113,501	69,381	0.6
Colorado	741,650	704,929	36,721	5.0	1,168,681	1,147,652	21,029	1.8	1,477,349	1,465,571	11,778	0.8
Connecticut	968,068	942,226	25,842	2.7	1,144,053	1,127,996	16,057	1.4	1,320,850	1,315,105	5,745	0.4
Delaware	174,743	165,887	8,856	5.1	230,107	225,402	4,705	2.0	289,919	288,197	1,722	0.6
District of Columbia	278,374	271,943	6,431	2.3	276,792	270,163	6,629	2.4	278,489	276,239	2,250	0.8
Florida	2,488,968	2,361,445	127,523	5.1	4,270,391	4,217,726	52,665	1.2	6,100,262	6,072,305	27,957	0.5
Georgia	1,466,268	1,272,520	193,748	13.2	2,012,640	1,937,022	75,618	3.8	2,638,418	2,609,956	28,462	1.1
Hawaii	215,897	203,856	12,041	5.6	332,213	324,511	7,702	2.3	389,810	385,498	4,312	1.1
Idaho	238,123	225,504	12,619	5.3	359,756	352,461	7,295	2.0	413,327	407,309	6,018	1.5
Illinois	3,692,915	3,515,960	176,955	4.8	4,302,863	4,216,890	85,973	2.0	4,506,275	4,476,959	29,316	0.7
Indiana	1,711,868	1,601,187	110,681	6.5	2,063,117	2,020,417	42,700	2.1	2,246,046	2,229,811	16,235	0.7
Iowa	954,801	882,981	71,820	7.5	1,121,199	1,094,789	26,410	2.4	1,143,669	1,133,898	9,771	0.9
Kansas	787,422	743,567	43,855	5.6	950,151	930,982	19,169	2.0	1,044,112	1,036,261	7,851	0.8
Kentucky	1,060,364	839,718	220,646	20.8	1,355,008	1,252,777	102,231	7.5	1,506,845	1,462,623	44,222	2.9
Louisiana	1,145,881	1,013,690	132,191	11.5	1,535,321	1,488,152	47,169	3.1	1,716,241	1,694,335	21,906	1.3
Maine	337,007	284,992	52,015	15.4	427,377	402,583	24,794	5.8	587,045	566,269	20,776	3.5
Maryland	1,234,509	1,179,739	54,770	4.4	1,549,219	1,515,988	33,231	2.1	1,891,917	1,879,232	12,685	0.7
Massachusetts	1,836,198	1,770,477	65,721	3.6	2,140,141	2,103,509	36,632	1.7	2,472,711	2,460,345	12,366	0.5
Michigan	2,841,827	2,718,000	123,827	4.4	3,448,335	3,385,095	63,240	1.8	3,847,926	3,815,434	32,492	0.8
Minnesota	1,218,700	1,119,240	99,460	8.2	1,529,363	1,486,413	42,950	2.8	1,848,445	1,824,081	24,364	1.3
Mississippi	697,094	527,732	169,362	24.3	904,078	838,834	65,244	7.2	1,010,423	988,572	21,851	2.2
Missouri	1,664,123	1,502,256	161,867	9.7	1,961,163	1,902,964	58,199	3.0	2,199,129	2,172,297	26,832	1.2
Montana	240,304	218,558	21,746	9.0	315,015	304,218	10,797	3.4	361,155	354,144	7,011	1.9
Nebraska	511,891	480,586	31,305	6.1	618,699	606,962	11,737	1.9	660,621	655,379	5,242	0.8
Nevada	171,635	166,150	5,485	3.2	337,491	332,814	4,677	1.4	518,858	516,156	2,702	0.5
New Hampshire	247,008	229,605	17,403	7.0	349,215	339,098	10,117	2.9	503,904	497,996	5,908	1.2
New Jersey	2,302,609	2,244,692	57,917	2.5	2,687,754	2,642,381	45,373	1.7	3,075,310	3,059,718	15,592	0.5
New Mexico	321,898	287,672	34,226	10.6	493,292	469,430	23,862	4.8	632,058	612,087	19,971	3.2
New York	6,152,263	5,957,098	195,165	3.2	6,699,084	6,507,921	191,163	2.9	7,226,891	7,159,544	67,347	0.9
North Carolina	1,618,103	1,365,784	252,319	15.6	2,223,007	2,107,079	115,928	5.2	2,818,193	2,775,231	42,962	1.5
North Dakota	200,334	172,699	27,635	13.8	252,618	241,950	10,668	4.2	276,340	270,763	5,577	2.0
Ohio	3,447,168	3,269,060	178,108	5.2	4,077,276	3,994,575	82,701	2.0	4,371,945	4,339,037	32,908	0.8
Oklahoma	937,640	871,214	66,426	7.1	1,228,679	1,203,675	25,004	2.0	1,406,499	1,392,742	13,757	1.0
Oregon	735,243	708,818	26,425	3.6	1,071,294	1,051,581	19,713	1.8	1,193,567	1,183,174	10,393	0.9
Pennsylvania	3,876,211	3,677,606	198,605	5.1	4,509,332	4,396,803	112,529	2.5	4,938,140	4,891,083	47,057	1.0
Rhode Island	306,501	296,855	9,646	3.1	362,633	355,765	6,868	1.9	414,572	412,319	2,253	0.5
South Carolina	804,755	655,455	149,300	18.6	1,121,448	1,064,227	57,221	5.1	1,424,155	1,403,978	20,177	1.4
South Dakota	221,720	191,661	30,059	13.6	269,494	257,887	11,607	4.3	292,436	286,513	5,923	2.0
Tennessee	1,297,006	1,104,463	192,543	14.8	1,736,847	1,657,075	79,772	4.6	2,026,067	1,993,707	32,360	1.6
Texas	3,808,406	3,517,023	291,383	7.7	5,480,416	5,338,780	141,636	2.6	7,008,999	6,923,924	85,075	1.2
Utah	311,814	303,257	8,557	2.7	480,744	475,359	5,385	1.1	598,388	592,522	5,866	1.0
Vermont	149,101	136,647	12,454	8.4	195,944	189,429	6,515	3.3	271,214	265,092	6,122	2.3
Virginia	1,484,151	1,284,834	199,317	13.4	1,998,693	1,897,362	101,331	5.1	2,496,334	2,450,215	46,119	1.8
Washington	1,204,187	1,162,677	41,510	3.4	1,650,411	1,623,003	27,408	1.7	2,032,378	2,013,760	18,618	0.9
West Virginia	592,371	483,693	108,678	18.3	736,352	685,896	50,456	6.9	781,295	756,226	25,069	3.2
Wisconsin	1,414,105	1,312,733	101,372	7.2	1,752,969	1,708,608	44,361	2.5	2,055,774	2,025,997	29,777	1.4
Wyoming	114,330	107,611	6,719	5.9	182,368	178,195	4,173	2.3	203,411	200,194	3,217	1.6

Source: U.S. Bureau of the Census, Census of Housing 1940-1990. Based on tables prepared by Robert Bonnette.

(1) Alaska and Hawaii are not included in the 1950 totals.

(2) The definition of "complete plumbing facilities" in 1990 is not strictly comparable to earlier censuses. See Appendix A for explanation.

Evolution of the Housing Stock

TABLE 2.6. SOURCE OF WATER BY STATE: 1970 TO 1990

AREA	1970			
	All year-round housing units	Public system or private company	Individual well [1]	Some other source
United States	67,693,842	55,293,575	11,102,324	1,297,943
Alabama	1,114,791	775,486	306,292	33,013
Alaska	88,563	59,962	17,111	11,490
Arizona	578,750	542,789	28,436	7,525
Arkansas	672,970	441,593	207,447	23,930
California	6,975,969	6,640,227	294,586	41,156
Colorado	742,638	662,623	65,730	14,285
Connecticut	968,821	769,707	194,154	4,960
Delaware	174,989	136,245	37,605	1,139
District of Columbia	278,393	278,141	122	130
Florida	2,490,777	2,085,329	394,965	10,483
Georgia	1,466,625	1,114,021	324,515	28,089
Hawaii	215,840	212,679	404	2,757
Idaho	238,303	166,793	62,149	9,361
Illinois	3,691,949	3,249,823	418,316	23,810
Indiana	1,711,797	1,188,856	494,075	28,866
Iowa	955,038	708,381	240,365	6,292
Kansas	787,484	649,692	126,095	11,697
Kentucky	1,060,572	711,561	244,402	104,609
Louisiana	1,145,973	938,039	189,390	18,544
Maine	339,201	219,311	101,893	17,997
Maryland	1,234,469	1,022,977	194,707	16,785
Massachusetts	1,838,789	1,738,290	94,792	5,707
Michigan	2,845,079	2,094,053	737,245	13,781
Minnesota	1,219,495	870,840	337,692	10,963
Mississippi	697,210	455,434	202,882	38,894
Missouri	1,665,583	1,331,445	277,068	57,070
Montana	240,753	172,442	56,088	12,223
Nebraska	511,446	400,485	108,965	1,996
Nevada	171,682	154,732	15,303	1,647
New Hampshire	248,721	172,822	68,136	7,763
New Jersey	2,305,341	2,067,567	232,224	5,550
New Mexico	322,240	255,084	56,149	11,007
New York	6,158,661	5,554,366	550,154	54,141
North Carolina	1,619,279	881,365	659,159	78,755
North Dakota	200,498	129,498	59,389	11,611
Ohio	3,447,393	2,767,639	612,505	67,249
Oklahoma	937,827	764,886	158,448	14,493
Oregon	735,470	587,236	124,666	23,568
Pennsylvania	3,880,038	3,168,255	613,197	98,586
Rhode Island	307,334	279,504	27,162	668
South Carolina	804,817	515,081	267,006	22,730
South Dakota	221,594	147,512	60,341	13,741
Tennessee	1,296,928	969,568	253,496	73,864
Texas	3,808,917	3,295,954	454,568	58,395
Utah	311,874	296,114	12,329	3,431
Vermont	149,844	92,236	32,169	25,439
Virginia	1,484,823	1,042,156	351,898	90,769
Washington	1,204,924	1,040,332	139,788	24,804
West Virginia	592,779	398,830	156,279	37,670
Wisconsin	1,416,042	984,446	420,488	11,108
Wyoming	114,549	91,168	19,979	3,402

See notes at end of table.

Evolution of the Housing Stock

AREA	All year-round housing units	Public system or private company	Individual well			Some other source
			Total	Drilled	Dug	
United States	86,758,717	72,528,131	13,101,922	11,227,722	1,874,200	1,128,664
Alabama	1,450,755	1,158,608	267,202	204,219	62,983	24,945
Alaska	154,051	107,768	32,391	30,171	2,220	13,892
Arizona	1,071,787	1,020,731	43,226	40,427	2,799	7,830
Arkansas	889,193	659,725	213,672	182,740	30,932	15,796
California	9,223,120	8,819,702	359,584	334,836	24,748	43,834
Colorado	1,169,574	1,074,680	84,459	76,836	7,623	10,435
Connecticut	1,144,520	899,330	241,130	203,602	37,528	4,060
Delaware	230,301	176,869	52,701	45,450	7,251	731
District of Columbia	276,857	276,646	76	62	14	135
Florida	4,278,634	3,698,274	573,059	542,716	30,343	7,301
Georgia	2,013,839	1,585,084	405,078	302,876	102,202	23,677
Hawaii	332,205	327,197	536	443	93	4,472
Idaho	360,031	261,496	88,853	83,013	5,840	9,682
Illinois	4,304,425	3,835,388	443,681	346,903	96,778	25,356
Indiana	2,065,115	1,495,026	546,381	494,918	51,463	23,708
Iowa	1,121,314	877,037	236,709	181,883	54,826	7,568
Kansas	950,511	825,134	116,567	97,143	19,424	8,810
Kentucky	1,355,434	1,003,974	247,506	188,758	58,748	103,954
Louisiana	1,537,183	1,328,035	200,446	165,258	35,188	8,702
Maine	428,245	261,322	149,331	105,262	44,069	17,592
Maryland	1,549,680	1,283,600	252,142	211,361	40,781	13,938
Massachusetts	2,141,364	2,003,575	132,119	104,153	27,966	5,670
Michigan	3,450,696	2,503,336	934,184	880,736	53,448	13,176
Minnesota	1,530,293	1,137,212	382,572	339,464	43,108	10,509
Mississippi	904,523	738,555	150,816	123,622	27,194	15,152
Missouri	1,962,576	1,620,506	305,853	264,551	41,302	36,217
Montana	315,098	223,211	80,817	72,119	8,698	11,070
Nebraska	618,833	504,320	112,740	103,037	9,703	1,773
Nevada	337,649	312,151	24,142	23,074	1,068	1,356
New Hampshire	349,172	230,811	110,712	72,774	39,938	7,649
New Jersey	2,690,377	2,408,624	277,326	248,691	28,635	4,427
New Mexico	493,489	415,179	70,157	63,659	6,498	8,153
New York	6,706,199	5,990,705	659,973	554,603	105,370	55,521
North Carolina	2,224,196	1,324,436	821,995	645,594	176,401	77,765
North Dakota	252,749	192,558	54,008	44,945	9,063	6,183
Ohio	4,078,064	3,317,852	692,062	616,358	75,704	68,150
Oklahoma	1,229,522	1,056,894	164,506	149,362	15,144	8,122
Oregon	1,071,613	867,896	178,407	163,299	15,108	25,310
Pennsylvania	4,512,674	3,613,011	800,292	725,001	75,291	99,371
Rhode Island	362,918	328,261	33,987	25,711	8,276	670
South Carolina	1,122,927	812,731	297,435	241,291	56,144	12,761
South Dakota	269,644	204,810	56,512	46,813	9,699	8,322
Tennessee	1,737,123	1,416,564	258,997	219,180	39,817	61,562
Texas	5,485,273	4,961,560	490,453	419,075	71,378	33,260
Utah	481,066	463,342	14,511	13,007	1,504	3,213
Vermont	196,459	113,673	58,380	41,744	16,636	24,406
Virginia	2,000,075	1,469,796	455,556	353,757	101,799	74,723
Washington	1,651,680	1,431,226	195,132	162,647	32,485	25,322
West Virginia	737,033	517,778	181,069	156,119	24,950	38,186
Wisconsin	1,756,311	1,223,745	521,579	485,183	36,396	10,987
Wyoming	182,347	148,187	30,900	29,276	1,624	3,260

See notes at end of table.

Evolution of the Housing Stock

TABLE 2.6. SOURCE OF WATER BY STATE: 1970 TO 1990 - Continued

AREA	1990					
	All housing units	Public system or private company	Individual well			Some other source
			Total	Drilled	Dug	
United States	102,263,678	86,068,766	15,131,691	13,467,148	1,664,543	1,063,221
Alabama	1,670,379	1,454,160	201,105	170,898	30,207	15,114
Alaska	232,608	152,550	56,116	52,697	3,419	23,942
Arizona	1,659,430	1,568,614	77,229	71,562	5,667	13,587
Arkansas	1,000,667	815,155	174,664	154,969	19,695	10,848
California	11,182,882	10,668,942	464,621	432,689	31,932	49,319
Colorado	1,477,349	1,344,307	119,898	110,516	9,382	13,144
Connecticut	1,320,850	1,026,900	289,885	252,669	37,216	4,065
Delaware	289,919	220,935	68,452	62,267	6,185	532
District of Columbia	278,489	278,190	181	151	30	118
Florida	6,100,262	5,298,184	794,558	745,506	49,052	7,520
Georgia	2,638,418	2,144,049	476,726	391,011	85,715	17,643
Hawaii	389,810	380,375	868	755	113	8,567
Idaho	413,327	289,502	112,333	105,860	6,473	11,492
Illinois	4,506,275	4,044,971	440,172	366,146	74,026	21,132
Indiana	2,246,046	1,664,281	564,286	516,561	47,725	17,479
Iowa	1,143,669	927,716	209,984	174,323	35,661	5,969
Kansas	1,044,112	934,508	104,107	90,689	13,418	5,497
Kentucky	1,506,845	1,214,664	206,523	171,220	35,303	85,658
Louisiana	1,716,241	1,527,872	182,931	156,538	26,393	5,438
Maine	587,045	312,299	245,831	190,639	55,192	28,915
Maryland	1,891,917	1,565,946	315,155	283,750	31,405	10,816
Massachusetts	2,472,711	2,265,229	200,314	171,182	29,132	7,168
Michigan	3,847,926	2,711,224	1,121,066	1,064,011	57,055	15,636
Minnesota	1,848,445	1,348,611	484,018	442,662	41,356	15,816
Mississippi	1,010,423	882,496	122,447	106,407	16,040	5,480
Missouri	2,199,129	1,839,532	336,598	309,678	26,920	22,999
Montana	361,155	236,532	109,273	100,222	9,051	15,350
Nebraska	660,621	548,285	110,754	102,092	8,662	1,582
Nevada	518,858	479,732	36,815	35,060	1,755	2,311
New Hampshire	503,904	303,911	188,825	141,959	46,866	11,168
New Jersey	3,075,310	2,756,133	314,868	288,970	25,898	4,309
New Mexico	632,058	525,244	97,045	90,385	6,660	9,769
New York	7,226,891	6,329,446	824,332	703,295	121,037	73,113
North Carolina	2,818,193	1,843,476	913,733	771,663	142,070	60,984
North Dakota	276,340	218,257	52,953	45,932	7,021	5,130
Ohio	4,371,945	3,603,499	707,886	644,790	63,096	60,560
Oklahoma	1,406,499	1,223,121	177,074	163,916	13,158	6,304
Oregon	1,193,567	963,096	204,470	189,423	15,047	26,001
Pennsylvania	4,938,140	3,854,953	978,220	905,420	72,800	104,967
Rhode Island	414,572	367,984	45,836	37,434	8,402	752
South Carolina	1,424,155	1,099,695	318,708	273,941	44,767	5,752
South Dakota	292,436	238,038	48,892	42,806	6,086	5,506
Tennessee	2,026,067	1,736,138	244,943	215,752	29,191	44,986
Texas	7,008,999	6,417,136	566,716	511,056	55,660	25,147
Utah	598,388	573,222	18,522	17,106	1,416	6,644
Vermont	271,214	137,953	99,781	83,366	16,415	33,480
Virginia	2,496,334	1,900,436	539,237	444,953	94,284	56,661
Washington	2,032,378	1,742,224	263,532	231,249	32,283	26,622
West Virginia	781,295	563,191	184,098	166,306	17,792	34,006
Wisconsin	2,055,774	1,367,925	674,510	626,299	48,211	13,339
Wyoming	203,411	157,927	40,600	38,397	2,203	4,884

Source: U.S. Bureau of the Census, Census of Housing 1970-1990. Based on tables prepared by Robert Bonnette.

(1) Includes both drilled and dug wells, which were not identified separately in the 1970 Census.

Evolution of the Housing Stock

	TABLE 2.7. SEWAGE DISPOSAL BY STATE: 1970 TO 1990							
AREA	1970				1980			
	All year-round housing units	Public sewer	Septic tank or cesspool	Other means	All year-round housing units	Public sewer	Septic tank or cesspool	Other means
United States	67,693,842	48,187,675	16,601,792	2,904,375	86,758,717	64,240,532	20,926,961	1,591,224
Alabama	1,114,791	566,307	385,345	163,139	1,450,755	771,748	607,358	71,649
Alaska	88,563	55,511	18,629	14,423	154,051	104,797	31,262	17,992
Arizona	578,750	446,304	114,433	18,013	1,071,787	869,862	180,665	21,260
Arkansas	672,970	355,684	220,287	96,999	889,193	514,653	336,712	37,828
California	6,975,969	6,084,632	853,013	38,324	9,223,120	8,251,415	920,690	51,015
Colorado	742,638	612,659	113,290	16,689	1,169,574	1,019,477	138,742	11,355
Connecticut	968,821	608,603	354,585	5,633	1,144,520	781,657	357,446	5,417
Delaware	174,989	130,259	39,860	4,870	230,301	172,294	54,970	3,037
District of Columbia	278,393	277,068	454	871	276,857	274,913	402	1,542
Florida	2,490,777	1,509,682	938,352	42,743	4,278,634	3,076,260	1,167,676	34,698
Georgia	1,466,625	848,516	474,455	143,654	2,013,839	1,214,548	737,539	61,752
Hawaii	215,840	161,438	50,558	3,844	332,205	270,701	57,576	3,928
Idaho	238,303	137,891	93,146	7,266	360,031	229,481	124,832	5,718
Illinois	3,691,949	3,072,266	554,603	65,080	4,304,425	3,656,245	614,499	33,681
Indiana	1,711,797	1,060,942	589,794	61,061	2,065,115	1,361,704	676,718	26,693
Iowa	955,038	662,320	257,889	34,829	1,121,314	830,489	273,536	17,289
Kansas	787,484	594,758	163,918	28,808	950,511	752,124	183,803	14,584
Kentucky	1,060,572	536,388	312,856	211,328	1,355,434	736,144	510,637	108,653
Louisiana	1,145,973	778,247	287,481	80,245	1,537,183	1,101,516	401,695	33,972
Maine	339,201	169,975	140,409	28,817	428,245	214,145	198,629	15,471
Maryland	1,234,469	953,470	243,728	37,271	1,549,680	1,232,785	294,286	22,609
Massachusetts	1,838,789	1,339,304	490,365	9,120	2,141,364	1,581,814	550,629	8,921
Michigan	2,845,079	1,947,137	847,433	50,509	3,450,696	2,463,078	954,965	32,653
Minnesota	1,219,495	864,984	307,441	47,070	1,530,293	1,144,993	362,120	23,180
Mississippi	697,210	338,581	209,115	149,514	904,523	510,732	319,285	74,506
Missouri	1,665,583	1,173,688	359,278	132,617	1,962,576	1,418,141	475,424	69,011
Montana	240,753	154,581	74,198	11,974	315,098	201,014	107,018	7,066
Nebraska	511,446	385,860	105,320	20,266	618,833	492,946	114,257	11,630
Nevada	171,682	147,743	21,988	1,951	337,649	294,758	41,241	1,650
New Hampshire	248,721	132,475	109,015	7,231	349,172	182,656	161,386	5,130
New Jersey	2,305,341	1,890,977	404,241	10,123	2,690,377	2,327,869	350,598	11,910
New Mexico	322,240	230,737	65,781	25,722	493,489	361,847	111,967	19,675
New York	6,158,661	4,824,525	1,289,253	44,883	6,706,199	5,279,298	1,375,362	51,539
North Carolina	1,619,279	733,848	687,572	197,859	2,224,196	1,040,451	1,084,336	99,409
North Dakota	200,498	128,967	53,074	18,457	252,749	182,570	62,357	7,822
Ohio	3,447,393	2,565,317	779,510	102,566	4,078,064	3,108,321	911,386	58,357
Oklahoma	937,827	686,240	203,174	48,413	1,229,522	908,666	301,354	19,502
Oregon	735,470	448,967	275,944	10,559	1,071,613	735,626	326,213	9,774
Pennsylvania	3,880,038	2,798,522	985,014	96,502	4,512,674	3,360,158	1,083,043	69,473
Rhode Island	307,334	197,947	107,544	1,843	362,918	248,174	112,663	2,081
South Carolina	804,817	363,611	334,210	106,996	1,122,927	596,811	480,455	45,661
South Dakota	221,594	140,258	62,366	18,970	269,644	189,988	71,743	7,913
Tennessee	1,296,928	671,248	457,008	168,672	1,737,123	979,399	687,054	70,670
Texas	3,808,917	2,989,684	654,283	164,950	5,485,273	4,461,444	938,671	85,158
Utah	311,874	258,649	49,249	3,976	481,066	421,923	56,700	2,443
Vermont	149,844	72,264	68,265	9,315	196,459	91,707	99,752	5,000
Virginia	1,484,823	906,030	408,213	170,580	2,000,075	1,315,815	593,912	90,348
Washington	1,204,924	786,551	403,909	14,464	1,651,680	1,117,544	520,354	13,782
West Virginia	592,779	304,151	187,028	101,600	737,033	381,110	297,401	58,522
Wisconsin	1,416,042	994,926	371,567	49,549	1,756,311	1,262,265	467,986	26,060
Wyoming	114,549	86,983	23,349	4,217	182,347	142,456	37,656	2,235

See notes at end of table.

Evolution of the Housing Stock

TABLE 2.7. SEWAGE DISPOSAL BY STATE: 1970 TO 1990 - Continued

AREA	1990			
	All housing units	Public sewer	Septic tank or cesspool	Other means
United States	102,263,678	76,455,211	24,670,877	1,137,590
Alabama	1,670,379	910,782	728,690	30,907
Alaska	232,608	144,905	59,886	27,817
Arizona	1,659,430	1,348,836	282,897	27,697
Arkansas	1,000,667	601,188	382,467	17,012
California	11,182,882	10,022,843	1,092,174	67,865
Colorado	1,477,349	1,283,186	183,817	10,346
Connecticut	1,320,850	935,541	378,382	6,927
Delaware	289,919	212,793	74,541	2,585
District of Columbia	278,489	276,481	575	1,433
Florida	6,100,262	4,499,793	1,559,113	41,356
Georgia	2,638,418	1,638,979	970,686	28,753
Hawaii	389,810	312,812	72,940	4,058
Idaho	413,327	264,618	142,879	5,830
Illinois	4,506,275	3,885,689	598,125	22,461
Indiana	2,246,046	1,525,810	703,032	17,204
Iowa	1,143,669	869,056	264,889	9,724
Kansas	1,044,112	847,767	187,398	8,947
Kentucky	1,506,845	849,491	600,182	57,172
Louisiana	1,716,241	1,246,678	442,758	26,805
Maine	587,045	266,344	301,373	19,328
Maryland	1,891,917	1,533,799	342,523	15,595
Massachusetts	2,472,711	1,803,176	659,120	10,415
Michigan	3,847,926	2,724,408	1,090,481	33,037
Minnesota	1,848,445	1,356,520	467,936	23,989
Mississippi	1,010,423	585,185	387,406	37,832
Missouri	2,199,129	1,617,996	532,844	48,289
Montana	361,155	218,372	135,371	7,412
Nebraska	660,621	534,692	117,460	8,469
Nevada	518,858	456,107	60,508	2,243
New Hampshire	503,904	250,060	246,692	7,152
New Jersey	3,075,310	2,703,489	357,890	13,931
New Mexico	632,058	452,934	161,068	18,056
New York	7,226,891	5,716,917	1,460,873	49,101
North Carolina	2,818,193	1,403,033	1,365,632	49,528
North Dakota	276,340	204,328	66,479	5,533
Ohio	4,371,945	3,392,785	940,943	38,217
Oklahoma	1,406,499	1,028,594	367,197	10,708
Oregon	1,193,567	835,545	349,122	8,900
Pennsylvania	4,938,140	3,670,338	1,210,054	57,748
Rhode Island	414,572	293,901	118,410	2,261
South Carolina	1,424,155	825,754	578,129	20,272
South Dakota	292,436	207,996	78,435	6,005
Tennessee	2,026,067	1,213,934	781,616	30,517
Texas	7,008,999	5,690,550	1,266,713	51,736
Utah	598,388	528,864	65,403	4,121
Vermont	271,214	115,201	149,125	6,888
Virginia	2,496,334	1,740,787	707,409	48,138
Washington	2,032,378	1,387,396	630,646	14,336
West Virginia	781,295	427,930	318,697	34,668
Wisconsin	2,055,774	1,440,024	580,836	34,914
Wyoming	203,411	151,004	49,055	3,352

Source: U.S. Bureau of the Census, Census of Housing 1970-1990. Based on tables prepared by Robert Bonnette.

Evolution of the Housing Stock

TABLE 2.8. TELEPHONES BY STATE: 1960 TO 1990

AREA	1960				1970			
	Occupied housing units	Telephone available	No telephone available		Occupied housing units	Telephone available	No telephone available	
			Number	Percent			Number	Percent
United States	53,023,875	41,618,040	11,405,835	21.5	63,449,747	55,176,700	8,273,047	13.0
Alabama	884,116	523,166	360,950	40.8	1,034,113	808,353	225,760	21.8
Alaska	57,250	34,368	22,882	40.0	79,059	57,602	21,457	27.1
Arizona	366,630	237,086	129,544	35.3	539,157	426,191	112,966	21.0
Arkansas	523,552	268,867	254,685	48.6	615,424	463,208	152,216	24.7
California	4,982,108	4,130,218	851,890	17.1	6,573,861	5,871,481	702,380	10.7
Colorado	529,419	445,380	84,039	15.9	690,928	616,911	74,017	10.7
Connecticut	752,736	688,136	64,600	8.6	933,269	873,698	59,571	6.4
Delaware	128,582	107,676	20,906	16.3	164,804	148,888	15,916	9.7
District of Columbia	252,066	209,042	43,024	17.1	262,538	228,878	33,660	12.8
Florida	1,550,414	1,055,151	495,263	31.9	2,284,786	1,859,031	425,755	18.6
Georgia	1,070,325	660,042	410,283	38.3	1,369,225	1,092,890	276,335	20.2
Hawaii	153,064	125,009	28,055	18.3	203,088	184,250	18,838	9.3
Idaho	193,839	147,294	46,545	24.0	218,960	185,079	33,881	15.5
Illinois	3,084,971	2,622,022	462,949	15.0	3,502,138	3,124,620	377,518	10.8
Indiana	1,387,878	1,125,890	261,988	18.9	1,609,494	1,420,380	189,114	11.7
Iowa	841,357	750,230	91,127	10.8	896,311	834,283	62,028	6.9
Kansas	672,899	573,120	99,779	14.8	727,364	655,260	72,104	9.9
Kentucky	851,867	523,494	328,373	38.5	983,665	768,357	215,308	21.9
Louisiana	892,344	619,655	272,689	30.6	1,052,038	860,070	191,968	18.2
Maine	280,355	202,775	77,580	27.7	302,923	258,443	44,480	14.7
Maryland	863,001	690,968	172,033	19.9	1,175,073	1,049,851	125,222	10.7
Massachusetts	1,534,985	1,340,000	194,985	12.7	1,759,692	1,623,653	136,039	7.7
Michigan	2,239,079	1,928,267	310,812	13.9	2,653,059	2,422,272	230,787	8.7
Minnesota	991,981	866,159	125,822	12.7	1,153,946	1,079,718	74,228	6.4
Mississippi	568,070	257,273	310,797	54.7	636,724	429,338	207,386	32.6
Missouri	1,360,054	1,058,409	301,645	22.2	1,520,567	1,333,934	186,633	12.3
Montana	202,240	159,478	42,762	21.1	217,304	186,632	30,672	14.1
Nebraska	433,448	366,855	66,593	15.4	473,721	434,354	39,367	8.3
Nevada	91,520	63,676	27,844	30.4	160,052	129,790	30,262	18.9
New Hampshire	180,020	139,758	40,262	22.4	225,378	199,923	25,455	11.3
New Jersey	1,806,439	1,536,962	269,477	14.9	2,218,182	2,007,048	211,134	9.5
New Mexico	251,209	160,239	90,970	36.2	289,389	220,275	69,114	23.9
New York	5,248,710	4,320,483	928,227	17.7	5,913,861	5,185,144	728,717	12.3
North Carolina	1,204,715	704,153	500,562	41.6	1,509,564	1,168,419	341,145	22.6
North Dakota	173,362	134,510	38,852	22.4	181,613	164,304	17,309	9.5
Ohio	2,852,557	2,418,525	434,032	15.2	3,289,432	2,982,472	306,960	9.3
Oklahoma	734,593	548,020	186,573	25.4	850,803	718,399	132,404	15.6
Oregon	558,214	461,440	96,774	17.3	691,631	615,041	76,590	11.1
Pennsylvania	3,350,839	2,864,941	485,898	14.5	3,705,410	3,385,893	319,517	8.6
Rhode Island	257,335	208,573	48,762	18.9	291,965	265,576	26,389	9.0
South Carolina	603,551	334,004	269,547	44.7	734,373	554,928	179,445	24.4
South Dakota	194,821	150,875	43,946	22.6	200,807	175,751	25,056	12.5
Tennessee	1,003,301	683,353	319,948	31.9	1,213,187	979,967	233,220	19.2
Texas	2,778,116	1,961,636	816,480	29.4	3,433,996	2,824,900	609,096	17.7
Utah	241,532	210,378	31,154	12.9	297,934	271,470	26,464	8.9
Vermont	110,732	84,774	25,958	23.4	132,098	116,511	15,587	11.8
Virginia	1,072,840	743,811	329,029	30.7	1,390,636	1,164,345	226,291	16.3
Washington	894,168	759,064	135,104	15.1	1,105,587	990,573	115,014	10.4
West Virginia	521,142	350,280	170,862	32.8	547,214	435,638	111,576	20.4
Wisconsin	1,146,342	985,422	160,920	14.0	1,328,804	1,232,317	96,487	7.3
Wyoming	99,187	77,133	22,054	22.2	104,600	90,391	14,209	13.6

See notes at end of table.

Evolution of the Housing Stock

TABLE 2.8. TELEPHONES BY STATE: 1960 TO 1990 - Continued

AREA	1980				1990			
	Occupied housing units	Telephone in unit	No telephone in unit		Occupied housing units	Telephone in unit	No telephone in unit	
			Number	Percent			Number	Percent
United States	80,389,673	74,719,996	5,669,677	7.1	91,947,410	87,129,953	4,817,457	5.2
Alabama	1,341,856	1,168,631	173,225	12.9	1,506,790	1,375,236	131,554	8.7
Alaska	131,463	109,507	21,956	16.7	188,915	173,185	15,730	8.3
Arizona	957,032	853,557	103,475	10.8	1,368,843	1,252,435	116,408	8.5
Arkansas	816,065	713,697	102,368	12.5	891,179	793,643	97,536	10.9
California	8,629,866	8,174,972	454,894	5.3	10,381,206	10,068,066	313,140	3.0
Colorado	1,061,249	994,689	66,560	6.3	1,282,489	1,228,907	53,582	4.2
Connecticut	1,093,678	1,056,371	37,307	3.4	1,230,479	1,198,163	32,316	2.6
Delaware	207,081	196,909	10,172	4.9	247,497	239,813	7,684	3.1
District of Columbia	253,143	241,032	12,111	4.8	249,634	239,105	10,529	4.2
Florida	3,744,254	3,376,613	367,641	9.8	5,134,869	4,864,627	270,242	5.3
Georgia	1,871,652	1,651,116	220,536	11.8	2,366,615	2,170,926	195,689	8.3
Hawaii	294,052	279,557	14,495	4.9	356,267	346,873	9,394	2.6
Idaho	324,107	301,052	23,055	7.1	360,723	339,644	21,079	5.8
Illinois	4,045,374	3,834,056	211,318	5.2	4,202,240	4,010,024	192,216	4.6
Indiana	1,927,050	1,799,517	127,533	6.6	2,065,355	1,943,603	121,752	5.9
Iowa	1,053,033	1,012,728	40,305	3.8	1,064,325	1,027,838	36,487	3.4
Kansas	872,239	828,047	44,192	5.1	944,726	902,993	41,733	4.4
Kentucky	1,263,355	1,113,514	149,841	11.9	1,379,782	1,238,901	140,881	10.2
Louisiana	1,411,788	1,258,433	153,355	10.9	1,499,269	1,374,814	124,455	8.3
Maine	395,184	365,813	29,371	7.4	465,312	447,930	17,382	3.7
Maryland	1,460,865	1,399,144	61,721	4.2	1,748,991	1,693,888	55,103	3.2
Massachusetts	2,032,717	1,945,944	86,773	4.3	2,247,110	2,199,728	47,382	2.1
Michigan	3,195,213	3,064,173	131,040	4.1	3,419,331	3,280,249	139,082	4.1
Minnesota	1,445,222	1,395,981	49,241	3.4	1,647,853	1,607,500	40,353	2.4
Mississippi	827,169	689,605	137,564	16.6	911,374	796,244	115,130	12.6
Missouri	1,793,399	1,695,833	97,566	5.4	1,961,206	1,858,481	102,725	5.2
Montana	283,742	261,413	22,329	7.9	306,163	285,040	21,123	6.9
Nebraska	571,400	549,694	21,706	3.8	602,363	580,681	21,682	3.6
Nevada	304,327	274,661	29,666	9.7	466,297	441,179	25,118	5.4
New Hampshire	323,493	304,692	18,801	5.8	411,186	397,119	14,067	3.4
New Jersey	2,548,594	2,427,891	120,703	4.7	2,794,711	2,708,860	85,851	3.1
New Mexico	441,466	379,742	61,724	14.0	542,709	475,177	67,532	12.4
New York	6,340,429	5,865,797	474,632	7.5	6,639,322	6,306,914	332,408	5.0
North Carolina	2,043,291	1,819,379	223,912	11.0	2,517,026	2,338,336	178,690	7.1
North Dakota	227,664	218,100	9,564	4.2	240,878	232,363	8,515	3.5
Ohio	3,833,828	3,607,319	226,509	5.9	4,087,546	3,895,552	191,994	4.7
Oklahoma	1,118,561	1,029,940	88,621	7.9	1,206,135	1,099,754	106,381	8.8
Oregon	991,593	926,855	64,738	6.5	1,103,313	1,053,261	50,052	4.5
Pennsylvania	4,219,606	4,044,249	175,357	4.2	4,495,966	4,379,187	116,779	2.6
Rhode Island	338,590	322,502	16,088	4.8	377,977	366,104	11,873	3.1
South Carolina	1,029,981	900,550	129,431	12.6	1,258,044	1,143,349	114,695	9.1
South Dakota	242,523	227,137	15,386	6.3	259,034	243,516	15,518	6.0
Tennessee	1,618,505	1,458,614	159,891	9.9	1,853,725	1,721,394	132,331	7.1
Texas	4,929,267	4,465,923	463,344	9.4	6,070,937	5,547,903	523,034	8.6
Utah	448,603	424,315	24,288	5.4	537,273	515,801	21,472	4.0
Vermont	178,325	166,292	12,033	6.7	210,650	201,258	9,392	4.5
Virginia	1,863,073	1,709,016	154,057	8.3	2,291,830	2,168,192	123,638	5.4
Washington	1,540,510	1,452,870	87,640	5.7	1,872,431	1,807,764	64,667	3.5
West Virginia	686,311	613,033	73,278	10.7	688,557	617,803	70,754	10.3
Wisconsin	1,652,261	1,597,741	54,520	3.3	1,822,118	1,771,278	50,840	2.8
Wyoming	165,624	151,780	13,844	8.4	168,839	159,352	9,487	5.6

Source: U.S. Bureau of the Census, Census of Housing 1960-1990. Based on tables prepared by Robert Bonnette.

In 1980 and 1990 the census collected data on the presence of a telephone within the housing unit, whereas in 1960 and 1970 data were collected on the availability of a telephone. See Appendix A for additional explanation.

Evolution of the Housing Stock

TABLE 2.9. SEASONAL, RECREATIONAL, AND OCCASIONAL USE HOUSING BY STATE: 1940 TO 1990

AREA	1940		1950 [1]	
	All housing units	Seasonal units	All housing units	Seasonal units
United States	37,325,470	739,594	45,983,398	1,050,466
Alabama	708,043	1,964	843,857	6,307
Alaska	....	....	33,072	263
Arizona	147,079	4,725	240,750	5,487
Arkansas	520,613	2,252	575,163	7,294
California	2,340,373	60,684	3,590,660	59,355
Colorado	354,660	14,806	436,226	19,924
Connecticut	488,543	23,293	611,162	22,658
Delaware	75,567	2,435	97,013	3,031
District of Columbia	185,128	37	229,738	129
Florida	590,451	22,572	952,131	25,121
Georgia	796,715	2,878	966,672	7,493
Hawaii	....	....	120,606	....
Idaho	152,835	2,626	188,328	5,408
Illinois	2,280,826	17,253	2,671,647	20,102
Indiana	1,005,952	14,994	1,232,314	21,710
Iowa	726,654	4,867	811,912	7,538
Kansas	545,721	1,295	625,148	3,890
Kentucky	729,206	1,110	820,141	4,586
Louisiana	619,233	2,231	777,672	6,269
Maine	260,659	26,220	311,441	37,754
Maryland	500,156	11,752	689,116	18,071
Massachusetts	1,221,252	46,366	1,400,185	56,916
Michigan	1,519,378	60,486	1,971,842	100,534
Minnesota	773,042	22,576	918,434	41,330
Mississippi	557,246	1,528	609,329	6,235
Missouri	1,140,493	9,169	1,268,354	12,639
Montana	177,443	3,302	194,256	5,504
Nebraska	387,368	1,431	417,245	3,036
Nevada	36,770	691	56,515	791
New Hampshire	158,044	15,838	190,563	24,184
New Jersey	1,223,887	65,801	1,501,473	78,320
New Mexico	145,642	4,656	199,706	4,248
New York	4,032,460	116,960	4,633,806	161,474
North Carolina	820,888	5,711	1,058,367	13,525
North Dakota	162,881	749	175,769	2,242
Ohio	1,977,693	18,401	2,402,565	23,522
Oklahoma	647,485	2,374	715,691	5,523
Oregon	369,811	8,890	524,003	12,657
Pennsylvania	2,618,056	26,376	3,036,494	43,071
Rhode Island	203,469	9,130	244,147	11,024
South Carolina	458,899	3,269	557,672	7,776
South Dakota	179,744	1,706	194,573	2,789
Tennessee	742,030	2,236	921,837	5,534
Texas	1,804,884	23,240	2,393,828	42,540
Utah	147,291	1,198	200,554	2,243
Vermont	106,362	7,052	121,911	10,582
Virginia	659,787	4,560	901,483	9,639
Washington	590,439	15,106	809,701	21,945
West Virginia	459,725	1,407	544,075	4,267
Wisconsin	897,719	39,666	1,055,843	52,107
Wyoming	76,868	1,725	92,086	2,142

See notes at end of table.

Evolution of the Housing Stock

TABLE 2.9. SEASONAL, RECREATIONAL, AND OCCASIONAL USE HOUSING BY STATE: 1940 TO 1990 - Continued

AREA	1960 All housing units	For seasonal or occasional use Total	For seasonal or occasional use Seasonal	For seasonal or occasional use Occasional use	1970 All housing units	For seasonal or occasional use Total	For seasonal or occasional use Seasonal	For seasonal or occasional use Occasional use
United States	58,326,357	2,024,381	1,742,465	281,916	68,679,030	2,020,087	1,022,464	997,623
Alabama	967,466	21,680	18,156	3,524	1,120,220	24,797	5,580	19,217
Alaska	67,193	4,157	3,079	1,078	90,729	5,187	2,386	2,801
Arizona	415,834	17,323	15,686	1,637	584,171	15,598	5,681	9,917
Arkansas	586,552	22,309	19,113	3,196	675,611	17,117	2,816	14,301
California	5,465,870	128,870	89,854	39,016	6,996,990	129,593	20,246	109,347
Colorado	594,522	28,690	24,523	4,167	757,070	31,610	15,420	16,190
Connecticut	818,544	31,550	28,237	3,313	981,158	19,678	13,090	6,588
Delaware	143,725	6,429	6,054	375	180,233	7,506	5,490	2,016
District of Columbia	262,641	610	354	256	278,444	1,073	70	1,003
Florida	1,776,961	73,926	63,531	10,395	2,526,612	84,921	37,644	47,277
Georgia	1,170,039	23,337	18,642	4,695	1,470,557	22,984	4,289	18,695
Hawaii	165,506	2,960	1,541	1,419	216,085	3,066	188	2,878
Idaho	223,533	14,837	13,668	1,169	244,695	13,166	6,572	6,594
Illinois	3,275,799	37,424	30,608	6,816	3,703,367	31,417	10,452	20,965
Indiana	1,503,148	39,780	33,955	5,825	1,730,099	36,070	18,231	17,839
Iowa	905,295	18,129	15,940	2,189	964,060	17,687	9,259	8,428
Kansas	740,335	12,100	9,877	2,223	789,196	10,888	1,774	9,114
Kentucky	925,572	17,078	12,858	4,220	1,064,451	20,039	4,087	15,952
Louisiana	978,452	22,114	17,514	4,600	1,150,235	24,285	4,354	19,931
Maine	364,617	64,718	61,102	3,616	397,169	76,062	60,162	15,900
Maryland	934,552	24,996	20,868	4,128	1,249,177	25,210	14,668	10,542
Massachusetts	1,690,998	87,019	80,525	6,494	1,890,400	68,382	54,202	14,180
Michigan	2,548,792	170,932	153,138	17,794	2,954,570	178,143	112,743	65,400
Minnesota	1,119,271	77,627	72,607	5,020	1,276,198	74,153	57,498	16,655
Mississippi	628,945	18,243	15,516	2,727	699,150	17,176	2,056	15,120
Missouri	1,491,397	37,125	29,195	7,930	1,673,361	46,514	9,238	37,276
Montana	233,310	14,091	12,766	1,325	246,603	13,297	6,299	6,998
Nebraska	472,950	10,003	8,263	1,740	515,069	9,294	3,178	6,116
Nevada	101,623	2,573	2,180	393	172,558	3,617	923	2,694
New Hampshire	224,440	33,882	31,590	2,292	280,962	44,045	33,954	10,091
New Jersey	1,998,940	122,152	113,189	8,963	2,388,011	108,292	85,402	22,890
New Mexico	281,976	10,110	8,961	1,149	325,722	11,072	3,824	7,248
New York	5,695,880	247,977	225,169	22,808	6,298,663	208,018	146,400	61,618
North Carolina	1,322,957	36,583	29,616	6,967	1,641,222	48,811	23,119	25,692
North Dakota	194,597	7,395	6,500	895	204,222	8,047	3,888	4,159
Ohio	3,041,151	41,790	33,670	8,120	3,465,356	38,505	18,188	20,317
Oklahoma	815,685	18,670	13,262	5,408	939,681	19,859	2,041	17,818
Oregon	622,853	23,612	16,924	6,688	744,616	19,403	9,373	10,030
Pennsylvania	3,581,877	85,121	75,403	9,718	3,924,757	84,114	48,546	35,568
Rhode Island	286,757	14,521	13,709	812	316,477	11,621	9,976	1,645
South Carolina	678,379	21,189	17,185	4,004	815,123	27,631	10,368	17,263
South Dakota	216,449	8,102	7,224	878	225,253	8,281	3,533	4,748
Tennessee	1,084,365	17,073	12,979	4,094	1,300,908	19,432	3,902	15,530
Texas	3,153,127	107,159	82,487	24,672	3,829,502	112,657	21,096	91,561
Utah	262,670	5,518	4,821	697	315,765	7,117	3,951	3,166
Vermont	136,307	18,171	16,517	1,654	165,068	25,324	15,967	9,357
Virginia	1,168,913	23,770	18,450	5,320	1,492,954	31,306	8,803	22,503
Washington	1,009,519	42,372	37,339	5,033	1,220,475	40,263	16,288	23,975
West Virginia	574,357	13,909	10,543	3,366	597,266	17,649	4,895	12,754
Wisconsin	1,288,620	88,130	81,581	6,549	1,472,466	94,932	58,361	36,571
Wyoming	113,096	6,545	5,996	549	116,323	5,178	1,993	3,185

See notes at end of table.

Evolution of the Housing Stock

TABLE 2.9. SEASONAL, RECREATIONAL, AND OCCASIONAL USE HOUSING BY STATE: 1940 TO 1990 - Continued

AREA	1980				1990			
	All housing units	For seasonal or occasional use			All housing units	For seasonal, recreational, or occasional use (Including units for migrant workers)		
		Total	Seasonal	Occasional use		Total	For seasonal, recreational, or occasional use	Units for migrant workers
United States	88,411,263	2,794,054	1,718,440	1,075,614	102,263,678	3,116,867	3,081,923	34,944
Alabama	1,467,374	30,283	17,363	12,920	1,670,379	35,904	35,609	295
Alaska	162,825	11,996	8,654	3,342	232,608	17,190	16,991	199
Arizona	1,110,558	66,498	44,121	22,377	1,659,430	97,030	96,104	926
Arkansas	898,593	20,965	9,853	11,112	1,000,667	18,667	18,224	443
California	9,279,036	181,620	58,615	123,005	11,182,882	198,436	195,385	3,051
Colorado	1,194,253	48,116	25,572	22,544	1,477,349	64,621	63,814	807
Connecticut	1,158,884	20,696	14,831	5,865	1,320,850	20,475	20,428	47
Delaware	238,611	16,243	8,504	7,739	289,919	19,365	19,328	37
District of Columbia	276,984	903	192	711	278,489	1,663	1,575	88
Florida	4,378,691	304,607	108,300	196,307	6,100,262	421,003	417,670	3,333
Georgia	2,028,350	31,025	15,710	15,315	2,638,418	34,254	33,637	617
Hawaii	334,235	6,431	2,022	4,409	389,810	12,888	12,806	82
Idaho	375,127	22,737	15,371	7,366	413,327	25,342	24,252	1,090
Illinois	4,319,672	31,610	16,809	14,801	4,506,275	25,263	25,056	207
Indiana	2,091,795	41,727	28,678	13,049	2,246,046	37,065	36,945	120
Iowa	1,131,299	15,803	10,100	5,703	1,143,669	14,696	14,644	52
Kansas	954,906	10,272	4,755	5,517	1,044,112	7,531	7,336	195
Kentucky	1,369,125	22,288	14,117	8,171	1,506,845	21,159	20,962	197
Louisiana	1,548,419	29,750	13,098	16,652	1,716,241	30,786	30,333	453
Maine	501,093	79,876	73,716	6,160	587,045	88,206	88,039	167
Maryland	1,570,907	34,269	21,688	12,581	1,891,917	42,486	42,268	218
Massachusetts	2,208,146	81,955	68,005	13,950	2,472,711	90,501	90,367	134
Michigan	3,589,912	215,958	141,577	74,381	3,847,926	226,621	223,549	3,072
Minnesota	1,612,960	97,753	83,597	14,156	1,848,445	105,659	105,122	537
Mississippi	911,627	20,036	7,549	12,487	1,010,423	16,348	16,002	346
Missouri	1,988,915	53,371	27,752	25,619	2,199,129	55,847	55,492	355
Montana	328,465	19,046	13,450	5,596	361,155	21,069	20,481	588
Nebraska	624,829	10,623	6,130	4,493	660,621	11,329	10,978	351
Nevada	339,949	7,494	2,458	5,036	518,858	11,522	11,258	264
New Hampshire	386,381	45,884	37,166	8,718	503,904	57,177	57,135	42
New Jersey	2,772,149	105,825	84,395	21,430	3,075,310	100,858	100,591	267
New Mexico	507,513	24,069	14,221	9,848	632,058	22,464	21,862	602
New York	6,867,638	215,920	168,554	47,366	7,226,891	213,436	212,625	811
North Carolina	2,274,737	84,233	51,730	32,503	2,818,193	100,143	98,714	1,429
North Dakota	258,772	9,353	6,154	3,199	276,340	7,746	7,236	510
Ohio	4,108,105	45,195	30,829	14,366	4,371,945	37,781	37,324	457
Oklahoma	1,237,040	20,265	8,361	11,904	1,406,499	25,547	25,169	378
Oregon	1,083,285	30,237	11,991	18,246	1,193,567	31,679	30,200	1,479
Pennsylvania	4,596,431	125,052	87,099	37,953	4,938,140	144,571	144,359	212
Rhode Island	372,672	12,057	10,039	2,018	414,572	12,053	12,037	16
South Carolina	1,153,709	43,992	32,261	11,731	1,424,155	50,203	49,843	360
South Dakota	276,997	10,706	7,503	3,203	292,436	8,484	8,391	93
Tennessee	1,747,422	21,676	10,575	11,101	2,026,067	23,689	23,389	300
Texas	5,549,352	154,974	68,936	86,038	7,008,999	157,649	151,919	5,730
Utah	490,006	12,602	9,262	3,340	598,388	21,203	21,023	180
Vermont	223,199	34,279	27,255	7,024	271,214	45,443	45,405	38
Virginia	2,020,941	39,589	22,248	17,341	2,496,334	42,209	41,742	467
Washington	1,689,450	56,304	39,039	17,265	2,032,378	58,342	55,832	2,510
West Virginia	747,810	18,923	11,458	7,465	781,295	22,526	22,403	123
Wisconsin	1,863,897	140,401	110,928	29,473	2,055,774	150,761	150,601	160
Wyoming	188,217	8,567	5,849	2,718	203,411	9,977	9,468	509

Source: U.S. Bureau of the Census, Census of Housing 1940-1990. Based on tables prepared by Robert Bonnette.

(1) Alaska and Hawaii are not included in U.S. total for 1950.

Evolution of the Housing Stock

TABLE 2.10. NEW HOUSING UNITS BY STATE: 1980 AND 1990

AREA	1980			1990		
	All year-round housing units	New homes (Built after 1974)		All housing units	New homes (Built after 1984)	
		Number	Percent of all year-round units		Number	Percent of all units
United States	86,758,717	11,396,168	13.1	102,263,678	11,193,801	10.9
Alabama	1,450,755	224,410	15.5	1,670,379	214,372	12.8
Alaska	154,051	48,745	31.6	232,608	31,161	13.4
Arizona	1,071,787	268,081	25.0	1,659,430	326,719	19.7
Arkansas	889,193	141,854	16.0	1,000,667	120,192	12.0
California	9,223,120	1,323,013	14.3	11,182,882	1,537,943	13.8
Colorado	1,169,574	230,035	19.7	1,477,349	146,245	9.9
Connecticut	1,144,520	88,834	7.8	1,320,850	126,994	9.6
Delaware	230,301	25,554	11.1	289,919	43,209	14.9
District of Columbia	276,857	9,351	3.4	278,489	6,380	2.3
Florida	4,278,634	866,336	20.3	6,100,262	1,130,062	18.5
Georgia	2,013,839	291,820	14.5	2,638,418	497,994	18.9
Hawaii	332,205	61,786	18.6	389,810	41,910	10.8
Idaho	360,031	82,640	23.0	413,327	30,715	7.4
Illinois	4,304,425	409,368	9.5	4,506,275	292,373	6.5
Indiana	2,065,115	220,048	10.7	2,246,046	179,289	8.0
Iowa	1,121,314	130,829	11.7	1,143,669	48,716	4.3
Kansas	950,511	120,411	12.7	1,044,112	86,579	8.3
Kentucky	1,355,434	193,615	14.3	1,506,845	157,191	10.4
Louisiana	1,537,183	250,776	16.3	1,716,241	133,010	7.8
Maine	428,245	50,199	11.7	587,045	74,859	12.8
Maryland	1,549,680	170,110	11.0	1,891,917	245,713	13.0
Massachusetts	2,141,364	131,728	6.2	2,472,711	204,718	8.3
Michigan	3,450,696	350,606	10.2	3,847,926	307,599	8.0
Minnesota	1,530,293	203,509	13.3	1,848,445	189,974	10.3
Mississippi	904,523	133,725	14.8	1,010,423	123,202	12.2
Missouri	1,962,576	225,900	11.5	2,199,129	229,831	10.5
Montana	315,098	55,924	17.8	361,155	23,450	6.5
Nebraska	618,833	76,003	12.3	660,621	39,797	6.0
Nevada	337,649	104,954	31.1	518,858	125,593	24.2
New Hampshire	349,172	46,611	13.4	503,904	87,665	17.4
New Jersey	2,690,377	193,721	7.2	3,075,310	274,298	8.9
New Mexico	493,489	101,553	20.6	632,058	84,385	13.4
New York	6,706,199	316,477	4.7	7,226,891	399,934	5.5
North Carolina	2,224,196	325,614	14.6	2,818,193	454,568	16.1
North Dakota	252,749	47,239	18.7	276,340	17,319	6.3
Ohio	4,078,064	383,074	9.4	4,371,945	294,708	6.7
Oklahoma	1,229,522	190,245	15.5	1,406,499	98,438	7.0
Oregon	1,071,613	209,381	19.5	1,193,567	93,963	7.9
Pennsylvania	4,512,674	357,566	7.9	4,938,140	345,892	7.0
Rhode Island	362,918	27,657	7.6	414,572	37,657	9.1
South Carolina	1,122,927	178,752	15.9	1,424,155	221,730	15.6
South Dakota	269,644	41,097	15.2	292,436	19,517	6.7
Tennessee	1,737,123	263,265	15.2	2,026,067	283,368	14.0
Texas	5,485,273	1,095,498	20.0	7,008,999	786,187	11.2
Utah	481,066	110,524	23.0	598,388	65,648	11.0
Vermont	196,459	23,684	12.1	271,214	35,325	13.0
Virginia	2,000,075	301,205	15.1	2,496,334	394,575	15.8
Washington	1,651,680	329,504	20.0	2,032,378	251,208	12.4
West Virginia	737,033	97,431	13.2	781,295	64,173	8.2
Wisconsin	1,756,311	217,102	12.4	2,055,774	156,969	7.6
Wyoming	182,347	48,804	26.8	203,411	10,484	5.2

Source: U.S. Bureau of the Census, Census of Housing 1980-1990.

Current Characteristics of the Housing Stock

TABLE 2.11. SELECTED INTRODUCTORY CHARACTERISTICS OF THE HOUSING STOCK: 1991
(In thousands, except as noted)

CHARACTERISTIC	Total housing units	Sea-sonal units	Year-round units Total	Occupied Total	Owner	Renter	Vacant Total	For rent	Rental vacancy rate (Percent)	For sale only	Rented or sold	Occa-sional use/ URE[1]	Other vacant	Con-struct-ed within 4 years	Mobile homes
TOTAL	104,592	2,728	101,864	93,147	59,796	33,351	8,717	2,684	7.4	1,026	754	2,611	1,643	5,840	6,983
UNITS IN STRUCTURE															
1, detached	62,646	1,637	61,009	57,485	49,084	8,401	3,524	444	5.0	692	364	1,108	915	3,360	...
1, attached	6,156	74	6,082	5,442	2,722	2,720	640	259	8.6	66	59	169	86	474	...
2 to 4	10,890	90	10,800	9,490	1,909	7,581	1,309	640	7.7	77	131	195	267	270	...
5 to 9	5,368	56	5,312	4,639	398	4,240	674	367	7.9	18	49	165	75	302	...
10 to 19	4,764	69	4,694	3,993	317	3,676	701	395	9.6	8	41	198	59	389	...
20 to 49	3,713	58	3,655	3,118	328	2,790	536	243	7.9	17	30	229	18	241	...
50 or more	4,073	98	3,975	3,350	505	2,845	625	227	7.3	49	50	263	35	225	...
Mobile home or trailer	6,983	645	6,338	5,630	4,532	1,098	708	108	8.9	98	31	284	187	580	6,983
STORIES IN STRUCTURE[2]															
1	3,015	25	2,990	2,606	290	2,316	384	241	9.3	14	26	67	35	127	...
2	10,398	118	10,280	8,920	929	7,992	1,360	714	8.1	49	111	334	151	646	...
3	8,110	116	7,994	6,938	1,254	5,684	1,056	505	8.1	46	73	284	149	393	...
4 to 6	4,724	58	4,666	4,024	628	3,396	642	302	8.1	27	48	170	95	175	...
7 or more	2,585	56	2,529	2,123	373	1,750	406	110	5.8	33	42	197	24	90	...
COOPERATIVES AND CONDOMINIUMS															
Cooperatives	742	21	721	630	396	234	91	20	7.8	21	9	36	5	11	34
Condominiums	4,516	291	4,225	3,357	2,310	1,047	868	131	11.1	121	45	524	47	448	14
YEAR STRUCTURE BUILT[3]															
1990 to 1994	2,389	42	2,346	2,041	1,539	501	306	70	12.1	108	50	54	24	2,389	299
1985 to 1989	8,951	157	8,794	8,043	5,433	2,610	751	239	8.3	99	46	326	43	3,451	965
1980 to 1984	8,292	230	8,061	7,290	4,671	2,619	771	216	7.5	93	88	289	85	...	1,099
1975 to 1979	12,146	312	11,834	11,023	7,300	3,724	810	244	6.1	76	65	355	70	...	1,490
1970 to 1974	11,452	377	11,074	9,982	6,077	3,905	1,092	337	7.9	97	84	432	141	...	1,675
1960 to 1969	16,161	468	15,693	14,523	9,570	4,953	1,170	409	7.5	100	101	326	235	...	1,171
1950 to 1959	13,836	420	13,416	12,512	8,982	3,530	904	240	6.3	143	72	241	209	...	243
1940 to 1949	8,607	226	8,381	7,668	4,742	2,926	713	228	7.2	88	64	154	179	...	26
1930 to 1939	6,768	188	6,579	5,984	3,355	2,629	595	169	6.0	52	57	124	193	...	15
1920 to 1929	5,677	76	5,601	5,062	2,872	2,190	539	209	8.6	60	37	101	132	...	-
1919 or earlier	10,314	230	10,084	9,019	5,257	3,762	1,065	322	7.8	111	91	209	331	...	-
Median (Year)	1964	1965	1964	1964	1965	1963	1965	1964	...	1966	1966	1972	1949	...	1976

See notes at end of table.

Current Characteristics of the Housing Stock

TABLE 2.11. SELECTED INTRODUCTORY CHARACTERISTICS OF THE HOUSING STOCK: 1991 - Continued
(In thousands, except as noted)

CHARACTERISTIC	Total housing units	Sea-sonal units	Year-round units Total	Occupied Total	Occupied Owner	Occupied Renter	Vacant Total	Vacant For rent	Vacant Rental vacancy rate (Percent)	Vacant For sale only	Vacant Rented or sold	Vacant Occa-sional use/ URE [1]	Vacant Other vacant	Construct-ed within 4 years	Mobile homes
METROPOLITAN/ NONMETROPOLITAN AREAS															
Inside metropolitan statistical areas	79,949	935	79,014	72,723	44,883	27,840	6,290	2,284	7.5	775	609	1,534	1,087	4,657	3,504
In central cities	32,925	132	32,793	29,687	14,422	15,265	3,106	1,314	7.8	283	310	657	542	1,042	382
Suburbs	47,024	804	46,221	43,036	30,461	12,575	3,184	971	7.1	492	299	878	545	3,615	3,123
Outside metropolitan statistical areas	24,643	1,792	22,850	20,424	14,913	5,510	2,427	399	6.7	251	145	1,076	555	1,183	3,478
REGIONS															
Northeast	21,093	774	20,319	18,962	11,869	7,093	1,358	497	6.5	165	132	302	261	783	599
Midwest	24,987	616	24,371	22,593	15,238	7,355	1,778	552	6.9	212	196	444	374	1,187	1,311
South	36,983	927	36,057	32,190	21,272	10,918	3,866	1,060	8.8	475	271	1,260	802	2,326	3,649
West	21,528	411	21,117	19,402	11,417	7,985	1,715	575	6.7	173	156	606	206	1,545	1,424
URBANIZED AREAS															
Inside urbanized areas	62,741	414	62,327	57,394	32,904	24,490	4,933	2,031	7.6	561	474	1,068	799	2,857	1,456
In central cities of (P)MSAs	32,353	126	32,227	29,165	14,127	15,038	3,062	1,299	7.9	276	304	645	538	982	374
Urban fringe	30,388	288	30,100	28,229	18,778	9,451	1,871	732	7.1	285	171	423	260	1,875	1,082
Outside urbanized areas	41,850	2,314	39,537	35,753	26,892	8,861	3,784	652	6.8	465	280	1,543	844	2,983	5,527
Other urban	12,446	222	12,224	11,102	7,048	4,054	1,122	318	7.2	145	95	378	187	631	679
Rural	29,405	2,092	27,312	24,650	19,844	4,807	2,662	335	6.4	320	185	1,165	657	2,352	4,847
PLACE SIZE															
Less than 2,500 persons	4,960	230	4,730	4,292	3,070	1,222	438	82	6.2	58	38	141	120	139	492
2,500 to 9,999 persons	10,213	220	9,993	9,102	6,185	2,917	891	244	7.7	109	61	315	161	420	681
10,000 to 19,999 persons	8,770	67	8,703	8,036	5,223	2,814	667	210	6.9	97	82	188	91	402	259
20,000 to 49,999 persons	13,243	98	13,146	12,303	7,565	4,738	843	339	6.6	119	81	168	135	591	309
50,000 to 99,999 persons	8,848	23	8,826	8,112	4,647	3,465	714	265	7.0	75	65	216	93	333	180
100,000 to 249,999 persons	8,151	22	8,129	7,464	3,917	3,547	665	297	7.7	76	54	144	94	353	136
250,000 to 499,999 persons	5,642	15	5,626	5,119	2,440	2,679	507	247	8.4	57	31	78	94	168	36
500,000 to 999,999 persons	4,995	11	4,984	4,455	2,197	2,258	530	223	8.8	36	68	114	89	140	47
1,000,000 persons or more	7,261	30	7,231	6,558	2,554	4,005	673	315	7.2	53	72	75	157	128	23

Source: U.S. Bureau of the Census and U.S. Department of Housing and Urban Development, "American Housing Survey for the United States in 1991." Current Housing Reports H150/91. Issued April 1993.

Consistent with the 1990 Census.

(1) URE means usual residence elsewhere. See Appendix A for additional explanation.
(2) Limited to multiunit structures.
(3) For mobile homes, oldest category is 1939 or earlier.
(-) means zero or rounds to zero.

Current Characteristics of the Housing Stock

TABLE 2.12. SELECTED INTRODUCTORY CHARACTERISTICS OF THE HOUSING STOCK: 1993
(In thousands, except as noted)

| CHARACTERISTIC | Total housing units | Sea-sonal units | Year-round units | | | | | | | | | | | Con-struct-ed within 4 years | Mobile homes |
| | | | Total | Occupied | | | Vacant | | | | | | | | |
				Total	Owner	Renter	Total	For rent	Rental vacancy rate (Percent)	For sale only	Rented or sold	Occa-sional use/ URE [1]	Other vacant		
TOTAL	106,611	3,088	103,522	94,724	61,252	33,472	8,799	2,651	7.3	889	882	2,506	1,870	5,605	7,072
UNITS IN STRUCTURE															
1, detached	64,283	1,808	62,475	58,918	50,490	8,428	3,557	388	4.4	624	396	1,114	1,035	3,405	....
1, attached	6,079	114	5,965	5,375	2,824	2,550	591	195	7.1	70	56	160	108	414	....
2 to 4	10,732	127	10,606	9,279	1,774	7,505	1,327	638	7.7	59	124	229	277	221	....
5 to 9	5,521	76	5,445	4,724	409	4,315	721	388	8.1	21	80	156	77	221	....
10 to 19	5,025	102	4,923	4,190	359	3,831	733	432	10.0	16	79	146	60	267	....
20 to 49	3,826	107	3,720	3,154	335	2,819	566	285	9.0	11	56	181	32	169	....
50 or more	4,072	93	3,979	3,429	579	2,850	551	217	7.0	18	42	218	55	133	....
Mobile home or trailer	7,072	663	6,409	5,655	4,482	1,173	754	107	8.3	69	50	302	226	776	7,072
STORIES IN STRUCTURE [2]															
1	2,807	32	2,775	2,424	266	2,158	350	212	8.9	16	22	43	58	122	....
2	10,742	173	10,570	9,101	976	8,125	1,469	793	8.8	54	141	325	156	438	....
3	8,373	166	8,207	7,137	1,204	5,934	1,070	511	7.8	29	128	250	152	307	....
4 to 6	4,543	61	4,481	3,829	595	3,234	652	323	9.0	10	65	161	94	89	....
7 or more	2,721	72	2,649	2,294	420	1,873	356	122	6.1	18	24	152	41	53	....
COOPERATIVES AND CONDOMINIUMS															
Cooperatives	872	33	839	729	419	311	109	16	5.0	20	12	54	7	12	57
Condominiums	4,806	386	4,420	3,621	2,532	1,089	799	104	8.6	92	79	453	71	407	18
YEAR STRUCTURE BUILT [3]															
1990 to 1994	5,134	100	5,034	4,576	3,720	855	458	96	10.0	114	89	121	39	5,134	746
1985 to 1989	8,951	237	8,714	7,969	5,324	2,645	745	214	7.4	58	103	291	78	471	879
1980 to 1984	8,143	195	7,948	7,171	4,593	2,579	776	226	7.9	55	88	298	110	....	919
1975 to 1979	11,915	373	11,542	10,708	7,161	3,547	834	221	5.8	89	81	331	112	....	1,425
1970 to 1974	11,559	486	11,073	10,110	6,129	3,981	963	331	7.6	89	89	325	129	....	1,663
1960 to 1969	16,070	538	15,532	14,405	9,482	4,923	1,127	371	6.9	122	110	297	227	....	1,169
1950 to 1959	13,633	406	13,227	12,360	8,855	3,505	867	269	7.1	92	72	216	218	....	214
1940 to 1949	8,529	252	8,276	7,539	4,696	2,843	737	209	6.8	62	64	165	237	....	32
1930 to 1939	6,747	222	6,525	5,853	3,293	2,560	673	184	6.6	73	52	156	208	....	25
1920 to 1929	5,677	98	5,579	5,047	2,819	2,228	532	175	7.2	49	49	92	167	....	-
1919 or earlier	10,252	182	10,071	8,986	5,178	3,808	1,085	353	8.4	87	85	214	346	....	-
Median (Year)	1965	1967	1965	1965	1966	1964	1964	1964	....	1967	1971	1972	1949	....	1977

See notes at end of table.

Current Characteristics of the Housing Stock

TABLE 2.12. SELECTED INTRODUCTORY CHARACTERISTICS OF THE HOUSING STOCK: 1993 - Continued
(In thousands, except as noted)

CHARACTERISTIC	Total housing units	Sea-sonal units	Year-round units											Con-struct-ed within 4 years	Mobile homes
				Occupied			Vacant								
			Total	Total	Owner	Renter	Total	For rent	Rental vacancy rate (Percent)	For sale only	Rented or sold	Occa-sional use/ URE [1]	Other vacant		
METROPOLITAN/ NONMETROPOLITAN AREAS															
Inside metropolitan statistical areas	81,293	1,036	80,257	73,898	46,081	27,817	6,359	2,248	7.4	666	718	1,463	1,263	4,204	3,559
In central cities	33,140	165	32,975	29,838	14,644	15,194	3,137	1,326	7.9	242	314	607	649	907	389
Suburbs	48,153	871	47,282	44,060	31,438	12,623	3,221	923	6.7	425	404	856	614	3,297	3,170
Outside metropolitan statistical areas	25,318	2,052	23,266	20,826	15,170	5,656	2,440	403	6.6	223	164	1,043	607	1,401	3,512
REGIONS															
Northeast	21,157	811	20,346	18,906	11,751	7,155	1,440	489	6.3	153	154	393	251	610	647
Midwest	25,480	725	24,755	23,031	15,617	7,415	1,724	552	6.8	176	210	433	352	1,214	1,338
South	37,886	1,092	36,794	32,936	21,841	11,096	3,857	977	8.0	374	298	1,211	998	2,368	3,603
West	22,088	460	21,627	19,850	12,043	7,808	1,777	633	7.4	187	220	469	268	1,412	1,483
URBANIZED AREAS															
Inside urbanized areas	63,355	491	62,863	57,837	33,534	24,303	5,026	2,023	7.6	494	539	1,004	967	2,438	1,427
In central cities of (P)MSAs	32,465	163	32,302	29,232	14,292	14,939	3,070	1,309	8.0	236	312	575	638	840	380
Urban fringe	30,890	329	30,561	28,606	19,241	9,364	1,956	714	7.0	258	227	428	329	1,598	1,046
Outside urbanized areas	43,256	2,597	40,659	36,887	27,718	9,169	3,772	629	6.3	395	343	1,503	903	3,167	5,645
Other urban	12,672	284	12,387	11,253	7,133	4,120	1,134	324	7.2	123	136	349	201	588	653
Rural	30,585	2,313	28,272	25,633	20,585	5,049	2,638	305	5.6	272	207	1,154	701	2,579	4,992
PLACE SIZE															
Less than 2,500 persons	5,174	286	4,888	4,443	3,184	1,259	446	81	6.0	64	39	146	114	222	530
2,500 to 9,999 persons	10,383	328	10,055	9,193	6,253	2,940	862	241	7.5	99	68	255	198	412	639
10,000 to 19,999 persons	8,827	74	8,752	8,089	5,284	2,805	663	197	6.4	90	102	170	105	356	246
20,000 to 49,999 persons	13,329	81	13,248	12,349	7,652	4,696	899	372	7.3	79	100	206	143	455	283
50,000 to 99,999 persons	8,991	30	8,961	8,246	4,757	3,489	715	295	7.7	60	81	178	100	292	193
100,000 to 249,999 persons	8,170	39	8,130	7,404	3,978	3,426	726	294	7.8	83	83	121	145	300	142
250,000 to 499,999 persons	5,704	34	5,670	5,153	2,482	2,672	516	231	7.9	38	51	79	117	147	47
500,000 to 999,999 persons	5,014	10	5,005	4,520	2,195	2,325	485	214	8.3	52	52	66	102	144	45
1,000,000 persons or more	7,207	29	7,178	6,478	2,538	3,940	700	321	7.5	34	58	125	162	79	18

Source: U.S. Bureau of the Census and U.S. Department of Housing and Urban Development, "American Housing Survey for the United States in 1993." Current Housing Reports H150/93. Issued February 1995.

Consistent with the 1990 Census.

(1) URE means usual residence elsewhere. See Appendix A for additional explanation.
(2) Limited to multiunit structures.
(3) For mobile homes, oldest category is 1939 or earlier.
(-) means zero or rounds to zero.

Current Characteristics of the Housing Stock

TABLE 2.13. SELECTED INTRODUCTORY CHARACTERISTICS OF THE HOUSING STOCK: 1995
(In thousands, except as noted)

CHARACTERISTIC	Total housing units	Sea-sonal units	Year-round units Total	Occupied Total	Owner	Renter	Vacant Total	For rent	Rental vacancy rate (Percent)	For sale only	Rented or sold	Occa-sional use/ URE [1]	Other vacant	Con-struct-ed within 4 years	Mobile homes
TOTAL	109,457	3,054	106,403	97,693	63,544	34,150	8,710	2,666	7.2	917	690	2,757	1,681	5,832	7,647
UNITS IN STRUCTURE															
1, detached	66,169	1,804	64,365	60,826	52,257	8,569	3,539	482	5.3	624	338	1,143	952	3,597	....
1, attached	6,213	41	6,172	5,545	2,936	2,609	627	197	7.0	77	34	209	110	462	....
2 to 4	10,700	124	10,576	9,299	1,734	7,565	1,277	626	7.6	55	98	237	260	161	....
5 to 9	5,594	102	5,492	4,803	520	4,283	690	391	8.3	19	48	167	65	179	....
10 to 19	5,092	93	4,999	4,342	368	3,974	657	369	8.4	14	39	208	27	252	....
20 to 49	3,901	74	3,827	3,244	342	2,903	583	247	7.7	14	56	218	48	127	....
50 or more	4,140	55	4,085	3,470	550	2,920	615	224	7.1	29	42	282	37	80	....
Mobile home or trailer	7,647	761	6,886	6,164	4,837	1,328	722	129	8.8	86	33	293	182	973	7,647
STORIES IN STRUCTURE [2]															
1	3,065	35	3,029	2,678	279	2,399	352	191	7.3	17	28	58	57	94	....
2	10,828	149	10,679	9,318	1,055	8,263	1,361	774	8.5	37	85	353	112	353	....
3	8,268	152	8,115	7,056	1,179	5,877	1,060	497	7.7	34	98	301	129	259	....
4 to 6	4,652	79	4,573	3,904	591	3,312	670	285	7.8	24	54	198	109	70	....
7 or more	2,627	32	2,594	2,213	415	1,799	381	111	5.8	18	19	203	30	25	....
COOPERATIVES AND CONDOMINIUMS															
Cooperatives	772	24	748	639	371	268	109	18	6.4	13	12	57	9	12	50
Condominiums	4,962	286	4,677	3,783	2,736	1,047	894	119	10.1	93	53	587	42	342	14
YEAR STRUCTURE BUILT [3]															
1995 to 1999	986	28	957	810	598	212	148	41	16.1	46	40	8	12	983	146
1990 to 1994	7,573	122	7,452	6,978	5,712	1,266	473	92	6.6	67	59	226	30	4,850	1,249
1985 to 1989	9,033	247	8,786	8,118	5,350	2,768	668	201	6.7	72	55	297	43	....	998
1980 to 1984	8,257	257	8,000	7,295	4,651	2,644	705	188	6.6	80	44	333	59	....	1,001
1975 to 1979	12,314	322	11,992	11,108	7,301	3,806	884	258	6.3	82	55	355	135	....	1,363
1970 to 1974	11,403	462	10,940	9,925	6,046	3,879	1,015	348	8.2	74	85	410	97	....	1,575
1960 to 1969	15,806	472	15,334	14,267	9,349	4,918	1,068	359	6.8	99	82	356	172	....	1,068
1950 to 1959	13,569	371	13,198	12,398	8,798	3,600	800	245	6.3	97	58	207	192	....	210
1940 to 1949	8,400	228	8,172	7,487	4,671	2,817	685	226	7.4	68	44	119	228	....	24
1930 to 1939	6,552	231	6,320	5,744	3,201	2,542	577	195	7.1	61	44	112	164	....	14
1920 to 1929	5,545	86	5,459	4,893	2,828	2,065	566	189	8.3	69	34	102	172	....	-
1919 or earlier	10,019	227	9,792	8,671	5,039	3,632	1,120	324	8.1	102	89	230	374	....	-
Median (Year)	1967	1968	1967	1967	1968	1965	1966	1964	....	1966	1969	1973	1946	....	1978

See notes at end of table.

Current Characteristics of the Housing Stock

TABLE 2.13. SELECTED INTRODUCTORY CHARACTERISTICS OF THE HOUSING STOCK: 1995 - Continued
(In thousands, except as noted)

CHARACTERISTIC	Total housing units	Sea-sonal units	Year-round units Total	Occupied Total	Owner	Renter	Vacant Total	For rent	Rental vacancy rate (Percent)	For sale only	Rented or sold	Occa-sional use/ URE [1]	Other vacant	Con-struct-ed within 4 years	Mobile homes
METROPOLITAN/ NONMETROPOLITAN AREAS															
Inside metropolitan statistical areas	83,349	1,021	82,327	76,107	47,689	28,418	6,220	2,168	7.0	684	546	1,640	1,182	4,381	3,830
In central cities	33,513	128	33,385	30,243	14,808	15,434	3,142	1,294	7.7	277	255	668	648	876	397
Suburbs	49,836	894	48,942	45,864	32,880	12,984	3,078	874	6.3	407	291	972	533	3,505	3,433
Outside metropolitan statistical areas	26,108	2,032	24,076	21,586	15,855	5,731	2,489	498	7.9	233	143	1,117	499	1,451	3,817
REGIONS															
Northeast	21,461	714	20,747	19,200	11,861	7,338	1,548	483	6.1	156	122	452	334	576	651
Midwest	26,056	646	25,410	23,662	16,567	7,096	1,748	555	.7.2	212	152	481	347	1,284	1,374
South	39,148	1,235	37,912	34,236	22,959	11,277	3,677	1,022	8.2	375	256	1,278	746	2,634	4,095
West	22,791	458	22,333	20,596	12,157	8,439	1,738	606	6.6	174	159	545	253	1,339	1,528
URBANIZED AREAS															
Inside urbanized areas	65,791	472	65,318	60,325	35,295	25,030	4,994	1,929	7.1	510	453	1,179	924	3,764	1,459
In central cities of (P)MSAs	32,854	128	32,726	29,654	14,460	15,194	3,072	1,270	7.7	275	239	647	641	849	389
Urban fringe	32,937	344	32,593	30,670	20,834	9,836	1,922	659	6.2	234	214	532	283	2,916	1,071
Outside urbanized areas	43,666	2,582	41,085	37,369	28,249	9,120	3,716	737	7.4	407	237	1,578	757	2,068	6,188
Other urban	12,689	325	12,365	11,226	7,179	4,047	1,139	347	7.8	115	98	390	187	271	666
Rural	30,977	2,257	28,720	26,143	21,070	5,073	2,577	390	7.1	292	138	1,187	570	1,797	5,522
PLACE SIZE															
Less than 2,500 persons	5,152	220	4,932	4,441	3,180	1,261	491	89	6.5	82	28	177	116	202	571
2,500 to 9,999 persons	10,542	317	10,225	9,366	6,411	2,955	859	251	7.8	92	79	282	155	405	674
10,000 to 19,999 persons	9,055	70	8,986	8,360	5,484	2,876	626	198	6.4	61	58	228	80	353	263
20,000 to 49,999 persons	13,599	65	13,534	12,604	7,723	4,881	930	333	6.3	81	83	263	171	491	270
50,000 to 99,999 persons	9,231	24	9,207	8,502	4,882	3,620	705	255	6.5	65	83	185	117	347	186
100,000 to 249,999 persons	8,374	33	8,341	7,638	4,062	3,576	702	285	7.3	81	49	163	124	236	158
250,000 to 499,999 persons	5,634	21	5,613	5,094	2,500	2,595	518	257	9.0	42	33	77	109	160	39
500,000 to 999,999 persons	5,036	22	5,014	4,555	2,277	2,278	459	202	8.1	45	25	69	118	138	34
1,000,000 persons or more	7,185	25	7,161	6,460	2,459	4,001	701	311	7.2	54	65	107	164	83	15

Source: U.S. Bureau of the Census and U.S. Department of Housing and Urban Development, "American Housing Survey for the United States in 1995." Current Housing Reports H150/95RV. Issued

Consistent with the 1990 Census.

(1) URE means usual residence elsewhere. See Appendix A for additional explanation.
(2) Limited to multiunit structures.
(3) For mobile homes, oldest category is 1939 or earlier.
(-) means zero or rounds to zero.

Current Characteristics of the Housing Stock

TABLE 2.14. SIZE OF UNIT AND LOT: 1991
(In thousands, except as noted)

CHARACTERISTIC	Total housing units	Sea-sonal units	Year-round units Total	Occupied Total	Owner	Renter	Vacant Total	For rent	Rental vacancy rate (Percent)	For sale only	Rented or sold	Occa-sional use/ URE [1]	Other vacant	Con-struct-ed within 4 years	Mobile homes
TOTAL	104,592	2,728	101,864	93,147	59,796	33,351	8,717	2,684	7.4	1,026	754	2,611	1,643	5,840	6,983
ROOMS															
1 room	969	105	864	637	37	600	227	101	14.0	2	19	68	37	24	29
2 rooms	1,485	198	1,287	1,020	54	967	267	120	11.0	8	15	79	45	44	71
3 rooms	10,078	452	9,626	8,066	881	7,185	1,560	734	9.2	52	98	439	236	382	473
4 rooms	20,843	972	19,871	17,131	6,284	10,847	2,740	937	7.9	241	190	864	507	957	2,901
5 rooms	23,673	570	23,103	21,189	13,664	7,525	1,913	507	6.2	248	182	548	429	1,218	2,202
6 rooms	20,745	255	20,490	19,465	15,681	3,784	1,025	185	4.6	209	104	296	231	1,194	877
7 rooms	12,986	105	12,882	12,397	10,928	1,469	485	63	4.1	119	61	160	82	758	243
8 rooms	7,781	32	7,749	7,484	6,876	608	265	17	2.7	81	51	74	42	693	126
9 rooms	3,489	22	3,467	3,355	3,122	233	112	14	5.7	25	21	36	16	315	35
10 rooms or more	2,542	16	2,526	2,404	2,270	134	123	4	3.2	41	12	47	18	254	28
Median (Rooms)	5.3	4.1	5.3	5.4	6.1	4.2	4.3	3.9	......	5.3	4.8	4.3	4.5	5.7	4.5
BEDROOMS															
None	1,756	171	1,586	1,220	70	1,151	365	172	12.8	6	28	116	43	50	38
1	14,195	596	13,599	11,510	1,696	9,814	2,089	989	9.1	80	141	570	310	578	594
2	33,869	1,280	32,589	28,871	14,717	14,155	3,718	1,151	7.4	381	294	1,129	763	1,487	3,911
3	39,937	534	39,404	37,492	30,770	6,722	1,911	307	4.3	403	181	602	419	2,534	2,260
4 or more	14,835	148	14,687	14,053	12,544	1,509	634	65	4.1	156	111	195	107	1,191	180
Median (Bedrooms)	2.6	2.0	2.6	2.6	2.9	1.9	2.0	1.7	......	2.6	2.2	2.0	2.1	2.8	2.2
COMPLETE BATHROOMS															
None	1,392	491	901	620	202	418	281	58	11.9	9	17	53	144	35	113
1	51,748	1,487	50,262	44,758	20,417	24,341	5,504	2,092	7.8	435	406	1,406	1,164	1,145	3,646
1 1/2	15,632	238	15,395	14,629	11,182	3,447	766	173	4.7	131	83	235	144	488	855
2 or more	35,819	512	35,307	33,140	27,994	5,146	2,167	361	6.5	451	248	917	190	4,173	2,368
SQUARE FOOTAGE OF UNIT Single detached and mobile homes	69,586	2,281	67,305	63,075	53,586	9,489	4,230	552	5.5	790	395	1,390	1,102	3,935	6,940
Less than 500	1,310	369	941	736	384	353	205	33	8.5	19	11	86	56	24	474
500 to 749	3,426	404	3,022	2,546	1,572	974	477	91	8.5	34	19	172	160	32	1,401
750 to 999	6,790	339	6,451	5,851	4,314	1,537	600	117	7.1	85	38	193	167	228	2,287
1,000 to 1,499	16,101	360	15,741	14,755	12,252	2,503	986	119	4.5	193	104	287	283	729	1,531
1,500 to 1,999	13,775	172	13,603	13,025	11,547	1,478	579	68	4.3	156	77	171	107	866	357
2,000 to 2,499	9,559	59	9,500	9,178	8,475	704	322	23	3.2	75	36	97	91	642	68
2,500 to 2,999	5,158	40	5,118	4,953	4,609	344	165	15	4.0	55	39	33	23	353	14
3,000 to 3,999	4,625	25	4,600	4,413	4,229	184	187	8	3.8	54	29	60	37	351	23
4,000 or more	2,700	16	2,684	2,574	2,373	201	110	8	4.0	35	15	35	17	275	45
Not reported (Includes don't know)	6,141	497	5,644	5,044	3,832	1,212	600	69	5.4	85	27	258	161	435	740
Median (Square feet)	1,649	838	1,672	1,697	1,775	1,255	1,270	998	......	1,571	1,577	1,202	1,154	1,925	884
LOT SIZE															
Less than 1/8 acre	6,708	38	6,669	6,362	5,377	985	307	110	9.9	115	50	32	-	307	1,076
1/8 up to 1/4 acre	12,672	39	12,633	12,216	10,974	1,243	417	107	7.8	200	65	45	-	640	481
1/4 up to 1/2 acre	9,606	34	9,572	9,323	8,573	750	249	55	6.8	96	54	43	-	680	317
1/2 up to 1 acre	7,081	18	7,064	6,926	6,144	782	138	27	3.4	59	26	26	-	519	419
1 to 4 acres	10,121	24	10,098	9,883	8,883	1,001	215	49	4.6	93	31	42	-	796	1,173
5 to 9 acres	1,719	5	1,714	1,673	1,507	166	41	10	5.5	20	3	8	-	139	260
10 acres or more	3,848	18	3,830	3,729	3,170	559	101	20	3.4	36	19	26	-	174	453
Don't know	18,070	38	18,031	17,052	10,497	6,555	979	419	5.9	233	204	124	-	815	1,697
Not reported	1,415	20	1,394	1,353	1,184	169	41	15	8.1	5	1	20	-	143	54
Median (Acres)	0.42	0.33	0.42	0.42	0.42	0.42	0.26	0.22	......	0.25	0.29	0.45	......	0.50	0.76

Source: U.S. Bureau of the Census and U.S. Department of Housing and Urban Development, "American Housing Survey for the United States in 1991." Current Housing Reports H150/91. Issued April 1993.

Consistent with the 1990 Census.
(-) means zero or rounds to zero.

(1) URE means usual residence elsewhere. See Appendix A for additional explanation.

Current Characteristics of the Housing Stock

TABLE 2.15. SIZE OF UNIT AND LOT: 1993
(In thousands, except as noted)

| CHARACTERISTIC | Total housing units | Sea-sonal units | Year-round units | | | | | | | | | | | Con-struct-ed within 4 years | Mobile homes |
| | | | Total | Occupied | | | Vacant | | | | | | | | |
				Total	Owner	Renter	Total	For rent	Rental vacancy rate (Percent)	For sale only	Rented or sold	Occa-sional use/ URE [1]	Other vacant		
TOTAL	106,611	3,088	103,522	94,724	61,252	33,472	8,799	2,651	7.3	889	882	2,506	1,870	5,605	7,072
ROOMS															
1 room	951	137	814	611	19	592	203	95	13.8	3	4	55	45	6	33
2 rooms	1,432	178	1,253	989	62	928	264	123	11.6	2	13	76	50	26	63
3 rooms	9,966	477	9,489	7,959	836	7,123	1,530	725	9.1	47	120	366	272	274	382
4 rooms	21,097	1,114	19,983	17,221	6,280	10,941	2,763	963	8.0	200	239	799	562	827	2,935
5 rooms	23,609	676	22,933	21,030	13,534	7,496	1,904	479	5.9	220	193	576	436	1,249	2,190
6 rooms	21,314	307	21,008	19,870	15,988	3,882	1,138	172	4.2	176	144	349	296	1,157	967
7 rooms	13,714	122	13,592	13,083	11,553	1,529	509	62	3.8	119	72	140	116	883	376
8 rooms	8,015	33	7,982	7,683	7,043	640	299	23	3.4	88	48	75	65	579	89
9 rooms	3,876	33	3,842	3,738	3,531	207	104	5	2.4	16	24	43	16	354	17
10 rooms or more	2,637	12	2,625	2,541	2,406	134	85	4	2.8	18	25	27	11	250	20
Median (Rooms)	5.3	4.2	5.4	5.5	6.1	4.2	4.4	3.9	....	5.4	4.8	4.4	4.5	5.9	4.6
BEDROOMS															
None	1,670	200	1,470	1,129	45	1,083	342	167	13.2	3	12	94	64	19	33
1	13,958	620	13,338	11,279	1,657	9,622	2,059	966	9.0	79	159	494	360	420	585
2	34,101	1,423	32,678	28,965	14,523	14,442	3,713	1,157	7.3	298	344	1,128	787	1,340	3,953
3	41,216	656	40,560	38,504	31,718	6,786	2,057	300	4.2	387	245	594	530	2,672	2,311
4 or more	15,666	190	15,476	14,848	13,309	1,539	628	61	3.7	121	122	196	129	1,154	189
Median (Bedrooms)	2.6	2.0	2.6	2.7	3.0	1.9	2.0	1.7	....	2.7	2.3	2.1	2.1	2.9	2.2
COMPLETE BATHROOMS															
None	1,291	462	828	526	171	354	303	44	10.9	26	9	73	151	21	108
1	51,050	1,677	49,373	43,944	19,604	24,339	5,429	2,068	7.7	377	465	1,258	1,262	924	3,499
1 1/2	15,821	274	15,547	14,740	11,345	3,395	807	188	5.2	132	85	259	144	485	864
2 or more	38,449	675	37,774	35,515	30,131	5,384	2,259	352	6.0	353	324	917	313	4,176	2,599
SQUARE FOOTAGE OF UNIT															
Single detached and mobile	71,355	2,471	68,884	64,574	54,972	9,601	4,311	495	4.9	693	446	1,416	1,261	4,181	7,072
Less than 500	1,275	360	915	697	395	302	218	35	10.5	5	7	97	73	29	478
500 to 749	3,311	445	2,866	2,381	1,425	956	486	81	7.8	52	15	158	179	14	1,335
750 to 999	6,688	377	6,311	5,704	4,158	1,546	607	91	5.5	72	54	178	212	247	2,226
1,000 to 1,499	16,417	398	16,019	15,084	12,398	2,686	935	102	3.6	165	97	297	275	755	1,572
1,500 to 1,999	14,235	212	14,024	13,414	11,888	1,526	609	58	3.6	128	90	178	155	886	425
2,000 to 2,499	10,127	79	10,048	9,653	8,923	730	395	32	4.1	104	49	114	95	682	104
2,500 to 2,999	5,585	34	5,551	5,374	5,012	361	177	6	1.7	36	35	57	43	436	19
3,000 to 3,999	4,971	31	4,940	4,799	4,545	254	141	10	3.9	39	21	41	31	343	30
4,000 or more	2,832	20	2,812	2,688	2,504	184	124	3	1.7	32	23	33	33	282	35
Not reported															
(Includes don't know)	5,913	515	5,398	4,780	3,723	1,057	618	77	6.7	60	55	262	164	507	847
Median (Square feet)	1,677	865	1,701	1,725	1,805	1,273	1,286	1,008	....	1,590	1,624	1,241	1,152	1,947	896
LOT SIZE															
Less than 1/8 acre	6,915	63	6,851	6,608	5,656	952	244	80	7.6	95	32	37	-	274	974
1/8 to 1/4 acre	12,415	41	12,374	11,976	10,876	1,099	398	102	8.4	165	81	49	-	714	512
1/4 to 1/2 acre	10,089	59	10,030	9,830	9,094	736	200	36	4.6	82	42	39	-	699	261
1/2 to 1 acre	7,165	49	7,117	6,958	6,291	667	159	32	4.5	41	47	39	-	479	383
1 to 4 acres	10,733	48	10,685	10,519	9,329	1,190	166	23	1.9	61	45	37	-	806	1,220
5 to 9 acres	1,669	3	1,667	1,633	1,518	115	34	12	9.6	10	11	-	-	142	252
10 acres or more	3,710	28	3,682	3,621	3,066	555	61	5	0.9	14	12	30	-	194	389
Don't know	14,120	95	14,025	13,186	7,737	5,449	838	303	5.2	227	182	126	-	901	1,718
Not reported	5,871	18	5,853	5,603	4,218	1,385	249	94	6.4	67	49	39	-	213	258
Median (Acres)	0.42	0.42	0.42	0.43	0.43	0.46	0.25	0.21	....	0.23	0.38	0.44	....	0.49	0.82

Source: U.S. Bureau of the Census and U.S. Department of Housing and Urban Development, "American Housing Survey for the United States in 1993." Current Housing Reports H150/93. Issued February 1995.

Consistent with the 1990 Census.
(-) means zero or rounds to zero.
(1) URE means usual residence elsewhere. See Appendix A for additional explanation.

Current Characteristics of the Housing Stock

TABLE 2.16. SIZE OF UNIT AND LOT: 1995
(In thousands, except as noted)

CHARACTERISTIC	Total housing units	Sea-sonal units	Year-round units											Con-struct-ed within 4 years	Mobile homes
				Occupied			Vacant								
			Total	Total	Owner	Renter	Total	For rent	Rental vacancy rate (Percent)	For sale only	Rented or sold	Occa-sional use/ URE [1]	Other vacant		
TOTAL	109,457	3,054	106,403	97,693	63,544	34,150	8,710	2,666	7.2	917	690	2,757	1,681	5,832	7,647
ROOMS															
1 room	862	104	758	550	22	528	208	97	15.5	10	3	40	58	8	30
2 rooms	1,422	215	1,207	958	60	898	249	100	9.9	5	13	95	36	16	69
3 rooms	10,166	484	9,682	8,311	859	7,452	1,371	667	8.2	42	71	366	225	229	455
4 rooms	20,789	1,070	19,718	17,062	6,069	10,993	2,656	927	7.7	205	180	852	493	654	2,883
5 rooms	24,328	660	23,668	21,600	13,895	7,705	2,068	555	6.7	209	147	724	433	1,250	2,481
6 rooms	22,151	327	21,824	20,700	16,686	4,014	1,125	209	4.9	196	114	349	256	1,370	1,108
7 rooms	14,183	88	14,096	13,560	12,007	1,554	536	68	4.2	124	77	175	92	1,014	461
8 rooms	8,381	59	8,321	8,041	7,447	594	280	33	5.2	63	51	94	40	607	103
9 rooms	4,110	15	4,096	3,984	3,734	250	111	7	2.8	28	12	37	28	366	42
10 rooms or more	3,064	32	3,032	2,927	2,765	162	105	2	1.4	36	23	24	20	317	14
Median (Rooms)	5.4	4.2	5.4	5.5	6.2	4.2	4.5	4.0	....	5.4	5.0	4.5	4.6	6.1	4.7
BEDROOMS															
None	1,519	147	1,373	1,047	52	995	325	157	13.6	10	8	80	69	16	39
1	14,334	639	13,695	11,777	1,734	10,043	1,918	890	8.1	62	120	529	317	347	631
2	34,260	1,446	32,814	29,146	14,532	14,613	3,668	1,165	7.3	313	255	1,215	719	1,277	3,991
3	43,071	650	42,421	40,302	33,332	6,970	2,118	396	5.3	378	198	715	430	2,972	2,815
4 or more	16,273	171	16,102	15,421	13,894	1,528	680	57	3.6	154	108	217	145	1,219	172
Median (Bedrooms)	2.6	2.0	2.6	2.7	3.0	1.9	2.1	1.7	....	2.7	2.3	2.1	2.1	2.9	2.3
COMPLETE BATHROOMS															
None	1,201	468	733	465	195	270	268	49	14.9	27	12	55	125	16	107
1	50,700	1,703	48,996	43,777	19,069	24,709	5,219	2,027	7.5	366	355	1,298	1,173	751	3,528
1 1/2	15,887	237	15,650	14,780	11,319	3,461	870	232	6.2	123	74	315	126	368	834
2 or more	41,669	645	41,023	38,671	32,961	5,710	2,353	358	5.9	400	249	1,089	256	4,696	3,178
SQUARE FOOTAGE OF UNIT															
Single detached and mobile homes	73,816	2,564	71,252	66,990	57,094	9,897	4,261	611	5.8	710	371	1,435	1,134	4,570	7,647
Less than 500	1,242	360	882	667	379	288	216	40	12.0	12	7	99	58	43	452
500 to 749	3,293	483	2,811	2,356	1,386	969	455	88	8.3	44	26	151	146	59	1,327
750 to 999	6,676	393	6,283	5,697	4,126	1,571	586	114	6.7	95	31	160	186	183	2,222
1,000 to 1,499	16,741	406	16,335	15,450	12,697	2,753	885	120	4.1	155	78	296	237	917	1,860
1,500 to 1,999	14,576	202	14,374	13,785	12,218	1,567	589	74	4.5	128	57	201	129	960	573
2,000 to 2,499	10,344	69	10,275	9,943	9,211	732	333	28	3.6	79	42	114	70	693	105
2,500 to 2,999	5,739	39	5,700	5,486	5,147	339	214	19	5.4	43	28	73	51	450	34
3,000 to 3,999	5,178	55	5,123	4,956	4,737	219	167	9	4.0	32	30	53	44	440	34
4,000 or more	2,938	31	2,907	2,785	2,597	189	121	2	0.9	33	21	36	29	285	27
Not reported (Includes don't know)	7,089	527	6,561	5,867	4,596	1,271	695	118	8.5	88	53	252	184	540	1,014
Median (Square feet)	1,686	862	1,710	1,732	1,814	1,270	1,297	1,020	....	1,516	1,661	1,307	1,179	1,924	923
LOT SIZE															
Less than 1/8 acre	6,497	-	6,497	6,292	5,367	924	205	82	8.1	80	33	10	-	332	916
1/8 to 1/4 acre	12,519	-	12,519	12,184	11,077	1,107	335	97	7.9	167	68	3	-	791	526
1/4 to 1/2 acre	10,245	-	10,245	10,077	9,303	774	168	50	6.0	73	37	8	-	780	351
1/2 to 1 acre	7,505	-	7,505	7,394	6,656	738	111	33	4.2	46	26	6	-	562	520
1 to 4 acres	10,608	-	10,608	10,450	9,398	1,051	158	52	4.7	56	40	10	-	814	1,294
5 to 9 acres	1,748	-	1,748	1,713	1,574	139	35	5	3.6	27	3	-	-	124	298
10 acres or more	3,716	-	3,716	3,670	3,185	485	46	14	2.8	15	14	4	-	226	416
Don't know	14,985	-	14,985	14,239	8,539	5,700	746	317	5.2	236	129	65	-	922	1,692
Not reported	7,337	153	7,184	6,503	4,921	1,582	681	159	9.1	86	56	381	-	338	504
Median (Acres)	0.43	....	0.43	0.43	0.43	0.44	0.25	0.23	....	0.24	0.32	0.49	....	0.47	0.85

Source: U.S. Bureau of the Census and U.S. Department of Housing and Urban Development, "American Housing Survey for the United States in 1995." Current Housing Reports H150/95RV. Issued July

Consistent with the 1990 Census.
(-) means zero or rounds to zero.
(1) URE means usual residence elsewhere. See Appendix A for additional explanation.

Current Characteristics of the Housing Stock

TABLE 2.17. UNIT, BUILDING, AND NEIGHBORHOOD CONDITIONS: 1991
(In thousands, except as noted)

CONDITION	Total housing units	Sea-sonal units	Year-round units											Con-struct-ed within 4 years	Mobile homes
			Total	Occupied			Vacant								
				Total	Owner	Renter	Total	For rent	Rental vacancy rate (Percent)	For sale only	Rented or sold	Occa-sional use/ URE[1]	Other vacant		
TOTAL	104,592	2,728	101,864	93,147	59,796	33,351	8,717	2,684	7.4	1,026	754	2,611	1,643	5,840	6,983
BUILDING CONDITIONS															
External building conditions [2, 3]															
Sagging roof	132	2	130	93	7	86	37	15	14.8	-	-	-	23	-	...
Missing roofing material	144	2	142	104	14	91	38	7	7.1	-	8	5	18	-	...
Hole in roof	29	-	29	26	5	21	3	-	-	-	-	-	3	-	...
Could not see roof	2,851	36	2,815	2,371	278	2,092	444	214	9.2	15	31	121	63	65	...
Missing bricks, siding, other outside wall material	484	2	482	369	29	340	113	65	15.8	2	9	12	26	2	...
Sloping outside walls	72	-	72	56	6	51	15	13	20.8	-	-	-	2	-	...
Boarded up windows	369	2	367	241	3	238	125	56	18.7	11	11	2	44	-	...
Broken windows	438	2	435	295	10	285	140	79	21.5	4	10	12	35	-	...
Bars on windows	567	-	567	492	59	433	74	40	8.4	8	7	5	13	3	...
Foundation crumbling or has open crack or hole	406	7	399	309	20	289	90	46	13.5	2	8	7	28	-	...
Could not see foundation	1,073	2	1,071	897	108	789	174	88	10.0	10	8	35	32	11	...
None of the above	21,199	267	20,932	18,313	2,545	15,768	2,618	1,313	7.6	111	225	723	247	1,224	...
Could not observe or not reported	3,647	59	3,588	3,041	553	2,488	547	231	8.5	28	18	192	78	137	...
UNIT CONDITIONS															
Kitchen facilities															
Lacking complete kitchen facilities	3,622	337	3,285	957	329	628	2,328	628	46.8	531	246	154	769	220	218
With complete kitchen (Sink, refrigerator, and burners)	100,970	2,391	98,579	92,190	59,467	32,723	6,389	2,056	5.9	495	508	2,457	873	5,620	6,765
Plumbing															
With all plumbing facilities	101,197	2,182	99,015	90,869	58,471	32,398	8,146	2,536	7.2	960	711	2,500	1,439	5,684	6,677
Lacking some plumbing facilities [3]	489	151	338	233	72	161	105	29	15.1	3	6	14	52	14	38
No hot piped water	104	39	65	38	23	14	27	-	-	2	2	2	22	5	3
No bathtub nor shower	420	136	284	194	51	143	90	29	16.5	2	6	12	41	7	28
No flush toilet	242	57	185	133	25	108	52	21	16.2	2	2	4	22	7	29
No plumbing facilities for exclusive use	2,905	394	2,511	2,045	1,253	792	466	119	12.8	62	37	97	151	143	267
Selected deficiencies [3]															
Holes in floors	1,489	96	1,392	1,139	465	674	253	42	5.8	17	16	27	151	9	178
Open cracks or holes (Interior)	5,700	222	5,478	4,705	2,016	2,689	773	144	5.1	58	44	108	419	87	308
Broken plaster or peeling paint (Interior)	4,751	136	4,615	3,847	1,808	2,039	768	149	6.8	68	43	108	400	21	169
No electrical wiring	161	95	67	31	26	4	36	1	25.0	-	2	4	28	13	15
Exposed wiring	1,813	160	1,653	1,491	660	831	162	12	1.5	10	19	24	96	64	86
Rooms without electric outlets	2,021	135	1,886	1,637	824	813	250	23	2.7	37	7	27	157	51	107

See notes at end of table.

Current Characteristics of the Housing Stock

TABLE 2.17. UNIT, BUILDING, AND NEIGHBORHOOD CONDITIONS: 1991 - Continued
(In thousands, except as noted)

| CONDITION | Total housing units | Sea-sonal units | Year-round units | | | | | | | | | | | Con-struct-ed within 4 years | Mobile homes |
| | | | Total | Occupied | | | Vacant | | | | | | | | |
				Total	Owner	Renter	Total	For rent	Rental vacancy rate (Percent)	For sale only	Rented or sold	Occa-sional use/ URE [1]	Other vacant		
NEIGHBORHOOD CONDITIONS															
Other buildings vandalized or with interior exposed [2]															
None	23,732	302	23,429	20,373	2,833	17,540	3,056	1,494	7.8	133	259	866	303	1,239	25
1 building	443	-	443	383	34	349	60	31	8.1	4	3	3	19	7	-
More than 1 building	840	10	829	670	71	599	160	88	12.7	6	16	5	45	9	-
No buildings within 300 feet	419	2	417	360	48	312	57	28	8.3	-	4	12	13	51	-
Not reported	3,399	58	3,340	2,825	488	2,337	515	230	8.9	27	18	166	74	125	-
Bars on windows of buildings [2] With other buildings within 300 feet	25,014	313	24,701	21,426	2,938	18,488	3,275	1,614	7.9	143	278	874	367	1,254	25
No bars on windows	20,994	290	20,704	17,943	2,543	15,400	2,761	1,325	7.8	112	243	812	269	1,168	22
1 building with bars	679	-	679	608	68	539	71	42	7.1	6	3	13	8	18	-
2 or more buildings with bars	3,167	21	3,147	2,729	305	2,424	418	229	8.6	24	30	45	90	61	2
Not reported	173	2	172	146	21	125	25	17	12.0	-	3	5	-	7	-
Condition of streets [2]															
No repairs needed	19,285	277	19,008	16,506	2,344	14,162	2,502	1,241	8.0	114	187	693	267	1,134	15
Minor repairs needed	5,623	35	5,588	4,802	578	4,224	786	397	8.4	27	94	161	108	145	4
Major repairs needed	559	3	555	479	68	410	76	37	8.2	6	5	20	8	18	6
No streets within 300 feet	367	11	356	305	48	258	51	17	6.1	-	-	30	4	31	-
Not reported	2,998	47	2,951	2,519	436	2,083	433	181	7.9	22	15	148	67	103	-
Trash, litter, or junk on streets or any properties [2]															
None	18,493	273	18,220	15,764	2,513	13,251	2,456	1,146	7.9	114	196	755	244	1,207	14
Minor accumulation	6,702	49	6,653	5,810	494	5,315	844	495	8.4	24	71	132	122	121	10
Major accumulation	678	2	675	554	35	519	121	52	8.9	8	21	19	22	8	-
Not reported	2,959	49	2,910	2,484	431	2,053	426	179	8.0	22	13	146	66	95	-

Source: U.S. Bureau of the Census and U.S. Department of Housing and Urban Development, "American Housing Survey for the United States in 1991." Current Housing Reports H150/91. Issued April 1993.

Consistent with the 1990 Census.

(-) means zero or rounds to zero.

(1) URE means usual residence elsewhere. See Appendix A for additional explanation.

(2) Limited to multiunit structures.

(3) Figures may not add to total because more than one category may apply.

Current Characteristics of the Housing Stock

| | | | Year-round units | | | | | | | | | | | Con-struct-ed within 4 years | Mobile homes |
| | | | | Occupied | | | Vacant | | | | | | | | |
CONDITION	Total housing units	Sea-sonal units	Total	Total	Owner	Renter	Total	For rent	Rental vacancy rate (Percent)	For sale only	Rented or sold	Occa-sional use/ URE [1]	Other vacant		
TOTAL	106,611	3,088	103,522	94,724	61,252	33,472	8,799	2,651	7.3	889	882	2,506	1,870	5,605	7,072
BUILDING CONDITIONS															
External building conditions [2,3]															
Sagging roof	115	-	115	87	9	79	27	14	15.5	2	-	-	11	-	....
Missing roofing material	199	11	187	143	22	121	44	15	10.8	4	-	2	23	-	....
Hole in roof	34	-	34	24	2	22	10	2	7.2	2	-	-	6	-	....
Could not see roof	3,492	13	3,479	2,958	419	2,538	521	266	9.4	11	49	97	99	36	....
Missing bricks, siding, other outside wall material	550	2	548	409	34	375	139	71	15.4	4	19	-	45	3	....
Sloping outside walls	85	-	85	64	4	60	21	6	8.4	-	-	5	11	-	....
Boarded up windows	286	-	286	161	12	149	126	56	27.4	5	3	-	60	-	....
Broken windows	384	4	380	256	8	248	124	68	21.3	6	6	-	43	-	....
Bars on windows	589	-	589	515	70	445	74	40	8.1	-	11	14	10	4	....
Foundation crumbling or has open crack or hole	413	-	413	326	23	303	87	44	12.3	6	7	2	28	-	....
Could not see foundation	1,295	7	1,288	1,068	219	849	220	94	9.8	2	19	57	48	25	....
None of the above	22,382	399	21,983	19,136	2,623	16,513	2,847	1,431	7.9	95	279	759	283	883	....
Could not observe or not reported	2,266	78	2,188	1,857	321	1,537	331	170	9.8	12	32	60	57	83	....
UNIT CONDITIONS															
Kitchen facilities															
Lacking complete kitchen facilities	3,757	325	3,431	1,107	461	647	2,324	627	47.1	415	261	140	881	183	165
With complete kitchen (Sink, refrigerator, and burners)	102,854	2,763	100,091	93,617	60,791	32,826	6,475	2,024	5.7	474	621	2,366	989	5,422	6,907
Plumbing															
With all plumbing facilities	104,302	2,594	101,708	93,345	60,441	32,905	8,363	2,550	7.1	853	871	2,401	1,688	5,547	6,899
Lacking some plumbing facilities [3]	455	131	324	227	60	167	97	18	9.5	2	5	28	44	4	55
No hot piped water	146	51	95	57	30	28	37	-	-	-	-	11	26	3	30
No bathtub nor shower	367	111	256	181	31	151	75	18	10.4	2	4	21	30	-	35
No flush toilet	208	30	178	131	28	103	47	12	10.4	-	5	10	20	4	19
No plumbing facilities for exclusive use	1,854	364	1,490	1,152	751	401	338	83	17.1	34	6	77	138	55	118
Selected deficiencies [3]															
Holes in floors	1,535	68	1,467	1,148	469	678	319	53	7.2	26	6	32	202	13	195
Open cracks or holes (Interior)	5,513	223	5,290	4,542	1,842	2,699	748	150	5.3	75	34	74	415	70	315
Broken plaster or peeling paint (Interior)	4,525	132	4,392	3,597	1,615	1,982	795	171	7.9	72	23	85	444	16	185
No electrical wiring	147	83	63	21	19	2	43	-	-	2	-	14	27	6	2
Exposed wiring	2,069	199	1,870	1,603	794	808	268	34	4.1	26	14	30	164	41	107
Rooms without electric outlets	2,162	104	2,059	1,721	808	913	338	25	2.7	29	6	49	229	52	122

See notes at end of table.

Current Characteristics of the Housing Stock

TABLE 2.18. UNIT, BUILDING, AND NEIGHBORHOOD CONDITIONS: 1993 - Continued
(In thousands, except as noted)

| CONDITION | Total housing units | Sea-sonal units | Year-round units | | | | | | | | | | | Con-struct-ed within 4 years | Mobile homes |
| | | | | Occupied | | | Vacant | | | | | | | | |
			Total	Total	Owner	Renter	Total	For rent	Rental vacancy rate (Percent)	For sale only	Rented or sold	Occa-sional use/ URE [1]	Other vacant		
NEIGHBORHOOD CONDITIONS															
Other buildings vandalized or with interior exposed [2]															
None	24,915	453	24,463	21,228	3,006	18,222	3,235	1,591	7.9	95	339	853	356	879	9
1 building	489	-	489	418	39	379	71	38	9.0	8	3	3	20	2	-
More than 1 building	1,008	4	1,005	821	44	776	184	105	11.8	7	5	5	62	9	-
No buildings within 300 feet	502	3	500	419	61	358	80	47	11.4	4	7	9	13	39	-
Not reported	2,271	45	2,226	1,898	309	1,589	327	180	10.0	11	26	61	49	80	-
Bars on windows of buildings [2]															
With other buildings within 300 feet	26,413	456	25,956	22,467	3,090	19,377	3,490	1,734	8.1	111	347	861	438	891	9
No bars on windows	21,909	432	21,478	18,538	2,577	15,961	2,939	1,433	8.1	96	302	774	334	852	9
1 building with bars	613	-	613	527	68	460	85	33	6.6	-	7	20	25	8	-
2 or more buildings with bars	3,749	18	3,731	3,286	426	2,859	446	257	8.2	14	35	64	76	28	-
Not reported	141	7	135	115	19	97	19	11	9.8	2	2	2	2	2	-
Condition of streets [2]															
No repairs needed	20,452	404	20,047	17,379	2,623	14,756	2,668	1,261	7.8	92	273	726	316	815	9
Minor repairs needed	5,701	41	5,660	4,863	497	4,366	797	453	9.3	30	66	135	114	107	-
Major repairs needed	686	6	680	589	37	552	91	55	9.0	-	4	7	25	14	-
No streets within 300 feet	536	16	520	453	54	399	67	38	8.6	-	14	15	-	18	-
Not reported	1,811	37	1,774	1,500	249	1,251	274	154	10.8	3	24	47	45	56	-
Trash, litter, or junk on streets or any properties [2]															
None	19,719	407	19,313	16,853	2,685	14,168	2,460	1,160	7.5	80	265	709	247	868	9
Minor accumulation	6,824	61	6,764	5,725	487	5,238	1,039	569	9.7	35	92	164	179	80	-
Major accumulation	838	-	838	720	37	683	117	81	10.6	4	-	1	31	6	-
Not reported	1,805	37	1,768	1,487	251	1,235	281	150	10.7	6	24	57	44	56	-

Source: U.S. Bureau of the Census and U.S. Department of Housing and Urban Development, "American Housing Survey for theb United States in 1993." Current Housing Reports H150/93. Issued February 1995.

Consistent with the 1990 Census.

(-) means zero or rounds to zero.

(1) URE means usual residence elsewhere. See Appendix A for additional explanation.

(2) Limited to multiunit structures.

(3) Figures may not add to total because more than one category may apply.

Current Characteristics of the Housing Stock

TABLE 2.19. UNIT, BUILDING, AND NEIGHBORHOOD CONDITIONS: 1995
(In thousands, except as noted)

| CONDITION | Total housing units | Sea-sonal units | Year-round units | | | | | | | | | | | Con-struct-ed within 4 years | Mobile homes |
| | | | Total | Occupied | | | Vacant | | | | | | | | |
				Total	Owner	Renter	Total	For rent	Rental vacancy rate (Percent)	For sale only	Rented or sold	Occa-sional use/ URE [1]	Other vacant		
TOTAL	109,457	3,054	106,403	97,693	63,544	34,150	8,710	2,666	7.2	917	690	2,757	1,681	5,832	7,647
BUILDING CONDITIONS															
External building conditions [2,3]															
Sagging roof	115	17	98	69	5	64	28	14	17.7	4	-	1	9	-	...
Missing roofing material	169	13	156	120	13	108	36	15	12.0	4	1	5	10	-	...
Hole in roof	33	13	20	12	2	10	7	4	26.2	-	-	-	4	-	...
Could not see roof	3,458	39	3,419	2,959	358	2,601	460	220	7.8	21	20	125	75	20	...
Missing bricks, siding, other outside wall material	561	20	541	406	27	379	135	60	13.6	10	1	7	57	5	...
Sloping outside walls	88	17	70	53	2	51	18	9	15.4	-	-	4	5	-	...
Boarded up windows	257	16	241	146	4	142	95	41	22.5	6	1	2	46	-	...
Broken windows	369	13	355	232	13	219	124	65	23.0	9	-	6	43	2	...
Bars on windows	606	3	603	539	71	468	65	36	7.0	2	8	6	13	4	...
Foundation crumbling or has open crack or hole	355	17	337	267	23	244	70	38	13.2	-	3	6	23	3	...
Could not see foundation	981	4	977	838	121	717	139	69	8.7	6	5	17	41	5	...
None of the above	22,479	312	22,167	19,402	2,743	16,659	2,765	1,388	7.6	92	228	826	230	710	...
Could not observe or not reported	2,400	77	2,323	1,919	308	1,611	403	159	8.9	9	26	153	56	53	...
UNIT CONDITIONS															
Kitchen facilities															
Lacking complete kitchen facilities	3,629	391	3,238	1,075	461	614	2,163	628	48.8	420	183	131	801	137	196
With complete kitchen (sink, refrigerator, and burners)	105,827	2,662	103,165	96,618	63,083	33,536	6,546	2,038	5.7	497	507	2,626	880	5,695	7,451
Plumbing															
With all plumbing facilities	106,942	2,532	104,410	96,234	62,572	33,663	8,176	2,510	6.9	865	650	2,627	1,524	5,774	7,451
Lacking some plumbing facilities [3]	424	136	288	188	80	107	100	20	15.3	9	7	10	55	13	38
No hot piped water	127	52	75	42	26	16	33	-	-	4	4	2	23	5	24
No bathtub nor shower	315	100	215	141	49	93	74	20	17.3	4	4	8	38	9	18
No flush toilet	202	60	142	85	24	62	56	14	17.9	7	3	6	27	10	20
No plumbing facilities for exclusive use	2,091	386	1,705	1,271	892	380	434	136	25.7	43	33	119	102	45	158
Selected deficiencies [3]															
Holes in floors	1,483	100	1,383	1,074	503	571	309	50	8.0	31	3	39	187	25	239
Open cracks or holes (Interior)	5,574	259	5,316	4,527	1,943	2,584	789	168	6.1	70	25	117	409	89	412
Broken plaster or peeling paint (Interior)	4,641	193	4,448	3,673	1,672	2,002	775	153	7.1	88	31	79	424	39	176
No electrical wiring	163	101	62	26	22	4	36	-	-	2	-	9	25	-	25
Exposed wiring	2,161	189	1,971	1,760	873	887	212	32	3.5	20	17	36	107	41	131
Rooms without electric outlets	2,240	141	2,099	1,816	891	925	283	47	4.8	26	12	42	157	47	170

See notes at end of table.

Current Characteristics of the Housing Stock

TABLE 2.19. UNIT, BUILDING, AND NEIGHBORHOOD CONDITIONS: 1995 - Continued
(In thousands, except as noted)

| CONDITION | Total housing units | Sea-sonal units | Year-round units | | | | | | | | | | | Con-struct-ed within 4 years | Mobile homes |
| | | | Total | Occupied | | | Vacant | | | | | | | | |
				Total	Owner	Renter	Total	For rent	Rental vacancy rate (Percent)	For sale only	Rented or sold	Occa-sional use/ URE [1]	Other vacant		
NEIGHBORHOOD CONDITIONS															
Other buildings vandalized or with interior exposed [2]															
None	25,577	350	25,228	22,065	3,070	18,995	3,162	1,531	7.4	113	250	932	336	711	12
1 building	548	19	530	443	44	399	87	54	11.8	4	7	4	18	4	-
More than 1 building	813	-	813	664	64	601	149	93	13.3	6	7	3	40	2	-
No buildings within 300 feet	480	6	474	390	59	332	84	30	8.2	1	11	31	10	32	-
Not reported	2,021	74	1,947	1,606	283	1,322	341	148	10.0	6	10	143	34	50	-
Bars on windows of buildings [2]															
With other buildings within 300 feet	26,938	369	26,570	23,172	3,177	19,995	3,398	1,679	7.7	123	263	940	393	717	12
No bars on windows	22,751	353	22,398	19,514	2,729	16,785	2,884	1,371	7.5	107	225	880	300	669	10
1 building with bars	616	2	615	544	79	465	70	43	8.4	-	8	13	6	9	-
2 or more buildings with bars	3,387	14	3,373	2,948	358	2,590	425	253	8.8	16	31	38	87	31	2
Not reported	184	-	184	166	11	155	18	11	6.6	-	-	7	-	9	-
Condition of streets [2]															
No repairs needed	20,798	327	20,471	17,909	2,676	15,233	2,562	1,215	7.3	102	224	759	263	664	9
Minor repairs needed	5,916	46	5,871	5,039	509	4,530	831	447	8.9	18	45	201	121	65	2
Major repairs needed	592	4	589	520	59	460	69	37	7.4	3	2	8	19	10	-
No streets within 300 feet	341	-	341	295	18	277	45	22	7.2	2	5	14	3	13	-
Not reported	1,792	72	1,720	1,405	257	1,149	315	137	10.6	6	9	131	31	48	-
Trash, litter, or junk on streets or any properties [2]															
None	20,142	325	19,817	17,367	2,754	14,614	2,450	1,106	7.0	105	205	821	214	664	12
Minor accumulation	6,782	34	6,748	5,808	462	5,346	940	543	9.1	18	62	150	166	80	-
Major accumulation	752	17	734	609	62	547	125	76	12.0	2	8	14	25	7	-
Not reported	1,763	72	1,691	1,384	242	1,142	308	133	10.4	5	9	128	32	48	-

Source: U.S. Bureau of the Census and U.S. Department of Housing and Urban Development, "American Housing Survey for the United States in 1995." Current Housing Reports H150/95RV.

Consistent with the 1990 Census.

(-) means zero or rounds to zero.

(1) URE means usual residence elsewhere. See Appendix A for additional explanation.

(2) Limited to multiunit structures.

(3) Figures may not add to total because more than one category may apply.

Current Characteristics of the Housing Stock

TABLE 2.20. SELECTED INTRODUCTORY CHARACTERISTICS OF OCCUPIED HOUSING UNITS: 1991

(In thousands, except as noted)

CHARACTERISTIC	Total occupied units	Tenure		Household characteristics					Regions			
		Owner	Renter	Black	Hispanic	Elderly (65+)	Moved in past year	Below poverty level	Northeast	Midwest	South	West
TOTAL	93,147	59,796	33,351	10,832	6,239	20,348	16,434	12,836	18,962	22,593	32,190	19,402
TENURE												
Owner-occupied	59,796	59,796	...	4,635	2,423	15,734	4,204	4,994	11,869	15,238	21,272	11,417
Percent of all occupied	64.2	100.0	...	42.8	38.8	77.3	25.6	38.9	62.6	67.4	66.1	58.8
Renter-occupied	33,351	...	33,351	6,197	3,816	4,613	12,230	7,843	7,093	7,355	10,918	7,985
RACE AND HISPANIC ORIGIN												
White	79,140	53,749	25,391	...	5,515	18,253	13,235	8,978	16,349	20,021	25,898	16,872
Non-Hispanic	73,625	51,465	22,160	...	...	17,632	11,787	7,674	15,505	19,669	24,060	14,390
Hispanic	5,515	2,284	3,231	...	5,515	621	1,448	1,304	844	352	1,838	2,482
Black	10,832	4,635	6,197	10,832	198	1,839	2,300	3,236	1,927	2,149	5,790	965
Other	3,175	1,412	1,763	...	526	256	899	622	686	423	502	1,564
Total Hispanic	6,239	2,423	3,816	198	6,239	669	1,720	1,501	1,140	414	1,977	2,708
UNITS IN STRUCTURE												
1, detached	57,485	49,084	8,401	5,002	2,846	13,571	5,904	5,797	9,761	15,092	20,954	11,678
1, attached	5,442	2,722	2,720	1,054	368	1,040	1,331	785	1,544	923	1,814	1,161
2 to 4	9,490	1,909	7,581	1,649	1,023	1,558	2,820	2,037	3,211	2,409	2,119	1,751
5 to 9	4,639	398	4,240	932	542	628	1,766	1,015	975	969	1,520	1,175
10 to 19	3,993	317	3,676	670	413	511	1,649	701	714	765	1,479	1,036
20 to 49	3,118	328	2,790	481	476	609	1,131	659	882	615	741	880
50 or more	3,350	505	2,845	670	363	1,204	878	705	1,373	726	682	569
Mobile home or trailer	5,630	4,532	1,098	374	208	1,227	955	1,136	502	1,095	2,882	1,151
STORIES IN STRUCTURE [1]												
1	2,606	290	2,316	464	376	591	924	733	145	418	1,216	827
2	8,920	929	7,992	1,528	1,095	1,171	3,541	1,835	947	1,347	3,434	3,193
3	6,938	1,254	5,684	1,078	509	1,217	2,311	1,157	2,475	2,414	1,205	844
4 to 6	4,024	628	3,396	810	557	810	1,075	918	2,265	954	386	419
7 or more	2,123	373	1,750	526	281	731	397	477	1,329	351	305	139
COOPERATIVES AND CONDOMINIUMS												
Cooperatives	630	396	234	99	41	190	55	50	440	70	72	48
Condominiums	3,357	2,310	1,047	149	205	866	753	221	638	611	1,095	1,013
YEAR STRUCTURE BUILT												
1990 to 1994	2,041	1,539	501	147	67	180	1,253	160	226	427	822	566
1985 to 1989	8,043	5,433	2,610	521	424	833	1,804	563	1,151	1,390	3,470	2,031
1980 to 1984	7,290	4,671	2,619	674	432	1,035	1,547	842	713	1,142	3,753	1,682
1975 to 1979	11,023	7,300	3,724	952	670	1,725	1,939	1,355	1,265	2,485	4,483	2,789
1970 to 1974	9,982	6,077	3,905	1,204	646	1,928	1,925	1,459	1,452	2,177	4,041	2,312
1960 to 1969	14,523	9,570	4,953	1,704	908	3,364	2,160	1,779	2,445	3,389	5,353	3,337
1950 to 1959	12,512	8,982	3,530	1,424	986	3,775	1,449	1,581	2,621	3,236	3,964	2,691
1940 to 1949	7,668	4,742	2,926	1,282	725	2,247	1,199	1,386	1,700	1,818	2,550	1,599
1930 to 1939	5,984	3,355	2,629	1,083	526	1,490	1,019	1,151	1,675	1,655	1,629	1,025
1920 to 1929	5,062	2,872	2,190	805	381	1,357	744	934	1,848	1,649	898	667
1919 or earlier	9,019	5,257	3,762	1,038	476	2,415	1,395	1,625	3,865	3,224	1,227	703
Median (Year)	1964	1965	1963	1958	1960	1957	1971	1958	1952	1959	1971	1969

See notes at end of table.

Current Characteristics of the Housing Stock

TABLE 2.20. SELECTED INTRODUCTORY CHARACTERISTICS OF OCCUPIED HOUSING UNITS: 1991 - Continued

(In thousands, except as noted)

CHARACTERISTIC	Total occupied units	Tenure Owner	Tenure Renter	Black	Hispanic	Elderly (65+)	Moved in past year	Below poverty level	Northeast	Midwest	South	West
METROPOLITAN/NONMETROPOLITAN AREAS												
Inside metropolitan statistical areas	72,723	44,883	27,840	9,295	5,589	14,896	13,439	9,059	16,638	16,073	23,608	16,404
In central cities	29,687	14,422	15,265	6,396	3,216	6,144	6,421	5,182	6,263	6,742	9,657	7,025
Suburbs	43,036	30,461	12,575	2,899	2,373	8,752	7,018	3,877	10,376	9,331	13,952	9,378
Outside metropolitan statistical areas	20,424	14,913	5,510	1,537	650	5,452	2,995	3,777	2,324	6,520	8,582	2,998
REGIONS												
Northeast	18,962	11,869	7,093	1,927	1,140	4,497	2,480	2,173	18,962	...	...	...
Midwest	22,593	15,238	7,355	2,149	414	5,105	3,672	3,021	...	22,593	...	...
South	32,190	21,272	10,918	5,790	1,977	6,985	6,102	5,455	...	...	32,190	...
West	19,402	11,417	7,985	965	2,708	3,762	4,180	2,187	...	...	...	19,402
URBANIZED AREAS												
Inside urbanized areas	57,394	32,904	24,490	8,527	4,987	11,774	11,251	7,457	13,321	12,840	17,143	14,091
In central cities of (P)MSAs	29,165	14,127	15,038	6,347	3,179	6,056	6,290	5,114	6,230	6,663	9,462	6,810
Urban fringe	28,229	18,778	9,451	2,180	1,808	5,717	4,960	2,343	7,091	6,177	7,680	7,281
Outside urbanized areas	35,753	26,892	8,861	2,305	1,252	8,574	5,183	5,379	5,641	9,753	15,048	5,311
Other urban	11,102	7,048	4,054	935	650	3,014	2,130	1,902	1,346	3,365	4,285	2,107
Rural	24,650	19,844	4,807	1,370	602	5,560	3,053	3,477	4,296	6,388	10,763	3,204
PLACE SIZE												
Less than 2,500 persons	4,292	3,070	1,222	178	111	1,285	582	720	633	1,771	1,403	485
2,500 to 9,999 persons	9,102	6,185	2,917	599	460	2,381	1,554	1,229	1,879	2,438	3,294	1,491
10,000 to 19,999 persons	8,036	5,223	2,814	731	474	2,046	1,455	1,024	1,577	2,331	2,740	1,388
20,000 to 49,999 persons	12,303	7,565	4,738	1,219	836	2,617	2,377	1,504	2,348	3,190	3,602	3,162
50,000 to 99,999 persons	8,112	4,647	3,465	836	753	1,836	1,608	1,012	2,017	2,130	1,521	2,443
100,000 to 249,999 persons	7,464	3,917	3,547	1,307	682	1,325	1,719	1,061	936	1,366	2,808	2,354
250,000 to 499,999 persons	5,119	2,440	2,679	1,128	526	999	1,327	916	431	1,124	2,084	1,480
500,000 to 999,999 persons	4,455	2,197	2,258	1,174	416	860	990	740	203	979	1,951	1,322
1,000,000 persons or more	6,558	2,554	4,005	1,945	1,150	1,455	991	1,320	3,239	1,481	600	1,238

Source: U.S. Bureau of the Census and U.S. Department of Housing and Urban Development, "American Housing Survey for the United States in 1991." Current Housing Reports H150/91. April 1993.

Consistent with the 1990 Census.

(1) Limited to multiunit structures.

Current Characteristics of the Housing Stock

TABLE 2.21. SELECTED INTRODUCTORY CHARACTERISTICS OF OCCUPIED HOUSING UNITS: 1993

(In thousands, except as noted)

CHARACTERISTIC	Total occupied units	Tenure		Household characteristics					Regions			
		Owner	Renter	Black	Hispanic	Elderly (65+)	Moved in past year	Below poverty level	North-east	Midwest	South	West
TOTAL	94,724	61,252	33,472	11,128	6,614	20,438	16,102	13,787	18,906	23,031	32,936	19,850
TENURE												
Owner-occupied	61,252	61,252	....	4,788	2,788	15,767	4,578	5,386	11,751	15,617	21,841	12,043
Percent of all occupied	64.7	100.0	....	43.0	42.2	77.1	28.4	39.1	62.2	67.8	66.3	60.7
Renter-occupied	33,472	....	33,472	6,340	3,826	4,671	11,524	8,400	7,155	7,415	11,096	7,808
RACE AND HISPANIC ORIGIN												
White	80,029	54,878	25,151	....	5,749	18,329	13,013	9,492	16,087	20,359	26,449	17,134
Non-Hispanic	74,280	52,280	22,001	....	....	17,687	11,659	7,984	15,331	19,971	24,385	14,593
Hispanic	5,749	2,598	3,151	....	5,749	642	1,354	1,508	757	387	2,064	2,542
Black	11,128	4,788	6,340	11,128	188	1,825	2,162	3,555	1,990	2,249	5,902	987
Other	3,567	1,586	1,981	....	677	285	926	740	828	423	586	1,729
Total Hispanic	6,614	2,788	3,826	188	6,614	696	1,629	1,793	1,133	474	2,197	2,810
UNITS IN STRUCTURE												
1, detached	58,918	50,490	8,428	5,232	3,107	13,681	5,898	6,180	9,749	15,411	21,668	12,091
1, attached	5,375	2,824	2,550	1,015	383	999	1,253	911	1,535	970	1,779	1,091
2 to 4	9,279	1,774	7,505	1,627	964	1,476	2,672	2,101	3,099	2,353	2,073	1,754
5 to 9	4,724	409	4,315	953	557	613	1,696	1,203	923	1,054	1,605	1,142
10 to 19	4,190	359	3,831	762	505	499	1,709	804	735	846	1,597	1,011
20 to 49	3,154	335	2,819	532	473	629	1,039	684	886	611	755	902
50 or more	3,429	579	2,850	671	363	1,274	758	806	1,432	676	692	628
Mobile home or trailer	5,655	4,482	1,173	337	261	1,266	1,077	1,098	547	1,110	2,766	1,232
STORIES IN STRUCTURE [1]												
1	2,424	266	2,158	445	384	537	834	717	82	387	1,156	799
2	9,101	976	8,125	1,619	1,130	1,170	3,458	2,040	1,009	1,328	3,627	3,137
3	7,137	1,204	5,934	1,180	549	1,198	2,244	1,397	2,432	2,564	1,204	937
4 to 6	3,829	595	3,234	749	506	769	960	877	2,125	895	407	402
7 or more	2,294	420	1,873	552	294	820	382	568	1,429	366	330	169
COOPERATIVES AND CONDOMINIUMS												
Cooperatives	729	419	311	114	39	219	76	106	465	103	102	59
Condominiums	3,621	2,532	1,089	211	215	923	693	263	688	661	1,190	1,082
YEAR STRUCTURE BUILT												
1990 to 1994	4,576	3,720	855	307	234	525	1,697	280	466	1,014	1,933	1,162
1985 to 1989	7,969	5,324	2,645	556	401	929	1,662	659	1,149	1,440	3,354	2,026
1980 to 1984	7,171	4,593	2,579	686	447	1,067	1,360	894	727	1,158	3,629	1,658
1975 to 1979	10,708	7,161	3,547	891	694	1,737	1,751	1,372	1,198	2,407	4,344	2,759
1970 to 1974	10,110	6,129	3,981	1,254	676	2,014	1,826	1,630	1,431	2,215	4,131	2,333
1960 to 1969	14,405	9,482	4,923	1,819	981	3,315	2,088	2,003	2,421	3,389	5,266	3,329
1950 to 1959	12,360	8,855	3,505	1,481	1,030	3,789	1,518	1,777	2,521	3,212	3,959	2,667
1940 to 1949	7,539	4,696	2,843	1,302	727	2,145	1,063	1,385	1,635	1,791	2,554	1,559
1930 to 1939	5,853	3,293	2,560	1,021	556	1,435	956	1,132	1,641	1,610	1,604	998
1920 to 1929	5,047	2,819	2,228	774	385	1,262	797	979	1,840	1,603	927	678
1919 or earlier	8,986	5,178	3,808	1,038	483	2,219	1,384	1,678	3,876	3,193	1,235	682
Median (Year)	1965	1966	1964	1960	1961	1958	1971	1960	1952	1960	1971	1970

See notes at end of table.

Current Characteristics of the Housing Stock

TABLE 2.21. SELECTED INTRODUCTORY CHARACTERISTICS OF OCCUPIED HOUSING UNITS: 1993 - Continued
(In thousands, except as noted)

CHARACTERISTIC	Total occupied units	Tenure		Household characteristics					Regions			
		Owner	Renter	Black	Hispanic	Elderly (65+)	Moved in past year	Below poverty level	Northeast	Midwest	South	West
METROPOLITAN/NONMETROPOLITAN AREAS												
Inside metropolitan statistical areas	73,898	46,081	27,817	9,662	5,999	14,885	13,024	10,222	16,460	16,397	24,352	16,689
In central cities	29,838	14,644	15,194	6,523	3,352	6,039	6,158	5,736	6,208	6,725	9,817	7,088
Suburbs	44,060	31,438	12,623	3,140	2,646	8,846	6,867	4,486	10,252	9,672	14,535	9,601
Outside metropolitan statistical areas	20,826	15,170	5,656	1,466	615	5,553	3,078	3,565	2,446	6,634	8,584	3,162
REGIONS												
Northeast	18,906	11,751	7,155	1,990	1,133	4,540	2,434	2,569	18,906	....	....	....
Midwest	23,031	15,617	7,415	2,249	474	4,976	3,773	3,256	....	23,031	....	....
South	32,936	21,841	11,096	5,902	2,197	7,048	5,965	5,551	....	....	32,936	....
West	19,850	12,043	7,808	987	2,810	3,874	3,930	2,410	....	....	....	19,850
URBANIZED AREAS												
Inside urbanized areas	57,837	33,534	24,303	8,870	5,282	11,674	10,736	8,473	13,125	12,967	17,454	14,292
In central cities of (P)MSAs	29,232	14,292	14,939	6,481	3,302	5,935	6,003	5,669	6,171	6,642	9,598	6,821
Urban fringe	28,606	19,241	9,364	2,389	1,980	5,739	4,733	2,804	6,954	6,325	7,856	7,471
Outside urbanized areas	36,887	27,718	9,169	2,258	1,332	8,764	5,366	5,314	5,781	10,064	15,482	5,558
Other urban	11,253	7,133	4,120	906	666	3,036	2,093	1,886	1,353	3,425	4,316	2,159
Rural	25,633	20,585	5,049	1,352	666	5,729	3,273	3,428	4,428	6,639	11,166	3,399
PLACE SIZE												
Less than 2,500 persons	4,443	3,184	1,259	189	120	1,276	655	677	663	1,763	1,466	551
2,500 to 9,999 persons	9,193	6,253	2,940	600	507	2,345	1,468	1,353	1,860	2,539	3,291	1,502
10,000 to 19,999 persons	8,089	5,284	2,805	745	485	1,988	1,438	1,024	1,572	2,367	2,768	1,383
20,000 to 49,999 persons	12,349	7,652	4,696	1,294	870	2,632	2,244	1,686	2,279	3,174	3,674	3,223
50,000 to 99,999 persons	8,246	4,757	3,489	880	859	1,851	1,475	1,133	1,915	2,199	1,563	2,568
100,000 to 249,999 persons	7,404	3,978	3,426	1,320	681	1,261	1,602	1,175	870	1,369	2,830	2,335
250,000 to 499,999 persons	5,153	2,482	2,672	1,157	540	998	1,162	989	380	1,141	2,108	1,525
500,000 to 999,999 persons	4,520	2,195	2,325	1,153	476	885	1,012	848	197	1,018	1,909	1,396
1,000,000 persons or more	6,478	2,538	3,940	1,997	1,127	1,361	1,072	1,550	3,351	1,367	659	1,101

Source: U.S. Bureau of the Census and U.S. Department of Housing and Urban Development, "American Housing Survey for the United States in 1993." Current Housing Reports H150/93. Issued February 1995.

Consistent with the 1990 Census.
(1) Limited to multiunit structures.

Current Characteristics of the Housing Stock

TABLE 2.22. SELECTED INTRODUCTORY CHARACTERISTICS OF OCCUPIED HOUSING UNITS: 1995
(In thousands, except as noted)

CHARACTERISTIC	Total occupied units	Tenure		Household characteristics					Regions			
		Owner	Renter	Black	Hispanic	Elderly (65+)	Moved in past year	Below poverty level	Northeast	Midwest	South	West
TOTAL	97,693	63,544	34,150	11,773	7,757	20,841	17,204	14,695	19,200	23,662	34,236	20,596
TENURE												
Owner-occupied	63,544	63,544	...	5,137	3,245	16,299	4,954	6,034	11,861	16,567	22,959	12,157
Percent of all occupied	65.0	100.0	...	43.6	41.8	78.2	28.8	41.1	61.8	70.0	67.1	59.0
Renter-occupied	34,150	...	34,150	6,637	4,512	4,542	12,251	8,661	7,338	7,096	11,277	8,439
RACE AND HISPANIC ORIGIN												
White	81,611	56,507	25,104	...	6,454	18,598	13,495	10,127	16,082	20,948	27,091	17,490
Non-Hispanic	75,157	53,627	21,530	...	...	17,869	11,920	8,402	15,241	20,533	24,764	14,619
Hispanic	6,454	2,880	3,574	...	6,454	729	1,574	1,726	841	415	2,328	2,871
Black	11,773	5,137	6,637	11,773	238	1,882	2,536	3,627	2,147	2,227	6,295	1,104
American Indian, Eskimo, Aleut	601	287	314	...	57	89	149	196	48	115	112	327
Asian and Pacific Islander	2,430	1,295	1,135	...	45	210	576	387	466	256	406	1,302
Other	1,278	318	960	...	963	62	449	358	456	116	332	372
Total Hispanic	7,757	3,245	4,512	238	7,757	838	2,002	2,089	1,294	510	2,686	3,267
UNITS IN STRUCTURE												
1, detached	60,826	52,257	8,569	5,601	3,699	13,992	6,297	6,810	9,818	16,175	22,406	12,427
1, attached	5,545	2,936	2,609	1,071	393	1,064	1,344	916	1,571	1,053	1,867	1,055
2 to 4	9,299	1,734	7,565	1,754	1,170	1,451	2,811	2,201	3,126	2,168	2,083	1,922
5 to 9	4,803	520	4,283	988	687	545	1,772	1,214	970	1,023	1,592	1,218
10 to 19	4,342	368	3,974	742	561	500	1,866	884	791	880	1,575	1,096
20 to 49	3,244	342	2,903	495	568	645	1,221	713	896	559	856	933
50 or more	3,470	550	2,920	724	387	1,322	754	833	1,470	668	641	691
Mobile home or trailer	6,164	4,837	1,328	398	292	1,320	1,140	1,123	557	1,136	3,216	1,254
STORIES IN STRUCTURE [1]												
1	2,678	279	2,399	475	502	583	944	850	158	374	1,204	942
2	9,318	1,055	8,263	1,748	1,461	1,150	3,654	2,207	1,065	1,321	3,594	3,338
3	7,056	1,179	5,877	1,117	612	1,134	2,419	1,279	2,363	2,451	1,249	992
4 to 6	3,904	591	3,312	811	554	778	1,030	922	2,287	793	395	429
7 or more	2,213	415	1,799	553	247	820	382	593	1,382	359	312	160
COOPERATIVES AND CONDOMINIUMS												
Cooperatives	639	371	268	118	32	221	81	90	414	86	93	46
Condominiums	3,783	2,736	1,047	235	226	1,030	731	271	712	732	1,277	1,063
YEAR STRUCTURE BUILT												
1995 to 1999	810	598	212	33	34	40	767	42	81	179	354	196
1990 to 1994	6,978	5,712	1,266	465	376	815	1,443	538	684	1,562	3,032	1,701
1985 to 1989	8,118	5,350	2,768	626	475	1,033	1,669	756	1,159	1,397	3,468	2,093
1980 to 1984	7,295	4,651	2,644	776	571	1,140	1,481	936	755	1,163	3,728	1,649
1975 to 1979	11,108	7,301	3,806	1,050	866	1,903	1,939	1,525	1,326	2,689	4,291	2,801
1970 to 1974	9,925	6,046	3,879	1,324	772	1,989	1,772	1,728	1,390	2,183	4,067	2,285
1960 to 1969	14,267	9,349	4,918	1,852	1,170	3,437	2,235	2,141	2,415	3,266	5,286	3,300
1950 to 1959	12,398	8,798	3,600	1,616	1,112	3,808	1,618	1,882	2,546	3,245	3,936	2,670
1940 to 1949	7,487	4,671	2,817	1,259	850	2,088	1,103	1,472	1,680	1,750	2,500	1,558
1930 to 1939	5,744	3,201	2,542	1,001	638	1,301	977	1,150	1,628	1,584	1,510	1,022
1920 to 1929	4,893	2,828	2,065	769	389	1,207	726	924	1,774	1,556	882	681
1919 or earlier	8,671	5,039	3,632	1,003	503	2,080	1,474	1,600	3,760	3,088	1,182	642
Median (Year)	1967	1968	1965	1961	1963	1960	1971	1961	1953	1962	1972	1971

See notes at end of table.

Current Characteristics of the Housing Stock

TABLE 2.22. SELECTED INTRODUCTORY CHARACTERISTICS OF OCCUPIED HOUSING UNITS: 1995 - Continued
(In thousands, except as noted)

CHARACTERISTIC	Total occupied units	Tenure		Household characteristics					Regions			
		Owner	Renter	Black	Hispanic	Elderly (65+)	Moved in past year	Below poverty level	Northeast	Midwest	South	West
METROPOLITAN/NONMETROPOLITAN AREAS												
Inside metropolitan statistical areas	76,107	47,689	28,418	10,155	7,037	15,084	14,064	10,928	16,735	16,879	25,208	17,284
In central cities	30,243	14,808	15,434	6,699	3,803	5,916	6,631	5,925	6,329	6,723	9,849	7,341
Suburbs	45,864	32,880	12,984	3,457	3,234	9,168	7,434	5,004	10,406	10,156	15,359	9,943
Outside metropolitan statistical areas	21,586	15,855	5,731	1,618	720	5,756	3,140	3,767	2,464	6,783	9,027	3,312
REGIONS												
Northeast	19,200	11,861	7,338	2,147	1,294	4,563	2,591	2,675	19,200	...	...	...
Midwest	23,662	16,567	7,096	2,227	510	5,112	3,915	3,282	...	23,662	...	...
South	34,236	22,959	11,277	6,295	2,686	7,230	6,295	5,725	...	...	34,236	...
West	20,596	12,157	8,439	1,104	3,267	3,935	4,403	3,014	...	...	...	20,596
URBANIZED AREAS												
Inside urbanized areas	60,325	35,295	25,030	9,317	6,159	11,893	12,167	9,086	13,458	13,476	18,356	15,035
In central cities of (P)MSAs	29,654	14,460	15,194	6,656	3,747	5,807	6,530	5,847	6,299	6,642	9,638	7,076
Urban fringe	30,670	20,834	9,836	2,660	2,412	6,086	5,637	3,239	7,159	6,834	8,718	7,959
Outside urbanized areas	37,369	28,249	9,120	2,457	1,598	8,948	5,037	5,609	5,742	10,186	15,880	5,561
Other urban	11,226	7,179	4,047	1,003	802	3,049	2,010	1,999	1,338	3,420	4,283	2,186
Rural	26,143	21,070	5,073	1,454	796	5,899	3,027	3,610	4,404	6,767	11,597	3,375
PLACE SIZE												
Less than 2,500 persons	4,441	3,180	1,261	191	109	1,261	629	745	656	1,774	1,460	551
2,500 to 9,999 persons	9,366	6,411	2,955	648	599	2,397	1,498	1,424	1,802	2,644	3,329	1,591
10,000 to 19,999 persons	8,360	5,484	2,876	850	583	2,061	1,479	1,204	1,611	2,466	2,823	1,461
20,000 to 49,999 persons	12,604	7,723	4,881	1,423	1,027	2,665	2,427	1,710	2,308	3,259	3,740	3,298
50,000 to 99,999 persons	8,502	4,882	3,620	901	987	1,813	1,741	1,315	1,938	2,271	1,632	2,661
100,000 to 249,999 persons	7,638	4,062	3,576	1,459	836	1,291	1,793	1,234	931	1,385	2,881	2,442
250,000 to 499,999 persons	5,094	2,500	2,595	1,157	585	945	1,265	998	393	1,084	2,098	1,519
500,000 to 999,999 persons	4,555	2,277	2,278	1,184	548	900	1,051	931	220	1,004	1,928	1,404
1,000,000 persons or more	6,460	2,459	4,001	1,958	1,257	1,301	1,089	1,471	3,325	1,331	619	1,185

Source: U.S. Bureau of the Census and U.S. Department of Housing and Urban Development, "American Housing Survey for the United States in 1995." Current Housing Reports H150/95RV.

Consistent with the 1990 Census.
(1) Limited to multiunit structures.

Current Characteristics of the Housing Stock

TABLE 2.23. SIZE OF UNIT AND LOT OF OCCUPIED HOUSING UNITS: 1991
(In thousands, except as noted)

CHARACTERISTIC	Total occupied units	Tenure — Owner	Tenure — Renter	Black	Hispanic	Elderly (65+)	Moved in past year	Below poverty level	Northeast	Midwest	South	West
TOTAL	93,147	59,796	33,351	10,832	6,239	20,348	16,434	12,836	18,962	22,593	32,190	19,402
ROOMS												
1 room	637	37	600	128	86	101	233	192	229	127	110	171
2 rooms	1,020	54	967	219	125	206	384	314	312	197	236	275
3 rooms	8,066	881	7,185	1,346	934	2,074	2,787	1,961	2,115	1,822	2,162	1,967
4 rooms	17,131	6,284	10,847	2,443	1,785	3,729	4,700	3,556	3,129	3,806	6,254	3,942
5 rooms	21,189	13,664	7,525	2,739	1,413	5,289	3,600	3,173	3,681	5,433	8,030	4,046
6 rooms	19,465	15,681	3,784	2,115	991	4,560	2,286	2,055	3,952	4,779	7,006	3,727
7 rooms	12,397	10,928	1,469	1,048	506	2,392	1,168	931	2,593	3,002	4,276	2,526
8 rooms	7,484	6,876	608	480	248	1,154	681	393	1,720	1,942	2,303	1,519
9 rooms	3,355	3,122	233	199	81	517	342	161	719	879	1,043	713
10 rooms or more	2,404	2,270	134	116	69	324	254	100	511	607	770	516
Median (Rooms)	5.4	6.1	4.2	5.0	4.6	5.3	4.5	4.6	5.5	5.5	5.4	5.3
BEDROOMS												
None	1,220	70	1,151	233	154	212	461	365	405	259	227	329
1	11,510	1,696	9,814	1,839	1,228	2,836	3,859	2,572	3,036	2,605	3,129	2,739
2	28,871	14,717	14,155	3,674	2,304	7,621	6,438	4,980	5,378	7,144	10,260	6,089
3	37,492	30,770	6,722	3,939	1,972	7,525	4,331	3,885	6,984	9,008	14,386	7,114
4 or more	14,053	12,544	1,509	1,148	581	2,153	1,345	1,034	3,158	3,577	4,188	3,130
Median (Bedrooms)	2.6	2.9	1.9	2.4	2.3	2.4	2.1	2.2	2.6	2.6	2.7	2.6
COMPLETE BATHROOMS												
None	620	202	418	173	72	154	135	287	189	139	204	88
1	44,758	20,417	24,341	6,886	3,982	10,786	9,869	9,171	10,710	11,999	13,882	8,167
1 1/2	14,629	11,182	3,447	1,611	585	3,489	1,865	1,417	3,605	4,574	4,056	2,394
2 or more	33,140	27,994	5,146	2,162	1,601	5,918	4,564	1,961	4,457	5,882	14,049	8,753
SQUARE FOOTAGE OF UNIT												
Single detached and mobile homes	63,075	53,586	9,489	5,373	3,052	14,778	6,852	6,925	10,249	16,187	23,829	12,810
Less than 500	736	384	353	99	96	183	200	235	67	137	339	194
500 to 749	2,546	1,572	974	403	213	703	442	705	269	580	1,227	470
750 to 999	5,851	4,314	1,537	655	401	1,531	882	1,164	577	1,388	2,777	1,109
1,000 to 1,499	14,755	12,252	2,503	1,411	920	3,888	1,611	1,830	1,453	3,241	6,593	3,468
1,500 to 1,999	13,025	11,547	1,478	935	582	2,948	1,281	982	1,827	3,090	4,963	3,144
2,000 to 2,499	9,178	8,475	704	526	285	1,918	847	561	1,886	2,758	2,795	1,740
2,500 to 2,999	4,953	4,609	344	280	110	1,026	400	272	1,205	1,570	1,354	824
3,000 to 3,999	4,413	4,229	184	208	105	843	280	186	1,132	1,373	1,236	672
4,000 or more	2,574	2,373	201	143	71	543	201	153	717	752	775	330
Not reported	5,044	3,832	1,212	713	268	1,195	708	839	1,117	1,298	1,771	859
Median (Square feet)	1,697	1,775	1,255	1,415	1,371	1,583	1,481	1,257	2,099	1,840	1,509	1,617
LOT SIZE												
Less than 1/8 acre	6,362	5,377	985	723	403	1,825	723	783	1,426	1,559	1,739	1,639
1/8 up to 1/4 acre	12,216	10,974	1,243	794	681	3,353	1,033	925	2,023	3,134	3,848	3,211
1/4 up to 1/2 acre	9,323	8,573	750	493	326	2,176	812	546	1,785	2,219	3,550	1,769
1/2 up to 1 acre	6,926	6,144	782	410	166	1,395	719	537	1,504	1,456	3,086	880
1 to 4 acres	9,883	8,883	1,001	635	209	1,957	843	1,016	2,071	2,089	4,542	1,181
5 to 9 acres	1,673	1,507	166	75	28	297	143	187	272	409	740	253
10 acres or more	3,729	3,170	559	150	50	1,103	264	570	442	1,228	1,631	428
Don't know	17,052	10,497	6,555	3,060	1,479	3,368	3,430	3,048	1,981	4,704	6,144	4,223
Not reported	1,353	1,184	169	87	77	345	216	98	291	313	362	388
Median (Acres)	0.42	0.42	0.42	0.31	0.22	0.35	0.41	0.53	0.43	0.40	0.57	0.24
PERSONS PER ROOM												
0.50 or less	62,846	42,762	20,084	6,097	2,565	18,841	9,834	7,499	12,644	15,773	21,927	12,502
0.51 to 1.00	27,773	16,151	11,622	4,170	2,757	1,420	5,929	4,369	5,907	6,435	9,479	5,952
1.01 to 1.50	2,010	768	1,242	449	651	69	515	731	339	338	654	680
1.51 or more	518	115	403	117	267	18	156	238	72	47	130	268

See notes at end of table.

Current Characteristics of the Housing Stock

TABLE 2.23. SIZE OF UNIT AND LOT OF OCCUPIED HOUSING UNITS: 1991 - Continued
(In thousands, except as noted)

CHARACTERISTIC	Total occupied units	Tenure		Household characteristics					Regions			
		Owner	Renter	Black	Hispanic	Elderly (65+)	Moved in past year	Below poverty level	Northeast	Midwest	South	West
SQUARE FEET PER PERSON												
Single detached and mobile homes	63,075	53,586	9,489	5,373	3,052	14,778	6,852	6,925	10,249	16,187	23,829	12,810
Less than 200	1,926	1,180	746	341	395	139	414	617	144	353	958	471
200 to 299	4,396	3,078	1,317	581	486	325	710	771	408	928	1,970	1,090
300 to 399	6,233	4,957	1,276	714	445	543	826	662	759	1,426	2,676	1,372
400 to 499	6,607	5,546	1,061	569	290	841	867	559	941	1,633	2,612	1,420
500 to 599	5,666	4,909	757	441	244	967	628	449	839	1,513	2,148	1,165
600 to 699	5,651	4,964	687	358	219	1,306	531	488	905	1,471	1,981	1,294
700 to 799	4,629	4,177	452	300	128	1,225	452	410	794	1,132	1,652	1,051
800 to 899	3,519	3,143	376	245	121	907	303	287	613	865	1,367	674
900 to 999	3,215	2,891	324	215	88	1,034	270	318	518	882	1,158	657
1,000 to 1,499	9,080	8,337	743	513	218	3,268	642	817	1,636	2,561	3,238	1,644
1,500 or more	7,110	6,572	538	384	151	3,029	500	708	1,574	2,126	2,297	1,113
Not reported	5,044	3,832	1,212	713	268	1,195	708	839	1,117	1,298	1,771	859
Median (Square feet)	674	706	475	528	423	952	540	597	772	711	634	635

Source: U.S. Bureau of the Census and U.S. Department of Housing and Urban Development, "American Housing Survey for the United States in 1991." Currnt Housing Reports H150/91. April

Consistent with the 1990 Census.

Current Characteristics of the Housing Stock

TABLE 2.24. SIZE OF UNIT AND LOT OF OCCUPIED HOUSING UNITS: 1993
(In thousands, except as noted)

CHARACTERISTIC	Total occupied units	Tenure		Household characteristics					Regions			
		Owner	Renter	Black	Hispanic	Elderly (65+)	Moved in past year	Below poverty level	North-east	Midwest	South	West
TOTAL	94,724	61,252	33,472	11,128	6,614	20,438	16,102	13,787	18,906	23,031	32,936	19,850
ROOMS												
1 room	611	19	592	121	64	109	225	195	261	98	87	165
2 rooms	989	62	928	168	124	242	328	305	288	193	216	293
3 rooms	7,959	836	7,123	1,283	900	1,973	2,516	2,021	2,139	1,758	2,155	1,907
4 rooms	17,221	6,280	10,941	2,535	1,905	3,763	4,696	3,779	3,079	3,969	6,331	3,841
5 rooms	21,030	13,534	7,496	2,754	1,508	5,147	3,484	3,349	3,659	5,298	7,991	4,082
6 rooms	19,870	15,988	3,882	2,194	1,145	4,557	2,362	2,252	3,827	4,828	7,278	3,937
7 rooms	13,083	11,553	1,529	1,132	564	2,496	1,276	1,064	2,602	3,254	4,548	2,678
8 rooms	7,683	7,043	640	546	234	1,231	726	496	1,749	1,968	2,439	1,526
9 rooms	3,738	3,531	207	221	119	524	307	204	794	975	1,090	879
10 rooms or more	2,541	2,406	134	175	50	396	182	122	508	690	800	542
Median (Rooms)	5.5	6.1	4.2	5.0	4.7	5.3	4.6	4.7	5.5	5.5	5.5	5.4
BEDROOMS												
None	1,129	45	1,083	193	129	222	399	353	400	217	174	338
1	11,279	1,657	9,622	1,740	1,196	2,789	3,544	2,623	2,944	2,562	3,151	2,623
2	28,965	14,523	14,442	3,753	2,485	7,324	6,431	5,203	5,374	7,214	10,200	6,178
3	38,504	31,718	6,786	4,124	2,174	7,813	4,432	4,300	6,973	9,339	14,863	7,329
4 or more	14,848	13,309	1,539	1,319	630	2,291	1,296	1,308	3,215	3,700	4,549	3,383
Median (Bedrooms)	2.7	3.0	1.9	2.5	2.3	2.5	2.1	2.3	2.6	2.7	2.7	2.6
COMPLETE BATHROOMS												
None	526	171	354	120	52	130	119	225	123	115	193	95
1	43,944	19,604	24,339	6,895	4,085	10,277	9,439	9,643	10,532	11,775	13,710	7,927
1 1/2	14,740	11,345	3,395	1,778	665	3,625	1,734	1,589	3,500	4,739	4,141	2,360
2 or more	35,515	30,131	5,384	2,335	1,811	6,406	4,810	2,329	4,751	6,402	14,892	9,469
SQUARE FOOTAGE OF UNIT												
Single detached and mobile homes	64,574	54,972	9,601	5,569	3,369	14,948	6,975	7,277	10,295	16,521	24,434	13,323
Less than 500	697	395	302	106	93	165	178	214	65	113	306	213
500 to 749	2,381	1,425	956	370	209	624	457	653	262	558	1,144	417
750 to 999	5,704	4,158	1,546	662	433	1,480	830	1,168	559	1,396	2,672	1,077
1,000 to 1,499	15,084	12,398	2,686	1,530	1,014	3,907	1,643	1,925	1,434	3,245	6,889	3,517
1,500 to 1,999	13,414	11,888	1,526	996	653	3,062	1,292	1,053	1,835	3,200	5,097	3,283
2,000 to 2,499	9,653	8,923	730	546	321	1,998	856	638	1,869	2,889	2,982	1,913
2,500 to 2,999	5,374	5,012	361	304	122	1,082	438	369	1,244	1,704	1,520	907
3,000 to 3,999	4,799	4,545	254	231	96	956	365	327	1,223	1,491	1,350	735
4,000 or more	2,688	2,504	184	139	84	570	209	158	724	775	829	360
Not reported	4,780	3,723	1,057	684	344	1,104	707	772	1,082	1,151	1,646	900
Median (Square feet)	1,725	1,805	1,273	1,426	1,384	1,622	1,510	1,316	2,121	1,871	1,538	1,650
LOT SIZE												
Less than 1/8 acre	6,608	5,656	952	689	526	1,829	621	766	1,477	1,513	1,759	1,859
1/8 up to 1/4 acre	11,976	10,876	1,099	876	627	3,253	1,155	967	1,805	3,363	3,781	3,027
1/4 up to 1/2 acre	9,830	9,094	736	637	348	2,265	808	694	1,755	2,421	3,716	1,938
1/2 up to 1 acre	6,958	6,291	667	404	182	1,376	569	564	1,526	1,486	3,005	940
1 to 4 acres	10,519	9,329	1,190	701	228	2,075	940	1,133	2,213	2,179	4,886	1,242
5 to 9 acres	1,633	1,518	115	50	12	320	116	122	239	462	685	247
10 acres or more	3,621	3,066	555	109	47	1,059	260	471	463	1,279	1,492	387
Don't know	13,186	7,737	5,449	2,159	1,309	2,465	3,208	2,507	1,553	3,378	5,066	3,190
Not reported	5,603	4,218	1,385	957	473	1,303	546	965	795	1,410	1,822	1,577
Median (Acres)	0.43	0.43	0.46	0.32	0.22	0.36	0.39	0.48	0.46	0.40	0.57	0.25
PERSONS PER ROOM												
0.50 or less	64,611	44,296	20,315	6,722	2,625	18,856	9,855	7,979	12,754	16,132	22,840	12,886
0.51 to 1.00	27,727	16,072	11,654	3,961	3,077	1,498	5,697	4,815	5,765	6,526	9,393	6,042
1.01 to 1.50	1,940	786	1,154	369	678	60	424	748	314	334	605	687
1.51 or more	446	97	349	76	234	24	126	244	73	40	98	235

See notes at end of table.

Current Characteristics of the Housing Stock

TABLE 2.24. SIZE OF UNIT AND LOT OF OCCUPIED HOUSING UNITS: 1993 - Continued
(In thousands, except as noted)

CHARACTERISTIC	Total occupied units	Tenure		Household characteristics					Regions			
		Owner	Renter	Black	Hispanic	Elderly (65+)	Moved in past year	Below poverty level	North-east	Midwest	South	West
SQUARE FEET PER PERSON												
Single detached and mobile homes	64,574	54,972	9,601	5,569	3,369	14,948	6,975	7,277	10,295	16,521	24,434	13,323
Less than 200	1,752	1,070	683	300	391	100	361	574	153	343	793	463
200 to 299	4,283	3,003	1,280	573	554	308	650	883	345	997	1,887	1,055
300 to 399	6,222	4,914	1,308	682	471	530	771	751	685	1,456	2,674	1,407
400 to 499	6,623	5,502	1,121	645	353	824	850	628	858	1,599	2,725	1,441
500 to 599	5,897	5,095	802	464	256	955	638	480	917	1,461	2,192	1,327
600 to 699	5,756	5,051	705	371	241	1,213	623	465	944	1,508	2,066	1,238
700 to 799	4,731	4,222	509	359	135	1,200	467	378	789	1,167	1,761	1,014
800 to 899	3,607	3,233	374	234	146	944	335	315	580	885	1,409	734
900 to 999	3,394	3,078	317	240	91	1,057	271	302	557	913	1,198	726
1,000 to 1,499	9,798	8,959	839	566	222	3,430	750	956	1,719	2,742	3,549	1,787
1,500 or more	7,729	7,122	607	450	164	3,282	551	774	1,666	2,299	2,533	1,231
Not reported	4,780	3,723	1,057	684	344	1,104	707	772	1,082	1,151	1,646	900
Median (Square feet)	689	723	489	552	427	980	579	587	789	727	654	642

Source: U.S. Bureau of the Census and U.S. Department of Housing and Urban Development, "American Housing Survey for the United States in 1993." Current Housing Reports H150/93. Issued February 1995.

Consistent with the 1990 Census.

Current Characteristics of the Housing Stock

TABLE 2.25. SIZE OF UNIT AND LOT OF OCCUPIED HOUSING UNITS: 1995
(In thousands, except as noted)

CHARACTERISTIC	Total occupied units	Tenure		Household characteristics					Regions			
		Owner	Renter	Black	Hispanic	Elderly (65+)	Moved in past year	Below poverty level	Northeast	Midwest	South	West
TOTAL	97,693	63,544	34,150	11,773	7,757	20,841	17,204	14,695	19,200	23,662	34,236	20,596
ROOMS												
1 room	550	22	528	93	73	95	211	164	246	109	72	123
2 rooms	958	60	898	162	135	181	365	313	279	139	235	305
3 rooms	8,311	859	7,452	1,411	1,109	2,020	2,800	2,164	2,299	1,691	2,240	2,081
4 rooms	17,062	6,069	10,993	2,591	2,087	3,614	4,704	3,837	3,124	3,858	6,135	3,945
5 rooms	21,600	13,895	7,705	3,004	1,808	5,269	3,793	3,648	3,749	5,292	8,380	4,178
6 rooms	20,700	16,686	4,014	2,378	1,381	4,829	2,461	2,462	3,797	5,122	7,725	4,055
7 rooms	13,560	12,007	1,554	1,160	670	2,665	1,453	1,177	2,606	3,467	4,781	2,706
8 rooms	8,041	7,447	594	541	263	1,268	778	488	1,690	2,162	2,518	1,672
9 rooms	3,984	3,734	250	254	134	525	381	274	802	1,067	1,201	915
10 rooms or more	2,927	2,765	162	180	96	375	258	168	608	756	948	615
Median (Rooms)	5.5	6.2	4.2	5.0	4.8	5.4	4.6	4.7	5.5	5.6	5.5	5.4
BEDROOMS												
None	1,047	52	995	153	129	174	402	300	383	180	171	313
1	11,777	1,734	10,043	1,925	1,441	2,804	3,866	2,823	3,124	2,546	3,255	2,853
2	29,146	14,532	14,613	3,864	2,862	7,141	6,746	5,526	5,343	7,090	10,417	6,296
3	40,302	33,332	6,970	4,517	2,566	8,376	4,696	4,681	7,149	9,871	15,641	7,642
4 or more	15,421	13,894	1,528	1,315	759	2,345	1,494	1,364	3,201	3,977	4,751	3,493
Median (Bedrooms)	2.7	3.0	1.9	2.5	2.3	2.5	2.1	2.3	2.6	2.7	2.7	2.6
COMPLETE BATHROOMS												
None	465	195	270	95	52	109	113	183	133	116	159	57
1	43,777	19,069	24,709	7,102	4,646	9,973	9,886	9,791	10,472	11,456	13,627	8,221
1 1/2	14,780	11,319	3,461	1,842	787	3,692	1,883	1,775	3,610	4,889	4,008	2,273
2 or more	38,671	32,961	5,710	2,734	2,272	7,066	5,322	2,946	4,984	7,201	16,442	10,044
SQUARE FOOTAGE OF UNIT												
Single detached and mobile homes	66,990	57,094	9,897	5,999	3,991	15,312	7,437	7,933	10,375	17,312	25,622	13,682
Less than 500	667	379	288	90	95	164	157	186	59	107	295	206
500 to 749	2,356	1,386	969	345	258	618	402	663	244	521	1,166	424
750 to 999	5,697	4,126	1,571	657	540	1,433	839	1,158	521	1,400	2,675	1,101
1,000 to 1,499	15,450	12,697	2,753	1,655	1,131	3,973	1,836	2,150	1,408	3,327	7,147	3,568
1,500 to 1,999	13,785	12,218	1,567	1,068	746	3,109	1,420	1,284	1,839	3,288	5,343	3,314
2,000 to 2,499	9,943	9,211	732	542	380	2,070	854	756	1,913	2,960	3,124	1,947
2,500 to 2,999	5,486	5,147	339	322	136	1,130	456	360	1,265	1,689	1,590	942
3,000 to 3,999	4,956	4,737	219	221	122	991	398	291	1,214	1,532	1,449	761
4,000 or more	2,785	2,597	189	151	82	576	200	183	739	814	879	353
Not reported	5,867	4,596	1,271	949	501	1,247	876	903	1,174	1,673	1,953	1,066
Median (Square feet)	1,732	1,814	1,270	1,433	1,377	1,636	1,516	1,351	2,139	1,875	1,552	1,652
LOT SIZE												
Less than 1/8 acre	6,292	5,367	924	634	540	1,750	617	766	1,324	1,528	1,710	1,730
1/8 up to 1/4 acre	12,184	11,077	1,107	821	789	3,309	1,057	1,085	1,777	3,212	3,725	3,470
1/4 up to 1/2 acre	10,077	9,303	774	581	410	2,336	851	737	1,707	2,643	3,741	1,986
1/2 up to 1 acre	7,394	6,656	738	486	225	1,466	663	610	1,537	1,635	3,275	947
1 to 4 acres	10,450	9,398	1,051	711	250	2,154	801	1,113	2,138	2,188	4,990	1,134
5 to 9 acres	1,713	1,574	139	60	22	307	144	176	225	477	768	244
10 acres or more	3,670	3,185	485	118	77	1,081	252	503	452	1,258	1,529	431
Don't know	14,239	8,539	5,700	2,524	1,602	2,349	3,696	2,636	1,840	3,934	5,170	3,294
Not reported	6,503	4,921	1,582	1,135	467	1,625	694	1,219	943	1,489	2,572	1,499
Median (Acres)	0.43	0.43	0.44	0.36	0.22	0.37	0.40	0.47	0.47	0.41	0.61	0.24
PERSONS PER ROOM												
0.50 or less	67,043	46,210	20,832	7,073	3,172	19,249	10,629	8,796	13,095	16,908	23,812	13,228
0.51 to 1.00	28,097	16,453	11,644	4,248	3,469	1,524	5,851	4,774	5,707	6,412	9,652	6,325
1.01 to 1.50	2,059	782	1,276	363	834	59	565	849	298	304	654	803
1.51 or more	495	98	397	89	281	8	159	275	100	39	118	238

See notes at end of table.

Current Characteristics of the Housing Stock

TABLE 2.25. SIZE OF UNIT AND LOT OF OCCUPIED HOUSING UNITS: 1995 - Continued
(In thousands, except as noted)

CHARACTERISTIC	Total occupied units	Tenure		Household characteristics					Regions			
		Owner	Renter	Black	Hispanic	Elderly (65+)	Moved in past year	Below poverty level	Northeast	Midwest	South	West
SQUARE FEET PER PERSON												
Single detached and mobile homes	66,990	57,094	9,897	5,999	3,991	15,312	7,437	7,933	10,375	17,312	25,622	13,682
Less than 200	1,779	1,070	709	268	469	102	371	609	133	324	798	524
200 to 299	4,223	2,889	1,334	540	578	299	709	790	384	974	1,742	1,123
300 to 399	6,403	5,019	1,384	779	571	538	882	818	660	1,447	2,889	1,407
400 to 499	6,741	5,627	1,114	616	430	883	877	654	871	1,614	2,795	1,461
500 to 599	5,906	5,222	684	489	295	993	596	571	882	1,425	2,357	1,242
600 to 699	5,882	5,161	721	422	276	1,214	610	517	980	1,473	2,205	1,224
700 to 799	4,966	4,450	516	337	165	1,275	522	443	780	1,267	1,849	1,069
800 to 899	3,696	3,321	375	264	146	904	387	383	619	922	1,393	763
900 to 999	3,490	3,187	302	246	101	1,065	346	352	534	1,020	1,242	694
1,000 to 1,499	10,005	9,150	854	617	278	3,437	742	1,040	1,724	2,724	3,671	1,886
1,500 or more	8,034	7,401	632	473	180	3,355	519	854	1,634	2,449	2,729	1,223
Not reported	5,867	4,596	1,271	949	501	1,247	876	903	1,174	1,673	1,953	1,066
Median (Square feet)	694	728	480	566	429	977	574	614	788	744	657	645

Source: U.S. Bureau of the Census and U.S. Department of Housing and Urban Development, "American Housing Survey for the United States in 1995." Current Housing Reports H150/95RV.

Consistent with the 1990 Census.

Current Characteristics of the Housing Stock

TABLE 2.26. SELECTED UNIT AND BUILDING CONDITIONS FOR OCCUPIED HOUSING UNITS: 1991

(In thousands, except as noted)

CHARACTERISTIC	Total occupied units	Tenure		Household characteristics					Regions			
		Owner	Renter	Black	Hispanic	Elderly (65+)	Moved in past year	Below poverty level	Northeast	Midwest	South	West
TOTAL	93,147	59,796	33,351	10,832	6,239	20,348	16,434	12,836	18,962	22,593	32,190	19,402
BUILDING CONDITIONS												
External building conditions [1,2]												
Sagging roof	93	7	86	21	18	2	38	38	14	44	17	17
Missing roofing material	104	14	91	38	12	8	33	44	29	42	13	20
Hole in roof	26	5	21	9	2	-	-	7	12	3	9	2
Could not see roof	2,371	278	2,092	565	403	402	765	641	631	662	485	592
Missing bricks, siding, other outside wall material	369	29	340	106	89	26	130	152	134	84	57	93
Sloping outside walls	56	6	51	16	14	9	17	37	20	22	7	7
Boarded up windows	241	3	238	128	73	11	86	128	91	83	32	36
Broken windows	295	10	285	150	55	14	80	143	72	111	47	65
Bars on windows	492	59	433	205	145	74	87	143	234	102	53	104
Foundation crumbling or has open crack or hole	309	20	289	116	55	32	101	132	91	108	51	59
Could not see foundation	897	108	789	209	208	144	276	257	252	193	234	218
None of the above	18,313	2,545	15,768	3,051	2,044	3,259	6,606	3,634	5,643	4,055	4,677	3,938
Could not observe or not reported	3,041	553	2,488	520	205	767	598	559	596	537	1,219	689
UNIT CONDITIONS												
Kitchen facilities												
Lacking complete kitchen facilities	957	329	628	243	117	178	311	286	243	220	296	197
With complete kitchen (Sink, refrigerator and burners)	92,190	59,467	32,723	10,589	6,122	20,170	16,123	12,550	18,718	22,373	31,894	19,205
Plumbing												
With all plumbing facilities	90,869	58,471	32,398	10,499	6,057	19,812	16,007	12,307	18,533	22,022	31,389	18,925
Lacking some plumbing facilities [2]	233	72	161	79	34	54	55	120	73	44	67	49
No hot piped water	38	23	14	11	6	15	4	18	4	5	25	5
No bathtub nor shower	194	51	143	71	27	46	50	101	72	32	51	39
No flush toilet	133	25	108	52	23	17	43	74	45	28	27	32
No plumbing facilities for exclusive use	2,045	1,253	792	255	148	482	372	410	356	527	734	428
Selected deficiencies [2]												
Signs of rats in last 3 months	3,341	1,554	1,787	1,190	597	577	650	1,120	637	332	1,850	522
Holes in floors	1,139	465	674	310	132	177	235	440	240	199	473	227
Open cracks or holes (Interior)	4,705	2,016	2,689	1,097	503	731	971	1,397	968	973	1,702	1,062
Broken plaster or peeling paint (Interior)	3,847	1,808	2,039	910	432	672	659	1,144	828	891	1,393	735
No electrical wiring	31	26	4	-	-	7	3	20	6	13	10	2
Exposed wiring	1,491	660	831	312	206	324	396	408	346	290	433	422
Rooms without electric outlets	1,637	824	813	326	154	370	355	460	355	443	528	310
Overall Opinion of Structure												
1 (Worst)	632	157	475	216	99	96	200	299	112	146	255	119
2	369	85	284	70	47	56	114	142	75	71	140	83
3	658	194	464	113	60	80	168	188	121	142	242	153
4	1,095	331	764	212	130	104	305	263	214	233	357	292
5	6,373	2,726	3,648	1,061	705	1,189	1,372	1,512	1,178	1,475	2,363	1,357
6	4,590	2,002	2,588	666	379	633	1,139	800	833	1,065	1,610	1,083
7	10,653	5,521	5,132	1,323	762	1,366	2,487	1,343	2,069	2,609	3,587	2,388
8	22,482	14,184	8,297	2,388	1,374	3,989	4,136	2,596	4,620	5,520	7,623	4,720
9	13,621	9,762	3,858	1,321	743	2,828	2,098	1,277	2,852	3,307	4,435	3,027
10 (Best)	31,924	24,390	7,534	3,341	1,869	9,688	4,316	4,209	6,756	7,813	11,321	6,033
Not reported	750	443	307	123	71	318	98	206	130	212	259	148

See notes at end of table.

Current Characteristics of the Housing Stock

TABLE 2.26. SELECTED UNIT AND BUILDING CONDITIONS FOR OCCUPIED HOUSING UNITS: 1991 - Continued

(In thousands, except as noted)

CHARACTERISTIC	Total occupied units	Tenure		Household characteristics					Regions			
		Owner	Renter	Black	Hispanic	Elderly (65+)	Moved in past year	Below poverty level	Northeast	Midwest	South	West
SELECTED PHYSICAL PROBLEMS												
Severe physical problems [2]	2,874	1,527	1,347	526	267	603	491	745	658	658	963	595
Plumbing	2,278	1,326	952	334	182	536	427	529	429	571	801	477
Heating	341	108	233	97	48	37	19	86	169	43	60	70
Electric	67	41	26	19	7	7	14	39	16	26	15	10
Upkeep	249	83	166	93	43	36	37	138	67	31	103	49
Hallways	3	-	3	-	-	-	3	3	3	-	-	-
Moderate physical problems [2]	4,531	2,156	2,375	1,358	564	972	917	1,491	561	655	2,614	700
Plumbing	295	105	190	74	44	39	72	103	52	42	141	61
Heating	1,977	1,129	848	700	271	617	344	751	33	62	1,723	160
Upkeep	1,914	815	1,099	557	224	266	360	645	379	432	750	353
Hallways	47	-	47	14	12	-	11	12	18	13	5	11
Kitchen	560	206	354	119	58	105	184	112	109	127	174	150

Source: U.S. Bureau of the Census and U.S. Department of Housing and Urban Development, "American Housing Survey for the United States in 1991." Current Housing Reports H150/91. Issued April 1993.

Consistent with the 1990 Census.

(-) means zero or rounds to zero.

(1) Limited to multiunit structures.

(2) Figures may not add to total because more than one category may apply.

Current Characteristics of the Housing Stock

TABLE 2.27. SELECTED UNIT AND BUILDING CONDITIONS FOR OCCUPIED HOUSING UNITS: 1993
(In thousands, except as noted)

CHARACTERISTIC	Total occupied units	Tenure		Household characteristics					Regions			
		Owner	Renter	Black	Hispanic	Elderly (65+)	Moved in past year	Below poverty level	North-east	Midwest	South	West
TOTAL	94,724	61,252	33,472	11,128	6,614	20,438	16,102	13,787	18,906	23,031	32,936	19,850
BUILDING CONDITIONS												
External building conditions [1,2]												
Sagging roof	87	9	79	33	8	-	22	48	19	37	25	7
Missing roofing material	143	22	121	27	23	13	40	42	35	32	55	21
Hole in roof	24	2	22	5	6	-	12	13	3	6	12	3
Could not see roof	2,958	419	2,538	652	484	522	814	763	1,169	630	482	678
Missing bricks, siding, other outside wall material	409	34	375	92	100	23	159	146	125	97	109	79
Sloping outside walls	64	4	60	29	12	4	20	29	19	18	16	11
Boarded up windows	161	12	149	80	47	11	40	90	42	50	52	16
Broken windows	256	8	248	99	72	13	85	125	78	65	83	31
Bars on windows	515	70	445	164	125	83	83	176	312	36	68	99
Foundation crumbling or has open crack or hole	326	23	303	96	71	24	94	123	78	122	74	53
Could not see foundation	1,068	219	849	217	202	184	247	268	508	196	204	161
None of the above	19,136	2,623	16,513	3,371	2,106	3,358	6,520	4,118	5,414	4,117	5,299	4,306
Could not observe or not reported	1,857	321	1,537	266	129	537	305	434	257	607	679	314
UNIT CONDITIONS												
Kitchen facilities												
Lacking complete kitchen facilities	1,107	461	647	193	128	207	315	325	260	261	368	218
With complete kitchen (Sink, refrigerator, and burners)	93,617	60,791	32,826	10,935	6,486	20,231	15,787	13,461	18,646	22,770	32,568	19,632
Plumbing												
With all plumbing facilities	93,345	60,441	32,905	10,906	6,499	20,049	15,922	13,442	18,606	22,701	32,498	19,540
Lacking some plumbing facilities [2]	227	60	167	45	23	47	62	87	69	40	71	47
No hot piped water	57	30	28	12	5	21	13	31	11	7	35	5
No bathtub nor shower	181	31	151	33	23	32	62	61	58	33	45	45
No flush toilet	131	28	103	36	11	11	37	50	50	23	25	33
No plumbing facilities for exclusive use	1,152	751	401	177	92	342	119	257	231	290	367	263
Selected deficiencies [2]												
Signs of rats in last 3 months	2,637	1,066	1,571	826	595	393	501	1,015	575	248	1,263	551
Holes in floors	1,148	469	678	278	230	188	246	441	240	204	494	210
Open cracks or holes (Interior)	4,542	1,842	2,699	1,055	619	573	945	1,450	937	957	1,594	1,053
Broken plaster or peeling paint (Interior)	3,597	1,615	1,982	827	475	537	621	1,120	802	873	1,232	690
No electrical wiring	21	19	2	2	-	4	-	10	-	11	7	3
Exposed wiring	1,603	794	808	297	280	352	334	472	395	325	468	415
Rooms without electric outlets	1,721	808	913	283	194	325	361	540	410	408	584	318
Overall Opinion of Structure												
1 (Worst)	550	106	444	168	101	64	144	267	133	98	212	106
2	334	67	267	87	45	34	85	109	58	77	118	80
3	714	223	491	140	82	103	212	238	128	154	280	152
4	967	232	735	202	118	108	282	260	160	236	333	238
5	6,073	2,616	3,457	1,004	651	1,105	1,313	1,567	1,074	1,403	2,272	1,324
6	4,600	1,958	2,642	753	454	623	1,030	845	864	1,098	1,645	994
7	10,700	5,536	5,164	1,392	802	1,429	2,319	1,496	2,102	2,636	3,518	2,443
8	22,862	14,443	8,419	2,580	1,397	4,138	3,906	2,893	4,541	5,667	7,787	4,867
9	14,638	10,518	4,120	1,480	888	2,792	2,364	1,579	3,077	3,536	4,920	3,105
10 (Best)	32,517	25,167	7,349	3,200	1,982	9,750	4,301	4,319	6,585	7,948	11,600	6,384
Not reported	769	384	385	123	93	292	145	215	186	179	249	156

See notes at end of table.

Current Characteristics of the Housing Stock

CHARACTERISTIC	Total occupied units	Tenure		Household characteristics					Regions			
		Owner	Renter	Black	Hispanic	Elderly (65+)	Moved in past year	Below poverty level	North-east	Midwest	South	West
TABLE 2.27. SELECTED UNIT AND BUILDING CONDITIONS FOR OCCUPIED HOUSING UNITS: 1993 - Continued (In thousands, except as noted)												
SELECTED PHYSICAL PROBLEMS												
Severe physical problems [2]	1,901	992	909	385	217	429	253	556	475	447	587	392
Plumbing	1,379	811	568	222	115	389	180	344	300	330	438	310
Heating	287	81	207	86	57	20	28	97	140	51	47	49
Electric	70	41	28	116	4	4	14	37	13	26	24	7
Upkeep	220	78	142	88	51	20	34	114	46	44	98	33
Hallways	6	-	6	2	-	2	-	4	4	2	-	-
Moderate physical problems [2]	4,225	1,971	2,254	1,154	591	785	815	1,380	628	718	2,253	627
Plumbing	287	88	199	92	31	31	67	98	63	52	115	57
Heating	1,528	888	640	543	242	419	223	582	40	46	1,365	78
Upkeep	1,880	735	1,145	497	281	217	368	645	381	468	671	360
Hallways	48	2	47	14	14	2	16	28	27	4	13	5
Kitchen	737	342	395	101	84	138	200	158	160	180	249	149

Source: U.S. Bureau of the Census and U.S. Department of Housing and Urban Development, "American Housing Survey for the United States in 1993." Current Housing Reports H150/93. Issued February 1995.

Consistent with the 1990 Census.

(-) means zero or rounds to zero.

(1) Limited to multiunit structures.

(2) Figures may not add to total because more than one category may apply.

Current Characteristics of the Housing Stock

TABLE 2.28. SELECTED UNIT AND BUILDING CONDITIONS FOR OCCUPIED HOUSING UNITS: 1995
(In thousands, except as noted)

CHARACTERISTIC	Total occupied units	Tenure		Household characteristics					Regions			
		Owner	Renter	Black	Hispanic	Elderly (65+)	Moved in past year	Below poverty level	Northeast	Midwest	South	West
TOTAL	97,693	63,544	34,150	11,773	7,757	20,841	17,204	14,695	19,200	23,662	34,236	20,596
BUILDING CONDITIONS												
External building conditions [1,2]												
Sagging roof	69	5	64	21	18	6	24	25	22	18	18	11
Missing roofing material	120	13	108	33	28	15	42	36	28	16	37	39
Hole in roof	12	2	10	6	4	1	-	7	5	2	5	-
Could not see roof	2,959	358	2,601	675	547	552	806	824	1,247	493	537	681
Missing bricks, siding, other outside wall material	406	27	379	122	98	32	151	153	125	95	92	95
Sloping outside walls	53	2	51	20	3	7	6	19	18	14	9	11
Boarded up windows	146	4	142	75	38	8	39	81	56	38	36	17
Broken windows	232	13	219	108	53	15	89	106	76	66	60	30
Bars on windows	539	71	468	206	166	92	125	213	232	35	103	169
Foundation crumbling or has open crack or hole	267	23	244	72	43	23	83	100	67	91	50	60
Could not see foundation	838	121	717	237	173	142	230	276	314	164	179	181
None of the above	19,402	2,743	16,659	3,436	2,411	3,404	6,861	4,334	5,195	4,336	5,293	4,578
Could not observe or not reported	1,919	308	1,611	314	239	413	482	375	554	303	687	374
UNIT CONDITIONS												
Kitchen facilities												
Lacking complete kitchen facilities	1,075	461	614	197	151	180	319	293	241	281	302	252
With complete kitchen (sink, refrigerator, and burners)	96,618	63,083	33,536	11,576	7,606	20,661	16,886	14,402	18,959	23,382	33,934	20,344
Plumbing												
With all plumbing facilities	96,234	62,572	33,663	11,522	7,637	20,466	16,977	14,329	18,875	23,258	33,729	20,372
Lacking some plumbing facilities [2]	188	80	107	33	16	52	58	70	58	43	67	20
No hot piped water	42	26	16	6	6	25	7	23	5	9	25	3
No bathtub nor shower	141	49	93	24	8	38	45	50	50	34	43	14
No flush toilet	85	24	62	15	8	6	36	33	29	20	22	13
No plumbing facilities for exclusive use	1,271	892	380	218	104	322	170	297	266	362	440	203
Selected deficiencies [2]												
Signs of rats in last 3 months	2,708	1,219	1,489	786	656	395	497	872	529	278	1,284	617
Holes in floors	1,074	503	571	283	195	119	258	348	274	159	444	198
Open cracks or holes (Interior)	4,527	1,943	2,584	1,106	594	523	960	1,267	910	974	1,653	989
Broken plaster or peeling paint (Interior)	3,673	1,672	2,002	857	478	542	713	1,033	785	888	1,233	766
No electrical wiring	26	22	4	-	-	5	4	15	2	14	5	5
Exposed wiring	1,760	873	887	328	255	366	410	410	472	407	522	358
Rooms without electric outlets	1,816	891	925	399	191	373	409	540	463	454	529	370
Overall Opinion of Structure												
1 (Worst)	540	159	381	175	96	94	146	228	100	105	221	114
2	399	122	276	110	49	70	122	146	93	92	162	52
3	751	213	537	158	97	95	202	261	170	138	267	176
4	1,088	379	709	201	126	115	309	282	199	223	384	283
5	5,844	2,374	3,470	985	721	1,098	1,284	1,407	1,134	1,241	2,134	1,335
6	4,738	2,091	2,647	813	433	689	1,279	877	885	1,021	1,666	1,166
7	10,998	5,632	5,366	1,491	932	1,375	2,483	1,699	2,080	2,628	3,673	2,618
8	24,256	15,274	8,982	2,842	1,884	4,257	4,495	3,151	4,650	5,931	8,487	5,187
9	15,173	10,994	4,179	1,486	1,091	2,979	2,403	1,695	3,041	3,935	4,958	3,239
10 (Best)	32,826	25,753	7,073	3,359	2,224	9,707	4,332	4,681	6,427	8,162	11,965	6,272
Not reported	1,080	551	530	155	104	361	150	268	421	186	319	155

See notes at end of table.

Current Characteristics of the Housing Stock

TABLE 2.28. SELECTED UNIT AND BUILDING CONDITIONS FOR OCCUPIED HOUSING UNITS: 1995 - Continued
(In thousands, except as noted)

CHARACTERISTIC	Total occupied units	Tenure		Household characteristics					Regions			
		Owner	Renter	Black	Hispanic	Elderly (65+)	Moved in past year	Below poverty level	Northeast	Midwest	South	West
SELECTED PHYSICAL PROBLEMS												
Severe physical problems [2]	2,022	1,173	849	448	227	431	313	584	545	512	648	317
Plumbing	1,459	972	487	251	120	374	228	366	324	405	507	223
Heating	361	116	245	124	66	33	46	119	180	65	50	67
Electric	61	36	25	7	7	9	12	31	9	21	20	11
Upkeep	182	67	115	76	38	18	33	87	45	34	85	18
Hallways	6	-	6	4	1	-	-	4	4	-	-	2
Moderate physical problems [2]	4,348	2,071	2,277	1,148	622	820	925	1,303	668	690	2,296	693
Plumbing	276	107	169	79	46	34	71	95	49	51	100	77
Heating	1,579	930	650	509	252	468	269	553	40	29	1,441	69
Upkeep	1,887	767	1,121	495	260	217	392	572	412	396	698	381
Hallways	36	2	34	15	10	3	9	11	14	15	5	2
Kitchen	794	355	438	133	97	141	240	182	170	218	204	201

Source: U.S. Bureau of the Census and U.S. Department of Housing and Urban Development, "American Housing Survey for the United States in 1995." Current Housing Reports H150/95RV. Issued July 1997.

Consistent with the 1990 Census.

(-) means zero or rounds to zero.

(1) Limited to multiunit structures.

(2) Figures may not add to total because more than one category may apply.

Current Characteristics of the Housing Stock

TABLE 2.29. SELECTED NEIGHBORHOOD CONDITIONS FOR OCCUPIED HOUSING UNITS: 1991
(In thousands, except as noted)

CHARACTERISTIC	Total occupied units	Tenure		Household characteristics					Regions			
		Owner	Renter	Black	Hispanic	Elderly (65+)	Moved in past year	Below poverty level	Northeast	Midwest	South	West
TOTAL	93,147	59,796	33,351	10,832	6,239	20,348	16,434	12,836	18,962	22,593	32,190	19,402
OVERALL OPINION OF NEIGHBORHOOD												
1 (Worst)	1,526	537	989	551	217	253	358	594	326	386	545	270
2	816	261	555	172	93	112	226	227	157	188	285	186
3	1,303	454	849	269	131	176	317	353	243	304	424	332
4	1,649	716	933	293	137	194	355	329	282	377	556	434
5	7,288	3,786	3,503	1,168	703	1,414	1,419	1,377	1,428	1,756	2,435	1,670
6	4,859	2,507	2,353	738	352	706	1,047	634	920	1,092	1,619	1,228
7	10,002	5,788	4,214	1,280	672	1,483	2,065	1,147	2,148	2,315	3,162	2,376
8	20,219	13,187	7,032	2,111	1,292	3,851	3,567	2,134	4,222	4,897	6,707	4,394
9	12,927	9,128	3,799	1,119	704	2,439	2,098	1,175	2,701	3,265	4,247	2,713
10 (Best)	30,706	22,232	8,474	2,888	1,818	9,074	4,679	4,447	6,260	7,551	11,423	5,471
No neighborhood	796	599	197	50	29	245	103	142	85	175	381	155
Not reported	1,055	600	455	193	92	400	199	278	190	285	407	173
NEIGHBORHOOD CONDITIONS												
With neighborhood	91,296	58,597	32,700	10,588	6,119	19,703	16,131	12,416	18,687	22,133	31,402	19,074
No problems	56,413	37,392	19,020	6,038	3,787	14,045	9,760	7,649	11,478	14,189	20,289	10,455
With problems [1]	34,548	20,997	13,551	4,524	2,308	5,580	6,291	4,726	7,114	7,894	10,995	8,545
Crime	6,701	2,710	3,991	1,754	737	859	1,310	1,470	1,629	1,267	2,127	1,678
Noise	7,017	3,311	3,706	1,074	616	1,272	1,620	1,079	1,653	1,367	1,793	2,203
Traffic	6,651	4,142	2,509	587	424	950	1,178	721	1,519	1,455	1,819	1,858
Litter or housing deterioration	4,147	2,806	1,341	666	270	820	505	567	786	989	1,335	1,038
Poor city or county services	1,484	1,010	474	279	107	231	173	219	400	306	511	267
Undesirable commercial, institutional, industrial uses	1,583	1,032	551	148	114	299	216	144	403	391	434	354
People	11,369	6,279	5,090	1,603	884	1,706	2,321	2,024	2,174	2,654	3,506	3,035
Other	8,376	5,913	2,463	821	380	1,344	1,309	833	1,589	1,965	2,899	1,923
Type of problem not reported	607	422	185	77	18	100	118	54	122	141	248	95
Presence of problems not reported	335	208	128	27	24	77	80	41	95	50	118	73
Other buildings vandalized or with interior exposed [2]												
None	20,373	2,833	17,540	3,338	2,370	3,618	7,311	4,133	6,027	4,547	5,194	4,606
1 building	383	34	349	152	87	41	93	153	184	105	55	39
More than 1 building	670	71	599	401	134	76	170	295	307	173	124	66
No buildings within 300 feet	360	48	312	28	45	76	131	67	81	56	154	68
Not reported	2,825	488	2,337	487	182	710	543	473	561	602	1,018	643

See notes at end of table.

Current Characteristics of the Housing Stock

TABLE 2.29. SELECTED NEIGHBORHOOD CONDITIONS FOR OCCUPIED HOUSING UNITS: 1991 - Continued

(In thousands, except as noted)

CHARACTERISTIC	Total occupied units	Tenure		Household characteristics					Regions			
		Owner	Renter	Black	Hispanic	Elderly (65+)	Moved in past year	Below poverty level	Northeast	Midwest	South	West
Bars on windows of buildings [2]												
With other buildings within 300 feet	21,426	2,938	18,488	3,891	2,591	3,734	7,574	4,580	6,518	4,825	5,373	4,711
No bars on windows	17,943	2,543	15,400	2,740	1,698	3,216	6,662	3,615	4,996	4,354	4,736	3,857
1 building with bars	608	68	539	146	149	103	188	159	178	93	121	215
2 or more buildings with bars	2,729	305	2,424	975	714	407	666	774	1,286	362	467	614
Not reported	146	21	125	30	30	8	59	32	57	15	48	25
Condition of streets [2]												
No repairs needed	16,506	2,344	14,162	2,595	1,872	2,995	5,992	3,195	4,756	3,679	4,229	3,843
Minor repairs needed	4,802	578	4,224	1,149	677	759	1,522	1,267	1,693	1,115	1,130	864
Major repairs needed	479	68	410	154	99	76	155	173	175	130	113	61
No streets within 300 feet	305	48	258	65	29	40	141	50	70	61	113	61
Not reported	2,519	436	2,083	444	140	651	438	435	467	498	961	593
Trash, litter, or junk on streets or any properties [2]												
None	15,764	2,513	13,251	2,062	1,448	3,046	5,725	2,621	4,303	3,785	4,153	3,524
Minor accumulation	5,810	494	5,315	1,661	1,075	764	1,933	1,817	2,212	1,099	1,303	1,196
Major accumulation	554	35	519	240	149	75	168	245	210	114	123	107
Not reported	2,484	431	2,053	443	145	635	423	437	435	486	967	596

Source: U.S. Bureau of the Census and U.S. Department of Housing and Urban Development, "American Housing Survey for the United States in 1991." Current Housing Reports H150/91. Issued April 1993.

Consistent with the 1990 Census.

(1) Figures may not add to total because more than one category may apply.

(2) Limited to multiunit structures.

Current Characteristics of the Housing Stock

TABLE 2.30. SELECTED NEIGHBORHOOD CONDITIONS FOR OCCUPIED HOUSING UNITS: 1993
(In thousands, except as noted)

CHARACTERISTIC	Total occupied units	Tenure		Household characteristics					Regions			
		Owner	Renter	Black	Hispanic	Elderly (65+)	Moved in past year	Below poverty level	North-east	Midwest	South	West
TOTAL	94,724	61,252	33,472	11,128	6,614	20,438	16,102	13,787	18,906	23,031	32,936	19,850
OVERALL OPINION OF NEIGHBORHOOD												
1 (Worst)	1,463	451	1,012	560	221	230	335	635	293	331	588	252
2	896	338	559	201	103	150	179	275	193	197	279	227
3	1,319	529	790	292	159	164	325	355	288	270	440	320
4	1,797	747	1,050	360	151	241	406	419	353	381	569	494
5	7,155	3,495	3,660	1,172	695	1,366	1,459	1,489	1,397	1,640	2,465	1,653
6	4,861	2,598	2,263	707	387	756	929	811	992	1,140	1,595	1,133
7	10,172	5,986	4,186	1,347	761	1,451	1,907	1,308	2,058	2,387	3,348	2,379
8	20,628	13,690	6,938	2,181	1,257	3,973	3,486	2,357	4,250	5,056	6,805	4,517
9	13,522	9,607	3,914	1,209	814	2,515	2,164	1,349	2,728	3,327	4,526	2,940
10 (Best)	31,192	22,785	8,407	2,924	1,942	9,006	4,633	4,384	6,075	7,860	11,620	5,637
No neighborhood	838	600	239	27	24	231	120	137	82	205	421	130
Not reported	880	425	455	149	99	354	161	269	196	237	279	168
NEIGHBORHOOD CONDITIONS												
With neighborhood	93,006	60,227	32,779	10,953	6,491	19,853	15,821	13,381	18,628	22,589	32,236	19,552
No problems	57,019	38,196	18,823	6,151	3,888	14,113	9,493	8,092	11,341	14,435	20,272	10,970
With problems [1]	35,799	21,906	13,892	4,763	2,593	5,681	6,295	5,244	7,261	8,111	11,883	8,544
Crime	6,828	2,811	4,017	1,659	790	846	1,414	1,543	1,465	1,130	2,288	1,944
Noise	7,607	3,669	3,938	1,120	738	1,203	1,682	1,364	1,822	1,602	2,068	2,115
Traffic	6,920	4,245	2,675	598	460	969	1,215	891	1,630	1,498	2,039	1,754
Litter or housing deterioration	3,980	2,699	1,281	640	302	812	574	605	828	892	1,426	834
Poor city or county services	1,272	858	414	250	116	187	197	182	305	260	484	223
Undesirable commercial, institutional, industrial uses	1,387	883	505	152	73	273	204	159	347	345	440	256
People	11,825	6,610	5,215	1,712	1,008	1,834	2,348	2,220	2,101	2,814	4,106	2,804
Other	9,898	6,963	2,935	1,125	607	1,555	1,421	1,115	1,873	2,246	3,303	2,476
Type of problem not reported	496	323	173	77	11	77	94	94	71	117	213	95
Presence of problems not reported	188	124	64	39	10	60	33	45	26	43	81	38
Other buildings vandalized or with interior exposed [2]												
None	21,228	3,006	18,222	3,573	2,443	3,710	6,976	4,591	6,222	4,472	5,680	4,853
1 building	418	39	379	173	77	72	136	163	197	67	94	61
More than 1 building	821	44	776	438	192	91	234	353	317	230	144	129
No buildings within 300 feet	419	61	358	76	31	104	189	74	77	94	195	53
Not reported	1,898	309	1,589	284	119	516	343	418	265	677	610	348

See notes at end of table.

Current Characteristics of the Housing Stock

TABLE 2.30. SELECTED NEIGHBORHOOD CONDITIONS FOR OCCUPIED HOUSING UNITS: 1993 - Continued

(In thousands, except as noted)

CHARACTERISTIC	Total occupied units	Tenure		Household characteristics					Regions			
		Owner	Renter	Black	Hispanic	Elderly (65+)	Moved in past year	Below poverty level	North-east	Midwest	South	West
Bars on windows of buildings [2]												
With other buildings within 300 feet	22,467	3,090	19,377	4,184	2,712	3,874	7,347	5,107	6,736	4,769	5,918	5,043
No bars on windows	18,538	2,577	15,961	2,879	1,812	3,235	6,469	3,940	4,872	4,347	5,231	4,089
1 building with bars	527	68	460	158	96	111	131	120	180	64	110	174
2 or more buildings with bars	3,286	426	2,859	1,118	790	503	718	1,017	1,635	341	549	761
Not reported	115	19	97	29	15	25	29	30	49	18	28	20
Condition of streets [2]												
No repairs needed	17,379	2,623	14,756	2,863	1,885	3,216	5,698	3,431	5,326	3,532	4,582	3,939
Minor repairs needed	4,863	497	4,366	1,207	736	713	1,586	1,505	1,376	1,210	1,218	1,058
Major repairs needed	589	37	552	186	137	57	200	240	161	153	189	85
No streets within 300 feet	453	54	399	76	21	52	196	61	65	79	196	113
Not reported	1,500	249	1,251	211	83	455	199	362	149	565	537	249
Trash, litter, or junk on streets or any properties [2]												
None	16,853	2,685	14,168	2,411	1,501	3,235	5,593	2,993	4,789	3,704	4,616	3,744
Minor accumulation	5,725	487	5,238	1,642	1,054	768	1,855	1,899	1,924	1,115	1,393	1,292
Major accumulation	720	37	683	290	223	46	235	352	210	163	185	162
Not reported	1,487	251	1,235	202	84	445	194	355	154	559	529	245

Source: U.S. Bureau of the Census and U.S. Department of Housing and Urban Development, "American Housing Survey for the United States in 1993." Current Housing Reports H150/93. Issued February 1995.

Consistent with the 1990 Census.
(1) Figures may not add to total because more than one category may apply.
(2) Limited to multiunit structures.

Current Characteristics of the Housing Stock

TABLE 2.31. SELECTED NEIGHBORHOOD CONDITIONS FOR OCCUPIED HOUSING UNITS: 1995
(In thousands, except as noted)

CHARACTERISTIC	Total occupied units	Tenure		Household characteristics					Regions			
		Owner	Renter	Black	Hispanic	Elderly (65+)	Moved in past year	Below poverty level	Northeast	Midwest	South	West
TOTAL	97,693	63,544	34,150	11,773	7,757	20,841	17,204	14,695	19,200	23,662	34,236	20,596
OVERALL OPINION OF NEIGHBORHOOD												
1 (Worst)	1,349	447	902	443	216	254	331	576	325	334	412	278
2	795	324	471	189	81	132	182	243	159	167	258	212
3	1,208	482	726	255	159	185	289	330	246	295	362	304
4	1,813	764	1,049	280	211	220	442	366	366	414	528	505
5	7,011	3,387	3,623	1,249	793	1,288	1,481	1,558	1,309	1,578	2,421	1,703
6	4,919	2,521	2,398	800	504	737	1,150	846	975	1,080	1,642	1,222
7	10,173	5,943	4,230	1,410	764	1,442	2,020	1,301	2,076	2,309	3,373	2,415
8	22,242	14,692	7,551	2,522	1,606	4,256	3,838	2,779	4,436	5,417	7,599	4,791
9	14,361	10,311	4,050	1,277	972	2,780	2,387	1,540	2,837	3,771	4,681	3,073
10 (Best)	31,623	23,354	8,269	3,125	2,264	8,842	4,764	4,695	5,881	7,871	12,109	5,762
No neighborhood	872	628	244	20	42	226	107	122	103	192	455	122
Not reported	1,326	691	636	205	144	480	214	340	487	233	398	209
NEIGHBORHOOD CONDITIONS												
With neighborhood	95,495	62,225	33,270	11,549	7,571	20,135	16,883	14,233	18,609	23,237	33,383	20,265
No problems	60,176	40,612	19,563	6,711	4,657	14,577	10,336	8,831	11,698	15,015	21,719	11,745
With problems [1]	34,852	21,308	13,543	4,756	2,892	5,458	6,432	5,325	6,850	8,172	11,353	8,477
Crime	6,926	2,920	4,007	1,649	871	812	1,503	1,554	1,349	1,417	2,168	1,993
Noise	7,396	3,505	3,891	1,148	751	1,166	1,758	1,333	1,663	1,540	2,145	2,050
Traffic	7,319	4,478	2,842	712	484	1,000	1,365	957	1,577	1,639	2,181	1,922
Litter or housing deterioration	4,058	2,680	1,378	750	398	832	639	696	789	941	1,371	957
Poor city or county services	1,179	777	402	206	128	152	214	199	299	230	384	266
Undesirable commercial, institutional, industrial uses	1,335	870	465	167	89	229	253	194	309	341	407	279
People	11,161	6,147	5,013	1,680	1,146	1,694	2,332	2,157	2,118	2,921	3,399	2,723
Other	9,441	6,683	2,758	1,113	623	1,571	1,341	1,176	1,938	2,062	3,227	2,215
Type of problem not reported	604	395	208	70	47	75	125	77	101	83	336	84
Presence of problems not reported	468	304	164	82	22	101	115	78	62	51	312	43
Other buildings vandalized or with interior exposed [2]												
None	22,065	3,070	18,995	3,878	2,940	3,855	7,575	4,956	6,275	4,674	5,751	5,365
1 building	443	44	399	160	102	52	121	146	208	94	73	68
More than 1 building	664	64	601	345	143	73	206	308	296	152	149	67
No buildings within 300 feet	390	59	332	80	26	125	134	110	128	78	139	45
Not reported	1,606	283	1,322	240	165	359	393	328	349	299	642	316
Bars on windows of buildings [2]												
With other buildings within 300 feet	23,172	3,177	19,995	4,383	3,185	3,981	7,902	5,411	6,779	4,921	5,973	5,500
No bars on windows	19,514	2,729	16,785	3,116	2,208	3,411	6,840	4,163	5,268	4,476	5,252	4,518
1 building with bars	544	79	465	133	136	74	163	187	176	83	93	192
2 or more buildings with bars	2,948	358	2,590	1,083	816	446	838	1,003	1,286	329	582	752
Not reported	166	11	155	51	25	50	61	58	49	33	45	39
Condition of streets [2]												
No repairs needed	17,909	2,676	15,233	2,925	2,277	3,244	6,093	3,788	5,128	3,727	4,653	4,401
Minor repairs needed	5,039	509	4,530	1,328	845	759	1,689	1,554	1,623	1,180	1,201	1,034
Major repairs needed	520	59	460	182	101	89	175	181	180	101	141	97
No streets within 300 feet	295	18	277	58	27	38	120	43	37	44	138	77
Not reported	1,405	257	1,149	211	126	333	351	283	288	246	621	251
Trash, litter, or junk on streets or any properties [2]												
None	17,367	2,754	14,614	2,453	1,976	3,337	5,865	3,323	4,870	3,783	4,665	4,050
Minor accumulation	5,808	462	5,346	1,769	1,101	727	2,018	1,960	1,866	1,181	1,354	1,407
Major accumulation	609	62	547	273	174	54	202	284	241	91	121	156
Not reported	1,384	242	1,142	208	126	346	345	283	279	243	614	247

Source: U.S. Bureau of the Census and U.S. Department of Housing and Urban Development, "American Housing Survey for the United States in 1995." Current Housing Reports H150/95RV.

Consistent with the 1990 Census.
(1) Figures may not add to total because more than one category may apply.
(2) Limited to multiunit structures.

Current Characteristics of the Housing Stock

CHARACTERISTIC	Total, all single-family	Single-family detached	Single-family attached	Single unit with business	Condominium	Cooperative	Mobile home
TABLE 2.32. SELECTED CHARACTERISTICS OF PRIVATELY-OWNED SINGLE-FAMILY RENTAL HOUSING BY TYPE OF PROPERTY: 1996 (Number of housing units)							
TOTAL	8,773,165	6,438,228	773,229	74,302	568,566	117,726	801,114
YEAR STRUCTURE BUILT							
1990 or later	175,305	85,340	45,181	0	29,460	0	15,324
1985 to 1989	533,188	214,640	79,106	0	95,391	0	144,051
1980 to 1984	648,702	335,470	73,709	2,991	130,780	0	105,752
1970 to 1979	1,477,096	756,098	211,797	2,496	168,750	32,739	305,216
1960 to 1969	1,074,959	776,483	56,962	0	72,584	38,373	130,557
1950 to 1959	1,261,931	1,121,518	73,856	14,886	17,305	10,688	23,678
1940 to 1949	973,857	909,274	30,787	6,406	11,284	16,106	0
1930 to 1939	591,941	532,779	39,343	13,209	0	3,966	2,644
1920 to 1929	523,756	442,723	71,529	0	9,504	0	0
1919 or earlier	744,137	630,588	67,685	30,920	4,946	7,442	2,556
Not reported	768,293	633,313	23,274	3,393	28,563	8,413	71,337
AMENITIES AVAILABLE TO TENANTS [1]							
Air conditioning	4,477,452	2,999,141	417,607	35,669	419,284	49,309	556,442
Covered off-street parking	4,189,988	3,468,215	267,149	17,364	261,777	25,862	149,621
Uncovered off-street parking	5,095,358	3,399,261	490,511	57,590	426,743	75,792	645,461
Swimming pool	908,977	314,906	133,673	6,064	389,253	19,836	45,245
Cable television	5,138,427	3,583,992	508,902	38,115	492,631	106,882	407,905
Laundry facilities	5,148,437	3,669,811	507,505	34,313	480,638	78,007	378,163
Security system or protective system	953,946	498,831	109,167	6,189	243,467	46,600	49,692
Specified amenities not available	377,307	263,511	28,117	2,991	20,573	21,564	40,551
Not reported	169,358	130,207	9,132	0	9,234	4,917	15,868

Source: U.S. Bureau of the Census, Property Owners and Managers Survey.

(1) Numbers of units for all amenity categories will sum to more than total because of multiple responses.

Current Characteristics of the Housing Stock

TABLE 2.33. SELECTED CHARACTERISTICS OF PRIVATELY-OWNED MULTIFAMILY RENTAL HOUSING BY NUMBER OF UNITS AT PROPERTY: 1996
(Number of housing units)

CHARACTERISTIC	Total, all multifamily	2 units	3 or 4 units	5-9 units	10-19 units	20-49 units	50 or more units
TOTAL	20,584,822	3,084,750	2,471,070	1,894,445	1,467,786	2,223,786	9,442,986
YEAR STRUCTURE BUILT							
1990 or later	750,351	81,859	50,711	44,233	52,722	56,721	464,105
1985 to 1989	2,301,360	122,502	113,329	154,135	82,089	195,555	1,633,750
1980 to 1984	1,915,560	134,754	131,104	73,915	167,836	244,322	1,163,629
1970 to 1979	5,005,780	337,820	297,269	266,586	242,758	500,178	3,361,169
1960 to 1969	3,025,402	285,904	248,152	270,547	228,115	381,381	1,611,303
1950 to 1959	1,294,410	307,845	214,460	153,405	124,232	135,552	358,916
1940 to 1949	1,094,959	328,255	201,392	146,508	94,824	83,557	240,423
1930 to 1939	978,457	311,678	233,874	120,269	75,307	133,700	103,629
1920 to 1929	1,266,807	339,522	257,005	160,198	109,543	188,143	212,396
1919 or earlier	1,910,132	593,638	547,829	313,228	178,179	158,263	118,995
Not reported	1,041,605	240,972	175,948	191,419	112,179	146,415	174,672
AMENITIES AVAILABLE TO TENANTS [1]							
Air conditioning	12,692,853	1,162,576	955,197	810,725	789,904	1,272,279	7,702,172
Covered off-street parking	6,577,898	1,035,976	614,810	518,966	379,585	587,765	3,440,796
Uncovered off-street parking	15,136,010	1,663,022	1,466,266	1,163,148	1,022,226	1,508,389	8,312,959
Swimming pool	6,615,524	85,322	72,900	149,373	206,428	440,175	5,661,326
Cable television	15,660,868	1,838,226	1,613,257	1,250,843	1,070,283	1,680,677	8,207,582
Secretarial/message service	1,216,054	15,392	43,271	23,628	33,530	90,944	1,009,289
Common room(s) for parties	5,222,674	23,205	40,102	91,551	118,416	320,512	4,628,888
Organized social events	5,174,333	12,529	37,198	87,480	101,295	264,279	4,671,552
Electronic security system for individual units	2,375,480	88,298	130,937	124,415	104,754	251,338	1,675,738
Shuttle bus service	1,570,718	72,740	79,906	62,002	72,880	127,990	1,155,200
Athletic facilities	4,236,409	30,178	58,844	109,186	95,101	154,796	3,788,304
Laundry appliances in unit	4,346,622	809,907	475,840	296,919	208,170	270,337	2,285,449
Common laundry room	12,581,075	533,794	653,071	796,362	926,594	1,661,508	8,009,746
Elevator	2,867,886	0	20,794	18,898	83,303	387,518	2,357,373
Security system or protective system	5,862,692	121,316	159,223	254,672	259,652	610,459	4,457,370
Automatic sprinkler system	3,579,528	60,103	136,604	138,433	190,928	383,117	2,670,343
Play area with equipment for children	4,340,609	135,425	134,142	140,665	118,408	275,945	3,536,024
Specified amenities not available	951,710	284,728	214,906	189,822	94,811	128,424	39,019
Not reported	276,269	73,057	41,234	70,833	44,646	23,215	23,284
STRUCTURES ON PROPERTY							
1 building	9,390,672	2,757,211	2,028,080	1,222,792	812,794	1,022,340	1,547,455
2 buildings	1,554,167	231,682	235,082	263,964	226,437	301,350	295,652
3 or 4 buildings	1,345,682	7,683	125,292	113,140	154,852	363,342	581,373
5 or more buildings	7,836,779	24,165	26,776	175,963	206,171	508,321	6,895,383
Not reported	457,521	64,009	55,840	118,585	67,530	28,433	123,124

Source: U.S. Bureau of the Census, Property Owners and Managers Survey.

(1) Numbers of units for all amenity categories will sum to more than total because of multiple responses.

The table shows housing units categorized by the number of units at a given property, not the number of units in the building.

Housing Production and Investment

TABLE 2.34. NEW PRIVATELY-OWNED HOUSING UNITS AUTHORIZED IN PERMIT-ISSUING PLACES BY REGION AND STRUCTURE TYPE: 1959 TO 1997
(Thousands of units)

YEAR		United States					Northeast	Midwest	South	West
		Total	Number of units in structure							
			1 unit	2 units	3 and 4 units	5 units or more				
10,000-place series	1959	1,208	938	77		193	222	286	356	344
	1960	998	746	65		187	199	228	283	288
	1961	1,064	723	68		274	229	226	299	309
	1962	1,187	716	87		383	243	238	343	363
12,000-place series	1963	1,335	750	51	68	466	239	269	403	423
	1964	1,286	720	49	52	465	243	287	401	354
	1965	1,240	710	47	38	445	253	311	408	269
	1966	972	563	36	25	348	210	251	331	180
13,000-place series	1967	1,141	651	43	31	418	223	310	391	218
	1968	1,353	695	45	39	574	235	350	477	291
	1969	1,324	626	45	41	613	216	317	471	320
	1970	1,352	647	43	45	617	218	287	503	343
	1971	1,925	906	62	71	886	304	421	725	475
14,000-place series	1972	2,219	1,033	68	81	1,037	333	441	905	539
	1973	1,820	882	54	63	820	272	361	763	423
	1974	1,074	644	33	32	366	165	241	390	278
	1975	939	675	34	30	200	130	242	293	275
	1976	1,296	894	48	46	309	152	326	402	416
	1977	1,690	1,126	62	59	443	182	402	561	545
16,000-place series	1978	1,801	1,183	64	66	487	194	388	668	551
	1979	1,552	982	60	66	445	167	289	628	468
	1980	1,191	710	54	61	366	118	192	562	319
	1981	986	564	45	57	319	110	133	491	251
	1982	1,000	546	38	50	366	107	126	543	224
	1983	1,605	901	58	76	570	164	188	863	390
17,000-place series	1984	1,682	922	62	81	617	201	212	812	457
	1985	1,733	957	54	66	657	260	237	753	484
	1986	1,769	1,078	50	58	584	283	290	687	510
	1987	1,535	1,024	41	49	421	272	282	575	406
	1988	1,456	994	35	41	386	230	266	544	416
	1989	1,338	932	32	35	340	179	252	505	402
	1990	1,111	794	27	28	263	126	234	426	325
	1991	949	754	22	21	152	110	215	376	248
	1992	1,095	911	23	23	138	125	259	443	269
	1993	1,199	987	27	26	160	134	277	501	288
19,000-place series	1994	1,372	1,069	31	31	241	139	305	586	342
	1995	1,333	997	32	32	272	124	297	583	329
	1996	1,426	1,070	34	32	290	137	318	623	347
	1997	1,441	1,062	35	34	310	142	300	636	364

Source: U.S. Bureau of the Census, Building Permits Survey.

Details may not add to totals because of rounding.

Housing Production and Investment

TABLE 2.35. NUMBER OF NEW PRIVATELY-OWNED HOUSING UNITS AUTHORIZED IN PERMIT-ISSUING PLACES BY STRUCTURE TYPE AND STATE: 1980 TO 1997

AREA	1980						1981					
		Number of units in structure						Number of units in structure				
	Total units	1 unit	2 units	3 and 4 units	5 units or more	Number of structures with 5 or more units	Total units	1 unit	2 units	3 and 4 units	5 units or more	Number of structures with 5 or more units
United States	1,190,600	710,390	53,768	60,712	365,730	24,717	985,533	564,313	44,586	57,214	319,420	22,360
Alabama	15,909	8,973	272	756	5,908	608	9,868	5,046	236	595	3,991	338
Alaska	2,230	1,621	214	97	298	42	4,514	3,025	504	248	737	77
Arizona	36,688	22,759	738	1,342	11,849	494	33,395	19,165	742	1,514	11,974	572
Arkansas	8,162	4,920	474	677	2,091	174	4,590	2,804	284	621	881	80
California	144,375	86,638	5,776	9,486	42,475	3,921	104,205	60,028	3,980	8,035	32,162	2,777
Colorado	30,129	19,184	860	1,568	8,517	549	29,391	18,547	846	1,680	8,318	717
Connecticut	10,088	6,211	420	249	3,208	254	9,321	5,522	346	356	3,097	233
Delaware	2,895	2,351	2	20	522	58	2,302	1,752	32	92	426	42
District of Columbia	2,661	478	34	0	2,149	46	981	88	14	0	879	27
Florida	174,247	88,821	10,810	10,512	64,104	3,482	146,163	69,155	8,320	9,988	58,700	3,479
Georgia	34,837	25,343	906	922	7,666	719	29,996	19,889	1,476	1,263	7,368	778
Hawaii	10,323	3,994	82	472	5,775	237	6,262	2,431	188	220	3,423	83
Idaho	5,795	4,434	318	361	682	52	3,382	2,633	154	127	468	45
Illinois	25,226	10,627	1,042	1,765	11,792	744	16,356	8,769	672	1,069	5,846	355
Indiana	20,919	10,716	520	850	8,833	612	13,900	7,479	416	760	5,245	410
Iowa	8,740	4,773	604	778	2,585	215	5,592	3,576	312	603	1,101	91
Kansas	10,886	6,126	1,286	1,179	2,295	153	8,153	5,314	944	733	1,162	91
Kentucky	10,188	5,947	570	681	2,990	285	7,609	4,017	346	365	2,881	191
Louisiana	20,509	11,941	1,054	2,580	4,934	291	19,627	10,627	1,040	2,930	5,030	351
Maine	3,406	2,213	212	256	725	68	2,521	2,036	48	166	271	32
Maryland	20,028	16,447	190	68	3,323	141	16,988	13,706	234	127	2,921	137
Massachusetts	16,480	10,514	526	424	5,016	207	16,669	10,269	524	614	5,262	262
Michigan	28,976	17,870	780	999	9,327	508	18,767	11,449	450	874	5,994	352
Minnesota	21,287	13,393	1,258	931	5,705	266	17,256	11,433	1,026	1,233	3,564	209
Mississippi	9,357	5,286	396	815	2,860	275	5,459	3,634	180	378	1,267	135
Missouri	13,621	8,412	776	849	3,584	294	9,879	6,330	528	750	2,271	135
Montana	2,314	1,339	120	345	510	35	1,876	1,000	148	291	437	55
Nebraska	6,666	4,928	386	317	1,035	75	3,783	2,628	208	217	730	63
Nevada	11,752	6,275	170	966	4,341	333	10,267	5,793	150	679	3,645	306
New Hampshire	5,278	3,678	248	167	1,185	92	4,368	2,969	316	176	907	69
New Jersey	22,270	14,780	1,598	296	5,596	332	20,676	12,329	1,422	419	6,506	372
New Mexico	8,665	6,090	254	890	1,431	75	7,952	5,630	92	938	1,292	138
New York	24,491	14,423	1,550	978	7,540	296	26,234	13,884	1,502	1,649	9,199	386
North Carolina	35,509	25,202	1,522	1,892	6,893	722	34,113	22,062	1,100	2,544	8,407	884
North Dakota	3,111	1,642	168	214	1,087	84	2,155	1,049	110	131	865	70
Ohio	31,227	16,264	1,874	2,415	10,674	977	21,820	11,156	966	1,721	7,977	802
Oklahoma	17,688	11,607	1,072	560	4,449	270	14,972	10,108	1,192	489	3,183	314
Oregon	19,253	13,607	1,376	849	3,421	324	12,887	8,786	604	565	2,932	254
Pennsylvania	30,037	20,409	1,450	931	7,247	408	24,345	15,880	1,086	754	6,625	454
Rhode Island	2,909	1,713	100	62	1,034	47	3,139	1,378	122	40	1,599	67
South Carolina	22,333	15,594	606	1,153	4,980	417	18,915	11,029	470	964	6,452	506
South Dakota	3,100	2,133	36	85	846	63	1,490	1,054	42	30	364	31
Tennessee	19,389	12,334	1,204	577	5,274	321	11,675	7,531	950	407	2,787	197
Texas	127,546	67,221	5,390	3,453	51,482	3,018	135,759	65,509	6,222	4,997	59,031	3,870
Utah	10,463	7,647	622	459	1,735	127	8,715	5,397	578	871	1,869	99
Vermont	2,918	1,786	100	88	944	85	2,574	1,440	170	155	809	73
Virginia	37,285	29,062	702	806	6,715	580	29,677	22,503	716	739	5,719	409
Washington	33,043	17,856	1,394	2,970	10,823	791	24,384	14,894	1,060	1,828	6,602	478
West Virginia	3,326	1,500	102	187	1,537	87	2,377	1,279	84	84	930	53
Wisconsin	18,220	11,005	1,430	1,001	4,784	381	14,160	8,088	1,112	750	4,210	326
Wyoming	3,845	2,303	174	414	954	82	4,074	2,213	322	435	1,104	85

See notes at end of table.

Housing Production and Investment

	1982						1983					
		Number of units in structure						Number of units in structure				
AREA	Total units	1 unit	2 units	3 and 4 units	5 units or more	Number of structures with 5 or more units	Total units	1 unit	2 units	3 and 4 units	5 units or more	Number of structures with 5 or more units
United States	1,000,485	546,433	38,366	49,917	365,769	26,537	1,605,221	901,460	57,516	76,134	570,111	42,456
Alabama	8,691	4,701	162	307	3,521	315	17,326	8,551	250	919	7,606	583
Alaska	8,242	4,273	776	745	2,448	177	11,248	4,568	668	2,136	3,876	294
Arizona	36,545	19,545	514	1,827	14,659	1,017	63,964	30,807	1,100	2,824	29,233	2,058
Arkansas	6,325	2,228	348	770	2,979	211	9,989	4,208	776	882	4,123	317
California	85,031	50,761	3,142	5,481	25,647	2,315	171,889	102,311	4,974	9,684	54,920	4,974
Colorado	31,788	19,207	520	1,074	10,987	822	51,290	29,968	884	1,722	18,716	1,587
Connecticut	10,276	6,403	224	317	3,332	201	15,672	11,661	328	300	3,383	243
Delaware	2,968	1,525	192	74	1,177	78	3,627	2,530	78	181	838	82
District of Columbia	432	29	12	0	391	17	164	54	2	0	108	7
Florida	103,813	56,448	5,942	7,511	33,912	2,552	188,986	100,020	8,812	14,050	66,104	5,574
Georgia	38,737	25,224	1,630	1,750	10,133	836	65,910	40,522	2,592	2,345	20,451	1,822
Hawaii	5,675	2,132	40	86	3,417	121	4,760	3,277	142	96	1,245	52
Idaho	2,536	2,176	68	53	239	15	4,225	3,359	110	246	510	39
Illinois	18,960	7,980	588	853	9,539	430	29,836	17,654	1,136	1,208	9,838	566
Indiana	12,482	6,022	360	844	5,256	466	16,027	10,125	508	780	4,614	494
Iowa	5,271	3,039	186	393	1,653	140	6,999	3,938	310	416	2,335	157
Kansas	8,572	4,226	870	975	2,501	201	14,168	7,562	1,798	1,315	3,493	283
Kentucky	7,514	4,107	298	487	2,622	225	11,675	6,000	472	780	4,423	416
Louisiana	20,316	11,351	832	2,825	5,308	426	33,847	17,649	916	3,329	11,953	916
Maine	3,146	2,178	78	233	657	68	4,162	3,224	62	192	684	67
Maryland	20,958	16,672	160	74	4,052	226	39,624	30,448	154	331	8,691	509
Massachusetts	15,435	9,851	482	295	4,807	293	22,836	16,688	794	527	4,827	318
Michigan	14,176	8,113	246	432	5,385	322	21,423	14,972	404	867	5,180	348
Minnesota	18,820	11,162	500	1,168	5,990	277	24,810	16,122	636	1,581	6,471	325
Mississippi	6,207	3,442	346	374	2,045	203	9,620	4,880	648	1,235	2,857	291
Missouri	11,544	6,076	438	1,175	3,855	265	18,687	12,318	852	1,266	4,251	378
Montana	2,022	983	110	239	690	65	3,001	1,661	190	365	785	87
Nebraska	3,614	2,412	168	203	831	58	5,465	3,969	284	164	1,048	75
Nevada	8,138	4,364	158	922	2,694	280	15,982	8,426	62	951	6,543	649
New Hampshire	4,508	3,042	186	127	1,153	87	7,727	5,324	446	153	1,804	117
New Jersey	21,297	14,005	960	499	5,833	341	35,897	25,539	1,346	567	8,445	594
New Mexico	8,600	5,540	96	451	2,513	285	10,742	8,009	120	572	2,041	224
New York	24,980	12,956	1,516	931	9,577	388	37,908	20,807	2,508	1,487	13,106	500
North Carolina	33,088	21,378	1,162	2,291	8,257	907	53,945	33,948	1,576	3,006	15,415	1,538
North Dakota	2,759	1,366	66	149	1,178	85	4,364	1,708	200	316	2,140	140
Ohio	16,600	9,059	632	979	5,930	515	26,567	16,451	994	1,301	7,821	768
Oklahoma	28,741	14,277	1,744	908	11,812	972	40,077	17,713	1,360	1,267	19,737	1,569
Oregon	7,458	4,975	314	301	1,868	148	8,593	6,748	320	345	1,180	78
Pennsylvania	22,201	14,427	1,084	599	6,091	420	33,208	24,579	1,484	866	6,279	450
Rhode Island	2,602	1,327	96	64	1,115	38	3,765	2,635	134	135	861	45
South Carolina	18,010	11,008	836	706	5,460	440	29,769	17,759	1,360	1,542	9,108	788
South Dakota	1,220	798	32	39	351	25	2,489	1,391	58	42	998	49
Tennessee	14,799	7,328	1,330	838	5,303	421	26,553	13,548	3,072	995	8,938	513
Texas	201,163	77,421	6,362	6,534	110,846	7,317	276,224	100,825	8,770	7,456	159,173	9,575
Utah	7,537	4,678	462	539	1,858	165	14,667	9,105	392	744	4,426	312
Vermont	2,210	1,539	74	77	520	45	2,881	1,867	116	149	749	67
Virginia	29,878	22,998	508	547	5,825	600	53,773	43,244	974	1,611	7,944	727
Washington	17,559	11,381	560	1,010	4,608	358	27,248	18,500	1,016	1,464	6,268	499
West Virginia	1,824	974	32	87	731	47	1,834	1,150	20	113	551	57
Wisconsin	12,280	7,343	802	511	3,624	273	16,962	11,234	1,188	881	3,659	300
Wyoming	2,937	1,983	122	243	589	38	2,816	1,904	120	430	362	35

TABLE 2.35. NUMBER OF NEW PRIVATELY-OWNED HOUSING UNITS AUTHORIZED IN PERMIT-ISSUING PLACES BY STRUCTURE TYPE AND STATE: 1980 TO 1997 - Continued

See notes at end of table.

Housing Production and Investment

TABLE 2.35. NUMBER OF NEW PRIVATELY-OWNED HOUSING UNITS AUTHORIZED IN PERMIT-ISSUING PLACES BY STRUCTURE TYPE AND STATE: 1980 TO 1997 - Continued

AREA	1984 Total units	1984 1 unit	1984 2 units	1984 3 and 4 units	1984 5 units or more	1984 Number of structures with 5 or more units	1985 Total units	1985 1 unit	1985 2 units	1985 3 and 4 units	1985 5 units or more	1985 Number of structures with 5 or more units
United States	1,681,822	922,447	61,852	80,716	616,807	47,262	1,733,266	956,595	54,024	66,052	656,595	48,081
Alabama	15,308	8,224	228	1,665	5,191	461	17,237	9,932	166	708	6,431	544
Alaska	6,486	3,649	484	1,004	1,349	128	4,029	2,233	272	598	926	90
Arizona	79,239	30,685	1,084	3,130	44,340	3,103	71,820	32,672	1,154	2,157	35,837	2,451
Arkansas	9,727	4,535	742	1,005	3,445	309	9,935	5,224	722	781	3,208	272
California	224,689	112,920	6,496	13,434	91,839	8,214	271,396	113,647	6,390	13,765	137,594	11,255
Colorado	44,329	23,359	856	1,716	18,398	1,372	32,824	20,071	606	856	11,291	763
Connecticut	17,778	13,292	520	468	3,498	228	24,545	16,762	622	540	6,621	517
Delaware	4,364	2,756	46	216	1,346	135	4,636	3,345	44	24	1,223	66
District of Columbia	393	88	30	4	271	12	590	152	24	31	383	4
Florida	204,884	103,072	8,474	12,164	81,174	6,464	202,615	104,642	6,742	9,068	82,163	6,284
Georgia	70,264	43,560	2,922	2,728	21,054	1,810	73,141	45,871	2,770	2,120	22,380	1,804
Hawaii	5,401	4,121	144	93	1,043	64	7,262	4,565	190	207	2,300	109
Idaho	4,308	3,370	168	292	478	50	4,307	2,963	136	328	880	59
Illinois	30,160	19,556	1,198	1,420	7,986	672	38,719	20,496	1,212	1,902	15,109	974
Indiana	18,904	11,012	776	796	6,320	523	23,016	12,654	756	797	8,809	743
Iowa	7,000	3,948	210	266	2,576	150	5,190	2,790	128	266	2,006	113
Kansas	16,727	7,098	1,298	1,100	7,231	557	13,267	6,042	956	901	5,368	403
Kentucky	13,043	6,198	452	746	5,647	520	13,770	6,346	440	810	6,174	591
Louisiana	28,073	14,985	758	2,505	9,825	657	18,766	11,133	584	1,247	5,802	417
Maine	6,570	4,347	132	376	1,715	167	8,113	5,672	244	554	1,643	178
Maryland	38,523	30,083	118	258	8,064	400	42,137	34,293	48	863	6,933	398
Massachusetts	29,288	21,184	1,358	887	5,859	418	39,196	25,594	1,746	1,250	10,606	693
Michigan	27,749	17,200	424	1,415	8,710	665	37,592	21,792	422	1,655	13,723	1,047
Minnesota	26,698	16,042	530	1,256	8,870	397	28,611	16,382	486	791	10,952	467
Mississippi	11,524	6,465	430	640	3,989	379	8,757	5,862	412	521	1,962	184
Missouri	24,817	12,376	1,274	1,713	9,454	815	27,236	13,706	1,312	1,971	10,247	817
Montana	2,837	1,551	182	399	705	82	2,034	954	106	158	816	53
Nebraska	5,786	3,895	284	174	1,433	96	5,001	3,268	256	137	1,340	84
Nevada	13,749	6,698	232	1,099	5,720	628	14,004	7,385	118	332	6,169	529
New Hampshire	11,051	7,212	724	337	2,778	204	17,769	10,500	1,060	694	5,515	407
New Jersey	43,824	32,518	1,684	608	9,014	714	55,027	39,216	2,088	752	12,971	856
New Mexico	16,525	7,955	132	722	7,716	663	11,790	7,150	80	317	4,243	306
New York	44,729	26,837	3,320	2,313	12,259	509	61,927	34,292	3,564	2,310	21,761	864
North Carolina	62,687	38,462	1,892	3,688	18,645	1,852	70,727	41,723	1,894	2,540	24,570	2,118
North Dakota	3,185	1,397	142	204	1,442	98	2,641	890	126	134	1,491	73
Ohio	29,641	16,320	1,094	2,032	10,195	952	33,024	18,199	1,204	1,454	12,167	1,144
Oklahoma	22,926	11,634	838	647	9,807	690	10,670	7,023	254	140	3,253	191
Oregon	7,994	6,129	182	259	1,424	86	11,297	6,407	178	399	4,313	343
Pennsylvania	39,415	30,160	1,478	1,261	6,516	565	43,566	34,617	1,460	1,215	6,274	525
Rhode Island	4,208	3,040	358	169	641	51	5,408	3,990	278	193	947	110
South Carolina	35,891	19,032	1,250	1,668	13,941	1,172	32,815	18,738	1,370	1,098	11,609	919
South Dakota	3,221	1,637	44	99	1,441	77	2,544	1,432	56	135	921	53
Tennessee	36,764	13,769	3,962	1,508	17,525	1,246	38,126	17,310	2,366	887	17,563	1,329
Texas	195,426	84,559	8,990	6,791	95,086	5,756	143,114	69,322	5,354	3,758	64,680	3,251
Utah	19,698	8,630	484	892	9,692	681	16,525	9,789	256	649	5,831	429
Vermont	3,900	2,620	182	289	809	69	4,161	2,859	160	199	943	99
Virginia	60,209	43,544	1,030	1,425	14,210	1,011	64,120	46,826	898	677	15,719	1,245
Washington	30,391	17,153	874	1,480	10,884	942	35,474	17,040	1,038	2,111	15,285	1,361
West Virginia	2,099	1,311	18	124	646	62	1,477	1,111	34	85	247	28
Wisconsin	17,771	11,035	1,306	1,104	4,326	362	20,151	10,913	1,216	888	7,134	495
Wyoming	1,649	1,224	18	127	280	24	1,167	800	26	79	262	26

See notes at end of table.

Housing Production and Investment

TABLE 2.35. NUMBER OF NEW PRIVATELY-OWNED HOUSING UNITS AUTHORIZED IN PERMIT-ISSUING PLACES BY STRUCTURE TYPE AND STATE: 1980 TO 1997 - Continued

AREA	1986 Total units	1 unit	2 units	3 and 4 units	5 units or more	Number of structures with 5 or more units	1987 Total units	1 unit	2 units	3 and 4 units	5 units or more	Number of structures with 5 or more units
United States	1,769,443	1,077,596	50,398	57,962	583,487	42,794	1,534,772	1,024,374	40,778	48,475	421,145	31,680
Alabama	19,180	11,520	240	534	6,886	608	14,523	10,649	138	291	3,445	346
Alaska	1,353	974	126	197	56	7	731	401	56	127	147	3
Arizona	61,614	33,642	538	1,271	26,163	1,862	40,181	27,680	224	665	11,612	817
Arkansas	8,719	5,055	532	636	2,496	205	6,476	5,042	288	278	868	98
California	314,641	145,692	6,366	14,498	148,085	11,811	251,824	134,691	4,924	11,822	100,387	8,152
Colorado	30,961	20,409	514	584	9,454	532	17,988	12,903	314	341	4,430	233
Connecticut	27,730	20,494	752	790	5,694	459	26,750	18,081	834	512	7,323	591
Delaware	5,527	4,210	24	89	1,204	85	7,058	4,986	70	4	1,998	113
District of Columbia	640	142	26	0	472	30	1,198	286	10	16	886	9
Florida	195,525	110,022	4,952	6,908	73,643	5,465	178,764	113,130	4,944	5,782	54,908	4,042
Georgia	76,896	50,705	2,136	1,701	22,354	1,707	64,217	46,415	1,348	1,007	15,447	1,200
Hawaii	7,217	4,488	146	186	2,397	152	6,909	5,348	162	60	1,339	103
Idaho	3,804	2,897	144	206	557	60	3,185	2,570	60	174	381	53
Illinois	51,876	30,635	1,438	1,992	17,811	1,135	50,447	32,972	1,118	2,218	14,139	890
Indiana	29,686	17,198	974	1,036	10,478	823	27,273	18,889	1,118	876	6,390	510
Iowa	5,472	3,085	196	174	2,017	117	5,778	3,815	112	206	1,645	105
Kansas	13,086	7,309	976	611	4,190	267	11,782	7,839	820	452	2,671	224
Kentucky	13,503	8,037	490	561	4,415	336	13,223	9,027	370	374	3,452	248
Louisiana	10,501	8,594	402	183	1,322	106	8,520	7,070	166	157	1,127	96
Maine	9,554	6,801	288	479	1,986	197	9,800	7,228	238	308	2,026	175
Maryland	42,378	34,318	262	347	7,451	401	41,130	33,642	146	476	6,866	473
Massachusetts	45,215	28,110	2,256	1,726	13,123	846	40,419	25,311	2,370	1,504	11,234	675
Michigan	47,230	26,982	742	2,560	16,946	1,226	46,593	28,494	704	1,627	15,768	1,244
Minnesota	33,215	20,694	514	725	11,282	429	33,376	21,333	278	700	11,065	444
Mississippi	8,289	5,864	392	376	1,657	191	6,632	5,182	324	342	784	87
Missouri	33,208	17,414	1,636	1,967	12,191	873	29,085	18,014	1,178	1,707	8,186	603
Montana	1,153	726	56	200	171	26	792	610	14	55	113	2
Nebraska	6,236	3,331	266	130	2,509	126	4,902	3,289	184	36	1,393	70
Nevada	15,655	9,940	190	369	5,156	479	16,345	10,178	144	343	5,680	508
New Hampshire	18,015	12,273	1,570	1,046	3,126	220	14,564	10,878	1,104	664	1,918	136
New Jersey	57,352	42,606	2,558	584	11,604	878	51,462	36,497	2,408	715	11,842	854
New Mexico	11,513	8,122	76	199	3,116	162	9,268	7,338	40	160	1,730	70
New York	60,198	41,322	4,306	2,644	11,926	839	62,186	41,672	4,118	2,812	13,584	724
North Carolina	62,995	42,729	1,502	1,884	16,880	1,495	54,270	40,862	1,318	1,201	10,889	987
North Dakota	1,702	874	102	112	614	40	1,970	913	70	98	889	43
Ohio	44,460	25,610	1,462	1,782	15,606	1,447	45,153	28,786	1,424	2,980	11,963	1,034
Oklahoma	8,984	6,304	214	135	2,331	175	6,247	5,200	60	46	941	67
Oregon	10,662	6,996	248	360	3,058	258	12,218	7,887	204	256	3,871	305
Pennsylvania	53,442	43,972	1,280	951	7,239	591	54,803	45,783	1,168	1,193	6,659	570
Rhode Island	7,274	4,699	454	353	1,768	164	7,201	4,804	592	329	1,476	137
South Carolina	26,840	19,128	820	621	6,271	524	23,520	18,518	470	563	3,969	367
South Dakota	1,981	1,257	46	76	602	28	1,874	1,214	42	55	563	37
Tennessee	34,356	21,607	1,708	777	10,264	836	29,919	21,686	874	942	6,417	506
Texas	96,737	59,117	2,780	983	33,857	1,331	50,455	43,949	912	343	5,251	346
Utah	13,827	9,137	232	369	4,089	232	7,660	6,838	134	138	550	32
Vermont	4,478	3,484	176	230	588	62	4,610	3,744	142	205	519	67
Virginia	73,511	54,432	1,018	1,159	16,902	1,328	66,650	46,153	956	1,027	18,514	1,389
Washington	36,434	19,262	822	1,464	14,886	1,175	38,341	19,962	800	1,081	16,498	1,379
West Virginia	1,918	1,444	32	61	381	34	1,859	1,328	52	74	405	35
Wisconsin	21,824	13,151	1,400	1,110	6,163	408	24,064	14,788	1,224	1,109	6,943	475
Wyoming	876	782	18	26	50	6	577	499	10	24	44	6

See notes at end of table.

Housing Production and Investment

TABLE 2.35. NUMBER OF NEW PRIVATELY-OWNED HOUSING UNITS AUTHORIZED IN PERMIT-ISSUING PLACES BY STRUCTURE TYPE AND STATE: 1980 TO 1997 - Continued

AREA	1988 Total units	1 unit	2 units	3 and 4 units	5 units or more	Number of structures with 5 or more units	1989 Total units	1 unit	2 units	3 and 4 units	5 units or more	Number of structures with 5 or more units
United States	1,455,623	993,772	35,026	40,684	386,141	28,674	1,338,423	931,662	31,664	35,265	339,832	25,132
Alabama	12,773	9,668	170	430	2,505	236	12,042	8,500	130	502	2,910	244
Alaska	802	485	112	205	0	0	637	446	50	117	24	3
Arizona	32,878	23,367	244	380	8,887	570	23,820	20,206	236	310	3,068	255
Arkansas	6,232	4,696	226	330	980	89	6,339	4,559	306	339	1,135	103
California	253,369	160,735	4,366	8,955	79,313	6,154	237,694	162,981	4,148	7,838	62,727	5,462
Colorado	12,864	9,742	230	309	2,583	140	11,131	9,026	208	177	1,720	143
Connecticut	18,865	12,759	602	442	5,062	348	11,969	8,012	506	177	3,274	175
Delaware	7,423	5,885	88	128	1,322	139	5,763	4,639	38	96	990	95
District of Columbia	852	253	32	21	546	18	410	91	20	0	299	15
Florida	170,597	110,318	4,014	4,714	51,551	3,638	164,985	107,049	3,324	4,359	50,253	3,344
Georgia	63,017	42,559	1,204	882	18,372	1,258	50,457	35,145	978	521	13,813	1,047
Hawaii	8,445	5,740	202	284	2,219	173	9,555	6,176	264	196	2,919	228
Idaho	3,211	2,806	34	167	204	24	4,776	3,582	96	203	895	92
Illinois	49,145	33,936	1,272	1,853	12,084	758	42,377	30,205	1,296	1,544	9,332	579
Indiana	25,248	19,219	1,066	583	4,380	353	26,473	18,981	1,076	577	5,839	387
Iowa	6,785	4,414	182	260	1,929	79	7,392	4,911	240	408	1,833	125
Kansas	9,684	7,286	688	351	1,359	123	8,627	6,832	418	246	1,131	101
Kentucky	13,363	8,955	422	386	3,600	321	12,656	8,875	358	460	2,963	260
Louisiana	7,270	5,425	262	95	1,488	146	6,116	5,196	112	75	733	34
Maine	8,801	6,839	196	235	1,531	137	6,382	5,233	170	178	801	70
Maryland	39,568	33,294	146	240	5,888	371	40,585	29,748	316	82	10,439	579
Massachusetts	30,482	20,112	2,152	989	7,229	470	21,283	14,521	1,626	695	4,441	366
Michigan	44,907	29,724	618	1,605	12,960	912	45,687	30,778	706	1,381	12,822	816
Minnesota	28,380	19,237	288	533	8,322	417	25,127	18,298	222	376	6,231	335
Mississippi	7,396	4,918	250	345	1,883	154	6,643	4,701	340	238	1,364	147
Missouri	23,473	16,097	1,122	1,149	5,105	362	17,970	13,847	830	838	2,455	182
Montana	789	561	10	34	184	15	706	542	18	55	91	6
Nebraska	5,739	3,498	138	136	1,967	97	6,040	3,836	162	94	1,948	106
Nevada	30,769	12,566	98	360	17,745	1,583	29,253	16,147	252	584	12,270	930
New Hampshire	11,692	7,714	668	716	2,594	157	7,260	5,537	350	221	1,152	72
New Jersey	40,909	28,452	1,708	522	10,227	674	30,337	20,880	1,198	334	7,925	502
New Mexico	6,401	5,337	22	52	990	44	6,658	5,349	76	189	1,044	43
New York	54,719	37,498	3,162	2,588	11,471	755	48,735	31,915	3,144	2,378	11,298	592
North Carolina	50,322	39,469	1,066	1,326	8,461	768	48,351	35,324	898	873	11,256	929
North Dakota	1,815	848	46	121	800	37	2,210	828	34	36	1,312	47
Ohio	45,105	27,631	1,208	1,484	14,782	1,384	41,228	26,957	1,370	1,564	11,337	987
Oklahoma	5,046	4,330	80	138	498	65	5,622	4,634	80	80	828	28
Oregon	14,049	9,163	240	437	4,209	382	23,089	11,398	536	719	10,436	925
Pennsylvania	53,833	45,293	788	941	6,811	555	45,483	37,653	582	910	6,338	492
Rhode Island	6,065	3,655	628	246	1,536	138	3,865	2,900	392	223	350	43
South Carolina	23,102	17,091	464	676	4,871	387	21,204	16,872	346	494	3,492	289
South Dakota	1,922	1,094	34	100	694	35	2,075	1,212	34	73	756	41
Tennessee	27,803	19,397	666	632	7,108	509	24,244	17,638	656	574	5,376	580
Texas	40,479	35,881	502	351	3,745	211	41,287	36,631	258	548	3,850	210
Utah	6,269	5,857	58	114	240	22	5,993	5,601	64	102	226	22
Vermont	4,810	3,703	150	179	778	98	3,642	3,018	120	198	306	51
Virginia	66,487	48,204	820	1,164	16,299	1,172	56,877	40,540	680	823	14,834	936
Washington	45,055	21,484	926	1,304	21,341	1,656	48,210	26,420	1,046	1,080	19,664	1,497
West Virginia	1,784	1,302	36	70	376	32	1,689	1,363	22	73	231	24
Wisconsin	24,122	14,774	1,308	1,118	6,922	504	26,914	15,408	1,318	1,087	9,101	593
Wyoming	707	501	12	4	190	4	555	521	14	20	0	0

See notes at end of table.

Housing Production and Investment

TABLE 2.35. NUMBER OF NEW PRIVATELY-OWNED HOUSING UNITS AUTHORIZED IN PERMIT-ISSUING PLACES BY STRUCTURE TYPE AND STATE: 1980 TO 1997 - Continued

AREA	1990 Total units	1 unit	2 units	3 and 4 units	5 units or more	Number of structures with 5 or more units	1991 Total units	1 unit	2 units	3 and 4 units	5 units or more	Number of structures with 5 or more units
United States	1,110,766	793,924	26,664	27,606	262,572	19,069	948,794	753,537	21,992	21,118	152,147	11,471
Alabama	12,525	8,817	160	188	3,360	253	11,277	8,840	138	309	1,990	171
Alaska	732	626	56	26	24	2	1,047	916	46	57	28	2
Arizona	23,030	18,723	208	317	3,782	300	23,521	21,448	240	346	1,487	127
Arkansas	5,915	4,784	270	164	697	60	6,881	4,966	394	167	1,354	120
California	163,175	104,843	3,926	5,746	48,660	3,991	105,956	73,885	2,342	4,554	25,175	2,036
Colorado	11,897	10,095	204	165	1,433	100	14,071	12,938	172	153	808	71
Connecticut	7,584	5,525	296	181	1,582	84	7,477	5,902	174	123	1,278	86
Delaware	5,142	4,152	76	12	902	58	4,300	3,795	60	3	442	35
District of Columbia	368	180	26	0	162	3	333	83	14	0	236	2
Florida	126,347	82,624	2,212	2,114	39,397	2,676	95,308	71,003	1,432	1,936	20,937	1,402
Georgia	41,251	33,009	778	343	7,121	355	37,580	33,592	448	280	3,260	230
Hawaii	8,718	5,535	192	213	2,778	214	9,238	4,703	112	146	4,277	318
Idaho	5,703	4,677	124	290	612	58	6,603	5,483	182	242	696	72
Illinois	38,255	27,401	1,284	1,239	8,331	482	32,846	26,045	1,112	1,173	4,516	400
Indiana	25,002	19,331	848	479	4,344	313	23,936	19,385	822	253	3,476	209
Iowa	7,637	5,249	162	383	1,843	118	8,025	5,926	190	252	1,657	110
Kansas	8,454	6,362	414	358	1,320	128	7,780	6,641	418	209	512	51
Kentucky	11,810	8,739	404	370	2,297	219	11,961	9,192	388	330	2,051	195
Louisiana	6,451	5,711	66	35	639	38	7,182	6,670	96	27	389	28
Maine	4,757	4,047	112	126	472	37	3,710	3,468	94	17	131	18
Maryland	32,004	23,667	116	133	8,088	312	25,223	21,014	136	54	4,019	250
Massachusetts	14,290	10,749	866	376	2,299	162	12,672	11,343	466	181	682	75
Michigan	38,871	28,298	640	924	9,009	581	33,806	28,152	492	570	4,592	282
Minnesota	23,473	18,052	160	273	4,988	252	21,117	18,071	186	361	2,499	153
Mississippi	5,923	4,452	204	167	1,100	115	5,160	4,418	132	95	515	53
Missouri	15,284	12,327	684	780	1,493	134	16,118	13,070	768	836	1,444	121
Montana	1,191	721	32	97	341	20	1,504	1,004	58	189	253	29
Nebraska	6,750	4,031	150	62	2,507	128	6,235	4,569	172	91	1,403	100
Nevada	25,096	14,544	240	694	9,618	844	20,976	15,344	126	348	5,158	429
New Hampshire	4,126	3,439	138	57	492	24	3,488	3,311	40	49	88	11
New Jersey	17,524	12,801	654	130	3,939	250	14,856	12,869	402	101	1,484	140
New Mexico	5,988	5,018	22	215	733	88	6,057	5,413	36	50	558	49
New York	34,950	24,444	2,746	1,300	6,460	314	28,580	21,664	2,556	814	3,546	219
North Carolina	40,777	32,603	920	964	6,290	534	39,034	33,220	1,042	579	4,193	392
North Dakota	1,512	858	10	23	621	32	2,106	1,041	20	15	1,030	44
Ohio	38,491	26,399	1,134	1,264	9,694	795	35,810	27,062	1,156	1,324	6,268	513
Oklahoma	5,284	4,740	34	59	451	35	5,918	5,686	24	44	164	14
Oregon	22,858	13,298	352	1,023	8,185	768	16,384	11,755	436	553	3,640	355
Pennsylvania	37,204	31,037	574	722	4,871	357	34,608	29,353	530	505	4,220	276
Rhode Island	3,042	2,350	342	43	307	34	2,377	2,045	94	27	211	18
South Carolina	21,251	17,099	438	300	3,414	291	18,712	16,187	428	381	1,716	152
South Dakota	2,830	1,414	118	763	535	38	2,507	1,625	34	73	775	45
Tennessee	20,194	16,373	472	332	3,017	251	19,265	16,916	484	390	1,475	128
Texas	47,103	38,141	228	461	8,273	403	51,866	41,654	310	606	9,296	536
Utah	7,324	6,444	92	184	604	58	8,945	8,058	118	297	472	45
Vermont	2,370	2,079	40	38	213	25	2,013	1,842	8	16	147	17
Virginia	42,116	31,492	874	663	9,087	688	33,706	29,539	524	329	3,314	265
Washington	48,447	28,672	1,048	1,670	17,057	1,339	33,012	23,737	904	747	7,624	593
West Virginia	1,766	1,477	34	44	211	22	1,954	1,658	28	22	246	16
Wisconsin	27,282	15,931	1,476	1,066	8,809	676	25,122	16,483	1,404	878	6,357	463
Wyoming	692	544	8	30	110	10	631	553	4	16	58	5

See notes at end of table.

Housing Production and Investment

TABLE 2.35. NUMBER OF NEW PRIVATELY-OWNED HOUSING UNITS AUTHORIZED IN PERMIT-ISSUING PLACES BY STRUCTURE TYPE AND STATE: 1980 TO 1997 - Continued

AREA	1992 Total units	1 unit	2 units	3 and 4 units	5 units or more	Number of structures with 5 or more units	1993 Total units	1 unit	2 units	3 and 4 units	5 units or more	Number of structures with 5 or more units
United States	1,094,933	910,679	23,340	22,475	138,439	10,815	1,199,063	986,549	26,742	25,616	160,156	12,417
Alabama	13,905	11,546	144	144	2,071	159	16,105	12,815	250	289	2,751	252
Alaska	1,104	1,034	42	11	17	2	1,657	1,352	60	81	164	12
Arizona	31,793	29,179	230	410	1,974	165	38,656	34,714	456	610	2,876	270
Arkansas	7,934	6,203	656	358	717	64	9,962	6,969	1,106	506	1,381	115
California	97,781	76,332	1,886	3,934	15,629	1,382	84,341	69,568	1,406	2,390	10,977	953
Colorado	23,484	20,691	302	232	2,259	161	29,913	25,855	480	350	3,228	276
Connecticut	8,011	7,208	118	82	603	37	9,247	7,831	86	60	1,270	59
Delaware	4,632	4,266	44	56	266	18	4,877	4,646	110	33	88	7
District of Columbia	132	92	14	0	26	2	305	99	0	43	163	1
Florida	102,022	83,710	1,532	1,722	15,058	1,083	115,103	91,261	1,970	2,006	19,866	1,336
Georgia	44,566	42,087	588	265	1,626	126	53,874	47,599	768	341	5,166	411
Hawaii	7,809	4,628	104	155	2,922	205	6,624	4,614	136	110	1,764	172
Idaho	9,597	7,540	278	601	1,178	117	11,567	8,770	326	907	1,564	147
Illinois	40,430	32,695	1,432	1,290	5,013	382	44,742	36,232	1,558	1,631	5,321	412
Indiana	28,739	24,410	908	380	3,041	220	30,803	25,883	950	370	3,600	274
Iowa	10,520	7,162	262	500	2,596	184	10,567	7,350	292	331	2,594	185
Kansas	9,804	8,543	434	145	682	80	11,035	8,940	446	236	1,413	94
Kentucky	14,689	11,608	488	618	1,975	190	15,907	12,357	498	719	2,333	224
Louisiana	9,750	8,859	72	29	790	51	11,226	10,363	168	70	625	23
Maine	4,327	4,004	92	62	169	9	3,844	3,638	34	26	146	16
Maryland	32,412	28,075	104	152	4,081	254	29,956	25,393	182	10	4,371	272
Massachusetts	16,411	15,162	376	103	770	65	17,460	15,820	418	149	1,073	78
Michigan	37,026	31,467	508	489	4,562	240	39,755	33,669	420	607	5,059	350
Minnesota	26,360	22,518	270	235	3,337	226	27,265	22,954	252	285	3,774	272
Mississippi	6,321	5,487	144	179	511	56	8,116	6,870	156	227	863	95
Missouri	20,078	16,624	914	730	1,810	152	21,702	18,318	988	944	1,452	107
Montana	2,084	1,700	156	119	109	17	2,872	1,912	220	205	535	67
Nebraska	6,745	5,115	192	68	1,370	65	7,751	5,463	224	194	1,870	108
Nevada	17,274	13,437	212	264	3,361	371	23,303	19,472	192	380	3,259	339
New Hampshire	4,012	3,652	54	46	260	23	4,191	3,724	52	39	376	22
New Jersey	19,072	16,506	510	74	1,982	146	25,188	21,340	758	129	2,961	170
New Mexico	7,240	6,898	18	69	255	9	8,874	8,145	58	212	459	22
New York	29,851	23,265	2,052	904	3,630	271	28,604	21,099	2,314	1,075	4,116	218
North Carolina	48,158	41,906	876	564	4,812	429	53,281	45,855	988	550	5,888	471
North Dakota	2,570	1,427	10	51	1,082	50	2,940	1,571	42	101	1,226	56
Ohio	42,610	31,315	1,226	1,820	8,249	742	44,235	34,051	1,356	2,070	6,758	648
Oklahoma	7,678	7,330	42	18	288	20	8,673	8,280	200	82	111	16
Oregon	16,994	13,121	436	609	2,828	269	20,529	15,215	628	644	4,042	361
Pennsylvania	38,282	34,477	526	512	2,767	179	40,126	35,916	568	589	3,053	214
Rhode Island	2,592	2,369	72	20	131	5	2,579	2,413	48	32	86	2
South Carolina	20,221	17,714	378	242	1,887	155	21,060	18,672	306	199	1,883	163
South Dakota	3,159	2,170	62	67	860	77	3,729	2,292	62	158	1,217	73
Tennessee	23,319	21,214	342	633	1,130	136	26,984	24,065	488	678	1,753	193
Texas	64,235	54,798	412	762	8,263	546	77,754	62,672	678	876	13,528	928
Utah	12,789	11,027	236	345	1,181	114	17,311	13,856	234	842	2,379	177
Vermont	2,255	1,825	38	37	355	28	2,282	1,967	32	60	223	24
Virginia	40,205	35,354	546	355	3,950	289	44,963	39,361	526	498	4,578	425
Washington	39,682	29,056	1,226	925	8,475	644	41,342	30,418	1,174	1,287	8,463	701
West Virginia	2,275	1,968	18	54	235	19	2,576	2,198	56	57	265	26
Wisconsin	30,995	20,964	1,744	999	7,288	580	32,114	21,652	1,982	1,275	7,205	579
Wyoming	999	941	14	36	8	1	1,193	1,060	40	53	40	1

See notes at end of table.

Housing Production and Investment

TABLE 2.35. NUMBER OF NEW PRIVATELY-OWNED HOUSING UNITS AUTHORIZED IN PERMIT-ISSUING PLACES BY STRUCTURE TYPE AND STATE: 1980 TO 1997 - Continued

AREA	1994						1995					
		Number of units in structure						Number of units in structure				
	Total units	1 unit	2 units	3 and 4 units	5 units or more	Number of structures with 5 or more units	Total units	1 unit	2 units	3 and 4 units	5 units or more	Number of structures with 5 or more units
United States	1,371,637	1,068,461	31,402	30,794	240,980	18,380	1,332,549	997,268	32,228	31,528	271,525	19,482
Alabama	19,136	14,443	346	299	4,048	304	20,114	13,412	386	252	6,064	423
Alaska	2,056	1,542	104	34	376	19	2,164	1,657	194	75	238	15
Arizona	51,832	42,124	694	797	8,217	740	52,714	39,879	410	799	11,626	989
Arkansas	12,374	7,768	1,220	606	2,780	247	11,707	7,295	936	610	2,866	235
California	96,982	77,795	1,382	3,100	14,705	1,178	83,864	68,148	1,170	2,880	11,666	1,002
Colorado	37,229	29,317	734	633	6,545	485	38,622	28,404	732	750	8,736	639
Connecticut	9,460	8,110	104	128	1,118	88	8,550	7,604	136	31	779	44
Delaware	4,966	4,666	30	20	250	15	4,608	4,252	18	35	303	24
District of Columbia	210	96	0	0	114	2	35	35	0	0	0	0
Florida	128,602	96,276	1,834	2,340	28,152	1,728	122,903	84,071	1,752	1,915	35,165	1,910
Georgia	64,860	52,530	876	584	10,870	765	72,225	55,027	806	657	15,735	858
Hawaii	7,328	4,452	146	81	2,649	258	6,614	3,866	110	113	2,525	174
Idaho	12,640	9,279	548	1,106	1,707	153	10,666	8,366	298	648	1,354	123
Illinois	49,290	38,532	1,492	2,028	7,238	580	47,467	35,392	1,856	1,990	8,229	667
Indiana	34,432	28,493	1,150	341	4,448	347	35,715	27,905	1,560	652	5,598	428
Iowa	12,470	7,893	366	527	3,684	246	11,341	7,313	338	384	3,306	237
Kansas	12,976	10,156	534	305	1,981	153	12,655	8,709	582	237	3,127	227
Kentucky	18,554	14,176	584	814	2,980	282	17,625	12,829	752	662	3,382	327
Louisiana	14,782	12,758	344	262	1,418	119	14,723	12,461	304	283	1,675	93
Maine	4,578	4,327	86	40	125	15	4,417	4,162	60	25	170	10
Maryland	28,987	25,034	110	40	3,803	244	26,576	23,194	134	72	3,176	192
Massachusetts	18,115	16,533	370	251	961	87	16,428	14,449	360	163	1,456	98
Michigan	46,475	38,491	768	725	6,491	463	47,226	39,289	798	800	6,339	409
Minnesota	25,629	21,338	312	497	3,482	261	25,494	20,675	324	709	3,786	315
Mississippi	10,933	7,976	204	229	2,524	253	10,753	7,267	284	647	2,555	237
Missouri	26,374	20,869	1,478	928	3,099	248	24,282	18,975	1,514	768	3,025	243
Montana	3,025	2,087	204	292	442	52	3,064	1,708	202	349	805	74
Nebraska	7,877	5,386	278	183	2,030	103	8,164	5,161	230	136	2,637	129
Nevada	31,071	22,924	124	510	7,513	822	32,804	22,470	230	739	9,365	937
New Hampshire	4,667	4,130	126	65	346	24	4,423	4,105	48	40	230	19
New Jersey	25,388	22,437	722	121	2,108	151	21,521	18,341	670	158	2,352	142
New Mexico	11,545	9,246	72	218	2,009	134	11,009	8,619	40	54	2,296	198
New York	31,135	22,173	2,488	1,201	5,273	365	28,060	19,864	2,520	885	4,791	292
North Carolina	62,859	49,116	906	673	12,164	927	60,923	47,703	966	944	11,310	887
North Dakota	3,379	1,638	38	90	1,613	82	3,185	1,458	28	84	1,615	74
Ohio	47,152	35,575	1,462	2,406	7,709	766	44,812	32,635	1,360	2,296	8,521	743
Oklahoma	9,507	8,175	310	155	867	68	10,066	7,775	320	116	1,855	111
Oregon	24,067	16,123	1,094	934	5,916	572	26,201	15,379	1,198	1,045	8,579	758
Pennsylvania	40,210	37,005	556	433	2,216	181	36,250	32,005	516	404	3,325	239
Rhode Island	2,539	2,330	74	24	111	9	2,331	2,065	90	26	150	9
South Carolina	24,586	19,963	326	304	3,993	374	23,959	19,274	412	287	3,986	329
South Dakota	4,563	2,440	118	156	1,849	108	3,832	2,203	108	138	1,383	86
Tennessee	31,874	26,824	616	873	3,561	364	35,096	27,695	770	1,078	5,553	502
Texas	102,580	70,355	1,004	1,067	30,154	1,818	105,102	70,418	1,374	2,029	31,281	1,830
Utah	18,591	14,691	446	972	2,482	230	20,898	15,246	562	1,233	3,857	293
Vermont	2,376	2,034	56	81	205	21	2,269	1,950	26	60	233	22
Virginia	46,830	39,520	564	428	6,318	453	43,129	34,677	644	661	7,147	505
Washington	44,034	31,464	1,516	1,382	9,672	780	38,160	26,772	1,564	1,361	8,463	708
West Virginia	3,873	3,321	38	62	452	55	3,691	2,932	80	56	623	45
Wisconsin	34,619	22,811	2,402	1,343	8,063	626	32,403	20,748	2,388	1,087	8,180	616
Wyoming	2,020	1,719	46	106	149	15	1,709	1,429	68	105	107	15

See notes at end of table.

Housing Production and Investment

TABLE 2.35. NUMBER OF NEW PRIVATELY-OWNED HOUSING UNITS AUTHORIZED IN PERMIT-ISSUING PLACES BY STRUCTURE TYPE AND STATE: 1980 TO 1997 - Continued

AREA	1996 Total units	1 unit	2 units	3 and 4 units	5 units or more	Number of structures with 5 or more units	1997 Total units	1 unit	2 units	3 and 4 units	5 units or more	Number of structures with 5 or more units
United States	1,425,616	1,069,472	33,608	32,230	290,306	20,994	1,441,136	1,062,396	34,850	33,588	310,302	21,127
Alabama	19,868	14,566	216	285	4,801	397	17,732	13,634	314	419	3,365	272
Alaska	2,640	1,810	212	101	517	38	2,560	1,889	238	131	302	37
Arizona	53,715	41,311	426	418	11,560	844	57,762	44,373	390	544	12,455	1,035
Arkansas	11,144	7,671	564	432	2,477	220	11,026	6,831	494	344	3,357	262
California	92,060	73,532	1,138	2,457	14,933	1,042	109,589	84,149	1,180	2,298	21,962	1,401
Colorado	41,135	30,361	862	1,128	8,784	744	43,053	31,941	858	856	9,398	665
Connecticut	8,537	7,590	86	129	732	44	9,311	7,811	138	153	1,209	79
Delaware	4,370	4,218	26	4	122	16	4,732	4,080	24	110	518	49
District of Columbia	0	0	0	0	0	0	15	11	0	4	0	0
Florida	125,020	91,040	1,488	2,411	30,081	1,948	133,990	90,309	1,638	2,594	39,449	2,364
Georgia	74,874	59,397	990	539	13,948	849	75,123	59,596	832	803	13,892	730
Hawaii	3,927	2,698	58	51	1,120	60	3,676	2,606	46	88	936	26
Idaho	10,755	9,180	294	559	722	74	10,337	8,838	238	335	926	88
Illinois	49,592	35,912	1,628	2,796	9,256	791	46,323	32,801	1,496	2,365	9,661	730
Indiana	37,219	29,863	1,288	576	5,492	412	35,241	28,118	1,408	473	5,242	380
Iowa	12,027	7,923	442	441	3,221	216	10,706	7,361	374	345	2,626	188
Kansas	14,676	10,121	872	422	3,261	259	13,590	9,689	750	285	2,866	191
Kentucky	18,778	14,056	748	652	3,322	357	18,114	13,734	1,034	677	2,669	253
Louisiana	17,998	14,422	426	272	2,878	183	15,144	13,189	338	237	1,380	79
Maine	4,685	4,463	46	41	135	14	4,706	4,304	106	59	237	19
Maryland	25,108	22,594	68	66	2,380	143	25,966	21,063	102	201	4,600	264
Massachusetts	17,261	15,077	466	144	1,574	135	17,186	15,152	466	298	1,270	67
Michigan	52,355	43,421	758	889	7,287	535	49,237	40,238	1,026	1,290	6,683	491
Minnesota	27,043	22,085	376	774	3,808	274	24,900	20,060	634	997	3,209	222
Mississippi	10,367	8,061	158	233	1,915	209	10,079	7,801	184	284	1,810	174
Missouri	26,298	20,107	2,004	1,458	2,729	230	25,156	18,811	2,158	931	3,256	211
Montana	2,678	1,494	214	259	711	56	2,472	1,501	214	201	556	39
Nebraska	10,091	5,717	342	90	3,942	193	9,880	5,637	382	145	3,716	195
Nevada	37,242	23,810	220	716	12,496	1,177	34,811	23,462	140	1,028	10,181	918
New Hampshire	4,926	4,233	88	36	569	42	5,404	4,598	78	107	621	49
New Jersey	24,173	20,853	880	211	2,229	155	28,018	23,472	916	324	3,306	155
New Mexico	10,180	8,842	26	83	1,229	83	10,265	8,182	36	87	1,960	96
New York	34,895	20,215	3,166	1,094	10,420	498	32,881	19,590	2,684	1,158	9,449	379
North Carolina	66,997	51,796	990	773	13,438	1,064	73,015	55,529	1,238	782	15,466	1,203
North Dakota	2,324	1,479	36	50	759	43	3,222	1,488	118	42	1,574	72
Ohio	49,280	35,719	1,736	2,392	9,433	907	46,487	32,728	1,882	3,069	8,808	892
Oklahoma	10,640	8,757	370	73	1,440	99	11,201	8,523	334	110	2,234	166
Oregon	27,814	17,232	1,156	918	8,508	702	26,999	16,250	1,370	1,290	8,089	581
Pennsylvania	37,895	32,439	544	796	4,116	358	39,877	32,250	678	865	6,084	429
Rhode Island	2,462	2,077	106	23	256	21	2,672	2,324	70	41	237	8
South Carolina	29,403	22,511	402	375	6,115	486	30,072	22,218	624	348	6,882	501
South Dakota	3,648	2,418	120	133	977	55	3,174	2,464	56	165	489	26
Tennessee	40,522	28,217	824	775	10,706	782	34,054	26,694	732	553	6,075	407
Texas	118,823	83,103	1,570	1,629	32,521	1,882	125,974	82,180	1,390	2,159	40,245	2,253
Utah	23,481	16,663	624	904	5,290	384	19,263	14,818	610	547	3,288	238
Vermont	2,070	1,872	68	7	123	9	1,831	1,649	46	29	107	14
Virginia	45,919	35,163	640	470	9,646	602	45,523	35,877	518	604	8,524	632
Washington	39,597	27,015	1,564	1,588	9,430	632	41,089	27,776	1,756	1,373	10,184	857
West Virginia	3,616	2,908	58	84	566	51	4,104	2,881	94	159	970	96
Wisconsin	33,296	21,811	2,140	1,334	8,011	644	31,925	20,628	2,356	1,204	7,737	625
Wyoming	2,192	1,649	84	139	320	35	1,669	1,288	62	77	242	19

Source: U.S. Bureau of the Census, Building Permits Survey and the Survey of the Use of Permits.

Table shows number of units authorized, except for the last column under each year. The last column under each year shows the number of multifamily (i.e., 5 or more units) structures authorized.

Housing Production and Investment

TABLE 2.36. VALUATION OF NEW PRIVATELY-OWNED HOUSING UNITS AUTHORIZED IN PERMIT-ISSUING PLACES BY STRUCTURE TYPE AND STATE: 1980 TO 1997
(Thousands of current dollars)

AREA	1980					1981				
		Number of units in structure					Number of units in structure			
	Total units	1 unit	2 units	3 and 4 units	5 units or more	Total units	1 unit	2 units	3 and 4 units	5 units or more
United States	47,156,287	33,072,632	1,580,293	1,704,395	10,798,967	41,910,159	28,707,080	1,470,506	1,723,990	10,008,583
Alabama	388,467	269,587	5,075	13,169	100,636	281,976	167,609	4,533	11,432	98,402
Alaska	155,011	121,186	11,124	4,690	18,011	339,951	257,802	30,089	13,623	38,437
Arizona	1,244,053	953,770	17,897	29,409	242,977	1,201,644	895,383	18,752	33,870	253,639
Arkansas	269,978	206,320	10,031	11,985	41,642	162,067	120,183	6,454	15,967	19,463
California	7,787,517	5,311,555	248,996	362,846	1,864,120	6,350,342	4,294,075	213,013	362,992	1,480,262
Colorado	1,153,971	859,245	34,110	43,134	217,482	1,351,336	965,587	41,677	55,031	289,041
Connecticut	411,996	317,017	11,082	7,462	76,435	398,951	306,224	10,989	10,874	70,864
Delaware	90,305	78,533	78	581	11,113	80,783	65,239	964	3,232	11,348
District of Columbia	82,124	23,139	471	0	58,514	42,352	5,699	365	0	36,288
Florida	6,471,134	3,508,862	261,126	282,635	2,418,511	5,806,611	3,008,478	227,356	276,995	2,293,782
Georgia	1,166,334	988,756	19,165	19,255	139,158	1,018,380	815,185	32,235	27,351	143,609
Hawaii	640,155	192,699	6,623	24,584	416,249	425,523	142,912	19,090	13,254	250,267
Idaho	219,264	181,504	10,241	10,701	16,818	154,299	128,453	6,077	4,635	15,134
Illinois	1,086,542	617,428	33,869	61,897	373,348	775,381	536,769	23,648	29,441	185,523
Indiana	767,982	548,913	14,867	25,137	179,065	540,854	391,937	13,629	21,870	113,418
Iowa	311,937	216,068	18,659	17,507	59,703	221,102	168,288	10,311	13,250	29,253
Kansas	434,523	319,952	42,519	28,123	43,929	361,540	288,158	32,595	20,102	20,685
Kentucky	351,415	255,157	12,993	16,083	67,182	268,702	177,115	8,394	7,962	75,231
Louisiana	682,419	490,584	26,138	57,826	107,871	673,658	458,114	26,769	69,822	118,953
Maine	113,411	81,546	3,626	6,471	21,768	92,561	76,363	1,803	5,621	8,774
Maryland	811,229	695,972	6,151	2,040	107,066	726,955	629,743	4,743	3,703	88,766
Massachusetts	634,128	470,925	12,613	11,673	138,917	712,455	504,116	15,584	18,448	174,307
Michigan	1,164,142	873,789	25,091	31,094	234,168	816,892	574,559	15,501	26,904	199,928
Minnesota	974,133	697,704	51,766	36,307	188,356	840,449	615,752	43,053	47,452	134,192
Mississippi	254,539	180,952	9,773	15,871	47,943	167,815	131,432	3,748	7,649	24,986
Missouri	458,742	338,007	21,016	18,827	80,892	361,178	270,675	16,599	17,624	56,280
Montana	71,361	49,442	2,903	7,058	11,958	68,086	45,396	5,608	6,312	10,770
Nebraska	207,765	173,586	9,125	6,155	18,899	138,223	114,911	5,405	4,657	13,250
Nevada	457,870	320,138	6,262	36,180	95,290	370,554	262,018	5,025	21,541	81,970
New Hampshire	197,639	158,586	5,648	5,010	28,395	188,951	144,605	12,553	7,236	24,557
New Jersey	985,353	758,222	46,024	7,841	173,266	1,005,209	673,634	49,208	15,131	267,236
New Mexico	329,753	275,757	6,365	18,269	29,362	324,095	270,123	2,540	21,799	29,633
New York	925,957	618,832	32,926	20,222	253,977	1,048,576	701,549	33,576	32,384	281,067
North Carolina	1,175,700	968,951	36,920	39,272	130,557	1,155,312	888,158	30,337	61,825	174,992
North Dakota	114,825	77,514	6,275	6,074	24,962	82,587	53,736	3,521	4,611	20,719
Ohio	1,283,053	899,589	59,735	64,505	259,224	960,358	658,301	33,305	43,925	224,827
Oklahoma	809,879	619,048	38,281	18,664	133,886	774,619	627,620	44,321	14,071	88,607
Oregon	828,482	682,951	41,585	20,430	83,516	588,354	478,524	19,261	20,879	69,690
Pennsylvania	1,118,425	849,865	34,123	23,670	210,767	956,344	702,421	30,155	21,376	202,392
Rhode Island	90,065	67,301	2,177	2,338	18,249	97,713	56,864	3,275	1,311	36,263
South Carolina	747,421	603,560	11,584	27,644	104,633	703,944	466,804	9,229	32,056	195,855
South Dakota	97,474	78,888	1,159	1,814	15,613	50,314	42,098	1,294	717	6,205
Tennessee	610,739	477,251	26,502	11,206	95,780	397,844	305,596	22,469	8,516	61,263
Texas	4,850,981	3,484,036	158,766	81,695	1,126,484	5,252,305	3,643,045	196,222	118,521	1,294,517
Utah	389,202	316,330	20,075	12,996	39,801	439,355	269,859	21,301	33,256	114,939
Vermont	97,597	69,391	2,182	1,682	24,342	92,233	60,171	7,225	3,506	21,331
Virginia	1,321,502	1,127,904	18,107	19,093	156,398	1,101,689	915,088	19,111	19,720	147,770
Washington	1,372,921	917,524	44,041	85,973	325,383	1,159,839	796,824	36,685	73,910	252,420
West Virginia	108,451	60,074	2,623	4,957	40,797	76,655	49,466	1,956	1,744	23,489
Wisconsin	689,816	508,690	45,879	30,997	104,250	551,490	379,584	38,060	23,735	110,111
Wyoming	148,605	110,032	5,926	11,343	21,304	151,753	104,835	10,893	12,147	23,878

See notes at end of table.

Housing Production and Investment

TABLE 2.36. VALUATION OF NEW PRIVATELY-OWNED HOUSING UNITS AUTHORIZED IN PERMIT-ISSUING PLACES BY STRUCTURE TYPE AND STATE: 1980 TO 1997 - Continued
(Thousands of current dollars)

AREA	1982 Total units	1 unit	2 units	3 and 4 units	5 units or more	1983 Total units	1 unit	2 units	3 and 4 units	5 units or more
United States	40,491,729	27,359,243	1,259,061	1,481,175	10,392,250	69,277,523	49,118,094	1,970,956	2,373,728	15,814,745
Alabama	228,764	148,657	3,301	6,650	70,156	481,118	311,466	6,776	17,271	145,605
Alaska	528,547	352,771	40,231	33,739	101,806	731,095	426,544	38,138	105,514	160,899
Arizona	1,231,154	841,420	13,456	43,332	332,946	2,317,210	1,549,844	27,708	70,157	669,501
Arkansas	195,897	100,535	8,210	18,745	68,407	327,743	201,623	18,044	21,831	86,245
California	5,002,721	3,506,723	160,525	232,760	1,102,713	10,256,052	7,403,104	261,948	426,079	2,164,921
Colorado	1,302,954	938,441	22,128	36,209	306,176	2,125,597	1,528,298	45,051	59,494	492,754
Connecticut	436,404	329,486	5,978	11,028	89,912	743,665	625,979	11,297	12,202	94,187
Delaware	100,157	62,785	1,912	3,194	32,266	144,134	105,301	1,942	7,420	29,471
District of Columbia	12,130	1,745	179	0	10,206	9,482	5,847	30	0	3,605
Florida	4,052,185	2,345,437	151,418	199,880	1,355,450	7,389,273	4,463,263	253,141	406,679	2,266,190
Georgia	1,387,196	1,050,231	41,691	43,470	251,804	2,367,445	1,797,470	64,210	47,581	458,184
Hawaii	309,202	116,086	4,005	3,737	185,374	291,486	196,316	12,974	10,140	72,056
Idaho	118,678	97,411	2,537	2,190	16,540	200,803	177,120	4,697	7,167	11,819
Illinois	909,727	486,414	21,673	30,593	371,047	1,610,253	1,165,497	41,379	40,289	363,088
Indiana	464,786	316,143	12,943	23,210	112,490	760,284	577,875	17,763	23,918	140,728
Iowa	195,663	137,935	6,810	10,526	40,392	284,826	204,909	12,064	14,833	53,020
Kansas	350,008	236,083	31,637	26,029	56,259	663,603	480,755	69,986	36,517	76,345
Kentucky	248,961	171,135	7,064	11,633	59,129	421,816	293,332	11,860	19,334	97,290
Louisiana	670,712	460,057	18,354	68,976	123,325	1,118,920	753,432	22,615	83,374	259,499
Maine	116,230	82,960	4,006	9,208	20,056	169,488	140,741	2,067	7,004	19,676
Maryland	913,209	783,724	3,653	2,809	123,023	1,736,465	1,442,632	5,439	11,932	276,462
Massachusetts	719,918	511,073	15,672	11,262	181,911	1,179,816	946,680	25,181	19,826	188,129
Michigan	586,950	388,161	8,655	13,625	176,509	1,006,407	820,796	14,603	30,141	140,867
Minnesota	909,185	621,144	20,547	45,480	222,014	1,321,444	994,762	29,130	60,582	236,970
Mississippi	189,738	130,698	9,113	9,688	40,239	313,134	211,530	15,275	28,107	58,222
Missouri	436,209	294,941	13,610	30,367	97,291	806,981	643,203	23,450	28,793	111,535
Montana	70,729	45,373	3,469	6,171	15,716	131,066	92,282	7,780	9,965	21,039
Nebraska	127,666	102,509	4,069	4,737	16,351	217,215	183,560	9,934	4,275	19,446
Nevada	293,128	210,192	5,374	21,142	56,420	572,296	396,795	2,723	23,900	148,878
New Hampshire	177,055	135,618	5,084	4,440	31,913	318,451	256,977	13,213	5,130	43,131
New Jersey	992,321	743,526	32,985	15,332	200,478	1,802,265	1,412,532	45,825	19,370	324,538
New Mexico	346,373	274,388	2,982	10,634	58,369	489,210	427,187	3,999	15,127	42,897
New York	1,097,328	664,036	37,308	21,596	374,388	1,657,815	1,130,051	67,540	45,216	415,008
North Carolina	1,135,596	874,506	28,803	54,165	178,122	2,003,768	1,528,132	42,102	76,037	357,497
North Dakota	105,422	73,107	2,724	5,648	23,943	166,827	100,496	8,031	11,189	47,111
Ohio	725,085	524,518	22,879	32,412	145,276	1,331,842	1,034,957	36,426	47,064	213,395
Oklahoma	1,249,372	812,043	64,884	27,163	345,282	1,592,936	1,009,320	47,591	52,101	483,924
Oregon	346,901	278,105	11,210	9,381	48,205	482,523	406,081	10,008	11,470	54,964
Pennsylvania	880,456	635,076	29,315	18,733	197,332	1,423,743	1,149,441	40,110	28,426	205,766
Rhode Island	80,965	54,727	2,441	1,578	22,219	142,557	111,494	4,166	4,047	22,850
South Carolina	651,727	456,907	19,186	19,210	156,424	1,124,487	785,836	35,230	45,071	258,350
South Dakota	41,758	31,093	923	1,132	8,610	94,053	70,278	1,691	1,087	20,997
Tennessee	482,849	304,137	38,487	18,345	121,880	985,500	647,478	94,072	23,887	220,063
Texas	6,903,043	4,165,969	233,941	186,323	2,316,810	10,464,192	6,402,663	331,690	190,066	3,539,773
Utah	338,462	241,585	14,767	16,283	65,827	671,977	488,814	16,475	24,494	142,194
Vermont	89,227	68,480	2,589	1,530	16,628	115,750	89,657	3,261	3,209	19,623
Virginia	1,218,517	1,018,797	14,431	16,718	168,571	2,236,462	1,989,906	27,295	40,554	178,707
Washington	859,772	653,206	19,094	34,387	153,085	1,536,863	1,211,089	38,423	52,369	234,982
West Virginia	58,201	37,670	643	1,786	18,102	61,007	45,902	359	2,009	12,737
Wisconsin	481,239	349,194	27,153	16,433	88,459	758,845	582,242	43,020	32,161	101,422
Wyoming	121,252	92,285	5,012	7,556	16,399	117,333	96,605	3,224	9,319	8,185

See notes at end of table.

Housing Production and Investment

TABLE 2.36. VALUATION OF NEW PRIVATELY-OWNED HOUSING UNITS AUTHORIZED IN PERMIT-ISSUING PLACES BY STRUCTURE TYPE AND STATE: 1980 TO 1997 - Continued

(Thousands of current dollars)

AREA	1984					1985				
	Total units	Number of units in structure				Total units	Number of units in structure			
		1 unit	2 units	3 and 4 units	5 units or more		1 unit	2 units	3 and 4 units	5 units or more
United States	77,661,313	54,320,124	2,243,562	2,674,463	18,423,164	84,904,249	59,492,732	2,105,295	2,493,792	20,812,430
Alabama	467,897	324,300	5,676	28,884	109,037	537,362	396,581	4,845	17,201	118,735
Alaska	484,247	325,590	31,793	54,826	72,038	319,493	214,977	18,485	32,781	53,250
Arizona	3,137,680	1,860,071	31,712	95,142	1,150,755	3,119,238	2,093,854	33,784	77,102	914,498
Arkansas	354,403	226,780	18,191	25,703	83,729	387,923	270,404	19,110	21,893	76,516
California	13,336,281	8,771,698	372,709	606,466	3,585,408	16,188,407	9,610,204	383,055	638,281	5,556,867
Colorado	1,980,019	1,346,445	38,296	60,211	535,067	1,570,156	1,196,964	29,746	29,349	314,097
Connecticut	956,390	788,150	15,612	19,011	133,617	1,288,617	1,042,923	20,313	20,508	204,873
Delaware	178,152	129,505	1,816	9,990	36,841	202,135	154,691	2,519	1,675	43,250
District of Columbia	30,871	8,680	768	600	20,823	23,810	8,646	732	946	13,486
Florida	8,179,450	4,991,204	253,694	381,815	2,552,737	8,464,320	5,435,771	224,956	310,730	2,492,863
Georgia	2,896,776	2,200,231	79,608	64,281	552,656	3,130,037	2,443,194	69,024	53,347	564,472
Hawaii	324,388	262,388	8,435	5,599	47,966	489,255	346,584	11,259	9,575	121,837
Idaho	225,047	195,760	6,568	9,342	13,377	217,154	178,059	5,876	10,706	22,513
Illinois	1,716,762	1,375,953	40,560	46,371	253,878	2,237,683	1,593,308	51,272	69,293	523,810
Indiana	905,282	680,907	31,337	31,318	161,720	1,099,993	818,736	30,124	28,539	222,594
Iowa	295,314	212,585	7,784	9,898	65,047	242,169	165,513	5,086	9,446	62,124
Kansas	716,454	479,866	54,235	31,488	150,865	609,297	424,345	41,384	27,997	115,571
Kentucky	482,752	334,448	11,437	16,553	120,314	522,626	358,697	11,561	21,062	131,306
Louisiana	1,099,107	766,927	20,960	66,314	244,906	803,829	598,812	17,419	40,667	146,931
Maine	276,077	201,002	5,575	14,114	55,386	382,208	295,875	8,299	20,765	57,269
Maryland	1,803,212	1,510,182	3,106	9,882	280,042	1,918,702	1,582,237	1,358	113,612	221,495
Massachusetts	1,627,938	1,339,752	44,573	28,498	215,115	2,341,631	1,767,246	68,265	48,259	457,861
Michigan	1,323,735	1,001,968	16,618	52,855	252,294	1,829,062	1,347,298	18,254	67,625	395,885
Minnesota	1,456,444	1,047,755	25,111	48,325	335,253	1,650,679	1,186,874	25,778	36,928	401,099
Mississippi	416,626	293,052	12,653	16,049	94,872	351,959	280,888	11,916	13,819	45,336
Missouri	1,018,073	681,835	41,782	45,394	249,062	1,180,603	791,349	43,440	56,172	289,642
Montana	129,018	90,596	6,901	10,942	20,579	86,924	54,416	3,921	4,130	24,457
Nebraska	254,373	211,939	11,256	4,910	26,268	221,357	184,735	9,188	3,567	23,867
Nevada	589,447	393,717	6,092	32,840	156,798	593,602	414,092	4,883	10,045	164,582
New Hampshire	509,913	402,435	22,743	12,285	72,450	892,106	663,973	41,088	29,457	157,588
New Jersey	2,321,262	1,888,124	71,229	26,271	335,638	3,129,816	2,400,066	99,017	31,595	599,138
New Mexico	683,631	474,800	4,314	16,936	187,581	567,041	457,343	2,179	8,111	99,408
New York	2,424,190	1,596,906	98,450	63,254	665,580	3,573,195	2,115,774	134,409	88,134	1,234,878
North Carolina	2,504,992	1,891,654	53,308	117,121	442,909	2,964,341	2,229,153	55,768	79,942	599,478
North Dakota	131,139	83,310	5,845	6,845	35,139	101,810	55,600	5,212	3,914	37,084
Ohio	1,517,326	1,117,170	51,200	74,536	274,420	1,724,225	1,308,906	53,721	49,562	312,036
Oklahoma	958,478	689,314	29,234	21,344	218,586	502,166	414,253	9,866	4,104	73,943
Oregon	452,804	402,613	6,699	8,004	35,488	589,766	452,602	7,329	13,407	116,428
Pennsylvania	1,781,968	1,514,427	40,828	32,293	194,420	2,183,613	1,885,409	43,229	42,115	212,860
Rhode Island	170,600	141,017	11,127	4,800	13,656	240,762	203,211	8,034	8,232	21,285
South Carolina	1,415,350	904,512	39,477	47,495	423,866	1,359,896	952,273	44,036	35,424	328,163
South Dakota	110,380	74,624	1,425	3,177	31,154	90,707	63,111	1,998	2,518	23,080
Tennessee	1,272,760	671,164	133,355	33,402	434,839	1,514,807	951,472	86,350	23,927	453,058
Texas	8,639,658	5,746,668	323,085	204,696	2,365,209	6,719,907	4,922,702	197,564	120,079	1,479,562
Utah	826,863	522,885	24,571	31,840	247,567	741,200	558,593	10,636	23,273	148,698
Vermont	174,654	137,300	7,250	7,279	22,825	217,876	170,252	7,207	6,708	33,709
Virginia	2,598,289	2,138,899	32,041	47,423	379,926	2,959,539	2,494,450	29,042	17,264	418,783
Washington	1,555,699	1,142,647	32,944	46,752	333,356	1,793,674	1,210,188	45,057	75,254	463,175
West Virginia	75,654	53,706	507	2,714	18,727	58,304	49,640	1,058	1,324	6,282
Wisconsin	802,149	610,086	48,400	35,123	108,540	917,254	632,290	45,749	32,091	207,124
Wyoming	71,339	62,577	672	3,252	4,838	52,013	44,198	894	1,337	5,584

See notes at end of table.

Housing Production and Investment

TABLE 2.36. VALUATION OF NEW PRIVATELY-OWNED HOUSING UNITS AUTHORIZED IN PERMIT-ISSUING PLACES BY STRUCTURE TYPE AND STATE: 1980 TO 1997 - Continued
(Thousands of current dollars)

AREA	1986					1987				
		Number of units in structure					Number of units in structure			
	Total units	1 unit	2 units	3 and 4 units	5 units or more	Total units	1 unit	2 units	3 and 4 units	5 units or more
United States	98,004,563	73,695,474	2,097,410	2,334,524	19,877,155	98,346,270	78,198,015	1,799,791	2,112,855	16,235,609
Alabama	686,046	526,119	5,978	12,866	141,083	648,482	559,019	3,796	6,435	79,232
Alaska	116,995	94,742	8,759	10,476	3,018	63,329	41,975	4,599	9,474	7,281
Arizona	3,082,559	2,326,370	18,534	38,682	698,973	2,774,721	2,275,712	9,268	30,706	459,035
Arkansas	375,826	290,654	13,696	16,445	55,031	319,721	287,111	7,148	6,467	18,995
California	20,865,183	13,205,531	418,019	749,866	6,491,767	19,559,979	13,711,376	313,536	658,573	4,876,494
Colorado	1,626,675	1,314,618	27,139	22,406	262,512	1,234,883	1,051,628	21,848	17,128	144,279
Connecticut	1,677,305	1,428,865	26,741	34,932	186,767	1,806,186	1,477,491	31,528	20,710	276,457
Delaware	235,011	204,388	1,076	6,017	23,530	318,720	253,776	2,364	185	62,395
District of Columbia	21,456	8,159	870	0	12,427	43,033	17,790	344	538	24,361
Florida	8,742,292	6,050,190	175,725	251,543	2,264,834	9,210,485	6,951,404	180,214	237,182	1,841,685
Georgia	3,868,204	3,126,359	61,507	49,060	631,278	3,722,607	3,215,840	41,907	27,614	437,246
Hawaii	465,328	321,869	8,223	19,465	115,771	469,993	403,789	10,244	3,872	52,088
Idaho	217,385	189,953	7,156	6,374	13,902	201,003	182,850	3,364	6,002	8,787
Illinois	3,390,808	2,539,981	59,667	76,810	714,350	3,806,505	3,091,275	58,258	94,080	562,892
Indiana	1,578,147	1,250,619	40,059	33,343	254,126	1,755,925	1,488,165	49,709	35,999	182,052
Iowa	268,434	199,797	6,765	5,959	55,913	313,706	261,467	4,869	7,988	39,382
Kansas	781,924	598,223	45,836	22,187	115,678	802,402	682,269	42,394	17,444	60,295
Kentucky	641,647	496,638	12,664	12,660	119,685	740,040	638,346	10,820	9,658	81,216
Louisiana	556,788	501,465	11,458	5,321	38,544	449,575	414,320	5,382	5,215	24,658
Maine	505,131	408,570	11,260	18,023	67,278	583,751	485,767	9,815	10,613	77,556
Maryland	2,269,303	2,029,426	9,558	7,020	223,299	2,484,738	2,206,862	4,045	9,424	264,407
Massachusetts	3,086,546	2,264,713	95,353	74,857	651,623	3,084,194	2,288,207	117,410	84,742	593,835
Michigan	2,436,559	1,819,201	31,838	108,190	477,330	2,625,514	2,050,356	30,297	76,796	468,065
Minnesota	2,141,579	1,618,748	28,102	36,620	458,109	2,421,528	1,842,607	17,077	30,492	531,352
Mississippi	355,789	303,398	12,016	9,104	31,271	324,157	289,483	9,483	8,442	16,749
Missouri	1,585,970	1,124,274	59,489	61,279	340,928	1,642,860	1,286,011	49,854	66,638	240,357
Montana	57,348	45,107	2,195	4,498	5,548	47,608	42,744	579	1,582	2,703
Nebraska	251,687	201,650	10,030	2,878	37,129	242,411	208,748	7,765	1,365	24,533
Nevada	758,243	593,747	8,389	12,966	143,141	785,850	611,138	5,699	12,691	156,322
New Hampshire	1,113,383	894,290	68,283	52,604	98,206	1,016,706	864,056	49,315	37,053	66,282
New Jersey	3,549,629	2,807,823	112,817	25,143	603,846	3,575,031	2,828,090	125,834	30,456	590,651
New Mexico	603,833	532,310	2,985	6,419	62,119	548,599	494,720	1,216	4,664	47,999
New York	3,729,937	2,874,850	179,905	114,851	560,331	4,417,092	3,182,107	177,188	129,570	928,227
North Carolina	3,053,807	2,496,046	46,523	59,589	451,649	3,103,702	2,744,994	43,340	41,348	274,020
North Dakota	82,623	58,302	4,925	3,702	15,694	93,280	64,188	4,041	3,015	22,036
Ohio	2,536,711	1,988,536	56,471	67,763	423,941	2,998,653	2,447,727	62,713	112,184	376,029
Oklahoma	465,716	380,320	8,206	4,195	72,995	363,197	338,863	2,315	924	21,095
Oregon	627,973	526,348	9,089	11,294	81,242	752,589	625,785	8,048	8,550	110,206
Pennsylvania	2,993,576	2,688,560	42,485	33,391	229,140	3,587,611	3,230,359	41,107	46,221	269,924
Rhode Island	349,706	279,741	13,790	12,600	43,575	395,503	325,733	17,240	10,093	42,437
South Carolina	1,356,764	1,123,729	25,286	19,355	188,394	1,405,182	1,236,492	16,585	19,066	133,039
South Dakota	80,812	62,820	1,662	1,456	14,874	84,541	67,250	1,307	864	15,120
Tennessee	1,700,923	1,323,069	67,907	23,894	286,053	1,765,406	1,530,277	32,013	37,517	165,599
Texas	5,180,382	4,265,847	95,067	28,210	791,258	3,570,307	3,416,208	29,003	11,427	113,669
Utah	697,684	570,448	9,453	12,884	104,899	509,078	478,331	5,476	5,214	20,057
Vermont	266,829	224,091	6,508	11,757	24,473	298,805	266,675	6,467	8,519	17,144
Virginia	3,663,092	3,106,446	34,144	39,139	483,363	3,697,312	3,082,806	31,144	28,079	555,283
Washington	2,042,947	1,437,406	34,487	54,570	516,484	2,224,222	1,507,391	34,946	39,408	642,477
West Virginia	83,328	71,665	1,002	1,274	9,387	88,006	74,288	1,794	1,707	10,217
Wisconsin	1,130,271	854,269	57,267	39,753	178,982	1,330,476	1,039,091	54,747	38,355	198,283
Wyoming	48,469	45,184	1,046	834	1,405	37,066	35,058	336	566	1,106

See notes at end of table.

Housing Production and Investment

TABLE 2.36. VALUATION OF NEW PRIVATELY-OWNED HOUSING UNITS AUTHORIZED IN PERMIT-ISSUING PLACES BY STRUCTURE TYPE AND STATE: 1980 TO 1997 - Continued
(Thousands of current dollars)

AREA	1988 Total units	1 unit	2 units	3 and 4 units	5 units or more	1989 Total units	1 unit	2 units	3 and 4 units	5 units or more
United States	101,624,891	82,814,685	1,728,284	1,877,376	15,204,546	100,697,657	83,002,084	1,641,216	1,723,310	14,331,047
Alabama	613,777	548,182	4,625	9,839	51,131	595,225	505,875	3,638	12,006	73,706
Alaska	78,477	52,482	9,313	16,682	0	64,205	49,520	4,642	8,543	1,500
Arizona	2,462,040	2,053,927	12,694	12,870	382,549	1,939,381	1,790,603	10,639	10,514	127,625
Arkansas	318,868	282,693	6,036	7,575	22,564	317,558	273,883	9,132	8,978	25,565
California	23,659,449	18,273,843	332,144	592,715	4,460,747	24,613,848	19,883,557	329,319	543,747	3,857,225
Colorado	980,240	852,807	14,881	21,786	90,766	1,057,198	949,238	14,545	19,090	74,325
Connecticut	1,365,113	1,145,194	23,434	19,595	176,890	902,339	770,421	21,749	6,976	103,193
Delaware	353,634	314,066	3,378	1,712	34,478	330,810	296,554	1,383	4,364	28,509
District of Columbia	34,706	16,879	1,117	754	15,956	16,977	6,745	721	0	9,511
Florida	9,669,841	7,408,438	188,113	179,751	1,893,539	10,434,172	7,965,635	155,690	191,234	2,121,613
Georgia	3,687,608	3,068,324	37,087	22,807	559,390	3,051,459	2,570,145	32,487	15,963	432,864
Hawaii	656,972	486,729	13,713	18,375	138,155	888,724	574,872	24,945	16,781	272,126
Idaho	225,598	213,522	2,076	5,325	4,675	342,494	308,143	4,030	6,075	24,246
Illinois	4,057,802	3,385,868	63,427	95,865	512,642	3,781,053	3,212,645	65,451	92,993	409,964
Indiana	1,825,313	1,628,566	45,985	18,875	131,887	1,972,245	1,723,805	49,125	21,703	177,612
Iowa	417,202	333,163	7,979	9,743	66,317	476,862	387,080	12,780	17,216	59,786
Kansas	758,755	662,262	38,350	15,197	42,946	697,965	637,849	17,833	9,224	33,059
Kentucky	786,711	673,552	12,671	10,126	90,362	779,383	684,553	10,206	12,647	71,977
Louisiana	401,988	353,173	6,681	3,182	38,952	374,869	349,099	2,814	1,963	20,993
Maine	547,846	472,440	8,583	9,261	57,562	427,878	379,911	7,292	6,473	34,202
Maryland	2,650,413	2,414,142	4,963	8,622	222,686	2,703,588	2,314,498	30,065	6,173	352,852
Massachusetts	2,524,335	1,995,319	105,158	50,925	372,933	1,853,727	1,492,476	84,460	42,087	234,704
Michigan	2,776,203	2,251,378	29,371	81,407	414,047	2,987,333	2,479,658	35,243	66,169	406,263
Minnesota	2,071,921	1,724,484	17,193	26,620	303,624	1,946,610	1,667,839	14,616	22,137	242,018
Mississippi	339,989	274,659	8,537	8,872	47,921	316,916	269,475	10,188	6,986	30,267
Missouri	1,448,463	1,202,752	47,941	40,003	157,767	1,221,655	1,082,644	33,503	28,203	77,305
Montana	52,759	43,806	704	1,374	6,875	53,505	46,772	959	3,089	2,685
Nebraska	293,758	246,015	7,252	2,926	37,565	313,027	271,291	7,246	2,574	31,916
Nevada	1,300,924	765,198	4,602	11,880	519,244	1,513,521	1,098,353	9,343	22,425	383,400
New Hampshire	826,056	659,573	36,695	31,926	97,862	561,511	483,121	19,006	10,609	48,775
New Jersey	2,932,170	2,293,732	103,390	26,392	508,656	2,272,460	1,738,355	72,371	18,025	443,709
New Mexico	420,612	396,783	930	1,944	20,955	443,484	408,640	3,184	6,753	24,907
New York	4,016,302	3,178,966	162,535	129,214	545,587	3,711,002	2,771,426	166,180	114,077	659,319
North Carolina	3,019,796	2,737,643	39,443	44,380	198,330	2,977,667	2,648,901	34,501	25,945	268,320
North Dakota	89,311	64,236	1,971	3,483	19,621	101,930	67,886	1,627	1,292	31,125
Ohio	3,075,962	2,529,975	57,025	64,472	424,490	3,079,963	2,600,937	70,475	68,607	339,944
Oklahoma	323,622	307,285	2,394	2,516	11,427	406,746	371,755	3,354	2,414	29,223
Oregon	929,093	765,127	10,312	17,465	136,189	1,400,856	1,028,292	25,451	24,122	322,991
Pennsylvania	3,863,109	3,537,172	32,731	41,289	251,917	3,424,442	3,097,316	24,974	46,847	255,305
Rhode Island	364,811	287,536	22,649	8,690	45,936	288,373	251,587	14,372	9,855	12,559
South Carolina	1,390,891	1,217,753	15,100	20,704	137,334	1,338,735	1,194,443	15,668	15,577	113,047
South Dakota	89,930	66,362	1,367	2,038	20,163	105,737	77,773	1,562	2,369	24,033
Tennessee	1,660,146	1,432,052	20,958	18,421	188,715	1,450,793	1,284,175	19,698	17,423	129,497
Texas	3,138,974	3,009,162	14,939	7,669	107,204	3,437,713	3,313,607	7,150	11,486	105,470
Utah	452,406	435,464	2,682	4,694	9,566	474,330	456,595	5,346	4,675	7,714
Vermont	343,922	297,862	9,304	8,536	28,220	273,867	246,388	4,848	10,487	12,144
Virginia	4,058,662	3,447,237	29,349	37,253	544,823	3,886,323	3,199,410	27,121	34,818	624,974
Washington	2,668,228	1,757,437	44,738	56,568	809,485	3,246,846	2,319,075	53,281	46,673	827,817
West Virginia	90,563	79,627	1,010	2,073	7,853	99,370	91,726	787	1,682	5,175
Wisconsin	1,459,951	1,127,570	60,368	42,745	229,268	1,689,181	1,257,193	65,504	42,535	323,949
Wyoming	49,669	42,268	386	240	6,775	51,801	50,344	712	706	39

See notes at end of table.

Housing Production and Investment

TABLE 2.36. VALUATION OF NEW PRIVATELY-OWNED HOUSING UNITS AUTHORIZED IN PERMIT-ISSUING PLACES BY STRUCTURE TYPE AND STATE: 1980 TO 1997 - Continued
(Thousands of current dollars)

AREA	1990 Total units	1990 Number of units in structure 1 unit	2 units	3 and 4 units	5 units or more	1991 Total units	1991 Number of units in structure 1 unit	2 units	3 and 4 units	5 units or more
United States	86,522,244	72,309,989	1,404,791	1,393,471	11,413,993	78,772,163	69,722,742	1,169,563	1,061,568	6,818,290
Alabama	682,706	578,194	4,726	5,946	93,840	692,350	623,937	3,833	8,357	56,223
Alaska	92,067	84,978	4,367	1,359	1,363	137,221	127,943	3,853	4,025	1,400
Arizona	1,962,919	1,772,611	9,412	12,483	168,413	2,262,288	2,172,314	10,505	15,204	64,265
Arkansas	332,679	304,715	8,137	4,182	15,645	385,805	339,741	13,464	3,960	28,640
California	17,233,077	13,298,405	309,989	416,182	3,208,501	11,990,089	9,677,346	197,698	335,280	1,779,765
Colorado	1,156,509	1,061,872	16,256	12,650	65,731	1,511,965	1,453,150	18,095	8,710	32,010
Connecticut	648,771	554,055	12,064	7,937	74,715	667,160	613,908	8,336	4,288	40,628
Delaware	274,462	245,729	2,592	246	25,895	237,953	224,649	1,892	60	11,352
District of Columbia	20,801	14,212	1,092	0	5,497	16,602	7,486	587	0	8,529
Florida	8,424,362	6,572,897	104,616	95,011	1,651,838	7,087,079	6,079,818	73,034	89,206	845,021
Georgia	2,720,399	2,398,572	25,145	8,961	287,721	2,701,199	2,567,793	15,961	7,073	110,372
Hawaii	1,007,598	652,770	32,443	41,006	281,379	1,138,072	571,212	17,130	17,597	532,133
Idaho	445,319	405,818	10,420	11,118	17,963	519,114	475,948	9,716	10,805	22,645
Illinois	3,514,914	2,940,355	68,161	63,492	442,906	3,188,748	2,865,115	62,948	67,030	193,655
Indiana	2,032,953	1,845,037	42,192	22,487	123,237	1,994,617	1,844,186	34,467	11,039	104,925
Iowa	530,766	443,213	7,740	16,100	63,713	603,443	523,804	11,148	12,918	55,573
Kansas	658,589	584,835	21,807	15,825	36,122	643,566	599,842	21,399	7,129	15,196
Kentucky	771,010	689,050	12,619	12,221	57,120	784,108	705,083	11,958	9,995	57,072
Louisiana	440,227	413,403	2,225	1,919	22,680	509,353	493,722	2,829	848	11,954
Maine	325,467	303,370	4,441	4,087	13,569	279,639	270,096	3,884	704	4,955
Maryland	2,180,056	1,904,160	4,436	4,774	266,686	1,914,763	1,744,467	5,883	3,923	160,490
Massachusetts	1,321,152	1,149,336	47,536	20,115	104,165	1,265,031	1,196,828	26,035	8,750	33,418
Michigan	2,747,707	2,336,667	33,285	51,847	325,908	2,597,467	2,357,603	26,181	34,873	178,810
Minnesota	1,867,065	1,636,082	10,499	14,729	205,755	1,882,328	1,746,453	13,032	20,777	102,066
Mississippi	298,015	264,465	6,459	3,854	23,237	285,476	267,323	3,685	1,951	12,517
Missouri	1,089,493	983,698	27,971	22,962	54,862	1,122,313	1,020,360	31,459	25,705	44,789
Montana	85,698	64,748	2,348	5,303	13,299	111,397	87,465	4,131	8,609	11,192
Nebraska	354,902	297,320	7,816	2,025	47,741	387,078	340,405	8,767	2,907	34,999
Nevada	1,427,079	1,083,370	9,779	30,355	303,575	1,280,425	1,094,359	5,010	15,272	165,784
New Hampshire	361,248	330,181	6,027	2,529	22,511	303,685	298,079	1,695	2,012	1,899
New Jersey	1,397,722	1,188,683	41,425	7,289	160,325	1,245,009	1,143,655	24,311	4,138	72,905
New Mexico	463,624	421,436	585	15,352	26,251	471,045	448,389	1,658	1,831	19,167
New York	2,782,142	2,139,242	146,388	76,199	420,313	2,420,679	2,001,622	143,166	38,268	237,623
North Carolina	2,753,493	2,522,410	32,046	33,774	165,263	2,803,354	2,622,200	43,293	18,458	119,403
North Dakota	88,505	72,008	449	856	15,192	111,811	85,476	1,039	525	24,771
Ohio	3,039,006	2,666,424	51,256	48,542	272,784	3,146,886	2,854,732	57,680	55,898	178,576
Oklahoma	400,621	385,728	868	1,503	12,522	488,344	481,822	1,164	1,164	4,194
Oregon	1,657,464	1,299,214	18,421	41,885	297,944	1,382,335	1,200,579	23,510	26,063	132,183
Pennsylvania	2,895,675	2,640,272	25,026	28,807	201,570	2,797,639	2,568,037	24,004	20,301	185,297
Rhode Island	233,137	209,296	11,830	1,500	10,511	180,904	171,258	3,546	693	5,407
South Carolina	1,445,118	1,302,763	16,655	10,510	115,190	1,352,573	1,267,511	16,921	13,263	54,878
South Dakota	139,722	94,721	4,889	23,338	16,774	146,771	114,364	1,493	2,181	28,733
Tennessee	1,317,082	1,203,761	18,998	8,745	85,578	1,358,757	1,282,330	16,908	9,732	49,787
Texas	3,869,099	3,642,062	7,758	14,562	204,717	4,300,778	4,009,967	8,799	15,700	266,312
Utah	594,481	557,317	5,682	9,548	21,934	777,650	736,868	6,767	13,945	20,070
Vermont	188,780	174,673	2,544	2,241	9,322	167,490	158,422	323	1,310	7,435
Virginia	2,797,762	2,441,522	28,372	22,173	305,695	2,489,945	2,336,658	19,818	10,922	122,547
Washington	3,486,985	2,598,042	56,935	80,717	751,291	2,644,122	2,200,475	49,969	39,819	353,859
West Virginia	110,034	101,788	1,685	1,248	5,313	126,282	119,660	790	520	5,312
Wisconsin	1,791,727	1,377,849	76,114	52,457	285,307	1,797,871	1,470,249	75,469	46,833	205,320
Wyoming	62,055	56,660	265	520	4,610	61,584	58,033	320	997	2,234

See notes at end of table.

Housing Production and Investment

TABLE 2.36. VALUATION OF NEW PRIVATELY-OWNED HOUSING UNITS AUTHORIZED IN PERMIT-ISSUING PLACES BY STRUCTURE TYPE AND STATE: 1980 TO 1997 - Continued
(Thousands of current dollars)

AREA	1992 Total units	1 unit	2 units	3 and 4 units	5 units or more	1993 Total units	1 unit	2 units	3 and 4 units	5 units or more
United States	95,539,025	87,071,455	1,272,157	1,126,252	6,069,161	106,800,971	97,118,621	1,478,601	1,281,696	6,922,053
Alabama	940,274	875,355	4,773	3,721	56,425	1,147,452	1,045,697	8,291	8,296	85,168
Alaska	139,483	134,644	3,183	618	1,038	228,406	196,478	4,418	8,978	18,532
Arizona	3,112,428	2,977,138	13,231	22,574	99,485	3,777,972	3,592,356	22,851	30,742	132,023
Arkansas	517,222	464,354	23,936	9,843	19,089	644,421	553,710	42,466	15,571	32,674
California	11,353,425	9,889,703	157,984	265,261	1,040,477	10,194,908	9,088,473	119,237	175,374	811,824
Colorado	2,439,174	2,290,533	29,068	19,146	100,427	3,095,858	2,882,752	47,696	25,621	139,789
Connecticut	820,039	782,929	5,561	5,763	25,786	929,664	873,057	3,712	2,398	50,497
Delaware	283,567	266,549	2,017	2,274	12,727	313,243	301,616	5,033	1,551	5,043
District of Columbia	16,459	14,806	740	0	913	20,557	15,761	0	3,796	1,000
Florida	8,557,562	7,535,854	78,316	101,600	841,792	9,658,404	8,291,202	119,973	122,671	1,124,558
Georgia	3,497,432	3,408,761	19,403	8,971	60,297	4,301,528	4,057,658	22,894	11,750	209,226
Hawaii	847,324	559,286	14,924	13,570	259,544	679,494	566,580	14,936	6,607	91,371
Idaho	750,633	672,379	13,939	24,227	40,088	928,542	815,856	17,882	38,085	56,719
Illinois	3,961,561	3,516,408	84,660	80,533	279,960	4,487,398	4,048,223	93,588	102,842	242,745
Indiana	2,594,830	2,442,151	43,899	22,591	86,189	2,896,209	2,715,278	49,047	21,292	110,592
Iowa	811,816	675,494	15,211	24,673	96,438	882,419	752,369	18,009	18,402	93,639
Kansas	885,228	836,165	22,619	5,043	21,401	1,027,807	932,945	25,085	9,760	60,017
Kentucky	1,023,682	932,920	16,658	21,310	52,794	1,172,971	1,060,457	18,444	22,805	71,265
Louisiana	710,381	683,838	2,870	670	23,003	859,373	831,074	5,969	2,272	20,058
Maine	333,990	318,465	5,038	3,317	7,170	308,569	295,412	1,729	969	10,459
Maryland	2,511,378	2,341,480	4,935	6,411	158,552	2,309,289	2,140,272	5,875	733	162,409
Massachusetts	1,747,349	1,674,713	20,466	8,493	43,677	1,890,560	1,787,774	25,344	10,070	67,372
Michigan	2,999,971	2,787,023	27,448	29,940	155,560	3,389,520	3,123,419	24,522	36,685	204,894
Minnesota	2,481,643	2,309,131	18,958	14,753	138,801	2,672,437	2,468,567	21,519	14,785	167,566
Mississippi	369,741	348,806	3,776	4,173	12,986	495,062	463,693	4,737	5,047	21,585
Missouri	1,525,889	1,404,675	38,728	25,409	57,077	1,749,829	1,626,393	44,487	33,254	45,695
Montana	168,928	147,479	9,982	5,462	6,005	212,314	171,176	13,679	10,614	16,845
Nebraska	461,970	419,024	10,210	3,376	29,360	551,055	480,510	11,725	7,007	51,813
Nevada	1,186,573	1,033,575	12,211	11,738	129,049	1,636,879	1,471,199	9,775	16,525	139,380
New Hampshire	357,746	340,033	3,371	3,032	11,310	381,486	358,984	3,171	2,905	16,426
New Jersey	1,648,211	1,529,943	27,639	3,947	86,682	2,087,085	1,926,452	38,680	6,772	115,181
New Mexico	612,714	604,010	819	2,441	5,444	775,187	749,587	1,431	10,413	13,756
New York	2,597,938	2,280,740	119,057	47,056	151,085	2,620,744	2,242,559	138,853	58,211	181,121
North Carolina	3,740,281	3,540,872	35,414	18,737	145,258	4,431,043	4,169,295	49,422	23,248	189,078
North Dakota	158,996	127,889	480	1,961	28,666	189,878	146,578	2,612	5,416	35,272
Ohio	3,926,554	3,535,187	65,859	71,546	253,962	4,318,975	3,937,698	75,657	91,030	214,590
Oklahoma	670,486	662,106	1,774	370	6,236	808,617	797,705	5,660	2,654	2,598
Oregon	1,542,725	1,379,528	24,820	24,993	113,384	1,956,405	1,708,555	35,895	32,959	178,996
Pennsylvania	3,308,453	3,143,698	24,976	23,219	116,560	3,546,851	3,363,249	27,505	26,388	129,709
Rhode Island	212,230	206,019	3,286	806	2,119	235,128	226,860	2,288	1,875	4,105
South Carolina	1,573,480	1,478,216	15,129	7,938	72,197	1,694,090	1,589,743	10,834	6,908	86,605
South Dakota	200,664	164,318	3,690	2,395	30,261	242,285	184,642	3,849	5,582	48,212
Tennessee	1,779,703	1,716,952	11,138	20,611	31,002	2,171,098	2,086,300	14,684	17,833	52,281
Texas	5,599,306	5,318,103	17,056	20,141	244,006	6,895,890	6,413,635	24,768	26,757	430,730
Utah	1,122,552	1,052,067	13,521	16,732	40,232	1,507,621	1,360,765	14,322	40,120	92,414
Vermont	189,906	165,880	2,008	1,814	20,204	201,902	185,610	1,894	2,981	11,417
Virginia	3,154,942	2,963,651	23,544	13,741	154,006	3,699,728	3,493,903	20,930	20,712	164,183
Washington	3,460,468	2,877,765	76,813	51,957	453,933	3,629,448	3,046,188	79,653	70,346	433,261
West Virginia	152,144	144,100	509	1,624	5,911	185,280	172,515	3,058	1,962	7,745
Wisconsin	2,376,686	1,996,102	95,506	44,739	240,339	2,624,031	2,177,761	118,387	60,031	267,852
Wyoming	102,888	100,638	1,004	992	254	136,059	130,080	2,125	2,091	1,763

See notes at end of table.

Housing Production and Investment

TABLE 2.36. VALUATION OF NEW PRIVATELY-OWNED HOUSING UNITS AUTHORIZED IN PERMIT-ISSUING PLACES BY STRUCTURE TYPE AND STATE: 1980 TO 1997 - Continued
(Thousands of current dollars)

AREA	1994 Total units	1994 1 unit	1994 2 units	1994 3 and 4 units	1994 5 units or more	1995 Total units	1995 1 unit	1995 2 units	1995 3 and 4 units	1995 5 units or more
United States	123,278,316	109,293,956	1,813,313	1,595,719	10,575,328	120,810,731	104,738,669	1,910,433	1,713,281	12,448,348
Alabama	1,357,145	1,167,942	13,875	8,001	167,327	1,429,234	1,142,496	14,352	7,964	264,422
Alaska	230,231	199,350	8,269	1,990	20,622	256,532	212,715	15,254	6,245	22,318
Arizona	5,075,302	4,560,316	37,171	45,961	431,854	5,132,542	4,430,994	26,777	48,138	626,633
Arkansas	794,774	647,692	52,980	19,067	75,035	765,593	614,442	40,475	20,081	90,595
California	11,936,670	10,568,958	118,466	230,925	1,018,321	10,835,567	9,686,577	102,807	228,336	817,847
Colorado	3,906,077	3,421,541	71,859	44,295	368,382	3,858,795	3,301,640	71,442	62,382	423,331
Connecticut	1,029,982	965,244	5,678	6,105	52,955	955,979	909,261	6,185	1,543	38,990
Delaware	336,757	326,214	1,204	2,044	7,295	331,607	320,957	636	785	9,229
District of Columbia	18,446	13,357	0	0	5,089	4,569	4,569	0	0	0
Florida	11,075,555	9,229,771	122,482	144,838	1,578,464	10,826,577	8,403,236	113,860	142,958	2,166,523
Georgia	5,094,970	4,627,467	29,143	18,606	419,754	5,580,684	4,903,574	31,435	24,746	620,929
Hawaii	800,944	603,059	18,012	7,687	172,186	752,018	498,189	13,447	10,641	229,741
Idaho	1,042,869	898,121	29,508	48,878	66,362	943,723	839,799	22,269	31,526	50,129
Illinois	5,011,762	4,442,020	93,246	126,773	349,723	4,844,287	4,220,262	118,557	127,554	377,914
Indiana	3,324,433	3,094,802	63,918	18,193	147,520	3,378,485	3,056,027	86,515	34,768	201,175
Iowa	997,805	810,832	22,197	26,118	138,658	975,602	798,706	21,264	18,311	137,321
Kansas	1,177,351	1,077,800	31,240	12,307	56,004	1,175,272	1,007,582	34,792	9,767	123,131
Kentucky	1,370,011	1,236,144	19,865	27,042	86,960	1,276,432	1,120,601	30,225	20,285	105,321
Louisiana	1,141,395	1,072,052	10,265	8,101	50,977	1,141,371	1,055,688	12,489	6,916	66,278
Maine	377,233	366,810	3,599	1,541	5,283	390,693	375,801	3,411	1,888	9,593
Maryland	2,394,571	2,235,552	6,277	1,718	151,024	2,293,152	2,141,810	6,456	3,359	141,527
Massachusetts	2,046,278	1,966,050	21,829	13,740	44,659	1,895,158	1,752,157	22,109	12,088	108,804
Michigan	4,149,392	3,813,670	48,530	48,414	238,778	4,411,432	4,065,083	55,797	57,462	233,090
Minnesota	2,557,844	2,328,581	25,515	34,035	169,713	2,589,746	2,303,668	27,139	49,381	209,558
Mississippi	659,896	572,115	6,407	6,989	74,385	650,920	537,551	7,262	22,732	83,375
Missouri	2,149,314	1,944,991	69,771	37,530	97,022	2,032,503	1,817,618	71,341	33,538	110,006
Montana	232,817	186,351	12,454	13,692	20,320	224,310	159,637	12,605	17,604	34,464
Nebraska	574,131	488,567	15,562	8,253	61,749	570,329	470,639	12,672	6,570	80,448
Nevada	2,185,076	1,818,065	7,997	26,520	332,494	2,737,942	2,246,323	13,838	39,853	437,928
New Hampshire	453,874	420,555	8,030	5,428	19,861	463,598	445,680	2,699	2,597	12,622
New Jersey	2,317,713	2,188,984	40,054	5,381	83,294	1,947,321	1,814,826	35,772	6,575	90,148
New Mexico	968,729	870,129	2,689	8,800	87,111	898,751	800,121	1,698	1,528	95,404
New York	2,787,332	2,347,689	141,360	69,095	229,188	2,616,323	2,188,947	153,327	57,522	216,527
North Carolina	5,276,528	4,774,319	45,221	30,019	426,969	5,274,682	4,774,038	53,798	40,798	406,048
North Dakota	211,088	153,258	3,151	5,110	49,569	200,828	140,883	2,093	4,669	53,183
Ohio	4,799,052	4,318,015	87,457	110,818	282,762	4,375,036	3,901,181	83,851	100,379	289,625
Oklahoma	903,271	846,849	11,891	4,941	39,590	877,781	793,554	12,617	3,626	67,984
Oregon	2,276,411	1,905,900	66,834	43,707	259,970	2,491,839	1,944,766	86,559	59,813	400,701
Pennsylvania	3,727,569	3,577,483	26,916	20,514	102,656	3,317,763	3,123,603	27,734	20,102	146,324
Rhode Island	233,472	224,349	2,766	1,259	5,098	213,930	203,006	3,648	807	6,469
South Carolina	2,018,997	1,798,423	13,353	11,199	196,022	1,983,985	1,784,397	14,893	9,647	175,048
South Dakota	287,955	202,448	6,944	6,112	72,451	257,644	188,521	6,294	5,681	57,148
Tennessee	2,538,773	2,367,548	21,241	26,666	123,318	2,838,290	2,581,085	29,398	35,750	192,057
Texas	8,098,055	7,007,787	38,705	32,636	1,018,927	8,324,089	7,066,127	50,329	62,079	1,145,554
Utah	1,716,988	1,523,876	33,305	50,806	109,001	1,870,447	1,563,595	39,635	77,647	189,570
Vermont	220,347	202,834	3,150	3,757	10,606	204,789	190,130	999	3,183	10,477
Virginia	3,965,418	3,700,412	27,368	15,792	221,846	3,658,118	3,354,415	29,285	20,008	254,410
Washington	4,017,867	3,329,542	104,105	81,768	502,452	3,578,229	2,917,843	109,824	87,832	462,730
West Virginia	282,927	265,222	1,459	1,966	14,280	261,145	232,101	3,898	2,427	22,719
Wisconsin	2,917,016	2,388,902	156,395	65,861	305,858	2,727,434	2,177,259	162,979	58,565	328,631
Wyoming	209,903	195,998	3,600	4,721	5,584	167,655	154,989	3,692	4,625	4,349

See notes at end of table.

Housing Production and Investment

TABLE 2.36. VALUATION OF NEW PRIVATELY-OWNED HOUSING UNITS AUTHORIZED IN PERMIT-ISSUING PLACES BY STRUCTURE TYPE AND STATE: 1980 TO 1997 - Continued
(Thousands of current dollars)

AREA	1996					1997				
		Number of units in structure					Number of units in structure			
	Total units	1 unit	2 units	3 and 4 units	5 units or more	Total units	1 unit	2 units	3 and 4 units	5 units or more
United States	134,175,811	116,535,045	2,069,137	1,861,424	13,710,205	141,004,397	121,194,486	2,304,007	2,057,673	15,448,231
Alabama	1,508,738	1,301,462	10,131	10,333	186,812	1,536,622	1,353,495	17,587	14,176	151,364
Alaska	316,425	249,435	21,770	10,540	34,680	334,123	271,617	24,903	13,592	24,011
Arizona	5,448,566	4,759,903	30,839	29,026	628,798	5,775,743	5,075,320	24,653	37,432	638,338
Arkansas	777,153	673,828	22,974	12,679	67,672	760,728	621,066	21,189	13,181	105,292
California	12,472,294	11,130,529	110,365	200,184	1,031,216	15,395,622	13,538,518	117,839	194,174	1,545,091
Colorado	4,274,869	3,621,681	81,568	85,941	485,679	4,658,596	3,973,564	101,830	78,937	504,265
Connecticut	987,222	941,093	6,786	7,541	31,802	1,100,557	1,023,486	8,920	10,383	57,768
Delaware	351,730	342,781	1,448	271	7,230	381,453	354,477	1,365	6,929	18,682
District of Columbia	0	0	0	0	0	1,317	1,103	0	214	0
Florida	11,471,660	9,361,145	99,500	186,202	1,824,813	12,205,450	9,550,594	118,944	200,128	2,335,784
Georgia	6,075,222	5,429,227	36,723	20,291	588,981	6,459,614	5,746,781	37,488	32,392	642,953
Hawaii	486,062	373,848	7,105	7,508	97,601	506,896	364,189	5,995	8,028	128,684
Idaho	1,058,954	983,104	22,387	25,428	28,035	1,041,831	963,727	17,029	17,579	43,496
Illinois	5,198,763	4,423,251	109,291	166,745	499,476	5,087,002	4,267,423	110,313	154,113	555,153
Indiana	3,719,252	3,428,866	80,660	32,859	176,867	3,705,711	3,380,983	90,880	30,036	203,812
Iowa	1,050,537	862,899	30,113	24,158	133,367	1,012,033	845,053	27,799	24,037	115,144
Kansas	1,322,385	1,124,060	52,382	16,639	129,304	1,349,982	1,155,203	54,220	15,889	124,670
Kentucky	1,484,079	1,314,348	32,251	23,328	114,152	1,483,895	1,320,525	44,521	24,072	94,777
Louisiana	1,436,403	1,308,078	14,246	7,778	106,301	1,332,274	1,256,623	12,704	8,652	54,295
Maine	436,422	425,650	1,879	2,116	6,777	451,158	428,602	7,070	2,222	13,264
Maryland	2,284,010	2,170,591	3,687	4,889	104,843	2,356,798	2,072,938	9,499	13,831	260,530
Massachusetts	2,055,225	1,927,960	32,361	11,063	83,841	2,172,003	2,024,472	32,641	26,558	88,332
Michigan	5,179,181	4,733,581	52,184	53,696	339,720	5,101,603	4,628,382	79,627	90,320	303,274
Minnesota	2,902,560	2,581,526	34,575	57,676	228,783	2,757,956	2,410,282	58,589	76,958	212,127
Mississippi	709,629	633,815	5,720	5,748	64,346	716,139	630,367	7,250	7,630	70,892
Missouri	2,275,667	2,008,419	101,620	55,071	110,557	2,265,005	1,966,818	118,190	48,706	131,291
Montana	209,026	149,625	16,066	13,664	29,671	204,445	151,770	15,943	11,789	24,943
Nebraska	681,359	540,899	19,531	4,443	116,486	711,145	547,877	23,316	6,402	133,550
Nevada	2,854,151	2,258,801	14,052	41,463	539,835	2,787,984	2,277,934	8,119	58,394	443,537
New Hampshire	516,839	473,734	5,430	4,257	33,418	571,675	529,606	4,534	6,544	30,991
New Jersey	2,134,126	1,985,727	47,616	14,716	86,067	2,533,450	2,332,346	45,538	13,548	142,018
New Mexico	1,083,501	1,029,456	1,114	3,473	49,458	887,175	794,950	1,651	4,260	86,314
New York	3,110,079	2,380,716	177,108	76,539	475,716	3,064,240	2,389,731	148,819	72,386	453,304
North Carolina	6,042,572	5,418,435	51,955	41,310	530,872	6,722,702	5,987,351	66,271	42,184	626,896
North Dakota	181,018	147,765	2,496	3,578	27,179	221,875	146,451	7,258	2,298	65,868
Ohio	5,000,781	4,430,635	112,136	109,762	348,248	4,795,483	4,186,968	125,479	165,944	317,092
Oklahoma	980,991	906,920	15,041	2,659	56,371	1,014,322	898,695	14,306	5,324	95,997
Oregon	2,759,925	2,225,636	86,248	54,988	393,053	2,837,727	2,182,713	100,294	93,073	461,647
Pennsylvania	3,549,886	3,299,216	27,673	39,251	183,746	3,801,783	3,420,307	38,037	48,363	295,076
Rhode Island	219,557	202,375	5,837	839	10,506	250,456	235,635	3,433	1,648	9,740
South Carolina	2,464,112	2,145,657	14,902	17,460	286,093	2,651,372	2,247,213	29,632	16,858	357,669
South Dakota	278,738	220,148	7,690	6,654	44,246	255,942	220,675	4,887	9,774	20,606
Tennessee	3,334,418	2,739,338	32,769	28,440	533,871	3,103,939	2,738,122	36,736	20,380	308,701
Texas	9,934,738	8,480,809	69,613	53,131	1,331,185	10,725,108	8,952,700	63,583	82,481	1,626,344
Utah	2,111,224	1,748,741	45,128	56,997	260,358	1,880,380	1,629,495	52,333	34,123	164,429
Vermont	201,383	190,788	3,740	362	6,493	191,864	182,016	2,731	1,678	5,439
Virginia	3,947,353	3,534,235	35,528	27,614	349,976	4,119,267	3,749,184	34,192	23,403	312,488
Washington	3,772,982	3,019,875	113,722	111,299	528,086	4,224,849	3,336,678	140,609	101,388	646,174
West Virginia	276,125	246,997	2,955	4,676	21,497	308,733	264,122	3,669	5,967	34,975
Wisconsin	3,047,212	2,472,467	153,535	77,446	343,764	2,998,203	2,394,410	177,788	75,970	350,035
Wyoming	200,707	174,970	4,687	8,693	12,357	190,163	171,928	3,805	3,321	11,109

Source: U.S. Bureau of the Census, Building Permits Survey and the Survey of the Use of Permits.

Housing Production and Investment

TABLE 2.37. NEW PRIVATELY-OWNED HOUSING UNITS AUTHORIZED, BUT NOT STARTED, IN PERMIT-ISSUING PLACES AT END OF PERIOD: 1973 TO 1997
(Thousands of units)

	YEAR	United States Total	1 unit	2-4 units	5 units or more	Northeast Total	1 unit	2-4 units	5 units or more	Midwest Total	1 unit	2-4 units	5 units or more	South Total	1 unit	2-4 units	5 units or more	West Total	1 unit	2-4 units	5 units or more
14,000-place series	1973	355	94	25	236	61	17	4	40	44	12	5	28	187	47	7	133	63	19	9	35
	1974	242	73	15	153	52	14	2	37	28	11	3	14	116	35	4	77	46	14	6	26
	1975	192	64	10	119	43	13	1	29	20	8	2	11	91	29	2	60	37	14	4	20
	1976	205	78	14	113	41	14	1	25	23	10	3	10	88	31	3	54	54	23	7	24
	1977	232	91	13	128	42	13	1	29	32	14	3	16	95	36	3	56	62	28	6	28
	1978	208	87	15	106	40	14	1	24	27	13	3	11	84	32	4	47	58	28	6	24
16,000-place series	1979	184	77	14	92	33	12	1	19	20	8	3	9	85	33	5	47	46	24	6	17
	1980	174	70	15	88	26	12	1	13	18	7	3	8	89	33	7	49	42	18	5	19
	1981	146	60	11	75	23	12	1	11	10	5	2	3	78	30	5	43	35	14	3	18
	1982	168	67	12	89	19	9	1	9	10	5	2	4	100	39	6	56	38	15	3	20
	1983	178	69	13	96	22	13	1	8	12	5	2	5	104	34	7	64	40	17	3	19
	1984	193	66	10	116	23	11	1	11	14	5	2	8	109	35	5	70	46	16	3	27
17,000-place series	1985	223	81	14	129	37	19	2	16	20	6	2	12	121	43	6	72	45	12	4	29
	1986	205	93	12	100	34	21	2	11	21	6	2	12	91	44	4	44	58	22	4	33
	1987	155	79	11	65	37	23	2	11	12	7	2	3	69	34	4	31	38	16	3	19
	1988	156	76	10	70	33	20	2	11	16	6	2	7	64	30	3	31	44	20	3	21
	1989	174	93	8	73	34	25	2	7	18	8	2	9	74	34	2	37	48	26	3	19
	1990	132	75	9	48	26	20	1	5	14	6	2	6	55	27	2	26	37	22	3	12
	1991	126	71	5	51	24	17	1	6	17	6	1	9	51	26	1	24	34	21	1	11
	1992	109	72	5	32	19	14	1	5	13	9	2	3	50	33	1	15	27	16	2	9
	1993	119	73	4	43	22	15	1	6	14	9	1	5	59	35	1	22	24	13	1	10
	1994	116	66	4	46	17	12	-	5	13	8	1	4	58	31	1	26	27	14	1	12
19,000-place series	1995	142	80	5	58	18	14	1	4	19	13	1	5	72	37	1	34	34	17	1	15
	1996	126	68	5	54	16	9	1	6	17	11	2	4	68	32	1	34	26	16	1	9
	1997	111	64	4	44	11	7	-	4	14	9	1	4	59	32	1	26	27	15	1	11

Source: U.S. Bureau of the Census, Survey of Construction.

Details may not add to totals because of rounding.

These backlog data represent the number of housing units authorized in all months up to and including the last day of the reporting period and not started as of that date without regard to the months of original permit issuance. Cancelled, abandoned, expired, and revoked permits are excluded fron the backlog.

(-) means rounds to zero.

Housing Production and Investment

TABLE 2.38. AVERAGE NUMBER OF MONTHS FROM AUTHORIZATION TO START OF NEW BUILDINGS STARTED BY REGION AND TYPE OF STRUCTURE: 1981 TO 1997

YEAR	United States			Northeast			Midwest			South			West		
	1 unit	2-4 units	5 units or more	1 unit	2-4 units	5 units or more	1 unit	2-4 units	5 units or more	1 unit	2-4 units	5 units or more	1 unit	2-4 units	5 units or more
1981	0.8	1.2	2.0	1.1	1.3	4.2	0.4	0.6	1.4	0.8	1.3	2.1	0.8	1.5	1.7
1982	0.8	0.9	1.9	1.3	1.2	2.9	0.4	0.6	0.9	0.8	0.8	2.2	0.8	0.8	1.4
1983	0.7	1.2	1.7	1.1	1.9	1.9	0.3	0.7	0.8	0.8	1.2	1.9	0.7	1.1	1.5
1984	0.8	1.1	1.6	1.0	1.7	2.1	0.4	0.6	0.8	0.8	0.9	2.1	0.7	1.5	1.1
1985	0.7	1.0	1.6	1.0	1.0	2.0	0.4	0.6	1.2	0.7	1.4	2.0	0.7	0.7	1.1
1986	0.8	1.1	1.7	1.0	1.5	2.4	0.5	0.7	1.3	0.9	1.1	2.3	0.6	1.0	1.2
1987	0.8	1.2	1.9	1.1	1.8	1.6	0.4	0.5	0.9	0.9	1.2	2.7	0.8	1.4	1.8
1988	0.8	1.3	1.6	1.1	2.2	1.3	0.4	0.4	0.6	0.8	1.2	2.2	0.7	1.4	1.5
1989	0.8	1.5	2.0	1.2	2.7	2.2	0.4	0.6	1.0	0.8	0.8	2.6	0.8	1.8	1.8
1990	0.8	1.5	2.2	1.4	2.7	3.7	0.4	0.5	1.1	0.9	2.0	2.7	0.9	1.6	2.0
1991	0.8	1.5	1.8	1.3	2.1	3.2	0.4	0.9	1.0	0.9	0.8	2.2	0.9	1.9	2.0
1992	0.8	0.9	2.0	1.3	1.5	2.4	0.4	0.5	1.6	0.8	1.0	2.1	0.9	0.8	2.2
1993	0.8	1.2	1.6	1.3	2.6	1.9	0.5	0.7	0.8	0.9	0.9	1.9	0.7	1.1	1.5
1994	0.7	1.1	1.8	1.2	1.7	2.4	0.4	0.7	1.1	0.9	0.8	2.2	0.6	1.0	1.5
1995	0.7	1.1	1.6	1.0	2.2	2.2	0.5	0.7	0.4	0.8	0.7	2.0	0.5	1.0	1.8
1996	0.7	1.3	1.8	1.0	1.8	1.2	0.6	0.5	1.3	0.9	1.0	2.3	0.6	1.2	1.4
1997	0.7	0.8	1.9	0.9	1.2	2.2	0.5	0.6	0.7	0.8	0.8	2.7	0.5	0.9	0.9

Source: U.S. Bureau of the Census, Survey of Construction.

Housing Production and Investment

TABLE 2.39. NEW PRIVATELY-OWNED HOUSING UNITS STARTED BY SELECTED CHARACTERISTICS: 1964 TO 1997
(In thousands)

YEAR	United States				Regions				Condominium Units [1]		
	Total	Structures with			Northeast	Midwest	South	West	Total	Structure type	
		1 unit	2-4 units	5 or more units						Single-family	Multi-family
1964	1,529	971	108	450	255	340	578	357	....	....	....
1965	1,473	964	87	423	270	362	575	266	....	....	....
1966	1,165	779	61	325	207	288	473	198	....	....	....
1967	1,292	844	72	376	215	337	520	220	....	....	....
1968	1,508	899	81	527	227	369	619	294	....	....	....
1969	1,467	811	85	571	206	349	588	324	....	....	....
1970	1,434	813	85	536	218	294	612	311	....	....	....
1971	2,052	1,151	120	781	264	434	869	486	....	....	....
1972	2,357	1,309	141	906	330	443	1,057	527	....	....	....
1973	2,045	1,132	118	795	277	440	899	429	241	69	172
1974	1,338	888	68	382	183	317	553	285	175	46	130
1975	1,160	892	64	204	149	294	442	275	65	20	45
1976	1,538	1,162	86	289	169	400	569	400	95	30	64
1977	1,987	1,451	122	414	202	465	783	538	118	41	77
1978	2,020	1,433	125	462	200	451	824	545	156	42	114
1979	1,745	1,194	122	429	178	349	748	470	198	43	156
1980	1,292	852	110	331	125	218	643	306	186	35	150
1981	1,084	705	91	288	117	165	562	240	181	36	145
1982	1,062	663	80	320	117	149	591	205	170	40	130
1983	1,703	1,068	113	522	168	218	935	382	276	77	199
1984	1,750	1,084	121	544	204	243	866	436	291	96	194
1985	1,742	1,072	93	576	252	240	782	468	225	79	146
1986	1,805	1,179	84	542	294	296	733	483	214	80	134
1987	1,620	1,146	65	409	269	298	634	420	196	73	123
1988	1,488	1,081	59	348	235	274	575	404	148	53	95
1989	1,376	1,003	55	318	179	266	536	396	118	37	82
1990	1,193	895	37	260	131	253	479	329	75	22	53
1991	1,014	840	36	138	113	233	414	254	60	21	39
1992	1,200	1,030	31	139	127	288	497	288	74	35	40
1993	1,288	1,126	29	133	126	298	562	302	86	45	41
1994	1,457	1,198	35	224	138	329	639	351	96	48	48
1995	1,354	1,076	34	244	118	290	615	331	93	47	47
1996	1,477	1,161	45	271	132	322	662	361	107	53	55
1997	1,474	1,134	45	296	137	304	670	363	110	56	55

Source: U.S. Bureau of the Census, Survey of Construction.

(1) Units intended for condominium use at the time of start. This category includes a small number of units to be cooperatively owned. See Appendix A for additional explanation.

Housing Production and Investment

TABLE 2.40. NEW PRIVATELY-OWNED HOUSING UNITS STARTED BY PURPOSE OF CONSTRUCTION: 1964 TO 1997
(Thousands of units)

YEAR	Total	Units in structure							
		1 unit					2 units or more		
		Total	For sale[1]	For owner occupancy on owner's land		For rent	Total	For sale[1]	For rent
				Contractor built	Owner built				
1964	1,529	970	571	185	190	24	558	....	....
1965	1,473	964	596	181	171	16	509	....	....
1966	1,165	779	445	176	144	13	386	....	....
1967	1,292	844	509	170	150	15	448	....	....
1968	1,508	899	544	181	160	14	608	....	....
1969	1,467	811	489	172	137	12	656	....	....
1970	1,434	813	502	168	134	9	621	....	....
1971	2,052	1,151	749	226	162	14	901	....	....
1972	2,357	1,309	859	256	180	14	1,047	....	....
1973	2,045	1,132	693	245	183	11	913	....	....
1974	1,338	888	501	205	174	8	450	131	319
1975	1,160	892	531	190	164	7	268	45	223
1976	1,538	1,162	705	240	209	8	375	63	312
1977	1,987	1,451	904	298	240	9	536	90	446
1978	2,020	1,433	901	287	231	14	587	131	456
1979	1,745	1,194	742	213	222	17	551	173	378
1980	1,292	852	526	149	164	12	440	163	277
1981	1,084	705	426	122	148	10	379	158	221
1982	1,062	663	409	108	133	12	400	140	259
1983	1,703	1,068	713	151	179	24	635	210	425
1984	1,750	1,084	728	157	165	33	665	206	459
1985	1,742	1,072	713	177	157	26	669	154	515
1986	1,805	1,179	782	204	166	27	626	143	483
1987	1,620	1,146	732	208	178	28	474	130	344
1988	1,488	1,081	709	196	154	22	407	99	307
1989	1,376	1,003	648	192	144	19	373	87	286
1990	1,193	895	529	196	147	22	298	56	241
1991	1,014	840	490	198	138	14	174	41	132
1992	1,200	1,030	618	224	168	19	170	41	128
1993	1,288	1,126	716	225	162	22	162	44	118
1994	1,457	1,198	763	245	169	22	259	52	206
1995	1,354	1,076	712	199	133	33	278	51	227
1996	1,477	1,161	774	218	144	25	316	59	257
1997	1,474	1,134	784	189	131	29	341	59	282

Source: U.S. Bureau of the Census, Survey of Construction.

(1) Includes houses already sold when construction started.

Housing units for which the purpose of construction is not reported are distributed proportionally to those for which information is reported.

Details may not add to totals because of rounding.

Housing Production and Investment

TABLE 2.41. NEW PRIVATELY-OWNED HOUSING UNITS UNDER CONSTRUCTION AT END OF PERIOD, BY SELECTED CHARACTERISTICS: 1969 TO 1997
(Thousands of units)

YEAR	United States					Regions			
	Total	Structures with				Northeast	Midwest	South	West
		1 unit	2 units	3-4 units	5 or more units				
1969	885	350	23	26	486	159	211	335	180
1970	922	381	23	27	491	197	189	359	176
1971	1,254	505	27	38	685	237	279	494	244
1972	1,542	613	36	46	847	264	307	669	302
1973	1,454	522	31	48	854	239	293	650	272
1974	1,001	441	19	29	511	178	219	419	185
1975	794	448	20	27	299	130	195	298	171
1976	922	563	23	32	305	125	232	333	231
1977	1,208	730	34	45	399	146	285	457	321
1978	1,310	765	36	47	462	158	309	498	345
1979	1,140	639	31	47	423	147	233	449	312
1980	896	515	28	40	313	120	171	377	228
1981	682	382	17	29	255	103	110	300	170
1982	720	400	17	25	279	99	112	344	165
1983	1,003	524	19	39	421	121	123	521	239
1984	1,051	556	21	43	431	153	137	489	272
1985	1,063	539	21	35	468	187	144	438	295
1986	1,074	583	19	28	443	219	166	387	302
1987	987	591	17	23	357	222	159	343	264
1988	919	570	16	24	310	202	148	308	262
1989	850	535	12	25	278	159	146	282	264
1990	711	449	11	15	236	122	133	242	214
1991	606	434	9	15	149	104	122	209	172
1992	612	473	6	11	123	81	138	228	165
1993	680	543	7	12	118	89	154	265	171
1994	762	558	9	13	183	96	174	312	180
1995	776	547	8	13	208	86	172	331	186
1996	792	550	9	19	214	85	178	338	191
1997	847	555	11	21	260	87	182	365	213

Source: U.S. Bureau of the Census, Survey of Construction.

Details may not add to totals because of rounding.

Table shows number of units under construction at the end of each year.

Housing Production and Investment

YEAR	United States				Regions			
	Total	Structures with			Northeast	Midwest	South	West
		1 unit	2-4 units	5 or more units				
	TABLE 2.42. NEW PRIVATELY-OWNED HOUSING UNITS COMPLETED BY SELECTED CHARACTERISTICS: 1968 TO 1997 (In thousands)							
1968	1,320	859	78	384	199	348	527	246
1969	1,399	808	79	512	220	345	553	281
1970	1,418	802	85	531	185	323	595	315
1971	1,706	1,014	106	586	226	348	727	405
1972	2,004	1,160	119	725	281	412	849	462
1973	2,101	1,197	124	780	294	442	906	459
1974	1,728	940	95	693	232	377	756	364
1975	1,317	875	61	382	186	313	531	287
1976	1,377	1,034	77	266	170	356	513	338
1977	1,657	1,258	95	304	177	400	636	444
1978	1,868	1,369	116	382	182	417	752	517
1979	1,871	1,301	125	445	188	415	762	506
1980	1,502	957	119	426	146	274	696	386
1981	1,266	819	112	336	127	218	626	294
1982	1,006	632	81	293	120	143	539	203
1983	1,390	924	92	374	139	201	746	305
1984	1,652	1,025	112	515	168	221	867	396
1985	1,703	1,072	97	534	214	230	812	447
1986	1,756	1,120	86	550	254	270	764	469
1987	1,669	1,123	71	475	257	302	660	449
1988	1,530	1,085	57	389	250	280	595	405
1989	1,423	1,026	59	338	219	267	549	387
1990	1,308	966	45	297	158	263	511	376
1991	1,091	838	37	217	120	240	439	291
1992	1,158	964	36	158	136	268	462	290
1993	1,193	1,039	26	127	118	273	512	290
1994	1,347	1,160	32	155	123	307	581	336
1995	1,313	1,066	35	212	127	288	581	317
1996	1,413	1,128	33	251	125	304	637	346
1997	1,401	1,116	37	247	134	296	634	336

Source: U.S. Bureau of the Census, Survey of Construction.

Components may not add to totals because of rounding.

Housing Production and Investment

CHARACTERISTIC															
TABLE 2.43. SELECTED CHARACTERISTICS OF NEW PRIVATELY-OWNED ONE-FAMILY HOUSES COMPLETED: 1970 TO 1997 (Percent distribution, except as indicated)															
	1970	1971	1972	1973	1974	1975	1976	1977	1978	1979	1980	1981	1982	1983	1984
One-family houses completed (Thousands)	793	1,014	1,143	1,197	940	875	1,034	1,258	1,369	1,301	957	819	632	924	1,025
Floor area	100	100	100	100	100	100	100	100	100	100	100	100	100	100	100
Under 1,200 square feet	36	36	32	25	24	25	22	19	18	18	21	24	25	22	19
1,200 to 1,599 square feet	28	29	30	31	29	30	29	30	28	28	29	29	30	31	30
1,600 to 2,399 square feet	37	26	29	33	34	34	37	38	40	38	35	32	30	33	33
2,400 square feet and over	(1)	9	9	12	13	11	12	13	14	15	15	15	15	15	17
Average (Square feet)	1,500	1,520	1,555	1,660	1,695	1,645	1,700	1,720	1,755	1,760	1,740	1,720	1,710	1,725	1,780
Median (Square feet)	1,385	1,375	1,405	1,525	1,560	1,535	1,590	1,610	1,655	1,645	1,595	1,550	1,520	1,565	1,605
Number of stories	100	100	100	100	100	100	100	100	100	100	100	100	100	100	100
1	74	73	72	67	65	65	63	63	61	59	60	61	61	58	54
2 or more [2]	17	17	18	23	25	23	25	26	28	31	31	32	33	36	40
Split level	10	10	9	10	10	12	12	11	11	11	8	8	6	6	6
Foundation	100	100	100	100	100	100	100	100	100	100	100	100	100	100	100
Full or partial basement	37	36	37	41	45	45	45	44	42	42	36	33	31	32	32
Slab	36	38	39	38	36	35	36	38	40	39	45	47	49	51	50
Crawl space	27	26	24	21	19	20	19	18	18	19	19	20	20	17	18
Bedrooms	100	100	100	100	100	100	100	100	100	100	100	100	100	100	100
2 or less	13	14	12	12	13	14	12	11	12	14	17	21	24	24	24
3	63	62	65	64	64	65	65	66	64	64	63	60	58	59	58
4 or more	24	24	23	23	23	21	23	23	24	23	20	20	18	18	18
Bathrooms	100	100	100	100	100	100	100	100	100	100	100	100	100	100	100
1 or less	32	31	27	21	22	24	20	17	15	16	18	20	22	18	14
1 1/2 [3]	20	21	20	19	18	17	13	13	11	11	10	10	11	10	10
2	32	33	37	41	40	40	45	47	48	48	48	46	45	48	48
2 1/2 or more	16	15	16	19	21	20	22	23	25	26	25	24	22	24	28
Heating fuel	100	100	100	100	100	100	100	100	100	100	100	100	100	100	100
Electricity	28	31	36	42	49	49	48	50	52	51	50	50	50	49	48
Gas	62	60	54	47	41	40	39	38	37	39	41	41	40	43	45
Oil	8	8	8	10	9	9	11	9	8	7	3	2	3	2	2
Other or none	1	1	1	1	1	2	2	2	3	3	5	7	8	6	5
Central air-conditioning	100	100	100	100	100	100	100	100	100	100	100	100	100	100	100
With	34	36	43	49	48	46	49	54	58	60	63	65	66	70	71
Without	66	64	57	51	52	54	51	46	42	40	37	35	34	30	29
Fireplaces	100	100	100	100	100	100	100	100	100	100	100	100	100	100	100
No fireplace	65	64	63	56	51	48	42	39	36	38	43	45	46	43	41
1 or more	35	36	38	44	49	52	58	61	64	62	56	54	54	57	59
Parking facilities	100	100	100	100	100	100	100	100	100	100	100	100	100	100	100
Garage	58	57	61	65	68	67	72	74	74	74	69	66	65	68	70
Carport	17	17	17	13	10	9	8	7	7	7	7	8	8	7	5
No garage or carport	25	26	22	22	22	24	20	19	18	20	24	25	27	25	25

See notes at end of table.

Housing Production and Investment

CHARACTERISTIC	TABLE 2.43. SELECTED CHARACTERISTICS OF NEW PRIVATELY-OWNED ONE-FAMILY HOUSES COMPLETED: 1970 TO 1997 - Continued (Percent distribution, except as indicated)												
	1985	1986	1987	1988	1989	1990	1991	1992	1993	1994	1995	1996	1997
One-family houses completed (Thousands)	1,072	1,120	1,123	1,085	1,026	966	838	964	1,039	1,160	1,066	1,129	1,116
Floor area	100	100	100	100	100	100	100	100	100	100	100	100	100
Under 1,200 square feet	20	17	14	12	13	11	12	10	9	9	10	9	8
1,200 to 1,599 square feet	30	30	27	25	23	22	22	22	21	21	22	21	21
1,600 to 2,399 square feet	33	35	38	38	38	39	38	40	40	42	40	41	41
2,400 square feet and over	17	18	21	25	26	29	28	29	30	29	28	30	31
Average (Square feet)	1,785	1,825	1,905	1,995	2,035	2,080	2,075	2,095	2,095	2,100	2,095	2,120	2,150
Median (Square feet)	1,605	1,660	1,755	1,810	1,850	1,905	1,890	1,920	1,945	1,940	1,920	1,950	1,975
Number of stories	100	100	100	100	100	100	100	100	100	100	100	100	100
1	52	51	49	46	46	46	48	48	48	49	49	49	49
2 or more [2]	42	44	46	49	49	49	47	47	48	47	48	47	49
Split level	6	5	5	4	4	4	5	5	4	3	3	3	3
Foundation	100	100	100	100	100	100	100	100	100	100	100	100	100
Full or partial basement	35	37	39	39	37	38	40	42	40	39	39	37	37
Slab	48	45	43	41	43	40	38	38	40	41	42	44	45
Crawl space	18	18	18	19	19	21	22	20	20	20	19	19	19
Bedrooms	100	100	100	100	100	100	100	100	100	100	100	100	100
2 or less	25	21	19	17	15	15	14	12	12	12	13	13	13
3	57	59	58	57	57	57	59	59	58	58	57	56	56
4 or more	18	20	23	26	28	29	28	29	30	30	30	31	31
Bathrooms	100	100	100	100	100	100	100	100	100	100	100	100	100
1 or less	13	10	10	8	8	....	....	....	....	....	....	....	....
1 1/2 [3]	11	9	7	7	6	13	14	13	12	11	11	9	9
2	48	47	45	44	42	42	43	40	40	40	41	41	41
2 1/2 or more	29	33	38	42	44	45	44	47	48	49	48	49	50
Heating fuel	100	100	100	100	100	100	100	100	100	100	100	100	100
Electricity	44	44	40	37	34	33	32	29	29	29	28	26	26
Gas	49	47	52	54	58	59	60	65	66	67	67	69	69
Oil	3	5	5	6	5	5	4	4	3	3	3	3	3
Other or none	4	4	3	3	3	3	4	2	2	1	1	1	1
Central air-conditioning	100	100	100	100	100	100	100	100	100	100	100	100	100
With	70	69	71	75	77	76	75	77	78	79	80	81	82
Without	30	31	29	25	23	24	25	23	22	21	20	19	18
Fireplaces	100	100	100	100	100	100	100	100	100	100	100	100	100
No fireplace	41	38	38	35	35	34	37	37	37	36	37	38	39
1 or more	59	62	62	65	65	66	63	63	63	64	63	62	61
Parking facilities	100	100	100	100	100	100	100	100	100	100	100	100	100
Garage	70	74	79	78	80	82	81	83	84	86	84	86	86
Carport	5	4	3	3	3	2	3	2	2	2	2	1	1
No garage or carport	25	21	18	18	17	16	17	15	14	13	14	13	13

Source: U.S. Bureau of the Census, Survey of Construction.

(1) Included with floor area of 1,600 to 2,399 square feet.
(2) May include a small number of houses with one and one-half, two and one-half, or three stories.
(3) One and one-half or less for 1990 and after.

Percentages may not add to 100 due to rounding.

Housing Production and Investment

YEAR	1 unit	2-4 units	Buildings with 5 or more units					
			Total	5-9 units	10-19 units	20-29 units	30-49 units	50 units or more
1981	6.6	6.7	8.8	8.5	8.4	9.0	11.5	14.8
1982	6.6	6.3	8.4	7.8	7.9	9.4	11.1	15.3
1983	5.8	5.9	7.3	7.0	7.1	7.6	9.2	13.0
1984	6.1	6.0	7.8	7.5	7.8	8.3	10.1	12.5
1985	6.2	6.6	8.4	7.8	8.6	9.0	10.6	13.1
1986	6.2	7.2	8.4	8.0	8.6	9.0	10.1	13.0
1987	6.2	7.3	9.2	8.7	9.3	9.6	10.6	13.4
1988	6.5	8.1	9.5	9.1	9.4	9.9	10.9	15.6
1989	6.4	8.0	9.3	8.9	9.3	9.4	10.3	13.7
1990	6.4	7.6	9.4	9.2	9.3	9.1	11.4	15.6
1991	6.3	8.5	9.7	9.2	10.4	8.8	10.5	14.2
1992	5.8	7.1	9.1	8.6	8.8	11.0	9.7	15.2
1993	5.6	7.4	8.6	7.6	9.5	9.3	11.0	14.7
1994	5.6	7.3	9.3	8.2	11.0	8.8	9.8	13.3
1995	5.9	6.8	9.1	8.6	9.5	9.4	9.8	12.9
1996	6.0	7.5	8.9	8.6	8.9	10.4	9.8	10.8
1997	6.0	7.5	9.2	8.5	9.3	10.1	11.2	12.7

TABLE 2.44. AVERAGE NUMBER OF MONTHS FROM START TO COMPLETION OF NEW RESIDENTIAL BUILDINGS BY NUMBER OF UNITS IN STRUCTURE: 1981 TO 1997

Source: U.S. Bureau of the Census, Survey of Construction.

Housing Production and Investment

CATEGORY OF HOUSE, REGION, AND CONSTRUCTION TYPE	TABLE 2.45. TYPE OF CONSTRUCTION METHOD BY CATEGORY OF HOUSE AND REGION: 1992 TO 1997											
	Number of houses (In thousands)						Percent distribution					
	1992	1993	1994	1995	1996	1997	1992	1993	1994	1995	1996	1997
ALL NEW HOUSES [1]												
United States	964	1,039	1,160	1,066	1,129	1,116	100	100	100	100	100	100
Stick-built	903	978	1,093	1,001	1,059	1,046	94	94	94	94	94	94
Modular	33	32	38	35	37	40	3	3	3	3	3	4
Other [2]	28	29	30	29	32	30	3	3	3	3	3	3
Northeast	114	105	113	108	108	115	100	100	100	100	100	100
Stick-built	98	91	98	92	92	102	86	87	87	85	85	88
Modular	12	9	10	10	9	10	10	9	9	9	9	9
Other [2]	4	5	5	6	6	4	4	4	4	5	6	3
Midwest	218	232	255	232	245	236	100	100	100	100	100	100
Stick-built	198	210	231	210	220	209	91	91	90	90	90	89
Modular	12	13	17	15	16	17	6	6	7	7	7	7
Other [2]	8	8	7	7	8	9	3	3	3	3	3	4
South	400	456	507	472	507	506	100	100	100	100	100	100
Stick-built	378	433	484	449	483	481	95	95	95	95	95	95
Modular	7	8	8	8	8	10	2	2	2	2	2	2
Other [2]	14	15	15	15	15	14	3	3	3	3	3	3
West	232	247	285	253	269	259	100	100	100	100	100	100
Stick-built	229	243	280	250	264	253	99	98	98	99	98	98
Modular	....	....	3	....	3	3	....	....	1	....	1	1
Other [2]	....	....	3	....	....	3	....	....	1	....	....	1
HOUSES BUILT FOR SALE												
United States	577	642	739	682	746	757	100	100	100	100	100	100
Stick-built	553	618	712	654	716	727	96	96	96	96	96	96
Modular	7	7	8	7	7	7	1	1	1	1	1	1
Other [2]	16	17	20	21	23	22	3	3	3	3	3	3
Northeast	62	58	65	64	68	72	100	100	100	100	100	100
Stick-built	57	53	59	57	61	67	91	91	91	89	90	92
Modular	3	3	3	3	....	3	5	5	5	5	....	4
Other [2]	....	....	3	4	5	3	....	....	5	6	7	4
Midwest	108	118	136	127	135	137	100	100	100	100	100	100
Stick-built	102	112	130	120	127	130	94	95	96	95	94	94
Modular	....	....	....	....	....	....						
Other [2]	4	4	4	4	5	7	4	3	3	3	4	5
South	245	287	326	306	335	344	100	100	100	100	100	100
Stick-built	233	276	313	292	321	330	95	96	96	96	96	96
Modular	....	....	....	....	....	....						
Other [2]	10	10	11	12	13	12	4	4	4	4	4	3
West	162	178	212	185	207	204	100	100	100	100	100	100
Stick-built	161	177	210	184	206	201	100	99	99	99	99	99
Modular	....	....	....	....	....	....						
Other [2]	....	....	....	....	....	....						

See notes at end of table.

Housing Production and Investment

CATEGORY OF HOUSE, REGION, AND CONSTRUCTION TYPE	Number of houses (In thousands)						Percent distribution					
TABLE 2.45. TYPE OF CONSTRUCTION METHOD BY CATEGORY OF HOUSE AND REGION: 1992 TO 1997 - Continued	1992	1993	1994	1995	1996	1997	1992	1993	1994	1995	1996	1997
CONTRACTOR-BUILT HOUSES												
United States	213	216	238	204	214	192	100	100	100	100	100	100
Stick-built	192	196	215	183	193	171	91	91	90	90	90	89
Modular	15	15	18	17	18	18	7	7	8	8	8	9
Other [2]	5	5	5	4	4	4	2	3	2	2	2	2
Northeast	30	27	29	27	23	22	100	100	100	100	100	100
Stick-built	25	23	24	22	18	18	82	83	82	81	79	83
Modular	4	3	4	4	4	3	15	13	14	16	17	15
Other [2]	....	....	....	....	....	....	....	....	....	....	....	....
Midwest	58	61	67	57	58	50	100	100	100	100	100	100
Stick-built	50	53	56	48	49	40	87	86	83	84	85	80
Modular	7	7	10	8	8	9	12	11	14	14	13	17
Other [2]	....	....	....	....	....	....	....	....	....	....	....	....
South	88	95	106	92	105	91	100	100	100	100	100	100
Stick-built	83	89	100	86	98	85	94	94	95	94	94	93
Modular	3	4	4	4	5	5	4	4	4	4	5	5
Other [2]	....	....	....	....	....	....	....	....	....	....	....	....
West	36	33	36	29	28	28	100	100	100	100	100	100
Stick-built	34	32	35	27	26	27	95	95	97	96	94	96
Modular	....	....	....	....	....	....	....	....	....	....	....	....
Other [2]	....	....	....	....	....	....	....	....	....	....	....	....
OWNER-BUILT HOUSES												
United States	155	159	160	146	136	137	100	100	100	100	100	100
Stick-built	140	143	144	132	122	121	90	90	90	90	90	88
Modular	10	11	12	10	10	13	7	7	7	7	8	9
Other [2]	5	5	4	4	3	4	3	3	3	3	2	3
Northeast	20	18	16	15	15	17	100	100	100	100	100	100
Stick-built	15	14	13	12	12	14	76	78	82	79	82	82
Modular	4	3	....	....	....	....	18	16	....	....	....	....
Other [2]	....	....	....	....	....	....	....	....	....	....	....	....
Midwest	48	47	47	42	42	41	100	100	100	100	100	100
Stick-built	42	41	40	36	35	33	87	86	84	85	84	80
Modular	4	5	6	5	6	7	8	11	12	11	14	17
Other [2]	3	....	....	....	....	....	5	....	....	....	....	....
South	56	63	66	59	51	55	100	100	100	100	100	100
Stick-built	52	58	62	55	48	51	93	93	93	94	95	93
Modular	3	3	3	....	....	3	5	4	5	....	....	5
Other [2]	....	....	....	....	....	....	....	....	....	....	....	....
West	31	31	31	30	28	25	100	100	100	100	100	100
Stick-built	30	30	29	29	26	23	98	97	95	96	95	95
Modular	....	....	....	....	....	....	....	....	....	....	....	....
Other [2]	....	....	....	....	....	....	....	....	....	....	....	....

Source: U.S. Bureau of the Census, Survey of Construction.

(1) Includes houses built for rent (not shown separately).

(2) Includes panelized and precut units. See Appendix A for definitions of construction type categories.

The table includes only privately-owned, one-family houses completed in each year.

Housing Production and Investment

YEAR	United States	Northeast	Midwest	South	West
	TABLE 2.46. NEW MOBILE HOMES PLACED FOR RESIDENTIAL USE BY REGION: 1974 TO 1997 (Thousands)				
1974	332.0	23.3	67.5	170.8	70.4
1975	229.3	14.7	48.5	110.8	55.2
1976	249.6	16.8	51.5	114.8	66.5
1977	257.5	16.7	50.7	112.5	77.7
1978	279.9	17.4	49.5	135.3	77.7
1979	279.9	16.9	47.3	145.2	70.5
1980	233.7	12.3	32.3	140.3	48.7
1981	229.2	12.0	30.1	143.5	43.6
1982	234.1	12.4	25.6	161.1	35.0
1983	278.1	16.3	34.3	186.0	41.4
1984	287.9	19.8	35.2	193.4	39.4
1985	283.4	20.2	38.6	187.6	36.9
1986	256.1	21.2	37.2	162.3	35.4
1987	239.2	23.6	40.0	145.5	30.1
1988	224.3	22.7	39.1	130.7	31.8
1989	202.8	20.2	39.1	112.8	30.6
1990	195.4	18.8	37.7	108.4	30.6
1991	174.3	14.3	35.4	97.6	27.0
1992	212.0	15.0	42.2	124.4	30.4
1993	242.5	15.4	44.5	146.7	35.9
1994	286.1	16.2	53.0	174.4	42.5
1995	310.7	14.6	56.0	198.3	41.8
1996	319.7	15.4	56.6	205.1	42.6
1997	296.5	13.7	50.9	188.8	43.1

Source: U.S. Bureau of the Census, Survey of New Mobile Home Placements.

Housing Production and Investment

TABLE 2.47. NEW MOBILE HOMES PLACED FOR RESIDENTIAL USE BY REGION AND NUMBER OF SECTIONS IN HOME: 1980 TO 1997
(In thousands)

YEAR	United States			Northeast			Midwest			South			West		
------	Total [1]	Single wide	Double wide	Total [1]	Single wide	Double wide	Total [1]	Single wide	Double wide	Total [1]	Single wide	Double wide	Total [1]	Single wide	Double wide
1980	233.7	165.0	65.8	12.3	10.9	1.4	32.3	27.8	4.5	140.3	104.7	35.5	48.7	21.7	24.3
1981	229.2	173.0	54.3	12.0	10.5	1.5	30.1	26.0	4.1	143.5	113.9	29.5	43.6	22.5	19.2
1982	234.1	182.5	50.7	12.4	11.0	1.3	25.6	21.6	4.0	161.1	130.4	30.7	35.0	19.5	14.7
1983	278.1	205.8	70.9	16.3	13.9	2.5	34.3	28.4	5.9	186.0	144.1	41.8	41.4	19.4	20.6
1984	287.9	204.0	82.5	19.8	16.6	3.2	35.2	28.1	7.2	193.4	141.9	51.4	39.4	17.4	20.7
1985	283.4	192.9	88.8	20.2	16.2	4.0	38.6	30.3	8.3	187.6	131.7	55.7	36.9	14.6	20.9
1986	256.1	165.0	89.8	21.2	15.3	5.9	37.2	27.6	9.6	162.3	109.6	52.5	35.4	12.4	21.8
1987	239.2	148.5	89.2	23.6	16.6	6.9	40.0	27.6	12.4	145.5	94.6	50.6	30.1	9.6	19.3
1988	224.3	128.4	94.2	22.7	14.9	7.8	39.1	25.6	13.5	130.7	80.6	49.9	31.8	7.4	23.1
1989	202.8	107.4	93.7	20.2	12.4	7.8	39.1	23.9	15.1	112.8	64.6	47.8	30.6	6.4	22.9
1990	195.4	103.8	89.5	18.8	12.1	6.7	37.7	22.9	14.7	108.4	62.7	44.8	30.6	6.1	23.3
1991	174.3	94.6	77.8	14.3	9.1	5.2	35.4	21.6	13.8	97.6	58.2	38.4	27.0	5.8	20.3
1992	212.0	114.5	95.5	15.0	8.3	6.7	42.2	25.3	16.9	124.4	73.4	50.1	30.4	7.4	21.9
1993	242.5	127.0	112.4	15.4	8.6	6.7	44.5	24.7	19.7	146.7	83.8	61.5	35.9	9.9	24.4
1994	286.1	146.0	135.9	16.2	9.0	7.1	53.0	27.5	25.3	174.4	98.8	73.9	42.5	10.6	29.5
1995	310.7	158.2	148.3	14.6	7.9	6.6	56.0	29.4	26.6	198.3	109.8	86.8	41.8	11.1	28.2
1996	319.7	154.1	160.3	15.4	7.8	7.6	56.6	27.0	29.4	205.1	108.3	94.2	42.6	11.0	29.2
1997	296.5	126.4	164.8	13.7	5.5	8.2	50.9	21.5	29.2	188.8	90.0	96.0	43.1	9.4	31.3

Source: U.S. Bureau of the Census, Survey of New Mobile Home Placements.

Details may not add to totals because of rounding.
(1) Includes mobile homes with more than two sections.

Housing Production and Investment

TABLE 2.48. NEW MOBILE HOMES PLACED FOR RESIDENTIAL USE BY STATE AND NUMBER OF SECTIONS IN HOME: 1980 TO 1997
(In thousands)

AREA	1980			1981			1982			1983			1984		
	Total[1]	Single wide	Double wide	Total[1]	Single wide	Double wide	Total[1]	Single wide	Double wide	Total[1]	Single wide	Double wide	Total[1]	Single wide	Double wide
United States	233.7	165.0	65.8	229.2	173.0	54.3	234.1	182.5	50.7	278.1	205.8	70.9	287.9	204.0	82.5
Northeast	12.3	10.9	1.4	12.0	10.5	1.5	12.4	11.0	1.3	16.3	13.9	2.5	19.8	16.6	3.2
Midwest	32.3	27.8	4.5	30.1	26.0	4.1	25.6	21.6	4.0	34.3	28.4	5.9	35.2	28.1	7.2
South	140.3	104.7	35.5	143.5	113.9	29.5	161.1	130.4	30.7	186.0	144.1	41.8	193.4	141.9	51.4
West	48.7	21.7	24.3	43.6	22.5	19.2	35.0	19.5	14.7	41.4	19.4	20.6	39.4	17.4	20.7
Alabama	5.7	4.6	1.1	4.9	4.1	0.8	6.0	5.1	0.9	9.1	7.7	1.4	12.0	9.7	2.4
Alaska	0.1	(S)	(S)	0.2	(S)	(S)	0.9	(S)	(S)	0.9	0.7	0.2	0.3	(S)	(S)
Arizona	5.4	2.8	2.5	6.0	4.1	1.9	4.8	2.9	1.9	5.7	2.7	2.9	7.1	3.7	3.3
Arkansas	3.0	2.4	0.6	2.6	2.2	0.4	2.6	2.3	0.3	5.7	5.0	0.7	6.3	5.5	0.8
California	14.4	2.3	9.8	11.4	2.4	7.5	7.4	2.0	4.8	11.7	2.7	7.8	10.2	2.4	6.8
Colorado	3.2	2.4	0.8	3.6	2.9	0.8	2.4	1.7	0.6	2.5	1.7	0.8	2.0	1.2	0.8
Connecticut	0.4	(S)	(S)	0.2	(S)	(S)	0.2	(S)	(S)	(S)	(S)	(S)	0.7	(S)	(S)
Delaware	0.9	(S)	(S)	1.0	0.8	0.2	1.1	1.0	0.2	2.3	1.9	0.4	2.0	1.6	0.4
District of Columbia	0.0	0.0	0.0	0.0	0.0	0.0	0.0	0.0	0.0	0.0	0.0	0.0	0.0	0.0	0.0
Florida	29.9	12.3	17.5	25.7	13.3	12.4	23.5	11.8	11.6	30.5	14.3	16.2	31.1	14.6	16.4
Georgia	9.5	6.4	3.1	9.2	6.0	3.2	11.7	7.7	4.0	14.1	9.2	4.9	15.7	8.7	7.0
Hawaii	0.0	0.0	0.0	0.0	0.0	0.0	0.0	0.0	0.0	0.0	0.0	0.0	0.0	0.0	0.0
Idaho	1.8	0.8	1.0	1.2	0.8	0.4	1.2	0.8	0.5	1.7	0.8	0.9	1.9	1.0	0.9
Illinois	3.4	2.6	0.8	3.9	3.4	0.5	2.8	2.0	0.8	3.7	3.0	0.7	3.1	2.4	0.8
Indiana	4.5	4.0	0.5	3.6	3.2	0.4	3.0	2.6	0.4	4.7	3.9	0.9	4.4	3.3	1.1
Iowa	1.0	0.8	0.2	0.8	0.7	0.2	1.0	0.8	0.2	1.0	0.9	0.1	1.3	1.1	0.2
Kansas	2.2	1.7	0.5	3.1	2.7	0.3	2.6	2.1	0.4	2.7	2.0	0.7	2.1	1.6	0.5
Kentucky	4.5	3.8	0.7	4.9	4.3	0.6	4.6	4.1	0.5	4.2	3.4	0.8	6.0	4.9	1.2
Louisiana	15.3	14.1	1.2	12.9	12.0	1.0	13.9	13.2	0.7	12.3	11.5	0.8	11.9	11.2	0.7
Maine	1.1	(S)	(S)	0.7	(S)	(S)	0.9	(S)	(S)	1.5	(S)	(S)	1.3	(S)	(S)
Maryland	1.4	(S)	(S)	1.3	(S)	(S)	1.2	1.1	0.2	1.4	1.2	0.2	1.8	1.5	0.4
Massachusetts	0.7	(S)	(S)	0.3	(S)	(S)	0.3	(S)	(S)	0.7	0.3	0.4	0.7	0.4	0.3
Michigan	5.2	4.6	0.6	4.1	3.3	0.7	3.9	3.2	0.7	5.0	3.6	1.4	7.2	5.5	1.7
Minnesota	2.1	1.9	0.2	1.7	1.5	0.5	1.6	(S)	(S)	2.2	2.0	0.1	2.0	1.7	0.3
Mississippi	4.6	4.0	0.6	4.1	3.7	0.5	5.1	4.8	0.4	6.8	6.1	0.7	5.4	4.9	0.5
Missouri	3.1	2.5	0.6	2.8	2.2	0.6	2.5	2.1	0.4	4.2	3.8	0.5	5.3	4.4	0.9
Montana	2.5	2.2	0.4	1.2	1.0	0.2	1.5	1.3	0.3	1.4	1.0	0.4	1.3	0.8	0.5
Nebraska	0.9	0.7	0.2	0.8	0.7	0.2	0.7	0.6	0.1	0.7	0.5	0.2	0.8	0.6	0.2
Nevada	1.9	0.8	1.0	2.0	0.8	1.2	1.4	0.4	1.0	2.1	1.1	1.0	1.8	0.7	1.0
New Hampshire	0.6	(S)	(S)	0.8	0.6	0.1	0.6	(S)	(S)	0.8	0.6	0.1	1.1	0.9	0.2
New Jersey	0.7	0.5	0.2	0.5	0.4	0.2	0.7	0.6	0.1	0.7	0.4	0.2	0.9	0.6	0.3
New Mexico	2.9	2.4	0.5	3.7	3.0	0.6	5.0	4.2	0.8	4.8	3.8	1.1	4.9	4.0	0.8
New York	2.9	2.3	0.6	3.6	3.0	0.6	4.1	3.7	0.5	6.3	5.5	0.8	6.8	5.7	1.1
North Carolina	11.7	9.8	2.0	12.8	10.4	2.4	16.0	13.4	2.6	21.3	17.0	4.3	24.1	18.2	6.0
North Dakota	1.3	1.1	0.2	1.0	0.8	0.3	1.2	1.0	0.2	0.6	0.4	0.2	0.4	(S)	(S)
Ohio	5.7	5.1	0.6	5.5	5.0	0.5	3.6	3.1	0.5	5.4	4.5	0.9	5.2	4.2	1.0
Oklahoma	7.5	6.6	0.9	10.8	10.1	0.7	12.4	11.2	1.2	10.5	9.5	1.0	7.3	6.0	1.3
Oregon	4.3	1.6	2.5	3.7	1.3	2.4	1.9	0.7	1.2	2.0	0.7	1.3	2.8	0.7	2.0
Pennsylvania	5.3	4.9	0.5	5.4	4.9	0.5	5.0	4.5	0.5	5.8	4.9	0.9	7.4	6.3	1.2
Rhode Island	0.1	(S)	(S)	0.1	(S)	(S)	0.1	(S)	(S)	(S)	(S)	(S)	0.3	(S)	(S)
South Carolina	6.2	4.3	1.8	7.9	6.1	1.8	8.0	6.0	2.0	10.9	8.0	2.9	14.9	10.4	4.5
South Dakota	0.6	0.4	0.2	0.3	(S)	(S)	0.7	0.6	0.1	0.8	(S)	(S)	0.8	0.6	0.2
Tennessee	4.7	4.1	0.6	3.9	3.6	0.3	3.6	3.1	0.5	5.1	4.6	0.6	7.3	6.2	1.1
Texas	25.8	21.8	4.1	33.6	29.3	4.3	42.3	38.2	4.1	41.9	36.5	5.4	36.4	29.6	6.8
Utah	1.0	0.7	0.3	1.2	0.8	0.4	1.2	0.7	0.5	1.3	0.7	0.6	0.8	0.6	0.2
Vermont	0.5	(S)	(S)	0.4	(S)	(S)	0.5	(S)	(S)	0.5	(S)	(S)	0.7	(S)	(S)
Virginia	5.0	4.1	0.9	4.7	4.2	0.5	5.6	4.9	0.7	5.8	4.8	0.9	7.4	6.2	1.2
Washington	8.7	3.7	4.8	6.5	3.2	3.2	5.9	3.0	2.8	6.1	2.6	3.4	5.8	2.0	3.7
West Virginia	4.7	4.2	0.4	3.1	2.8	0.3	3.3	2.7	0.6	4.1	3.3	0.8	3.8	2.9	0.9
Wisconsin	2.3	(S)	(S)	2.5	2.4	0.2	2.0	(S)	(S)	3.4	3.2	0.2	2.6	2.3	0.2
Wyoming	2.5	1.9	0.6	2.9	2.2	0.7	1.4	1.0	0.3	1.3	1.0	0.3	0.6	(S)	(S)

See notes at end of table.

Housing Production and Investment

TABLE 2.48. NEW MOBILE HOMES PLACED FOR RESIDENTIAL USE BY STATE AND NUMBER OF SECTIONS IN HOME: 1980 TO 1997 - Continued
(In thousands)

AREA	1985 Total[1]	1985 Single wide	1985 Double wide	1986 Total[1]	1986 Single wide	1986 Double wide	1987 Total[1]	1987 Single wide	1987 Double wide	1988 Total[1]	1988 Single wide	1988 Double wide	1989 Total[1]	1989 Single wide	1989 Double wide
United States	283.4	192.9	88.8	256.1	165.0	89.8	239.2	148.5	89.2	224.3	128.4	94.2	202.8	107.4	93.7
Northeast	20.2	16.2	4.0	21.2	15.3	5.9	23.6	16.6	6.9	22.7	14.9	7.8	20.2	12.4	7.8
Midwest	38.6	30.3	8.3	37.2	27.6	9.6	40.0	27.6	12.4	39.1	25.6	13.5	39.1	23.9	15.1
South	187.6	131.7	55.7	162.3	109.6	52.5	145.5	94.6	50.6	130.7	80.6	49.9	112.8	64.6	47.8
West	36.9	14.6	20.9	35.4	12.4	21.8	30.1	9.6	19.3	31.8	7.4	23.1	30.6	6.4	22.9
Alabama	12.4	9.7	2.7	12.0	9.5	2.4	11.2	9.1	2.1	11.9	8.8	3.1	8.6	6.6	2.0
Alaska	0.2	(S)	(S)	(S)	(S)	(S)	(S)	(S)	(S)	(S)	(S)	(S)	(S)	(S)	(S)
Arizona	5.1	2.6	2.5	5.9	3.4	2.4	5.5	2.9	2.5	4.7	1.8	2.8	3.2	0.8	2.4
Arkansas	6.6	5.8	0.8	5.8	4.8	0.9	5.4	4.5	0.9	4.0	3.2	0.8	3.2	2.2	1.1
California	9.9	2.1	6.6	10.8	1.7	8.1	9.1	1.9	6.3	11.1	1.6	8.4	11.3	1.7	8.5
Colorado	1.7	0.9	0.7	1.4	0.7	0.7	1.1	0.5	0.6	0.8	0.4	0.4	0.7	(S)	(S)
Connecticut	(S)	(S)	(S)	0.4	(S)	(S)	0.6	0.5	0.1	(S)	(S)	(S)	(S)	(S)	(S)
Delaware	1.7	1.4	0.3	2.2	1.8	0.3	1.7	1.1	0.5	1.7	1.1	0.6	1.7	1.0	0.7
District of Columbia	0.0	0.0	0.0	0.0	0.0	0.0	0.0	0.0	0.0	0.0	0.0	0.0	0.0	0.0	0.0
Florida	29.8	12.7	17.1	25.7	10.4	15.3	25.6	9.5	16.0	23.3	8.2	15.0	23.4	8.1	15.2
Georgia	21.0	12.0	9.0	17.8	10.6	7.1	15.2	8.8	6.4	14.7	8.2	6.5	10.7	5.1	5.4
Hawaii	0.0	0.0	0.0	0.0	0.0	0.0	0.0	0.0	0.0	0.0	0.0	0.0	0.0	0.0	0.0
Idaho	1.5	0.8	0.6	1.2	0.6	0.6	0.8	0.3	0.5	0.8	(S)	(S)	0.7	(S)	(S)
Illinois	4.0	3.0	1.0	3.0	2.2	0.8	3.7	2.8	0.9	3.0	2.0	1.0	2.9	1.8	1.1
Indiana	5.2	4.0	1.3	5.9	4.3	1.6	5.3	3.6	1.7	7.0	4.6	2.4	6.1	3.8	2.3
Iowa	1.2	(S)	(S)	0.7	0.5	0.1	0.8	0.5	0.3	1.0	0.8	0.2	1.8	1.3	0.4
Kansas	2.2	1.7	0.5	1.7	1.3	0.3	1.6	0.9	0.7	1.6	0.8	0.7	1.6	0.9	0.8
Kentucky	5.9	4.7	1.2	5.3	3.9	1.4	5.4	4.0	1.4	5.8	4.6	1.1	6.4	4.9	1.5
Louisiana	8.4	7.8	0.7	5.4	4.9	0.5	3.0	2.8	0.3	1.7	1.5	0.2	1.3	1.1	0.3
Maine	1.6	(S)	(S)	2.5	2.3	0.2	2.9	2.4	0.5	2.8	2.3	0.5	2.8	2.2	0.6
Maryland	1.5	1.0	0.5	1.8	1.3	0.5	1.7	1.1	0.5	1.6	0.9	0.7	1.5	0.7	0.8
Massachusetts	1.1	0.8	0.3	1.1	0.6	0.5	0.9	0.5	0.4	0.6	0.2	0.4	0.7	(S)	(S)
Michigan	8.8	6.7	2.1	10.1	6.9	3.2	10.6	6.4	4.2	10.4	5.8	4.7	10.9	5.0	5.8
Minnesota	2.0	1.7	0.3	1.5	1.2	0.3	1.4	1.0	0.4	1.4	1.1	0.4	1.8	1.2	0.5
Mississippi	6.9	5.9	1.0	6.2	5.3	0.9	5.0	3.8	1.2	4.4	3.5	0.9	4.5	3.0	1.4
Missouri	5.8	4.7	1.1	4.9	3.7	1.1	5.3	4.1	1.2	4.6	3.4	1.3	3.6	2.4	1.3
Montana	1.4	0.8	0.5	0.8	0.4	0.5	0.7	(S)	(S)	0.6	(S)	(S)	0.5	(S)	(S)
Nebraska	0.6	0.4	0.1	0.6	0.5	0.1	0.3	(S)	(S)	0.4	(S)	(S)	0.4	(S)	(S)
Nevada	1.5	0.5	0.9	1.7	0.5	1.1	1.8	0.6	1.2	2.2	0.5	1.6	2.2	0.5	1.6
New Hampshire	1.2	0.8	0.4	1.4	1.1	0.3	1.4	1.0	0.4	1.3	0.9	0.5	1.1	0.9	0.2
New Jersey	0.8	0.3	0.4	1.2	0.7	0.5	0.9	(S)	(S)	0.8	0.4	0.4	0.6	0.3	0.3
New Mexico	4.5	3.0	1.4	4.2	3.2	0.9	2.8	1.9	0.9	2.6	1.3	1.3	2.4	1.3	1.2
New York	7.4	6.0	1.4	6.7	4.6	2.1	8.6	6.1	2.5	7.8	5.1	2.7	7.2	4.0	3.2
North Carolina	27.3	21.6	5.7	27.9	20.2	7.7	24.2	16.7	7.5	23.5	16.1	7.3	18.1	11.4	6.6
North Dakota	0.3	(S)	(S)	0.2	(S)	(S)	0.2	(S)	(S)	(S)	(S)	(S)	0.2	(S)	(S)
Ohio	5.7	4.4	1.3	6.5	5.0	1.5	7.9	5.6	2.3	6.5	4.6	1.9	6.2	4.3	1.9
Oklahoma	3.9	3.0	0.9	2.8	1.8	1.0	2.2	1.7	0.4	0.9	0.6	0.4	1.0	0.5	0.5
Oregon	2.7	0.5	2.1	2.6	0.4	2.1	2.8	0.4	2.3	3.6	0.7	2.8	3.8	0.8	2.9
Pennsylvania	7.3	6.1	1.2	6.8	4.7	2.0	7.2	5.0	2.2	8.1	5.1	3.0	6.8	4.2	2.6
Rhode Island	0.2	(S)	(S)	0.2	(S)	(S)	(S)	(S)	(S)	(S)	(S)	(S)	(S)	(S)	(S)
South Carolina	14.7	10.0	4.7	14.9	10.2	4.7	15.1	10.7	4.4	13.9	8.6	5.3	12.3	6.9	5.4
South Dakota	0.7	0.5	0.2	0.6	0.5	0.1	0.9	0.6	0.3	0.5	(S)	(S)	0.7	0.4	0.3
Tennessee	8.8	7.2	1.6	8.1	6.0	2.0	9.0	6.4	2.6	9.2	6.7	2.5	7.7	5.2	2.5
Texas	27.7	20.6	7.0	16.0	10.9	5.1	9.6	6.0	3.5	5.5	3.1	2.3	3.7	2.2	1.5
Utah	1.1	0.5	0.5	0.8	0.4	0.4	0.5	(S)	(S)	(S)	(S)	(S)	0.4	(S)	(S)
Vermont	0.6	(S)	(S)	0.9	0.7	0.2	1.1	0.9	0.2	1.1	0.8	0.3	0.8	0.6	0.2
Virginia	6.5	5.3	1.2	6.8	5.1	1.7	7.4	5.4	2.0	4.7	3.1	1.6	6.2	4.0	2.2
Washington	6.7	2.2	4.4	5.4	0.8	4.6	4.8	0.8	3.9	5.1	0.7	4.2	5.2	0.5	4.6
West Virginia	4.2	3.0	1.3	3.6	2.7	0.9	3.8	2.8	0.9	3.8	2.3	1.4	2.7	1.8	0.9
Wisconsin	2.1	1.9	0.2	1.5	1.3	0.2	2.0	1.8	0.2	2.5	2.0	0.5	2.9	2.5	0.4
Wyoming	0.9	0.6	0.3	0.5	(S)	(S)	0.2	(S)	(S)	0.3	(S)	(S)	0.3	(S)	(S)

See notes at end of table.

Housing Production and Investment

TABLE 2.48. NEW MOBILE HOMES PLACED FOR RESIDENTIAL USE BY STATE AND NUMBER OF SECTIONS IN HOME: 1980 TO 1997 - Continued
(In thousands)

AREA	1990			1991			1992			1993			1994		
	Total [1]	Single wide	Double wide	Total [1]	Single wide	Double wide	Total [1]	Single wide	Double wide	Total [1]	Single wide	Double wide	Total [1]	Single wide	Double wide
United States	195.4	103.8	89.5	174.3	94.6	77.8	212.0	114.5	95.5	242.5	127.0	112.4	286.1	146.0	135.9
Northeast	18.8	12.1	6.7	14.3	9.1	5.2	15.0	8.3	6.7	15.4	8.6	6.7	16.2	9.0	7.1
Midwest	37.7	22.9	14.7	35.4	21.6	13.8	42.2	25.3	16.9	44.5	24.7	19.7	53.0	27.5	25.3
South	108.4	62.7	44.8	97.6	58.2	38.4	124.4	73.4	50.1	146.7	83.8	61.5	174.4	98.8	73.9
West	30.6	6.1	23.3	27.0	5.8	20.3	30.4	7.4	21.9	35.9	9.9	24.4	42.5	10.6	29.5
Alabama	8.5	6.5	1.9	7.9	5.8	2.0	9.7	6.7	3.0	11.1	7.4	3.6	14.4	10.1	4.2
Alaska	(S)	(S)	(S)	(S)	(S)	(S)	(S)	(S)	(S)	0.1	(S)	(S)	(S)	(S)	(S)
Arizona	3.2	1.2	2.0	2.6	0.8	1.9	3.5	1.3	2.2	4.3	1.6	2.6	5.7	2.0	3.7
Arkansas	2.7	1.8	0.9	3.3	2.4	0.9	3.5	2.2	1.3	5.1	3.6	1.5	5.3	3.3	2.0
California	10.4	1.2	8.4	6.2	0.7	5.1	5.6	0.8	4.4	3.8	(S)	(S)	3.7	0.5	2.9
Colorado	0.9	0.5	0.4	1.1	0.6	0.6	1.5	0.8	0.7	2.7	1.5	1.2	3.8	1.9	1.9
Connecticut	(S)	(S)	(S)	(S)	(S)	(S)	(S)	(S)	(S)	(S)	(S)	(S)	(S)	(S)	(S)
Delaware	1.3	0.8	0.6	1.1	0.6	0.5	1.6	1.2	0.4	1.6	0.9	0.7	1.1	0.7	0.4
District of Columbia	0.0	0.0	0.0	0.0	0.0	0.0	0.0	0.0	0.0	0.0	0.0	0.0	0.0	0.0	0.0
Florida	18.6	6.4	12.0	14.6	5.0	9.3	19.9	8.7	11.0	17.7	5.6	11.6	16.7	5.3	10.9
Georgia	10.9	4.9	5.8	9.5	4.8	4.5	10.6	4.6	5.8	12.9	6.3	6.4	17.2	8.1	8.9
Hawaii	(S)	(S)	(S)	(S)	(S)	(S)	(S)	(S)	(S)	(S)	(S)	(S)	(S)	(S)	(S)
Idaho	1.1	0.3	0.9	1.2	0.4	0.8	1.6	0.3	1.4	2.1	0.5	1.6	3.2	0.8	2.3
Illinois	3.6	2.2	1.4	3.3	1.9	1.4	3.5	1.9	1.6	4.2	2.4	1.8	5.2	3.0	2.1
Indiana	6.4	4.0	2.4	5.9	3.5	2.3	5.8	3.4	2.3	6.0	3.1	3.0	7.4	3.5	3.9
Iowa	1.7	1.2	0.5	1.5	1.1	0.5	2.8	2.1	0.7	2.0	1.3	0.7	2.0	1.1	0.9
Kansas	1.4	0.9	0.6	1.5	1.0	0.5	1.3	0.7	0.6	2.1	1.3	0.8	3.2	2.0	1.2
Kentucky	5.8	4.1	1.6	6.2	4.5	1.6	8.0	5.8	2.3	7.8	5.2	2.6	9.3	5.9	3.4
Louisiana	1.6	1.3	0.2	1.6	1.1	0.5	3.2	2.7	0.5	4.7	4.0	0.7	6.4	5.2	1.2
Maine	2.6	2.2	0.5	1.9	1.6	0.3	1.8	1.2	0.5	1.3	1.0	0.3	1.5	1.1	0.4
Maryland	1.1	0.6	0.6	1.5	1.0	0.5	0.6	0.2	0.4	1.2	0.5	0.7	0.8	0.3	0.5
Massachusetts	0.2	(S)	(S)	(S)	(S)	(S)	0.1	(S)	(S)	0.3	(S)	(S)	0.4	(S)	(S)
Michigan	10.0	4.6	5.4	8.6	4.2	4.4	9.9	4.2	5.7	9.2	3.6	5.5	10.4	3.2	7.2
Minnesota	1.6	0.8	0.8	1.1	0.7	0.5	1.9	1.3	0.6	2.1	1.3	0.8	1.9	0.9	1.0
Mississippi	3.9	3.0	0.9	3.6	2.9	0.6	4.9	3.7	1.2	6.0	4.5	1.5	7.7	5.3	2.3
Missouri	3.1	2.3	0.8	3.5	2.5	1.0	4.8	3.1	1.6	5.7	3.6	2.1	8.0	5.2	2.8
Montana	0.5	(S)	(S)	0.6	(S)	(S)	1.1	0.5	0.6	1.7	0.8	0.8	1.7	0.7	1.1
Nebraska	0.5	0.4	0.1	0.7	0.5	0.2	0.6	0.4	0.2	0.5	0.2	0.2	0.5	0.3	0.2
Nevada	2.2	0.4	1.8	2.1	0.3	1.7	1.9	0.3	1.5	1.7	0.2	1.4	2.2	(S)	(S)
New Hampshire	0.8	0.5	0.3	0.3	(S)	(S)	0.3	0.2	0.1	0.3	(S)	(S)	0.6	0.4	0.2
New Jersey	0.5	(S)	(S)	(S)	(S)	(S)	0.3	(S)	(S)	0.2	(S)	(S)	0.4	0.2	0.2
New Mexico	1.7	0.9	0.8	1.9	1.0	0.9	3.2	1.7	1.4	5.1	3.0	2.1	4.5	2.2	2.3
New York	6.9	3.9	3.0	4.8	3.0	1.8	5.1	2.5	2.6	5.6	2.9	2.6	5.3	2.7	2.6
North Carolina	19.0	12.1	6.7	16.9	10.6	6.0	20.5	12.0	8.3	24.3	14.3	9.8	30.4	17.0	13.2
North Dakota	(S)	(S)	(S)	0.3	(S)	(S)	0.5	0.3	0.2	0.4	0.2	0.1	0.7	0.3	0.3
Ohio	5.6	3.8	1.8	5.9	3.9	2.0	7.3	4.9	2.3	7.2	4.0	3.3	7.7	3.8	3.9
Oklahoma	1.3	0.8	0.4	1.0	0.7	0.3	1.5	0.7	0.7	3.0	1.6	1.4	3.2	2.1	1.1
Oregon	4.2	0.5	3.5	4.4	0.8	3.5	5.2	0.8	4.1	6.4	0.9	4.8	8.0	0.7	6.4
Pennsylvania	6.9	4.6	2.3	6.4	3.8	2.6	6.7	3.9	2.8	7.0	4.0	3.0	7.3	4.0	3.3
Rhode Island	(S)	(S)	(S)	(S)	(S)	(S)	(S)	(S)	(S)	(S)	(S)	(S)	(S)	(S)	(S)
South Carolina	12.3	7.1	5.1	8.7	4.9	3.8	11.4	6.5	4.8	13.8	7.1	6.5	14.1	6.1	7.8
South Dakota	0.6	0.4	0.3	0.8	0.5	0.3	0.9	0.6	0.3	1.3	0.8	0.5	1.8	1.2	0.5
Tennessee	7.5	5.0	2.5	7.6	5.2	2.4	10.8	7.7	3.1	12.0	7.9	4.0	14.3	9.1	5.1
Texas	4.2	2.0	2.2	5.2	3.0	2.2	9.0	5.4	3.6	14.8	8.7	6.1	21.8	13.5	8.1
Utah	0.4	(S)	(S)	0.1	(S)	(S)	0.7	(S)	(S)	0.8	0.2	0.6	1.3	0.4	0.9
Vermont	0.6	0.3	0.3	0.5	0.2	0.3	0.6	0.3	0.3	0.6	0.4	0.2	0.5	0.4	0.2
Virginia	6.1	3.9	2.1	5.7	3.5	2.1	5.5	3.3	2.2	6.1	3.5	2.6	6.0	3.1	2.8
Washington	5.8	0.7	4.8	6.4	0.9	5.3	5.9	0.7	4.9	6.8	0.8	5.5	7.0	0.8	5.5
West Virginia	3.7	2.4	1.3	3.2	2.1	1.1	3.8	2.2	1.5	4.6	2.9	1.7	5.8	3.7	2.0
Wisconsin	2.9	2.4	0.4	2.3	1.7	0.6	3.1	2.3	0.7	3.8	3.0	0.8	4.1	2.9	1.2
Wyoming	(S)	(S)	(S)	0.3	(S)	(S)	0.2	(S)	(S)	0.4	(S)	(S)	1.0	0.6	0.5

See notes at end of table.

Housing Production and Investment

TABLE 2.48. NEW MOBILE HOMES PLACED FOR RESIDENTIAL USE BY STATE AND NUMBER OF SECTIONS IN HOME: 1980 TO 1997 - Continued
(In thousands)

AREA	1995			1996			1997		
	Total [1]	Single wide	Double wide	Total [1]	Single wide	Double wide	Total [1]	Single wide	Double wide
United States	310.7	158.2	148.3	319.7	154.1	160.3	296.5	126.4	164.8
Northeast	14.6	7.9	6.6	15.4	7.8	7.6	13.7	5.5	8.2
Midwest	56.0	29.4	26.6	56.6	27.0	29.4	50.9	21.5	29.2
South	198.3	109.8	86.8	205.1	108.3	94.2	188.8	90.0	96.0
West	41.8	11.1	28.2	42.6	11.0	29.2	43.1	9.4	31.3
Alabama	14.4	9.6	4.6	15.5	9.2	6.1	16.4	8.7	7.5
Alaska	(S)	(S)	(S)	(S)	(S)	(S)	(S)	(S)	(S)
Arizona	6.5	2.2	4.3	7.0	2.2	4.7	6.9	2.0	4.8
Arkansas	6.3	3.8	2.5	6.8	4.4	2.4	6.3	3.7	2.5
California	3.2	(S)	(S)	3.7	(S)	(S)	4.9	0.4	4.2
Colorado	3.9	1.8	2.1	4.5	1.9	2.5	5.2	1.9	3.2
Connecticut	(S)	(S)	(S)	(S)	(S)	(S)	0.1	(S)	(S)
Delaware	1.5	0.8	0.8	1.5	0.7	0.8	1.1	0.4	0.6
District of Columbia	0.0	0.0	0.0	(S)	(S)	(S)	0.0	0.0	0.0
Florida	15.3	3.9	10.9	15.1	3.9	10.4	16.5	4.4	11.3
Georgia	19.1	8.5	10.3	19.4	8.0	11.0	19.8	6.9	12.4
Hawaii	(S)	(S)	(S)	(S)	(S)	(S)	(S)	(S)	(S)
Idaho	2.6	0.6	1.9	2.2	(S)	1.6	2.0	0.4	1.5
Illinois	5.4	2.6	2.9	4.3	1.8	2.5	4.8	2.0	2.9
Indiana	8.0	4.2	3.8	8.0	3.7	4.3	7.4	2.8	4.6
Iowa	2.3	1.5	0.8	2.5	1.3	1.2	1.6	0.9	0.7
Kansas	3.2	1.9	1.4	3.4	2.2	1.2	2.9	1.3	1.6
Kentucky	11.4	7.5	3.8	10.4	6.4	4.0	9.2	5.1	4.1
Louisiana	9.1	7.3	1.8	8.2	6.2	1.9	8.5	5.8	2.7
Maine	1.4	1.0	0.5	2.0	1.2	0.7	1.8	0.9	0.9
Maryland	1.4	0.6	0.8	0.8	(S)	(S)	1.1	0.4	0.7
Massachusetts	0.3	(S)	(S)	(S)	(S)	(S)	0.2	(S)	(S)
Michigan	11.2	3.9	7.3	12.1	3.9	8.2	11.8	3.5	8.3
Minnesota	3.0	1.8	1.2	3.1	1.9	1.3	2.9	1.3	1.5
Mississippi	10.3	7.3	3.0	10.4	7.3	3.1	9.4	5.7	3.6
Missouri	8.1	5.1	3.0	7.6	4.3	3.3	6.0	3.1	2.8
Montana	1.4	0.6	0.8	1.6	0.6	1.0	2.0	0.7	1.2
Nebraska	1.0	0.6	0.4	1.4	0.6	0.8	1.4	0.7	0.7
Nevada	2.2	(S)	(S)	2.7	(S)	2.3	2.8	0.4	2.3
New Hampshire	0.6	0.3	0.3	0.7	(S)	(S)	0.9	0.4	0.5
New Jersey	0.4	(S)	(S)	(S)	(S)	(S)	0.3	(S)	(S)
New Mexico	6.4	3.8	2.5	6.3	3.5	2.8	5.5	2.3	3.1
New York	4.6	2.2	2.4	5.4	2.5	2.9	5.2	2.1	3.1
North Carolina	29.3	14.6	14.5	33.2	16.3	16.7	23.5	9.3	13.9
North Dakota	0.6	0.4	0.2	0.7	(S)	(S)	0.7	0.5	0.2
Ohio	8.4	4.9	3.4	8.2	4.3	3.8	6.6	3.0	3.6
Oklahoma	4.9	2.9	2.0	5.5	3.1	2.4	7.5	4.5	3.0
Oregon	6.3	0.3	5.1	6.3	(S)	5.1	5.4	0.3	4.4
Pennsylvania	6.6	3.7	3.0	6.3	3.1	3.2	4.4	1.5	2.9
Rhode Island	(S)	(S)	(S)	(S)	(S)	(S)	(S)	(S)	(S)
South Carolina	16.7	8.5	8.0	19.8	8.7	10.8	16.4	7.0	9.1
South Dakota	1.3	0.6	0.7	1.5	0.9	0.6	1.5	0.9	0.5
Tennessee	14.8	9.0	5.7	15.4	8.8	6.4	16.4	8.5	7.8
Texas	31.6	18.9	12.5	32.2	19.3	12.6	26.5	14.3	11.9
Utah	1.6	0.5	1.0	1.7	(S)	1.3	1.7	0.2	1.5
Vermont	0.5	0.3	0.2	0.5	(S)	(S)	0.8	0.3	0.4
Virginia	6.7	3.4	3.3	5.5	2.8	2.7	5.0	2.4	2.6
Washington	6.6	0.6	5.3	5.4	(S)	4.3	5.6	0.3	4.6
West Virginia	5.5	3.2	2.3	5.3	2.9	2.4	5.3	2.9	2.4
Wisconsin	3.6	1.9	1.7	3.8	2.0	1.7	3.3	1.5	1.7
Wyoming	1.0	0.5	0.4	1.1	(S)	0.6	1.1	0.6	0.5

Source: U.S. Bureau of the Census, Survey of New Mobile Home Placements.

Details may not add to totals because of rounding.

(1) Includes mobile homes with more than two sections.

(S) Suppressed because estimate or complimentary estimate was based on fewer than five responses.

Housing Production and Investment

TABLE 2.49. NEW MOBILE HOMES ON DEALER LOTS AT END OF YEAR BY REGION AND NUMBER OF SECTIONS IN HOME: 1980 TO 1997
(In thousands)

YEAR	United States			Northeast			Midwest			South			West		
	Total [1]	Single wide	Double wide	Total [1]	Single wide	Double wide	Total [1]	Single wide	Double wide	Total [1]	Single wide	Double wide	Total [1]	Single wide	Double wide
1980	56.0	42.2	13.5	2.8	2.5	0.3	8.6	7.6	1.0	33.1	26.3	6.7	11.5	5.7	5.6
1981	57.9	44.8	12.7	2.4	2.2	0.3	8.8	7.9	1.0	36.0	29.1	6.9	10.6	5.6	4.6
1982	58.3	46.1	11.9	2.9	2.6	0.4	7.7	6.7	1.0	38.4	31.7	6.7	9.2	5.1	3.9
1983	73.2	55.0	17.9	4.2	3.7	0.5	10.1	8.2	1.9	48.5	37.7	10.8	10.4	5.4	4.7
1984	81.7	61.3	20.2	4.3	3.7	0.6	11.0	9.3	1.7	55.9	44.0	12.0	10.5	4.4	6.0
1985	77.6	56.8	20.6	4.3	3.6	0.7	9.6	7.8	1.8	55.1	41.8	13.1	8.6	3.6	4.9
1986	67.1	46.5	20.2	5.3	4.2	1.1	10.0	7.8	2.3	45.3	32.3	13.0	6.4	2.2	3.9
1987	60.6	38.5	21.7	5.5	4.0	1.5	9.3	6.5	2.7	39.2	26.2	12.9	6.6	1.8	4.5
1988	58.0	35.1	22.5	5.7	3.7	2.0	10.9	7.6	3.3	34.9	21.8	12.9	6.5	2.0	4.3
1989	55.5	33.3	22.0	5.5	3.6	1.9	10.6	7.1	3.5	33.1	20.7	12.3	6.3	1.9	4.3
1990	49.0	28.3	20.1	4.1	2.8	1.3	9.9	6.3	3.6	29.2	18.2	10.8	5.8	1.1	4.5
1991	49.3	28.9	20.1	4.4	2.8	1.6	10.0	6.7	3.2	29.1	18.0	10.9	5.9	1.4	4.4
1992	50.9	28.7	21.7	3.9	2.4	1.5	9.1	5.2	4.0	31.7	19.4	11.9	6.2	1.7	4.3
1993	61.4	34.6	26.1	4.2	2.4	1.8	10.6	6.2	4.4	39.2	24.3	14.7	7.3	1.7	5.2
1994	72.3	38.6	32.6	3.9	2.3	1.5	12.4	6.8	5.5	47.4	27.0	20.0	8.6	2.4	5.5
1995	91.0	48.2	41.7	4.6	2.5	2.1	15.9	8.2	7.6	58.0	33.8	23.7	12.5	3.6	8.3
1996	110.2	55.6	52.8	4.8	2.6	2.1	16.3	7.9	8.4	75.5	41.6	33.1	13.6	3.6	9.2
1997	143.4	66.7	74.2	4.8	2.6	2.2	19.2	9.2	9.9	105.1	51.4	52.3	14.4	3.6	9.8

Source: U.S. Bureau of the Census, Survey of New Mobile Home Placements.

Details may not add to totals because of rounding.

(1) Includes mobile homes with more than two sections.

Housing Production and Investment

	TABLE 2.50. APARTMENTS COMPLETED IN NEWLY CONSTRUCTED BUILDINGS WITH FIVE UNITS OR MORE: 1970 TO 1996					
YEAR	Total	Unfurnished apartments	Furnished apartments	Cooperatives and condominiums	Federally-subsidized	Other
1970	526,000	328,400	48,200	72,500	55,900	21,000
1971	583,400	334,400	32,200	49,100	104,800	63,000
1972	718,200	497,900	37,700	57,300	93,800	31,400
1973	774,800	531,700	36,200	98,100	82,000	26,800
1974	685,400	405,500	20,700	159,000	75,400	25,000
1975	371,400	223,100	11,100	84,600	38,900	13,800
1976	258,200	157,000	12,800	46,300	32,000	10,000
1977	289,400	195,600	16,200	43,000	26,000	8,700
1978	362,700	228,700	11,200	54,500	54,100	14,300
1979	439,300	241,200	12,100	91,800	87,500	6,700
1980	418,900	196,100	9,700	122,800	79,900	10,500
1981	332,500	135,400	6,000	112,600	66,100	12,500
1982	288,200	117,000	5,400	107,900	48,000	10,000
1983	370,700	191,500	4,700	111,800	47,700	15,100
1984	506,000	313,200	9,800	143,600	28,500	10,700
1985	533,300	364,500	7,400	135,800	12,000	13,700
1986	550,200	407,600	11,600	101,700	23,300	6,000
1987	474,200	345,600	7,900	92,300	17,000	11,300
1988	388,600	284,500	4,300	76,200	15,200	8,400
1989	337,900	246,400	4,900	59,700	19,800	7,200
1990 [1]	294,400	214,300	2,900	52,600	13,800	10,800
1991	216,500	165,300	2,800	35,300	9,600	3,500
1992	155,200	110,200	700	31,100	7,000	6,000
1993	124,800	77,200	2,700	32,000	7,700	5,200
1994	154,900	104,000	1,100	34,400	11,800	3,600
1995	212,400	155,000	1,600	36,400	13,700	5,700
1996	251,300	191,300	2,400	36,900	14,200	6,400

Source: U.S. Bureau of the Census and U.S. Department of Housing and Urban Development, Survey of Market Absorption.

(1) New ratio estimation procedures were adopted in 1990 to derive more accurate estimates of completions. Caution should be used when comparing numbers of completions in 1990 and later years with those in earlier years.

Details may not add to totals due to rounding.

Housing Production and Investment

YEAR	Total	No bedrooms	1 bedroom	2 bedrooms	3 or more bedrooms
TABLE 2.51. UNFURNISHED APARTMENTS COMPLETED IN NEWLY CONSTRUCTED BUILDINGS WITH FIVE UNITS OR MORE, BY NUMBER OF BEDROOMS: 1970 TO 1996					
1970	328,400	8,200	130,800	171,100	18,300
1971	334,400	8,800	134,300	168,600	22,700
1972	497,900	18,200	193,400	249,900	36,400
1973	531,700	23,600	221,500	256,300	30,100
1974	405,500	17,500	167,000	197,000	24,200
1975	223,100	8,000	93,300	109,000	12,700
1976	157,000	6,200	68,900	74,500	7,400
1977	195,600	6,700	81,100	100,600	7,200
1978	228,700	8,700	103,900	107,800	8,300
1979	241,200	7,800	111,400	113,300	8,700
1980	196,100	5,500	88,200	95,100	7,300
1981	135,400	4,900	60,800	63,000	6,700
1982	117,000	3,600	54,100	53,300	6,000
1983	191,500	5,800	83,600	93,700	8,300
1984	313,200	8,700	142,000	153,600	8,900
1985	364,500	8,600	158,000	187,100	10,800
1986	407,600	14,700	172,100	208,500	12,400
1987	345,600	11,200	140,400	181,700	12,400
1988	284,500	11,700	112,300	147,800	12,800
1989	246,400	6,100	93,700	130,300	16,100
1990 [1]	214,300	4,100	77,000	114,200	19,000
1991	165,300	5,000	57,300	88,400	14,700
1992	110,200	2,200	37,200	59,800	11,100
1993	77,200	1,100	21,400	44,000	10,800
1994	104,000	2,000	32,900	56,000	13,100
1995	155,000	4,400	48,400	82,100	20,100
1996	191,300	2,200	59,300	101,000	28,700

Source: U.S. Bureau of the Census and U.S. Department of Housing and Urban Development, Survey of Market Absorption.

(1) New ratio estimation procedures were adopted in 1990 to derive more accurate estimates of completions. Caution should be used when comparing numbers of completions in 1990 and later years with those in earlier years.

Privately financed, nonsubsidized, unfurnished rental apartments with five units or more.

Components may not add to totals due to rounding.

Housing Production and Investment

TABLE 2.52. UNFURNISHED APARTMENTS COMPLETED IN NEWLY CONSTRUCTED BUILDINGS WITH FIVE UNITS OR MORE, BY REGION: 1970 TO 1996

YEAR	Total	Northeast	Midwest	South	West
1970	328,400	37,600	84,100	142,300	64,400
1971	334,400	35,800	78,300	125,400	94,900
1972	497,900	65,200	123,300	183,500	126,000
1973	531,700	64,600	141,100	211,600	114,400
1974	405,500	37,500	91,700	197,900	78,400
1975	223,100	31,100	55,600	91,800	44,500
1976	157,000	16,000	54,500	48,300	38,200
1977	195,600	11,200	59,800	60,800	63,800
1978	228,700	13,400	66,800	89,500	59,000
1979	241,200	20,500	54,000	111,200	55,400
1980	196,100	14,200	43,800	91,500	46,600
1981	135,400	4,900	36,900	68,400	25,100
1982	117,000	4,600	21,900	66,800	23,700
1983	191,500	3,500	41,100	115,100	31,800
1984	313,200	3,800	41,200	194,400	73,900
1985	364,500	8,200	53,900	166,400	135,900
1986	407,600	16,900	64,500	171,700	154,500
1987	345,600	11,300	66,000	124,500	143,900
1988	284,500	8,700	60,400	91,700	123,800
1989	246,400	13,100	45,200	85,900	102,000
1990 [1]	214,300	12,700	44,300	77,200	80,000
1991	165,300	6,800	37,900	63,600	57,000
1992	110,200	10,900	34,000	37,400	28,000
1993	77,200	3,700	25,300	27,700	20,500
1994	104,000	3,700	32,200	44,500	23,600
1995	155,000	7,100	31,700	78,500	37,700
1996	191,300	6,100	37,200	96,900	51,100

Source: U.S. Bureau of the Census and U.S. Department of Housing and Urban Development, Survey of Market Absorption.

(1) New ratio estimation procedures were adopted in 1990 to derive more accurate estimates of completions. Caution should be used when comparing numbers of completions in 1990 and later years with those in earlier years.

Privately financed, nonsubsidized, unfurnished rental apartments with five units or more.

Components may not add to totals due to rounding.

Housing Production and Investment

YEAR	Total	Less than $150	$150-$174	$175-$199	$200-$249	$250-$299	$300-$349	$350-$399
				TABLE 2.53. UNFURNISHED APARTMENTS COMPLETED IN NEWLY CONSTRUCTED BUILDINGS WITH FIVE UNITS OR MORE, BY RENT CLASS: 1970 TO 1996				
1970	328,400	46,100	78,800	77,900	80,100	45,500 [1]	....	....
1971	334,400	55,000	72,800	84,900	83,200	38,500 [1]	....	....
1972	497,900	66,400	102,100	124,500	133,500	71,500 [1]	....	....
1973	531,700	71,600	109,400	132,100	138,800	79,800 [1]	....	....
1974	405,500	33,600	81,700	101,600	111,400	77,400 [1]	....	....
1975	223,100	14,700	34,700	47,600	63,800	62,100 [1]	....	....
1976	157,000	6,800	14,400	35,000	56,900	30,300	13,500 [2]	....
1977	195,600	6,400	14,500	30,400	72,500	47,600	24,200 [2]	....
1978	228,700	3,600	13,100	25,200	71,600	64,800	50,400 [2]	....
1979	241,200	2,500	6,100	15,100	66,000	69,000	82,500 [2]	....
1980	196,100	....	....	6,900 [3]	32,900	51,100	44,500	30,900
1981	135,400	....	....	2,500 [3]	9,900	27,800	29,000	23,800
1982	117,000	....	....	1,400 [3]	5,100	12,600	22,200	24,500
1983	191,500	....	....	....	....	25,300 [4]	37,400	45,400
1984	313,200	....	....	....	....	36,700 [4]	54,100	75,600
1985	364,500	....	....	....	....	30,500 [4]	41,600	72,000
1986	407,600	....	....	....	....	30,300 [4]	34,400	66,700
1987	345,600	....	....	....	....	....	23,600 [7]	42,000
1988	284,500	....	....	....	....	....	16,800 [7]	22,100
1989	246,400	....	....	....	....	....	14,100 [7]	....
1990 [11]	214,300	....	....	....	....	....	14,000 [7]	....
1991	165,300	....	....	....	....	....	13,200 [7]	....
1992	110,200	....	....	....	....	....	10,500 [7]	....
1993	77,200	....	....	....	....	....	4,900 [7]	....
1994	104,000	....	....	....	....	....	6,700 [7]	....
1995	155,000	....	....	....	....	....	9,300 [7]	....
1996	191,300	....	....	....	....	....	4,300 [7]	....

See notes at end of table.

Housing Production and Investment

YEAR	TABLE 2.53. UNFURNISHED APARTMENTS COMPLETED IN NEWLY CONSTRUCTED BUILDINGS WITH FIVE UNITS OR MORE, BY RENT CLASS: 1970 TO 1996 - Continued						
	$400-$449	$450-$499	$500-$549	$550-$649	$650-$749	$750 or more	Median rent
1970	....	....	....	....	....	....	$188
1971	....	....	....	....	....	....	$187
1972	....	....	....	....	....	....	$191
1973	....	....	....	....	....	....	$191
1974	....	....	....	....	....	....	$197
1975	....	....	....	....	....	....	$211
1976	....	....	....	....	....	....	$219
1977	....	....	....	....	....	....	$232
1978	....	....	....	....	....	....	$251
1979	....	....	....	....	....	....	$272
1980	29,800 [5]	....	....	....	....	....	$308
1981	42,300 [5]	....	....	....	....	....	$347
1982	51,300 [5]	....	....	....	....	....	$385
1983	30,900	22,800	29,700 [6]	....	....	....	$386
1984	50,800	42,800	53,100 [6]	....	....	....	$393
1985	60,500	57,400	102,500 [6]	....	....	....	$432
1986	63,900	61,600	150,800 [6]	....	....	....	$457
1987	42,800	51,700	38,100	147,500 [10]	....	....	$517
1988	28,300	36,600	31,900	148,800 [10]	....	....	$550+
1989	33,700 [8]	....	54,400 [9]	144,000 [10]	....	....	$550+
1990 [11]	25,300 [8]	....	45,700 [9]	43,900	32,300	53,000	$600
1991	13,700 [8]	....	32,500 [9]	36,100	22,600	47,100	$614
1992	13,100 [8]	....	23,900 [9]	21,200	12,300	29,300	$586
1993	11,900 [8]	....	18,500 [9]	13,800	8,900	19,300	$573
1994	14,500 [8]	....	25,100 [9]	21,900	15,200	20,700	$576
1995	12,000 [8]	....	26,700 [9]	28,000	27,600	51,400	$654
1996	14,700 [8]	....	32,700 [9]	36,200	34,700	68,800	$672

Source: U.S. Bureau of the Census and U.S. Department of Housing and Urban Development, Survey of Market Absorption.

All rents are asking rents.

(1) $250 or more. (2) $300 or more. (3) Less than $200. (4) Less than $300. (5) $400 or more. (6) $500 or more. (7) Less than $350. (8) $350 to $449.

(9) $450 to $549. (10) $550 or more. (11) New ratio estimation procedures were adopted in 1990 to derive more accurate estimates of completions. Caution should be used when comparing numbers of completions in 1990 and later years with those in earlier years.

Privately financed, nonsubsidized, unfurnished rental apartments with five units or more.

Components may not add to totals because of rounding.

Housing Production and Investment

YEAR	TABLE 2.54. COOPERATIVE AND CONDOMINIUM APARTMENTS COMPLETED, BY REGION: 1970 TO 1996				
	Total	Northeast	Midwest	South	West
1970	72,500	....	....	....	....
1971	49,100	....	....	....	....
1972	57,300	6,900	11,400	27,200	11,600
1973	98,100	12,500	12,000	56,300	17,400
1974	159,000	16,400	17,700	91,500	33,300
1975	84,600	7,300	7,000	45,700	24,600
1976	46,300	9,200	6,700	17,100	13,300
1977	43,000	6,800	6,900	17,400	11,900
1978	54,500	2,400	8,900	22,300	20,900
1979	91,800	3,300	21,000	38,900	28,600
1980	122,800	5,500	18,000	64,500	34,800
1981	112,600	10,500	10,000	60,000	32,000
1982	107,900	8,600	9,500	64,500	25,300
1983	111,800	8,200	11,500	69,700	22,400
1984	143,600	10,100	13,600	90,800	29,100
1985	135,800	18,900	10,500	80,400	26,000
1986	101,700	28,400	7,700	42,700	22,900
1987	92,300	32,500	9,100	29,800	20,900
1988	76,200	34,200	5,200	23,400	13,400
1989	59,700	19,300	6,400	17,500	16,300
1990 [1]	52,600	9,300	5,600	21,300	16,300
1991	35,300	6,300	2,900	12,400	13,800
1992	31,100	3,300	3,000	10,100	14,700
1993	32,000	4,600	3,200	13,500	10,600
1994	34,400	2,600	5,400	13,200	13,200
1995	36,400	4,800	7,400	11,800	12,400
1996	36,900	6,600	5,100	15,200	10,000

Source: U.S. Bureau of the Census and U.S. Department of Housing and Urban Development, Survey of Market Absorption.

(1) New ratio estimation procedures were adopted in 1990 to derive more accurate estimates of completions. Caution should be used when comparing numbers of completions in 1990 and later years with those in earlier years.

Privately financed, nonsubsidized, unfurnished apartments in newly constructed buildings with five units or more.

Components may not add to totals due to rounding.

Housing Production and Investment

TABLE 2.55. ANNUAL VALUE OF NEW PRIVATE RESIDENTIAL CONSTRUCTION PUT IN PLACE: 1974 TO 1997

(Millions of dollars)

YEAR	Total [1]	New housing units			Improvements
		Total	1 unit	2 or more units	
1974	55,967	43,420	29,700	13,720	12,547
1975	51,581	36,317	29,639	6,679	15,264
1976	68,273	50,771	43,860	6,910	17,502
1977	92,004	72,231	62,214	10,017	19,773
1978	109,838	85,601	72,769	12,832	24,237
1979	116,444	89,272	72,257	17,015	27,172
1980	100,381	69,629	52,921	16,708	30,752
1981	99,241	69,424	51,965	17,460	29,817
1982	84,676	57,001	41,462	15,838	27,675
1983	125,521	94,649	72,203	22,447	30,872
1984 [2]	153,849	113,826	85,605	28,221	40,023
1985	158,474	114,662	86,123	28,539	43,812
1986	187,148	133,192	102,154	31,038	53,956
1987	194,656	139,915	114,463	25,452	54,741
1988	198,101	138,947	116,649	22,298	59,154
1989	196,551	139,202	116,898	22,304	57,349
1990	182,856	127,987	108,737	19,250	54,869
1991	157,835	110,592	95,444	15,148	47,243
1992	187,819	129,600	116,505	13,094	58,219
1993	210,455	144,071	133,282	10,788	66,384
1994	238,874	167,919	153,838	14,081	70,955
1995	230,688	162,898	145,009	17,889	67,790
1996	256,460	179,448	159,124	20,324	77,012
1997	265,610	187,075	164,444	22,631	78,535

Source: U.S. Bureau of the Census, Value of New Construction Put in Place.

(1) Monthly totals include residential improvements, which are not shown separately.
(2) Beginning in January 1984, estimates of private residential improvements on owner-occupied units were based on a new data source. See Appendix B, "Value of New Construction Put in Place."

Housing Production and Investment

TABLE 2.56. EXPENDITURES BY RESIDENTIAL PROPERTY OWNERS FOR IMPROVEMENTS AND MAINTENANCE AND REPAIRS, BY TYPE OF PROPERTY AND ACTIVITY: 1970 to 1996
(In millions of dollars)

YEAR	Total expenditures	By property type		Construction improvements and maintenance and repairs					Maintenance and repairs
				Construction improvements					
					Additions and alterations				
		1-unit properties with owner occupant	Other properties	Total	To structures		To property outside of structures	Major replacements	
					Additions	Alterations			
1970	14,770	9,469	5,301	6,246	1,411	3,539	1,296	2,629	5,895
1971	16,299	10,234	6,065	6,818	1,685	3,699	1,433	3,120	6,361
1972	17,498	11,128	6,370	7,526	1,378	4,447	1,701	3,255	6,717
1973	18,512	11,297	7,215	7,386	1,360	4,694	1,332	3,202	7,924
1974	21,114	13,578	7,536	8,060	1,529	4,836	1,695	4,563	8,491
1975	25,239	15,684	9,556	10,997	1,971	6,844	2,182	4,484	9,758
1976	29,034	18,854	10,180	12,314	3,493	6,367	2,454	5,341	11,379
1977	31,280	21,761	9,519	14,237	2,655	8,505	3,077	5,699	11,344
1978	37,461	24,189	13,272	16,458	3,713	8,443	4,302	8,094	12,909
1979	42,231	28,280	13,951	18,285	3,280	9,642	5,363	8,996	14,950
1980	46,338	31,481	14,857	21,336	4,183	11,193	5,960	9,816	15,187
1981	46,351	30,201	16,150	20,414	3,164	11,947	5,303	9,915	16,022
1982	45,291	29,779	15,512	18,774	2,641	10,711	5,423	9,707	16,810
1983	49,295	32,524	16,771	20,271	4,739	11,673	3,859	10,895	18,128
1984 [1]	69,784	43,781	26,003	27,822	6,007	14,486	7,329	13,067	28,894
1985	80,267	47,742	32,525	28,775	3,966	17,599	7,211	16,134	35,358
1986	91,274	54,298	36,976	38,608	7,377	21,192	10,040	16,695	35,971
1987	94,082	54,791	39,291	39,978	9,557	21,641	8,779	15,875	38,229
1988	101,117	60,822	40,295	43,339	11,333	22,703	9,303	16,893	40,885
1989	100,891	59,858	41,033	39,786	6,828	23,129	9,828	18,415	42,689
1990	106,773	59,683	47,090	37,253	8,561	21,920	6,771	18,215	51,305
1991	97,528	58,083	39,445	30,944	7,914	16,076	6,954	16,744	49,840
1992	103,734	67,316	36,418	40,186	6,783	22,700	10,704	18,393	45,154
1993 [2]	108,304	70,746	37,558	45,797	12,757	24,782	8,259	20,809	41,699
1994	115,030	77,270	37,760	48,828	9,647	28,673	10,509	23,248	42,953
1995	111,683	75,362	36,321	44,726	7,936	26,893	9,897	24,910	42,047
1996	114,919	76,094	38,825	53,456	12,035	30,064	11,357	24,465	36,997

Source: U.S. Bureau of the Census, Consumer Expenditure Survey and Residential Improvement and Repairs Mail Survey.

(1) Beginning in 1984, estimates of private residential improvements on owner-occupied units were based on the Consumer Expenditure Survey. Prior to 1984, they were based on the Survey of Residential Alterations and Repairs.

(2) Beginning in 1993, doors and windows were moved from the Maintenance and Repairs category to the Major Replacements category.

PART 3: MARKET OUTCOMES

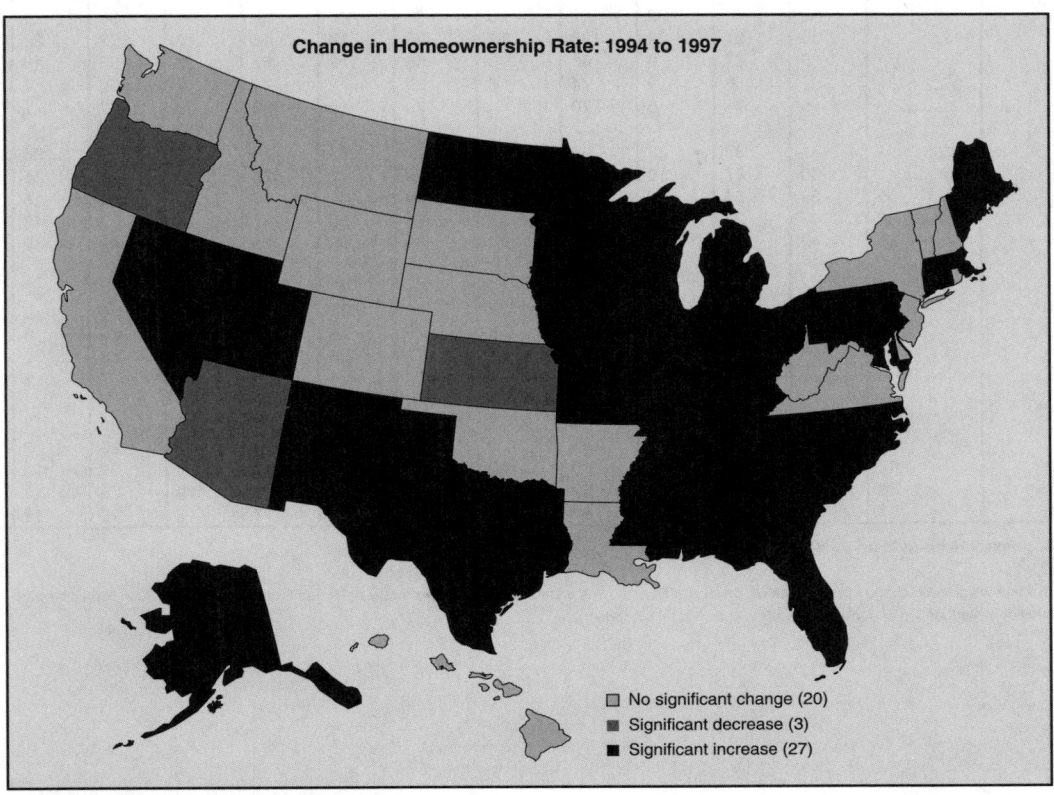

Change in Homeownership Rate: 1994 to 1997

☐ No significant change (20)
■ Significant decrease (3)
■ Significant increase (27)

Source: State homeownership rate data from Table 3.29.

Supported by a strong economy and low interest rates, the nation's homeownership rate reached an all-time annual high of 65.7 percent in 1997. The U.S. homeownership rate has increased by almost two percentage points in the past 3 years and the number of homeowners has increased by 4 million.[1]

---

[1]*The State of the Nation's Housing 1998*, recently published by Harvard's Joint Center for Housing Studies, notes that this is the largest 3-year increase in homeowners on record.

[2]Standard errors used to conduct statistical tests were obtained from U.S. Bureau of the Census, "Housing Vacancies and Homeownership: Annual Statistics 1997," <http://www.census. gov/ftp/pub/hhes/www/housing/hvs/annual97/ann97ind.html>; and Robert R. Callis, *Housing Vacancies and Homeownership: Annual Statistics 1994*, Current Housing Reports H111/94-A. Tests were performed at the 0.10 level of significance.

Between 1994 and 1997, homeownership rates increased significantly in 27 of the 50 states (see figure).[2] Most of the states that experienced gains are located in the Midwest and South, which together accounted for all but eight of the states with rising homeownership rates. Within these regions, states with homeownership rate increases are concentrated in the East North Central and East South Central divisions. Every state in each of these divisions experienced a significant homeownership gain during the period. Only three states—Oregon, Arizona, and Kansas—have experienced significant decreases in homeownership rates during the current homebuying boom.

Market Conditions and Outlook

YEAR	Composite housing market index [1]	Current sales						Sales expectations						Buyer traffic (Detached units)	
		Single-family				Condominiums		Single-family				Condominiums			
		Detached		Attached				Detached		Attached					
		Good	Poor	Good	Poor	Good	Poor	Good	Poor	Good	Poor	Good	Poor	High	Low
1978	....	59	10	32	27	26	36	40	9	24	30	21	38	31	18
1979	....	30	34	29	36	32	32	17	43	17	52	22	41	15	51
1980	....	5	67	8	61	9	56	9	57	13	53	16	49	7	73
1981	....	2	86	2	74	6	69	2	71	4	66	7	62	4	77
1982	....	5	76	5	70	4	70	8	52	8	52	7	54	9	73
1983	....	31	27	23	36	21	42	38	19	27	31	26	36	30	35
1984	....	30	27	19	43	15	48	29	25	18	42	15	48	21	39
1985	55	39	24	20	47	16	56	41	17	21	44	16	51	27	34
1986	60	47	23	18	53	15	63	50	17	18	52	13	62	36	31
1987	56	42	22	19	49	13	60	39	19	17	49	12	61	25	35
1988	53	37	24	15	53	12	61	37	19	13	51	11	60	24	38
1989	48	29	29	10	61	8	69	33	18	10	56	9	65	20	46
1990	34	16	44	6	70	5	75	18	34	6	65	6	72	11	58
1991	36	16	44	3	73	4	77	23	26	6	63	6	70	13	55
1992	48	27	27	7	63	4	73	34	16	8	53	5	66	22	44
1993	59	41	18	12	49	6	68	37	9	19	28	12	46	30	33
1994	56	38	16	14	39	8	59	39	7	17	25	12	40	22	35
1995	47	26	26	12	43	10	57	29	17	13	37	10	53	15	45
1996	56	36	16	20	32	14	50	37	9	19	28	12	46	21	30
1997	57	34	14	17	30	13	44	39	7	17	25	12	40	16	27

TABLE 3.1. HOME BUILDERS' PERCEPTIONS OF CURRENT HOME SALES, SALES EXPECTATIONS, AND BUYER TRAFFIC: 1978 TO 1997

Source: National Association of Home Builders, Builders Economic Council Survey.

(1) The composite index is a weighted average of current sales, buyer traffic, and sales expectations for single-family detached homes. A value of 50 indicates average market conditions. See Appendix A for additional explanation of composite index and individual components.

Market Conditions and Outlook

MARKET PERCEPTION	TABLE 3.2. CONSUMERS' PERCEPTIONS OF THE HOME BUYING MARKET: 1992 TO 1997 (Percent)					
	1992	1993	1994	1995	1996	1997
Very good time to buy a home	38	50	45	18	28	26
Just a somewhat good time to buy a home	24	22	31	37	33	37
Just a somewhat bad time to buy a home	11	12	9	16	14	14
Very bad time to buy a home	7	7	6	9	8	8
Neither good nor bad/depends	11	4	4	9	8	6
Not sure	9	5	5	11	9	9

Source: Fannie Mae, National Housing Survey.

See Appendix A for a description of the survey question.

Based on a sample survey of adults in the contiguous United States.

Market Conditions and Outlook

MONTH AND YEAR	TABLE 3.3. SUMMARY INDEX OF RESIDENTIAL REAL ESTATE TRENDS: 1991 TO 1997				
	United States	Northeast	Midwest	South	West
1991					
April	70	58	69	70	76
July	73	63	78	72	76
October	63	58	66	67	59
1992					
January	69	64	65	73	70
May	81	74	84	86	79
July	69	68	73	75	61
October	63	61	62	71	52
1993					
January	73	74	77	87	55
April	74	74	84	86	54
July	73	74	84	85	52
October	72	76	80	82	55
1994					
January	77	77	77	89	64
April	82	86	83	86	73
July	71	77	68	78	64
October	64	63	62	67	63
1995					
January	58	60	49	62	60
April	57	60	57	56	54
July	64	65	69	68	48
October	63	63	65	67	53
1996					
January	57	52	59	61	50
April	68	58	68	71	71
July	69	64	62	69	81
October	63	64	53	65	75
1997					
January	65	66	58	64	76
April	69	72	64	67	76
July	73	81	62	72	84
October	67	76	59	64	75

Source: Federal Deposit Insurance Corporation, Survey of Real Estate Trends.

The index is a summary measure of perceived changes in residential market conditions expressed by a sample of senior examiners and asset managers at federal bank and thrift regulatory agencies. An index value greater than 50 indicates improving market conditions; a value below 50 indicates declining conditions. See Appendix A for additional explanation.

Sales, Prices, and Rents

YEAR AND QUARTER	TABLE 3.4. MEDIAN ASKING SALES PRICE FOR SPECIFIED HOMEOWNER UNITS, THE U.S. AND REGIONS: 1988 TO 1997 (Current dollars)				
	United States	Northeast	Midwest	South	West
1988, annual	59,200	124,500	38,100	56,400	81,300
First quarter	57,000	136,700	38,000	52,200	79,200
Second quarter	63,500	124,000	44,500	56,300	91,100
Third quarter	60,300	114,000	38,400	58,500	74,400
Fourth quarter	59,100	125,000	32,100	57,200	73,900
1989, annual	59,500	108,100	36,800	57,900	72,700
First quarter	61,600	108,100	40,100	59,300	70,700
Second quarter	64,300	108,900	42,600	62,600	73,200
Third quarter	57,600	119,700	41,200	53,500	71,600
Fourth quarter	57,400	115,800	34,400	59,200	85,900
1989 [r], annual	54,200	102,400	33,100	52,300	64,600
First quarter	55,700	95,600	37,800	55,200	59,500
Second quarter	56,000	93,900	32,200	53,200	67,100
Third quarter	53,300	116,800	32,600	49,800	63,600
Fourth quarter	51,900	113,600	32,300	52,100	68,200
1990, annual	62,700	109,900	39,200	50,400	120,500
First quarter	48,900	97,700	33,500	41,900	100,100
Second quarter	65,900	112,300	39,300	49,500	131,800
Third quarter	69,000	125,900	42,900	56,600	120,700
Fourth quarter	64,600	103,600	41,900	52,500	127,500
1991, annual	63,700	101,600	48,300	49,700	120,900
First quarter	68,700	99,300	48,500	54,100	125,700
Second quarter	65,000	115,700	46,300	51,300	105,600
Third quarter	58,600	73,600	47,000	46,100	99,800
Fourth quarter	63,700	109,900	51,400	50,600	137,400
1992, annual	73,300	96,800	41,500	57,700	134,900
First quarter	68,700	102,000	47,300	52,000	133,500
Second quarter	72,500	97,400	33,900	59,700	153,700
Third quarter	75,200	99,300	43,500	57,200	123,100
Fourth quarter	76,800	91,500	41,200	63,200	133,300
1993, annual	69,900	99,700	46,900	58,600	125,800
First quarter	72,600	101,600	49,800	60,500	135,700
Second quarter	70,300	99,500	42,700	61,800	119,000
Third quarter	67,300	91,200	46,800	54,400	122,300
Fourth quarter	69,400	107,900	48,500	57,700	124,200

See notes at end of table.

Sales, Prices, and Rents

TABLE 3.4. MEDIAN ASKING SALES PRICE FOR SPECIFIED HOMEOWNER UNITS, THE U.S. AND REGIONS: 1988 TO 1997 - Continued
(Current dollars)

YEAR AND QUARTER	United States	Northeast	Midwest	South	West
1993 [r], annual	69,600	99,900	46,900	59,800	124,900
First quarter	71,500	102,700	50,500	63,500	135,300
Second quarter	70,200	99,600	42,700	62,000	118,000
Third quarter	67,200	91,400	46,800	54,400	121,200
Fourth quarter	69,200	107,700	48,100	57,600	124,000
1994, annual	72,200	107,100	51,000	63,200	105,100
First quarter	77,300	113,900	49,800	67,300	104,600
Second quarter	69,300	110,000	49,800	61,600	107,200
Third quarter	70,700	98,400	47,600	63,400	114,600
Fourth quarter	72,800	108,600	61,200	61,900	98,200
1995, annual	77,500	102,600	61,400	65,400	128,300
First quarter	77,800	100,000	55,400	65,200	143,200
Second quarter	79,900	90,100	57,800	70,200	138,100
Third quarter	77,200	107,000	65,500	64,700	100,000
Fourth quarter	75,200	114,100	65,700	62,200	119,100
1996, annual	81,200	95,700	66,800	70,300	121,900
First quarter	80,600	93,300	69,600	67,500	128,600
Second quarter	79,300	112,800	67,700	68,400	108,900
Third quarter	82,800	98,200	62,000	72,300	123,200
Fourth quarter	81,500	92,400	63,600	71,500	123,100
1997, annual	87,700	97,700	79,800	77,000	119,200
First quarter	87,900	117,200	86,400	73,900	110,300
Second quarter	88,600	101,700	72,000	81,500	116,200
Third quarter	87,300	93,500	83,900	74,700	127,700
Fourth quarter	86,300	83,300	77,600	77,500	123,300

Source: U.S. Bureau of the Census, Current Population Survey/Housing Vacancy Survey.

(r) Revised.

Specified homeowner units are one-unit structures located on properties of less than 10 acres and without a commercial establishment, medical office, or other housing units on the property.

Sales, Prices, and Rents

YEAR AND QUARTER	TABLE 3.5. MEDIAN ASKING MONTHLY RENT FOR SPECIFIED RENTAL UNITS, THE U.S. AND REGIONS: 1988 TO 1997 (Current dollars)				
	United States	Northeast	Midwest	South	West
1988, annual	343	417	301	311	428
First quarter	330	416	300	303	390
Second quarter	344	406	304	317	431
Third quarter	347	420	304	308	429
Fourth quarter	350	424	297	316	476
1989, annual	358	459	320	316	456
First quarter	345	437	300	314	419
Second quarter	358	447	331	312	456
Third quarter	355	445	325	315	468
Fourth quarter	370	483	334	317	474
1989 [r], annual	346	453	304	304	444
First quarter	331	440	297	299	410
Second quarter	344	442	297	298	458
Third quarter	345	457	298	308	465
Fourth quarter	358	477	324	309	450
1990, annual	371	487	319	318	500
First quarter	368	475	336	309	511
Second quarter	363	456	305	312	497
Third quarter	374	518	316	329	455
Fourth quarter	380	499	320	325	525
1991, annual	398	498	339	347	523
First quarter	385	522	337	325	509
Second quarter	395	476	356	353	508
Third quarter	402	487	314	354	516
Fourth quarter	414	504	346	357	556
1992, annual	411	476	347	354	533
First quarter	401	469	338	344	505
Second quarter	404	489	349	347	518
Third quarter	409	479	348	359	528
Fourth quarter	430	482	352	366	571
1993, annual	431	483	360	372	548
First quarter	422	473	365	367	529
Second quarter	436	502	361	387	539
Third quarter	427	480	351	362	563
Fourth quarter	444	482	363	377	559

See notes at end of table.

Sales, Prices, and Rents

TABLE 3.5. MEDIAN ASKING MONTHLY RENT FOR SPECIFIED RENTAL UNITS, THE U.S. AND REGIONS: 1988 TO 1997 - Continued
(Current dollars)

YEAR AND QUARTER	United States	Northeast	Midwest	South	West
1993 [r], annual	430	483	360	370	547
First quarter	420	473	367	363	526
Second quarter	435	502	361	385	536
Third quarter	426	480	351	361	562
Fourth quarter	444	482	363	375	562
1994, annual	429	467	367	375	536
First quarter	431	481	362	377	544
Second quarter	430	478	363	379	531
Third quarter	425	445	369	363	529
Fourth quarter	427	462	372	380	551
1995, annual	438	473	371	393	541
First quarter	433	510	364	385	539
Second quarter	419	436	351	386	540
Third quarter	437	486	387	390	537
Fourth quarter	445	441	390	413	550
1996, annual	444	457	377	417	535
First quarter	428	434	387	402	524
Second quarter	435	454	365	409	535
Third quarter	449	476	371	422	536
Fourth quarter	458	470	383	441	547
1997, annual	442	487	383	404	533
First quarter	436	488	381	396	535
Second quarter	431	450	380	401	539
Third quarter	448	496	375	408	522
Fourth quarter	455	516	395	411	543

Source: U.S. Bureau of the Census, Current Population Survey/Housing Vacancy Survey.

(r) Revised.

Specified rental units exclude single-family units on parcels of 10 acres or more.

Sales, Prices, and Rents

YEAR	United States	Northeast	Midwest	South	West
	TABLE 3.6. NEW PRIVATELY-OWNED SINGLE-FAMILY HOUSES SOLD, BY REGION: 1963 TO 1997 (Thousands)				
1963	560	37	134	199	141
1964	565	90	146	200	129
1965	575	94	142	210	129
1966	461	84	113	166	99
1967	487	77	112	179	119
1968	490	73	119	177	121
1969	448	62	97	175	114
1970	485	61	100	203	121
1971	656	82	127	270	176
1972	718	96	130	305	187
1973	634	95	120	257	161
1974	519	69	103	207	139
1975	549	71	106	222	150
1976	646	72	128	247	199
1977	819	86	162	317	255
1978	817	78	145	331	262
1979	709	67	112	304	225
1980	545	50	81	267	145
1981	436	46	60	219	112
1982	412	47	48	219	99
1983	623	76	71	323	152
1984	639	94	76	309	160
1985	688	112	82	323	170
1986	750	136	96	322	196
1987	671	117	97	271	186
1988	676	101	97	276	202
1989	650	86	102	260	202
1990	534	71	89	225	149
1991	509	57	93	215	144
1992	610	65	116	259	170
1993	666	60	123	295	188
1994	670	61	123	295	191
1995	667	55	125	300	187
1996	757	74	137	337	209
1997	804	78	140	363	223

Source: U.S. Bureau of the Census, Survey of Construction/Housing Sales Survey.

Components may not add to totals because of rounding.

Sales, Prices, and Rents

TABLE 3.7. EXISTING SINGLE-FAMILY HOUSES SOLD, BY REGION: 1968 TO 1997
(Thousands)

YEAR	United States	Northeast	Midwest	South	West
1968	1,569	243	490	529	308
1969	1,594	240	508	538	308
1970	1,612	251	501	568	292
1971	2,018	311	583	735	389
1972	2,252	361	630	788	473
1973	2,334	367	674	847	446
1974	2,272	354	645	839	434
1975	2,476	370	701	862	543
1976	3,064	439	881	1,033	712
1977	3,650	515	1,101	1,231	803
1978	3,986	516	1,144	1,416	911
1979	3,827	526	1,061	1,353	887
1980	2,973	403	806	1,092	672
1981	2,419	353	632	917	516
1982	1,990	354	490	780	366
1983	2,697	477	692	1,004	524
1984	2,829	478	720	1,006	624
1985	3,134	561	806	1,063	704
1986	3,474	635	922	1,145	773
1987	3,436	618	892	1,163	763
1988	3,513	606	865	1,224	817
1989	3,346	531	855	1,185	775
1990	3,211	469	831	1,202	709
1991	3,220	479	840	1,199	702
1992	3,520	534	939	1,292	755
1993	3,802	571	1,007	1,416	808
1994	3,967	595	1,038	1,469	865
1995	3,812	577	992	1,431	813
1996	4,087	611	1,048	1,516	912
1997	4,215	632	1,067	1,575	942

Source: National Association of Realtors®, Existing Home Sales Survey.

Components may not add to totals because of rounding.

Sales, Prices, and Rents

AREA	1981	1982	1983	1984	1985	1986
TABLE 3.8. SALES OF EXISTING SINGLE-FAMILY HOMES AND APARTMENT CONDOMINIUMS AND COOPERATIVES, BY STATE: 1981 TO 1997 (Thousands)						
United States	2,580	2,120	2,880	3,030	3,380	3,770
Northeast	390	390	520	520	630	720
Midwest	670	520	740	760	850	980
South	970	820	1,060	1,070	1,140	1,230
West	550	390	570	670	770	840
Alabama	29.4	32.1	40.8	51.5	54.8	57.2
Alaska	6.7	5.5	9.4	7.7	9.5	7.3
Arizona	47.2	37.0	51.1	63.7	83.6	86.9
Arkansas	38.0	31.5	42.3	42.0	49.9	56.0
California	336.1	234.3	343.2	381.8	405.3	488.0
Colorado	47.3	38.4	49.7	54.6	64.4	64.9
Connecticut	26.8	21.3	34.3	36.7	42.6	41.4
Delaware	8.4	7.3	9.1	9.7	11.3	11.5
District of Columbia	6.1	5.5	7.3	7.6	9.2	11.4
Florida	150.2	100.9	124.5	133.0	142.7	158.3
Georgia	54.6	36.0	50.0	58.1	58.7	69.1
Hawaii	4.8	4.6	9.7	9.6	12.3	15.1
Idaho	9.3	8.1	10.5	12.2	14.2	14.4
Illinois	101.3	77.8	110.2	116.0	130.2	165.0
Indiana	53.3	40.1	54.9	61.0	88.4	85.7
Iowa	39.3	27.8	37.3	39.7	36.4	43.1
Kansas	41.4	32.6	47.1	47.1	45.6	54.0
Kentucky	37.0	37.2	55.2	55.4	51.8	52.7
Louisiana	40.7	45.7	61.8	48.6	36.4	24.1
Maine	13.6	14.8	19.1	19.3	21.8	26.1
Maryland	47.2	43.8	59.4	64.5	71.3	80.8
Massachusetts	42.9	42.6	59.2	54.9	60.2	67.0
Michigan	118.8	92.4	128.8	131.9	153.4	165.7
Minnesota	57.5	43.1	56.3	62.0	67.4	87.3
Mississippi	22.9	23.0	32.1	30.9	34.7	35.7
Missouri	59.1	47.2	69.2	76.7	78.9	83.9
Montana	7.2	6.7	10.0	11.1	11.7	12.6
Nebraska	18.2	16.2	23.5	23.6	22.6	23.2
Nevada	13.1	10.5	13.9	13.9	16.8	18.6
New Hampshire	10.2	7.9	13.8	13.9	14.5	15.2
New Jersey	68.6	78.4	117.7	132.2	160.2	173.3
New Mexico	17.8	13.4	16.3	18.4	22.2	21.7
New York	120.5	121.4	135.1	123.0	150.0	170.0
North Carolina	69.7	70.0	91.4	99.7	107.9	123.7
North Dakota	8.4	6.2	9.0	9.5	8.8	9.6
Ohio	101.6	81.0	122.6	130.9	147.6	171.5
Oklahoma	58.5	52.1	63.5	50.2	42.3	43.6
Oregon	26.8	18.7	26.9	28.6	36.1	41.3
Pennsylvania	103.8	106.6	142.9	140.7	157.5	205.8
Rhode Island	6.0	6.2	8.0	9.1	10.3	10.6
South Carolina	31.3	30.1	39.0	44.5	48.4	53.0
South Dakota	9.4	8.4	12.7	11.1	10.5	12.5
Tennessee	50.2	47.0	69.7	76.1	89.3	104.3
Texas	220.1	165.6	187.2	190.2	183.5	186.2
Utah	16.2	13.4	16.9	18.9	22.1	22.1
Vermont	6.2	6.0	6.8	6.8	7.5	8.8
Virginia	77.2	71.7	101.1	94.9	116.0	141.7
Washington	46.5	33.7	47.7	50.6	61.8	77.1
West Virginia	21.8	21.9	31.6	33.5	31.1	24.7
Wisconsin	51.5	35.1	51.6	52.0	61.9	75.5
Wyoming	5.7	5.0	5.8	7.0	8.0	7.8

See notes at end of table.

Sales, Prices, and Rents

TABLE 3.8. SALES OF EXISTING SINGLE-FAMILY HOMES AND APARTMENT CONDOMINIUMS AND COOPERATIVES, BY STATE: 1981 TO 1997 - Continued

(Thousands)

AREA	1987	1988	1989	1990	1991	1992
United States	3,770	3,860	3,710	3,560	3,559	3,886
Northeast	710	690	610	530	545	612
Midwest	950	920	920	890	901	1,006
South	1,260	1,330	1,290	1,310	1,308	1,407
West	850	920	890	830	805	861
Alabama	61.6	61.5	59.4	61.1	64.0	72.5
Alaska	7.6	9.1	6.6	....	....	....
Arizona	74.8	80.3	77.7	86.3	79.7	89.8
Arkansas	47.6	47.5	47.5	44.8	43.4	47.8
California	511.6	562.2	539.3	453.0	425.4	427.3
Colorado	61.4	60.9	53.9	54.2	59.6	71.4
Connecticut	40.7	49.2	41.0	34.3	37.6	40.0
Delaware	12.2	12.4	11.8	9.7	10.4	10.0
District of Columbia	9.1	8.0	15.5	13.1	12.5	12.4
Florida	168.7	179.2	177.6	183.3	176.0	179.2
Georgia	79.1	78.2	73.6	73.2	70.7	....
Hawaii	20.7	20.4	21.2	19.2	12.2	11.6
Idaho	13.5	13.1	15.0	18.1	19.0	21.6
Illinois	162.7	168.1	162.7	160.9	168.1	186.2
Indiana	86.5	81.6	81.6	80.1	76.0	84.8
Iowa	54.4	57.9	54.6	51.9	54.1	53.1
Kansas	52.1	47.6	45.1	38.8	37.1	46.2
Kentucky	54.7	60.9	62.2	66.4	67.8	78.7
Louisiana	42.4	39.8	40.8	41.6	47.1	47.0
Maine	21.8	18.4	9.0	....	....	10.3
Maryland	68.5	81.6	76.8	67.1	66.8	69.0
Massachusetts	76.3	76.5	67.4	44.0	49.6	57.6
Michigan	149.9	147.6	151.6	145.0	145.0	157.3
Minnesota	79.2	70.8	62.7	64.8	66.3	75.7
Mississippi	37.3	36.6	36.5	34.7	35.2	39.2
Missouri	79.6	73.0	81.0	84.1	82.7	98.8
Montana	12.3	12.5	13.0	12.7	13.9	16.6
Nebraska	21.2	20.0	20.9	19.3	19.9	22.4
Nevada	20.4	20.9	21.4	26.2	25.6	25.6
New Hampshire	15.4	13.8	9.7	7.9	9.3	12.0
New Jersey	158.4	133.6	126.6	114.8	118.8	132.1
New Mexico	22.9	20.5	21.9	23.6	24.4	29.2
New York	171.4	160.5	140.2	125.5	127.2	136.3
North Carolina	129.1	134.7	127.5	135.9	139.9	160.2
North Dakota	10.6	10.2	10.3	10.4	10.3	11.9
Ohio	168.3	160.6	163.4	151.6	149.8	167.4
Oklahoma	39.3	46.8	49.1	53.4	52.5	57.6
Oregon	44.8	48.9	53.2	56.6	48.1	52.5
Pennsylvania	209.0	225.2	193.8	182.7	179.2	204.4
Rhode Island	10.5	11.0	9.5	7.8	7.8	10.0
South Carolina	53.7	55.0	52.2	57.8	53.9	58.9
South Dakota	9.6	11.4	10.8	11.6	11.3	12.7
Tennessee	95.9	93.9	95.2	92.7	92.0	102.2
Texas	200.3	225.2	213.1	240.0	242.0	242.7
Utah	20.9	20.7	20.3	22.1	26.3	31.5
Vermont	9.6	9.5	6.2	6.1	8.1	9.5
Virginia	123.6	130.7	116.0	96.9	90.3	101.3
Washington	68.0	73.4	90.8	87.7	86.9	91.3
West Virginia	33.1	36.4	36.8	42.0	43.3	46.8
Wisconsin	77.3	75.2	74.1	74.2	82.8	91.5
Wyoming	7.6	7.4	7.3	7.4	8.2	9.9

See notes at end of table.

Sales, Prices, and Rents

TABLE 3.8. SALES OF EXISTING SINGLE-FAMILY HOMES AND APARTMENT CONDOMINIUMS AND COOPERATIVES, BY STATE: 1981 TO 1997 - Continued

(Thousands)

AREA	1993	1994	1995	1996	1997
United States	4,203	4,404	4,240	4,559	4,730
Northeast	657	691	676	723	758
Midwest	1,080	1,113	1,065	1,129	1,156
South	1,547	1,614	1,574	1,669	1,737
West	919	985	926	1,038	1,081
Alabama	77.9	77.4	74.2	76.8	82.2
Alaska	....	....	....	....	....
Arizona	107.9	123.8	122.0	128.2	135.1
Arkansas	52.8	52.3	57.5	59.7	58.7
California	435.0	482.5	425.6	505.4	555.4
Colorado	82.1	80.6	76.9	81.6	86.6
Connecticut	45.9	49.8	51.4	49.2	55.0
Delaware	9.4	10.4	10.2	....	....
District of Columbia	12.3	12.3	11.6	10.8	14.2
Florida	208.9	229.7	220.3	225.5	234.4
Georgia	....	....	....	....	....
Hawaii	12.5	13.1	10.0	9.8	11.1
Idaho	23.4	23.1	20.5	20.2	20.7
Illinois	193.9	188.4	183.5	191.6	199.7
Indiana	100.8	103.3	100.6	103.5	111.5
Iowa	53.5	54.3	51.6	56.4	57.7
Kansas	53.7	55.7	54.4	59.9	61.6
Kentucky	83.3	81.1	78.2	78.8	81.1
Louisiana	49.3	51.4	50.4	50.9	52.9
Maine	11.6	13.1	13.1	14.2	14.7
Maryland	73.4	69.5	58.7	60.3	66.4
Massachusetts	66.0	68.7	68.1	81.9	94.3
Michigan	170.6	184.2	176.3	179.8	180.3
Minnesota	81.8	82.1	76.7	85.8	88.0
Mississippi	43.6	43.5	46.1	46.7	47.7
Missouri	106.4	110.2	108.3	113.7	115.9
Montana	16.2	15.6	13.8	14.2	14.9
Nebraska	23.2	23.3	21.1	20.3	23.4
Nevada	30.5	32.9	29.6	31.8	29.7
New Hampshire	13.6	16.2	....	....	....
New Jersey	139.0	145.4	138.3	147.8	157.3
New Mexico	31.0	30.4	28.9	26.7	25.5
New York	143.0	156.3	150.4	165.8	171.0
North Carolina	185.0	204.1	201.0	212.5	228.0
North Dakota	11.8	10.9	10.6	12.0	11.9
Ohio	179.1	186.4	182.8	192.7	187.3
Oklahoma	61.5	59.7	57.7	60.6	64.2
Oregon	58.8	58.1	59.0	58.9	60.1
Pennsylvania	216.1	216.4	217.2	224.3	233.3
Rhode Island	11.0	11.6	11.5	12.9	14.3
South Carolina	62.2	67.3	68.9	74.2	81.5
South Dakota	13.7	13.2	13.3	13.9	15.2
Tennessee	120.5	129.8	133.6	142.9	149.9
Texas	258.8	266.9	256.8	275.0	293.1
Utah	31.2	32.4	31.6	33.8	30.0
Vermont	11.0	10.9	8.8	8.4	8.1
Virginia	104.2	99.5	92.2	92.2	98.5
Washington	97.0	101.2	95.5	101.5	116.5
West Virginia	45.7	45.8	44.2	43.8	45.2
Wisconsin	94.6	94.3	93.2	101.0	104.6
Wyoming	10.9	11.0	9.4	8.6	9.5

Sources: California data provided by California Association of Realtors®. All other data provided by National Association of Realtors®.

Sales, Prices, and Rents

TABLE 3.9. MEDIAN SALES PRICE OF NEW PRIVATELY-OWNED SINGLE-FAMILY HOUSES SOLD, BY REGION: 1963 TO 1997
(Current dollars)

YEAR	United States	Region			
		Northeast	Midwest	South	West
1963	18,000	20,300	17,900	16,100	18,800
1964	18,900	20,300	19,400	16,700	20,400
1965	20,000	21,500	21,600	17,500	21,600
1966	21,400	23,500	23,200	18,200	23,200
1967	22,700	25,400	25,100	19,400	24,100
1968	24,700	27,700	27,400	21,500	25,100
1969	25,600	31,600	27,600	22,800	25,300
1970	23,400	30,300	24,400	20,300	24,000
1971	25,200	30,600	27,200	22,500	25,500
1972	27,600	31,400	29,300	25,800	27,500
1973	32,500	37,100	32,900	30,900	32,400
1974	35,900	40,100	36,100	34,500	35,800
1975	39,300	44,000	39,600	37,300	40,600
1976	44,200	47,300	44,800	40,500	47,200
1977	48,800	51,600	51,500	44,100	53,500
1978	55,700	58,100	59,200	50,300	61,300
1979	62,900	65,500	63,900	57,300	69,600
1980	64,600	69,500	63,400	59,600	72,300
1981	68,900	76,000	65,900	64,400	77,800
1982	69,300	78,200	68,900	66,100	75,000
1983	75,300	82,200	79,500	70,900	80,100
1984	79,900	88,600	85,400	72,000	87,300
1985	84,300	103,300	80,300	75,000	92,600
1986	92,000	125,000	88,300	80,200	95,700
1987	104,500	140,000	95,000	88,000	111,000
1988	112,500	149,000	101,600	92,000	126,500
1989	120,000	159,600	108,800	96,400	139,000
1990	122,900	159,000	107,900	99,000	147,500
1991	120,000	155,900	110,000	100,000	141,100
1992	121,500	169,000	115,600	105,500	130,400
1993	126,500	162,600	125,000	115,000	135,000
1994	130,000	169,000	132,900	116,900	140,400
1995	133,900	180,000	134,000	124,500	141,000
1996	140,000	186,000	138,000	126,200	153,900
1997	146,000	190,000	149,900	129,600	160,000

Source: U.S. Bureau of the Census, Survey of Construction/Housing Sales Survey.

Sales, Prices, and Rents

TABLE 3.10. MEDIAN SALES PRICE OF EXISTING SINGLE-FAMILY HOUSES SOLD, BY REGION: 1968 TO 1997
(Current dollars)

YEAR	United States	Region			
		Northeast	Midwest	South	West
1968	20,100	21,400	18,200	19,000	22,900
1969	21,800	23,700	19,000	20,300	23,900
1970	23,000	25,200	20,100	22,200	24,300
1971	24,800	27,100	22,100	24,300	26,500
1972	26,700	29,800	23,900	26,400	28,400
1973	28,900	32,800	25,300	29,000	31,000
1974	32,000	35,800	27,700	32,300	34,800
1975	35,300	39,300	30,100	34,800	39,600
1976	38,100	41,800	32,900	36,500	46,100
1977	42,900	44,400	36,700	39,800	57,300
1978	48,700	47,900	42,200	45,100	66,700
1979	55,700	53,600	47,800	51,300	77,400
1980	62,200	60,800	51,900	58,300	89,300
1981	66,400	63,700	54,300	64,400	96,200
1982	67,800	63,500	55,100	67,100	98,900
1983	70,300	72,200	56,600	69,200	94,900
1984	72,400	78,700	57,100	71,300	95,800
1985	75,500	88,900	58,900	75,200	95,400
1986	80,300	104,800	63,500	78,200	100,900
1987	85,600	133,300	66,000	80,400	113,200
1988	89,300	143,000	68,400	82,200	124,900
1989	93,100	145,200	71,300	84,500	139,900
1990	95,500	141,200	74,000	85,900	139,600
1991	100,300	141,900	77,800	88,900	147,200
1992	103,700	140,000	81,700	92,100	143,800
1993	106,800	139,500	85,200	95,000	142,600
1994	109,900	139,100	87,900	96,000	147,000
1995	113,100	136,900	93,600	97,800	148,300
1996	118,200	140,900	99,800	102,800	152,900
1997	124,100	145,100	106,100	109,000	160,400

Source: National Association of Realtors®, Existing Home Sales Survey.

Sales, Prices, and Rents

YEAR	United States	Region			
		Northeast	Midwest	South	West
TABLE 3.11. AVERAGE SALES PRICE OF NEW MOBILE HOMES PLACED FOR RESIDENTIAL USE, BY REGION: 1974 TO 1997 (Current dollars)					
1974	9,300	9,400	9,300	8,300	11,600
1975	10,600	10,500	10,700	9,000	13,600
1976	12,300	11,600	11,600	10,600	16,000
1977	14,200	12,900	13,500	12,100	18,100
1978	15,900	14,300	15,100	13,700	20,600
1979	17,600	15,800	16,100	15,600	23,100
1980 [1]	19,800	18,500	18,600	18,200	25,400
1981	19,900	19,000	18,900	18,400	25,600
1982	19,700	19,800	20,000	18,500	24,700
1983	21,000	21,400	20,400	19,700	27,000
1984	21,500	22,200	21,100	20,200	27,400
1985	21,800	22,700	21,500	20,400	28,700
1986	22,400	24,400	21,800	20,700	29,900
1987	23,700	25,600	23,700	21,900	31,000
1988	25,100	27,000	24,600	22,700	33,900
1989	27,200	30,200	26,700	24,100	37,800
1990	27,800	30,000	27,000	24,500	39,300
1991	27,700	30,400	27,600	24,500	38,600
1992	28,400	30,900	28,800	25,400	39,000
1993	30,500	32,000	31,400	27,700	40,500
1994	33,500	33,900	34,600	30,500	44,600
1995	36,300	37,600	36,600	34,000	46,800
1996	38,400	40,200	39,600	36,100	47,700
1997	41,100	43,900	41,600	38,700	50,900

Source: U.S. Bureau of the Census, Survey of New Mobile Home Placements.

(1) Beginning in 1980, the data no longer reflect the prices (values) of mobile homes sold (leased) after placement. See Appendix A.

Sales, Prices, and Rents

TABLE 3.12. CONSUMER PRICE INDEX FOR ALL ITEMS, HOUSING, AND SHELTER, BY REGION: 1967 TO 1997

YEAR	United States city average			Northeast			North Central			South			West		
	All items	Housing	Shelter	All items	Housing	Shelter	All items	Housing	Shelter	All items	Housing	Shelter	All items	Housing	Shelter
(CPI-U, 1982-84=100)															
1967	33.4	30.8	28.8	34.0	....	....	33.4	....	....	32.6	....	....	33.3	....	....
1968	34.8	32.0	30.1	35.4	....	....	34.8	....	....	34.0	....	....	34.6	....	....
1969	36.7	34.0	32.6	37.5	....	....	36.8	....	....	36.0	....	....	36.3	....	....
1970	38.8	36.4	35.5	40.0	....	....	38.8	....	....	37.9	....	....	38.2	....	....
1971	40.5	38.0	37.0	42.1	....	....	40.3	....	....	39.5	....	....	39.5	....	....
1972	41.8	39.4	38.7	43.8	....	....	41.5	....	....	40.7	....	....	40.8	....	....
1973	44.4	41.2	40.5	46.5	....	....	43.9	....	....	43.3	....	....	43.1	....	....
1974	49.3	45.8	44.4	51.7	....	....	48.7	....	....	48.6	....	....	47.7	....	....
1975	53.8	50.7	48.8	55.8	....	....	53.0	....	....	53.3	....	....	52.6	....	....
1976	56.9	53.8	51.5	59.0	....	....	56.1	....	....	56.3	....	....	55.8	....	....
1977	60.6	57.4	54.9	62.3	....	....	59.9	....	....	60.0	....	....	59.9	....	....
1978	65.2	62.4	60.5	66.2	63.6	62.5	64.7	60.6	58.2	65.0	62.6	59.7	65.0	63.2	62.2
1979	72.6	70.1	68.9	72.8	70.2	68.8	72.6	69.2	68.0	72.4	70.2	68.6	72.6	70.8	70.6
1980	82.4	81.1	81.0	82.2	80.7	79.5	82.4	80.0	80.3	81.9	80.8	80.7	83.3	83.3	83.9
1981	90.9	90.4	90.5	91.0	90.7	89.3	90.1	87.7	87.7	90.7	90.4	90.9	91.9	92.6	93.8
1982	96.5	96.9	96.9	95.8	95.7	94.3	96.5	96.3	96.7	96.5	97.5	97.8	97.4	98.4	98.9
1983 [1]	99.6	99.5	99.1	99.8	99.7	100.0	99.9	100.3	99.7	99.7	99.6	99.3	99.0	98.2	97.6
1984	103.9	103.6	104.0	104.5	104.6	105.8	103.6	103.5	103.6	103.8	103.0	102.9	103.6	103.3	103.5
1985	107.6	107.7	109.8	108.4	109.0	113.0	106.8	107.0	108.4	107.1	106.3	106.9	108.0	108.8	110.7
1986	109.6	110.9	115.8	111.1	112.7	121.3	108.0	109.4	113.3	108.9	109.0	111.0	110.5	113.0	116.9
1987	113.6	114.2	121.3	116.0	117.3	129.3	111.9	112.4	118.8	112.4	111.0	113.9	114.3	116.5	122.2
1988	118.3	118.5	127.1	121.8	124.0	139.4	116.1	115.9	123.9	116.4	113.9	117.1	119.0	120.7	127.2
1989	124.0	123.0	132.8	128.6	130.8	148.2	121.5	119.9	128.9	121.5	117.2	121.0	124.6	124.8	132.6
1990	130.7	128.5	140.0	136.3	138.0	157.2	127.4	124.1	135.1	127.9	121.8	126.7	131.5	130.9	140.3
1991	136.2	133.6	146.3	142.5	144.4	165.3	132.4	128.5	140.6	132.9	125.6	131.2	137.3	136.9	147.3
1992	140.3	137.5	151.2	147.3	149.0	171.4	136.1	132.1	145.3	136.5	128.8	135.2	142.0	141.2	152.3
1993	144.5	141.2	155.7	151.4	152.6	175.9	140.0	135.8	150.0	140.8	132.8	139.9	146.2	144.6	156.3
1994	148.2	144.8	160.5	155.1	156.4	181.0	144.0	139.2	155.6	144.7	136.4	144.7	149.6	148.0	160.3
1995	152.4	148.5	165.7	159.1	159.9	185.8	148.4	143.1	161.8	149.0	140.0	150.2	153.5	151.8	164.5
1996	156.9	152.8	171.0	163.6	164.2	190.6	153.0	147.8	167.5	153.6	145.0	155.8	157.6	155.2	169.5
1997	160.5	156.8	176.3	167.6	168.3	196.5	156.7	151.9	172.9	156.9	148.4	160.3	161.4	159.5	174.8

See notes at end of table.

Sales, Prices, and Rents

YEAR	TABLE 3.12. CONSUMER PRICE INDEX FOR ALL ITEMS, HOUSING, AND SHELTER, BY REGION: 1967 TO 1997 - Continued														
	United States city average			Northeast			North Central			South			West		
	All items	Housing	Shelter	All items	Housing	Shelter	All items	Housing	Shelter	All items	Housing	Shelter	All items	Housing	Shelter
PERCENT CHANGE [2]															
1968	4.2	3.9	4.5	4.1	....	....	4.2	....	....	4.3	....	....	3.9	....	....
1969	5.5	6.3	8.3	5.9	....	....	5.7	....	....	5.9	....	....	4.9	....	....
1970	5.7	7.1	8.9	6.7	....	....	5.4	....	....	5.3	....	....	5.2	....	....
1971	4.4	4.4	4.2	5.3	....	....	3.9	....	....	4.2	....	....	3.4	....	....
1972	3.2	3.7	4.6	4.0	....	....	3.0	....	....	3.0	....	....	3.3	....	....
1973	6.2	4.6	4.7	6.2	....	....	5.8	....	....	6.4	....	....	5.6	....	....
1974	11.0	11.2	9.6	11.2	....	....	10.9	....	....	12.2	....	....	10.7	....	....
1975	9.1	10.7	9.9	7.9	....	....	8.8	....	....	9.7	....	....	10.3	....	....
1976	5.8	6.1	5.5	5.7	....	....	5.8	....	....	5.6	....	....	6.1	....	....
1977	6.5	6.7	6.6	5.6	....	....	6.8	....	....	6.6	....	....	7.3	....	....
1978	7.6	8.7	10.2	6.3	....	....	8.0	....	....	8.3	....	....	8.5	....	....
1979	11.3	12.3	13.9	10.0	10.4	10.1	12.2	14.2	16.8	11.4	12.1	14.9	11.7	12.0	13.5
1980	13.5	15.7	17.6	12.9	15.0	15.6	13.5	15.6	18.1	13.1	15.1	17.6	14.7	17.7	18.8
1981	10.3	11.5	11.7	10.7	12.4	12.3	9.3	9.6	9.2	10.7	11.9	12.6	10.3	11.2	11.8
1982	6.2	7.2	7.1	5.3	5.5	5.6	7.1	9.8	10.3	6.4	7.9	7.6	6.0	6.3	5.4
1983 [1]	3.2	2.7	2.3	4.2	4.2	6.0	3.5	4.2	3.1	3.3	2.2	1.5	1.6	-0.2	-1.3
1984	4.3	4.1	4.9	4.7	4.9	5.8	3.7	3.2	3.9	4.1	3.4	3.6	4.6	5.2	6.0
1985	3.6	4.0	5.6	3.7	4.2	6.8	3.1	3.4	4.6	3.2	3.2	3.9	4.2	5.3	7.0
1986	1.9	3.0	5.5	2.5	3.4	7.3	1.1	2.2	4.5	1.7	2.5	3.8	2.3	3.9	5.6
1987	3.6	3.0	4.7	4.4	4.1	6.6	3.6	2.7	4.9	3.2	1.8	2.6	3.4	3.1	4.5
1988	4.1	3.8	4.8	5.0	5.7	7.8	3.8	3.1	4.3	3.6	2.6	2.8	4.1	3.6	4.1
1989	4.8	3.8	4.5	5.6	5.5	6.3	4.7	3.5	4.0	4.4	2.9	3.3	4.7	3.4	4.2
1990	5.4	4.5	5.4	6.0	5.5	6.1	4.9	3.5	4.8	5.3	3.9	4.7	5.5	4.9	5.8
1991	4.2	4.0	4.5	4.5	4.6	5.2	3.9	3.5	4.1	3.9	3.1	3.6	4.4	4.6	5.0
1992	3.0	2.9	3.3	3.4	3.2	3.7	2.8	2.8	3.3	2.7	2.5	3.0	3.4	3.1	3.4
1993	3.0	2.7	3.0	2.8	2.4	2.6	2.9	2.8	3.2	3.2	3.1	3.5	3.0	2.4	2.6
1994	2.6	2.5	3.1	2.4	2.5	2.9	2.9	2.5	3.7	2.8	2.7	3.4	2.3	2.4	2.6
1995	2.8	2.6	3.2	2.6	2.2	2.7	3.1	2.8	4.0	3.0	2.6	3.8	2.6	2.6	2.6
1996	3.0	2.9	3.2	2.8	2.7	2.6	3.1	3.3	3.5	3.1	3.6	3.7	2.7	2.2	3.0
1997	2.3	2.6	3.1	2.4	2.5	3.1	2.4	2.8	3.2	2.1	2.3	2.9	2.4	2.8	3.1

Source: U.S. Bureau of Labor Statistics, Consumer Price Index.

Annual averages of monthly figures.

(1) In 1983 the Bureau of Labor Statistics switched from an asset price approach to a rental equivalence approach for estimating homeowner costs. See Appendix A for explanation.
(2) Percent change from immediate prior year.

Sales, Prices, and Rents

YEAR	TABLE 3.13. CONSUMER PRICE INDEX FOR SELECTED HOUSING ITEMS, BY REGION: 1978 TO 1997											
	United States city average				Northeast				North Central			
	Renters		Homeowners		Renters		Homeowners		Renters		Homeowners	
	Renters' costs [1]	Rent, residential [2]	Home-owners' costs [1]	Owners' equivalent rent [1]	Renters' costs [1]	Rent, residential [2]	Home-owners' costs [1]	Owners' equivalent rent [1]	Renters' costs [1]	Rent, residential [2]	Home-owners' costs [1]	Owners' equivalent rent [1]
CPI-U												
1978	....	69.3	....	....	....	70.9	....	....	....	73.3	....	....
1979	....	74.3	....	....	....	74.8	....	....	....	78.4	....	....
1980	....	80.9	....	....	....	80.7	....	....	....	84.5	....	....
1981	....	87.9	....	....	....	87.5	....	....	....	90.5	....	....
1982	....	94.6	....	....	....	94.1	....	....	....	95.8	....	....
1983 [3]	103.0	100.1	102.5	102.5	103.2	100.2	103.4	103.4	102.5	100.0	101.6	101.6
1984	108.6	105.3	107.3	107.3	109.2	105.7	109.5	109.5	107.4	104.2	105.4	105.3
1985	115.4	111.8	113.1	113.2	116.7	112.8	117.1	117.3	113.2	109.4	110.1	110.0
1986	121.9	118.3	119.4	119.4	125.2	121.6	126.0	126.4	118.5	114.7	115.1	115.0
1987	128.1	123.1	124.8	124.8	133.9	129.0	134.2	134.6	125.4	119.1	120.5	120.4
1988	133.6	127.8	131.1	131.1	142.3	136.4	145.7	146.2	129.7	123.4	126.0	126.0
1989	138.9	132.8	137.3	137.4	149.4	144.0	155.7	156.4	134.7	127.5	131.1	131.2
1990	146.7	138.4	144.6	144.8	159.9	150.8	164.6	165.4	139.4	132.3	138.0	138.2
1991	155.6	143.3	150.2	150.4	173.1	155.6	171.0	171.9	145.3	137.5	143.6	143.8
1992	160.9	146.9	155.3	155.5	180.2	159.5	177.0	178.0	150.0	141.0	148.5	148.7
1993	165.0	150.3	160.2	160.5	183.6	162.9	182.3	183.3	154.5	144.8	153.5	153.8
1994	169.4	154.0	165.5	165.8	188.0	166.0	188.1	189.2	159.8	149.2	159.3	159.6
1995	174.3	157.8	171.0	171.3	192.3	169.9	193.4	194.4	166.4	154.2	165.6	165.8
1996	180.2	162.0	176.5	176.8	198.4	174.1	198.0	199.1	172.4	158.7	171.4	171.8
1997	186.4	166.7	181.5	181.9	206.4	179.3	203.4	204.5	178.1	163.7	176.8	177.3
PERCENT CHANGE [4]												
1979	....	7.2	....	....	....	5.5	....	....	....	7.0	....	....
1980	....	8.9	....	....	....	7.9	....	....	....	7.8	....	....
1981	....	8.7	....	....	....	8.4	....	....	....	7.1	....	....
1982	....	7.6	....	....	....	7.5	....	....	....	5.9	....	....
1983	....	5.8	....	....	....	6.5	....	....	....	4.4	....	....
1984	5.4	5.2	4.7	4.7	5.8	5.5	5.9	5.9	4.8	4.2	3.7	3.6
1985	6.3	6.2	5.4	5.5	6.9	6.7	6.9	7.1	5.4	5.0	4.5	4.5
1986	5.6	5.8	5.6	5.5	7.3	7.8	7.6	7.8	4.7	4.8	4.5	4.5
1987	5.1	4.1	4.5	4.5	6.9	6.1	6.5	6.5	5.8	3.8	4.7	4.7
1988	4.3	3.8	5.0	5.0	6.3	5.7	8.6	8.6	3.4	3.6	4.6	4.7
1989	4.0	3.9	4.7	4.8	5.0	5.6	6.9	7.0	3.9	3.3	4.0	4.1
1990	5.6	4.2	5.3	5.4	7.0	4.7	5.7	5.8	3.5	3.8	5.3	5.3
1991	6.1	3.5	3.9	3.9	8.3	3.2	3.9	3.9	4.2	3.9	4.1	4.1
1992	3.4	2.5	3.4	3.4	4.1	2.5	3.5	3.5	3.2	2.5	3.4	3.4
1993	2.5	2.3	3.2	3.2	1.9	2.1	3.0	3.0	3.0	2.7	3.4	3.4
1994	2.7	2.5	3.3	3.3	2.4	1.9	3.2	3.2	3.4	3.0	3.8	3.8
1995	2.9	2.5	3.3	3.3	2.3	2.3	2.8	2.7	4.1	3.4	4.0	3.9
1996	3.4	2.7	3.2	3.2	3.2	2.5	2.4	2.4	3.6	2.9	3.5	3.6
1997	3.4	2.9	2.8	2.9	4.0	3.0	2.7	2.7	3.3	3.2	3.2	3.2

See notes at end of table.

Sales, Prices, and Rents

TABLE 3.13. CONSUMER PRICE INDEX FOR SELECTED HOUSING ITEMS, BY REGION: 1978 TO 1997 - Continued

YEAR	United States city average — Renters — Renters' costs [1]	Rent, residential [2]	Homeowners — Home-owners' costs [1]	Owners' equivalent rent [1]	South — Renters — Renters' costs [1]	Rent, residential [2]	Homeowners — Home-owners' costs [1]	Owners' equivalent rent [1]	West — Renters — Renters' costs [1]	Rent, residential [2]	Homeowners — Home-owners' costs [1]	Owners' equivalent rent [1]
CPI-U												
1978	....	69.3	....	....	....	69.1	....	....	....	64.6	....	....
1979	....	74.3	....	....	....	74.4	....	....	....	70.8	....	....
1980	....	80.9	....	....	....	81.2	....	....	....	78.3	....	....
1981	....	87.9	....	....	....	88.3	....	....	....	86.3	....	....
1982	....	94.6	....	....	....	95.2	....	....	....	93.8	....	....
1983 [3]	103.0	100.1	102.5	102.5	102.6	100.4	101.7	101.7	103.3	99.7	103.3	103.3
1984	108.6	105.3	107.3	107.3	107.2	104.5	105.0	104.9	110.2	106.5	109.3	109.4
1985	115.4	111.8	113.1	113.2	111.9	109.1	108.8	108.7	118.7	114.6	116.6	116.7
1986	121.9	118.3	119.4	119.4	116.8	113.5	113.0	112.7	125.3	121.4	123.2	123.1
1987	128.1	123.1	124.8	124.8	120.6	116.0	115.6	115.2	130.6	126.1	128.9	128.8
1988	133.6	127.8	131.1	131.1	124.3	118.6	118.7	118.3	136.0	130.5	134.2	134.0
1989	138.9	132.8	137.3	137.4	128.5	121.7	122.7	122.2	141.0	135.3	140.2	140.1
1990	146.7	138.4	144.6	144.8	135.1	125.9	128.2	127.8	149.4	141.6	148.4	148.4
1991	155.6	143.3	150.2	150.4	140.9	130.3	132.5	132.1	159.3	146.8	154.6	154.8
1992	160.9	146.9	155.3	155.5	145.1	133.8	136.5	136.1	164.5	150.2	160.0	160.2
1993	165.0	150.3	160.2	160.5	150.5	137.5	141.2	140.8	167.6	153.2	164.8	165.0
1994	169.4	154.0	165.5	165.8	155.3	141.9	146.2	145.6	170.8	156.2	169.4	169.6
1995	174.3	157.8	171.0	171.3	161.3	146.1	151.6	151.1	174.1	158.7	174.6	174.8
1996	180.2	162.0	176.5	176.8	167.1	150.9	157.4	157.0	179.4	162.1	179.7	179.9
1997	186.4	166.7	181.5	181.9	172.1	154.9	161.9	161.6	185.7	166.8	185.0	185.0
PERCENT CHANGE [4]												
1979	....	7.2	....	....	....	7.7	....	....	....	9.6	....	....
1980	....	8.9	....	....	....	9.1	....	....	....	10.6	....	....
1981	....	8.7	....	....	....	8.7	....	....	....	10.2	....	....
1982	....	7.6	....	....	....	7.8	....	....	....	8.7	....	....
1983 [3]	....	5.8	....	....	....	5.5	....	....	....	6.3	....	....
1984	5.4	5.2	4.7	4.7	4.5	4.1	3.2	3.1	6.7	6.8	5.8	5.9
1985	6.3	6.2	5.4	5.5	4.4	4.4	3.6	3.6	7.7	7.6	6.7	6.7
1986	5.6	5.8	5.6	5.5	4.4	4.0	3.9	3.7	5.6	5.9	5.7	5.5
1987	5.1	4.1	4.5	4.5	3.3	2.2	2.3	2.2	4.2	3.9	4.6	4.6
1988	4.3	3.8	5.0	5.0	3.1	2.2	2.7	2.7	4.1	3.5	4.1	4.0
1989	4.0	3.9	4.7	4.8	3.4	2.6	3.4	3.3	3.7	3.7	4.5	4.6
1990	5.6	4.2	5.3	5.4	5.1	3.5	4.5	4.6	6.0	4.7	5.8	5.9
1991	6.1	3.5	3.9	3.9	4.3	3.5	3.4	3.4	6.6	3.7	4.2	4.3
1992	3.4	2.5	3.4	3.4	3.0	2.7	3.0	3.0	3.3	2.3	3.5	3.5
1993	2.5	2.3	3.2	3.2	3.7	2.8	3.4	3.5	1.9	2.0	3.0	3.0
1994	2.7	2.5	3.3	3.3	3.2	3.2	3.5	3.4	1.9	2.0	2.8	2.8
1995	2.9	2.5	3.3	3.3	3.9	3.0	3.7	3.8	1.9	1.6	3.1	3.1
1996	3.4	2.7	3.2	3.2	3.6	3.3	3.8	3.9	3.0	2.1	2.9	2.9
1997	3.4	2.9	2.8	2.9	3.0	2.7	2.9	2.9	3.5	2.9	2.9	2.8

Source: U.S. Bureau of Labor Statistics, Consumer Price Index.

Annual averages of monthly figures.
(1) December 1982=100.
(2) 1982-84=100.
(3) In 1983 the Bureau of Labor Statistics switched from an asset price approach to a rental equivalence approach for estimating homeowner costs. See Appendix A for explanation.
(4) Percent change from immediate prior year.

Sales, Prices, and Rents

TABLE 3.14. FIXED-WEIGHTED PRICE INDEX (LASPEYRES) OF NEW ONE-FAMILY HOUSES SOLD INCLUDING LOT AND AVERAGE SALES PRICE OF KINDS OF ONE-FAMILY HOUSES SOLD IN 1992: 1979 TO 1997

PERIOD	Price index (1992=100.0; index based on kinds of houses sold in 1992)					Average sales price of kinds of houses sold in 1992 (Estimated from price index)	Average sales price of houses actually sold
	United States	Region					
		Northeast	Midwest	South	West		
1979	61.8	46.3	64.0	62.9	61.1	89,100	71,800
1980	68.1	50.5	67.1	70.2	68.2	98,100	76,400
1981	73.5	55.3	73.9	76.7	72.9	105,900	83,000
1982	75.2	56.7	75.1	79.5	73.5	108,400	83,900
1983	76.8	60.3	75.2	81.4	75.2	110,700	89,800
1984	79.9	66.0	80.2	84.6	77.3	115,100	97,600
1985	80.9	74.5	78.4	86.6	78.0	116,600	100,800
1986	84.1	84.5	82.5	89.4	80.9	121,200	111,900
1987	88.6	97.6	88.8	92.3	84.8	127,700	127,200
1988	91.9	100.5	92.8	94.3	87.6	132,400	138,300
1989	95.6	102.1	94.9	97.2	92.2	137,800	148,800
1990	97.4	99.3	95.5	97.4	98.1	140,400	149,800
1991	98.7	96.4	97.7	98.9	99.1	142,200	147,200
1992	100.0	100.0	100.0	100.0	100.0	144,100	144,100
1993	104.3	97.1	106.7	104.7	103.6	150,300	147,700
1994	109.3	98.4	112.0	108.5	110.9	157,500	154,500
1995	112.4	100.7	116.3	111.9	112.7	161,900	158,700
1996	114.5	104.1	118.6	112.6	116.8	165,100	166,400
1997	118.4	106.6	122.9	116.5	120.5	170,600	176,200

Source: U.S. Bureau of the Census, Survey of Construction/Housing Sales Survey.

See Appendix A for description of Laspeyres index.

Sales, Prices, and Rents

TABLE 3.15. CHAIN-TYPE ANNUAL-WEIGHTED PRICE INDEX (FISHER IDEAL) OF NEW ONE-FAMILY HOUSES SOLD INCLUDING LOT: 1979 TO 1997

PERIOD	United States	Price index (1992=100.0; index based on kinds of houses sold in 1992)			
		Region			
		Northeast	Midwest	South	West
1979	59.5	47.1	64.4	63.6	59.6
1980	65.4	51.2	67.6	70.7	66.1
1981	70.3	56.0	72.3	76.3	70.1
1982	73.2	58.4	75.5	80.3	71.5
1983	75.3	61.7	75.0	82.6	73.8
1984	78.1	67.1	79.2	84.7	76.2
1985	80.1	73.6	78.5	86.6	77.2
1986	83.8	84.8	83.0	88.9	78.7
1987	88.7	96.8	88.6	91.8	82.6
1988	92.1	99.8	92.7	94.0	87.2
1989	95.8	102.1	94.8	97.0	92.9
1990	97.4	98.1	95.4	97.3	98.3
1991	98.6	96.2	97.8	98.9	99.2
1992	100.0	100.0	100.0	100.0	100.0
1993	104.5	98.0	107.0	104.7	103.8
1994	109.6	100.0	112.8	108.4	111.1
1995	112.5	103.0	116.5	111.7	113.2
1996	114.9	104.7	119.3	113.0	117.2
1997	118.2	107.5	123.3	115.8	120.8

Source: U.S. Bureau of the Census, Survey of Construction/Housing Sales Survey.

See Appendix A for description of Fisher Ideal index.

Sales, Prices, and Rents

PERIOD	TABLE 3.16. OFFICE OF FEDERAL HOUSING ENTERPRISE OVERSIGHT REPEAT SALES HOUSE PRICE INDEX: 1980 TO 1997									
	United States	New England	Middle Atlantic	South Atlantic	East South Central	West South Central	West North Central	East North Central	Mountain	Pacific
1980										
First quarter	100.0	100.0	100.0	100.0	100.0	100.0	100.0	100.0	100.0	100.0
Second quarter	100.7	102.3	100.1	99.0	97.3	102.3	102.4	100.8	98.9	102.4
Third quarter	104.0	108.0	105.7	103.6	100.3	103.3	103.5	102.3	104.3	106.4
Fourth quarter	104.2	109.7	106.1	104.4	98.1	104.1	102.6	101.4	105.0	107.9
1981										
First quarter	105.0	109.5	105.0	106.9	100.8	104.3	102.4	102.2	103.2	109.4
Second quarter	106.8	113.8	104.8	107.0	103.0	109.4	101.0	103.2	109.4	112.8
Third quarter	108.3	115.8	108.0	106.9	103.3	113.0	100.1	103.5	113.4	115.3
Fourth quarter	108.2	115.9	106.2	108.6	98.1	116.4	102.7	101.7	111.8	114.9
1982										
First quarter	109.3	117.2	109.1	111.6	103.1	119.6	101.6	98.4	112.7	115.5
Second quarter	110.5	119.2	113.1	113.0	102.5	121.8	100.8	98.9	116.1	114.9
Third quarter	110.2	120.5	110.2	112.8	101.7	121.4	100.8	99.2	116.1	115.4
Fourth quarter	110.9	121.8	110.2	113.4	103.3	123.5	102.0	98.5	119.4	115.8
1983										
First quarter	112.9	124.8	111.2	115.8	106.8	124.0	104.4	101.3	121.0	117.0
Second quarter	114.2	131.7	116.6	115.9	108.4	125.1	106.0	101.5	118.8	117.1
Third quarter	115.0	136.9	118.9	117.2	109.0	124.1	107.2	101.9	118.1	116.6
Fourth quarter	115.2	140.4	121.5	118.3	108.0	123.5	106.0	101.5	115.9	116.9
1984										
First quarter	116.6	148.2	124.5	119.8	102.2	122.7	108.3	102.5	117.8	119.4
Second quarter	118.7	154.6	130.8	121.0	105.1	123.0	109.8	104.1	118.0	120.6
Third quarter	117.6	161.4	133.5	113.8	93.4	123.4	111.0	104.1	117.5	121.8
Fourth quarter	119.9	166.1	136.9	119.3	104.2	122.1	111.1	104.3	117.0	122.2
1985										
First quarter	122.1	174.2	140.9	122.6	109.3	121.5	112.1	104.7	119.8	123.2
Second quarter	123.3	185.9	145.1	119.5	114.6	122.0	113.5	106.6	119.9	121.4
Third quarter	125.9	195.7	149.4	125.1	113.5	121.4	109.6	108.1	119.5	127.3
Fourth quarter	127.8	207.1	154.2	126.5	116.7	119.2	114.7	109.0	117.6	127.9
1986										
First quarter	130.8	215.6	158.0	129.7	118.9	122.2	116.7	111.2	123.7	128.7
Second quarter	134.2	226.4	167.8	132.3	121.6	125.1	116.6	113.1	123.9	131.3
Third quarter	137.5	238.7	177.2	135.0	122.5	122.5	120.0	115.9	124.7	134.5
Fourth quarter	140.4	250.9	184.9	137.5	127.2	120.4	121.6	118.1	122.9	137.5
1987										
First quarter	143.2	260.6	191.9	139.2	128.6	120.9	122.5	119.3	126.7	141.2
Second quarter	146.4	270.2	201.2	142.8	130.8	115.9	125.7	123.6	126.4	143.7
Third quarter	149.7	279.4	211.5	146.1	133.0	113.7	127.1	126.7	123.8	147.8
Fourth quarter	151.3	283.8	217.2	148.2	133.8	110.7	126.5	128.5	121.9	151.2
1988										
First quarter	154.0	288.8	221.0	151.3	136.0	110.4	127.7	130.4	123.2	156.9
Second quarter	157.4	293.6	227.3	155.1	136.6	111.5	129.4	133.6	123.8	162.9
Third quarter	159.2	293.4	230.0	157.1	137.7	109.0	129.3	135.9	123.3	169.7
Fourth quarter	160.9	295.3	231.0	158.8	137.5	108.5	130.0	137.0	122.6	177.2
1989										
First quarter	163.1	294.1	232.4	160.9	138.7	109.0	130.2	138.9	122.9	185.3
Second quarter	165.4	292.7	232.2	163.1	139.9	110.3	131.9	141.3	123.3	194.1
Third quarter	169.1	297.1	235.0	165.5	141.2	112.1	133.3	144.3	125.6	205.1
Fourth quarter	170.8	297.9	236.8	167.1	142.3	111.7	134.2	145.4	126.0	211.6
1990										
First quarter	171.6	293.7	236.7	167.9	142.7	111.6	134.5	147.2	126.3	214.8
Second quarter	171.6	285.9	234.4	167.9	143.1	112.5	134.9	149.1	126.7	216.0
Third quarter	172.1	281.9	233.4	168.2	143.5	112.9	135.3	150.6	128.0	217.9
Fourth quarter	171.4	275.5	231.3	167.5	143.1	112.5	135.1	151.0	128.3	217.8

See notes at end of table.

Sales, Prices, and Rents

TABLE 3.16. OFFICE OF FEDERAL HOUSING ENTERPRISE OVERSIGHT REPEAT SALES HOUSE PRICE INDEX: 1980 TO 1997 - Continued

PERIOD	United States	New England	Middle Atlantic	South Atlantic	East South Central	West South Central	West North Central	East North Central	Mountain	Pacific
1991										
First quarter	172.6	274.3	231.4	168.9	145.1	113.6	136.7	152.5	130.1	219.4
Second quarter	173.6	270.8	232.1	170.5	146.4	115.1	137.8	154.7	131.8	219.0
Third quarter	173.6	267.8	232.1	169.9	146.9	115.3	138.2	155.9	132.2	218.7
Fourth quarter	175.9	270.1	235.0	172.8	149.0	116.7	140.2	157.8	134.5	221.2
1992										
First quarter	177.1	269.6	237.2	174.1	150.5	118.3	141.1	159.2	136.3	220.9
Second quarter	176.8	266.0	235.4	173.9	151.1	118.2	142.0	160.8	137.7	219.2
Third quarter	178.4	267.0	237.9	175.7	153.1	120.1	143.4	162.2	139.6	219.6
Fourth quarter	179.3	267.6	238.9	176.6	154.2	120.8	144.5	163.9	141.9	218.8
1993										
First quarter	179.2	265.9	238.0	176.4	155.0	121.5	145.3	164.7	143.8	216.3
Second quarter	180.7	267.3	240.4	178.1	157.0	122.9	146.7	166.4	147.1	215.9
Third quarter	181.9	268.2	240.9	179.2	159.0	124.6	148.4	168.2	150.3	215.0
Fourth quarter	183.4	269.6	242.7	180.6	160.8	125.9	150.2	170.0	154.0	215.3
1994										
First quarter	184.6	269.6	242.4	181.5	163.2	127.1	152.4	172.6	157.8	214.5
Second quarter	185.5	265.4	241.1	181.4	165.6	128.0	156.5	176.1	163.1	211.8
Third quarter	185.9	263.1	238.7	181.6	167.8	128.4	158.7	178.7	167.0	209.9
Fourth quarter	185.7	262.0	235.9	181.7	169.1	127.8	159.6	180.0	169.4	208.1
1995										
First quarter	186.8	263.7	235.6	182.7	170.7	128.3	161.0	182.3	172.2	208.2
Second quarter	190.2	268.0	239.6	185.9	174.1	131.1	163.8	185.5	175.9	211.9
Third quarter	193.4	272.8	243.8	188.9	177.2	132.8	166.4	188.6	180.2	215.3
Fourth quarter	195.3	275.2	244.8	191.1	179.5	134.1	168.3	191.3	183.4	216.1
1996										
First quarter	197.8	278.4	247.9	193.6	182.4	136.0	170.4	193.6	186.6	218.1
Second quarter	198.7	276.7	246.4	194.2	184.3	136.5	172.9	197.7	187.7	217.5
Third quarter	199.6	276.6	245.3	194.7	185.7	136.5	174.6	200.4	190.2	217.4
Fourth quarter	202.3	281.3	247.1	197.3	188.8	138.2	177.0	203.4	194.2	220.3
1997										
First quarter	204.3	283.6	249.2	199.6	191.0	139.1	178.7	206.0	196.7	222.0
Second quarter	205.8	285.8	249.0	200.2	192.0	139.9	180.6	209.1	197.3	224.2
Third quarter	209.0	290.8	252.3	203.2	195.3	141.4	183.3	211.6	201.1	229.4
Fourth quarter	211.7	296.0	254.7	206.6	197.8	143.1	185.0	214.0	204.6	232.9

Source: Office of Federal Housing Enterprise Oversight, House Price Index.

See Appendix A for description of index.

Vacancy Rates

TABLE 3.17. QUARTERLY VACANCY RATES BY TENURE: 1960 TO 1997
(Percent)

YEAR	Homeowner vacancy rate				Rental vacancy rate			
	First quarter	Second quarter	Third quarter	Fourth quarter	First quarter	Second quarter	Third quarter	Fourth quarter
1960	1.2	1.3	1.3	1.3	8.0	8.0	8.3	8.4
1965	1.7	1.5	1.6	1.5	8.5	8.2	7.8	8.5
1966	1.5	1.5	1.4	1.3	8.3	7.4	7.4	7.7
1967	1.4	1.3	1.4	1.3	7.3	6.9	7.0	6.2
1968	1.1	1.1	1.2	1.2	6.1	6.2	5.9	5.4
1969	1.0	1.0	1.1	1.0	5.6	5.7	5.5	5.1
1970	1.0	1.0	1.1	1.1	5.4	5.4	5.3	5.2
1971	1.0	0.9	1.0	1.0	5.3	5.3	5.6	5.6
1972	1.0	1.0	0.9	1.0	5.3	5.5	5.8	5.6
1973	1.0	0.9	1.1	1.2	5.7	5.8	5.8	5.8
1974	1.2	1.1	1.2	1.3	6.2	6.3	6.2	6.0
1975	1.2	1.2	1.4	1.2	6.1	6.3	6.2	5.4
1976	1.2	1.2	1.3	1.2	5.5	5.8	5.7	5.3
1977	1.3	1.3	1.1	1.0	5.1	5.3	5.4	5.1
1978	1.0	0.9	1.0	1.1	5.0	5.1	5.0	5.0
1979	1.0	1.1	1.1	1.1	4.8	5.0	5.2	5.0
1979 [1]	1.1	1.1	1.2	1.3	5.1	5.5	5.7	5.4
1980	1.3	1.4	1.4	1.4	5.2	5.6	5.7	5.0
1981	1.3	1.3	1.5	1.4	5.2	5.0	5.0	5.0
1982	1.4	1.6	1.5	1.6	5.3	5.1	5.3	5.5
1983	1.4	1.5	1.6	1.6	5.7	5.5	5.8	5.5
1984	1.6	1.7	1.7	1.7	5.6	5.5	6.0	6.3
1985	1.8	1.9	1.8	1.6	6.3	6.2	6.8	6.7
1986	1.5	1.7	1.6	1.6	6.9	7.3	7.5	7.7
1987	1.7	1.7	1.7	1.6	7.4	7.5	8.1	7.8
1988	1.6	1.6	1.6	1.6	8.0	7.7	7.8	7.3
1989	1.5	1.6	1.8	1.6	7.3	7.3	7.3	6.8
1989 [2]	1.7	1.7	1.9	1.8	7.5	7.4	7.6	7.1
1990	1.7	1.7	1.7	1.7	7.5	7.0	7.2	7.2
1991	1.7	1.8	1.8	1.6	7.5	7.3	7.6	7.3
1992	1.5	1.6	1.6	1.5	7.4	7.7	7.3	7.1
1993	1.4	1.4	1.4	1.4	7.9	7.6	7.1	6.9
1993 [3]	1.4	1.4	1.4	1.4	7.8	7.6	7.0	6.9
1994	1.4	1.4	1.4	1.6	7.5	7.4	7.2	7.4
1995	1.5	1.6	1.5	1.6	7.4	7.7	7.7	7.7
1996	1.6	1.5	1.7	1.7	7.9	7.8	8.0	7.7
1997	1.7	1.6	1.5	1.7	7.5	7.9	7.9	7.7

Source: U.S. Bureau of the Census, Current Population Survey/Housing Vacancy Survey.

(1) Revised to reflect a supplemental sample and refined estimation procedures.
(2) Revised to reflect new edit procedures that allocate cases that would have been recorded as "not reported" under previous procedures. Also reflects the inclusion of year-round vacant mobile homes for the first time.
(3) Revised using weights based on the 1990 Census.

Vacancy Rates

TABLE 3.18. ANNUAL VACANCY RATES BY TENURE AND UNITS IN STRUCTURE: 1970 TO 1997
(Percent)

YEAR	Homeowner units			Rental units		
	1-unit structures	2 or more units in structure	5 or more units in structure	1-unit structures	2 or more units in structure	5 or more units in structure
1970	1.0	2.1	4.3	3.6	6.2	7.1
1971	0.9	2.4	8.5	3.6	6.4	7.9
1972	1.0	2.2	3.6	4.0	7.0	8.3
1973	1.0	3.3	9.3	4.3	7.0	8.1
1974	1.0	4.7	12.6	3.8	7.5	8.8
1975	1.0	5.4	14.4	3.6	7.3	8.3
1976	1.0	5.3	14.4	3.2	6.8	7.8
1977	0.9	5.4	16.3	3.1	6.4	7.1
1978	0.9	3.2	9.2	3.1	6.1	6.7
1979	1.0	3.8	6.1	3.1	5.9	6.6
1979 [1]	1.0	3.7	6.6	3.2	6.6	7.6
1980	1.2	4.3	8.7	3.4	6.4	7.1
1981	1.1	5.4	10.8	3.3	6.0	6.4
1982	1.2	6.1	12.2	3.6	6.2	6.5
1983	1.3	5.2	8.8	3.7	6.7	7.1
1984	1.4	6.1	10.6	3.8	7.0	7.5
1985	1.4	6.6	10.1	3.8	7.9	8.8
1986	1.3	5.6	8.3	3.9	9.2	10.4
1987	1.4	5.8	8.6	4.0	9.7	11.2
1988	1.3	6.1	9.7	3.6	9.8	11.4
1989 [2]	1.4	7.1	9.6	4.2	9.2	10.1
1990	1.4	7.1	8.4	4.0	9.0	9.6
1991	1.4	6.8	7.9	3.9	9.4	10.4
1992	1.3	5.8	7.4	3.8	9.4	10.0
1993	1.1	5.2	6.7	3.8	9.4	10.3
1993 [3]	1.2	5.3	6.8	3.7	9.4	10.2
1994	1.3	4.9	5.6	4.5	9.1	9.8
1995	1.4	4.8	5.1	5.4	9.0	9.5
1996	1.4	5.1	6.0	5.5	9.2	9.6
1997	1.5	4.4	4.6	5.8	9.0	9.1

Source: U.S. Bureau of the Census, Current Population Survey/Housing Vacancy Survey.

(1) Revised to reflect a supplemental sample and refined estimation procedures.
(2) Revised to reflect new edit procedures that allocate cases that would have been recorded as "not reported" under previous procedures. Also reflects the inclusion of year-round vacant mobile homes for the first time.
(3) Revised using weights based on the 1990 Census.

Vacancy Rates

TABLE 3.19. QUARTERLY VACANCY RATES BY TENURE AND REGION: 1986 TO 1997
(Percent)

YEAR AND QUARTER	Homeowner vacancy rates					Rental vacancy rates				
	United States	Northeast	Midwest	South	West	United States	Northeast	Midwest	South	West
1986										
First quarter	1.5	0.9	1.3	2.1	1.4	6.9	3.9	6.6	9.5	6.4
Second quarter	1.7	0.9	1.7	2.3	2.2	7.3	3.6	6.7	10.3	7.2
Third quarter	1.6	1.0	1.5	2.0	1.7	7.5	3.8	7.1	10.3	7.2
Fourth quarter	1.6	1.1	1.5	2.1	1.7	7.7	4.1	7.2	10.3	7.7
1987										
First quarter	1.7	1.2	1.5	2.0	1.6	7.4	4.2	6.6	10.5	6.9
Second quarter	1.7	1.2	1.5	1.9	1.9	7.5	4.0	6.4	10.6	7.5
Third quarter	1.7	1.2	1.3	2.1	2.0	8.1	4.1	7.4	11.2	7.8
Fourth quarter	1.6	1.3	1.2	2.0	1.6	7.8	4.3	6.7	11.4	6.9
1988										
First quarter	1.6	1.5	1.2	1.9	1.6	8.0	4.9	7.1	10.7	7.7
Second quarter	1.6	1.4	1.3	1.8	1.9	7.7	4.4	7.0	10.1	8.0
Third quarter	1.6	1.7	1.2	2.0	1.3	7.8	4.9	6.7	9.9	8.4
Fourth quarter	1.6	1.8	1.1	2.0	1.5	7.3	4.9	6.7	9.9	6.5
1989										
First quarter	1.5	1.4	1.1	2.0	1.4	7.3	4.7	7.0	9.4	6.9
Second quarter	1.6	1.5	1.2	1.9	1.4	7.3	4.6	6.9	9.5	6.9
Third quarter	1.8	1.7	1.4	2.3	1.5	7.3	4.8	6.9	9.2	7.3
Fourth quarter	1.6	1.5	1.4	2.0	1.4	6.8	5.2	5.8	8.5	6.6
1989 [1]										
First quarter	1.7	1.5	1.2	2.1	1.6	7.5	4.5	7.2	9.8	7.2
Second quarter	1.7	1.6	1.3	2.2	1.6	7.4	4.6	7.1	9.9	7.0
Third quarter	1.9	1.7	1.6	2.5	1.6	7.6	4.9	6.9	9.9	7.4
Fourth quarter	1.8	1.5	1.6	2.2	1.6	7.1	5.2	6.1	9.2	6.9
1990										
First quarter	1.7	1.6	1.4	2.2	1.6	7.5	6.0	6.7	9.3	7.1
Second quarter	1.7	1.8	1.2	2.1	1.8	7.0	6.4	6.0	8.4	6.4
Third quarter	1.7	1.5	1.2	2.2	1.8	7.2	6.1	6.5	8.7	6.6
Fourth quarter	1.7	1.5	1.4	2.0	1.8	7.2	6.2	6.6	8.9	6.4
1991										
First quarter	1.7	1.5	1.2	2.2	1.8	7.5	7.0	6.9	8.8	6.6
Second quarter	1.8	1.5	1.2	2.2	1.9	7.3	6.8	6.4	9.2	6.1
Third quarter	1.8	1.6	1.4	2.3	1.5	7.6	7.3	6.8	8.8	7.0
Fourth quarter	1.6	1.3	1.3	2.1	1.4	7.3	6.3	6.8	8.9	6.5
1992										
First quarter	1.5	1.5	1.1	1.8	1.8	7.4	6.4	7.0	8.2	7.6
Second quarter	1.6	1.3	1.3	1.8	1.9	7.7	7.1	6.9	8.8	7.2
Third quarter	1.6	1.2	1.3	1.7	2.1	7.3	6.7	6.8	7.9	7.4
Fourth quarter	1.5	1.3	1.1	1.7	1.7	7.1	7.4	6.1	8.0	6.4
1993										
First quarter	1.4	1.4	1.1	1.6	1.4	7.9	8.4	6.8	8.3	7.9
Second quarter	1.4	1.3	1.1	1.7	1.3	7.6	7.0	6.6	8.5	7.9
Third quarter	1.4	1.3	1.1	1.6	1.4	7.1	6.5	6.9	7.7	7.0
Fourth quarter	1.4	1.3	1.1	1.5	1.4	6.9	6.5	6.3	7.5	7.0

See notes at end of table.

Vacancy Rates

TABLE 3.19. QUARTERLY VACANCY RATES BY TENURE AND REGION: 1986 TO 1997 - Continued
(Percent)

YEAR AND QUARTER	Homeowner vacancy rates					Rental vacancy rates				
	United States	Northeast	Midwest	South	West	United States	Northeast	Midwest	South	West
1993 [2]										
First quarter	1.4	1.4	1.1	1.7	1.4	7.8	8.3	6.7	8.3	7.9
Second quarter	1.4	1.3	1.1	1.7	1.4	7.6	6.9	6.5	8.4	7.8
Third quarter	1.4	1.3	1.1	1.6	1.4	7.0	6.5	6.8	7.6	6.9
Fourth quarter	1.4	1.4	1.1	1.5	1.5	6.9	6.4	6.2	7.4	7.1
1994										
First quarter	1.4	1.4	0.9	1.7	1.6	7.5	7.3	7.0	8.2	7.2
Second quarter	1.4	1.4	1.1	1.6	1.5	7.4	7.1	7.1	7.7	7.3
Third quarter	1.4	1.5	1.0	1.6	1.7	7.2	7.0	6.5	7.8	7.2
Fourth quarter	1.6	1.6	1.2	1.9	1.6	7.4	7.1	6.8	8.3	6.8
1995										
First quarter	1.5	1.6	1.4	1.6	1.6	7.4	7.3	6.7	8.3	6.8
Second quarter	1.6	1.5	1.3	1.8	1.8	7.7	7.5	7.1	8.2	7.7
Third quarter	1.5	1.5	1.2	1.6	1.6	7.7	7.1	7.4	8.2	7.9
Fourth quarter	1.6	1.5	1.3	1.7	1.8	7.7	6.9	7.6	8.5	7.5
1996										
First quarter	1.6	1.7	1.5	1.6	1.7	7.9	6.9	8.3	8.5	7.6
Second quarter	1.5	1.4	1.1	1.9	1.3	7.8	7.6	7.2	8.6	7.2
Third quarter	1.7	1.6	1.4	1.8	1.8	8.0	7.8	7.8	8.7	7.4
Fourth quarter	1.7	1.8	1.4	1.8	1.9	7.7	7.1	8.2	8.5	6.7
1997										
First quarter	1.7	1.8	1.3	1.9	1.8	7.5	6.1	8.5	8.7	6.2
Second quarter	1.6	1.6	1.1	1.9	1.9	7.9	6.7	8.2	9.3	6.8
Third quarter	1.5	1.5	1.2	1.7	1.7	7.9	7.2	7.9	9.1	6.8
Fourth quarter	1.7	1.6	1.3	2.1	1.7	7.7	6.9	7.3	9.3	6.5

Source: U.S. Bureau of the Census, Current Population Survey/Housing Vacancy Survey.

(1) Revised to reflect new edit procedures that allocate cases that would have been recorded as "not reported" under previous procedures. Also reflects the inclusion of year-round vacant mobile homes for the first time.

(2) Revised using weights based on the 1990 Census.

Vacancy Rates

AREA	1986	1987	1988	1989	1989 [1]	1990	1991	1992	1993	1993 [2]	1994	1995	1996	1997
United States	1.6	1.7	1.6	1.6	1.8	1.7	1.7	1.5	1.4	1.4	1.5	1.5	1.6	1.6
Alabama	2.8	2.0	1.7	1.8	1.9	1.5	2.7	1.3	1.3	1.4	1.4	1.5	1.8	1.7
Alaska	2.4	4.5	5.6	3.8	3.8	2.6	2.4	1.5	1.3	1.2	1.3	1.3	1.7	1.3
Arizona	2.2	3.6	2.5	2.8	3.4	2.5	2.1	2.1	1.3	1.3	1.5	1.9	1.7	2.8
Arkansas	1.8	1.7	1.9	1.7	2.3	2.5	3.0	1.7	0.9	0.9	1.2	1.5	1.4	1.4
California	1.1	1.2	1.1	0.9	1.0	1.8	1.6	2.1	1.6	1.7	2.0	2.1	2.0	1.8
Colorado	2.6	2.9	2.7	3.7	3.8	2.2	2.1	1.8	1.4	1.5	0.8	0.9	0.9	0.6
Connecticut	0.4	0.5	1.5	2.7	2.7	2.4	1.6	1.4	1.1	1.1	1.4	1.8	2.0	1.5
Delaware	1.2	0.8	1.1	1.6	1.6	2.1	2.3	2.0	1.6	1.6	1.8	2.8	1.4	2.6
District of Columbia	2.5	2.0	1.4	1.9	1.9	2.4	2.9	3.3	2.3	2.1	3.5	3.9	3.5	3.3
Florida	2.5	2.5	2.3	2.7	3.2	2.7	3.4	3.0	2.7	2.8	2.4	2.1	2.4	2.5
Georgia	1.4	1.5	2.0	2.0	2.0	1.8	1.4	1.7	1.2	1.2	1.8	1.2	2.0	1.5
Hawaii	0.8	1.1	0.4	1.0	1.0	0.8	1.4	2.5	3.1	3.0	2.0	2.0	1.4	1.6
Idaho	2.6	3.2	1.9	1.5	1.5	1.5	1.7	1.0	0.9	0.8	0.9	0.9	1.1	0.8
Illinois	1.2	1.2	1.3	1.8	1.9	1.3	1.3	1.3	1.1	1.1	1.2	1.1	1.4	1.6
Indiana	1.8	2.1	1.3	1.1	1.3	1.5	1.3	1.1	0.9	0.9	0.7	1.2	1.1	1.4
Iowa	2.0	1.7	1.4	1.5	1.8	0.8	0.9	0.8	0.5	0.5	0.8	1.0	0.8	1.2
Kansas	2.0	1.7	1.9	2.8	3.2	2.0	1.6	1.4	1.5	1.6	1.2	2.3	1.8	1.9
Kentucky	1.7	1.8	1.4	0.9	1.0	1.7	1.6	1.1	1.2	1.2	0.6	0.6	1.2	1.3
Louisiana	2.3	2.1	2.2	2.4	2.4	1.7	1.9	1.1	0.9	0.9	1.5	0.8	1.1	1.3
Maine	1.1	1.3	1.4	0.9	1.1	1.0	1.5	2.3	2.0	1.9	1.5	1.1	1.1	1.6
Maryland	0.8	0.9	0.6	0.8	0.8	1.7	1.7	1.1	2.0	2.0	2.3	2.3	2.3	2.1
Massachusetts	0.7	1.7	1.8	1.3	1.3	1.4	1.2	1.0	1.2	1.2	1.4	1.2	1.1	0.8
Michigan	1.1	1.1	0.8	0.9	1.0	1.1	1.2	1.2	1.1	1.1	0.9	1.3	1.4	1.2
Minnesota	1.5	1.3	0.8	0.6	0.9	1.2	1.0	1.0	1.0	0.9	1.2	1.5	1.1	0.8
Mississippi	1.3	1.5	1.6	1.9	1.9	1.6	1.5	1.0	0.9	0.9	0.8	0.9	1.0	1.1
Missouri	1.3	1.7	2.0	1.7	1.9	1.8	1.7	1.4	1.6	1.7	2.0	2.2	2.0	1.3
Montana	2.0	2.3	2.9	2.3	2.3	3.0	2.2	2.2	2.4	2.6	1.8	1.0	1.4	2.0
Nebraska	2.9	1.9	1.6	1.4	1.4	1.6	1.4	0.8	1.0	1.0	0.8	0.7	2.0	1.5
Nevada	3.3	3.4	3.8	2.4	2.4	2.7	3.0	2.3	1.9	1.9	2.3	2.4	2.0	2.3
New Hampshire	1.6	1.4	1.2	1.4	1.4	1.7	2.2	1.8	2.1	2.2	1.8	1.1	1.6	2.2
New Jersey	0.7	1.1	1.6	1.8	1.8	1.8	1.1	1.2	1.2	1.3	1.2	1.5	1.6	2.0
New Mexico	1.7	2.3	2.4	1.9	2.4	2.4	1.8	1.4	1.0	0.9	1.1	1.1	1.3	2.2
New York	1.1	1.3	1.6	1.6	1.6	1.8	1.8	1.7	1.7	1.7	1.9	1.6	1.7	2.0
North Carolina	1.3	1.5	1.5	1.3	1.5	1.6	1.6	1.7	1.4	1.3	1.1	1.2	1.4	1.8
North Dakota	2.5	2.9	2.3	2.4	2.4	3.6	2.3	1.7	1.2	1.2	1.2	1.4	1.8	1.9
Ohio	1.2	1.1	0.9	1.0	1.1	1.2	1.2	1.0	1.0	1.0	0.9	1.2	1.1	1.0
Oklahoma	4.6	3.2	2.8	3.3	3.7	3.1	2.2	1.9	1.5	1.5	1.7	1.5	1.6	2.3
Oregon	1.5	1.2	1.3	1.1	1.1	0.8	0.8	0.8	0.4	0.4	1.0	0.8	1.4	1.8
Pennsylvania	1.3	1.2	1.6	1.1	1.2	1.1	1.3	1.0	0.9	1.0	1.1	1.4	1.6	1.4
Rhode Island	0.4	0.8	1.3	1.3	1.3	2.1	1.5	0.7	1.6	1.7	2.0	1.9	1.6	1.2
South Carolina	1.4	1.7	1.7	1.1	1.2	1.0	1.2	1.2	1.2	1.1	2.4	2.6	1.7	1.5
South Dakota	1.7	1.6	1.8	1.1	1.7	1.2	1.1	0.9	0.7	0.7	1.4	1.9	1.7	1.9
Tennessee	1.5	1.0	1.3	1.2	1.3	2.4	1.7	1.1	1.0	1.0	1.4	1.5	1.6	1.3
Texas	2.9	3.0	2.9	2.9	3.2	2.5	2.4	1.6	1.8	1.9	1.8	1.9	1.4	1.8
Utah	2.9	2.3	2.1	1.8	2.1	1.9	1.7	1.1	0.9	1.0	1.3	1.2	1.0	2.0
Vermont	0.8	0.8	0.9	1.3	1.3	1.9	1.4	1.8	1.3	1.3	1.9	1.9	1.4	1.5
Virginia	0.8	1.1	1.0	1.6	1.6	1.7	1.9	2.0	1.6	1.7	1.5	1.6	2.2	2.4
Washington	1.6	1.4	1.2	0.7	0.9	0.8	1.4	1.5	0.7	0.7	0.8	1.2	1.4	1.2
West Virginia	2.2	1.9	2.0	1.6	1.8	2.9	2.2	1.3	1.4	1.5	1.9	1.9	2.2	2.5
Wisconsin	1.8	1.1	1.2	0.7	0.8	0.9	1.3	1.6	1.1	1.0	0.8	0.9	1.0	0.6
Wyoming	3.3	3.2	2.8	1.7	2.5	2.0	2.0	1.5	1.2	1.3	1.3	1.4	1.4	2.6

TABLE 3.20. ANNUAL HOMEOWNER VACANCY RATES BY STATE: 1986 TO 1997
(Percent)

Source: U.S. Bureau of the Census, Current Population Survey/Housing Vacancy Survey.

(1) Revised to reflect new edit procedures that allocate cases that would have been recorded as "not reported" under previous procedures. Also reflects the inclusion of year-round vacant mobile homes for the first time.

(2) Revised using weights based on the 1990 Census.

Vacancy Rates

AREA	1986	1987	1988	1989	1989 [1]	1990	1991	1992	1993	1993 [2]	1994	1995	1996	1997
TABLE 3.21. ANNUAL RENTAL VACANCY RATES BY STATE: 1986 TO 1997 (Percent)														
United States	7.3	7.7	7.7	7.1	7.4	7.2	7.4	7.4	7.4	7.3	7.4	7.6	7.8	7.7
Alabama	5.0	5.0	6.8	6.0	6.9	8.1	7.2	6.4	6.3	6.8	7.2	8.5	8.7	7.3
Alaska	15.3	15.9	14.3	11.0	11.0	6.8	5.7	5.8	5.4	4.9	4.5	6.0	5.9	7.4
Arizona	13.1	12.7	11.8	10.2	10.5	10.7	9.6	9.5	7.6	7.4	8.8	7.2	10.2	9.1
Arkansas	7.4	7.8	8.5	6.4	8.0	7.9	8.6	6.9	7.1	7.2	6.8	7.4	7.2	8.1
California	4.9	5.4	6.2	5.8	5.9	6.0	6.2	7.5	8.2	8.2	7.9	8.5	7.2	6.5
Colorado	13.6	11.6	13.0	11.7	12.4	10.2	5.8	5.8	4.7	4.9	5.3	4.3	6.1	3.7
Connecticut	5.0	4.8	5.8	5.9	5.9	7.5	7.7	8.3	11.2	11.1	11.4	15.2	10.7	7.7
Delaware	4.9	5.5	6.9	5.6	6.7	6.0	8.0	9.1	8.3	8.4	8.3	10.6	7.7	8.5
District of Columbia	3.5	4.8	5.2	5.1	5.1	7.7	8.8	9.7	8.5	7.7	10.3	12.9	13.4	13.2
Florida	11.0	11.0	10.5	9.1	9.5	9.0	9.1	8.7	8.2	8.3	8.0	7.8	9.0	9.5
Georgia	6.2	6.1	7.5	9.3	10.0	9.4	9.7	8.9	7.3	7.3	9.1	11.3	11.6	11.2
Hawaii	5.7	6.5	6.3	6.6	6.6	6.6	5.8	5.8	7.1	6.8	7.4	6.3	6.0	7.1
Idaho	8.8	9.0	6.4	6.0	6.0	5.4	3.9	2.7	4.4	3.7	3.6	4.5	5.8	6.8
Illinois	6.9	5.9	6.9	7.0	7.2	6.1	6.5	7.0	6.2	6.3	6.8	7.4	7.9	8.5
Indiana	7.5	8.2	7.9	6.0	6.2	5.3	6.2	7.0	7.3	7.2	5.0	5.2	6.9	7.2
Iowa	9.5	8.0	8.1	8.5	8.5	7.8	7.0	3.9	4.3	4.3	4.9	5.3	5.5	6.4
Kansas	10.3	9.4	10.1	8.5	9.3	7.8	6.9	5.9	6.1	6.2	9.0	6.2	9.9	9.4
Kentucky	6.5	7.9	6.5	6.7	7.2	5.8	7.6	8.7	8.6	8.5	7.6	5.1	5.8	9.4
Louisiana	12.1	15.6	13.6	12.4	13.2	13.1	9.5	7.8	7.1	7.2	9.4	9.6	7.8	8.4
Maine	5.1	5.4	5.1	6.0	6.0	9.7	10.8	10.7	10.4	10.4	11.0	8.6	7.2	6.1
Maryland	5.3	6.9	5.0	5.5	5.5	5.2	6.7	7.2	8.8	8.7	8.1	5.7	6.7	8.0
Massachusetts	3.8	3.6	4.4	5.0	5.0	6.9	8.3	8.8	7.9	7.8	7.1	6.2	5.8	5.2
Michigan	5.0	6.8	7.3	7.4	7.5	7.3	7.2	7.7	8.0	7.9	8.9	8.8	10.2	8.9
Minnesota	4.9	4.9	5.5	5.8	5.8	6.5	6.6	5.4	5.5	4.9	5.2	6.7	5.5	4.7
Mississippi	9.1	10.7	9.8	9.6	10.5	8.7	7.8	7.4	8.1	8.0	7.9	13.2	13.2	11.5
Missouri	9.7	8.8	7.5	7.7	8.3	9.6	11.1	9.9	9.1	9.4	10.1	10.0	8.6	8.9
Montana	8.1	10.3	9.3	8.9	9.7	8.1	6.6	4.2	3.3	3.4	3.5	3.6	5.1	5.0
Nebraska	8.3	6.7	7.0	6.2	6.6	6.5	8.1	7.5	5.9	5.9	5.5	5.5	6.6	6.3
Nevada	11.8	9.5	9.3	10.9	10.9	8.4	8.5	9.0	9.5	9.1	6.1	6.8	7.1	7.5
New Hampshire	4.9	7.7	6.7	7.7	7.7	9.7	11.0	9.5	6.6	6.7	7.7	5.4	5.6	6.2
New Jersey	4.0	3.9	5.1	4.6	4.6	5.9	7.7	6.9	8.3	8.2	7.1	6.6	7.7	5.5
New Mexico	9.3	10.7	8.8	11.1	12.7	13.7	13.2	7.8	3.7	3.5	5.1	4.8	7.1	9.5
New York	2.9	3.3	4.1	3.7	3.7	4.9	5.5	5.8	5.6	5.5	5.9	6.3	6.9	6.2
North Carolina	7.0	6.1	7.0	6.7	7.4	7.2	7.7	7.0	6.0	5.6	6.1	8.2	8.0	9.7
North Dakota	9.3	8.9	7.0	7.9	7.9	8.0	6.2	5.1	5.0	4.8	5.1	6.7	8.5	8.3
Ohio	6.3	6.5	6.4	5.8	5.9	5.5	5.4	6.2	7.0	7.1	6.8	7.4	8.1	8.9
Oklahoma	17.2	18.9	15.8	13.2	14.7	14.6	9.5	9.7	11.6	11.5	8.9	10.3	11.0	11.4
Oregon	7.0	6.1	6.0	4.0	4.2	3.3	5.1	4.9	5.5	5.6	3.9	4.0	5.9	5.4
Pennsylvania	5.4	5.7	6.0	5.9	6.0	7.2	7.1	7.0	7.3	7.5	8.0	8.0	8.7	10.1
Rhode Island	4.9	4.8	5.0	7.4	7.4	9.6	9.6	8.7	8.6	8.6	8.0	7.1	7.2	6.0
South Carolina	6.2	9.1	10.6	8.4	9.1	8.4	11.1	10.0	11.2	10.6	12.3	9.3	14.1	15.1
South Dakota	8.4	6.9	6.8	6.1	7.1	5.3	4.5	3.1	4.4	4.3	5.3	5.9	9.9	12.6
Tennessee	6.0	7.6	7.2	8.0	9.1	9.5	8.5	6.0	4.7	4.6	4.6	5.4	5.4	7.2
Texas	16.2	17.1	14.5	12.2	12.5	9.7	9.6	8.9	9.1	8.9	7.9	8.2	8.0	8.4
Utah	21.5	21.5	25.8	10.1	10.6	12.6	14.9	14.6	13.1	15.7	7.1	12.3	13.4	14.4
Vermont	4.7	4.8	2.6	2.9	2.9	6.2	6.5	5.3	5.1	5.2	10.3	5.3	4.2	3.7
Virginia	6.0	7.0	7.3	6.2	6.6	5.8	10.3	8.2	7.5	7.7	8.9	7.6	7.4	6.3
Washington	4.2	4.7	4.2	5.4	5.5	3.3	4.1	4.1	5.6	5.0	5.9	6.0	5.6	4.4
West Virginia	9.1	8.8	10.6	10.7	11.5	8.2	6.3	5.4	5.6	6.0	8.5	7.6	5.8	7.5
Wisconsin	4.7	4.7	4.2	3.9	4.1	3.3	4.6	4.9	4.6	4.0	4.6	5.7	5.5	4.9
Wyoming	15.0	16.8	12.0	10.5	12.1	7.9	7.7	6.7	5.0	5.5	6.7	5.0	6.4	8.2

Source: U.S. Bureau of the Census, Current Population Survey/Housing Vacancy Survey.

(1) Revised to reflect new edit procedures that allocate cases that would have been recorded as "not reported" under previous procedures. Also reflects the inclusion of year-round vacant mobile homes for the first time.
(2) Revised using weights based on the 1990 Census.

Market Absorption of Apartments

YEAR OF COMPLETION	Completions	TABLE 3.22. UNFURNISHED RENTAL APARTMENT COMPLETIONS AND ABSORPTION RATES: 1970 TO 1996			
		Percent rented within...			
		3 months	6 months	9 months	12 months
1970	328,400	73	87	93	96
1971	334,400	68	85	92	95
1972	497,900	68	84	92	96
1973	531,700	70	85	93	96
1974	405,500	68	83	90	94
1975	223,100	70	85	92	95
1976	157,000	80	93	97	99
1977	195,600	80	94	97	99
1978	228,700	82	93	97	99
1979	241,200	82	93	97	99
1980	196,100	75	90	95	98
1981	135,400	80	92	96	97
1982	117,000	72	87	93	96
1983	191,500	69	85	92	96
1984	313,200	67	84	92	96
1985	364,500	65	84	92	95
1986	407,600	66	84	92	96
1987	345,600	63	82	90	94
1988	284,500	66	84	91	95
1989	246,400	70	86	93	96
1990 [1]	214,300	67	85	93	96
1991	165,300	70	87	93	97
1992	110,200	74	91	96	98
1993	77,200	75	88	94	96
1994	104,000	80	93	97	98
1995	155,000	73	89	94	97
1996	191,300	72	88	95	98

Source: U.S. Bureau of the Census, Survey of Market Absorption.

Includes only privately-financed, nonsubsidized, unfurnished apartments completed in newly constructed buildings with five units or more.
(1) New ratio estimation procedures were adopted in 1990 to derive more accurate estimates of completions. Caution should be used in comparing numbers of completions in 1990 and later years with those in earlier years.

Market Absorption of Apartments

YEAR OF COMPLETION	Completions	Percent absorbed within...			
		3 months	6 months	9 months	12 months
	TABLE 3.23. COOPERATIVE AND CONDOMINIUM APARTMENT COMPLETIONS AND ABSORPTION RATES: 1970 TO 1996				
1970	72,500	....	....	....	....
1971	49,100	....	....	....	....
1972	57,300	....	....	....	....
1973	98,100	....	....	....	....
1974	159,000	57	....	....	....
1975	84,600	44	....	....	....
1976	46,300	53	....	....	....
1977	43,000	71	....	....	....
1978	54,500	77	....	....	....
1979	91,800	74	....	....	....
1980	122,800	72	....	....	....
1981	112,600	62	....	....	....
1982	107,900	54	....	....	....
1983	111,800	66	....	....	....
1984	143,600	69	82	87	91
1985	135,800	65	77	85	89
1986	101,700	74	82	87	91
1987	92,300	74	83	88	92
1988	76,200	64	76	83	86
1989	59,700	66	77	82	86
1990 [1]	52,600	60	74	80	85
1991	35,300	60	74	80	86
1992	31,100	68	81	87	90
1993	32,000	76	85	90	93
1994	34,400	77	87	91	93
1995	36,400	74	83	89	92
1996	36,900	80	90	94	97

Source: U.S. Bureau of the Census, Survey of Market Absorption.

Includes only apartments completed in buildings with five units or more.

(1) New ratio estimation procedures were adopted in 1990 to derive more accurate estimates of completions. Caution should be used in comparing numbers of completions in 1990 and later years with those in earlier years.

Tenure

TABLE 3.24. HOMEOWNERSHIP RATES BY STATE: 1900 TO 1990
(Percent)

AREA	1900	1910	1920	1930	1940	1950 [1]	1960	1970	1980	1990
United States	46.5	45.9	45.6	47.8	43.6	55.0	61.9	62.9	64.4	64.2
Alabama	34.4	35.1	35.0	34.2	33.6	49.4	59.7	66.7	70.1	70.5
Alaska	....	....	....	....	....	54.5	48.3	50.3	58.3	56.1
Arizona	57.5	49.2	42.8	44.8	47.9	56.4	63.9	65.3	68.3	64.2
Arkansas	47.7	46.6	45.1	40.1	39.7	54.5	61.4	66.7	70.5	69.6
California	46.3	49.5	43.7	46.1	43.4	54.3	58.4	54.9	55.9	55.6
Colorado	46.6	51.5	51.6	50.7	46.3	58.1	63.8	63.4	64.5	62.2
Connecticut	39.0	37.3	37.6	44.5	40.5	51.1	61.9	62.5	63.9	65.6
Delaware	36.3	40.7	44.7	52.1	47.1	58.9	66.9	68.0	69.1	70.2
District of Columbia	24.0	25.2	30.3	38.6	29.9	32.3	30.0	28.2	35.5	38.9
Florida	46.8	44.2	42.5	42.0	43.6	57.6	67.5	68.6	68.3	67.2
Georgia	30.6	30.5	30.9	30.6	30.8	46.5	56.2	61.1	65.0	64.9
Hawaii	....	....	....	....	....	33.0	41.1	46.9	51.7	53.9
Idaho	71.6	68.1	60.9	57.0	57.9	65.5	70.5	70.1	72.0	70.1
Illinois	45.0	44.1	43.8	46.5	40.3	50.1	57.8	59.4	62.6	64.2
Indiana	56.1	54.8	54.8	57.3	53.1	65.5	71.1	71.7	71.7	70.2
Iowa	60.5	58.4	58.1	54.7	51.5	63.4	69.1	71.7	71.8	70.0
Kansas	59.1	59.1	56.9	56.0	51.0	63.9	68.9	69.1	70.2	67.9
Kentucky	51.5	51.6	51.6	51.3	48.0	58.7	64.3	66.9	70.0	69.6
Louisiana	31.4	32.2	33.7	35.0	36.9	50.3	59.0	63.1	65.5	65.9
Maine	64.8	62.5	59.6	61.7	57.3	*62.8	66.5	70.1	70.9	70.5
Maryland	40.0	44.0	49.9	55.2	47.4	56.3	64.5	58.8	62.0	65.0
Massachusetts	35.0	33.1	34.8	43.5	38.1	47.9	55.9	57.5	57.5	59.3
Michigan	62.3	61.7	58.9	59.0	55.4	67.5	74.4	74.4	72.7	71.0
Minnesota	63.5	61.9	60.7	58.9	55.2	66.4	72.1	71.5	71.7	71.8
Mississippi	34.5	34.0	34.0	32.5	33.3	47.8	57.7	66.3	71.0	71.5
Missouri	50.9	51.1	49.5	49.9	44.3	57.7	64.3	67.2	69.6	68.8
Montana	56.6	60.0	60.5	54.5	52.0	60.3	64.0	65.7	68.6	67.3
Nebraska	56.8	59.1	57.4	54.3	47.1	60.6	64.8	66.4	68.4	66.5
Nevada	66.2	53.4	47.6	47.1	46.1	48.7	56.3	58.5	59.6	54.8
New Hampshire	53.9	51.2	49.8	55.0	51.7	58.1	65.1	68.2	67.6	68.2
New Jersey	34.3	35.0	38.3	48.4	39.4	53.1	61.3	60.9	62.0	64.9
New Mexico	68.5	70.6	59.4	57.4	57.3	58.8	65.3	66.4	68.1	67.4
New York	33.2	31.0	30.7	37.1	30.3	37.9	44.8	47.3	48.6	52.2
North Carolina	46.6	47.3	47.4	44.5	42.4	53.3	60.1	65.4	68.4	68.0
North Dakota	80.0	75.7	65.3	58.6	49.8	66.2	68.4	68.4	68.7	65.6
Ohio	52.5	51.3	51.6	54.4	50.0	61.1	67.4	67.7	68.4	67.5
Oklahoma	54.2	45.4	45.5	41.3	42.8	60.0	67.0	69.2	70.7	68.1
Oregon	58.7	60.1	54.8	59.1	55.4	65.3	69.3	66.1	65.1	63.1
Pennsylvania	41.2	41.6	45.2	54.4	45.9	59.7	68.3	68.8	69.9	70.6
Rhode Island	28.6	28.3	31.1	41.2	37.4	45.3	54.5	57.9	58.8	59.5
South Carolina	30.6	30.8	32.2	30.9	30.6	45.1	57.3	66.1	70.2	69.8
South Dakota	71.2	68.2	61.5	53.1	45.0	62.2	67.2	69.6	69.3	66.1
Tennessee	46.3	47.0	47.7	46.2	44.1	56.5	63.7	66.7	68.6	68.0
Texas	46.5	45.1	42.8	41.7	42.8	56.7	64.8	64.7	64.3	60.9
Utah	67.8	64.8	60.0	60.9	61.1	65.3	71.7	69.3	70.7	68.1
Vermont	60.4	58.5	57.5	59.8	55.9	61.3	66.0	69.1	68.7	69.0
Virginia	48.8	51.5	51.1	52.4	48.9	55.1	61.3	62.0	65.6	66.3
Washington	54.5	57.3	54.7	59.4	57.0	65.0	68.5	66.8	65.6	62.6
West Virginia	54.6	49.5	46.8	45.9	43.7	55.0	64.3	68.9	73.6	74.1
Wisconsin	66.4	64.6	63.6	63.2	54.4	63.5	68.6	69.1	68.2	66.7
Wyoming	55.2	54.5	51.9	48.3	48.6	54.0	62.2	66.4	69.2	67.8

Source: U.S. Bureau of the Census, 1900-1990 Censuses. Table prepared by Robert Bonnette.

(1) Alaska and Hawaii are not included in the 1950 national homeownership rate. The national homeownership rate does not change if they are included.

Tenure

TABLE 3.25. HOMEOWNERSHIP RATES BY HOUSEHOLD CHARACTERISTIC AND STATE: 1950 TO 1990
(Percent)

| | | | | 1950[1] | | | |
| | | | | Age of householder | | | |
AREA	Total, all occupied units	One-person households	Recent movers	Under 35	65 and older	Black householder	Hispanic householder[2]
United States	55.0	42.1	....	....	67.9	34.5	....
Alabama	49.4	42.1	....	....	....	35.6	....
Alaska	54.5	53.1	....	....	....	....	....
Arizona	56.4	40.7	....	....	....	40.4	....
Arkansas	54.5	49.6	....	....	....	39.8	....
California	54.3	33.6	....	....	....	36.5	....
Colorado	58.1	40.9	....	....	....	44.7	....
Connecticut	51.1	36.7	....	....	....	19.5	....
Delaware	58.9	46.3	....	....	....	36.0	....
District of Columbia	32.3	13.7	....	....	....	30.3	....
Florida	57.6	47.0	....	....	....	39.6	....
Georgia	46.5	40.1	....	....	....	29.2	....
Hawaii	33.0	14.7	....	....	....	....	....
Idaho	65.5	55.9	....	....	....	41.7	....
Illinois	50.1	35.7	....	....	....	21.0	....
Indiana	65.5	56.5	....	....	....	45.0	....
Iowa	63.4	58.3	....	....	....	61.0	....
Kansas	63.9	58.8	....	....	....	62.9	....
Kentucky	58.7	52.6	....	....	....	43.2	....
Louisiana	50.3	38.7	....	....	....	36.1	....
Maine	62.8	54.3	....	....	....	57.0	....
Maryland	56.3	42.9	....	....	....	33.0	....
Massachusetts	47.9	33.6	....	....	....	25.5	....
Michigan	67.5	52.8	....	....	....	39.5	....
Minnesota	66.4	49.2	....	....	....	46.2	....
Mississippi	47.8	41.3	....	....	....	30.8	....
Missouri	57.7	45.3	....	....	....	30.1	....
Montana	60.3	46.0	....	....	....	53.6	....
Nebraska	60.6	54.6	....	....	....	56.2	....
Nevada	48.7	36.4	....	....	....	45.8	....
New Hampshire	58.1	46.6	....	....	....	41.9	....
New Jersey	53.1	39.0	....	....	....	31.9	....
New Mexico	58.8	47.7	....	....	....	42.5	....
New York	37.9	22.7	....	....	....	11.0	....
North Carolina	53.3	50.0	....	....	....	36.3	....
North Dakota	66.2	58.1	....	....	....	51.8	....
Ohio	61.1	49.6	....	....	....	36.0	....
Oklahoma	60.0	53.5	....	....	....	54.8	....
Oregon	65.3	46.7	....	....	....	37.7	....
Pennsylvania	59.7	43.2	....	....	....	31.5	....
Rhode Island	45.3	34.0	....	....	....	24.0	....
South Carolina	45.1	40.6	....	....	....	33.2	....
South Dakota	62.2	55.7	....	....	....	56.4	....
Tennessee	56.5	46.8	....	....	....	35.4	....
Texas	56.7	48.9	....	....	....	47.1	....
Utah	65.3	50.9	....	....	....	37.9	....
Vermont	61.3	51.1	....	....	....	54.3	....
Virginia	55.1	47.5	....	....	....	46.5	....
Washington	65.0	44.5	....	....	....	36.7	....
West Virginia	55.0	48.0	....	....	....	35.4	....
Wisconsin	63.5	55.2	....	....	....	31.0	....
Wyoming	54.0	43.1	....	....	....	24.1	....

See notes at end of table.

Tenure

TABLE 3.25. HOMEOWNERSHIP RATES BY HOUSEHOLD CHARACTERISTIC AND STATE: 1950 TO 1990 - Continued
(Percent)

AREA	Total, all occupied units	One-person households	Recent movers	Age of householder Under 35	Age of householder 65 and older[3]	Black householder[4]	Hispanic householder[4]
United States	61.9	40.8	34.0	....	68.8	....	....
Alabama	59.7	47.7	31.9	....	66.3	....	....
Alaska	48.3	37.2	26.9	....	72.1	....	....
Arizona	63.9	44.6	42.0	....	71.1	....	....
Arkansas	61.4	54.0	30.7	....	71.2	....	....
California	58.4	31.3	32.3	....	61.9	....	....
Colorado	63.8	39.5	35.5	....	68.9	....	....
Connecticut	61.9	37.4	35.0	....	66.8	....	....
Delaware	66.9	46.2	39.2	....	73.8	....	....
District of Columbia	30.0	11.9	10.0	....	43.7	....	....
Florida	67.5	50.4	45.3	....	76.4	....	....
Georgia	56.2	43.7	29.7	....	64.0	....	....
Hawaii	41.1	17.5	18.3	....	52.9	....	....
Idaho	70.5	53.8	41.0	....	78.4	....	....
Illinois	57.8	34.7	30.7	....	66.9	....	....
Indiana	71.1	55.8	39.4	....	80.0	....	....
Iowa	69.1	57.2	39.6	....	80.0	....	....
Kansas	68.9	59.4	36.3	....	81.7	....	....
Kentucky	64.3	51.8	33.2	....	74.9	....	....
Louisiana	59.0	43.7	32.0	....	66.2	....	....
Maine	66.5	49.8	33.6	....	72.7	....	....
Maryland	64.5	40.0	35.1	....	70.7	....	....
Massachusetts	55.9	29.9	30.1	....	55.8	....	....
Michigan	74.4	51.4	41.0	....	79.8	....	....
Minnesota	72.1	46.7	40.7	....	76.3	....	....
Mississippi	57.7	51.1	29.6	....	67.9	....	....
Missouri	64.3	44.6	35.8	....	70.9	....	....
Montana	64.0	44.2	32.9	....	71.1	....	....
Nebraska	64.8	54.0	34.5	....	78.6	....	....
Nevada	56.3	34.7	34.4	....	63.7	....	....
New Hampshire	65.1	44.1	37.4	....	68.2	....	....
New Jersey	61.3	36.7	36.3	....	64.8	....	....
New Mexico	65.3	50.5	39.0	....	77.5	....	....
New York	44.8	21.4	25.1	....	47.2	....	....
North Carolina	60.1	50.1	30.0	....	73.6	....	....
North Dakota	68.4	52.6	37.0	....	78.7	....	....
Ohio	67.4	48.1	36.5	....	74.9	....	....
Oklahoma	67.0	55.3	35.3	....	76.1	....	....
Oregon	69.3	46.4	39.4	....	75.2	....	....
Pennsylvania	68.3	44.5	36.2	....	73.2	....	....
Rhode Island	54.5	33.4	28.0	....	59.1	....	....
South Carolina	57.3	46.9	30.1	....	66.4	....	....
South Dakota	67.2	56.9	38.6	....	78.3	....	....
Tennessee	63.7	48.5	33.8	....	72.1	....	....
Texas	64.8	50.3	35.2	....	75.4	....	....
Utah	71.7	48.9	39.2	....	77.4	....	....
Vermont	66.0	46.2	34.8	....	69.6	....	....
Virginia	61.3	44.4	32.1	....	75.0	....	....
Washington	68.5	42.4	36.5	....	71.1	....	....
West Virginia	64.3	51.0	30.7	....	74.2	....	....
Wisconsin	68.6	49.1	35.5	....	76.5	....	....
Wyoming	62.2	42.5	35.2	....	72.9	....	....

See notes at end of table.

Tenure

TABLE 3.25. HOMEOWNERSHIP RATES BY HOUSEHOLD CHARACTERISTIC AND STATE: 1950 TO 1990 - Continued
(Percent)

AREA	1970						
	Total, all occupied units	One-person households	Recent movers	Age of householder		Black householder	Hispanic householder[5]
				Under 35	65 and older		
United States	62.9	42.4	31.4	41.2	67.5	41.6	43.7
Alabama	66.7	53.4	35.7	....	69.5	50.4	53.0
Alaska	50.3	35.5	27.6	....	68.9	25.2	28.4
Arizona	65.3	47.5	39.6	....	72.9	49.3	59.8
Arkansas	66.7	56.6	35.0	....	73.2	52.9	49.6
California	54.9	30.7	24.2	....	59.9	39.1	46.4
Colorado	63.4	39.8	32.0	....	68.3	47.1	54.6
Connecticut	62.5	37.8	28.6	....	63.6	22.9	26.8
Delaware	68.0	46.2	34.7	....	71.4	49.9	42.4
District of Columbia	28.2	13.4	8.6	....	41.9	27.3	17.0
Florida	68.6	53.5	42.2	....	74.7	48.7	49.2
Georgia	61.1	44.9	33.1	....	65.3	41.3	41.7
Hawaii	46.9	25.0	20.0	....	58.5	11.4	34.5
Idaho	70.1	55.7	36.8	....	78.7	29.1	48.1
Illinois	59.4	37.4	28.8	....	64.2	29.0	29.1
Indiana	71.7	56.6	37.2	....	78.6	51.0	50.7
Iowa	71.7	58.9	36.9	....	79.8	55.5	57.9
Kansas	69.1	58.8	31.7	....	81.0	54.1	55.6
Kentucky	66.9	53.5	33.1	....	74.4	48.2	43.0
Louisiana	63.1	49.0	31.1	....	69.1	47.1	48.6
Maine	70.1	51.5	36.2	....	72.6	30.8	39.6
Maryland	58.8	36.2	25.0	....	64.4	37.7	45.3
Massachusetts	57.5	31.7	24.9	....	54.8	24.7	25.3
Michigan	74.4	52.5	41.0	....	78.0	53.4	60.7
Minnesota	71.5	46.8	34.9	....	74.1	41.9	51.0
Mississippi	66.3	57.0	37.6	....	71.7	49.1	50.6
Missouri	67.2	49.2	34.6	....	71.9	43.3	53.7
Montana	65.7	47.4	30.7	....	71.6	24.3	42.9
Nebraska	66.4	52.4	31.8	....	75.9	48.3	49.8
Nevada	58.5	35.0	33.5	....	61.9	38.7	55.2
New Hampshire	68.2	46.1	38.2	....	67.5	32.2	47.1
New Jersey	60.9	35.0	31.5	....	60.0	33.6	26.2
New Mexico	66.4	50.3	33.2	....	75.4	46.4	68.5
New York	47.3	24.4	24.4	....	45.9	19.7	14.1
North Carolina	65.4	53.8	34.6	....	73.5	45.5	44.6
North Dakota	68.4	51.3	29.6	....	75.4	6.8	21.6
Ohio	67.7	46.4	33.3	....	71.3	44.6	52.8
Oklahoma	69.2	57.6	34.0	....	77.9	59.6	53.7
Oregon	66.1	47.1	32.5	....	73.7	45.5	46.8
Pennsylvania	68.8	46.2	33.4	....	70.2	46.1	45.4
Rhode Island	57.9	34.4	24.9	....	56.0	24.7	29.8
South Carolina	66.1	54.1	38.7	....	70.4	49.7	34.5
South Dakota	69.6	57.2	33.5	....	78.0	23.1	36.9
Tennessee	66.7	51.1	33.9	....	72.2	43.7	49.1
Texas	64.7	50.1	31.0	....	74.8	53.8	59.6
Utah	69.3	50.9	30.2	....	78.4	43.9	50.5
Vermont	69.1	48.2	39.3	....	69.0	38.4	60.0
Virginia	62.0	42.8	29.0	....	72.5	51.5	39.6
Washington	66.8	42.9	32.0	....	70.3	49.1	50.3
West Virginia	68.9	55.9	35.7	....	74.1	58.7	62.0
Wisconsin	69.1	48.0	33.3	....	74.0	34.2	40.3
Wyoming	66.4	49.9	34.7	....	73.8	37.8	50.9

See notes at end of table.

Tenure

TABLE 3.25. HOMEOWNERSHIP RATES BY HOUSEHOLD CHARACTERISTIC AND STATE: 1950 TO 1990 - Continued
(Percent)

AREA	Total, all occupied units	One-person households	Recent movers	Age of householder Under 35	Age of householder 65 and older	Black householder	Hispanic householder
United States	64.4	43.5	33.5	43.8	70.1	44.4	43.4
Alabama	70.1	53.7	38.3	52.2	74.8	56.4	56.4
Alaska	58.3	41.1	32.5	42.9	71.0	31.0	39.5
Arizona	68.3	51.8	41.6	46.4	79.5	47.6	60.2
Arkansas	70.5	56.5	39.5	50.4	76.8	55.7	54.2
California	55.9	35.8	28.5	32.5	64.6	39.6	42.4
Colorado	64.5	42.6	36.5	44.8	71.3	43.0	55.1
Connecticut	63.9	38.9	30.9	40.3	65.9	28.9	25.0
Delaware	69.1	47.8	35.2	48.2	72.5	50.4	46.3
District of Columbia	35.5	22.3	16.5	15.3	48.6	33.1	20.7
Florida	68.3	53.6	42.2	43.5	77.0	49.6	50.7
Georgia	65.0	46.2	34.5	46.5	70.2	47.1	47.6
Hawaii	51.7	33.7	24.5	27.6	64.5	13.4	37.8
Idaho	72.0	54.3	40.4	52.5	81.0	36.0	47.7
Illinois	62.6	40.4	31.2	42.7	67.3	35.3	33.1
Indiana	71.7	51.8	37.3	52.6	76.8	50.5	55.7
Iowa	71.8	53.1	37.4	51.6	77.5	45.6	56.3
Kansas	70.2	53.0	36.1	47.9	79.4	48.0	53.5
Kentucky	70.0	53.2	37.0	52.4	76.0	47.9	56.6
Louisiana	65.5	48.2	35.2	47.0	74.3	51.0	54.9
Maine	70.9	49.9	34.1	52.9	71.9	34.3	51.7
Maryland	62.0	40.0	30.5	40.4	67.0	40.8	48.7
Massachusetts	57.5	31.8	24.7	35.6	56.4	26.3	21.8
Michigan	72.7	50.4	39.0	53.4	76.9	52.5	58.8
Minnesota	71.7	45.5	37.3	53.5	71.8	36.6	49.2
Mississippi	71.0	58.2	40.2	53.3	77.1	58.9	57.7
Missouri	69.6	49.0	36.7	49.3	73.2	48.8	56.9
Montana	68.6	47.4	38.0	49.3	73.8	29.1	48.7
Nebraska	68.4	48.0	35.2	47.1	76.4	45.3	51.2
Nevada	59.6	39.1	34.3	41.7	66.0	41.5	48.6
New Hampshire	67.6	44.1	35.6	49.0	68.5	37.4	48.0
New Jersey	62.0	36.4	31.1	39.8	63.7	35.9	27.3
New Mexico	68.1	50.9	38.7	48.2	77.6	45.3	67.9
New York	48.6	25.6	22.5	29.9	49.1	22.1	14.8
North Carolina	68.4	52.6	36.5	49.0	75.4	51.0	49.4
North Dakota	68.7	45.7	36.5	49.7	72.4	14.1	36.1
Ohio	68.4	45.1	33.4	48.2	72.0	44.8	53.4
Oklahoma	70.7	55.8	38.3	49.7	79.8	55.0	49.1
Oregon	65.1	45.5	33.8	42.5	75.6	41.3	42.1
Pennsylvania	69.9	47.1	34.2	49.7	71.8	49.7	42.8
Rhode Island	58.8	33.0	26.4	38.9	56.1	27.3	31.1
South Carolina	70.2	55.2	39.0	52.9	75.9	59.2	54.5
South Dakota	69.3	48.6	37.2	50.6	72.3	22.9	44.8
Tennessee	68.6	50.2	35.5	48.5	74.7	48.4	55.5
Texas	64.3	45.9	31.8	41.7	77.1	51.1	56.1
Utah	70.7	51.2	37.4	50.9	82.7	35.5	51.3
Vermont	68.7	47.5	34.3	49.5	71.0	42.1	60.6
Virginia	65.6	46.2	34.4	44.1	74.4	51.2	46.1
Washington	65.6	43.8	34.4	43.8	72.5	42.0	44.5
West Virginia	73.6	57.9	42.1	57.0	78.2	60.7	69.0
Wisconsin	68.2	43.5	31.8	46.7	71.5	34.9	41.2
Wyoming	69.2	49.4	45.7	53.5	77.6	39.3	59.1

See notes at end of table.

Tenure

TABLE 3.25. HOMEOWNERSHIP RATES BY HOUSEHOLD CHARACTERISTIC AND STATE: 1950 TO 1990 - Continued
(Percent)

AREA	Total, all occupied units	One-person households	Recent movers	1990 Age of householder Under 35	65 and older	Black householder	Hispanic householder
United States	64.2	48.7	28.8	39.6	75.2	43.4	42.4
Alabama	70.5	57.2	32.8	48.5	79.4	56.9	52.0
Alaska	56.1	43.2	22.5	34.6	74.3	28.0	37.1
Arizona	64.2	50.7	28.4	37.7	81.1	41.1	54.0
Arkansas	69.6	58.1	31.6	45.1	79.9	53.0	47.7
California	55.6	43.7	26.1	29.7	72.5	36.5	40.4
Colorado	62.2	45.1	25.8	37.2	75.4	38.7	50.7
Connecticut	65.6	47.8	27.0	41.0	71.6	31.4	25.9
Delaware	70.2	55.5	37.4	47.9	79.1	48.4	44.1
District of Columbia	38.9	29.7	15.4	17.0	54.4	35.7	20.5
Florida	67.2	57.4	33.4	39.7	81.9	46.9	50.4
Georgia	64.9	50.8	28.6	41.9	76.6	46.1	40.6
Hawaii	53.9	40.8	22.5	24.6	71.9	12.4	38.1
Idaho	70.1	56.3	34.0	43.8	83.2	38.2	46.5
Illinois	64.2	46.8	30.4	39.9	73.9	38.0	39.8
Indiana	70.2	53.5	32.9	47.2	78.4	45.9	56.6
Iowa	70.0	54.6	31.9	43.2	79.8	38.8	50.3
Kansas	67.9	53.2	28.1	41.6	80.7	42.9	51.5
Kentucky	69.6	56.1	32.7	47.0	79.2	43.1	47.8
Louisiana	65.9	53.2	24.8	42.8	79.1	50.8	53.8
Maine	70.5	51.9	31.1	48.6	73.6	29.9	47.0
Maryland	65.0	49.6	33.0	42.7	73.7	43.3	46.2
Massachusetts	59.3	39.7	22.3	33.7	64.0	26.4	18.7
Michigan	71.0	53.7	34.6	47.6	78.8	47.7	56.0
Minnesota	71.8	50.9	33.7	50.6	75.2	30.9	46.7
Mississippi	71.5	61.9	33.1	49.5	82.1	60.0	56.2
Missouri	68.8	52.0	30.9	45.1	76.7	45.3	54.7
Montana	67.3	51.3	30.0	41.1	77.9	30.5	46.7
Nebraska	66.5	50.3	26.9	39.0	79.4	39.7	48.8
Nevada	54.8	40.1	28.5	32.7	68.2	33.6	40.1
New Hampshire	68.2	48.2	29.2	46.4	72.9	34.4	40.6
New Jersey	64.9	46.6	30.8	42.1	71.2	37.3	31.2
New Mexico	67.4	53.4	30.1	43.9	81.2	43.0	67.5
New York	52.2	34.6	24.1	32.3	57.2	24.7	17.1
North Carolina	68.0	55.4	31.0	44.2	79.2	49.6	41.4
North Dakota	65.6	46.4	25.9	38.7	74.1	13.4	32.9
Ohio	67.5	49.5	29.9	42.7	76.4	42.0	50.3
Oklahoma	68.1	56.4	26.9	41.5	82.9	47.4	46.7
Oregon	63.1	47.6	30.6	33.1	78.0	37.5	38.4
Pennsylvania	70.6	52.4	32.3	47.2	76.1	50.7	43.0
Rhode Island	59.5	39.5	23.5	35.8	62.0	26.5	23.0
South Carolina	69.8	58.4	32.5	46.8	81.5	58.8	47.7
South Dakota	66.1	48.2	29.7	42.5	73.3	24.1	40.9
Tennessee	68.0	53.0	30.9	43.7	78.8	47.2	48.6
Texas	60.9	45.3	22.1	34.3	79.8	45.2	53.2
Utah	68.1	52.2	27.8	42.1	84.9	36.3	49.5
Vermont	69.0	51.1	32.7	45.3	75.0	40.0	55.8
Virginia	66.3	53.4	31.6	41.6	78.1	49.2	40.9
Washington	62.6	45.8	28.8	35.4	76.7	35.8	40.4
West Virginia	74.1	61.7	33.2	50.3	82.2	54.4	63.1
Wisconsin	66.7	46.8	28.3	40.7	74.0	30.2	39.0
Wyoming	67.8	53.2	29.7	44.0	80.6	41.4	58.1

Source: U.S. Bureau of the Census, Census of Housing 1950-1990. Table prepared by Robert Bonnette.

(1) Alaska and Hawaii are not included in the 1950 national homeownership rate. (2) Hispanic households were not separately identified in 1950. (3) In 1960, homeownership rates for householders 65 and over were estimated from the report "Housing of Senior Citizens" (Volume VII). (4) Black and Hispanic households were not separately identified in 1960. (5) Hispanic in 1970 was restricted to householder of "Spanish language"; that is, one who reported Spanish as his or her mother tongue.

Persons of Hispanic origin may be of any race.

Tenure

TABLE 3.26. HOMEOWNERSHIP RATES BY UNITS IN STRUCTURE AND STATE: 1950 TO 1990
(Percent)

AREA	1950[1] Total, all occupied units	Units in structure 1 unit, detached	5 or more units	Mobile home	1960 Total, all occupied units	Units in structure 1 unit, detached	5 or more units	Mobile home
United States	55.0	73.0	4.1	79.4	61.9	78.3	4.6	88.3
Alabama	49.4	57.8	3.2	78.4	59.7	67.7	4.1	88.3
Alaska	54.5	....	....	....	48.3	71.4	2.5	85.1
Arizona	56.4	65.0	5.6	77.7	63.9	71.5	9.1	83.7
Arkansas	54.5	59.2	7.2	62.1	61.4	65.8	12.7	86.3
California	54.3	72.1	4.8	74.9	58.4	75.6	4.2	83.5
Colorado	58.1	73.6	5.1	84.1	63.8	78.4	4.9	90.6
Connecticut	51.1	84.2	4.1	88.1	61.9	88.2	4.7	92.1
Delaware	58.9	72.8	5.6	89.0	66.9	79.4	7.5	82.5
District of Columbia	32.3	80.4	3.4	75.2	30.0	80.7	3.9	89.6
Florida	57.6	69.5	6.6	86.7	67.5	79.6	9.3	89.5
Georgia	46.5	56.3	3.4	76.7	56.2	66.8	3.5	84.2
Hawaii	33.0	....	....	....	41.1	57.3	5.6	36.0
Idaho	65.5	73.4	7.1	79.2	70.5	77.3	8.5	92.2
Illinois	50.1	77.0	5.3	80.8	57.8	82.2	5.3	89.6
Indiana	65.5	78.3	5.7	81.4	71.1	81.0	5.5	88.8
Iowa	63.4	72.4	7.5	80.9	69.1	76.6	6.1	90.8
Kansas	63.9	73.5	8.3	84.2	68.9	75.9	8.2	90.4
Kentucky	58.7	68.0	5.8	78.8	64.3	72.2	7.6	86.0
Louisiana	50.3	61.4	4.8	86.6	59.0	70.4	6.2	91.4
Maine	62.8	83.2	6.1	83.7	66.5	85.4	7.8	90.1
Maryland	56.3	75.8	3.0	82.9	64.5	81.8	5.3	86.7
Massachusetts	47.9	86.8	3.5	86.1	55.9	88.8	4.2	94.4
Michigan	67.5	85.2	3.8	82.8	74.4	87.4	4.3	91.2
Minnesota	66.4	82.3	6.3	82.0	72.1	86.3	4.6	92.7
Mississippi	47.8	52.5	5.4	72.7	57.7	62.6	5.8	90.5
Missouri	57.7	75.8	5.5	80.7	64.3	79.5	4.9	86.1
Montana	60.3	71.8	6.1	77.4	64.0	74.3	7.5	91.0
Nebraska	60.6	69.6	6.0	82.5	64.8	73.8	6.0	90.8
Nevada	48.7	58.7	7.9	72.8	56.3	70.3	8.3	85.6
New Hampshire	58.1	83.6	5.7	84.0	65.1	86.0	6.9	92.9
New Jersey	53.1	84.8	3.6	83.1	61.3	88.8	3.9	93.4
New Mexico	58.8	67.0	9.1	83.6	65.3	71.7	18.6	87.6
New York	37.9	84.4	2.8	78.9	44.8	88.5	4.0	92.4
North Carolina	53.3	60.3	3.9	75.6	60.1	65.9	3.1	83.3
North Dakota	66.2	74.8	7.4	77.0	68.4	77.3	8.2	92.3
Ohio	61.1	80.3	4.4	81.5	67.4	83.2	3.7	89.6
Oklahoma	60.0	67.7	5.2	80.7	67.0	73.3	6.8	87.3
Oregon	65.3	77.4	4.3	81.4	69.3	79.1	5.0	92.3
Pennsylvania	59.7	79.1	6.6	83.8	68.3	83.6	6.0	90.1
Rhode Island	45.3	81.8	5.5	87.3	54.5	85.6	5.1	82.3
South Carolina	45.1	51.2	3.4	83.1	57.3	62.5	3.6	84.5
South Dakota	62.2	69.9	6.3	80.7	67.2	73.6	7.7	90.5
Tennessee	56.5	66.3	3.8	68.6	63.7	72.3	3.8	83.5
Texas	56.7	65.8	4.9	77.9	64.8	72.6	4.2	87.7
Utah	65.3	83.2	5.5	70.8	71.7	86.0	4.1	89.1
Vermont	61.3	81.1	5.9	80.8	66.0	83.1	5.9	91.7
Virginia	55.1	70.0	2.9	81.2	61.3	73.9	2.2	87.1
Washington	65.0	79.2	3.8	78.4	68.5	81.3	4.7	89.8
West Virginia	55.0	63.6	6.6	79.1	64.3	70.6	11.1	87.8
Wisconsin	63.5	80.9	4.8	71.8	68.6	84.3	3.7	91.7
Wyoming	54.0	65.3	5.4	74.3	62.2	71.1	7.4	89.8

See notes at end of table.

Tenure

TABLE 3.26. HOMEOWNERSHIP RATES BY UNITS IN STRUCTURE AND STATE: 1950 TO 1990 - Continued
(Percent)

AREA	1970				1980[2]			
		Units in structure				Units in structure		
	Total, all occupied units	1 unit, detached	5 or more units	Mobile home	Total, all occupied units	1 unit, detached	5 or more units	Mobile home
United States	62.9	81.6	5.2	84.5	64.4	85.6	10.2	79.8
Alabama	66.7	74.8	2.6	82.9	70.1	81.9	10.5	80.4
Alaska	50.3	74.9	3.0	80.1	58.3	82.5	10.9	78.0
Arizona	65.3	76.4	10.9	82.2	68.3	83.7	13.3	79.6
Arkansas	66.7	72.5	6.0	78.9	70.5	79.8	12.9	73.6
California	54.9	75.5	4.9	87.0	55.9	80.2	9.2	83.3
Colorado	63.4	80.4	5.3	85.8	64.5	84.6	12.5	80.8
Connecticut	62.5	90.9	4.3	87.5	63.9	92.4	9.7	81.8
Delaware	68.0	85.1	1.3	80.4	69.1	89.0	8.0	79.4
District of Columbia	28.2	79.3	3.5	63.4	35.5	84.8	11.4	25.1
Florida	68.6	82.9	19.4	86.2	68.3	86.2	33.3	80.6
Georgia	61.1	74.2	2.0	80.3	65.0	82.0	8.1	75.3
Hawaii	46.9	66.5	11.6	49.7	51.7	73.8	27.0	59.2
Idaho	70.1	77.5	7.4	84.2	72.0	83.2	11.4	81.6
Illinois	59.4	85.7	5.2	84.0	62.6	88.8	13.7	78.1
Indiana	71.7	83.7	4.7	84.9	71.7	87.2	6.0	80.1
Iowa	71.7	81.5	4.7	87.5	71.8	85.4	6.4	83.7
Kansas	69.1	78.4	7.1	85.5	70.2	83.6	7.4	75.7
Kentucky	66.9	76.7	3.8	82.1	70.0	83.0	8.9	77.9
Louisiana	63.1	74.7	3.3	83.5	65.5	81.2	10.7	81.0
Maine	70.1	88.6	5.4	87.9	70.9	89.9	5.2	84.9
Maryland	58.8	85.2	1.5	83.3	62.0	88.8	8.3	78.2
Massachusetts	57.5	92.3	2.8	87.3	57.5	93.1	5.9	82.8
Michigan	74.4	89.4	5.5	88.7	72.7	89.9	7.7	83.8
Minnesota	71.5	89.5	2.5	90.2	71.7	92.1	7.8	86.8
Mississippi	66.3	71.8	4.3	80.2	71.0	80.3	14.3	79.3
Missouri	67.2	83.0	5.1	81.6	69.6	86.3	8.1	77.9
Montana	65.7	76.3	6.9	84.2	68.6	81.7	11.4	80.3
Nebraska	66.4	77.6	3.7	84.7	68.4	83.2	5.7	77.6
Nevada	58.5	77.2	5.3	82.6	59.6	83.9	8.4	79.8
New Hampshire	68.2	90.4	5.2	86.9	67.6	91.3	6.0	86.8
New Jersey	60.9	91.8	3.1	85.3	62.0	93.1	5.7	83.7
New Mexico	66.4	74.0	7.9	83.5	68.1	80.7	13.6	80.2
New York	47.3	90.7	6.5	86.6	48.6	91.6	6.1	78.9
North Carolina	65.4	72.6	3.2	78.6	68.4	79.8	12.5	73.0
North Dakota	68.4	82.5	5.0	87.2	68.7	87.1	10.4	88.5
Ohio	67.7	85.9	2.6	85.5	68.4	88.8	6.3	82.3
Oklahoma	69.2	76.5	4.0	85.1	70.7	82.0	9.1	80.7
Oregon	66.1	77.9	4.6	87.6	65.1	81.9	7.2	83.9
Pennsylvania	68.8	87.7	3.8	86.0	69.9	90.3	7.1	81.2
Rhode Island	57.9	88.9	4.0	86.7	58.8	91.2	3.9	82.1
South Carolina	66.1	72.0	5.0	79.8	70.2	80.7	15.9	75.7
South Dakota	69.6	78.2	5.8	85.5	69.3	83.3	8.0	78.8
Tennessee	66.7	77.6	2.2	81.0	68.6	83.7	8.4	72.5
Texas	64.7	76.3	2.6	84.0	64.3	81.7	9.5	78.0
Utah	69.3	84.9	5.6	84.4	70.7	88.8	12.4	83.2
Vermont	69.1	87.7	5.6	87.0	68.7	88.1	8.1	81.3
Virginia	62.0	78.9	1.4	84.4	65.6	84.4	10.6	79.4
Washington	66.8	81.2	4.2	85.7	65.6	83.0	10.5	82.8
West Virginia	68.9	76.2	6.3	84.9	73.6	82.8	12.5	81.1
Wisconsin	69.1	87.8	2.6	88.5	68.2	89.9	6.0	81.5
Wyoming	66.4	74.4	7.7	86.2	69.2	82.1	13.1	80.6

See notes at end of table.

Tenure

TABLE 3.26. HOMEOWNERSHIP RATES BY UNITS IN STRUCTURE AND STATE: 1950 TO 1990 - Continued
(Percent)

AREA	Total, all occupied units	1990 Units in structure		
		1 unit, detached	5 or more units	Mobile home
United States	64.2	85.5	9.6	79.8
Alabama	70.5	83.8	3.0	81.0
Alaska	56.1	80.5	9.1	71.4
Arizona	64.2	84.4	5.5	80.6
Arkansas	69.6	80.9	2.5	75.2
California	55.6	79.9	7.7	82.8
Colorado	62.2	82.7	9.4	77.5
Connecticut	65.6	92.4	15.8	87.5
Delaware	70.2	90.8	7.0	83.9
District of Columbia	38.9	86.0	13.7	48.4
Florida	67.2	85.9	30.5	82.7
Georgia	64.9	83.5	4.0	74.8
Hawaii	53.9	73.7	30.0	64.1
Idaho	70.1	82.1	3.4	77.4
Illinois	64.2	89.1	14.4	78.0
Indiana	70.2	86.9	2.1	81.3
Iowa	70.0	84.3	4.3	81.4
Kansas	67.9	83.1	2.7	75.0
Kentucky	69.6	84.7	4.2	78.3
Louisiana	65.9	82.2	3.4	81.5
Maine	70.5	90.6	3.7	85.6
Maryland	65.0	89.9	10.8	79.1
Massachusetts	59.3	92.5	11.5	88.6
Michigan	71.0	88.1	4.7	84.9
Minnesota	71.8	92.8	7.9	86.9
Mississippi	71.5	82.7	2.0	80.4
Missouri	68.8	86.0	5.6	77.6
Montana	67.3	80.3	3.5	77.3
Nebraska	66.5	82.2	2.9	73.6
Nevada	54.8	82.8	3.9	79.4
New Hampshire	68.2	91.7	8.3	88.9
New Jersey	64.9	92.8	12.2	89.9
New Mexico	67.4	81.1	2.7	80.2
New York	52.2	91.1	12.9	82.6
North Carolina	68.0	82.1	5.3	74.4
North Dakota	65.6	86.2	5.0	86.0
Ohio	67.5	88.1	4.2	81.1
Oklahoma	68.1	80.6	2.5	79.5
Oregon	63.1	80.2	2.8	80.9
Pennsylvania	70.6	91.1	6.0	80.9
Rhode Island	59.5	91.1	5.7	88.3
South Carolina	69.8	83.2	6.3	77.2
South Dakota	66.1	81.0	2.2	78.1
Tennessee	68.0	85.2	3.4	74.8
Texas	60.9	81.1	2.7	77.9
Utah	68.1	87.6	7.4	80.9
Vermont	69.0	89.4	6.3	82.2
Virginia	66.3	85.6	11.0	78.1
Washington	62.6	82.4	7.1	80.1
West Virginia	74.1	84.6	3.2	79.3
Wisconsin	66.7	89.5	4.2	82.4
Wyoming	67.8	80.4	3.2	78.1

Source: U.S. Bureau of the Census, Census of Housing 1950-1990. Table prepared by Robert Bonnette.

(1) Alaska and Hawaii are not included in the 1950 national homeownership rate.
(2) Mobile homes in 1980 included a small number of units that were classified as "A boat, tent, van, etc."

Tenure

	TABLE 3.27. ANNUAL AND QUARTERLY HOMEOWNERSHIP RATES: 1966 TO 1997 (Percent)				
YEAR	First quarter	Second quarter	Third quarter	Fourth quarter	Annual
1966	63.5	63.2	63.3	63.8	63.4
1967	63.3	63.9	63.8	63.5	63.6
1968	63.6	64.1	64.1	63.6	63.9
1969	64.1	64.4	64.4	64.4	64.3
1970	64.3	64.0	64.4	64.0	64.2
1971	64.0	64.1	64.4	64.5	64.3
1972	64.3	64.5	64.3	64.4	64.4
1973	64.9	64.4	64.4	64.4	64.5
1974	64.8	64.8	64.6	64.4	64.6
1975	64.4	64.9	64.6	64.5	64.6
1976	64.6	64.6	64.9	64.8	64.7
1977	64.8	64.5	65.0	64.9	64.8
1978	64.8	64.4	65.2	65.4	65.0
1979	65.3	65.1	66.0	65.8	65.6
1979 [1]	64.8	64.9	65.8	65.4	65.2
1980	65.5	65.5	65.8	65.5	65.6
1981	65.6	65.3	65.6	65.2	65.4
1982	64.8	64.9	64.9	64.5	64.8
1983	64.7	64.7	64.8	64.4	64.6
1984	64.6	64.6	64.6	64.1	64.5
1985	64.1	64.1	63.9	63.5	63.9
1986	63.6	63.8	63.8	63.9	63.8
1987	63.8	63.8	64.2	64.1	64.0
1988	63.7	63.7	64.0	63.8	63.8
1989	63.9	63.8	64.1	63.8	63.9
1990	64.0	63.7	64.0	64.1	63.9
1991	63.9	63.9	64.2	64.2	64.1
1992	64.0	63.9	64.3	64.4	64.1
1993	64.2	64.4	64.7	64.6	64.5
1993 [2]	63.7	63.9	64.2	64.2	64.0
1994	63.8	63.8	64.1	64.2	64.0
1995	64.2	64.7	65.0	65.1	64.7
1996	65.1	65.4	65.6	65.4	65.4
1997	65.4	65.7	66.0	65.7	65.7

Source: U.S. Bureau of the Census, Current Population Survey/Housing Vacancy Survey.

(1) Revised to reflect a supplemental sample and refined estimation procedures.
(2) Revised using new weights based on the 1990 Census.

Tenure

YEAR/AREA	TABLE 3.28. ANNUAL AND QUARTERLY HOMEOWNERSHIP RATES BY REGION: 1976 TO 1997 (Percent)				
	First quarter	Second quarter	Third quarter	Fourth quarter	Annual
1976					
United States	64.6	64.6	64.9	64.8	64.7
Northeast	59.4	59.7	60.1	60.1	59.8
Midwest	70.0	69.8	69.7	69.2	69.7
South	66.1	66.2	66.6	66.5	66.4
West	60.9	60.4	61.1	61.1	60.9
1977					
United States	64.8	64.5	65.0	64.9	64.8
Northeast	60.2	59.7	60.5	60.7	60.3
Midwest	69.0	69.3	69.8	69.4	69.4
South	67.2	66.7	67.2	67.4	67.1
West	60.1	59.7	60.0	59.3	59.8
1978					
United States	64.8	64.4	65.2	65.4	65.0
Northeast	60.3	59.9	61.5	60.5	60.6
Midwest	69.4	68.9	69.8	69.5	69.3
South	67.5	67.3	67.7	68.7	67.9
West	59.2	58.7	59.1	59.6	59.2
1979					
United States	65.3	65.1	66.0	65.8	65.6
Northeast	60.9	60.3	61.0	60.8	60.7
Midwest	69.1	69.2	69.9	70.3	69.6
South	68.4	68.3	69.1	68.6	68.6
West	59.9	59.5	61.0	60.7	60.3
1979 [1]					
United States	64.8	64.9	65.8	65.4	65.2
Northeast	60.4	60.2	60.8	60.7	60.5
Midwest	68.9	69.4	70.2	70.0	69.6
South	68.1	67.8	68.8	68.3	68.3
West	58.9	59.4	60.6	59.9	59.7
1980					
United States	65.5	65.5	65.8	65.5	65.6
Northeast	60.7	60.8	61.1	60.5	60.8
Midwest	69.6	69.4	70.0	70.1	69.8
South	69.1	68.6	68.9	68.3	68.7
West	59.4	60.2	60.3	60.1	60.0
1981					
United States	65.6	65.3	65.6	65.2	65.4
Northeast	60.2	60.4	61.7	60.8	60.8
Midwest	70.1	69.7	69.6	69.6	69.7
South	69.1	68.0	68.0	67.8	68.2
West	59.8	60.3	60.8	59.9	60.2
1982					
United States	64.8	64.9	64.9	64.5	64.8
Northeast	60.7	60.8	61.9	61.1	61.1
Midwest	69.5	69.8	69.3	69.1	69.4
South	67.1	66.8	66.5	66.5	66.7
West	59.3	59.8	60.0	58.7	59.4

See notes at end of table.

Tenure

TABLE 3.28. ANNUAL AND QUARTERLY HOMEOWNERSHIP RATES BY REGION: 1976 TO 1997 - Continued (Percent)				
YEAR/AREA	First quarter	Second quarter	Third quarter	Fourth quarter	Annual
1983					
United States	64.7	64.7	64.8	64.4	64.6
Northeast	61.6	61.4	61.8	61.2	61.5
Midwest	69.6	69.6	69.3	68.9	69.3
South	66.7	66.7	67.0	67.4	67.0
West	58.4	59.0	58.3	57.2	58.2
1984					
United States	64.6	64.6	64.6	64.1	64.5
Northeast	61.1	61.1	61.7	60.9	61.2
Midwest	69.0	68.6	68.5	67.7	68.4
South	67.2	66.8	66.8	67.2	67.0
West	58.3	59.4	59.0	57.5	58.5
1985					
United States	64.1	64.1	63.9	63.5	63.9
Northeast	60.8	60.9	60.8	60.8	60.8
Midwest	67.3	67.3	66.8	66.4	66.9
South	66.7	66.7	66.3	66.0	66.4
West	59.0	59.2	59.3	58.5	59.0
1986					
United States	63.6	63.8	63.8	63.9	63.8
Northeast	61.0	61.4	61.2	61.9	61.4
Midwest	66.5	67.0	67.2	67.0	66.9
South	66.4	66.1	66.1	65.9	66.1
West	57.7	58.5	58.6	58.6	58.3
1987					
United States	63.8	63.8	64.2	64.1	64.0
Northeast	61.3	61.7	61.8	61.9	61.7
Midwest	66.8	67.3	67.8	67.2	67.3
South	66.5	66.0	66.2	66.4	66.3
West	58.1	58.3	58.9	58.6	58.4
1988					
United States	63.7	63.7	64.0	63.8	63.8
Northeast	61.5	61.3	61.5	60.8	61.3
Midwest	67.2	67.3	67.6	67.8	67.5
South	65.5	65.7	66.1	66.0	65.8
West	58.7	58.4	58.7	58.2	58.5
1989					
United States	63.9	63.8	64.1	63.8	63.9
Northeast	61.2	62.0	62.2	62.6	62.0
Midwest	67.8	67.8	67.9	67.0	67.7
South	66.2	65.9	66.0	65.6	65.9
West	58.2	57.7	58.0	57.5	57.8
1990					
United States	64.0	63.7	64.0	64.1	63.9
Northeast	62.2	62.2	63.1	62.8	62.6
Midwest	67.2	67.4	67.8	67.8	67.5
South	66.3	65.8	65.2	65.7	65.7
West	58.3	57.3	58.3	58.3	58.0

See notes at end of table.

Tenure

TABLE 3.28. ANNUAL AND QUARTERLY HOMEOWNERSHIP RATES BY REGION: 1976 TO 1997 - Continued
(Percent)

YEAR/AREA	First quarter	Second quarter	Third quarter	Fourth quarter	Annual
1991					
United States	63.9	63.9	64.2	64.2	64.1
Northeast	62.0	62.1	62.7	62.7	62.3
Midwest	67.1	66.8	67.2	67.2	67.2
South	65.9	66.3	66.2	66.2	66.1
West	58.5	58.3	58.9	58.9	58.6
1992					
United States	64.0	63.9	64.3	64.4	64.1
Northeast	62.3	62.5	62.6	62.8	62.5
Midwest	67.5	66.5	67.5	67.3	67.2
South	65.8	65.7	65.8	66.2	65.8
West	58.7	59.1	59.6	59.9	59.3
1993					
United States	64.2	64.4	64.7	64.6	64.5
Northeast	62.6	62.6	62.3	62.1	62.4
Midwest	66.9	67.1	67.8	67.8	67.4
South	65.8	66.0	66.4	66.3	66.1
West	59.8	60.4	60.6	60.7	60.4
1993 [2]					
United States	63.7	63.9	64.2	64.2	64.0
Northeast	62.0	62.0	61.7	61.5	61.8
Midwest	66.6	66.8	67.4	67.5	67.1
South	65.3	65.5	66.0	65.8	65.7
West	59.2	59.9	60.1	60.2	59.9
1994					
United States	63.8	63.8	64.1	64.2	64.0
Northeast	61.7	61.3	61.4	61.4	61.5
Midwest	66.8	67.5	67.9	68.6	67.7
South	65.6	65.2	66.0	65.7	65.6
West	59.5	59.7	59.0	59.6	59.4
1995					
United States	64.2	64.7	65.0	65.1	64.7
Northeast	61.9	62.3	62.2	61.6	62.0
Midwest	67.9	68.5	70.1	70.1	69.2
South	66.1	66.5	66.6	67.5	66.7
West	58.9	59.8	59.1	59.0	59.2
1996					
United States	65.1	65.4	65.6	65.4	65.4
Northeast	61.4	62.3	62.8	62.3	62.2
Midwest	70.4	70.5	70.7	70.8	70.6
South	67.5	67.2	67.5	67.6	67.5
West	58.9	59.8	59.2	58.9	59.2
1997					
United States	65.4	65.7	66.0	65.7	65.7
Northeast	61.6	62.4	63.0	62.7	62.4
Midwest	70.6	70.3	70.7	70.4	70.5
South	67.8	68.1	68.2	67.8	68.0
West	59.0	59.9	59.8	59.8	59.6

Source: U.S. Bureau of the Census, Current Population Survey/Housing Vacancy Survey

(1) Revised to reflect a supplemental sample and refined estimation procedures.
(2) Revised using new weights based on the 1990 Census.

Tenure

TABLE 3.29. HOMEOWNERSHIP RATES BY STATE: 1984 TO 1997
(Percent)

AREA	1984	1985	1986	1987	1988	1989	1990	1991	1992	1993	1993 [1]	1994	1995	1996	1997
United States	64.5	63.9	63.8	64.0	63.8	63.9	63.9	64.1	64.1	64.5	64.0	64.0	64.7	65.4	65.7
Alabama	73.7	70.4	70.3	67.9	66.5	67.6	68.4	69.9	70.3	70.5	70.2	68.5	70.1	71.0	71.3
Alaska	57.6	61.2	61.5	59.7	57.0	58.7	58.4	57.1	55.5	56.0	55.4	58.8	60.9	62.9	67.2
Arizona	65.2	64.7	62.5	63.3	66.1	63.9	64.5	66.3	69.3	69.6	69.1	67.7	62.9	62.0	63.0
Arkansas	65.9	66.6	67.5	68.1	67.0	66.3	67.8	68.6	70.3	70.8	70.5	68.1	67.2	66.6	66.7
California	53.7	54.2	53.8	54.3	54.4	53.6	53.8	54.5	55.3	56.8	56.0	55.5	55.4	55.0	55.7
Colorado	64.7	63.6	63.7	61.8	60.1	58.6	59.0	59.8	60.9	62.3	61.8	62.9	64.6	64.5	64.1
Connecticut	67.8	69.0	68.1	67.0	66.5	66.4	67.9	65.5	66.1	65.0	64.5	63.8	68.2	69.0	68.1
Delaware	70.4	70.3	71.0	71.1	70.1	68.7	67.7	70.2	73.8	74.4	74.1	70.5	71.7	71.5	69.2
District of Columbia	37.3	37.4	34.6	35.8	37.5	38.7	36.4	35.1	35.0	36.4	35.7	37.8	39.2	40.4	42.5
Florida	66.5	67.2	66.5	66.3	64.9	64.4	65.1	66.1	66.0	66.0	65.5	65.7	66.6	67.1	66.9
Georgia	63.6	62.7	62.4	63.9	64.8	64.7	64.3	65.7	66.9	66.8	66.5	63.4	66.6	69.3	70.9
Hawaii	50.7	51.0	50.9	50.7	53.2	54.7	55.5	55.2	53.8	53.2	52.8	52.3	50.2	50.6	50.2
Idaho	69.7	71.0	69.8	71.6	71.5	70.2	69.4	68.4	70.3	72.5	72.1	70.7	72.0	71.4	72.3
Illinois	62.4	60.6	60.9	61.0	61.4	61.9	63.0	63.0	62.4	62.3	61.8	64.2	66.4	68.2	68.1
Indiana	69.9	67.6	67.6	69.1	68.3	68.2	67.0	66.1	67.6	69.0	68.7	68.4	71.0	74.2	74.1
Iowa	71.3	69.9	69.2	67.7	68.3	69.6	70.7	68.4	66.3	68.6	68.2	70.1	71.4	72.8	72.7
Kansas	72.7	68.3	66.4	67.9	68.6	68.1	69.0	69.7	69.8	69.3	68.9	69.0	67.5	67.5	66.5
Kentucky	70.2	68.5	68.1	67.6	65.4	64.9	65.8	67.2	69.0	69.0	68.8	70.6	71.2	73.2	75.0
Louisiana	70.1	70.2	70.4	71.0	68.5	66.3	67.8	68.9	66.7	65.8	65.4	65.8	65.3	64.9	66.4
Maine	74.1	73.7	74.0	73.2	72.2	73.6	74.2	72.0	72.0	72.1	71.9	72.6	76.7	76.5	74.9
Maryland	67.8	65.6	62.8	62.7	63.5	65.5	64.9	63.8	64.8	65.8	65.5	64.1	65.8	66.9	70.5
Massachusetts	61.7	60.5	60.3	60.6	60.0	58.9	58.6	60.2	61.8	61.2	60.7	60.6	60.2	61.7	62.3
Michigan	72.7	70.7	70.9	71.7	72.5	73.2	72.3	70.6	70.6	72.6	72.3	72.0	72.2	73.3	73.3
Minnesota	72.6	70.0	68.0	68.9	69.1	68.3	68.0	68.9	66.7	66.2	65.8	68.9	73.3	75.4	75.4
Mississippi	72.3	69.6	70.4	72.5	73.7	72.2	69.4	71.8	70.4	69.9	69.7	69.2	71.1	73.0	73.7
Missouri	69.5	69.2	67.8	66.1	64.8	63.7	64.0	64.2	65.2	66.8	66.4	68.4	69.4	70.2	70.5
Montana	66.4	66.5	64.4	65.0	65.4	67.9	69.1	69.6	69.9	70.0	69.7	68.8	68.7	68.6	67.5
Nebraska	69.3	68.5	68.3	66.8	66.6	67.2	67.3	67.5	68.4	68.0	67.7	68.0	67.1	66.8	66.7
Nevada	58.9	57.0	54.5	54.1	54.3	54.3	55.8	55.8	55.1	56.2	55.8	55.8	58.6	61.1	61.2
New Hampshire	67.1	65.5	64.8	66.4	67.9	67.0	65.0	66.8	66.6	65.7	65.4	65.1	66.0	65.0	66.8
New Jersey	63.4	62.3	63.3	64.0	64.8	65.7	65.0	64.8	64.6	65.2	64.5	64.1	64.9	64.6	63.1
New Mexico	68.0	68.2	67.8	67.2	65.4	65.5	68.6	69.5	70.5	69.5	69.1	66.8	67.0	67.1	69.6
New York	51.1	50.3	51.3	52.0	50.7	52.3	53.3	52.6	53.3	53.5	52.8	52.5	52.7	52.7	52.6
North Carolina	68.8	68.0	68.2	68.4	68.3	69.4	69.0	69.3	68.6	69.1	68.8	68.7	70.1	70.4	70.2
North Dakota	70.1	69.9	69.2	68.9	67.7	67.1	67.2	65.4	63.7	63.1	62.7	63.3	67.3	68.2	68.1
Ohio	67.7	67.9	68.2	68.6	69.6	69.6	68.7	68.7	69.1	68.8	68.5	67.4	67.9	69.2	69.0
Oklahoma	71.0	70.5	69.7	70.9	72.1	71.4	70.3	69.2	68.9	70.7	70.3	68.5	69.8	68.4	68.5
Oregon	61.9	61.5	63.9	64.6	64.0	63.4	64.4	65.2	64.3	64.1	63.8	63.9	63.2	63.1	61.0
Pennsylvania	71.1	71.6	72.3	71.8	72.1	72.8	73.8	74.0	73.1	72.3	72.0	71.8	71.5	71.7	73.3
Rhode Island	60.9	61.4	62.2	60.4	62.0	61.2	58.5	58.2	56.8	58.1	57.6	56.5	57.9	56.6	58.7
South Carolina	69.1	72.0	70.3	72.8	73.8	71.0	71.4	73.1	71.0	71.4	71.1	72.0	71.3	72.9	74.1
South Dakota	69.6	67.6	65.9	66.8	66.4	65.8	66.2	66.1	66.5	66.1	65.6	66.4	67.5	67.8	67.6
Tennessee	67.6	67.6	67.4	67.2	66.9	67.3	68.3	68.0	67.4	64.4	64.1	65.2	67.0	68.8	70.2
Texas	62.5	60.5	61.0	61.1	59.9	61.0	59.7	59.0	58.3	59.3	58.7	59.7	61.4	61.8	61.5
Utah	69.9	71.5	68.0	69.0	70.2	70.4	70.1	70.7	70.0	69.4	68.9	69.3	71.5	72.7	72.5
Vermont	66.9	69.5	69.8	70.5	68.7	69.7	72.6	70.8	70.8	68.5	68.5	69.4	70.4	70.3	69.1
Virginia	68.3	68.5	68.2	69.0	69.8	70.2	69.8	68.9	67.8	68.8	68.5	69.3	68.1	68.5	68.4
Washington	65.7	66.8	65.1	64.4	64.2	64.2	61.8	61.8	62.5	63.5	63.1	62.4	61.6	63.1	62.9
West Virginia	72.0	75.9	76.4	72.5	73.2	74.8	72.0	72.4	73.3	73.6	73.3	73.7	73.1	74.3	74.6
Wisconsin	65.2	63.8	66.5	68.2	68.0	69.3	68.3	68.9	69.4	66.0	65.7	64.2	67.5	68.2	68.3
Wyoming	68.8	73.2	72.0	68.9	67.8	69.6	68.9	68.7	67.9	67.6	67.1	65.8	69.0	68.0	67.6

Source: U.S. Bureau of the Census, Current Population Survey/Housing Vacancy Survey.

(1) Revised using new weights based on the 1990 Census.

Tenure

AGE OF HOUSEHOLDER	1982	1983	1984	1985	1986	1987	1988	1989	1990	1991	1992	1993	1993[1]	1994	1995	1996	1997

TABLE 3.30. HOMEOWNERSHIP RATES BY AGE OF HOUSEHOLDER AND REGION: 1982 TO 1997
(Percent)

AGE OF HOUSEHOLDER	1982	1983	1984	1985	1986	1987	1988	1989	1990	1991	1992	1993	1993[1]	1994	1995	1996	1997
UNITED STATES	64.8	64.6	64.5	63.9	63.8	64.0	63.8	63.9	63.9	64.1	64.1	64.5	64.0	64.0	64.7	65.4	65.7
Less than 25 years	19.3	18.8	17.9	17.2	17.2	16.0	15.8	16.6	15.7	15.3	14.9	15.0	14.8	14.9	15.9	18.0	17.7
25 to 29 years	38.6	38.3	38.6	37.7	36.7	36.4	35.9	35.3	35.2	33.8	33.6	34.0	33.6	34.1	34.4	34.7	35.0
30 to 34 years	57.1	55.4	54.8	54.0	53.6	53.5	53.2	53.2	51.8	51.2	50.5	51.0	50.8	50.6	53.1	53.0	52.6
35 to 39 years	67.6	66.5	66.1	65.4	64.8	64.1	63.6	63.4	63.0	62.2	61.4	62.1	61.8	61.2	62.1	62.1	62.6
40 to 44 years	73.0	72.8	72.3	71.4	70.5	70.8	70.7	70.2	69.8	69.5	69.1	69.0	68.6	68.2	68.6	69.0	69.7
45 to 49 years	76.0	75.3	74.6	74.3	74.1	74.6	74.4	74.1	73.9	73.7	74.2	73.9	73.7	73.8	73.7	74.4	74.2
50 to 54 years	78.8	78.8	78.4	77.5	78.1	77.8	77.1	77.2	76.8	76.1	76.2	77.1	77.2	76.8	77.0	77.2	77.7
55 to 59 years	80.0	80.1	80.1	79.2	80.0	80.0	79.3	79.1	78.8	79.5	79.3	78.8	78.9	78.4	78.8	79.4	79.7
60 to 64 years	80.1	79.8	79.9	79.9	79.8	80.4	79.8	80.1	79.8	80.5	81.2	80.9	80.9	80.1	80.3	80.7	80.5
65 to 69 years	77.9	78.7	79.3	79.5	79.4	79.5	80.0	80.0	80.0	81.4	80.8	80.6	80.7	80.6	81.0	82.4	81.9
70 to 74 years	75.2	75.4	75.5	76.8	77.2	77.7	77.7	77.8	78.4	78.8	79.0	79.9	79.9	80.1	80.9	81.4	82.0
75 years and over	71.0	71.9	71.5	69.8	70.0	70.8	70.8	71.2	72.3	73.1	73.3	73.3	73.4	73.5	74.6	75.3	75.8
Less than 35 years	41.2	40.7	40.5	39.9	39.6	39.5	39.3	39.1	38.5	37.8	37.6	37.9	37.3	37.3	38.6	39.1	38.7
35 to 44 years	70.0	69.3	68.9	68.1	67.3	67.2	66.9	66.6	66.3	65.8	65.1	65.4	65.1	64.5	65.2	65.5	66.1
45 to 54 years	77.4	77.0	76.5	75.9	76.0	76.1	75.6	75.5	75.2	74.8	75.1	75.4	75.3	75.2	75.2	75.6	75.8
55 to 64 years	80.0	79.9	80.0	79.5	79.9	80.2	79.5	79.6	79.3	80.0	80.2	79.8	79.9	79.3	79.5	80.0	80.1
65 years and over	74.4	75.0	75.1	74.8	75.0	75.5	75.6	75.8	76.3	77.2	77.1	77.3	77.3	77.4	78.1	78.9	79.1
NORTHEAST	61.1	61.5	61.2	60.8	61.4	61.7	61.3	62.0	62.6	62.3	62.5	62.4	61.8	61.5	62.0	62.2	62.4
Less than 25 years	13.1	13.8	13.2	13.7	15.0	15.0	14.0	16.8	14.6	12.3	12.8	12.8	12.3	11.7	13.1	13.3	13.7
25 to 29 years	32.3	32.3	34.8	34.4	33.4	34.2	34.8	35.0	35.5	33.7	32.2	31.4	31.0	31.9	30.6	30.2	30.3
30 to 34 years	53.3	52.2	51.2	50.6	51.0	51.6	51.8	53.8	53.7	50.0	49.6	49.8	49.3	47.5	50.2	50.2	49.8
35 to 39 years	62.2	63.0	63.9	63.0	62.7	61.8	61.9	62.5	61.8	61.1	61.2	61.1	60.5	58.2	59.2	58.3	58.3
40 to 44 years	69.3	69.3	69.1	67.9	68.8	68.8	68.1	68.6	68.4	68.6	68.0	66.9	66.2	65.8	65.7	66.6	66.8
45 to 49 years	70.9	70.3	69.3	69.7	70.4	70.5	70.3	70.9	71.7	71.0	72.4	72.1	71.7	71.2	71.7	71.3	70.5
50 to 54 years	73.5	75.3	74.2	73.7	74.8	74.1	73.1	72.3	71.5	72.8	72.3	72.7	72.7	72.7	72.2	73.3	73.6
55 to 59 years	75.4	76.4	75.7	74.7	76.4	75.1	74.6	74.2	74.6	74.5	75.4	73.4	73.2	74.8	72.9	73.3	74.2
60 to 64 years	74.8	73.2	73.1	74.2	74.7	75.0	74.5	74.7	74.7	75.7	75.1	75.9	75.8	74.1	74.0	73.6	73.8
65 to 69 years	70.0	71.6	72.2	71.8	73.3	74.6	73.7	74.7	75.4	76.3	75.8	75.1	75.0	75.7	75.2	75.5	74.7
70 to 74 years	68.0	67.6	66.8	67.0	66.5	68.5	69.5	70.5	72.1	73.2	73.5	74.5	74.4	72.4	74.1	75.5	74.6
75 years and over	61.3	62.9	60.8	59.6	60.7	60.8	60.3	61.3	64.5	65.5	66.0	65.8	65.8	65.4	66.3	66.9	67.6
Less than 35 years	37.4	37.6	38.0	37.9	38.1	38.7	39.0	40.5	40.7	38.0	37.6	37.1	36.4	36.0	37.0	37.0	36.7
35 to 44 years	65.4	65.9	66.3	65.3	65.5	65.1	64.9	65.4	65.0	64.8	64.5	64.0	63.3	61.9	62.4	62.4	62.5
45 to 54 years	72.3	72.8	71.8	71.7	72.6	72.2	71.6	71.5	71.6	71.8	72.4	72.4	72.2	71.9	71.9	72.1	71.9
55 to 64 years	75.1	74.8	74.4	74.4	75.6	75.1	74.6	74.5	74.7	75.1	75.2	74.7	74.5	74.5	73.4	73.4	74.0
65 years and over	66.0	67.0	66.1	65.6	66.4	67.3	67.0	68.0	70.0	71.0	71.1	71.0	70.9	70.2	70.9	71.5	71.3
MIDWEST	69.4	69.3	68.4	66.9	66.9	67.3	67.5	67.7	67.5	67.2	67.2	67.4	67.1	67.7	69.2	70.6	70.5
Less than 25 years	21.7	20.3	19.3	17.8	16.7	16.0	16.1	16.5	16.5	17.5	16.2	14.9	14.7	16.4	18.2	20.0	19.5
25 to 29 years	45.1	44.5	42.9	40.3	40.0	40.4	40.5	38.9	38.6	37.2	37.6	38.4	38.2	39.1	40.5	41.0	42.8
30 to 34 years	62.5	62.9	60.6	58.9	59.2	58.3	59.1	59.4	57.1	56.8	56.6	57.3	57.1	57.2	60.0	61.3	60.0
35 to 39 years	74.9	72.9	71.4	70.7	70.2	69.4	68.6	69.7	69.6	68.4	68.3	67.8	67.6	67.0	68.8	69.6	70.6
40 to 44 years	78.7	78.6	77.5	75.7	75.2	75.6	76.8	76.9	76.1	74.2	73.5	74.2	73.9	74.1	75.7	75.8	76.4
45 to 49 years	81.2	80.6	80.0	78.8	79.2	79.5	79.6	79.1	78.1	78.6	78.7	79.3	79.2	79.2	79.9	80.6	79.6
50 to 54 years	83.9	83.1	82.8	81.2	81.3	82.2	81.3	82.0	82.7	79.2	79.8	82.0	82.1	82.0	81.4	82.7	82.8
55 to 59 years	84.4	84.4	84.1	83.7	84.5	83.7	81.9	82.1	82.8	84.0	83.2	82.0	82.2	81.7	83.7	85.0	84.6
60 to 64 years	83.0	83.8	83.4	82.1	82.5	84.3	83.9	83.4	82.9	83.4	84.2	84.3	84.4	84.2	82.7	83.9	83.8
65 to 69 years	83.4	83.3	83.6	82.2	82.0	81.4	82.0	82.3	82.1	83.1	82.7	82.7	82.9	83.4	83.6	85.0	84.7
70 to 74 years	78.7	78.9	78.5	78.7	79.5	79.3	79.1	79.4	79.2	78.6	77.5	79.4	79.4	81.6	82.8	84.3	84.0
75 years and over	74.5	74.6	74.0	69.2	69.4	70.8	71.2	71.6	71.3	71.6	72.0	71.9	72.0	72.2	74.0	75.2	75.2
Less than 35 years	45.8	45.8	44.4	42.8	42.6	42.9	43.2	43.0	41.8	41.6	41.6	41.5	41.1	41.7	43.8	44.9	44.5
35 to 44 years	76.6	75.4	74.1	73.0	72.4	72.2	72.3	73.0	72.6	71.2	70.8	70.9	70.6	70.4	72.1	72.6	73.5
45 to 54 years	82.5	81.9	81.4	80.0	80.3	80.8	80.4	80.4	80.2	78.9	79.2	80.6	80.5	80.5	80.6	81.5	81.0
55 to 64 years	83.7	84.1	83.7	82.9	83.5	84.0	83.0	82.8	82.9	83.7	83.7	83.1	83.3	82.9	83.2	84.5	84.2
65 years and over	78.5	78.6	78.3	75.9	76.0	76.3	76.5	76.9	76.7	76.9	76.5	77.0	77.1	77.9	78.9	80.2	80.0

See notes at end of table.

Tenure

AGE OF HOUSEHOLDER	TABLE 3.30. HOMEOWNERSHIP RATES BY AGE OF HOUSEHOLDER AND REGION: 1982 TO 1997 - Continued (Percent)																
	1982	1983	1984	1985	1986	1987	1988	1989	1990	1991	1992	1993	1993[1]	1994	1995	1996	1997
SOUTH	66.7	67.0	67.0	66.4	66.1	66.3	65.8	65.9	65.7	66.1	65.8	66.1	65.7	65.6	66.7	67.5	68.0
Less than 25 years	23.5	23.4	21.8	21.4	22.6	19.9	19.1	19.8	18.4	18.3	17.5	18.8	18.7	18.0	18.7	21.9	21.6
25 to 29 years	41.2	41.5	41.6	40.8	39.9	39.4	37.9	37.9	37.2	35.7	36.2	35.8	35.4	35.1	36.8	38.0	37.7
30 to 34 years	58.3	56.2	56.8	55.8	54.9	54.9	54.5	53.6	51.2	52.4	51.2	51.7	51.5	52.0	54.6	53.7	53.9
35 to 39 years	68.3	67.8	67.4	66.6	66.3	65.6	64.4	64.6	63.9	62.6	60.2	61.9	61.5	61.7	63.4	62.4	63.2
40 to 44 years	73.4	74.3	74.1	72.7	71.6	72.5	72.2	69.9	70.4	70.2	69.8	69.7	69.3	68.6	69.1	70.1	70.8
45 to 49 years	76.4	76.2	77.0	77.2	75.4	76.1	76.3	75.7	75.0	74.9	75.0	74.4	74.2	74.3	73.9	75.5	76.2
50 to 54 years	80.2	80.3	80.2	79.6	80.0	79.0	79.4	79.9	78.8	78.4	78.0	77.9	78.0	77.8	78.6	78.2	79.7
55 to 59 years	81.5	81.8	82.1	80.7	80.9	81.7	80.8	80.9	80.2	81.3	80.6	80.5	80.7	79.6	80.6	81.4	81.9
60 to 64 years	82.6	82.7	82.6	82.8	82.6	82.4	81.1	82.0	82.2	83.1	84.2	83.0	83.2	82.0	82.8	83.9	83.5
65 to 69 years	81.1	81.7	82.4	82.1	81.1	81.8	82.9	82.8	82.5	84.3	83.0	83.3	83.2	83.2	84.2	86.3	85.8
70 to 74 years	78.6	79.2	79.7	81.5	82.6	82.9	81.4	82.6	83.0	82.5	83.1	83.7	83.7	84.3	84.1	85.4	85.7
75 years and over	76.9	78.1	77.6	76.7	76.5	77.4	77.3	77.3	78.7	79.4	78.7	78.4	78.4	79.4	80.5	81.1	82.1
Less than 35 years	43.2	43.0	42.9	42.2	42.1	41.6	40.9	40.6	39.3	39.4	39.1	39.4	39.0	38.8	40.6	41.1	40.8
35 to 44 years	70.7	70.8	70.5	69.4	68.7	68.8	68.0	67.2	67.0	66.3	64.8	65.6	65.2	64.9	66.1	62.4	63.2
45 to 54 years	78.4	78.3	78.6	78.4	77.6	77.5	77.8	77.7	76.7	76.5	76.3	76.0	75.9	75.9	76.0	76.6	77.8
55 to 64 years	82.0	82.3	82.4	81.8	81.7	82.1	80.9	81.4	81.2	82.2	82.4	81.8	81.9	80.8	81.7	82.6	82.7
65 years and over	78.8	79.6	79.7	79.8	79.7	80.3	80.2	80.5	81.0	81.7	81.2	81.3	81.3	81.9	82.6	83.8	84.1
WEST	59.4	58.2	58.5	59.0	58.3	58.4	58.5	57.8	58.0	58.6	59.3	60.4	59.9	59.4	59.2	59.2	59.6
Less than 25 years	13.9	13.0	13.2	11.7	10.9	9.9	11.4	11.6	11.0	10.1	10.5	10.6	10.5	10.5	10.9	12.9	12.4
25 to 29 years	32.0	30.8	31.9	31.9	30.3	28.6	28.1	27.1	27.8	26.7	26.1	27.9	27.6	28.4	27.0	26.4	25.9
30 to 34 years	52.3	48.7	48.3	48.4	47.6	47.2	45.8	45.0	44.9	44.5	43.4	44.1	44.0	43.8	45.8	46.1	45.4
35 to 39 years	63.3	60.6	60.2	59.7	58.2	57.9	58.3	55.3	55.6	56.0	56.4	57.2	57.2	56.8	55.2	56.8	57.0
40 to 44 years	69.0	67.0	66.8	67.4	65.3	64.6	64.4	65.0	63.8	64.3	64.4	64.6	64.3	63.5	62.9	62.3	63.5
45 to 49 years	74.1	72.5	69.6	68.5	69.7	71.0	69.8	69.2	69.7	69.0	69.8	69.2	69.1	69.7	68.8	68.8	68.4
50 to 54 years	75.7	74.6	73.7	73.7	73.8	74.2	71.7	71.9	71.7	72.1	73.0	74.7	74.7	73.6	74.1	73.4	73.1
55 to 59 years	76.8	75.7	76.5	75.5	76.9	78.0	78.6	77.8	75.7	76.1	76.4	77.5	77.5	76.6	75.8	75.3	75.6
60 to 64 years	78.1	77.3	79.2	78.7	77.7	78.5	78.3	78.5	77.1	77.5	79.1	78.5	78.5	77.9	79.5	78.2	77.7
65 to 69 years	75.0	75.4	76.1	80.6	80.3	78.9	79.7	78.1	78.4	80.1	80.2	80.0	80.2	77.9	78.3	79.2	79.4
70 to 74 years	73.5	73.2	74.6	77.6	76.4	77.4	79.2	76.5	76.3	79.5	79.8	79.8	80.0	79.1	80.2	77.1	80.8
75 years and over	67.1	67.8	69.9	71.2	70.4	71.7	71.8	71.4	70.7	72.3	73.9	74.9	75.0	74.7	74.5	75.1	74.8
Less than 35 years	35.6	33.9	34.4	34.1	33.2	32.5	32.2	31.3	31.6	31.1	30.7	31.8	31.3	31.2	31.5	31.5	30.8
35 to 44 years	65.8	63.4	63.1	63.1	61.4	61.0	61.1	59.8	59.4	60.0	60.1	60.7	60.6	60.0	58.9	59.5	60.2
45 to 54 years	74.9	73.5	71.6	71.0	71.6	72.5	70.6	70.4	70.6	70.4	71.2	71.6	71.6	71.4	71.0	70.8	70.5
55 to 64 years	77.5	76.5	77.8	77.1	77.3	78.2	78.4	78.1	76.4	76.8	77.7	78.0	78.0	77.2	77.5	76.7	76.6
65 years and over	71.4	71.8	73.2	76.0	75.3	75.6	76.4	75.0	74.7	76.8	77.4	77.8	77.9	76.8	77.1	76.8	77.6

Source: U.S. Bureau of the Census, Current Population Survey/Housing Vacancy Survey.

(1) Revised using new weights based on the 1990 Census.

Tenure

TABLE 3.31. HOMEOWNERSHIP RATES BY AGE OF HOUSEHOLDER AND FAMILY STATUS: 1982 TO 1997

(Percent)

FAMILY STATUS AND AGE OF HOUSEHOLDER	1982	1983	1984	1985	1986	1987	1988	1989	1990	1991	1992	1993	1993 [1]	1994	1995	1996	1997
FAMILY HOUSEHOLDS																	
Married-couple families	78.5	78.3	78.2	78.2	78.4	78.7	78.9	78.3	78.1	78.5	78.7	79.1	78.7	78.8	79.6	80.2	80.8
Less than 35 years	58.2	57.7	57.7	57.6	57.4	57.9	58.0	56.6	56.0	55.6	55.7	56.3	55.7	55.8	57.2	58.1	58.2
35 to 44 years	82.0	81.2	81.0	80.9	80.7	80.4	80.5	80.2	79.7	79.6	79.2	79.6	79.3	79.1	79.8	79.6	80.6
45 to 54 years	87.4	86.8	86.8	86.3	86.6	86.6	86.8	86.6	86.3	86.2	86.6	86.4	86.3	86.6	87.1	87.5	87.8
55 to 64 years	89.5	89.4	89.5	89.2	89.8	90.1	89.7	89.9	89.7	90.2	90.2	90.4	90.3	89.6	89.8	90.3	90.5
65 years and over	86.6	87.3	87.2	87.8	88.1	88.5	88.8	89.1	89.2	90.0	90.2	90.2	90.2	90.4	90.8	91.3	91.6
Other family households	49.6	49.5	49.5	48.4	47.8	48.2	47.8	46.5	46.4	46.1	45.8	46.7	46.0	46.0	47.3	48.3	48.0
Male householder, no wife present	59.3	59.2	59.2	57.8	56.8	56.5	56.1	55.7	55.2	54.3	53.6	54.6	53.7	52.8	55.3	55.5	54.0
Less than 35 years	35.8	36.1	36.2	34.4	33.3	32.3	31.8	31.8	31.8	33.4	31.2	32.3	31.5	32.9	36.7	36.4	35.1
35 to 44 years	62.3	62.9	61.6	61.3	58.9	59.6	60.0	59.0	58.7	54.2	53.9	56.5	56.1	52.0	54.4	56.7	56.0
45 to 54 years	72.2	70.2	70.9	70.7	68.7	66.9	66.8	68.3	67.1	63.2	65.1	65.6	65.6	64.9	66.4	66.2	64.7
55 to 64 years	77.7	73.2	74.7	72.3	71.9	75.1	77.0	74.8	74.9	74.4	69.5	73.0	73.3	69.5	74.0	74.5	73.6
65 years and over	75.3	79.1	78.4	78.3	80.0	80.7	80.0	79.5	80.7	82.7	83.4	83.1	82.8	83.5	83.9	85.6	85.5
Female householder, no husband present	47.1	47.0	46.9	45.8	45.3	45.8	45.3	44.1	44.0	43.9	43.6	44.5	43.9	44.2	45.1	46.1	46.1
Less than 35 years	20.9	19.8	20.4	19.2	18.4	18.0	18.5	17.1	17.2	16.9	16.8	17.0	16.8	16.6	19.2	21.0	20.6
35 to 44 years	48.3	48.1	46.8	45.1	44.4	45.7	44.7	43.0	42.6	41.9	41.0	42.5	42.2	42.0	42.4	42.8	44.1
45 to 54 years	61.7	61.4	59.5	59.6	59.0	60.0	57.5	57.7	58.3	59.2	57.8	60.0	59.8	59.7	59.8	60.2	60.4
55 to 64 years	68.7	69.1	70.5	70.4	71.4	69.6	69.0	68.7	67.9	68.8	71.0	68.9	68.8	69.7	69.8	69.2	67.5
65 years and over	75.1	75.2	76.7	76.7	77.0	78.1	78.3	77.6	76.9	78.6	77.2	78.8	78.7	79.9	80.3	81.1	80.7
NONFAMILY HOUSEHOLDS																	
1-person households	45.6	46.2	46.5	45.8	45.9	46.3	46.3	48.2	49.0	49.4	49.8	50.0	49.8	49.8	50.5	51.4	51.8
Male householder	38.0	38.3	38.9	38.8	40.0	39.9	39.9	41.8	42.4	43.1	43.5	43.2	42.8	43.1	43.8	44.9	45.2
Less than 35 years	23.7	23.9	23.4	23.1	24.8	23.3	24.0	26.4	25.0	25.1	26.1	25.2	24.8	25.2	25.0	25.4	24.8
35 to 44 years	37.6	37.4	39.0	39.4	38.0	38.2	39.0	40.6	41.3	40.8	40.1	40.0	39.8	39.5	40.8	43.3	42.3
45 to 54 years	39.5	41.4	41.5	42.3	43.3	43.5	44.4	46.7	47.4	47.7	47.1	48.4	48.3	48.3	47.0	48.6	49.6
55 to 64 years	49.1	47.2	48.7	49.4	51.8	52.9	49.6	50.3	51.7	53.1	54.1	53.5	53.9	53.0	54.5	55.1	56.0
65 years and over	58.6	59.6	60.3	59.6	61.3	61.0	60.1	61.1	62.4	65.1	65.3	63.8	64.1	63.7	64.8	65.2	65.3
Female householder	51.2	52.0	52.2	51.3	50.9	51.6	51.8	52.6	53.6	53.8	54.1	54.8	54.6	54.5	55.4	56.0	56.7
Less than 35 years	15.1	15.0	15.6	15.7	16.4	17.1	17.8	19.3	19.1	16.9	17.0	19.0	18.8	18.6	17.8	18.8	18.1
35 to 44 years	37.0	37.1	38.4	38.7	36.8	37.1	38.1	38.3	38.7	42.8	42.9	41.7	41.8	42.0	42.0	40.4	41.5
45 to 54 years	49.1	49.6	50.6	52.8	52.4	52.1	52.1	51.7	53.9	53.5	55.1	55.6	55.6	55.0	55.6	55.5	56.8
55 to 64 years	62.4	64.2	63.3	61.2	60.6	62.0	62.7	63.8	62.8	63.4	64.5	64.2	64.3	63.5	62.5	63.8	64.6
65 years and over	62.2	62.7	63.0	61.7	61.2	62.0	62.0	62.6	64.0	64.1	63.9	64.5	64.5	64.6	66.0	67.2	67.9
2-or-more-person households	30.1	30.6	30.4	31.1	31.2	31.6	31.5	31.2	32.0	32.5	33.0	34.1	33.5	33.9	33.8	35.7	37.3
Male householder	28.3	29.5	28.8	30.1	29.8	31.1	31.3	31.5	31.7	31.8	32.4	33.2	32.6	33.6	34.2	35.5	35.9
Less than 35 years	19.9	20.6	19.6	20.1	18.6	20.3	20.6	21.1	19.9	20.9	20.8	20.8	20.3	20.8	20.9	21.0	21.9
35 to 44 years	43.0	43.4	43.8	44.3	45.9	47.2	46.2	43.8	47.9	44.2	46.0	45.2	44.9	44.7	44.9	47.4	46.4
45 to 54 years	46.8	50.0	46.3	49.1	54.5	54.1	54.1	58.3	53.6	53.3	53.4	57.0	57.0	56.4	57.3	58.8	58.5
55 to 64 years	50.0	56.3	58.9	64.5	62.0	55.3	55.0	59.3	58.7	56.2	59.7	59.0	59.6	62.7	60.6	64.9	63.7
65 years and over	61.1	67.4	64.1	67.0	68.2	66.7	67.5	67.0	65.5	64.3	67.0	67.8	67.3	69.3	70.9	70.6	73.6
Female householder	30.1	29.7	30.0	30.6	31.4	30.7	30.5	30.8	32.5	33.8	34.0	35.6	35.0	34.3	33.0	35.9	39.5
Less than 35 years	12.7	12.9	14.1	14.2	14.1	14.8	14.3	15.3	15.0	15.2	14.9	15.7	15.4	17.1	16.1	15.4	18.4
35 to 44 years	37.9	36.3	44.0	45.8	49.4	44.0	45.4	44.7	49.0	49.1	45.8	48.6	48.3	48.0	48.0	52.9	52.1
45 to 54 years	60.2	57.8	55.8	52.9	56.9	63.0	62.9	54.0	60.4	63.0	61.2	63.6	63.4	58.7	52.4	62.1	64.2
55 to 64 years	72.6	70.8	64.7	70.0	66.3	65.4	65.9	66.3	62.4	67.6	70.6	74.8	75.0	66.7	66.7	68.0	78.6
65 years and over	77.2	77.0	75.2	75.5	75.7	73.9	71.6	70.4	74.8	70.8	72.7	73.9	73.6	68.3	71.2	70.8	69.1

Source: U.S. Bureau of the Census, Current Population Survey/Housing Vacancy Survey.

(1) Revised using new weights based on the 1990 Census.

Tenure

TABLE 3.32. HOMEOWNERSHIP RATES BY RACE AND HISPANIC ORIGIN OF HOUSEHOLDER: 1983 TO 1997
(Percent)

DATA SOURCE AND PERIOD	All households	Non-Hispanic householder			Hispanic householder [1]
		White	Black	Other race	
MARCH SUPPLEMENT TO THE CURRENT POPULATION SURVEY					
1983	64.9	69.1	45.6	53.3	41.2
1984	64.5	69.0	46.0	50.9	40.1
1985	64.3	69.0	44.4	50.7	41.1
1986	63.8	68.4	44.8	49.7	40.6
1987	64.0	68.7	45.8	48.7	40.6
1988	64.0	69.1	42.9	49.7	40.6
1989	64.0	69.3	42.1	50.6	41.6
1990	64.1	69.4	42.6	49.2	41.2
1991	64.0	69.5	42.7	51.3	39.0
1992	64.1	69.6	42.6	52.5	39.9
1993[2]	64.1	70.2	42.0	50.6	39.4
1994	64.2	70.1	42.8	51.7	41.6
1995	64.7	70.8	42.2	51.0	42.4
1996	65.4	71.6	44.3	50.5	41.2
1997	65.7	71.7	46.0	52.8	43.1
CURRENT POPULATION SURVEY/ HOUSING VACANCY SURVEY					
1994	64.0	70.0	42.5	50.8	41.2
First quarter	63.8	69.8	42.4	52.5	40.3
Second quarter	63.8	69.9	42.0	48.5	41.1
Third quarter	64.1	70.0	42.9	51.0	41.4
Fourth quarter	64.2	70.2	42.9	51.2	42.2
1995	64.7	70.9	42.9	51.5	42.0
First quarter	64.2	70.4	41.5	51.5	41.8
Second quarter	64.7	70.9	42.3	50.6	42.8
Third quarter	65.0	71.1	43.3	52.0	42.5
Fourth quarter	65.1	71.2	44.6	52.1	41.1
1996	65.4	71.7	44.5	51.5	42.8
First quarter	65.1	71.4	44.2	51.5	41.4
Second quarter	65.4	71.7	44.0	50.4	43.9
Third quarter	65.6	71.8	44.9	52.0	43.5
Fourth quarter	65.4	71.8	44.8	52.1	42.3
1997	65.7	72.0	45.4	53.3	43.3
First quarter	65.4	71.6	45.0	52.6	42.6
Second quarter	65.7	72.1	44.9	53.4	43.3
Third quarter	66.0	72.3	45.8	54.1	43.0
Fourth quarter	65.7	71.9	45.7	53.3	44.0

Sources: U.S. Bureau of the Census, Current Population Survey - March Supplement and Current Population Survey/Housing Vacancy Survey.

(1) Persons of Hispanic origin may be of any race.
(2) Beginning in 1993, weighted based on the 1990 Census.

Annual statistics for the Current Population Survey/Housing Vacancy Survey are annual averages of quarterly data.

Characteristics of Recent Homebuyers

TABLE 3.33. CHARACTERISTICS OF RECENT HOMEBUYERS: 1976 TO 1997

YEAR	Median purchase price (Dollars)			Average monthly mortgage payment		Percent buying					Average age of buyer (Years)		Downpayment/sales price (Percent)		
	All	First-time buyers	Repeat buyers	Amount (Dollars)	Percent of after-tax income	New houses	Existing houses	Single-family houses	Condo-miniums	For the first time	First-time buyers	Repeat buyers	All	First-time buyers	Repeat buyers
1976	43,340	37,670	50,090	329	24.0	15.1	84.9	88.8	11.2	44.8	28.1	35.9	25.2	18.0	30.8
1980	68,714	61,450	75,750	599	32.4	22.4	77.6	82.4	17.6	32.9	28.3	36.4	28.0	20.5	32.7
1981	78,220	63,180	82,220	694	35.5	25.2	74.8	78.3	20.3	39.4	28.4	36.4	24.1	19.4	27.1
1982	82,500	58,900	98,300	732	33.0	23.2	76.8	76.6	23.4	40.6	28.6	37.1	22.4	15.1	27.3
1983	90,000	73,100	101,800	794	32.5	26.4	73.6	87.8	12.2	40.5	28.9	37.3	22.9	15.7	27.8
1984	89,400	81,500	100,400	868	30.3	22.3	77.7	89.9	10.1	37.7	29.1	37.8	20.9	13.2	25.6
1985	90,400	75,100	106,200	896	30.0	23.8	76.2	87.0	10.6	36.6	28.4	38.4	24.8	11.4	32.7
1986	93,680	74,700	114,860	852	28.6	25.7	74.3	85.1	14.2	35.5	30.9	39.5	23.4	13.4	28.9
1987	99,260	84,730	115,430	939	29.3	23.8	76.2	87.3	12.5	36.8	29.6	39.1	27.2	20.4	31.3
1988	121,910	97,100	141,400	1,008	32.8	26.2	73.8	83.3	12.4	37.8	30.3	38.9	24.0	14.6	29.7
1989	129,800	105,200	144,700	1,054	31.8	21.8	78.2	84.8	13.5	40.2	29.6	39.4	24.4	15.8	30.3
1990	131,200	106,000	149,400	1,127	33.8	21.2	78.8	83.8	13.1	41.9	30.5	39.1	23.3	15.7	28.9
1991	134,300	118,700	152,500	1,144	34.0	19.7	80.3	85.3	11.5	45.1	30.7	39.8	22.6	14.7	29.1
1992	141,000	122,400	158,000	1,064	33.2	20.5	79.5	85.0	13.1	47.7	31.0	40.8	21.4	14.3	28.0
1993	141,900	121,100	159,600	1,015	31.5	22.3	77.7	84.2	12.8	46.0	31.6	41.0	20.2	14.0	25.4
1994	145,400	125,000	163,500	1,028	31.4	22.0	78.0	83.9	12.1	47.1	31.6	41.7	20.2	13.7	26.1
1995	147,700	128,300	164,300	1,062	32.6	21.5	78.5	83.1	14.0	46.2	32.1	40.7	20.4	13.3	26.8
1996	153,200	130,100	170,700	1,087	32.6	22.7	77.3	82.6	14.2	44.7	32.4	41.1	19.5	12.4	25.3
1997	159,700	135,400	178,700	1,114	32.8	20.9	79.1	81.6	15.5	46.8	32.1	41.1	20.3	13.7	26.1

Source: Chicago Title and Trust Family of Title Insurers, Survey of Recent Home Buyers.

As of October. Based on a sample of homebuyers in metropolitan areas.

Ownership of Private Rental Properties

TYPE OF OWNER	TABLE 3.34. TYPES OF OWNERS OF PRIVATELY-OWNED SINGLE-FAMILY RENTAL HOUSING BY TYPE OF PROPERTY: 1996							
	Total, all single-family		Single-family detached		Single-family attached		Single unit with business	
	Number	Percent [1]	Number	Percent [1]	Number	Percent [1]	Number	Percent [1]
TOTAL	8,773,165	....	6,438,228	....	773,229	....	74,302	....
TYPE OF OWNER								
Individual investors	7,347,982	88	5,473,068	89	587,587	79	57,594	80
Trustee for estate	186,294	2	157,231	3	14,282	2	0	0
Limited partnership	99,706	1	44,517	1	27,634	4	2,991	4
General partnership	112,375	1	77,137	1	24,207	3	2,496	3
Joint venture	58,747	1	38,257	1	17,499	2	0	0
Real estate investment trust	29,712	0	8,710	0	8,802	1	0	0
Life insurance company	0	0	0	0	0	0	0	0
Financial institution	8,895	0	5,982	0	0	0	0	0
Real estate corporation	127,898	2	64,897	1	33,711	5	0	0
Other corporation	136,548	2	99,661	2	12,002	2	2,533	4
Housing cooperative organization	34,427	0	0	0	0	0	0	0
Non-profit/church-related institution	214,384	3	183,419	3	15,364	2	5,942	8
Fraternal organization	3,835	0	0	0	0	0	0	0
Other	0	0	0	0	0	0	0	0
Not reported	412,362	5	285,348	4	32,140	4	2,746	4

See notes at end of table.

Ownership of Private Rental Properties

TYPE OF OWNER	TABLE 3.34. TYPES OF OWNERS OF PRIVATELY-OWNED SINGLE-FAMILY RENTAL HOUSING BY TYPE OF PROPERTY: 1996 - Continued					
	Condominium		Cooperative		Mobile home	
	Number	Percent [1]	Number	Percent [1]	Number	Percent [1]
TOTAL	568,566	....	117,726	....	801,114	....
TYPE OF OWNER						
Individual investors	487,771	90	48,675	52	693,287	91
Trustee for estate	9,885	2	0	0	4,896	1
Limited partnership	4,766	1	7,442	8	12,356	2
General partnership	3,566	1	0	0	4,969	1
Joint venture	2,991	1	0	0	0	0
Real estate investment trust	12,200	2	0	0	0	0
Life insurance company	0	0	0	0	0	0
Financial institution	0	0	2,913	3	0	0
Real estate corporation	11,459	2	0	0	17,831	2
Other corporation	5,555	1	3,966	4	12,831	2
Housing cooperative organization	3,107	1	31,320	33	0	0
Non-profit/church-related institution	0	0	0	0	9,659	1
Fraternal organization	0	0	0	0	3,835	1
Other	0	0	0	0	0	0
Not reported	27,267	5	23,410	20	41,451	5

Source: U.S. Bureau of the Census, Property Owners and Managers Survey.

(1) Percent distributions for type of owner are calculated on the basis of the number of units of a given type reporting ownership. Percentages for "not reported" are calculated based on the total number of units of a given type.

Ownership of Private Rental Properties

TYPE OF OWNER	TABLE 3.35. TYPES OF OWNERS OF PRIVATELY-OWNED MULTIFAMILY RENTAL HOUSING BY NUMBER OF UNITS AT PROPERTY: 1996							
	Total, all multifamily		2 units		3-4 units		5-9 units	
	Number	Percent [1]	Number	Percent [1]	Number	Percent [1]	Number	Percent [1]
TOTAL	20,584,822	....	3,084,750	....	2,471,070	....	1,894,445	....
TYPE OF OWNER								
Individual investors	9,728,474	55	2,672,697	91	2,040,897	87	1,326,467	78
Trustee for estate	304,887	2	46,475	2	73,971	3	38,861	2
Limited partnership	2,697,569	15	44,842	2	52,375	2	65,737	4
General partnership	1,436,466	8	52,942	2	65,706	3	77,458	5
Joint venture	394,725	2	23,092	1	48,884	2	27,721	2
Real estate investment trust	417,612	2	24,075	1	9,035	0	29,064	2
Life insurance company	85,618	0	3,674	0	3,945	0	3,305	0
Financial institution	129,347	1	0	0	0	0	2,506	0
Real estate corporation	1,178,757	7	36,353	1	18,329	1	53,807	3
Other corporation	706,937	4	30,348	1	18,729	1	35,306	2
Housing cooperative organization	36,259	0	0	0	8,818	0	0	0
Non-profit/church-related institution	702,636	4	6,209	0	16,013	1	27,558	2
Fraternal organization	10,711	0	8,279	0	0	0	2,432	0
Other	7,145	0	0	0	0	0	0	0
Not reported	2,747,680	13	135,763	4	114,370	5	204,224	11

See notes at end of table.

Ownership of Private Rental Properties

TYPE OF OWNER	TABLE 3.35. TYPES OF OWNERS OF PRIVATELY-OWNED MULTIFAMILY RENTAL HOUSING BY NUMBER OF UNITS AT PROPERTY: 1996 - Continued					
	10-19 units		20-49 units		50 or more units	
	Number	Percent [1]	Number	Percent [1]	Number	Percent [1]
TOTAL	1,467,786	....	2,223,786	....	9,442,986	....
TYPE OF OWNER						
Individual investors	871,394	68	1,006,137	51	1,810,882	24
Trustee for estate	36,077	3	52,211	3	57,292	1
Limited partnership	84,029	7	340,678	17	2,109,908	28
General partnership	57,572	4	205,051	10	977,737	13
Joint venture	25,208	2	27,227	1	242,593	3
Real estate investment trust trust	8,074	1	27,044	1	320,320	4
Life insurance company	0	0	7,811	0	66,883	1
Financial institution	26,520	2	3,231	0	97,090	1
Real estate corporation	71,749	6	96,489	5	902,030	12
Other corporation	72,151	6	117,564	6	432,839	6
Housing cooperative organization	0	0	7,932	0	19,509	0
Non-profit/church-related institution	27,928	2	78,541	4	546,387	7
Fraternal organization	0	0	0	0	0	0
Other	0	0	0	0	7,145	0
Not reported	187,083	13	253,870	11	1,852,370	20

Source: U.S. Bureau of the Census, Property Owners and Managers Survey.

(1) Percent distributions for type of owner are calculated on the basis of the number of units of a given type reporting ownership. Percentages for "not reported" are calculated based on the total number of units of a given type.

Housing Problems and Costs

TABLE 3.36. INCIDENCE OF UNFAVORABLE TREATMENT AND HOUSING MARKET DISCRIMINATION FOR BLACK AND HISPANIC HOMESEEKERS: 1989
(Percent)

TYPE OF UNFAVORABLE TREATMENT	Rentals		Sales	
	Blacks	Hispanics	Blacks	Hispanics
HOUSING AVAILABILITY				
No appointment or no units available	15.1	12.1	7.6	7.5
Availability of advertised unit	17.2	15.5	11.1	9.5
Availability of similar units	13.7	15.2	19.7	17.1
Number of units shown	31.7	26.9	31.1	31.3
Number of units recommended but not shown	22.3	18.5	26.2	32.5
Composite index of unfavorable treatment in housing availability	39.0	35.5	35.7	38.0
CONTRIBUTIONS TO COMPLETING THE HOUSING TRANSACTION				
Sales effort	41.1	36.4	30.5	32.9
Terms and conditions	23.9	24.6	....	....
Financing assistance	....	....	39.2	37.3
Composite index of unfavorable treatment in completing the housing transaction	44.5	42.1	45.9	46.7
RACIAL AND ETHNIC STEERING [1]				
Neighborhood percent minority	....	....	11.8	12.4
Neighborhood per capita income	....	....	10.6	10.8
Neighborhood median house value	....	....	17.2	16.8
Composite index of racial/ethnic steering	....	....	20.9	21.3
OVERALL INCIDENCE OF UNFAVORABLE TREATMENT	45.7	42.7	50.4	44.6
OVERALL INCIDENCE OF DISCRIMINATION	56.0	50.0	59.0	56.0

Source: U.S. Department of Housing and Urban Development, Housing Discrimination Study.

With the exception of the overall incidence of discrimination, all values reflect the gross incidence of unfavorable treatment using weighted data and are statistically significant at the 95 percent confidence level.

(1) Incidence of unfavorable treatment in which agents identified addresses for both minority and majority homeseekers.

Housing Problems and Costs

RACIAL OR ETHNIC GROUP AND METROPOLITAN AREA SIZE GROUP	TABLE 3.37. MEAN RESIDENTIAL SEGREGATION INDEXES FOR METROPOLITAN AREAS BY SIZE:				
	Mean			Segregation measure	
	Total population	Racial or ethnic group population	Racial or ethnic group as percent of total population	Dissimilarity	Interaction
ALL METROPOLITAN AREAS					
American Indian, Eskimo, or Aleut	772,571	21,759	3.3	0.353	0.874
Asian or Pacific Islander	3,796,396	364,803	13.6	0.416	0.690
Black	2,859,378	589,417	19.5	0.686	0.376
Hispanic [1]	3,595,930	1,010,828	27.4	0.507	0.474
Non-Hispanic Black	2,800,017	546,193	19.1	0.688	0.377
METROPOLITAN SIZE GROUP					
1 million or more persons					
American Indian, Eskimo, or Aleut	1,938,362	29,171	1.5	0.390	0.864
Asian or Pacific Islander	4,655,816	396,562	8.9	0.423	0.723
Black	4,090,985	845,342	19.5	0.730	0.321
Hispanic [1]	4,862,438	1,362,489	25.4	0.536	0.456
Non-Hispanic Black	4,022,905	783,901	18.8	0.732	0.323
500,000 to 1 million persons					
American Indian, Eskimo, or Aleut	768,093	36,540	4.7	0.316	0.853
Asian or Pacific Islander	768,933	370,001	44.9	0.379	0.427
Black	787,022	156,995	19.4	0.638	0.437
Hispanic [1]	664,798	186,405	29.9	0.470	0.509
Non-Hispanic Black	788,262	156,765	19.3	0.639	0.437
Less than 500,000 Persons					
American Indian, Eskimo, or Aleut	239,068	6,520	3.0	0.366	0.895
Asian or Pacific Islander	306,801	21,785	6.1	0.405	0.812
Black	280,530	55,069	19.6	0.574	0.517
Hispanic [1]	293,262	100,243	34.2	0.411	0.525
Non-Hispanic Black	280,253	55,002	19.6	0.575	0.517

Source: U.S. Bureau of the Census, 1990 Census.

Only metropolitan areas with 2 percent or more of their total population in a given racial or ethnic group are included. (The requirement is 1 percent for American Indian, Eskimo, or Aleut.)

(1) Persons of Hispanic origin may be of any race.

See Appendix A for a description of the segregation indices.

Housing Problems and Costs

TENURE AND PROBLEM	TABLE 3.38. HOUSING PROBLEMS BY TENURE: 1978 TO 1995											
	Number of households (Thousands)						Percent					
	1978	1983	1989	1991	1993	1995	1978	1983	1989	1991	1993	1995
RENTERS	26,919	29,952	33,767	33,351	33,472	34,150	....	....	....	....	....	....
Rent burden greater than 50% of income	3,661	5,481	5,187	5,426	5,948	6,187	14	18	15	16	18	18
Rent burden 31-50% of income	4,765	5,661	6,983	6,938	7,163	7,385	18	19	21	21	21	22
Severely inadequate housing	1,677	1,617	1,587	1,347	910	849	6	5	5	4	3	2
Moderately inadequate housing	2,105	2,037	2,441	2,375	2,253	2,277	8	7	7	7	7	7
Crowded	1,548	1,692	1,722	1,644	1,503	1,673	6	6	5	5	4	5
Priority problems	4,695	5,999	5,622	5,691	5,824	5,886	17	20	17	17	17	17
Other problems	5,976	6,479	7,466	7,479	7,431	7,773	22	22	22	22	22	23
No problems	13,529	14,077	16,370	15,965	15,765	15,837	50	47	48	48	47	46
Assisted	2,719	3,474	4,309	4,216	4,452	4,654	10	12	13	13	13	14
OWNERS	50,470	54,889	59,916	59,796	61,251	63,544	....	....	....	....	....	....
Cost burden greater than 50% of income	1,645	2,360	3,170	3,432	3,798	4,913	3	4	5	6	6	8
Cost burden 31-50% of income	2,423	3,376	6,351	7,171	7,166	8,053	5	6	11	12	12	13
Severely inadequate housing	939	933	1,576	1,527	980	1,173	2	2	3	3	2	2
Moderately inadequate housing	2,019	1,927	2,001	2,156	1,960	2,071	4	4	3	4	3	3
Crowded	1,625	1,153	953	883	858	881	3	2	2	2	1	1
Priority problems	2,524	3,206	4,643	4,838	4,655	5,957	5	6	8	8	8	9
Other problems	5,501	5,780	8,358	9,268	9,126	10,042	11	11	14	16	15	16
No problems	42,395	45,904	46,914	45,684	47,470	47,545	84	84	78	76	78	75

Source: Analysis of data from American/Annual Housing Surveys in U.S. Department of Housing and Urban Development, Office of Policy Development and Research, "Rental Housing Assistance - The Crisis Continues: The 1997 Report to Congress on Worst Case Housing Needs." April 1998.

See Appendix A for definitions of housing problems.

Housing Problems and Costs

PRESENCE OF CHILDREN AND PROBLEM	TABLE 3.39. HOUSING PROBLEMS OF VERY LOW-INCOME RENTERS BY PRESENCE OF CHILDREN: 1978 TO 1995											
	Number of households (Thousands)						Percent					
	1978	1983	1989	1991	1993	1995	1978	1983	1989	1991	1993	1995
ALL VERY LOW-INCOME RENTERS	10,682	12,138	13,384	14,013	14,749	14,562	....	....	....	....	....	....
Priority problems	3,963	5,122	4,805	4,954	5,349	5,320	37	42	36	35	36	37
Severe physical problems	961	874	716	615	470	400	9	7	5	4	3	3
Rent burden greater than 50% of income	3,226	4,564	4,363	4,588	5,048	5,057	30	38	33	33	34	35
Rent burden only	2,596	3,641	3,407	3,643	4,170	4,181	24	30	25	26	28	29
Other problems	3,087	2,792	3,291	3,321	3,687	3,521	29	23	25	24	25	24
Moderate physical problems	691	540	625	673	627	591	6	4	5	5	4	4
Rent burden 31-50% of income	2,500	2,355	2,781	3,069	3,208	3,046	23	19	21	22	22	21
Crowded	470	461	504	462	479	558	4	4	4	3	3	4
No problems	1,538	1,457	1,779	2,004	1,947	1,945	14	12	13	14	13	13
Assisted	2,094	2,767	3,509	3,447	3,770	3,774	20	23	26	25	26	26
VERY LOW-INCOME RENTERS WITH CHILDREN	4,166	5,091	5,892	6,149	6,653	6,509	....	....	....	....	....	....
Priority problems	1,383	2,151	1,928	2,033	2,282	2,106	33	42	33	33	34	32
Severe physical problems	312	346	262	203	175	143	8	7	4	3	3	2
Rent burden greater than 50% of income	1,166	1,940	1,768	1,921	2,187	2,014	28	38	30	31	33	31
Rent burden only	825	1,375	1,232	1,316	1,601	1,464	20	27	21	21	24	23
Other problems	1,321	1,303	1,606	1,691	1,738	1,780	32	26	27	28	26	27
Moderate physical problems	306	229	298	285	278	269	7	5	5	5	4	4
Rent burden 31-50% of income	954	1,033	1,273	1,347	1,441	1,463	23	20	22	22	22	22
Crowded	450	450	482	448	451	535	11	9	8	7	7	8
No problems	500	453	648	758	762	762	12	9	11	12	11	12
Assisted	962	1,181	1,712	1,666	1,870	1,861	23	23	29	27	28	29

Source: Analysis of data from American/Annual Housing Surveys in U.S. Department of Housing and Urban Development, Office of Policy Development and Research, "Rental Housing Assistance - The Crisis Continues: The 1997 Report to Congress on Worst Case Housing Needs." April 1998.

See Appendix A for definitions of housing problems.

Housing Problems and Costs

RACE/HISPANIC ORIGIN AND PROBLEM	TABLE 3.40. HOUSING PROBLEMS OF VERY LOW-INCOME RENTERS BY RACE AND HISPANIC ORIGIN: 1978 TO 1995											
	Number of households (Thousands)						Percent					
	1978	1983	1989	1991	1993	1995	1978	1983	1989	1991	1993	1995
NON-HISPANIC WHITE	6,673	7,395	7,626	7,908	8,127	7,579	....	....	....	....	....	....
Priority problems	2,602	3,213	2,877	2,940	3,020	2,884	39	43	38	37	37	38
Severe physical problems	500	429	368	335	228	171	8	6	5	4	3	2
Rent burden greater than 50% of income	2,215	2,928	2,665	2,736	2,869	2,758	33	40	35	35	35	36
Rent burden only	1,908	2,544	2,280	2,388	2,576	2,480	29	34	30	30	32	33
Other problems	1,915	1,661	1,876	1,983	2,105	1,805	29	22	25	25	26	24
Moderate physical problems	314	251	279	281	252	276	5	3	4	4	3	4
Rent burden 31-50% of income	1,682	1,479	1,685	1,782	1,918	1,640	25	20	22	23	24	22
Crowded	133	137	144	97	132	97	2	2	2	1	2	1
No problems	1,088	1,087	1,205	1,344	1,292	1,241	16	15	16	17	16	16
Assisted	1,068	1,435	1,670	1,639	1,715	1,648	16	19	22	21	21	22
NON-HISPANIC BLACK	2,643	2,842	3,343	3,525	3,725	3,676	....	....	....	....	....	....
Priority problems	936	1,102	1,033	1,033	1,114	1,167	35	39	31	29	30	32
Severe physical problems	367	296	198	158	104	121	14	10	6	4	3	3
Rent burden greater than 50% of income	655	912	906	929	1,043	1,096	25	32	27	26	28	30
Rent burden only	423	614	610	652	786	814	16	22	18	19	21	22
Other problems	673	587	663	796	771	734	25	21	20	23	21	20
Moderate physical problems	256	190	195	259	238	161	10	7	6	7	6	4
Rent burden 31-50% of income	484	486	538	626	626	638	18	17	16	18	17	17
Crowded	119	97	79	97	83	80	5	3	2	3	2	2
No problems	285	199	312	365	369	336	11	7	9	10	10	9
Assisted	748	954	1,334	1,329	1,471	1,439	28	34	40	38	39	39
HISPANIC ORIGIN [1]	1,123	1,460	1,915	2,010	2,214	2,584	....	....	....	....	....	....
Priority problems	358	597	697	753	920	964	32	41	36	37	42	37
Severe physical problems	88	107	119	95	108	92	8	7	6	5	5	4
Rent burden greater than 50% of income	292	539	617	709	852	914	26	37	32	35	39	35
Rent burden only	191	345	383	451	592	650	17	24	20	22	27	25
Other problems	420	432	613	683	651	807	37	30	32	34	29	31
Moderate physical problems	108	85	129	100	101	122	10	6	7	5	5	5
Rent burden 31-50% of income	279	312	450	550	522	612	25	21	23	27	24	24
Crowded	190	181	241	232	215	356	17	12	13	12	10	14
No problems	118	133	205	228	209	301	11	9	11	11	9	12
Assisted	227	298	399	346	434	512	20	20	21	17	20	20

Source: Analysis of data from American/Annual Housing Surveys in U.S. Department of Housing and Urban Development, Office of Policy Development and Research, "Rental Housing Assistance - The Crisis Continues: The 1997 Report to Congress on Worst Case Housing Needs." April 1998.

(1) Persons of Hispanic origin may be of any race.

See Appendix A for definitions of housing problems.

Housing Problems and Costs

TABLE 3.41. HOUSING PROBLEMS OF VERY LOW-INCOME RENTERS BY REGION: 1978 TO 1995

REGION AND PROBLEM	Number of households (Thousands)						Percent					
	1978	1983	1989	1991	1993	1995	1978	1983	1989	1991	1993	1995
NORTHEAST	2,723	3,189	2,914	3,076	3,288	3,319	....	....	....	....	....	....
Priority problems	1,146	1,333	1,137	1,140	1,295	1,300	42	42	39	37	39	39
Severe physical problems	289	275	192	187	148	143	11	9	7	6	5	4
Rent burden greater than 50% of income	956	1,186	1,037	1,038	1,213	1,214	35	37	36	34	37	37
Rent burden only	762	925	819	835	977	1,006	28	29	28	27	30	30
Other problems	664	702	516	638	631	587	24	22	18	21	19	18
Moderate physical problems	98	83	54	98	53	75	4	3	2	3	2	2
Rent burden 31-50% of income	596	638	466	572	598	537	22	20	16	19	18	16
Crowded	84	88	45	59	66	46	3	3	2	2	2	1
No problems	312	332	303	430	381	362	11	10	10	14	12	11
Assisted	599	826	962	867	980	1,070	22	26	33	28	30	32
MIDWEST	2,443	2,924	3,255	3,342	3,446	3,014	....	....	....	....	....	....
Priority problems	859	1,199	1,074	1,000	1,151	1,006	35	41	33	30	33	33
Severe physical problems	177	155	156	135	90	81	7	5	5	4	3	3
Rent burden greater than 50% of income	716	1,099	977	906	1,089	944	29	38	30	27	32	31
Rent burden only	630	944	810	763	958	814	26	32	25	23	28	27
Other problems	662	649	796	872	779	663	27	22	24	26	23	22
Moderate physical problems	42	47	113	78	77	81	2	2	3	2	2	3
Rent burden 31-50% of income	606	591	719	802	710	593	25	20	22	24	21	20
Crowded	56	67	78	74	75	42	2	2	2	2	2	1
No problems	471	409	501	547	551	444	19	14	15	16	16	15
Assisted	451	664	882	923	965	901	18	23	27	28	28	30
SOUTH	3,327	3,338	4,392	4,535	4,768	4,534	....	....	....	....	....	....
Priority problems	1,211	1,425	1,373	1,476	1,516	1,454	36	43	31	33	32	32
Severe physical problems	429	340	224	174	134	109	13	10	5	4	3	2
Rent burden greater than 50% of income	858	1,165	1,217	1,366	1,411	1,377	26	35	28	30	30	30
Rent burden only	599	816	894	1,046	1,178	1,120	18	24	20	23	25	25
Other problems	1,058	728	1,217	1,298	1,349	1,219	32	22	28	29	28	27
Moderate physical problems	472	324	386	384	381	322	14	10	9	8	8	7
Rent burden 31-50% of income	705	541	953	1,005	1,078	1,006	21	16	22	22	23	22
Crowded	173	117	145	151	132	161	5	4	3	3	3	4
No problems	416	394	663	664	677	732	12	12	15	15	14	16
Assisted	642	791	1,142	1,097	1,225	1,129	19	24	26	24	26	25
WEST	2,189	2,688	2,822	3,060	3,246	3,696	....	....	....	....	....	....
Priority problems	746	1,167	1,221	1,338	1,386	1,560	34	43	43	44	43	42
Severe physical problems	74	99	144	119	97	67	3	4	5	4	3	2
Rent burden greater than 50% of income	692	1,110	1,132	1,278	1,334	1,523	32	41	40	42	41	41
Rent burden only	598	954	883	1,002	1,058	1,239	27	36	31	33	33	34
Other problems	705	707	763	796	925	1,053	32	26	27	26	28	28
Moderate physical problems	83	89	73	114	98	113	4	3	3	4	3	3
Rent burden 31-50% of income	587	586	643	693	831	911	27	22	23	23	26	25
Crowded	162	194	231	175	201	310	7	7	8	6	6	8
No problems	335	325	313	360	325	407	15	12	11	12	10	11
Assisted	401	489	525	566	604	676	18	18	19	19	19	18

Source: Analysis of data from American/Annual Housing Surveys in U.S. Department of Housing and Urban Development, Office of Policy Development and Research, "Rental Housing Assistance - The Crisis Continues: The 1997 Report to Congress on Worst Case Housing Needs." April 1998.

See Appendix A for definitions of housing problems.

Housing Problems and Costs

TABLE 3.42. PRIORITY HOUSING PROBLEMS AND ASSISTANCE FOR RENTERS BY PRESENCE OF CHILDREN AND RELATIVE INCOME: 1978 TO 1995

PRESENCE OF CHILDREN AND INCOME AS A PERCENT OF HUD-ADJUSTED AREA MEDIAN INCOME	1978					1993					1995				
	Total	With priority problems		Assisted		Total	With priority problems		Assisted		Total	With priority problems		Assisted	
		Number	Percent of income category	Number	Percent of income category		Number	Percent of income category	Number	Percent of income category		Number	Percent of income category	Number	Percent of income category
ALL RENTERS	26,919	4,688	17	2,729	10	33,472	5,825	17	4,459	13	34,149	5,886	17	4,654	14
0 to 30 percent	5,895	3,015	51	1,425	24	8,731	4,176	48	2,856	33	8,617	3,997	46	2,884	33
31 to 50	4,792	953	20	670	14	6,025	1,175	19	916	15	5,946	1,323	22	892	15
51 to 60	2,261	156	7	167	7	2,443	147	6	210	9	2,585	173	7	225	9
61 to 80	3,822	203	5	218	6	3,916	145	4	195	5	4,579	160	4	238	5
81 to 100	3,257	130	4	114	4	4,010	58	1	118	3	3,896	94	2	184	5
101 percent or more	6,891	231	3	134	2	8,375	124	2	163	2	8,527	139	2	171	2
RENTERS WITH CHILDREN	9,667	1,604	17	1,315	14	12,635	2,442	19	2,211	18	12,991	2,261	17	2,243	17
0 to 30 percent	2,178	1,092	50	626	29	4,075	1,927	47	1,454	36	3,893	1,692	43	1,459	37
31 to 50	1,998	297	15	338	17	2,578	356	14	419	16	2,615	414	16	402	15
51 to 60	967	55	6	105	11	1,049	50	5	108	10	1,082	55	5	110	10
61 to 80	1,547	59	4	133	9	1,453	45	3	103	7	1,753	30	2	127	7
81 to 100	1,141	39	3	59	5	1,290	26	2	63	5	1,274	32	2	68	5
101 percent or more	1,837	62	3	53	3	2,197	38	2	65	3	2,375	37	2	78	3

Source: Analysis of data from American/Annual Housing Surveys in U.S. Department of Housing and Urban Development, Office of Policy Development and Research, "Rental Housing Assistance - The Crisis Continues: The 1997 Report to Congress on Worst Case Housing Needs." April 1998.

See Appendix A for definitions of priority housing problems and HUD-adjusted area median income.

Housing Problems and Costs

TABLE 3.43. CROWDED AND SEVERELY CROWDED HOUSING UNITS BY STATE: 1940 TO 1990

AREA	1940 Occupied units reporting persons per room	Crowded units Number	Crowded units Percent	Severely crowded units Number	Severely crowded units Percent	1950[1] Occupied units reporting persons per room	Crowded units Number	Crowded units Percent	Severely crowded units Number	Severely crowded units Percent
United States	34,447,032	6,964,894	20.2	3,085,922	9.0	42,154,443	6,628,292	15.7	2,607,717	6.2
Alabama	664,342	271,795	40.9	151,995	22.9	774,350	236,381	30.5	118,871	15.4
Alaska	....	....	....	....	....	28,214	9,585	34.0	6,442	22.8
Arizona	129,315	50,775	39.3	35,154	27.2	205,895	56,794	27.6	32,381	15.7
Arkansas	489,654	185,066	37.8	101,391	20.7	513,675	136,897	26.7	66,529	13.0
California	2,112,988	276,057	13.1	118,009	5.6	3,286,242	403,360	12.3	153,081	4.7
Colorado	311,232	71,533	23.0	37,024	11.9	384,684	69,216	18.0	30,737	8.0
Connecticut	442,790	57,092	12.9	14,795	3.3	561,985	54,437	9.7	12,047	2.1
Delaware	69,801	7,828	11.2	2,386	3.4	89,089	8,573	9.6	2,668	3.0
District of Columbia	170,860	34,318	20.1	14,579	8.5	220,074	31,035	14.1	11,709	5.3
Florida	512,628	125,719	24.5	63,890	12.5	805,885	144,887	18.0	65,343	8.1
Georgia	741,877	271,138	36.5	143,466	19.3	873,424	237,277	27.2	114,220	13.1
Hawaii	....	....	....	....	....	111,394	34,364	30.8	13,174	11.8
Idaho	139,296	42,622	30.6	22,787	16.4	165,994	36,933	22.2	15,104	9.1
Illinois	2,172,101	330,425	15.2	120,011	5.5	2,541,472	324,876	12.8	121,187	4.8
Indiana	950,905	139,123	14.6	53,083	5.6	1,152,649	159,069	13.8	56,569	4.9
Iowa	693,860	81,364	11.7	30,456	4.4	767,732	79,371	10.3	26,223	3.4
Kansas	505,187	75,885	15.0	29,779	5.9	576,512	67,118	11.6	23,517	4.1
Kentucky	690,299	232,135	33.6	125,579	18.2	766,080	192,270	25.1	90,032	11.8
Louisiana	586,762	208,067	35.5	110,154	18.8	712,475	186,975	26.2	88,428	12.4
Maine	215,788	30,576	14.2	11,037	5.1	250,993	30,351	12.1	10,166	4.1
Maryland	459,377	65,420	14.2	20,891	4.5	632,109	77,580	12.3	23,399	3.7
Massachusetts	1,105,354	129,275	11.7	29,787	2.7	1,289,544	126,495	9.8	25,099	1.9
Michigan	1,383,109	179,193	13.0	56,676	4.1	1,763,830	192,930	10.9	56,925	3.2
Minnesota	720,426	121,902	16.9	48,333	6.7	831,232	108,690	13.1	35,807	4.3
Mississippi	525,315	211,323	40.2	113,745	21.7	543,568	174,704	32.1	89,856	16.5
Missouri	1,056,293	232,034	22.0	111,419	10.5	1,173,885	197,396	16.8	84,447	7.2
Montana	157,317	40,314	25.6	20,974	13.3	172,170	32,736	19.0	14,126	8.2
Nebraska	357,331	53,731	15.0	21,519	6.0	384,930	48,549	12.6	17,157	4.5
Nevada	32,532	7,399	22.7	3,983	12.2	48,941	7,999	16.3	3,309	6.8
New Hampshire	131,287	14,437	11.0	4,297	3.3	153,208	13,564	8.9	3,620	2.4
New Jersey	1,086,639	131,670	12.1	33,380	3.1	1,359,323	138,323	10.2	34,131	2.5
New Mexico	127,186	61,109	48.0	41,882	32.9	171,959	58,453	34.0	34,393	20.0
New York	3,615,727	508,945	14.1	120,331	3.3	4,257,492	526,049	12.4	141,043	3.3
North Carolina	778,285	274,476	35.3	138,596	17.8	976,516	245,304	25.1	107,420	11.0
North Dakota	150,007	41,891	27.9	20,409	13.6	158,803	32,587	20.5	13,473	8.5
Ohio	1,880,099	231,487	12.3	79,132	4.2	2,284,265	248,404	10.9	80,507	3.5
Oklahoma	601,338	199,671	33.2	114,233	19.0	649,755	130,199	20.0	60,046	9.2
Oregon	332,483	44,082	13.3	19,375	5.8	471,471	59,823	12.7	23,241	4.9
Pennsylvania	2,491,353	379,277	15.2	118,299	4.7	2,879,311	306,791	10.7	82,493	2.9
Rhode Island	186,085	24,462	13.1	6,572	3.5	223,538	21,756	9.7	4,798	2.1
South Carolina	430,403	170,996	39.7	91,973	21.4	505,616	146,231	28.9	69,491	13.7
South Dakota	162,950	33,362	20.5	15,739	9.7	179,850	27,607	15.4	11,144	6.2
Tennessee	706,731	250,318	35.4	135,145	19.1	857,614	217,252	25.3	102,776	12.0
Texas	1,660,787	530,343	31.9	297,272	17.9	2,148,625	499,564	23.3	252,014	11.7
Utah	138,330	41,880	30.3	18,559	13.4	184,586	43,271	23.4	12,563	6.8
Vermont	91,428	8,986	9.8	2,541	2.8	102,089	9,183	9.0	2,606	2.6
Virginia	621,217	161,265	26.0	77,187	12.4	830,216	158,788	19.1	65,691	7.9
Washington	529,562	69,165	13.1	27,939	5.3	722,533	81,826	11.3	27,691	3.8
West Virginia	440,099	135,012	30.7	66,759	15.2	510,467	115,401	22.6	49,706	9.7
Wisconsin	819,863	100,460	12.3	33,120	4.0	955,062	106,662	11.2	31,867	3.3
Wyoming	68,434	19,491	28.5	10,280	15.0	82,725	18,355	22.2	8,066	9.8

See notes at end of table.

Housing Problems and Costs

TABLE 3.43. CROWDED AND SEVERELY CROWDED HOUSING UNITS BY STATE: 1940 TO 1990 - Continued

AREA	1960 Occupied housing units	Crowded units Number	Crowded units Percent	Severely crowded units Number	Severely crowded units Percent	1970 Occupied housing units	Crowded units Number	Crowded units Percent	Severely crowded units Number	Severely crowded units Percent
United States	53,023,875	6,113,473	11.5	1,902,923	3.6	63,449,747	5,210,874	8.2	1,408,416	2.2
Alabama	884,116	171,113	19.4	77,551	8.8	1,034,113	114,680	11.1	40,922	4.0
Alaska	57,250	16,090	28.1	8,053	14.1	79,059	15,490	19.6	7,715	9.8
Arizona	366,630	69,884	19.1	32,616	8.9	539,157	68,220	12.7	28,318	5.3
Arkansas	523,552	93,077	17.8	40,346	7.7	615,424	65,747	10.7	22,173	3.6
California	4,982,108	475,287	9.5	121,173	2.4	6,573,861	521,952	7.9	156,429	2.4
Colorado	529,419	61,283	11.6	17,824	3.4	690,928	47,971	6.9	12,100	1.8
Connecticut	752,736	56,004	7.4	9,003	1.2	933,269	58,048	6.2	10,343	1.1
Delaware	128,582	10,122	7.9	2,524	2.0	164,804	9,277	5.6	1,875	1.1
District of Columbia	252,066	30,725	12.2	11,018	4.4	262,538	32,160	12.2	12,501	4.8
Florida	1,550,414	191,526	12.4	71,956	4.6	2,284,786	204,871	9.0	78,462	3.4
Georgia	1,070,325	197,130	18.4	85,402	8.0	1,369,225	148,737	10.9	50,621	3.7
Hawaii	153,064	39,331	25.7	13,088	8.6	203,088	40,462	19.9	15,804	7.8
Idaho	193,839	29,997	15.5	8,225	4.2	218,960	20,249	9.2	4,912	2.2
Illinois	3,084,971	309,350	10.0	82,830	2.7	3,502,138	273,536	7.8	59,468	1.7
Indiana	1,387,878	158,017	11.4	40,204	2.9	1,609,494	129,318	8.0	26,471	1.6
Iowa	841,357	67,286	8.0	13,826	1.6	896,311	52,582	5.9	8,721	1.0
Kansas	672,899	63,523	9.4	14,509	2.2	727,364	43,153	5.9	8,209	1.1
Kentucky	851,867	145,771	17.1	55,004	6.5	983,665	104,292	10.6	30,659	3.1
Louisiana	892,344	188,035	21.1	80,423	9.0	1,052,038	152,440	14.5	53,560	5.1
Maine	280,355	28,958	10.3	7,452	2.7	302,923	22,833	7.5	5,011	1.7
Maryland	863,001	83,471	9.7	20,059	2.3	1,175,073	77,384	6.6	15,462	1.3
Massachusetts	1,534,985	103,072	6.7	15,473	1.0	1,759,692	104,706	6.0	17,322	1.0
Michigan	2,239,079	220,263	9.8	44,108	2.0	2,653,059	202,116	7.6	36,440	1.4
Minnesota	991,981	102,733	10.4	21,534	2.2	1,153,946	84,979	7.4	15,349	1.3
Mississippi	568,070	133,428	23.5	68,975	12.1	636,724	96,344	15.1	42,647	6.7
Missouri	1,360,054	161,096	11.8	52,878	3.9	1,520,567	124,181	8.2	31,364	2.1
Montana	202,240	30,043	14.9	8,891	4.4	217,304	20,777	9.6	5,327	2.5
Nebraska	433,448	39,936	9.2	8,439	1.9	473,721	29,307	6.2	5,320	1.1
Nevada	91,520	12,619	13.8	4,268	4.7	160,052	14,131	8.8	3,929	2.5
New Hampshire	180,020	13,286	7.4	2,395	1.3	225,378	14,826	6.6	2,732	1.2
New Jersey	1,806,439	131,194	7.3	26,485	1.5	2,218,182	136,436	6.2	27,345	1.2
New Mexico	251,209	59,299	23.6	28,103	11.2	289,389	45,171	15.6	19,384	6.7
New York	5,248,710	488,423	9.3	131,418	2.5	5,913,861	447,602	7.6	108,615	1.8
North Carolina	1,204,715	207,234	17.2	76,186	6.3	1,509,564	153,718	10.2	44,483	2.9
North Dakota	173,362	26,666	15.4	7,550	4.4	181,613	16,549	9.1	3,864	2.1
Ohio	2,852,557	270,759	9.5	63,993	2.2	3,289,432	215,805	6.6	38,065	1.2
Oklahoma	734,593	87,365	11.9	28,533	3.9	850,803	61,924	7.3	15,302	1.8
Oregon	558,214	48,317	8.7	11,237	2.0	691,631	38,629	5.6	8,666	1.3
Pennsylvania	3,350,839	242,146	7.2	46,928	1.4	3,705,410	203,203	5.5	35,277	1.0
Rhode Island	257,335	17,740	6.9	2,596	1.0	291,965	17,604	6.0	2,670	0.9
South Carolina	603,551	125,317	20.8	53,482	8.9	734,373	90,623	12.3	31,208	4.2
South Dakota	194,821	25,399	13.0	7,541	3.9	200,807	18,042	9.0	5,082	2.5
Tennessee	1,003,301	162,692	16.2	64,492	6.4	1,213,187	117,441	9.7	36,825	3.0
Texas	2,778,116	451,873	16.3	186,688	6.7	3,433,996	387,530	11.3	137,527	4.0
Utah	241,532	40,246	16.7	9,221	3.8	297,934	31,601	10.6	6,766	2.3
Vermont	110,732	8,696	7.9	1,910	1.7	132,098	8,647	6.5	1,677	1.3
Virginia	1,072,840	147,590	13.8	49,772	4.6	1,390,636	110,869	8.0	30,172	2.2
Washington	894,168	74,025	8.3	15,832	1.8	1,105,587	60,290	5.5	13,539	1.2
West Virginia	521,142	78,878	15.1	27,628	5.3	547,214	49,829	9.1	13,321	2.4
Wisconsin	1,146,342	101,676	8.9	18,602	1.6	1,328,804	95,423	7.2	16,284	1.2
Wyoming	99,187	15,482	15.6	4,679	4.7	104,600	9,169	8.8	2,178	2.1

See notes at end of table.

Housing Problems and Costs

	TABLE 3.43. CROWDED AND SEVERELY CROWDED HOUSING UNITS BY STATE: 1940 TO 1990 - Continued									
	1980					1990				
AREA	Occupied housing units	Crowded units		Severely crowded units		Occupied housing units	Crowded units		Severely crowded units	
		Number	Percent	Number	Percent		Number	Percent	Number	Percent
United States	80,389,673	3,648,445	4.5	1,134,619	1.4	91,947,410	4,548,799	4.9	1,911,867	2.1
Alabama	1,341,856	72,668	5.4	19,709	1.5	1,506,790	52,927	3.5	13,786	0.9
Alaska	131,463	13,225	10.1	6,625	5.0	188,915	16,201	8.6	7,284	3.9
Arizona	957,032	69,307	7.2	30,526	3.2	1,368,843	101,636	7.4	46,721	3.4
Arkansas	816,065	42,650	5.2	10,607	1.3	891,179	33,197	3.7	7,977	0.9
California	8,629,866	638,333	7.4	302,704	3.5	10,381,206	1,275,377	12.3	737,247	7.1
Colorado	1,061,249	30,216	2.8	8,893	0.8	1,282,489	38,139	3.0	13,500	1.1
Connecticut	1,093,678	28,595	2.6	5,318	0.5	1,230,479	28,237	2.3	7,796	0.6
Delaware	207,081	5,351	2.6	1,161	0.6	247,497	5,624	2.3	1,556	0.6
District of Columbia	253,143	20,518	8.1	9,279	3.7	249,634	20,587	8.2	11,060	4.4
Florida	3,744,254	199,529	5.3	82,330	2.2	5,134,869	297,557	5.8	135,722	2.6
Georgia	1,871,652	99,423	5.3	27,114	1.4	2,366,615	95,828	4.0	28,771	1.2
Hawaii	294,052	44,905	15.3	20,706	7.0	356,267	56,708	15.9	27,810	7.8
Idaho	324,107	14,462	4.5	3,673	1.1	360,723	15,199	4.2	4,468	1.2
Illinois	4,045,374	169,056	4.2	42,745	1.1	4,202,240	166,805	4.0	57,081	1.4
Indiana	1,927,050	60,009	3.1	10,582	0.5	2,065,355	45,376	2.2	9,277	0.4
Iowa	1,053,033	21,590	2.1	3,810	0.4	1,064,325	16,009	1.5	3,797	0.4
Kansas	872,239	20,679	2.4	4,495	0.5	944,726	23,690	2.5	6,958	0.7
Kentucky	1,263,355	58,788	4.7	12,375	1.0	1,379,782	35,873	2.6	7,150	0.5
Louisiana	1,411,788	99,965	7.1	27,544	2.0	1,499,269	89,268	6.0	27,024	1.8
Maine	395,184	12,137	3.1	2,354	0.6	465,312	7,998	1.7	1,671	0.4
Maryland	1,460,865	44,824	3.1	10,987	0.8	1,748,991	53,139	3.0	18,920	1.1
Massachusetts	2,032,717	53,192	2.6	10,049	0.5	2,247,110	56,700	2.5	17,970	0.8
Michigan	3,195,213	99,929	3.1	18,631	0.6	3,419,331	90,551	2.6	23,813	0.7
Minnesota	1,445,222	32,832	2.3	6,910	0.5	1,647,853	34,126	2.1	11,048	0.7
Mississippi	827,169	66,385	8.0	21,643	2.6	911,374	52,890	5.8	16,116	1.8
Missouri	1,793,399	60,097	3.4	12,790	0.7	1,961,206	48,264	2.5	11,158	0.6
Montana	283,742	10,784	3.8	2,954	1.0	306,163	8,886	2.9	2,462	0.8
Nebraska	571,400	12,052	2.1	2,273	0.4	602,363	10,512	1.7	2,762	0.5
Nevada	304,327	14,255	4.7	5,440	1.8	466,297	29,890	6.4	13,353	2.9
New Hampshire	323,493	7,826	2.4	1,416	0.4	411,186	6,610	1.6	1,213	0.3
New Jersey	2,548,594	89,564	3.5	20,709	0.8	2,794,711	108,771	3.9	37,250	1.3
New Mexico	441,466	38,031	8.6	15,153	3.4	542,709	42,810	7.9	17,644	3.3
New York	6,340,429	311,848	4.9	90,086	1.4	6,639,322	431,733	6.5	183,651	2.8
North Carolina	2,043,291	91,854	4.5	19,163	0.9	2,517,026	72,635	2.9	16,549	0.7
North Dakota	227,664	6,178	2.7	1,175	0.5	240,878	4,762	2.0	1,119	0.5
Ohio	3,833,828	95,646	2.5	15,153	0.4	4,087,546	71,771	1.8	13,647	0.3
Oklahoma	1,118,561	41,073	3.7	9,182	0.8	1,206,135	39,941	3.3	10,432	0.9
Oregon	991,593	28,967	2.9	9,030	0.9	1,103,313	40,135	3.6	15,086	1.4
Pennsylvania	4,219,606	101,290	2.4	18,965	0.4	4,495,966	82,518	1.8	21,800	0.5
Rhode Island	338,590	8,600	2.5	1,340	0.4	377,977	8,676	2.3	2,323	0.6
South Carolina	1,029,981	61,508	6.0	14,956	1.5	1,258,044	51,061	4.1	13,500	1.1
South Dakota	242,523	8,739	3.6	2,482	1.0	259,034	7,660	3.0	2,466	1.0
Tennessee	1,618,505	70,744	4.4	16,205	1.0	1,853,725	50,767	2.7	12,134	0.7
Texas	4,929,267	356,539	7.2	124,859	2.5	6,070,937	494,578	8.1	216,949	3.6
Utah	448,603	25,824	5.8	5,001	1.1	537,273	29,577	5.5	7,728	1.4
Vermont	178,325	4,534	2.5	873	0.5	210,650	3,595	1.7	764	0.4
Virginia	1,863,073	64,081	3.4	15,422	0.8	2,291,830	65,042	2.8	20,875	0.9
Washington	1,540,510	44,380	2.9	15,293	1.0	1,872,431	72,798	3.9	29,409	1.6
West Virginia	686,311	28,232	4.1	5,469	0.8	688,557	13,123	1.9	2,115	0.3
Wisconsin	1,652,261	40,270	2.4	6,706	0.4	1,822,118	38,340	2.1	9,745	0.5
Wyoming	165,624	6,961	4.2	1,754	1.1	168,839	4,702	2.8	1,210	0.7

Source: U.S. Bureau of the Census, Census of Housing 1940-1990. Tables prepared by Robert Bonnette.

Crowded units have 1.01 or more persons per room. Severely crowded units have 1.51 or more persons per room.

(1) Alaska and Hawaii are not included in 1950 U.S. total.

Housing Problems and Costs

TABLE 3.44. SELECTED HOUSING COSTS FOR OCCUPIED HOUSING UNITS: 1991
(In thousands, except as noted)

CHARACTERISTIC	Total occupied units	Tenure — Owner	Tenure — Renter	Household characteristics — Black	Hispanic	Elderly (65+)	Moved in past year	Below poverty level	Regions — North-east	Midwest	South	West
TOTAL	93,147	59,796	33,351	10,832	6,239	20,348	16,434	12,836	18,962	22,593	32,190	19,402
MONTHLY HOUSING COSTS												
Less than $100	2,119	1,505	615	538	147	918	282	1,032	150	335	1,352	282
$100 to $199	11,239	8,987	2,252	1,558	630	5,759	782	2,869	1,249	2,845	5,384	1,761
$200 to $249	5,969	4,549	1,420	684	322	2,687	634	1,137	942	1,879	2,197	950
$250 to $299	5,831	3,828	2,003	751	320	2,096	805	1,004	1,101	1,832	2,036	863
$300 to $349	5,701	3,110	2,591	767	406	1,672	1,084	1,096	1,114	1,733	1,943	911
$350 to $399	5,494	2,651	2,843	775	414	1,218	1,280	898	1,112	1,520	1,960	903
$400 to $449	5,455	2,435	3,019	791	403	891	1,367	807	1,095	1,542	1,878	939
$450 to $499	5,198	2,337	2,861	669	432	774	1,227	568	1,073	1,384	1,753	988
$500 to $599	8,707	4,066	4,641	1,029	781	1,130	2,077	825	1,936	2,111	2,803	1,857
$600 to $699	6,866	3,614	3,252	784	520	714	1,633	459	1,546	1,654	2,110	1,557
$700 TO $799	5,236	3,157	2,078	529	412	441	1,226	263	1,195	1,082	1,554	1,405
$800 to $999	6,802	4,856	1,945	492	431	463	1,275	287	1,650	1,348	1,965	1,839
$1,000 to $1,249	4,364	3,599	765	296	256	245	703	116	1,155	763	1,147	1,299
$1,250 to $1,499	2,458	2,162	296	113	131	136	350	36	684	374	565	835
$1,500 or more	3,990	3,746	244	128	209	173	576	75	1,217	482	794	1,496
No cash rent	2,526	...	2,526	450	231	482	605	968	468	502	1,082	474
Mortgage payment not reported	5,192	5,192	...	479	195	548	528	395	1,276	1,207	1,668	1,041
Median (In dollars; excludes no cash rent)	459	455	462	392	481	257	509	285	540	410	396	572
MEDIAN MONTHLY HOUSING COSTS FOR OWNERS												
Monthly costs including all mortgages plus maintenance costs (In dollars)	480	480	...	403	520	251	727	232	611	443	384	643
Monthly costs excluding 2nd and subsequent mortgages and maintenance costs (In dollars)	439	439	...	367	479	239	697	220	555	407	353	556
MONTHLY HOUSING COSTS AS PERCENT OF CURRENT INCOME												
Less than 5 percent	2,759	2,538	221	164	109	622	196	32	362	549	1,281	566
5 to 9 percent	9,801	8,771	1,030	772	446	2,746	640	130	1,636	2,582	3,913	1,669
10 to 14 percent	12,260	9,525	2,735	1,040	465	3,059	1,313	263	2,188	3,557	4,480	2,035
15 to 19 percent	13,193	8,928	4,265	1,277	702	2,667	2,038	515	2,528	3,540	4,622	2,504
20 to 24 percent	11,247	7,022	4,225	1,269	708	2,003	2,112	758	2,294	2,790	3,922	2,242
25 to 29 percent	9,103	5,197	3,906	1,083	625	1,762	2,042	893	2,085	2,122	2,890	2,007
30 to 34 percent	6,244	3,362	2,882	903	530	1,414	1,373	773	1,453	1,364	1,940	1,487
35 to 39 percent	4,212	2,213	2,000	563	357	991	1,026	673	948	849	1,277	1,138
40 to 49 percent	5,175	2,506	2,669	810	601	1,278	1,241	1,227	1,121	1,116	1,663	1,275
50 to 59 percent	2,917	1,210	1,707	509	297	775	788	932	692	591	836	798
60 to 69 percent	1,786	715	1,071	303	229	490	524	737	448	326	514	498
70 to 99 percent	2,563	967	1,596	444	324	658	719	1,307	585	563	714	701
100 percent or more [1]	3,181	1,210	1,971	585	332	696	980	2,319	725	717	1,010	729
Zero or negative income	987	440	547	180	89	157	311	914	153	218	379	238
No cash rent	2,526	...	2,526	450	231	482	605	968	468	502	1,082	474
Mortgage payment not reported	5,192	5,192	...	479	195	548	528	395	1,276	1,207	1,668	1,041
Median (In percent; excludes 3 previous lines)	22	18	28	27	28	21	28	50	24	20	20	25
Median (In percent; excludes 4 lines before medians)	21	18	27	25	27	20	27	41	23	20	20	24

Source: U.S. Bureau of the Census and U.S. Department of Housing and Urban Development, "American Housing Survey for the United States in 1991." Current Housing Reports H150/91. April 1993.

Consistent with the 1990 Census.
(1) May reflect a temporary situation, living off savings, or response error.

Housing Problems and Costs

TABLE 3.45. SELECTED HOUSING COSTS FOR OCCUPIED HOUSING UNITS: 1993
(In thousands, except as noted)

CHARACTERISTIC	Total occupied units	Tenure		Household characteristics					Regions			
		Owner	Renter	Black	Hispanic	Elderly (65+)	Moved in past year	Below poverty level	North-east	Midwest	South	West
TOTAL	94,724	61,252	33,472	11,128	6,614	20,438	16,102	13,787	18,906	23,031	32,936	19,850
MONTHLY HOUSING COSTS												
Less than $100	1,606	1,055	551	419	113	626	257	832	126	284	956	240
$100 to $199	9,600	7,521	2,079	1,373	585	4,963	813	2,704	993	2,422	4,684	1,502
$200 to $249	5,860	4,437	1,424	722	286	2,762	506	1,162	852	1,742	2,254	1,012
$250 to $299	5,546	3,818	1,728	721	283	2,182	705	1,012	1,099	1,662	2,006	779
$300 to $349	5,285	3,214	2,071	658	352	1,801	861	902	1,005	1,523	1,896	860
$350 to $399	5,324	2,583	2,741	862	382	1,267	1,114	979	1,007	1,512	1,943	862
$400 to $449	5,306	2,456	2,850	717	418	1,061	1,233	872	947	1,615	1,926	818
$450 to $499	5,152	2,302	2,851	654	465	832	1,203	717	1,002	1,402	1,821	927
$500 to $599	9,295	4,478	4,817	1,159	847	1,215	2,100	1,097	1,951	2,373	3,096	1,875
$600 to $699	7,698	4,015	3,683	938	690	833	1,680	716	1,764	1,824	2,388	1,721
$700 TO $799	5,861	3,479	2,382	610	435	504	1,313	388	1,363	1,253	1,819	1,426
$800 to $999	7,737	5,480	2,257	667	570	600	1,414	452	1,873	1,592	2,227	2,045
$1,000 to $1,249	5,263	4,292	971	369	292	318	878	184	1,226	942	1,501	1,595
$1,250 to $1,499	3,044	2,665	379	132	188	141	401	127	837	556	709	941
$1,500 or more	4,222	3,946	275	156	198	272	475	112	1,260	516	863	1,582
No cash rent	2,414	....	2,414	473	226	469	544	922	408	514	1,062	430
Mortgage payment not reported	5,512	5,512	....	498	282	593	604	606	1,193	1,301	1,785	1,234
Median (In dollars; excludes no cash rent)	497	511	487	423	520	281	537	323	583	445	434	613
MEDIAN MONTHLY HOUSING COSTS FOR OWNERS												
Monthly costs including all mortgages plus maintenance costs (In dollars)	536	536	....	464	579	276	735	279	661	495	442	702
Monthly costs excluding 2nd and subsequent mortgages and maintenance costs (In dollars)	494	494	....	415	529	261	706	270	605	460	409	629
MONTHLY HOUSING COSTS AS PERCENT OF CURRENT INCOME												
Less than 5 percent	2,393	2,237	156	140	81	570	198	18	293	586	1,043	470
5 to 9 percent	8,961	8,072	889	629	369	2,590	574	104	1,365	2,444	3,581	1,570
10 to 14 percent	12,601	9,753	2,848	1,077	563	3,164	1,426	245	2,239	3,507	4,727	2,128
15 to 19 percent	13,976	9,892	4,083	1,280	691	2,767	2,090	490	2,624	3,671	5,149	2,532
20 to 24 percent	11,625	7,511	4,114	1,299	761	1,988	2,174	614	2,253	2,902	4,112	2,359
25 to 29 percent	8,915	5,204	3,710	1,105	649	1,774	1,717	877	1,986	2,045	2,768	2,116
30 to 34 percent	6,352	3,368	2,984	913	550	1,383	1,342	844	1,493	1,439	1,999	1,421
35 to 39 percent	4,204	2,109	2,095	599	415	985	972	644	943	799	1,352	1,109
40 to 49 percent	5,186	2,406	2,781	795	512	1,213	1,265	1,308	1,126	1,112	1,657	1,291
50 to 59 percent	2,906	1,291	1,615	551	363	698	760	946	686	574	853	793
60 to 69 percent	1,965	829	1,136	348	243	571	480	776	484	388	563	530
70 to 99 percent	2,854	1,008	1,846	539	350	729	762	1,450	656	611	788	798
100 percent or more [1]	3,694	1,401	2,293	634	473	780	1,032	2,820	885	856	1,103	851
Zero or negative income	1,166	659	507	248	86	165	162	1,121	271	281	393	221
No cash rent	2,414	....	2,414	473	226	469	544	922	408	514	1,062	430
Mortgage payment not reported	5,512	5,512	....	498	282	593	604	606	1,193	1,301	1,785	1,234
Median (In percent; excludes 3 previous lines)	22	19	29	27	29	21	28	54	24	20	20	25
Median (In percent; excludes 4 lines before medians)	21	18	28	26	27	20	26	42	23	20	20	24

Source: U.S. Bureau of the Census and U.S. Department of Housing and Urban Development, "American Housing Survey for the United States in 1993." Current Housing Reports H150/93. Issued February 1995.

Consistent with the 1990 Census.
(1) May reflect a temporary situation, living off savings, or response error.

Housing Problems and Costs

TABLE 3.46. SELECTED HOUSING COSTS FOR OCCUPIED HOUSING UNITS: 1995
(In thousands, except as noted)

CHARACTERISTIC	Total occupied units	Tenure		Household characteristics					Regions			
		Owner	Renter	Black	Hispanic	Elderly (65+)	Moved in past year	Below poverty level	North-east	Midwest	South	West
TOTAL	97,693	63,544	34,150	11,773	7,757	20,841	17,204	14,695	19,200	23,662	34,236	20,596
MONTHLY HOUSING COSTS												
Less than $100	1,537	1,049	488	353	134	637	190	746	133	287	935	181
$100 to $199	9,055	7,269	1,786	1,389	676	4,610	699	2,701	917	2,214	4,489	1,436
$200 to $249	5,859	4,675	1,183	731	364	2,725	457	1,270	756	1,835	2,350	918
$250 to $299	5,393	4,034	1,358	671	259	2,226	584	980	891	1,616	1,999	887
$300 to $349	5,265	3,375	1,890	752	378	1,725	808	1,056	998	1,585	1,857	825
$350 to $399	5,379	2,985	2,395	808	438	1,394	993	959	1,011	1,518	2,010	841
$400 to $449	5,507	2,702	2,805	804	485	1,174	1,309	963	1,045	1,528	1,989	945
$450 to $499	5,406	2,566	2,840	822	526	889	1,387	893	1,053	1,522	1,841	990
$500 to $599	9,997	4,921	5,076	1,358	1,024	1,432	2,492	1,294	2,019	2,522	3,420	2,036
$600 to $699	8,544	4,356	4,188	1,079	870	975	1,952	879	1,863	1,997	2,771	1,914
$700 TO $799	7,052	4,142	2,910	731	597	695	1,560	647	1,477	1,551	2,304	1,720
$800 to $999	9,540	6,684	2,856	912	664	827	1,774	591	2,162	2,009	3,032	2,338
$1,000 to $1,249	6,721	5,477	1,244	486	482	440	1,134	329	1,633	1,390	1,889	1,809
$1,250 to $1,499	3,938	3,518	420	231	260	245	559	175	1,061	709	936	1,232
$1,500 or more	6,156	5,791	365	236	333	368	766	305	1,730	938	1,396	2,092
No cash rent	2,344	...	2,344	408	265	481	540	908	451	442	1,017	435
Mortgage payment not reported	-	-	....	-	-	-	-	-	-	-	-	-
Median (in dollars; excludes no cash rent)	543	563	523	461	547	300	576	357	630	484	477	653
MEDIAN MONTHLY HOUSING COSTS FOR OWNERS												
Monthly costs including all mortgages plus maintenance costs (In dollars)	593	593	....	497	614	299	794	320	736	542	499	756
Monthly costs excluding 2nd and subsequent mortgages and maintenance costs (In dollars)	549	549	....	451	577	282	765	299	677	504	464	695
MONTHLY HOUSING COSTS AS PERCENT OF CURRENT INCOME												
Less than 5 percent	3,036	2,845	191	190	123	683	199	32	419	720	1,348	549
5 to 9 percent	10,508	9,570	938	798	542	2,816	713	143	1,519	2,976	4,196	1,815
10 to 14 percent	14,002	11,260	2,741	1,274	660	3,351	1,563	339	2,451	4,053	5,269	2,228
15 to 19 percent	14,673	10,637	4,035	1,482	894	2,575	2,462	490	2,720	3,960	5,463	2,530
20 to 24 percent	12,318	8,174	4,144	1,464	879	2,105	2,425	645	2,552	3,084	4,096	2,586
25 to 29 percent	9,519	5,523	3,996	1,163	810	1,752	2,063	896	2,031	2,202	3,075	2,211
30 to 34 percent	6,514	3,586	2,928	837	615	1,351	1,375	810	1,461	1,355	2,145	1,553
35 to 39 percent	4,703	2,402	2,301	648	534	987	1,120	680	1,060	953	1,434	1,255
40 to 49 percent	5,481	2,688	2,793	932	648	1,237	1,354	1,247	1,235	1,011	1,759	1,477
50 to 59 percent	3,174	1,525	1,649	510	411	783	807	931	735	589	949	900
60 to 69 percent	2,118	950	1,168	389	267	521	557	808	441	447	619	611
70 to 99 percent	2,988	1,185	1,803	547	474	748	727	1,627	744	544	828	873
100 percent or more [1]	4,473	2,029	2,444	805	489	1,050	1,079	3,394	1,089	935	1,330	1,120
Zero or negative income	1,843	1,169	674	326	146	401	220	1,746	291	393	707	452
No cash rent	2,344	....	2,344	408	265	481	540	908	451	442	1,017	435
Mortgage payment not reported	-	-	....	-	-	-	-	-	-	-	-	-
Median (In percent; excludes 3 previous lines)	22	19	29	26	29	21	27	58	24	20	20	25
Median (In percent; excludes 4 lines before medians)	21	18	28	25	27	20	26	42	23	19	19	24

Source: U.S. Bureau of the Census and U.S. Department of Housing and Urban Development, "American Housing Survey for the United States in 1995." Current Housing Reports H150/95RV. Issued July 1997.

Consistent with the 1990 Census.

(1) May reflect a temporary situation, living off savings, or response error.

(-) means zero or rounds to zero.

Housing Problems and Costs

	Monthly income (1997 dollars)		Owner costs (1997 dollars, except as noted)				Renter costs (1997 dollars)		Cost as a percent of income			
									Owners		Renters	
YEAR	Owner	Renter	Home price	Mortgage rate (Percent)	Mortgage payment	After-tax mortgage payment	Contract rent	Gross rent	Before-tax mortgage payment	After-tax mortgage payment	Contract rent	Gross rent
1975	2,888	1,805	97,827	8.92	703	580	398	457	24.4	20.1	22.0	25.3
1976	2,937	1,835	99,604	8.87	713	589	399	462	24.3	20.1	21.8	25.2
1977	2,949	1,843	104,935	8.82	748	662	401	467	25.4	22.5	21.8	25.4
1978	2,970	1,856	112,931	9.37	845	728	404	472	28.4	24.5	21.8	25.4
1979	2,936	1,835	117,768	10.59	977	831	399	467	33.3	28.3	21.7	25.4
1980	2,884	1,802	114,806	12.46	1,100	911	393	464	38.1	31.6	21.8	25.7
1981	2,874	1,796	110,068	14.39	1,204	981	393	467	41.9	34.1	21.9	26.0
1982	2,888	1,805	107,008	14.73	1,197	991	402	481	41.4	34.3	22.3	26.6
1983	2,910	1,819	106,218	12.26	1,002	832	411	493	34.4	28.6	22.6	27.1
1984	2,934	1,834	105,823	11.99	979	818	418	500	33.4	27.9	22.8	27.3
1985	2,970	1,857	107,205	11.17	931	780	431	512	31.4	26.3	23.2	27.6
1986	3,037	1,898	112,635	9.79	874	736	451	531	28.8	24.2	23.8	28.0
1987	3,061	1,913	116,090	8.95	837	732	456	531	27.3	23.9	23.8	27.8
1988	3,086	1,929	118,360	8.98	856	766	457	530	27.7	24.8	23.7	27.5
1989	3,044	1,903	119,742	9.81	931	828	455	527	30.6	27.2	23.9	27.7
1990	3,039	1,900	117,274	9.74	906	807	453	522	29.8	26.5	23.8	27.5
1991	3,014	1,884	114,708	9.07	836	749	452	521	27.7	24.8	24.0	27.6
1992	3,078	1,924	114,412	7.83	743	674	452	520	24.2	21.9	23.5	27.1
1993	3,040	1,900	113,622	6.93	676	619	452	520	22.2	20.4	23.8	27.4
1994	3,033	1,895	113,819	7.31	703	645	454	521	23.2	21.3	23.9	27.5
1995	3,050	1,907	114,708	7.69	735	671	455	520	24.1	22.0	23.9	27.3
1996	3,080	1,925	116,485	7.58	739	674	456	521	24.0	21.9	23.7	27.1
1997	3,080	1,925	118,854	7.52	749	684	461	526	24.3	22.2	24.0	27.3

TABLE 3.47. OWNER AND RENTER COSTS AND COSTS RELATIVE TO INCOME: 1975 to 1997

Source: Joint Center for Housing Studies of Harvard University, "The State of the Nation's Housing: 1998."

All dollar amounts are expressed in 1997 constant dollars using the Bureau of Labor Statistics' Consumer Price Index (CPI-UX) for All Items.
See Appendix B under "Consumer Price Index" (CPI) for a discussion on the use of the CPI as a price deflator.

Housing Problems and Costs

TABLE 3.48. NATIONAL ASSOCIATION OF REALTORS® HOUSING AFFORDABILITY INDICES: 1977 TO 1997

YEAR	Composite	Fixed [1]	ARM [2]	First-time buyer
1977	120.6	....	....	93.7
1978	111.4	....	....	83.8
1979	97.2	....	....	73.4
1980	79.9	....	....	58.8
1981	68.9	....	....	50.7
1982	69.5	69.4	69.7	50.6
1983	83.2	82.0	85.6	59.4
1984	89.1	84.6	92.1	64.9
1985	94.8	89.6	100.6	68.3
1986	108.9	105.7	116.3	75.6
1987	114.2	107.6	122.4	79.0
1988	113.5	103.6	122.0	77.7
1989	106.1	101.8	112.3	72.5
1990	109.5	106.5	118.3	72.4
1991	112.9	109.9	124.2	75.0
1992	124.7	120.1	145.0	80.1
1993	133.3	128.4	154.9	86.4
1994	131.8	122.2	149.5	83.8
1995	129.3	123.7	140.0	82.2
1996	130.5	127.0	140.0	83.2
1997	129.5	126.6	140.5	82.9

Source: National Association of Realtors®, Housing Affordability Index.

(1) Based on purchase using fixed-rate mortgage.
(2) Based on purchase using adjustable-rate mortgage.
See Appendix A for descriptions of indices.

Housing Problems and Costs

YEAR AND QUARTER	TABLE 3.49. NATIONAL ASSOCIATION OF HOME BUILDERS HOUSING OPPORTUNITY INDEX: 1991 TO 1997
	Index value
1991	
First quarter	....
Second quarter	....
Third quarter	....
Fourth quarter	37.9
1992	
First quarter	53.9
Second quarter	55.5
Third quarter	57.5
Fourth quarter	60.0
1993	
First quarter	64.7
Second quarter	65.1
Third quarter	65.1
Fourth quarter	66.8
1994	
First quarter	67.5
Second quarter	60.5
Third quarter	61.7
Fourth quarter	62.3
1995	
First quarter	61.2
Second quarter	60.5
Third quarter	61.3
Fourth quarter	63.4
1996	
First quarter	67.5
Second quarter	63.1
Third quarter	61.2
Fourth quarter	64.1
1997	
First quarter	66.5
Second quarter	64.3
Third quarter	63.7
Fourth quarter	64.8

Source: National Association of Home Builders, Housing Opportunity Index.

See Appendix A for description of Housing Opportunity Index.

Housing Problems and Costs

TABLE 3.50. AFFORDABILITY STATUS OF FAMILIES AND UNRELATED INDIVIDUALS FOR A MEDIAN-PRICED HOME, BY CURRENT TENURE AND TYPE OF FINANCING: 1984, 1988, 1991, AND 1993
(Numbers in thousands)

YEAR, TENURE, AND TYPE OF FINANCING	Families												Unrelated individuals		
	Total			Married-couple			Male householder, no wife present			Female householder, no husband present					
	Total	Cannot afford median-priced home in area		Total	Cannot afford median-priced home in area		Total	Cannot afford median-priced home in area		Total	Cannot afford median-priced home in area		Total	Cannot afford median-priced home in area	
		Number	Percent		Number	Percent		Number	Percent		Number	Percent		Number	Percent
USING CONVENTIONAL, FIXED-RATE, 30-YEAR FINANCING															
Total															
1984	65,708	31,893	48.5	51,744	20,763	40.1	2,371	1,559	65.8	11,593	9,571	82.6	28,979	22,233	76.7
1988	67,958	33,015	48.6	52,445	20,835	39.7	2,919	2,008	68.8	12,593	10,171	80.8	32,635	24,643	75.5
1991	69,543	35,668	51.3	53,249	22,449	42.2	2,810	1,904	67.8	13,484	11,314	83.9	36,010	27,433	76.2
1993	71,344	35,329	49.5	53,822	21,185	39.4	3,062	2,129	69.5	14,461	12,015	83.1	36,749	27,557	75.0
Current owners															
1984	46,884	14,699	31.4	39,973	10,445	26.1	1,377	640	46.4	5,534	3,615	65.3	12,455	6,957	55.9
1988	48,541	15,440	31.8	40,588	10,593	26.1	1,797	975	54.3	6,155	3,871	62.9	14,374	7,888	54.9
1991	49,881	17,742	35.6	41,875	12,591	30.1	1,804	967	53.6	6,202	4,185	67.5	16,311	9,291	57.0
1993	50,623	16,386	32.4	42,051	11,013	26.2	1,936	1,051	54.3	6,636	4,322	65.1	16,566	8,833	53.3
Current renters															
1984	18,825	17,194	91.3	11,771	10,318	87.7	994	920	92.5	6,060	5,956	98.3	16,524	15,276	92.4
1988	19,417	17,575	90.5	11,857	10,242	86.4	1,122	1,033	92.1	6,438	6,300	97.9	18,261	16,755	91.8
1991	19,662	17,926	91.2	11,373	9,859	86.7	1,007	937	93.1	7,282	7,130	97.9	19,699	18,142	92.1
1993	20,721	18,943	91.4	11,771	10,172	86.4	1,126	1,078	95.7	7,825	7,693	98.3	20,182	18,723	92.8
USING FHA, FIXED-RATE, 30-YEAR FINANCING															
Total															
1984	65,708	31,015	47.2	51,744	19,975	38.6	2,371	1,539	64.9	11,593	9,501	82.0	28,979	22,033	76.0
1988	67,958	31,347	46.1	52,445	19,326	36.9	2,919	1,973	67.6	12,593	10,048	79.8	32,635	24,216	74.2
1991	69,543	34,362	49.4	53,249	21,256	39.9	2,810	1,874	66.7	13,484	11,232	83.3	36,010	27,173	75.5
1993	71,344	34,868	48.9	53,822	20,664	38.4	3,062	2,148	70.1	14,461	12,056	83.4	36,749	27,477	74.8
Current owners															
1984	46,884	14,016	29.9	39,973	9,846	24.6	1,377	620	45.0	5,534	3,550	64.2	12,455	6,882	55.3
1988	48,541	14,223	29.3	40,588	9,469	23.3	1,797	950	52.8	6,155	3,805	61.8	14,374	7,704	53.6
1991	49,881	16,724	33.5	41,875	11,667	27.9	1,804	937	52.0	6,202	4,119	66.4	16,311	9,141	56.0
1993	50,623	16,045	31.7	42,051	10,620	25.3	1,936	1,070	55.3	6,636	4,354	65.6	16,566	8,822	53.3
Current renters															
1984	18,825	16,999	90.3	11,771	10,129	86.1	994	919	92.4	6,060	5,951	98.2	16,524	15,152	91.7
1988	19,417	17,124	88.2	11,857	9,858	83.1	1,122	1,023	91.2	6,438	6,243	97.0	18,261	16,512	90.4
1991	19,662	17,639	89.7	11,373	9,589	84.3	1,007	937	93.1	7,282	7,113	97.7	19,699	18,032	91.5
1993	20,721	18,824	90.8	11,771	10,044	85.3	1,126	1,078	95.7	7,825	7,702	98.4	20,182	18,655	92.4

Source: Analysis of data from the Survey of Income and Program Participation in Savage, Howard A., "Who Can Afford to Buy a House in 1993?" U.S. Bureau of the Census, Current Housing Reports, H121/97-1.

Details may not add to totals due to rounding.

Housing Problems and Costs

TABLE 3.51. AFFORDABILITY STATUS OF FAMILIES AND UNRELATED INDIVIDUALS FOR A MODESTLY-PRICED HOME, BY CURRENT TENURE AND TYPE OF FINANCING: 1984, 1988, 1991, AND 1993
(Numbers in thousands)

YEAR, TENURE, AND TYPE OF FINANCING	Families												Unrelated individuals		
	Total			Married-couple			Male householder, no wife present			Female householder, no husband present					
	Total	Cannot afford modestly-priced home in area		Total	Cannot afford modestly-priced home in area		Total	Cannot afford modestly-priced home in area		Total	Cannot afford modestly-priced home in area		Total	Cannot afford modestly-priced home in area	
		Number	Percent		Number	Percent		Number	Percent		Number	Percent		Number	Percent
USING CONVENTIONAL, FIXED-RATE, 30-YEAR FINANCING															
Total															
1984	65,708	25,998	39.6	51,744	16,090	31.1	2,371	1,323	55.8	11,593	8,586	74.1	28,979	19,272	66.5
1988	67,958	27,355	40.3	52,445	16,584	31.6	2,919	1,655	56.7	12,593	9,117	72.4	32,635	21,557	66.1
1991	69,543	29,461	42.4	53,249	17,583	33.0	2,810	1,616	57.5	13,484	10,262	76.1	36,010	23,994	66.6
1993	71,344	30,188	42.3	53,822	17,360	32.3	3,062	1,843	60.2	14,461	10,985	76.0	36,749	24,427	66.5
Current owners															
1984	46,884	9,553	20.4	39,973	6,403	16.0	1,377	440	32.0	5,534	2,709	49.0	12,455	4,958	39.8
1988	48,541	10,654	21.9	40,588	6,980	17.2	1,797	667	37.1	6,155	3,007	48.8	14,374	5,637	39.2
1991	49,881	12,374	24.8	41,875	8,454	20.2	1,804	694	38.5	6,202	3,226	52.0	16,311	6,691	41.0
1993	50,623	11,881	23.5	42,051	7,696	18.3	1,936	798	41.2	6,636	3,387	51.0	16,566	6,500	39.2
Current renters															
1984	18,825	16,445	87.4	11,771	9,686	82.3	994	883	88.8	6,060	5,876	97.0	16,524	14,314	86.6
1988	19,417	16,701	86.0	11,857	9,604	81.0	1,122	987	88.0	6,438	6,110	94.9	18,261	15,920	87.2
1991	19,662	17,087	86.9	11,373	9,129	80.3	1,007	922	91.6	7,282	7,036	96.6	19,699	17,304	87.8
1993	20,721	18,307	88.3	11,771	9,664	82.1	1,126	1,045	92.8	7,825	7,598	97.1	20,182	17,927	88.8
USING FHA, FIXED-RATE, 30-YEAR FINANCING															
Total															
1984	65,708	24,731	37.6	51,744	14,907	28.8	2,371	1,303	55.0	11,593	8,521	73.5	28,979	18,863	65.1
1988	67,958	25,336	37.3	52,445	14,760	28.1	2,919	1,596	54.7	12,593	8,980	71.3	32,635	20,885	64.0
1991	69,543	27,301	39.3	53,249	15,643	29.4	2,810	1,572	55.9	13,484	10,087	74.8	36,010	23,324	64.8
1993	71,344	28,912	40.5	53,822	16,168	30.0	3,062	1,822	59.5	14,461	10,923	75.5	36,749	24,158	65.7
Current owners															
1984	46,884	8,813	18.8	39,973	5,717	14.3	1,377	426	30.9	5,534	2,670	48.2	12,455	4,810	38.6
1988	48,541	9,346	19.3	40,588	5,809	14.3	1,797	620	34.5	6,155	2,917	47.4	14,374	5,391	37.5
1991	49,881	10,781	21.6	41,875	7,019	16.8	1,804	663	36.8	6,202	3,099	50.0	16,311	6,440	39.5
1993	50,623	10,985	21.7	42,051	6,843	16.3	1,936	786	40.6	6,636	3,357	50.6	16,566	6,417	38.7
Current renters															
1984	18,825	15,918	84.6	11,771	9,190	78.1	994	877	88.2	6,060	5,851	96.6	16,524	14,053	85.0
1988	19,417	15,990	82.3	11,857	8,951	75.5	1,122	976	87.0	6,438	6,063	94.2	18,261	15,494	84.8
1991	19,662	16,520	84.0	11,373	8,624	75.8	1,007	909	90.3	7,282	6,988	96.0	19,699	16,884	85.7
1993	20,721	17,927	86.5	11,771	9,325	79.2	1,126	1,037	92.1	7,825	7,566	96.7	20,182	17,741	87.9

Source: Analysis of data from the Survey of Income and Program Participation in Savage, Howard A., "Who Can Afford to Buy a House in 1993?" U.S. Bureau of the Census, Current Housing Reports, H121/97-1.

Details may not add to totals due to rounding.

Housing Problems and Costs

TABLE 3.52. AFFORDABILITY STATUS OF FAMILIES AND UNRELATED INDIVIDUALS, BY VALUE AND INCOME QUINTILES AND CURRENT TENURE, USING CONVENTIONAL, FIXED-RATE, 30-YEAR FINANCING: 1984, 1988, 1991, AND 1993

(Numbers in thousands)

CURRENT TENURE AND VALUE AND INCOME QUINTILE	Families and unrelated individuals that cannot afford median-priced home in value quintile															
	Married-couple families								Male/female householder, no spouse present families							
	1984		1988		1991		1993		1984		1988		1991		1993	
	Total in quintile	Percent cannot afford	Total in quintile	Percent cannot afford	Total in quintile	Percent cannot afford	Total in quintile	Percent cannot afford	Total in quintile	Percent cannot afford	Total in quintile	Percent cannot afford	Total in quintile	Percent cannot afford	Total in quintile	Percent cannot afford
CURRENT OWNERS																
Lowest value quintile																
Lowest income quintile	2,023	33.0	1,960	37.3	1,899	46.1	1,918	44.6	2,226	58.0	2,528	56.4	2,521	60.8	2,667	63.4
Second income quintile	5,154	15.4	5,371	13.5	5,503	15.5	5,190	17.3	2,002	33.5	1,963	30.3	1,970	37.2	2,335	37.0
Third income quintile	7,606	12.8	7,867	12.4	8,034	15.6	8,152	13.7	1,426	21.3	1,725	32.0	1,794	29.3	1,754	28.3
Fourth income quintile	11,040	10.4	10,878	13.9	10,925	15.6	11,261	15.2	819	8.8	1,151	16.8	1,213	21.0	1,243	18.3
Fifth income quintile	14,150	5.1	14,511	8.4	15,514	11.1	15,531	9.7	439	8.6	586	12.0	508	13.1	572	15.8
Second value quintile																
Lowest income quintile	2,023	48.2	1,960	52.8	1,899	61.4	1,918	59.3	2,226	73.3	2,528	72.8	2,521	75.4	2,667	77.7
Second income quintile	5,154	33.6	5,371	32.9	5,503	33.5	5,190	33.3	2,002	52.0	1,963	49.9	1,970	56.5	2,335	57.3
Third income quintile	7,606	25.6	7,867	20.3	8,034	24.1	8,152	20.0	1,426	37.1	1,725	42.2	1,794	43.1	1,754	37.2
Fourth income quintile	11,040	14.0	10,878	17.2	10,925	19.6	11,261	17.7	819	12.6	1,151	19.5	1,213	25.5	1,243	23.5
Fifth income quintile	14,150	6.5	14,511	10.2	15,514	13.4	15,531	11.6	439	12.1	586	15.1	508	16.6	572	16.4
Third value quintile																
Lowest income quintile	2,023	57.9	1,960	60.5	1,899	66.1	1,918	68.1	2,226	82.3	2,528	82.7	2,521	84.3	2,667	85.5
Second income quintile	5,154	47.8	5,371	47.2	5,503	50.1	5,190	49.1	2,002	66.6	1,963	65.2	1,970	70.9	2,335	71.6
Third income quintile	7,606	41.3	7,867	34.0	8,034	38.8	8,152	31.9	1,426	53.8	1,725	61.3	1,794	59.3	1,754	51.8
Fourth income quintile	11,040	23.2	10,878	23.2	10,925	28.1	11,261	22.3	819	31.2	1,151	28.0	1,213	38.0	1,243	32.0
Fifth income quintile	14,150	7.9	14,511	11.5	15,514	15.4	15,531	13.2	439	15.0	586	16.6	508	20.7	572	20.0
Fourth value quintile																
Lowest income quintile	2,023	66.3	1,960	72.1	1,899	76.6	1,918	78.0	2,226	87.2	2,528	88.7	2,521	91.0	2,667	90.9
Second income quintile	5,154	61.2	5,371	62.5	5,503	67.1	5,190	67.0	2,002	78.5	1,963	80.8	1,970	81.9	2,335	85.4
Third income quintile	7,606	59.0	7,867	54.6	8,034	56.8	8,152	52.6	1,426	72.7	1,725	74.1	1,794	76.9	1,754	74.2
Fourth income quintile	11,040	44.5	10,878	39.3	10,925	45.5	11,261	34.7	819	55.5	1,151	47.4	1,213	55.4	1,243	48.9
Fifth income quintile	14,150	13.6	14,511	16.5	15,514	20.9	15,531	16.0	439	22.0	586	23.4	508	24.0	572	25.6
Fifth value quintile																
Lowest income quintile	2,023	82.0	1,960	82.1	1,899	85.9	1,918	88.7	2,226	94.3	2,528	93.8	2,521	95.4	2,667	96.3
Second income quintile	5,154	79.5	5,371	80.4	5,503	84.6	5,190	86.2	2,002	91.4	1,963	90.9	1,970	93.0	2,335	94.9
Third income quintile	7,606	82.8	7,867	78.1	8,034	81.8	8,152	80.9	1,426	88.8	1,725	86.8	1,794	91.6	1,754	94.3
Fourth income quintile	11,040	77.3	10,878	73.2	10,925	76.8	11,261	70.5	819	87.8	1,151	84.3	1,213	83.1	1,243	84.0
Fifth income quintile	14,150	43.1	14,511	39.0	15,514	41.8	15,531	31.5	439	46.4	586	49.9	508	55.9	572	43.9

See notes at end of table.

Housing Problems and Costs

TABLE 3.52. AFFORDABILITY STATUS OF FAMILIES AND UNRELATED INDIVIDUALS, BY VALUE AND INCOME QUINTILES AND CURRENT TENURE, USING CONVENTIONAL, FIXED-RATE, 30-YEAR FINANCING: 1984, 1988, 1991, AND 1993 - Continued
(Numbers in thousands)

CURRENT TENURE AND VALUE AND INCOME QUINTILE	Families and unrelated individuals that cannot afford median-priced home in value quintile							
	Unrelated individuals							
	1984		1988		1991		1993	
	Total in quintile	Percent cannot afford	Total in quintile	Percent cannot afford	Total in quintile	Percent cannot afford	Total in quintile	Percent cannot afford
CURRENT OWNERS								
Lowest value quintile								
Lowest income quintile	4,194	39.0	4,711	36.6	4,879	44.4	4,644	45.5
Second income quintile	3,844	23.8	3,778	25.5	4,802	24.3	4,882	23.9
Third income quintile	2,161	21.5	2,878	23.8	3,130	24.0	3,152	27.7
Fourth income quintile	1,454	18.0	1,984	22.3	2,280	28.9	2,428	20.5
Fifth income quintile	803	8.8	1,024	9.1	1,219	16.8	1,460	12.4
Second value quintile								
Lowest income quintile	4,194	59.7	4,711	58.1	4,879	61.9	4,644	65.8
Second income quintile	3,844	44.0	3,778	41.7	4,802	42.7	4,882	40.2
Third income quintile	2,161	36.2	2,878	38.5	3,130	37.0	3,152	36.0
Fourth income quintile	1,454	26.7	1,984	29.6	2,280	33.5	2,428	25.7
Fifth income quintile	803	11.8	1,024	12.2	1,219	17.6	1,460	15.4
Third value quintile								
Lowest income quintile	4,194	70.4	4,711	68.6	4,879	76.4	4,644	75.2
Second income quintile	3,844	58.0	3,778	56.7	4,802	56.0	4,882	57.0
Third income quintile	2,161	50.7	2,878	55.0	3,130	51.5	3,152	48.1
Fourth income quintile	1,454	38.4	1,984	38.9	2,280	43.8	2,428	32.5
Fifth income quintile	803	15.2	1,024	15.7	1,219	21.4	1,460	17.2
Fourth value quintile								
Lowest income quintile	4,194	79.6	4,711	79.2	4,879	84.8	4,644	84.3
Second income quintile	3,844	74.1	3,778	72.0	4,802	70.3	4,882	74.2
Third income quintile	2,161	64.5	2,878	71.1	3,130	64.8	3,152	65.9
Fourth income quintile	1,454	60.2	1,984	52.0	2,280	57.2	2,428	45.4
Fifth income quintile	803	24.0	1,024	22.8	1,219	29.1	1,460	21.2
Fifth value quintile								
Lowest income quintile	4,194	89.3	4,711	89.2	4,879	92.5	4,644	93.6
Second income quintile	3,844	88.1	3,778	85.5	4,802	86.3	4,882	87.8
Third income quintile	2,161	83.8	2,878	85.9	3,130	84.0	3,152	88.6
Fourth income quintile	1,454	82.3	1,984	82.4	2,280	85.3	2,428	76.6
Fifth income quintile	803	48.9	1,024	47.8	1,219	56.8	1,460	40.3

See notes at end of table.

Housing Problems and Costs

TABLE 3.52. AFFORDABILITY STATUS OF FAMILIES AND UNRELATED INDIVIDUALS, BY VALUE AND INCOME QUINTILES AND CURRENT TENURE, USING CONVENTIONAL, FIXED-RATE, 30-YEAR FINANCING: 1984, 1988, 1991, AND 1993 - Continued

(Numbers in thousands)

CURRENT TENURE AND VALUE AND INCOME QUINTILE	Families and unrelated individuals that cannot afford median-priced home in value quintile															
	Married-couple families								Male/female householder, no spouse present families							
	1984		1988		1991		1993		1984		1988		1991		1993	
	Total in quintile	Percent cannot afford	Total in quintile	Percent cannot afford	Total in quintile	Percent cannot afford	Total in quintile	Percent cannot afford	Total in quintile	Percent cannot afford	Total in quintile	Percent cannot afford	Total in quintile	Percent cannot afford	Total in quintile	Percent cannot afford
CURRENT RENTERS																
Lowest value quintile																
Lowest income quintile	1,260	94.7	1,326	96.9	1,334	94.8	1,392	97.6	3,670	98.4	3,860	99.3	4,067	99.4	4,434	99.7
Second income quintile	2,371	86.0	2,192	84.1	2,000	87.3	2,150	88.6	1,574	93.5	1,570	94.9	1,954	95.5	2,184	95.7
Third income quintile	3,060	78.6	2,807	83.2	2,732	78.2	2,983	83.2	1,245	91.6	1,399	83.5	1,437	88.5	1,456	86.9
Fourth income quintile	2,982	76.3	3,300	71.3	3,099	75.3	3,020	75.4	436	78.8	565	64.5	656	80.4	734	80.8
Fifth income quintile	2,097	47.6	2,233	52.8	2,209	53.9	2,225	52.1	129	41.6	165	41.3	174	74.5	143	51.9
Second value quintile																
Lowest income quintile	1,260	96.4	1,326	98.2	1,334	96.1	1,392	98.8	3,670	98.7	3,860	99.3	4,067	99.6	4,434	99.8
Second income quintile	2,371	94.2	2,192	93.2	2,000	91.1	2,150	93.9	1,574	96.9	1,570	97.1	1,954	97.4	2,184	99.0
Third income quintile	3,060	90.0	2,807	88.1	2,732	86.2	2,983	88.5	1,245	96.2	1,399	91.0	1,437	92.9	1,456	92.8
Fourth income quintile	2,982	84.3	3,300	77.9	3,099	80.8	3,020	81.3	436	85.2	565	73.1	656	84.4	734	89.1
Fifth income quintile	2,097	56.2	2,233	61.1	2,209	61.0	2,225	58.6	129	49.9	165	61.7	174	76.1	143	56.1
Third value quintile																
Lowest income quintile	1,260	97.6	1,326	99.5	1,334	97.6	1,392	99.3	3,670	98.8	3,860	99.8	4,067	99.7	4,434	99.9
Second income quintile	2,371	95.5	2,192	95.6	2,000	93.4	2,150	96.1	1,574	98.4	1,570	98.3	1,954	98.5	2,184	99.9
Third income quintile	3,060	94.0	2,807	92.1	2,732	91.7	2,983	92.1	1,245	98.6	1,399	97.6	1,437	94.0	1,456	95.6
Fourth income quintile	2,982	89.2	3,300	84.5	3,099	87.2	3,020	85.7	436	94.0	565	83.2	656	90.5	734	92.3
Fifth income quintile	2,097	61.5	2,233	65.1	2,209	67.1	2,225	62.4	129	49.9	165	61.7	174	80.8	143	63.0
Fourth value quintile																
Lowest income quintile	1,260	98.6	1,326	99.5	1,334	99.0	1,392	99.8	3,670	99.2	3,860	99.8	4,067	99.7	4,434	100.0
Second income quintile	2,371	96.1	2,192	95.9	2,000	94.7	2,150	98.1	1,574	99.7	1,570	98.3	1,954	98.9	2,184	99.9
Third income quintile	3,060	96.0	2,807	95.3	2,732	95.4	2,983	96.3	1,245	99.0	1,399	98.4	1,437	98.1	1,456	98.5
Fourth income quintile	2,982	95.3	3,300	93.6	3,099	91.0	3,020	90.8	436	96.7	565	93.9	656	94.9	734	97.1
Fifth income quintile	2,097	68.8	2,233	74.6	2,209	74.8	2,225	67.9	129	64.5	165	66.9	174	86.2	143	72.1
Fifth value quintile																
Lowest income quintile	1,260	98.9	1,326	99.5	1,334	99.7	1,392	99.8	3,670	99.5	3,860	99.8	4,067	99.9	4,434	100.0
Second income quintile	2,371	98.8	2,192	96.8	2,000	97.9	2,150	99.3	1,574	100.0	1,570	98.9	1,954	99.8	2,184	100.0
Third income quintile	3,060	98.3	2,807	97.8	2,732	98.9	2,983	98.4	1,245	99.5	1,399	99.1	1,437	99.7	1,456	99.6
Fourth income quintile	2,982	98.1	3,300	97.8	3,099	97.2	3,020	97.3	436	98.1	565	95.6	656	98.4	734	99.6
Fifth income quintile	2,097	86.9	2,233	83.4	2,209	85.9	2,225	80.3	129	78.7	165	80.3	174	91.8	143	87.0

See notes at end of table.

Housing Problems and Costs

TABLE 3.52. AFFORDABILITY STATUS OF FAMILIES AND UNRELATED INDIVIDUALS, BY VALUE AND INCOME QUINTILES AND CURRENT TENURE, USING CONVENTIONAL, FIXED-RATE, 30-YEAR FINANCING: 1984, 1988, 1991, AND 1993 - Continued
(Numbers in thousands)

CURRENT TENURE AND VALUE AND INCOME QUINTILE	Families and unrelated individuals that cannot afford median-priced home in value quintile							
	Unrelated individuals							
	1984		1988		1991		1993	
	Total in quintile	Percent cannot afford	Total in quintile	Percent cannot afford	Total in quintile	Percent cannot afford	Total in quintile	Percent cannot afford
CURRENT RENTERS								
Lowest value quintile								
Lowest income quintile	5,065	93.7	6,379	90.9	6,199	93.1	6,551	95.0
Second income quintile	5,033	86.6	5,091	84.9	5,617	85.0	6,120	87.6
Third income quintile	3,596	73.0	3,631	80.3	4,355	78.5	4,058	79.8
Fourth income quintile	2,053	61.1	2,192	63.4	2,568	66.0	2,458	70.7
Fifth income quintile	777	40.4	970	38.1	960	50.6	995	42.2
Second value quintile								
Lowest income quintile	5,065	95.6	6,379	95.0	6,199	96.1	6,551	97.2
Second income quintile	5,033	93.0	5,091	92.4	5,617	92.6	6,120	93.8
Third income quintile	3,596	87.9	3,631	88.2	4,355	88.7	4,058	88.4
Fourth income quintile	2,053	71.8	2,192	74.2	2,568	75.1	2,458	80.2
Fifth income quintile	777	48.7	970	53.1	960	58.2	995	48.4
Third value quintile								
Lowest income quintile	5,065	96.5	6,379	96.7	6,199	96.9	6,551	98.0
Second income quintile	5,033	96.1	5,091	95.0	5,617	94.7	6,120	96.4
Third income quintile	3,596	93.4	3,631	92.4	4,355	93.2	4,058	92.6
Fourth income quintile	2,053	84.8	2,192	83.7	2,568	83.1	2,458	85.5
Fifth income quintile	777	58.3	970	57.6	960	64.8	995	54.8
Fourth value quintile								
Lowest income quintile	5,065	97.6	6,379	98.3	6,199	98.0	6,551	98.5
Second income quintile	5,033	97.4	5,091	96.9	5,617	96.6	6,120	97.9
Third income quintile	3,596	96.4	3,631	96.1	4,355	95.0	4,058	96.0
Fourth income quintile	2,053	92.0	2,192	91.7	2,568	91.3	2,458	91.4
Fifth income quintile	777	65.1	970	67.6	960	71.4	995	63.8
Fifth value quintile								
Lowest income quintile	5,065	98.5	6,379	98.7	6,199	99.1	6,551	99.3
Second income quintile	5,033	98.8	5,091	98.3	5,617	98.6	6,120	99.2
Third income quintile	3,596	98.6	3,631	98.6	4,355	98.1	4,058	98.6
Fourth income quintile	2,053	96.9	2,192	98.6	2,568	98.0	2,458	97.1
Fifth income quintile	777	84.1	970	88.3	960	87.5	995	79.4

Source: Analysis of data from the Survey of Income and Program Participation in Savage, Howard A. "Who Can Afford to Buy a House in 1993?" U.S. Bureau of the Census, Current Housing Reports, H121/97-1.

Housing Problems and Costs

TABLE 3.53. AFFORDABILITY STATUS OF FAMILIES AND UNRELATED INDIVIDUALS, BY VALUE AND INCOME QUINTILES AND CURRENT TENURE, USING FHA, FIXED-RATE, 30-YEAR FINANCING: 1984, 1988, 1991, AND 1993

(Numbers in thousands)

CURRENT TENURE AND VALUE AND INCOME QUINTILE	Families and unrelated individuals that cannot afford median-priced home in value quintile															
	Married-couple families								Male/female householder, no spouse present families							
	1984		1988		1991		1993		1984		1988		1991		1993	
	Total in quintile	Percent cannot afford	Total in quintile	Percent cannot afford	Total in quintile	Percent cannot afford	Total in quintile	Percent cannot afford	Total in quintile	Percent cannot afford	Total in quintile	Percent cannot afford	Total in quintile	Percent cannot afford	Total in quintile	Percent cannot afford
CURRENT OWNERS																
Lowest value quintile																
Lowest income quintile	2,023	33.0	1,960	36.9	1,899	46.1	1,918	44.3	2,226	58.0	2,528	56.0	2,521	60.4	2,667	63.8
Second income quintile	5,154	14.1	5,371	12.6	5,503	13.9	5,190	17.1	2,002	33.5	1,963	28.8	1,970	34.1	2,335	36.6
Third income quintile	7,606	10.8	7,867	9.6	8,034	12.4	8,152	11.9	1,426	18.0	1,725	26.5	1,794	22.9	1,754	25.2
Fourth income quintile	11,040	7.4	10,878	9.4	10,925	12.0	11,261	11.1	819	7.0	1,151	12.1	1,213	16.7	1,243	16.9
Fifth income quintile	14,150	3.3	14,511	5.4	15,514	7.3	15,531	7.2	439	5.8	586	3.0	508	10.8	572	12.2
Second value quintile																
Lowest income quintile	2,023	48.2	1,960	52.1	1,899	60.6	1,918	59.3	2,226	73.0	2,528	72.8	2,521	74.8	2,667	77.5
Second income quintile	5,154	33.1	5,371	32.0	5,503	32.8	5,190	34.7	2,002	51.4	1,963	49.4	1,970	56.3	2,335	57.8
Third income quintile	7,606	24.4	7,867	18.1	8,034	21.7	8,152	19.5	1,426	35.8	1,725	38.3	1,794	40.3	1,754	36.7
Fourth income quintile	11,040	11.6	10,878	12.7	10,925	15.1	11,261	14.6	819	11.7	1,151	17.5	1,213	21.3	1,243	21.4
Fifth income quintile	14,150	4.3	14,511	6.6	15,514	9.0	15,531	8.6	439	8.8	586	5.8	508	10.7	572	14.4
Third value quintile																
Lowest income quintile	2,023	57.9	1,960	60.5	1,899	65.7	1,918	68.3	2,226	82.0	2,528	82.4	2,521	84.2	2,667	85.5
Second income quintile	5,154	47.2	5,371	46.9	5,503	49.7	5,190	50.7	2,002	66.2	1,963	64.7	1,970	69.9	2,335	72.2
Third income quintile	7,606	40.2	7,867	32.4	8,034	37.3	8,152	33.1	1,426	51.9	1,725	59.5	1,794	58.4	1,754	54.0
Fourth income quintile	11,040	21.2	10,878	19.0	10,925	24.3	11,261	20.1	819	28.1	1,151	24.9	1,213	35.2	1,243	33.4
Fifth income quintile	14,150	5.9	14,511	8.0	15,514	13.1	15,531	11.1	439	11.1	586	15.1	508	16.3	572	16.8
Fourth value quintile																
Lowest income quintile	2,023	66.1	1,960	71.8	1,899	75.7	1,918	77.9	2,226	87.2	2,528	87.7	2,521	90.2	2,667	90.8
Second income quintile	5,154	61.1	5,371	61.7	5,503	66.0	5,190	67.4	2,002	78.3	1,963	80.4	1,970	81.5	2,335	85.7
Third income quintile	7,606	58.8	7,867	53.6	8,034	55.6	8,152	55.0	1,426	70.7	1,725	73.4	1,794	76.2	1,754	75.9
Fourth income quintile	11,040	43.3	10,878	36.6	10,925	42.8	11,261	35.5	819	54.9	1,151	43.8	1,213	54.1	1,243	52.5
Fifth income quintile	14,150	11.5	14,511	13.3	15,514	21.2	15,531	16.5	439	20.0	586	20.1	508	21.6	572	25.5
Fifth value quintile																
Lowest income quintile	2,023	81.8	1,960	82.1	1,899	84.9	1,918	88.2	2,226	94.3	2,528	93.2	2,521	95.2	2,667	96.2
Second income quintile	5,154	79.3	5,371	80.3	5,503	84.5	5,190	86.1	2,002	91.1	1,963	90.9	1,970	92.7	2,335	94.8
Third income quintile	7,606	82.4	7,867	77.4	8,034	81.3	8,152	81.6	1,426	88.7	1,725	86.4	1,794	91.6	1,754	94.5
Fourth income quintile	11,040	76.6	10,878	72.2	10,925	76.4	11,261	72.7	819	87.8	1,151	83.6	1,213	82.5	1,243	86.0
Fifth income quintile	14,150	41.0	14,511	35.3	15,514	49.0	15,531	41.3	439	45.4	586	48.0	508	60.1	572	49.0

See notes at end of table.

Housing Problems and Costs

TABLE 3.53. AFFORDABILITY STATUS OF FAMILIES AND UNRELATED INDIVIDUALS, BY VALUE AND INCOME QUINTILES AND CURRENT TENURE, USING FHA, FIXED-RATE, 30-YEAR FINANCING: 1984, 1988, 1991, AND 1993 - Continued
(Numbers in thousands)

CURRENT TENURE AND VALUE AND INCOME QUINTILE	Families and unrelated individuals that cannot afford median-priced home in value quintile							
	Unrelated individuals							
	1984		1988		1991		1993	
	Total in quintile	Percent cannot afford	Total in quintile	Percent cannot afford	Total in quintile	Percent cannot afford	Total in quintile	Percent cannot afford
CURRENT OWNERS								
Lowest value quintile								
Lowest income quintile	4,194	38.6	4,711	35.9	4,879	44.2	4,644	45.9
Second income quintile	3,844	23.1	3,778	24.7	4,802	23.3	4,882	24.1
Third income quintile	2,161	19.2	2,878	21.3	3,130	20.3	3,152	25.2
Fourth income quintile	1,454	13.1	1,984	17.4	2,280	23.6	2,428	15.9
Fifth income quintile	803	7.2	1,024	7.9	1,219	12.0	1,460	10.9
Second value quintile								
Lowest income quintile	4,194	59.5	4,711	58.1	4,879	61.5	4,644	65.8
Second income quintile	3,844	43.3	3,778	41.5	4,802	42.0	4,882	41.6
Third income quintile	2,161	35.1	2,878	34.5	3,130	34.4	3,152	36.2
Fourth income quintile	1,454	21.1	1,984	24.9	2,280	30.7	2,428	23.7
Fifth income quintile	803	9.6	1,024	8.4	1,219	15.4	1,460	12.5
Third value quintile								
Lowest income quintile	4,194	70.1	4,711	67.8	4,879	75.5	4,644	75.2
Second income quintile	3,844	57.7	3,778	56.3	4,802	55.5	4,882	57.9
Third income quintile	2,161	50.3	2,878	53.8	3,130	51.0	3,152	48.9
Fourth income quintile	1,454	37.2	1,984	35.7	2,280	41.4	2,428	31.1
Fifth income quintile	803	12.4	1,024	12.3	1,219	20.6	1,460	14.1
Fourth value quintile								
Lowest income quintile	4,194	79.4	4,711	79.1	4,879	84.6	4,644	84.1
Second income quintile	3,844	73.9	3,778	71.3	4,802	69.7	4,882	74.4
Third income quintile	2,161	64.5	2,878	71.1	3,130	63.6	3,152	67.8
Fourth income quintile	1,454	59.0	1,984	50.8	2,280	55.1	2,428	46.3
Fifth income quintile	803	21.6	1,024	17.3	1,219	29.2	1,460	22.0
Fifth value quintile								
Lowest income quintile	4,194	89.3	4,711	89.2	4,879	92.5	4,644	93.2
Second income quintile	3,844	88.0	3,778	85.5	4,802	85.9	4,882	87.7
Third income quintile	2,161	83.3	2,878	85.6	3,130	83.8	3,152	88.7
Fourth income quintile	1,454	82.3	1,984	81.6	2,280	85.3	2,428	78.4
Fifth income quintile	803	49.0	1,024	48.5	1,219	62.3	1,460	48.4

See notes at end of table.

Housing Problems and Costs

TABLE 3.53. AFFORDABILITY STATUS OF FAMILIES AND UNRELATED INDIVIDUALS, BY VALUE AND INCOME QUINTILES AND CURRENT TENURE, USING FHA, FIXED-RATE, 30-YEAR FINANCING: 1984, 1988, 1991, AND 1993 - Continued

(Numbers in thousands)

CURRENT TENURE AND VALUE AND INCOME QUINTILE	Families and unrelated individuals that cannot afford median-priced home in value quintile															
	Married-couple families								Male/female householder, no spouse present families							
	1984		1988		1991		1993		1984		1988		1991		1993	
	Total in quintile	Percent cannot afford	Total in quintile	Percent cannot afford	Total in quintile	Percent cannot afford	Total in quintile	Percent cannot afford	Total in quintile	Percent cannot afford	Total in quintile	Percent cannot afford	Total in quintile	Percent cannot afford	Total in quintile	Percent cannot afford
CURRENT RENTERS																
Lowest value quintile																
Lowest income quintile	1,260	94.7	1,326	96.7	1,334	94.8	1,392	97.6	3,670	98.4	3,860	99.3	4,067	99.4	4,434	99.7
Second income quintile	2,371	85.3	2,192	82.7	2,000	85.2	2,150	86.8	1,574	93.2	1,570	93.4	1,954	95.3	2,184	95.5
Third income quintile	3,060	72.9	2,807	77.4	2,732	72.1	2,983	79.9	1,245	89.6	1,399	78.9	1,437	80.6	1,456	84.9
Fourth income quintile	2,982	63.1	3,300	57.8	3,099	65.0	3,020	67.7	436	70.7	565	58.8	656	68.4	734	74.5
Fifth income quintile	2,097	36.1	2,233	31.8	2,209	39.2	2,225	40.5	129	35.6	165	30.5	174	60.9	143	39.6
Second value quintile																
Lowest income quintile	1,260	96.0	1,326	98.2	1,334	96.1	1,392	98.8	3,670	98.7	3,860	99.3	4,067	99.6	4,434	99.8
Second income quintile	2,371	94.2	2,192	93.2	2,000	91.1	2,150	93.9	1,574	96.4	1,570	97.1	1,954	97.4	2,184	98.9
Third income quintile	3,060	89.2	2,807	86.7	2,732	84.1	2,983	87.8	1,245	95.0	1,399	88.3	1,437	91.7	1,456	92.3
Fourth income quintile	2,982	79.3	3,300	71.0	3,099	75.6	3,020	77.1	436	83.6	565	67.0	656	81.2	734	84.6
Fifth income quintile	2,097	44.4	2,233	47.9	2,209	49.6	2,225	51.3	129	41.6	165	50.5	174	72.5	143	50.2
Third value quintile																
Lowest income quintile	1,260	97.6	1,326	99.5	1,334	97.6	1,392	99.3	3,670	98.8	3,860	99.8	4,067	99.7	4,434	99.9
Second income quintile	2,371	95.3	2,192	95.6	2,000	93.2	2,150	96.1	1,574	98.4	1,570	98.3	1,954	98.5	2,184	99.9
Third income quintile	3,060	93.7	2,807	92.0	2,732	91.3	2,983	91.9	1,245	98.6	1,399	96.8	1,437	94.0	1,456	96.4
Fourth income quintile	2,982	89.0	3,300	79.9	3,099	83.1	3,020	84.3	436	93.9	565	75.1	656	88.2	734	93.1
Fifth income quintile	2,097	53.4	2,233	54.9	2,209	61.3	2,225	58.8	129	46.0	165	55.8	174	79.6	143	57.0
Fourth value quintile																
Lowest income quintile	1,260	98.6	1,326	99.5	1,334	98.9	1,392	99.5	3,670	99.2	3,860	99.8	4,067	99.7	4,434	100.0
Second income quintile	2,371	96.1	2,192	95.9	2,000	94.7	2,150	97.9	1,574	99.7	1,570	98.3	1,954	98.9	2,184	99.9
Third income quintile	3,060	96.0	2,807	95.3	2,732	95.4	2,983	96.5	1,245	99.0	1,399	98.4	1,437	97.9	1,456	98.9
Fourth income quintile	2,982	94.7	3,300	91.4	3,099	90.3	3,020	90.0	436	96.7	565	93.9	656	93.6	734	97.1
Fifth income quintile	2,097	64.3	2,233	66.5	2,209	70.5	2,225	66.1	129	64.5	165	61.7	174	82.2	143	66.0
Fifth value quintile																
Lowest income quintile	1,260	98.9	1,326	99.5	1,334	99.7	1,392	99.8	3,670	99.5	3,860	99.8	4,067	99.9	4,434	100.0
Second income quintile	2,371	98.8	2,192	96.8	2,000	97.9	2,150	99.2	1,574	100.0	1,570	98.9	1,954	99.8	2,184	100.0
Third income quintile	3,060	98.3	2,807	97.8	2,732	98.9	2,983	98.5	1,245	99.5	1,399	99.1	1,437	99.7	1,456	99.6
Fourth income quintile	2,982	98.1	3,300	97.3	3,099	97.2	3,020	97.6	436	98.1	565	95.6	656	97.7	734	99.6
Fifth income quintile	2,097	86.4	2,233	82.4	2,209	88.0	2,225	84.8	129	78.7	165	80.3	174	96.5	143	86.6

See notes at end of table.

Housing Problems and Costs

TABLE 3.53. AFFORDABILITY STATUS OF FAMILIES AND UNRELATED INDIVIDUALS, BY VALUE AND INCOME QUINTILES AND CURRENT TENURE, USING FHA, FIXED-RATE, 30-YEAR FINANCING: 1984, 1988, 1991, AND 1993 - Continued
(Numbers in thousands)

CURRENT TENURE AND VALUE AND INCOME QUINTILE	Families and unrelated individuals that cannot afford median-priced home in value quintile							
	Unrelated individuals							
	1984		1988		1991		1993	
	Total in quintile	Percent cannot afford	Total in quintile	Percent cannot afford	Total in quintile	Percent cannot afford	Total in quintile	Percent cannot afford
CURRENT RENTERS								
Lowest value quintile								
Lowest income quintile	5,065	93.7	6,379	90.9	6,199	93.1	6,551	95.1
Second income quintile	5,033	86.4	5,091	83.4	5,617	83.4	6,120	87.2
Third income quintile	3,596	67.0	3,631	72.3	4,355	70.4	4,058	75.7
Fourth income quintile	2,053	47.1	2,192	49.3	2,568	52.3	2,458	64.1
Fifth income quintile	777	30.4	970	29.8	960	37.4	995	34.2
Second value quintile								
Lowest income quintile	5,065	95.6	6,379	95.0	6,199	96.1	6,551	97.2
Second income quintile	5,033	92.9	5,091	92.4	5,617	92.3	6,120	94.3
Third income quintile	3,596	87.3	3,631	87.7	4,355	87.0	4,058	87.5
Fourth income quintile	2,053	66.6	2,192	65.7	2,568	69.9	2,458	75.9
Fifth income quintile	777	38.6	970	36.2	960	46.9	995	43.2
Third value quintile								
Lowest income quintile	5,065	96.5	6,379	96.7	6,199	96.9	6,551	98.0
Second income quintile	5,033	96.1	5,091	94.8	5,617	94.5	6,120	96.4
Third income quintile	3,596	93.4	3,631	92.1	4,355	93.2	4,058	93.0
Fourth income quintile	2,053	83.0	2,192	79.9	2,568	80.6	2,458	83.3
Fifth income quintile	777	47.4	970	43.5	960	61.4	995	51.7
Fourth value quintile								
Lowest income quintile	5,065	97.5	6,379	98.1	6,199	97.9	6,551	98.5
Second income quintile	5,033	97.4	5,091	96.9	5,617	96.6	6,120	97.9
Third income quintile	3,596	96.3	3,631	95.9	4,355	95.0	4,058	96.3
Fourth income quintile	2,053	92.0	2,192	91.6	2,568	90.0	2,458	90.7
Fifth income quintile	777	59.4	970	63.8	960	71.0	995	62.4
Fifth value quintile								
Lowest income quintile	5,065	98.4	6,379	98.7	6,199	99.0	6,551	99.3
Second income quintile	5,033	98.8	5,091	98.3	5,617	98.4	6,120	99.2
Third income quintile	3,596	98.6	3,631	98.6	4,355	98.1	4,058	98.6
Fourth income quintile	2,053	96.9	2,192	98.6	2,568	98.0	2,458	97.5
Fifth income quintile	777	86.5	970	88.4	960	91.2	995	82.8

Source: Analysis of data from the Survey of Income and Program Participation in Savage, Howard A., "Who Can Afford to Buy a House in 1993?" U.S. Bureau of the Census, Current Housing Reports, H121/97-1.

Housing Problems and Costs

TABLE 3.54. AFFORDABILITY STATUS OF FAMILIES AND UNRELATED INDIVIDUALS FOR A MEDIAN-PRICED HOME, BY RACE AND HISPANIC ORIGIN, CURRENT TENURE, AND TYPE OF FINANCING: 1988
(Numbers in thousands)

RACE AND HISPANIC ORIGIN, TENURE, AND TYPE OF FINANCING	Families — Total	Cannot afford median-priced home in area — Number	Percent	Married-couple Total	Cannot afford median-priced home in area — Number	Percent	Male householder, no wife present Total	Cannot afford median-priced home in area — Number	Percent	Female householder, no husband present Total	Cannot afford median-priced home in area — Number	Percent	Unrelated individuals Total	Cannot afford median-priced home in area — Number	Percent
USING CONVENTIONAL, FIXED-RATE, 30-YEAR FINANCING															
Total	67,957	32,581	47.9	52,445	20,622	39.3	2,919	1,942	66.5	12,593	10,017	79.5	32,636	24,348	74.6
White	58,012	25,130	43.3	47,255	17,471	37.0	2,442	1,562	64.0	8,315	6,097	73.3	28,000	20,297	72.5
Black	8,045	6,166	76.6	3,725	2,224	59.7	343	295	86.0	3,977	3,647	91.7	3,875	3,415	88.1
Other race	1,901	1,286	67.6	1,465	928	63.3	135	85	(s)	301	273	90.7	760	636	83.7
Hispanic origin[1]	5,026	3,727	74.2	3,366	2,203	65.4	284	227	79.9	1,377	1,297	94.2	1,875	1,690	90.1
Not of Hispanic origin[1]	62,931	28,854	45.9	49,079	18,419	37.5	2,636	1,715	65.1	11,216	8,720	77.7	30,761	22,658	73.7
Current owners	48,540	15,023	30.9	40,588	10,368	25.5	1,797	897	49.9	6,155	3,757	61.0	14,374	7,614	53.0
White	43,541	12,392	28.5	37,423	9,129	24.4	1,519	717	47.2	4,599	2,546	55.4	12,858	6,549	50.9
Black	4,000	2,203	55.1	2,345	913	38.9	192	144	(s)	1,463	1,146	78.3	1,225	863	70.4
Other race	1,000	428	42.8	820	326	39.8	86	36	(s)	94	66	(s)	290	203	70.0
Hispanic origin[1]	2,541	1,294	50.9	1,929	818	42.4	87	31	(s)	524	445	84.9	473	329	69.6
Not of Hispanic origin[1]	46,000	13,729	29.8	38,659	9,550	24.7	1,710	867	50.7	5,631	3,313	58.8	13,901	7,285	52.4
Current renters	19,418	17,558	90.4	11,857	10,254	86.5	1,122	1,044	93.0	6,438	6,260	97.2	18,261	16,734	91.6
White	14,471	12,738	88.0	9,832	8,341	84.8	923	845	91.5	3,716	3,552	95.6	15,142	13,748	90.8
Black	4,045	3,963	98.0	1,380	1,311	95.0	151	151	(s)	2,514	2,501	99.5	2,650	2,552	96.3
Other race	901	858	95.2	645	602	93.3	49	49	(s)	207	207	100.0	470	434	92.3
Hispanic origin[1]	2,486	2,434	97.9	1,437	1,385	96.4	196	196	(s)	852	852	100.0	1,402	1,361	97.1
Not of Hispanic origin[1]	16,931	15,124	89.3	10,420	8,869	85.1	926	848	91.6	5,585	5,407	96.8	16,860	15,373	91.2
USING FHA, FIXED-RATE, 30-YEAR FINANCING															
Total	67,957	30,970	45.6	52,445	19,203	36.6	2,919	1,883	64.5	12,593	9,884	78.5	32,636	23,925	73.3
White	58,012	23,756	41.0	47,255	16,248	34.4	2,442	1,504	61.6	8,315	6,004	72.2	28,000	19,899	71.1
Black	8,045	5,937	73.8	3,725	2,036	54.7	343	295	86.0	3,977	3,606	90.7	3,875	3,404	87.8
Other race	1,901	1,278	67.2	1,465	920	62.8	135	85	(s)	301	273	90.7	760	620	81.6
Hispanic origin[1]	5,026	3,650	72.6	3,366	2,126	63.2	284	227	79.9	1,377	1,297	94.2	1,875	1,690	90.1
Not of Hispanic origin[1]	62,931	27,319	43.4	49,079	17,077	34.8	2,636	1,656	62.8	11,216	8,586	76.6	30,761	22,236	72.3
Current owners	48,540	13,936	28.7	40,588	9,396	23.1	1,797	849	47.2	6,155	3,691	60.0	14,374	7,432	51.7
White	43,541	11,443	26.3	37,423	8,286	22.1	1,519	669	44.0	4,599	2,488	54.1	12,858	6,374	49.6
Black	4,000	2,073	51.8	2,345	792	33.8	192	144	(s)	1,463	1,137	77.7	1,225	863	70.4
Other race	1,000	420	42.0	820	318	38.8	86	36	(s)	94	66	(s)	290	194	66.9
Hispanic origin[1]	2,541	1,233	48.5	1,929	757	39.2	87	31	(s)	524	445	84.9	473	329	69.6
Not of Hispanic origin[1]	46,000	12,703	27.6	38,659	8,639	22.3	1,710	818	47.8	5,631	3,246	57.6	13,901	7,103	51.1
Current renters	19,418	17,034	87.7	11,857	9,807	82.7	1,122	1,034	92.2	6,438	6,193	96.2	18,261	16,493	90.3
White	14,471	12,313	85.1	9,832	7,962	81.0	923	835	90.5	3,716	3,516	94.6	15,142	13,525	89.3
Black	4,045	3,864	95.5	1,380	1,244	90.1	151	151	(s)	2,514	2,469	98.2	2,650	2,541	95.9
Other race	901	858	95.2	645	602	93.3	49	49	(s)	207	207	99.8	470	426	90.6
Hispanic origin[1]	2,486	2,417	97.2	1,437	1,369	95.3	196	196	(s)	852	852	99.9	1,402	1,361	97.1
Not of Hispanic origin[1]	16,931	14,616	86.3	10,420	8,438	81.0	926	838	90.5	5,585	5,340	95.6	16,860	15,133	89.8

Source: Analysis of data from the Survey of Income and Program Participation in Fronczek, Peter J., and Howard A. Savage, "Who Can Afford to Buy a House?" U.S. Bureau of the Census, Current Housing Reports, H121/91-1.

(1) Persons of Hispanic origin may be of any race.
(s) Data suppressed.
Details may not add to totals due to rounding.

Housing Problems and Costs

TABLE 3.55. AFFORDABILITY STATUS OF FAMILIES AND UNRELATED INDIVIDUALS FOR A MEDIAN-PRICED HOME, BY RACE AND HISPANIC ORIGIN, CURRENT TENURE, AND TYPE OF FINANCING: 1991
(Numbers in thousands)

RACE AND HISPANIC ORIGIN, TENURE, AND TYPE OF FINANCING	Families													Unrelated individuals		
	Total			Married-couple			Male householder, no wife present			Female householder, no husband present					
	Total	Cannot afford median-priced home in area		Total	Cannot afford median-priced home in area		Total	Cannot afford median-priced home in area		Total	Cannot afford median-priced home in area		Total	Cannot afford median-priced home in area	
		Number	Percent		Number	Percent		Number	Percent		Number	Percent		Number	Percent
USING CONVENTIONAL, FIXED-RATE, 30-YEAR FINANCING															
Total	69,543	35,668	51.3	53,249	22,449	42.2	2,810	1,904	67.8	13,484	11,314	83.9	36,010	27,433	76.2
White	59,038	27,755	47.0	47,892	19,243	40.2	2,277	1,474	64.7	8,868	7,039	79.4	30,786	22,739	73.9
Black	8,388	6,560	78.2	3,709	2,275	61.3	409	323	79.0	4,270	3,962	92.8	4,339	3,926	90.5
Other race	2,118	1,352	63.9	1,648	932	56.6	124	107	86.5	346	313	90.6	885	767	86.7
Hispanic origin[1]	5,519	4,347	78.8	3,578	2,541	71.0	302	262	86.6	1,638	1,544	94.3	2,117	1,971	93.1
Not of Hispanic origin[1]	64,024	31,321	48.9	49,671	19,908	40.1	2,508	1,642	65.5	11,846	9,770	82.5	33,894	25,462	75.1
Current owners	49,881	17,742	35.6	41,875	12,591	30.1	1,804	967	53.6	6,202	4,185	67.5	16,311	9,291	57.0
White	44,492	14,800	33.3	38,319	11,082	28.9	1,546	806	52.2	4,626	2,911	62.9	14,538	7,982	54.9
Black	4,074	2,353	57.8	2,459	1,091	44.4	199	118	59.6	1,417	1,144	80.7	1,458	1,085	74.4
Other race	1,316	590	44.8	1,097	417	38.0	59	42	71.7	159	130	81.6	314	224	71.2
Hispanic origin[1]	2,482	1,403	56.5	1,922	964	50.1	121	83	68.2	438	357	81.4	557	426	76.4
Not of Hispanic origin[1]	47,400	16,339	34.5	39,953	11,627	29.1	1,683	884	52.6	5,764	3,828	66.4	15,754	8,865	56.3
Current renters	19,662	17,926	91.2	11,373	9,859	86.7	1,007	937	93.1	7,282	7,130	97.9	19,699	18,142	92.1
White	14,546	12,956	89.1	9,573	8,160	85.2	731	667	91.3	4,242	4,128	97.3	16,247	14,757	90.8
Black	4,314	4,207	97.5	1,250	1,184	94.7	210	205	97.4	2,853	2,819	98.8	2,881	2,841	98.6
Other race	802	763	95.1	551	515	93.4	65	65	100.0	186	183	98.3	571	543	95.2
Hispanic origin[1]	3,037	2,943	96.9	1,656	1,577	95.2	181	179	98.8	1,200	1,187	98.9	1,559	1,545	99.1
Not of Hispanic origin[1]	16,625	14,982	90.1	9,718	8,282	85.2	825	758	91.8	6,082	5,943	97.7	18,140	16,597	91.5
USING FHA, FIXED-RATE, 30-YEAR FINANCING															
Total	69,543	34,362	49.4	53,249	21,256	39.9	2,810	1,874	66.7	13,484	11,232	83.3	36,010	27,173	75.5
White	59,038	26,566	45.0	47,892	18,150	37.9	2,277	1,450	63.7	8,868	6,966	78.6	30,786	22,502	73.1
Black	8,388	6,437	76.7	3,709	2,161	58.3	409	317	77.6	4,270	3,958	92.7	4,339	3,909	90.1
Other race	2,118	1,360	64.2	1,648	945	57.4	124	107	86.5	346	307	88.9	885	762	86.2
Hispanic origin[1]	5,519	4,281	77.6	3,578	2,483	69.4	302	262	86.6	1,638	1,537	93.8	2,117	1,954	92.3
Not of Hispanic origin[1]	64,024	30,081	47.0	49,671	18,774	37.8	2,508	1,613	64.3	11,846	9,695	81.8	33,894	25,219	74.4
Current owners	49,881	16,724	33.5	41,875	11,667	27.9	1,804	937	52.0	6,202	4,119	66.4	16,311	9,141	56.0
White	44,492	13,869	31.2	38,319	10,235	26.7	1,546	783	50.6	4,626	2,851	61.6	14,538	7,850	54.0
Black	4,074	2,255	55.4	2,459	999	40.6	199	112	56.6	1,417	1,144	80.7	1,458	1,068	73.2
Other race	1,316	600	45.6	1,097	433	39.5	59	42	71.7	159	124	78.0	314	224	71.2
Hispanic origin[1]	2,482	1,350	54.4	1,922	919	47.8	121	83	68.2	438	349	79.7	557	413	74.1
Not of Hispanic origin[1]	47,400	15,373	32.4	39,953	10,749	26.9	1,683	855	50.8	5,764	3,770	65.4	15,754	8,728	55.4
Current renters	19,662	17,639	89.7	11,373	9,589	84.3	1,007	937	93.1	7,282	7,113	97.7	19,699	18,032	91.5
White	14,546	12,697	87.3	9,573	7,914	82.7	731	667	91.3	4,242	4,115	97.0	16,247	14,652	90.2
Black	4,314	4,181	96.9	1,250	1,162	93.0	210	205	97.4	2,853	2,814	98.6	2,881	2,841	98.6
Other race	802	760	94.8	551	512	93.0	65	65	100.0	186	183	98.3	571	539	94.4
Hispanic origin[1]	3,037	2,931	96.5	1,656	1,564	94.5	181	179	98.8	1,200	1,187	98.9	1,559	1,541	98.8
Not of Hispanic origin[1]	16,625	14,708	88.5	9,718	8,025	82.6	825	758	91.8	6,082	5,925	97.4	18,140	16,491	90.9

Source: Analysis of data from the Survey of Income and Program Participation in Savage, Howard A., and Peter J. Fronczek, "Who Can Afford to Buy a House in 1991?" U.S. Bureau of the Census, Current Housing Reports, H121/93-3.

(1) Persons of Hispanic origin may be of any race.
Details may not add to totals due to rounding.

Housing Problems and Costs

TABLE 3.56. AFFORDABILITY STATUS OF FAMILIES AND UNRELATED INDIVIDUALS FOR A MEDIAN-PRICED HOME, BY RACE AND HISPANIC ORIGIN, CURRENT TENURE, AND TYPE OF FINANCING: 1993
(Numbers in thousands)

RACE AND HISPANIC ORIGIN, TENURE, AND TYPE OF FINANCING	Families												Unrelated individuals		
	Total			Married-couple			Male householder, no wife present			Female householder, no husband present					
	Total	Cannot afford median-priced home in area		Total	Cannot afford median-priced home in area		Total	Cannot afford median-priced home in area		Total	Cannot afford median-priced home in area		Total	Cannot afford median-priced home in area	
		Number	Percent		Number	Percent		Number	Percent		Number	Percent		Number	Percent
USING CONVENTIONAL, FIXED-RATE, 30-YEAR FINANCING															
Total	71,344	35,329	49.5	53,822	21,185	39.4	3,062	2,129	69.5	14,461	12,015	83.1	36,749	27,557	75.0
White	59,992	26,948	44.9	48,067	17,891	37.2	2,484	1,634	65.8	9,441	7,424	78.6	31,381	22,936	73.1
Black	8,777	6,843	78.0	3,806	2,259	59.4	420	374	89.1	4,550	4,210	92.5	4,314	3,726	86.4
Other race	2,577	1,537	59.7	1,949	1,035	53.1	158	121	76.5	470	381	81.2	1,054	895	84.9
Hispanic origin[1]	6,342	5,000	78.8	4,019	2,879	71.6	400	336	83.9	1,923	1,785	92.9	2,524	2,343	92.8
Not of Hispanic origin[1]	65,003	30,328	46.7	49,804	18,306	36.8	2,661	1,793	67.4	12,538	10,230	81.6	34,225	25,213	73.7
Current owners	50,623	16,386	32.4	42,051	11,013	26.2	1,936	1,051	54.3	6,636	4,322	65.1	16,566	8,833	53.3
White	44,799	13,350	29.8	38,298	9,564	25.0	1,659	856	51.6	4,842	2,930	60.5	14,713	7,645	52.0
Black	4,232	2,401	56.7	2,444	978	40.0	210	164	78.1	1,578	1,259	79.7	1,533	987	64.4
Other race	1,593	635	39.9	1,310	471	35.9	67	32	47.2	215	133	61.8	320	201	62.9
Hispanic origin[1]	2,912	1,651	56.7	2,176	1,115	51.2	172	110	63.7	564	427	75.7	676	518	76.6
Not of Hispanic origin[1]	47,711	14,734	30.9	39,876	9,898	24.8	1,764	942	53.4	6,072	3,895	64.1	15,890	8,315	52.3
Current renters	20,721	18,943	91.4	11,771	10,172	86.4	1,126	1,078	95.7	7,825	7,693	98.3	20,182	18,723	92.8
White	15,192	13,599	89.5	9,769	8,327	85.2	824	778	94.4	4,599	4,494	97.7	16,668	15,291	91.7
Black	4,545	4,443	97.8	1,362	1,281	94.0	210	210	100.0	2,972	2,951	99.3	2,781	2,739	98.5
Other race	984	902	91.6	639	565	88.3	91	89	98.1	254	248	97.6	734	694	94.5
Hispanic origin[1]	3,430	3,349	97.6	1,843	1,764	95.7	228	226	99.2	1,358	1,358	100.0	1,848	1,825	98.8
Not of Hispanic origin[1]	17,292	15,594	90.2	9,928	8,408	84.7	897	851	94.9	6,467	6,335	98.0	18,335	16,898	92.2
USING FHA, FIXED-RATE, 30-YEAR FINANCING															
Total	71,344	34,868	48.9	53,822	20,664	38.4	3,062	2,148	70.1	14,461	12,056	83.4	36,749	27,477	74.8
White	59,992	26,524	44.2	48,067	17,425	36.3	2,484	1,653	66.5	9,441	7,446	78.9	31,381	22,854	72.8
Black	8,777	6,812	77.6	3,806	2,206	58.0	420	374	89.1	4,550	4,232	93.0	4,314	3,729	86.4
Other race	2,577	1,533	59.5	1,949	1,033	53.0	158	121	76.5	470	379	80.7	1,054	895	84.9
Hispanic origin[1]	6,342	4,971	78.4	4,019	2,843	70.7	400	342	85.5	1,923	1,786	92.9	2,524	2,337	92.6
Not of Hispanic origin[1]	65,002	29,897	46.0	49,804	17,821	35.8	2,661	1,805	67.8	12,538	10,271	81.9	34,225	25,141	73.5
Current owners	50,623	16,045	31.7	42,051	10,620	25.3	1,936	1,070	55.3	6,636	4,354	65.6	16,566	8,822	53.3
White	44,799	13,026	29.1	38,298	9,212	24.1	1,659	875	52.7	4,842	2,940	60.7	14,713	7,631	51.9
Black	4,232	2,397	56.6	2,444	949	38.8	210	164	78.1	1,578	1,284	81.3	1,533	990	64.6
Other race	1,593	622	39.0	1,310	460	35.1	67	32	47.2	215	131	60.6	320	201	62.9
Hispanic origin[1]	2,912	1,643	56.4	2,176	1,100	50.6	172	116	67.4	564	427	75.7	676	516	76.3
Not of Hispanic origin[1]	47,711	14,401	30.2	39,876	9,520	23.9	1,764	954	54.1	6,072	3,927	64.7	15,890	8,306	52.3
Current renters	20,721	18,824	90.8	11,771	10,044	85.3	1,126	1,078	95.7	7,825	7,702	98.4	20,182	18,655	92.4
White	15,192	13,497	88.8	9,769	8,213	84.1	824	778	94.4	4,599	4,506	98.0	16,668	15,223	91.3
Black	4,545	4,415	97.2	1,362	1,257	92.3	210	210	100.0	2,972	2,948	99.2	2,781	2,739	98.5
Other race	984	911	92.6	639	574	89.8	91	89	98.1	254	248	97.6	734	694	94.5
Hispanic origin[1]	3,430	3,327	97.0	1,843	1,743	94.5	228	226	99.2	1,358	1,358	100.0	1,848	1,821	98.5
Not of Hispanic origin[1]	17,292	15,496	89.6	9,928	8,301	83.6	897	851	94.9	6,467	6,344	98.1	18,335	16,835	91.8

Source: Analysis of data from the Survey of Income and Program Participation in Savage, Howard A., "Who Can Afford to Buy a House in 1993?" U.S. Bureau of the Census, Current Housing Reports, H121/97-1.

(1) Persons of Hispanic origin may be of any race.
Details may not add to totals due to rounding.

Housing Problems and Costs

TABLE 3.57. AFFORDABILITY STATUS OF FAMILIES AND UNRELATED INDIVIDUALS FOR A MEDIAN-PRICED HOME, BY AGE OF HOUSEHOLDER, CURRENT TENURE, AND TYPE OF FINANCING: 1988
(Numbers in thousands)

AGE OF HOUSEHOLDER, TENURE, AND TYPE OF FINANCING	Families												Unrelated individuals		
	Total			Married-couple			Male householder, no wife present			Female householder, no husband present					
	Total	Cannot afford median-priced home in area		Total	Cannot afford median-priced home in area		Total	Cannot afford median-priced home in area		Total	Cannot afford median-priced home in area		Total	Cannot afford median-priced home in area	
		Number	Percent		Number	Percent		Number	Percent		Number	Percent		Number	Percent
USING CONVENTIONAL, FIXED-RATE, 30-YEAR FINANCING															
Total	67,957	32,581	47.9	52,445	20,622	39.3	2,919	1,942	66.5	12,593	10,017	79.5	32,636	24,348	74.6
Under 25 years	3,669	3,453	94.1	2,075	1,859	89.6	131	131	(s)	1,463	1,463	100.0	4,064	3,994	98.3
25 to 34 years	16,026	11,413	71.2	11,945	7,564	63.3	674	562	83.4	3,407	3,287	96.5	8,226	7,175	87.2
35 to 44 years	16,867	7,962	47.2	12,653	4,840	38.3	765	562	73.5	3,449	2,560	74.2	4,074	2,934	72.0
45 to 54 years	11,197	3,938	35.2	8,693	2,342	26.9	652	352	54.0	1,852	1,244	67.2	2,973	2,054	69.1
55 to 64 years	9,744	2,651	27.2	8,183	1,764	21.6	419	208	49.6	1,142	679	59.5	3,726	2,242	60.2
65 years or older	10,454	3,164	30.3	8,896	2,252	25.3	278	128	46.0	1,280	784	61.3	9,573	5,949	62.1
Median (Years)	43.5	36.8	....	44.6	36.8	....	43.6	39.9	....	39.1	36.0	....	44.9	38.4	....
Current owners	48,540	15,023	30.9	40,588	10,368	25.5	1,797	897	49.9	6,155	3,757	61.0	14,374	7,614	53.0
Under 25 years	1,274	1,102	86.5	722	550	76.2	41	41	(s)	511	511	100.0	744	705	94.8
25 to 34 years	8,644	4,624	53.5	7,235	3,398	47.0	353	253	71.7	1,056	973	92.1	2,306	1,574	68.3
35 to 44 years	12,220	3,773	30.9	10,174	2,712	26.7	422	238	56.4	1,624	823	50.7	1,808	948	52.4
45 to 54 years	8,942	1,896	21.2	7,412	1,238	16.7	448	159	35.5	1,082	499	46.1	1,446	784	54.2
55 to 64 years	8,358	1,545	18.5	7,233	1,059	14.6	318	142	44.7	807	344	42.6	2,203	896	40.7
65 years or older	9,102	2,082	22.9	7,811	1,411	18.1	214	64	29.9	1,077	607	56.4	5,868	2,706	46.1
Median (Years)	47.4	39.7	....	47.9	39.6	....	46.8	41.5	....	44.3	39.8	....	59.0	52.4	....
Current renters	19,418	17,558	90.4	11,857	10,254	86.5	1,122	1,044	93.0	6,438	6,260	97.2	18,261	16,734	91.6
Under 25 years	2,394	2,351	98.2	1,353	1,310	96.8	89	89	(s)	952	952	100.0	3,320	3,289	99.1
25 to 34 years	7,381	6,789	92.0	4,709	4,166	88.5	321	309	96.3	2,351	2,314	98.4	5,920	5,601	94.6
35 to 44 years	4,646	4,188	90.1	2,478	2,128	85.9	343	323	94.2	1,825	1,737	95.2	2,266	1,986	87.6
45 to 54 years	2,255	2,042	90.6	1,281	1,104	86.2	203	193	95.1	771	745	96.6	1,527	1,270	83.2
55 to 64 years	1,387	1,106	79.7	950	705	74.2	101	66	(s)	335	335	100.0	1,523	1,346	88.4
65 years or older	1,353	1,083	80.0	1,085	842	77.6	64	64	(s)	204	177	86.8	3,705	3,243	87.5
Median (Years)	34.9	34.5	....	34.7	34.2	....	39.4	38.8	....	34.8	34.4	....	34.8	34.1	....
USING FHA, FIXED-RATE, 30-YEAR FINANCING															
Total	67,957	30,970	45.6	52,445	19,203	36.6	2,919	1,884	64.5	12,593	9,884	78.5	32,636	23,925	73.3
Under 25 years	3,669	3,393	92.5	2,075	1,814	87.4	131	130	(s)	1,463	1,449	99.0	4,064	3,978	97.9
25 to 34 years	16,026	10,716	66.9	11,944	6,922	58.0	674	562	83.4	3,407	3,232	94.9	8,226	6,960	84.6
35 to 44 years	16,867	7,343	43.5	12,652	4,302	34.0	765	527	68.9	3,449	2,514	72.9	4,074	2,841	69.7
45 to 54 years	11,197	3,814	34.1	8,693	2,240	25.8	652	341	52.3	1,852	1,233	66.6	2,973	2,002	67.3
55 to 64 years	9,744	2,589	26.6	8,183	1,715	21.0	419	195	46.5	1,142	679	59.5	3,726	2,203	59.1
65 years or older	10,454	3,113	29.8	8,896	2,209	24.8	278	128	46.0	1,280	776	60.6	9,573	5,941	62.1
Median (Years)	43.5	36.9	....	44.6	37.0	....	43.6	39.7	....	39.1	36.0	....	44.9	38.6	....
Current owners	48,540	13,936	28.7	40,588	9,396	23.1	1,797	849	47.2	6,155	3,691	60.0	14,374	7,432	51.7
Under 25 years	1,274	1,075	84.4	722	532	73.7	41	41	(s)	511	502	98.2	744	705	94.8
25 to 34 years	8,644	4,184	48.4	7,235	2,984	41.2	353	253	71.7	1,056	947	89.7	2,306	1,478	64.1
35 to 44 years	12,220	3,308	27.1	10,174	2,296	22.6	422	213	50.5	1,624	799	49.2	1,808	912	50.4
45 to 54 years	8,942	1,821	20.4	7,412	1,174	15.8	448	148	33.0	1,082	499	46.1	1,446	761	52.6
55 to 64 years	8,358	1,497	17.9	7,233	1,024	14.2	318	129	40.6	807	344	42.6	2,203	877	39.8
65 years or older	9,102	2,048	22.5	7,811	1,385	17.7	214	64	29.9	1,077	599	55.6	5,868	2,698	46.0
Median (Years)	47.4	40.2	....	47.9	40.1	....	46.8	41.1	....	44.3	40.0	....	59.0	53.2	....
Current renters	19,418	17,034	87.7	11,857	9,807	82.7	1,122	1,034	92.2	6,438	6,193	96.2	18,261	16,493	90.3
Under 25 years	2,394	2,318	96.8	1,353	1,282	94.8	89	89	(s)	952	947	99.5	3,320	3,273	98.6
25 to 34 years	7,381	6,532	88.5	4,709	3,938	83.6	321	309	96.3	2,351	2,285	97.2	5,920	5,482	92.6
35 to 44 years	4,646	4,035	86.8	2,478	2,006	81.0	343	314	91.5	1,825	1,715	94.0	2,266	1,929	85.1
45 to 54 years	2,255	1,993	88.4	1,281	1,066	83.2	203	193	95.1	771	734	95.2	1,527	1,241	81.3
55 to 64 years	1,387	1,092	78.7	950	691	72.7	101	66	(s)	335	335	99.9	1,523	1,326	87.1
65 years or older	1,353	1,065	78.7	1,085	824	75.9	64	64	(s)	204	177	86.8	3,705	3,243	87.5
Median (Years)	34.9	34.5	....	34.7	34.2	....	39.4	38.6	....	34.8	34.4	....	34.8	34.1	....

Source: Analysis of data from the Survey of Income and Program Participation in Fronczek, Peter J., and Howard A. Savage, "Who Can Afford to Buy a House?" U.S. Bureau of the Census, Current Housing Reports, H121/91-1.

(s) Data suppressed.
Details may not add to totals due to rounding.

Housing Problems and Costs

TABLE 3.58. AFFORDABILITY STATUS OF FAMILIES AND UNRELATED INDIVIDUALS FOR A MEDIAN-PRICED HOME, BY AGE OF HOUSEHOLDER, CURRENT TENURE, AND TYPE OF FINANCING: 1991
(Numbers in thousands)

AGE OF HOUSEHOLDER, TENURE, AND TYPE OF FINANCING	Families												Unrelated individuals		
	Total			Married-couple			Male householder, no wife present			Female householder, no husband present					
	Total	Cannot afford median-priced home in area		Total	Cannot afford median-priced home in area		Total	Cannot afford median-priced home in area		Total	Cannot afford median-priced home in area		Total	Cannot afford median-priced home in area	
		Number	Percent		Number	Percent		Number	Percent		Number	Percent		Number	Percent
USING CONVENTIONAL, FIXED-RATE, 30-YEAR FINANCING															
Total	69,543	35,668	51.3	53,249	22,449	42.2	2,810	1,904	67.8	13,484	11,314	83.9	36,010	27,433	76.2
Under 25 years	3,693	3,563	96.5	1,739	1,629	93.7	176	173	97.8	1,777	1,761	99.1	4,124	4,030	97.7
25 to 34 years	15,666	11,839	75.6	11,128	7,519	67.6	581	484	83.3	3,957	3,836	96.9	8,957	8,079	90.2
35 to 44 years	17,748	9,085	51.2	13,594	5,686	41.8	802	591	73.8	3,353	2,808	83.8	5,509	4,335	78.7
45 to 54 years	12,067	4,809	39.9	9,679	3,192	33.0	490	283	57.7	1,898	1,334	70.3	3,594	2,447	68.1
55 to 64 years	9,403	3,011	32.0	7,891	2,088	26.5	352	174	49.5	1,160	748	64.5	3,595	2,402	66.8
65 years or older	10,967	3,360	30.6	9,219	2,335	25.3	410	199	48.6	1,338	826	61.7	10,232	6,140	60.0
Median (Years)	43.7	37.7	....	45.2	38.7	....	43.1	40.0	....	38.0	35.2	....	43.9	38.7	....
Current owners	49,881	17,742	35.6	41,875	12,591	30.1	1,804	967	53.6	6,202	4,185	67.5	16,311	9,291	57.0
Under 25 years	1,080	989	91.6	581	503	86.6	37	37	100.0	462	450	97.3	738	694	94.1
25 to 34 years	8,224	4,844	58.9	6,741	3,552	52.7	316	223	70.6	1,168	1,069	91.6	2,520	1,983	78.7
35 to 44 years	12,995	4,757	36.6	10,991	3,409	31.0	517	331	64.2	1,488	1,017	68.4	2,447	1,544	63.1
45 to 54 years	9,902	2,914	29.4	8,339	2,078	24.9	354	163	45.9	1,209	673	55.6	1,907	963	50.5
55 to 64 years	8,093	1,909	23.6	7,045	1,416	20.1	255	97	38.1	793	396	49.9	2,072	1,056	51.0
65 years or older	9,587	2,329	24.3	8,179	1,633	20.0	325	116	35.6	1,083	580	53.6	6,629	3,051	46.0
Median (Years)	47.7	41.4	....	48.1	41.6	....	45.9	41.8	....	44.9	40.6	....	57.6	49.4	....
Current renters	19,662	17,926	91.2	11,373	9,859	86.7	1,007	937	93.1	7,282	7,130	97.9	19,699	18,142	92.1
Under 25 years	2,613	2,574	98.5	1,158	1,126	97.2	140	136	97.2	1,315	1,312	99.7	3,386	3,336	98.5
25 to 34 years	7,442	6,995	94.0	4,387	3,967	90.4	265	261	98.4	2,789	2,767	99.2	6,438	6,096	94.7
35 to 44 years	4,753	4,328	91.1	2,603	2,277	87.5	285	260	91.2	1,865	1,791	96.0	3,062	2,791	91.1
45 to 54 years	2,165	1,896	87.6	1,340	1,114	83.2	135	120	88.6	690	662	96.0	1,687	1,484	88.0
55 to 64 years	1,310	1,102	84.1	846	673	79.5	96	77	79.8	367	353	96.1	1,523	1,346	88.4
65 years or older	1,380	1,031	74.7	1,039	701	67.5	85	84	98.2	256	246	96.1	3,603	3,089	85.7
Median (Years)	34.7	34.1	....	35.5	34.6	....	38.5	37.8	....	33.3	33.1	....	35.1	34.4	....
USING FHA, FIXED-RATE, 30-YEAR FINANCING															
Total	69,543	34,362	49.4	53,249	21,256	39.9	2,810	1,874	66.7	13,484	11,232	83.3	36,010	27,173	75.5
Under 25 years	3,693	3,507	95.0	1,739	1,573	90.5	176	173	97.8	1,777	1,761	99.1	4,124	4,019	97.5
25 to 34 years	15,666	11,386	72.7	11,128	7,092	63.7	581	484	83.3	3,957	3,810	96.3	8,957	7,966	88.9
35 to 44 years	17,748	8,651	48.7	13,594	5,293	38.9	802	581	72.4	3,353	2,777	82.8	5,509	4,302	78.1
45 to 54 years	12,067	4,612	38.2	9,679	3,013	31.1	490	277	56.7	1,898	1,322	69.6	3,594	2,428	67.6
55 to 64 years	9,403	2,931	31.2	7,891	2,022	25.6	352	164	46.7	1,160	744	64.2	3,595	2,383	66.3
65 years or older	10,967	3,275	29.9	9,219	2,262	24.5	410	196	47.7	1,338	817	61.0	10,232	6,075	59.4
Median (Years)	43.7	37.6	....	45.2	38.7	....	43.1	39.8	....	38.0	35.2	....	43.9	38.7	....
Current owners	49,881	16,724	33.5	41,875	11,667	27.9	1,804	937	52.0	6,202	4,119	66.4	16,311	9,141	56.0
Under 25 years	1,080	946	87.7	581	460	79.2	37	37	100.0	462	450	97.3	738	694	94.1
25 to 34 years	8,224	4,526	55.0	6,741	3,255	48.3	316	223	70.6	1,168	1,048	89.7	2,520	1,938	76.9
35 to 44 years	12,995	4,402	33.9	10,991	3,089	28.1	517	321	62.1	1,488	993	66.7	2,447	1,521	62.2
45 to 54 years	9,902	2,753	27.8	8,339	1,929	23.1	354	158	44.5	1,209	666	55.1	1,907	950	49.8
55 to 64 years	8,093	1,852	22.9	7,045	1,373	19.5	255	87	34.2	793	392	49.4	2,072	1,044	50.4
65 years or older	9,587	2,246	23.4	8,179	1,562	19.1	325	112	34.4	1,083	571	52.8	6,629	2,994	45.2
Median (Years)	47.7	41.6	....	48.1	41.9	....	45.9	41.5	....	44.9	40.7	....	57.6	49.4	....
Current renters	19,662	17,639	89.7	11,373	9,589	84.3	1,007	937	93.1	7,282	7,113	97.7	19,699	18,032	91.5
Under 25 years	2,613	2,561	98.0	1,158	1,113	96.1	140	136	97.2	1,315	1,312	99.7	3,386	3,325	98.2
25 to 34 years	7,442	6,861	92.2	4,387	3,837	87.5	265	261	98.4	2,789	2,763	99.0	6,438	6,028	93.6
35 to 44 years	4,753	4,249	89.4	2,603	2,205	84.7	285	260	91.2	1,865	1,785	95.7	3,062	2,781	90.8
45 to 54 years	2,165	1,859	85.9	1,340	1,084	80.9	135	120	88.6	690	656	95.1	1,687	1,478	87.6
55 to 64 years	1,310	1,079	82.4	846	650	76.8	96	77	79.8	367	353	96.1	1,523	1,339	87.9
65 years or older	1,380	1,029	74.6	1,039	700	67.4	85	84	98.2	256	246	96.1	3,603	3,082	85.5
Median (Years)	34.7	34.1	....	35.5	34.6	....	38.5	37.8	....	33.3	33.1	....	35.1	34.4	....

Source: Analysis of data from the Survey of Income and Program Participation in Savage, Howard A., and Peter J. Fronczek, "Who Can Afford to Buy a House in 1991?" U.S. Bureau of the Census, Current Housing Reports, H121/93-3.

Details may not add to totals due to rounding.

Housing Problems and Costs

TABLE 3.59. AFFORDABILITY STATUS OF FAMILIES AND UNRELATED INDIVIDUALS FOR A MEDIAN-PRICED HOME, BY AGE OF HOUSEHOLDER, CURRENT TENURE, AND TYPE OF FINANCING: 1993
(Numbers in thousands)

AGE OF HOUSEHOLDER, TENURE, AND TYPE OF FINANCING	Families												Unrelated individuals		
	Total			Married-couple			Male householder, no wife present			Female householder, no husband present					
	Total	Cannot afford median-priced home in area		Total	Cannot afford median-priced home in area		Total	Cannot afford median-priced home in area		Total	Cannot afford median-priced home in area		Total	Cannot afford median-priced home in area	
		Number	Percent		Number	Percent		Number	Percent		Number	Percent		Number	Percent
USING CONVENTIONAL, FIXED-RATE, 30-YEAR FINANCING															
Total	71,344	35,329	49.5	53,822	21,185	39.4	3,062	2,129	69.5	14,461	12,015	83.1	36,749	27,557	75.0
Under 25 years	3,785	3,644	96.3	1,602	1,470	91.7	193	193	100.0	1,990	1,981	99.6	4,028	3,970	98.5
25 to 34 years	15,766	11,619	73.7	11,114	7,220	65.0	744	658	88.4	3,908	3,741	95.7	8,584	7,627	88.9
35 to 44 years	18,710	9,522	50.9	13,974	5,702	40.8	845	569	67.3	3,890	3,251	83.6	5,982	4,611	77.1
45 to 54 years	12,777	4,706	36.8	10,173	3,018	29.7	627	331	52.9	1,978	1,357	68.6	4,374	3,037	69.4
55 to 64 years	9,074	2,563	28.2	7,614	1,606	21.1	299	179	60.0	1,161	778	67.0	3,722	2,226	59.8
65 years or older	11,233	3,275	29.2	9,345	2,169	23.2	354	199	56.1	1,534	906	59.1	10,058	6,087	60.5
Median (Years)	43.6	37.5	....	45.2	38.4	....	42.0	38.7	....	38.4	35.9	....	44.6	39.7	....
Current owners	50,623	16,386	32.4	42,051	11,013	26.2	1,936	1,051	54.3	6,636	4,322	65.1	16,566	8,833	53.3
Under 25 years	1,196	1,075	89.8	528	413	78.2	77	77	100.0	591	585	98.9	593	575	96.9
25 to 34 years	8,255	4,599	55.7	6,736	3,299	49.0	361	284	78.5	1,158	1,016	87.7	2,268	1,700	74.9
35 to 44 years	13,124	4,436	33.8	10,902	3,060	28.1	530	272	51.3	1,692	1,105	65.3	2,611	1,514	58.0
45 to 54 years	10,258	2,495	24.3	8,668	1,770	20.4	450	171	37.9	1,140	554	48.6	2,366	1,215	51.4
55 to 64 years	7,847	1,562	19.9	6,825	1,026	15.0	211	97	45.9	811	439	54.2	2,378	1,028	43.2
65 years or older	9,943	2,220	22.3	8,393	1,445	17.2	307	151	49.4	1,244	623	50.1	6,351	2,802	44.1
Median (Years)	47.7	40.7	....	48.3	40.9	....	45.0	41.0	....	44.3	40.1	....	56.9	50.2	....
Current renters	20,721	18,943	91.4	11,771	10,172	86.4	1,126	1,078	95.7	7,825	7,693	98.3	20,182	18,723	92.8
Under 25 years	2,589	2,570	99.3	1,074	1,057	98.4	116	116	100.0	1,398	1,397	99.9	3,435	3,395	98.8
25 to 34 years	7,510	7,020	93.5	4,378	3,921	89.6	382	374	97.8	2,750	2,725	99.1	6,317	5,928	93.8
35 to 44 years	5,585	5,086	91.1	3,072	2,643	86.0	316	297	94.2	2,198	2,147	97.7	3,372	3,098	91.9
45 to 54 years	2,519	2,212	87.8	1,505	1,248	82.9	176	161	91.1	838	803	95.8	2,008	1,821	90.7
55 to 64 years	1,228	1,001	81.5	789	580	73.5	88	82	93.6	351	339	96.6	1,344	1,198	89.1
65 years or older	1,290	1,055	81.8	952	724	76.0	47	47	100.0	290	283	97.7	3,707	3,285	88.6
Median (Years)	35.5	34.8	....	36.4	35.4	....	37.1	36.6	....	34.1	34.0	....	36.0	35.1	....
USING FHA, FIXED-RATE, 30-YEAR FINANCING															
Total	71,344	34,868	48.9	53,821	20,664	38.4	3,062	2,148	70.1	14,461	12,056	83.4	36,749	27,477	74.8
Under 25 years	3,785	3,608	95.3	1,602	1,434	89.5	193	193	100.0	1,990	1,981	99.6	4,028	3,966	98.5
25 to 34 years	15,766	11,369	72.1	11,114	6,958	62.6	744	659	88.7	3,908	3,751	96.0	8,584	7,578	88.3
35 to 44 years	18,710	9,269	49.5	13,974	5,447	39.0	845	579	68.5	3,890	3,243	83.4	5,982	4,565	76.3
45 to 54 years	12,777	4,660	36.5	10,173	2,943	28.9	627	337	53.8	1,978	1,380	69.8	4,373	3,001	68.6
55 to 64 years	9,074	2,607	28.7	7,614	1,638	21.5	299	178	59.6	1,161	791	68.1	3,722	2,257	60.6
65 years or older	11,233	3,356	29.9	9,345	2,245	24.0	354	201	56.8	1,534	910	59.3	10,058	6,111	60.8
Median (Years)	43.6	37.7	....	45.2	38.6	....	42.0	38.8	....	38.4	35.9	....	44.6	39.8	....
Current owners	50,623	16,045	31.7	42,051	10,620	25.3	1,936	1,070	55.3	6,636	4,354	65.6	16,566	8,822	53.3
Under 25 years	1,196	1,052	88.0	528	390	74.0	77	77	100.0	591	585	98.9	593	574	96.7
25 to 34 years	8,255	4,412	53.4	6,736	3,103	46.1	361	285	78.9	1,158	1,024	88.4	2,268	1,668	73.5
35 to 44 years	13,124	4,223	32.2	10,902	2,842	26.1	530	281	53.1	1,692	1,100	65.0	2,611	1,491	57.1
45 to 54 years	10,258	2,465	24.0	8,668	1,718	19.8	450	176	39.2	1,140	571	50.1	2,366	1,198	50.6
55 to 64 years	7,847	1,599	20.4	6,825	1,051	15.4	211	96	45.5	811	452	55.8	2,378	1,060	44.6
65 years or older	9,944	2,293	23.1	8,393	1,516	18.1	307	154	50.1	1,244	623	50.1	6,351	2,832	44.6
Median (Years)	47.7	41.2	....	48.3	41.5	....	45.0	41.2	....	44.3	40.2	....	56.9	50.7	....
Current renters	20,721	18,824	90.8	11,771	10,044	85.3	1,126	1,078	95.7	7,825	7,702	98.4	20,182	18,655	92.4
Under 25 years	2,589	2,556	98.7	1,074	1,044	97.1	116	116	100.0	1,398	1,397	99.9	3,435	3,393	98.8
25 to 34 years	7,510	6,957	92.6	4,378	3,855	88.1	382	374	97.8	2,750	2,728	99.2	6,317	5,911	93.6
35 to 44 years	5,585	5,045	90.3	3,072	2,604	84.8	316	297	94.2	2,198	2,144	97.6	3,372	3,074	91.2
45 to 54 years	2,519	2,194	87.1	1,505	1,225	81.4	176	161	91.1	838	809	96.5	2,008	1,803	89.8
55 to 64 years	1,228	1,008	82.1	789	587	74.4	88	82	93.6	351	339	96.6	1,344	1,197	89.0
65 years or older	1,290	1,062	82.4	952	728	76.5	47	47	100.0	290	287	98.8	3,707	3,279	88.4
Median (Years)	35.5	34.9	....	36.4	35.5	....	37.1	36.7	....	34.1	34.0	....	36.0	35.1	....

Source: Analysis of data from the Survey of Income and Program Participation in Savage, Howard A., "Who Can Afford to Buy a House in 1993?" U.S. Bureau of the Census, Current Housing Reports, H121/97-1.

Details may not add to totals due to rounding.

Housing Problems and Costs

OBSTACLE	All adults						Whites						African Americans						Hispanics					
TABLE 3.60. PERCEIVED OBSTACLES TO HOMEOWNERSHIP BY RACE/ETHNICITY: 1992 TO 1997 (Percent)	1992	1993	1994	1995	1996	1997	1992	1993	1994	1995	1996	1997	1992	1993	1994	1995	1996	1997	1992	1993	1994	1995	1996	1997
Having enough money for a downpayment and closing costs	51	45	51	44	52	44	47	41	50	44	52	44	66	58	56	47	54	49	59	59	55	50	50	50
Earning enough income to meet monthly mortgage payments	44	25	30	41	50	34	39	24	30	40	48	32	59	28	31	44	48	45	55	30	31	41	59	34
Being able to find a home that you like and can afford	....	....	43	40	49	42	....	....	41	39	47	40	....	....	57	52	55	47	....	....	42	43	54	49
Having enough confidence in job security	29	16	25	26	48	36	25	15	23	24	47	35	38	17	39	32	45	37	46	21	23	-	44	41
Finding a neighborhood in which you feel confident investing in a home	....	....	29	25	43	35	....	....	26	23	42	32	....	....	50	33	45	36	....	....	31	-	40	43
Finding a real estate agent you can trust	....	....	29	29	39	....	....	....	26	27	38	....	....	....	38	41	53	....	....	....	44	-	38	....
Having a good enough credit record to get a mortgage	25	19	24	21	38	30	21	17	23	20	36	29	37	30	28	-	46	36	36	24	30	30	29	34
Not knowing how to get started buying a home	....	....	23	25	32	25	....	....	20	21	29	22	....	....	34	-	35	36	....	....	37	33	40	38
The expense of maintaining or repairing a home	....	....	21	21	28	....	....	....	19	19	25	....	....	....	18	-	41	....	....	....	30	24	28	....
Facing discrimination or social barriers that might prevent you from buying the home you would want to buy	9	10	14	12	18	15	6	7	11	8	14	11	21	27	42	32	34	39	14	20	17	14	24	23

Source: Fannie Mae, National Housing Survey.

The table shows the percent of respondents indicating that a given item is a "major obstacle" to buying a home. See Appendix A for wording of the survey question.
Based on a sample survey of adults in the contiguous United States.
(-) Results not reported due to high margin of error within subgroup.

PART 4: HOUSING FINANCE

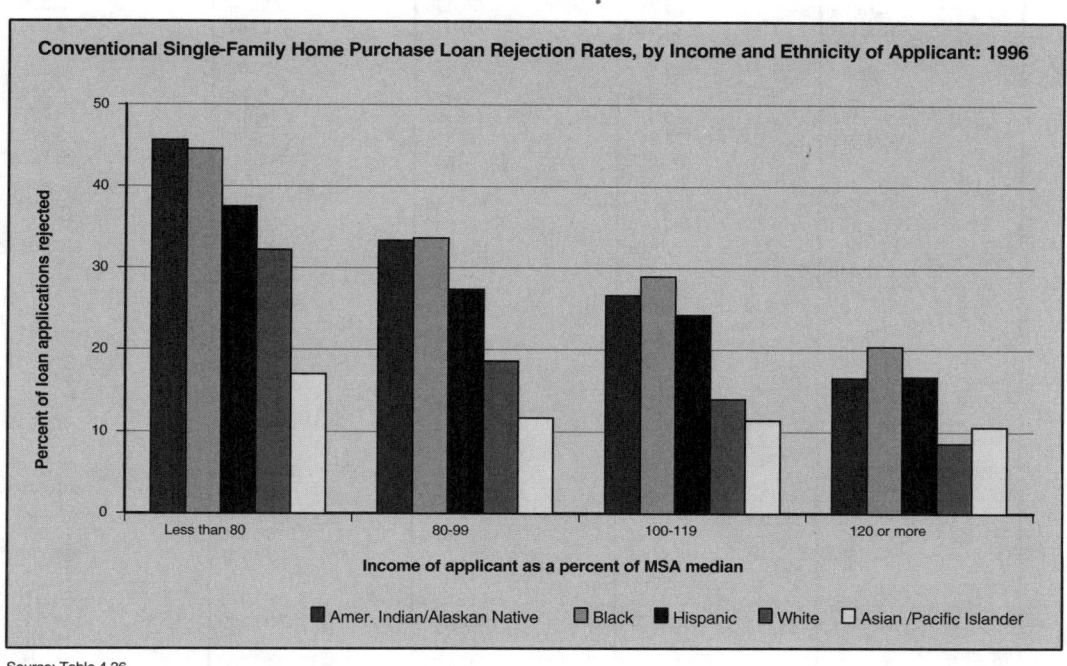

Conventional Single-Family Home Purchase Loan Rejection Rates, by Income and Ethnicity of Applicant: 1996

Source: Table 4.36.

Beginning in 1990 the Home Mortgage Disclosure Act (HMDA) required that certain home mortgage lenders report information on the characteristics of home loan applicants and the disposition of loan applications. These data reveal considerable variability in loan denial rates by applicant ethnicity and income (see figure).

Controlling for income does not remove differences in denial rates across ethnic groups.[1] Within each of the income categories denial rates vary by at least a factor of two, although these gaps narrow as income increases. Interethnic disparities are even more powerfully demonstrated by selected comparisons across income and ethnic categories simultaneously. For example, Black applicants with incomes of 120 percent of area median income or more had a denial rate in 1996 that was higher than the rate for Asians and Pacific Islanders with incomes of less than 80 percent of area median. Hispanic, American Indian, and Alaskan Native applicants in the highest income category experienced denial rates roughly equal to the rate for Asians and Pacific Islanders in the lowest income category.

---

[1]Differences in denial rates across groups do not prove discrimination on the part of mortgage lenders covered by HMDA. Even after controlling for income, differences in denial rates might be explained by intergroup differences in characteristics such as credit histories and assets that are critical to the loan underwriting decision but not reported under HMDA.

283

Mortgage Debt Outstanding

TABLE 4.1. MORTGAGE DEBT OUTSTANDING, BY TYPE OF PROPERTY: 1949 TO 1997
(In millions of dollars)

YEAR	Total mortgage debt outstanding	Residential nonfarm			Commercial	Farm
		Total	1-4-family homes	Multifamily		
1949	62,318	45,916	37,272	8,644	10,829	5,573
1950	72,679	55,193	45,077	10,116	11,451	6,035
1951	82,144	63,100	51,643	11,457	12,450	6,594
1952	91,254	70,734	58,438	12,296	13,355	7,165
1953	101,161	78,973	66,037	12,936	14,520	7,668
1954	113,580	89,157	75,677	13,480	16,268	8,155
1955	129,893	102,554	88,249	14,305	18,316	9,023
1956	144,452	113,880	99,001	14,879	20,737	9,835
1957	156,519	122,947	107,617	15,330	23,175	10,397
1958	171,767	134,535	117,687	16,848	26,123	11,109
1959	190,818	149,522	130,854	18,668	29,195	12,101
1960	207,498	162,289	141,940	20,349	32,371	12,838
1961	227,967	177,569	154,598	22,971	36,481	13,917
1962	251,440	195,115	169,302	25,813	41,132	15,193
1963	278,478	215,439	186,396	29,043	46,217	16,822
1964	305,909	236,925	203,358	33,567	50,042	18,942
1965	333,306	257,662	220,479	37,183	54,457	21,187
1966	356,476	273,251	232,944	40,307	60,148	23,077
1967	381,206	291,240	247,330	43,910	64,824	25,142
1968	411,064	312,129	264,783	47,346	71,390	27,545
1969	441,584	335,342	283,163	52,179	76,889	29,353
1970	473,663	357,542	297,431	60,111	85,629	30,492
1971	524,201	395,952	325,890	70,062	95,868	32,381
1972	597,354	449,328	366,488	82,840	112,665	35,361
1973	672,593	501,062	407,930	93,132	131,725	39,806
1974	732,468	540,669	440,693	99,976	146,877	44,922
1975	791,858	582,673	482,064	100,609	159,332	49,853
1976	878,599	651,980	546,314	105,666	171,207	55,412
1977	1,010,303	756,646	642,652	113,994	189,708	63,949
1978	1,163,002	878,467	753,542	124,925	211,778	72,757
1979	1,328,448	1,005,393	870,532	134,861	236,300	86,755
1980	1,464,787	1,111,171	970,205	140,966	256,129	97,487
1981	1,588,901	1,189,270	1,050,339	138,931	292,402	107,229
1982	1,673,995	1,238,152	1,097,383	140,769	324,532	111,311
1983	1,866,960	1,374,417	1,220,418	153,999	378,822	113,721
1984	2,110,434	1,538,515	1,361,550	176,965	459,497	112,422
1985	2,373,861	1,742,107	1,536,895	205,212	525,903	105,850
1986	2,657,158	1,981,333	1,742,916	238,417	580,659	95,166
1987	2,993,904	2,238,789	1,977,942	260,847	667,396	87,720
1988	3,310,022	2,496,624	2,219,105	277,519	730,445	82,953
1989	3,579,678	2,749,326	2,461,055	288,271	749,870	80,482
1990	3,793,874	2,961,141	2,674,206	286,935	753,831	78,903
1991	3,947,718	3,133,975	2,850,512	283,463	734,550	79,193
1992	4,063,023	3,292,868	3,019,450	273,418	690,417	79,738
1993	4,205,844	3,447,831	3,178,444	269,387	677,274	80,739
1994	4,392,093	3,632,100	3,357,475	274,625	677,022	82,971
1995	4,606,303	3,820,592	3,533,295	287,297	701,150	84,561
1996	4,929,430	4,074,269	3,761,711	312,558	768,027	87,134
1997	5,277,185	4,357,363	4,019,228	338,135	829,476	90,346

Source: Board of Governors of the Federal Reserve System, Federal Reserve Bulletin, monthly.

All data as of December 31.
Includes Puerto Rico and Guam.

Mortgage Debt Outstanding

TABLE 4.2. RESIDENTIAL NONFARM MORTGAGE DEBT OUTSTANDING, BY PROPERTY TYPE AND TYPE OF HOLDER: 1968 TO 1997
(In millions of dollars)

YEAR	Total residential nonfarm mortgage debt outstanding	1 to 4-family homes												
		Total, 1 to 4 family	Commer-cial banks	Savings institutions	Life insurance companies	Mortgage pools or trusts					Federal and related agencies			Individuals and others
						Total [1]	Government National Mortgage Association	Fannie Mae	Freddie Mac	Private mortgage conduits	Total [2]	Fannie Mae	Freddie Mac	
1968	312,129	264,783	38,765	149,788	29,030	994	0	0	0	0	13,306	7,151	0	32,900
1969	335,342	283,163	41,356	158,995	27,964	1,369	0	0	0	0	17,280	10,919	0	36,199
1970	357,542	297,431	42,329	167,119	26,739	2,532	347	0	0	0	21,772	15,181	357	36,940
1971	395,952	325,890	48,020	185,100	24,645	6,717	3,074	0	48	0	23,230	16,681	934	38,178
1972	449,328	366,488	57,004	212,639	22,315	10,701	5,353	0	331	0	24,455	17,697	1,754	39,374
1973	501,062	407,930	67,998	235,889	20,426	13,636	7,561	0	617	0	27,150	20,370	2,446	42,831
1974	540,669	440,693	74,758	250,200	19,026	18,639	11,249	0	608	0	33,457	23,778	4,217	44,613
1975	582,673	482,064	77,018	273,928	17,590	28,081	17,538	0	1,349	0	37,860	25,813	4,588	47,587
1976	651,980	546,314	86,234	313,883	16,088	42,084	29,583	0	2,282	0	35,530	26,934	3,889	52,495
1977	756,646	642,652	105,115	368,753	14,740	60,573	43,555	0	5,621	0	35,719	28,504	2,738	57,752
1978	878,467	753,542	129,167	419,374	14,436	75,789	52,732	0	9,657	0	43,780	37,579	2,428	70,996
1979	1,005,393	870,532	149,460	460,485	16,144	100,886	73,853	0	12,149	0	53,263	45,488	3,072	90,294
1980	1,111,171	970,205	161,598	487,252	17,943	125,419	91,602	0	13,471	3,663	61,429	51,775	3,864	116,564
1981	1,189,270	1,050,339	171,576	501,329	17,201	146,762	103,209	717	19,501	4,957	67,886	55,986	5,181	145,585
1982	1,238,152	1,097,383	174,829	457,811	16,751	200,821	116,038	14,450	42,560	7,768	77,755	66,500	4,686	169,416
1983	1,374,417	1,220,418	183,574	481,573	15,319	271,097	155,950	25,121	57,273	12,349	87,367	73,045	7,559	181,489
1984	1,538,515	1,361,550	197,348	528,791	14,120	322,232	175,589	35,965	70,253	18,612	97,272	81,698	9,654	201,787
1985	1,742,107	1,536,895	214,699	554,301	12,381	406,951	207,198	54,036	99,515	24,016	109,553	91,898	11,881	239,010
1986 [3]	1,981,333	1,742,916	237,134	559,067	12,827	536,137	256,920	95,791	166,667	16,617	125,471	89,050	10,010	272,281
1987	2,238,789	1,977,942	277,075	602,408	13,226	681,692	309,806	137,988	205,977	27,800	119,662	85,473	11,430	283,879
1988	2,496,624	2,219,105	336,029	671,722	11,164	758,467	331,257	172,331	219,988	34,865	125,749	87,737	15,077	315,974
1989	2,749,326	2,461,055	391,494	669,220	12,231	887,125	358,142	219,577	266,060	43,325	131,353	90,575	18,248	369,633
1990	2,961,141	2,674,206	457,974	600,154	13,005	1,046,493	391,505	291,194	308,369	55,408	153,286	94,323	19,185	403,293
1991	3,133,975	2,850,512	485,667	538,358	10,642	1,230,461	415,767	362,667	351,906	100,110	163,488	100,584	24,125	421,896
1992	3,292,868	3,019,450	510,754	489,622	11,215	1,400,120	410,675	435,979	401,525	151,933	193,514	124,219	31,032	414,227
1993	3,447,831	3,178,444	560,796	470,000	8,593	1,519,081	404,864	486,804	442,612	184,796	229,697	150,698	44,345	390,276
1994	3,632,100	3,357,475	615,861	477,626	7,018	1,658,189	441,198	520,763	487,725	208,500	228,425	158,766	38,882	370,356
1995	3,820,592	3,533,295	669,434	482,353	7,316	1,771,202	461,438	569,724	512,238	227,800	227,309	161,665	39,901	375,682
1996	4,074,269	3,761,711	698,508	513,712	6,772	1,940,781	494,158	633,210	551,513	261,900	225,445	160,751	41,758	376,493
1997	4,357,363	4,019,228	762,421	518,976	7,186	2,105,983	523,156	687,981	576,846	318,000	221,135	156,245	42,629	403,526

See notes at end of table.

Mortgage Debt Outstanding

TABLE 4.2. RESIDENTIAL NONFARM MORTGAGE DEBT OUTSTANDING, BY PROPERTY TYPE AND TYPE OF HOLDER: 1968 TO 1997 - Continued
(In millions of dollars)

YEAR	Total residential nonfarm mortgage debt outstanding	Multifamily						
		Total multifamily	Commercial banks	Savings institutions	Life insurance companies	Mortgage pools or trusts	Federal and related agencies	Individuals and others
1968	312,129	47,346	2,668	17,799	12,754	18	1,916	12,191
1969	335,342	52,179	3,217	19,345	14,119	35	2,612	12,851
1970	357,542	60,111	3,311	21,618	15,969	60	3,408	15,745
1971	395,952	70,062	3,984	27,185	16,747	114	4,626	17,406
1972	449,328	82,840	5,778	31,961	17,347	392	5,897	21,465
1973	501,062	93,132	6,932	35,122	18,451	616	8,029	23,982
1974	540,669	99,976	7,619	36,731	19,625	785	10,940	24,276
1975	582,673	100,609	5,915	39,339	19,629	1,263	12,315	22,148
1976	651,980	105,666	8,082	42,602	19,178	1,910	12,313	21,581
1977	756,646	113,994	9,215	47,550	18,823	3,089	12,409	22,908
1978	878,467	124,925	10,266	51,982	19,000	4,966	12,979	25,732
1979	1,005,393	134,861	11,180	54,136	19,215	7,128	13,343	29,859
1980	1,111,171	140,966	12,870	54,200	19,514	8,267	14,881	31,233
1981	1,189,270	138,931	14,950	53,659	19,283	6,359	13,737	30,943
1982	1,238,152	140,769	16,480	53,759	18,856	7,650	12,378	31,646
1983	1,374,417	153,999	18,410	61,580	19,107	9,612	11,223	34,067
1984	1,538,515	176,965	20,264	75,567	18,938	11,052	11,113	40,031
1985	1,742,107	205,212	23,373	89,739	19,894	13,445	12,170	46,591
1986 [3]	1,981,333	238,417	31,173	97,059	20,952	11,865	19,842	57,526
1987	2,238,789	260,847	32,756	106,359	22,524	16,574	19,905	62,728
1988	2,496,624	277,519	33,912	110,775	24,560	21,979	21,342	64,951
1989	2,749,326	288,271	38,876	106,014	26,907	26,152	24,295	66,027
1990	2,961,141	286,935	37,015	91,806	28,979	29,468	36,131	63,535
1991	3,133,975	283,463	36,932	79,881	29,342	29,800	46,054	61,455
1992	3,292,868	273,418	38,053	69,791	27,221	30,135	43,451	64,766
1993	3,447,831	269,387	38,657	67,366	25,376	31,159	42,068	64,761
1994	3,632,100	274,625	39,346	64,343	23,902	37,367	40,360	69,306
1995	3,820,592	287,297	43,837	61,987	23,435	48,172	36,332	73,533
1996	4,074,269	312,558	46,675	61,570	23,197	66,188	33,368	81,560
1997	4,357,363	338,135	51,100	59,527	23,755	86,055	29,875	87,823

Source: Board of Governors of the Federal Reserve System, Federal Reserve Bulletin, monthly.

All data as of December 31.
Includes Puerto Rico and Guam.

(1) Includes mortgage pools backed by the Rural Housing Service (formerly, Farmers Home Administration), not shown separately.
(2) Includes other federal and related agencies, not shown separately.
(3) Securities that were guaranteed by the Farmers Home Administration (FmHA) and sold to the Federal Financing Bank were reallocated from mortgage pools to federal and related agencies' mortgage holdings in 1986 because of accounting changes at FmHA.

Mortgage Debt Outstanding

TABLE 4.3. REAL ESTATE LOANS OF DOMESTIC OFFICES OF FDIC-INSURED COMMERCIAL BANKS AND TRUST COMPANIES AT YEAR END: 1934 TO 1996
(Millions of current dollars)

YEAR	Total	Construction and land development	1- to 4-family residential properties	Multifamily residential properties	Farmland	Nonfarm non-residential
1934	3,336	....	2,836	....	499	....
1935	3,323	....	2,835	....	488	....
1936	3,447	....	2,959	....	488	....
1937	3,641	....	3,139	....	502	....
1938	3,859	....	2,417	....	519	923
1939	4,137	....	2,597	....	534	1,006
1940	4,470	....	2,883	....	544	1,044
1941	4,776	....	3,209	....	535	1,031
1942	4,647	....	3,263	....	477	907
1943	4,438	....	3,204	....	449	786
1944	4,344	....	3,157	....	450	738
1945	4,679	....	3,332	....	507	840
1946	7,106	....	5,058	....	684	1,365
1947	9,271	....	6,816	....	794	1,661
1948	10,671	....	7,913	....	848	1,911
1949	11,413	....	8,513	....	886	2,014
1950	13,416	....	10,250	....	946	2,219
1951	14,487	....	11,081	....	983	2,423
1952	15,616	....	11,996	....	1,037	2,583
1953	16,613	....	12,744	....	1,062	2,806
1954	18,347	....	13,979	....	1,139	3,229
1955	20,767	....	15,715	....	1,279	3,773
1956	22,484	....	16,836	....	1,317	4,331
1957	23,104	....	16,990	....	1,349	4,766
1958	25,267	....	18,420	....	1,453	5,394
1959	28,031	....	20,247	....	1,571	6,214
1960	28,694	....	20,288	....	1,631	6,775
1961	30,330	....	21,150	....	1,731	7,449
1962	34,309	....	23,368	....	2,003	8,939
1963	39,088	....	26,245	....	2,303	10,540
1964	43,733	....	28,739	....	2,617	12,378
1965	49,394	....	32,159	....	2,888	14,346
1966	54,102	....	34,660	....	3,112	16,330
1967	58,674	....	37,370	....	3,419	17,885
1968	65,328	....	41,144	....	3,735	20,449

See notes at end of table.

Mortgage Debt Outstanding

TABLE 4.3. REAL ESTATE LOANS OF DOMESTIC OFFICES OF FDIC-INSURED COMMERCIAL BANKS AND TRUST COMPANIES AT YEAR END: 1934 TO 1996 - Continued
(Millions of current dollars)

YEAR	Total	Construction and land development	1 to 4-family residential properties	Multifamily residential properties	Farmland	Nonfarm non-residential
1969	70,325	....	41,068	3,210	3,993	22,053
1970	73,083	....	42,217	3,308	4,319	23,239
1971	82,314	....	47,881	3,982	4,174	26,278
1972	99,086	....	56,843	5,776	4,752	31,715
1973	118,787	....	67,796	6,929	5,420	38,642
1974	131,751	....	74,552	7,591	6,031	43,577
1975	136,187	....	77,019	5,915	6,371	46,882
1976	150,905	17,273	81,080	4,582	6,717	41,253
1977	178,606	21,395	96,765	4,911	7,732	47,803
1978	212,740	27,024	117,944	5,694	8,474	53,604
1979	243,927	32,720	136,776	6,281	8,563	59,587
1980	262,378	36,591	146,865	6,498	8,549	63,875
1981	282,590	44,946	154,971	7,098	8,318	67,257
1982	298,859	52,305	158,473	7,636	8,373	72,072
1983	327,957	60,577	167,339	9,297	9,313	81,431
1984	374,891	76,140	181,639	10,798	10,181	96,133
1985	425,384	89,234	198,751	12,590	11,359	113,450
1986	498,299	106,744	222,590	15,894	12,709	140,362
1987	582,785	119,911	263,222	17,681	14,433	167,538
1988	653,021	128,441	301,767	18,260	15,517	189,036
1989	738,888	135,987	350,843	19,980	16,696	215,382
1990	803,198	126,160	400,625	20,899	17,294	238,220
1991	825,309	102,645	430,695	23,879	18,509	249,581
1992	847,052	78,618	463,470	27,237	19,950	257,777
1993	900,615	66,415	515,864	29,693	20,944	267,699
1994	971,246	64,506	568,955	31,928	22,649	283,208
1995	1,052,905	68,696	625,982	35,788	23,907	298,532
1996	1,111,926	76,402	656,421	38,148	24,960	315,995

Source: Federal Deposit Insurance Corporation: Historical Statistics on Banking, 1934-1996.

Includes U.S. territories and possessions.
See Appendix A for discussion of important changes over time in loan-type categories.

Mortgage Debt Outstanding

YEAR	Total	Construction and land development	1- to 4-family residential properties	Multifamily residential properties	Nonresidential properties
	TABLE 4.4. REAL ESTATE LOANS OF FDIC-INSURED SAVINGS INSTITUTIONS AT YEAR END: 1984 TO 1996 (Millions of current dollars)				
1984	720,471	25,141	517,786	76,199	101,344
1985	785,048	64,535	542,636	88,192	89,684
1986	805,443	96,384	528,476	79,331	101,253
1987	852,444	89,930	561,131	89,260	112,122
1988 [1]	922,815	88,164	625,568	92,083	116,999
1989	846,902	65,907	592,339	83,832	104,825
1990	755,717	44,403	544,269	77,448	89,598
1991	678,083	26,571	506,432	70,586	74,495
1992	616,095	19,441	469,251	66,109	61,294
1993	595,433	19,026	455,760	64,282	56,366
1994	602,917	20,023	467,893	62,673	52,328
1995	609,955	21,723	477,715	59,922	50,596
1996	637,314	25,429	502,169	59,530	50,186

Source: Federal Deposit Insurance Corporation: Historical Statistics on Banking, 1934-1996.

Includes U.S. territories and possessions.

(1) There was a slight change in the "1-4-Family Residential Property" category in 1988. See Appendix A.

Mortgage Debt Outstanding

TABLE 4.5. FIRST MORTGAGE DEBT OUTSTANDING ON PRIVATE NONFARM RESIDENTIAL PROPERTIES, BY PROPERTY TYPE: 1981 AND 1991

	1981		1991	
	Amount (Billions of dollars)	Percent distribution	Amount (Billions of dollars)	Percent distribution
HOMEOWNER PROPERTIES				
1 unit	646.5	70.3	1,618.8	64.0
2 to 4 units	21.7	2.4	55.3	2.2
Condominiums	22.2	2.4	133.5	5.3
Mobile homes	....	....	28.8	1.1
RENTAL AND VACANT PROPERTIES				
1 to 4 units	103.8	11.3	301.8	11.9
5 to 49 units	43.9	4.8	120.2	4.8
50 or more units	81.0	8.8	195.9	7.7
Condominiums	....	....	69.3	2.7
Mobile homes	....	....	5.6	0.2
TOTAL	919.1	100.0	2,529.2	100.0

Source: U.S. Bureau of the Census and U.S. Department of Housing and Urban Development, Residential Finance Survey.

Components may not add to totals due to rounding.

Mortgage Debt Outstanding

TYPE OF HOLDER	TABLE 4.6. FIRST MORTGAGE DEBT OUTSTANDING ON PRIVATE NONFARM RESIDENTIAL PROPERTIES, BY TYPE OF HOLDER: 1981 AND 1991			
	1981		1991	
	Amount (Billions of dollars)	Percent distribution	Amount (Billions of dollars)	Percent distribution
Commercial bank or trust company	122.9	13.4	367.9	14.5
Savings and loan association, federal savings bank	380.1	41.4	611.0	24.2
Mutual savings bank	73.5	8.0	48.3	1.9
Life insurance company	35.6	3.9	60.3	2.4
Mortgage banker or mortgage company	23.6	2.6	227.2	9.0
Federally-sponsored secondary market agency or pool	143.3	15.6	769.0	30.4
Federal agency	32.1	3.5	86.4	3.4
Conventional mortgage pool	....	....	76.6	3.0
Real estate investment trust	....	....	5.6	0.2
Pension or retirement fund	....	....	14.9	0.6
Credit union	....	....	28.1	1.1
Finance company	....	....	35.8	1.4
State or municipal government or housing finance agency	....	....	67.2	2.7
Individual or individual's estate	45.6	5.0	79.5	3.1
Other	62.4	6.8	51.4	2.0
TOTAL	919.1	100.0	2,529.2	100.0

Source: U.S. Bureau of the Census and U.S. Department of Housing and Urban Development, Residential Finance Survey.

Components may not add to totals due to rounding.

Mortgage Debt Outstanding

TABLE 4.7. FIRST MORTGAGE DEBT OUTSTANDING ON PRIVATE NONFARM RESIDENTIAL PROPERTIES BY PROPERTY TYPE, REGION, AND FIRST MORTGAGE INSURANCE: 1991
(Millions of dollars)

REGION AND MORTGAGE INSURANCE STATUS OF FIRST MORTGAGE	All properties	Homeowner properties					Rental and vacant properties						
		Total	1 housing unit	2-4 housing units	Condo-miniums	Mobile homes	Total	1 housing unit	2-4 housing units	5-49 housing units	50 or more housing units	Condo-miniums	Mobile homes
UNITED STATES													
All mortgaged properties	2,529,237	1,836,486	1,618,846	55,340	133,478	28,822	692,751	200,505	101,313	120,197	195,914	69,270	5,552
FHA-insured	371,064	287,142	257,538	7,120	21,283	1,201	83,922	26,224	8,477	8,213	34,070	6,363	574
VA-guaranteed	136,253	124,734	117,917	1,249	4,802	766	11,519	8,797	1,800	35	-	742	144
FmHA-insured	26,629	18,236	17,677	53	342	163	8,393	729	195	6,134	1,335	-	-
Insured by state agency	29,689	17,025	14,562	377	2,085	-	12,664	1,929	317	2,595	7,722	101	-
Conventional insured	291,600	244,530	212,455	6,505	22,500	3,070	47,071	18,195	8,604	6,938	4,218	8,852	263
Conventional uninsured	1,674,002	1,144,820	998,697	40,036	82,465	23,622	529,183	144,632	81,919	96,281	148,569	53,212	4,570
NORTHEAST													
All mortgaged properties	553,604	392,724	326,343	27,340	35,433	3,609	160,880	35,998	30,186	31,163	46,149	17,032	352
FHA-insured	42,966	31,465	25,556	2,940	2,969	-	11,501	757	1,149	1,990	7,208	110	288
VA-guaranteed	11,337	11,000	10,005	456	538	-	337	296	42	-	-	-	-
FmHA-insured	3,826	3,051	3,028	24	-	-	775	-	-	612	163	-	-
Insured by state agency	2,681	1,475	1,458	17	-	-	1,206	-	29	210	967	-	-
Conventional insured	61,726	48,573	38,385	3,539	6,137	511	13,153	2,447	3,247	4,801	1,124	1,534	-
Conventional uninsured	431,069	297,161	247,912	20,363	25,788	3,098	133,908	32,499	25,720	23,550	36,687	15,388	64
MIDWEST													
All mortgaged properties	438,664	333,606	308,514	8,746	12,045	4,300	105,058	21,919	16,535	22,866	38,282	4,919	538
FHA-insured	77,005	59,958	56,685	1,790	1,324	159	17,047	2,569	2,420	1,365	10,474	165	55
VA-guaranteed	22,211	20,281	19,522	476	251	32	1,929	857	750	35	-	239	47
FmHA-insured	5,734	3,245	3,220	25	-	-	2,489	110	105	2,079	195	-	-
Insured by state agency	2,101	626	626	-	-	-	1,475	73	10	114	1,278	-	-
Conventional insured	52,634	48,021	42,565	1,824	2,615	1,017	4,613	1,619	1,300	368	680	646	-
Conventional uninsured	278,980	201,475	185,897	4,633	7,854	3,092	77,505	16,691	11,950	18,904	25,655	3,868	436
SOUTH													
All mortgaged properties	723,952	534,047	484,226	4,588	32,309	12,924	189,905	68,850	15,219	20,237	59,214	24,230	2,155
FHA-insured	138,923	109,743	99,214	869	8,618	1,042	29,180	11,224	2,195	2,208	11,016	2,509	28
VA-guaranteed	57,464	52,059	50,840	317	766	136	5,405	4,587	316	-	-	503	-
FmHA-insured	12,418	8,887	8,718	5	-	163	3,532	369	58	2,445	660	-	-
Insured by state agency	4,423	1,325	1,171	-	154	-	3,098	-	-	346	2,752	-	-
Conventional insured	99,535	80,705	71,884	237	7,264	1,320	18,830	9,361	2,351	1,003	1,303	4,650	162
Conventional uninsured	411,189	281,329	252,400	3,160	15,506	10,263	129,860	43,310	10,300	14,235	43,483	16,567	1,964
WEST													
All mortgaged properties	813,016	576,108	499,762	14,666	53,691	7,989	236,908	73,737	39,372	45,931	52,270	23,090	2,507
FHA-insured	112,170	85,976	76,083	1,521	8,372	-	26,194	11,674	2,714	2,651	5,372	3,579	204
VA-guaranteed	45,241	41,394	37,550	-	3,246	597	3,847	3,057	693	-	-	-	97
FmHA-insured	4,651	3,053	2,711	-	342	-	1,597	249	32	999	317	-	-
Insured by state agency	20,484	13,599	11,308	360	1,931	-	6,885	1,856	278	1,925	2,725	101	-
Conventional insured	77,706	67,232	59,621	905	6,484	222	10,475	4,768	1,706	765	1,112	2,022	102
Conventional uninsured	552,764	364,854	312,489	11,880	33,317	7,169	187,910	52,132	33,949	39,592	42,743	17,389	2,105

Source: U.S. Bureau of the Census and U.S. Department of Housing and Urban Development, 1991 Residential Finance Survey.

(-) Indicates less than $500,000.

Data show first mortgage debt outstanding only.

Components may not add to totals due to rounding.

Mortgage Debt Outstanding

TABLE 4.8. TOTAL MORTGAGE DEBT OUTSTANDING ON PRIVATE NONFARM RESIDENTIAL PROPERTIES BY PROPERTY TYPE, REGION, AND TYPE OF HOLDER: 1991
(Millions of dollars)

REGION AND TYPE OF HOLDER	All properties	Homeowner properties					Rental and vacant properties						
		Total	1 housing unit	2-4 housing units	Condo-miniums	Mobile homes	Total	1 housing unit	2-4 housing units	5-49 housing units	50 or more housing units	Condo-miniums	Mobile homes
UNITED STATES	2,678,152	1,960,483	1,735,801	58,964	136,527	29,190	717,670	207,086	105,550	125,780	203,409	69,989	5,854
Commercial bank or trust company	427,151	290,635	257,509	9,284	15,473	8,368	136,517	40,786	20,699	26,034	35,847	11,110	2,040
Savings and loan association, federal savings bank	635,806	440,527	389,356	12,406	34,768	3,998	195,279	54,183	36,462	42,541	31,598	30,271	224
Mutual savings bank	51,668	36,646	31,093	3,169	1,551	833	15,022	3,180	2,145	4,730	3,294	1,673	-
Life insurance company	61,050	14,545	13,751	324	348	122	46,506	1,360	6,396	5,578	33,126	46	-
Mortgage banker or mortgage company	232,221	181,611	159,601	6,265	13,233	2,512	50,610	20,453	5,357	4,380	15,078	4,962	381
Federally-sponsored secondary market agency or pool	771,610	657,079	588,751	17,032	49,220	2,076	114,531	48,863	18,457	10,183	24,460	12,360	208
Conventional mortgage pool	76,758	65,751	57,042	2,135	6,000	575	11,007	4,828	2,422	531	1,399	1,827	-
Federal agency	88,559	59,431	55,667	497	2,978	289	29,128	5,574	1,150	8,999	12,631	745	28
Real estate investment trust	5,846	2,931	2,786	92	52	-	2,915	653	53	173	1,842	194	-
Pension or retirement fund	15,472	7,227	5,696	69	1,210	253	8,245	401	258	938	5,850	798	-
Credit union	42,716	37,434	33,904	1,329	1,297	905	5,281	3,596	865	158	10	246	407
Finance company	48,711	35,551	28,800	632	945	5,174	13,160	3,278	973	5,013	2,625	473 *	798
State or municipal government or housing finance agency	68,996	40,199	34,568	1,814	3,319	499	28,797	2,868	317	2,904	22,000	653	55
Individual or individual's estate	93,122	56,291	47,345	2,269	3,634	3,043	36,831	12,092	7,661	10,317	3,073	2,246	1,441
Other	58,466	34,625	29,932	1,649	2,500	544	23,842	4,971	2,337	3,303	10,575	2,385	271
NORTHEAST	591,372	424,860	356,175	29,019	35,997	3,669	166,512	37,231	31,342	32,424	47,852	17,311	352
Commercial bank or trust company	114,546	76,618	66,130	3,982	4,954	1,552	37,927	10,260	8,800	7,390	8,705	2,772	-
Savings and loan association, federal savings bank	115,542	84,482	71,926	4,373	7,317	866	31,060	6,859	8,656	5,494	4,607	5,444	-
Mutual savings bank	41,348	29,153	24,672	2,854	1,385	242	12,195	1,644	1,987	4,247	2,645	1,673	-
Life insurance company	9,660	3,143	2,752	144	248	-	6,516	-	135	531	5,851	-	-
Mortgage banker or mortgage company	57,418	42,925	33,991	3,766	5,085	84	14,493	6,366	1,603	1,225	3,009	2,003	288
Federally-sponsored secondary market agency or pool	141,766	123,060	103,137	9,005	10,794	124	18,706	4,388	5,233	2,002	4,811	2,271	-
Conventional mortgage pool	14,436	12,224	9,723	1,539	962	-	2,211	706	883	77	266	279	-
Federal agency	10,679	7,399	6,575	271	552	-	3,280	79	209	1,201	1,765	26	-
Real estate investment trust	902	538	446	92	-	-	364	-	-	2	295	67	-
Pension or retirement fund	4,377	2,080	1,078	69	829	103	2,297	-	48	586	1,112	550	-
Credit union	8,277	7,192	6,179	822	184	8	1,085	316	610	102	5	52	-
Finance company	15,919	9,223	8,662	372	-	189	6,695	1,057	351	4,623	644	20	-
State or municipal government or housing finance agency	19,817	7,600	4,484	1,033	1,753	330	12,217	425	27	1,145	10,489	131	-
Individual or individual's estate	14,829	6,377	4,736	393	1,174	73	8,452	4,010	1,428	2,032	698	220	64
Other	21,856	12,844	11,683	303	760	98	9,012	1,121	1,372	1,766	2,951	1,803	-
MIDWEST	459,299	351,224	325,493	9,142	12,231	4,358	108,075	22,558	16,994	23,706	39,361	4,919	538
Commercial bank or trust company	91,971	65,883	60,468	1,824	2,303	1,288	26,088	7,000	4,481	5,944	6,877	1,523	263
Savings and loan association, federal savings bank	111,144	86,114	79,879	1,965	3,744	527	25,029	6,654	4,892	6,642	4,849	1,898	94
Mutual savings bank	1,576	683	462	190	31	-	894	722	70	65	37	-	-
Life insurance company	11,821	2,251	2,086	165	-	-	9,570	114	61	2,334	7,062	-	-
Mortgage banker or mortgage company	31,464	25,742	23,712	626	878	526	5,722	830	707	1,093	2,813	280	-
Federally-sponsored secondary market agency or pool	137,758	122,474	115,579	3,364	3,531	-	15,284	3,601	4,033	1,054	5,703	892	-
Conventional mortgage pool	7,068	6,343	5,844	230	185	84	725	102	-	193	429	-	-
Federal agency	18,623	11,836	11,673	105	58	-	6,787	571	293	3,036	2,887	-	-
Real estate investment trust	1,083	309	309	-	-	-	774	-	53	16	705	-	-
Pension or retirement fund	3,140	1,018	637	-	381	-	2,122	85	73	54	1,663	248	-
Credit union	6,587	6,048	5,450	203	77	317	539	423	105	10	1	-	-
Finance company	5,816	4,922	3,812	146	333	631	894	149	156	187	355	-	47
State or municipal government or housing finance agency	11,002	5,430	5,175	31	224	-	5,572	512	199	783	4,077	-	-
Individual or individual's estate	15,601	10,067	8,512	282	330	943	5,534	1,435	1,401	1,971	516	78	133
Other	4,646	2,103	1,895	11	156	42	2,542	361	471	323	1,388	-	-

See notes at end of table.

Mortgage Debt Outstanding

TABLE 4.8. TOTAL MORTGAGE DEBT OUTSTANDING ON PRIVATE NONFARM RESIDENTIAL PROPERTIES BY PROPERTY TYPE, REGION, AND TYPE OF HOLDER: 1991 - Continued
(Millions of dollars)

REGION AND TYPE OF HOLDER	All properties	Homeowner properties					Rental and vacant properties						
		Total	1 housing unit	2-4 housing units	Condo-miniums	Mobile homes	Total	1 housing unit	2-4 housing units	5-49 housing units	50 or more housing units	Condo-miniums	Mobile homes
SOUTH	758,555	562,744	511,912	4,933	32,831	13,068	195,810	70,526	15,640	21,358	61,526	24,360	2,401
Commercial bank or trust company	114,816	73,846	65,927	908	3,685	3,327	40,970	14,978	3,595	7,431	10,282	3,800	885
Savings and loan association, federal savings bank	140,137	99,002	89,699	1,260	6,606	1,436	41,135	14,542	4,668	4,025	7,697	10,162	41
Mutual savings bank	2,043	1,473	1,377	8	88	-	570	158	89	59	265	-	-
Life insurance company	19,511	5,335	5,124	-	89	122	14,176	1,190	7	1,111	11,821	46	-
Mortgage banker or mortgage company	74,631	57,280	51,611	206	3,774	1,690	17,350	6,990	1,100	1,128	6,343	1,736	53
Federally-sponsored secondary market agency or pool	256,470	221,083	204,424	1,501	14,302	856	35,386	18,463	3,114	1,013	7,091	5,706	-
Conventional mortgage pool	26,642	22,304	20,038	110	1,759	397	4,338	2,997	333	58	486	464	-
Federal agency	33,416	22,004	20,861	59	795	289	11,413	3,011	265	3,059	4,823	227	28
Real estate investment trust	1,375	710	658	-	52	-	665	71	-	127	467	-	-
Pension or retirement fund	2,395	178	178	-	-	-	2,217	316	-	13	1,888	-	-
Credit union	12,065	10,242	9,588	190	108	357	1,822	1,419	137	45	-	194	27
Finance company	14,957	11,349	7,988	59	200	3,102	3,608	1,221	203	101	1,157	369	557
State or municipal government or housing finance agency	17,086	10,853	10,384	-	462	7	6,233	1,024	32	120	4,536	522	-
Individual or individual's estate	31,316	20,643	18,285	580	599	1,179	10,673	3,580	1,985	2,498	974	849	788
Other	11,695	6,443	5,772	53	313	306	5,252	567	112	571	3,696	284	23
WEST	868,927	621,655	542,222	15,871	55,468	8,095	247,272	76,772	41,575	48,292	54,670	23,400	2,563
Commercial bank or trust company	105,818	74,287	64,984	2,570	4,532	2,201	31,530	8,548	3,823	5,269	9,983	3,015	892
Savings and loan association, federal savings bank	268,983	170,930	147,853	4,808	17,101	1,168	98,054	26,129	18,245	26,379	14,445	12,767	89
Mutual savings bank	6,700	5,337	4,582	117	47	591	1,363	657	-	359	347	-	-
Life insurance company	20,058	3,816	3,789	15	11	-	16,243	56	6,193	1,602	8,392	-	-
Mortgage banker or mortgage company	68,709	55,664	50,287	1,668	3,497	212	13,045	6,267	1,947	935	2,913	943	40
Federally-sponsored secondary market agency or pool	235,616	190,461	165,610	3,162	20,592	1,097	45,155	22,411	6,077	6,114	6,855	3,491	208
Conventional mortgage pool	28,613	24,880	21,436	256	3,095	93	3,734	1,024	1,205	202	219	1,084	-
Federal agency	25,840	18,192	16,558	62	1,572	-	7,648	1,913	383	1,704	3,156	492	-
Real estate investment trust	2,486	1,374	1,374	-	-	-	1,112	582	-	28	375	127	-
Pension or retirement fund	5,561	3,952	3,803	-	-	149	1,609	-	137	285	1,187	-	-
Credit union	15,787	13,952	12,687	115	927	223	1,835	1,438	13	-	4	-	380
Finance company	12,019	10,056	8,338	54	411	1,253	1,963	850	262	102	470	84	195
State or municipal government or housing finance agency	21,091	16,317	14,525	749	880	162	4,774	907	59	855	2,898	-	55
Individual or individual's estate	31,377	19,204	15,812	1,013	1,532	847	12,172	3,068	2,847	3,817	885	1,099	456
Other	20,269	13,234	10,583	1,282	1,270	98	7,035	2,923	382	643	2,541	298	248

Source: U.S. Bureau of the Census and U.S. Department of Housing and Urban Development, 1991 Residential Finance Survey.

(-) Indicates less than $500,000.

Data include both first and junior mortgage debt outstanding.

Components may not add to totals due to rounding.

Mortgage Credit Flows

TABLE 4.9. VOLUME OF LONG-TERM RESIDENTIAL MORTGAGE LOANS ORIGINATED, BY TYPE OF PROPERTY: 1970 TO 1996
(Millions of current dollars)

YEAR	1 to 4-unit family home			Multifamily residential			Total		
	Total	New properties	Existing properties	Total	New properties	Existing properties	Total	New properties	Existing properties
1970	35,587	12,601	22,986	8,787	6,981	1,806	44,374	19,582	24,792
1971	57,788	20,456	37,332	12,455	8,223	4,232	70,243	28,679	41,564
1972	75,864	25,832	50,031	15,427	9,214	6,212	91,289	35,046	56,243
1973	79,126	27,970	51,157	14,022	8,684	5,337	93,148	36,654	56,494
1974	67,508	24,131	43,377	12,277	8,417	3,860	79,785	32,548	47,237
1975	77,913	24,585	53,328	10,642	5,770	4,872	88,555	30,355	58,200
1976	112,785	32,158	80,627	12,293	4,473	7,820	125,078	36,631	88,447
1977	161,973	46,423	115,550	15,826	5,668	10,158	177,799	52,091	125,708
1978	185,036	58,015	127,021	16,373	6,776	9,596	201,408	64,791	136,617
1979	187,091	60,701	126,390	15,209	7,786	7,422	202,299	68,487	133,812
1980	133,762	49,138	84,624	12,497	8,633	3,864	146,259	57,771	88,488
1981	98,212	37,303	60,910	11,971	7,979	3,991	110,183	45,282	64,901
1982	96,951	30,588	66,363	11,633	6,250	5,383	108,584	36,838	71,746
1983	201,863	47,388	154,475	21,441	8,791	12,650	223,304	56,179	167,125
1984	203,705	53,731	149,974	27,576	11,144	16,432	231,281	64,875	166,406
1985	289,783	58,956	230,827	31,931	10,617	21,314	321,714	69,573	252,141
1986	499,412	72,488	426,924	49,868	15,250	34,618	549,280	87,738	461,542
1987	507,231	79,015	428,216	45,092	14,068	31,024	552,323	93,083	459,240
1988	446,263	85,198	361,065	38,158	8,962	29,196	484,421	94,160	390,261
1989	452,907	90,382	362,525	31,147	8,307	22,840	484,054	98,689	385,365
1990	458,404	110,678	347,726	32,563	6,517	26,046	490,967	117,195	373,772
1991	562,074	119,977	442,097	25,501	6,076	19,425	587,575	126,053	461,522
1992	893,681	132,386	761,295	25,731	4,866	20,865	919,412	137,252	782,160
1993	1,019,861	117,344	902,517	31,702	4,419	27,283	1,051,563	121,763	929,800
1994	768,748	114,551	654,197	32,685	4,535	28,150	801,433	119,086	682,347
1995	639,436	110,701	528,735	39,184	5,411	33,773	678,620	116,112	562,508
1996	785,233	178,165	607,068	47,138	8,386	38,752	832,371	186,551	645,820

Source: U.S. Department of Housing and Urban Development, Survey of Mortgage Lending Activity.

Sum of components may not add to totals due to rounding.

Excludes loans on farm properties.

Includes loans secured by real property located in U.S. territories and possessions.

Mortgage Credit Flows

TABLE 4.10. VOLUME OF LONG-TERM RESIDENTIAL MORTGAGE LOANS ORIGINATED, BY LENDER TYPE AND PROPERTY TYPE: 1970 TO 1996
(Millions of current dollars)

YEAR	Total, all lender types			Commercial banks			Mutual savings banks			Savings and loan associations			Mortgage companies		
	1 to 4-unit family home	Multi-family	Total	1 to 4-unit family home	Multi-family	Total	1 to 4-unit family home	Multi-family	Total	1 to 4-unit family home	Multi-family	Total	1 to 4-unit family home	Multi-family	Total
1970	35,587	8,787	44,374	7,797	324	8,121	2,147	1,140	3,287	14,814	1,927	16,741	8,906	1,433	10,339
1971	57,788	12,455	70,243	12,598	726	13,324	3,540	1,870	5,410	26,603	3,711	30,314	12,487	1,960	14,447
1972	75,864	15,427	91,291	17,710	1,347	19,057	5,052	1,929	6,981	36,739	5,285	42,024	13,326	2,698	16,024
1973	79,126	14,022	93,148	18,782	1,122	19,904	5,912	2,088	8,000	38,441	4,171	42,612	12,657	928	13,585
1974	67,508	12,277	79,785	16,128	749	16,877	3,929	1,532	5,461	30,932	3,262	34,194	13,026	595	13,621
1975	77,913	10,642	88,555	14,450	767	15,217	4,333	1,459	5,792	41,242	3,562	44,804	13,992	778	14,770
1976	112,785	12,293	125,078	24,501	1,987	26,488	6,428	1,356	7,784	61,900	5,113	67,013	15,744	609	16,353
1977	161,973	15,826	177,799	36,675	1,890	38,565	8,660	1,492	10,152	86,304	6,837	93,141	25,651	1,965	27,616
1978	185,036	16,373	201,409	43,924	2,136	46,060	9,379	1,195	10,574	89,952	6,225	96,177	34,448	1,848	36,296
1979	187,091	15,209	202,300	41,415	2,032	43,447	8,963	906	9,869	82,825	4,906	87,731	45,260	1,980	47,240
1980	133,762	12,497	146,259	28,778	1,247	30,025	5,435	543	5,978	61,095	3,100	64,195	29,419	1,633	31,052
1981	98,212	11,971	110,183	21,689	1,491	23,180	4,022	593	4,615	41,980	2,339	44,319	23,958	2,051	26,009
1982	96,951	11,633	108,584	25,189	1,660	26,849	4,001	561	4,562	34,783	3,171	37,954	27,995	960	28,955
1983	201,863	21,441	223,304	44,830	3,517	48,347	10,775	1,968	12,743	81,524	8,521	90,045	59,762	566	60,328
1984	203,705	27,576	231,281	41,941	3,466	45,407	12,685	2,053	14,738	96,187	13,160	109,347	47,589	443	48,032
1985	289,783	31,931	321,714	57,031	4,498	61,529	7,477	870	8,347	109,276	15,612	124,888	110,004	2,746	112,750
1986	499,412	49,868	549,280	108,613	7,176	115,789	31,109	2,892	34,001	176,073	19,877	195,950	175,986	7,172	183,158
1987	507,231	45,092	552,323	124,551	8,299	132,850	34,232	4,773	39,005	174,549	17,830	192,379	167,053	2,409	169,462
1988	446,263	38,158	484,421	101,863	6,920	108,783	28,425	3,065	31,490	160,446	17,486	177,932	148,004	4,526	152,530
1989	452,907	31,147	484,054	123,193	7,669	130,862	23,196	2,059	25,255	134,480	11,410	145,890	166,494	4,443	170,937
1990	458,404	32,563	490,967	153,285	10,966	164,251	17,956	1,529	19,485	121,034	9,225	130,259	161,153	5,536	166,689
1991	562,074	25,501	587,575	153,323	12,162	165,485	18,516	977	19,493	121,900	6,328	128,228	263,917	2,032	265,949
1992	893,681	25,731	919,412	232,065	11,742	243,807	34,246	1,055	35,301	184,546	7,346	191,892	437,604	2,058	439,662
1993	1,019,861	31,702	1,051,563	268,985	18,820	287,805	39,411	1,112	40,523	179,339	6,181	185,520	526,502	2,000	528,502
1994	768,748	32,685	801,433	199,996	20,924	220,920	29,260	2,141	31,401	123,121	5,840	128,961	408,141	0	408,141
1995	639,436	39,184	678,620	155,359	23,118	178,477	23,258	1,825	25,083	95,598	3,875	99,473	358,705	6,108	364,813
1996	785,233	47,138	832,371	178,548	22,619	201,167	33,911	1,898	35,809	121,700	4,933	126,633	445,739	12,321	458,060

See notes at end of table.

Mortgage Credit Flows

TABLE 4.10. VOLUME OF LONG-TERM RESIDENTIAL MORTGAGE LOANS ORIGINATED, BY LENDER TYPE AND PROPERTY TYPE: 1970 TO 1996 - Continued
(Millions of current dollars)

YEAR	Total, all lender types			Life insurance companies			Federal credit agencies			State and local credit agencies			Other lenders		
	1-4-unit family home	Multi-family	Total	1-4-unit family home	Multi-family	Total	1-4-unit family home	Multi-family	Total	1-4-unit family home	Multi-family	Total	1-4-unit family home	Multi-family	Total
1970	35,587	8,787	44,374	334	2,238	2,572	1,366	1,077	2,443	139	316	455	83	332	415
1971	57,788	12,455	70,243	333	1,708	2,041	1,798	1,372	3,170	183	520	703	247	586	833
1972	75,864	15,427	91,291	401	1,826	2,227	2,044	1,444	3,488	188	476	664	404	422	826
1973	79,126	14,022	93,148	380	2,293	2,673	2,351	2,218	4,569	345	500	845	258	701	959
1974	67,508	12,277	79,785	359	2,046	2,405	2,467	2,870	5,337	538	759	1,297	130	464	594
1975	77,913	10,642	88,555	251	1,139	1,390	2,867	1,725	4,592	594	749	1,343	183	464	647
1976	112,785	12,293	125,078	365	756	1,121	2,652	1,114	3,766	987	955	1,942	208	404	612
1977	161,973	15,826	177,799	440	997	1,437	3,093	1,029	4,122	822	1,239	2,061	327	375	702
1978	185,036	16,373	201,409	848	1,845	2,693	4,843	1,715	6,558	1,321	874	2,195	321	535	856
1979	187,091	15,209	202,300	2,024	1,597	3,621	4,445	2,632	7,077	1,877	607	2,484	282	548	830
1980	133,762	12,497	146,259	1,711	1,427	3,138	4,378	2,932	7,310	2,600	1,356	3,956	346	260	606
1981	98,212	11,971	110,183	478	753	1,231	4,464	3,215	7,679	1,453	1,382	2,835	168	147	315
1982	96,951	11,633	108,584	544	438	982	3,504	3,364	6,868	871	1,395	2,266	64	84	148
1983	201,863	21,441	223,304	726	1,597	2,323	3,180	2,837	6,017	1,053	2,415	3,468	13	20	33
1984	203,705	27,576	231,281	826	1,466	2,292	3,223	2,407	5,630	1,241	4,563	5,804	14	18	32
1985	289,783	31,931	321,714	1,306	2,772	4,078	3,154	2,000	5,154	1,508	3,362	4,870	27	71	98
1986	499,412	49,868	549,280	3,814	3,723	7,537	2,676	1,739	4,415	1,038	7,270	8,308	104	19	123
1987	507,231	45,092	552,323	3,209	3,547	6,756	2,890	1,120	4,010	724	7,087	7,811	23	27	50
1988	446,263	38,158	484,421	3,331	3,732	7,063	2,858	1,155	4,013	1,286	1,158	2,444	50	116	166
1989	452,907	31,147	484,054	1,443	2,786	4,229	2,687	1,194	3,881	1,209	1,538	2,747	205	48	253
1990	458,404	32,563	490,967	606	2,172	2,778	3,022	1,565	4,587	1,272	1,524	2,796	76	46	122
1991	562,074	25,501	587,575	564	1,575	2,139	3,050	918	3,968	797	1,509	2,306	7	0	7
1992	893,681	25,731	919,412	697	1,406	2,103	3,362	1,049	4,411	619	859	1,478	542	216	758
1993	1,019,861	31,702	1,051,563	807	1,486	2,293	4,073	933	5,006	388	976	1,364	356	194	550
1994	768,748	32,685	801,433	662	1,257	1,919	5,502	627	6,129	1,072	1,149	2,221	994	747	1,741
1995	639,436	39,184	678,620	670	1,611	2,281	3,595	733	4,328	1,083	973	2,056	1,168	941	2,109
1996	785,233	47,138	832,371	444	1,629	2,073	2,928	482	3,410	884	2,059	2,943	1,079	1,197	2,276

Source: U.S. Department of Housing and Urban Development, Survey of Mortgage Lending Activity.

Sum of components may not add to totals due to rounding.

Excludes loans on farm properties.

Includes loans secured by real property located in U.S. territories and possessions.

Mortgage Credit Flows

	TABLE 4.11. VOLUME OF LONG-TERM RESIDENTIAL MORTGAGE LOANS ORIGINATED ON ONE-TO-FOUR-UNIT HOMES, BY LENDER TYPE AND LOAN TYPE: 1970 TO 1996 (Millions of current dollars)											
	Total				Commercial banks				Mutual savings banks			
YEAR	FHA-insured	VA-guaranteed	Conventional	Total	FHA-insured	VA-guaranteed	Conventional	Total	FHA-insured	VA-guaranteed	Conventional	Total
1970	8,769	3,846	22,972	35,587	1,528	425	5,844	7,797	401	168	1,578	2,147
1971	10,994	6,830	39,964	57,788	1,458	810	10,330	12,598	425	319	2,797	3,540
1972	8,456	7,749	59,659	75,864	1,003	873	15,834	17,710	374	479	4,200	5,052
1973	5,185	7,577	66,364	79,126	725	797	17,261	18,782	308	524	5,080	5,912
1974	4,532	7,889	55,088	67,508	262	671	15,195	16,128	187	303	3,440	3,929
1975	6,265	8,836	62,811	77,913	613	773	13,064	14,450	267	355	3,710	4,333
1976	6,998	10,426	95,361	112,785	790	1,146	22,565	24,501	322	474	5,632	6,428
1977	10,469	14,882	136,622	161,973	999	1,096	34,580	36,675	356	499	7,805	8,660
1978	14,581	16,026	154,429	185,036	1,385	1,272	41,267	43,924	402	578	8,399	9,379
1979	20,710	18,876	147,505	187,091	1,228	1,147	39,041	41,415	378	355	8,229	8,963
1980	14,955	12,102	106,704	133,762	996	745	27,037	28,778	136	89	5,210	5,435
1981	10,538	7,534	80,141	98,212	831	409	20,449	21,689	70	50	3,903	4,022
1982	11,482	7,687	77,782	96,951	1,008	912	23,268	25,189	64	35	3,902	4,001
1983	28,753	18,880	154,229	201,863	3,735	2,529	38,566	44,830	380	94	10,300	10,775
1984	16,600	12,024	175,081	203,705	2,338	1,675	37,927	41,941	165	130	12,390	12,685
1985	28,767	15,246	245,771	289,783	3,509	2,594	50,928	57,031	85	63	7,329	7,477
1986	64,770	23,149	411,493	499,412	4,901	2,790	100,922	108,613	323	148	30,637	31,109
1987	77,822	30,176	399,232	507,231	8,099	4,072	112,380	124,551	397	114	33,720	34,232
1988	46,655	15,875	383,733	446,263	4,421	1,627	95,815	101,863	582	283	27,560	28,425
1989	45,108	13,681	394,118	452,907	5,157	701	117,335	123,193	886	453	21,857	23,196
1990	59,803	21,901	376,700	458,404	11,267	4,606	137,412	153,285	1,233	302	16,421	17,956
1991	46,914	15,285	499,875	562,074	4,151	1,208	147,964	153,323	1,128	719	16,669	18,516
1992	50,275	24,543	818,863	893,681	5,104	1,694	225,267	232,065	1,128	846	32,272	34,246
1993	83,457	41,023	895,381	1,019,861	7,276	2,341	259,368	268,985	1,760	1,068	36,583	39,411
1994	94,913	48,190	625,645	768,748	6,636	1,695	191,665	199,996	1,149	782	27,329	29,260
1995	48,424	26,262	564,750	639,436	4,504	2,571	148,284	155,359	1,162	797	21,299	23,258
1996	72,727	35,211	677,295	785,233	3,472	3,325	171,751	178,548	1,022	671	32,218	33,911

See notes at end of table.

Mortgage Credit Flows

TABLE 4.11. VOLUME OF LONG-TERM RESIDENTIAL MORTGAGE LOANS ORIGINATED ON ONE-TO-FOUR-UNIT HOMES, BY LENDER TYPE AND LOAN TYPE: 1970 TO 1996 - Continued
(Millions of current dollars)

YEAR	Savings and loan associations				Mortgage companies				Life insurance companies			
	FHA-insured	VA-guaranteed	Conventional	Total	FHA-insured	VA-guaranteed	Conventional	Total	FHA-insured	VA-guaranteed	Conventional	Total
1970	944	491	13,379	14,814	5,768	2,719	419	8,906	110	32	192	334
1971	1,438	1,323	23,842	26,603	7,531	4,332	624	12,487	103	37	193	333
1972	765	1,244	34,731	36,739	6,125	5,030	2,171	13,326	133	87	181	401
1973	391	1,158	36,892	38,441	3,606	4,962	4,090	12,657	58	109	214	380
1974	412	989	29,530	30,932	3,600	5,770	3,656	13,026	36	94	229	359
1975	666	1,266	39,310	41,242	4,601	6,326	3,065	13,992	52	75	125	251
1976	580	1,305	60,015	61,900	5,096	7,381	3,267	15,744	70	88	207	365
1977	616	1,462	84,226	86,304	8,228	11,624	5,798	25,651	90	138	213	440
1978	791	1,534	87,627	89,952	11,587	12,372	10,489	34,448	148	175	525	848
1979	1,180	1,614	80,031	82,825	17,397	15,544	12,319	45,260	301	153	1,570	2,024
1980	1,260	1,511	58,324	61,095	12,161	9,567	7,691	29,419	185	111	1,415	1,711
1981	758	916	40,306	41,980	8,736	6,044	9,178	23,958	113	84	281	478
1982	394	448	33,941	34,783	9,808	6,158	12,029	27,995	160	105	279	544
1983	1,405	1,930	78,189	81,524	22,936	14,148	22,678	59,762	266	163	297	726
1984	1,340	1,538	93,309	96,187	12,532	8,553	26,504	47,589	154	99	573	826
1985	1,344	1,285	106,647	109,276	23,434	11,140	75,430	110,004	240	115	951	1,306
1986	3,386	1,485	171,202	176,073	55,594	18,522	101,870	175,986	429	189	3,196	3,814
1987	6,114	2,133	166,302	174,549	62,716	23,703	80,634	167,053	359	124	2,726	3,209
1988	3,675	1,614	155,157	160,446	37,518	12,230	98,256	148,004	253	83	2,995	3,331
1989	3,683	1,292	129,505	134,480	34,739	11,086	120,669	166,494	352	94	997	1,443
1990	4,626	1,107	115,301	121,034	42,310	15,825	103,018	161,153	162	33	411	606
1991	4,256	1,160	116,484	121,900	36,991	12,141	214,785	263,917	213	37	314	564
1992	4,031	1,665	178,850	184,546	39,474	20,266	377,864	437,604	214	47	436	697
1993	5,487	2,701	171,151	179,339	68,483	34,830	423,189	526,502	219	63	525	807
1994	6,183	2,757	114,181	123,121	80,071	42,191	285,879	408,141	171	41	450	662
1995	3,110	1,309	91,179	95,598	38,848	20,118	299,739	358,705	169	47	454	670
1996	4,513	1,490	115,697	121,700	63,003	28,461	354,275	445,739	121	22	301	444

See notes at end of table.

Mortgage Credit Flows

TABLE 4.11. VOLUME OF LONG-TERM RESIDENTIAL MORTGAGE LOANS ORIGINATED ON ONE-TO-FOUR-UNIT HOMES, BY LENDER TYPE AND LOAN TYPE: 1970 TO 1996 - Continued
(Millions of current dollars)

YEAR	Federal credit agencies				State and local credit agencies				Other lenders			
	FHA-insured	VA-guaranteed	Conventional	Total	FHA-insured	VA-guaranteed	Conventional	Total	FHA-insured	VA-guaranteed	Conventional	Total
1970	0	0	1,366	1,366	0	0	139	139	18	10	55	83
1971	0	0	1,798	1,798	3	0	179	183	36	10	200	247
1972	0	0	2,044	2,044	10	2	176	188	46	34	323	404
1973	0	0	2,351	2,351	12	9	324	345	85	20	153	258
1974	0	0	2,467	2,467	17	26	494	538	17	36	77	130
1975	0	0	2,867	2,867	21	6	567	594	44	36	103	183
1976	0	0	2,652	2,652	62	9	916	987	79	23	106	208
1977	0	0	3,093	3,093	111	17	694	822	69	46	213	327
1978	0	0	4,843	4,843	219	48	1,053	1,321	48	48	226	321
1979	0	0	4,445	4,445	172	32	1,673	1,877	54	31	197	282
1980	0	0	4,378	4,378	182	75	2,343	2,600	35	5	306	346
1981	0	0	4,464	4,464	26	31	1,396	1,453	4	0	164	168
1982	0	0	3,504	3,504	40	28	803	871	7	1	56	64
1983	0	0	3,180	3,180	31	16	1,006	1,053	0	0	13	13
1984	0	0	3,223	3,223	69	29	1,143	1,241	1	0	13	14
1985	0	0	3,154	3,154	141	47	1,320	1,508	14	1	12	27
1986	0	0	2,676	2,676	136	15	887	1,038	0	0	104	104
1987	0	0	2,890	2,890	137	30	557	724	0	0	23	23
1988	0	0	2,858	2,858	207	38	1,041	1,286	0	0	50	50
1989	0	0	2,687	2,687	278	49	882	1,209	13	6	186	205
1990	0	0	3,022	3,022	196	25	1,051	1,272	9	3	64	76
1991	0	0	3,050	3,050	175	20	602	797	0	0	7	7
1992	0	0	3,362	3,362	137	25	457	619	187	0	355	542
1993	0	0	4,073	4,073	105	19	264	388	127	1	228	356
1994	0	675	4,827	5,502	229	34	809	1,072	474	15	505	994
1995	0	1,354	2,241	3,595	264	43	776	1,083	367	23	778	1,168
1996	0	1,197	1,731	2,928	229	41	614	884	367	4	708	1,079

Source: U.S. Department of Housing and Urban Development, Survey of Mortgage Lending Activity.

Sum of components may not add to totals due to rounding.

Excludes loans on farm properties.

Includes loans secured by real property located in U.S. territories and possessions.

Mortgage Credit Flows

TABLE 4.12. VOLUME OF LONG-TERM RESIDENTIAL MORTGAGE LOANS ORIGINATED ON MULTIFAMILY PROPERTIES, BY LENDER TYPE AND LOAN TYPE: 1970 TO 1996
(Millions of current dollars)

YEAR	Total			Commercial banks			Mutual savings banks			Savings and loan associations			Mortgage companies		
	FHA-insured	Conven-tional	Total	FHA-insured	Conven-tional	Total	FHA-insured	Conven-tional	Total	FHA-insured	Conven-tional	Total	FHA-insured	Conven-tional	Total
1970	1,921	6,866	8,787	15	309	324	61	1,078	1,140	94	1,833	1,927	646	787	1,433
1971	2,837	9,618	12,455	98	627	726	124	1,746	1,870	128	3,584	3,711	997	963	1,960
1972	3,247	12,179	15,427	136	1,211	1,347	105	1,825	1,929	259	5,026	5,285	1,340	1,358	2,698
1973	3,060	10,962	14,022	156	966	1,122	193	1,895	2,088	175	3,996	4,171	286	642	928
1974	3,350	8,928	12,277	51	698	749	287	1,246	1,532	158	3,105	3,262	92	502	595
1975	2,142	8,501	10,642	12	755	767	269	1,190	1,459	37	3,525	3,562	248	530	778
1976	1,972	10,321	12,293	153	1,833	1,987	450	905	1,356	81	5,032	5,113	362	247	609
1977	2,208	13,618	15,826	179	1,711	1,890	165	1,327	1,492	83	6,754	6,837	968	997	1,965
1978	3,225	13,147	16,373	160	1,977	2,136	258	937	1,195	130	6,095	6,225	1,117	731	1,848
1979	3,868	11,340	15,209	136	1,896	2,032	134	772	906	123	4,783	4,906	1,218	762	1,980
1980	3,888	8,609	12,497	37	1,210	1,247	96	446	543	108	2,992	3,100	1,231	402	1,633
1981	3,879	8,092	11,971	65	1,426	1,491	132	460	593	68	2,271	2,339	721	1,330	2,051
1982	4,081	7,552	11,633	64	1,595	1,660	26	535	561	95	3,076	3,171	663	297	960
1983	3,968	17,474	21,441	60	3,457	3,517	29	1,939	1,968	120	8,401	8,521	165	401	566
1984	4,651	22,925	27,576	17	3,449	3,466	11	2,042	2,053	122	13,038	13,160	132	311	443
1985	3,482	28,449	31,931	1	4,497	4,498	6	865	870	223	15,389	15,612	359	2,387	2,746
1986	8,740	41,127	49,868	43	7,133	7,176	12	2,880	2,892	318	19,559	19,877	2,905	4,267	7,172
1987	6,831	38,261	45,092	9	8,291	8,299	6	4,767	4,773	279	17,551	17,830	1,363	1,046	2,409
1988	2,960	35,198	38,158	21	6,899	6,920	28	3,037	3,065	264	17,222	17,486	2,001	2,525	4,526
1989	950	30,197	31,147	15	7,654	7,669	4	2,055	2,059	166	11,244	11,410	149	4,294	4,443
1990	2,004	30,559	32,563	280	10,686	10,966	15	1,514	1,529	135	9,090	9,225	853	4,683	5,536
1991	916	24,585	25,501	74	12,088	12,162	1	976	977	89	6,239	6,328	138	1,894	2,032
1992	576	25,155	25,731	108	11,634	11,742	0	1,055	1,055	102	7,244	7,346	0	2,058	2,058
1993	1,659	30,043	31,702	23	18,797	18,820	0	1,112	1,112	84	6,097	6,181	866	1,134	2,000
1994	963	31,722	32,685	4	20,920	20,924	0	2,141	2,141	76	5,764	5,840	0	0	0
1995	1,279	37,905	39,184	9	23,109	23,118	12	1,813	1,825	49	3,826	3,875	573	5,535	6,108
1996	3,440	43,698	47,138	520	22,099	22,619	0	1,898	1,898	58	4,875	4,933	1,931	10,390	12,321

See notes at end of table.

Mortgage Credit Flows

TABLE 4.12. VOLUME OF LONG-TERM RESIDENTIAL MORTGAGE LOANS ORIGINATED ON MULTIFAMILY PROPERTIES, BY LENDER TYPE AND LOAN TYPE: 1970 TO 1996 - Continued
(Millions of current dollars)

YEAR	Total			Life insurance companies			Federal credit agencies			State and local credit agencies			Other lenders		
	FHA-insured	Conven-tional	Total	FHA-insured	Conven-tional	Total	FHA-insured	Conven-tional	Total	FHA-insured	Conven-tional	Total	FHA-insured	Conven-tional	Total
1970	1,921	6,866	8,787	114	2,124	2,238	860	217	1,077	38	278	316	93	239	332
1971	2,837	9,618	12,455	73	1,636	1,708	1,231	141	1,372	81	440	520	105	481	586
1972	3,247	12,179	15,427	67	1,760	1,826	1,302	142	1,444	9	467	476	31	391	422
1973	3,060	10,962	14,022	92	2,201	2,293	2,096	122	2,218	6	494	500	55	645	701
1974	3,350	8,928	12,277	45	2,001	2,046	2,669	201	2,870	28	730	759	21	445	464
1975	2,142	8,501	10,642	5	1,134	1,139	1,419	306	1,725	28	721	749	124	339	464
1976	1,972	10,321	12,293	2	754	756	794	320	1,114	33	922	955	97	307	404
1977	2,208	13,618	15,826	0	997	997	663	366	1,029	12	1,227	1,239	139	236	375
1978	3,225	13,147	16,373	35	1,810	1,845	1,255	461	1,715	30	844	874	241	295	535
1979	3,868	11,340	15,209	45	1,552	1,597	1,684	948	2,632	146	461	607	382	166	548
1980	3,888	8,609	12,497	1	1,426	1,427	1,981	951	2,932	310	1,046	1,356	124	136	260
1981	3,879	8,092	11,971	1	752	753	2,327	888	3,215	497	885	1,382	67	80	147
1982	4,081	7,552	11,633	0	438	438	2,570	794	3,364	643	752	1,395	20	64	84
1983	3,968	17,474	21,441	0	1,597	1,597	1,962	875	2,837	1,617	798	2,415	15	5	20
1984	4,651	22,925	27,576	0	1,466	1,466	984	1,423	2,407	3,384	1,179	4,563	1	17	18
1985	3,482	28,449	31,931	0	2,772	2,772	353	1,647	2,000	2,538	824	3,362	2	69	71
1986	8,740	41,127	49,868	0	3,723	3,723	114	1,625	1,739	5,348	1,922	7,270	0	19	19
1987	6,831	38,261	45,092	0	3,547	3,547	0	1,120	1,120	5,175	1,912	7,087	0	27	27
1988	2,960	35,198	38,158	0	3,732	3,732	2	1,153	1,155	631	527	1,158	13	103	116
1989	950	30,197	31,147	0	2,786	2,786	0	1,194	1,194	603	935	1,538	13	35	48
1990	2,004	30,559	32,563	0	2,172	2,172	0	1,565	1,565	719	805	1,524	2	44	46
1991	916	24,585	25,501	0	1,575	1,575	0	918	918	614	895	1,509	0	0	0
1992	576	25,155	25,731	0	1,406	1,406	0	1,049	1,049	358	501	859	8	208	216
1993	1,659	30,043	31,702	0	1,486	1,486	0	933	933	642	334	976	44	150	194
1994	963	31,722	32,685	0	1,257	1,257	0	627	627	791	358	1,149	92	655	747
1995	1,279	37,905	39,184	0	1,611	1,611	0	733	733	485	488	973	151	790	941
1996	3,440	43,698	47,138	0	1,629	1,629	78	404	482	665	1,394	2,059	188	1,009	1,197

Source: U.S. Department of Housing and Urban Development, Survey of Mortgage Lending Activity.

Sum of components may not add to totals due to rounding.

Excludes loans on farm properties.

Includes loans secured by real property located in U.S. territories and possessions.

Mortgage Credit Flows

MONTH	TABLE 4.13. MONTHLY REFINANCE SHARE OF TOTAL MORTGAGE ORIGINATIONS: 1987 TO 1997 (Percent)										
	1987	1988	1989	1990	1991	1992	1993	1994	1995	1996	1997
January	....	21	19	32	39	66	42	58	10	46	31
February	....	26	19	29	45	60	50	55	10	47	27
March	56	27	20	28	46	54	54	42	12	36	25
April	51	24	19	23	41	43	53	35	14	29	23
May	26	23	20	22	40	38	51	25	18	21	23
June	25	22	21	23	37	40	58	21	21	19	25
July	25	20	26	25	32	55	63	19	23	21	27
August	19	15	27	....	37	56	65	17	24	21	30
September	21	17	26	23	46	61	64	14	25	24	34
October	....	19	32	25	55	52	69	10	33	26	40
November	18	21	34	29	58	50	64	16	33	32	41
December	19	21	30	32	64	43	59	11	40	34	48

Source: Freddie Mac, Primary Mortgage Market Survey.

Mortgage Characteristics

TABLE 4.14. CHARACTERISTICS OF CONVENTIONAL FIRST MORTGAGE LOANS FOR PURCHASE OF NEW AND EXISTING SINGLE-FAMILY HOMES: 1963 TO 1997
(In percent, except as indicated)

YEAR	Contract interest rate	Initial fees, charges	Effective interest rate	Term to maturity (Years)	Mortgage amount ($1,000)	Purchase price ($1,000)	Loan-to-price ratio	Percent distribution of estimated number of loans by loan-to-price ratio				Percent of number of loans with adjustable rates
								70 percent or less	70 to 80 percent	80 to 90 percent	More than 90 percent	
1963	5.9	0.6	6.0	21.3	14.8	20.6	71.7	....	....	....	....	....
1964	5.9	0.6	6.0	22.1	15.7	21.8	72.1	....	....	....	....	....
1965	5.8	0.5	5.9	22.6	16.4	22.5	73.0	....	....	....	....	....
1966	6.3	0.7	6.4	22.5	16.9	23.3	72.3	....	....	....	....	....
1967	6.4	0.8	6.5	23.1	18.3	25.1	72.9	....	....	....	....	....
1968	6.9	0.8	7.0	23.4	19.7	26.9	73.2	....	....	....	....	....
1969	7.7	0.9	7.8	23.5	21.5	29.9	71.9	....	....	....	....	....
1970	8.2	1.0	8.4	23.5	22.5	31.5	71.3	....	....	....	....	....
1971	7.6	0.8	7.7	24.7	24.2	32.8	74.0	....	....	....	....	....
1972	7.4	0.8	7.5	26.1	26.1	34.3	76.2	....	....	....	....	....
1973	7.8	1.0	8.0	24.0	24.6	33.7	74.8	24	40	23	14	....
1974	8.8	1.2	9.0	24.1	26.8	37.6	72.9	27	42	20	12	....
1975	8.9	1.3	9.1	24.9	29.7	41.2	73.7	27	42	19	14	....
1976	8.9	1.2	9.1	25.2	31.9	44.3	73.9	28	41	21	11	....
1977	8.8	1.2	9.0	26.3	36.3	49.6	75.0	26	43	21	11	....
1978	9.4	1.3	9.6	26.7	41.4	57.1	74.6	29	42	19	11	....
1979	10.6	1.5	10.9	27.4	48.2	67.7	73.5	33	43	17	9	....
1980	12.5	2.0	12.8	27.2	51.7	73.4	72.9	34	41	16	10	....
1981	14.4	2.4	14.9	26.4	53.7	76.3	73.1	32	37	17	15	....
1982	14.7	2.7	15.3	25.6	55.0	78.4	72.9	29	31	20	21	41
1983	12.3	2.4	12.7	26.0	59.9	83.1	74.5	26	34	19	21	40
1984	12.0	2.6	12.5	26.8	64.5	86.6	77.0	24	30	20	27	62
1985	11.2	2.5	11.6	25.9	70.2	96.1	75.8	26	34	19	21	51
1986	9.8	2.2	10.2	25.6	79.3	110.6	74.1	28	41	20	11	30
1987	9.0	2.1	9.3	26.8	89.1	121.8	75.2	28	42	23	8	43
1988	9.0	2.0	9.3	27.7	97.4	131.6	76.0	25	44	23	8	58
1989	9.8	1.9	10.1	27.7	104.5	142.8	74.8	28	46	20	7	38
1990	9.7	1.8	10.1	27.0	104.0	142.6	74.7	29	45	18	8	28
1991	9.1	1.6	9.3	26.5	106.3	146.7	74.4	32	41	18	9	23
1992	7.8	1.6	8.1	25.4	108.7	146.4	76.6	26	38	21	14	20
1993	6.9	1.2	7.1	25.5	107.0	143.1	77.2	25	37	20	17	20
1994	7.3	1.1	7.5	27.1	109.9	142.0	79.9	20	34	21	25	39
1995	7.7	1.0	7.9	27.4	110.4	142.8	79.9	20	34	18	27	32
1996	7.6	1.0	7.7	26.9	118.7	155.1	79.0	21	36	17	25	27
1997	7.5	1.0	7.7	27.5	126.6	164.5	79.4	20	38	17	25	22

Source: U.S. Federal Housing Finance Board, Monthly Interest Rate Survey.

Mortgage Characteristics

	TABLE 4.15. CHARACTERISTICS OF CONVENTIONAL FIRST MORTGAGE LOANS FOR PURCHASE OF NEW SINGLE-FAMILY HOMES: 1963 TO 1997 (In percent, except as indicated)											
YEAR	Contract interest rate	Initial fees, charges	Effective interest rate	Term to maturity (Years)	Mortgage amount ($1,000)	Purchase price ($1,000)	Loan-to-price ratio	Percent distribution of estimated number of loans by loan-to-price ratio				Percent of number of loans with adjustable rates
								70 percent or less	70 to 80 percent	80 to 90 percent	More than 90 percent	
1963	5.8	0.6	5.9	24.1	16.9	23.1	72.9	....	....	....	....	....
1964	5.8	0.5	5.8	24.7	17.8	24.3	73.3	....	....	....	....	....
1965	5.7	0.5	5.8	25.0	18.5	25.1	73.9	....	....	....	....	....
1966	6.1	0.7	6.3	24.7	19.4	26.6	73.0	....	....	....	....	....
1967	6.3	0.8	6.5	25.2	20.6	28.0	73.6	....	....	....	....	....
1968	6.8	0.9	7.0	25.5	22.6	30.7	73.9	....	....	....	....	....
1969	7.7	0.9	7.8	25.5	24.9	34.1	72.8	....	....	....	....	....
1970	8.3	1.0	8.5	25.1	25.5	35.5	71.7	....	....	....	....	....
1971	7.6	0.9	7.7	26.2	27.0	36.3	74.3	....	....	....	....	....
1972	7.5	0.9	7.6	27.2	28.6	37.3	76.8	....	....	....	....	....
1973	7.8	1.1	8.0	26.2	27.9	37.0	76.9	24	40	23	14	....
1974	8.7	1.3	8.9	26.4	29.9	40.1	75.9	27	42	20	12	....
1975	8.8	1.5	9.0	27.0	33.4	44.7	76.2	26	42	19	14	....
1976	8.8	1.4	9.0	27.3	36.4	49.1	75.7	28	41	21	11	....
1977	8.8	1.3	9.0	27.9	40.5	54.4	76.3	26	43	21	11	....
1978	9.3	1.4	9.6	28.0	46.0	62.8	75.2	29	42	19	11	....
1979	10.5	1.7	10.8	28.5	53.3	74.4	73.8	33	43	17	9	....
1980	12.3	2.1	12.7	28.1	59.1	83.2	73.2	34	41	16	10	....
1981	14.1	2.7	14.7	27.7	65.2	90.3	74.8	32	37	17	15	....
1982	14.5	3.0	15.1	27.5	69.5	94.1	76.6	29	31	20	21	41
1983	12.1	2.4	12.6	26.7	70.6	93.9	77.3	26	34	19	21	37
1984	11.9	2.7	12.4	27.8	73.7	96.8	78.6	24	30	20	27	59
1985	11.1	2.5	11.6	27.0	78.2	105.0	77.1	26	34	19	21	51
1986	9.7	2.5	10.2	26.8	87.6	119.8	75.3	28	41	20	11	27
1987	8.9	2.3	9.3	27.8	100.6	137.2	75.2	28	42	23	8	41
1988	8.8	2.2	9.2	28.0	110.9	150.5	75.6	27	42	23	8	19
1989	9.8	2.1	10.1	28.1	117.4	160.1	74.6	29	45	20	7	35
1990	9.7	2.0	10.1	27.3	113.2	154.1	74.9	29	44	17	10	31
1991	9.0	1.7	9.3	26.8	114.2	155.2	75.0	30	40	18	12	25
1992	8.0	1.6	8.2	25.6	118.1	158.1	76.6	26	35	20	19	17
1993	7.0	1.3	7.2	26.1	123.2	163.7	78.0	23	34	21	22	18
1994	7.3	1.3	7.5	27.5	130.9	170.7	78.7	23	32	20	25	41
1995	7.7	1.2	7.9	27.7	134.3	175.4	78.6	22	34	18	26	37
1996	7.6	1.2	7.8	27.1	139.1	182.6	78.1	22	35	17	25	26
1997	7.6	1.0	7.7	28.2	141.2	181.4	80.4	19	36	15	30	21

Source: U.S. Federal Housing Finance Board, Monthly Interest Rate Survey.

Mortgage Characteristics

TABLE 4.16. CHARACTERISTICS OF CONVENTIONAL FIRST MORTGAGE LOANS FOR PURCHASE OF EXISTING SINGLE-FAMILY HOMES: 1963 TO 1997
(In percent, except as indicated)

YEAR	Contract interest rate	Initial fees, charges	Effective interest rate	Term to maturity (Years)	Mortgage amount ($1,000)	Purchase price ($1,000)	Loan-to-price ratio	Percent distribution of estimated number of loans by loan-to-price ratio				Percent of number of loans with adjustable rates
								70 percent or less	70 to 80 percent	80 to 90 percent	More than 90 percent	
1963	5.9	0.6	6.0	20.4	14.0	19.7	71.2	....	....	....	....	....
1964	5.9	0.6	6.0	21.3	15.0	20.9	71.7	....	....	....	....	....
1965	5.9	0.6	6.0	21.8	15.7	21.6	72.7	....	....	....	....	....
1966	6.3	0.7	6.4	21.7	16.0	22.2	72.0	....	....	....	....	....
1967	6.4	0.8	6.5	22.4	17.5	24.1	72.7	....	....	....	....	....
1968	6.9	0.8	7.0	22.7	18.7	25.6	73.0	....	....	....	....	....
1969	7.7	0.9	7.8	22.7	20.2	28.3	71.5	....	....	....	....	....
1970	8.2	0.9	8.4	22.8	21.3	30.0	71.1	....	....	....	....	....
1971	7.5	0.8	7.7	24.2	23.4	31.7	73.9	....	....	....	....	....
1972	7.4	0.8	7.5	25.7	25.4	33.4	76.0	....	....	....	....	....
1973	7.8	1.0	8.0	23.3	23.1	31.5	75.0	28	44	20	8	....
1974	8.8	1.1	9.0	23.3	25.0	35.5	72.4	35	45	16	4	....
1975	9.0	1.2	9.2	24.2	28.2	39.2	73.5	31	47	17	5	....
1976	8.9	1.1	9.1	24.6	30.2	42.0	73.8	30	47	18	5	....
1977	8.8	1.2	9.0	25.8	34.8	47.6	75.1	27	48	20	6	....
1978	9.4	1.3	9.6	26.4	39.6	54.5	75.0	28	45	21	7	....
1979	10.6	1.4	10.9	27.1	46.4	64.8	74.0	31	43	19	6	....
1980	12.5	1.9	12.9	26.9	48.4	68.3	73.5	34	41	17	9	....
1981	14.5	2.3	15.0	25.9	47.7	68.5	72.9	36	38	16	10	....
1982	14.8	2.6	15.3	24.9	48.7	70.7	71.9	37	36	16	11	39
1983	12.3	2.4	12.8	25.9	56.8	79.3	74.3	33	36	17	15	41
1984	12.0	2.5	12.5	26.5	60.9	82.2	76.8	27	35	19	20	64
1985	11.2	2.5	11.6	25.5	67.5	92.7	75.7	28	38	19	16	50
1986	9.8	2.1	10.2	25.4	77.4	108.5	73.9	30	43	19	8	31
1987	8.9	2.0	9.3	26.6	86.4	117.7	75.4	27	45	22	8	44
1988	9.0	1.9	9.3	27.7	94.3	126.6	76.4	25	44	24	8	24
1989	9.8	1.8	10.1	27.7	101.6	138.4	75.2	27	47	20	6	37
1990	9.8	1.7	10.1	27.0	102.5	140.3	74.9	29	45	18	8	27
1991	9.1	1.5	9.3	26.5	105.2	145.8	74.4	32	41	19	9	22
1992	7.8	1.6	8.1	25.4	106.9	144.1	76.5	26	39	22	13	21
1993	6.9	1.2	7.1	25.4	104.2	139.6	77.1	25	38	20	17	20
1994	7.3	1.1	7.5	27.1	105.9	136.4	80.1	20	34	21	25	39
1995	7.7	0.9	7.8	27.4	106.4	137.3	80.1	20	34	19	28	31
1996	7.6	0.9	7.7	26.8	115.1	150.2	79.1	21	36	17	25	27
1997	7.5	1.0	7.7	27.3	123.5	161.0	79.2	21	39	17	24	22

Source: U.S. Federal Housing Finance Board, Monthly Interest Rate Survey.

Mortgage Characteristics

TABLE 4.17. CHARACTERISTICS OF CONVENTIONAL FIXED-RATE FIRST MORTGAGE LOANS FOR PURCHASE OF SINGLE-FAMILY HOMES: 1985 TO 1997
(In percent, except as indicated)

PROPERTY TYPE AND YEAR	Contract interest rate	Initial fees, charges	Effective interest rate	Term to maturity (Years)	Mortgage amount ($1,000)	Purchase price ($1,000)	Loan-to-price ratio
ALL PROPERTY TYPES							
1985	11.9	2.6	12.4	24.1	65.3	93.3	73.5
1986	10.1	2.3	10.5	24.9	75.5	107.7	73.2
1987	9.5	2.2	9.9	25.5	81.9	114.8	73.9
1988	10.0	2.1	10.4	26.0	82.8	117.3	73.7
1989	10.2	1.9	10.5	27.0	96.7	135.2	73.7
1990	10.1	1.9	10.4	26.1	97.4	136.1	73.9
1991	9.4	1.6	9.7	25.8	101.0	141.7	73.8
1992	8.2	1.6	8.5	24.4	104.4	141.4	76.5
1993	7.3	1.2	7.5	24.7	101.9	136.7	77.3
1994	8.0	1.1	8.2	25.8	96.1	125.3	79.7
1995	8.0	1.0	8.2	26.5	99.4	129.9	79.5
1996	7.8	1.0	8.0	26.1	107.2	141.6	78.6
1997	7.7	1.0	7.9	26.9	118.7	155.0	79.3
NEW HOMES							
1985	11.9	2.6	12.4	25.4	74.3	103.2	75.4
1986	10.0	2.6	10.5	26.4	85.0	118.0	74.7
1987	9.5	2.4	9.9	26.8	93.2	129.9	74.0
1988	10.0	2.4	10.4	26.1	97.2	140.7	71.9
1989	10.2	2.2	10.6	27.5	110.8	153.9	73.4
1990	10.1	2.1	10.4	26.4	104.0	144.3	74.2
1991	9.3	1.8	9.6	26.1	107.3	147.8	74.4
1992	8.3	1.6	8.5	25.1	115.8	154.6	77.0
1993	7.3	1.3	7.5	25.8	120.0	158.4	78.4
1994	7.9	1.4	8.1	26.4	118.2	155.1	78.4
1995	8.0	1.3	8.2	26.7	120.8	159.7	78.0
1996	7.8	1.3	8.0	26.4	129.0	170.3	77.9
1997	7.7	1.0	7.9	27.8	132.8	170.9	80.4
EXISTING HOMES							
1985	11.9	2.6	12.4	23.6	62.0	89.3	73.3
1986	10.1	2.2	10.5	24.5	73.0	104.8	72.9
1987	9.5	2.1	9.9	25.2	78.8	110.4	74.1
1988	10.1	2.0	10.4	26.1	79.3	111.3	74.4
1989	10.2	1.8	10.5	26.9	93.1	129.9	74.1
1990	10.1	1.8	10.4	26.1	96.1	134.2	74.0
1991	9.4	1.6	9.7	25.8	100.3	141.0	73.8
1992	8.2	1.6	8.5	24.3	102.1	138.7	76.4
1993	7.3	1.2	7.5	24.5	98.7	132.8	77.1
1994	8.0	1.1	8.2	25.7	92.0	119.9	80.0
1995	8.0	1.0	8.2	26.5	96.2	125.4	79.8
1996	7.8	1.0	8.0	26.1	103.3	136.4	78.8
1997	7.7	1.0	7.9	26.7	115.7	151.7	79.0

Source: U.S. Federal Housing Finance Board, Monthly Interest Rate Survey.

Mortgage Characteristics

TABLE 4.18. CHARACTERISTICS OF CONVENTIONAL ADJUSTABLE-RATE FIRST MORTGAGE LOANS FOR PURCHASE OF SINGLE-FAMILY HOMES: 1985 TO 1997
(In percent, except as indicated)

PROPERTY TYPE AND YEAR	Contract interest rate	Initial fees, charges	Effective interest rate	Term to maturity (Years)	Mortgage amount ($1,000)	Purchase price ($1,000)	Loan-to-price ratio
ALL PROPERTY TYPES							
1985	10.4	2.5	10.9	27.7	75.0	98.7	78.0
1986	9.1	2.0	9.4	27.3	88.0	117.7	76.1
1987	8.2	2.0	8.5	28.6	98.5	130.8	76.9
1988	8.2	1.9	8.5	28.9	107.9	141.7	77.7
1989	9.2	1.8	9.4	28.9	117.4	155.5	76.7
1990	8.9	1.6	9.2	29.3	122.3	160.4	77.1
1991	8.0	1.4	8.3	28.7	122.6	163.3	76.3
1992	6.4	1.4	6.6	29.1	125.3	165.9	76.7
1993	5.6	1.2	5.7	28.8	127.5	168.8	76.9
1994	6.3	1.1	6.4	29.2	131.3	167.7	80.1
1995	7.0	0.9	7.1	29.3	134.1	170.6	80.6
1996	6.9	0.8	7.1	29.0	150.5	192.1	79.9
1997	6.8	0.9	6.9	29.4	155.2	198.9	79.7
NEW HOMES							
1985	10.4	2.5	10.8	28.5	81.9	106.8	78.9
1986	9.0	2.1	9.4	28.0	94.4	124.5	77.0
1987	8.2	2.1	8.5	29.2	111.1	147.6	77.0
1988	8.1	2.1	8.5	29.2	119.3	156.4	77.8
1989	9.0	1.8	9.3	29.2	129.7	171.6	76.7
1990	8.9	1.7	9.2	29.3	133.8	176.2	76.4
1991	8.1	1.5	8.4	28.8	135.1	177.6	76.6
1992	6.6	1.5	6.9	27.7	128.9	174.5	74.7
1993	5.8	1.1	5.9	27.7	137.8	187.8	76.4
1994	6.5	1.2	6.6	29.0	149.2	193.4	79.2
1995	7.2	1.1	7.4	29.3	157.1	201.9	79.7
1996	7.0	1.0	7.2	29.2	168.5	217.9	78.9
1997	6.9	1.0	7.0	29.6	172.1	219.8	80.1
EXISTING HOMES							
1985	10.5	2.4	10.9	27.4	72.8	95.9	78.1
1986	9.1	1.9	9.4	27.3	87.5	117.1	76.0
1987	8.2	1.9	8.5	28.4	96.0	127.1	77.1
1988	8.2	1.8	8.5	28.9	105.5	138.0	77.9
1989	9.2	1.8	9.4	29.0	116.0	152.6	77.2
1990	8.9	1.5	9.2	29.2	119.7	156.8	77.2
1991	8.0	1.4	8.2	28.8	122.1	162.5	76.5
1992	6.3	1.4	6.5	29.3	124.7	164.5	77.1
1993	5.5	1.2	5.7	28.9	125.9	165.9	77.0
1994	6.2	1.0	6.4	29.3	127.7	162.5	80.2
1995	7.0	0.8	7.1	29.3	129.4	164.3	80.7
1996	6.9	0.8	7.1	29.0	147.5	187.8	80.1
1997	6.7	0.9	6.9	29.4	151.7	194.6	79.7

Source: U.S. Federal Housing Finance Board, Monthly Interest Rate Survey.

Mortgage Characteristics

TABLE 4.19. MORTGAGE INTEREST RATES AND POINTS ON CONVENTIONAL CONFORMING LOANS: 1972 TO 1997
(Percent)

PERIOD	30-year fixed-rate		15-year fixed-rate		1-year ARMs [1]	
	Rate	Points	Rate	Points	Rate	Points
1972	7.38	0.9	....	....	....	....
1973	8.04	1.0	....	....	....	....
1974	9.19	1.2	....	....	....	....
1975	9.05	1.1	....	....	....	....
1976	8.87	1.2	....	....	....	....
1977	8.85	1.1	....	....	....	....
1978	9.64	1.3	....	....	....	....
1979	11.20	1.6	....	....	....	....
1980	13.74	1.8	....	....	....	....
1981	16.63	2.1	....	....	....	....
1982	16.04	2.2	....	....	....	....
1983	13.24	2.1	....	....	....	....
1984	13.88	2.5	....	....	11.51	2.5
1985	12.43	2.5	....	....	10.05	2.5
1986	10.19	2.2	....	....	8.43	2.3
1987	10.21	2.2	....	....	7.83	2.2
1988	10.34	2.1	....	....	7.90	2.3
1989	10.32	2.1	....	....	8.80	2.3
1990	10.13	2.1	....	....	8.36	2.1
1991	9.25	2.0	....	....	7.09	1.9
1992	8.39	1.7	7.96	1.7	5.62	1.7
1993	7.31	1.6	6.83	1.6	4.58	1.5
1994	8.38	1.8	7.86	1.8	5.36	1.5
1995	7.93	1.8	7.48	1.8	6.06	1.5
1996	7.81	1.7	7.32	1.7	5.67	1.4
1997	7.60	1.7	7.13	1.7	5.61	1.4

Source: Freddie Mac, Primary Mortgage Market Survey.

(1) Before April 1986, the Adjustable-Rate Mortgage (ARM) Index was not specified. Beginning that month, the average rate is for contracts indexed to the 1-year Treasury.

Mortgage Characteristics

TABLE 4.20. MORTGAGE INSURANCE ACTIVITY ON ONE-TO-FOUR-FAMILY HOMES, BY TYPE OF INSURANCE: 1968 TO 1997

PERIOD	Federal Housing Administration [1]			Department of Veterans Affairs guarantees	Private mortgage insurance certificates
	Applications	Total endorsements	Purchase endorsements		
1968	751,982	425,339	....	211,025	....
1969	788,874	450,079	....	213,940	....
1970	941,566	475,176	....	167,734	....
1971	998,365	565,417	....	284,358	....
1972	655,747	427,858	....	375,485	....
1973	359,941	240,004	....	321,522	....
1974	383,993	195,850	....	313,156	....
1975	445,350	255,061	....	301,443	....
1976	491,981	250,808	....	330,442	....
1977	550,168	321,118	....	392,557	....
1978	627,971	334,108	....	368,648	....
1979	652,435	457,054	....	364,656	....
1980	516,938	381,169	359,151	274,193	392,808
1981	299,889	224,829	204,376	151,811	334,565
1982	461,129	166,734	143,931	103,354	315,868
1983	776,893	503,425	455,189	300,568	652,214
1984	476,888	267,831	235,847	210,366	946,408
1985	900,119	409,547	328,639	201,313	729,597
1986	1,907,316	921,370	634,491	351,242	585,987
1987	1,210,257	1,319,987	866,962	455,616	511,058
1988	949,353	698,990	622,873	212,671	423,470
1989	989,724	726,359	649,596	183,209	365,497
1990	957,302	780,329	726,028	192,992	367,120
1991	898,859	685,905	620,050	186,561	494,259
1992	1,090,392	680,278	522,738	290,003	907,511
1993	1,740,504	1,065,832	591,243	457,596	1,198,307
1994	961,466	1,217,685	686,487	536,931	1,148,696
1995	857,364	568,399	516,380	243,719	960,756
1996	1,064,324	849,861	719,517	326,458	1,068,707
1997	1,115,434	839,712	745,524	254,780	974,698

Sources: Office of Housing, Department of Housing and Urban Development; Department of Veterans Affairs; and Mortgage Insurance Companies of America.

(1) These operational numbers differ slightly from adjusted accounting numbers.

Mortgage Characteristics

TABLE 4.21. MORTGAGE ORIGINATIONS ON ONE-TO-FOUR-FAMILY HOMES BY PRESENCE AND TYPE OF MORTGAGE INSURANCE: 1970 TO 1996
(Billions of current dollars)

PERIOD	Federal Housing Administration-insured	Department of Veterans Affairs-guaranteed	Private insurance	Not insured [1]	Totals
1970	8.769	3.846	0.116	22.856	35.587
1971	10.994	6.830	3.526	36.438	57.788
1972	8.456	7.749	9.158	50.501	75.864
1973	5.185	7.577	12.627	53.737	79.126
1974	4.532	7.889	9.220	45.867	67.508
1975	6.265	8.836	10.024	52.788	77.913
1976	6.998	10.426	14.600	80.761	112.785
1977	10.469	14.882	21.595	115.027	161.973
1978	14.581	16.026	27.327	127.102	185.036
1979	20.710	18.876	25.327	122.178	187.091
1980	14.955	12.102	19.035	87.670	133.762
1981	10.538	7.534	18.079	62.061	98.212
1982	11.482	7.687	18.953	58.829	96.951
1983	28.753	18.880	42.363	111.867	201.863
1984	16.600	12.024	63.403	111.678	203.705
1985	28.767	15.246	50.475	195.296	289.784
1986	64.770	23.149	46.138	365.355	499.412
1987	77.822	30.176	44.475	354.758	507.231
1988	46.655	15.875	39.664	344.069	446.263
1989	45.108	13.681	37.117	357.001	452.907
1990	59.803	21.901	38.956	337.744	458.404
1991	46.914	15.285	53.997	445.878	562.074
1992	50.275	24.543	101.047	717.817	893.681
1993	83.457	41.023	136.767	758.615	1,019.861
1994	94.913	48.190	131.402	494.243	768.748
1995	48.424	26.262	109.625	455.125	639.436
1996	72.768	35.211	126.972	550.373	785.324

Sources: Mortgage Insurance Companies of America and U.S. Department of Housing and Urban Development, Survey of Mortgage Lending Activity.

(1) Includes a small number of loans backed by the Rural Housing Service (formerly Farmers Home Administration).

Mortgage Characteristics

	TABLE 4.22. FEDERAL HOUSING ADMINISTRATION UNASSISTED MULTIFAMILY MORTGAGE INSURANCE ACTIVITY: 1980 TO 1997								
	Construction of new rental units			Purchase or refinance of existing rental units			Congregate housing, nursing homes, assisted living, and board and care facilities		
PERIOD	Projects	Units	Mortgage amount (Millions of dollars)	Projects	Units	Mortgage amount (Millions of dollars)	Projects	Units [1]	Mortgage amount (Millions of dollars)
1980	79	14,671	560.8	32	6,459	89.1	25	3,187	78.1
1981	94	14,232	415.1	12	2,974	43.0	35	4,590	130.0
1982	98	14,303	460.4	28	7,431	95.2	50	7,096	200.0
1983	74	14,353	543.9	94	22,118	363.0	65	9,231	295.8
1984	96	14,158	566.2	88	21,655	428.2	45	5,697	175.2
1985	144	23,253	954.1	135	34,730	764.3	41	5,201	179.1
1986	154	22,006	1,117.5	245	32,554	1,550.1	22	3,123	111.2
1987	171	28,300	1,379.4	306	68,000	1,618.0	45	6,243	225.7
1988	140	21,180	922.2	234	49,443	1,402.3	47	5,537	197.1
1989	101	15,240	750.9	144	32,995	864.6	41	5,183	207.9
1990	61	9,910	411.4	69	13,848	295.3	53	6,166	263.2
1991	72	13,098	590.2	185	40,640	1,015.1	81	10,150	437.2
1992	54	7,823	358.5	119	24,960	547.1	66	8,229	367.4
1993	56	9,321	428.6	262	50,140	1,209.4	77	9,036	428.6
1994	84	12,988	658.5	321	61,416	1,587.0	94	13,688	701.7
1995	89	17,113	785.0	192	32,383	822.3	103	12,888	707.2
1996	128	23,554	1,178.8	268	51,760	1,391.1	152	20,069	927.5
1997	147	23,880	1,362.2	186	31,538	1,098.5	143	16,819	820.0

Source: U.S. Department of Housing and Urban Development, Office of Housing - Federal Housing Administration Comptroller.

(1) Includes both housing units and beds.

Mortgage Characteristics

REGION AND MORTGAGE CHARACTERISTIC	All properties	Homeowner properties					Rental and vacant properties						
		Total	1 housing unit	2-4 housing units	Condo-miniums	Mobile homes	Total	1 housing unit	2-4 housing units	5-49 housing units	50 or more housing units	Condo-miniums	Mobile homes
UNITED STATES													
Mortgage status													
All properties	70,907	56,058	47,578	1,581	2,636	4,263	14,849	8,964	2,320	557	65	1,587	1,355
Mortgaged	42,033	34,533	30,070	901	1,959	1,602	7,500	4,255	1,449	391	57	1,068	281
Nonmortgaged	28,874	21,525	17,507	680	676	2,661	7,349	4,710	871	166	8	520	1,074
Type of first mortgage instrument													
Fixed-rate, level-payment	33,180	27,920	24,481	692	1,405	1,343	5,259	3,117	979	226	36	671	232
Short-term with balloon payment	1,403	946	778	22	40	106	456	266	84	40	12	33	20
Graduated-payment (GPM)	287	227	190	14	20	4	60	50	3	1	1	6	-
Adjustable-rate (ARM)	7,006	5,319	4,526	167	487	138	1,688	808	371	121	8	350	29
Other type	158	120	96	6	7	11	37	13	12	3	1	9	-
NORTHEAST													
Mortgage status													
All properties	13,506	11,237	9,478	804	540	414	2,269	1,110	622	145	15	311	65
Mortgaged	8,093	6,839	5,815	456	434	133	1,254	521	386	97	14	225	12
Nonmortgaged	5,413	4,399	3,663	348	107	281	1,014	589	236	48	2	86	53
Type of first mortgage instrument													
Fixed-rate, level-payment	6,189	5,396	4,690	350	248	109	793	349	267	54	9	104	12
Short-term with balloon payment	168	85	63	10	9	3	83	43	10	13	4	13	-
Graduated-payment (GPM)	87	81	59	7	12	4	6	4	1	-	-	-	-
Adjustable-rate (ARM)	1,607	1,252	987	88	160	17	355	124	99	29	1	102	-
Other type	41	24	17	2	5	-	17	2	9	-	-	6	-
MIDWEST													
Mortgage status													
All properties	17,236	13,951	12,416	375	386	773	3,285	2,103	625	126	13	154	263
Mortgaged	9,758	8,286	7,560	214	244	268	1,473	862	368	89	12	96	45
Nonmortgaged	7,477	5,665	4,857	161	142	505	1,812	1,241	257	37	1	58	218
Type of first mortgage instrument													
Fixed-rate, level-payment	7,589	6,613	6,026	171	188	228	975	571	246	55	9	65	29
Short-term with balloon payment	542	377	339	6	12	19	166	101	42	9	2	3	8
Graduated-payment (GPM)	45	40	37	3	-	-	5	5	-	-	-	-	-
Adjustable-rate (ARM)	1,518	1,204	1,111	31	44	18	314	177	79	24	1	25	7
Other type	65	52	47	2	-	3	13	8	-	2	-	3	-
SOUTH													
Mortgage status													
All properties	25,948	19,848	16,632	205	951	2,059	6,101	3,904	565	112	21	719	779
Mortgaged	14,526	11,823	10,213	106	638	866	2,703	1,693	318	71	17	449	155
Nonmortgaged	11,422	8,025	6,420	100	313	1,193	3,397	2,211	247	41	4	270	624
Type of first mortgage instrument													
Fixed-rate, level-payment	11,909	9,867	8,535	86	500	746	2,042	1,333	224	44	11	295	135
Short-term with balloon payment	481	331	273	3	9	45	150	91	27	11	4	14	4
Graduated-payment (GPM)	73	47	42	-	5	-	26	21	2	-	-	2	-
Adjustable-rate (ARM)	2,028	1,544	1,341	15	122	66	484	249	65	15	2	138	16
Other type	34	34	22	1	2	8	1	-	-	-	-	-	-
WEST													
Mortgage status													
All properties	14,217	11,022	9,051	197	757	1,018	3,195	1,847	508	173	15	404	248
Mortgaged	9,656	7,585	6,483	125	643	335	2,070	1,178	377	134	14	298	69
Nonmortgaged	4,562	3,437	2,568	72	115	683	1,125	668	131	40	1	106	179
Type of first mortgage instrument													
Fixed-rate, level-payment	7,492	6,044	5,230	85	469	260	1,449	864	241	73	8	207	56
Short-term with balloon payment	210	154	103	2	9	39	57	31	5	7	3	2	8
Graduated-payment (GPM)	83	59	52	4	3	-	24	20	-	-	-	3	-
Adjustable-rate (ARM)	1,853	1,319	1,087	33	162	36	534	259	128	53	4	85	5
Other type	17	11	11	-	-	-	6	4	2	-	-	-	-

TABLE 4.23. MORTGAGE STATUS AND TYPE OF FIRST MORTGAGE INSTRUMENT ON PRIVATE NONFARM RESIDENTIAL PROPERTIES, BY PROPERTY TYPE AND REGION: 1991
(Thousands of properties)

Source: U.S. Bureau of the Census and U.S. Department of Housing and Urban Development, 1991 Residential Finance Survey.

(-) Indicates less than 500 properties.

Components may not add to totals due to rounding.

Mortgage Characteristics

TABLE 4.24. SELECTED MORTGAGE CHARACTERISTICS FOR OWNER-OCCUPIED HOUSING UNITS: 1991
(In thousands, except as noted)

	Total owner-occupied units	Housing unit characteristics		Household characteristics					Regions			
		New construc-tion (within 4 years)	Mobile homes	Black	Hispanic	Elderly (65+)	Moved in past year	Below poverty level	North-east	Midwest	South	West
TOTAL	59,796	3,824	4,532	4,635	2,423	15,734	4,204	4,994	11,869	15,238	21,272	11,417
MORTGAGES CURRENTLY ON PROPERTY												
None, owned free and clear	24,454	700	2,727	1,812	852	12,969	867	3,303	4,816	6,595	9,350	3,694
With mortgage or land contract	35,342	3,125	1,805	2,823	1,571	2,765	3,337	1,691	7,053	8,644	11,922	7,723
One mortgage or land contract	29,753	2,822	1,700	2,365	1,355	2,450	3,105	1,437	5,712	7,419	10,388	6,234
Two mortgages	4,746	250	58	349	172	161	109	127	1,205	1,017	1,259	1,266
Three or more mortgages	92	6	2	5	3	3	6	4	13	13	23	43
Number of mortgages not reported	750	46	45	105	41	151	117	123	123	195	253	179
TOTAL OWNERS WITH ONE OR MORE MORTGAGES	35,342	3,125	1,805	2,823	1,571	2,765	3,337	1,691	7,053	8,644	11,922	7,723
TYPE OF PRIMARY MORTGAGE												
FHA	5,282	400	55	785	334	298	642	255	520	1,204	2,204	1,354
VA	2,576	121	40	355	111	216	182	96	210	490	1,141	734
Farmers Home Administration	447	25	7	52	25	32	14	64	63	97	214	72
Other types	25,180	2,459	1,626	1,384	997	1,950	2,293	1,043	5,922	6,463	7,690	5,105
Don't know	753	42	28	88	49	80	55	65	139	133	285	195
Not reported	1,104	78	49	158	54	189	151	168	197	257	388	262
MORTGAGE ORIGINATION												
Placed new mortgage(s)	28,618	2,880	1,643	2,265	1,287	2,265	3,005	1,359	5,720	7,224	9,773	5,902
Primary obtained when property acquired	23,293	2,768	1,501	1,876	1,130	1,605	2,940	1,101	4,485	5,883	8,230	4,695
Obtained later	5,204	103	140	371	155	646	53	247	1,212	1,317	1,492	1,183
Date not reported	121	10	2	18	2	14	12	11	22	23	51	25
Assumed	1,676	34	89	123	99	172	174	91	92	308	773	502
Wrap-around	32	2	3	5	-	4	1	3	5	-	13	14
Combination of the above	3,977	152	21	303	125	150	18	105	1,080	875	979	1,043
Origin not reported	1,038	57	49	128	59	174	138	134	156	237	385	261
PAYMENT PLAN OF PRIMARY MORTGAGE												
Fixed-payment, self-amortizing	27,008	2,347	1,318	2,105	1,248	1,921	2,588	1,080	5,372	6,558	9,228	5,850
Adjustable-rate mortgage	3,103	366	100	156	136	175	213	87	748	757	808	790
Adjustable-term mortgage	69	7	5	9	-	15	2	10	11	17	22	19
Graduated-payment mortgage	434	74	9	37	37	18	75	18	114	71	122	127
Balloon	273	28	29	15	2	9	69	9	38	92	87	56
Other	455	43	3	59	19	27	34	60	74	103	178	100
Combination of the above	283	48	8	18	-	41	25	12	64	59	76	84
Not reported	3,716	213	334	425	129	559	332	415	631	988	1,402	696
LENDERS OF PRIMARY AND SECONDARY MORTGAGES												
Only borrowed from firm(s)	30,919	2,910	1,554	2,324	1,331	2,389	2,869	1,319	6,384	7,631	10,332	6,573
Only borrowed from seller	1,003	28	128	63	81	70	193	102	88	302	390	223
Only borrowed from other individual(s)	394	25	29	33	10	33	54	33	69	110	143	73
Borrowed from a firm and a seller	219	11	15	15	17	2	23	7	22	31	87	79
Borrowed from a firm and other individual	118	13	1	15	5	5	8	4	21	15	38	44
Borrowed from seller and other individual	4	-	-	-	-	-	-	-	-	-	4	-
One or both sources not reported	2,684	137	78	373	127	266	191	226	470	555	929	730
ITEMS INCLUDED IN PRIMARY MORTGAGE PAYMENT[1]												
Principal and interest only	12,651	1,148	1,341	744	504	1,237	1,057	803	2,285	3,259	3,917	3,191
Property taxes	19,932	1,710	143	1,699	915	1,157	1,981	604	4,214	4,822	6,931	3,965
Property insurance	16,739	1,551	310	1,594	815	937	1,774	567	2,540	4,052	6,676	3,472
Other	1,466	136	49	126	66	71	144	48	368	302	523	273
Not reported	1,702	113	73	225	103	272	200	200	391	380	570	362
YEAR PRIMARY MORTGAGE ORIGINATED												
1990 to 1994	7,017	1,552	496	450	336	341	3,026	304	1,173	1,738	2,297	1,809
1985 to 1989	14,632	1,513	923	932	680	705	119	559	2,998	3,592	4,922	3,120
1980 to 1984	4,095	....	273	368	178	284	33	190	818	963	1,539	775
1975 to 1979	4,690	....	45	431	178	494	12	222	993	1,202	1,526	969
1970 to 1974	2,276	....	6	305	104	340	4	131	549	549	716	462
1960 to 1969	1,296	....	2	150	40	334	4	96	283	272	447	294
1950 to 1959	71	....	-	5	2	37	-	7	13	19	17	22
1949 or earlier	11	....	-	-	-	9	-	4	1	1	4	4
Not reported	1,254	60	60	182	52	221	138	177	224	308	455	267
Median (Year)	1987	....	1988	1985	1987	1981	1990+	1986	1986	1987	1987	1987

See notes at end of table.

Mortgage Characteristics

**TABLE 4.24. SELECTED MORTGAGE CHARACTERISTICS FOR OWNER-OCCUPIED HOUSING UNITS:
1991 - Continued**

(In thousands, except as noted)

CHARACTERISTIC	Total owner-occupied units	Housing unit characteristics		Household characteristics					Regions			
		New construc-tion (within 4 years)	Mobile homes	Black	Hispanic	Elderly (65+)	Moved in past year	Below poverty level	North-east	Midwest	South	West
TERM OF PRIMARY MORTGAGE AT ORIGINATION OR ASSUMPTION												
Less than 8 years	777	84	320	53	29	33	217	93	86	248	355	88
8 to 12	1,019	80	375	78	48	63	153	99	123	240	507	150
13 to 17	3,346	488	650	142	148	199	380	194	614	960	1,245	527
18 to 22	2,352	137	101	182	87	222	139	130	500	673	892	287
23 to 27	2,388	71	20	116	88	178	103	96	752	619	652	364
28 to 32	16,820	1,985	58	1,510	896	956	2,002	478	3,095	3,757	5,630	4,338
33 years or more	469	32	4	72	11	36	38	47	82	111	179	98
Variable	369	21	17	33	2	86	26	35	92	97	95	84
Not reported	7,802	226	260	636	260	992	281	520	1,708	1,938	2,368	1,788
Median (Years)	29	29	14	30	29	29	29	26	29	29	29	30
REMAINING YEARS MORTGAGED												
Less than 8 years	4,590	109	791	431	166	653	262	384	896	1,212	1,825	658
8 to 12	4,966	152	475	377	184	455	141	252	1,091	1,392	1,606	877
13 to 17	4,983	445	234	403	245	419	384	229	993	1,224	1,780	986
18 to 22	2,946	135	79	248	124	185	144	132	579	724	1,019	623
23 to 27	6,593	498	39	461	362	185	129	142	1,371	1,401	2,233	1,587
28 to 32	6,188	1,569	21	413	342	170	1,963	125	1,092	1,372	1,757	1,968
33 years or more	128	17	4	10	2	4	34	6	26	32	24	45
Variable	928	55	17	59	6	113	28	43	248	252	235	193
Not reported	4,021	145	146	421	138	581	253	377	757	1,035	1,443	785
Median (Years)	19	28	8	18	23	12	29	13	18	17	18	24
CURRENT INTEREST RATE												
Less than 6 percent	846	83	32	74	51	124	83	46	127	151	313	255
6 to 7.9	1,561	42	12	120	63	235	107	54	354	372	502	333
8 to 9.9	8,633	1,081	77	517	401	452	1,532	222	1,650	2,187	2,864	1,933
10 to 11.9	6,206	807	233	351	275	270	588	201	1,232	1,595	2,038	1,341
12 to 13.9	928	112	240	89	65	58	51	51	148	246	388	146
14 to 15.9	221	24	141	21	12	11	36	38	30	39	103	47
16 to 17.9	70	1	38	6	13	5	3	15	11	14	37	8
18 to 19.9	47	-	28	7	9	4	8	4	5	6	30	7
20 percent or more	20	-	11	11	-	-	3	8	-	-	20	-
Not reported	16,810	975	993	1,628	681	1,607	926	1,053	3,494	4,036	5,627	3,652

See notes at end of table.

Mortgage Characteristics

TABLE 4.24. SELECTED MORTGAGE CHARACTERISTICS FOR OWNER-OCCUPIED HOUSING UNITS: 1991 - Continued

(In thousands, except as noted)

CHARACTERISTIC	Total owner-occupied units	Housing unit characteristics		Household characteristics					Regions			
		New construction (within 4 years)	Mobile homes	Black	Hispanic	Elderly (65+)	Moved in past year	Below poverty level	North-east	Midwest	South	West
TOTAL OUTSTANDING PRINCIPAL AMOUNT												
Less than $10,000	2,002	56	241	187	74	338	95	160	426	509	734	332
$10,000 to 19,999	2,294	159	367	176	97	240	134	146	435	675	868	316
$20,000 to 29,999	2,167	100	119	171	106	184	159	115	406	656	723	381
$30,000 to 39,999	2,023	101	45	140	101	94	184	76	334	657	691	340
$40,000 to 49,999	1,801	135	14	108	126	87	188	29	273	520	697	311
$50,000 to 59,999	1,564	155	19	111	63	50	262	39	236	424	600	304
$60,000 to 69,999	1,317	189	2	72	58	37	206	21	197	298	505	316
$70,000 to 79,999	1,148	172	2	58	54	34	209	15	215	241	398	294
$80,000 to 99,999	1,492	346	-	88	55	42	283	4	316	297	459	420
$100,000 to 119,999	930	229	-	25	50	24	197	10	238	149	247	296
$120,000 to 149,999	800	188	2	32	62	12	208	6	271	102	170	257
$150,000 to 199,999	495	165	2	19	27	9	153	7	105	42	120	228
$200,000 to 249,999	209	69	-	2	10	5	48	7	62	8	29	109
$250,000 to 299,999	103	36	-	4	4	-	28	-	16	6	33	48
$300,000 or more	187	50	-	4	2	3	56	3	28	22	20	116
Not reported	16,810	975	993	1,628	681	1,607	926	1,053	3,494	4,036	5,627	3,652
Median (Dollars)	44,334	80,463	14,495	34,594	45,329	20,106	68,882	21,163	46,511	37,047	41,877	61,599
CURRENT TOTAL LOAN AS PERCENT OF VALUE												
Less than 20 percent	3,227	112	73	220	136	540	80	141	917	662	929	720
20 to 39	2,880	188	67	183	118	262	123	105	704	738	870	568
40 to 59	3,630	451	107	188	183	173	318	146	638	1,028	1,155	808
60 to 79	4,586	699	144	266	209	130	766	110	677	1,252	1,593	1,065
80 to 89	2,081	383	142	161	122	25	530	61	279	472	841	489
90 to 99	1,266	209	83	122	51	7	425	29	133	290	602	240
100 percent or more	862	108	196	56	69	22	169	47	211	165	305	180
Not reported	16,810	975	993	1,628	681	1,607	926	1,053	3,494	4,036	5,627	3,652
Median (Percent)	57.4	69.3	81.0	60.6	60.7	23.0	77.9	50.1	45.0	57.6	62.4	58.5

Source: U.S. Bureau of the Census and U.S. Department of Housing and Urban Development, "American Housing Survey for the United States in 1991." Current Housing Reports H150/91. April 1993.

(1) Figures may not add to total because more than one category may apply to a unit.

(-) means zero or rounds to zero.

Mortgage Characteristics

TABLE 4.25. SELECTED MORTGAGE CHARACTERISTICS FOR OWNER-OCCUPIED HOUSING UNITS: 1993
(In thousands, except as noted)

CHARACTERISTIC	Total owner-occupied units	Housing unit characteristics		Household characteristics					Regions			
		New construction (Within 4 years)	Mobile homes	Black	Hispanic	Elderly (65+)	Moved in past year	Below poverty level	North-east	Midwest	South	West
TOTAL	61,252	4,056	4,482	4,788	2,788	15,767	4,578	5,386	11,751	15,617	21,841	12,043
MORTGAGES CURRENTLY ON PROPERTY												
None, owned free and clear	24,068	762	2,677	1,804	929	12,873	890	3,169	4,779	6,300	9,266	3,724
With mortgage or land contract	37,183	3,295	1,805	2,984	1,859	2,894	3,688	2,217	6,973	9,317	12,575	8,319
One mortgage or land contract	32,302	3,110	1,704	2,489	1,604	2,553	3,472	1,846	5,857	8,258	11,133	7,054
Two mortgages	3,975	115	57	389	164	189	100	174	956	864	1,168	987
Three or more mortgages	71	3	-	9	2	4	5	2	7	13	7	45
Number of mortgages not reported	835	67	44	97	89	148	112	196	153	182	267	234
TOTAL OWNERS WITH ONE OR MORE MORTGAGES	37,183	3,295	1,805	2,984	1,859	2,894	3,688	2,217	6,973	9,317	12,575	8,319
TYPE OF PRIMARY MORTGAGE												
FHA	5,367	431	30	887	374	290	578	362	535	1,233	2,253	1,346
VA	2,545	186	42	394	143	188	232	106	213	483	1,155	694
Farmers Home Administration	451	42	5	64	14	38	37	68	48	115	229	59
Other types	26,793	2,483	1,617	1,418	1,126	2,098	2,634	1,367	5,798	7,050	8,240	5,704
Don't know	844	62	55	84	90	102	55	79	148	163	328	206
Not reported	1,183	91	55	137	111	178	152	235	231	272	369	311
MORTGAGE ORIGINATION												
Placed new mortgage(s)	31,288	3,137	1,623	2,389	1,556	2,417	3,395	1,736	5,863	8,097	10,487	6,840
Primary obtained when property acquired	21,311	2,737	1,426	1,909	1,224	1,481	3,318	1,299	3,746	5,433	7,914	4,218
Obtained later	9,814	389	193	461	321	926	59	423	2,076	2,638	2,528	2,572
Date not reported	163	11	5	20	10	11	18	13	41	26	45	50
Assumed	1,401	23	95	130	90	137	126	120	69	220	744	369
Wrap-around	24	-	2	-	4	-	2	4	-	3	13	9
Combination of the above	3,433	65	31	346	117	182	34	152	880	784	946	823
Origin not reported	1,038	69	53	119	92	158	131	206	160	214	385	278
PAYMENT PLAN OF PRIMARY MORTGAGE												
Fixed-payment, self-amortizing	28,147	2,580	1,351	2,292	1,397	1,970	2,777	1,431	5,240	7,021	9,732	6,154
Adjustable-rate mortgage	3,670	327	71	163	134	195	417	154	762	892	1,083	934
Adjustable-term mortgage	79	-	2	10	9	17	7	3	11	28	20	20
Graduated-payment mortgage	332	58	2	23	14	13	53	9	88	41	88	116
Balloon	305	36	22	10	21	24	60	16	23	124	57	101
Other	562	27	6	55	27	42	40	44	106	157	167	132
Combination of the above	272	37	4	6	7	17	33	15	70	75	62	65
Not reported	3,816	229	347	425	250	616	301	545	673	979	1,366	798
LENDERS OF PRIMARY AND SECONDARY MORTGAGES												
Only borrowed from firm(s)	32,873	3,076	1,507	2,472	1,521	2,510	3,169	1,711	6,389	8,352	10,961	7,170
Only borrowed from seller	950	11	155	80	94	40	198	123	55	269	431	195
Only borrowed from other individual(s)	534	55	55	31	45	52	89	54	73	126	227	108
Borrowed from a firm and a seller	162	5	17	10	11	5	21	12	16	23	63	60
Borrowed from a firm and other individual	133	11	8	12	-	9	12	4	20	18	28	67
Borrowed from seller and other individual	17	-	2	-	3	-	7	-	4	-	7	5
One or both sources not reported	2,516	136	60	379	186	279	191	313	416	528	858	714
ITEMS INCLUDED IN PRIMARY MORTGAGE PAYMENT [1]												
Principal and interest only	13,957	1,353	1,405	773	607	1,469	1,178	912	2,454	3,585	4,359	3,559
Property taxes	20,558	1,687	150	1,895	1,051	1,101	2,212	950	4,017	5,153	7,227	4,161
Property insurance	17,775	1,588	265	1,782	965	894	2,039	820	2,638	4,419	7,021	3,697
Other	1,533	148	47	146	84	78	169	40	359	304	575	295
Not reported	1,713	134	65	188	150	252	210	285	365	394	549	405
YEAR PRIMARY MORTGAGE ORIGINATED												
1990 to 1994	17,815	3,086	998	926	874	857	3,457	700	2,993	4,669	5,684	4,469
1985 to 1989	9,124	123	544	801	466	568	56	519	1,938	2,135	3,239	1,812
1980 to 1984	2,861	....	156	305	164	269	15	262	538	708	1,071	544
1975 to 1979	3,459	....	44	393	131	396	10	256	665	910	1,249	635
1970 to 1974	1,699	....	-	278	77	299	2	127	383	417	576	322
1960 to 1969	795	....	2	116	22	240	4	95	173	173	266	183
1950 to 1959	56	....	-	7	3	32	-	10	15	9	18	15
1949 or earlier	5	....	-	-	-	5	-	-	-	2	-	2
Not reported	1,370	86	61	160	122	226	143	248	268	293	472	338
Median (Year)	1990	....	1990+	1987	1990+	1986	1990+	1987	1989	1990+	1989	1990+

See notes at end of table.

Mortgage Characteristics

CHARACTERISTIC	Total owner-occupied units	Housing unit characteristics		Household characteristics					Regions			
		New con-struction (Within 4 years)	Mobile homes	Black	His-panic	Elderly (65+)	Moved in past year	Below poverty level	North-east	Mid-west	South	West
TERM OF PRIMARY MORTGAGE AT ORIGINATION OR ASSUMPTION												
Less than 8 years	751	107	294	33	67	47	216	84	64	242	305	140
8 to 12	935	128	350	74	52	63	151	93	114	240	491	91
13 to 17	3,201	489	566	172	142	198	472	165	525	915	1,346	415
18 to 22	1,878	166	137	165	112	152	182	132	399	501	717	261
23 to 27	1,792	53	11	108	74	146	99	99	551	450	539	251
28 to 32	15,313	1,755	84	1,612	874	911	2,240	761	2,605	3,503	5,410	3,795
33 years or more	405	32	2	55	23	54	27	55	51	85	187	82
Variable	520	27	8	33	20	102	33	27	121	162	134	103
Not reported	12,389	538	354	733	495	1,220	268	802	2,544	3,217	3,446	3,182
Median (Years)	29	29	14	30	29	29	29	29	29	29	29	30
REMAINING YEARS MORTGAGED												
Less than 8 years	4,749	161	791	437	241	693	234	399	870	1,346	1,825	709
8 to 12	4,657	211	393	383	167	462	166	288	956	1,209	1,758	734
13 to 17	6,388	511	232	457	241	405	478	320	1,219	1,874	2,003	1,293
18 to 22	2,742	178	113	290	186	174	191	182	554	616	993	579
23 to 27	5,925	398	38	540	347	205	123	276	1,183	1,321	1,918	1,504
28 to 32	7,882	1,628	48	400	409	235	2,204	204	1,211	1,778	2,386	2,507
33 years or more	96	17	-	2	16	-	23	3	22	5	24	46
Variable	1,073	30	10	68	27	132	40	43	274	298	293	210
Not reported	3,672	160	181	407	225	587	229	503	685	872	1,376	739
Median (Years)	19	28	8	18	22	12	29	15	18	17	18	24
CURRENT INTEREST RATE												
Less than 6 percent	999	140	8	49	52	108	276	48	152	171	342	333
6 to 7.9	4,582	705	49	243	192	298	1,337	158	852	1,205	1,499	1,026
8 to 9.9	7,740	974	200	507	459	450	899	265	1,305	1,897	2,921	1,617
10 to 11.9	2,599	228	237	259	162	121	181	165	485	674	957	483
12 to 13.9	571	82	225	77	36	43	44	77	89	143	245	95
14 to 15.9	126	23	66	21	10	21	9	8	12	21	74	19
16 to 17.9	59	12	33	15	2	2	4	9	10	5	41	3
18 to 19.9	32	5	21	2	3	2	7	-	5	4	23	-
20 percent or more	10	-	7	2	-	-	2	2	-	8	2	-
Not reported	20,464	1,127	959	1,809	941	1,849	929	1,486	4,062	5,189	6,470	4,743
Median (Percent)	8.7	8.4	11.4	9.1	8.9	8.5	7.6	9.2	8.6	8.7	8.8	8.5

See notes at end of table.

Mortgage Characteristics

TABLE 4.25. SELECTED MORTGAGE CHARACTERISTICS FOR OWNER-OCCUPIED HOUSING UNITS: 1993 - Continued
(In thousands, except as noted)

CHARACTERISTIC	Total owner-occupied units	Housing unit characteristics		Household characteristics					Regions			
		New construction (Within 4 years)	Mobile homes	Black	His-panic	Elderly (65+)	Moved in past year	Below poverty level	North-east	Mid-west	South	West
TOTAL OUTSTANDING PRINCIPAL AMOUNT												
Less than $10,000	1,633	37	236	158	60	278	77	122	307	454	601	271
$10,000 to 19,999	1,850	171	316	159	82	212	153	136	336	559	683	272
$20,000 to 29,999	1,889	109	153	155	124	130	167	145	311	608	736	235
$30,000 to 39,999	1,697	89	76	128	81	129	163	83	202	520	693	282
$40,000 to 49,999	1,513	123	39	116	94	86	214	77	240	415	594	264
$50,000 to 59,999	1,465	147	10	109	102	61	271	53	175	384	626	281
$60,000 to 69,999	1,371	222	2	85	74	26	310	26	215	311	584	260
$70,000 to 79,999	1,036	190	-	83	50	25	239	15	186	246	391	212
$80,000 to 99,999	1,529	364	2	73	87	35	407	17	278	321	514	416
$100,000 to 119,999	881	206	-	43	39	27	228	18	255	144	218	263
$120,000 to 149,999	798	217	5	26	83	14	237	19	200	70	216	311
$150,000 to 199,999	626	175	2	32	35	15	196	9	135	63	155	273
$200,000 to 249,999	216	67	-	2	7	2	46	7	40	14	47	115
$250,000 to 299,999	88	28	-	-	-	3	24	2	9	7	18	53
$300,000 or more	129	21	2	5	-	2	26	2	20	11	27	70
Not reported	20,464	1,127	959	1,809	941	1,849	929	1,486	4,062	5,189	6,470	4,743
Median (Dollars)	48,537	79,746	15,895	39,070	51,723	22,486	70,994	27,444	53,376	38,528	45,710	67,096
CURRENT TOTAL LOAN AS PERCENT OF VALUE												
Less than 20 percent	2,511	48	88	158	118	395	72	155	656	593	733	529
20 to 39	2,308	150	58	178	111	244	141	110	438	644	823	403
40 to 59	2,911	340	150	205	162	177	294	143	476	805	986	644
60 to 79	4,351	663	166	251	229	141	808	150	663	1,097	1,640	951
80 to 89	2,329	499	115	175	128	25	687	52	296	504	917	612
90 to 99	1,521	327	111	141	112	34	568	64	217	320	672	312
100 percent or more	788	141	158	68	57	30	189	59	164	165	334	126
Not reported	20,464	1,127	959	1,809	941	1,849	929	1,486	4,062	5,189	6,470	4,743
Median (Percent)	62.9	76.5	75.3	63.7	65.9	30.5	80.9	54.2	55.2	60.4	66.2	64.5

Source: U.S. Bureau of the Census and U.S. Department of Housing and Urban Development, "American Housing Survey for the United States in 1993." Current Housing Reports H150/93. Issued February 1995.

(1) Figures may not add to total because more than one category may apply to a unit.

(-) means zero or rounds to zero.

Mortgage Characteristics

TABLE 4.26. SELECTED MORTGAGE CHARACTERISTICS FOR OWNER-OCCUPIED HOUSING UNITS: 1995

(In thousands, except as noted)

CHARACTERISTIC	Total owner-occupied units	Housing unit characteristics New construction (Within 4 years)	Mobile homes	Black	His-panic	Elderly (65+)	Moved in past year	Below poverty level	North-east	Mid-west	South	West
TOTAL	63,544	4,439	4,837	5,137	3,245	16,299	4,954	6,034	11,861	16,567	22,959	12,157
MORTGAGES CURRENTLY ON PROPERTY												
None, owned free and clear	24,518	838	2,903	1,879	1,126	13,060	940	3,647	4,607	6,479	9,666	3,765
With mortgage or land contract	39,026	3,601	1,933	3,257	2,120	3,239	4,013	2,387	7,254	10,088	13,292	8,392
One mortgage or land contract	34,730	3,382	1,872	2,939	1,947	3,036	3,893	2,192	6,326	8,913	12,183	7,307
Two mortgages	4,244	219	61	315	170	203	116	190	914	1,167	1,102	1,062
Three or more mortgages	52	-	-	4	3	-	4	4	14	7	7	23
Number of mortgages not reported	-	-	-	-	-	-	-	-	-	-	-	-
TOTAL OWNERS WITH ONE OR MORE MORTGAGES	39,026	3,601	1,933	3,257	2,120	3,239	4,013	2,387	7,254	10,088	13,292	8,392
TYPE OF PRIMARY MORTGAGE												
FHA	5,172	392	44	815	450	263	526	294	514	1,182	2,252	1,225
VA	2,356	232	43	398	118	165	239	113	170	467	1,086	632
Farmers Home Administration	381	40	11	47	22	43	29	54	47	114	158	62
Other types	27,906	2,733	1,650	1,579	1,276	2,265	2,881	1,426	5,732	7,793	8,583	5,798
Don't know	1,336	111	119	164	149	172	111	146	265	202	585	284
Not reported	1,875	93	65	255	104	331	227	353	527	330	628	390
MORTGAGE ORIGINATION												
Placed new mortgages(s)	34,241	3,432	1,816	2,853	1,915	2,955	3,862	2,165	6,351	8,907	11,805	7,179
Primary obtained when property acquired	24,393	3,262	1,574	2,272	1,592	1,843	3,787	1,669	4,240	6,298	9,074	4,781
Obtained later	9,848	171	241	582	323	1,112	76	496	2,111	2,608	2,731	2,398
Date not reported	-	-	-	-	-	-	-	-	-	-	-	-
Assumed	1,014	15	69	118	67	103	118	58	67	153	524	270
Wrap-around	19	-	-	4	-	-	-	-	8	-	11	-
Combination of the above	3,682	154	48	278	129	178	28	162	822	1,021	916	923
Origin not reported	69	-	-	4	9	2	5	2	6	7	37	19
PAYMENT PLAN OF PRIMARY MORTGAGE												
Fixed-payment, self-amortizing	30,002	2,753	1,648	2,574	1,671	2,296	3,016	1,661	5,392	7,925	10,519	6,166
Adjustable-rate mortgage	4,473	486	113	231	184	335	517	188	900	1,116	1,233	1,224
Adjustable-term mortgage	-	-	-	-	-	-	-	-	-	-	-	-
Graduated-payment mortgage	370	80	4	24	27	19	74	18	67	79	114	109
Balloon	586	68	61	19	28	48	69	35	53	244	178	112
Other	567	23	14	46	41	68	24	53	102	144	200	121
Combination of the above	336	28	5	3	16	32	22	2	71	93	103	69
Not reported	2,691	162	88	361	152	441	292	429	669	486	946	590

See notes at end of table.

Mortgage Characteristics

TABLE 4.26. SELECTED MORTGAGE CHARACTERISTICS FOR OWNER-OCCUPIED HOUSING UNITS: 1995 - Continued

(In thousands, except as noted)

CHARACTERISTIC	Total owner-occupied units	New construction (Within 4 years)	Mobile homes	Black	His-panic	Elderly (65+)	Moved in past year	Below poverty level	North-east	Mid-west	South	West
LENDERS OF PRIMARY AND SECONDARY MORTGAGES												
Only borrowed from firm(s)	34,375	3,381	1,730	2,734	1,817	2,786	3,516	1,819	6,408	9,107	11,554	7,306
Only borrowed from seller	766	3	78	56	90	18	141	98	46	216	359	146
Only borrowed from other individual(s)	435	51	31	30	23	27	41	23	51	116	181	88
Borrowed from a firm and a seller	105	-	6	1	15	3	8	2	11	13	39	43
Borrowed from a firm and other individual	81	4	-	4	8	4	8	-	17	15	19	31
Borrowed from seller and other individual	16	-	-	2	-	-	2	3	4	5	3	5
One or both sources not reported	3,247	162	87	429	167	401	297	442	718	615	1,140	774
ITEMS INCLUDED IN PRIMARY MORTGAGE PAYMENT [1]												
Principal and interest only	18,338	1,640	1,551	1,362	836	2,164	1,676	1,470	3,651	4,781	5,615	4,291
Property taxes	19,461	1,814	176	1,719	1,214	995	2,166	826	3,458	5,084	7,045	3,874
Property insurance	17,016	1,708	281	1,667	1,122	818	1,925	717	2,384	4,331	6,895	3,406
Other	1,261	140	36	92	88	51	146	46	254	272	484	250
Not reported	330	41	49	31	18	9	75	14	45	60	169	55
YEAR PRIMARY MORTGAGE ORIGINATED												
1995 to 1999	3,851	793	301	297	191	174	2,715	158	615	993	1,396	846
1990 to 1994	21,174	2,802	1,093	1,409	1,204	1,210	1,243	1,076	3,614	5,680	7,077	4,803
1985 to 1989	6,677	....	408	588	356	546	27	479	1,511	1,634	2,248	1,284
1980 to 1984	2,323	....	104	285	143	290	13	171	483	555	858	427
1975 to 1979	2,812	....	18	336	129	364	10	228	521	739	974	578
1970 to 1974	1,358	....	6	239	80	304	3	156	292	327	470	269
1960 to 1969	587	....	2	79	12	229	2	87	153	106	190	137
1950 to 1959	106	....	-	16	4	82	-	13	35	23	34	14
1949 or earlier	26	....	-	4	-	26	-	4	8	4	6	7
Not reported	113	6	1	4	1	14	-	16	23	26	39	25
Median (Year)	1991	....	1992	1990	1991	1988	1995+	1990	1991	1991	1991	1992

See notes at end of table.

Mortgage Characteristics

TABLE 4.26. SELECTED MORTGAGE CHARACTERISTICS FOR OWNER-OCCUPIED HOUSING UNITS: 1995 - Continued
(In thousands, except as noted)

CHARACTERISTIC	Total owner-occupied units	Housing unit characteristics		Household characteristics					Regions			
		New con-struction (Within 4 years)	Mobile homes	Black	Hispanic	Elderly (65+)	Moved in past year	Below poverty level	North-east	Midwest	South	West
TERM OF PRIMARY MORTGAGE AT ORIGINATION OR ASSUMPTION												
Less than 8 years	981	127	286	77	67	70	220	115	76	331	384	191
8 to 12	1,012	90	325	80	66	86	137	106	124	264	478	146
13 to 17	4,149	592	726	275	196	286	578	279	804	1,145	1,717	482
18 to 22	2,058	255	204	169	91	220	260	144	385	662	774	236
23 to 27	1,556	78	38	117	49	178	105	109	403	389	531	233
28 to 32	17,972	2,248	96	1,852	1,268	1,175	2,608	1,049	3,050	4,299	6,291	4,333
33 years or more	418	31	5	59	24	54	26	50	57	96	177	89
Variable	-	-	-	-	-	-	-	-	-	-	-	-
Not reported	10,879	180	253	628	358	1,170	80	536	2,356	2,902	2,940	2,682
Median (Years)	29	29	15	30	30	29	29	29	29	29	29	30
REMAINING YEARS MORTGAGED												
Less than 8 years	5,712	164	827	523	276	937	260	535	1,098	1,648	2,112	854
8 to 12	5,503	255	405	464	231	559	159	351	1,150	1,518	1,956	880
13 to 17	5,930	491	362	476	269	435	576	375	1,117	1,659	2,076	1,079
18 to 22	4,027	243	194	412	220	310	278	227	836	991	1,398	802
23 to 27	7,116	511	56	548	470	318	133	422	1,330	1,646	2,292	1,848
28 to 32	9,588	1,909	62	714	617	363	2,582	325	1,459	2,339	3,065	2,724
33 years or more	100	20	5	2	11	4	24	7	11	19	23	47
Variable	-	-	-	-	-	-	-	-	-	-	-	-
Not reported	1,049	9	23	108	25	313	2	144	253	267	372	158
Median (Years)	20	28	10	19	24	13	29	16	19	18	19	24
CURRENT INTEREST RATE												
Less than 6 percent	1,089	123	25	84	71	86	159	63	218	250	367	255
6 to 7.9	9,430	1,564	191	699	525	729	1,496	541	1,621	2,375	3,263	2,172
8 to 9.9	11,211	1,265	510	1,112	804	804	1,835	725	1,814	2,936	4,394	2,068
10 to 11.9	2,618	223	402	304	196	194	300	235	540	653	990	434
12 to 13.9	723	70	314	107	47	71	96	91	91	155	390	87
14 to 15.9	228	33	117	48	12	31	17	40	20	48	127	33
16 to 17.9	49	-	25	2	1	7	3	6	3	17	27	2
18 to 19.9	81	-	35	26	9	13	3	17	6	10	60	5
20 percent or more	42	-	25	9	4	2	-	7	2	9	24	7
Not reported	13,553	324	290	867	452	1,302	104	662	2,940	3,635	3,650	3,328
Median (Percent)	8.3	7.9	10.4	8.7	8.5	8.3	8.3	8.7	8.3	8.4	8.5	8.1

See notes at end of table.

Mortgage Characteristics

TABLE 4.26. SELECTED MORTGAGE CHARACTERISTICS FOR OWNER-OCCUPIED HOUSING UNITS: 1995 - Continued

(In thousands, except as noted)

CHARACTERISTIC	Total owner-occupied units	Housing unit characteristics		Household characteristics					Regions			
		New construction (Within 4 years)	Mobile homes	Black	Hispanic	Elderly (65+)	Moved in past year	Below poverty level	North-east	Mid-west	South	West
TOTAL OUTSTANDING PRINCIPAL AMOUNT												
Less than $10,000	3,566	114	686	452	211	633	212	473	637	973	1,421	535
$10,000 to 19,999	2,638	213	477	361	152	289	256	231	460	722	1,112	344
$20,000 to 29,999	2,484	192	266	266	150	217	316	223	345	835	988	316
$30,000 to 39,999	2,231	120	120	207	145	191	251	163	291	737	903	300
$40,000 to 49,999	2,145	169	55	244	157	148	283	140	310	607	904	325
$50,000 to 59,999	1,945	193	16	209	104	104	258	91	283	496	809	358
$60,000 to 69,999	1,828	292	7	151	132	97	307	86	250	433	846	298
$70,000 to 79,999	1,614	268	-	138	113	48	343	68	246	414	661	292
$80,000 to 99,999	2,403	545	15	153	166	71	524	71	461	523	803	616
$100,000 to 119,999	1,385	304	-	75	95	43	320	58	332	269	367	418
$120,000 to 149,999	1,406	403	-	75	143	40	399	50	294	236	401	475
$150,000 to 199,999	1,077	298	-	44	65	24	259	55	259	135	255	428
$200,000 to 249,999	294	61	-	5	22	11	64	10	67	19	79	128
$250,000 to 299,999	205	50	-	6	7	9	53	6	35	20	39	111
$300,000 or more	251	54	-	4	5	12	64	1	42	36	53	121
Not reported	13,553	324	290	867	452	1,302	104	662	2,940	3,635	3,650	3,328
Median (Dollars)	48,466	82,818	12,836	35,593	51,814	22,110	72,069	27,095	53,968	39,468	44,382	71,937
CURRENT TOTAL LOAN AS PERCENT OF VALUE												
Less than 20 percent	4,637	148	304	438	265	830	209	470	1,061	1,123	1,528	925
20 to 39	3,567	286	223	379	231	380	266	298	623	988	1,332	624
40 to 59	4,504	547	232	340	269	300	447	301	690	1,296	1,614	903
60 to 79	6,682	1,127	322	553	402	262	1,228	351	1,019	1,772	2,583	1,307
80 to 89	3,112	549	195	319	230	90	737	144	473	679	1,328	632
90 to 99	2,125	483	189	270	185	50	793	103	274	419	952	480
100 percent or more	846	136	178	91	86	25	230	58	175	176	304	191
Not reported	13,553	324	290	867	452	1,302	104	662	2,940	3,635	3,650	3,328
Median (Percent)	60.1	71.7	63.9	61.3	63.4	27.3	76.8	46.3	53.7	57.2	62.7	61.2

Source: U.S. Bureau of the Census and U.S. Department of Housing and Urban Development, "American Housing Survey for the United States in 1995." Current Housing Reports H150/95RV. Issued July 1997.

(1) Figures may not add to totals because more than one category may apply to a unit.

(-) means zero or rounds to zero.

Mortgage Delinquency and Foreclosure

TABLE 4.27. MORTGAGE DELINQUENCY RATES AND FORECLOSURES STARTED: 1986 TO 1997 (Percent)											
	Delinquency rates								Foreclosures started during period			
PERIOD	Total past due				90 days or more past due							
	All loans	Conven-tional loans	FHA loans	VA loans	All loans	Conven-tional loans	FHA loans	VA loans	All loans	Conven-tional loans	FHA loans	VA loans
1986												
First quarter	5.74	4.05	7.44	6.68	0.98	0.67	1.26	1.18	0.24	0.18	0.30	0.27
Second quarter	5.69	3.92	7.29	6.63	1.04	0.71	1.32	1.25	0.25	0.18	0.31	0.29
Third quarter	5.51	3.72	7.08	6.63	1.02	0.67	1.30	1.29	0.27	0.20	0.32	0.31
Fourth quarter	5.31	3.49	6.83	6.36	0.99	0.61	1.29	1.24	0.26	0.19	0.33	0.31
1987												
First quarter	5.23	3.40	6.73	6.31	1.01	0.65	1.28	1.27	0.26	0.19	0.31	0.31
Second quarter	5.06	3.34	6.53	6.20	0.95	0.65	1.19	1.17	0.25	0.18	0.32	0.29
Third quarter	4.69	2.85	6.35	6.04	0.85	0.57	1.11	1.07	0.26	0.15	0.35	0.32
Fourth quarter	4.89	3.01	6.62	6.27	0.89	0.55	1.18	1.16	0.27	0.18	0.36	0.35
1988												
First quarter	4.88	2.93	6.66	6.26	0.87	0.54	1.17	1.13	0.27	0.17	0.36	0.33
Second quarter	4.90	2.95	6.71	6.36	0.88	0.53	1.21	1.19	0.27	0.16	0.36	0.32
Third quarter	4.70	2.87	6.39	6.00	0.83	0.53	1.10	1.09	0.27	0.17	0.36	0.31
Fourth quarter	4.69	2.99	6.47	6.27	0.83	0.55	1.09	1.14	0.27	0.19	0.38	0.31
1989												
First quarter	4.74	2.97	6.61	6.43	0.82	0.52	1.12	1.13	0.29	0.18	0.41	0.37
Second quarter	4.56	2.90	6.28	6.17	0.79	0.51	1.07	1.11	0.30	0.19	0.43	0.40
Third quarter	4.91	3.14	6.94	6.47	0.78	0.50	1.08	1.06	0.28	0.18	0.39	0.35
Fourth quarter	5.03	3.11	7.12	6.74	0.76	0.46	1.07	1.04	0.28	0.18	0.40	0.35
1990												
First quarter	4.54	2.84	6.48	6.17	0.70	0.38	1.04	1.03	0.31	0.21	0.44	0.39
Second quarter	4.52	2.87	6.54	6.19	0.70	0.37	1.10	1.04	0.31	0.21	0.41	0.38
Third quarter	4.83	3.13	6.84	6.58	0.71	0.41	1.10	1.03	0.33	0.21	0.47	0.44
Fourth quarter	4.75	3.12	6.85	6.46	0.73	0.41	1.16	1.06	0.29	0.21	0.41	0.40
1991												
First quarter	5.13	3.42	7.29	6.69	0.78	0.47	1.17	1.05	0.31	0.24	0.42	0.38
Second quarter	5.26	3.44	7.55	7.04	0.79	0.46	1.21	1.09	0.34	0.26	0.43	0.40
Third quarter	4.87	3.02	7.22	6.73	0.82	0.44	1.31	1.16	0.35	0.28	0.44	0.45
Fourth quarter	4.85	3.16	7.17	6.62	0.81	0.46	1.29	1.13	0.35	0.31	0.43	0.44

See notes at end of table.

Mortgage Delinquency and Foreclosure

TABLE 4.27. MORTGAGE DELINQUENCY RATES AND FORECLOSURES STARTED: 1986 TO 1997 - Continued
(Percent)

| PERIOD | Delinquency rates | | | | | | | | Foreclosures started during period | | | |
| | Total past due | | | | 90 days or more past due | | | | | | | |
	All loans	Conven-tional loans	FHA loans	VA loans	All loans	Conven-tional loans	FHA loans	VA loans	All loans	Conven-tional loans	FHA loans	VA loans
1992												
First quarter	4.69	3.08	7.05	6.54	0.80	0.47	1.32	1.13	0.33	0.26	0.42	0.41
Second quarter	4.69	3.06	7.12	6.51	0.83	0.49	1.38	1.17	0.33	0.25	0.43	0.40
Third quarter	4.60	2.90	7.19	6.53	0.83	0.48	1.39	1.20	0.33	0.25	0.45	0.38
Fourth quarter	4.29	2.76	8.91	6.25	0.76	0.45	1.31	1.09	0.34	0.26	0.48	0.41
1993												
First quarter	4.31	2.74	6.99	6.30	0.78	0.46	1.35	1.14	0.32	0.23	0.47	0.43
Second quarter	4.26	2.66	7.21	6.37	0.78	0.45	1.41	1.15	0.32	0.25	0.48	0.42
Third quarter	4.22	2.71	7.13	6.27	0.77	0.46	1.40	1.17	0.31	0.24	0.46	0.38
Fourth quarter	4.09	2.52	7.22	6.25	0.76	0.42	1.45	1.17	0.31	0.22	0.49	0.43
1994												
First quarter	4.13	2.62	7.29	6.30	0.76	0.44	1.45	1.19	0.31	0.22	0.51	0.44
Second quarter	4.17	2.67	7.29	6.34	0.81	0.50	1.46	1.22	0.34	0.24	0.56	0.49
Third quarter	3.93	2.49	7.04	6.04	0.74	0.43	1.43	1.16	0.34	0.22	0.61	0.53
Fourth quarter	4.15	2.63	7.40	6.35	0.73	0.42	1.43	1.18	0.33	0.22	0.54	0.47
1995												
First quarter	3.96	2.49	7.12	6.09	0.72	0.42	1.37	1.15	0.32	0.21	0.56	0.49
Second quarter	4.15	2.68	7.36	6.35	0.76	0.44	1.46	1.19	0.33	0.21	0.54	0.51
Third quarter	4.44	2.94	7.89	6.68	0.78	0.45	1.56	1.23	0.32	0.23	0.51	0.48
Fourth quarter	4.44	2.96	7.83	6.64	0.71	0.40	1.46	1.10	0.33	0.25	0.51	0.51
1996												
First quarter	4.47	2.88	8.17	6.74	0.70	0.35	1.57	1.10	0.37	0.28	0.56	0.53
Second quarter	4.35	2.81	8.09	6.78	0.63	0.31	1.44	1.07	0.34	0.23	0.58	0.47
Third quarter	4.18	2.70	7.89	6.68	0.59	0.30	1.33	1.08	0.33	0.24	0.58	0.43
Fourth quarter	4.31	2.74	8.03	6.77	0.61	0.32	1.28	1.12	0.33	0.24	0.58	0.42
1997												
First quarter	4.35	2.89	8.19	6.96	0.56	0.31	1.20	1.10	0.37	0.26	0.66	0.51
Second quarter	4.24	2.76	7.94	6.87	0.58	0.32	1.19	1.12	0.34	0.25	0.57	0.47
Third quarter	4.26	2.78	8.13	6.88	0.57	0.30	1.21	1.14	0.35	0.26	0.59	0.49
Fourth quarter	4.36	2.86	8.27	7.02	0.62	0.34	1.32	1.22	0.37	0.27	0.65	0.58

Source: Mortgage Bankers Association of America, National Delinquency Survey.

Data are for one-to-four-family residential nonfarm mortgage loans.

All data are seasonally adjusted to annual rates using the X-11Q Variant of the Census Method II seasonal adjustment program.

Secondary Mortgage Market

TABLE 4.28. PURCHASES AND SALES OF LONG-TERM RESIDENTIAL MORTGAGE LOANS BY INSTITUTION AND PROPERTY TYPE: 1970 TO 1996
(Millions of current dollars)

INSTITUTION AND PROPERTY TYPE	1970		1971		1972		1973		1974	
	Purchases	Sales	Purchases	Sales	Purchases	Sales	Purchases	Sales	Purchases	Sales
COMMERCIAL BANKS										
1-4-family homes	521	1,674	1,130	1,971	1,046	2,245	925	2,010	372	1,623
Multifamily	34	74	6	34	40	93	24	75	144	60
Total	555	1,748	1,136	2,005	1,086	2,338	949	2,085	516	1,683
MUTUAL SAVINGS BANKS										
1-4-family homes	1,408	254	1,874	175	2,708	202	1,958	161	1,039	228
Multifamily	285	16	266	59	263	59	275	64	261	77
Total	1,693	270	2,140	234	2,971	261	2,233	225	1,300	305
SAVINGS AND LOAN ASSOCIATIONS										
1-4-family homes	3,397	804	6,635	1,654	9,502	2,886	5,862	2,759	4,824	3,093
Multifamily	229	92	467	187	622	425	539	414	433	228
Total	3,626	896	7,102	1,841	10,124	3,311	6,401	3,173	5,257	3,321
LIFE INSURANCE COMPANIES										
1-4-family homes	198	19	185	37	207	5	247	8	179	24
Multifamily	281	3	149	8	107	1	124	1	128	5
Total	479	22	334	45	314	6	371	9	307	29
PRIVATE NON-INSURED PENSION FUNDS										
1-4-family homes	11	64	15	235	3	405	6	131	25	1
Multifamily	29	22	0	270	1	286	4	79	6	5
Total	40	86	15	505	4	691	10	210	31	6
MORTGAGE COMPANIES										
1-4-family homes	60	9,613	403	12,394	1,431	14,315	1,382	14,980	880	14,886
Multifamily	0	1,438	12	1,583	18	2,257	11	1,871	9	639
Total	60	11,051	415	13,977	1,449	16,572	1,393	16,851	889	15,525
PRIVATE MORTGAGE-BACKED CONDUITS [1]										
1-4-family homes	132	0	155	17	266	111	13	39	9	0
Multifamily	0	0	5	0	20	0	17	0	11	0
Total	132	0	160	17	286	111	30	39	20	0
STATE AND LOCAL RETIREMENT FUNDS										
1-4-family homes	453	13	192	1	96	5	302	24	250	28
Multifamily	52	11	69	0	29	3	71	41	98	18
Total	505	24	261	1	125	8	373	65	348	46
FEDERAL CREDIT AGENCIES										
1-4-family homes	5,371	1,631	3,733	1,853	4,996	3,799	7,396	4,315	8,801	2,534
Multifamily	88	96	242	56	346	204	701	306	805	395
Total	5,459	1,727	3,975	1,909	5,342	4,003	8,097	4,621	9,606	2,929
MORTGAGE POOLS										
1-4-family homes	1,841	119	3,947	197	4,756	157	4,178	436	6,305	692
Multifamily	25	9	52	8	322	9	268	15	316	35
Total	1,866	128	3,999	205	5,078	166	4,446	451	6,621	727
STATE AND LOCAL CREDIT AGENCIES										
1-4-family homes	14	0	24	0	65	1	302	0	354	0
Multifamily	4	0	6	14	53	1	109	0	173	8
Total	18	0	30	14	118	2	411	0	527	8
TOTAL										
1-4-family homes	13,406	14,192	18,292	18,534	25,076	24,129	22,573	24,862	23,039	23,111
Multifamily	1,027	1,760	1,275	2,220	1,820	3,339	2,144	2,866	2,383	1,471
Total	14,433	15,952	19,567	20,754	26,896	27,468	24,717	27,728	25,422	24,582

See notes at end of table.

Secondary Mortgage Market

TABLE 4.28. PURCHASES AND SALES OF LONG-TERM RESIDENTIAL MORTGAGE LOANS BY INSTITUTION AND PROPERTY TYPE: 1970 TO 1996 - Continued
(Millions of current dollars)

INSTITUTION AND PROPERTY TYPE	1975		1976		1977		1978		1979	
	Purchases	Sales	Purchases	Sales	Purchases	Sales	Purchases	Sales	Purchases	Sales
COMMERCIAL BANKS										
1-4-family homes	236	2,932	839	4,023	1,756	5,839	1,674	6,773	2,112	6,526
Multifamily	30	27	18	153	16	104	15	109	46	85
Total	266	2,959	857	4,176	1,772	5,943	1,689	6,882	2,158	6,611
MUTUAL SAVINGS BANKS										
1-4-family homes	1,103	235	2,127	457	2,947	221	2,800	296	2,633	521
Multifamily	343	32	290	65	324	33	290	33	129	26
Total	1,446	267	2,417	522	3,271	254	3,090	329	2,762	547
SAVINGS AND LOAN ASSOCIATIONS										
1-4-family homes	7,167	4,726	11,106	7,714	13,155	12,955	10,283	14,999	11,608	18,108
Multifamily	393	102	820	388	665	610	366	381	323	287
Total	7,560	4,828	11,926	8,102	13,820	13,565	10,649	15,380	11,931	18,395
LIFE INSURANCE COMPANIES										
1-4-family homes	126	25	114	3	194	5	814	20	1,454	237
Multifamily	76	0	34	0	45	12	59	24	59	0
Total	202	25	148	3	239	17	873	44	1,513	237
PRIVATE NON-INSURED PENSION FUNDS										
1-4-family homes	11	10	12	5	77	34	184	15	293	79
Multifamily	8	25	0	12	90	77	0	65	16	11
Total	19	35	12	17	167	111	184	80	309	90
MORTGAGE COMPANIES										
1-4-family homes	785	14,451	2,221	17,332	4,116	27,327	3,826	35,037	5,693	44,412
Multifamily	24	807	4	593	53	1,461	162	1,771	29	1,471
Total	809	15,258	2,225	17,925	4,169	28,788	3,988	36,808	5,722	45,883
PRIVATE MORTGAGE-BACKED CONDUITS [1]										
1-4-family homes	6	4	12	7	4	51	24	48	8	11
Multifamily	8	9	8	24	15	60	3	87	3	31
Total	14	13	20	31	19	111	27	135	11	42
STATE AND LOCAL RETIREMENT FUNDS										
1-4-family homes	138	87	157	27	302	44	423	46	480	42
Multifamily	156	21	122	3	94	4	510	11	496	13
Total	294	108	279	30	396	48	933	57	976	55
FEDERAL CREDIT AGENCIES										
1-4-family homes	10,732	6,722	9,573	10,831	9,295	7,575	18,779	9,088	15,759	5,825
Multifamily	1,261	892	728	1,202	1,410	1,363	1,873	2,668	1,511	3,022
Total	11,993	7,614	10,301	12,033	10,705	8,938	20,652	11,756	17,270	8,847
MORTGAGE POOLS										
1-4-family homes	11,156	454	16,367	534	23,433	1,309	23,202	1,427	27,990	775
Multifamily	594	32	679	24	1,428	81	2,018	63	2,430	0
Total	11,750	486	17,046	558	24,861	1,390	25,220	1,490	30,420	775
STATE AND LOCAL CREDIT AGENCIES										
1-4-family homes	420	7	311	0	432	0	945	9	1,740	0
Multifamily	263	250	38	58	25	18	72	277	159	72
Total	683	257	349	58	457	18	1,017	286	1,899	72
TOTAL										
1-4-family homes	31,881	29,652	42,840	40,934	55,712	55,361	62,953	67,758	69,771	76,536
Multifamily	3,154	2,196	2,741	2,524	4,162	3,821	5,369	5,489	5,201	5,018
Total	35,035	31,848	45,581	43,458	59,874	59,182	68,322	73,247	74,972	81,554

See notes at end of table.

Secondary Mortgage Market

TABLE 4.28. PURCHASES AND SALES OF LONG-TERM RESIDENTIAL MORTGAGE LOANS BY INSTITUTION AND PROPERTY TYPE: 1970 TO 1996 - Continued
(Millions of current dollars)

INSTITUTION AND PROPERTY TYPE	1980		1981		1982		1983		1984	
	Purchases	Sales	Purchases	Sales	Purchases	Sales	Purchases	Sales	Purchases	Sales
COMMERCIAL BANKS										
1-4-family homes	4,280	7,500	3,120	4,497	1,913	7,888	3,484	14,842	5,116	12,682
Multifamily	116	26	209	36	327	8	197	127	205	23
Total	4,396	7,526	3,329	4,533	2,240	7,896	3,681	14,969	5,321	12,705
MUTUAL SAVINGS BANKS										
1-4-family homes	966	725	245	446	1,425	2,179	2,412	2,617	2,961	2,530
Multifamily	122	35	28	25	9	21	104	241	193	423
Total	1,088	760	273	471	1,434	2,200	2,516	2,858	3,154	2,953
SAVINGS AND LOAN ASSOCIATIONS										
1-4-family homes	12,440	15,523	10,037	12,402	20,156	50,776	32,919	50,173	44,660	54,169
Multifamily	253	331	192	159	608	1,761	3,834	1,511	4,236	2,463
Total	12,693	15,854	10,229	12,561	20,764	52,537	36,753	51,684	48,896	56,632
LIFE INSURANCE COMPANIES										
1-4-family homes	1,329	134	159	255	234	238	213	703	214	841
Multifamily	56	4	40	53	21	3	45	9	20	27
Total	1,385	138	199	308	255	241	258	712	234	868
PRIVATE NON-INSURED PENSION FUNDS										
1-4-family homes	183	5	41	21	133	17	87	5	81	41
Multifamily	2	12	6	0	11	2	51	1	138	3
Total	185	17	47	21	144	19	138	6	219	44
MORTGAGE COMPANIES										
1-4-family homes	3,422	31,500	4,348	26,607	4,947	29,635	13,092	70,084	10,885	55,232
Multifamily	10	1,322	114	1,781	5	682	35	443	212	545
Total	3,432	32,822	4,462	28,388	4,952	30,317	13,127	70,527	11,097	55,777
PRIVATE MORTGAGE-BACKED CONDUITS [1]										
1-4-family homes	2	10	0	13	3,049	0	5,500	0	7,658	0
Multifamily	11	7	0	0	0	21	0	0	0	0
Total	13	17	0	13	3,049	21	5,500	0	7,658	0
STATE AND LOCAL RETIREMENT FUNDS										
1-4-family homes	405	9	424	15	207	12	226	9	163	0
Multifamily	513	1	1,029	3	900	29	868	0	264	27
Total	918	10	1,453	18	1,107	41	1,094	9	427	27
FEDERAL CREDIT AGENCIES										
1-4-family homes	14,381	7,226	11,189	5,853	18,411	7,973	25,332	9,646	23,842	7,853
Multifamily	918	1,552	580	2,415	143	3,028	227	2,655	1,043	2,021
Total	15,299	8,778	11,769	8,268	18,554	11,001	25,559	12,301	24,885	9,874
MORTGAGE POOLS										
1-4-family homes	26,717	3,203	21,415	3,085	57,070	2,849	85,419	4,044	64,080	4,133
Multifamily	949	6	836	4	438	5	1,252	7	1,767	9
Total	27,666	3,209	22,251	3,089	57,508	2,854	86,671	4,051	65,847	4,142
STATE AND LOCAL CREDIT AGENCIES										
1-4-family homes	5,842	0	5,021	0	2,792	0	5,218	0	5,443	0
Multifamily	155	40	60	4	122	0	88	0	28	0
Total	5,997	40	5,081	4	2,914	0	5,306	0	5,471	0
TOTAL										
1-4-family homes	69,967	65,835	55,999	53,194	110,337	101,567	173,902	152,123	165,102	137,481
Multifamily	3,105	3,336	3,095	4,480	2,584	5,560	6,702	4,994	8,106	5,541
Total	73,072	69,171	59,094	57,674	112,921	107,127	180,604	157,117	173,208	143,022

See notes at end of table.

Secondary Mortgage Market

TABLE 4.28. PURCHASES AND SALES OF LONG-TERM RESIDENTIAL MORTGAGE LOANS BY INSTITUTION AND PROPERTY TYPE: 1970 TO 1996 - Continued
(Millions of current dollars)

INSTITUTION AND PROPERTY TYPE	1985 Purchases	1985 Sales	1986 Purchases	1986 Sales	1987 Purchases	1987 Sales	1988 Purchases	1988 Sales	1989 Purchases	1989 Sales
COMMERCIAL BANKS										
1-4-family homes	6,276	21,730	10,922	39,087	21,246	50,258	24,301	39,475	26,565	46,166
Multifamily	432	54	115	48	161	95	81	80	544	186
Total	6,708	21,784	11,037	39,135	21,407	50,353	24,382	39,555	27,109	46,352
MUTUAL SAVINGS BANKS										
1-4-family homes	1,190	8,325	3,298	12,650	3,329	12,568	4,115	10,428	1,432	12,451
Multifamily	89	1,371	49	225	79	164	164	332	22	1,535
Total	1,279	9,696	3,347	12,875	3,408	12,732	4,279	10,760	1,454	13,986
SAVINGS AND LOAN ASSOCIATIONS										
1-4-family homes	48,843	93,748	62,076	156,944	56,726	116,059	49,492	97,858	38,318	100,827
Multifamily	3,543	3,040	2,359	3,218	2,795	4,039	2,340	4,043	1,040	3,800
Total	52,386	96,788	64,435	160,162	59,521	120,098	51,832	101,901	39,358	104,627
LIFE INSURANCE COMPANIES										
1-4-family homes	209	1,521	883	1,538	1,336	1,071	2,266	3,668	2,085	1,447
Multifamily	110	53	79	35	266	89	141	7	214	76
Total	319	1,574	962	1,573	1,602	1,160	2,407	3,675	2,299	1,523
PRIVATE NON-INSURED PENSION FUNDS										
1-4-family homes	127	0	55	40	90	238	98	34	419	3
Multifamily	132	72	265	4	196	210	188	117	15	1
Total	259	72	320	44	286	448	286	151	434	4
MORTGAGE COMPANIES										
1-4-family homes	31,252	138,423	61,819	226,790	86,812	265,704	60,197	203,247	105,429	251,722
Multifamily	561	2,997	275	6,519	664	3,937	229	4,425	13	4,573
Total	31,813	141,420	62,094	233,309	87,476	269,641	60,426	207,672	105,442	256,295
PRIVATE MORTGAGE-BACKED CONDUITS [1]										
1-4-family homes	7,870	0	16,179	0	21,166	0	23,411	0	16,396	0
Multifamily	0	0	0	0	0	0	0	0	0	0
Total	7,870	0	16,179	0	21,166	0	23,411	0	16,396	0
STATE AND LOCAL RETIREMENT FUNDS										
1-4-family homes	200	9	323	242	928	3	650	222	973	146
Multifamily	186	0	270	9	162	16	73	13	229	21
Total	386	9	593	251	1,090	19	723	235	1,202	167
FEDERAL CREDIT AGENCIES										
1-4-family homes	27,348	4,952	35,403	13,307	23,691	6,134	29,135	6,326	27,139	4,041
Multifamily	4,359	892	3,563	2,118	1,445	1,100	1,962	402	3,728	0
Total	31,707	5,844	38,966	15,425	25,136	7,234	31,097	6,728	30,867	4,041
MORTGAGE POOLS										
1-4-family homes	109,584	2,139	253,527	1,008	225,251	232	142,769	258	192,261	148
Multifamily	2,594	2,150	6,457	0	5,424	0	5,667	0	4,236	0
Total	112,178	4,289	259,984	1,008	230,675	232	148,436	258	196,497	148
STATE AND LOCAL CREDIT AGENCIES										
1-4-family homes	5,976	0	5,651	1	4,173	0	6,055	20	6,346	0
Multifamily	29	0	26	0	62	0	61	1	28	0
Total	6,005	0	5,677	1	4,235	0	6,116	21	6,374	0
TOTAL										
1-4-family homes	238,875	270,847	450,136	451,607	444,748	452,267	342,489	361,536	417,363	416,951
Multifamily	12,035	10,629	13,458	12,176	11,254	9,650	10,905	9,421	10,069	10,192
Total	250,910	281,476	463,594	463,783	456,002	461,917	353,394	370,957	427,432	427,143

See notes at end of table.

Secondary Mortgage Market

TABLE 4.28. PURCHASES AND SALES OF LONG-TERM RESIDENTIAL MORTGAGE LOANS BY INSTITUTION AND PROPERTY TYPE: 1970 TO 1996 - Continued
(Millions of current dollars)

INSTITUTION AND PROPERTY TYPE	1990		1991		1992		1993		1994	
	Purchases	Sales	Purchases	Sales	Purchases	Sales	Purchases	Sales	Purchases	Sales
COMMERCIAL BANKS										
1-4-family homes	33,275	68,803	26,553	67,242	42,239	101,877	59,134	136,015	49,699	85,728
Multifamily	402	962	185	24	598	1	736	275	670	122
Total	33,677	69,765	26,738	67,266	42,837	101,878	59,870	136,290	50,369	85,850
MUTUAL SAVINGS BANKS										
1-4-family homes	3,564	12,095	4,243	10,751	4,205	16,544	6,448	22,205	1,999	12,241
Multifamily	115	45	61	82	0	4	48	208	0	293
Total	3,679	12,140	4,304	10,833	4,205	16,548	6,496	22,413	1,999	12,534
SAVINGS AND LOAN ASSOCIATIONS										
1-4-family homes	37,512	108,614	50,036	120,359	53,733	166,370	58,219	147,435	44,851	88,872
Multifamily	1,101	2,084	1,035	5,232	1,192	3,871	1,176	2,171	1,261	2,579
Total	38,613	110,698	51,071	125,591	54,925	170,241	59,395	149,606	46,112	91,451
LIFE INSURANCE COMPANIES										
1-4-family homes	774	442	418	491	537	678	849	1,183	588	666
Multifamily	432	58	70	71	44	96	61	74	57	106
Total	1,206	500	488	562	581	774	910	1,257	645	772
PRIVATE NON-INSURED PENSION FUNDS										
1-4-family homes	41	0	0	0	0	0	116	0	636	0
Multifamily	0	47	0	0	30	0	85	0	0	0
Total	41	47	0	0	30	0	201	0	636	0
MORTGAGE COMPANIES										
1-4-family homes	51,265	213,367	38,125	290,790	79,981	518,003	139,134	666,107	147,767	579,872
Multifamily	276	4,859	1,105	3,225	0	1,773	0	1,890	0	0
Total	51,541	218,226	39,230	294,015	79,981	519,776	139,134	667,997	147,767	579,872
PRIVATE MORTGAGE-BACKED CONDUITS [1]										
1-4-family homes	20,147	0	38,782	0	78,187	0	90,609	0	61,855	0
Multifamily	0	0	0	0	0	0	2,244	0	3,715	0
Total	20,147	0	38,782	0	78,187	0	92,853	0	65,570	0
STATE AND LOCAL RETIREMENT FUNDS										
1-4-family homes	243	16	953	33	1,119	56	298	0	505	0
Multifamily	14	11	20	0	61	0	199	0	121	0
Total	257	27	973	33	1,180	56	497	0	626	0
FEDERAL CREDIT AGENCIES										
1-4-family homes	63,890	27,955	68,805	26,895	95,766	22,951	116,238	12,863	85,259	6,681
Multifamily	15,350	4,259	14,604	4,521	8,700	5,811	4,888	2,381	3,991	2,252
Total	79,240	32,214	83,409	31,416	104,466	28,762	121,126	15,244	89,250	8,933
MORTGAGE POOLS										
1-4-family homes	229,740	0	271,732	5	463,158	6	561,754	0	353,348	13
Multifamily	3,135	0	4,638	0	3,996	0	2,486	0	4,070	0
Total	232,875	0	276,370	5	467,154	6	564,240	0	357,418	13
STATE AND LOCAL CREDIT AGENCIES										
1-4-family homes	4,948	1	4,190	14	3,422	0	2,853	113	4,391	67
Multifamily	49	44	173	0	243	0	336	0	360	29
Total	4,997	45	4,363	14	3,665	0	3,189	113	4,751	96
TOTAL										
1-4-family homes	445,399	431,293	503,837	516,580	822,347	826,485	1,035,652	985,921	750,898	774,140
Multifamily	20,874	12,369	21,891	13,155	14,864	11,556	12,259	6,999	14,245	5,381
Total	466,273	443,662	525,728	529,735	837,211	838,041	1,047,911	992,920	765,143	779,521

See notes at end of table.

Secondary Mortgage Market

TABLE 4.28. PURCHASES AND SALES OF LONG-TERM RESIDENTIAL MORTGAGE LOANS BY INSTITUTION AND PROPERTY TYPE: 1970 TO 1996 - Continued
(Millions of current dollars)

INSTITUTION AND PROPERTY TYPE	1995		1996	
	Purchases	Sales	Purchases	Sales
COMMERCIAL BANKS				
1-4-family homes	81,612	72,862	86,499	106,620
Multifamily	3,428	213	1,662	697
Total	85,040	73,075	88,161	107,317
MUTUAL SAVINGS BANKS				
1-4-family homes	6,867	8,933	3,750	11,970
Multifamily	11	42	43	0
Total	6,878	8,975	3,793	11,970
SAVINGS AND LOAN ASSOCIATIONS				
1-4-family homes	35,364	66,524	44,190	86,226
Multifamily	1,015	1,595	1,596	2,651
Total	36,379	68,119	45,786	88,877
LIFE INSURANCE COMPANIES				
1-4-family homes	892	897	800	640
Multifamily	91	117	52	307
Total	983	1,014	852	947
PRIVATE NON-INSURED PENSION FUNDS				
1-4-family homes	887	0	1,526	0
Multifamily	0	0	0	0
Total	887	0	1,526	0
MORTGAGE COMPANIES				
1-4-family homes	130,706	493,929	154,518	592,031
Multifamily	101	4,967	86	12,483
Total	130,807	498,896	154,604	604,514
PRIVATE MORTGAGE-BACKED CONDUITS [1]				
1-4-family homes	37,424	0	38,756	0
Multifamily	1,071	0	1,002	0
Total	38,495	0	39,758	0
STATE AND LOCAL RETIREMENT FUNDS				
1-4-family homes	512	0	700	0
Multifamily	102	0	234	0
Total	614	0	934	0
FEDERAL CREDIT AGENCIES				
1-4-family homes	92,423	5,554	99,516	2,025
Multifamily	3,454	1,989	3,912	1,099
Total	95,877	7,543	103,428	3,124
MORTGAGE POOLS				
1-4-family homes	263,388	23	357,914	0
Multifamily	5,902	0	7,917	0
Total	269,290	23	365,831	0
STATE AND LOCAL CREDIT AGENCIES				
1-4-family homes	5,764	57	4,836	40
Multifamily	347	0	176	0
Total	6,111	57	5,012	40
TOTAL				
1-4-family homes	655,839	648,779	793,005	799,552
Multifamily	15,522	8,923	16,680	17,237
Total	671,361	657,702	809,685	816,789

Source: U.S. Department of Housing and Urban Development, Survey of Mortgage Lending Activity.

(1) This category included real estate investment trusts (REITs) prior to 1982.

Sum of components may not add to totals due to rounding.

Secondary Mortgage Market

TABLE 4.29. ISSUES OF PASSTHROUGH MORTGAGE-BACKED SECURITIES BY FREDDIE MAC AND FANNIE MAE: 1984 TO 1996
(Millions of current dollars)

AGENCY AND YEAR	Conventional 1-4-family fixed-rate	Conventional 1-4-family adjustable-rate mortgages	FHA/VA[1]	Multifamily	Total
FREDDIE MAC					
1984	17,860	0	438	386	18,684
1985	36,081	250	1,253	1,245	38,829
1986	93,708	1,619	1,471	3,400	100,198
1987	67,040	4,993	833	2,152	75,018
1988	31,354	7,287	849	287	39,777
1989	54,492	17,864	575	587	73,518
1990	55,398	16,194	406	1,817	73,815
1991	84,622	7,574	144	0	92,340
1992	163,960	15,181	61	5	179,207
1993	187,876	20,052	20	0	207,948
1994	100,297	16,591	14	209	117,111
1995	71,253	14,267	2	355	85,877
1996	112,433	6,446	53	770	119,702
FANNIE MAE					
1984	9,381	2,684	1,022	459	13,546
1985	19,017	3,670	455	507	23,649
1986	43,102	6,197	10,718	549	60,566
1987	50,665	7,969	3,433	1,162	63,229
1988	32,144	18,407	569	3,758	54,878
1989	52,239	13,501	749	3,275	69,764
1990	84,171	11,703	132	689	96,695
1991	97,919	12,411	1,158	1,415	112,903
1992	180,776	12,108	303	850	194,037
1993	205,920	14,300	265	959	221,444
1994	112,879	15,305	201	2,237	130,622
1995	86,834	18,807	630	4,187	110,457
1996	128,393	15,273	535	5,668	149,869

Source: Fannie Mae and Freddie Mac, as published in Freddie Mac, "Secondary Mortgage Markets" (14, 2), July 1997.

(1) Mortgages backed by the Federal Housing Administration or Department of Veterans Affairs.

Column headings indicate the types of mortgages included in the pools funding the mortgage-backed securities.

Secondary Mortgage Market

TABLE 4.30. ISSUES OF PASSTHROUGH MORTGAGE-BACKED SECURITIES BY GINNIE MAE: 1984 TO 1996
(Millions of current dollars)

YEAR	FHA/VA 1- to 4-family fixed rates	FHA adjustable-rate mortgages	Mobile homes	FHA multifamily	Total
1984	26,584	16	623	874	28,097
1985	44,418	101	512	949	45,980
1986	97,634	962	896	1,941	101,433
1987	89,802	2,067	824	2,197	94,890
1988	50,659	1,777	482	2,263	55,181
1989	54,529	520	543	1,482	57,074
1990	61,781	716	598	1,300	64,395
1991	57,477	3,516	653	984	62,630
1992	69,371	11,211	434	901	81,917
1993	115,299	20,208	454	2,028	137,989
1994	80,304	28,798	139	1,944	111,185
1995	47,888	22,712	86	2,140	72,826
1996	75,538	22,960	56	2,653	101,207

Source: Ginnie Mae, as published in Freddie Mac, "Secondary Mortgage Markets" (14, 2). July 1997.

FHA is the Federal Housing Administration. VA is the Department of Veterans Affairs.

Column headings indicate the types of mortgages included in the pools funding the mortgage-backed securities.

Secondary Mortgage Market

TABLE 4.31. ISSUES OF MULTICLASS MORTGAGE SECURITIES BY FREDDIE MAC, FANNIE MAE, AND GINNIE MAE: 1984 TO 1996 (Millions of dollars)			
YEAR	Freddie Mac	Fannie Mae	Ginnie Mae
1984	1,805	0	0
1985	2,625	0	0
1986	2,233	0	0
1987	0	916	0
1988	12,986	11,199	0
1989	39,754	37,583	0
1990	40,479	60,917	0
1991	72,032	101,805	0
1992	131,284	154,781	0
1993	143,336	167,992	0
1994	73,131	56,316	3,111
1995	15,372	8,191	2,226
1996	34,145	26,560	7,863

Source: Fannie Mae, Freddie Mac, and Ginnie Mae as published in Freddie Mac, "Secondary Mortgage Markets" (14, 2). July 1997.

Secondary Mortgage Market

TABLE 4.32. SELECTED BALANCE SHEET AND MORTGAGE-BACKED SECURITY DATA FOR FANNIE MAE AND FREDDIE MAC: 1971 TO 1997
(Millions of current dollars)

| | Fannie Mae | | | | | Freddie Mac | | | | |
| | Assets | | Debt outstanding | Mortgage-backed securties outstanding | | Assets | | Debt outstanding[4] | Mortgage-backed securties outstanding | |
END OF YEAR	Total	Retained mortgage portfolio outstanding		Total[1]	Multiclass[2]	Total	Retained mortgage portfolio outstanding[3]		Total[1]	Multiclass
1971	18,591	17,886	17,672	....	....	1,038	935	915	64	....
1972	20,346	19,652	19,239	....	....	1,778	1,726	1,639	444	....
1973	24,318	23,589	23,003	....	....	2,873	2,521	2,696	791	....
1974	29,671	28,666	28,168	....	....	4,901	4,469	3,989	780	....
1975	31,596	30,820	29,963	....	....	5,899	4,878	4,050	1,643	....
1976	32,393	31,775	30,565	....	....	4,832	4,175	3,351	2,765	....
1977	33,980	33,252	31,890	....	....	3,501	3,204	3,110	6,765	....
1978	43,506	42,103	40,985	....	....	3,697	3,038	3,066	12,017	....
1979[5]	51,300	49,777	48,424	....	....	4,648	4,003	3,981	15,316	....
1980	57,879	55,589	54,880	....	....	5,478	5,006	4,686	16,962	....
1981	61,578	59,629	58,551	717	....	6,326	5,178	5,480	19,897	....
1982	72,981	69,356	69,614	14,450	....	6,029	4,679	4,521	42,952	....
1983	78,383	75,247	74,594	25,121	....	8,954	7,485	6,782	57,720	....
1984	87,798	84,135	83,719	35,738	....	13,175	10,018	10,186	70,025	....
1985	99,076	94,609	93,985	54,552	....	16,299	13,547	11,754	99,908	....
1986	99,621	94,123	93,563	95,568	....	23,229	13,093	13,378	169,186	....
1987	103,459	93,665	97,057	135,734	11,359	25,674	12,354	17,461	212,635	....
1988	112,258	100,099	105,459	170,097	26,660	34,352	16,918	24,846	226,406	10,877
1989	124,315	107,981	116,064	216,512	64,826	35,462	21,448	24,102	272,870	47,573
1990	133,113	114,066	123,403	288,075	127,278	40,579	21,520	28,375	316,359	83,437
1991	147,072	126,679	133,937	355,284	224,806	46,860	26,667	28,300	359,163	142,960
1992	180,978	156,260	166,300	424,444	312,369	59,502	33,629	28,173	407,514	217,030
1993	216,979	190,169	201,112	471,306	381,865	83,880	55,938	48,510	439,029	264,122
1994	272,508	220,815	257,230	486,345	378,733	106,199	73,171	92,053	460,656	263,662
1995	316,550	252,868	299,174	513,230	353,528	137,181	107,706	119,328	459,045	246,969
1996	351,041	286,527	331,270	548,173	339,798	173,866	137,826	156,491	473,065	231,539
1997	391,673	316,592	369,774	579,138	388,360	194,597	164,543	168,574	475,985	233,591

Source: Office of Federal Housing Enterprise Oversight, "1998 Report to Congress."

(1) Excludes mortgage-backed securities held in portfolio.
(2) Includes multiclass mortgage-backed securities held in portfolio.
(3) Beginning in 1995, the data reflects adoption of SFAS 114. Data for prior periods have not been restated.
(4) Does not include subordinated borrowings.
(5) For Fannie Mae, figures for 1979 and prior years are not restated for December 1987 FAS 91 change.

Fair Lending

RACIAL OR ETHNIC IDENTITY OF APPLICANT	TABLE 4.33. PERCENTAGE OF ONE-TO-FOUR-FAMILY HOME PURCHASE LOAN APPLICATIONS DENIED, BY LOAN TYPE AND RACIAL OR ETHNIC IDENTITY OF APPLICANT, 1990-1996					
	1990		1991		1992	
	Government-backed	Conventional	Government-backed	Conventional	Government-backed	Conventional
American Indian or Alaskan Native	22.5	22.4	22.1	27.3	17.5	26.6
Asian or Pacific Islander	12.8	12.9	12.5	15.0	13.5	15.3
Black	26.3	33.9	26.4	37.6	23.8	35.9
Hispanic	18.4	21.4	18.9	26.6	18.5	27.3
White	12.1	14.4	16.3	17.3	12.8	15.9
Other	18.4	19.0	16.3	19.9	16.0	21.0
Joint [1]	14.1	14.9	15.9	17.5	14.8	17.6

See notes at end of table.

Fair Lending

RACIAL OR ETHNIC IDENTITY OF APPLICANT	1993		1994		1995		1996	
	Government-backed	Conventional	Government-backed	Conventional	Government-backed	Conventional	Government-backed	Conventional
American Indian or Alaskan Native	17.5	27.8	15.3	31.6	13.3	41.4	12.7	50.2
Asian or Pacific Islander	11.7	14.6	10.5	12.0	8.7	12.5	9.9	13.8
Black	22.2	34.0	18.8	33.4	15.3	40.5	15.5	48.8
Hispanic	14.6	25.1	12.7	24.6	9.5	29.5	10.2	34.4
White	11.8	15.3	10.4	16.4	8.5	20.6	8.6	24.1
Other	17.8	23.1	15.0	23.8	10.7	29.6	12.4	30.0
Joint [1]	14.7	17.3	11.7	17.2	10.1	22.4	10.5	32.3

TABLE 4.33. PERCENTAGE OF ONE-TO-FOUR-FAMILY HOME PURCHASE LOAN APPLICATIONS DENIED, BY LOAN TYPE AND RACIAL OR ETHNIC IDENTITY OF APPLICANT, 1990-1996 - Continued

Source: U.S. General Accounting Office: "Fair Lending: Federal Oversight and Enforcement Improved but Some Challenges Remain" (GAO/GGD-96-145) and Federal Reserve Bulletin, September 1996 and 1997.

(1) An application with White and minority co-applicants.

All denial rates are for one-to-four family home purchase loan applications reported under the Home Mortgage Disclosure Act.

Fair Lending

TABLE 4.34. APPLICATIONS FOR ONE-TO-FOUR-FAMILY HOME LOANS REPORTED UNDER THE HOME MORTGAGE DISCLOSURE ACT, BY SELECTED CHARACTERISTICS: 1994 TO 1996

CHARACTERISTIC	1994							
	Home purchase loans				Home refinancing loans		Home improvement loans	
	Government-backed		Conventional					
	Number	Percent	Number	Percent	Number	Percent	Number	Percent
APPLICANT								
Racial or ethnic identity								
American Indian or Alaskan Native	4,813	0.5	21,887	0.5	17,151	0.5	9,163	0.7
Asian or Pacific Islander	15,508	1.6	128,992	3.2	131,306	3.9	21,154	1.5
Black	140,900	14.3	250,267	6.2	221,910	6.7	155,848	11.1
Hispanic [1]	101,919	10.4	219,844	5.5	210,231	6.3	119,093	8.5
White	681,071	69.3	3,290,026	81.6	2,641,947	79.3	1,055,069	75.5
Other	5,233	0.5	33,041	0.8	33,898	1.0	13,983	1.0
All	33,809	3.4	89,021	2.2	74,162	2.2	23,805	1.7
Total	983,253	100.0	4,033,078	100.0	3,330,605	100.0	1,398,115	100.0
Income ratio [2]								
Less than 80	335,912	41.0	809,920	27.6	689,658	25.3	476,650	37.1
80-99	175,207	21.4	402,921	13.7	375,005	13.8	189,000	14.7
100-119	124,250	15.2	372,468	12.7	353,399	13.0	164,184	12.8
120 or more	183,607	22.4	1,345,089	45.9	1,307,272	48.0	456,154	35.5
Total	818,976	100.0	2,930,398	100.0	2,725,334	100.0	1,285,988	100.0
CENSUS TRACT								
Racial or ethnic composition								
(Minorities as percentage of population)								
Less than 10	305,923	37.6	1,536,461	52.6	1,367,155	45.3	607,071	48.6
10-19	189,742	23.3	629,939	21.6	637,288	21.1	218,633	17.5
20-49	211,458	26.0	496,869	17.0	594,298	19.7	208,429	16.7
50-79	64,801	8.0	160,091	5.5	228,933	7.6	94,344	7.6
80-100	41,538	5.1	96,042	3.3	188,931	6.3	120,853	9.7
Total	813,462	100.0	2,919,402	100.0	3,016,605	100.0	1,249,330	100.0
Income [3]								
Low or moderate	139,723	17.0	354,253	12.1	435,193	14.3	272,252	21.3
Middle	481,747	58.5	1,449,151	49.6	1,543,198	50.7	671,206	52.4
Upper	201,450	24.5	1,118,982	38.3	1,064,330	35.0	337,594	26.4
Total	822,920	100.0	2,922,386	100.0	3,042,721	100.0	1,281,052	100.0
Location [4]								
Central city	385,292	46.3	1,145,411	38.5	1,215,509	39.4	579,087	44.2
Non-central city	447,405	53.7	1,829,464	61.5	1,872,041	60.6	730,295	55.8
Total	832,697	100.0	2,974,875	100.0	3,087,550	100.0	1,309,382	100.0

See notes at end of table.

Fair Lending

TABLE 4.34. APPLICATIONS FOR ONE-TO-FOUR-FAMILY HOME LOANS REPORTED UNDER THE HOME MORTGAGE DISCLOSURE ACT, BY SELECTED CHARACTERISTICS: 1994 TO 1996 - Continued

CHARACTERISTIC	1995							
	Home purchase loans				Home refinancing loans		Home improvement loans	
	Government-backed		Conventional					
	Number	Percent	Number	Percent	Number	Percent	Number	Percent
APPLICANT								
Racial or ethnic identity								
American Indian or Alaskan Native	4,051	0.4	27,351	0.6	10,578	0.5	9,617	0.7
Asian or Pacific Islander	15,172	1.6	121,089	2.8	65,964	3.0	20,414	1.4
Black	146,717	15.4	325,849	7.5	189,379	8.6	171,075	12.1
Hispanic [1]	106,687	11.2	257,826	6.0	128,399	5.8	115,237	8.2
White	643,050	67.4	3,462,366	80.0	1,740,552	78.9	1,054,827	74.7
Other	5,933	0.6	41,107	0.9	27,321	1.2	14,633	1.0
All	32,652	3.4	94,386	2.2	44,033	2.0	25,527	1.8
Total	954,262	100.0	4,329,974	100.0	2,206,226	100.0	1,411,330	100.0
Income ratio [2]								
Less than 80	314,092	39.1	890,953	29.3	541,331	27.8	482,376	35.7
80-99	172,951	21.5	420,408	13.8	272,217	14.0	196,614	14.6
100-119	126,099	15.7	374,235	12.3	251,248	12.9	174,783	12.9
120 or more	189,610	23.6	1,357,489	44.6	885,912	45.4	496,706	36.8
Total	802,752	100.0	3,043,085	100.0	1,950,708	100.0	1,350,479	100.0
CENSUS TRACT								
Racial or ethnic composition								
(Minorities as percentage of population)								
Less than 10	295,903	37.1	1,562,872	52.1	975,894	47.4	617,724	46.9
10-19	186,689	23.4	641,595	21.4	396,944	19.3	233,098	17.7
20-49	206,070	25.8	518,268	17.3	366,150	17.8	228,549	17.3
50-79	64,117	8.0	168,716	5.6	155,564	7.6	103,062	7.8
80-100	44,770	5.6	108,084	3.6	163,603	7.9	135,092	10.3
Total	797,549	100.0	2,999,535	100.0	2,058,155	100.0	1,317,525	100.0
Income [3]								
Low or moderate	144,546	17.9	409,030	13.6	358,685	17.4	296,817	22.1
Middle	463,961	57.5	1,500,430	50.0	1,033,298	50.0	694,042	51.8
Upper	197,731	24.5	1,092,905	36.4	674,890	32.7	349,440	26.1
Total	806,238	100.0	3,002,365	100.0	2,066,873	100.0	1,340,299	100.0
Location [4]								
Central city	379,043	46.3	1,186,518	38.6	833,506	39.5	606,417	44.2
Non-central city	439,447	53.7	1,886,593	61.4	1,276,772	60.5	765,234	55.8
Total	818,490	100.0	3,073,111	100.0	2,110,278	100.0	1,371,651	100.0

See notes at end of table.

Fair Lending

TABLE 4.34. APPLICATIONS FOR ONE-TO-FOUR-FAMILY HOME LOANS REPORTED UNDER THE HOME MORTGAGE DISCLOSURE ACT, BY SELECTED CHARACTERISTICS: 1994 TO 1996 - Continued

CHARACTERISTIC	1996							
	Home purchase loans				Home refinancing loans		Home improvement loans	
	Government-backed		Conventional					
	Number	Percent	Number	Percent	Number	Percent	Number	Percent
APPLICANT								
Racial or ethnic identity								
American Indian or Alaskan Native	5,107	0.5	35,626	0.7	14,780	0.4	10,322	0.7
Asian or Pacific Islander	17,967	1.6	132,581	2.7	96,734	2.7	24,150	1.5
Black	158,862	14.5	386,805	7.8	297,244	8.3	181,665	11.6
Hispanic [1]	143,734	13.2	289,780	5.9	191,018	5.3	133,427	8.5
White	723,690	66.2	3,909,737	79.3	2,862,904	79.8	1,169,544	74.7
Other	6,885	0.6	48,070	1.0	53,805	1.5	18,058	1.2
All	36,394	3.3	125,036	2.5	70,087	2.0	28,466	1.8
Total	1,092,639	100.0	4,927,635	100.0	3,586,572	100.0	1,565,632	100.0
Income ratio [2]								
Less than 80	401,326	41.8	1,104,236	31.0	994,536	29.3	610,570	36.2
80-99	205,039	21.4	490,525	13.8	496,362	14.6	254,899	15.1
100-119	142,297	14.8	430,426	12.1	446,152	13.2	220,344	13.1
120 or more	210,724	22.0	1,539,747	43.2	1,453,606	42.9	600,560	35.6
Total	959,386	100.0	3,564,934	100.0	3,390,656	100.0	1,686,373	100.0
CENSUS TRACT								
Racial or ethnic composition								
(Minorities as percentage of population)								
Less than 10	363,776	37.5	1,862,839	51.8	1,818,366	49.7	752,526	44.2
10-19	223,969	23.1	777,714	21.6	696,220	19.0	316,004	18.6
20-49	247,606	25.5	636,157	17.7	622,544	17.0	327,076	19.2
50-79	78,115	8.1	201,602	5.6	253,381	6.9	137,692	8.1
80-100	56,892	5.9	119,853	3.3	267,725	7.3	169,277	9.9
Total	970,358	100.0	3,598,165	100.0	3,658,236	100.0	1,702,575	100.0
Income [3]								
Low or moderate	179,887	18.3	501,023	13.9	619,444	16.9	382,286	22.1
Middle	560,903	57.2	1,798,183	49.9	1,880,950	51.3	905,699	52.3
Upper	240,397	24.5	1,301,405	36.1	1,166,120	31.8	442,967	25.6
Total	981,187	100.0	3,600,611	100.0	3,666,514	100.0	1,730,952	100.0
Location [4]								
Central city	456,154	46.0	1,423,485	38.8	1,465,266	39.4	782,096	44.4
Non-central city	536,052	54.0	2,244,134	61.2	2,256,574	60.6	978,297	55.6
Total	992,206	100.0	3,667,619	100.0	3,721,840	100.0	1,760,393	100.0

Source: Board of Governors of the Federal Reserve System, Federal Reserve Bulletin, September 1995, September 1996, and September 1997.

Lenders reported 10,719,915 home loan applications under the Home Mortgage Disclosure Act in 1994; 9,926,444 in 1995; and 13,009,405 in 1996. Not all characteristics were reported for all applications; thus the total number of applications for each characteristic varies.

(1) Persons of Hispanic origin may be of any race.
(2) Applicant income as a percentage of the median family income of the metropolitan statistical area in which the property related to the loan is located.
(3) Median family income of the tract relative to that of the metropolitan statistical area in which the tract is located. See Appendix A for additional explanation.
(4) For census tracts located in metropolitan statistical areas.

Fair Lending

TABLE 4.35. DENIAL RATES FOR ONE-TO-FOUR-FAMILY HOME LOAN APPLICATIONS REPORTED UNDER THE HOME MORTGAGE DISCLOSURE ACT, BY SELECTED CHARACTERISTICS: 1994 TO 1996
(Percent)

CHARACTERISTIC	1994				1995				1996			
	Home purchase loans		Home refinancing loans	Home improvement loans	Home purchase loans		Home refinancing loans	Home improvement loans	Home purchase loans		Home refinancing loans	Home improvement loans
	Government-backed	Conventional			Government-backed	Conventional			Government-backed	Conventional		
APPLICANT												
Racial or ethnic identity												
American Indian or Alaskan Native	15.3	31.6	16.9	29.9	13.3	41.4	19.7	32.6	12.7	50.2	21.0	42.9
Asian or Pacific Islander	10.5	12.0	16.5	26.2	8.7	12.5	19.3	29.4	9.9	13.8	19.7	33.2
Black	18.8	33.4	20.4	36.0	15.3	40.5	24.9	38.8	15.5	48.8	25.8	42.8
Hispanic [1]	12.7	24.6	19.6	40.7	9.5	29.5	23.7	40.1	10.2	34.4	24.3	40.6
White	10.4	16.4	11.4	18.6	8.5	20.6	13.3	20.4	8.6	24.1	14.7	23.3
Other	15.0	23.8	23.6	30.0	10.7	29.6	25.3	33.7	12.4	30.0	32.4	36.5
Joint [2]	11.7	17.2	14.9	21.3	10.1	22.4	17.7	23.6	10.5	32.3	18.3	26.5
Income ratio [3]												
Less than 80	13.1	22.7	20.9	34.8	10.9	29.9	26.5	38.7	11.2	34.2	26.2	42.2
80-99	9.3	13.7	15.7	25.4	7.6	18.0	20.0	29.6	8.0	20.5	20.6	32.4
100-119	8.5	11.0	14.3	22.5	6.8	13.9	18.0	25.9	7.3	15.8	18.8	28.4
120 or more	8.2	7.8	12.5	18.1	6.4	8.7	14.7	19.9	7.0	9.8	15.6	21.9
CENSUS TRACT												
Racial or ethnic composition												
(Minorities as percentage of population)												
Less than 10	9.0	10.5	11.4	18.8	7.4	13.2	14.8	20.7	7.5	15.8	16.5	24.4
10-19	10.0	13.0	14.7	24.6	8.0	16.1	18.7	27.3	8.5	18.9	19.7	31.2
20-49	11.6	16.8	17.3	30.2	9.3	20.8	22.6	33.9	10.0	24.8	23.2	37.2
50-79	14.3	20.4	21.0	36.8	11.1	24.0	27.0	40.9	12.2	29.2	26.7	44.4
80-100	15.9	24.3	25.7	41.6	11.6	28.1	30.3	45.1	12.9	33.1	28.9	48.9
Income [4]												
Low or moderate	13.9	21.6	21.3	36.7	10.9	26.3	26.9	39.9	11.6	31.7	26.6	43.7
Middle	10.3	14.4	14.5	24.6	8.3	18.0	18.6	27.3	8.8	21.4	19.7	31.2
Upper	9.2	8.7	12.5	20.3	7.4	10.1	15.5	21.8	7.8	11.7	16.4	25.2
Location [5]												
Central city	11.8	14.3	16.0	29.1	9.5	17.6	21.2	32.1	10.0	21.1	21.7	36.0
Non-central city	9.7	12.5	13.9	23.6	7.8	15.7	17.5	25.8	8.3	18.6	18.6	29.4

Source: Board of Governors of the Federal Reserve System, Federal Reserve Bulletin, September 1995, September 1996, and September 1997.

(1) Persons of Hispanic origin may be of any race.
(2) An application with White and minority co-applicants.
(3) Applicant income as a percentage of the median family income of the metropolitan statistical area in which the property related to the loan is located.
(4) Median family income of the tract relative to that of the metropolitan statistical area in which the tract is located. See Appendix A for additional explanation.
(5) For census tracts located in metropolitan statistical areas.

Fair Lending

TABLE 4.36. DENIAL RATES FOR ONE-TO-FOUR-FAMILY HOME LOAN APPLICATIONS REPORTED UNDER THE HOME MORTGAGE DISCLOSURE ACT, BY INCOME AND RACE/ETHNICITY OF APPLICANT: 1994 TO 1996
(Percent)

INCOME RATIO[1] AND RACE/ETHNICITY OF APPLICANT	1994				1995				1996			
	Home purchase loans		Home refinancing loans	Home improvement loans	Home purchase loans		Home refinancing loans	Home improvement loans	Home purchase loans		Home refinancing loans	Home improvement loans
	Government-backed	Conventional			Government-backed	Conventional			Government-backed	Conventional		
Less than 80	13.1	22.7	20.9	34.8	10.9	29.9	26.5	38.7	11.2	34.2	26.2	42.2
American Indian or Alaskan Native	15.8	30.5	21.6	35.7	14.1	40.8	23.6	39.1	13.5	45.6	25.1	40.8
Asian or Pacific Islander	11.1	15.0	20.9	36.3	9.6	16.5	24.1	41.4	10.3	17.0	24.7	45.7
Black	19.1	30.5	25.5	41.3	15.6	37.3	28.3	44.6	15.9	44.5	28.1	48.9
Hispanic[2]	13.9	27.0	26.3	44.0	10.0	32.4	28.9	46.5	10.7	37.5	29.1	49.0
White	11.0	21.0	15.3	25.3	9.2	28.4	18.0	28.3	9.5	32.1	19.4	31.8
Other	14.5	27.9	31.4	41.9	12.0	37.4	32.7	41.6	14.0	39.1	38.4	47.8
Joint[3]	14.4	27.6	21.0	31.9	12.3	35.6	25.7	38.8	13.1	50.9	24.7	40.2
80-99	9.3	13.7	15.7	25.4	7.6	18.0	20.0	29.6	8.0	20.5	20.6	32.4
American Indian or Alaskan Native	11.3	19.2	17.2	25.8	10.2	26.4	19.8	25.7	11.2	33.3	19.7	33.0
Asian or Pacific Islander	8.9	11.1	16.5	27.6	7.4	11.2	19.4	30.9	8.2	11.7	19.3	34.2
Black	15.0	22.2	21.7	34.3	11.8	27.9	24.6	37.4	12.6	33.6	26.2	41.3
Hispanic[2]	10.8	20.7	23.8	40.0	8.2	24.6	25.9	39.9	8.8	27.3	25.4	40.2
White	7.7	11.9	11.6	18.0	6.3	16.4	13.3	21.2	6.6	18.6	14.9	24.0
Other	15.0	17.8	23.6	32.5	9.3	22.7	24.1	33.9	9.0	25.7	32.3	36.7
Joint[3]	9.7	17.1	16.5	22.8	8.4	24.1	18.8	28.9	9.1	29.7	21.0	31.1
100-119	8.5	11.0	14.3	22.5	6.8	13.9	18.0	25.9	7.3	15.8	18.8	28.4
American Indian or Alaskan Native	10.4	15.8	16.6	23.1	9.4	19.6	18.4	23.6	9.3	26.6	19.9	26.7
Asian or Pacific Islander	8.3	10.4	16.4	22.5	6.0	10.4	18.4	28.1	8.4	11.4	18.5	29.4
Black	14.3	19.0	20.2	31.2	11.3	23.9	23.8	35.0	12.3	28.9	24.6	38.1
Hispanic[2]	10.0	18.6	23.0	40.8	7.4	22.4	25.3	38.5	8.7	24.2	25.1	37.3
White	7.1	9.5	10.8	15.7	5.7	12.3	12.1	18.2	6.0	14.0	13.5	20.8
Other	9.7	15.0	23.0	29.5	9.1	19.2	23.8	33.7	9.8	21.2	29.6	31.2
Joint[3]	8.9	12.6	15.3	20.5	7.1	17.5	18.7	23.6	7.9	20.0	18.7	26.7
120 or more	8.2	7.8	12.5	18.1	6.4	8.7	14.7	19.9	7.0	9.8	15.6	21.9
American Indian or Alaskan Native	12.4	12.3	16.6	20.1	7.6	13.4	15.6	19.9	8.5	16.6	18.1	22.5
Asian or Pacific Islander	9.0	10.0	16.2	20.8	6.7	9.5	17.4	22.5	8.9	10.6	17.9	25.8
Black	13.3	15.1	19.6	26.6	10.5	17.5	22.9	29.5	11.4	20.4	23.4	31.7
Hispanic[2]	10.0	14.1	17.3	37.5	7.0	15.6	19.4	33.1	8.3	16.7	20.5	30.9
White	6.7	6.7	10.2	12.0	5.4	7.6	10.8	13.6	5.8	8.6	11.8	15.6
Other	11.9	12.3	20.9	23.5	7.1	13.6	21.8	26.1	11.6	14.5	25.8	26.2
Joint[3]	8.4	9.2	14.8	16.5	7.2	10.7	16.0	18.0	7.7	11.4	16.6	20.7

Source: Board of Governors of the Federal Reserve System, Federal Reserve Bulletin, September 1995, September 1996, and September 1997.

(1) Applicant income as a percentage of the median family income of the metropolitan statistical area in which the property related to the loan is located.
(2) Persons of Hispanic origin may be of any race.
(3) An application with White and minority co-applicants.

Fair Lending

CHARACTERISTIC	TABLE 4.37. HOME LOANS SOLD BY TYPE OF PURCHASER AND CHARACTERISTICS OF BORROWER AND CENSUS TRACT: 1994									
	Fannie Mae		Ginnie Mae		Freddie Mac		Farmers Home Administration		Commercial bank	
	Number	Percent	Number	Percent	Number	Percent	Number	Percent	Number	Percent
ALL	1,025,443	....	961,032	....	760,122	....	1,603	....	125,283	....
BORROWER										
Racial or ethnic identity										
American Indian or Alaskan Native	4,543	0.5	3,035	0.5	2,269	0.3	176	11.4	308	0.3
Asian or Pacific Islander	38,623	4.1	11,899	1.8	29,862	4.4	73	4.7	2,045	2.1
Black	38,223	4.1	74,361	11.1	20,748	3.0	62	4.0	8,750	9.2
Hispanic [1]	47,891	5.1	68,891	10.3	29,906	4.4	168	10.9	6,000	6.3
White	773,373	83.1	483,374	72.5	582,623	85.1	999	65.0	75,391	78.9
Other	7,092	0.8	3,299	0.5	4,754	0.7	19	1.2	710	0.7
Joint [2]	21,073	2.3	22,097	3.3	14,655	2.1	41	2.7	2,337	2.4
Total	930,818	100.0	666,956	100.0	684,817	100.0	1,538	100.0	95,541	100.0
Income ratio [3]										
Less than 80	174,989	22.7	160,818	37.0	123,004	22.0	413	37.1	27,543	29.4
80-99	119,941	15.6	92,930	21.4	82,417	14.7	242	21.7	15,219	16.2
100-119	116,102	15.1	69,980	16.1	84,394	15.1	142	12.8	13,300	14.2
120 or more	359,939	46.7	111,192	25.6	270,028	48.2	316	28.4	37,606	40.1
Total	770,971	100.0	434,920	100.0	559,843	100.0	1,113	100.0	93,668	100.0
CENSUS TRACT										
Racial or ethnic composition (Minorities as percentage of population)										
Less than 10	441,011	52.4	306,164	37.3	328,303	54.7	451	35.4	51,608	47.5
10-19	181,678	21.6	199,736	24.3	127,269	21.2	284	22.3	22,723	20.9
20-49	144,495	17.2	214,820	26.2	98,616	16.4	313	24.6	21,260	19.6
50-79	47,231	5.6	63,633	7.7	30,035	5.0	122	9.6	6,817	6.3
80-100	27,525	3.3	36,909	4.5	16,187	2.7	104	8.2	6,287	5.8
Total	841,940	100.0	821,262	100.0	600,410	100.0	1,274	100.0	108,695	100.0
Income [4]										
Low or moderate	80,809	9.6	124,825	15.0	52,230	8.7	239	18.7	14,940	13.7
Middle	427,108	50.7	492,475	59.1	304,182	50.6	746	58.5	57,247	52.5
Upper	334,407	39.7	216,330	26.0	244,843	40.7	290	22.7	36,927	33.8
Total	842,324	100.0	833,630	100.0	601,255	100.0	1,275	100.0	109,114	100.0
Location [5]										
Central city	323,485	38.4	380,302	45.6	215,715	35.8	561	43.9	42,338	38.8
Non-central city	519,449	61.6	453,733	54.4	386,040	64.2	716	56.1	66,883	61.2
Total	842,934	100.0	834,035	100.0	601,755	100.0	1,277	100.0	109,221	100.0

See notes at end of table.

Fair Lending

TABLE 4.37. HOME LOANS SOLD BY TYPE OF PURCHASER AND CHARACTERISTICS OF BORROWER AND CENSUS TRACT: 1994 - Continued

CHARACTERISTIC	Savings bank or savings and loan association		Life insurance company		Affiliate [6]		Other	
	Number	Percent	Number	Percent	Number	Percent	Number	Percent
ALL	63,459	....	16,868	....	497,015	....	1,045,211	....
BORROWER								
Racial or ethnic identity								
American Indian or Alaskan Native	219	0.4	58	0.4	1,673	0.4	5,290	0.6
Asian or Pacific Islander	1,905	3.3	350	2.3	10,498	2.5	31,220	3.3
Black	3,077	5.3	1,618	10.9	26,779	6.3	76,879	8.1
Hispanic [1]	2,894	4.9	796	5.3	19,312	4.5	63,234	6.6
White	48,673	83.2	11,642	78.1	356,188	83.6	740,792	77.8
Other	343	0.6	79	0.5	2,763	0.6	8,822	0.9
Joint [2]	1,394	2.4	361	2.4	9,049	2.1	25,981	2.7
Total	58,505	100.0	14,904	100.0	426,262	100.0	952,218	100.0
Income ratio [3]								
Less than 80	11,788	23.4	3,831	28.2	80,604	23.8	208,939	27.2
80-99	7,159	14.2	2,527	18.6	46,062	13.6	112,094	14.6
100-119	6,994	13.9	2,028	14.9	41,872	12.4	96,334	12.5
120 or more	24,456	48.5	5,212	38.3	169,502	50.1	350,578	45.7
Total	50,397	100.0	13,598	100.0	338,040	100.0	767,945	100.0
CENSUS TRACT								
Racial or ethnic composition								
(Minorities as percentage of population)								
Less than 10	28,596	54.6	6,981	44.6	206,424	57.3	361,905	43.5
10-19	10,982	21.0	3,909	25.0	76,841	21.3	197,205	23.7
20-49	8,609	16.4	3,354	21.4	53,075	14.7	176,732	21.2
50-79	2,656	5.1	867	5.5	14,589	4.1	55,183	6.6
80-100	1,564	3.0	553	3.5	9,277	2.6	41,639	5.0
Total	52,407	100.0	15,664	100.0	360,206	100.0	832,664	100.0
Income [4]								
Low or moderate	5,556	10.5	1,852	11.8	37,484	10.3	111,394	13.4
Middle	25,614	48.3	8,529	54.6	171,518	47.3	407,196	48.8
Upper	21,843	41.2	5,249	33.6	153,729	42.4	315,349	37.8
Total	53,013	100.0	15,630	100.0	362,731	100.0	833,939	100.0
Location [5]								
Central city	18,593	35.0	6,043	38.6	135,175	37.2	337,948	40.5
Non-central city	34,534	65.0	9,622	61.4	227,929	62.8	497,479	59.5
Total	53,127	100.0	15,665	100.0	363,104	100.0	835,427	100.0

Source: Board of Governors of the Federal Reserve System, Federal Reserve Bulletin, September 1995. Data reported under the Home Mortgage Disclosure Act.

(1) Persons of Hispanic origin may be of any race.
(2) An application with White and minority co-applicants.
(3) Applicant income as a percentage of the median family income of the metropolitan statistical area in which the property related to the loan is located.
(4) Median family income of the tract relative to that of the metropolitan statistical area in which the tract is located. See Appendix A for additional explanation.
(5) For census tracts located in metropolitan statistical areas.
(6) Refers to an affiliate of the institution reporting the loan.

Fair Lending

TABLE 4.38. HOME LOANS SOLD BY TYPE OF PURCHASER AND CHARACTERISTICS OF BORROWER AND CENSUS TRACT: 1995

CHARACTERISTIC	Fannie Mae		Ginnie Mae		Freddie Mac		Farmers Home Administration		Commercial bank	
	Number	Percent	Number	Percent	Number	Percent	Number	Percent	Number	Percent
ALL	974,528	....	630,742	....	589,130	....	4,832	....	109,889	....
BORROWER										
Racial or ethnic identity										
American Indian or Alaskan Native	3,300	0.4	1,984	0.4	1,566	0.3	13	0.3	384	0.4
Asian or Pacific Islander	33,327	3.8	7,648	1.6	16,320	3.1	116	2.7	1,996	2.0
Black	39,457	4.6	64,647	13.7	18,289	3.5	299	7.0	9,931	10.1
Hispanic [1]	48,216	5.6	50,380	10.6	20,412	3.9	516	12.0	7,427	7.5
White	716,818	82.7	329,672	69.7	458,543	86.7	3,224	75.3	75,839	77.0
Other	6,444	0.7	2,961	0.6	3,370	0.6	30	0.7	710	0.7
Joint [2]	19,379	2.2	15,860	3.4	10,639	2.0	85	2.0	2,151	2.2
Total	866,941	100.0	473,152	100.0	529,139	100.0	4,283	100.0	98,438	100.0
Income ratio [3]										
Less than 80	153,849	20.9	135,399	35.4	80,395	19.3	1,197	43.4	23,040	25.4
80-99	112,007	15.2	83,691	21.9	60,698	14.6	711	25.8	14,534	16.0
100-119	110,791	15.1	65,105	17.0	63,857	15.3	352	12.8	12,920	14.2
120 or more	359,305	48.8	98,646	25.8	212,033	50.8	499	18.1	40,296	44.4
Total	735,952	100.0	382,841	100.0	416,983	100.0	2,759	100.0	90,790	100.0
CENSUS TRACT										
Racial or ethnic composition (Minorities as percentage of population)										
Less than 10	427,204	53.7	200,880	37.6	271,474	60.3	1,779	47.2	46,625	49.6
10-19	168,129	21.1	127,528	23.9	90,454	20.1	983	26.1	19,570	20.8
20-49	130,785	16.4	136,795	25.6	62,239	13.8	702	18.6	17,851	19.0
50-79	42,855	5.4	41,075	7.7	16,789	3.7	175	4.6	5,291	5.6
80-100	26,561	3.3	27,526	5.2	9,162	2.0	134	3.6	4,681	5.0
Total	795,534	100.0	533,804	100.0	450,118	100.0	3,773	100.0	94,018	100.0
Income [4]										
Low or moderate	80,537	10.1	88,904	16.4	38,772	8.6	638	16.9	12,459	13.1
Middle	397,045	49.9	315,846	58.4	228,226	50.7	2,223	58.9	47,562	50.0
Upper	317,978	40.0	135,715	25.1	183,183	40.7	916	24.3	35,158	36.9
Total	795,560	100.0	540,465	100.0	450,181	100.0	3,777	100.0	95,179	100.0
Location [5]										
Central city	299,737	37.6	242,436	44.8	158,869	35.3	979	25.9	37,672	39.5
Non-central city	496,568	62.4	298,320	55.2	291,712	64.7	2,799	74.1	57,636	60.5
Total	796,305	100.0	540,756	100.0	450,581	100.0	3,778	100.0	95,308	100.0

See notes at end of table.

Fair Lending

TABLE 4.38. HOME LOANS SOLD BY TYPE OF PURCHASER AND CHARACTERISTICS OF BORROWER AND CENSUS TRACT: 1995 - Continued

CHARACTERISTIC	Savings bank or savings and loan association		Life insurance company		Affiliate[6]		Other	
	Number	Percent	Number	Percent	Number	Percent	Number	Percent
ALL	44,587	....	6,433	....	389,980	....	1,036,012	....
BORROWER								
Racial or ethnic identity								
American Indian or Alaskan Native	86	0.2	18	0.3	1,741	0.5	4,193	0.4
Asian or Pacific Islander	766	1.9	123	2.0	7,530	2.2	24,089	2.6
Black	2,782	7.0	726	11.7	26,491	7.7	94,321	10.0
Hispanic[1]	1,568	3.9	406	6.6	18,268	5.3	70,252	7.4
White	33,549	84.4	4,757	76.8	279,339	81.1	716,203	75.8
Other	233	0.6	34	0.5	3,356	1.0	10,302	1.1
Joint[2]	753	1.9	128	2.1	7,628	2.2	25,228	2.7
Total	39,737	100.0	6,192	100.0	344,353	100.0	944,588	100.0
Income ratio[3]								
Less than 80	8,377	23.0	1,605	28.3	71,678	27.6	236,104	30.4
80-99	5,361	14.7	968	17.1	34,586	13.3	127,709	16.5
100-119	5,036	13.8	843	14.9	29,687	11.4	104,946	13.5
120 or more	17,606	48.4	2,246	39.7	123,716	47.6	307,577	39.6
Total	36,380	100.0	5,662	100.0	259,667	100.0	776,336	100.0
CENSUS TRACT								
Racial or ethnic composition (Minorities as percentage of population)								
Less than 10	24,295	63.8	3,069	52.7	156,068	53.9	362,771	43.4
10-19	6,498	17.1	1,214	20.9	65,387	22.6	188,767	22.6
20-49	4,562	12.0	928	15.9	47,479	16.4	176,808	21.2
50-79	1,448	3.8	359	6.2	12,651	4.4	57,415	6.9
80-100	1,253	3.3	252	4.3	8,038	2.8	49,423	5.9
Total	38,056	100.0	5,822	100.0	289,623	100.0	835,184	100.0
Income[4]								
Low or moderate	4,573	12.0	783	13.5	36,422	12.4	132,639	15.8
Middle	18,334	48.0	3,076	52.9	137,963	47.0	436,930	52.1
Upper	15,302	40.0	1,956	33.6	119,015	40.6	269,138	32.1
Total	38,209	100.0	5,815	100.0	293,400	100.0	838,707	100.0
Location[5]								
Central city	12,941	33.8	2,181	37.5	115,675	39.4	345,319	41.1
Non-central city	25,314	66.2	3,641	62.5	177,954	60.6	494,282	58.9
Total	38,255	100.0	5,822	100.0	293,629	100.0	839,601	100.0

Source: Board of Governors of the Federal Reserve System, Federal Reserve Bulletin, September 1996. Data reported under the Home Mortgage Disclosure Act.

(1) Persons of Hispanic origin may be of any race.
(2) An application with White and minority co-applicants.
(3) Applicant income as a percentage of the median family income of the metropolitan statistical area in which the property related to the loan is located.
(4) Median family income of the tract relative to that of the metropolitan statistical area in which the tract is located. See Appendix A for additional explanation.
(5) For census tracts located in metropolitan statistical areas.
(6) Refers to an affiliate of the institution reporting the loan.

Fair Lending

TABLE 4.39. HOME LOANS SOLD BY TYPE OF PURCHASER AND CHARACTERISTICS OF BORROWER AND CENSUS TRACT: 1996

CHARACTERISTIC	Fannie Mae		Ginnie Mae		Freddie Mac		Farmers Home Administration		Commercial bank	
	Number	Percent	Number	Percent	Number	Percent	Number	Percent	Number	Percent
ALL	1,092,445	....	824,445	....	843,859	....	3,444	....	116,675	....
BORROWER										
Racial or ethnic identity										
American Indian or Alaskan Native	2,877	0.3	2,267	0.4	1,740	0.2	38	1.2	275	0.3
Asian or Pacific Islander	33,501	3.7	8,736	1.6	20,189	2.9	76	2.4	2,225	2.4
Black	35,624	3.9	68,130	12.7	21,447	3.1	386	12.1	7,714	8.2
Hispanic [1]	46,711	5.1	64,146	12.0	25,363	3.6	422	13.2	7,368	7.8
White	772,148	84.1	374,431	69.8	612,093	87.5	2,156	67.7	73,830	78.1
Other	7,579	0.8	3,530	0.7	4,886	0.7	21	0.7	732	0.8
Joint [2]	19,228	2.1	14,987	2.8	13,483	1.9	86	2.7	2,329	2.5
Total	917,668	100.0	536,227	100.0	699,201	100.0	3,185	100.0	94,473	100.0
Income ratio [3]										
Less than 80	176,873	21.6	140,033	38.7	127,580	20.6	1,146	40.9	21,241	24.9
80-99	127,591	15.6	78,882	21.8	94,046	15.2	557	19.9	13,234	15.5
100-119	123,771	15.1	57,412	15.9	95,269	15.4	363	12.9	11,782	13.8
120 or more	390,102	47.7	85,632	23.7	302,177	48.8	739	26.3	39,142	45.8
Total	818,337	100.0	361,959	100.0	619,072	100.0	2,805	100.0	85,399	100.0
CENSUS TRACT										
Racial or ethnic composition (Minorities as percentage of population)										
Less than 10	512,872	54.8	268,952	36.5	429,231	59.9	1,360	45.1	48,249	47.3
10-19	201,014	21.5	175,616	23.9	145,551	20.3	643	21.3	22,430	22.0
20-49	150,895	16.1	192,339	26.1	101,211	14.1	620	20.5	20,858	20.5
50-79	45,387	4.8	59,212	8.0	27,171	3.8	188	6.2	5,674	5.6
80-100	26,257	2.8	39,901	5.4	13,896	1.9	207	6.9	4,717	4.6
Total	936,425	100.0	736,020	100.0	717,060	100.0	3,018	100.0	101,928	100.0
Income [4]										
Low or moderate	87,520	9.3	123,376	16.6	59,853	8.3	659	21.9	13,710	13.3
Middle	468,804	50.0	430,471	58.0	365,890	51.0	1,694	56.3	51,083	49.5
Upper	380,803	40.6	188,483	25.4	291,249	40.6	654	21.7	38,440	37.2
Total	937,127	100.0	742,330	100.0	716,992	100.0	3,007	100.0	103,233	100.0
Location [5]										
Central city	350,330	37.4	328,997	44.3	253,414	35.3	1,341	44.4	41,827	40.5
Non-central city	587,447	62.6	413,644	55.7	464,003	64.7	1,677	55.6	61,485	59.5
Total	937,777	100.0	742,641	100.0	717,417	100.0	3,018	100.0	103,312	100.0

See notes at end of table.

Fair Lending

TABLE 4.39. HOME LOANS SOLD BY TYPE OF PURCHASER AND CHARACTERISTICS OF BORROWER AND CENSUS TRACT: 1996 - Continued

CHARACTERISTIC	Savings bank or savings and loan association		Life insurance company		Affiliate [6]		Other	
	Number	Percent	Number	Percent	Number	Percent	Number	Percent
ALL	59,616	....	6,761	....	484,759	....	1,422,144	....
BORROWER								
Racial or ethnic identity								
American Indian or Alaskan Native	149	0.3	13	0.2	2,175	0.5	6,139	0.5
Asian or Pacific Islander	1,140	2.2	154	2.4	18,952	4.3	30,153	2.6
Black	3,203	6.2	570	8.7	31,459	7.1	120,071	10.2
Hispanic [1]	2,256	4.3	172	2.6	19,624	4.4	92,545	7.9
White	43,828	84.4	5,462	83.6	357,428	80.2	885,935	75.3
Other	317	0.6	33	0.5	4,117	0.9	11,345	1.0
Joint [2]	1,023	2.0	130	2.0	11,947	2.7	29,670	2.5
Total	51,916	100.0	6,534	100.0	445,702	100.0	1,175,858	100.0
Income ratio [3]								
Less than 80	11,189	22.5	1,599	29.1	96,767	27.3	332,835	32.8
80-99	6,950	14.0	959	17.5	45,156	12.8	165,163	16.3
100-119	6,350	12.8	769	14.0	38,890	11.0	134,129	13.2
120 or more	25,287	50.8	2,161	39.4	173,022	48.9	383,310	37.7
Total	49,776	100.0	5,488	100.0	353,835	100.0	1,015,437	100.0
CENSUS TRACT								
Racial or ethnic composition (Minorities as percentage of population)								
Less than 10	33,274	62.3	3,990	64.2	205,063	52.2	499,606	42.7
10-19	9,825	18.4	1,061	17.1	89,275	22.7	262,766	22.5
20-49	6,523	12.2	770	12.4	65,388	16.6	244,674	20.9
50-79	2,015	3.8	239	3.8	20,060	5.1	84,527	7.2
80-100	1,753	3.3	154	2.5	13,309	3.4	78,279	6.7
Total	53,390	100.0	6,214	100.0	393,095	100.0	1,169,852	100.0
Income [4]								
Low or moderate	6,099	11.4	703	11.3	46,515	11.8	196,004	16.7
Middle	24,267	45.3	3,304	53.2	181,652	46.0	597,756	51.0
Upper	23,209	43.3	2,203	35.5	167,050	42.3	378,351	32.3
Total	53,575	100.0	6,210	100.0	395,217	100.0	1,172,111	100.0
Location [5]								
Central city	16,976	31.6	2,254	36.3	150,373	38.0	490,394	41.8
Non-central city	36,668	68.4	3,960	63.7	245,060	62.0	682,933	58.2
Total	53,644	100.0	6,214	100.0	395,433	100.0	1,173,327	100.0

Source: Board of Governors of the Federal Reserve System, Federal Reserve Bulletin, September 1997. Data reported under the Home Mortgage Disclosure Act.

(1) Persons of Hispanic origin may be of any race.
(2) An application with White and minority co-applicants.
(3) Applicant income as a percentage of the median family income of the metropolitan statistical area in which the property related to the loan is located.
(4) Median family income of the tract relative to that of the metropolitan statistical area in which the tract is located. See Appendix A for additional explanation.
(5) For census tracts located in metropolitan statistical areas.
(6) Refers to an affiliate of the institution reporting the loan.

Fair Lending

TABLE 4.40. PRIVATE MORTGAGE INSURANCE APPLICATIONS AND POLICIES WRITTEN ON SINGLE-FAMILY HOMES, BY PURPOSE OF LOAN AND INSURANCE COMPANY: 1994 TO 1996
(Percent, except as noted)

COMPANY	1994				1995				1996			
	Home purchase		Home refinance		Home purchase		Home refinance		Home purchase		Home refinance	
	Applica-tions	Policies written	Applica-tions	Policies written	Applica-tions	Policies written	Applica-tions	Policies written	Applica-tions	Policies written	Applica-tions	Policies written
Number of applications or policies, all companies	1,176,044	941,803	307,532	205,819	1,108,512	884,745	127,725	94,244	1,134,947	897,108	242,460	172,652
Percent distribution												
Amerin Guaranty	1.8	2.0	0.8	1.0	3.8	4.8	4.5	6.1	4.5	5.7	4.1	5.8
Commonwealth Mortgage Assurance	7.2	6.7	9.5	8.8	10.1	9.6	12.2	11.2	10.8	9.9	11.9	10.5
GE Capital Mortgage Insurance	27.0	27.1	28.8	28.6	23.2	23.0	19.4	19.0	19.6	18.6	19.4	19.0
Mortgage Guaranty Insurance	26.5	27.9	24.8	26.5	26.8	27.3	27.2	27.9	26.2	26.7	26.0	25.9
PMI Mortgage Insurance	14.3	13.6	14.5	13.7	12.7	12.1	13.7	13.0	13.1	13.3	13.5	13.4
Republic Mortgage Insurance	9.4	9.6	7.2	8.3	9.6	9.6	9.5	9.3	11.6	11.6	11.2	11.4
Triad Guaranty Insurance	1.4	1.4	1.1	1.1	1.5	1.5	1.4	1.4	1.7	1.8	1.8	1.8
United Guaranty	12.4	11.7	13.2	11.9	12.2	12.1	12.0	12.0	12.5	12.5	12.1	12.1
Total	100.0	100.0	100.0	100.0	100.0	100.0	100.0	100.0	100.0	100.0	100.0	100.0

Source: Board of Governors of the Federal Reserve System, Federal Reserve Bulletin, November 1995, December 1996, and September 1997.

Fair Lending

TABLE 4.41. PRIVATE MORTGAGE INSURANCE APPLICATIONS ON SINGLE-FAMILY HOMES, BY SELECTED CHARACTERISTICS: 1994 TO 1996

CHARACTERISTIC	1994				1995				1996			
	Home purchase		Home refinance		Home purchase		Home refinance		Home purchase		Home refinance	
	Number	Percent	Number	Percent	Number	Percent	Number	Percent	Number	Percent	Number	Percent
APPLICANT												
Racial or ethnic identity												
American Indian or Alaskan Native	3,669	0.4	1,609	0.7	3,102	0.3	399	0.4	2,920	0.3	628	0.3
Asian or Pacific Islander	30,201	3.1	12,229	5.1	28,881	3.1	4,159	3.9	29,102	3.0	6,973	3.5
Black	57,124	6.0	12,305	5.1	67,261	7.2	7,248	6.8	59,740	6.2	11,772	5.9
Hispanic [1]	65,928	6.9	14,794	6.1	72,406	7.8	6,645	6.2	68,826	7.2	10,673	5.4
White	776,939	80.9	193,832	80.2	733,187	78.6	85,293	79.5	768,437	79.9	161,407	81.3
Other	4,645	0.5	1,476	0.6	6,364	0.7	1,009	0.9	9,287	1.0	2,111	1.1
Joint	21,527	2.2	5,324	2.2	22,189	2.4	2,478	2.3	23,151	2.4	4,932	2.5
Total	960,033	100.0	241,569	100.0	933,390	100.0	107,231	100.0	961,463	100.0	198,496	100.0
Income ratio [2]												
Less than 80	160,795	20.2	28,453	11.3	148,557	20.4	11,291	11.8	148,589	20.7	24,349	13.9
80-99	127,930	16.0	34,306	13.6	114,329	15.7	12,982	13.5	113,054	15.7	26,242	15.0
100-119	127,404	16.0	39,983	15.9	112,316	15.4	14,873	15.5	111,289	15.5	28,593	16.4
120 or more	381,597	47.8	149,432	59.3	353,964	48.5	56,724	59.2	346,208	48.1	95,424	54.7
Total	797,726	100.0	252,174	100.0	729,166	100.0	95,870	100.0	719,140	100.0	174,608	100.0
CENSUS TRACT												
Racial or ethnic composition (Minorities as percentage of population)												
Less than 10	408,009	50.3	103,009	40.7	371,013	49.6	41,234	42.8	368,371	50.8	83,212	47.4
10-19	181,964	22.4	61,111	24.2	164,676	22.0	21,962	22.8	162,465	22.4	40,157	22.9
20-49	146,265	18.0	59,651	23.6	136,585	18.3	21,090	21.9	127,427	17.6	34,425	19.6
50-79	47,151	5.8	19,138	7.6	46,649	6.2	7,292	7.6	42,171	5.8	11,159	6.3
80-100	27,335	3.4	10,084	4.0	28,776	3.8	4,651	4.8	24,978	3.4	6,784	3.9
Total	810,724	100.0	252,993	100.0	747,699	100.0	96,229	100.0	725,412	100.0	175,737	100.0
Income [3]												
Lower	84,800	10.5	23,893	9.5	89,662	12.0	10,389	10.8	81,194	11.2	17,775	10.1
Middle	405,210	50.0	130,170	51.5	371,199	49.7	49,752	51.8	357,261	49.3	93,090	53.0
Upper	320,077	39.5	98,632	39.0	286,223	38.3	35,996	37.4	286,435	39.5	64,701	36.9
Total	810,087	100.0	252,695	100.0	747,084	100.0	96,137	100.0	724,890	100.0	175,566	100.0
Location [4]												
Central city	324,738	40.1	92,667	36.6	305,980	40.9	34,316	35.7	295,268	40.7	62,660	35.7
Non-central city	486,018	59.9	160,329	63.4	441,749	59.1	61,914	64.3	430,200	59.3	113,079	64.3
Total	810,756	100.0	252,996	100.0	747,729	100.0	96,230	100.0	725,468	100.0	175,739	100.0

Source: Board of Governors of the Federal Reserve System, Federal Reserve Bulletin, November 1995, December 1996, and September 1997.

Not all characteristics were reported for all applications.

(1) Persons of Hispanic origin may be of any race.
(2) Applicant income as a percentage of the median family income of the metropolitan statistical area in which the property related to the loan is located. In 1994, the two upper income categories were 100-120 percent and more than 120 percent.
(3) Median family income of the tract relative to that of the metropolitan statistical area in which the tract is located. See Appendix A for additional explanation.
(4) For census tracts located in metropolitan statistical areas.

Fair Lending

TABLE 4.42. DENIAL RATES FOR PRIVATE MORTGAGE INSURANCE APPLICATIONS ON SINGLE-FAMILY HOMES, BY SELECTED CHARACTERISTICS: 1994 TO 1996
(Percent)

CHARACTERISTIC	1994		1995		1996	
	Home purchase	Home refinance	Home purchase	Home refinance	Home purchase	Home refinance
TOTAL	9.7	8.5	9.3	11.5	8.8	8.2
APPLICANT						
Racial or ethnic identity						
American Indian or Alaskan Native	9.9	6.5	10.5	9.8	11.6	13.4
Asian or Pacific Islander	16.3	14.3	13.8	15.8	11.5	10.4
Black	18.4	12.9	19.3	19.7	18.2	14.9
Hispanic [1]	19.4	17.9	17.6	19.3	16.8	13.6
White	9.3	8.2	8.5	10.9	8.0	8.0
Other	16.1	14.2	12.6	10.0	8.0	7.1
Joint	12.7	12.3	11.0	13.0	9.4	7.1
Income ratio [2]						
Less than 80	13.5	13.1	13.7	18.0	12.8	12.4
80-99	9.5	9.2	9.4	12.6	8.3	8.5
100-119	8.3	8.2	7.8	11.1	6.9	7.6
120 or more	7.6	7.5	7.0	10.2	6.1	6.8
CENSUS TRACT						
Racial or ethnic composition						
(Minorities as percentage of population)						
Less than 10	6.0	4.9	5.8	8.8	5.6	6.2
10-19	9.4	8.4	8.6	11.1	7.8	7.7
20-49	13.1	11.7	12.1	13.6	10.8	9.3
50-79	16.5	13.9	15.5	16.8	14.3	12.7
80-100	19.1	16.5	18.7	21.9	17.4	15.7
Income [3]						
Lower	14.2	12.5	13.8	16.2	13.0	11.9
Middle	9.2	8.5	8.6	11.6	8.0	7.9
Upper	7.6	7.6	7.1	10.3	6.4	7.0
Location [4]						
Central city	9.6	8.7	9.2	11.7	8.5	8.5
Non-central city	8.8	8.3	8.3	11.5	7.5	7.6

Source: Board of Governors of the Federal Reserve System, Federal Reserve Bulletin, November 1995, December 1996, and September 1997.

Not all characteristics were reported for all applications.

(1) Persons of Hispanic origin may be of any race.
(2) Applicant income as a percentage of the median family income of the metropolitan statistical area in which the property related to the loan is located. In 1994, the two upper income categories were 100-120 percent and more than 120 percent.
(3) Median family income of the tract relative to that of the metropolitan statistical area in which the tract is located. See Appendix A for additional explanation.
(4) For census tracts located in metropolitan statistical areas.

Fair Lending

YEAR	Bank regulatory agencies					Department of Housing and Urban Development	Total
	Federal Reserve Board	Federal Deposit Insurance Corporation	Office of the Comptroller of the Currency	Office of Thrift Supervision	National Credit Union Administration		
TABLE 4.43. NUMBER OF REFERRALS BY BANK REGULATORY AGENCIES AND THE U.S. DEPARTMENT OF HOUSING AND URBAN DEVELOPMENT TO THE DEPARTMENT OF JUSTICE FOR VIOLATIONS OF FAIR LENDING LAWS, BY AGENCY, 1990-1995							
1990	0	0	1	0	0	0	1
1991	0	0	0	0	0	0	0
1992	1	3	0	0	0	0	4
1993	0	7	4	1	0	1	13
1994	1	12	7	5	0	0	25
1995	5	0	5	0	0	0	10
Total, 1990-95	7	22	17	6	0	1	53

Source: U.S. Department of Justice data as reported in U.S. General Accounting Office, "Fair Lending: Federal Oversight and Enforcement Improved but Some Challenges Remain" (GAO/GGD-96-145).

Fair Lending

RESPONDENT GROUP AND SURVEY YEAR	TABLE 4.44. PERCEPTIONS OF DISCRIMINATION IN MORTGAGE AVAILABILITY: 1993 TO 1997			
	Group discriminated against			
	African Americans	Asian Americans	Hispanic Americans	Women
ALL ADULTS				
1993	36	17	31	24
1994	30	14	29	21
1995	16	7	14	16
1996	17	8	16	14
1997	23	11	21	17
BY RACE/HISPANIC ORIGIN				
Whites				
1993	32	16	29	22
1994	26	13	26	19
1995	12	7	12	15
1996	14	6	14	12
1997	18	10	17	14
African Americans				
1993	59	23	44	39
1994	54	16	40	28
1995	37	11	29	26
1996	33	15	26	25
1997	46	19	42	31
Hispanic Americans [1]				
1993	47	18	40	31
1994	41	18	39	25
1995	22	7	20	14
1996	25	10	23	17
1997	29	15	29	27
BY SEX				
Women				
1993	37	16	32	29
1994	31	15	28	25
1995	15	7	14	18
1996	19	9	18	18
1997	24	12	23	22
Men				
1993	34	17	29	19
1994	29	12	29	16
1995	17	8	15	15
1996	15	8	13	10
1997	21	10	19	11

Source: Fannie Mae, National Housing Survey.

(1) Persons of Hispanic origin may be of any race.

Table shows percent of persons in given respondent group and survey year who believe that the group listed in column heading is discriminated against all or most of the time in getting access to mortgage credit. See Appendix A for wording of the survey questions.

Based on a sample survey of adults in the contiguous United States.

PART 5: FEDERAL HOUSING ASSISTANCE

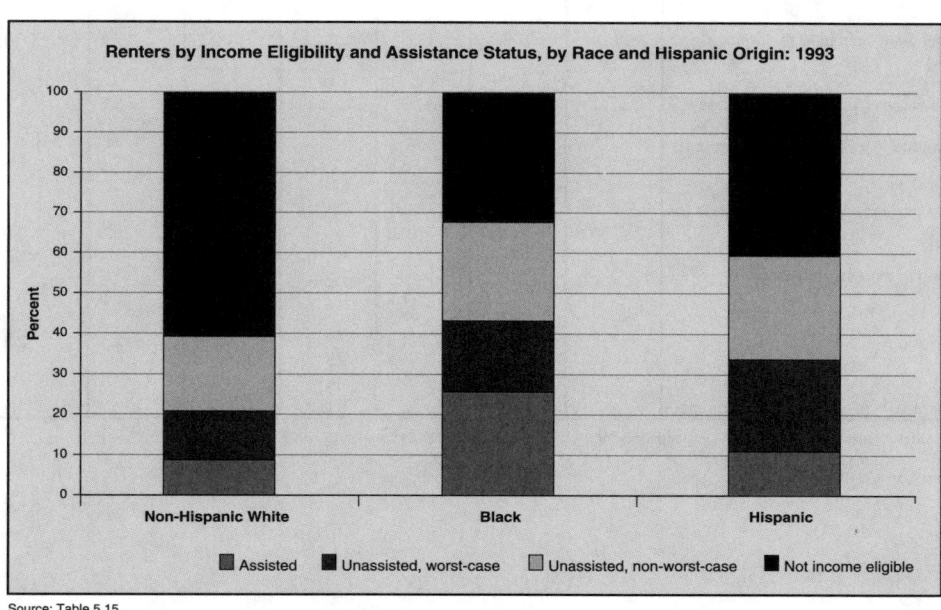

Renters by Income Eligibility and Assistance Status, by Race and Hispanic Origin: 1993

Source: Table 5.15.

Oॖne-half of all renters in the United States qualify for federal low-income housing assistance on the basis of their incomes.[1] Only one-quarter of these income-eligible renters are assisted under one of the rental housing assistance programs administered by the U.S. Department of Housing and Urban Development (HUD). These programs include conventional public housing, Section 8 certificates and vouchers, and several programs that provide subsidies directly to private owners of rental properties in exchange for reduced rents.

Eligibility for and receipt of federal low-income rental housing assistance vary substantially by race and Hispanic origin (see figure). Whereas 40 percent of renters with a non-Hispanic White householder have incomes that qual-

ify them for rental assistance, 68 percent of Black renters and 59 percent of Hispanic renters qualify. Within the population of income-eligible renters, percentages of persons receiving assistance and the incidence of worst-case housing needs substantially differ across groups.[2] Only 18 percent of income-eligible Hispanic renters receive HUD rental assistance, compared with 22 percent of non-Hispanic Whites and 38 percent of Blacks. In 1993, there were 2.1 unassisted Hispanic renters with worst-case housing needs for every Hispanic renter receiving HUD rental assistance. The corresponding ratios for non-Hispanic Whites and Blacks were 1.4:1 and 0.7:1.

---

[1]Income-eligible renters are those households with incomes at 50 percent or less of area median family income, adjusted for family size.

[2]Unassisted renters with incomes at or below 50 percent of area median are deemed to have a worst-case housing need if they pay over 50 percent of their income in rent or live in severely substandard housing.

355

Housing Tax Expenditures in the Income Tax

	TABLE 5.1. PROJECTED FEDERAL TAX EXPENDITURES ON HOUSING: FISCAL YEARS 1998 TO 2002 (Billions of dollars)									
TAX PROVISION	Corporations					Individuals				
	1998	1999	2000	2001	2002	1998	1999	2000	2001	2002
Deduction of mortgage interest on owner-occupied residences	....	....	....	....	....	43.0	44.7	46.4	48.3	50.2
Deduction of property tax on owner-occupied residences	....	....	....	....	....	16.6	17.3	17.9	18.7	19.5
Exclusion of capital gains on sales of principal residences	....	....	....	....	....	5.6	5.7	5.9	6.1	6.3
Exclusion of interest on state and local government bonds for owner-occupied housing	0.6	0.6	0.7	0.7	0.7	1.6	1.7	1.8	1.9	1.9
Exclusion of interest on state and local government bonds for rental housing	0.3	0.3	0.3	0.3	0.3	0.8	0.8	0.9	0.9	0.9
Depreciation of rental housing in excess of alternative depreciation system	1.1	1.0	1.0	1.0	1.0	0.8	0.7	0.7	0.7	0.7
Tax credit for low-income housing	1.1	1.2	1.4	1.5	1.6	2.1	2.3	2.5	2.8	3.0
Tax credit for first-time homebuyers in the District of Columbia	....	....	....	....	....	[1]	[1]	[1]	[1]	[1]

Source: Joint Committee on Taxation, "Estimates of Federal Tax Expenditures for Fiscal Years 1998-2002." December 15, 1997.

(1) Positive tax expenditure of less than $50 million.

Major Programs for Low- and Moderate-Income Households

TABLE 5.2. HOUSEHOLDS RECEIVING FEDERAL HOUSING ASSISTANCE BY TYPE OF SUBSIDY: 1977 TO 1997
(Thousands)

BEGINNING OF FISCAL YEAR	Assisted renters					Assisted homeowners	Total assisted renters and owners
	Existing housing			New construction	Total		
	Household-based	Project-based	Total				
1977	162	105	268	1,825	2,092	1,071	3,164
1978	297	126	423	1,977	2,400	1,082	3,482
1979	427	175	602	2,052	2,654	1,095	3,749
1980 [1]	521	185	707	2,189	2,895	1,112	4,007
1981	599	221	820	2,379	3,012	1,127	4,139
1982	651	194	844	2,559	3,210	1,201	4,411
1983	691	265	955	2,702	3,443	1,226	4,668
1984	728	357	1,086	2,836	3,700	1,219	4,920
1985	749	431	1,180	2,931	3,887	1,193	5,080
1986	797	456	1,253	2,986	3,998	1,176	5,174
1987	893	473	1,366	3,047	4,175	1,126	5,301
1988 [2]	956	490	1,446	3,085	4,296	918	5,213
1989	1,025	509	1,534	3,117	4,402	892	5,295
1990	1,090	527	1,616	3,141	4,515	875	5,390
1991	1,137	540	1,678	3,180	4,613	853	5,465
1992	1,166	554	1,721	3,204	4,680	826	5,506
1993	1,326	574	1,900	3,196	4,851	774	5,625
1994	1,392	593	1,985	3,213	4,962	751	5,714
1995	1,487	595	2,081	3,242	5,087	705	5,792
1996	1,413	608	2,021	3,293	5,079	670	5,748
1997	1,465	586	2,051	3,305	5,120	631	5,751

Source: Congressional Budget Office based on data provided by the U.S. Department of Housing and Urban Development and the Farmers Home Administration/Rural Housing Service.

(1) Figures for total assisted renters have been adjusted since 1980 to avoid double-counting households receiving more than one subsidy.

(2) Starting with 1988, the number of assisted homeowners reflects a one-time decrease of 141,000 because of asset sales by the Farmers Home Administration to private investors.

Major Programs for Low- and Moderate-Income Households

FISCAL YEAR	TABLE 5.3. NET NEW COMMITMENTS FOR RENTERS AND NEW COMMITMENTS FOR HOMEBUYERS: 1977 TO 1997			
	Net new commitments for renters			New commitments for homebuyers
	Existing housing	New construction	Total	
1977	127,581	247,667	375,248	112,234
1978	126,472	214,503	340,975	112,214
1979	102,669	231,156	333,825	107,871
1980	58,402	155,001	213,403	140,564
1981	83,520	94,914	178,434	74,636
1982	37,818	48,157	85,975	66,711
1983	54,071	23,861	77,932	54,550
1984	78,648	36,719	115,367	44,409
1985	85,741	42,667	128,408	45,387
1986	85,476	34,375	119,851	25,479
1987	72,788	37,247	110,035	24,132
1988	65,295	36,456	101,751	26,200
1989	68,858	30,049	98,907	25,264
1990	61,309	23,491	84,800	24,968
1991	55,900	28,478	84,378	23,879
1992	62,595	38,324	100,919	25,690
1993	50,593	34,065	84,658	30,982
1994	66,907	29,194	96,101	38,588
1995	25,822	19,440	45,262	31,985
1996	33,696	16,259	49,955	40,838
1997[1]	36,134	14,027	50,161	48,360

Source: Congressional Budget Office based on data provided by the U.S. Department of Housing and Urban Development and the Farmers Home Administration/Rural Housing Service.

(1) Estimated.

Because of data limitations, figures for 1992 to 1997 are not adjusted for units for which funds were de-obligated.

Major Programs for Low- and Moderate-Income Households

| FISCAL YEAR | TABLE 5.4. NET BUDGET AUTHORITY APPROPRIATED FOR HOUSING AID ADMINISTERED BY THE U.S. DEPARTMENT OF HOUSING AND URBAN DEVELOPMENT: 1977 TO 1997 (In millions of current and 1997 dollars) | |
	Current dollars	Constant 1997 CPI-U-X1 adjusted dollars [1]
1977	28,579	73,356
1978	32,169	77,558
1979	25,123	55,622
1980	27,435	54,657
1981	26,022	47,112
1982	14,766	24,981
1983	10,001	16,201
1984	11,425	17,757
1985	11,071	16,595
1986	10,032	14,673
1987	8,979	12,765
1988	8,592	11,732
1989	8,879	11,576
1990	10,557	13,109
1991	19,239	22,741
1992	16,883	19,375
1993	18,466	20,564
1994	18,414	19,981
1995	11,840	12,497
1996	13,229	13,586
1997 [2]	12,020	12,020

Source: Congressional Budget Office based on data provided by the U.S. Department of Housing and Urban Development.

(1) See Appendix B under "Consumer Price Index" (CPI) for a discussion of the use of the CPI-U-X1 as a price deflator.
(2) Estimate.

All figures are net of funding rescissions, exclude reappropriations of funds, but include supplemental appropriations. See Appendix A for additional notes.

Major Programs for Low- and Moderate-Income Households

FISCAL YEAR	TABLE 5.5. TOTAL OUTLAYS AND PER UNIT OUTLAYS FOR HOUSING AID ADMINISTERED BY THE U.S. DEPARTMENT OF HOUSING AND URBAN DEVELOPMENT: 1977 TO 1997			
	Total outlays		Per unit outlays	
	Current dollars (Millions)	Constant 1997 CPI-U-X1 adjusted dollars (Millions) [1]	Current dollars	Constant 1997 CPI-U-X1 adjusted dollars [1]
1977	2,928	7,515	1,160	2,980
1978	3,592	8,660	1,310	3,160
1979	4,189	9,275	1,430	3,160
1980	5,364	10,687	1,750	3,480
1981	6,733	12,189	2,100	3,810
1982	7,846	13,273	2,310	3,900
1983	9,419	15,257	2,600	4,220
1984	11,000	17,096	2,900	4,500
1985 [2]	25,064	37,569	6,420	9,620
1986	12,179	17,813	3,040	4,440
1987	12,509	17,784	3,040	4,320
1988	13,684	18,684	3,270	4,460
1989	14,466	18,860	3,390	4,420
1990	15,690	19,484	3,610	4,480
1991	16,898	19,973	3,830	4,530
1992	18,243	20,936	4,060	4,670
1993	20,490	22,817	4,450	4,960
1994	22,191	24,079	4,720	5,120
1995 [3]	24,059	25,394	5,080	5,360
1996 [3]	25,349	26,032	5,350	5,490
1997 [4]	26,110	26,110	5,490	5,490

Source: Congressional Budget Office based on data provided by the U.S. Department of Housing and Urban Development.

(1) See Appendix B under "Consumer Price Index" (CPI) for a discussion of the use of the CPI-U-X1 as a price deflator.

(2) A change in the method of financing public housing caused almost $14 billion in one-time expenditures in 1985. See Appendix A for additional explanation.

(3) Data for 1995 and 1996 have been adjusted to account for $1.2 billion of advance spending that occurred in 1995 but should have occurred in 1996.

(4) Estimate.

Major Programs for Low- and Moderate-Income Households

PROGRAM	TABLE 5.6. DOLLARS OBLIGATED AND UNITS ASSISTED UNDER SELECTED FARMERS HOME ADMINISTRATION PROGRAMS FROM INCEPTION THROUGH FISCAL YEAR 1997		
	Year of inception	Dollars obligated (Billions)	Units assisted (Thousands)
Section 502 direct homeownership loans	1950	50.389	1,884.1
Section 502 guaranteed homeownership loans	1977	6.305	96.8
Section 504 very low-income repair loans	1950	0.359	113.6
Section 504 very low-income repair grants	1950	0.341	101.6
Section 514/516 farm labor housing loans and grants	1962, 1966	0.678	29.7
Section 515 rural rental housing	1963	14.236	517.2
Section 533 housing preservation grants	1986	0.228	49.8
Section 538 guaranteed multifamily housing loans	1996	0.044	1.3
Section 521 rental assistance	1978	6.717	497.2

Source: Housing Assistance Council.

Major Programs for Low- and Moderate-Income Households

TABLE 5.7. OBLIGATIONS FOR FARMERS HOME ADMINISTRATION/RURAL HOUSING SERVICE HOUSING PROGRAMS: FISCAL YEARS 1980 TO 1997
(Millions of dollars)

YEAR	502 home-ownership loans	504 low-income repair loans	504 low-income repair grants	Credit sales	306C individual water and waste disposal grants	514 farm labor housing loans	516 farm labor housing grants	515 rural rental housing	523 self-help tech. ass. grants	523 and 524 site loans	509(f) and 525 grants	Rental assist. contracts	509(c) compensation for constr. defects	533 housing preserv. grants	538 guaranteed multi-family housing	Total
1980	2,843.4	21.9	24.0	....	....	24.6	22.3	881.3	6.2	1.3	1.5	393.0	0.6	....	....	4,220.1
1981	2,589.3	17.9	22.7	....	....	18.5	10.5	864.8	12.4	0.9	1.0	403.0	0.7	....	....	3,941.7
1982	2,476.4	10.0	13.6	....	....	11.9	14.9	953.7	4.7	0.4	0.0	398.0	0.3	....	....	3,883.9
1983	2,137.1	7.1	12.5	....	....	4.0	7.5	802.0	10.2	0.3	0.0	123.7	0.3	....	....	3,105.5
1984	1,849.4	7.2	12.5	....	....	5.5	9.8	919.0	5.1	0.2	0.0	111.0	0.2	0.0	....	2,919.9
1985	1,789.9	7.9	12.5	....	....	17.6	12.2	903.3	10.8	1.3	0.0	168.2	0.5	0.0	....	2,923.9
1986	1,155.4	7.0	13.9	....	....	10.7	10.9	652.3	5.9	0.6	0.0	160.3	0.3	19.1	....	2,036.4
1987	1,144.4	5.9	12.5	....	....	10.7	7.6	554.9	8.4	0.7	0.0	275.3	0.2	19.1	....	2,039.7
1988	1,270.9	7.6	12.5	....	....	11.4	11.2	554.9	5.7	0.0	0.0	275.3	0.3	19.1	....	2,168.9
1989	1,266.9	11.3	12.5	....	....	11.4	9.7	554.9	10.2	0.9	0.0	275.4	0.3	19.1	....	2,172.6
1990	1,308.1	11.6	12.6	....	....	11.3	11.1	571.9	6.4	0.6	0.0	296.4	0.2	19.1	....	2,252.3
1991	1,308.1	11.2	12.7	....	....	13.8	10.7	576.3	13.2	1.1	0.0	311.1	0.2	23.0	....	2,281.4
1992	1,649.6	11.3	12.8	....	....	15.9	12.8	573.9	7.8	0.9	0.0	319.8	0.2	23.0	....	2,628.0
1993	2,561.2	11.8	16.3	....	....	16.3	15.9	573.9	18.0	0.6	0.0	404.0	0.3	23.0	....	3,641.3
1994	2,382.7	25.2	27.5	123.4	3.1	15.7	40.6	512.4	12.8	0.1	1.8	449.6	0.4	23.0	....	3,618.3
1995	1,982.7	29.5	27.8	....	2.4	15.1	11.0	183.3	14.5	....	0.5	523.0	0.3	22.0	....	2,812.1
1996	2,716.4	35.1	25.7	....	1.7	15.0	10.0	151.0	12.9	0.6	3.4	540.5	0.3	11.0	23.7	3,547.3
1997	2,706.3	30.9	17.6	23.9	1.2	15.0	8.4	151.5	26.2	0.4	1.0	520.2	0.3	7.6	28.1	3,538.6

Source: Housing Assistance Council, "The RHCDS Housing Program in Fiscal Year 1996: 'A Year of Serious Consequences'," and 1997 updates provided by the Housing Assistance Council.

See Appendix A for program descriptions.

Major Programs for Low- and Moderate-Income Households

TABLE 5.8. UNITS PRODUCED AND HOUSEHOLDS ASSISTED UNDER FARMERS HOME ADMINISTRATION/RURAL HOUSING SERVICE HOUSING PROGRAMS: FISCAL YEARS 1980 TO 1997

YEAR	Assisted units												Rental assistance con-tracts [2,3]	Total [4]
	502 sub-sidized	502 un-subsidized	502 guaran-teed	Credit sales	504 loans	504 grants	514 farm labor housing loans and 516 farm labor housing grants [1]	515 sub-sidized	515 un-subsidized	533 housing preserv. grants	538 guaran-teed multi-family housing	Total		
1980	62,739	18,918	590	0	6,934	8,013	1,606	33,564	2,227	....	....	134,642	20,000	154,642
1981	61,544	7,990	172	0	5,296	7,014	913	29,643	784	....	....	113,356	17,655	131,011
1982	56,850	5,107	0	0	2,711	3,937	565	30,616	0	....	....	99,846	14,280	114,126
1983	51,211	709	0	0	1,993	3,670	301	23,406	0	....	....	81,290	11,750	93,040
1984	43,459	20	0	0	2,057	3,416	775	29,772	0	0	....	79,499	11,750	91,249
1985	40,813	1	0	0	2,315	3,464	653	28,218	0	0	....	75,464	15,250	90,714
1986	25,474	4	0	0	2,018	3,897	731	21,252	0	4,106	....	57,483	14,511	71,994
1987	24,077	8	0	0	1,707	3,403	413	17,434	0	4,055	....	51,097	24,921	76,018
1988	25,869	334	0	0	2,145	3,384	421	16,489	0	4,450	....	53,092	24,921	78,013
1989	24,788	476	0	0	3,041	3,430	404	15,996	0	4,401	....	52,536	24,929	77,465
1990	24,269	700	0	0	3,372	2,611	170	16,063	0	5,349	....	52,534	26,467	79,001
1991	22,517	605	660	0	2,557	3,385	281	15,396	0	4,560	....	49,961	29,240	79,201
1992	21,181	681	3,828	0	2,467	3,376	574	14,798	0	3,981	....	50,886	29,735	80,621
1993	21,430	651	8,901	4,595	2,627	3,670	641	15,251	0	4,702	....	62,468	33,662	96,130
1994	26,302	1,049	11,523	2,925	5,067	6,773	807	11,542	0	5,009	....	70,997	36,476	107,473
1995	15,351	0	16,580	0	5,444	6,199	617	2,853	0	4,878	....	51,922	41,760	93,682
1996	15,883	0	24,955	0	6,006	5,400	399	1,913	0	2,651	450	57,657	40,012	97,669
1997	11,403	0	29,161	359	4,726	3,470	337	2,468	0	1,707	813	54,444	39,495	93,939

Source: Housing Assistance Council, "The RHCDS Housing Program in Fiscal Year 1996: 'A Year of Serious Consequences'," and 1997 updates provided by the Housing Assistance Council.

(1) Does not include 535 rehabilitated existing 514/516 units in fiscal year 1990, 472 rehabilitated units in fiscal year 1991, and 77 rehabilitated units in fiscal year 1997.

(2) Includes new, renewal, and servicing rental assistance units.

(3) Farmers Home Administration converted to state average contract costs in fiscal year 1991.

(4) Not unduplicated units; that is, counts twice some units that receive more than one Rural Housing Service loan, grant, or other type of assistance. Housing unit production contained in total under assisted units.

See Appendix A for program descriptions.

Major Programs for Low- and Moderate-Income Households

TABLE 5.9. HUD-SUBSIDIZED UNITS AND LOW-INCOME HOUSING TAX CREDIT UNITS, BY STATE

AREA	HUD-subsidized units								Low-Income Housing Tax Credit	Total, HUD-subsidized and Low-Income Housing Tax Credit
	Indian Housing	Public Housing	Section 8 Certificates and Vouchers	Section 8 Moderate Rehabilitation	Section 8 New Construction or Substantial Rehabilitation	Section 236	Other FHA projects with subsidies	Total, HUD-subsidized		
United States	69,755	1,321,717	1,433,191	109,859	894,684	447,606	292,229	4,569,041	332,085	4,901,126
Alabama	155	44,651	19,795	1,805	13,758	5,184	1,555	86,903	8,738	95,641
Alaska	5,354	1,628	2,640		887	642	238	11,389	387	11,776
Arizona	13,574	6,911	14,552	890	6,209	3,726	1,641	47,503	2,857	50,360
Arkansas	0	15,661	18,943	206	7,864	2,955	3,880	49,509	3,734	53,243
California	2,640	46,544	207,583	7,962	61,103	53,382	20,909	400,123	15,189	415,312
Colorado	565	8,581	17,313	2,277	11,839	7,068	2,631	50,274	3,011	53,285
Connecticut	60	18,728	22,495	2,142	16,057	10,229	7,626	77,337	2,261	79,598
Delaware	0	3,388	3,410	152	3,830	709	563	12,052	1,299	13,351
District of Columbia	0	11,788	4,012	1,271	6,190	4,462	3,904	31,627	1,157	32,784
Florida	418	43,874	66,187	8,272	25,751	18,509	11,928	174,939	14,144	189,083
Guam	0	751	1,423	75	50	0	0	2,299	0	2,299
Georgia	0	57,559	28,953	1,425	17,182	13,346	7,325	125,790	10,525	136,315
Hawaii	0	5,263	8,695	58	2,591	2,205	1,587	20,399	651	21,050
Idaho	792	816	4,917	121	3,497	820	399	11,362	2,394	13,756
Illinois	0	78,845	47,926	5,567	46,912	12,632	16,760	208,642	17,067	225,709
Indiana	0	18,363	26,848	1,274	21,224	14,999	9,780	92,488	4,015	96,503
Iowa	20	4,759	15,625	1,055	11,667	3,133	1,495	37,754	2,927	40,681
Kansas	412	9,294	7,396	351	9,082	3,209	3,266	33,010	6,660	39,670
Kentucky	0	25,699	20,967	1,738	18,258	6,531	5,856	79,049	3,781	82,830
Louisiana	78	32,086	27,346	2,482	11,789	6,131	6,539	86,451	11,164	97,615
Maine	429	4,188	9,122	1,486	7,308	1,655	624	24,812	2,606	27,418
Maryland	0	26,430	28,398	2,808	17,869	14,904	5,753	96,162	9,219	105,381
Massachusetts	18	35,043	49,114	4,306	36,232	20,497	12,776	157,986	8,857	166,843
Michigan	833	29,395	26,851	950	40,635	23,257	17,092	139,013	10,903	149,916
Minnesota	1,869	22,000	24,604	901	23,841	10,243	4,355	87,813	6,877	94,690
Mississippi	721	15,541	13,072	1,082	11,932	3,234	4,170	49,752	4,922	54,674
Missouri	0	21,316	31,737	3,495	21,167	8,277	7,121	93,113	12,384	105,497
Montana	5,386	2,068	3,785	823	2,741	2,222	1,135	18,160	998	19,158
Nebraska	682	7,349	9,898	718	5,597	1,789	835	26,868	3,786	30,654
Nevada	1,916	4,500	5,331	834	2,255	1,627	1,354	17,817	2,301	20,118
New Hampshire	0	4,344	6,060	403	4,938	1,969	398	18,112	1,060	19,172
New Jersey	0	48,027	43,542	3,351	36,776	11,694	7,681	151,071	3,957	155,028
New Mexico	3,127	4,865	9,841	494	3,173	1,968	2,449	25,917	2,708	28,625
New York	513	197,043	143,409	10,654	81,450	38,132	15,747	486,948	6,498	493,446
North Carolina	1,281	39,960	38,869	3,758	21,086	6,750	5,318	117,022	8,071	125,093
North Dakota	2,817	1,919	6,207	549	3,146	859	384	15,881	1,046	16,927
Northern Mariana Islands	0	0	61	0	192	0	0	253	0	253
Ohio	0	56,920	55,671	5,010	46,411	26,061	18,558	208,631	16,905	225,536
Oklahoma	12,942	13,413	19,328	2,710	6,721	4,725	3,894	63,733	7,755	71,488
Oregon	462	6,168	22,303	1,382	7,364	3,375	1,832	42,886	7,237	50,123
Pennsylvania	0	80,620	55,384	4,783	45,714	19,980	6,631	213,112	13,290	226,402
Puerto Rico	0	57,047	30,764	4,549	18,388	4,511	4,328	119,587	3,957	123,544
Rhode Island	0	10,045	7,016	611	11,922	3,588	941	34,123	1,676	35,799
South Carolina	0	16,867	15,521	2,029	12,876	5,030	4,869	57,192	3,591	60,783
South Dakota	5,742	1,691	3,985	604	3,582	1,099	2,130	18,833	2,234	21,067
Tennessee	0	42,552	19,807	1,918	21,650	8,530	7,984	102,441	8,493	110,934
Texas	240	66,746	91,247	5,590	27,721	21,936	27,437	240,917	35,903	276,820
Utah	451	2,194	6,621	830	3,339	859	402	14,696	1,760	16,456
Vermont	0	1,791	3,795	292	3,045	292	279	9,494	950	10,444
Virgin Islands	0	4,368	448	163	124	0	0	5,103	157	5,260
Virginia	0	22,946	25,765	822	23,306	14,697	6,818	94,354	10,391	104,745
Washington	3,206	17,237	24,336	742	9,879	5,353	6,315	67,068	8,118	75,186
West Virginia	0	7,397	11,822	1,014	9,030	1,891	1,004	32,158	1,624	33,782
Wisconsin	2,407	13,822	20,956	894	25,500	6,278	3,509	73,366	9,812	83,178
Wyoming	645	716	1,495	181	2,034	452	224	5,747	78	5,825

Source: Burke, Paul, "A Picture of Subsidized Households in 1997: United States: Totals and Agencies with over 500 Units." U.S. Department of Housing and Urban Development. December 15, 1997.

The table shows the number of Public and Indian Housing, Section 8 Certificate and Voucher, and Section 8 Moderate Rehabilitation units under contract and available for occupancy as of June 1, 1997. For other HUD-subsidized programs, the unit counts are as of September 30, 1995. Low-Income Housing Tax Credit counts are for units in service as of December 1994.

Characteristics of Assisted Households, Their Housing, and Their Neighborhoods

TABLE 5.10. AVERAGE INCOME AND RENT FOR SELECTED HUD-RENTAL HOUSING PROGRAMS

AREA	Public Housing			Section 8 Certificates and Vouchers			Section 8 New Construction or Substantial Rehabilitation			Total, HUD-subsidized [1]		
	Percent reported [2]	Average monthly rent (Dollars)	Average annual income ($1,000s)	Percent reported [2]	Average monthly rent (Dollars)	Average annual income ($1,000s)	Percent reported [2]	Average monthly rent (Dollars)	Average annual income ($1,000s)	Percent reported [2]	Average monthly rent (Dollars)	Average annual income ($1,000s)
United States	80	192	8.9	84	204	9.1	83	190	8.9	80	202	9.2
Alabama	91	148	7.1	92	151	6.8	90	147	7.4	90	152	7.2
Alaska	91	363	16.0	95	338	14.0	66	318	14.0	66	300	19.0
Arizona	96	180	8.6	97	189	8.7	95	171	8.0	85	184	10.0
Arkansas	93	143	7.0	87	151	7.1	91	146	7.1	89	153	7.3
California	82	239	11.0	86	269	11.0	87	222	9.8	84	256	11.0
Colorado	89	189	8.9	85	203	8.9	83	183	8.7	85	193	8.8
Connecticut	71	229	10.0	68	256	11.0	60	224	10.0	67	258	12.0
Delaware	25	....	....	87	209	9.0	90	202	9.5	73	205	9.3
District of Columbia	91	180	8.3	0	....	....	68	188	8.5	57	207	9.2
Florida	77	160	7.5	71	180	8.1	96	169	7.8	78	176	7.9
Guam	56	337	14.0	94	302	12.0	0	....	....	77	313	12.0
Georgia	76	151	7.1	76	180	7.9	86	165	8.1	78	169	7.8
Hawaii	99	257	11.0	98	279	12.0	91	220	9.6	92	289	12.0
Idaho	97	185	9.0	99	199	8.7	96	174	8.4	93	188	8.9
Illinois	57	150	7.3	87	195	9.2	48	196	9.5	61	182	8.7
Indiana	85	163	8.1	73	182	8.2	93	174	8.7	82	193	9.1
Iowa	95	195	9.5	99	193	8.7	98	185	9.1	95	192	9.1
Kansas	90	173	8.5	85	196	8.6	92	176	9.0	88	188	9.5
Kentucky	93	150	7.2	98	156	7.3	97	148	7.2	92	157	7.5
Louisiana	87	128	6.6	77	150	6.8	91	143	7.1	83	147	7.0
Maine	98	202	9.3	99	189	8.4	35	....	....	75	202	9.1
Maryland	87	178	8.2	58	199	8.8	75	200	9.4	71	212	9.4
Massachusetts	70	223	9.9	94	250	11.0	76	240	11.0	75	245	11.0
Michigan	85	192	9.1	81	204	9.6	93	201	9.5	79	213	10.0
Minnesota	94	196	9.4	90	220	9.6	42	200	9.7	73	211	9.7
Mississippi	87	161	7.6	97	164	7.2	82	136	6.6	86	154	7.3
Missouri	85	163	7.7	88	175	7.5	95	170	8.3	83	173	7.9
Montana	83	165	8.0	97	184	8.1	94	172	8.6	73	174	9.1
Nebraska	96	191	9.4	93	201	8.8	95	178	8.8	92	192	9.1
Nevada	47	216	10.0	96	229	10.0	85	195	8.9	74	217	10.0
New Hampshire	95	235	11.0	99	248	11.0	93	213	10.0	94	245	11.0
New Jersey	59	223	9.9	77	242	10.0	83	230	10.0	72	235	10.0
New Mexico	78	177	8.2	86	169	7.6	92	162	7.6	81	177	9.0
New York	91	295	13.0	84	214	10.0	87	243	10.0	84	263	12.0
North Carolina	94	161	7.6	90	172	7.8	87	161	7.7	89	170	7.9
North Dakota	98	176	8.9	92	173	8.4	88	159	8.1	82	165	8.7
Northern Mariana Islands	....	....	....	99	194	9.0	17	....	....	37	....	....
Ohio	91	169	8.0	90	188	8.3	93	174	8.3	91	178	8.2
Oklahoma	78	142	7.1	91	163	7.4	86	153	7.7	82	147	8.5
Oregon	99	211	9.6	99	217	9.2	59	178	8.3	89	209	9.1
Pennsylvania	67	183	8.4	84	196	8.8	94	198	9.3	80	197	9.0
Puerto Rico	34	....	....	54	91	5.0	86	100	5.5	49	85	4.7
Rhode Island	76	210	9.7	84	229	9.9	94	217	10.0	84	219	9.9
South Carolina	92	152	7.4	96	163	7.6	92	153	7.3	91	161	7.6
South Dakota	95	196	9.9	99	191	8.7	93	170	8.5	75	181	9.2
Tennessee	88	142	6.8	86	165	7.5	92	155	7.5	87	154	7.3
Texas	86	141	6.8	80	151	7.2	91	153	7.4	82	156	7.4
Utah	96	210	9.8	95	220	9.1	92	187	8.7	91	207	9.1
Vermont	96	228	10.0	98	239	9.9	98	216	9.8	94	233	10.0
Virgin Islands	32	....	....	0	....	....	90	167	7.1	29	....	....
Virginia	81	167	8.0	62	213	9.3	93	181	8.6	74	202	9.1
Washington	82	200	9.0	81	229	9.3	94	187	8.7	80	210	9.1
West Virginia	87	145	6.9	98	147	6.5	94	156	7.7	92	151	7.0
Wisconsin	92	213	9.8	97	244	10.0	51	204	9.7	75	225	10.0
Wyoming	92	175	8.7	99	172	7.8	91	154	7.8	87	160	8.1

Source: Burke, Paul, "A Picture of Subsidized Households in 1997: United States: Totals and Agencies with over 500 Units." U.S. Department of Housing and Urban Development. December 15, 1997.

Characteristics are based on reports received in the 30-month period prior to June/July of 1997.

(1) Includes other programs, not shown separately.

(2) Overall percent of occupied units reporting for given program. Percent of units reporting may vary for individual characteristic.

Characteristics of Assisted Households, Their Housing, and Their Neighborhoods

TABLE 5.11. HOUSEHOLD DEMOGRAPHIC AND SOCIAL CHARACTERISTICS FOR SELECTED HUD-RENTAL HOUSING PROGRAMS
(Percent)

AREA	Public Housing				Section 8 Certificates and Vouchers			
	Percent reported [2]	Head or spouse age 62 or older	Head is minority	Households with spouse absent and children under 18	Percent reported [2]	Head or spouse age 62 or older	Head is minority	Households with spouse absent and children under 18
United States	80	32	68	39	84	16	58	57
Alabama	91	26	73	51	92	12	70	68
Alaska	91	25	58	48	95	8	41	56
Arizona	96	17	78	51	97	15	66	60
Arkansas	93	34	54	42	87	16	43	59
California	82	24	82	46	86	22	69	48
Colorado	89	29	64	40	85	12	48	54
Connecticut	71	36	72	41	68	14	68	64
Delaware	25	....	....	....	87	10	75	67
District of Columbia	91	30	99	35	0	....	....	....
Florida	77	31	86	50	71	21	77	61
Guam	56	9	98	48	94	6	99	55
Georgia	76	27	81	53	76	11	85	70
Hawaii	99	35	87	34	98	13	76	52
Idaho	97	44	11	17	99	4	13	54
Illinois	57	35	61	39	87	13	70	63
Indiana	85	34	51	42	73	14	38	57
Iowa	95	53	8	25	99	16	16	53
Kansas	90	44	31	28	85	10	43	61
Kentucky	93	27	39	42	98	10	30	56
Louisiana	87	20	88	61	77	12	82	67
Maine	98	44	5	33	99	21	2	45
Maryland	87	35	81	43	58	14	73	62
Massachusetts	70	43	47	28	94	15	41	57
Michigan	85	44	48	29	81	5	50	64
Minnesota	94	44	32	16	90	15	29	59
Mississippi	87	25	79	54	97	8	81	77
Missouri	85	39	48	34	88	11	49	65
Montana	83	18	20	48	97	14	20	47
Nebraska	96	49	25	23	93	15	36	58
Nevada	47	29	49	52	96	23	49	55
New Hampshire	95	58	7	20	99	25	4	40
New Jersey	59	43	73	35	77	24	57	51
New Mexico	78	26	82	43	86	10	78	63
New York	91	34	86	19	84	26	57	50
North Carolina	94	23	84	54	90	17	66	60
North Dakota	98	45	14	23	92	21	13	44
Northern Mariana Islands	....	....	....	....	99	3	97	36
Ohio	91	26	65	42	90	10	52	60
Oklahoma	78	35	37	33	91	14	46	62
Oregon	99	26	24	33	99	17	20	44
Pennsylvania	67	36	46	37	84	16	36	56
Puerto Rico	34	....	....	....	54	11	99	48
Rhode Island	76	54	31	21	84	15	28	61
South Carolina	92	21	86	59	96	13	77	68
South Dakota	95	67	12	15	99	18	16	47
Tennessee	88	25	55	46	86	9	43	65
Texas	86	30	78	44	80	12	82	66
Utah	96	40	26	39	95	10	21	57
Vermont	96	58	3	17	98	21	2	39
Virgin Islands	32	....	....	....	0	....	....	....
Virginia	81	21	85	57	62	11	70	64
Washington	82	27	44	24	81	14	30	49
West Virginia	87	33	23	32	98	9	10	51
Wisconsin	92	45	36	25	97	13	42	57
Wyoming	92	34	19	43	99	14	20	53

See notes at end of table.

Characteristics of Assisted Households, Their Housing, and Their Neighborhoods

TABLE 5.11. HOUSEHOLD DEMOGRAPHIC AND SOCIAL CHARACTERISTICS FOR SELECTED HUD-RENTAL HOUSING PROGRAMS - Continued
(Percent)

AREA	Section 8 New Construction or Substantial Rehabilitation				Total, HUD-subsidized [1]			
	Percent reported [2]	Head or spouse age 62 or older	Head is minority	Households with spouse absent and children under 18	Percent reported [2]	Head or spouse age 62 or older	Head is minority	Households with spouse absent and children under 18
United States	83	60	37	20	80	31	57	42
Alabama	90	50	39	29	90	26	66	52
Alaska	66	32	46	33	66	18	62	45
Arizona	95	71	29	14	85	23	67	46
Arkansas	91	54	27	16	89	29	45	45
California	87	67	49	16	84	33	66	38
Colorado	83	63	29	17	85	30	49	39
Connecticut	60	69	32	12	67	34	57	42
Delaware	90	51	44	32	73	31	62	50
District of Columbia	68	50	96	33	57	34	99	39
Florida	96	69	52	16	78	35	74	47
Guam	0	....	....	....	77	7	99	53
Georgia	86	48	47	34	78	25	77	54
Hawaii	91	65	77	10	92	29	81	37
Idaho	96	49	5	27	93	24	14	39
Illinois	48	68	38	14	61	31	63	44
Indiana	93	60	18	22	82	30	37	43
Iowa	98	65	7	17	95	37	12	37
Kansas	92	69	10	9	88	38	30	33
Kentucky	97	44	15	27	92	27	30	41
Louisiana	91	57	54	24	83	21	80	57
Maine	35	....	....	....	75	35	4	35
Maryland	75	63	49	19	71	29	71	47
Massachusetts	76	71	24	9	75	37	41	36
Michigan	93	64	29	17	79	38	42	36
Minnesota	42	66	5	14	73	34	28	34
Mississippi	82	40	70	38	86	22	76	58
Missouri	95	61	34	20	83	31	46	45
Montana	94	61	7	20	73	30	30	35
Nebraska	95	65	9	17	92	36	27	38
Nevada	85	58	24	24	74	28	49	46
New Hampshire	93	78	1	6	94	47	4	27
New Jersey	83	71	50	13	72	43	62	34
New Mexico	92	58	46	18	81	21	76	49
New York	87	58	56	20	84	35	70	32
North Carolina	87	52	44	25	89	25	71	52
North Dakota	88	56	6	19	82	31	19	35
Northern Mariana Islands	17	....	....	....	37	....	....	....
Ohio	93	55	29	24	91	29	50	43
Oklahoma	86	61	24	18	82	24	49	44
Oregon	59	60	10	13	89	27	19	34
Pennsylvania	94	71	24	15	80	39	37	37
Puerto Rico	86	34	99	29	49	18	99	42
Rhode Island	94	73	16	7	84	48	24	27
South Carolina	92	35	55	41	91	21	76	58
South Dakota	93	56	6	18	75	34	27	33
Tennessee	92	58	26	19	87	29	46	44
Texas	91	59	50	22	82	24	76	52
Utah	92	51	13	24	91	24	21	45
Vermont	98	69	2	13	94	44	2	27
Virgin Islands	90	42	95	28	29	....	....	....
Virginia	93	50	50	32	74	26	69	50
Washington	94	61	16	16	80	30	31	32
West Virginia	94	53	7	19	92	28	12	37
Wisconsin	51	66	15	13	75	37	35	36
Wyoming	91	48	11	24	87	30	23	38

Source: Burke, Paul, "A Picture of Subsidized Households in 1997: United States: Totals and Agencies with over 500 Units." U.S. Department of Housing and Urban Development. December 15, 1997.

Characteristics are based on reports received in the 30-month period prior to June/July of 1997.

(1) Includes other programs, not shown separately.

(2) Overall percent of occupied units reporting for given program. Percent of units reporting may vary for individual characteristic.

Characteristics of Assisted Households, Their Housing, and Their Neighborhoods

AREA	TABLE 5.12. CENSUS TRACT CHARACTERISTICS FOR SELECTED HUD-RENTAL HOUSING PROGRAMS AND FOR THE LOW-INCOME HOUSING TAX CREDIT PROGRAM (Percent)									
	Public Housing		Section 8 Certificates and Vouchers		Section 8 New Construction or Substantial Rehabilitation		Low-Income Housing Tax Credit		Total, HUD-subsidized and Low-Income Housing Tax Credit [1]	
	Average proportion of tract population that is poor	Average proportion of tract population that is minority	Average proportion of tract population that is poor	Average proportion of tract population that is minority	Average proportion of tract population that is poor	Average proportion of tract population that is minority	Average proportion of tract population that is poor	Average proportion of tract population that is minority	Average proportion of tract population that is poor	Average proportion of tract population that is minority
United States	37	59	20	39	20	34	21	37	26	45
Alabama	40	60	26	47	24	35	24	45	33	52
Alaska	12	34	11	26	11	26	9	19	10	29
Arizona	42	68	21	41	22	36	20	39	26	45
Arkansas	34	48	25	26	22	23	15	11	26	32
California	30	68	18	56	18	50	23	56	20	57
Colorado	31	49	19	32	19	26	16	25	22	35
Connecticut	26	52	15	37	15	32	17	37	18	40
Delaware	34	69	14	35	14	31	17	42	21	46
District of Columbia	34	91	....	....	29	92	31	99	31	92
Florida	35	62	20	45	24	46	18	38	25	50
Guam	....	....	....	....	....	....	....	....	....	....
Georgia	41	63	21	48	23	41	20	46	31	56
Hawaii	30	84	12	71	12	79	13	69	17	77
Idaho	20	12	15	8	16	7	12	7	16	8
Illinois	49	65	20	48	23	42	29	63	33	56
Indiana	29	37	19	25	16	17	14	16	20	26
Iowa	19	7	17	8	16	7	11	8	17	8
Kansas	27	35	17	21	13	12	11	15	17	21
Kentucky	44	38	25	21	24	16	25	20	31	25
Louisiana	59	77	32	53	32	50	32	51	41	61
Maine	19	3	15	3	16	3	14	2	16	3
Maryland	39	69	15	49	16	42	15	47	22	54
Massachusetts	26	39	15	24	17	26	22	42	19	31
Michigan	40	56	....	....	19	27	22	31	25	36
Minnesota	31	26	16	13	14	8	13	8	19	15
Mississippi	35	49	31	53	33	54	25	45	32	52
Missouri	38	46	20	26	21	31	23	30	25	33
Montana	20	7	20	9	19	6	20	7	20	8
Nebraska	24	26	19	21	15	11	22	20	19	19
Nevada	25	51	15	29	17	32	15	27	19	37
New Hampshire	13	6	10	4	11	3	15	6	11	4
New Jersey	27	68	14	43	20	55	20	50	21	58
New Mexico	26	60	25	57	20	42	20	54	24	55
New York	38	80	23	51	27	57	33	69	31	66
North Carolina	32	62	20	42	18	35	19	41	24	49
North Dakota	20	3	14	4	16	4	12	3	15	4
Northern Mariana Islands	....	....	....	....	....	....	....	....	....	....

See notes at end of table.

Characteristics of Assisted Households, Their Housing, and Their Neighborhoods

	TABLE 5.12. CENSUS TRACT CHARACTERISTICS FOR SELECTED HUD-RENTAL HOUSING PROGRAMS AND FOR THE LOW-INCOME HOUSING TAX CREDIT PROGRAM - Continued (Percent)									
AREA	Public Housing		Section 8 Certificates and Vouchers		Section 8 New Construction or Substantial Rehabilitation		Low-Income Housing Tax Credit		Total, HUD-subsidized and Low-Income Housing Tax Credit [1]	
	Average proportion of tract population that is poor	Average proportion of tract population that is minority	Average proportion of tract population that is poor	Average proportion of tract population that is minority	Average proportion of tract population that is poor	Average proportion of tract population that is minority	Average proportion of tract population that is poor	Average proportion of tract population that is minority	Average proportion of tract population that is poor	Average proportion of tract population that is minority
Ohio	43	51	22	26	23	25	25	25	31	36
Oklahoma	35	42	22	28	22	26	26	37	26	32
Oregon	19	14	16	11	21	14	18	11	18	12
Pennsylvania	35	44	17	21	20	22	25	39	26	33
Puerto Rico	....	....	....	....	....	....	....	....	....	....
Rhode Island	19	20	14	18	15	18	17	23	17	19
South Carolina	31	59	21	45	19	37	18	43	24	50
South Dakota	....	....	15	7	15	5	13	6	15	7
Tennessee	41	49	21	27	23	25	21	34	30	39
Texas	43	72	25	56	23	47	22	52	30	60
Utah	24	22	17	14	22	17	18	15	20	17
Vermont	16	3	14	3	16	2	9	2	14	3
Virgin Islands	....	....	....	....	....	....	....	....	....	....
Virginia	43	71	17	43	17	38	17	40	24	50
Washington	27	34	16	19	18	16	19	18	21	23
West Virginia	26	13	23	6	24	8	20	6	24	9
Wisconsin	33	40	18	22	14	10	15	9	18	19
Wyoming	14	15	15	14	13	8	12	13	14	11

Source: Burke, Paul, "A Picture of Subsidized Households in 1997: United States: Totals and Agencies with over 500 Units." U.S. Department of Housing and Urban Development. December 15, 1997.

Census tract characteristics are as of April 1990.

(1) Includes other HUD programs, not shown separately.

Characteristics of Assisted Households, Their Housing, and Their Neighborhoods

TABLE 5.13. CHARACTERISTICS OF RENTER HOUSEHOLDERS BY INCOME-ELIGIBILITY AND HOUSING ASSISTANCE PROGRAM: 1989
(Numbers in thousands, except as noted)

CHARACTERISTIC	Total renters	Income-eligible renters		Assisted			
		Total	Unassisted	Total	Public housing	Certificate or voucher programs	Private project-based
TOTAL HOUSEHOLDS	33,767	13,808	9,738	4,070	1,360	1,060	1,650
RACE AND HISPANIC ORIGIN							
White	26,143	9,267	6,983	2,284	596	600	1,087
Non-Hispanic	22,884	7,593	5,702	1,891	463	482	946
Hispanic	3,258	1,673	1,281	392	133	118	142
Black	6,070	3,882	2,242	1,640	721	427	491
Other	1,554	660	513	147	43	32	72
Total Hispanic	3,701	1,902	1,460	442	163	126	153
AGE							
Under 25 years	3,552	1,516	1,268	248	47	87	114
25 to 29	6,207	1,906	1,443	463	85	188	189
30 to 34	6,199	1,960	1,487	473	162	175	135
35 to 44	6,845	2,298	1,633	665	212	171	282
45 to 54	3,581	1,256	900	356	156	111	89
55 to 64	2,610	1,295	847	448	184	89	175
65 to 74	2,364	1,634	975	659	243	101	315
75 and older	2,410	1,943	1,184	759	270	138	351
Median (Years)	36	41	39	50	56	40	56
EDUCATION							
No years completed	196	140	118	22	5	12	5
Elementary							
Less than 8 years	2,083	1,630	1,089	541	266	109	166
8 years	1,370	959	657	302	142	72	88
High school							
1 to 3 years	4,710	3,156	2,159	997	357	254	386
4 years	12,067	4,914	3,439	1,475	393	413	669
College							
1 to 3 years	6,582	2,019	1,497	522	157	140	226
4 years	6,759	991	780	211	39	61	111
Median (Years)	12.7	12.2	12.2	12.1	11.4	12.2	12.3
YEAR MOVED IN							
1985 to 1989	25,283	9,402	6,934	2,468	720	714	1,034
1980 to 1984	4,146	2,117	1,273	844	272	185	388
1975 to 1979	1,975	1,095	683	412	151	101	159
1970 to 1974	951	535	334	201	110	28	64
1960 to 1969	847	408	311	97	64	27	6
1950 to 1959	327	154	109	45	43	2	0
1940 to 1949	155	82	79	3	0	3	0
1939 or earlier	83	16	16	0	0	0	0

See notes at end of table.

Characteristics of Assisted Households, Their Housing, and Their Neighborhoods

TABLE 5.13. CHARACTERISTICS OF RENTER HOUSEHOLDERS BY INCOME-ELIGIBILITY AND HOUSING ASSISTANCE PROGRAM: 1989 - Continued
(Percent)

| CHARACTERISTIC | Total renters | Income-eligible renters | | | | | |
| | | Total | Unassisted | Assisted | | | |
				Total	Public housing	Certificate or voucher programs	Private project-based
TOTAL HOUSEHOLDS	100	100	100	100	100	100	100
RACE AND HISPANIC ORIGIN							
White	77	67	72	56	44	57	66
Non-Hispanic	68	55	59	46	34	45	57
Hispanic	10	12	13	10	10	11	9
Black	18	28	23	40	53	40	30
Other	5	5	5	4	3	3	4
Total Hispanic	11	14	15	11	12	12	9
AGE							
Under 25 years	11	11	13	6	3	8	7
25 to 29	18	14	15	11	6	18	11
30 to 34	18	14	15	12	12	17	8
35 to 44	20	17	17	16	16	16	17
45 to 54	11	9	9	9	11	10	5
55 to 64	8	9	9	11	14	8	11
65 to 74	7	12	10	16	18	10	19
75 and older	7	14	12	19	20	13	21
Median (Years)	....	....	....	....	....	....	....
EDUCATION							
No years completed	1	1	1	1	0	1	0
Elementary							
Less than 8 years	6	12	11	13	20	10	10
8 years	4	7	7	7	10	7	5
High school							
1 to 3 years	14	23	22	24	26	24	23
4 years	36	36	35	36	29	39	41
College							
1 to 3 years	19	15	15	13	12	13	14
4 years	20	7	8	5	3	6	7
Median (Years)	....	....	....	....	....	....	....
YEAR MOVED IN							
1985 to 1989	75	68	71	61	53	67	63
1980 to 1984	12	15	13	21	20	17	24
1975 to 1979	6	8	7	10	11	10	10
1970 to 1974	3	4	3	5	8	3	4
1960 to 1969	3	3	3	2	5	3	0
1950 to 1959	1	1	1	1	3	0	0
1940 to 1949	0	1	1	0	0	0	0
1939 or earlier	0	0	0	0	0	0	0

Source: Casey, Connie H. "Characteristics of HUD-Assisted Renters and Their Units in 1989." U.S. Department of Housing and Urban Development, Office of Policy Development and Research, HUD-1346-PDR. March 1992.

Characteristics of Assisted Households, Their Housing, and Their Neighborhoods

TABLE 5.14. CHARACTERISTICS OF RENTER HOUSEHOLDERS BY INCOME-ELIGIBILITY AND HOUSING ASSISTANCE PROGRAM: 1991
(Numbers in thousands, except as noted)

| CHARACTERISTIC | Total renters | Income-eligible renters | | | | | |
| | | Total | Unassisted | Assisted | | | |
				Total	Public housing	Certificate or voucher programs	Private project-based
TOTAL HOUSEHOLDS	33,351	16,194	12,158	4,036	1,146	1,141	1,749
RACE AND HISPANIC ORIGIN							
White	25,391	10,765	8,299	2,466	514	733	1,219
Non-Hispanic	22,160	8,930	6,811	2,119	408	618	1,093
Hispanic	3,231	1,835	1,488	347	107	114	125
Black	6,197	4,803	3,182	1,398	589	353	456
Other	1,763	853	676	172	43	55	74
Total Hispanic	3,816	2,134	1,729	405	142	129	135
AGE							
Under 25 years	4,227	2,222	1,835	326	74	99	153
25 to 29	5,550	2,147	1,679	443	64	171	208
30 to 34	5,570	2,136	1,633	477	117	195	165
35 to 44	7,180	2,728	2,118	603	168	188	228
45 to 54	3,835	1,496	1,131	365	146	127	93
55 to 64	2,376	1,297	917	380	124	96	159
65 to 74	2,219	1,934	1,304	630	210	119	300
75 and older	2,394	2,353	1,541	812	243	126	443
Median (Years)	37	41	39	50	55	40	57
EDUCATION							
No years completed	182	161	132	27	5	17	5
Elementary							
Less than 8 years	1,948	1,785	1,238	558	248	128	181
8 years	1,252	1,055	767	288	91	93	105
High school							
1 to 3 years	4,469	3,518	2,520	998	318	244	436
4 years	11,944	5,925	4,406	1,472	345	453	674
College							
1 to 3 years	6,835	2,448	1,945	503	100	167	236
4 years	6,721	1,338	1,149	189	38	39	112
Median (Years)	12.7	12.3	12.3	12.1	11.3	12.2	12.2
YEAR MOVED IN							
1990 or later	16,908	7,256	5,873	1,358	286	510	561
1985 to 1989	10,408	5,245	3,625	1,579	443	426	711
1980 to 1984	2,784	1,734	1,155	579	163	102	314
1975 to 1979	1,363	890	596	294	111	54	129
1970 to 1974	772	501	363	138	85	24	29
1960 to 1969	666	373	306	67	37	25	6
1950 to 1959	260	149	128	21	21	0	0
1940 to 1949	120	68	68	0	0	0	0
1939 or earlier	69	44	44	0	0	0	0

See notes at end of table.

Characteristics of Assisted Households, Their Housing, and Their Neighborhoods

TABLE 5.14. CHARACTERISTICS OF RENTER HOUSEHOLDERS BY INCOME-ELIGIBILITY AND HOUSING ASSISTANCE PROGRAM: 1991 - Continued
(Percent)

CHARACTERISTIC	Total renters	Income-eligible renters		Assisted			
		Total	Unassisted	Total	Public housing	Certificate or voucher programs	Private project-based
TOTAL HOUSEHOLDS	100	100	100	100	100	100	100
RACE AND HISPANIC ORIGIN							
White	76	66	68	61	45	64	70
Non-Hispanic	66	55	56	53	36	54	62
Hispanic	10	11	12	9	9	10	7
Black	19	30	26	35	51	31	26
Other	5	5	6	4	4	5	4
Total Hispanic	11	13	14	10	12	11	8
AGE							
Under 25 years	13	14	15	8	6	9	9
25 to 29	17	13	14	11	6	15	12
30 to 34	17	13	13	12	10	17	9
35 to 44	22	17	17	15	15	16	13
45 to 54	11	9	9	9	13	11	5
55 to 64	7	8	8	9	11	8	9
65 to 74	7	12	11	16	18	10	17
75 and older	7	15	13	20	21	11	25
Median (Years)	....	....	....	....	....	....	....
EDUCATION							
No years completed	1	1	1	1	0	1	0
Elementary							
Less than 8 years	6	11	10	14	22	11	10
8 years	4	7	6	7	8	8	6
High school							
1 to 3 years	13	22	21	25	28	21	25
4 years	36	37	36	36	30	40	39
College							
1 to 3 years	20	15	16	12	9	15	13
4 years	20	8	9	5	3	3	6
Median (Years)	....	....	....	....	....	....	....
YEAR MOVED IN							
1990 or later	51	45	48	34	25	45	32
1985 to 1989	31	32	30	39	39	37	41
1980 to 1984	8	11	9	14	14	9	18
1975 to 1979	4	5	5	7	10	5	7
1970 to 1974	2	3	3	3	7	2	2
1960 to 1969	2	2	3	2	3	2	0
1950 to 1959	1	1	1	1	2	0	0
1940 to 1949	0	0	1	0	0	0	0
1939 or earlier	0	0	0	0	0	0	0

Source: Casey, Connie H. "Characteristics of HUD-Assisted Renters and Their Units in 1991." U.S. Department of Housing and Urban Development, Office of Policy Development and Research, May 1997.

Characteristics of Assisted Households, Their Housing, and Their Neighborhoods

TABLE 5.15. CHARACTERISTICS OF RENTER HOUSEHOLDERS BY INCOME-ELIGIBILITY AND HOUSING ASSISTANCE PROGRAM: 1993
(Numbers in thousands, except as noted)

| CHARACTERISTIC | Total renters | Income-eligible renters | | | | | | |
| | | Total | Unassisted | | Assisted | | | |
			Total	Worst-case needs	Total	Public housing	Certificate or voucher programs	Private project-based
TOTAL HOUSEHOLDS	33,472	15,795	11,741	4,849	4,054	1,138	1,200	1,716
RACE AND HISPANIC ORIGIN								
White	25,151	10,462	8,279	3,354	2,183	475	674	1,034
Non-Hispanic	22,001	8,594	6,725	2,644	1,869	378	564	927
Hispanic	3,151	1,869	1,555	710	314	97	110	107
Black	6,340	4,281	2,656	1,104	1,625	610	413	601
Other	1,981	1,052	805	391	246	53	113	80
Total Hispanic[1]	3,826	2,270	1,852	871	418	142	147	129
AGE								
Under 25 years	4,184	2,189	1,771	841	417	114	122	181
25 to 29	5,351	2,051	1,597	640	454	115	169	170
30 to 34	5,326	1,995	1,475	600	520	83	221	215
35 to 44	7,573	2,993	2,303	926	691	186	243	262
45 to 54	4,008	1,561	1,174	484	386	97	145	144
55 to 64	2,359	1,239	948	385	291	128	87	75
65 to 74	2,193	1,641	1,120	442	521	193	90	238
75 and older	2,478	2,126	1,352	530	774	222	122	431
Median (Years)	37	41	39	39	44	52	39	47
EDUCATION								
No years completed	188	159	125	60	33	16	17	0
Elementary								
Less than 8 years	1,812	1,516	1,057	457	459	212	111	136
8 years	1,194	967	711	266	256	87	64	105
High school								
1 to 3 years	4,348	3,249	2,250	944	1,000	314	262	424
4 years	11,923	5,785	4,223	1,718	1,562	348	474	740
College								
1 to 3 years	6,935	2,614	2,072	887	542	118	194	230
4 years	7,072	1,506	1,303	518	202	43	78	81
Median (Years)	12.8	12.3	12.4	12.4	12.2	11.6	12.3	12.3
YEAR MOVED IN								
1990 to 1994	23,079	9,990	7,807	3,434	2,183	539	760	884
1985 to 1989	5,767	2,938	1,902	687	1,036	325	279	432
1980 to 1984	2,013	1,227	749	272	479	117	65	296
1975 to 1979	1,059	670	480	179	190	68	40	82
1970 to 1974	595	363	265	104	98	51	25	22
1960 to 1969	583	342	294	116	47	22	26	0
1950 to 1959	209	146	129	30	17	17	0	0
1940 to 1949	104	67	65	15	2	0	2	0
1939 or earlier	63	52	49	12	2	0	2	0

See notes at end of table.

Characteristics of Assisted Households, Their Housing, and Their Neighborhoods

TABLE 5.15. CHARACTERISTICS OF RENTER HOUSEHOLDERS BY INCOME-ELIGIBILITY AND HOUSING ASSISTANCE PROGRAM: 1993 - Continued
(Percent)

| CHARACTERISTIC | Total renters | Income-eligible renters | | | | | | |
| | | Total | Unassisted | | Assisted | | | |
			Total	Worst-case needs	Total	Public housing	Certificate or voucher programs	Private project-based
TOTAL HOUSEHOLDS	100	100	100	100	100	100	100	100
RACE AND HISPANIC ORIGIN								
White	75	66	71	69	54	42	56	60
Non-Hispanic	66	54	57	55	46	33	47	54
Hispanic	9	12	13	15	8	9	9	6
Black	19	27	23	23	40	54	34	35
Other	6	7	7	8	6	5	9	5
Total Hispanic[1]	11	14	16	18	10	12	12	8
AGE								
Under 25 years	13	14	15	17	10	10	10	11
25 to 29	16	13	14	13	11	10	14	10
30 to 34	16	13	13	12	13	7	18	13
35 to 44	23	19	20	19	17	16	20	15
45 to 54	12	10	10	10	10	9	12	8
55 to 64	7	8	8	8	7	11	7	4
65 to 74	7	10	10	9	13	17	8	14
75 and older	7	13	12	11	19	20	10	25
Median (Years)	....	....	....	....	....	....	....	....
EDUCATION								
No years completed	1	1	1	1	1	1	1	0
Elementary								
Less than 8 years	5	10	9	9	11	19	9	8
8 years	4	6	6	5	6	8	5	6
High school								
1 to 3 years	13	21	19	19	25	28	22	25
4 years	36	37	36	35	39	31	40	43
College								
1 to 3 years	21	17	18	18	13	10	16	13
4 years	21	10	11	11	5	4	7	5
Median (Years)	....	....	....	....	....	....	....	....
YEAR MOVED IN								
1990 to 1994	69	63	66	71	54	47	63	52
1985 to 1989	17	19	16	14	26	29	23	25
1980 to 1984	6	8	6	6	12	10	5	17
1975 to 1979	3	4	4	4	5	6	3	5
1970 to 1974	2	2	2	2	2	4	2	1
1960 to 1969	2	2	3	2	1	2	2	0
1950 to 1959	1	1	1	1	0	1	0	0
1940 to 1949	0	0	1	0	0	0	0	0
1939 or earlier	0	0	0	0	0	0	0	0

Source: McGough, Duane T. "Characteristics of HUD-Assisted Renters and Their Units in 1993." U.S. Department of Housing and Urban Development, Office of Policy Development and Research. May 1997.

(1) Persons of Hispanic origin may be of any race.

Characteristics of Assisted Households, Their Housing, and Their Neighborhoods

TABLE 5.16. HOUSEHOLD COMPOSITION AND SIZE AND PERSONS PER ROOM FOR RENTER HOUSEHOLDS BY INCOME-ELIGIBILITY AND HOUSING ASSISTANCE PROGRAM: 1989

(Numbers in thousands, except as noted)

| CHARACTERISTIC | Total renters | Income-eligible renters | | Assisted | | | |
		Total	Unassisted	Total	Public housing	Certificate or voucher programs	Private project-based
TOTAL HOUSEHOLDS	33,767	13,808	9,738	4,070	1,360	1,060	1,650
HOUSEHOLD COMPOSITION							
2 or more persons	21,947	8,163	5,839	2,324	722	769	833
Married couples	10,535	2,654	2,110	544	121	168	255
Elderly (65 and older)	910	412	288	124	36	33	55
Other male	3,621	894	720	174	40	35	99
Elderly (65 and older)	173	105	72	33	6	3	25
Other female	7,791	4,614	3,008	1,606	562	565	479
Elderly (65 and older)	430	267	184	83	48	17	18
1 person	11,820	5,645	3,899	1,746	638	291	817
Male	5,488	1,868	1,446	422	173	73	176
Elderly (65 and older)	721	510	327	183	83	32	68
Female	6,332	3,777	2,453	1,324	465	218	642
Elderly (65 and older)	2,541	2,281	1,287	994	341	154	499
Total female	14,123	8,391	5,461	2,930	1,027	783	1,121
Total elderly	4,775	3,575	2,158	1,417	514	239	665
Total elderly female	2,971	2,548	1,471	1,077	389	171	517
PERSONS IN HOUSEHOLD							
1 person	11,820	5,645	3,899	1,746	638	291	817
2 persons	9,357	2,873	2,062	811	230	282	300
3 persons	5,314	2,106	1,447	659	171	196	293
4 persons	4,018	1,587	1,131	456	164	144	148
5 persons	1,969	906	658	248	90	76	81
6 persons	813	411	336	75	30	44	0
7 persons or more	476	281	206	75	37	27	11
Median (Number of persons)	2.0	1.9	2.0	1.9	1.7	2.3	1.5
PERSONS PER ROOM							
0.50 or less	20,128	7,785	5,387	2,398	786	535	1,078
0.51 to 1.00	11,918	5,041	3,526	1,515	502	467	547
1.01 to 1.50	1,258	716	603	113	40	48	25
1.51 or more	464	266	222	44	33	11	0

See notes at end of table.

Characteristics of Assisted Households, Their Housing, and Their Neighborhoods

TABLE 5.16. HOUSEHOLD COMPOSITION AND SIZE AND PERSONS PER ROOM FOR RENTER HOUSEHOLDS BY INCOME-ELIGIBILITY AND HOUSING ASSISTANCE PROGRAM: 1989 - Continued

(Percent)

| CHARACTERISTIC | Total renters | Income-eligible renters | | Assisted | | | |
		Total	Unassisted	Total	Public housing	Certificate or voucher programs	Private project-based
TOTAL HOUSEHOLDS	100	100	100	100	100	100	100
HOUSEHOLD COMPOSITION							
2 or more persons	65	59	60	57	53	73	50
Married couples	31	19	22	13	9	16	15
Elderly (65 and older)	3	3	3	3	3	3	3
Other male	11	6	7	4	3	3	6
Elderly (65 and older)	1	1	1	1	0	0	2
Other female	23	33	31	39	41	53	29
Elderly (65 and older)	1	2	2	2	4	2	1
1 person	35	41	40	43	47	27	50
Male	16	14	15	10	13	7	11
Elderly (65 and older)	2	4	3	4	6	3	4
Female	19	27	25	33	34	21	39
Elderly (65 and older)	8	17	13	24	25	15	30
Total female	42	61	56	72	76	74	68
Total elderly	14	26	22	35	38	23	40
Total elderly female	9	18	15	26	29	16	31
PERSONS IN HOUSEHOLD							
1 person	35	41	40	43	47	27	50
2 persons	28	21	21	20	17	27	18
3 persons	16	15	15	16	13	18	18
4 persons	12	11	12	11	12	14	9
5 persons	6	7	7	6	7	7	5
6 persons	2	3	3	2	2	4	0
7 persons or more	1	2	2	2	3	3	1
Median (Number of persons)	....	....	....	....	....	....	....
PERSONS PER ROOM							
0.50 or less	60	56	55	59	58	50	65
0.51 to 1.00	35	37	36	37	37	44	33
1.01 to 1.50	4	5	6	3	3	5	2
1.51 or more	1	2	2	1	2	1	0

Source: Casey, Connie H. "Characteristics of HUD-Assisted Renters and Their Units in 1989." U.S. Department of Housing and Urban Development, Office of Policy Development and Research, HUD-1346-PDR. March 1992.

Characteristics of Assisted Households, Their Housing, and Their Neighborhoods

TABLE 5.17. HOUSEHOLD COMPOSITION AND SIZE AND PERSONS PER ROOM FOR RENTER HOUSEHOLDS BY INCOME-ELIGIBILITY AND HOUSING ASSISTANCE PROGRAM: 1991

(Numbers in thousands, except as noted)

| CHARACTERISTIC | Total renters | Income-eligible renters | | Assisted | | | |
		Total	Unassisted	Total	Public housing	Certificate or voucher programs	Private project-based
TOTAL HOUSEHOLDS	33,351	16,194	12,158	4,036	1,146	1,141	1,749
HOUSEHOLD COMPOSITION							
2 or more persons	21,766	9,612	7,258	2,241	596	786	859
Married couples	10,292	3,109	2,516	593	119	217	256
Elderly (65 and older)	817	500	363	137	34	33	70
Other male	3,778	1,094	917	177	29	54	94
Elderly (65 and older)	146	70	67	3	0	3	0
Other female	7,696	5,296	3,825	1,471	448	514	509
Elderly (65 and older)	452	293	220	73	19	20	34
1 person	11,585	6,695	4,900	1,795	550	355	890
Male	5,322	2,296	1,783	513	168	124	221
Elderly (65 and older)	721	695	444	256	99	46	111
Female	6,263	4,399	3,117	1,282	382	232	669
Elderly (65 and older)	2,477	2,724	1,751	973	301	144	528
Total female	13,959	9,695	6,942	2,753	830	746	1,178
Total elderly	4,613	4,287	2,845	1,442	453	246	743
Total elderly female	2,929	3,017	1,971	1,046	320	164	562
PERSONS IN HOUSEHOLD							
1 person	11,585	6,695	4,900	1,795	550	355	890
2 persons	9,275	3,378	2,587	791	177	258	356
3 persons	5,569	2,519	1,897	622	156	261	204
4 persons	3,811	1,832	1,402	430	110	150	170
5 persons	1,905	1,026	760	242	90	63	89
6 persons	657	379	302	77	32	28	17
7 persons or more	550	389	310	79	31	26	22
Median (Number of persons)	2.0	1.9	2.0	1.8	1.6	2.3	1.5
PERSONS PER ROOM							
0.50 or less	20,084	9,434	6,981	2,453	666	625	1,162
0.51 to 1.00	11,622	5,736	4,299	1,437	434	472	530
1.01 to 1.50	1,242	773	652	121	34	36	50
1.51 or more	403	251	225	26	12	7	7

See notes at end of table.

Characteristics of Assisted Households, Their Housing, and Their Neighborhoods

TABLE 5.17. HOUSEHOLD COMPOSITION AND SIZE AND PERSONS PER ROOM FOR RENTER HOUSEHOLDS BY INCOME-ELIGIBILITY AND HOUSING ASSISTANCE PROGRAM: 1991 - Continued

(Percent)

CHARACTERISTIC	Total renters	Income-eligible renters					
		Total	Unassisted	Assisted			
				Total	Public housing	Certificate or voucher programs	Private project-based
TOTAL HOUSEHOLDS	100	100	100	100	100	100	100
HOUSEHOLD COMPOSITION							
2 or more persons	65	59	60	56	52	69	49
Married couples	31	19	21	15	10	19	15
Elderly (65 and older)	2	3	3	3	3	3	4
Other male	11	7	8	4	3	5	5
Elderly (65 and older)	0	0	1	0	0	0	0
Other female	23	33	31	36	39	45	29
Elderly (65 and older)	1	2	2	2	2	2	2
1 person	35	41	40	44	48	31	51
Male	16	14	15	13	15	11	13
Elderly (65 and older)	2	4	4	6	9	4	6
Female	19	27	26	32	33	20	38
Elderly (65 and older)	7	17	14	24	26	13	30
Total female	42	60	57	68	72	65	67
Total elderly	14	26	23	36	40	22	42
Total elderly female	9	19	16	26	28	14	32
PERSONS IN HOUSEHOLD							
1 person	35	41	40	44	48	31	51
2 persons	28	21	21	20	15	23	20
3 persons	17	16	16	15	14	23	12
4 persons	11	11	12	11	10	13	10
5 persons	6	6	6	6	8	6	5
6 persons	2	2	2	2	3	2	1
7 persons or more	2	2	3	2	3	2	1
Median (Number of persons)	....	....	....	....	....	....	....
PERSONS PER ROOM							
0.50 or less	60	58	57	61	58	55	66
0.51 to 1.00	35	35	35	36	38	41	30
1.01 to 1.50	4	5	5	3	3	3	3
1.51 or more	1	2	2	1	1	1	0

Source: Casey, Connie H. "Characteristics of HUD-Assisted Renters and Their Units in 1991." U.S. Department of Housing and Urban Development, Office of Policy Development and Research, May 1997.

Characteristics of Assisted Households, Their Housing, and Their Neighborhoods

TABLE 5.18. HOUSEHOLD COMPOSITION AND SIZE AND PERSONS PER ROOM FOR RENTER HOUSEHOLDS BY INCOME-ELIGIBILITY AND HOUSING ASSISTANCE PROGRAM: 1993

(Numbers in thousands, except as noted)

| CHARACTERISTIC | Total renters | Income-eligible renters | | | | | | |
| | | Total | Unassisted | | Assisted | | | |
			Total	Worst-case needs	Total	Public housing	Certificate or voucher programs	Private project-based
TOTAL HOUSEHOLDS	33,472	15,795	11,741	4,849	4,054	1,138	1,200	1,716
HOUSEHOLD COMPOSITION								
2 or more persons	21,836	9,526	7,179	3,085	2,348	620	876	852
Married couples	9,952	3,176	2,652	798	524	116	192	217
Elderly (65 and older)	824	433	330	105	103	26	24	53
Other male	3,910	1,120	995	513	125	23	51	52
Elderly (65 and older)	171	83	71	30	13	0	7	5
Other female	7,974	5,230	3,532	1,773	1,698	482	633	583
Elderly (65 and older)	402	284	205	86	80	44	22	14
1 person	11,636	6,268	4,562	1,765	1,706	518	324	864
Male	5,548	2,313	1,792	667	522	174	88	260
Elderly (65 and older)	751	601	373	135	228	90	31	106
Female	6,089	3,955	2,770	1,098	1,185	343	237	605
Elderly (65 and older)	2,523	2,365	1,493	617	872	255	128	490
Total female	14,063	9,185	6,302	2,871	2,883	825	870	1,188
Total elderly	4,671	3,768	2,472	973	1,296	415	212	668
Total elderly female	2,925	2,650	1,698	703	952	299	150	504
PERSONS IN HOUSEHOLD								
1 person	11,636	6,268	4,562	1,765	1,706	518	324	864
2 persons	9,351	3,362	2,605	1,203	757	176	292	289
3 persons	5,655	2,607	1,881	801	726	202	264	259
4 persons	3,813	1,821	1,348	535	473	115	178	180
5 persons	1,840	994	755	280	239	81	87	71
6 persons	695	412	317	143	95	27	32	36
7 persons or more	482	331	272	122	59	20	22	17
Median (Number of persons)	2.0	2.0	2.0	2.0	1.9	1.8	2.4	1.5
PERSONS PER ROOM								
0.50 or less	20,315	8,969	6,650	2,651	2,319	641	619	1,060
0.51 to 1.00	11,654	5,851	4,247	1,807	1,604	454	524	626
1.01 to 1.50	1,154	715	600	249	115	39	53	23
1.51 or more	349	259	243	143	16	4	5	7

See notes at end of table.

Characteristics of Assisted Households, Their Housing, and Their Neighborhoods

TABLE 5.18. HOUSEHOLD COMPOSITION AND SIZE AND PERSONS PER ROOM FOR RENTER HOUSEHOLDS BY INCOME-ELIGIBILITY AND HOUSING ASSISTANCE PROGRAM: 1993 - Continued

(Percent)

CHARACTERISTIC	Total renters	Income-eligible renters						
		Total	Unassisted		Assisted			
			Total	Worst-case needs	Total	Public housing	Certificate or voucher programs	Private project-based
TOTAL HOUSEHOLDS	100	100	100	100	100	100	100	100
HOUSEHOLD COMPOSITION								
2 or more persons	65	60	61	64	58	54	73	50
Married couples	30	20	23	16	13	10	16	13
Elderly (65 and older)	2	3	3	2	3	2	2	3
Other male	12	7	8	11	3	2	4	3
Elderly (65 and older)	1	1	1	1	0	0	1	0
Other female	24	33	30	37	42	42	53	34
Elderly (65 and older)	1	2	2	2	2	4	2	1
1 person	35	40	39	36	42	46	27	50
Male	17	15	15	14	13	15	7	15
Elderly (65 and older)	2	4	3	3	6	8	3	6
Female	18	25	24	23	29	30	20	35
Elderly (65 and older)	8	15	13	13	22	22	11	29
Total female	42	58	54	59	71	72	73	69
Total elderly	14	24	21	20	32	36	18	39
Total elderly female	9	17	14	14	23	26	13	29
PERSONS IN HOUSEHOLD								
1 person	35	40	39	36	42	46	27	50
2 persons	28	21	22	25	19	15	24	17
3 persons	17	17	16	17	18	18	22	15
4 persons	11	12	11	11	12	10	15	10
5 persons	5	6	6	6	6	7	7	4
6 persons	2	3	3	3	2	2	3	2
7 persons or more	1	2	2	3	1	2	2	1
Median (Number of persons)	....	....	....	....	....	....	....	....
PERSONS PER ROOM								
0.50 or less	61	57	57	55	57	56	52	62
0.51 to 1.00	35	37	36	37	40	40	44	36
1.01 to 1.50	3	5	5	5	3	3	4	1
1.51 or more	1	2	2	3	0	0	0	0

Source: McGough, Duane T. "Characteristics of HUD-Assisted Renters and Their Units in 1993." U.S. Department of Housing and Urban Development, Office of Policy Development and Research. May 1997.

Characteristics of Assisted Households, Their Housing, and Their Neighborhoods

TABLE 5.19. NUMBER OF CHILDREN, INCOME, AND RENT FOR RENTER HOUSEHOLDS BY INCOME-ELIGIBILITY AND HOUSING ASSISTANCE PROGRAM: 1989
(Numbers in thousands, except as noted)

| CHARACTERISTIC | Total renters | Income-eligible renters | | Assisted | | | |
		Total	Unassisted	Total	Public housing	Certificate or voucher programs	Private project-based
TOTAL HOUSEHOLDS	33,767	13,808	9,738	4,070	1,360	1,060	1,650
NUMBER OF CHILDREN UNDER 18							
None	20,867	7,754	5,521	2,233	797	417	1,018
1	5,394	2,120	1,388	732	173	241	318
2	4,338	2,052	1,427	625	211	211	203
3	2,083	1,133	844	289	95	102	92
4	731	485	386	99	41	50	8
5	213	154	101	53	23	25	5
6 or more	141	111	72	39	20	13	6
Median	0.5	0.5	0.5	0.5	0.5	1.0	0.5
MEDIAN INCOME (Dollars)	18,192	7,901	8,145	7,320	6,571	7,060	8,074
MEDIAN RENT (Dollars)	418	295	334	189	168	185	224
RENT/INCOME RATIO							
Less than 20 percent	7,550	1,116	561	555	167	143	246
20 to 24 percent	4,000	960	574	386	126	103	157
25 to 29 percent	3,455	1,525	793	732	271	160	301
30 to 34 percent	2,641	1,394	802	592	219	135	239
35 to 39 percent	1,736	1,089	796	293	81	92	120
40 percent or more	7,268	5,961	5,126	835	243	270	322
No cash rent or negative income	2,367	278	110	168	51	61	56
Not reported	4,750	1,483	975	508	203	96	209
Median (Percent) [1]	28	39	46	30	30	32	30
INCOME SOURCE							
Wages and salaries	26,097	7,347	5,700	1,647	480	459	708
Business	1,913	339	268	71	22	21	27
Social security/pensions	6,601	4,651	2,877	1,774	634	334	807
Interest/dividends	3,327	731	572	159	30	36	93
Rental income	1,138	169	119	50	6	11	33
Welfare or SSI	4,273	4,099	2,547	1,552	608	543	402
Alimony/child support	1,880	915	586	329	69	134	126
Other	3,189	1,079	824	255	82	70	103
FOOD STAMPS	4,706	4,619	2,955	1,664	660	590	414

See notes at end of table.

Characteristics of Assisted Households, Their Housing, and Their Neighborhoods

| CHARACTERISTIC | Total renters | Income-eligible renters | | Assisted | | | |
		Total	Unassisted	Total	Public housing	Certificate or voucher programs	Private project-based
TOTAL HOUSEHOLDS	100	100	100	100	100	100	100
NUMBER OF CHILDREN UNDER 18							
None	62	56	57	55	59	39	62
1	16	15	14	18	13	23	19
2	13	15	15	15	16	20	12
3	6	8	9	7	7	10	6
4	2	4	4	2	3	5	0
5	1	1	1	1	2	2	0
6 or more	0	1	1	1	1	1	0
Median	....	....	....	....	....	....	....
MEDIAN INCOME (Dollars)	....	....	....	....	....	....	....
MEDIAN RENT (Dollars)	....	....	....	....	....	....	....
RENT/INCOME RATIO							
Less than 20 percent	22	8	6	14	12	13	15
20 to 24 percent	12	7	6	9	9	10	10
25 to 29 percent	10	11	8	18	20	15	18
30 to 34 percent	8	10	8	15	16	13	14
35 to 39 percent	5	8	8	7	6	9	7
40 percent or more	22	43	53	21	18	25	20
No cash rent or negative income	7	2	1	4	4	6	3
Not reported	14	11	10	12	15	9	13
Median (Percent) [1]	....	....	....	....	....	....	....
INCOME SOURCE							
Wages and salaries	77	53	59	40	35	43	43
Business	6	2	3	2	2	2	2
Social security/pensions	20	34	30	44	47	32	49
Interest/dividends	10	5	6	4	2	3	6
Rental income	3	1	1	1	0	1	2
Welfare or SSI	13	30	26	38	45	51	24
Alimony/child support	6	7	6	8	5	13	8
Other	9	8	8	6	6	7	6
FOOD STAMPS	14	33	30	41	49	56	25

TABLE 5.19. NUMBER OF CHILDREN, INCOME, AND RENT FOR RENTER HOUSEHOLDS BY INCOME-ELIGIBILITY AND HOUSING ASSISTANCE PROGRAM: 1989 - Continued
(Percent)

Source: Casey, Connie H. "Characteristics of HUD-Assisted Renters and Their Units in 1989." U.S. Department of Housing and Urban Development, Office of Policy Development and Research, HUD-1346-PDR. March 1992.

(1) Excludes two preceding lines.

Characteristics of Assisted Households, Their Housing, and Their Neighborhoods

TABLE 5.20. NUMBER OF CHILDREN, INCOME, AND RENT FOR RENTER HOUSEHOLDS BY INCOME-ELIGIBILITY AND HOUSING ASSISTANCE PROGRAM: 1991
(Numbers in thousands, except as noted)

| CHARACTERISTIC | Total renters | Income-eligible renters | | Assisted | | | |
		Total	Unassisted	Total	Public housing	Certificate or voucher programs	Private project-based
TOTAL HOUSEHOLDS	33,351	16,194	12,158	4,036	1,146	1,141	1,749
NUMBER OF CHILDREN UNDER 18							
None	20,700	9,195	6,871	2,324	649	528	1,148
1	5,495	2,560	1,888	611	179	203	229
2	4,229	2,411	1,780	631	170	247	213
3	1,913	1,200	956	244	56	97	92
4	660	576	415	145	57	40	48
5	214	194	139	55	19	18	18
6 or more	140	134	109	25	17	8	0
Median	0.5	0.5	0.5	0.5	0.5	0.7	0.5
MEDIAN INCOME (Dollars)	18,917	8,180	8,290	7,983	7,338	7,906	8,504
MEDIAN RENT (Dollars)	457	327	362	220	171	261	260
RENT/INCOME RATIO							
Less than 20 percent	6,909	1,166	641	489	132	128	230
20 to 24 percent	3,656	1,152	642	491	163	112	215
25 to 29 percent	3,466	1,804	1,106	690	246	177	266
30 to 34 percent	2,513	1,565	1,002	563	186	127	251
35 to 39 percent	1,732	1,230	889	341	112	102	127
40 percent or more	7,819	6,862	5,842	989	218	373	399
No cash rent or negative income	2,761	1,964	1,626	328	60	101	166
Not reported	4,495	583	429	144	28	21	95
Median (Percent) [1]	27	36	45	31	30	34	31
INCOME SOURCE							
Wages and salaries	25,206	8,017	6,386	1,592	343	542	707
Business	1,738	336	303	33	0	23	10
Social security/pensions	6,515	5,406	3,627	1,779	529	338	913
Interest/dividends	3,000	808	619	185	42	24	119
Rental income	1,170	217	167	50	12	19	19
Welfare or SSI	4,640	4,944	3,351	1,505	520	510	475
Alimony/child support	1,776	1,006	704	302	62	119	120
Other	3,546	1,530	1,237	300	73	118	109
FOOD STAMPS	5,228	5,756	4,113	1,643	594	558	491

See notes at end of table.

Characteristics of Assisted Households, Their Housing, and Their Neighborhoods

CHARACTERISTIC	Total renters	Income-eligible renters		Assisted			
		Total	Unassisted	Total	Public housing	Certificate or voucher programs	Private project-based

TABLE 5.20. NUMBER OF CHILDREN, INCOME, AND RENT FOR RENTER HOUSEHOLDS BY INCOME-ELIGIBILITY AND HOUSING ASSISTANCE PROGRAM: 1991 - Continued
(Percent)

CHARACTERISTIC	Total renters	Total	Unassisted	Total	Public housing	Certificate or voucher programs	Private project-based
TOTAL HOUSEHOLDS	100	100	100	100	100	100	100
NUMBER OF CHILDREN UNDER 18							
None	62	57	57	58	57	46	66
1	16	16	16	15	16	18	13
2	13	15	15	16	15	22	12
3	6	7	8	6	5	9	5
4	2	4	3	4	5	4	3
5	1	1	1	1	2	2	1
6 or more	0	1	1	1	1	1	0
Median	....	....	....	....	....	....	....
MEDIAN INCOME (Dollars)	....	....	....	....	....	....	....
MEDIAN RENT (Dollars)	....	....	....	....	....	....	....
RENT/INCOME RATIO							
Less than 20 percent	21	7	5	12	12	11	13
20 to 24 percent	11	7	5	12	14	10	12
25 to 29 percent	10	11	9	17	21	16	15
30 to 34 percent	8	10	8	14	16	11	14
35 to 39 percent	5	8	7	8	10	9	7
40 percent or more	23	42	48	25	19	33	23
No cash rent or negative income	8	12	13	8	5	9	9
Not reported	13	4	4	4	2	2	5
Median (Percent) [1]	....	....	....	....	....	....	....
INCOME SOURCE							
Wages and salaries	76	50	53	39	30	48	40
Business	5	2	2	1	0	2	1
Social security/pensions	20	33	30	44	46	30	52
Interest/dividends	9	5	5	5	4	2	7
Rental income	4	1	1	1	1	2	1
Welfare or SSI	14	31	28	37	45	45	27
Alimony/child support	5	6	6	7	5	10	7
Other	11	9	10	7	6	10	6
FOOD STAMPS	16	36	34	41	52	49	28

Source: Casey, Connie H. "Characteristics of HUD-Assisted Renters and Their Units in 1991." U.S. Department of Housing and Urban Development, Office of Policy Development and Research, May 1997.

(1) Excludes two preceding lines and 100 percent or more.

Characteristics of Assisted Households, Their Housing, and Their Neighborhoods

TABLE 5.21. NUMBER OF CHILDREN, INCOME, AND RENT FOR RENTER HOUSEHOLDS BY INCOME-ELIGIBILITY AND HOUSING ASSISTANCE PROGRAM: 1993

(Numbers in thousands, except as noted)

| CHARACTERISTIC | Total renters | Income-eligible renters | | | | | | |
| | | Total | Unassisted | | Assisted | | | |
			Total	Worst-case needs	Total	Public housing	Certificate or voucher programs	Private project-based
TOTAL HOUSEHOLDS	33,472	15,795	11,741	4,849	4,054	1,138	1,200	1,716
NUMBER OF CHILDREN UNDER 18								
None	20,848	8,798	6,695	2,751	2,103	626	472	1,005
1	5,423	2,574	1,927	803	647	144	257	246
2	4,291	2,397	1,679	666	718	187	239	293
3	1,865	1,208	854	371	354	115	149	90
4	703	536	378	169	158	38	57	64
5	225	181	138	56	43	12	20	11
6 or more	118	101	71	34	30	16	7	7
Median	0.5	0.5	0.5	0.5-	0.5	0.5	1.0	0.5
MEDIAN INCOME (Dollars)	19,606	8,792	9,157	7,740	7,948	7,267	8,119	8,385
MEDIAN RENT (Dollars)	482	375	419	478	211	168	282	227
RENT/INCOME RATIO								
Less than 20 percent	7,766	1,106	479	28	627	200	137	289
20 to 24 percent	3,991	950	482	38	468	124	118	226
25 to 29 percent	3,549	1,474	790	44	684	229	158	297
30 to 34 percent	2,909	1,518	958	52	561	209	138	213
35 to 39 percent	2,013	1,155	862	53	293	71	102	120
40 percent or more	9,090	7,175	6,262	4,533	914	193	372	350
No cash rent or negative income	2,843	1,784	1,445	79	340	76	119	144
Not reported	1,311	633	464	22	168	36	55	77
Median (Percent) [1]	28	38	43	65	29	29	32	28
INCOME SOURCE								
Wages and salaries	2,479	7,911	6,379	2,284	1,532	327	549	656
Business	1,921	390	350	146	40	4	16	20
Social security/pensions	6,464	4,823	3,254	1,355	1,568	507	298	764
Interest/dividends	10,537	2,868	2,234	980	634	178	114	342
Rental income	3,879	916	818	555	98	7	49	43
Welfare or SSI	4,434	4,179	2,644	1,399	1,536	503	558	475
Alimony/child support	1,951	1,063	739	344	324	56	156	112
Other	4,886	2,183	1,695	732	488	129	154	204
FOOD STAMPS	5,714	5,677	3,692	1,846	1,985	636	688	661

See notes at end of table.

Characteristics of Assisted Households, Their Housing, and Their Neighborhoods

TABLE 5.21. NUMBER OF CHILDREN, INCOME, AND RENT FOR RENTER HOUSEHOLDS BY INCOME-ELIGIBILITY AND HOUSING ASSISTANCE PROGRAM: 1993 - Continued
(Percent)

CHARACTERISTIC	Total renters	Income-eligible renters						
		Total	Unassisted		Assisted			
			Total	Worst-case needs	Total	Public housing	Certificate or voucher programs	Private project-based
TOTAL HOUSEHOLDS	100	100	100	100	100	100	100	100
NUMBER OF CHILDREN UNDER 18								
None	62	56	57	57	52	55	39	59
1	16	16	16	17	16	13	21	14
2	13	15	14	14	18	16	20	17
3	6	8	7	8	9	10	12	5
4	2	3	3	3	4	3	5	4
5	1	1	1	1	1	1	2	1
6 or more	0	1	1	1	1	1	1	0
Median	....	....	....	....	....	....	....	....
MEDIAN INCOME (Dollars)	....	....	....	....	....	....	....	....
MEDIAN RENT (Dollars)	....	....	....	....	....	....	....	....
RENT/INCOME RATIO								
Less than 20 percent	23	7	4	1	15	18	11	17
20 to 24 percent	12	6	4	1	12	11	10	13
25 to 29 percent	11	9	7	1	17	20	13	17
30 to 34 percent	9	10	8	1	14	18	12	12
35 to 39 percent	6	7	7	1	7	6	9	7
40 percent or more	27	45	53	93	23	17	31	20
No cash rent or negative income	8	11	12	2	8	7	10	8
Not reported	4	4	4	0	4	3	5	4
Median (Percent) [1]	....	....	....	....	....	....	....	....
INCOME SOURCE								
Wages and salaries	74	50	54	47	38	29	46	38
Business	6	2	3	3	1	0	1	1
Social security/pensions	19	31	28	28	39	45	25	45
Interest/dividends	31	18	19	20	16	16	10	20
Rental income	12	6	7	11	2	1	4	3
Welfare or SSI	13	26	23	29	38	44	47	28
Alimony/child support	6	7	6	7	8	5	13	7
Other	15	14	14	15	12	11	13	12
FOOD STAMPS	17	36	31	38	49	56	57	39

Source: McGough, Duane T. "Characteristics of HUD-Assisted Renters and Their Units in 1993." U.S. Department of Housing and Urban Development, Office of Policy Development and Research. May 1997.

(1) Excludes two preceding lines and 100 percent or more.

Characteristics of Assisted Households, Their Housing, and Their Neighborhoods

TABLE 5.22. STRUCTURAL CHARACTERISTICS FOR UNITS WITH RENTER HOUSEHOLDS BY INCOME-ELIGIBILITY AND HOUSING ASSISTANCE PROGRAM: 1989
(Numbers in thousands, except as noted)

| CHARACTERISTIC | Total renters | Income-eligible renters | | | | | |
| | | Total | Unassisted | Assisted | | | |
				Total	Public housing	Certificate or voucher programs	Private project-based
TOTAL HOUSEHOLDS	33,767	13,808	9,738	4,070	1,360	1,060	1,650
UNITS IN STRUCTURE							
1, detached	8,659	2,523	2,217	306	48	228	30
1, attached	2,435	1,019	607	412	185	109	118
2 to 4	8,010	3,517	2,755	762	270	268	224
5 to 9	4,340	1,839	1,261	578	132	162	284
10 to 19	3,815	1,543	958	585	178	110	297
20 to 49	2,704	1,134	789	345	93	66	186
50 or more	2,771	1,847	772	1,075	453	111	511
Mobile home	1,033	385	379	6	0	6	0
YEAR BUILT							
1985 to 1989	2,405	493	377	116	6	55	54
1980 to 1984	2,675	1,081	590	491	41	109	341
1975 to 1979	4,043	1,738	1,078	660	132	143	385
1970 to 1974	3,954	1,907	1,009	898	359	138	400
1960 to 1969	5,146	2,089	1,482	607	220	181	206
1950 to 1959	3,621	1,529	1,036	493	291	94	108
1940 to 1949	2,996	1,404	1,059	345	206	107	33
1930 to 1939	2,725	1,178	999	179	78	87	14
1920 to 1929	2,238	844	722	122	6	55	62
1919 or earlier	3,965	1,546	1,387	159	20	93	46
Median (Year)	1963	1967	1957	1971	1964	1965	1974
REGION							
Northeast	7,281	3,191	2,035	1,156	544	193	418
Midwest	7,400	3,404	2,513	891	256	235	400
South	11,072	4,377	2,986	1,391	464	394	533
West	8,014	2,837	2,205	632	96	238	299
METROPOLITAN LOCATION							
Inside MSA	28,318	11,510	8,078	3,432	1,132	860	1,440
In central cities	15,532	7,288	4,921	2,367	940	526	900
In suburbs	12,787	4,223	3,157	1,066	191	334	540
Outside MSA	5,449	2,299	1,661	638	228	200	210
NUMBER OF BEDROOMS							
None	1,247	713	516	197	89	39	70
1	9,866	4,870	3,277	1,593	564	280	749
2	14,426	5,310	4,009	1,301	355	437	509
3	6,720	2,430	1,611	819	264	258	296
4 or more	1,509	486	326	160	88	46	26
Median	1.9	1.8	1.8	1.7	1.6	2.0	1.5
COMPLETE BATHROOMS							
None	463	279	244	35	18	11	6
1	24,744	11,467	8,033	3,434	1,254	863	1,317
1 1/2	3,647	1,225	786	439	56	109	274
2 or more	4,913	837	675	162	33	77	52

See notes at end of table.

Characteristics of Assisted Households, Their Housing, and Their Neighborhoods

TABLE 5.22. STRUCTURAL CHARACTERISTICS FOR UNITS WITH RENTER HOUSEHOLDS BY INCOME-ELIGIBILITY AND HOUSING ASSISTANCE PROGRAM: 1989 - Continued
(Percent)

| CHARACTERISTIC | Total renters | Income-eligible renters | | Assisted | | | |
		Total	Unassisted	Total	Public housing	Certificate or voucher programs	Private project-based
TOTAL HOUSEHOLDS	100	100	100	100	100	100	100
UNITS IN STRUCTURE							
1, detached	26	18	23	8	4	22	2
1, attached	7	7	6	10	14	10	7
2 to 4	24	25	28	19	20	25	14
5 to 9	13	13	13	14	10	15	17
10 to 19	11	11	10	14	13	10	18
20 to 49	8	8	8	8	7	6	11
50 or more	8	13	8	26	33	10	31
Mobile home	3	3	4	0	0	1	0
YEAR BUILT							
1985 to 1989	7	4	4	3	0	5	3
1980 to 1984	8	8	6	12	3	10	21
1975 to 1979	12	13	11	16	10	13	23
1970 to 1974	12	14	10	22	26	13	24
1960 to 1969	15	15	15	15	16	17	12
1950 to 1959	11	11	11	12	21	9	7
1940 to 1949	9	10	11	8	15	10	2
1930 to 1939	8	9	10	4	6	8	1
1920 to 1929	7	6	7	3	0	5	4
1919 or earlier	12	11	14	4	1	9	3
Median (Year)	....	....	....	....	....	....	....
REGION							
Northeast	22	23	21	28	40	18	25
Midwest	22	25	26	22	19	22	24
South	33	32	31	34	34	37	32
West	24	21	23	16	7	22	18
METROPOLITAN LOCATION							
Inside MSA	84	83	83	84	83	81	87
In central cities	46	53	51	58	69	50	55
In suburbs	38	31	32	26	14	32	33
Outside MSA	16	17	17	16	17	19	13
NUMBER OF BEDROOMS							
None	4	5	5	5	7	4	4
1	29	35	34	39	41	26	45
2	43	38	41	32	26	41	31
3	20	18	17	20	19	24	18
4 or more	4	4	3	4	6	4	2
Median	....	....	....	....	....	....	....
COMPLETE BATHROOMS							
None	1	2	3	1	1	1	0
1	73	83	82	84	92	81	80
1 1/2	11	9	8	11	4	10	17
2 or more	15	6	7	4	2	7	3

Source: Casey, Connie H. "Characteristics of HUD-Assisted Renters and Their Units in 1989." U.S. Department of Housing and Urban Development, Office of Policy Development and Research, HUD-1346-PDR. March 1992.

Characteristics of Assisted Households, Their Housing, and Their Neighborhoods

TABLE 5.23. STRUCTURAL CHARACTERISTICS FOR UNITS WITH RENTER HOUSEHOLDS BY INCOME-ELIGIBILITY AND HOUSING ASSISTANCE PROGRAM: 1991
(Numbers in thousands, except as noted)

| CHARACTERISTIC | Total renters | Income-eligible renters | | Assisted | | | |
		Total	Unassisted	Total	Public housing	Certificate or voucher programs	Private project-based
TOTAL HOUSEHOLDS	33,351	16,194	12,158	4,036	1,146	1,141	1,749
UNITS IN STRUCTURE							
1, detached	8,401	3,195	2,768	427	67	348	12
1, attached	2,720	1,246	915	331	153	73	105
2 to 4	7,581	3,591	2,939	652	212	289	151
5 to 9	4,240	2,224	1,573	651	139	146	366
10 to 19	3,676	1,760	1,203	557	90	102	365
20 to 49	2,790	1,386	1,032	321	70	75	177
50 or more	2,845	2,360	1,232	1,063	416	75	573
Mobile home	1,098	530	497	33	0	33	0
YEAR BUILT							
1990 to 1994	501	144	141	3	0	3	0
1985 to 1989	2,610	754	613	141	5	78	58
1980 to 1984	2,619	1,413	873	491	31	91	369
1975 to 1979	3,724	1,981	1,325	656	81	152	424
1970 to 1974	3,905	2,379	1,470	899	328	134	436
1960 to 1969	4,953	2,344	1,779	565	209	150	206
1950 to 1959	3,530	1,812	1,331	417	205	107	105
1940 to 1949	2,926	1,572	1,228	344	197	119	28
1930 to 1939	2,629	1,327	1,124	209	78	105	27
1920 to 1929	2,190	962	853	109	0	59	50
1919 or earlier	3,762	1,607	1,420	200	11	142	47
Median (Year)	1963	1964	1961	1971	1964	1963	1975
REGION							
Northeast	7,093	3,101	2,137	964	380	162	422
Midwest	7,355	3,782	2,886	896	214	265	418
South	10,918	5,756	4,261	1,495	455	446	594
West	7,985	3,555	2,874	681	97	269	315
METROPOLITAN LOCATION							
Inside MSA	27,840	13,278	10,014	3,264	958	811	1,495
In central cities	15,265	8,325	6,166	2,159	793	455	911
In suburbs	12,575	4,952	3,848	1,104	164	356	584
Outside MSA	5,510	2,916	2,144	772	188	330	254
NUMBER OF BEDROOMS							
None	1,151	745	563	182	96	32	55
1	9,814	5,754	4,138	1,609	449	290	870
2	14,155	6,292	4,892	1,324	282	530	512
3	6,722	2,919	2,121	798	263	238	297
4 or more	1,509	567	444	123	56	51	15
Median	1.9	1.8	1.8	1.7	1.6	2.0	1.4
COMPLETE BATHROOMS							
None	418	219	206	13	0	8	5
1	24,341	13,414	9,960	3,454	1,092	938	1,425
1 1/2	3,447	1,347	984	363	16	82	265
2 or more	5,146	1,214	1,008	206	38	113	55

See notes at end of table.

Characteristics of Assisted Households, Their Housing, and Their Neighborhoods

CHARACTERISTIC	Total renters	Income-eligible renters					
		Total	Unassisted	Assisted			
				Total	Public housing	Certificate or voucher programs	Private project-based
TOTAL HOUSEHOLDS	100	100	100	100	100	100	100
UNITS IN STRUCTURE							
1, detached	25	20	23	11	6	30	1
1, attached	8	8	8	8	13	6	6
2 to 4	23	22	24	16	18	25	9
5 to 9	13	14	13	16	12	13	21
10 to 19	11	11	10	14	8	9	21
20 to 49	8	9	8	8	6	7	10
50 or more	9	15	10	26	36	7	33
Mobile home	3	3	4	1	0	3	0
YEAR BUILT							
1990 to 1994	2	1	1	0	0	0	0
1985 to 1989	8	5	5	3	0	7	3
1980 to 1984	8	9	7	12	3	8	21
1975 to 1979	11	12	11	16	7	13	24
1970 to 1974	12	15	12	22	29	12	25
1960 to 1969	15	14	15	14	18	13	12
1950 to 1959	11	11	11	10	18	9	6
1940 to 1949	9	10	10	9	17	10	2
1930 to 1939	8	8	9	5	7	9	2
1920 to 1929	7	6	7	3	0	5	3
1919 or earlier	11	10	12	5	1	12	3
Median (Year)	....	....	....	....	....	....	....
REGION							
Northeast	21	19	18	24	33	14	24
Midwest	22	23	24	22	19	23	24
South	33	36	35	37	40	39	34
West	24	22	24	17	8	24	18
METROPOLITAN LOCATION							
Inside MSA	83	82	82	81	84	71	85
In central cities	46	51	51	53	69	40	52
In suburbs	38	31	32	27	14	31	33
Outside MSA	17	18	18	19	16	29	15
NUMBER OF BEDROOMS							
None	3	5	5	5	8	3	3
1	29	36	34	40	39	25	50
2	42	39	40	33	25	46	29
3	20	18	17	20	23	21	17
4 or more	5	4	4	3	5	4	1
Median	....	....	....	....	....	....	....
COMPLETE BATHROOMS							
None	1	1	2	0	0	1	0
1	73	83	82	86	95	82	81
1 1/2	10	8	8	9	1	7	15
2 or more	15	7	8	5	3	10	3

Table title: **TABLE 5.23. STRUCTURAL CHARACTERISTICS FOR UNITS WITH RENTER HOUSEHOLDS BY INCOME-ELIGIBILITY AND HOUSING ASSISTANCE PROGRAM: 1991 - Continued** (Percent)

Source: Casey, Connie H. "Characteristics of HUD-Assisted Renters and Their Units in 1991." U.S. Department of Housing and Urban Development, Office of Policy Development and Research, May 1997.

Characteristics of Assisted Households, Their Housing, and Their Neighborhoods

TABLE 5.24. STRUCTURAL CHARACTERISTICS FOR UNITS WITH RENTER HOUSEHOLDS BY INCOME-ELIGIBILITY AND HOUSING ASSISTANCE PROGRAM: 1993
(Numbers in thousands, except as noted)

CHARACTERISTIC	Total renters	Income-eligible renters						
		Total	Unassisted		Assisted			
			Total	Worst-case needs	Total	Public housing	Certificate or voucher programs	Private project-based
TOTAL HOUSEHOLDS	33,472	15,795	11,741	4,849	4,054	1,138	1,200	1,716
UNITS IN STRUCTURE								
1, detached	8,428	3,103	2,768	1,007	335	31	288	16
1, attached	2,550	1,231	796	325	435	172	97	167
2 to 4	7,505	3,558	2,911	1,187	647	187	297	163
5 to 9	4,315	2,191	1,544	681	648	143	168	336
10 to 19	3,831	1,783	1,283	587	499	100	93	307
20 to 49	2,819	1,382	999	496	383	105	115	164
50 or more	2,850	2,005	937	395	1,068	401	104	563
Mobile home	1,173	541	502	171	39	0	39	0
YEAR BUILT								
1990 to 1993	855	266	244	106	23	0	23	0
1985 to 1989	2,645	786	627	282	159	13	88	58
1980 to 1984	2,579	1,230	708	253	521	50	83	389
1975 to 1979	3,547	1,717	1,162	403	554	79	132	343
1970 to 1974	3,981	2,248	1,340	548	908	294	140	474
1960 to 1969	4,923	2,276	1,687	672	590	227	154	209
1950 to 1959	3,505	1,668	1,240	504	428	208	131	90
1940 to 1949	2,843	1,419	1,109	440	310	160	114	35
1930 to 1939	2,560	1,308	1,068	450	240	93	120	27
1920 to 1929	2,228	1,056	918	431	138	0	92	46
1919 or earlier	3,808	1,820	1,638	759	183	15	122	45
Median (Year)	1964	1963	1959	1957	1971	1964	1961	1974
REGION								
Northeast	7,155	3,583	2,481	1,155	1,103	396	286	421
Midwest	7,415	3,727	2,816	1,122	911	237	230	443
South	11,096	5,126	3,691	1,295	1,435	413	409	613
West	7,808	3,358	2,753	1,278	605	92	274	238
METROPOLITAN LOCATION								
Inside MSA	27,817	13,093	9,762	4,179	3,331	949	911	1,471
In central cities	15,194	8,075	5,802	2,604	2,273	769	566	938
In suburbs	12,623	5,017	3,960	1,575	1,058	180	345	534
Outside MSA	5,656	2,702	1,979	670	723	189	289	245
NUMBER OF BEDROOMS								
None	1,083	698	538	272	160	79	13	68
1	9,622	5,311	3,776	1,497	1,535	444	298	793
2	14,442	6,334	4,895	2,066	1,439	314	568	556
3	6,786	2,822	2,057	824	765	238	255	271
4 or more	1,539	630	475	190	155	62	66	27
Median	1.9	1.8	1.8	1.8	1.7	1.6	2.0	1.5
COMPLETE BATHROOMS								
None	354	241	227	189	14	4	6	5
1	24,339	12,931	9,479	3,781	3,452	1,056	986	1,409
1 1/2	3,395	1,276	888	376	388	55	113	220
2 or more	5,384	1,347	1,146	504	201	23	96	81

See notes at end of table.

Characteristics of Assisted Households, Their Housing, and Their Neighborhoods

TABLE 5.24. STRUCTURAL CHARACTERISTICS FOR UNITS WITH RENTER HOUSEHOLDS BY INCOME-ELIGIBILITY AND HOUSING ASSISTANCE PROGRAM: 1993 - Continued
(Percent)

CHARACTERISTIC	Total renters	Income-eligible renters						
		Total	Unassisted		Assisted			
			Total	Worst-case needs	Total	Public housing	Certificate or voucher programs	Private project-based
TOTAL HOUSEHOLDS	100	100	100	100	100	100	100	100
UNITS IN STRUCTURE								
1, detached	25	20	24	21	8	3	24	1
1, attached	8	8	7	7	11	15	8	10
2 to 4	22	23	25	24	16	16	25	9
5 to 9	13	14	13	14	16	13	14	20
10 to 19	11	11	11	12	12	9	8	18
20 to 49	8	9	9	10	9	9	10	10
50 or more	9	13	8	8	26	35	9	33
Mobile home	4	3	4	4	1	0	3	0
YEAR BUILT								
1990 to 1993	3	2	2	2	1	0	2	0
1985 to 1989	8	5	5	6	4	1	7	3
1980 to 1984	8	8	6	5	13	4	7	23
1975 to 1979	11	11	10	8	14	7	11	20
1970 to 1974	12	14	11	11	22	26	12	28
1960 to 1969	15	14	14	14	15	20	13	12
1950 to 1959	10	11	11	10	11	18	11	5
1940 to 1949	8	9	9	9	8	14	10	2
1930 to 1939	8	8	9	9	6	8	10	2
1920 to 1929	7	7	8	9	3	0	8	3
1919 or earlier	11	12	14	16	5	1	10	3
Median (Year)	....	....	....	....	....	....	....	....
REGION								
Northeast	21	23	21	24	27	35	24	25
Midwest	22	24	24	23	22	21	19	26
South	33	32	31	27	35	36	34	36
West	23	21	23	26	15	8	23	14
METROPOLITAN LOCATION								
Inside MSA	83	83	83	86	82	83	76	86
In central cities	45	51	49	54	56	68	47	55
In suburbs	38	32	34	32	26	16	29	31
Outside MSA	17	17	17	14	18	17	24	14
NUMBER OF BEDROOMS								
None	3	4	5	6	4	7	1	4
1	29	34	32	31	38	39	25	46
2	43	40	42	43	35	28	47	32
3	20	18	18	17	19	21	21	16
4 or more	5	4	4	4	4	5	6	2
Median	....	....	....	....	....	....	....	....
COMPLETE BATHROOMS								
None	1	2	2	4	0	0	1	0
1	73	82	81	78	85	93	82	82
1 1/2	10	8	8	8	10	5	9	13
2 or more	16	9	10	10	5	2	8	5

Source: McGough, Duane T. "Characteristics of HUD-Assisted Renters and Their Units in 1993." U.S. Department of Housing and Urban Development, Office of Policy Development and Research. May 1997.

Characteristics of Assisted Households, Their Housing, and Their Neighborhoods

TABLE 5.25. HOUSING AND NEIGHBORHOOD PROBLEMS FOR RENTERS BY INCOME-ELIGIBILITY AND HOUSING ASSISTANCE PROGRAM: 1989
(Numbers in thousands, except as noted)

PROBLEM	Total renters	Income-eligible renters		Assisted			
		Total	Unassisted	Total	Public housing	Certificate or voucher programs	Private project-based
TOTAL HOUSEHOLDS	33,767	13,808	9,738	4,070	1,360	1,060	1,650
FAILURES IN EQUIPMENT							
Within last 3 months:							
Water supply stop	2,010	813	544	269	86	63	120
No working toilet	2,549	1,253	871	382	169	99	113
Public sewage disposal	703	375	224	151	35	38	78
Electric fuses/breakers	4,628	1,758	1,286	472	204	120	148
Past winter:							
Heating equipment	1,028	525	367	158	73	46	38
WATER LEAKAGE							
From inside	5,540	2,404	1,644	760	242	230	288
From outside	4,742	1,755	1,344	411	107	124	180
SELECTED DEFICIENCIES							
Signs of rats	1,935	1,119	811	308	163	73	72
Holes in floor	634	319	263	56	17	19	20
Open cracks/holes	2,932	1,466	1,168	298	109	95	94
Broken plaster/paint	2,316	1,173	915	258	140	56	63
No electric wiring	5	5	5	0	0	0	0
Exposed wiring	911	497	423	74	18	22	34
Rooms without electric outlets	966	483	385	98	26	22	50
SEVERE PROBLEMS	1,588	837	665	172	60	49	63
Plumbing	1,134	602	470	132	35	39	58
Heating	279	122	91	31	11	15	5
Electric	63	43	43	0	0	0	0
Upkeep	161	100	83	17	15	2	0
Hallways	0	0	0	0	0	0	0
MODERATE PROBLEMS	2,443	1,317	1,069	248	112	85	51
Plumbing	179	108	67	41	21	8	12
Heating	824	447	397	50	19	31	0
Upkeep	1,178	640	514	126	54	50	22
Hallways	62	30	30	0	0	0	0
Kitchen	417	219	181	38	19	3	16
NEIGHBORHOOD PROBLEM	14,044	5,642	3,907	1,735	640	439	656
Crime	3,721	1,833	1,163	670	279	141	250
Noise	3,616	1,438	1,051	387	127	116	144
Traffic	2,764	829	630	199	63	80	56
Litter or housing rundown	1,366	656	464	192	90	58	44
Poor local services	418	174	122	52	31	9	12
Undesirable commercial, industrial, or institutional uses	623	185	147	38	10	15	13
People	5,269	2,510	1,713	797	247	229	322
Other	2,821	1,015	701	314	156	46	112
NEARBY BUILDINGS VANDALIZED OR INTERIORS EXPOSED	908	606	415	191	127	47	17
NEARBY BUILDINGS WITH BARS ON WINDOWS	2,228	1,173	855	318	151	78	88
TRASH, LITTER, JUNK ON STREETS OR PROPERTIES	5,685	3,229	2,208	1,021	433	227	361

See notes at end of table.

Characteristics of Assisted Households, Their Housing, and Their

TABLE 5.25. HOUSING AND NEIGHBORHOOD PROBLEMS FOR RENTERS BY INCOME-ELIGIBILITY AND HOUSING ASSISTANCE PROGRAM: 1989 - Continued
(Percent)

PROBLEM	Total renters	Income-eligible renters					
		Total	Unassisted	Assisted			
				Total	Public housing	Certificate or voucher programs	Private project-based
TOTAL HOUSEHOLDS	100	100	100	100	100	100	100
FAILURES IN EQUIPMENT							
Within last 3 months:							
Water supply stop	6	6	6	7	6	6	7
No working toilet	8	9	9	9	12	9	7
Public sewage disposal	2	3	2	4	3	4	5
Electric fuses/breakers	14	13	13	12	15	11	9
Past winter:							
Heating equipment	3	4	4	4	5	4	2
WATER LEAKAGE							
From inside	16	17	17	19	18	22	17
From outside	14	13	14	10	8	12	11
SELECTED DEFICIENCIES							
Signs of rats	6	8	8	8	12	7	4
Holes in floor	2	2	3	1	1	2	1
Open cracks/holes	9	11	12	7	8	9	6
Broken plaster/paint	7	8	9	6	10	5	4
No electric wiring	0	0	0	0	0	0	0
Exposed wiring	3	4	4	2	1	2	2
Rooms without electric outlets	3	3	4	2	2	2	3
SEVERE PROBLEMS	5	6	7	4	4	5	4
Plumbing	3	4	5	3	3	4	4
Heating	1	1	1	1	1	1	0
Electric	0	0	0	0	0	0	0
Upkeep	0	1	1	0	1	0	0
Hallways	0	0	0	0	0	0	0
MODERATE PROBLEMS	7	10	11	6	8	8	3
Plumbing	1	1	1	1	2	1	1
Heating	2	3	4	1	1	3	0
Upkeep	3	5	5	3	4	5	1
Hallways	0	0	0	0	0	0	0
Kitchen	1	2	2	1	1	0	1
NEIGHBORHOOD PROBLEM	42	41	40	43	47	41	40
Crime	11	13	12	16	21	13	15
Noise	11	10	11	10	9	11	9
Traffic	8	6	6	5	5	8	3
Litter or housing rundown	4	5	5	5	7	5	3
Poor local services	1	1	1	1	2	1	1
Undesirable commercial, industrial, or institutional uses	2	1	2	1	1	1	1
People	16	18	18	20	18	22	20
Other	8	7	7	8	11	4	7
NEARBY BUILDINGS VANDALIZED OR INTERIORS EXPOSED	3	4	4	5	9	4	1
NEARBY BUILDINGS WITH BARS ON WINDOWS	7	8	9	8	11	7	5
TRASH, LITTER, JUNK ON STREETS OR PROPERTIES	17	23	23	25	32	21	22

Source: Casey, Connie H. "Characteristics of HUD-Assisted Renters and Their Units in 1989." U.S. Department of Housing and Urban Development, Office of Policy Development and Research, HUD-1346-PDR. March 1992.

Characteristics of Assisted Households, Their Housing, and Their Neighborhoods

TABLE 5.26. HOUSING AND NEIGHBORHOOD PROBLEMS FOR RENTERS BY INCOME-ELIGIBILITY AND HOUSING ASSISTANCE PROGRAM: 1991
(Numbers in thousands, except as noted)

PROBLEM	Total renters	Income-eligible renters		Assisted			
		Total	Unassisted	Total	Public housing	Certificate or voucher programs	Private project-based
TOTAL HOUSEHOLDS	33,351	16,194	12,158	4,036	1,146	1,141	1,749
FAILURES IN EQUIPMENT							
Within last 3 months:							
Water supply stop	1,797	876	612	268	124	60	84
No working toilet	2,359	1,334	1,038	296	115	79	102
Public sewage disposal	563	326	234	92	22	25	45
Electric fuses/breakers	4,182	1,675	1,337	319	104	111	104
Past winter:							
Heating equipment	974	514	364	140	51	35	53
WATER LEAKAGE							
From inside	5,478	2,813	2,042	711	205	191	315
From outside	4,140	1,628	1,362	266	54	117	94
SELECTED DEFICIENCIES							
Signs of rats	1,787	1,228	951	277	111	70	96
Holes in floor	674	382	330	49	15	16	18
Open cracks/holes	2,689	1,501	1,190	311	129	89	93
Broken plaster/paint	2,039	1,209	950	259	116	74	69
No electric wiring	4	4	4	0	0	0	0
Exposed wiring	831	479	398	81	20	29	32
Rooms without electric outlets	813	408	367	41	12	21	8
SEVERE PROBLEMS	1,347	717	597	98	49	29	20
Plumbing	952	501	432	69	27	22	20
Heating	233	94	67	27	22	6	0
Electric	26	22	22	0	0	0	0
Upkeep	166	97	95	2	0	2	0
Hallways	3	3	3	0	0	0	0
MODERATE PROBLEMS	2,375	1,475	1,171	304	120	94	89
Plumbing	190	123	88	35	24	5	6
Heating	848	536	474	62	16	39	7
Upkeep	1,099	703	535	168	62	46	60
Hallways	47	22	14	8	5	3	0
Kitchen	354	195	158	37	17	4	16
NEIGHBORHOOD PROBLEM	13,551	6,635	4,800	1,739	555	448	735
Crime	3,991	2,355	1,652	703	296	126	282
Noise	3,706	1,878	1,360	518	144	132	242
Traffic	2,509	964	778	186	56	75	55
Litter or housing rundown	1,341	713	544	169	74	41	53
Poor local services	474	257	181	76	47	17	12
Undesirable commercial, industrial, or institutional uses	551	206	162	34	14	11	8
People	5,090	2,838	2,064	774	249	208	317
Other	2,463	1,040	760	280	93	85	102
NEARBY BUILDINGS VANDALIZED OR INTERIORS EXPOSED	948	807	504	261	162	50	49
NEARBY BUILDINGS WITH BARS ON WINDOWS	2,963	1,798	1,289	454	181	91	181
TRASH, LITTER, JUNK ON STREETS OR PROPERTIES	5,834	3,938	2,751	1,094	461	246	386

See notes at end of table.

Characteristics of Assisted Households, Their Housing, and Their Neighborhoods

PROBLEM	Total renters	Income-eligible renters		Assisted			
		Total	Unassisted	Total	Public housing	Certificate or voucher programs	Private project-based
TABLE 5.26. HOUSING AND NEIGHBORHOOD PROBLEMS FOR RENTERS BY INCOME-ELIGIBILITY AND HOUSING ASSISTANCE PROGRAM: 1991 - Continued (Percent)							
TOTAL HOUSEHOLDS	100	100	100	100	100	100	100
FAILURES IN EQUIPMENT							
Within last 3 months:							
Water supply stop	5	5	5	7	11	5	5
No working toilet	7	8	9	7	10	7	6
Public sewage disposal	2	2	2	2	2	2	3
Electric fuses/breakers	13	10	11	8	9	10	6
Past winter:							
Heating equipment	3	3	3	3	4	3	3
WATER LEAKAGE							
From inside	16	17	17	18	18	17	18
From outside	12	10	11	7	5	10	5
SELECTED DEFICIENCIES							
Signs of rats	5	8	8	7	10	6	5
Holes in floor	2	2	3	1	1	1	1
Open cracks/holes	8	9	10	8	11	8	5
Broken plaster/paint	6	7	8	6	10	6	4
No electric wiring	0	0	0	0	0	0	0
Exposed wiring	2	3	3	2	2	3	2
Rooms without electric outlets	2	3	3	1	1	2	0
SEVERE PROBLEMS	4	4	5	2	4	3	1
Plumbing	3	3	4	2	2	2	1
Heating	1	1	1	1	2	1	0
Electric	0	0	0	0	0	0	0
Upkeep	0	1	1	0	0	0	0
Hallways	0	0	0	0	0	0	0
MODERATE PROBLEMS	7	9	10	8	10	8	5
Plumbing	1	1	1	1	2	0	0
Heating	3	3	4	2	1	3	0
Upkeep	3	4	4	4	5	4	3
Hallways	0	0	0	0	0	0	0
Kitchen	1	1	1	1	1	0	1
NEIGHBORHOOD PROBLEM	41	41	39	43	48	39	42
Crime	12	15	14	17	26	11	16
Noise	11	12	11	13	13	12	14
Traffic	8	6	6	5	5	7	3
Litter or housing rundown	4	4	4	4	6	4	3
Poor local services	1	2	1	2	4	1	1
Undesirable commercial, industrial, or institutional uses	2	1	1	1	1	1	0
People	15	18	17	19	22	18	18
Other	7	6	6	7	8	7	6
NEARBY BUILDINGS VANDALIZED OR INTERIORS EXPOSED	3	5	4	6	14	4	3
NEARBY BUILDINGS WITH BARS ON WINDOWS	9	11	11	11	16	8	10
TRASH, LITTER, JUNK ON STREETS OR PROPERTIES	17	24	23	27	40	22	22

Source: Casey, Connie H. "Characteristics of HUD-Assisted Renters and Their Units in 1991." U.S. Department of Housing and Urban Development, Office of Policy Development and Research, May 1997.

Characteristics of Assisted Households, Their Housing, and Their Neighborhoods

TABLE 5.27. HOUSING AND NEIGHBORHOOD PROBLEMS FOR RENTERS BY INCOME-ELIGIBILITY AND HOUSING ASSISTANCE PROGRAM: 1993
(Numbers in thousands, except as noted)

| PROBLEM | Total renters | Income-eligible renters | | | | | | |
| | | Unassisted | | | Assisted | | | |
		Total	Total	Worst-case needs	Total	Public housing	Certificate or voucher programs	Private project-based
TOTAL HOUSEHOLDS	33,472	15,795	11,741	4,849	4,054	1,138	1,200	1,716
FAILURES IN EQUIPMENT								
Within last 3 months:								
Water supply stop	1,990	904	675	292	229	74	75	80
No working toilet	2,476	1,371	990	466	381	139	115	127
Public sewage disposal	629	292	245	119	48	19	18	11
Electric fuses/breakers	4,165	1,694	1,336	562	359	123	139	97
Past winter:								
Heating equipment	954	507	372	217	135	51	63	21
WATER LEAKAGE								
From inside	5,190	2,467	1,828	638	638	156	202	281
From outside	4,987	2,171	1,757	414	414	93	153	169
SELECTED DEFICIENCIES								
Signs of rats	1,571	1,125	820	444	305	148	74	84
Holes in floor	678	411	368	234	43	4	19	21
Open cracks/holes	2,699	1,511	1,234	671	277	103	105	69
Broken plaster/paint	1,982	1,172	943	519	229	130	51	48
No electric wiring	2	2	2	2	0	0	0	0
Exposed wiring	808	500	396	206	105	39	36	29
Rooms without electric outlets	913	528	433	228	95	22	36	36
SEVERE PROBLEMS	909	570	489	489	81	32	33	16
Plumbing	568	341	308	308	33	6	16	11
Heating	207	135	90	90	45	26	14	5
Electric	28	22	22	22	0	0	0	0
Upkeep	142	102	100	100	2	0	2	0
Hallways	6	4	4	4	0	0	0	0
MODERATE PROBLEMS	2,254	1,263	1,046	420	217	98	73	45
Plumbing	199	114	70	39	45	21	17	6
Heating	640	365	343	97	22	10	11	0
Upkeep	1,145	670	539	252	132	62	39	31
Hallways	47	30	28	9	2	0	2	0
Kitchen	395	186	156	49	30	8	7	14
NEIGHBORHOOD PROBLEM	13,892	6,542	4,767	2,068	1,774	568	514	693
Crime	4,017	2,191	1,502	685	689	301	156	233
Noise	3,938	1,987	1,458	663	529	181	153	195
Traffic	2,675	1,053	878	379	175	43	90	42
Litter or housing rundown	1,281	660	491	230	169	62	55	52
Poor local services	414	213	166	71	47	32	10	5
Undesirable commercial, industrial, or institutional uses	505	187	157	87	30	21	2	7
People	5,215	2,816	2,016	874	800	248	230	322
Other	2,935	1,177	905	394	272	98	91	83
NEARBY BUILDINGS VANDALIZED OR INTERIORS EXPOSED	1,155	897	634	310	263	134	58	72
NEARBY BUILDINGS WITH BARS ON WINDOWS	3,319	2,009	1,512	757	498	233	161	104
TRASH, LITTER, JUNK ON STREETS OR PROPERTIES	5,921	3,881	2,732	1,326	1,150	469	269	412

See notes at end of table.

Characteristics of Assisted Households, Their Housing, and Their Neighborhoods

TABLE 5.27. HOUSING AND NEIGHBORHOOD PROBLEMS FOR RENTERS BY INCOME-ELIGIBILITY AND HOUSING ASSISTANCE PROGRAM: 1993 - Continued
(Percent)

PROBLEM	Total renters	Income-eligible renters						
		Total	Unassisted		Assisted			
			Total	Worst-case needs	Total	Public housing	Certificate or voucher programs	Private project-based
TOTAL HOUSEHOLDS	100	100	100	100	100	100	100	100
FAILURES IN EQUIPMENT								
Within last 3 months:								
Water supply stop	6	6	6	6	6	7	6	5
No working toilet	7	9	8	10	9	12	10	7
Public sewage disposal	2	2	2	2	1	2	2	1
Electric fuses/breakers	12	11	11	12	9	11	12	6
Past winter:								
Heating equipment	3	3	3	4	3	4	5	1
WATER LEAKAGE								
From inside	16	16	16	13	16	14	17	16
From outside	15	14	15	9	10	8	13	10
SELECTED DEFICIENCIES								
Signs of rats	5	7	7	9	8	13	6	5
Holes in floor	2	3	3	5	1	0	2	1
Open cracks/holes	8	10	11	14	7	9	9	4
Broken plaster/paint	6	7	8	11	6	11	4	3
No electric wiring	0	0	0	0	0	0	0	0
Exposed wiring	2	3	3	4	3	3	3	2
Rooms without electric outlets	3	3	4	5	2	2	3	2
SEVERE PROBLEMS	3	4	4	10	2	3	3	1
Plumbing	2	2	3	6	1	1	1	1
Heating	1	1	1	2	1	2	1	0
Electric	0	0	0	0	0	0	0	0
Upkeep	0	1	1	2	0	0	0	0
Hallways	0	0	0	0	0	0	0	0
MODERATE PROBLEMS	7	8	9	9	5	9	6	3
Plumbing	1	1	1	1	1	2	1	0
Heating	2	2	3	2	1	1	1	0
Upkeep	3	4	5	5	3	5	3	2
Hallways	0	0	0	0	0	0	0	0
Kitchen	1	1	1	1	1	1	1	1
NEIGHBORHOOD PROBLEM	42	41	41	43	44	50	43	40
Crime	12	14	13	14	17	26	13	14
Noise	12	13	12	14	13	16	13	11
Traffic	8	7	7	8	4	4	8	2
Litter or housing rundown	4	4	4	5	4	5	5	3
Poor local services	1	1	1	1	1	3	1	0
Undesirable commercial, industrial, or institutional uses	2	1	1	2	1	2	0	0
People	16	18	17	18	20	22	19	19
Other	9	7	8	8	7	9	8	5
NEARBY BUILDINGS VANDALIZED OR INTERIORS EXPOSED	3	6	5	6	6	12	5	4
NEARBY BUILDINGS WITH BARS ON WINDOWS	10	13	13	16	12	20	13	6
TRASH, LITTER, JUNK ON STREETS OR PROPERTIES	18	25	23	27	28	41	22	24

Source: McGough, Duane T. "Characteristics of HUD-Assisted Renters and Their Units in 1993." U.S. Department of Housing and Urban Development, Office of Policy Development and Research. May 1997.

Characteristics of Assisted Households, Their Housing, and Their Neighborhoods

TABLE 5.28. RENTER OPINIONS OF HOUSING AND NEIGHBORHOOD BY INCOME-ELIGIBILITY AND HOUSING ASSISTANCE PROGRAM: 1989
(Numbers in thousands, except as noted)

CHARACTERISTIC	Total renters	Income-eligible renters					
		Total	Unassisted	Assisted			
				Total	Public housing	Certificate or voucher programs	Private project-based
TOTAL HOUSEHOLDS	33,767	13,808	9,738	4,070	1,360	1,060	1,650
OPINION OF STRUCTURE							
1 (Worst)	514	373	297	76	39	12	25
2	310	171	115	56	25	17	14
3	535	296	215	81	44	18	19
4	778	332	250	82	42	16	24
5	3,746	1,725	1,354	371	112	89	170
6	2,718	972	772	200	47	59	93
7	5,037	1,644	1,186	458	133	126	199
8	8,056	2,677	1,933	744	268	213	263
9	3,850	1,330	952	378	110	121	147
10 (Best)	7,835	4,091	2,522	1,569	498	386	685
Not reported	388	199	144	55	42	2	11
OPINION OF NEIGHBORHOOD							
1 (Worst)	1,147	905	532	373	171	59	143
2	646	434	284	150	43	31	77
3	811	408	286	122	48	34	41
4	970	415	253	162	70	45	47
5	3,519	1,698	1,245	453	175	127	152
6	2,161	744	557	187	45	49	92
7	3,939	1,319	970	349	101	111	137
8	7,063	2,340	1,754	586	134	192	260
9	3,797	1,167	855	312	86	100	126
10 (Best)	9,002	4,041	2,812	1,229	424	297	507
No neighborhood	192	65	27	38	15	5	18
Not reported	520	271	163	108	48	9	50

See notes at end of table.

Characteristics of Assisted Households, Their Housing, and Their Neighborhoods

CHARACTERISTIC	Total renters	Income-eligible renters					
		Total	Unassisted	Assisted			
				Total	Public housing	Certificate or voucher programs	Private project-based
TABLE 5.28. RENTER OPINIONS OF HOUSING AND NEIGHBORHOOD BY INCOME-ELIGIBILITY AND HOUSING ASSISTANCE PROGRAM: 1989 - Continued (Percent)							
TOTAL HOUSEHOLDS	100	100	100	100	100	100	100
OPINION OF STRUCTURE							
1 (Worst)	2	3	3	2	3	1	2
2	1	1	1	1	2	2	1
3	2	2	2	2	3	2	1
4	2	2	3	2	3	2	1
5	11	12	14	9	8	8	10
6	8	7	8	5	3	6	6
7	15	12	12	11	10	12	12
8	24	19	20	18	20	20	16
9	11	10	10	9	8	11	9
10 (Best)	23	30	26	39	37	36	42
Not reported	1	1	1	1	3	0	1
OPINION OF NEIGHBORHOOD							
1 (Worst)	3	7	5	9	13	6	9
2	2	3	3	4	3	3	5
3	2	3	3	3	4	3	2
4	3	3	3	4	5	4	3
5	10	12	13	11	13	12	9
6	6	5	6	5	3	5	6
7	12	10	10	9	7	10	8
8	21	17	18	14	10	18	16
9	11	8	9	8	6	9	8
10 (Best)	27	29	29	30	31	28	31
No neighborhood	1	0	0	1	1	0	1
Not reported	2	2	2	3	4	1	3

Source: Casey, Connie H. "Characteristics of HUD-Assisted Renters and Their Units in 1989." U.S. Department of Housing and Urban Development, Office of Policy Development and Research, HUD-1346-PDR. March 1992.

Characteristics of Assisted Households, Their Housing, and Their Neighborhoods

TABLE 5.29. RENTER OPINIONS OF HOUSING AND NEIGHBORHOOD BY INCOME-ELIGIBILITY AND HOUSING ASSISTANCE PROGRAM: 1991
(Numbers in thousands, except as noted)

| CHARACTERISTIC | Total renters | Income-eligible renters | | | | | |
| | | Total | Unassisted | Assisted | | | |
				Total	Public housing	Certificate or voucher programs	Private project-based
TOTAL HOUSEHOLDS	33,351	16,194	12,158	4,036	1,146	1,141	1,749
OPINION OF STRUCTURE							
1 (Worst)	475	368	293	75	29	32	14
2	284	206	155	51	32	19	0
3	464	244	202	42	10	16	16
4	764	362	306	56	18	19	19
5	3,648	1,924	1,477	447	143	131	173
6	2,588	1,114	882	238	87	80	71
7	5,132	2,007	1,609	398	98	125	175
8	8,297	3,386	2,591	795	194	238	363
9	3,858	1,611	1,168	443	101	111	230
10 (Best)	7,534	4,767	3,324	1,443	418	356	670
Not reported	307	197	151	46	16	12	18
OPINION OF NEIGHBORHOOD							
1 (Worst)	989	870	621	249	129	56	63
2	555	361	258	107	34	34	38
3	849	521	388	133	27	36	70
4	933	533	397	137	65	29	43
5	3,503	2,020	1,440	545	182	165	198
6	2,353	949	789	160	29	38	93
7	4,214	1,727	1,290	437	96	126	215
8	7,032	2,782	2,172	585	131	188	266
9	3,799	1,464	1,076	388	108	86	194
10 (Best)	8,474	4,634	3,431	1,203	318	358	527
No neighborhood	197	79	77	4	0	4	0
Not reported	455	307	218	89	27	20	42

See notes at end of table.

Characteristics of Assisted Households, Their Housing, and Their Neighborhoods

CHARACTERISTIC	Total renters	Income-eligible renters		Assisted			
		Total	Unassisted	Total	Public housing	Certificate or voucher programs	Private project-based
TOTAL HOUSEHOLDS	100	100	100	100	100	100	100
OPINION OF STRUCTURE							
1 (Worst)	1	2	2	2	3	3	1
2	1	1	1	1	3	2	0
3	1	2	2	1	1	1	1
4	2	2	3	1	2	2	1
5	11	12	12	11	12	11	10
6	8	7	7	6	8	7	4
7	15	12	13	10	9	11	10
8	25	21	21	20	17	21	21
9	12	10	10	11	9	10	13
10 (Best)	23	29	27	36	36	31	38
Not reported	1	1	1	1	1	1	1
OPINION OF NEIGHBORHOOD							
1 (Worst)	3	5	5	6	11	5	4
2	2	2	2	3	3	3	2
3	3	3	3	3	2	3	4
4	3	3	3	3	6	3	2
5	11	12	12	14	16	14	11
6	7	6	6	4	3	3	5
7	13	11	11	11	8	11	12
8	21	17	18	14	11	16	15
9	11	9	9	10	9	8	11
10 (Best)	25	29	28	30	28	31	30
No neighborhood	1	0	1	0	0	0	0
Not reported	1	2	2	2	2	2	2

TABLE 5.29. RENTER OPINIONS OF HOUSING AND NEIGHBORHOOD BY INCOME-ELIGIBILITY AND HOUSING ASSISTANCE PROGRAM: 1991 - Continued (Percent)

Source: Casey, Connie H. "Characteristics of HUD-Assisted Renters and Their Units in 1991." U.S. Department of Housing and Urban Development, Office of Policy Development and Research, May 1997.

Characteristics of Assisted Households, Their Housing, and Their Neighborhoods

TABLE 5.30. RENTER OPINIONS OF HOUSING AND NEIGHBORHOOD BY INCOME-ELIGIBILITY AND HOUSING ASSISTANCE PROGRAM: 1993
(Numbers in thousands, except as noted)

| CHARACTERISTIC | Total renters | Income-eligible renters | | | | | | |
| | | Total | Unassisted | | Assisted | | | |
			Total	Worst-case needs	Total	Public housing	Certificate or voucher programs	Private project-based
TOTAL HOUSEHOLDS	33,472	15,795	11,741	4,849	4,054	1,138	1,200	1,716
OPINION OF STRUCTURE								
1 (Worst)	444	325	261	144	64	30	20	14
2	267	154	101	56	53	28	13	11
3	491	275	222	123	53	17	17	19
4	735	334	273	131	61	25	24	11
5	3,457	1,834	1,437	629	397	146	108	143
6	2,642	1,178	920	399	258	77	87	95
7	5,164	2,031	1,589	611	442	114	151	177
8	8,419	3,398	2,613	1,011	784	159	272	353
9	4,120	1,751	1,265	544	486	130	150	205
10 (Best)	7,349	4,280	2,871	1,127	1,408	395	341	673
Not reported	385	236	187	75	49	17	16	16
OPINION OF NEIGHBORHOOD								
1 (Worst)	1,012	868	506	233	362	178	69	115
2	559	349	248	120	101	32	31	39
3	790	461	339	151	122	46	35	41
4	1,050	569	389	186	180	88	53	40
5	3,660	1,984	1,459	605	525	157	129	239
6	2,263	1,050	787	337	262	80	74	109
7	4,186	1,724	1,361	529	363	53	117	193
8	6,938	2,762	2,116	881	646	107	216	322
9	3,914	1,461	1,134	461	328	94	119	115
10 (Best)	8,407	4,151	3,085	1,234	1,066	266	330	469
No neighborhood	239	116	98	30	18	7	2	9
Not reported	455	300	219	80	80	31	24	25

See notes at end of table.

Characteristics of Assisted Households, Their Housing, and Their Neighborhoods

TABLE 5.30. RENTER OPINIONS OF HOUSING AND NEIGHBORHOOD BY INCOME-ELIGIBILITY AND HOUSING ASSISTANCE PROGRAM: 1993 - Continued
(Percent)

| CHARACTERISTIC | Total renters | Income-eligible renters | | | | | | |
| | | Total | Unassisted | | Assisted | | | |
			Total	Worst-case needs	Total	Public housing	Certificate or voucher programs	Private project-based
TOTAL HOUSEHOLDS	100	100	100	100	100	100	100	100
OPINION OF STRUCTURE								
1 (Worst)	1	2	2	3	2	3	2	1
2	1	1	1	1	1	2	1	1
3	1	2	2	3	1	1	1	1
4	2	2	2	3	2	2	2	1
5	10	12	12	13	10	13	9	8
6	8	7	8	8	6	7	7	6
7	15	13	14	13	11	10	13	10
8	25	22	22	21	19	14	23	21
9	12	11	11	11	12	11	13	12
10 (Best)	22	27	24	23	35	35	28	39
Not reported	1	1	2	2	1	1	1	1
OPINION OF NEIGHBORHOOD								
1 (Worst)	3	5	4	5	9	16	6	7
2	2	2	2	2	2	3	3	2
3	2	3	3	3	3	4	3	2
4	3	4	3	4	4	8	4	2
5	11	13	12	12	13	14	11	14
6	7	7	7	7	6	7	6	6
7	13	11	12	11	9	5	10	11
8	21	17	18	18	16	9	18	19
9	12	9	10	10	8	8	10	7
10 (Best)	25	26	26	25	26	23	28	27
No neighborhood	1	1	1	1	0	1	0	1
Not reported	1	2	2	2	2	3	2	1

Source: McGough, Duane T. "Characteristics of HUD-Assisted Renters and Their Units in 1993." U.S. Department of Housing and Urban Development, Office of Policy Development and Research. May 1997.

Characteristics of Assisted Households, Their Housing, and Their Neighborhoods

CHARACTERISTIC	TABLE 5.31. CHARACTERISTICS OF LOW-INCOME HOUSING TAX CREDIT PROPERTIES: 1990 TO 1994	
	Number	Percent
TOTAL PROJECTS	6,142	....
TOTAL UNITS	247,480	....
TOTAL ASSISTED UNITS	224,446	....
AVERAGE PROJECT SIZE (UNITS)	40.6	....
DISTRIBUTION BY PROJECT SIZE (PERCENT)		
0-10 units	....	26.2
11-50 units	....	53.1
51-99 units	....	11.1
100 or more units	....	9.6
DISTRIBUTION OF UNITS BY QUALIFYING RATIO [1] (PERCENT)		
0-20	....	1.5
21-40	....	3.5
41-60	....	2.7
61-80	....	2.3
81-90	....	1.6
91-95	....	1.0
96-100	....	87.3
DISTRIBUTION OF UNITS BY NUMBER OF BEDROOMS (PERCENT)		
No bedrooms	....	4.4
1 bedroom	....	41.1
2 bedrooms	....	40.5
3 bedrooms	....	13.0
4 or more bedrooms	....	1.0
DISTRIBUTION OF UNITS BY CONSTRUCTION TYPE (PERCENT)		
Existing	....	0.3
New	....	60.5
Rehabilitation	....	38.3
Both new and rehabilitation	....	0.9
PERCENTAGE OF UNITS WITH NONPROFIT SPONSOR	....	19.5
PERCENTAGE OF UNITS WITH RURAL HOUSING SERVICE SECTION 515 FINANCING	....	26.8
DISTRIBUTION OF UNITS BY REGION (PERCENT)		
Northeast	....	12.5
Midwest	....	27.0
South	....	43.3
West	....	17.2
DISTRIBUTION OF UNITS BY PLACE (PERCENT)		
Central city	....	53.6
Suburbs	....	26.6
Nonmetropolitan	....	19.8

Source: U.S. Department of Housing and Urban Development. "U.S. Housing Market Conditions." August 1996.

(1) Ratio of low-income units that qualify for tax credit to total units. See Appendix A.

Excludes units placed in service from 1990 to 1994 for which the precise year is unavailable.

Characteristics of Assisted Households, Their Housing, and Their Neighborhoods

CHARACTERISTIC	TABLE 5.32. CHARACTERISTICS OF LOW-INCOME HOUSING TAX CREDIT PROJECTS BY REGION: 1992-1994				
	Total	Northeast	Midwest	South	West
	N=166,685	N=21,525	N=44,708	N=69,291	N=31,161
REGION'S SHARE OF ALL UNITS (PERCENTAGE)	100.0	12.9	26.8	41.6	18.7
AVERAGE PROJECT SIZE (UNITS)	42.1	39.7	34.7	44.8	53.4
AVERAGE PERCENTAGE OF QUALIFYING UNITS [1]	97.8	95.7	97.4	99.1	97.0
AVERAGE NUMBER OF BEDROOMS PER UNIT [2]	1.7	1.6	1.7	1.6	1.7
DISTRIBUTION OF UNITS BY NUMBER OF BEDROOMS					
Studio/Efficiency	5.6	3.5	1.5	3.2	15.6
1 bedroom	40.5	42.9	43.4	44.8	28.0
2 bedrooms	38.5	43.5	40.9	39.4	33.1
3 bedrooms	13.9	8.9	13.3	11.6	20.3
4 bedrooms	1.3	1.1	0.8	0.9	2.9
PERCENTAGE OF UNITS WITH NON-PROFIT SPONSOR [3]	23.3	27.7	20.7	13.0	41.6
DISTRIBUTION OF UNITS BY CONSTRUCTION TYPE [4]					
New Construction	60.4	39.5	68.3	53.9	82.5
Rehab	38.2	57.5	31.4	45.5	16.2
Both New/Rehab	1.2	3.0	0.3	1.2	1.3
Existing	0.2	0.0	0.1	0.4	0.0
DISTRIBUTION BY CREDIT PERCENTAGE [5,6]					
4 percent	31.5	23.0	31.1	40.9	19.8
9 percent	57.0	55.9	55.2	47.0	76.6
Both	11.5	21.2	13.8	12.2	3.7
PERCENT OF UNITS WITH FmHA FINANCING [7]	25.1	15.3	22.7	32.8	14.1

Source: Abt Associates, "Development and Analysis of the National Low-Income Housing Tax Credit Database." July 1996.

(1) Qualifying units are reserved for low-income use, have restricted rents, and can be claimed for tax credits.
(2) Percent of units missing data: Total (53%); Northeast (87%); Midwest (53%); South (43%); West (52%).
(3) Percent of units missing data: Total (24%); Northeast (16%); Midwest (32%); South (27%); West (9%).
(4) Percent of units missing data: Total (29%); Northeast (35%); Midwest (31%); South (23%); West (34%).
(5) Two different tax credit rates - 4 and 9% - are applicable to LIHTC projects. See Appendix A.
(6) Percent of units missing data: Total (49%); Northeast (54%); Midwest (60%); South (48%); West (33%).
(7) Percent of units missing data: Total (27%); Northeast (46%); Midwest (34%); South (19%); West (25%).

Excludes 20 properties for which no information on the number of units was available and 29 properties in the Virgin Islands and Puerto Rico.

Characteristics of Assisted Households, Their Housing, and Their Neighborhoods

TABLE 5.33. CHARACTERISTICS OF LOW-INCOME HOUSING TAX CREDIT PROJECTS BY TYPE OF LOCATION: 1992-1994

CHARACTERISTIC	Total	Metropolitan areas		Non-metropolitan areas
		Central city	Non-central city	
	N=122,606	N=66,692	N=31,962	N=23,952
LOCATION TYPE'S SHARE OF ALL UNITS (PERCENTAGE)	100.0	54.4	26.1	19.5
AVERAGE PROJECT SIZE (UNITS)	43.3	48.4	53.7	28.2
AVERAGE PERCENTAGE OF QUALIFYING UNITS [1]	97.4	97.2	96.1	98.6
AVERAGE NUMBER OF BEDROOMS PER UNIT [2]	1.6	1.7	1.7	1.5
DISTRIBUTION OF UNITS BY NUMBER OF BEDROOMS				
Studio/Efficiency	6.4	9.8	3.0	2.2
1 bedroom	40.0	32.7	39.5	58.2
2 bedrooms	38.7	41.3	39.8	31.0
3 bedrooms	13.5	14.3	16.3	8.2
4 bedrooms	1.3	1.8	1.3	0.4
PERCENTAGE OF UNITS WITH NON-PROFIT SPONSOR [3]	25.7	30.4	28.9	7.9
DISTRIBUTION OF UNITS BY CONSTRUCTION TYPE [4]				
New Construction	54.9	42.1	63.5	76.9
Rehab	43.6	55.2	35.9	23.1
Both New/Rehab	1.3	2.3	0.5	0.0
Existing	0.2	0.4	0.1	0.0
DISTRIBUTION BY CREDIT PERCENTAGE [5, 6]				
4 percent	29.3	11.2	29.4	72.9
9 percent	57.5	70.1	60.3	22.9
Both	13.2	18.8	10.3	4.2
PERCENT OF UNITS WITH FmHA FINANCING [7]	20.6	2.7	19.0	69.4

Source: Abt Associates, "Development and Analysis of the National Low-Income Housing Tax Credit Database." July 1996.

(1) Qualifying units are reserved for low-income use, have restricted rents, and can be claimed for tax credits.
(2) Percent of units missing data: Total (52%); central city (52%); metro, non-central-city (55%); non-metro (50%).
(3) Percent of units missing data: Total (24%); central city (25%); metro, non-central-city (23%); non-metro (26%).
(4) Percent of units missing data: Total (27%); central city (29%); metro, non-central-city (23%); non-metro (26%).
(5) Two different tax credit rates - 4 and 9% - are applicable to LIHTC projects. See Appendix A.
(6) Percent of units missing data: Total (48%); central city (53%); metro, non-central-city (38%); non-metro (46%).
(7) Percent of units missing data: Total (26%); central city (28%); metro, non-central-city (26%); non-metro (22%).

Includes only geocoded projects (that is, projects that could be linked to a census tract) and excludes 25 projects with missing unit or census data.

Appendix A

Table Notes

This appendix provides detailed notes to accompany the data tables. It includes definitions of subject characteristics, descriptions of data limitations, and a discussion of factors that might affect comparability across data series and within a given data series over time. Although this appendix covers many of the important characteristics of the data, the reader should consult the publications referenced with each table for additional information. For descriptions of the principal sources for housing data, see Appendix B.

Area Definitions

Standard definitions for geographic regions and divisions are used in this book. States contained in each of the regions and divisions are as follows:

Northeast Region

New England—Connecticut, Maine, Massachusetts, New Hampshire, Rhode Island, Vermont

Middle Atlantic—New Jersey, New York, Pennsylvania

Midwest (North Central) Region

East North Central—Illinois, Indiana, Michigan, Ohio, Wisconsin

West North Central—Iowa, Kansas, Minnesota, Missouri, Nebraska, North Dakota, South Dakota

South Region

South Atlantic—Delaware, District of Columbia, Florida, Georgia, Maryland, North Carolina, South Carolina, Virginia, West Virginia

East South Central—Alabama, Kentucky, Mississippi, Tennessee

West South Central—Arkansas, Louisiana, Oklahoma, Texas

West Region

Mountain—Arizona, Colorado, Idaho, Montana, Nevada, New Mexico, Utah, Wyoming

Pacific—Alaska, California, Hawaii, Oregon, Washington

Part 1: Demographics and Housing Demand

Table 1.1

Data Source:

Current Population Survey/Housing Vacancy Survey
References:

U.S. Bureau of the Census, "Housing Vacancy Survey: Historical Tables (Table 13) Monthly Household Estimates," January 13, 1997; <http://www.census.gov/ftp/pub/hhes/www/housing/hvs/historic/histt13.html>. See also U.S. Bureau of the Census, "Using Different Census Bureau Sources for Estimating the Number of Households," April 24, 1996; <http://www.census.gov/population/methodshousecon.txt.>. U.S. Bureau of the Census, "Housing Vacancy Survey: Definitions and Explanations," <http://www.census.gov/ftp/pub/hhes/www/hvs.html>. U.S. Bureau of the Census, "Housing Vacancy Survey: Source and Accuracy of Estimates," <http://www.census.gov/ftp/pub/hhes/www/hvs.html>.

Definitions

Household. A household consists of all persons who occupy a housing unit. This includes related family members and all unrelated persons who share the housing unit. A person living alone in a housing unit, or a group of unrelated persons sharing a housing unit, is also counted as a household. Prior to 1983, a living arrangement consisting of five or more persons, none of whom was related to the person in charge, was classified as noninstitutional group quarters rather than a household. Beginning in 1983, the definition of noninstitutional group quarters was changed to nine or more persons not related to the person in charge. The latter definition was also used in the 1980 and 1990 Censuses.

The count of households is equal to the count of occupied housing units.

Housing unit. A housing unit is a house, an apartment, a mobile home, a group of rooms, or a single room occupied or intended for occupancy as separate living quarters. Separate living quarters are those in which the occupants do not live and eat with other persons in the structure and that have direct access from the outside of the building or through a common hall. Recreational vehicles, boats, vans, tents, railroad cars, and the like are counted as housing units if they are occupied by households as usual places of residence.

For vacant units, the criteria of separateness and direct access are applied to the intended occupants whenever possible. If the information cannot be obtained, the criteria are applied to the previous occupants. Tents and boats are excluded if vacant, used for business, or used for extra sleeping space or vacations. Vacant seasonal/migratory mobile homes are included in the count of vacant seasonal/migratory housing units.

Living quarters of the following types are excluded from the housing unit inventory: living quarters occupied by nine or more persons not related to the person in charge; dormitories, bunkhouses, and barracks; quarters in predominantly transient hotels, motels, and the like, except those occupied by persons who consider the hotel their usual place of residence; quarters in institutions, general hospitals, and military installations, except those occupied by staff members or resident employees who have separate living arrangements.

Occupied housing units. A housing unit is occupied if a person or group of persons is living in it at the time of the interview or if the occupants are only temporarily absent, as for example, on vacation. The persons living in the unit must consider it their usual place of residence or have no usual place of residence elsewhere.

Notes

Beginning in January 1982, the Current Population Survey/Housing Vacancy Survey (CPS/HVS) weighting procedures changed to reflect results of the 1980 Census. These weighting changes increased the estimated number of households by approximately 2 percent.

The second row of entries for 1993 is revised using 1990 Census–based population controls with adjustment for net undercount. The new 1990 population controls were introduced in the CPS beginning in January 1994. As discussed in Appendix B under "Current Population Survey," this change and other changes instituted in the CPS in January 1994 affect historical comparability.

March estimates in this table differ from the CPS March Supplement household estimates in Tables 1.4–1.7. There are also differences between the household estimates presented in this table and those from the decennial census, the American Housing Survey, and the Census Bureau's state household estimates developed from administrative data ("administrative records estimates"). There are several reasons for this variability, including differences in data collection and estimation methodologies, sampling frames and reference months, and treatment of population and housing unit undercount. The Census Bureau briefly summarizes the differences among various sources of current household estimates as follows:

- The Current Population Survey household estimates are based on a national sample of about 47,000 households. They are controlled to estimates that include the 1990 Census population coverage adjustment as measured by the Post Enumeration Survey (PES). They do not include a housing unit coverage adjustment. Each sampled householder has a 1990 Census population weight applied to him/her. The sum of these initial householder population weights is then adjusted to be consistent with postcensal population estimates that include the PES-measured undercount. The weighting methodology assumes that the survey coverage rate of all persons is the same. However, because householders have better coverage rates than the general population, the weighting factors for householders (and, therefore, households) are too high. This results in household estimates that are too high relative to other estimates. The estimation procedure for the CPS March Supplement includes a further adjustment so that a husband and a wife in a household receive the same weight.
- The CPS/HVS is based on the Current Population Survey sample. It is further adjusted to incorporate the housing unit undercount.
- The CPS estimates are based on a national survey and on national population estimates, whereas administrative records estimates are built up from state-level data. The estimates based on administrative records do not include either the population coverage adjustment or the housing unit coverage adjustment in the 1990 Census. They begin with

state-by-state 1990 Census universe data on householder rates by broad age group. They are updated by controlling to state-by-state age estimates as well as to any U.S. trends in householder rates by age (as measured by the CPS).

- The American Housing Survey (AHS) is based on a national sample of housing units. It does not include the 1990 Census population coverage adjustment but is controlled to estimates that include the housing unit coverage adjustment. The AHS controls begin with state-by-state 1990 Census housing unit data adjusted for coverage. These data are updated by measuring trends in state-level residential construction, residential mobile home placements, and residential housing loss.

The most appropriate source for current household estimates depends in part on the type of information needed. For national or state total household estimates, comparisons with the 1990 Census enumeration showed that the administrative records estimates were most accurate. For U.S. or state household estimates by age of householder, the Census Bureau recommends the administrative records estimates because they are directly controlled to state-level age detail. If additional demographic and socioeconomic detail beyond age is required, the CPS March Supplement and AHS are the best sources of information.

Table 1.2

Data Sources:
U.S. Bureau of the Census State Housing Unit and Household Estimates Program; Census of Housing
References:
Ron Prevost, *State Housing Unit and Household Estimates: April 1, 1980, to July 1, 1993*, U.S. Bureau of the Census, Current Population Reports, P25-1123, October 1994. U.S. Bureau of the Census, "Household and Housing Unit Estimates: Intercentsal Estimates of Total Households for States: April 1, 1980, to April 1, 1990," September 1995; <http://www.census.gov/population/estimates/housing/hh8090.txt>. U.S. Bureau of the Census, "Housing and Housing Unit Estimates: Estimates of Housing Units, Households, and Persons per Household for the United States, Regions and States: 1990 to 1995," <http://www/census.gov/population/estimates/housing/hsehld95.txt>.

Definitions

See Table 1.3 Definitions.

Notes

See the Notes section to Table 1.1 for a discussion of the differences in current household estimates produced from different sources.

The Census Bureau began producing housing unit and household estimates from administrative data series in 1989. What follows is a brief overview of the methods used to produce household estimates. For a more detailed description, see Prevost (1994).

For the period 1991 to 1996, the household estimates for each state are developed first by applying the change in national household formation rates by age of householder (as measured through CPS data) to the 1990 Census state-specific household formation rates by age. This process produces current estimates of state household formation rates by age. Next, the updated state household formation rates are applied to state population estimates by age to develop estimates of households by age of householder. The estimate of a state's total households is the summation of that state's households by age of householder.

The methodology used to produce household estimates for 1981 to 1989 was different than that used for 1991 to 1996. To develop 1981 to 1989 estimates, intercensal estimates of the population 18 years old and older were used in conjunction with estimates of the group-quarters population to produce intercensal estimates of the adult household population. Intercensal estimates of the adult population per household were developed using census data for states for 1980 and 1990 in conjunction with annual national trends in the adult population per household from the CPS. The intercensal estimates of the adult population in households were then divided by the intercensal estimates of the adult population per household to obtain preliminary household estimates.

These preliminary estimates then received small pro rata adjustments to make the total for each year equal to the national intercensal household estimate. National intercensal household estimates were obtained by adjusting the pattern of annual household change from 1980 to 1990 from the CPS, which was consistent with the 1980 Census, to be consistent with the national census counts of households in both the 1980 and 1990 Censuses.

The 1990 Census data used to develop these estimates were created by special age and race edits, commonly referred to as MARS (modified age, race, sex tabulations). These edit procedures not only affect the characteristics of the population, but also have a minor impact on the counts of housing units, households, and population living in group quarters.

Table 1.3

Data Source:
  Census of Housing
References:
  U.S. Bureau of the Census, "Housing: Then and Now, 50 Years of Decennial Censuses," <http://www. census.gov/hhes/www/censhsg. html>. Tables prepared by Robert Bonnette. For a discussion of changes over time in the definition of a household, see U.S. Bureau of the Census, *200 Years of U.S. Census Taking: Population and Housing Questions, 1790–1990*, November 1989.

Definition

Household. A household includes all the persons who occupy a housing unit. A housing unit is a house, an apartment, a mobile home, a group of rooms, or a single room that is occupied (or if vacant, is intended for occupancy) as separate living quarters. Separate living quarters are those in which the occupants live and eat separately from any other persons in the building and that have direct access from the outside of the building or through a common hall. The occupants may be a single family, one person living alone, two or more families living together, or any other group of related or unrelated persons who share living arrangements.

In the 1980 and 1990 Censuses, a living arrangement with nine or more persons unrelated to the person in charge was not considered to be a household; rather, such persons were included in the noninstitutional group quarters population. For the 1950 to 1970 Censuses, living arrangements with five or more persons unrelated to the person in charge were considered to be living in group quarters. In 1940, living arrangements with 10 or more unrelated lodgers were considered to be "quasi-households" and are not included in the table.

Tables 1.4–1.15

Data Source:
  Current Population Survey March Supplement

References:
  U.S. Bureau of the Census, *Household and Family Characteristics and Marital Status and Living Arrangements*, Current Population Reports, Series P20.

Definitions

Household. See Table 1.1 Definitions.

Householder. The householder refers to the person (or one of the persons) in whose name the housing unit is owned or rented. If there is no such person, any adult member of the household may be designated as the householder, excluding roomers, boarders, or paid employees. If the house is owned or rented jointly by a married couple, the householder may be either the husband or the wife. The number of householders is equal to the number of households and the number of family householders is equal to the number of families.

Reference person. The reference person is the person to whom the relationship of other persons in the household is recorded. The household reference person is the person listed as the householder (see definition). The subfamily reference person is either the single parent or the husband/wife in a married-couple situation.

Family. A family is a group of two or more persons (one of whom is the householder) related by birth, marriage, or adoption and residing together; all such persons (including related subfamily members) are considered as members of one family. Beginning with the 1980 Current Population Survey (CPS), unrelated subfamilies (referred to in the past as secondary families) are no longer included in the count of families, nor are the members of unrelated subfamilies included in the count of family members.

Family household. A family household is a household maintained by a family (as defined above), and any unrelated persons (unrelated subfamily members and/or secondary individuals) who may be residing there. Since 1980, when the Census Bureau stopped counting unrelated subfamilies as families, the number of family households is equal to the number of families. Prior to 1980, there were slight differences in estimates of families and family households caused by the inclusion of unrelated subfamilies in the count of families. (These differences can be seen by comparing the pre-1980 estimates of family households in Table 1.4 with the pre-1980 estimates of families in Tables 1.5 and 1.8.)

The count of family household members differs from

the count of family members in that the family household members include all persons living in the household. The count of family members, however, includes only the householder and his/her relatives.

Family group. A family group is any two or more persons (not necessarily including a householder) residing together, and related by birth, marriage, or adoption. A household may be composed of one such group, more than one, or none at all. The count of family groups includes family households, related subfamilies, and unrelated subfamilies.

Related subfamily. A related subfamily is a married couple with or without children, or one parent with one or more own, never-married children (see "own children" definition) under 18 years old, living in a household and related to, but not including, the person or couple who maintains the household. One example of a related subfamily is a young married couple sharing the home of the husband's or wife's parents. The number of related subfamilies is not included in the count of families.

Unrelated subfamily. An unrelated subfamily (formerly called a secondary family) is a married couple with or without children, or a single parent with one or more own, never-married children under 18 years old living in a household. Unrelated subfamily members are not related to the householder. An unrelated subfamily may include persons such as guests, partners, roommates, or resident employees and their spouses and/or children. The number of unrelated subfamily members is included in the total number of household members but is not included in the count of family members.

Nonfamily household. A nonfamily household consists of a person living alone or a householder who shares the home exclusively with persons to whom he/she is not related.

Size of household or family. The term "size of household" includes all persons occupying a housing unit. "Size of family" includes the family householder and all other persons in the living quarters who are related to the householder by birth, marriage, or adoption.

Race. The concept of race as used by the Census Bureau reflects self-identification; it does not denote any clear-cut scientific definition of biological stock. The data for race represent self-classification by people according to the race with which they most closely identify. The cat-

egories of race include both racial and national origin or sociocultural groups.

Householders are divided into three groups on the basis of race including White, Black, and other races. The last category includes Indians, Japanese, Chinese, and any other race except White and Black.

Persons of Hispanic origin. In the CPS, persons of Hispanic origin are determined on the basis of a question that asked for self-identification of the person's origin or descent. Respondents were asked to select their origin (or the origin of some other household member) from a "flash card" listing ethnic origins. Persons of Hispanic origin were those who indicated that their origin was Mexican, Puerto Rican, Cuban, Central or South American, or some other Hispanic origin. Persons of Hispanic origin may be of any race.

Age of householder. The age classification is based on the age of the person at the person's last birthday. The adult universe (i.e., population of marriageable age) now comprises persons 15 years old and over. Prior to 1980 the adult universe was 14 years old and over.

Own children. "Own" children in a family are sons and daughters, including stepchildren and adopted children, of the householder. The count of own children under 18 years old is limited to never-married children.

One-parent family with children under 18. These families include mothers and fathers living with their children, but without spouses at home.

Marital status. The marital status classification identifies four major categories including never married, married, widowed, and divorced. These terms refer to the marital status at the time of the enumeration. The category "married" is further divided into "married, spouse present," "separated," and "other married, spouse absent." A person was classified as "married, spouse present" if the husband or wife was reported as a member of the household, even though he or she may have been temporarily absent on business or on vacation, visiting, in a hospital, etc., at the time of the enumeration. Persons reported as "separated" included those with legal separations, those living apart with intentions of obtaining a divorce, and other persons permanently or temporarily separated because of marital discord. The group "other married, spouse absent" included married persons living apart because either the husband or wife was employed and living at a considerable distance from home, was serving away from home in the Armed Forces, had moved to another area, or had a different place of residence for any other reason except separation as defined above.

Married couple. A married couple, as defined for census purposes, is a husband and wife enumerated as members of the same household. The married couple may or may not have children living with them. The expression "husband-wife" or "married-couple" before the term "household," "family," or "subfamily" indicates that the household, family, or subfamily is maintained by a husband and wife. The number of married couples equals the count of married-couple families plus related and unrelated married-couple subfamilies.

Unmarried couple. An unmarried couple is composed of two unrelated adults of the opposite sex (one of whom is the householder) who share a housing unit with or without the presence of children under 15 years old.

Age at first marriage. The median age at first marriage is an approximation derived indirectly from tabulations of marital status and age. In computing this median, several steps are involved. First, the expected proportion of young people who will ever marry during their lifetime is computed. Second, one-half of this expected proportion is calculated. And third, the current age of young people who are at this halfway mark is computed. From the assumptions made and the procedures used, it follows that the date of the survey is also the date when this halfway mark is reached. Half of the young people of the given age who will ever get married had done so prior to the survey date and half are expected to marry in years to come.

Notes

See the Notes section to Table 1.1 for a discussion of household estimates produced from different data sources. See Appendix B under "Current Population Survey" for a discussion of recent major changes in the CPS that affect historical comparability.

Because no independent-population-control totals for persons of Hispanic origin were used before 1985, use caution in comparing changes over time for the Hispanic population in Tables 1.6 and 1.10.

Beginning in March 1980, the minimum age for householders was increased from 14 years to 15 years.

Table 1.16

Data Source:
   Joint Center for Housing Studies of Harvard University Household Projections
Reference:
   George S. Masnick, Nancy McArdle, and William C. Apgar Jr., *U.S. Household Trends: The 1990s and Beyond*, Joint Center for Housing Studies of Harvard University, July 1996.

Definitions

See Definitions for Tables 1.4–1.15.

Notes

The Joint Center uses a PC-based household projection model named the Potential Housing Demand (PHD) model. It was originally developed by the Research Division of the Canada Mortgage and Housing Corporation. The PHD was revised in 1995 in collaboration with Joint Center staff to introduce cohort-based trending and to be more compatible with U.S. data sources and household typologies. The PHD uses population projections, projected rates of family and nonfamily household formation for 5-year age groups, and projected household proportions to produce projections of households by 5-year age group and household type.

To produce these household projections, the Joint Center used population projections released by the Census Bureau in February 1996 (Day, Jennifer Cheeseman, *Population Projections of the United States by Age, Sex, Race, and Hispanic Origin: 1995 to 2050*, U.S. Bureau of the Census, 1996, Current Population Reports, P25-1130); benchmarks for family and nonfamily headship rates based on the 1995 Current Population Survey (CPS); 1990 to 1995 family and nonfamily headship trends developed by the Joint Center based on the CPS; and detailed household-type shares from the 1995 CPS. Projections of age-specific family and nonfamily headship rates were applied to the Census Bureau's population projections to produce projections of the number of family and nonfamily households to 2010. Once the numbers of family and nonfamily households were projected, they were further partitioned by detailed household type (e.g., married couples with children under 18 at home, lone parents with children under 18 at home, etc.). Detailed household-type shares within the family and nonfamily categories were held constant at their 1995 levels, with the exception that lone-parent shares were trended to reflect the pattern of the early 1990s. Because the"other family" category is a residual within the family category, the other family share also changes over time.

Tables 1.17–1.23

Data Source:

U.S. Bureau of the Census Household and Family Projections

Reference:

Jennifer Cheeseman Day, *Projections of the Number of Households and Families in the United States: 1995 to 2010*, U.S. Bureau of the Census, Current Population Reports, P25-1129.

Definitions

See Definitions for Tables 1.4–1.15.

Notes

In April of 1996 the Census Bureau released household and family projections for the first time in nearly a decade. Included in the projections are the numbers of households and families by type of household, sex of householder (if the householder is not married, spouse present), and age of householder. Also projected are the average size of households and families, marital status of the population, and the number of families with children. One series also includes projections of households and families disaggregated by four race groups—White; Black; American Indian, Eskimo, and Aleut; and Asian and Pacific Islander—and by Hispanic origin.

Three alternative projection series were produced to illuminate alternative patterns of future household change. All three household projection series are based on the middle series in the Census Bureau's most recent population projections (Day, Jennifer Cheeseman, *Population Projections of the United States by Age, Sex, Race, and Hispanic Origin: 1995 to 2050*, U.S. Bureau of the Census, Current Population Reports, P25-1130).

Series one, based on a time-series model, is the preferred projection in light of past and possible future trends in household change. It reflects projected trends by age and sex in the proportion of persons maintaining households of different types and projected changes in the age/sex structure of the population. Series two reflects the consequences of projected change in only the age/sex structure of the population, assuming no change from the 1990 proportions of persons maintaining households of

specific types by age and sex. Series three reflects the consequences of projected change in both the age/sex structure and race/origin composition of the population, assuming no change in the 1990 proportions maintaining specific types of households by age, sex, race, and Hispanic origin.

These household projections differ from previous Census Bureau projections based on the Current Population Survey (CPS), since independently derived household estimates began only recently and were not available for previous projections. These household projections are based on 1990 Census data and postcensal estimates and are not comparable with post-1990 results from the CPS or reports generated by the Census Bureau based on the CPS. The projections were not adjusted to reflect the population undercount in the 1990 Census.

Table 1.24

Data Source:

Census of Population

Reference:

U.S. Bureau of the Census, *1990 Census of Population and Housing: Population and Housing Unit Counts: United States*, 1990 CPH-2-1.

Definitions

Resident population. The resident population of an area includes all residents (both civilian and Armed Forces) living in the area. A resident of a specified area is defined as a person "usually resident" in that area. The resident population excludes the United States Armed Forces overseas, as well as civilian United States citizens whose usual place of residence is outside the United States.

Notes

The Census data presented in the table have not been adjusted for underenumeration. Figures for 1970 and 1980 have been revised since the Census publications were released.

In 1907 the Territory of Oklahoma and the remaining part of the Indian Territory were combined and admitted to the Union as the state of Oklahoma with boundaries substantially as at present. In 1930, part of Oklahoma was acquired by Texas upon settlement of a boundary dispute.

Table 1.25

Data Source:
U.S. Bureau of the Census, Population Estimates Program.

References:
Edwin R. Byerly, *State Population Estimates by Age and Sex: 1980 to 1992,* U.S. Bureau of the Census, Current Population Reports, P20-1106, U.S. Government Printing Office, Washington, DC, 1993. Edwin R. Byerly, and Kevin Deardorff, *National and State Population Estimates: 1990 to 1994*, U.S. Bureau of the Census, Current Population Reports, P25-1127, U.S. Government Printing Office, Washington, DC, 1995. U.S. Bureau of the Census, "State Population Estimates"; data tables and methodology description located at <http://www.census.gov/population/www/estimates/statepop.html>.

Definitions

Resident population. See Table 1.24 Definitions.

Notes

The Census Bureau's state population estimates are consistent with official decennial census figures and do not incorporate an adjustment for estimated census underenumeration.

Methodology for 1990 to 1997 estimates. In the production of state population estimates, the Census Bureau treats states as a tabulation geography rather than an estimates geography. This means the methodology used for state estimates is actually the methodology for counties, and the state population estimates are derived by summing the county estimates to the state level. The population of the District of Columbia is estimated as if the District of Columbia were a county.

The Census Bureau develops county estimates with a demographic procedure called a "component change" method. A major assumption underlying this approach is that the components that constitute population change can be represented by administrative data series in a statistical model. In order to build the model, Census Bureau demographers estimated each component of population change separately. For the population residing in households, the components of change are births, deaths, and net migration, including net immigration from abroad. For the nonhousehold population, change is represented by net change in the population in group quarters.

To develop county population estimates, the Census Bureau uses a component change procedure called the Tax Return method (formerly called the Administrative Records method). Each component in the model is represented with data that are symptomatic of some aspect of population change. For example, birth certificate(s) are symptomatic of additions to the population resulting from births, so these data are used to estimate the birth component for a county.

Except for the net migration component, the change components for a July 1 county estimate are calculated from data items that are extrapolated. Extrapolation is necessary because data needed for the estimate year, covering the period from July 1 of the previous year to June 30 of the current estimate year, are not always available for counties at the time an estimate is developed.

When data are not available for all counties for the current estimate year, an estimate of the data component is developed through one or more simplifying assumptions. In the simplest case, no change in the data is assumed between the current estimate year and the prior estimate year. In other cases, data may be available at the state level but not at the county level. In this case, the distribution of data by county is assumed to have remained the same as in the prior year. The county distribution is then applied to the current state total data to estimate current year data for counties. When initial population estimates are prepared, the same variant of the component model is used for all states. A year later, these initial estimates are replaced with "revised" estimates based on the actual data for all components of population change.

For additional information on the 1990–1997 estimation methodology, see Byerly and Deardorff (1995).

Methodology for 1980 to 1989 estimates. The July 1980 to 1989 intercensal state total population estimates are consistent with both the 1980 Census counts and the 1990 Census modified counts. The latest set of 1980-based postcensal state estimates were used in the following intercensal formula:

$$P_t = Q_t (P_{10}/Q_{10})^{t/10}$$

Where

t = time (years) elapsed since April 1, 1980, $0 \leq t \leq 10$
Q_t = postcensal estimate at time t
P_t = intercensal estimate at time t

And

$Q_0 = P_0$ = actual census count as of April 1, 1980
P_{10} = actual census count as of April 1, 1990
Q_{10} = postcensal estimate for April 1, 1990

This procedure was also used in developing the annual intercensal population estimates for the United States. The sum of intercensal state estimates for each year was adjusted to be consistent with the independent national intercensal estimates of population.

Table 1.26

Data Source:

U.S. Bureau of the Census, State Population Projections

References:

Paul R. Campbell, *Population Projections for States by Age, Sex, Race, and Hispanic Origin: 1995 to 2025*, U.S. Bureau of the Census, Population Division, PPL-47, 1996. Paul Campbell, *Population Projections: States, 1995–2025*, U.S. Bureau of the Census, Current Population Reports, P25-1131, May 1997. U.S. Bureau of the Census, "State Population Projections: 1995 to 2025," data tables located at <http://www.census.gov/population/www/projections/stproj.html>.

Definitions

Resident population. See Table 1.24 Definitions.

Notes

The Census Bureau's state population projections are consistent with official decennial census figures and do not incorporate an adjustment for estimated census underenumeration.

Methodology. The projections use the cohort-component method. The cohort-component method requires separate assumptions for each component of population change: births, deaths, internal migration, and international migration. These components, by race and Hispanic origin, come from various sources. State differentials in fertility are based on 1989 to 1993 births, 1994 estimated population distributions of females in childbearing ages for states, and 1994 national fertility data. State differentials in survival rates are based on 1989 to 1993 deaths, 1994 estimated population for states, and 1994 national life tables. The projections use Internal Revenue Service (IRS) data on interstate migration flows from 1975 to 1976 through 1993 to 1994. International migration for states is further disaggregated by age, sex, race, and Hispanic origin using the foreign-born population immigrating during the 5-year period 1985 to 1990 as enumerated in the 1990 Census.

Data in the table are from projection Series A, which is a time-series model that uses state-to-state migration observed from 1975–76 through 1993–94.

For additional information on the projection methodology, see Campbell (1996).

Tables 1.27–1.37

Data Source:

Current Population Survey March Supplement

References:

U.S. Bureau of the Census, *Money Income in the United States: 1996 (With Separate Data on Valuation of Noncash Benefits)*, Current Population Reports, P60-197, U.S. Government Printing Office, Washington, DC, 1997. See earlier reports in the P60 series also. U.S. Bureau of the Census, "Historical Income Tables—Households," data tables located at <http://www.census.gov/hhes/income/histinc/inchhdet.html>. U.S. Bureau of the Census, "Historical Income Tables—Families," data tables located at <http://www.census.gov/hhes/income/histinc/incfamdet.html>.

Definitions

See the Definitions for Tables 1.4–1.15 in addition to those provided here.

Income. For each person 15 years old and over in the Current Population Survey (CPS) sample, questions were asked about the amount of money income received in the preceding calendar year from each of the following sources: (1) earnings from longest job (or self-employment); (2) earnings from jobs other than longest job; (3) unemployment compensation; (4) worker's compensation; (5) Social Security; (6) Supplemental Security income; (7) public assistance; (8) veterans' payments; (9) survivor benefits; (10) disability benefits; (11) pension or retirement income; (12) interest; (13) dividends; (14) rents, royalties, and estates and trusts; (15) educational assistance; (16) alimony; (17) child support; (18) financial assistance from outside of the household and other periodic income. Capital gains and lump-sum or one-time payments are excluded.

Consumer income data collected in the CPS cover money income received before payments for personal income taxes, Social Security, union dues, Medicare deductions, etc. In addition, money income does not reflect the fact that some families receive part of their income in the form of noncash benefits such as food stamps, health benefits, rent-free housing, and goods produced and consumed on the farm, or that noncash benefits are also received by some nonfarm residents, which often take the form of the use of business transportation and facilities, full or partial payments by business for retirement programs, medical and educational expenses, etc.

It should be noted that although the income statistics refer to receipts during the preceding calendar year, the demographic characteristics such as age and family or household composition are as of the survey date. The income of the family/household does not include amounts received by persons who were members during all or part of the income year if those persons no longer resided in the family/household at the time of interview. However, income data are collected for persons who are current residents but did not reside in the household during the income year.

Users of these data should also be aware that for many different reasons there is a tendency in household surveys for respondents to underreport their income.

Mean income. Mean income is the amount obtained by dividing the total aggregate income of a group by the number of units in that group. The means for households, families, and unrelated individuals are based on all households, families, and unrelated individuals.

Median income. Median income is the amount that divides the income distribution into two equal groups, half having incomes above the median, half having incomes below the median. The medians for households, families, and unrelated individuals are based on all households, families, and unrelated individuals.

Gini ratio. The Gini ratio (or index of income concentration) is a statistical measure of income equality ranging from 0 to 1. A measure of 1 indicates perfect inequality (e.g., one person has all the income and the rest have none). A measure of 0 indicates perfect equality (e.g., all persons have equal shares of income).

Notes

The CPS has been used to collect annual income data since 1948, when only two supplementary questions were asked in April: "How much did ... earn in wages and salaries in 1947?" and "How much income from all sources did ... receive in 1947?" Over the years the number of income questions has expanded, questions on work experience and other characteristics have been added, and the month of interview has moved to March. Today, information is gathered on more than 50 different sources of income including noncash income sources such as food stamps, school lunch programs, employer-provided group health insurance plans, employer-provided pension plans, personal health insurance, Medicaid, Medicare, CHAMPUS or military health care, and energy assistance.

The upper reportable limit of earnings in the CPS March Supplement was increased from $99,999 to $299,999 in March 1986 and from $299,999 to $999,999 in March 1994. These changes affected estimates of mean income, the distribution of aggregate income, and the index of income concentration (Gini ratio) in 1985 and 1993.

See Appendix B under "Current Population Survey" for a discussion of recent major changes in the CPS that affect historical comparability.

Table 1.38

Data Source:
  Survey of Consumer Finances
Reference:
  Arthur B. Kennickell, Martha Starr-McCluer, and Annika E. Sunden, "Family Finances in the U.S.: Recent Evidence from the Survey of Consumer Finances," *Federal Reserve Bulletin*, January 1997.

Definitions

Family net worth. Net worth equals family assets minus family liabilities. Asset values do not include any adjustments for future tax liabilities.

Family income. The income measure is the family's total cash income, before taxes, for the calendar year preceding the year of the interview.

Family. The family is defined as the primary economic unit in a given household (see next definition). The definition of family used here is substantially different from that used by the Census Bureau, and it includes persons living alone.

Primary economic unit. In the Survey of Consumer Finances, a household is divided into a primary economic unit (PEU) and everyone else in the household. The PEU is the economically dominant single individual or pair of individuals (who may be married or living as partners) and all other persons who are financially dependent on that person or those persons.

Head. In a PEU containing only a single economically dominant individual, the head is taken to be that individual. In other PEUs, the head is taken to be the male in the core couple of the PEU or the older person in a same-sex couple. The use of the term "head" is not intended to imply any judgment regarding family structure.

Other not working. This category includes unemployed workers, students, and individuals not working outside of the home.

Tables 1.39–1.40

Data Source:
Survey of Income and Program Participation
Reference:
T. J. Eller, and Wallace Fraser, *Asset Ownership of Households: 1993*, U.S. Bureau of the Census, Current Population Reports, P70-47, U.S. Government Printing Office, Washington, DC, 1995.

Definitions

See Definitions for Tables 1.4–1.15 for additional information.

Measured net worth. The household measured net worth estimates are based on the sum of the market value of assets owned by every member of the household minus liabilities (secured or unsecured) owed by household members. The estimates represent the net worth of households as of the end of the appropriate reference period. The "measured net worth" concept is based on the value of all assets minus all liabilities. The major assets not covered are equities in pension plans, cash value of life insurance policies, and value of home furnishings and jewelry. These items were not covered because it is particularly difficult to obtain reliable estimates of the value of these assets in a household survey. See Eller and Fraser (1995) for a detailed list of assets and liabilities included in the calculation of net worth.

Other financial investments. These include mortgages held from sale of real estate, amount due from the sale of a business, unit trusts, and other financial investments.

Interest-earning assets at financial institutions. These include passbook savings accounts, money market deposit accounts, certificates of deposit, and interest-earning checking accounts.

Other interest-earning assets. These include money market funds, U.S. government securities, municipal and corporate bonds, and other interest-earning assets.

Other assets. See the definition of "Other financial investments."

Monthly household income. The monthly household income on which the quintile distribution is based represents the sum of the monthly income received by each member of the household age 15 years old or over at the date of interview. Monthly household income is an average of monthly amounts received during a 4-month reference period. To calculate the monthly income figures, the composition of the household was fixed at the date of the interview and the total cash income of household members 15 years and older for the 4-month reference period was divided by four. See Eller and Fraser (1995) for a detailed list of the income sources included in the calculation of income.

The monthly income quintile upper limits for 1993 were lowest quintile—$1,071; second quintile—$1,963; third quintile—$2,995; fourth quintile—$4,635.

Notes

Wealth data in the Survey of Income and Program Participation (SIPP). While SIPP was designed primarily to provide estimates of income and government program participation, its asset and liability data provide additional indicators of economic well-being. These data, collected on a regular basis in a supplement to the Survey, are also useful for modeling eligibility for government assistance programs.

Few household surveys provide information on asset accumulation and debt holdings. The only other ongoing survey that provides wealth information is the Survey of Consumer Finances (SCF) (see Table 1.35). The SCF, which is designed specifically to analyze the financial portfolios of U.S. families, is much more detailed in the classification of assets and liabilities than SIPP.

Household surveys provide data on the asset and debt holdings of the population, but it should be noted that asset accumulation tends to be underreported in household surveys. Further, the distribution of asset accumulation is known to be highly concentrated among households with large asset holdings. The concentration of asset accumulation and the paucity of observations for high-income households may bias various asset accumulation statistics.

Specifically, SIPP likely provides biased estimates of the aggregate of asset holdings and of mean amounts. The SIPP sample frame contains few observations for high-income households, while the SCF makes a special attempt to survey respondents who are likely to have high incomes or to be wealthy. For example, the 1993 SIPP–estimated total aggregate net worth of $9.6 trillion was 44 percent of the $21.8 trillion (in 1993 dollars) measured by the 1992 SCF. The 1993 SIPP–estimated mean measured net worth was $99,772, while the 1992 SCF-estimated mean measured net worth was $226,900 (in 1993 dollars).

In the presence of this pattern of underreporting, median values are better indicators of the asset accumulation of typical households than are mean values. The distribution of measured wealth is skewed, with a concentration of households at the low end of the distribution and a tail of households with high values. In this case, the median is lower than the mean of the distribution but less sensitive to outliers. Therefore, estimates of median measured net worth (measured assets less measured debts) from the two surveys are much closer than the estimates of mean measured net worth. The 1993 SIPP estimate of measured median net worth was $37,587, and the 1991 SIPP estimate of measured median net worth was $38,500 (in 1993 dollars), 71 percent of the 1992 SCF estimate of median net worth of $53,800 (in 1993 dollars).

Population coverage. The estimates in the tables are restricted to the civilian, noninstitutional population of the United States and members of the Armed Forces living off post or with their families on post. The estimates exclude group quarters.

All demographic surveys, including SIPP, suffer from undercoverage of the population. This undercoverage results from missed housing units and missed persons within sample households. The weighting procedures used by the Census Bureau partially correct for the bias due to undercoverage. However, its final impact on estimates is unknown.

Table 1.41

Data Source:
  Census of Population
Reference:
  U.S. Bureau of the Census, "Census Historical Poverty Tables: CPH-L-162, Persons by Poverty Status in 1969, 1979, and 1989, by State"; table located at <http://www.census.gov/hhes/poverty/census/cphl162.html>.

Definitions

Poverty status. Poverty statistics presented in census publications were based on a definition originated by the So-

cial Security Administration in 1964 and subsequently modified by federal interagency committees in 1969 and 1980 and prescribed by the Office of Management and Budget in Directive 14 as the standard to be used by federal agencies for statistical purposes.

At the core of this definition was the 1961 economy food plan, the least costly of four nutritionally adequate food plans designed by the Department of Agriculture. It was determined from the Agriculture Department's 1955 survey of food consumption that families of three or more persons spend approximately one-third of their income on food; hence, the poverty level for these families was set at three times the cost of the economy food plan. For smaller families and persons living alone, the cost of the economy food plan was multiplied by factors that were slightly higher to compensate for the relatively larger fixed expenses for these smaller households.

The income cutoffs used by the Census Bureau to determine the poverty status of families and unrelated individuals included a set of 48 thresholds arranged in a two-dimensional matrix consisting of family size (from one person to nine or more persons) cross-classified by presence and number of family members under 18 years old (from no children present to eight or more children present). Unrelated individuals and two-person families were further differentiated by age of the householder (under 65 years old and 65 years old and over).

The total income of each family or unrelated individual in the sample was tested against the appropriate poverty threshold to determine the poverty status of that family or unrelated individual. If the total income was less than the corresponding cutoff, the family or unrelated individual was classified as "below the poverty level." The number of persons below the poverty level was the sum of the number of persons in families with incomes below the poverty level and the number of unrelated individuals with incomes below the poverty level.

The poverty thresholds are revised annually to allow for changes in the cost of living as reflected in the Consumer Price Index. The average poverty threshold for a family of four persons was $12,674 in 1989. Poverty thresholds were applied on a national basis and were not adjusted for regional, state, or local variations in the cost of living.

Persons for Whom Poverty Status Is Determined. Poverty status was determined for all persons except institutionalized persons, persons in military group quarters and in college dormitories, and unrelated individuals under 15 years old. These groups also were excluded from the denominator when calculating poverty rates.

Notes

The poverty definition used in the 1990 and 1980 Censuses differed slightly from the one used in the 1970 Census. Three technical modifications were made to the definition used in the 1970 Census as described below:

- Separate thresholds for families with a female householder with no husband present and all other families were eliminated. For the 1980 and 1990 Censuses, the weighted average of the poverty thresholds for these two types of families was applied to all types of families, regardless of the sex of the householder.
- Farm families and farm unrelated individuals no longer had a set of poverty thresholds that were lower than the thresholds applied to nonfarm families and unrelated individuals. The farm thresholds were 85 percent of the corresponding levels for nonfarm families in the 1970 Census. The same thresholds were applied to all families and unrelated individuals regardless of residence in 1980 and 1990.
- The thresholds by size of family were extended from seven or more persons in 1970 to nine or more persons in 1980 and 1990.

These changes resulted in a minimal increase in the number of poor at the national level.

The population covered in the poverty statistics derived from the 1980 and 1990 Censuses was essentially the same as in the 1970 Census. The only difference was that in 1980 and 1990, unrelated individuals under 15 years old were excluded from the poverty universe, while in 1970, only those under 14 years old were excluded. The poverty data from the 1960 Census excluded all persons in group quarters and included all unrelated individuals regardless of age. It was unlikely that these differences in population coverage would have had significant impact when comparing the poverty data for persons since the 1960 Ccensus.

Comparability with the Current Population Survey. Because of differences in questionnaires and data collection procedures, estimates of the number of persons below the poverty level by various characteristics from the decennial census may differ from those reported in the Current Population Survey March Supplement.

Table 1.42

Data Source:
    Census of Housing
Reference:
    U.S. Bureau of the Census, "Housing: Then and Now, 50 Years of Decennial Censuses. Recent Movers," <http://www.census.gov/hhes/housing/census/movers.html>. Table prepared by Robert Bonnette.

Definitions

Tenure. All occupied housing units are classified as either owner-occupied or renter-occupied. A housing unit is owner-occupied if the owner or co-owner lives in the unit even if it is mortgaged or not fully paid for. The owner or co-owner must live in the unit. All occupied units that are not owner-occupied, whether they are rented for cash rent or occupied without payment of cash rent, are classified as renter-occupied.

In the 1990 Census, the question on tenure was modified to include separate categories for homes owned with a mortgage or a loan and those owned free and clear. This distinction was added because of concerns that respondents who had a mortgage were not reporting themselves as owners in previous censuses.

Recent mover. Recent mover householders are those who moved into their unit in the 15 months prior to the decennial census. These data refer to the year of the latest move by the householder. If a householder moved back into a housing unit that he or she previously occupied, the year of the latest move was reported. If the householder moved from one apartment to another within the same building, the year the householder moved into the present apartment was reported. The intent is to establish the year the present occupancy by the householder began. The year that the householder moved in is not necessarily the same year other members of the household moved, although in the great majority of cases an entire household moves at the same time.

Notes

Information on the year that the householder moved into his/her unit has been collected in the decennial census since 1960. In 1960 and 1970 the question on "year moved into unit" was asked of every person and included in population reports. In 1980 and 1990 the question was asked only of the householder.

Tables 1.43–1.47

Data Source:

Current Population Survey March Supplement

References:

Kristin A. Hansen, *Geographical Mobility: March 1993 to March 1994*, U.S. Bureau of the Census, Current Population Reports, P20-485, U.S. Government Printing Office, Washington, DC, 1995. U.S. Bureau of the Census, "Geographic Mobility/Migration"; tables located at <http://www.census.gov/population/www/socdemo/migrate.html>.

Definitions

See Definitions for Table 1.42 for definitions of owner-occupied and renter-occupied housing and Tables 1.4–1.15 for definitions of other terms used in the Current Population Survey March Supplement.

Mobility status. The population was classified according to mobility status on the basis of a comparison between the place of residence of each individual at the time of the survey and the place of residence 1 year earlier. Nonmovers are all persons who were living in the same house at both points in time. Movers are all persons who were living in a different house at these points in time. Movers are further classified as to whether they were living in the same or different county, state, or region, or were movers from abroad.

Notes

See Appendix B under "Current Population Survey" (CPS) for a discussion of recent major changes in the CPS that affect historical comparability.

The mobility questions in the CPS are asked for all members of the survey household who are 1 year old and older on the survey date. See Hansen (1995) for a discussion of the allocation of mobility data for persons for whom no response or only partial responses to the mobility questions were given.

The data in these tables differ from data in Table 1.42, which is based on the decennial census, in two important ways. First, as noted above, these tables provide mobility status for all household members at least 1 year old, whereas Table 1.42 shows mobility status for the householder only. Second, persons in these tables are considered movers if they lived in a different place 1 year prior to the survey. In Table 1.42, a recent mover is defined as a householder who moved into his/her current residence within the previous 15 months. Data for recent movers in

the American Housing Survey, shown elsewhere in this book, are for householders who moved into their unit in the 12 months prior to the interview.

Tables 1.48–1.49

Data Source:

National Housing Survey

Reference:

Fannie Mae, *Fannie Mae National Housing Survey*, annual.

Notes

The following question was used to collect the data presented in Table 1.48:

"Generally speaking, would you say that people are better off owning a residence or better off renting?"

This question was not asked in the 1995 or 1997 National Housing Surveys.

The following question was used to collect the data presented in Table 1.49:

"I'd like to read you descriptions of general types of residences. Thinking about your own situation and circumstances, let us suppose for a moment that you had to move to a new residence today. For each item I read, if you were faced with that housing situation, how would you feel about living there—would you consider that ideal, would it be a place you could accept with some reservations, would it be a place you could accept with major reservations, or would that be a place you could not live with?"

Respondents were then read a list of residence types and asked to rate the desirability of each.

Part 2: Housing Stock, Production, and Investment

Tables 2.1–2.2

Data Source:

Current Population Survey/Housing Vacancy Survey

Reference:

U.S. Bureau of the Census, "Housing Vacancy Survey"; various tables located at <http://www.census.gov/ ftp/pub/hhes/www/hvs.html>.

Definitions

Housing unit. A housing unit is a house, an apartment, a mobile home, a group of rooms, or a single room occupied or intended for occupancy as separate living quarters. Separate living quarters are those in which the occupants do not live and eat with other persons in the structure and that have direct access from the outside of the building or through a common hall. Recreational vehicles, boats, vans, tents, railroad cars, etc. are counted as housing units if they are occupied by households as usual places of residence.

For vacant units, the criteria of separateness and direct access are applied to the intended occupants whenever possible. If the information cannot be obtained, the criteria are applied to the previous occupants. Tents and boats are excluded if vacant, used for business, or used for extra sleeping space or vacations. Vacant seasonal/migratory mobile homes are included in the count of vacant seasonal/migratory housing units.

Living quarters of the following types are excluded from the housing unit inventory: living quarters occupied by nine or more persons not related to the person in charge; dormitories, bunkhouses, and barracks; quarters in predominantly transient hotels, motels, and the like, except those occupied by persons who consider the hotel their usual place of residence; quarters in institutions, general hospitals, and military installations, except those occupied by staff members or resident employees who have separate living arrangements. Prior to 1983 living quarters occupied by five or more persons not related to the person in charge were classified as noninstitutional group quarters and were not counted as housing units.

Occupied housing units. A housing unit is occupied if a person or group of persons is living in it at the time of the interview or if the occupants are only temporarily absent, as for example, on vacation. The persons living in the unit must consider it their usual place of residence or have no usual place of residence elsewhere. The count of occupied housing units is the same as the count of households.

Tenure. A unit is owner-occupied if the owner or co-owner lives in the unit, even if it is mortgaged or not fully paid for. A cooperative or condominium unit is owner-occupied only if the owner or co-owner lives in it. All other occupied units are classified as renter-occupied, including units rented for cash rent and those occupied without payment of cash rent.

Vacant housing units. A housing unit is vacant if no one is living in it at the time of the interview, unless its occupants are only temporarily absent. In addition, a vacant unit may be one that is entirely occupied by persons who have a usual residence elsewhere.

New units not yet occupied are classified as vacant housing units if construction has reached a point where all exterior windows and doors are installed and final usable floors are in place. Vacant units are excluded if they are exposed to the elements, that is, if the roof, walls, windows, or doors no longer protect the interior from the elements, or if there is positive evidence (such as a sign on the house or block) that the unit is to be demolished or is condemned. Also excluded are quarters being used entirely for nonresidential purposes such as a store, an office, or quarters used for the storage of business supplies or inventory, machinery, or agricultural products.

Vacant sleeping rooms in lodging houses, transient accommodations, barracks, and other quarters not defined as housing units are not included in the statistics in these tables.

Year-round vacant units. Year-round units are those intended for occupancy at any time of the year, even though they may not be in use the year round. In resort areas, a housing unit that is usually occupied on a year-round basis is considered a year-round unit. As indicated, year-round units temporarily occupied by persons with usual residence elsewhere are included with year-round vacant units. Beginning in 1990, year-round vacant mobile homes were included as part of the year-round vacant count of housing units.

Year-round vacant units are classified in the following categories:

Vacant units for rent. This group consists of vacant units offered for rent and those offered both for rent and sale.

Vacant units for sale only. This group is limited to units for sale only; it excludes units both for rent and sale. If a unit is located in a multiunit structure that is for sale as an entire structure and if the unit is not for rent, it is reported as "held off market." However, if the individual unit is intended to be occupied by the new owner, it is reported as "for sale."

Vacant units rented or sold. This group consists of year-round vacant units that have been rented or sold but the new renters or owners have not moved in as of the day of interview.

Vacant units held off the market. Included in this category are units held for occasional use, temporarily occupied by persons with usual residence elsewhere, and vacant for other reasons. These classifications are described as follows:

For occasional use. If the vacant unit is not for rent or for sale only but is held for weekends or occasional use throughout the year, the unit is included in this category. Timeshared units are classified in this category if the vacant unit is not for rent or for sale only, but held for use for an individual during the time of interview.

Units occupied by persons with usual residence elsewhere (URE). A housing unit that is occupied temporarily by persons who usually live elsewhere is classified as a vacant unit provided that a usual place of residence that is not offered for rent or for sale is held for the household. For example, a beach cottage occupied at the time of the interview by a family with a usual place of residence in the city is included in the count of vacant units. Their house in the city would be reported "occupied" and would be included in the count of occupied units since the occupants are only temporarily absent. Units occupied by persons with URE are further classified as seasonal vacant or year-round vacant units.

Other vacant. Included in this category are year-round units that were vacant for reasons other than those mentioned, for example, units held for occupancy of a caretaker or janitor, for settlement of an estate, or for personal reasons of the owner.

Seasonal vacant units. Seasonal housing units are those intended for occupancy only during certain seasons of the year and primarily in resort areas. Housing units held for occupancy by migratory labor employed in farm work during the crop season are tabulated as seasonal. Since the first quarter of 1986, vacant seasonal mobile homes have been counted as a part of the seasonal housing inventory.

Notes

Several major changes were introduced to the Current Population Survey/Housing Vacancy Survey (CPS/HVS) beginning in January 1994 that necessitate caution in comparing data for 1994 and later with earlier data. These changes, which are described in Appendix B under "Current Population Survey," included the introduction of 1990 Census–based population controls adjusted for net undercount and the implementation of Computer Assisted Survey Information Collection (CASIC). The Census Bureau estimates that the new population controls reduced estimates of the total housing inventory by about

0.1 percent. The Census Bureau was unable to determine the quantitative effects of the implementation of CASIC.

Comparability with Census of Housing. Most of the concepts and definitions are the same for items that appear in both the 1980 and 1990 Censuses and the CPS/HVS. However, there is one minor difference in the housing unit definition between the CPS/HVS and the 1980 and 1990 Censuses. The difference is that, in the CPS/HVS prior to 1983, living arrangements containing five or more persons, not related to the person in charge, were classified as group quarters; for the 1980 and 1990 Censuses, the requirement was nine or more persons not related to the person in charge.

Prior to the first quarter of 1990, there were significant differences between the CPS/HVS and the decennial censuses. The 1980 and 1990 Censuses included vacant seasonal and year-round mobile homes as housing units, whereas prior to 1986 the CPS/HVS did not. However, beginning in the first quarter of 1986, vacant seasonal mobile homes were counted as housing units in the CPS/HVS. In addition, year-round vacant mobile homes were counted as housing units beginning in the first quarter of 1990 in the CPS/HVS.

Another difference in the housing unit definition between the CPS/HVS (prior to 1986) and the 1980 and 1990 Censuses was that the CPS/HVS required units to be separate living quarters and to have direct access or complete kitchen facilities. For the 1980 and 1990 Censuses, the complete kitchen facilities alternative was dropped along with direct access required of all units. However, the CPS/HVS dropped those requirements beginning in 1990. Thus, the earlier definitional differences were eliminated.

In addition, there are differences between the methodologies used to collect data for the CPS/HVS and the censuses. These differences include interviewing procedures and staff experience and training; processing procedures and sample designs; the sampling variability associated with the CPS/HVS and the sample data from the census; and the nonsampling errors associated with the CPS/HVS and census data.

Research has shown that the CPS/HVS and the 1990 Census produced significant differences for vacancy characteristics. The rental vacancy rate from the April 1990 Census was 8.5 percent, whereas the CPS/HVS reported a rental vacancy rate of 7.2 percent for the first half of 1990. The April 1990 Census had a homeowner vacancy rate of 2.1 percent, while the CPS/HVS had a vacancy rate of approximately 1.7 percent for the first half of 1990. For occupied housing, the April 1990 Census produced a homeownership rate of 64.2 percent, while for the first half of 1990 the CPS/HVS produced a rate of 63.9 percent.

These differences illustrate that, for these characteristics as well as others, caution should be used when making comparisons between the 1990 Census and the CPS/HVS.

Table 2.3

Data Sources:
  U.S. Bureau of the Census State Housing Unit and Household Estimates Program, Census of Housing
References:
  Ron Prevost, *State Housing Unit and Household Estimates: April 1, 1980, to July 1, 1993*. U.S. Bureau of the Census, Current Population Reports, P25-1123, October 1994. U.S. Bureau of the Census, "Household and Housing Unit Estimates," <http://www.census.gov/population/www/estimates/housing.html>.

Definitions

Housing unit. See Definitions for Table 2.4.

Notes

The Census Bureau began producing housing unit and household estimates from administrative data series in 1989. What follows is a brief overview of the methods used to produce housing unit estimates. For a more detailed description, see Prevost (1994) .

Housing unit estimates for each state were developed by a component model that adds to the count of housing units from the 1990 Census estimates of new residential construction and mobile home placements, and subtracts an estimate of housing unit losses for the period between the census and the date of the estimate. New construction is estimated from building permit data, with adjustments to account for the lag time between permitting and completion and for permits that never result in actual construction. Estimates of new residential mobile home placements are based on data for mobile homes shipped to states, with adjustments for nonresidential use and lag times between shipment and placement. Estimates of residential housing loss are developed from demolition permits and information on nonpermitted losses from the American Housing Survey Components of Inventory Change.

Intercensal estimates for the 1980s were developed by adjusting the pattern of estimated annual housing unit change from 1980 to 1990 to be consistent with both the 1980 and 1990 Census counts of housing units.

The 1990 Census data used to develop these estimates were created by special age and race edits, commonly referred to as MARS (modified age, race, sex tabulations). These editing procedures not only affect the characteristics of the population, but also have a minor impact on the counts of housing units, households, and population living in group quarters.

Table 2.4

Data Source:
  Census of Housing
References:
  U.S. Bureau of the Census, "Housing: Then and Now, 50 Years of Decennial Censuses, Units in Structure," <http://www.census.gov/ hhes/housing/census/ units.html>. Tables prepared by Robert Bonnette. For information on housing unit concepts and definitions, see U.S. Bureau of the Census, *1990 Census of Population and Housing: Guide, Part A. Text*, 1990 CPH-R-1A, September 1992; and U.S. Bureau of the Census, *200 Years of U.S. Census Taking: Population and Housing Questions, 1790–1990*, November 1989. The "Definitions of Subject Characteristics" appendix of many 1990 Census publications also contains definitions of housing items and notes on comparability across censuses.

Definitions

Subject characteristics are defined as of the 1990 Census. See the Notes section, which follows the Definitions list, for information on historical comparability of definitions and concepts.

Housing unit. A housing unit is a house, an apartment, a mobile home or trailer, a group of rooms or a single room occupied as separate living quarters or, if vacant, intended for occupancy as separate living quarters. Separate living quarters are those in which the occupants live and eat separately from any other persons in the building and that have direct access from outside the building or through a common hall.

The occupants may be a single family, one person living alone, two or more families living together, or any other group of related or unrelated persons who share living arrangements. For vacant units, the criteria of separateness and direct access are applied to the intended occupants whenever possible. If that information cannot be obtained, the criteria are applied to the previous occupants.

Both occupied and vacant housing units are included in the housing unit inventory, except that recreational vehicles, boats, vans, tents, railroad cars, and the like are included only if they are occupied as someone's usual place of residence. Vacant mobile homes are included provided they are intended for occupancy on the site where they stand. Vacant mobile homes on dealers' sales lots, at the factory, or in storage yards are excluded from the housing inventory.

If the living quarters contains nine or more persons unrelated to the householder or person in charge (a total of at least 10 unrelated persons), it is classified as group quarters. If the living quarters contains eight or fewer persons unrelated to the householder or person in charge, it is classified as a housing unit.

Structure. A structure is a separate building that either has open spaces on all sides or is separated from other structures by dividing walls that extend from ground to roof. In determining the number of units in a structure, all housing units, both occupied and vacant, are counted. Stores and office space are excluded.

One-unit, detached. This is a one-unit structure detached from any other house (e.g., with open space on all four sides). Such structures are considered detached even if they have an adjoining shed or garage. A one-family house that contains a business is considered detached as long as the building has open space on all four sides. Mobile homes or trailers to which one or more permanent rooms have been added or built on also are included in this category.

One-unit, attached. This is a one-unit structure that has one or more walls extending from ground to roof separating it from adjoining structures. In row houses (sometimes called townhouses), double houses, or houses attached to nonresidential structures, each house is a separate, attached structure if the dividing or common wall goes from ground to roof.

Two or more units. These are units in structures containing two or more housing units, further categorized as units in structures with two to four units or five or more units.

Mobile home or trailer. Mobile homes to which no permanent rooms have been added are counted in this category. Those with a permanent room attached are counted in the one-unit, detached category. Mobile homes or trailers used only for business purposes or for extra sleeping space and mobile homes or trailers for sale on a dealer's lot, at the factory, or in storage are not counted in the housing inventory. In the 1970 and earlier censuses, mobile homes had to be occupied to be counted as housing units.

Notes

Data in this table represent the number of housing units in structures of specified type and size, not the number of residential buildings. There are some variations among censuses in the universe to which the tabulations apply. In 1970 and 1980, structure type is presented only for year-round housing units (i.e., seasonal and migratory vacant units are excluded).

In addition, there are slight variations over time in the definition of a housing unit and in structure-type categories. These differences are described as follows.

Changes in housing unit definition. The first census of housing in 1940 established the "dwelling unit" concept. A dwelling unit was defined as "living quarters occupied by, or intended for occupancy by, one household." In turn, a household was defined in terms of the group of people using "one set of cooking facilities or housekeeping arrangements." Living quarters with 10 or more lodgers were excluded from the count of dwelling units. The housing inventory included vacant, habitable dwelling units.

In 1950 the dwelling unit concept was continued, but expanded to include living quarters with separate cooking facilities or a separate entrance. In addition, any residence with five or more lodgers was categorized as a "nondwelling unit" and excluded from the housing inventory. Vacant trailers, boats, etc. were not enumerated as housing units.

The 1960 Census began use of the term "housing unit," but essentially maintained the definition used in 1950. As in 1950, residences with five or more lodgers were not included in the housing inventory, but in 1960 such living arrangements were called "group quarters."

The separate cooking facilities requirement was changed to "complete kitchen facilities" in 1970. Complete kitchen facilities included a sink with piped water, a range or cook stove, and a refrigerator.

Several significant changes in the housing unit definition were introduced with the 1980 Census. The complete kitchen facilities requirement of 1970 was dropped. Living quarters occupied by nine or more persons unrelated to the renter or owner, or with 10 or more unrelated people living together, were classified as noninstitutional group quarters and were not counted as housing units. For the first time, vacant mobile homes were counted as housing units, provided that they were intended for occupancy on the site where they were enumerated.

In 1990 the housing unit definition was unchanged from 1980. A question on direct access to the unit, which had been asked in the 1980 Census, was dropped from the 1990 Census questionnaire. In 1980 this question was used for analytical purposes only and was not used to identify housing units. (That is, if respondents indicated that they did not have direct access to their living quarters, this did not disqualify their residences from being counted as housing units.)

Changes in structure type categories. The "other" category in 1940 included trailers/mobile homes, tourist cabins, and boats whose occupants had no other usual place of residence. In 1940 and 1950, the "one-unit, attached" category included row houses (three or more attached houses) and semidetached (two units side-by-side); in the latter case, the units might not be completely separated by a dividing wall from the basement to the attic. In 1990, the "other" category was intended to describe living quarters such as houseboats, railroad cars, campers, vans, and caves. However, this category was far overstated, as can be seen by comparing the other category for 1990 to the "boat, tent, van, etc." category for 1980.

Table 2.5

Data Source:
   Census of Housing
References:
   U.S. Bureau of the Census, "Housing: Then and Now, 50 Years of Decennial Censuses, Plumbing Facilities"; <http://www.census.gov/hhes/housing/census/plumbing.html>. Table prepared by Robert Bonnette. For information on housing concepts and definitions, see U.S. Bureau of the Census, *1990 Census of Population and Housing: Guide, Part A Text*, 1990 CPH-R-1A, September 1992; and U.S. Bureau of the Census, *200 Years of U.S. Census Taking: Population and Housing Questions, 1790–1990*, November 1989.

The "Definitions of Subject Characteristics" appendix of many 1990 Census publications also contains definitions of housing items and notes on comparability across censuses.

Definitions

Subject characteristics are defined as of the 1990 Census. See the Notes section for information on historical comparability of definitions and concepts.

Housing unit. See Table 2.4 Definitions.

Complete plumbing facilities. Complete plumbing facilities include hot and cold piped water, a flush toilet, and a bathtub or shower. All three facilities must be located inside the house, apartment, or mobile home, but not necessarily in the same room. Housing units are classified as lacking complete plumbing facilities when any of the three facilities are not present.

Notes

The 1990 data on complete plumbing facilities are not strictly comparable with the 1980 and earlier data. In 1980 and preceding censuses, complete plumbing facilities were defined to be for the exclusive use of the residents of a given unit. Units in which occupants shared plumbing facilities with occupants of other units were tabulated as "lacking complete plumbing." In 1990, the requirement of exclusive use was dropped from the definition of complete plumbing facilities and units having complete plumbing not for exclusive use of their inhabitants were counted as having complete plumbing. Of the 2.3 million year-round housing units classified in 1980 as lacking complete plumbing for exclusive use, approximately 25 percent of these units had complete plumbing, but the facilities were also used by members of another household.

From 1940 to 1970, separate and more detailed questions were asked on piped water, bathing, and toilet facilities. In 1940, the question on water supply did not refer to hot and cold piped water, but simply to "running water" within the dwelling unit.

The universe for this item in the various census years is defined as follows: all housing units reporting plumbing facilities in 1940 and 1950, all housing units in 1960 and 1990, and year-round housing units in 1970 and 1980.

Table 2.6

Data Source:
   Census of Housing

References:

U.S. Bureau of the Census, "Housing: Then and Now, 50 Years of Decennial Censuses. Source of Water," <http://www.census.gov/ hhes/housing/census/water.html>. Tables prepared by Robert Bonnette. For information on housing concepts and definitions, see U.S. Bureau of the Census, *1990 Census of Population and Housing: Guide, Part A Text*, 1990 CPH-R-1A, September 1992; and U.S. Bureau of the Census, *200 Years of U.S. Census Taking: Population and Housing Questions, 1790–1990*, November 1989. The "Definitions of Subject Characteristics" appendix of many 1990 Census publications also contains definitions of housing items and notes on comparability across censuses.

Definitions

Housing unit. See Definitions for Table 2.4.

Source of water. Housing units may receive their water supply from a number of sources. A common source supplying water to five or more units is classified as a "public system or private company." The water may be supplied by a city, county, water district, water company, etc., or it may be obtained from a well that supplies water to five or more housing units. If the water is supplied from a well serving four or fewer housing units, in 1980 and 1990 the units are classified as having water supplied by either an "individual drilled well" or an "individual dug well." (In 1970, the individual wells category was not disaggregated into separate categories for dug and drilled wells.) Drilled wells or small-diameter wells are usually less than 1 1/2 feet in diameter. Dug wells are usually larger than 1 1/2 feet wide and generally hand dug. The category "some other source" includes water obtained from springs, creeks, rivers, lakes, cisterns, etc.

Notes

In 1970 and 1980, data are for yearround housing units only. In 1990, data are for all housing units.

Table 2.7

Data Source:

Census of Housing

References:

U.S. Bureau of the Census, "Housing: Then and Now, 50 Years of Decennial Censuses, Sewage Disposal," <http://www.census.gov/ hhes/housing/census/sew-

age.html>. Tables prepared by Robert Bonnette. For information on housing concepts and definitions, see U.S. Bureau of the Census, *1990 Census of Population and Housing: Guide, Part A Text*, 1990 CPH-R-1A, September 1992; and U.S. Bureau of the Census, *200 Years of U.S. Census Taking: Population and Housing Questions, 1790–1990*, November 1989. The "Definitions of Subject Characteristics" appendix of many 1990 Census publications also contains definitions of housing items and notes on comparability across censuses.

Definitions

Housing unit. See Definitions for Table 2.4.

Sewage disposal. Housing units are either connected to a public sewer, or to a septic tank or cesspool, or they dispose of sewage by other means. A public sewer may be operated by a government body or by a private organization. A housing unit is considered to be connected to a septic tank or cesspool when the unit is provided with an underground pit or tank for sewage disposal. The category "other means" includes housing units that dispose of sewage in some other way.

Notes

The question on sewage disposal was identical in the 1970, 1980, and 1990 Censuses. In 1970 and 1980, data are for year-round housing units only. In 1990, data are for all housing units.

Table 2.8

Data Source:

Census of Housing

References:

U.S. Bureau of the Census, "Housing: Then and Now, 50 Years of Decennial Censuses, Telephones," <http://www.census.gov/hhes/ housing/census/phone.html>. Tables prepared by Robert Bonnette. For information on housing concepts and definitions, see U.S. Bureau of the Census, *1990 Census of Population and Housing: Guide, Part A Text*, 1990 CPH-R-1A, September 1992; and U.S. Bureau of the Census, *200 Years of U.S. Census Taking: Population and Housing Questions, 1790–1990*, November 1989. The "Definitions of Subject Characteristics" appendix of many 1990 Census publications also contains definitions of housing items and notes on comparability across censuses.

Definitions

Housing unit. See Table 2.4 Definitions.

Telephone in unit. In 1980 and 1990, the census asked about the presence of a telephone inside the housing unit. Housing units where the respondent used a telephone located inside the building but not in the respondent's living quarters were classified as having no telephone.

Telephone availability. The 1960 and 1970 Censuses collected data on telephone availability rather than the presence of a telephone in the dwelling unit. A unit was classified as having a telephone available if there was a telephone number on which occupants of the unit could be reached. The telephone could have been in another unit, in a common hall, or outside the building.

Notes

For all years, the universe is occupied housing units.

Table 2.9

Data Source:
Census of Housing
References:
U.S. Bureau of the Census, "Housing: Then and Now, 50 Years of Decennial Censuses, Vacation Homes," <http://www.census.gov/hhes/housing/census/vacation.html>. Tables prepared by Robert Bonnette. For information on housing concepts and definitions, see U.S. Bureau of the Census, *1990 Census of Population and Housing: Guide, Part A Text*, 1990 CPH-R-1A, September 1992; and U.S. Bureau of the Census, *200 Years of U.S. Census Taking: Population and Housing Questions, 1790–1990*, November 1989. The "Definitions of Subject Characteristics" appendix of many 1990 Census publications also contains definitions of housing items and notes on comparability across censuses.

Definitions

Subject characteristics are defined as of the 1990 Census. See the following Notes section for information on historical comparability of definitions and concepts.

Housing unit. See Table 2.4 Definitions.

For seasonal, recreational, or occasional use. These are vacant units used or intended for use only in certain seasons or for weekend or other occasional use throughout the year. Seasonal units include those used for summer or winter sports or recreation, such as beach cottages and hunting cabins. Seasonal units also may include quarters for such workers as herders and loggers. Interval ownership units, sometimes called shared-ownership or time-sharing condominiums, also are included here.

For migrant workers. These include vacant units intended for occupancy by migratory workers employed in farm work during the crop season.

Notes

In order to make the data consistent over the decades, "seasonal," "held for occasional use," and "for migrant workers" are combined. The occasional use category was not used in the Census of 1940 or 1950. Counts of seasonal and occasional use vacant units are provided separately from 1960 to 1980, but are combined in 1990 because evidence indicated enumerators had great difficulty telling them apart. Housing for migrant workers is included with seasonal before 1990.

Counts of seasonal vacants are from 100-percent data for 1980, while estimates of occasional use vacants are from sample data. This is a result of a 100-percent computer edit that shifted many "occasional use" to "other" vacant units.

Any occasional-use vacants enumerated as "dilapidated" are not included in the vacant counts for 1960.

For all years, the universe is all housing units.

Table 2.10

Data Source:
Census of Housing
Reference:
U.S. Bureau of the Censu, *New Homes*, Statistical Brief SB/9414, July 1994.

Definitions

Housing unit. See Table 2.4 Definitions.

New homes. In 1990, new homes include units built after 1984. In 1980, new homes are those built after 1974.

Notes

The universe is all housing units for 1990 and year-round housing units for 1980.

Tables 2.11-2.31

Data Source:

American Housing Survey for the United States

References:

U.S. Bureau of the Census and U.S. Department of Housing and Urban Development, *American Housing Survey for the United States in 1991*, Current Housing Reports H150/91, April 1993; *American Housing Survey for the United States in 1993*, Current Housing Reports H150/93, February 1995, and *American Housing Survey for the United States in 1995*, Current Housing Reports H150/95RV, July 1997.

Definitions

Definitions for these tables are first presented for column headers and then for row headers.

Housing units. A housing unit is a house, an apartment, a group of rooms, or a single room occupied or intended for occupancy as separate living quarters. Separate living quarters are those in which the occupants do not live and eat with any other persons in the structure and that have direct access from the outside of the building or through a common hall that is used or intended for use by the occupants of another unit or by the general public. The occupants may be a single family, one person living alone, two or more families living together, or any other group of related or unrelated persons who share living arrangements (except as described in the following section on group quarters). For vacant units, the criteria of separateness and direct access are applied to the intended occupants whenever possible. If the information cannot be obtained, the criteria are applied to the previous occupants. Both occupied and vacant housing units are included in the housing inventory except that tents, caves, boats, railroad cars, and the like are included only if they are occupied.

Group quarters. Group quarters are any living quarters that are not classified as housing units. Institutional group quarters are living quarters occupied by one or more persons under care or custody, such as children in an orphanage, persons in a nursing home, and prisoners in a penitentiary. Noninstitutional group quarters include living quarters such as college-owned and/or operated dormitories, fraternity and sorority houses, nurses' dormitories, and boarding houses. In addition, noninstitutional group quarters include any living quarters that are occupied by nine or more persons unrelated to the householder, or by 10 or more unrelated persons.

Seasonal units. Seasonal units are units that are intended by the owner to be occupied during only certain seasons of the year. They are not anyone's usual residence and include units occupied entirely by persons with a usual residence elsewhere and vacant units. A seasonal unit may be used in more than one season. For example, it may be used both in the summer for summer sports and in the winter for winter sports. Counts of seasonal units also include housing units held for occupancy by migratory farm workers.

Year-round units. Year-round housing units include all units occupied by one or more persons for whom it is their usual residence and all vacant units that are intended by the owner for occupancy at any time of the year. If a unit in a resort area is intended for occupancy on a year-round basis, it is a year-round housing unit, even if vacant.

Occupied housing units. A housing unit is classified as occupied if a person or group of persons is living in it at the time of the interview or if the occupants are only temporarily absent, for example, on vacation. However, if the unit is occupied entirely by persons with a usual place of residence elsewhere, the unit is classified as vacant. By definition, the count of occupied housing units equals the count of households.

Tenure (owner- or renter-occupied). A housing unit is owner-occupied if the owner or co-owner lives in the unit, even if it is mortgaged or not fully paid for. Also, a cooperative or condominium unit is owner-occupied only if the owner or co-owner lives in it. All other occupied housing units are classified as renter-occupied, including housing units rented for cash rent and those occupied without payment of cash rent.

Vacant housing units. A housing unit is vacant if no one is living in it at the time of the interview, unless its occupants are only temporarily absent. In addition, a vacant housing unit may be one that is occupied entirely by persons who have a usual residence elsewhere (URE). New housing units not yet occupied are classified as vacant housing units if construction has reached a point where all exterior windows and doors are installed and final usable floors are in place. Vacant units are excluded if unfit for human habitation, that is if the roof, walls, windows, or doors no longer protect the interior from the elements, or if there is positive evidence (such as a sign on the house or block) that the unit is to be demolished or is condemned. Also excluded are quarters being used entirely for nonresidential purposes such as a store, an office, or quarters used for storing business supplies or inventory, machinery, or agricultural products.

Vacancy status. Vacant housing units are classified as either "seasonal" or "year-round." Year-round vacant housing units are subdivided as follows:

For sale only. Vacant year-round units "for sale only" also include vacant units in a cooperative or condominium building if the individual units are offered for sale only.

For rent. Vacant year-round units "for rent" also include vacant units offered either for rent or for sale.

Rented or sold, not occupied. If any money rent has been paid or agreed upon but the new renter has not moved in as of the date of the interview, or if the unit has recently been sold but the new owner has not yet moved in, the year-round vacant unit is classified as "rented or sold, not occupied."

Held for occasional use. This category consists of vacant year-round units that are held for weekend or other occasional use throughout the year. The intent of this question is to identify homes reserved by their owners as second homes. Because of the difficulty of distinguishing between this category and seasonal vacancies, it is possible that some second homes are classified as seasonal and vice versa.

Temporarily occupied by persons with usual residence elsewhere (URE). If all the persons in a housing unit usually live elsewhere, that unit is classified as vacant, provided the usual place of residence is held for the household and is not offered for rent or for sale. For example, a beach cottage occupied at the time of the interview by a family that has a usual place of residence in the city is included in the count of vacant units. If the house in the city was in the survey sample, the house would be reported occupied and would be included in the count of occupied units since the occupants are only temporarily absent.

Held for other reasons. If a vacant year-round unit does not fall into any of the classifications specified, it is classified as "held for other reasons." For example, this category includes units held for settlement of an estate, units held for occupancy by a caretaker or janitor, and units held for personal reasons of the owner. The "other vacant" category includes all housing units held for other reasons.

Rental vacancy rate. The rental vacancy rate is the number of vacant year-round units for rent as a percent of the total rental inventory (i.e., all renter-occupied housing units and all year-round vacant housing units for rent, or those rented, not occupied).

Constructed within four years. This is the American Housing Survey (AHS) category for new construction and refers to date of construction related to the date of the interview.

Manufactured (mobile) homes. Manufactured homes and trailers are shown as a separate category under "mobile homes." When one or more rooms have been added to a mobile home or trailer, it is still classified as a mobile home. In years before 1993, the American Housing Survey classified these units as a house, apartment, or flat.

Race. The classification of "race" refers to the race of the householder occupying the housing unit. The concept of race as used by the Census Bureau does not denote a clear-cut scientific definition of biological stock. Race was determined on the basis of a question that asked for self-identification of a person's race. In 1991 and 1993, "Other" races includes Asian, Pacific Islander, American Indian, Aleut, Eskimo, and any other race reported. "American Indian, Eskimo, and Aleut" and "Asian and Pacific Islander" were added as separate race categories beginning in 1995.

Hispanic. The classification "Hispanic" refers to the origin of the householder occupying the housing unit. Hispanic origin was determined on the basis of a question that asked for self-identification of persons living in the unit who were Hispanic or Spanish American. Hispanic persons may be of any race.

Elderly. Data for elderly include all households with a householder 65 years of age or over. The age classification refers to the age reported for the householder as of that person's last birthday.

Moved in past year. Data are shown for households that moved into the present unit during the 12 months prior to the date of the interview.

Poverty status. The poverty classification used here differs from official poverty estimates in two important respects. The first important difference is the use of a poverty definition that is based on household income in place of the official method that is based on the income of the family or the unrelated individual. Under the official approach, the poverty status of two unrelated individuals living together would be determined by comparing the income of each individual to the poverty threshold for an unrelated individual. The result might be that both were in poverty, both were out of poverty, or one was in poverty and one was not. Under the approach used in the AHS, the two unrelated individuals were treated as members of a two-person family and their poverty status was determined by comparing their combined income to the poverty threshold for a two-person family. The effect of using a poverty concept that is based on household income is to undercount the number of persons in poverty relative to the official estimate. A study based on the March 1975 Current Population Survey found that poverty estimates based on a household income concept were about 6 percent lower than official estimates.

A second important difference between the poverty estimates in the AHS and the official poverty estimates has to do with the method used to measure income. The official annual poverty estimates are based on data collected in the March supplement to the Current Population Survey. The income questions asked in that survey are very detailed and measure the amount of income received during the previous calendar year. The income questions asked in the AHS are much less detailed and measure the amount received during the previous 12 months. Because interviews were conducted during the period July through December, the income measures do not pertain to a fixed period. Many of the income questions in the AHS were asked on a household rather than an individual income basis. The lack of data for individuals made it necessary to adopt a poverty definition based on household income.

Officially, families and unrelated individuals are classified as being above or below the poverty level using the poverty index originated at the Social Security Administration in 1964 and revised by the Federal Interagency Committees in 1969 and 1980. The poverty index is based solely on money income and does not reflect the fact that many low-income persons receive noncash benefits such as food stamps, Medicaid, and public housing. The index is based on the Department of Agriculture's 1961 Economy Food Plan and reflects the different consumption requirements of families based on their size and composition. The poverty thresholds are updated every year to reflect changes in the Consumer Price Index.

Units in structure. In determining the number of housing units in a structure, all units, both occupied and vacant, were counted. The statistics are presented for the number of housing units in structures of specified type and size, not for the number of residential structures.

A structure is a separate building if it either has open space on all sides or is separated from other structures by dividing walls that extend from ground to roof. Structures containing only one housing unit are further classified as detached or attached.

A one-unit structure is detached if it has open space on all four sides even though it has an adjoining shed or garage. A one-unit structure is attached if it has one or more walls extending from ground to roof that divide it from other adjoining structures and does not share a furnace or boiler with adjoining structures such as in rowhouses, townhouses, etc.

Mobile homes and trailers are shown as a separate category. When one or more rooms have been added to a mobile home or trailer, it is classified as a mobile home. In years before 1993, the AHS classified these units as a house, apartment, or flat.

Stories in structure. The statistics presented are restricted to multiunits. Finished attics are included in the number of stories. Unfinished attics are not. For split levels and bilevels, the number of stories is determined by the highest number of floors that are physically over each other.

Cooperatives and condominiums. A cooperative is a type of ownership whereby a group of housing units are owned by a corporation of member-owners. Each individual member is entitled to occupy or rent an individual housing unit and is a shareholder in the corporation that owns the property.

A condominium is a type of ownership that enables a person to own an apartment or house in a project of similarly owned units. The owner has the deed and very likely the mortgage on the unit occupied. The owner may also hold common or joint ownership in some or all common areas such as grounds, hallways, entrances, elevators, etc.

Cooperative or condominium ownership may apply to various types of structures, including single-family houses, rowhouses, townhouses, etc., as well as apartment units.

Year structure built. "Year structure built" refers to when the building was first constructed, not when it was remodeled, added to, or converted. The figures refer to the number of housing units in structures built during the specified periods and in existence at the time of the interview. For mobile homes and trailers, the manufacturer's model year was assumed to be the year built. Median year built is rounded to the nearest year.

Metropolitan statistical areas. Metropolitan statistical areas (MSAs) shown in the AHS are defined by the Office of Management and Budget. An area qualifies for recognition as an MSA in one of two ways: if there is a city of at least 50,000 population or a Census Bureau–defined urbanized area of at least 50,000 with a total metropolitan population of at least 100,000 (75,000 in New England). Except in the New England states, an MSA is defined in terms of entire counties. In New England, MSAs are composed of cities and towns. In addition to the county containing the main city, additional counties are included in an MSA if they are socially and economically integrated with the central county. An MSA may contain more than one city of 50,000 population and may cross state lines.

Central cities. Every MSA has at least one central city, which is usually its largest city. Smaller cities are also identified as central cities if they have at least 25,000 population and meet the following two commuting requirements. First, the city must have at least 75 jobs for each 100 residents who are employed. Second, no more than 60 percent of the city's resident workers may commute to jobs outside the city limits. In addition, any city with at least 250,000 population or at least 100,000 persons working within its corporate limits qualifies as a central city even if it fails to meet the above two commuting requirements. Finally, in certain smaller MSAs, there are places with between 15,000 and 25,000 population that also qualify as central cities, because they are at least one-third the size of the MSA's largest city and meet the two commuting requirements.

Suburbs. Suburbs are defined as the areas inside of MSAs that are not within central cities.

Urban and rural residence. Urban housing comprises all housing units in urbanized areas and in places of 2,500 or more inhabitants outside urbanized areas. More specifically, urban housing consists of all housing units in (1) places of 2,500 or more inhabitants incorporated as cities, villages, boroughs (except in Alaska and New York), and towns (except in the New England states, New York, and Wisconsin), but excluding those housing units in the rural portions of extended cities; (2) census-designated places of 2,500 or more inhabitants; and (3) other territory, incorporated or unincorporated, included in urbanized areas. Housing units not classified as urban constitute rural housing.

Urbanized areas. The major objective of the Census Bureau in delineating urbanized areas is to provide a better separation of urban and rural housing in the vicinity of large cities. An urbanized area comprises an incorporated place and an adjacent, densely settled (1.6 or more people per acre) surrounding area that together have a minimum population of 50,000.

Places. Two types of places are recognized by the Census Bureau: incorporated places and census-designated places as defined here.

Incorporated places. Incorporated places are those that are incorporated under the laws of their respective states as cities, boroughs, towns, and villages.

Census designated places (CDPs). The Census Bureau has delineated boundaries for closely settled population centers without corporate limits. To be recognized for the census, CDPs must have a minimum population. If located in urbanized areas that have one or more cities of 50,000 or more population, CDPs must have a minimum population of 5,000. All other areas except for areas in Alaska and Hawaii require a minimum population of 1,000. The requirements are a population of 25 in Alaska and 300 in Hawaii.

Rooms. The statistics on rooms are for the number of housing units with a specified number of rooms. Rooms counted include whole rooms used for living purposes such as bedrooms, living rooms, dining rooms, kitchens, recreation rooms, permanently enclosed porches that are suitable for year-round use, lodgers' rooms, and other finished and unfinished rooms. Also included are rooms used for offices by a person living in the unit. The median for rooms is rounded to the nearest 10th.

A dining room, to be counted, must be a separate room. It must be separated from adjoining rooms by built-in floor-to-ceiling walls extending at least a few inches from the intersecting walls. Movable or collapsible partitions or partitions consisting solely of shelves or cabinets are not considered built-in walls. Bathrooms are not counted as rooms.

Bedrooms. The number of bedrooms in the housing unit is the count of rooms used mainly for sleeping, even if also used for other purposes. Rooms reserved for sleeping, such as guest rooms, even though used infrequently, are counted as bedrooms. On the other hand, rooms used mainly for other purposes, even though used also for sleeping, such as a living room with a hideaway bed, are not considered bedrooms. A housing unit consisting of only one room, such as a one-room efficiency apartment, is classified by definition as having no bedroom.

Complete bathrooms. A housing unit is classified as having a complete bathroom if it has a room with a flush toilet, a bathtub or shower, a sink, and hot and cold piped water. All facilities must be in the same room to be a complete bathroom. A half bathroom has either a flush toilet or a bathtub or shower but does not have all the facilities for a complete bathroom.

Square footage of unit. Housing size is shown for single-family, detached housing units and mobile homes. Excluded from the calculation of square footage are unfinished attics, carports, attached garages, porches that are not protected from the elements (e.g., screened porches), and mobile home hitches. Both finished and unfinished basements are included. Median square footage is rounded to the nearest foot. Square footage is based on the respondent's estimate of the size of the unit. If the respondent did not know the square footage, the interviewer measured the outside dimensions of the unit. Preliminary evaluation indicates that this item is somewhat unreliable.

Lot size. Lot size includes all connecting land that is owned or rented with the home. Excluded are buildings and mobile homes with two or more units. Median lot size is shown to hundredths of an acre.

External building conditions. The statistics presented are restricted to multiunits. The external condition of the building that contains the sample unit was determined by interviewer observation, as visible from the front of the building or the roadway. The categories are grouped into the following: roof, walls, windows, and foundation.

Roof. A "sagging roof" is a critical defect indicating continuous neglect or deep or serious damage to the structure. Only roofs with substantial sagging were included. "Missing roofing material" includes rotted, broken, loose, or missing shingles, tiles, slate, shake, tin, etc., caused by extensive damage from fire, storm, or serious neglect. "Hole in roof" occurs when the missing roof materials expose the interior of the unit directly to the elements. Holes caused by construction activity were not counted unless the construction had been abandoned. "Could not see roof" occurs when possible situations like a high tree, evening interviews, or a flat roof prevent the roof from being visible.

Walls. "Missing bricks, siding, other outside wall material" applies to the exterior walls (including chimney)

of the structure. Those defects may have been caused by storm, fire, flood, extensive neglect, vandalism, and so forth. Materials may include clapboard siding, shingles, boards, brick, concrete stucco, etc. The missing materials do not necessarily expose the interior of the unit openly to the elements. Missing materials resulting from construction activity were not counted unless construction had been abandoned. "Sloping outside walls" are a critical defect indicating continuous neglect or serious damage to the structure. Only walls with substantial sagging were included.

Windows. "Boarded-up windows" have been sealed off to protect against weather or entry and include windows and/or doors covered by board, brick, metal, or some other material. "Broken windows" indicate several broken or missing window panes. "Bars on windows" are to protect against unlawful entry. The condition of the windows has no bearing on this item. The bars can be vertical, horizontal, a metal grating, etc. Windows completely covered with metal sheeting are not included in this category.

Foundation crumbling or has open crack or hole. This category includes large cracks, holes, and rotted, loose, or missing foundation material.

Could not see foundation. This occurs when landscaping, night interviewing, or some other reason prevents visibility for observation.

Complete kitchen facilities. A housing unit has complete kitchen facilities when it has all of the following for the exclusive use of the occupants of the unit: (1) an installed kitchen sink, (2) burners, and (3) a mechanical refrigerator. Quarters with only portable cooking equipment are not considered as having a range or cookstove. An icebox is not included as a mechanical refrigerator. The kitchen facilities are for the exclusive use of the occupants when they are used only by the occupants of one housing unit, including lodgers or other unrelated persons living in the unit.

Beginning in 1993, the same criteria were used for occupied and vacant units in determining complete kitchen facilities. In previous years, for vacant units from which one or all of the kitchen facilities had been removed, the kitchen facilities used by the last occupant were reported. As a result, the total vacant units lacking complete kitchen facilities in these tables may appear higher than in survey years before 1993.

Plumbing facilities. The category "with all plumbing facilities" consists of housing units that have hot and cold piped water as well as a flush toilet and a bathtub or shower for the exclusive use of the occupants of the unit. All plumbing facilities must be located in the housing unit but they need not be in the same room. Lacking some plumbing facilities or no plumbing facilities for exclusive use means that the housing unit does not have all three specified plumbing facilities (hot and cold piped water, flush toilet, and bathtub or shower) inside the housing unit, or that the toilet or bathing facilities are also for the use of the occupants of other housing units.

In 1993, there were 1,854,000 housing units that reported a complete lack of plumbing facilities. The total number of units that reported such a lack decreased by about one-third between 1991 and 1993. A decrease in these units also was reported between 1989 and 1991. Total housing units with no plumbing facilities for exclusive use went from 3,135,000 in 1989 to 2,905,000 in 1991. In 1993, the questionnaire item on bathrooms for exclusive use was modified to provide more accurate estimates. The wording of the "answer options" to this question was changed to specify whether or not there was exclusive use of the facilities. Although the decrease between 1991 and 1993 seems unrealistic, the Census Bureau feels that the change in the 1993 questionnaire resulted in a better estimate. Caution should be used when making comparisons with the 1991 AHS-N survey and the 1993 and later surveys. The drop in the number of units with no plumbing facilities also caused a drop in the number of occupied units with severe physical problems, from 2,874,000 in 1991 to 1,901,000 in 1993.

Selected deficiencies.

Signs of rats. The statistics on signs of rats refer to respondents who reported seeing rats or signs of rats inside the house or building during the past 3 months or while the household was living in the unit if less than 3 months. Signs of rats include droppings, holes in the wall, or ripped or torn food containers.

Holes in floors. Data are shown on whether there are holes in the interior floors of a housing unit. The holes do not have to go all the way through to a lower floor or to the exterior of the unit. The holes must be large enough to cause someone to trip.

Open cracks or holes (interior). Statistics are presented on whether or not there are open cracks or holes in the interior walls or ceilings of the housing unit. Included are cracks or holes that do not go all the way through to the next room or to the exterior of the housing unit. Hairline cracks or cracks that appear in the walls or ceilings, but that are not large enough to insert the edge of a dime, and very small holes caused by nails or other similar objects are not considered to be open cracks or holes.

Broken plaster or peeling paint (interior). The area of peeling paint or broken plaster must be on the inside walls or ceilings and at least one area of broken plaster or peeling paint must be larger than 8 inches by 11 inches.

Electric wiring. A housing unit is classified as having exposed electric wiring if the unit has any wiring that is not enclosed, either in the walls or in metal coverings, or if the unit has any wiring outside the walls enclosed in some material other than metal. Excluded from the tabulation are appliance cords, extension cords, chandelier cords, and telephone, antenna, or cable TV wires.

Electric wall outlets. A housing unit is classified as having rooms without electric wall outlets if there is not at least one working electric wall outlet in each room of the unit. A working electric wall outlet is one that is in operating condition (e.g., can be used when needed). If a room does not have an electric wall outlet, an extension cord used in place of a wall outlet is not considered to be an electric wall outlet.

Persons per room. Persons per room is computed for each occupied housing unit by dividing the number of persons in the unit by the number of rooms in the unit. The figures shown refer, therefore, to the number of housing units having the specified ratio of persons per room.

Square feet per person. Square feet per person is computed for each single-family detached housing unit and manufactured home by dividing the number of persons in the unit by the square footage of the unit. The figures shown refer to the number of housing units having the specified square feet per person. Median square footage is rounded to the nearest foot.

Overall opinion of structure. The data presented are based on the respondent's overall opinion of the house or apartment as a place to live. The respondent was asked to rate the structure based on a scale from 1 to 10, where 10 is the best and 1 is the worst.

Severe physical problems. A unit has severe physical problems if it has any of the following five problems:

Plumbing. The unit lacks hot or cold piped water or a flush toilet, or lacks both bathtub and shower, all inside the structure for the exclusive use of the unit.

Heating. The respondent reports having been uncomfortably cold last winter for 24 hours or more because the heating equipment broke, and it broke at least three times last winter for at least 6 hours each time.

Electric. The unit has no electricity, or all of the following three electric problems: exposed wiring, a room with no working wall outlet, and three blown fuses or tripped circuit breakers in the past 90 days.

Upkeep. The structure or unit has any five of the following six maintenance problems: water leaks from the outside, such as from the roof, basement, windows, or doors; leaks from inside the structure such as pipes or plumbing fixtures; holes in the floors; holes or open cracks in the walls or ceilings; more than 8 inches by 11 inches of peeling paint or broken plaster; or signs of rats or mice in the past 90 days.

Hallways. Severe problems include having all of the following four problems in public areas: no working light fixtures, loose or missing steps, loose or missing railings, and no elevator.

A substantial decline in the number of housing units with no plumbing facilities between 1991 and 1993 also caused a drop in the number of occupied units with severe physical problems, from 2,874,000 in 1991 to 1,901,000 in 1993. See definition of plumbing facilities for additional explanation.

Moderate physical problems. A unit has moderate physical problems if it has any of the following five problems, but none of the severe problems.

Plumbing. On at least three occasions during the past 3 months or while the household was living in the unit if less than 3 months, all the flush toilets were broken at the same time for 6 hours or more.

Heating. The unit has unvented gas, oil, or kerosene heaters as the primary heating equipment.

Upkeep. The structure has any three or four of the overall list of six upkeep problems mentioned above under severe physical problems.

Hallways. The structure has any three of the four hallway problems mentioned under severe physical problems.

Kitchen. The unit lacks a kitchen sink, refrigerator, or burners inside the structure for the exclusive use of the unit.

Overall opinion of neighborhood. The data presented are based on the respondent's overall opinion of the neighborhood. The respondent defines neighborhood. The respondent was asked to rate the neighborhood based on a scale from 1 to 10, where 10 is the best and 1 is the worst.

Neighborhood conditions. The statistics presented are based on the respondent's opinion and attitude toward the neighborhood. The respondent defines "neighborhood." The respondent was asked a two-part question: Does anything about the neighborhood bother the respondent and if so, what? The interviewer coded the responses into the following categories: crime; noise; traffic; litter or housing deterioration; poor city/county services; undesirable commercial, institutional, or industrial property; people; and other. Multiple responses were allowed. The respondent may not have the same opinion as a neighbor about neighborhood conditions. The respondent's opinion may or may not reflect the actual neighborhood situation.

Other buildings vandalized or with interior exposed. The statistics presented are restricted to multiunits. The statistics presented are based on the interviewer's personal observation. A unit is considered to be vandalized if it has most of the visible windows broken, doors pulled off, been badly burned, words or symbols printed on it, or portions of the roof missing or gone, or in some other way has the interior exposed to the elements.

Bars on windows of buildings. The statistics presented are restricted to multiunits. The statistics presented are based on the interviewer's personal observation. The condition of the windows has no bearing on this item. The windows might be in perfect condition but the bars might be there to protect against vandalism. Windows that are boarded up or covered with tin are not included.

Condition of streets. The statistics presented are restricted to multiunits. The statistics presented are based on the interviewer's personal observation. Major repairs include large potholes, badly crumbling or deteriorating shoulders and roadsides, deep ruts, etc. Minor repairs include small cracks, shallow holes, or missing minor surfacing.

Trash, litter, or junk on streets or any properties. The statistics presented are restricted to multiunits. The statistics presented are based on the interviewer's personal observations. Major accumulation includes tires, appliances or large amounts of trash accumulated over a period of time. Minor accumulation includes small amounts of paper, cans, or bottles but does not give the impression of long neglect. The building in which the sample unit is located is included.

Notes

Historical changes in the American Housing Survey. Changes in the American Housing Survey (AHS) between 1991 and 1995 that might affect historical comparability are described in the Definitions section.

Comparability with 1990 Census of Population and Housing data. The concepts and definitions are essentially the same for items that appear in both the 1990 Census and the AHS. There is a major difference, however, in the time period of the "recent mover" classification. In the AHS, recent movers are households that moved into their unit during the 12 months prior to interview, a period of 1 year or less. In publications for the 1990 Census of Housing on mover households, the time period was from January 1, 1989, through March 31, 1990, a period of 15 months or less.

In the AHS, units are classified as new construction if constructed 4 years or less from the date of interview. In publications from the 1990 Census of Housing, units are classified as new construction if constructed in 1985 through 1990.

Data on poverty level in the 1990 Census of Housing do not contain the income of household members unrelated to the householder. In the American Housing Survey, data on poverty level include the income of all household members whether or not they are related to the householder.

Income data in the AHS are based on income for the 12 months prior to interview for those household members 14 years and older. The 1990 Census of Housing income data are for calendar year 1989 and for income of household members 15 years old and older.

In the 1990 Census of Population, data for years of school completed were based on responses to two questions: the highest grade or year of regular school each household member attended, and whether or not that grade was completed. The response categories for persons who have attended college were modified from earlier censuses because there was some ambiguity in interpreting responses in terms of number of years of college completed. This modification enhances the reporting of the number of college graduates. In the AHS, data for years of school completed were based on responses to a single question—the highest grade or year of regular school completed by the householder. Therefore, the AHS may overstate the education level of the householder. That is, respondents may have reported the grade or year the householder was currently enrolled in or had last been enrolled in whether or not the grade or year was completed.

Differences between the American Housing Survey data and the 1990 Census may also be attributed to several other factors. These include the extensive use of self-enumeration in the census in contrast to personal interview in the AHS, differences in processing procedures and sample designs, the sampling variability associated with the sample data from both the AHS and the census, the nonsampling errors associated with the AHS estimates, and the nonsampling errors associated with census data.

Comparability with the Survey of Construction. The Survey of Construction provides current data on housing starts and completions, construction authorized by building permits, new one-unit structures sold and for sale, characteristics of new housing, and value of new construction put in place. (See Appendix B for a description of the Survey of Construction.) The concepts and definitions used in this report differ from some of those used in the Survey of Construction. The major difference is that the Survey of Construction shows counts and characteristics of housing units in various stages of construction through completion. The AHS shows counts and characteristics of the existing housing inventory. Additional differences between the American Housing Survey and the Survey of Construction may be attributed to factors such as the sampling variability and nonsampling errors of the data from the two surveys, survey procedures and techniques, and processing procedures.

Comparability with housing vacancy surveys. There may be differences between the AHS and federal, state, local, and other surveys that present vacancy rates. (For a description of one such federal survey, the Current Population Survey/Housing Vacancy Survey, see Appendix B.) The differences may be attributed to such factors as differing interview periods, survey designs, survey techniques, and processing procedures, as well as differences in concepts and definitions. In addition, there may be differential sampling and nonsampling errors associated with the various surveys that produce information on vacancy rates.

Tables 2.32–2.33

Data Source:
  Property Owners and Managers Survey
References:
  U.S. Bureau of the Census, "Property Owners and Managers Survey"; various tables located at <http://www.census.gov/hhes/www/poms.html>.

Definitions

Property. Property means real estate, that is, land and anything permanently affixed to the land, such as buildings and those things attached to the buildings such as light fixtures, plumbing and heating fixtures, or other such items that would be personal property if not attached. A property may consist of a single-family house (attached or detached), a multifamily house, a condominium unit, a single mobile home, a mobile home park, an apartment building, or a group of apartment buildings. In the Property Owners and Managers Survey (POMS), the property is defined by the owner or manager.

Rental housing unit. This category includes housing units rented for cash rent, occupied by someone other than the owner without payment of cash rent, and vacant but available for rent.

Single-family rental housing. This category includes single-family detached houses, single-family attached houses, a single-unit house with an attached business, condominiums, cooperative apartments, and mobile homes.

Multifamily rental housing. This category includes apartment buildings or complexes (noncondominium or cooperative); single-family houses with an extra unit such as a garage, attic, or basement apartment; units in duplexes or triplexes; and units in any other property with two or more housing units.

Notes

The following types of units (and the properties containing these units) were either excluded from the original POMS sample, or were identified as being out of the scope of the survey when it was conducted:

- Units owned by a public housing authority
- Units owned by the United States military or any other federal agency
- Units that were owner-occupied
- Units that were vacant but were available for sale only
- Units that were vacant but were not available for rent or sale
- Units used primarily as second or vacation homes
- Units that were rental at the time of the 1993 American Housing Survey (AHS-N) but were no longer rental at the time of the POMS (November 1995 to June 1996)
- Units that became rental after the 1993 AHS-N (i.e., new construction and units converted from owner to rental)

Table 2.34–2.45

Data Sources:
  Building Permits Survey, Survey of Construction
References:
  U.S. Bureau of the Census, *Housing Starts*, Series C20, *Housing Completions*, Series C22, and *Characteristics of New Housing: 1997*, Current Construction Reports C25/97A, July 1998.

Definitions

Number and valuation of units authorized by building permit. The tables show only those units authorized by permit in the permit-issuing places included in the Building Permits Survey universe at a given time. The data are for new privately owned housing units intended for occupancy on a housekeeping basis (see definition within this Definitions list). They exclude hotels, motels, and other group residential structures such as nursing homes and college dormitories. The permit data also exclude mobile homes.

Current surveys indicate that construction is ultimately undertaken for all but a very small percentage of housing units authorized by building permits. A major portion typically get under way during the month of permit issuance and most of the remainder begin within the following 3 months. Because of this lag, private housing units authorized by building permit do not represent the number of units actually put into construction for a given period and therefore are not directly comparable to data on housing starts presented in other tables. In addition, the housing starts data include construction activity in both permit-issuing and non-permit-issuing areas, whereas the data reported on housing units authorized by permit pertain only to areas with building permit systems.

Detailed recent evidence is lacking as to how closely the valuation recorded for building permit purposes approximates the dollar amount of construction work involved.

Units authorized but not started. These "backlog" data represent the number of housing units authorized in all months up to and including the last day of the reporting period and not started as of that date without regard to the months of original permit issuance. Canceled, abandoned, expired, and revoked permits are excluded from the backlog.

Start of construction ("start"). The start of construction of a privately owned housing unit is when excavation begins for the footings or foundation of a building intended primarily as a housekeeping residential structure and designed for nontransient occupancy. All housing units in a multifamily building are defined as started when excavation for the building has begun. Beginning with statistics for September 1992, estimates of housing starts include units in residential structures being totally rebuilt on an existing foundation.

Completion of construction ("completion"). One-unit structures are defined as completed when all finish flooring has been installed (or carpeting, if used in place of finish flooring). If the building is occupied before all construction is finished, it is classified as completed at the time of occupancy. In buildings with two or more housing units, all the units in the building are counted as completed when 50 percent or more of the units are occupied or available for occupancy.

Under construction. Housing units are counted as under construction between start and completion, as defined here.

Housing unit. A housing unit is a single room or group of rooms intended for occupancy as separate living quarters by a family, by a group of unrelated persons living together, or by a person living alone. Separate living quarters are those in which the occupants do not live and eat with any other persons in the structure and that have direct access from the outside of the building or through a common hall that is used or intended to be used by the occupants of another unit or by the general public. Housing units include conventional "stick-built," prefabricated, panelized, componentized, sectional, and modular units. Mobile homes—single-wide and multi-wide—are excluded from the statistics in these tables.

Publicly owned housing units (contract awards) are excluded from the statistics. Units that are in structures built by private developers with partial public subsidies or that are for sale upon completion to local public housing authorities under the Department of Housing and Urban Development's "Turnkey" program are both classified as private housing.

Condominium unit. A condominium refers not to a housing unit in a particular type of structure, but rather to a type of ownership in which the owners of the individual housing units are also joint owners of the common areas of the building or community.

Housekeeping residential building. A housekeeping residential building is one consisting primarily of housing units. The data presented here exclude group quarters (such as dormitories and rooming houses), transient accommodations (such as transient hotels, motels, and tourist courts), mobile homes (trailers), moved or relocated buildings, and housing units created in an existing residential or nonresidential structure. However, in a building combining substantial residential and nonresidential floor areas, every effort is made to include the residential units in these statistics, even though the primary function of the entire building is for nonresidential purposes.

Units in structure (structure type). The statistics by units in structure refer to the structural characteristics of the building. The one-unit structure category (also referred to as "single-family" or "one-family" houses) includes fully detached, semidetached (semiattached, side-by-side), rowhouses, and townhouses. In the case of attached units, each must be separated from the adjacent unit by a ground-to-roof wall in order to be classified as a one-unit structure. Also, these units must not share heating/air-conditioning systems or interstructural public utilities, such as water supply, power supply, or sewage disposal lines. Manufactured homes are not covered in the Building Permits Survey or the Survey of Construction, and are therefore excluded from this category.

Units built one on top of another and those built side-by-side that do not have a ground-to-roof wall and/or have common facilities (e.g., attic, basement, heating plant, plumbing, etc.) are classified by the number of units in the structure (e.g., two-unit structure, three-unit structure, etc.). In these statistics, apartment buildings are defined as buildings containing five units or more. Apartments in a conventional-type apartment building may share a common basement, heating plant, stairs, entrance halls, and water supply and sewage disposal facilities. Townhouse apartments, though attached, are not separated by a ground-to-roof wall and/or share some interstructural facilities, such as water supply, sewage disposal, etc.

Type of ownership is not a criterion for structural classifications in the tables. A condominium apartment building is classified with apartment buildings in structures with five units or more, despite the fact that each unit is individually owned. Condominium townhouses may be in the one-unit category if each unit is separated from its neighbor by a ground-to-roof wall (no shared interstructural facilities), or in the multiunit building categories if they are not separated from each other by a ground-to-roof wall (shared interstructural facilities).

Contractor-built houses. This category includes all houses built for owner occupancy on the owner's land with construction supervised by a single general contractor.

Owner-built houses. This category includes houses built for owner occupancy, on the owner's land, under the supervision of the owner acting as his/her own general contractor. In most cases, owner-built houses are constructed partly by the owner and partly with paid help, but are sometimes built entirely with the employment of subcontractors. In a smaller number of cases, houses in this category are built on a "do-it-yourself" basis.

Stick-built. A stick-built home is built on site. It can include some factory components such as roof and floor trusses, wall panels, and door frames.

Modular. In this method, finished three-dimensional sections of the dwelling, built in a factory, are transported to the site to be joined together on a permanent foundation.

Other construction methods. This category includes panelized and precut construction methods, which are defined as follows:

Panelized. In this method, a package of wall panels, roof trusses, and other components are shipped from the factory to be assembled on site. The package may include all materials required to finish the house.

Precut. In this method a package of lumber or timber (logs), precut to exact size, length, and quantity, is assembled on site. The package may also include plumbing, wiring, and/or heating system elements.

Notes

In the tables on housing units authorized by building permit, starts, and completions, the definition of a housing unit differs from that used in tables on the housing stock. The primary definitional differences are that the tables related to housing production do not include publicly owned units or mobile homes. Housing stock statistics include both of these types of living quarters.

The tables on new privately owned housing units authorized and authorized but not started are divided into sections reflecting the number of permit-issuing places covered in the Building Permits Survey. The number of permit-issuing places has gradually expanded as more local areas have adopted building permit systems.

Relationship between authorizations, starts, and completions. In comparing data on permit issuance, housing starts, and housing completions, keep in mind the following:

- There are time lags between permit issuance and the start of construction and between the start of construction and completion. Tables 2.38 and 2.44 provide data on the average lengths of these lags.
- Permit data reflect only those permit-issuing places covered by the Building Permits Survey, whereas the data on starts and completions cover the entire United States. The difference in geographic coverage is relatively minor, however, as about 96 percent of new private housing units are constructed in permit-issuing places.
- A small percentage of units authorized by permit are never started and a small percentage of units are started in permit-issuing places without authorization.
- Approximately 15 percent of multifamily units in the building permit data are reclassified as single-family units in the starts data. This is part of the reason why multifamily starts are significantly lower than multifamily permits and why single-family starts sometimes exceed single-family permits. (Single-family starts also exceed single-family permits because, as noted previously, some single-family units are constructed outside of permit-issuing places and some units are started in permit-issuing places without authorization.)
- About 2 to 3 percent of single-family units are abandoned after start. That is, they do not proceed to completion.

Tables 2.46–2.49

Data Source:

Survey of New Mobile Home Placements

Reference:

U.S. Bureau of the Census, *Housing Starts*, Series C20, monthly.

Definitions

Mobile home. A mobile home is defined as a movable dwelling, 8 feet or more wide and 40 feet or more long, designed to be towed on its own chassis, with transportation gear integral to the unit when it leaves the factory, and without need of a permanent foundation. There are two general types of units. A single-wide is any unit so designated by a dealer and consisting of only one section and only one U.S. Department of Housing and Urban Development (HUD) label number. A double-wide is any unit so designated by a dealer and consisting of more than one section and more than one HUD label number.

Notes

These tabulations of mobile homes include multi-wides, which are counted as single units, and expandable mobile homes. Travel trailers, motor homes, and modular housing are excluded.

Increasingly, the term "manufactured housing" is being used in place of "mobile homes."

Tables 2.50–2.54

Data Source:

Survey of Market Absorption

References:

U.S. Bureau of the Census and U.S. Department of Housing and Urban Development. *Market Absorption of Apartments*, Current Housing Reports H130/97-A.

Definitions

Cooperatives and condominiums. In a cooperative, each member purchases shares in a nonprofit corporation that owns title to the cooperative building and the land upon which it is located. In return, the cooperative member receives the right to occupy a given unit within the cooperative. Each cooperative member is also responsible for paying rent to the corporation based on the unit's proportionate share of costs associated with operating the cooperative.

In contrast, the condominium resident owns his or her individual housing unit (e.g., owns the fee simple to the unit). The condominium owner also owns an undivided percentage interest in the common areas, including grounds and parts of the building not included in individual units, of the condominium development.

Federally subsidized apartments. Units categorized as federally subsidized are those built under the following programs of the U.S. Department of Housing and Urban Development: Low Income Housing Assistance (Section 8), Senior Citizens Housing Direct Loans (Section 202), and all units in buildings containing apartments in the Federal Housing Administration rent supplement program. The data on privately financed units include privately owned housing subsidized by state and local government.

Other apartments. Other apartments include timesharing units, continuing care retirement units, and turnkey housing (privately built for and sold to local public housing authorities subsequent to completion).

Notes

The Survey of Market Absorption adopted new ratio estimation procedures in 1990 to derive more accurate estimates of completions. The new procedures were used for the first time for processing annual data for 1990. Caution must be used in comparing completions in 1990 and later years with those in earlier years.

Table 2.55

Data Source:

Value of New Construction Put in Place

References:

U.S. Bureau of the Census, *Value of New Construction Put in Place*, Current Construction Reports, Series C30.

Definitions

Value of new construction put in place. This is a measure of the value of construction installed or erected at the site during a given period. For an individual project, it includes the following:

1. Cost of materials installed or erected
2. Cost of labor (both by contractors and force account) and a proportionate share of the cost of construction equipment rental
3. Contractor's profit

4. Project owner's overhead and office costs
5. Cost of architectural and engineering work
6. Miscellaneous costs chargeable to the project on the owner's books
7. Interest and taxes paid during construction

The total value-in-place for a given period is the sum of the value of work done on all projects under way during this period, regardless of when work on each individual project was started or when payment was made to the contractors.

Private residential construction. Private residential construction includes construction of new housing units and improvements. New housing units include new houses, apartments, condominiums, and townhouses. The classification excludes residential units in buildings that are primarily nonresidential. It also excludes mobile homes and houseboats. Improvements include remodeling, additions, and major replacements to properties subsequent to completion of the original building. The classification also includes construction of additional housing units in existing residential structures, finishing of basements and attics, modernization of kitchens, bathrooms, etc. Also included are improvements outside of residential structures, such as the addition of swimming pools and garages, and replacement of major equipment items such as water heaters, furnaces, and central air conditioners. Maintenance and repair work is not included.

Notes

See Appendix B, "Value of New Construction Put in Place," for a discussion of how the statistics in this table are developed.

Table 2.56

Data Sources:
   Consumer Expenditure Survey and Residential Improvement and Repairs Mail Survey
References:
   U.S. Bureau of the Census. *Expenditures for Residential Improvements and Repairs*, Current Construction Reports, Series C50, quarterly.

Definitions

Residential property. Residential properties are defined as those having half or more of the enclosed space devoted to nontransient residential use. A residential property consists of the land in one ownership unit, all residential structures on this land, and any facilities attached to the land. It includes the house and additional residential structures on the land, and auxiliary nonresidential structures such as a garage or a workshop. For the nonresident owners and owners of properties with five housing units or more, property identification is generally determined by bookkeeping practices. Groups of buildings owned by one person or organization can be classified as one or more properties depending on whether separate expenditure data are kept by the owner.

Construction improvements. Expenditures for construction improvements are capital expenditures that add to the value or useful life of a property. Since the classification is based on the concept of additions, alterations, and major replacements rather than dollar value, some very small expenditures that may not be considered capital investments are included among the improvements, such as installing a new electrical socket or garbage disposal. Construction improvements cover additions to residential structures, alterations within residential structures, additions and alterations on properties outside residential structures, and major replacements.

Additions to residential structures. These refer to the actual enlargement of the structure either by adding a wing, room, porch, attached garage, shed, or carport, or by raising the roof or digging a basement.

Alterations within residential structures. This category includes changes or improvements made within or on the structure. The changes or improvements range from a complete restructuring, which involves removal of the entire interior of the structure and remodeling it, to the installation of a new electric service outlet, wall switch, or new shelves.

Additions and alterations on property outside residential structures. These improvements include laying or improving walks or driveways; building walls or fences; creating or improving recreational facilities such as swimming pools, tennis courts, or barbecue fireplaces; constructing detached garages, sheds, patios, green houses, or improving these by the installation of electricity, drains, or new storage facilities. Grading and filling are included, but landscaping is not.

Major replacements. The following is a list of relatively expensive items that, when replaced, are considered to be construction improvements as opposed to repairs:

- Complete furnace or boiler
- Entire roof
- Central air conditioner
- All siding
- Water heater
- Entire electrical wiring
- Doors
- Plumbing fixtures
- All water pipes
- Windows
- Septic tank or cesspool
- Sink or laundry tub
- Complete walks or driveways
- Garbage disposal unit

In general, the distinction between major replacements and additions and alterations is that major replacements are not innovations. Installation of a bathtub where there had not been one before is an alteration, but the substitution of a new bathtub for an old one is a major replacement.

Doors and windows were moved from the maintenance and repairs category to the major replacements category in 1993.

Maintenance and repairs. These expenditures represent current costs for incidental maintenance and repairs that keep a property in ordinary working condition, rather than additional investment in the property.

Maintenance includes expenses for painting, papering, floor sanding, furnace cleaning or adjustment, etc. Repairs include many kinds of expenditures for plumbing, heating, electrical work, and other kinds of activity involved in the upkeep of residential properties. Repairs also include replacements of parts and of whole units except for a select list specified above as major replacement expenditures. For example, roof repairs (including replacement of shingles, gutters, etc.) are classified under maintenance and repairs, but a complete reroofing is classified as a major replacement. Plumbing repairs may include extensive replacement of water pipes, but if the entire piping system is removed and a new one put in, the expenditures for the work are classified as major replacements. Maintenance and repairs do not include expenses for trash and snow removal, lawn maintenance and landscaping, or cleaning and janitorial services.

Notes

New survey methods were used to develop estimates of expenditures for residential improvements and repairs beginning in January 1984. A description of the earlier method appears in Current Construction Reports C50/84A, issued April 1985.

Types of expenditures covered. The expenditures covered in the table are those connected with construction activity intended to maintain or improve the property. The expenditures involve expenses for maintenance and repairs, additions, alterations, and major replacements (see preceding definitions) that are made on the property by the owners. Included are all costs, for both the inside and outside of the house, whether on the main dwelling, on other structures on the property incidental to the residential use of the main dwellings, or for the grounds on which the structures are erected.

As a general principle, expenses connected with items not permanently attached or firmly affixed to some part of the house or property are not included in the table. Thus, expenses connected with the repair or replacement of household appliances, such as stoves, refrigerators, television sets, room air conditioners, etc., are excluded, as are costs connected with house furnishings such as furniture, rugs, and draperies. While the cost of appliances is excluded, the construction cost of building-in such appliances (e.g., the cost of building-in a wall oven) is included in the table. Everyday household and housekeeping expenses such as waxing floors and furniture, cleaning walls and windows, etc., are not included. Expenditures for grading, draining, fencing, and paving are included, but costs of landscaping (e.g., planting of flowers, trees, shrubs, etc.) are not included.

Expenditures included in the table cover work done under contract or by hired labor, materials purchased by owners, and the cost of purchasing or renting tools and equipment for purposes of carrying on the work. However, no attempt is made to estimate or include the value of labor in do-it-yourself jobs.

Types of properties covered. This table covers improvement and repair expenditures by property owners for residential properties in the 50 states and the District of Columbia with the exceptions noted later. These data cover single and multiunit structures, publicly and privately owned structures, nonfarm and farm properties, and residential properties that are occupied by owners or renters or are vacant.

Information on properties classified as primarily nonresidential is excluded even though such properties may contain some residential space. Also excluded are residential structures on the grounds of institutions, schools, convents, Armed Forces installations, etc.; hotels, motels, tourist cabins, mobile homes, and boarding houses; and unusual living quarters, such as tents, boats, etc.

Expenditures made by renters are not included in the table. A study of renters' expenditures in 1989 showed that they accounted for less than 1 percent of all expenditures for improvements and repairs.

Part 3: Market Outcomes

Table 3.1

Data Source:
    Builders Economic Council Survey
Reference:
    National Association of Home Builders, *Housing Market Statistics*, monthly.

Definitions

Composite housing market index. The composite housing market index is a weighted average of current sales, buyer traffic, and sales expectations for single-family detached homes reported in a survey of home builders. The index can range from zero to 100 with 50 representing average. If all the respondents say their sales are "good" (or "high" for buyer traffic), the index is 100. If all the respondents say "poor" (or "low" for buyer traffic), the index is zero.

Notes

With the exception of the composite index, the numbers in the table represent the percent of respondents who indicate that sales or expected sales in the given housing type category are "good" or "poor" ("high" or "low" for buyer traffic). The table does not show the "average" response category, which can be obtained by subtracting the "good" and "poor" (or "high" and "low" for buyer traffic) categories from the total of 100 percent.

Annual data are the average of 12 months.

Table 3.2

Data Source:
    National Housing Survey
Reference:
    Fannie Mae, *Fannie Mae National Housing Survey*, annual.

Notes

The following questions from the National Housing Survey are used to collect the data presented in the table:

"In general, is this a good time or a bad time to buy a home?" For those responding "good time" or "bad time," the survey asks, "Would you say it is a very (good time/bad time) or just a somewhat (good time/bad time) to buy a home?"

Table 3.3

Data Source:
    Survey of Real Estate Trends
Reference:
    Federal Deposit Insurance Corporation, *Survey of Real Estate Trends*, quarterly.

Definitions

Summary index of real estate trends. Each regional index is a summary measure of opinions about changes in residential market conditions in the past 3 months expressed by a sample of examiners and asset managers at lending regulatory agencies. The index is based on respondents' answers to the question: "What would you say is the general direction of the residential market now compared with 3 months ago?" Possible responses are: "a lot better," "a little better," "same," "a little worse," "a lot worse," and "not sure." In constructing the summary index, a value of 100 is assigned to responses indicating that conditions are "better," and a value of zero is given to responses saying conditions are "worse." A "no change" answer is assigned a value of 50. The summary index at the regional level is the sum of these values for respondents from the region divided by the number of respondents from the region. The national index is calculated as the weighted average of the regional indexes. An index above 50 generally indicates that, in the opinion of most respondents, the residential market has improved over the past 3 months; conversely, a summary index below 50 is an indication of declining market conditions.

Notes

In addition to the question on recent residential market trends, the Survey of Real Estate Trends also asks the following questions:

- "In general, how would you characterize the residential real estate market?"

- "How would you characterize the current volume of home sales?"
- "How would you characterize sales prices of existing homes?"
- "How would you characterize the current volume of new home construction?"
- "How would you characterize the current volume of rental apartment construction?"

See "Survey of Real Estate Trends" in Appendix B for data on responses to individual questions.

Tables 3.4–3.5

Data Source:
Current Population Survey/Housing Vacancy Survey
Reference:
U.S. Bureau of the Census, Current Population Survey/Housing Vacancy Survey, Series H111.

Definitions

Asking sales price. The asking sales price is at the time of the interview and may differ from the price at which the property is actually sold. It includes the price of a one-unit structure and the land on which it is located and may also include additional structures such as garages, sheds, barns, and so forth.

Asking rent. The asking rent applies to the amount asked for the unit at the time of interview and may differ from the rent contracted for when the unit is occupied. The table excludes data on vacant, for-rent single-family structures on lots of 10 acres or more.

Notes

See Appendix B under "Current Population Survey" for a discussion of major recent changes to the Current Population Survey/Housing Vacancy Survey (CPS/HVS) beginning in January 1994 that necessitate caution in comparing data for 1994 and later with earlier data.

See the Notes section to Tables 2.1–2.2 for a discussion of comparability of the CPS/HVS to other data sources.

Tables 3.6–3.10

Data Sources:
U.S. Bureau of the Census, Survey of Construction/Housing Sales Survey, and National Association of Realtors®, Existing Home Sales Survey

References:
U.S. Bureau of the Census and U.S. Department of Housing and Urban Development, New One-Family Houses Sold, Current Construction Reports, Series C25, monthly. National Association of Realtors, *Real Estate Outlook*, monthly. For a comparison of new and existing home sales data, see Michael S. Carliner, "New and Existing Sales," *Housing Economics*, June 1992.

Definitions

New single-family house. Single-family (one-family, one-unit) houses include fully detached, semidetached (semiattached, side-by-side), rowhouses, and townhouses. In the case of attached units, each must be separated from the adjacent unit by an unbroken ground-to-roof wall to be classified as single-family or one-unit. In addition, attached units must not share heating/air-conditioning systems or interstructural public utilities such as water supply, power supply, or sewage disposal lines. Units built one on top of another and those built side-by-side that do not have a ground-to-roof wall and/or have common facilities (e.g., attic, basement, heating plant, plumbing, etc.) are not considered one-family and are classified by the number of units in the structure (two-unit structure, three-unit structure, etc.) Tables 3.6 and 3.8 only include sales of one-family houses that are either not yet completed or, if completed, have not been previously occupied.

Existing single-family house. An existing single-family home is a house that has been previously occupied prior to sale.

Cooperatives and condominiums. In a cooperative, each member purchases shares in a nonprofit corporation that owns title to the cooperative building and the land upon which it is located. In return, the cooperative member receives the right to occupy a given unit within the cooperative. Each cooperative member is also responsible for paying rent to the corporation based on the unit's proportionate share of costs associated with operating the cooperative.

In contrast, the condominium resident owns his or her individual housing unit (e.g., owns the fee simple to the unit). The condominium owner also owns an undivided percentage interest in the common areas, including grounds and parts of the building not included in individual units, of the condominium development.

New houses sold. The category "new houses sold" includes all houses for which a sales contract has been signed or a deposit accepted. This includes houses for which a sales contract is signed or deposit accepted before construction is actually started. For instance, the category includes houses sold from a model or from plans before any work is started on the footings or foundations. It also includes houses sold while under construction or after completion (e.g., houses built on speculation). The data on new homes sold exclude contractor-built houses, owner-built houses, houses built to be rented, out-of-scope types (such as non-residential buildings), and mobile homes (trailers).

The Housing Sales Survey does not follow through to completion of the sales transaction (e.g., settlement). Land must be included in the transaction.

Existing houses sold. The majority of existing home sales reflect closings of sales contracts. However, some of the sales represent "pendings," that is, sales contracts that have not yet closed.

New home sales price. The sales price in the Housing Sales Survey is the price agreed upon between the purchaser and the seller at the time the first sales contract is signed or deposit made. It includes the price of the improved lot. The sales price does not reflect any subsequent price changes resulting from change orders or from any other factors affecting the price of the house. Furthermore, the sales price does not include the cost of any extras or options paid for in cash by the purchaser or otherwise not included in the original sales price reported.

Notes

Relationship between new single-family homes sold and single-family homes started and completed. New single-family home sales are significantly less than new single-family homes started or completed because of differences in unit coverage. All new single-family residential units (not including mobile homes) are reflected in starts and completions data. These construction data include units built for rent, those built by a contractor on the owner's land, and those built by the owner. New home sales data, on the other hand, include only those units that are built to be sold where the purchase of the lot is included in the transaction. Therefore, the sales data exclude contractor-built houses, owner-built houses, and houses built to be rented.

Comparison of new and existing single-family home sales data. As indicated in the definitions above, new sin-

gle-family home sales are based on sales contracts, whereas existing sales include a mix of contracts and closings. Because most of the existing sales data are based on closings, movements in existing sales tend to lag behind movements in new home sales and are not as timely an indicator of changes in the market.

New home sales data, which are based primarily on a sample of building permits in permit-issuing places, are subject to sampling error. In addition, preliminary new home sales estimates may be substantially revised in subsequent months because of late reports of home sales and because of sales that occur prior to the issuance of building permits.

Existing home sales data, on the other hand, cover virtually all of the existing home sales handled by real estate agents in the localities covered by the Existing Home Sales Survey and are therefore subject to little sampling error. Because the existing home sales data are limited to those transactions handled by real estate agents, and therefore do not represent the universe of existing home sales, weights based on homeowner mobility observed in the decennial census are applied to the agent-reported sales to develop estimates of total existing home sales.

For additional discussion of the characteristics of new and existing sales data, see Carliner (1992).

Table 3.11

Data Source:
  Survey of New Mobile Home Placements

Reference:
  U.S. Bureau of the Census, *Housing Starts*, Current Construction Reports Series C20, monthly.

Definitions

Mobile home. A mobile home is defined as a movable dwelling, 8 feet or more wide and 40 feet or more long, designed to be towed on its own chassis, with transportation gear integral to the unit when it leaves the factory, and without need of a permanent foundation. The data include multi-wide mobile homes, which are counted as single units, and expandable mobile homes. Excluded are travel trailers, motor homes, and modular housing.

Sales price. The sales prices of new mobile homes shown in this table are reported by dealers who are instructed to include dealer setup costs. In some cases, there may be additional costs to prepare units for occupancy not included in the sales prices reported.

Beginning in 1980, the average sales prices are computed from data for mobile homes sold at or before the time they are placed on a site. Prices (values) of mobile homes leased or sold after placement are not collected. The average sales price computation for mobile homes placed prior to 1980 included not only the sales price of those sold, but also the intended sales price of those for sale and the value of leased mobile homes.

Notes

Note that these data show the average sales prices of mobile homes sold, whereas the data in Tables 3.9 and 3.10 for new and existing single-family home sales show the median sales price.

Tables 3.12–3.13

Data Source:

Consumer Price Index

References:

Historical and current data are available at the Bureau of Labor Statistics' Web site via "Selective Access," <http://146.142.4.24/cgi-bin/dsrv?mu>. See also their monthly Consumer Price Index news releases. For historical data, see also Eva E. Jacobs, ed. *Handbook of U.S. Labor Statistics: Employment, Earnings, Prices, Productivity, and Other Labor Data,* and Courtenay M. Slater, ed. *Business Statistics of the United States.*

Definitions

Housing component. The housing item includes expenditures made by owners and renters for shelter and for household-related expenses including fuel and other utilities, household furnishings, household services, and household supplies.

Shelter component. These are expenditures directly related to housing services. Renter costs include rental payments and other rental costs, such as tenant insurance. Changes in renter costs are measured directly from a sample of approximately 35,000 renter-occupied units.

The Bureau of Labor Statistics (BLS) estimates owner costs by matching each house in a sample of about 30,000 owner-occupied units with two or more rental units that are similar in terms of location, structure type (e.g., single-family, mobile home, etc.), and general characteristics (e.g., size of unit, number of rooms, air conditioning, etc.). The change in rent charged for these matched rental units is used to estimate the change in the implicit rent for the homeowners; that is, the rent that homeowners could receive for leasing their units to others. This estimated rent for homeowners is called "owners' equivalent rent." In addition to owners' equivalent rent, homeowner costs also include expenditures for insurance and maintenance and repairs.

Notes

BLS switched to the rental equivalence approach in 1983. This approach measures the consumption value of a home (i.e., its value as a place to sleep, fix meals, relax, entertain, garden, etc.) and not its value as an investment. Prior to 1983, the homeowner cost component of the Consumer Price Index reflected both the consumption and the investment value of homeownership. Under this earlier method, BLS treated the purchase of a home similarly to the purchase of other consumer goods or services. In addition to changes in home prices, the pre-1983 homeownership component attempted to measure the change in expected financing costs resulting from the purchase of a home. The pre-1983 homeowner cost component also reflected changes in expenses incurred by all existing homeowners for property taxes, property insurance, and maintenance and repairs.

BLS adopted another revision in the shelter series for owners in January 1995 to correct a flaw in calculation procedures that overstated changes in owners' equivalent rent by about 0.6 percent a year.

Effective with the release of January 1998 data, the Consumer Price Index reflects several revisions, including an updated area sample based on the population distribution from the 1990 Census and new expenditure weights based on 1993–95 spending patterns. In addition to changes to the composition of some group and subgroup indexes, there were also changes in the availability of, and item codes for, published item and area indexes. The tables contained herein were constructed using the old item structure and coding system.

Table 3.14–3.15

Data Source:

Survey of Construction/Housing Sales Survey

References:

U.S. Bureau of the Census and U.S. Department of Housing and Urban Development. *New One-Family Houses Sold,* Current Construction Reports Series C25.

Definitions

Fixed-weighted price index (Laspeyres). The Laspeyres Index measures price changes over time of a home with the average characteristics of new homes built during some period in the past (in the current index series, houses built during 1992). Because the Laspeyres Index is used to estimate changes in the price of a house of fixed characteristics, it does not permit substitution of house features that may accompany changes in consumer preferences. Such substitution may permit consumers to maintain constant house quality as the mix of characteristics in the average house changes over time.

Chain-type annual-weighted price index (Fisher Ideal). The Fisher Ideal Index, which was published by the Census Bureau for the first time in May 1997, is designed to accommodate a changing mix of characteristics in the average house while holding house quality constant. For this index, the price change between two succeeding periods is not measured for a house of fixed characteristics, but rather for a house with the average characteristics of those houses built during the two periods. The index is calculated as the geometric mean in two succeeding time periods of the Laspeyres Index and the Paasche Index, which is another fixed-weighted index that measures the price change of a house with average characteristics from some period in the past to the current period.

Notes

The price indexes are computed using data from the Census Bureau's Housing Sales Survey, which collects data on the contract prices of houses built for sale. The Housing Sales Survey excludes houses built by the owner on the owner's land, contractor-built houses, and houses built for rent. For a discussion of the procedures and formulae used to compute the Laspeyres, Paasche, and Fisher Ideal price indexes, see U.S. Bureau of the Census, *New One-Family Houses Sold: March 1997*, Current Construction Reports C25/973, May 1997.

Comparing the price index with average sales price movements. Unlike the price indexes, which hold house quality constant, the average sales price of new houses actually sold may change from one period to the next not only because of price changes that are independent of quality, but also because of shifts in quality (e.g., the proportions of new houses with different characteristics). For example, the Laspeyres Index for the United States increased 4.3 percent from 1992 to 1993 whereas the average price of new houses actually sold during this period increased 2.5 percent. This difference is due to an overall shift toward the construction of smaller houses, houses with fewer amenities, or houses located in less expensive geographical areas. This comparison may be clearer if one were to think of the Laspeyres price index in terms of the prices shown in the next-to-last column of Table 3.14. The price index indicates that the kinds of new houses sold in 1992, which had an average sales price of $144,100, would have sold for $150,300 in 1993. However, the average price of new houses actually sold in 1993 was $147,700. As stated above, the difference of $2,600 may be attributed to the shift toward smaller houses, houses with fewer amenities, or houses built in less expensive areas.

Limitations of the price indexes. Although the price indexes are designed to measure price changes, keeping quality constant, houses may vary from one time period to the next because of changes in workmanship, materials, and mechanical equipment that are not measured by the characteristics used to estimate the index. Hence, some of the movement in a price index over time may be attributable to unmeasured changes in house quality.

Table 3.16

Data Source:
    Office of Federal Housing Enterprise Oversight
References:
    Office of Federal Housing Enterprise Oversight, *House Price Index. Fourth Quarter 1997*. See also Charles A. Calhoun, *OFHEO House Price Indexes: HPI Technical Description*, Office of Federal Housing Enterprise Oversight, March 1996. See also Dan Mercer, "State and Regional Home Price Growth," *Housing Economics*, January 1997.

Definitions

OFHEO house price index. The Office of Federal Housing Enterprise Oversight's (OFHEO) house price index (HPI) measures changes in house values for single-family detached homes on which at least two mortgages were originated and subsequently purchased or securitized by Fannie Mae or Freddie Mac (the government-sponsored enterprises, or GSEs). Because the HPI measures changes in the value of the same single-family property observed at two or more different points in time, the index helps to control for differences in quality across homes and therefore is referred to as a "constant quality" house price index. The value of the home at each observed transaction is measured either by the sales price for purchase transactions or by the appraised value for refinancing transactions.

The mortgages included in the database are both conforming and conventional, indicating that they meet the underwriting requirements for purchase by the GSEs, do not exceed the conforming loan limit for single-family homes, and are not backed by the Federal Housing Administration or the Department of Veterans Affairs. OFHEO produces the index quarterly for the nation, the nine Census divisions, and the 50 states and the District of Columbia.

Each quarterly release produces new data for the most recent quarter and also results in changes in the historical data. Historical data for the subnational indexes may be substantially revised with each new release.

Notes

Availability of other repeat-transaction house price indexes based on GSE data. Fannie Mae and Freddie Mac jointly publish a Conventional Mortgage Home Price Index (CMHPI) based on essentially the same database used by the Office of Federal Housing Enterprise Oversight to produce its house price index. Index values from the two series differ, however, because of differences in methodology. The CMHPI is available at the national and census division levels. Freddie Mac also produces its own state- and metropolitan-level indexes based on the same data.

Limitations of repeat-transaction house price indexes. House price indexes based on GSE data are attractive because they are based on a very large sample (over 7 million repeat transactions in the national sample as of the fourth quarter of 1997) and help to control for changes over time in the quality of homes sold. However, these indexes have several limitations that include the following:

- The GSE database does not include all types of homes. It excludes very expensive homes that have mortgages exceeding the conforming loan limit. It also excludes homes with mortgages that do not meet the GSE underwriting guidelines, are backed by the federal government, or are sold without mortgages. Mortgage transactions on attached or multiunit properties are also excluded.
- The sample is biased toward high-turnover homes, which may have physical characteristics and pat-

terns of price change that differ from those of all homes.
- Some unobserved changes in quality occur for the repeat-transaction properties over time.
- For refinancing transactions, the GSE collects information on appraised value rather than purchase price. The appraised value may not represent the actual market value of the home.

For additional discussion of these and other limitations of house price indexes that are based on the GSE data, see Mercer (1997).

Tables 3.17–3.21

Data Source:
Current Population Survey/Housing Vacancy Survey
References:
U.S. Bureau of the Census, Current Population Survey/Housing Vacancy Survey, Series H111. See also U.S. Bureau of the Census, "Housing Vacancy Survey," <http://www.census.gov/ftp/pub/hhes/www/hvs.html>.

Definitions

See description for Tables 2.1–2.2 for additional definitions.

Vacant housing units. A housing unit is vacant if no one is living in it at the time of the interview, unless its occupants are only temporarily absent. In addition, a vacant unit may be one that is occupied entirely by persons who have a usual residence elsewhere.

New units not yet occupied are classified as vacant housing units if construction has reached a point where all exterior windows and doors are installed and final usable floors are in place. Vacant units are excluded if they are exposed to the elements, that is, if the roof, walls, windows, or doors no longer protect the interior from the elements, or if there is positive evidence (such as a sign on the house or block) that the unit is to be demolished or is condemned. Also excluded are quarters being used entirely for nonresidential purposes, such as a store or an office, or quarters used for the storage of business supplies or inventory, machinery, or agricultural products.

Vacant sleeping rooms in lodging houses, transient accommodations, barracks, and other quarters not defined as housing units are not included in these statistics.

Rental vacancy rate. The rental vacancy rate is the proportion of the year-round rental inventory that is vacant for rent. The rate is computed using the following formula:

$$\text{Rental vacancy rate} = \frac{\text{Vacant year-round units for rent}}{\substack{\text{Rental occupied units}} + \substack{\text{Vacant year-round units rented but awaiting occupancy}} + \substack{\text{Vacant year-round units for rent}}}$$

Rental vacancy rates by units in structure. The rental vacancy rates in Table 3.18 are derived by dividing vacant year-round units for rent in structures with a given number of units (such as five or more unit structures) by all rental units in buildings of that size. Excluded from the denominator are year-round units rented but awaiting occupancy. For example, the numerator for the rental vacancy rate for units in structures with five or more units is all vacant year-round units for rent in buildings with five or more units. The denominator is (1) all renter-occupied units in buildings with five or more units; and (2) vacant year-round units for rent in buildings with five or more units.

Homeowner vacancy rate. The homeowner vacancy rate is the proportion of the year-round homeowner inventory that is vacant for sale. The rates are computed using the following formula:

$$\text{Homeowner vacancy rate} = \frac{\text{Vacant year-round units for sale only}}{\substack{\text{Owner occupied units}} + \substack{\text{Vacant year-round units sold but awaiting occupancy}} + \substack{\text{Vacant year-round units for sale only}}}$$

Homeowner vacancy rates by units in structure. The homeowner vacancy rates in Table 3.18 are derived by dividing vacant year-round units for sale in structures with a given number of units (such as five-or-more-unit structures) by all homeowner units in buildings of that size. Excluded from the denominator are year-round units sold but awaiting occupancy. For example, the numerator for the homeowner vacancy rate for units in structures with five or more units is all vacant year-round units for sale only in structures with five-or-more-units. The denominator is, (1) all owner-occupied units in buildings with five or more units; and (2) vacant year-round units for sale in buildings with five or more units.

Number of housing units in structure. A structure is a separate building that either has open space on all four sides or is separated from other structures by dividing walls that extend from ground to roof. In double houses, rowhouses, and houses attached to nonresidential structures, each building is a structure if the common wall between them goes from ground to roof. Sheds and private garages that adjoin houses are not counted as separate structures. In apartment developments, each building with open space on all sides is considered a separate structure. The count of housing units in a structure is the total number of units in the structure, including both occupied and vacant units. Occupied mobile homes or trailers, tents, and boats are included in the one-unit structure category.

Notes

See Tables 2.1–2.2 for notes on comparability between the Current Population Survey/Housing Vacancy Survey (CPS/HVS) and the decennial census. Research has shown that the CPS/HVS and the 1990 Census produced significant differences for vacancy characteristics. The rental vacancy rate from the April 1990 Census was 8.5 percent, whereas the CPS/HVS reported the rental vacancy rate of 7.2 percent for the first half of 1990. The April 1990 Census had a homeowner vacancy rate of 2.1 percent, while the CPS/HVS had a vacancy rate of approximately 1.7 percent for the first half of 1990.

These differences illustrate that, for these characteristics as well as others, caution should be used when making comparisons between the 1990 Census and the CPS/HVS.

Several major changes were introduced to the CPS/HVS beginning in January 1994 that necessitate caution in comparing data for 1994 and later with earlier data. The Census Bureau estimates that the introduction of 1990 Census–based population controls had a minimal effect on vacancy rate estimates from the CPS/HVS. The Census Bureau was unable to determine the quantitative effects of the implementation of Computer Assisted Survey Information Collection on vacancy rate estimates. See Appendix B under "Current Population Survey" for additional discussion of the survey changes.

Tables 3.22–3.23

Data Source:
Survey of Market Absorption

References:
U.S. Bureau of the Census and U.S. Department of Housing and Urban Development, *Market Absorption of Apartments*, Current Housing Reports H130/97-A. See also U.S. Bureau of the Census, "Survey of Market Absorption," <http://www.census.gov/hhes/www/soma.html>.

Definitions

See Definitions for Tables 2.50–2.54 for additional definitions.

Absorption rates. Absorption rates are calculated based on the first time an apartment offered for rent is rented after completion, or the first time a cooperative or condominium apartment is sold after completion. If apartments initially intended to be sold as cooperative or condominium units are offered by the builder or building owner for rent, they are counted as rental apartments.

Notes

The Survey of Market Absorption adopted new ratio estimation procedures in 1990 to derive more accurate estimates of completions. The new procedures were used for the first time for processing annual data for 1990. Caution must be used in comparing completions in 1990 and later years with those in earlier years.

Table 3.24–3.26

Data Source:
Decennial Census
References:
U.S. Bureau of the Census, "Housing: Then and Now, 50 Years of Decennial Censuses. Homeownership," <http://www.census.gov/hhes/housing/census/owner.html>; and "Housing: Then and Now, 50 Years of Decennial Censuses. Ownership Rates," <http://www.census.gov/hhes/housing/census/ownrate.html>. Tables prepared by Robert Bonnette. For information on housing unit concepts and definitions, see U.S. Bureau of the Census, *1990 Census of Population and Housing: Guide, Part A. Text* 1990 CPH-R-1A, September 1992; and U.S. Bureau of the Census, *200 Years of U.S. Census Taking: Population and Housing Questions, 1790–1990*, November 1989. The "Definitions of Subject Characteristics" appendix of many 1990 Census publications

also contains definitions of housing items and notes on comparability across censuses.

Definitions

Homeownership rate. The homeownership rate is the proportion of households that are owners. It is calculated by dividing the number of households that are owners (owner-occupied housing units) by the total number of households (total occupied housing units).

Recent mover. See Definitions for Table 1.42.

Age of householder. The age classification is based on the age of the person in complete years as of April 1, 1990. The age response to the census question was usually used to represent a person's age. However, when the age response was unacceptable or unavailable, a person's age was derived from an acceptable year-of-birth response in a separate question. Tabulations by the age of the householder are derived from the age responses for each householder.

Review of detailed 1990 Census information indicated that respondents tended to provide their age as of the date of completion of the questionnaire, not their age as of April 1, 1990. In addition, there may have been a tendency for respondents to round their age up if they were close to having a birthday. It is likely that approximately 10 percent of persons in most age groups are actually 1 year younger.

In each census since 1940, the age of a person was assigned when it was not reported. Since 1960, assignment of unknown age has been performed by a general procedure known as "imputation." The specific procedures for imputing age have been different in each census.

Race. The concept of race as used by the Census Bureau reflects self-identification; it does not denote any clear-cut scientific definition of biological stock. The data for race represent self-classification by people according to the race with which they most closely identify. Furthermore, it is recognized that the categories of the race item include both racial and national origin or sociocultural groups.

During direct interviews conducted by enumerators, if a person could not provide a single response to the race question, he or she was asked to select, using self-identification, the group that best described his or her racial identity. If a person could not provide a single race response, the race of the mother was used. If a single race response could not be provided for the person's mother, the first race reported by the person was used. In all cases where occupied housing units, households, or families are classified by race, the race of the householder is used.

The Black race category includes persons who indicated their race as "Black or Negro" or reported entries such as African American, Afro-American, Black Puerto Rican, Jamaican, Nigerian, West Indian, or Haitian.

Hispanic origin. Persons of Hispanic origin are those who classified themselves in one of the specific Hispanic origin categories listed on the census questionnaire—"Mexican," "Puerto Rican," or "Cuban"—as well as those who indicated that they were of "other Spanish/Hispanic" origin. Persons of "Other Spanish/Hispanic" origin are those whose origins are from Spain, the Spanish-speaking countries of Central or South America, or the Dominican Republic, or they are persons of Hispanic origin identifying themselves generally as Spanish, Spanish-American, Hispanic, Hispano, Latino, and so on.

Origin can be viewed as the ancestry, nationality group, lineage, or country of birth of the person or the person's parents or ancestors before their arrival in the United States. Persons of Hispanic origin may be of any race.

During direct interviews conducted by enumerators, if a person could not provide a single origin response, he or she was asked to select, based on self-identification, the group that best described his or her origin or descent. If a person could not provide a single group, the origin of the person's mother was used. If a single group could not be provided for the person's mother, the first origin reported by the person was used.

If any household member failed to respond to the Spanish/Hispanic origin question, a response was assigned by the computer according to the reported entries of other household members by using specific rules of precedence of household relationship. In the processing of sample questionnaires, responses to other questions on the questionnaire, such as ancestry and place of birth, were used to assign an origin before any reference was made to the origin reported by other household members. If an origin was not entered for any household member, an origin was assigned from another household according to the race of the householder.

The 1990 data on Hispanic origin are generally comparable with those for the 1980 Census. However, there are some differences in the format of the Hispanic origin question between the two censuses. For 1990, the word "descent" was deleted from the 1980 wording. In addition, the term "Mexican-Amer." used in 1980 was short-

ened further to "Mexican-Am." to reduce misreporting (of "American") in this category detected in the 1980 Census. Finally, the 1990 question allowed those who reported as "other Spanish/Hispanic" to write in their specific Hispanic origin group.

Misreporting in the "Mexican-Amer." category of the 1980 Census item on Spanish/Hispanic origin may affect the comparability of 1980 and 1990 Census data for persons of Hispanic origin for certain areas of the country. An evaluation of the 1980 Census item on Spanish/Hispanic origin indicated that there was misreporting in the Mexican origin category by White and Black persons in certain areas. The study results showed evidence that the misreporting occurred in the South (excluding Texas), the Northeast (excluding the New York City area), and a few states in the Midwest region. Also, results based on available data suggest that the impact of possible misreporting of Mexican origin in the 1980 Census was severe in those portions of the above-mentioned regions where the Hispanic origin population was generally sparse. However, national 1980 Census data on the Mexican origin population or total Hispanic origin population at the national level was not seriously affected by the reporting problem.

The 1990 and 1980 Census data on the Hispanic population are not directly comparable with 1970 Spanish-origin data because of a number of factors: (1) overall improvements in the 1980 and 1990 Censuses, (2) better coverage of the population, (3) improved question designs, and (4) an effective public relations campaign by the Census Bureau with the assistance of national and community ethnic groups.

Specific changes in question design between the 1970 and 1980 Censuses included the placement of the category "No, not Spanish/Hispanic" as the first category in that question. (The corresponding category appeared last in the 1970 question.) Also, the 1970 category "Central or South American" was deleted because in 1970 some respondents misinterpreted the category; furthermore, the designations "Mexican-American" and "Chicano" were added to the Spanish/Hispanic origin question in 1980. In the 1970 Census, the question on Spanish origin was asked of only a 5-percent sample of the population.

Structure type (units in structure). See Definitions for Table 2.4.

Notes

Homeownership rates for 1900 to 1930 are limited to households reporting tenure.

The rates for 1900 will not exactly match those given in some Census Bureau reports and briefs. The 1900 rates include some families living in institutions, boarding rooms, and other such living quarters that have not been counted as households from 1930 to the present and that were not counted as households in some earlier reports that included 1900 homeownership rates. Because families living in these types of living quarters were counted as households in 1910 and 1920, the 1900 data were made consistent with these other early censuses. If persons living in these types of living quarters were not included as households, the national homeownership rate in 1900 was only marginally higher—46.7 percent.

Tables 3.27–3.31

Data Source:
Current Population Survey/Housing Vacancy Survey
References:
U.S. Bureau of the Census, Current Population Survey/Housing Vacancy Survey, Series H111. See also U.S. Bureau of the Census, "Housing Vacancy Survey," <http://www.census.gov/ftp/pub/hhes/www/hvs.html>.

Definitions

Homeownership rate. See Definition at Tables 3.24–3.26.

Householder. The householder refers to the person (or one of the persons) in whose name the housing unit is owned or rented or, if there is no such person, any adult member, excluding roomers, boarders, or paid employees. If the house is jointly owned by a married couple, either the husband or the wife may be listed first, thereby becoming the reference person, or householder, to whom the relationship of the other household members is recorded. One person in each household is designated as the householder.

Homeownership rate by age of householder. This homeownership rate is calculated by dividing the number of owner households with a householder in a particular age group by the total number of households with a householder in that age group.

Homeownership rate by family status. This homeownership rate is calculated by dividing the number of owners in households of a particular type (e.g., married-couple families) by the total number of households of that type.

See Tables 1.4–1.15 for definitions of specific household types.

Notes

See notes on Tables 2.1–2.2 for comparability between the Current Population Survey/Housing Vacancy Survey (CPS/HVS) and the decennial census. The April 1990 Census recorded a homeownership rate of 64.2 percent, whereas the CPS/HVS estimated the homeownership rate at 63.9 percent for the first half of 1990.

Several major changes were introduced to the CPS/HVS beginning in January 1994 that necessitate caution in comparing data for 1994 and later with earlier data. The Census Bureau estimates that the introduction of 1990 Census–based population controls lowered the CPS/HVS estimate of the national homeownership rate by about one-half of a percentage point. The Census Bureau was unable to determine the quantitative effects of the implementation of Computer Assisted Survey Information Collection on homeownership rate estimates. See Appendix B under "Current Population Survey" for additional discussion of the survey changes.

Table 3.32

Data Sources:
Current Population Survey March Supplement and Current Population Survey/Housing Vacancy Survey
References:
Data provided by U.S. Bureau of the Census, Housing and Household Economics Statistics Division.

Definitions

Homeownership rate. See Definitions for Tables 3.24–3.26 for a definition of the homeownership rate and Tables 1.4–1.15 for definitions of race and Hispanic origin classifications.

Notes

The annual homeownership rate estimates from the Current Population Survey (CPS) March Supplement differ from those produced by the Current Population Survey/Housing Vacancy Survey (CPS/HVS) for several reasons. First, the CPS March Supplement estimates are based on data for a single month, whereas the CPS/HVS data are averages of monthly data for a quarter or an entire year. Another factor that might contribute to the difference is that the March Supplement sample includes an additional 2,500 housing units with at least one person of Hispanic origin that are not included in the basic monthly CPS sample, which is the basis for the CPS/HVS. Finally, the CPS/HVS includes an adjustment for housing unit undercount, whereas the CPS March Supplement does not.

See Notes for Tables 3.27–3.31 and Appendix B under "Current Population Survey" for discussions of recent changes in the CPS that may affect historical comparability of homeownership rate estimates.

Table 3.33

Data Source:
    Survey of Recent Home Buyers
Reference:
    Chicago Title and Trust Family of Title Insurers, *Who's Buying Homes in America*, annual.

Definitions

First-time and repeat buyers. First-time buyers are recent home purchasers who have never previously owned their own home. Repeat buyers are recent purchasers who have previously owned a home.

Mortgage payment. This includes the monthly payment for principal, interest, and taxes.

Single-family houses. Single-family houses include fully detached, semidetached (semiattached, side-by-side), rowhouses, and townhouses. In the case of attached units, each must be separated from the adjacent unit by a ground-to-roof wall in order to be classified as a one-unit structure. Also, these units must not share heating/air-conditioning systems or interstructural public utilities, such as water supply, power supply, or sewage disposal lines.

Condominiums. A condominium refers not to a housing unit in a particular type of structure, but rather to a type of ownership in which the owners of the individual housing units are also joint owners of the common areas of the building or community. Condominiums include homes in multiple-unit structures.

Down payment. The part of the purchase price of a property that the buyer pays in cash and does not finance with a mortgage.

Tables 3.34–3.35

Data Source:
    Property Owners and Managers Survey

References:
    U.S. Bureau of the Census, "Property Owners and Managers Survey Single-Family Properties: Type of Owner (Table 96)," <http://www.census.gov/hhes/www/housing/poms/singlefam/sfowner/sftab96.html>; and "Property Owners and Managers Survey Multi-family Properties: Type of Owner (Table 96)," <http://www.census.gov/hhes/www/housing/poms/multifam/ mfowner/mftab96.html>.

Definitions

Also see Definitions for Tables 2.32–2.33 for additional definitions.

The following owner-type categories are used in the tables:

Individual investor(s). This category includes ownership by only one person as well as joint ownership by two or more individuals, including husband and wife. Also included are cases where ownership is held by a group of individuals who have not signed a partnership agreement.

Trustee for estate. This is a person or agent, such as a bank, that holds legal title to property in order to administer it for an estate.

Limited partnership. A limited partnership is one in which there is at least one partner whose liability is limited to the amount invested and at least one general partner whose liability extends beyond monetary investment.

General partnership. This partnership is made up of general partners without special (limited) partners; that is, no partner's liability is limited.

Joint venture. This is an agreement between two or more parties who invest in a single property.

Real estate investment trust (REIT). A REIT pools funds from individuals for investing in real estate or mortgages. If it meets certain requirements, it is exempt from corporate income tax.

A life insurance company may use premiums received from policyholders and other earnings to make loans secured by real estate or to invest directly in real estate.

Financial institution. This category includes properties that were in the portfolio of a bank, savings and loan, or other financial institution at the time of the survey.

Real estate corporation. This is a corporation organized chiefly for the purpose of building, buying, selling, investing in, or managing property.

Other corporations. These include those not included in the real estate corporation category.

Housing cooperative organizations. Housing cooperatives (co-ops) are usually incorporated and own properties for the benefit of their members who purchase shares in the cooperative. The cooperative organization is the owner of the property. A member of the co-op has the right to occupy a specific housing unit and pays a proportionate share of the mortgage payment (if any), taxes, insurance, and operating costs.

Nonprofit or church-related institutions. These include such entities as schools, charitable organizations, churches, and other such institutions.

Fraternal organizations. These include organizations of persons who associate for some common purpose or interest.

Other. This category includes all types of owners not covered by the categories described above.

Table 3.36

Data Source:
  Housing Discrimination Study
Reference:
  U.S. Department of Housing and Urban Development, *Housing Discrimination Study: Synthesis*, August 1991.

Definitions

Incidence of unfavorable treatment. In audit tests that matched equally qualified minority (Black or Hispanic) and majority home seekers, the incidence of unfavorable treatment represents the share of cases in which the minority partner received less-favorable treatment than his/her majority partner. This measure does not distinguish random acts of differential treatment from systematic discrimination against minority home seekers. The actual incidence of discrimination against minority home seekers may be either greater than or less than the incidence of unfavorable treatment.

The overall incidence of unfavorable treatment measures the extent to which unfavorable treatment occurs at any stage of the audit process. For renters, this measure combines outcomes from the housing availability and contributions to the transaction stages. For owners, the overall incidence of unfavorable treatment combines outcomes from housing availability, contributions to the

transaction, and steering. (See the Notes section for a more detailed description of the audit stages.)

Incidence of discrimination. In the Housing Discrimination Study (HDS), researchers used a statistical technique called multinomial logit analysis to separate random effects from systematic unfavorable treatment of minority home seekers. The result of this procedure is a "best estimate" of the incidence of discrimination against minority home seekers.

Notes

The HDS was a national fair housing audit study sponsored by the U.S. Department of Housing and Urban Development and conducted by the Urban Institute and Syracuse University. Results are based on 3,800 fair housing audits (paired tests) conducted in 25 metropolitan areas during the late spring and early summer of 1989. The data gathering period for the HDS coincided with initial implementation of the 1988 Fair Housing Act Amendments. Therefore, the HDS results can be regarded as a benchmark against which the effects of the amendments can be measured.

The HDS audit methodology consisted of four basic steps.

1. A sample of metropolitan areas was selected to yield nationally representative estimates of differential treatment for minority (Black and Hispanic) home seekers in major urban areas.
2. Advertisements were randomly selected from the major newspaper in each sampled metropolitan area.
3. Teams of paired minority and majority auditors were sent to the sampled sales and rental agents to inquire about the availability of housing units. Audit teammates posed as otherwise identical home seekers, with income and other household characteristics that were the same and that qualified both team members for the advertised housing unit.
4. Minority and majority auditors independently recorded their treatment by sales and rental agents on structured data collection forms.

The HDS, like most other audit studies, focuses on the interaction between an agent and home seeker from the time a home seeker responds to an advertisement until the home seeker commits to renting or purchasing the unit. This encounter consists of up to three basic stages, and at each of these stages, minority and majority home seekers may receive differential treatment.

In stage one, housing availability, a home seeker inquires about the availability of an advertised unit and about other comparable units. Unfavorable treatment occurs when minority customers are denied information about the availability of some or all of the units that are available to comparable Whites. The most serious unfavorable treatment is complete denial of information about the availability of sale or rental units.

In stage two, contributions to completing a transaction, the audit seeks to determine if agents constrain access to housing opportunity for minorities through a reduced level of "sales effort" invested in the transaction, less favorable rental terms and conditions offered, or less assistance provided to homebuyers in obtaining financing.

Stage three, steering, only applies to homebuyer audits. Steering occurs when minority home seekers are offered houses, but in systematically different neighborhoods than their White counterparts. Steering can only occur when an agent identifies houses that would be of interest to a customer. Steering evidence is presented in the table only for cases in which both auditors were shown or recommended one or more houses.

Table 3.37

Data Source:

1990 Decennial Census

References:

U.S. Bureau of the Census, "Residential Segregation, Summary Tables, Table 1. Mean Residential Segregation Indexes for All Metropolitan Areas by Group: 1990; and Table 2. Mean Residential Segregation Indexes for Metropolitan Areas by Size and Group: 1990," <http://www.census.gov/hhes/www/housing/resseg/sumtabs.html>. For definitions of segregation measures, see Douglas S. Massey and Nancy A. Denton, 1988, "The Dimensions of Residential Segregation," *Social Forces* 67: 281–315.

Definitions

Dissimilarity. Evenness measures of segregation, of which dissimilarity is the most widely used, compare the spatial distributions of different groups. Segregation is smallest when majority and minority populations have the same spatial distribution. Conceptually, dissimilarity measures "the proportion of minority members that would have to change their area of residence to achieve an even distri-

bution, with the number of minority members moving being expressed as a proportion of the number that would have to move under conditions of maximum segregation" (Massey and Denton 1988). The index ranges from 0.0 (when no minorities would have to move) to 1.0 (when all would), with 1.0 being maximum segregation.

Interaction. The interaction index is categorized as an exposure measure of segregation. "Exposure measures the degree of potential contact, or possibility of interaction, between minority and majority group members" (Massey and Denton, 1988). Exposure thus depends on the extent to which two groups share common residential areas, and hence on the degree to which the average minority group member "experiences" segregation. Indexes of evenness and exposure are correlated but measure different things—exposure measures depend on the relative sizes of the two groups being compared, while evenness measures do not. The interaction index measures the exposure of minority group members to members of the majority group as the minority-weighted average of the majority proportion of the population in each areal unit.

Tables 3.38–3.42

Data Source:

American (Annual) Housing Survey

Reference:

U.S. Department of Housing and Urban Development, Office of Policy Development and Research, *Rental Housing Assistance—The Crisis Continues: The 1997 Report to Congress on Worst Case Housing Needs,* April 1998.

Definitions

Rent or cost burden. The rent or cost burden is the ratio between payments for housing (including utilities) and reported household income. This calculation is based on gross income. It does not make the adjustments to income required by housing assistance programs before percentage-of-income rents are determined.

Burdens are reported in two categories: cost burdens between 31 and 50 percent of income ("moderate rent or cost burden") and cost burdens exceeding 50 percent of income ("severe cost burden"). Any household with a housing-payment-to-income ratio of 31 percent or more is considered to be "rent burdened" or "cost burdened."

For owners, payments for housing include mortgage payments and property taxes. To the extent that American Housing Survey (AHS) respondents underreport total income, the tables may overestimate the number of households with cost burdens.

Inadequate housing. Housing with severe or moderate physical problems is considered inadequate. See Definitions for Tables 2.11–2.31.

Crowded. Housing is crowded if it has more than one person per room.

Priority problems. Problems qualifying for federal preference in admission to assisted housing programs include paying more than half of income for rent (severe rent burden), living in severely substandard housing (including being homeless or in a homeless shelter), or being involuntarily displaced. Because the AHS sample tracks housing units and thus cannot count the homeless, AHS-based estimates of priority problems include only households with cost burdens above 50 percent of income or living in severely inadequate housing.

Other problems. These include moderate physical problems, rent burden of 31 to 50 percent of income, or crowding without priority problems among unassisted households.

Assisted. Assisted households include those responding yes to the following AHS questions: "Is the building owned by a public housing authority? Does the federal government pay some of the cost of the unit? Do the people living here have to report the household's income to someone every year so they can set the rent?"

Very low-income. The term refers to households with income not in excess of 50 percent of U.S. Department of Housing and Urban Development (HUD)–adjusted area median family income.

HUD-adjusted area median family income. In 1974, Congress defined "low-income" and "very low-income" for HUD rental programs as incomes not exceeding 80 and 50 percent, respectively, of the area median family income, as adjusted by HUD. Statutory adjustments now include upper and lower caps for areas with low or high ratios of housing costs to income, and, for each nonmetropolitan county, a lower cap equal to its state's nonmetropolitan average. Estimates of the median family income and the official income cutoffs for each metropolitan area and nonmetropolitan county are based on the most recent decennial census results and then updated each year by HUD. Each base income cutoff is assumed to apply to a

household of four, and official cutoffs are further adjusted by household size: one person, 70 percent of base; two persons, 80 percent; three persons, 90 percent; five persons, 108 percent; six persons, 116 percent; etc.

Presence of children. This refers to households with a child under age 18 present.

Race. The classifications of "race" in the tables refer to the race of the householder occupying the housing unit. The concept of race as used by the Census Bureau does not denote a clear-cut scientific definition of biological stock. Race was determined on the basis of a question that asked for self-identification of a person's race.

Hispanic. The classification "Hispanic" in the tables refers to the origin of the householder occupying the housing unit. Hispanic origin was determined on the basis of a question that asked for self-identification of persons living in the unit who were Hispanic or Spanish American. Hispanic persons may be of any race.

Table 3.43

Data Source:
  Census of Housing
Reference:
  U.S. Bureau of the Census, "Housing: Then and Now, 50 Years of Decennial Censuses. Crowding," <http://www.census.gov/hhes/housing/census/crowding.html>. Table prepared by Robert Bonnette.

Definitions

Crowded and severely crowded units. Crowded units have 1.01 or more persons per room. Severely crowded units have 1.51 or more persons per room.

Notes

The states do not quite add up to the national total in 1950. The reason for this is unclear.

Tables 3.44–3.46

Data Source:
  American Housing Survey
References:
  U.S. Bureau of the Census and U.S. Department of Housing and Urban Development, *American Housing Survey for the United States in 1991*, Current Housing Reports H150/91, April 1993; *American*

Housing Survey for the United States in 1993, Current Housing Reports H150/93, February 1995; *and American Housing Survey for the United States in 1995*, Current Housing Reports H150/95RV, July 1997.

Definitions

See Definitions for Tables 2.11–2.31 for terms used in column heads.

Monthly housing costs. The data are presented for owner- and renter-occupied housing units. Monthly housing costs for owner-occupied units is the sum of monthly payments for all mortgages or installment loans or contracts, real estate taxes (including taxes on mobile homes or trailer sites if the site is owned), property insurance, homeowners association fee, cooperative or condominium fee, mobile home park fee, land rent, utilities (electricity, gas, water, and sewage disposal), fuels (oil, coal, kerosene, wood, etc.), and garbage and trash collection. Monthly housing costs are not computed for households with a mortgage or similar debt that failed to report the amount of their loan or contract payment.

For renter-occupied housing units, monthly housing costs include the contract rent plus the estimated average monthly cost of utilities (electricity, gas, water, and sewage disposal) and fuels (oil, coal, kerosene, wood, etc.), property insurance, mobile home land rent, and garbage and trash collection, if these items are paid for by the renter (or paid for by someone else, such as a relative, welfare agency, or friend) in addition to rent. Renter housing units occupied without payment of cash rent are shown separately as noncash rent. Monthly housing costs for vacant for-rent housing units include rent asked. For rental units subsidized by a public housing authority, the federal government, or state or local governments, the monthly rental costs reflect only the portion paid by the household and not the portion subsidized.

Monthly housing costs are shown for all renters and all owners. Medians for monthly housing costs are rounded to the nearest dollar.

Median monthly housing costs for owners. Two additional medians are shown separately for owner-occupied units. The first median includes maintenance costs in addition to those items included in "Monthly housing costs" (see previous item). The second excludes second and subsequent mortgages, installment loans or contracts, and maintenance costs, but includes all remaining items listed in "Monthly housing costs."

Monthly housing costs as percentage of current income. The yearly housing costs (monthly housing costs multiplied by 12) are expressed as a percentage of the total current income (see the following definition of "Current income"). This percentage is calculated for the same owner- and renter-occupied housing units for which monthly housing costs were computed (for exclusions see "Monthly housing costs"). The percentage was computed separately for each unit and rounded to the nearest percent. The measure was not computed for units where occupants reported no income or a net loss.

Monthly costs for electricity and gas. Beginning in 1989, two procedures were introduced that attempt to correct the overreporting of electricity and gas costs in the American Housing Survey. In the first procedure, respondents were asked the amount of their electricity and/or gas bill for the previous months of January, April, August, and December. These months are the best predictors of annual costs. If the respondent provided data for at least 3 of the 4 months, the results were used to provide an annual estimate of costs. This estimate was then divided by 12 to provide average monthly costs.

The second procedure was applied to the remaining units. If the respondents did not know the amount of their electricity and/or gas bill for at least 3 of the 4 months, their estimate of average monthly costs was used. A factor was then applied that, in effect, lowered these costs to make them consistent with electricity and gas costs reported in the Residential Energy Consumption Survey (RECS) sponsored by the U.S. Department of Energy.

Beginning in 1993, the procedures introduced in 1989 were improved and expanded from two to three procedures. All respondents were asked if they had records available showing their costs for electricity (or gas) separate from other utilities. If they responded "yes," they were asked the amount of their electricity (or gas) bill for the most recent months of January, April, August, and December. Depending on the number of months for which data were provided, one of two procedures was used. If the respondents answered "no" to the original question (that is, they did not have separate records for the electricity or gas), a third procedure was used. On average, more than one-third of respondents provided answers for at least 1 of the 4 months.

If the respondent provided data for only 1 month, the first procedure was used. The data for the month were adjusted using regression formulas to estimate yearly costs, which were then divided by 12. These formulas were modeled after the results of the RECS and took into account the following characteristics of the unit: electric home heating, natural gas home heating, electric water heating, natural gas water heating, year built, type of unit, number of rooms, number of bathrooms, number of appliances, and number of household members.

The second procedure was applied if the respondent provided data for 2, 3, or 4 months. As with the first procedure, the monthly data were adjusted using regression formulas, modeled after the results of RECS, to estimate yearly costs, which were then divided by 12. Because more than 1 month's worth of real costs were available, it was not necessary to take into account detailed characteristics of the unit as was done in the first procedure.

If the respondent answered "no," that he or she did not have separate records for the electricity (or gas), the third procedure was used. The respondent was asked to provide an estimate of the average monthly costs and a factor was then applied to make them consistent with electricity and gas costs in RECS.

Before 1989, respondents were only asked to provide an estimate of average monthly costs. Research done using the 1993 American Housing Survey has shown that this approach produces 0 to 10 percent overestimates of electricity costs and 15 to 25 percent overestimates of gas costs. The new procedures introduced in 1989 and 1993 produced lower and more accurate estimates.

Current income. Upon completion of the detailed income questions, respondents were asked, "Is your total family income this month about the same as it was a year ago?" "About the same" was defined as within 10 percent, or equal to cost-of-living adjustments. If the respondent answered "No," a second question was asked, "What do you expect your total family income to be in the next 12 months?" Current income for families whose most recent month's income was not about the same as a year ago is tabulated as the "total expected family income in the next 12 months." Current income for families whose most recent month's income was about the same as a year ago is "family and primary individual income." For the majority of families, current income equals "income of families and primary individuals." Data on current income is not published separately. Current income is used in the calculation of "Ratio of value to current income" and "Monthly housing costs as percent of current income." It is felt that respondents who have only recently entered the job market and those who changed jobs during the past year often report a previous year's income that is too low to accurately reflect their current financial situation as it relates to the value of their home and their housing costs.

Notes

See Tables 2.11–2.31 for notes on comparability.

Table 3.47

Data Sources:
   Several data sources were used in the preparation of this table. See the following Definitions and Notes sections.
Reference:
   Joint Center for Housing Studies of Harvard University, *The State of the Nation's Housing: 1998.*

Definitions

Monthly income. Income is the 1990 median family income estimated by the U.S. Department of Housing and Urban Development, indexed as follows. First, the Bureau of Economic Analysis' measure of wage and salary earnings per job, 1975–1995 was converted to an index format. Two Bureau of Labor Statistics news releases, "Average Annual Pay by State and Industry, 1996," and "Average Annual Pay Levels in Metropolitan Areas, 1996," were used to extend the index through 1996. The index was held constant in 1997.

Monthly owner incomes are defined as 80 percent of the indexed median family income divided by 12.

Monthly renter incomes are defined as 50 percent of the indexed median family income divided by 12.

Home price. Home price is the 1990 median sales price of existing single-family homes reported by the National Association of Realtors, indexed by the Freddie Mac Conventional Mortgage Home Price Index, deflated by the Bureau of Labor Statistics' Consumer Price Index for All Items.

Mortgage rate. Mortgage rates are from the Federal Housing Finance Board's Monthly Interest Rate Survey.

Mortgage payment. Mortgage payments assume a 30-year fixed-rate mortgage with 10 percent down. The after-tax mortgage payment equals the mortgage payment less tax savings of homeownership. Tax savings are based on the excess of housing deductions (mortgage interest and real estate taxes) plus nonhousing deductions over the standard deduction. Nonhousing deductions are set at 5 percent of income through 1986. They decrease to 4.25 percent in 1987 and 3.5 percent thereafter, reflecting the effects of tax reform.

Contract and gross rent. Contract rent is set equal to the median 1977 contract rent from the American Housing Survey, indexed by the Consumer Price Index residential rent index with adjustments for depreciation of the stock. Gross rent equals contract rent plus fuel and utilities.

Cost as a percent of income. For owners, this variable is either the before-tax or after-tax mortgage payments as a percent of monthly owner income. Cost as a percent of income for renters is monthly contract rent or gross rent as a percent of monthly renter income.

Table 3.48

Data Source:
    National Association of Realtors® Housing
    Affordability Index
References:
    National Association of Realtors®, *Real Estate Outlook*, monthly. Descriptions of the indexes are from Eileen A. Neely, "Housing Affordability: Understanding the NAR Indices," *Real Estate Outlook*, April 1994. See also Michael Feroli, "Measuring Housing Affordability: NAR's Housing Affordability Index," *Real Estate Outlook*, January 1998.

Definitions

Housing affordability. The commonly used housing affordability index from the National Association of Realtors measures whether or not a typical family could qualify for a mortgage loan on a typical home. The index has four variants: composite, fixed-rate (FRM), adjustable-rate (ARM), and first-time homebuyer. The first three indices correspond to three different financing assumptions. The fourth index—the first-time homebuyer affordability index—is designed to measure affordability conditions for potential first-time homebuyers.

The first three indices are calculated first by determining the minimum qualifying income for a 20 percent down-payment mortgage loan on a median-priced home from the NAR's existing single-family home price series at the relevant interest rate (composite, FRM, or ARM, depending on the index being calculated) using a 25 percent qualifying ratio. In other words, a potential homebuyer is qualified for a loan if the principal and in-

terest payment does not exceed 25 percent of his pretax income. The index is then calculated by dividing the median family income by the qualifying income and multiplying by 100. To interpret the index, a value of 100 means that a family with the median income has exactly enough income to qualify for a median-priced home using a 25 percent qualifying ratio (principal and interest payment does not exceed 25 percent of pretax income) and assuming a 20 percent down payment. For example, a housing affordability index of 117.2 means that a family earning the median income has 17.2 percent more income than necessary to qualify for a conventional loan covering 80 percent of the median price of an existing single-family home. For the first-time buyer index, the same general procedure is applied, but using the income, house price, down payment, and interest rate assumptions described below.

Fixed-rate, ARM, and composite indices. The fixed-rate index is based on the current effective interest rate on 30-year fixed-rate mortgages. The adjustable-rate index is calculated using the prevailing effective interest rate on adjustable-rate mortgages. Effective interest rates include closing fees and charges, which are amortized over the average life of such mortgages, which is approximately 7 years.

The composite index is established using a weighted average of the interest rates on FRMs and ARMs. The weights are determined by the relative proportion of FRMs and ARMs closed on existing homes. The composite index is the most widely quoted number and is often referred to generically as the "Housing Affordability Index."

First-time buyer index. The first-time homebuyer index recognizes the special characteristics of first-time homebuyers and the homes they purchase. The group most likely to purchase a first home consists of young families (with head of household ages 25 to 44). This group has a lower median income than the overall population. The first-time homebuyer index uses this lower median income in its calculation.

Also, prospective first-time homebuyers generally have less savings because they are younger. Lower savings, coupled with the absence of home equity, means that first-time buyers typically make lower down payments. The first-time homebuyer index considers these factors and assumes a 10 percent down payment and adds one-quarter of a percentage point to the mortgage rate for the requisite private mortgage insurance.

Survey data from the National Association of Realtors' Home Buyer and Selling Process: 1991 suggest that the median price of existing homes purchased by first-time buyers is about 85 percent of the median price of all existing homes purchased. The first-time homebuyer index, therefore, is calculated by using a sales price of 85 percent of the existing single-family home price estimated from the Existing Sales Survey.

Table 3.49

Data Source:
National Association of Home Builders' Housing Opportunity Index

References:
National Association of Home Builders, *Housing Economics*, monthly. Historical data are available at National Association of Home Builders, "Housing Opportunity Index: National," <http://www.nahb.com/housingopindex.html>. Description of the Housing Opportunity Index is from Ashok Chaluvadi, "Housing Opportunity Index: Fourth Quarter 1996," *Housing Economics*, April 1997.

Definitions

Housing Opportunity Index. The National Association of Home Builders' Housing Opportunity Index measures the proportion of homes sold during a given quarter that a family with the median income in the area of residence could afford to buy. The index assumes that a home is affordable to the median-income family if the combined total of mortgage payments, property taxes, and property insurance does not exceed 28 percent of that income. A down payment of 10 percent of the home price is assumed in calculating the index.

The index uses annual estimates of median family income produced by the Department of Housing and Urban Development and home price data (including sales of both new and existing homes) collected by Experian, Inc. Property tax and insurance data are from the decennial census. The interest rate is a weighted average of adjustable-rate and fixed-rate loans.

Because the price data used to calculate the national index come primarily from large metropolitan areas, and prices in small metropolitan areas and nonmetropolitan areas are generally lower, the national index probably understates the proportion of homes that are affordable to the median-income family in the nation. Data for individual metropolitan areas are published quarterly in *Housing Economics*.

Tables 3.50–3.59

Data Source:
Survey of Income and Program Participation (SIPP)

References:
Howard A. Savage, *Who Can Afford to Buy a House in 1993?* U.S. Bureau of the Census, Current Housing Reports, H121/97-1, July 1997. For detailed tables, see U.S. Bureau of the Census, "Housing Affordability 1993," <http://www.census.gov/hhes/www/hsgaffrd.html>.

Definitions

Affordability. For each family and unrelated individual, calculations are made using data on income, assets, and debt to determine if the family or individual can afford to purchase the criterion home (defined below) in the area where they live. Two criterion homes are used to measure affordability—a median-priced home and a modestly priced home. (See the Notes section for a discussion of the determination of affordability.)

Mortgage type. Affordability calculations are made using two types of mortgage loans: (1) conventional fixed-rate 30-year loans, and (2) Federal Housing Administration (FHA)–insured 30-year loans.

Interest rates. For conventional fixed-rate 30-year loans the interest rate used is the average contract interest rate on conventional loans closed during the survey period, determined from the Federal Housing Finance Board's Monthly Interest Rate Survey (MIRS). The rate for these loans was estimated at 7.17 percent in 1993, 9.51 percent in 1991, 9.79 percent in 1988, and 12.91 percent in 1984.

For FHA-insured loans, the rate was determined based on information from the U.S. Department of Housing and Urban Development's (HUD's) report on *Average Prices for FHA-Insured Home Mortgages* (Section 203) during the survey period. This assessment estimated that FHA-insured loans were 7.55 percent in 1993, 9.50 percent in 1991, 9.67 percent in 1988, and 13.00 percent in 1984.

Criterion home. The criterion home is the home whose value is used to determine affordability status. Two criterion homes are used in the tables. The median-priced home has the median value of new or existing owner-occupied (non–mobile home) units in each area based on value data collected in the Survey of Income and Program Participation (SIPP). Half of the homes in the area are below this value and half are above. The modestly priced home has the value of new or existing owner-occupied (non–mobile home) units at the upper limit of the first quartile of the cases in the area, based on SIPP. Twenty-five percent of the homes in the area are below this value and 75 percent are above.

Income. "Available money" family income (pretransfer) is used in all the affordability calculations. It is the income of the husband and wife only in a married-couple family, and the male or female only in a family with a male or female householder. The income data were collected during the 4-month reference period for each survey and converted to an annual amount by multiplying by three. The income amounts represent amounts actually received during the 4-month reference period, before deductions for income and payroll taxes, union dues, Part B Medicare premiums, etc. See Savage (1997) for detailed lists of the types of income that are included in or excluded from available money income.

Real estate taxes. Real estate taxes are estimated for each region based on data from the American Housing Survey.

Property insurance. Property insurance is estimated at $3 per $1,000 value for homes in all areas in each year based on guidelines set forth in the "Guide to Residential Financing."

Closing costs. Closing costs include costs for transfer taxes, title fees, and appraisal fees, and prepayment items such as real estate taxes and property insurance. Although closing costs can vary from area to area, for conventional loans they are estimated to be 3 percent of the total value of the property based on guidelines in the "Guide to Residential Financing." For conventional fixed-rate mortgages these fees must be paid up-front and they cannot be financed. For FHA-insured loans, the administrative part of the closing costs (transfer taxes, title fees, etc.), as well as the loan origination fee can be financed. (Based on HUD studies, the administrative closing costs are estimated to be 1.2 percent of the purchase price of the home.)

Fees and charges. Fees and charges include all fees, commissions, discounts, and "points" paid by the borrower or seller in order to obtain a loan. They exclude charges for mortgage credit, life or property insurance, transfer taxes, and title fees. Fees and charges were estimated for conventional loans based on data for conventional loans closed during the survey period, determined from the Federal Housing Finance Board's MIRS. This estimate produced fees and charges of 1.30 percent of the mortgage amount in 1993, 1.62 percent in 1991, 1.98 percent in 1988, and 2.58 percent in 1984. For FHA-insured loans, fees and charges were estimated from HUD's report on *Average Prices for FHA-Insured Home Mortgages* (Section 203). They were estimated at 1.59 percent of the mortgage amount in 1993, 1.63 percent in 1991, 2.00 percent in 1988, and 2.90 percent in 1984. For FHA-insured loans, the discount part of the fees and charges must be paid up-front. The remaining part—the loan origination fee—can be financed.

Down payment. The down payment is the cash portion of the price of the house that the buyer must pay from his/her own funds. The minimum down payment needed for conventional loans is 5 percent of the purchase price of the home and the amount cannot be financed.

For FHA-insured loans, the administrative part of the closing costs and the loan origination fee are added to the purchase price of the home to derive "total acquisition costs." The homebuyer is required to pay 3 percent of the first $25,000 of the total acquisition costs and 5 percent of the amount over $25,000.

Assets. Assets include all cash available in savings accounts, money market deposit accounts, certificates of deposit, money market funds, government securities, bonds, checking accounts, and the net value of stock and mutual funds. The net value of stock is the gross asset value of the stock portfolio minus the amount borrowed on stocks in a margin account.

Assets also include the net equity available, after selling costs and discounts are subtracted, in rental income property owned, non–rental income property owned, debt owed from businesses owned, and mortgages owned, as well as the equity available in any currently owned home. The following discounts were applied:

Equity in owned home and from sale of rental income property (10 percent). Typical selling costs include brokerage fees of 7 percent and fixup and transfer costs of three percent.

Non–rental income property (15 percent). This includes property such as vacation homes and undeveloped lots.

Typical selling costs include brokerage fees of 10 percent and fix-up and transfer costs of 5 percent.

Owned mortgages and debt from the sale of owned businesses (25 percent). Both of these are debt instruments that are not very liquid. Typically they are sold to investors who require high rates of return on their investments.

Debts. Debt is the amount owed on credit cards, automobile loans, bank loans, outstanding home mortgages, and all other loans.

Total allowable debt. Under Fannie Mae guidelines for a standard conventional loan, total allowable debt for a family or unrelated individual is 8 percent of "available" monthly family income for consumer debt and 28 percent for mortgage debt. For an FHA-insured loan the total allowable debt is 41 percent for consumer and mortgage debt, with a maximum of 29 percent allowed for mortgage debt.

Total monthly payment on outstanding debts. Monthly debt payments are estimated at 3 percent of total outstanding debt (2 percent principal, 1 percent interest), a typical minimum payment required of consumers.

Excess debt. A family or unrelated individual has excess debt if the monthly payment on outstanding debts is greater than the total allowable debt. This excess debt must be paid down to the total allowable debt level using available cash in order to qualify for a mortgage.

Age of householder. The age of the householder is based on the householder's age at his/her last birthday.

Race. Families and unrelated individuals are divided into three groups based on the race of the householder: White, Black, and "other races." The last category includes Native Americans, Japanese, Chinese, and any other race except White and Black.

Hispanic origin. Families and unrelated individuals are classified as Hispanic origin based on a question that asked for self-identification of the householder's origin or descent. Persons of Hispanic origin may be of any race.

Family. The term "family" refers to a group of two or more persons related by birth, marriage, or adoption who reside together. Every family must include a householder. A household may contain a primary family and one or more subfamilies.

Family status. Persons were classified in the following ways: as members of a married-couple family; a family with male householder, no wife present; a family with female householder, no husband present; or as unrelated individuals based on their most common status during the calender year. For example, a person who was in a married-couple family for 7 months but was an unrelated individual for 5 months was classified as being in a married-couple family.

Unrelated individuals. The term "unrelated individuals" refers to persons 15 years old or older who are not living with any relatives. An unrelated individual may (1) constitute a one-person household, or (2) be part of a household including one or more other families or unrelated individuals. Thus, a widow living by herself or with one or more other persons not related to her, a lodger not related to the householder or to anyone else in the household, or a servant living in an employer's household with no relatives are examples of unrelated individuals. The affordability status of unrelated individuals is determined independently of other household members.

Tenure. A family or unrelated individual is considered to be a "current owner" if the unrelated individual or a member of the family is an owner or co-owner of the unit in which they live, even if the unit is mortgaged or not fully paid for. A family or unrelated individual is a "current renter" if the individual or a member of the family is one of the persons who rents the unit. Subfamilies (both related and unrelated) are given the same tenure status as the primary family with whom they live.

Notes

There are two principal determinants of whether a family or unrelated individual can afford a criterion home: (1) they have the necessary cash available to pay the minimum down payment, closing costs, excess debt, if any, and fees and charges associated with purchasing the home; and (2) after all available cash has been exhausted, they have the necessary income needed to make the required monthly mortgage payments. If the answer to either question is "no," then they cannot afford the criterion home.

Conventional loans. The following specific steps go into the calculation of homeownership affordability for each family or unrelated individual for conventional loans:

1. Total "available" money family income, assets (transformed into available cash), debt level, and excess debt, if any, are determined.
2. If there is excess consumer debt (over 8 percent of

"available" monthly family income), the excess debt is paid down using available cash. If the available cash is not enough to pay the excess debt down to an acceptable level, the family or unrelated individual is not able to afford the criterion home.

3. The total amount needed for the minimum down payment, closing costs, fees and charges (including points) on the criterion home is determined. This amount is compared to the total remaining available cash (after any excess debt was paid down). If the available cash is not equal to or greater than the amount required, the family or unrelated individual is not able to afford the criterion home.

4. Any available cash still remaining is added to the minimum down payment to reduce the amount of the criterion home that has to be financed.

5. The mortgage needed to purchase the criterion home after all available cash is applied to the down payment is determined. The total mortgage needed is transformed into monthly payments of principal and interest based on the average interest rate for a conventional, 30-year fixed-payment mortgage.

6. Monthly payments for real estate taxes, property insurance, private mortgage insurance (if the down payment is less than 20 percent of the criterion home) are determined. These amounts plus the amount for principal and interest become the total monthly mortgage payment required.

7. According to standard Fannie Mae guidelines, the maximum amount of income that can be allocated to mortgage payments is 28 percent. If the total monthly mortgage payment required exceeds 28 percent of income, then the family or unrelated individual is not able to afford the criterion home.

FHA-insured loans. The specific steps involved in the calculation of affordability for FHA-insured loans are identical to those for conventional loans except for the following:

1. For FHA-insured loans, the excess debt that must be paid down is debt greater than 41 percent of available monthly family income for consumer and mortgage debt combined, with a maximum of 29 percent allocated to mortgage debt.

2. The total amount needed for the minimum down payment, closing costs, fees and charges (including points) on the criterion home is determined. For FHA-insured loans, the homebuyer is required to pay up-front 3 percent of the first $25,000 of total acquisition costs (purchase price, plus the administrative part of the closing costs, plus the loan origination fee), and 5 percent of the amount over $25,000. In addition, the buyer is required to pay prepaid items and any discount points. If the available cash is not equal to or greater than the amount required, the family or unrelated individual is not able to afford the criterion home using an FHA-insured loan.

In 1984, the maximum allowable FHA-insured mortgage for high-cost areas was $90,000. In 1988 and 1991, the maximum allowable FHA-insured mortgage for these areas was $124,875. In 1993, it was $151,000. If the required mortgage for the criterion home was above this amount, the homebuyer would have to pay the difference between the required mortgage and the maximum allowable mortgage from available cash.

3. The monthly payments of principal and interest are based on the interest rates for an FHA-insured, 30-year fixed-payment mortgage for each of the survey periods. This rate was estimated to be 7.55 percent in 1993, 9.50 percent in 1991, 9.67 percent in 1988, and 13.00 percent in 1984.

4. The total monthly mortgage payment includes payments for principal and interest, real estate taxes, property insurance, and FHA mortgage insurance premium (regardless of the amount of the down payment).

5. For FHA-insured loans, the maximum amount of income that can be allocated to mortgage payments is 29 percent.

There were several changes in the FHA regulations in 1991. In February 1991, the FHA implemented a new maximum loan-to-value ratio of 97.75 percent for properties appraised at $50,000 or more, and a ratio of 98.75 percent for properties appraised at less than $50,000. This change is implemented in the analysis of affordability for 1991.

In July 1991, FHA implemented two other changes in policy. They added an annual mortgage insurance premium of 50 basis points and limited the amount of closing costs that could be financed to 57 percent of the total. Since these changes occurred after data was collected in 1991 (February to May), and since the approach used in this analysis was to use the underwriting policy in effect at the time the data was collected, these two changes are reflected only in the affordability analysis for 1993.

See Savage (1997) for affordability calculations involving other criterion homes, including a low-priced home (at the 10th percentile of the area value distribution), a new single-family home, a price-adjusted home (the median home value in 1984 converted to 1993 constant dollars), and a condominium home.

Table 3.60

Data Source:
National Housing Survey
Reference:
Fannie Mae, *Fannie Mae National Housing Survey*, annual.

Notes

The following question from the National Housing Survey is used to collect the data presented in the table:

"I'd like to read you a list of some obstacles people may face in trying to buy a home. If you wanted to buy a home today, would [ITEM] present a major obstacle for you to overcome, a minor obstacle, or would it not be an obstacle to you buying a home?"

The data in the table show the proportion of adults responding that the given item would represent a major obstacle to them if they were buying a home at the time of the interview.

The racial/ethnic identity of the respondent is based on the following two questions: (1) "Is any member of your family, including yourself, of Hispanic or Spanish-speaking origin?" and (2) "And what is your race?" Hispanics include adults who either say they or a member of their family is of Hispanic or Spanish-speaking origin or say they are Hispanic in response to the race question.

Part 4: Housing Finance

Tables 4.1–4.2

Data Sources:
Board of Governors of the Federal Reserve System, based on data from various government and private organizations

Reference:
Board of Governors of the Federal Reserve System, *Federal Reserve Bulletin*, monthly.

Definitions

Mortgage debt outstanding. This is the unpaid principal balance on mortgage loans at the end of the specified time period.

Multifamily. This category includes mortgages on structures with five or more housing units.

Savings institution. This term includes mutual savings banks and savings and loan associations. The former category consists of mutually owned depository financial intermediaries chartered under state or federal laws. Savings and loans are depository financial institutions that may be either mutually or stockholder owned. Traditionally, their deposits have been invested in residential mortgage loans.

Commercial banks. Commercial banks are depository financial intermediaries chartered under either state or federal laws. In addition to their residential mortgage lending activities, commercial banks have traditionally played an important role in construction financing. This category includes loans held by nondeposit trust companies, but not loans held by bank trust departments.

Life insurance companies. These are nondepository financial intermediaries chartered at the state level that sell insurance policies and annuities and use the premiums plus reinvested dividends to make investments.

Mortgage pools or trusts. These are outstanding principal balances of mortgage pools backing securities insured or guaranteed by the agency indicated. The totals for this category include other pools not shown separately.

Fannie Mae. Fannie Mae is a private, stockholder-owned corporation chartered by Congress to provide liquidity to the U.S. residential mortgage markets. It does so by purchasing residential mortgages for its investment portfolio and by receiving pools of mortgage loans from lenders and exchanging them for mortgage-backed securities, which it guarantees. Fannie Mae was created by Congress in 1938 as a subsidiary of the Reconstruction Finance Corporation and became a fully private corporation as a result of the 1968 Housing Act.

Freddie Mac. Freddie Mac is a private, stockholder-owned corporation chartered by Congress and performing the same functions in the secondary market for residential mortgages as does Fannie Mae. Freddie Mac was created by the Emergency Home Finance Act of 1970 and was originally part of the Federal Home Loan Bank System. In 1989, the Financial Institutions Reform, Recovery, and Enforcement Act modified Freddie Mac's charter to make it essentially the same as that governing Fannie Mae.

Ginnie Mae (Government National Mortgage Association). A wholly owned government corporation within the U.S. Department of Housing and Urban Development, Ginnie Mae guarantees mortgage-backed securities with the full faith and credit of the federal government. Ginnie Mae mortgage pools consist of loans insured by the Federal Housing Administration or guaranteed by the Veterans Administration or by the Rural Housing Service (formerly the Farmers Home Administration). Ginnie Mae was created by the 1968 Housing Act.

Private mortgage conduits. These are mortgage pools that are not issued or guaranteed by Ginnie Mae, Fannie Mae, or Freddie Mac.

Individuals and others. This category includes individuals, mortgage companies, real estate investment trusts, state and local retirement funds, noninsured pension funds, state and local credit agencies, credit unions, and finance companies.

Table 4.3

Data Source:
   Federal Deposit Insurance Corporation (FDIC)
Reference:
   Federal Deposit Insurance Corporation, *Historical Statistics on Banking, 1934–1996.*

Definitions

Insured commercial bank and trust companies. The category of insured commercial banks includes all commercial banks insured by the Federal Deposit Insurance Corporation (FDIC) through the Bank Insurance Fund. It also includes all commercial banks insured by the FDIC through the Savings Association Insurance Fund that are regulated by and submit financial data to one of the three federal commercial bank regulators (Board of Governors of the Federal Reserve System, Federal De-

posit Insurance Corporation, or Office of the Comptroller of the Currency).

Construction and land development. The definition of this category has varied over time as follows:

1984 to the present. This category represents loans with maturities of 60 months or less that are secured by real estate and made to finance land development or the onsite construction of industrial, commercial, residential, or farm buildings. It includes new construction, additions, or alterations to existing structures and razing of existing structures to make way for new structures. Industrial development bonds are not included here any longer. They are reported as securities of states, counties, and municipalities (if rated) or in loans to states and political subdivisions if not rated.

1976 to 1983. This category represents loans secured primarily by real estate, the proceeds of which will be used to finance the construction of industrial, commercial, residential, or farm buildings; the acquisition, conversion and development of property into improved real estate; the construction of additions or alterations to existing structures; the demolition of existing structures in preparation for new construction; and loans to regional or local industrial development authorities who supply credit to business firms to assist in relocation or expansion.

1934 to 1975. Loans for the above purposes could have been included in any of the other categories of loans in this table during this period.

One- to four-family residential properties. The definition of this category has varied over time as follows:

1969 to the present. This category represents permanent loans secured by real estate as evidenced by mortgages (Federal Housing Administration, Department of Veterans Affairs, or conventional) or other liens on one- to four-family dwelling units, mobile homes, individual condominiums and co-ops, and vacant lots in established single-family residential sections.

1934 to 1968. This category includes permanent loans secured by real estate on both one- to four-family and on multifamily residential properties.

Multifamily residential properties. The definition of this category has varied over time as follows:

1969 to the present. Represents permanent nonfarm residential loans secured by real estate as evidenced by mortgages (Federal Housing Administration and conventional) or other liens on nonfarm properties with five or more dwelling units in apartments, housekeeping dwellings, cooperative-type apartment buildings, and vacant lots in established multifamily residential sections.

1934 to 1968. Multifamily residential real estate loans are included in the category "one- to four-family residential properties."

Farmland. From 1934 to the present, this category represents loans secured by farmland, including improvements, and other land known to be used or usable for agricultural purposes, as evidenced by mortgages or other liens. It includes loans secured by farmland that are guaranteed by the Farmers Home Administration or by the Small Business Administration.

Nonfarm nonresidential. The definition of this category has varied over time as follows:

1938 to the present. This category represents loans secured by real estate, as evidenced by mortgages or other liens on business and industrial properties, hotels, motels, churches, hospitals, educational and charitable institutions, dormitories, clubs, lodges, association buildings, homes for aged persons, golf courses, recreational facilities and other similar properties.

1934 to 1937. These loans are included in the category "one- to four-family residential properties."

Tables 4.4

Data Source:
    Federal Deposit Insurance Corporation (FDIC)
Reference:
    Federal Deposit Insurance Corporation, *Historical Statistics on Banking: 1934–1996.*

Definitions

FDIC-insured savings institutions. The category of Federal Deposit Insurance Corporation (FDIC)-insured savings institutions includes all institutions insured by either the Bank Insurance Fund or the Savings Association Insurance Fund operating under state or federal banking codes applicable to thrift institutions. Data on savings institutions that have been placed in Resolution Trust Corporation conservatorship are not aggregated with other savings institutions since they do not operate as privately held entities and their resolution costs do not accrue to the FDIC. The institutions covered in this category are regulated by and submit financial reports to one of two federal regulators—the FDIC or the Office of Thrift Supervision (OTS). Data for the savings institutions regulated by the FDIC are from the Federal Financial Institution Examination Council Reports of Income and Condition submitted to the FDIC (Call Reports). Data for savings institutions regulated by the OTS are from the Thrift Financial Reports.

Construction and land development. For 1984 to the present, this category represents loans secured by real estate made to finance land development preparatory to erecting new structures or the onsite construction of industrial, commercial, residential, or farm buildings. For Thrift Financial Reports filers, this category also includes loans made to acquire and improve developed and undeveloped land.

One- to four-family residential properties. The definition of this category has varied over time as follows:

1988 to the present. This period represents loans secured by real estate as evidenced by mortgages (government-backed and conventional) or other liens on one- to four-family dwelling units, mobile homes, individual condominiums and co-ops, and vacant lots in established single-family residential sections.

1984 to 1987. This period represents loans secured by real estate as evidenced by mortgages (government-backed or conventional) or other liens on one- to four-family dwelling units, mobile homes, individual condominiums and co-ops, and vacant lots in established single-family residential sections. For Thrift Financial Reports filers, this figure excludes home equity loans based on the creditworthiness of the borrower.

Multifamily residential properties. For 1984 to the present, this category represents permanent nonfarm residential loans secured by real estate with five or more dwelling units as evidenced by mortgages (Federal Housing Administration–insured and conventional) or other liens on apartments, housekeeping dwellings, cooperative-type apartment buildings, and vacant lots in established multifamily residential sections.

Nonresidential properties. For 1984 to the present, this category represents loans secured by real estate as evidenced by mortgages or other liens on business and industrial properties, farm properties, hotels, motels, churches, hospitals, educational and charitable institutions, dormitories, clubs, lodges, association buildings, homes for aged persons, golf courses, recreational facilities, and other similar properties.

Tables 4.5–4.8

Data Source:
  Residential Finance Survey
Reference:
  U.S. Bureau of the Census and U.S. Department of Housing and Urban Development, *1990 Census of Housing: Residential Finance*, 1990 CH-4-1, August 1994.

Definitions

Property. As defined in the 1991 Residential Finance Survey (RFS), property means real estate; that is, land and anything permanently affixed to the land, such as buildings and those things attached to the buildings, including light fixtures, plumbing and heating fixtures, or other such items that would be personal property if not attached. A property may consist of a single-family house (attached or detached), a multifamily house, a condominium unit, a single mobile home, a mobile home park, an apartment building, or a group of apartment buildings. If a property is mortgaged, the property is all land and buildings covered by a single first mortgage. If a property is not mortgaged, the property is the land and buildings identified by the address that appeared on the questionnaire label.

If a rental project or development is divided into sections or phases, each securing a separate first mortgage, each section or phase is considered a separate property. In the case of mortgaged properties, the number of properties is equal to the number of first mortgages.

Nonfarm. Properties classified as farms were not included in the RFS. A property was classified as nonfarm if it had one to four housing units and was on a place of fewer than 10 acres or if it had five or more units.

Residential. A property is considered residential if 50 percent or more of the floor space is used for residential purposes. If the owner indicated that the property consisted primarily of buildings or land that were essentially nonresidential in character, the property was classified as nonresidential and was out of the scope of the RFS.

Homeowner property. A homeowner property has one, two, three, or four housing units, at least one of which is occupied by the owner. Persons buying property and still owing money are considered owners, whether or not they hold legal title to the property. Homeowner data are presented for one-unit properties, two- to four-unit properties, mobile homes, and condominiums.

Rental and vacant properties. The term "rental and vacant" applies to properties with five or more housing units (even though one of the units may be occupied by an owner) and to properties with one to four housing units, all of which are either renter-occupied or vacant.

One-unit. A property consisting of one housing unit may be a single-family house (attached or detached), a condominium unit, or a single mobile home or trailer. Data are presented separately for one-unit properties, condominium properties, and mobile home properties.

Condominium. A condominium is a form of ownership in which a person owns a house or apartment in a development of similar units, and also holds a common or joint ownership in common areas or facilities that serve the project, such as land, roofs, hallways, entrances, elevators, etc. The owner has title to, and possibly a mortgage on, the unit. Although condominiums are one-unit properties by definition, data are presented separately for condominiums and other one-unit properties.

Mobile home or manufactured home. A mobile or manufactured home is a housing unit manufactured in a factory and designed to be transported, and perhaps permanently attached to, a site as opposed to conventional onsite construction. Individually owned mobile (manufactured) homes, as opposed to mobile homes owned and let to renters by a mobile home park, are one-unit properties by definition. However, data are presented separately for mobile homes and other one-unit properties.

Multiunit. This is a property consisting of more than one housing unit, regardless of the number of buildings and may be a multifamily house, a rental or cooperative apartment building or complex, or a mobile home park. Data are presented for 1- to 4-unit, 5- to 49-unit, or 50-unit or more properties.

Mortgage status. In the RFS, properties are classified mortgaged or nonmortgaged on the basis of information furnished by the owner and the lender. To ensure that all mortgage-type debts on the property were reported, the owner (or agent) was asked to report all of the various types of debt outstanding on the property. However, only mortgages were included in the survey. If there was any doubt about mortgage status of the property, confirmation was requested from the lender.

Mortgage. Mortgage refers to all forms of debt where the property is pledged as security for repayment of the debt. The following types of debt instruments or arrangements are classified as mortgages:

Mortgages, deeds of trust, trust deeds, mortgage bonds, and vendor liens. In such arrangements, the borrower generally has title to the property.

Contracts to purchase, contracts for deeds, and land contracts. These differ from mortgages or deeds of trust in that title to the property remains with the lender, who often is also the seller (i.e., the former owner) of the property. The buyer has the right to occupy the property so long as the payments on the debt are made. Title to the property passes to the buyer when the full or stipulated amount on the loan has been paid. For purposes of the RFS, the buyer is considered the "owner."

Nonmortgaged: The following types of debt are not mortgages and properties with only these types of debt are classified as nonmortgaged in the RFS: property improvement loans, such as Federal Housing Administration Title I loans not secured by the property; chattel mortgages (for example, mortgages on furniture, equipment, or other personal possessions that are not real estate); mechanics and tax liens; and judgment liens arising from a lawsuit against the property owner.

First mortgage. This is a mortgage having priority over all other voluntary liens against the property. A first mortgage gives the lender a first claim against the owner's rights in the property if the owner fails to meet the required payments on the mortgage.

First mortgage debt outstanding. This is the sum of unpaid principal balances on primary mortgages at the time the RFS was conducted. In some instances, it includes overdue or deferred interest.

Total mortgage debt outstanding. This is the sum of the unpaid balances of all mortgages (including home equity lines of credit) at the time of the survey.

Holder of mortgage. This term refers to the organization, institution, or person that has the legal right to the interest and principal due on the mortgage. The following categories of mortgage holders are included in the tables:

Commercial bank or trust company. This is a financial institution authorized to provide a variety of financial services. Although commercial banks have substantially increased their long-term mortgage lending in recent years, they have traditionally concentrated on short-term loans. They are good sources for construction loans, home improvement loans, junior loans secured by home equity, and home equity lines of credit.

Savings and loan association, federal savings bank. This is an association chartered to hold savings and make real estate loans. Such institutions are active in long-term financing rather than construction loans.

Mutual savings bank. This is a state-chartered savings institution owned by its depositors and operated for their benefit. These banks provide essentially the same financial services as commercial banks. Most of these banks are in the Northeastern United States and hold a large portion of their assets in home mortgage loans.

Life insurance company. The companies may use premiums received from policyholders and earnings received from investments to make loans secured by real estate.

Mortgage banker or mortgage company. This is a party or company providing mortgage financing with its own funds. Although the mortgage banker or company uses its own funds, these funds are generally borrowed and the financing is either short-term or long-term, but if long-term, the mortgages are sold to investors within a short time.

Mortgage pools. These are a collection of loans of similar characteristics that are sold as units in the secondary mortgage market or used to back securities, which are then sold in the capital markets.

Federally sponsored secondary market agency or pool. These refer to mortgages held or mortgage securities guaranteed by federally sponsored agencies such as the Farmers Home Administration (now the Rural Housing Service) and Ginnie Mae, and government-sponsored enterprises such as Fannie Mae and Freddie Mac.

Conventional mortgage pools. These are collections of loans not guaranteed by a federally sponsored or regulated agency.

Federal agency. This category includes mortgages that are held directly by an agency of the federal government often but not always as a result of foreclosure. The agencies include the Farmers Home Administration, U.S. Department of Housing and Urban Development, Resolution

Trust Corporation, Small Business Administration, and Department of Veterans Affairs.

Real estate investment trust. The trust sells shares of ownership and must invest in real estate or mortgages. If it meets certain requirements, it is exempt from corporate income tax.

Pension or retirement funds. These include state and local government retirement funds as well as private corporation pension or retirement funds.

Credit union. A credit union is an association governed by its members that performs many of the same services as a commercial bank.

Finance company. This type of lender makes loans primarily for consumer purchases. In many states, finance companies make home equity loans primarily, but not exclusively, as junior mortgages.

State or municipal government or housing finance agency. This category includes all nonfederal government agencies but excludes pension or retirement funds administered by such agencies.

Individual or individual's estate. Mortgages can be held directly (i.e., not as shares in a mortgage pool) by individual persons or estates of individuals that are not being administered as trust accounts by commercial banks.

Other. This category includes all organizations or institutions not listed above, such as nonprofit organizations, insurance companies not classified as life insurance companies, and trust accounts administered by a bank. This category also includes a few cases wherein the holder was not reported by the respondent or the type of holder could not be coded from the name provided.

Mortgage insurance status. This refers to the presence or absence of guaranty or insurance on a mortgage. Under a mortgage insurance program, the mortgage holder is assured of full or partial compensation of the unpaid principal balance if the borrower defaults on the mortgage payments. Mortgages may be insured or guaranteed by an agency of the federal or state government or by a private mortgage insurer. The following mortgage insurance categories are included in the tables:

FHA-insured first mortgages. These mortgages are made by private lending institutions and insured by the Federal Housing Administration (FHA) in the U.S. Department of Housing and Urban Development.

VA-guaranteed mortgages. VA-backed mortgages are made by private lending institutions and guaranteed or insured by the Department of Veterans Affairs.

FmHA-insured mortgages. These are made by private lenders and insured by the Farmer's Home Administration (now the Rural Housing Service) in the Department of Agriculture. Such mortgages are made to eligible purchasers of homes and farms in small towns and rural areas.

State bonding agencies. Bonding agencies act similarly to the FHA in insuring mortgages on large apartment properties as well as smaller residential properties.

Insured conventional mortgages. A private mortgage insurance company will, for a fee, issue insurance on mortgage loans similar to that offered by the FHA and Department of Veterans Affairs but usually not covering as great a proportion of the loan.

Uninsured conventional mortgages. These include mortgages other than government-insured or privately insured conventional mortgages.

Notes

Tables 4.5–4.6. In 1981, data were not collected for rental condominiums and homeowner and rental mobile homes, and data were not collected separately for the following types of holders of mortgages: conventional mortgage pools, real estate investment trusts, pension or retirement funds, credit unions, finance companies, and state or municipal governments or housing finance agencies.

Tables 4.9–4.12

Data Source:
    Survey of Mortgage Lending Activity
References:
    U.S. Department of Housing and Urban Development, monthly and quarterly press releases based on the Survey of Mortgage Lending Activity. HUD, "Survey of Mortgage Lending Activity: Annual Reports," <http://www.hud.gov/fha/comp/rpts/smla/gflistan.html>. HUD, *Instructions and Definitions for HUD136.1, Gross Flow of Mortgage Loans, and HUD136.2, Mortgage Loan Commitments.*

Definitions

Long-term mortgage loan. The term "mortgage loan" means indebtedness, regardless of purpose, incurred by a private borrower and secured by a mortgage or other lien (first or inferior) on completed real property.

Origination. Mortgage origination is the process by which a lender makes a mortgage secured by real property. The tables show the dollar volume of residential mortgage credit extended in a given period of time.

One- to four-family nonfarm home. Refers to nonfarm properties containing one, two, three, or four units. This category includes condominium apartments.

Multifamily residential. These are properties consisting of five or more dwelling units. The units may be situated in apartment houses, apartment hotels designed primarily to house persons on a more or less permanent basis, and housekeeping dwellings in properties that also contain commercial uses but that are primarily residential use.

Existing properties. This refers to any property that has been previously occupied. Included in this category are loans used to finance the purchase of an existing structure, to refinance an outstanding loan, to pay for improvements or alterations on an existing property (including those recently constructed), and to pay for nonrealty acquisitions or expenditures. It also includes add-on loans to finance property improvements, payments of taxes and insurance, and other nonrealty purposes.

New properties. This refers to completed newly constructed properties that have not been previously occupied and includes substantial additions made to an existing property.

Commercial banks. These are depository financial intermediaries chartered under either state or federal laws. In addition to their residential mortgage lending activities, commercial banks have traditionally played an important role in construction financing.

Savings and loan associations (S&Ls). S&Ls are depository financial institutions that may be either mutually or stockholder owned. S&Ls are chartered and regulated by either the federal government or a state government. Traditionally, S&L deposits have been invested in residential mortgage loans.

Mortgage companies. Mortgage companies are nondepository financial institutions that originate residential mortgage loans for sale to investors.

Mutual savings banks. These are mutually owned depository financial intermediaries chartered under state or federal laws.

Life insurance companies. These are nondepository financial intermediaries chartered at the state level that sell insurance policies and annuities and use the premiums plus reinvested dividends to make investments.

Federal credit agencies. This category includes the Rural Housing Service (formerly the Farmers Home Administration), Federal Housing Administration (FHA), Fannie Mae, Freddie Mac, Farm Credit Funding Corporation (Federal Land Banks), Ginnie Mae, and the Department of Veterans Affairs. Loans made pursuant to certain elderly and housing rehabilitation programs administered by HUD are also included in this category.

FHA-insured. These are loans insured by the Federal Housing Administration.

VA-guaranteed. VA-guaranteed loans are loans guaranteed by the Department of Veterans Affairs.

Conventional. This category refers to loans that are not insured or guaranteed by the Federal Housing Administration or the Department of Veterans Affairs. The Survey of Mortgage Lending Activity counts loans guaranteed by the Rural Housing Service as conventional loans.

Notes

The samples for commercial banks and mutual savings banks in the Survey of Mortgage Lending Activity were recently redrawn and new benchmark expansion weighting factors were created. In some instances, the changed methodology resulted in substantial revisions to the 1996 data and a significant shift in the level of lending activity compared with historical data. See *Survey of Mortgage Lending Activity Report: Fourth Quarter/Annual, 1996,* U.S. Department of Housing and Urban Development No. 9782, for additional information.

Table 4.13

Data Source:
  Primary Mortgage Market Survey
Reference:
  Freddie Mac, *Secondary Mortgage Markets: Mortgage Market Trends: 1997,* v.14, no. 2, July 1997. Updates provided by Freddie Mac, Financial Research.

Definitions

Refinance. A refinance is a type of loan transaction in which the existing mortgage is satisfied and replaced by a new obligation secured by the same property.

Tables 4.14–4.18

Data Source:
 Monthly Interest Rate Survey (Monthly Survey of Rates and Terms on Conventional One-Family Nonfarm Mortgage Loans)
References:
 U.S. Federal Housing Finance Board, *Federal Housing Finance Board News*, monthly, and *Rates and Terms on Conventional Home Mortgages, Annual Summary*. Historical data are available from U.S. Federal Housing Finance Board, "Monthly Interest Rate Survey," <http://www.fhfb.gov/mirs.htm>.

Definitions

New single-family home. This refers to a single-family home that has not been previously occupied prior to the sale. Single-family homes include fully detached, semidetached (semiattached, side-by-side), rowhouses, and townhouses. In the case of attached units, each must be separated from the adjacent unit by a ground-to-roof wall in order to be classified as a one-unit structure. Also, these units must not share heating/air-conditioning systems or interstructural public utilities, such as water supply, power supply, or sewage disposal lines.

Existing single-family home. This is a single-family home that has been occupied prior to the sale.

Conventional mortgage. A conventional mortgage loan is not insured or guaranteed by the federal government.

First mortgage. A first mortage creates a lien against real property and gives the holder first claim over other lienholders if the borrower defaults.

Home purchase loan. This refers to any loan secured by and made for the purpose of purchasing a dwelling.

Contract interest rate. This is the initial interest rate paid by the borrower as specified in the loan contract. For both adjustable-rate and fixed-rate loans, the contract rate reported is the initial rate on the mortgage.

Effective interest rate. The effective rate is the contract interest rate plus fees and charges amortized over a 10-year period, which is the assumed average life of a conventional mortgage loan.

Fixed-rate loan. With this type of mortgage the interest rate does not change during the life of the loan.

Adjustable-rate loan. The interest rate for this type of mortgage is periodically adjusted based on the movement in an index specified in the loan contract.

Initial fees, charges. These refer to all fees, commissions, discounts, and points paid by the borrower or seller in order to obtain the loan. The category excludes charges for mortgage, credit, life, or property insurance; for property transfer; and for title search and insurance. These charges are expressed as a percentage of the loan amount.

Term to maturity. The term of the loan is the total number of years for which the lender is obligated to provide funds.

Mortgage amount. This refers to the principal amount of the loan.

Purchase price. The purchase price is the estimated current market value of the loan collateral. Refinancing loans are excluded from the scope of coverage.

Loan-to-price ratio. The ratio is the dollar amount of the mortgage loan at origination divided by the purchase price of the home.

Notes

The tables reflect annual average terms and conditions on conventional, single-family, fully amortized, nonfarm, purchase money mortgage loans closed during the last five working days of each month. The data exclude multi-family loans, refinancing loans, nonamortized and balloon loans, loans insured by the Federal Housing Administration, and loans guaranteed by the Department of Veterans Affairs.

Table 4.19

Data Source:
 Primary Mortgage Market Survey
References:
 Freddie Mac, *Secondary Mortgage Markets: Mortgage Market Trends 1997*, vol. 14, no. 2, July 1997; historical data tables at <http://www.freddiemac.com/ function/fm-news/fm-pmms/pmms.htm#Historical>; and

weekly Primary Mortgage Market Survey news releases.

Definitions

Conventional conforming loan. This refers to a loan that is not insured or guaranteed by the federal government (conventional) and that meets the purchasing requirements of Fannie Mae and Freddie Mac (conforming).

Fixed-rate mortgage. The interest rate in this type of mortgage does not change during the life of the loan.

One-year adjustable-rate mortgage (ARM). An ARM has an interest rate that is periodically adjusted based on the movement in an index specified in the loan contract. For a 1-year ARM, the interest rate is adjusted annually. Before April 1986, the ARM index in the Primary Mortgage Market Survey was not specified. Since that time, the reported interest rate is for those ARMs indexed to the 1-year Treasury rate.

Commitment rate. This is the rate at which a lender would commit to lend mortgage money to a qualified borrower. It does not include fees, points, or private mortgage insurance. The commitment rates reported in the table apply only to conventional conforming mortgages with loan-to-value ratios of 80 percent or less.

Points. The points reported in the table represent all origination fees and discount points charged to the buyer and/or seller at settlement, expressed as a percentage of the loan amount.

Notes

The regional weights used to develop national estimates in the Primary Mortgage Market Survey were adjusted in July 1994 based on 1992 estimated dollar volumes of mortgage originations from the U.S. Department of Housing and Urban Development. The weights were adjusted again in October 1997 to reflect the dollar volume of mortgage originations reported under the Home Mortgage Disclosure Act for 1996.

Tables 4.20–4.21

Data Sources:
> Survey of Mortgage Lending Activity and data provided by the U.S. Department of Housing and Urban Development, Office of Housing; Department of Veterans Affairs; and Mortgage Insurance Companies of America

Reference:
> U.S. Department of Housing and Urban Development, Office of Policy Development and Research, *U.S. Housing Market Conditions,* quarterly.

Definitions

Mortgage insurance. Mortgage insurance protects the lender against loss in the event that a borrower defaults on a mortgage loan. Mortgage insurance is provided by private mortgage insurers, the Federal Housing Administration (FHA) within the U.S. Department of Housing and Urban Development, the Department of Veterans Affairs, and, to a much lesser degree, the Rural Housing Service.

FHA-insured. The term refers to mortgages that are insured by the FHA, an agency within the U.S. Department of Housing and Urban Development. One- to four-family mortgages are insured by the FHA under authority of Section 203(b) of the National Housing Act.

VA-guaranteed. This refers to loans guaranteed by the Department of Veterans Affairs and made to eligible veterans, their spouses, active-duty military personnel, and reservists.

Private insurance. Private mortgage insurance is provided by private companies that are regulated at the state level.

Not insured. This category includes a small number of loans backed by the Rural Housing Service (RHS). In 1994, the RHS backed less than 1 percent of all home purchase loans made.

Notes

The samples for commercial banks and mutual savings banks in the Survey of Mortgage Lending Activity were recently redrawn and new benchmark expansion weighting factors were created. In some instances, the changed methodology resulted in substantial revisions to the 1996 data and might affect historical comparability. See the Survey of Mortgage Lending Activity Report: Fourth Quarter/Annual, 1996 (U.S. Department of Housing and Urban Development No. 9782) for additional information.

Table 4.22

Data Source:
> U.S. Department of Housing and Urban Development, Office of Housing, FHA Comptroller

Reference:

U.S. Department of Housing and Urban Development, Office of Policy Development and Research, *U.S. Housing Market Conditions*, quarterly.

Definitions

Mortgage insurance activity. The table shows the number of projects for which mortgage insurance was written under the various insurance programs listed below.

Unassisted. The term refers to multifamily developments that are not receiving U.S. Department of Housing and Urban Development project-based rental assistance.

Construction of new rental units. This category includes insurance for loans made by private lenders and used to finance both new construction and substantial rehabilitation under Sections 207, 220, and 221(d).

Purchase or refinance of existing rental units. This category includes insurance for loans made by private lenders and used to purchase or refinance existing rental housing under Section 223.

Congregate housing, nursing home, assisted living, and board and care facilities. This category includes U.S. Department of Housing and Urban Development mortgage insurance for congregate rental housing for the elderly provided under Section 231, and nursing homes, board and care homes, assisted-living facilities, and intermediate-care facilities under Section 232. Loans may be for new construction, substantial rehabilitation, or purchase or refinancing of existing projects. The "units" column for this category includes both housing units and beds.

Table 4.23

Data Source:

1991 Residential Finance Survey

Reference:

U.S. Bureau of the Census and U.S. Department of Housing and Urban Development, *1990 Census of Housing: Residential Finance*, 1990 CH-4-1, August 1994.

Definitions

See Tables 4.5–4.8 for additional definitions.

The following types of first mortgage instruments are included in the table:

Fixed-rate mortgage (FRM). This instrument has an interest rate that is constant for the term of the loan. While a graduated-payment mortgage may be fixed-rate, such loans are not included in this category in these tabulations.

A short-term mortgage with a balloon payment. This instrument calls for periodic payments that are insufficient to fully amortize the face amount of the mortgage by the maturity date so that the remaining principal balance, known as the "balloon," is due at maturity.

An adjustable-rate mortgage (ARM). This allows the interest rate to change, usually based on an established index, at specified intervals over the term of the loan. This type of loan may be amortizing or nonamortizing.

Graduated-payment mortgages (GPM). This is a mortgage that allows lower payments in the early years of the mortgage. Payments increase in steps until the installments are sufficient to amortize the loan. A GPM allows for negative amortization in the early years of the loan; that is, the unpaid interest is added to the principal, thereby allowing the outstanding principal balance to exceed the face amount of the mortgage for a period of time.

Other type. This category includes loans, such as cash flow mortgages, that do not fit into the above categories.

Tables 4.24–4.26

Data Source:

American Housing Survey

References:

U.S. Bureau of the Census and U.S. Department of Housing and Urban Development, *American Housing Survey for the United States in 1991*, Current Housing Reports H150/91, April 1993, *American Housing Survey for the United States in 1993*, Current Housing Reports H150/93, February 1995, and *American Housing Survey for the United States in 1995*, Current Housing Reports H150/95RV, July 1997.

Definitions

See Definitions for Tables 2.11–2.31 for column heads.

Mortgages currently on property. The owner or the owner's spouse was asked the number of mortgages or similar loans (including home equity loans) currently in effect on the home. For mobile homes, if there was a separate loan for the mobile home and for the land, two mortgages were recorded. A mortgage or similar debt refers to all forms of debt where the property is pledged as security for payment of the debt. It includes such debt instruments as deeds of trust, trust deeds, mortgage bonds, and vendors' liens. In the first three arrangements, usually a third party, known as the trustee, holds the title to the property until the debt is paid. In the vendor lien arrangement, the title is kept by the buyer but the seller (vendor) reserves, in the deed to the buyer, a lien on the property to secure payment of the balance of the purchase price. Also included as a mortgage or similar debt are contracts to purchase, land contracts, and lease-purchase agreements where the title to the property remains with the seller until the agreed-upon payments have been made by the buyer.

Primary mortgage. Data are shown for primary mortgages and secondary mortgages. A mortgage is primary if it is the only one on the property. If two or more mortgages exist, one was designated as the primary mortgage. Detailed information on mortgages was collected in the AHS on the first two mortgages reported even if the unit had three or more mortgages. On the basis of this information, one of the first two mortgages was considered to be the primary mortgage. The definition of the primary mortgage may not in all cases totally agree with legal definitions of a "first mortgage." The following hierarchy was used to determine primary mortgage: (1) A Department of Veterans Affairs (VA), Federal Housing Administration (FHA), or Farmers Home Administration (FmHA) mortgage was automatically considered to be the primary mortgage. (2) If neither mortgage was a VA, FHA, or FmHA mortgage, an assumed mortgage was considered to be the primary mortgage. (3) If none of the above conditions existed, the mortgage obtained the year the home was purchased was considered to be the primary mortgage. (4) If both mortgages were obtained after the year of purchase, the one taken out first was considered to be the primary mortgage. (5) If all the above failed to designate a primary mortgage, the mortgage for the largest initial amount borrowed was considered the primary mortgage. All other mortgages were considered to be secondary.

Type of primary mortgage. Mortgage insurance is financial protection provided to the lender in case the borrower fails to keep up the required mortgage payments and defaults on the loan. Such insurance protection is offered both by the government, acting as an insurance agent, and by private mortgage insurance companies. The federal government agencies that currently insure or guarantee mortgages or similar debts include the Federal Housing Administration (FHA), the Department of Veterans Affairs (VA), and the Rural Housing Service (formerly the Farmers Home Administration). The FHA insures home loans made by private lenders. The Rural Housing Service provides much the same service as the FHA but confines its assistance to rural areas. The VA guarantees or insures loans under the Servicemen's Readjustment Act (GI Bill). Mortgage loans that are not insured by the FHA, VA, or Rural Housing Service are referred to as "conventional" mortgages. Conventional mortgages and mortgage debts insured or guaranteed by state or local government agencies are shown in the tables as "Other types."

Lower-cost state and local mortgages. Data are shown for owners with one or more mortgages. These are loans generally 1 to 3 percent below the current mortgage interest rate at the time the loan was made. The loans are managed through state or local governments. Excluded are federally funded VA programs.

Mortgage origination. Data are shown for owner-occupied units with one or more mortgages. For units with new mortgages, data are classified by the date the new mortgage was obtained in relation to the date the property was acquired. An assumed mortgage indicates that the present mortgage is the same mortgage that was assumed from the previous owner when the property was acquired and it has not been refinanced. A wraparound mortgage is a mortgage whose face value encompasses the unpaid balance of the first mortgage(s) plus the amount of any new funds extended by the wraparound lender. "Combination of the above" means that there was more than one method of origination for the outstanding mortgages on the property.

Payment plans of primary mortgage. The term "payment" refers to regular principal and interest payments only, and not to payments for real estate taxes, property insurance, etc. Fixed-payment, self-amortizing mortgages have payments that do not change during the term of the loan, with the principal payments sufficient to pay off the loan completely within the stated term. Adjustable-rate mortgages are mortgages whose interest rates could be changed during the life of the mortgage, thereby changing the amount of the payments required. In adjustable-term mortgages, the amount of the payments stays constant, but the number of payments required to pay off the loan can change over time as interest rates change. Graduated-payment mortgages allow monthly payments to change during the term of the mortgage by means other than a change in interest rate. These mortgages begin with lower payments that rise later in the life of the mortgage. Balloon mortgages are mortgages in which only part or none of the principal is paid off during the term of the loan (which commonly is about 5 years). At the end of the term the principal is paid off in one lump sum, refinanced with a new loan, or extended by renewal of the loan.

Lenders of primary and secondary mortgages. This item is restricted to units with two or more mortgages. The data are classified by whether the money was borrowed from a firm (bank or other organization), the seller of the property, or from another individual. Other organizations consist of mortgage corporations, pension plans, credit unions, savings and loan associations, etc. Individuals include anyone who was not the most recent owner.

Items included in primary mortgage payment. The respondent was asked to indicate which items were included in the monthly mortgage payment besides principal and interest. These items included property taxes, property insurance, and other charges. Other charges, which may include insurance premiums, disability insurances, life insurances, etc., may tally in more than one category.

Year primary mortgage originated. The year the primary mortgage was originated is the year the mortgage was signed. Medians for year primary mortgage originated are rounded to the nearest year.

Term of primary mortgage at origination or assumption. The term is the number of years from the date the new owners first obtained the present mortgage to the date the last payment is due according to the terms of the contract. Medians for term of primary mortgage are rounded to the nearest year.

Remaining years mortgaged. The owner or owner's spouse was asked the length of time it would take to pay off the loan at the current payments. The response reflects the amortization schedule. Medians for remaining years mortgaged are rounded to the nearest year.

Current interest rate. This item refers to the annual percentage rate in effect as of the date of the interview, not the rate when the mortgage was made, nor any imminent changes of which the respondent may be aware. Medians for current interest rate are rounded to the nearest 10th.

In 1993, a programming error was discovered and corrected involving the computation of the median for the current interest rate. The medians presented in the 1991 American Housing Survey national report (U.S. Bureau of the Census and U.S. Department of Housing and Urban Development, H150/91) are calculated incorrectly. However, the data distributions are correct and can be used to compute corrected medians.

Total outstanding principal amount. The statistics shown represent the total amount of principal that would have to be paid off if the loan were paid off in full on the date of interview. The formula used to calculate the outstanding principal amount does not take into account the fact that some households make additional principal payments. The resulting data, therefore, may be an overestimate of the total outstanding principal. Medians for outstanding principal amount are rounded to the nearest dollar.

Current total loan as percent of value. This percentage is computed by dividing the outstanding principal amount by the value of the housing unit. Medians for loan as a percent of value are rounded to the nearest tenth of a percent.

Notes

A variety of data on mortgages and homeowner properties are presented in publications from the Residential Finance Survey (RFS). Differences in the concepts and definitions in this survey and the American Housing Survey (AHS) include the following: the basic unit of tabulation in AHS is the housing unit; in the RFS, it is the property. All the data in AHS are provided by the occupant; in the RFS, mortgage information is reconciled with responses from the lender.

Table 4.27

Data Source:
National Delinquency Survey
References:
Mortgage Bankers Association of America, *National Delinquency Survey*, quarterly. These data are also published in U.S. Department of Housing and Urban Development, *U.S. Housing Market Conditions*, quarterly.

Definitions

Delinquency rate. The total past-due column shows the proportion of outstanding loans in the National Delinquency Survey that have an installment 30 days or more past due. Loans in foreclosure are not included in the count of delinquent mortgages.

Foreclosures started during period. This category includes loans placed in the process of foreclosure during the period. Foreclosure is a legal process by which a lender seeks to take possession of a property that is securing a defaulted mortgage. This category also includes deeds in lieu of foreclosure and loans assigned to the Federal Housing Administration, Department of Veterans Affairs, or other insurers or investors.

Conventional loans. A conventional mortgage loan is not insured or guaranteed by the federal government.

FHA loans. FHA loans are loans insured by the Federal Housing Administration.

VA loans. VA loans are loans guaranteed by the Department of Veterans Affairs.

Notes

These national data include loans in Puerto Rico.

Table 4.28

Data Source:
    Survey of Mortgage Lending Activity
References:
    U.S. Department of Housing and Urban Development, monthly and quarterly press releases based on the *Survey of Mortgage Lending Activity*; and, "Survey of Mortgage Lending Activity: Annual Reports," <http://www.hud.gov/fha/comp/rpts/smla/gflistan.html>.

Definitions

See Definitions for Tables 4.5–4.8 and 4.9–4.12 for additional explanations of the institutional categories included in the tables.

Pension funds. This category includes private and state and local retirement funds.

Private mortgage-backed conduits. These are private, nonagency (i.e., not Fannie Mae, Freddie Mac, or Ginnie Mae) issuers of mortgage-backed securities. In general,

private conduits securitize conventional mortgages that do not meet the purchasing requirements of Fannie Mae and Freddie Mac. Prior to 1982, this category included Real Estate Investment Trusts.

Mortgage pools. The mortgage pools category includes purchases and sales of loans by the Rural Housing Service (formerly the Farmers Home Administration), Freddie Mac, Fannie Mae, and Ginnie Mae for their mortgage-backed securities.

Notes

The samples for commercial banks and mutual savings banks in the Survey of Mortgage Lending Activity were recently redrawn and new benchmark expansion weighting factors were created. In some instances, the changed methodology resulted in substantial revisions to the 1996 data and a significant shift in the level of lending activity compared with historical data. See *Survey of Mortgage Lending Activity Report: Fourth Quarter/Annual, 1996* (U.S. Department of Housing and Urban Development No. 9782) for additional information.

Tables 4.29–4.31

Data Sources:
    Fannie Mae, Freddie Mac, and Ginnie Mae
Reference:
    Freddie Mac, *Secondary Mortgage Markets: Mortgage Market Trends 1997*, vol. 14, no. 2, July 1997.

Definitions

See Definitions for Tables 4.1–4.2 for descriptions of Fannie Mae, Freddie Mac, and Ginnie Mae.

Pass-through mortgage-backed securities. Holders of pass-through mortgage-backed securities (MBS) own an undivided interest in a pool of underlying mortgages and receive a monthly pro rata "pass-through" of principal and interest payments from the pool. Any prepayments on the underlying mortgages are also passed through to MBS holders on a pro rata basis. Freddie Mac, Fannie Mae, and Ginnie Mae provide guarantees of timely payments of principal and interest in exchange for retaining a guaranty fee.

Multiclass mortgage securities. These are security instruments, collateralized by pass-through mortgage-backed securities or groups of mortgage loans, that redistribute cash flows from the underlying collateral into different classes, or "tranches," of bonds with different risk profiles, payment structures, and maturities.

Conventional one- to four-family fixed-rate loans. These are loans on one- to four-unit residential properties that are not insured or backed by the federal government and that have a fixed rate of interest for the life of the loan.

Conventional one- to four-family ARMs (adjustable-rate mortgages). These are loans on one- to four-unit residential properties that are not insured or backed by the federal government and that have an interest rate that adjusts periodically based on the movement in an index specified in the loan contract.

FHA/VA loans. These are loans insured by the Federal Housing Administration or guaranteed by the Department of Veterans Affairs.

Multifamily loans. These are loans on residential properties with five or more units.

Table 4.32

Data Sources:
Fannie Mae and Freddie Mac
Reference:
Office of Federal Housing Enterprise Oversight, *1998 Report to Congress.*

Definitions

Total assets. This category includes the net retained mortgage portfolio plus loss reserves, cash and cash equivalents, investments, real estate owned, and other assets.

Retained mortgage portfolio outstanding. This category is the gross unpaid principal balance on mortgages and mortgage-backed securities held in portfolio net of unamortized purchase premiums, discounts, and fees.

Mortgage-backed securities (MBS) and multiclass MBS. See Tables 4.29–4.31.

Notes

For detailed breakdowns of each asset or liability class, see Freddie Mac's *Investor Analyst Report,* and Fannie Mae's *Investor/Analyst Report.*

Tables 4.33–4.39

Data Source:
Home Mortgage Disclosure Act data

References:
Board of Governors of the Federal Reserve System, *Federal Reserve Bulletin*, September 1995, September 1996, and September 1997. U.S. General Accounting Office, *Fair Lending: Federal Oversight and Enforcement Improved but Some Challenges Remain* (GAO/GGD-96-145).

Definitions

Application. An application means an oral or written request for a home purchase or home improvement loan that is made in accordance with procedures established by a financial institution for the type of credit requested.

Government-backed. The term refers to a loan insured or guaranteed by the Federal Housing Administration, Department of Veterans Affairs, or the Farmers Home Administration/Rural Housing Service.

Conventional. This refers to any loan other than those insured or guaranteed by the Federal Housing Administration, Department of Veterans Affairs, or the Farmers Home Administration/Rural Housing Service.

Home purchase loan. A home purchase loan is any loan secured by and made for the purpose of purchasing a dwelling.

Home improvement loan. A home improvement loan is a loan that will be used for repairing, rehabilitating, remodeling, or improving a dwelling (or the real property on which it is located) and that is classified by the reporting institution as a home improvement loan. The term covers both secured and unsecured loans.

Refinancing. Refinancing is a loan transaction in which the existing obligation, involving either a home purchase or a home improvement loan, is satisfied and replaced by a new obligation.

Income of applicant. The income of the applicant is the gross annual income that the reporting institution relied upon in making the credit decision. In calculating the income ratio, the applicant's income is divided by the metropolitan statistical area (MSA) median, which is the median family income of the MSA in which the property related to the loan is located.

Joint application. A joint application is one with White and non-White coapplicants.

Census tract income. Census tracts are categorized by the median family income for the tract relative to the median family income for the MSA in which the tract is located. The categories are as follows. Low or moderate: median family income for the census tract is less than 80 percent of the median family income for the MSA. Middle income: median family income of the tract is at least 80 percent of and less than 120 percent of MSA median. Upper income: median family income of the tract is 120 percent or greater of the MSA median.

Location. The location category applies to those census tracts located in MSA. Tracts are identified as being located inside or outside of a central city, as designated by the Office of Management and Budget.

Type of purchaser. See Definitions for Tables 4.1–4.2 for institution types.

Affiliate. The term refers to an affiliate of the institution reporting the loan.

Notes

The following transactions are excluded from reporting under the Home Mortgage Disclosure Act:

- Loans made or purchased in a fiduciary capacity
- Loans on unimproved land
- Construction loans and other temporary financing (but construction-permanent loans are reported)
- Purchase of an interest in a pool of mortgages, such as a mortgage participation certificate, a Real Estate Mortgage Investment Conduit, or a mortgage-backed security
- Purchases solely of servicing rights to loans
- Loans that, although secured by real estate, are made for purposes other than home purchase or home improvement or for refinancing (for example, loans to finance tuition, a vacation, or goods)
- The acquisition of only a partial interest in a home purchase or a home improvement loan by the reporting institution, even if the institution participated in the underwriting and origination of the loan
- Prequalification requests for mortgage loans

Tables 4.40–4.42

Data Source:

Data from private mortgage insurers submitted to the Federal Financial Institutions Examination Council through the Mortgage Insurance Companies of America

References:

Board of Governors of the Federal Reserve System, *Federal Reserve Bulletin*, September 1997, special tables 4.42–4.45. Glenn B. Canner, Wayne Passmore, and Brian J. Surette, "Distribution of Credit Risk Among Providers of Mortgages to Lower-Income and Minority Homebuyers," *Federal Reserve Bulletin*, December 1996. Glenn B. Canner, and Wayne Passmore, "Credit Risk and the Provision of Mortgages to Lower-Income and Minority Homebuyers," *Federal Reserve Bulletin*, December 1995. The notes provided below are taken from Canner, Passmore, and Surette (1996).

Definitions

See Definitions for Tables 4.33–4.39.

Private mortgage insurance application. The table shows data for mortgage insurance applications acted on by a private mortgage insurer during a given period.

Policies written. This represents the number of loans insured.

Notes

In 1993, the Mortgage Insurance Companies of America (MICA), which is the trade association for the private mortgage insurance (PMI) industry, asked the Federal Financial Institutions Examination Council (FFIEC) to process data from private mortgage insurance companies on applications for mortgage insurance and to produce public disclosure reports based on the data. The MICA request was a response to public and congressional interest in the activities of PMI companies as they relate to issues of fair lending, affordable housing, and community development.

PMI companies record data on each application for private mortgage insurance they act on during a given period. The data include the action taken on the application (approved, denied, withdrawn, or file closed because of incomplete information); the purpose of the mortgage for which insurance was sought (home purchase or refinance); the race or ethnic group, sex, and annual income of the applicant(s); the amount of the mortgage; and the geographic location of the property securing the mortgage.

The FFIEC summarizes the information in disclosure statements similar to those created for financial institutions covered by the Home Mortgage Disclosure Act (HMDA). Disclosure statements for each PMI company are publicly available at the company's headquarters and at a central depository in each metropolitan statistical area (MSA) in which HMDA data are held. The central depository also holds aggregate data for all the PMI companies active in the MSA. In addition, the PMI data are available from the Federal Reserve Board.

Table 4.43

Data Source:
   U.S. Department of Justice
Reference:
   U.S. General Accounting Office, *Fair Lending: Federal Oversight and Enforcement Improved but Some Challenges Remain.* (GAO/GGD-96-145).

Definitions

Fair lending laws. The Equal Credit Opportunity Act and Fair Housing Act, enacted in 1974 and 1968, respectively, comprise the federal civil rights statutes applicable to extensions of credit by banks and other lending institutions. Together, these statutes—referred to as the "fair lending laws" in the table—prohibit discrimination in all forms of credit transactions, including consumer and business loans as well as mortgage loans.

Referral. A referral occurs when a bank regulatory agency or the U.S. Department of Housing and Urban Development turns over an apparent fair lending violation to the Department of Justice (DOJ), which then assesses the nature of the case to determine if the apparent violation warrants a full investigation. If not, the case is returned to the appropriate agency to be handled administratively. In practice, this process can be informal, with DOJ and the banking regulatory agencies engaged in two-way discussions regarding the merits of individual cases so as to ascertain how best to pursue enforcement.

Table 4.44

Data Source:
   National Housing Survey
Reference:
   Fannie Mae, *Fannie Mae National Housing Survey,* annual.

Notes

The following question from the National Housing Survey is used to collect the data presented in the table:

"How often do you feel each of the following groups suffers from discrimination in the availability of mortgages—all of the time, most of the time, some of the time, rarely, or never?"

The table shows the proportion of respondents answering that a given group (African Americans, Hispanic Americans, Asian Americans, or women) experiences discrimination "all of the time" or "most of the time." The racial/ethnic identity of the respondent is based on the following two questions: first, "Is any member of your family, including yourself, of Hispanic or Spanish-speaking origin?" and second, "And what is your race?" Hispanics include adults who either say they or a member of their family is of Hispanic or Spanish-speaking origin or who say they are Hispanic in response to the race question.

Part 5: Federal Housing Assistance

Table 5.1

Data Source:
   Estimates of federal tax expenditures prepared by the U.S. Congress, Joint Committee on Taxation
Reference:
   U.S. Congress, Joint Committee on Taxation, *Estimates of Federal Tax Expenditures for Fiscal Years 1998–2002,* JCS-22-97, December 15, 1997.

Definitions

Tax expenditure. Tax expenditures are defined by the Congressional Budget and Impoundment Control Act of 1974 as "... those revenue losses attributable to provisions of the federal tax laws which allow a special exclusion, exemption, or deduction from gross income or which provide a special credit, a preferential rate of tax, or a deferral of tax liability." The legislative history of the act further indicates that tax expenditures are identified with reference to "normal tax law." In identifying tax expenditures, the Joint Committee on Taxation staff must exercise their judgment in distinguishing between those income tax provisions (and regulations) that can be viewed as part of normal tax law and those special provisions that result in tax expenditures.

Deductibility of mortgage interest on owner-occupied residences. A taxpayer may take an itemized deduction for "qualified residence interest," which includes interest paid on a mortgage secured by a principal residence and a second residence. The underlying mortgage loans can represent acquisition indebtedness of up to $1 million, plus home equity indebtedness of up to $100,000.

Deductibility of property tax on owner-occupied residences. Taxpayers may claim an itemized deduction for property taxes paid on owner-occupied residences.

Exclusion of capital gains on sales of principal residence. As of May 6, 1997, a taxpayer generally is able to exclude up to $250,000 (single taxpayers) or $500,000 (married taxpayers filing joint returns) of gain realized on the sale or exchange of a principal residence. The exclusion is allowed each time a taxpayer meets the eligibility requirements, but generally no more frequently than once every two years.

Exclusion of interest on state and local government bonds for owner-occupied housing. Interest income on state and local bonds issued to provide mortgages at below-market interest rates on owner-occupied principal residences of first-time homebuyers is tax exempt. The issuer of mortgage bonds typically uses bond proceeds to purchase mortgages made by a private lender. The homeowners make their monthly payments to the private lender, which passes them through as payments to the bondholders. Numerous limitations have been imposed on state and local Mortgage Revenue Bond programs, including restrictions on purchase prices of the houses that can be financed, on the income of the homebuyers, and on the portion of the bond proceeds that must be expended for mortgages in targeted (lower income) areas.

Exclusion of interest on state and local government bonds for rental housing. Interest income on state and local bonds used to finance the construction of multifamily residential rental housing units for low- and moderate-income families is tax exempt. Several requirements have been imposed on these projects, primarily on the share of the rental units that must be occupied by low-income families and the length of time over which the income restrictions must be satisfied.

Depreciation of rental housing in excess of alternative depreciation system. Taxpayers are allowed to deduct the costs of acquiring depreciable assets (assets that wear out or become obsolete over a period of years) as depreciation deductions. Since 1986, the tax code has allowed new rental housing to be written off over 27.5 years, using a "straight line" method where equal amounts are deducted each period. The tax expenditure measures the revenue loss from current depreciation deductions in excess of the deductions that would have been allowed under a 40-year write-off period.

Low-income housing tax credit. This program allows for tax credits equal to a portion of acquisition costs for qualified housing units. The credit rate is set so that the present value of the tax credit is equal to 70 percent for new construction and 30 percent for substantially rehabilitated housing or housing receiving other federal benefits (such as tax-exempt bond financing). Credits are permitted only for the fraction of units serving low-income tenants and these units are subject to maximum rent restrictions. To qualify for tax credits, a rental housing project must have 20 percent of its units occupied by families with less than 50 percent of area median income or 40 percent of its units occupied by families with less than 60 percent of area median income. Low-income housing tax credits are allocated through state housing agencies.

Tax credit for first-time homebuyers in the District of Columbia. The Taxpayer Relief Act of 1997 provides a tax credit of up to $5,000 to first-time homebuyers of a principal residence in the District of Columbia. The credit is phased out for taxpayers with adjusted gross incomes above certain levels. The credit is available for property purchased after August 5, 1997, and prior to January 1, 2001.

Notes

Some of the tax expenditure estimates presented in the table, which were first published in December 1997, may differ from estimates for the same years published before 1997. The reasons for these differences are changes in tax laws and economic conditions, the availability of better data, and improved estimating techniques. The estimates are based on the provisions in tax law as enacted through December 12, 1997.

The Taxpayer Relief Act of 1997, signed by President Clinton on August 5, 1997, changed the tax treatment of gains on the sale of a principal residence. Under the act, a taxpayer generally is able to exclude up to $250,000 (single taxpayers) or $500,000 (married taxpayers filing joint returns) of gain realized on the sale or exchange of a principal residence. The exclusion is allowed each time a taxpayer meets the eligibility requirements, but generally no more frequently than once every two years. The provision is effective for sales or exchanges occurring after May 6, 1997. This tax expenditure is listed as "exclusion of capital gains on sales of principal residences" in the table. It replaces two tax expenditure provisions from prior law, the "deferral of capital gains on sales of principal residences," and "exclusion of capital gains on sales of principal residences for persons aged 55 and over ($125,000 exclusion)," which are no longer listed in the table.

Tables 5.2–5.5

Data Source:
  Congressional Budget Office tabulations of data provided by the U.S. Department of Housing and Urban Development and the Rural Housing Service
Reference:
  U.S. House of Representatives, Committee on Ways and Means, *1998 Green Book: Background Material and Data on Programs within the Jurisdiction of the Committee on Ways and Means*, Ways and Means Committee Print WMCP: 105–7.

Definitions

New construction. These programs involve federal subsidies for the production of new assisted rental housing. They include the Department of Housing and Urban Development (HUD)–administered Public Housing Program, Section 8 New Construction and Substantial Rehabilitation Program, and Section 236 Mortgage Interest Subsidy Program. They also include the Section 515 Mortgage Interest Subsidy Program administered by the Rural Housing Service (formerly Farmers Home Administration). Commitments for the production of new units are still being funded through a modified version of the Section 8 New Construction Program for elderly and disabled families only and the Section 515 program. Some assistance has also been funded annually under two small HUD programs authorized in 1983—the rental housing development action grants (HoDAG) and the Rental Rehabilitation Block Grant Programs. The Housing and Community Development Act of 1987 terminated the HoDAG program at the end of fiscal year 1989, and the 1990 Housing Act repealed the Rental Rehabilitation Block Grant Program at the end of fiscal year 1991. A small number of renters continue to receive project-based subsidies through the now inactive Section 221(d)(3) below-market interest rate and rent supplement programs.

Existing housing. In contrast to the new construction programs, existing housing programs provide subsidies that are used in the existing private rental stock. Household-based subsidies are provided through two components of the Section 8 Existing Housing Program—Section 8 rental certificates and vouchers. These programs, both of which are currently active, tie aid to households that choose standard units in the private housing stock. Certificate holders generally must occupy units with rents that are within guidelines—the so-called fair market rents—established by the HUD. Voucher recipients, however, are allowed to occupy units with rents above the HUD guidelines, provided they pay the difference.

Some project-based aid is also provided through several components of HUD's Section 8 Existing Housing Program, which tie subsidies to specific units in the existing housing stock, many of which have received other forms of aid or mortgage insurance through HUD. These components, all of which are currently active, include the Section 8 loan management set-aside and property disposition components, which are designed to improve cash flows in selected financially troubled projects that are or were insured by the Federal Housing Administration. Other components include the Section 8 conversion assistance component, which subsidizes units that were previously aided through other programs, and the Section 8 Moderate Rehabilitation Program, which provides subsidies tied to units that are brought up to standard by the owner. The 1990 Housing Act repealed the Section 8 Moderate Rehabilitation Program at the end of fiscal year 1991, except for single-room-occupancy units for the homeless.

Assisted homeowners. This category includes programs that assist some low- and moderate-income households in becoming homeowners. Although a small number of very low-income homeowners receive grants or loans each year from the Rural Housing Service (RHS) for housing repairs, most programs help households become homeowners by making long-term commitments to reduce their interest rates. Most of this aid has been provided through the Section 502 program administered by the RHS. This program supplies direct mortgage loans at low interest rates roughly equal to the long-term government borrowing rates or provides guarantees for private loans with interest rates that may not exceed those set by the Department of Veterans Affairs. Many homebuyers, however, receive much deeper subsidies through the interest-credit component of this program, which reduces their effective interest rate to as low as 1 percent.

A number of homebuyers have received aid through the Section 235 program administered by HUD. This program provides interest subsidies for mortgages financed by private lenders. New commitments are now being made only through the Section 502 program, but a small number of homeowners continue to receive aid from prior commitments made under the Section 235 program.

New commitments. Net new commitments for renters represent net additions to the available pool of rental aid and are defined as the total number of commitments for which new funds are appropriated in any year. To avoid double-counting, these numbers are adjusted for the number of commitments for which such funds are deobligated or canceled that year (except where noted otherwise); the number of commitments for units converted from one type of assistance to another; in the RHS Section 515 program, the number of units that receive more than one subsidy; starting in 1985, the number of commitments specifically designed to replace those lost because private owners of assisted housing opt out of the programs or because public housing units are demolished; and, starting in 1989, the number of commitments for units whose Section 8 contracts expire.

New commitments for homebuyers are defined as the total number of new loans that the RHS or HUD makes or subsidizes each year. This measure of program activity is meant to indicate how many new homebuyers can be helped each year and is therefore not adjusted to account for homeowners who leave the programs in any year because of mortgage repayments, prepayments, or foreclosures. Thus, it does not represent net additions to the total number of assisted homeowners and therefore cannot be added to net new commitments for renters.

Net budget authority. Traditionally, funding for most additional commitments for housing assistance is provided each year through appropriations of long-term budget authority for subsidies to households and through appropriations of budget authority for grants, direct loans, and loan guarantees to public housing agencies, homebuyers, and developers of rental housing. Today, new rental subsidies are funded for either 1 or 5 years at a time, depending on program type. The figures are net of funding rescissions, exclude reappropriations of funds, but include supplemental appropriations.

Outlays. Outlays are expenditures on behalf of all households actually receiving aid in a given year.

Notes

Table 5.4. Net budget authority includes $99 million, $1,164 million, $8,814 million, $7,585 million, $6,926 mil-

lion, $5,202 million, $2,197 million, $4,008 million, and $3,550 million for renewing expiring Section 8 contracts in 1989, 1990, 1991, 1992, 1993, 1994, 1995, 1996, and 1997 respectively. Totals include funds appropriated for various public housing programs, including modernization and operating subsidies, drug elimination, and severely distressed public housing. Totals exclude budget authority for the HUD's Section 202 loan fund and for programs administered by the RHS.

Table 5.5. The bulge in total outlays and outlays per unit in 1985 is caused by a change in the method of financing public housing, which generated close to $14 billion in one-time expenditures. Without this change, outlays per unit would have amounted to around $2,860. The one-time expenditure paid off—all at once—the capital cost of public housing construction and modernization activities undertaken between 1974 and 1985, which otherwise would have been paid off over periods of up to 40 years. Because of this one-time expenditure, however, outlays for public housing since that time have been lower than they would have been otherwise.

Tables 5.6–5.8

Data Source:
   Housing Assistance Council tabulations of Rural
   Housing Service/Farmers Home Administration data
References:
   Housing Assistance Council, Inc. *The RHCDS Housing Program in Fiscal Year 1996: A Year of Serious Consequences*, April 1997. Updates for 1997 were provided by Arthur Collings of the Housing Assistance Council. Definitions are from Housing Assistance Council, Inc., *The RHCDS Housing Program in Fiscal Year 1995: A Year of Less*, March 1996, and Housing Assistance Council, Inc., "Information Sheets," <http://www.ruralhome.org/pubs/infoshts/>.

Definitions

Rural. With the exception of its farm labor housing program, which is also available in urban areas, the Rural Housing Service (RHS) makes housing loans and grants only in rural areas. RHS defines "rural" as open country that is not part of or associated with an urban area, or any town, village, city, or place, including an immediately adjacent densely settled area, that (1) is not part of, or associated with an urban area, has a population not in excess of 10,000, and is rural in character; (2) has a population under 20,000, is outside a metropolitan statistical area, and has a serious lack of mortgage credit for low-income families, as agreed to by the Secretaries of Agriculture and Housing and Urban Development; or (3) was determined to be rural prior to October 1, 1990, and whose population on or after the 1990 decennial census does not exceed 25,000, is rural in character, and has a serious lack of mortgage credit as determined by the Secretaries of Agriculture and Housing and Urban Development.

Dollars obligated. Obligations are commitments to spend appropriated funds. The expenditures need not occur in the year in which the obligated dollars are listed, but instead may be spent out over a number of years.

Units produced and households assisted. The term refers to units produced with RHS loans or grants and households receiving rural rental housing assistance payments in a given year. They are not cumulative. The grand total for each year is not unduplicated; that is, it may count some units twice that are receiving more than one RHS housing loan, grant, or tenant-based assistance payments.

Program descriptions. The major RHS loan, grant, and rental assistance programs included in the tables are described as follows:

Section 502 homeownership loans. Under this program, the RHS makes direct loans that enable low- and very low-income households to purchase, build, repair, renovate, or relocate houses, including manufactured homes. Loans may also be used to purchase and prepare sites, provide water supply or sewage disposal to the site, or refinance debts to avoid loss of the home or make rehabilitation affordable.

The RHS also has a growing guaranteed loan program under Section 502 whereby loans are made by private lenders and guaranteed by the RHS. These loans are made under a separate appropriation and are available to families with incomes up to 115 percent of area median family income.

Section 504 housing repair loans and grants. Section 504 provides loans and grants to very low-income homeowners to repair, improve, or modernize their dwellings or to remove health or safety hazards. Grants are available only to very low-income (income below 50 percent of area median) homeowners 62 years of age or older and only to pay for removal of health or safety hazards or to make the dwelling more safe and sanitary.

Section 515 rural rental housing and cooperative housing loans. Under Section 515, RHS provides direct loans to finance modest rental or cooperatively owned housing for very low-, low-, and moderate-income families, the elderly, and persons with disabilities. Funds may be used to construct new housing or to purchase and rehabilitate existing structures. Funds may also be used to buy and improve land and to provide necessary facilities such as water and waste disposal systems. RHS rental assistance, or Section 8 or state rental assistance, may also be used in combination with Section 515 loans to make rents affordable. The rural cooperative housing loan program is a variant of the Section 515 rural rental housing loan program that is designed for cooperative housing corporations.

Section 514 farm labor housing loans and Section 516 farm labor housing grants. Loans and grants under these programs are used to build, buy, improve, or repair housing for farm laborers, including persons whose income is earned in aquaculture (fish and oyster farms) and those engaged in on-farm processing. Funds can be used to purchase a site or a leasehold interest in a site, to construct the housing, to construct day care facilities and community rooms, to pay fees, to purchase durable household furnishings, and to pay construction loan interest.

Section 521 rural rental assistance payments. This program enables low-income families or individuals to reside in RHS rural rental, cooperative, or farm labor housing without paying over 30 percent of their income for rent. The RHS pays the owner of the property the difference between the tenant's contribution and the monthly rental rate, including the cost of all utilities and services. Rental assistance contracts between the RHS and the owner are for 5 years and are renewable.

Section 533 rural housing preservation grants. Rural housing preservation grants enable sponsoring organizations to assist low- and very low-income homeowners and landlords serving low-income populations to repair or rehabilitate their properties. For rental properties, landlords must agree to maintain the units for low-income use for a minimum of 5 years. The grants are competitive and made available in areas where there is a concentration of need.

Section 523 rural self-help housing technical assistance grants. The self-help technical assistance program provides administrative funding to organizations sponsoring self-help housing development. Under self-help, a group of families jointly contribute labor to build their own homes, which are usually financed under the RHS's Section 502 loan program (see definition under Section 502 homeownership loans). Individual families also participate to rehabilitate their own homes. The purposes of the program are to lower the cost of housing and provide skills enhancement to participating families.

Section 523 and 524 rural housing site loans. Loans are made to nonprofit organizations and public agencies to purchase and develop building sites and to construct streets and utilities. Section 523 loans are for self-help housing sites and Section 524 loans are for other sites for low- and moderate-income families.

Section 509(f) rural housing packaging grants. Rural housing packaging grants are made to eligible organizations to assist RHS to make loans and grants in targeted communities. Grant recipients include nonprofit organizations or corporations, states, state agencies, or units of local government that participate in state training programs and are certified by the Rural Economic and Community Development Agency.

Tables 5.9–5.12

Data Sources:

U.S. Department of Housing and Urban Development, Administrative Databases and Low-Income Housing Tax Credit Database

Reference:

Paul Burke, *A Picture of Subsidized Households: United States: Totals and Agencies with over 500 Units*, December 15, 1997, U.S. Department of Housing and Urban Development, Office of Policy Development and Research.

Definitions

Public and Indian Housing. Under the Public and Indian Housing program, the U.S. Department of Housing and Urban Development (HUD) gives grants to public housing agencies (PHAs) (including Indian housing authorities) to finance the capital cost of the construction, rehabilitation, or acquisition of public housing developed by PHAs. Eligible families and individuals must qualify as "low-income families," which are those with incomes no higher than 80 percent of the median income for the area. To cover the shortfall between tenant rents and operating expenses, HUD pays operating subsidies to many PHAs. To cover modernization of existing public housing, HUD makes modernization grants to PHAs.

Section 8 Certificate and Vouchers. HUD established the certificate and voucher programs under Section 8 of the U.S. Housing Act of 1937. Under the certificate program, PHAs issue certificates of family participation to very low-income families (and a limited number of families with incomes up to 80 percent of the area median). These families may select any decent, safe, and sanitary unit within the jurisdiction of the PHA that rents for an amount within the Fair Market Rent (FMR) limitations for the area. The voucher program, like the certificate program, permits families to select their own units from the housing stock available within the jurisdiction of the PHA and is otherwise functionally the same as the certificate program, except for a few key differences:

1. Vouchers may be issued only to very low-income families, families already assisted under the 1937 Act, families with incomes up to 80 percent of area median that are displaced by rental rehabilitation program activities, and families that qualify to receive a voucher in connection with one of the HOPE homeownership programs.
2. There is no limit on the rent for the unit a family selects, thereby giving families more freedom in choosing units.
3. Assistance is equal to the difference between the tenant contribution (30 percent of adjusted income) and the payment standard (which is usually the Section 8 FMR for existing housing for the area). If the family selects a unit renting for more than the payment standard, it pays the excess. Its rent-to-income ratio would then exceed 30 percent of adjusted income. If the family selects a unit renting for less than the payment standard, it, in effect, keeps the difference by paying a lower percentage of its income for rent. (Families are subject to a minimum rent of 10 percent of their gross income.)

Section 8 Moderate Rehabilitation. The purpose of the Moderate Rehabilitation Program was to upgrade substandard rental housing and to provide rental subsidies for low-income families that occupy the rehabilitated units. This program was repealed by the 1990 Housing Act, except for provisions for single-room occupancy units for the homeless.

Section 8 New Construction or Substantial Rehabilitation. Authority for the various Section 8 new construction and substantial rehabilitation programs was repealed by the Housing and Urban-Rural Recovery Act of 1983, except in connection with the old Section 202 direct loan program and projects in the pipeline. Under the program HUD approved applications for projects and agreed to provide Section 8 assistance upon completion of the construction or substantial rehabilitation. Assistance is provided to public housing authorities or private owners and in some instances through State Housing Finance and Development Agencies.

Section 236. The Section 236 Mortgage-Interest-Subsidy program was established by the 1968 Housing Act and combined federal mortgage insurance with subsidized mortgage interest rates to produce low-cost rental housing. The interest-rate subsidy lowered the effective interest rate on Section 236 loans to as low as 1 percent. New commitments are no longer being funded under this program. Some of the households counted in the total numbers of Section 236 units have incomes high enough to pay full rent without subsidy and are not included in the characteristics tabulations.

Other Federal Housing Administration (FHA) projects with subsidies. These include FHA-insured properties with subsidies under the Section 8 Loan Management, Rental Assistance, Rent Supplement, Property Disposition, and other programs.

Low-income Housing Tax Credit. These are housing developments subsidized through the Low-Income Housing Tax Credit (LIHTC), which was created by the Tax Reform Act of 1986. The act eliminated a variety of tax provisions that had favored rental housing and replaced them with a program of credits for the production of rental housing targeted to lower income households. Under the LIHTC program, the states were authorized to issue federal tax credits for the acquisition, rehabilitation, or new construction of affordable rental housing. The credits can be used by property owners to offset taxes on other income, and are generally sold to outside investors to raise initial development funds for a project.

To qualify for credits a project must have a specific proportion of its units set aside for lower income households. The rents on these units are limited to 30 percent of qualifying income. To qualify for credits, owners may elect to set aside at least 20 percent of the units for households at or below 50 percent of area median income or at least 40 percent for households with incomes below 60 percent of area median. Rents in qualifying units are limited to 30 percent of the elected 50 or 60 percent of income.

The amount of the credit that can be provided for a project is a function of development cost (excluding land), the proportion of units set aside, and the credit rate (which varies based on development method and whether other federal subsidies are used). The credit percentages are adjusted monthly but fall in the neighborhood of 4 percent or 9 percent of the qualifying basis. The 4 percent credit is used for the acquisition of an existing building or for federally subsidized new construction or rehabilitation. The 9 percent credit is used for nonfederally subsidized rehabilitation or construction. Credits are provided for a period of 10 years.

Average monthly rent. This is the average gross household rent per month. It includes rent the household pays to the agency or landlord and an estimate of any utilities paid by the household and not included in the rent.

Annual income. This is the average of annual household income expected for the next 12 months for households participating in a given program. It represents total income before adjustments, with the exception that it excludes certain incomes that the U.S. Department of Housing and Urban Development does not count, such as earnings of minors and scholarships.

Head. A family may pick as the head any adult in the household who is wholly or partly responsible for paying the rent.

Minority. The term refers to persons who are Black, Asian, Pacific Islander, Native American, and/or Hispanic.

Census tract. A census tract is an area of about 1,500 homes, chosen by local communities in cooperation with the Census Bureau as an area that is somewhat homogeneous socioeconomically. Tract characteristics presented in the table include the subsidized households living there, so that large projects can dominate the census tract statistics.

Notes

The data in these tables are derived from several HUD administrative databases and the LIHTC database. Because of the constantly changing nature of the HUD- and LIHTC-subsidized inventories, timing of the updates of various databases, and multiple subsidies in the same projects, these figures may deviate from the precise size and characteristics of the actual inventories at any given point in time.

For multistate agencies, Indian housing units are counted in the state in which the main office is located. Therefore, the number of Indian housing units listed for a given state may not equal the actual number of units located in that state.

When households take Section 8 certificates or vouchers to a new area (portability), they are counted against the original agency that issued the certificate or voucher and not against the receiving agency.

Tables 5.13–5.30

Data Sources:
U.S. Department of Housing and Urban Development, Housing Subsidy/American Housing Survey Data Base

References:
Connie H. Casey, *Characteristics of HUD-Assisted Renters and Their Units in 1989,* U.S. Department of Housing and Urban Development (HUD), Office of Policy Development and Research, HUD1346PDR, March 1992. Connie H. Casey, *Characteristics of HUD-Assisted Renters and Their Units in 1991,* HUD, Office of Policy Development and Research, May 1997. Duane T. McGough, *Characteristics of HUD-Assisted Renters and Their Units in 1993,* HUD, Office of Policy Development and Research, May 1997.

Definitions

See Definitions for Tables 2.11–2.31 for additional definitions.

Income-eligible renter households. These are households that would qualify for admission to assisted rental housing on the basis of their reported income. This group includes households that are living in assisted housing and households that receive no housing assistance but qualify on the basis of income. In 1991 and 1993, the latter group is restricted to households with incomes of 50 percent or less of median family income for their area, adjusted for family size.

Unassisted. These households are income-eligible, but are not receiving housing assistance from HUD.

Worst-case needs. A renter household has worst-case needs if it does not receive federal housing assistance; has income below 50 percent of area median income, as ad-

justed by HUD; and pays more than 50 percent of its income for rent and utilities or lives in severely substandard housing.

Public housing. Under the Public and Indian Housing program, HUD gives grants to public housing agencies (PHAs) (including Indian housing authorities) to finance the capital cost of the construction, rehabilitation, or acquisition of public housing developed by PHAs. Eligible families and individuals must qualify as "low-income families," which are those with incomes no higher than 80 percent of the median income for the area. To cover the shortfall between tenant rents and operating expenses, HUD pays operating subsidies to many PHAs. To cover modernization of existing public housing, HUD makes modernization grants to PHAs.

Section 8 Certificate and Voucher Programs. HUD established the Certificate and Voucher programs under Section 8 of the U.S. Housing Act of 1937. Under the certificate program, PHAs issue certificates of family participation to very low-income families (and a limited number of families with incomes up to 80 percent of the area median). Families may select any decent, safe, and sanitary unit within the jurisdiction of the PHA that rents for an amount within the Fair Market Rent (FMR) limitations for the area. The voucher program, like the certificate program, permits families to select their own units from the housing stock available within the jurisdiction of the PHA, and is otherwise functionally the same as the certificate program, except for a few key differences:

1. Vouchers may be issued only to very low-income families, families already assisted under the 1937 Act, families with incomes up to 80 percent of area median that are displaced by rental rehabilitation program activities, and families that qualify to receive a voucher in connection with one of the HOPE homeownership programs.
2. There is no limit on the rent for the unit a family selects, thereby giving families more freedom in choosing units.
3. Assistance is equal to the difference between the tenant contribution (30 percent of adjusted income) and the payment standard (which is usually the Section 8 FMR for existing housing for the area). If the family selects a unit renting for more than the payment standard, it pays the excess. Its rent-to-income ratio would then exceed 30 percent of adjusted income. If the family selects a unit rent-

ing for less than the payment standard, it, in effect, keeps the difference by paying a lower percentage of its income for rent. (Families are subject to a minimum rent of 10 percent of their gross income.)

Private project-based assistance. This includes several programs, some of which are now inactive, in which assistance is given directly to privately owned projects that contain a number of units and that are subsequently rented to low-income households at subsidized rents. The category includes the following programs: rent supplement; Section 221(d)(3) Below Market Interest Rate; Section 202 elderly; Section 236; Section 8 new construction, substantial rehabilitation, and moderate rehabilitation; and some other smaller programs.

Household. A household consists of all the persons who occupy a housing unit. By definition, the count of households is the same as the count of occupied housing units.

Householder. The householder is the first household member 18 years old or older who is the owner or renter of the sample unit. If no household member occupying the sample unit owns or rents the unit, the householder is the first household member listed who is 18 years old or older. In cases where no household member listed owns or rents the unit or is 18 or older, the first household member listed is the householder.

Age of householder. The age classification refers to the age reported for the householder as of that person's last birthday.

Education. The statistics refer to the highest grade of regular school completed by the householder, not to the highest grade attended. For persons still attending school, the highest grade completed is one less than the one in which they are currently enrolled. Regular school refers to formal education obtained in graded public, private, or parochial schools, colleges, universities, or professional schools, whether day or night school, and whether attendance was full- or part-time. That is, regular schooling is formal education that may advance a person toward an elementary or high school diploma, college, university, or professional school degree. Schooling or tutoring in other than regular schools is counted only if the credits obtained are regarded as transferable to a school in the regular school system. Householders whose highest grade completed was in a foreign school system or in an ungraded school were instructed to report the approximate equivalent grade (or years) in the regular United States

school system. Householders were not reported as having completed a given grade if they dropped out or failed to pass the last grade attended. Education received in the following types of schools is not counted as regular schooling: vocational schools, trade schools, business schools, and noncredit adult education classes.

Year householder moved into unit. The data are based on the information reported for the householder and refer to the year of latest move. Thus, if the householder moved back into a housing unit previously occupied, the year of the latest move was to be reported; if the householder moved from one apartment to another in the same building, the year the householder moved into the present unit was to be reported. The intent is to establish the year the present occupancy by the householder began. The year the householder moves is not necessarily the same year other members of the household move, although in the great majority of cases the entire household moves at the same time.

Household composition. Statistics are presented separately for two-person-or-more households and for one-person households. Households consisting of only one person are shown separately for male householder and female householder under the category "one-person households." Households having two or more persons are further subdivided as follows:

Married-couple families, no nonrelatives. Each household in this group consists of the householder and spouse, and other persons, if any, all of whom are related to the householder.

Other male householder. This category includes households with male householders who are married, but with wife absent because of separation or other reason, where husband and wife maintain separate residences, and male householders who are widowed, divorced, or single. Also included are households with male householder, wife present, and nonrelatives living with them.

Other female householder. This category includes households with female householders who are married, but with husband absent because of separation or other reason, where husband and wife maintain separate residences, and female householders who are widowed, divorced, or single. Also included are households with female householder, husband present, and nonrelatives living with them.

Persons in household. All persons occupying the housing unit are counted. These persons include not only occupants related to the householder but also any lodgers, roomers, boarders, partners, wards, foster children, and resident employees who share the living quarters of the householder. The data on persons show categories of the number of one-person through seven-person-or-more households. The median for persons is rounded to the nearest tenth.

A person is counted at the usual place of residence for that person. This refers to the place where the person lives and sleeps most of the time. This place is not necessarily the same as a legal residence, voting residence, or domicile.

Elderly. Data for elderly include all households with a householder of 65 years of age or over.

Number of single children under 18. Single children include all persons under 18 years of age, who may or may not be related to the householder and who are not married (e.g., widowed, divorced, separated, or never married) at the time of the interview.

Income. The statistics on income in the American Housing Survey are based on the respondent's reply to questions on income for the 12 months prior to the interview and are the sum of the amounts reported for wage and salary income, self-employment income, interest or dividends, stock dividends, Social Security or railroad retirement income, public assistance or welfare payments, alimony or child support, and all other money income. The figure represents the amount of income received, before deductions for personal income taxes, Social Security, union dues, bond purchases, health insurance premiums, Medicare deductions, etc., and consumed in the home. The figure also represents money received from the sale of property (unless the recipient was engaged in the business of selling such property); money borrowed; tax refund; withdrawal of bank deposits; accrued interest on uncashed savings bonds; exchange of money between relatives living in the same household; gifts of money; and lump-sum payments from inheritances, insurance policies, estates, trusts, gifts, etc.

Beginning in 1993, the questions on income sources of families and primary individuals were revised with the purpose of improved income reporting. The 1991 question, which reported interest or dividend income of $400 or more, was divided into two separate questions in 1993. One new question reports interest income from different sources and one reports dividends from stocks. Neither of these two questions have an amount limitation. Also,

starting in 1993, income from education loans, grants, and scholarships was included in the "Other" income category. Prior to 1993, these sources of income were not collected. Caution should be used in comparing household income and income source from the 1989 and 1991 surveys with those from the 1993 survey.

Rent. The statistics are for gross rent, which includes not only the portion of the contract rent paid by the household, but also utility and fuel (e.g., oil, coal, kerosene, wood, etc.) payments made by the household and not included in the contract rent.

Food stamps. Food stamps are government-issued coupons that can be used to purchase food. The food stamp program is a joint federal-state program that is administered by state and local governments.

Failures in equipment. Statistics for the following types of equipment failure are provided:

Water supply stoppage. Water supply stoppage means that the housing unit was completely without running water from its regular source. Completely without running water means that the water system servicing the unit supplied no water at all, that is, no equipment or facility using running water (in kitchen and bathroom sinks, shower, bathtub, flush toilet, dishwasher, and other similar items) had water supplied to it, or all were inoperable. The reason could vary from a stoppage because of a flood or storm, to a broken pipe, to a shutdown of the water system, to a failure to pay the bill, or other reasons. Data on water supply stoppage are shown if they occurred in the 3 months prior to the interview, or while the household was living in the unit, if less than 3 months.

No working toilet. The statistics on breakdowns of flush toilet are shown for housing units with at least one flush toilet for the household's use only. The flush toilet may be completely unusable because of a faulty flushing mechanism, broken pipes, stopped up soil pipe, lack of water supplied to the flush toilet, or some other reason. Data on breakdowns are provided in instances where none of the flush toilets were working in the 3 months prior to the interview, or while the household was living in the unit, if less than 3 months.

Public sewage disposal. The data on breakdowns in the means of sewage disposal are limited to housing units in which the means of sewage disposal was a public sewer, septic tank, or cesspool. Breakdowns refer to situations in which the system was completely unusable. Examples include the septic tank being pumped because it no longer perked, tank collapsed, tank exploded, sewer main broken, sewer treatment plant not operating as a result of electrical failure or water service interruption, etc. Data on breakdowns are shown if they occurred in the 3 months prior to the interview or while the household was living in the unit, if less than 3 months.

Electric fuses/breakers. The data show whether an electric fuse has blown or circuit breaker has tripped in the home in the 3 months prior to the interview or while the household was living in the unit, if less than 3 months. A blown fuse or tripped breaker switch results in the temporary loss of electricity until the fuse is replaced or the breaker switch reset. Blown fuses inside major pieces of installed equipment (such as some air conditioners) are counted as blown fuses or tripped breaker switches.

Heating equipment. For breakdowns of heating equipment, statistics are shown for housing units occupied by the householder during the winter prior to the interview. The data are classified by whether the housing unit was uncomfortably cold for 24 hours or more, by the number of times equipment breakdowns occurred lasting 6 hours or more, and by causes for the breakdowns. The heating equipment is broken if it is not providing heat at its normal heating capacity through some fault in the equipment. Utility interruptions occur when there is a cutoff in the gas, electricity, or other fuel supplying the heat. Inadequate heating capacity refers to heating equipment that is providing heat at its normal capacity, but the housing unit is still too cold for the occupants. Inadequate insulation refers to air drafts through window frames, electrical outlets, or walls that are cold.

Water leakage. Data on water leakage are shown if the leakage occurred in the 12 months prior to the interview or while the household was living in the unit, if less than 12 months. Housing units with water leakage are classified by whether the water leaked in from inside or outside the building and by the most common areas (roof, basement, walls, closed windows, or doors, etc.) or reasons (fixtures backed up or overflowed, pipes leaked, etc.) of water leakage.

Notes

Comparability of 1989, 1991, and 1993 data. Caution should be exercised when comparing 1991 and 1993 data with the 1989 data. The 1991 and 1993 data are benchmarked to the 1990 Census, while the 1989 data are benchmarked to the 1980 Census. Using 1990-based weights produced lower estimates of total households than 1980 weights, making comparison between 1989 and the later years difficult.

Another factor that should be considered in comparing data across years is the high error rates caused by small sample sizes. High sampling errors frequently render apparent differences between years statistically insignificant. The reports referenced above contain sampling errors that can be used to calculate statistical significance of apparent differences. In addition, the texts of McGough (1997) and Casey (1997) provide useful commentaries on changes over time.

Tables 5.31–5.33

Data Source:
    Low-Income Housing Tax Credit Database
References:
    Abt Associates, *Development and Analysis of the National Low-Income Housing Tax Credit Database*, July 1996. U.S. Department of Housing and Urban Development, U.S. Housing Market Conditions, August 1996.

Definitions

Low-Income Housing Tax Credit projects. These are housing developments subsidized through the Low-Income Housing Tax Credit (LIHTC), which was created by the Tax Reform Act of 1986. The act eliminated a variety of tax provisions that had favored rental housing and replaced them with a program of credits for the production of rental housing targeted to lower income households. Under the LIHTC program, the states were authorized to issue federal tax credits for the acquisition, rehabilitation, or new construction of affordable rental housing. The credits can be used by property owners to offset taxes on other income, and are generally sold to outside investors to raise initial development funds for a project.

To qualify for credits, a project must have a specific proportion of its units set aside for lower income households and the rents on those units must be limited to 30 percent of qualifying income. To qualify for credits, owners may elect to set aside at least 20 percent of the units for households at or below 50 percent of area median income or at least 40 percent for households with incomes below 60 percent of area median. Rents in qualifying units are limited to 30 percent of the elected 50 or 60 percent of income.

The amount of the credit that can be provided for a project is a function of development cost (excluding land), the proportion of units set aside, and the credit rate (which varies based on development method and whether other federal subsidies are used). The credit percentages are adjusted monthly, but fall in the neighborhood of 4 percent or 9 percent of the qualifying basis. The 4 percent credit is used for the acquisition of an existing building or for federally subsidized new construction or rehab. The 9 percent credit is used for nonfederally subsidized rehab or construction. Credits are provided for a period of 10 years.

Placed in service. Placed-in-service projects are those that have received a certificate of occupancy and for which the state has submitted an IRS Form 8609 indicating that the property owner is eligible to claim low-income housing tax credits.

Qualifying units. Qualifying units are those that are reserved for low-income use, have restricted rents, and can be claimed for tax credits. The qualifying ratio is the ratio of qualifying units to total units in a project.

Credit percentage. This refers to whether the 4 percent credit rate, 9 percent credit rate, or both are used. See definition under Low-Income Housing Tax Credit projects.

Notes

The percent distributions in the "Total" columns of tables 5.32 and 5.33 differ slightly because the two tables apply to different subsets of tax credit projects put in service between 1992 and 1994. Table 5.32 excludes 20 properties for which no information on the number of units was available and 29 properties in the Virgin Islands and Puerto Rico. Table 5.33 includes only geocoded projects (that is, projects that could be linked with a census tract) and excludes 25 projects for which unit or census data were missing.

In late 1996, additional efforts were made to improve the coverage of the Low-Income Housing Tax Credit database, from which the data presented in the tables are extracted. These efforts resulted in the addition of 1,989 projects containing 67,056 units to the database. The expanded data are available on the HUD Users Web site at <http://www.huduser.org/>.

Appendix B

Descriptions of Data Sources

This appendix describes the surveys, censuses, and other data collection programs that are the primary sources for the data presented in this book. These descriptions are arranged in alphabetical order by title of the data source. The publications and other sources from which these descriptions are taken or adapted are cited at the end of each description.

Definitions and notes related to the individual tables are provided in Appendix A. Appendix A also lists the data source for each table, which permits cross-references to this appendix.

American Housing Survey

U.S. Bureau of the Census

The main objective of the American Housing Survey (AHS) is to provide current, consistent, comprehensive, and accurate information on housing conditions and housing markets in the United States. With its inception in 1973, the AHS filled a significant gap in the federal statistical program by providing detailed housing statistics between the decennial censuses of housing. The AHS includes a variety of information on the size and composition of the housing stock and on housing and household characteristics. These statistics include age, sex, and race of householders; household composition; income; tenure; housing and neighborhood quality; housing costs and value; structural and equipment characteristics; and size and age of housing units. The AHS also collects data on homeowners' repairs and mortgages, rent control, rent subsidies, previous unit of recent movers, and reasons for moving. In 1995, questions were added regarding rooms used only for business; telecommuting; remodeling, alterations, and repairs; and home equity loans.

The AHS is actually two separate and independent data collection efforts consisting of a national sample (AHS-N) and a metropolitan sample (AHS-MS). The AHS-N, which is the source for all of the AHS data contained in this book, was conducted by the Census Bureau each year from 1973 to 1981, during which time it was called the Annual Housing Survey. Since 1981 the Census Bureau has been conducting the AHS-N only in odd-numbered years. The name was changed to the American Housing Survey in 1985.

In 1995, the AHS-N included an original sample of approximately 60,000 housing units. About 3,600 of these units were ineligible because the unit no longer existed or because the unit did not qualify as a housing unit. Approximately 4,200 of the remaining units (both occupied and vacant) were not interviewed because no one was at home after repeated visits, the respondent refused to be interviewed, or the interviewer was unable to find the unit.

The AHS-MS has been conducted every year since 1974. Originally, the Census Bureau surveyed 20 metropolitan areas each year over a 3-year cycle, for a total of 60 metropolitan areas in the AHS-MS. In 1977, the survey cycle was extended to 4 years to reduce costs. Beginning in 1984, the sample was reduced to 44 metropolitan areas over a 4-year cycle, with 11 areas surveyed each year. Currently, 47 metropolitan areas are included in the AHS-MS.

Beginning in 1995, the Census Bureau began conducting the New York, Northern New Jersey, Philadelphia, Chicago, Los Angeles, and Detroit metropolitan surveys in conjunction with the AHS-N. Supplemental interviews for these six areas will be conducted with every other AHS-N, resulting in a 4-year release cycle for the data for these metropolitan areas. As in the past, the results from these metropolitan surveys will be published separately from the results of the national survey.

A new plan for conducting surveys in the remainder of the AHS-MS metropolitan areas was introduced in 1996. With the exception of the six areas that will be surveyed with the AHS-N, all AHS-MS surveys are now being conducted only in even-numbered years to spread out interviewing costs. With 13 or 14 metropolitan surveys conducted in each even-numbered year, this will produce a 6-year release cycle for these metropolitan areas.

The AHS is currently conducted by three different interviewing methods: personal visit, decentralized telephone interviewing, and computer-assisted telephone interviewing (CATI). Prior to 1983 and in 1985 all interviews were collected through personal visits. (In 1983, an experiment was conducted using decentralized telephone interviewing.) The introduction of CATI beginning with the 1987 AHS-N affects longitudinal comparability of the AHS data. Experiments conducted by the Census Bureau on the effects of telephone interviewing produced evidence that differences exist in data collected from CATI and non-CATI methods. Although studies of the CATI and non-CATI methods were inconclusive regarding effects on data quality, it is believed that CATI improves income estimates because the computer ensures that all income questions are asked.

One of the unique features of the AHS is its longitudinal sample design. The same addresses generally remain in the AHS sample from year to year, thereby permitting analyses of changes in the characteristics and occupancy of housing units over time. Because a new sample for the AHS-N based on the 1980 Census was selected in 1985, longitudinal links are not available between 1983 and 1985; however, such links are available prior to 1983 and from 1985 to later years.

Beginning in 1995, new samples based on the 1990 Census are being introduced for the metropolitan areas in the AHS-MS. Only the eight metropolitan areas surveyed in 1994 (Anaheim, Buffalo, Dallas, Fort Worth, Milwaukee, Phoenix, Riverside, and San Diego) still retain a 1970 Census–based sample design.

The primary user of the AHS is the Department of Housing and Urban Development (HUD), which sponsors the survey and employs the data for a wide variety of policy and program uses. The AHS data are essential for evaluating trends in housing supply, costs, and affordability and for identifying where and for whom federal housing assistance may be most needed. For example, the AHS is the basis for an annual report to Congress on "worst-case" housing needs prepared by HUD's Office of Policy Development and Research. HUD also uses the AHS data to develop and evaluate the Fair Market Rents for the Section 8 rental certificate and voucher programs. The AHS is also widely used by academic and industry researchers to conduct a variety of housing research.

Sources: 1. U.S. Bureau of the Census and U.S. Department of Housing and Urban Development, *American Housing Survey for the United States in 1995*, Current Housing Reports H150/95RV, July 1997. 2. Personal communication with Barbara Williams, U.S. Bureau of the Census, Housing and Household Economics Statistics Division, May 12, 1997. 3. Fannie Mae Office of Housing Policy Research, *Proceedings: Roundtable Discussion on 1990 Census, Ongoing Survey Work, and Analysis Plans*, April 5, 1991.

Builders Economic Council Survey
National Association of Home Builders

The National Association of Home Builders' Builders Economic Council is a mail survey of the attitudes and expectations of approximately 450 builders that is conducted at the beginning of each month. The builders are asked questions about current sales and sales expectations for single-family and condominium units. They are also asked about the volume of potential buyer traffic.

Source: National Association of Home Builders, *Housing Market Statistics*, April 1998.

Building Permits Survey
U.S. Bureau of the Census

Monitoring building permits is a long-standing federal data collection activity that dates back to 1889. Responsibility for collecting permit data has rested with several federal agencies, including the U.S. Geological Survey and the Bureau of Labor Statistics. The Census Bureau assumed responsibility for the nation's building permit data collection system in 1959.

The Building Permits Survey (BPS) collects statistics on authorizations of new residential construction.[1] Although the BPS covers only those geographic areas with building permit systems, it captures the vast majority of all residential construction in the United States. For the country as a whole, approximately 96 percent of new private housing units are constructed in permit-issuing places.

The BPS has two components: the monthly mail survey and the annual survey. The monthly mail survey produces estimates of construction authorized by building permits for the nation, census regions and divisions, states, and selected metropolitan statistical areas. These monthly estimates are based on reports from a stratified probability sample of 8,500 out of the 19,000 local permit-issuing jurisdictions that are currently in the BPS universe.

The annual survey provides data on permits for all geographic levels and all of the individual permit-issuing places. Annual data is tabulated from reports collected directly from all 19,000 permit-issuing places.

The number of permit-issuing jurisdictions covered by the BPS has increased over time. Beginning in 1994, data are based on 19,000 places. Data for 1984 through 1993 are for 17,000 places; data for 1978 through 1983 are for 16,000 places; data for 1972 through 1977 are for 14,000 places; data for 1967 through 1971 are for 13,000 places;

data for 1963 to 1966 are for 12,000 places; and data for 1959 through 1962 are for 10,000 places.

BPS data, the only construction statistics that the federal government provides on an ongoing basis for small geographic units such as counties and places, are used extensively by federal, state, and local government agencies and numerous private organizations to monitor and anticipate trends in housing production. The residential permit data are a component of the index of leading economic indicators. Monthly permit estimates from the BPS are also key inputs to the compilations of housing starts, completions, and sales in the Survey of Construction (see description elsewhere in this appendix).

Sources: 1. U.S. Bureau of the Census, Survey of Construction, technical paper draft, October 26, 1990. 2. U.S. Bureau of the Census, "Housing Units Authorized by Building Permits," <http://www.census.gov/const/www/C40/c40text. html>. 3. Personal communication with Steven Berman, U.S. Bureau of the Census, Manufacturing and Construction Division, May 20, 1997. 4. U.S. Bureau of the Census, "Housing Units Authorized by Building Permits—Survey Changes," <http://www.census.gov/pub/const/www/C40/c40chnge.html>.

Census of Housing[2]

U.S. Bureau of the Census

The decennial population census, mandated by Article I, Section 2, of the United States Constitution has been conducted since 1790. Early censuses were limited to simple counts of persons by age, sex, and race and did not include any housing information. The census first collected information on housing in 1850, when enumerators counted "dwelling houses occupied by free inhabitants." In addition to housing units, dwelling houses included "hotels, poorhouses, garrisons, hospitals, asylums, jails, penitentiaries, and other similar institutions." In 1890, the census also began collecting information on tenure.

The first extensive battery of housing questions was asked in the 1940 Census for the purpose of assessing the general condition of the nation's housing stock and determining the need for public housing programs. In every decennial census since then, information has been collected on a variety of housing characteristics such as tenure, structure type, plumbing and kitchen facilities, value, rent, fuels, and heating equipment.

The types of housing questions asked in the decennial census have varied in response to the perceived needs of data users and to the changing characteristics of the nation's housing stock. Questions have been added or subtracted and others have been modified. For example, in 1990 a single question asked if the plumbing facilities of a housing unit were either complete or not complete. As recently as 1970, information on plumbing was compiled in three separate categories related to water supply, toilet facilities, and bathing facilities.

The concept of a housing unit has undergone only relatively minor changes between 1940 and 1990. Although the term "dwelling unit" was used originally, the concept that a housing unit is a living quarters where the occupants live and eat separately from the occupants of other living quarters has varied little from census to census. Perhaps the most significant changes occurred in 1980 when the requirement of separate kitchen facilities was dropped from the definition. Additionally, vacant mobile homes were counted as housing units provided that they were located where they were intended for occupancy. (For a description of other changes in the definition of a housing unit, see the notes to Table 2.4 in Appendix A.)

Since 1970, the decennial census has been conducted principally through a mailed questionnaire rather than field enumeration. There are two types of census questionnaires, the short form and the long form. In 1990, the short-form questionnaire was sent to about 83 percent of households and collected information on six housing-related items:

- Structure type/number of units in structure
- Number of rooms in unit
- Tenure (owned or rented)
- Acreage and the presence of a commercial establishment on the property
- Value of owner-occupied units
- Contract rent and inclusion of meals in rent for renter-occupied units

In 1990, the long-form questionnaire was used to collect more detailed demographic, economic, and housing information from about one in six households. In addition to the short-form information, the long-form questionnaire collected additional data on the following housing-related items:

- Year householder moved into unit
- Number of bedrooms
- Presence of complete plumbing facilities
- Presence of complete kitchen facilities
- Presence of telephone in unit
- Vehicles available

- House heating fuel
- Source of water
- Sewage disposal
- Year structure built
- Condominium status
- Farm/nonfarm status
- Cost of utilities and fuels
- Selected shelter costs for owner-occupied units
  - Real estate taxes
  - Insurance
  - Mortgage status and mortgage payments
  - Condominium fee (for condominium units)
  - Mobile home costs (for mobile home owners)

By combining various questions from the population and housing censuses, the following items were calculated by the Census Bureau from 1990 Census data:

- Gross rent
- Gross rent as a percentage of household income in 1989
- Persons per unit
- Persons per room
- Selected monthly owner costs
- Selected monthly owner costs as a percentage of household income in 1989

Census enumerators also collect information for vacant units, such as vacancy status, duration of vacancy, and boarded-up status.

The Census Bureau's proposal for the Census 2000 questionnaire calls for dropping three housing-related subjects: source of water, sewage disposal, and condominium status. In addition, the proposal would move questions on number of units in structure, home value, monthly rent, and rooms from the short form to the long form. Tenure would be the only housing item retained on the short form.

Congress, the U.S. Department of Housing and Urban Development (HUD), and the private sector use information from the decennial census in a variety of ways. For example, Community Development Block Grant funds are allocated based on a formula that uses data from the census. For much of the country, the census of housing is also the only source of information on rents from which HUD calculates Fair Market Rents used in its Section 8 rental certificate and voucher programs and several other low-income rental housing programs. The decennial census is also the primary source of information on housing characteristics and housing market con-

ditions in small geographic areas. In addition, national and regional estimates of households and housing units are often benchmarked to the decennial census of population and housing.

Sources: 1. U.S. Bureau of the Census, *1990 Census of Population and Housing: Guide, Part A, Text,* 1990 CPH-R-1A, September 1992. 2. U.S. Bureau of the Census, *200 Years of U.S. Census Taking: Population and Housing Questions, 1790–1990,* November 1989. 3. Fannie Mae Office of Housing Policy Research, *Proceedings: Roundtable Discussion on 1990 Census, Ongoing Survey Work, and Analysis Plans,* April 5, 1991. 4. John Weicher, *Statement before the House Subcommittee on Policy Research and Insurance of the Committee on Banking, Finance and Urban Affairs,* May 22, 1990. 5. U.S. Bureau of the Census, "Census Bureau Submits Subjects for Census 2000 to Congress," press release CB97-C.04, March 31, 1997.

Consumer Expenditure Survey and Residential Improvements and Repairs Mail Survey

U.S. Bureau of the Census

Data on expenditures for residential improvements and repairs are compiled by the Census Bureau from two sources: the Consumer Expenditure (CE) Survey, a household survey of a sample of consumer units, and a mail survey of owners of a sample of rental or vacant properties from the CE Survey.[3]

The CE Survey, conducted by the Census Bureau for the Bureau of Labor Statistics, is a national probability sample that generates interviews with about 4,200 urban households per quarter and collects data on major items of consumer expense, household characteristics, and income. The expenditures covered by the survey are those that respondents can be expected to recall fairly accurately for three months or longer, including expenditures for maintenance and repairs and improvement of properties. Estimates of expenditures for improvements and repairs are tabulated for owner occupants of one- to four-unit properties and condominiums.

Nonresident owners of rental or vacant properties with one to four housing units and owners of rental or vacant properties containing five housing units or more, as identified in the CE household survey, are mailed a questionnaire to report detailed maintenance and repairs and improvement expenditures for their entire property. Approximately 2,000 such owners are queried each quarter.

Source: U.S. Bureau of the Census, *Expenditures for*

Residential Improvements and Repairs: Third Quarter 1997, Current Construction Reports C50/97-Q3, March 1998.

Consumer Price Index

U.S. Bureau of Labor Statistics

The Bureau of Labor Statistics (BLS) produces the Consumer Price Index (CPI) by measuring the average change over time in the prices paid by urban consumers for a fixed "market basket" of consumer goods and services. Through December 1997, the composition of the market basket and the weights for each good and service included were determined from spending patterns recorded in the 1982–1984 Consumer Expenditure Survey. Beginning in January 1998, a new market basket and expenditure weights were developed based on Consumer Expenditure Survey data from 1993–1995. The items selected for the market basket are priced each month at retail outlets in urban areas throughout the country. According to the BLS, approximately 23,000 retail and service establishments are visited each month, with prices collected for about 90,000 items.

The CPI was initiated during World War I, when rapid increases in the prices of goods and services, particularly in shipbuilding centers, made such an index essential for calculating cost-of-living adjustments in wages. In 1921, the BLS began regular publication of an index representing the expenditures of urban wage and clerical workers, which was then called the Cost-of-Living Index. The name of the index was changed to the CPI following controversy during World War II over the index's validity as a measure of the cost of living. According to the BLS, it has always been a measure of the changes in prices for goods and services purchased for family living.

Major revisions are made to the CPI about every 10 years to update the fixed market basket of goods and services that compose the index. The most recent such change occurred in January 1998. This most recent revision also involves other important changes that will be implemented over time, such as the reselection and reclassification of areas, items, and outlets and the development of new data collection and processing systems. Other major revisions to the CPI were made in 1940, 1953, 1964, 1978, and 1987.

The 1978 revisions introduced a new index for all urban consumers—CPI-U. The CPI-U, which represents the expenditures of about 80 percent of the population, takes into account the buying patterns of almost all urban residents including professional employees, part-time workers, the self-employed, the unemployed, and retired persons, as well as those previously covered in the CPI. The BLS continued publication of the original index, the CPI-W, which represents the expenditures of urban wage and clerical workers, about 32 percent of the population.

The CPI has three major uses: (1) as an indicator of inflation for policymaking and economic decision making; (2) as an escalator for wages, income payments, and tax brackets to preserve the purchasing power of people receiving government transfer payments and to adjust the tax burden so that people pay in inflation-adjusted dollars; and (3) as a deflator of selected economic statistical data series to make adjustments to show real changes in the data over time.

Shelter components of the CPI-U

Residential Rent and Owner's Equivalent Rent are the two main shelter components of the CPI-U. Data for these components, collected from BLS' Housing Survey, measure monthly changes in the cost of shelter for renter- and owner-occupants, respectively. The Housing Survey interviews 35,000 renter-occupants on a rotating basis, over a 6-month period. About 30,000 owner-occupants are interviewed, also on a rotating basis, over a 2-year period. The housing units may be of any type: single-family, multifamily, or mobile homes.

The change in the monthly costs for renters is measured directly from the Housing Survey data. It reflects changes in economic rent, which is payment in exchange for all services provided by the landlord as well as the value of certain rent reductions.

The CPI-U uses a "rental equivalence" approach for owners, which measures the change in the monthly value of the shelter services provided by homeownership—the owner's equivalent rent. Because owners' equivalent rent is not an actual financial transaction, the BLS estimates changes in owner costs by matching each owner-occupied unit in the Housing Survey sample with two or more rental units that are similar in terms of location, structure type (e.g., single-family, mobile home, etc.), and general characteristics (e.g., size of unit, number of rooms, air conditioning, etc.). The change in rent charged for these matched rental units is used to estimate the change in owners' equivalent rent.

The rental equivalence approach was adopted by the BLS in 1983. Prior to 1983, the homeowner cost component of the CPI-U reflected both the consumption and the investment value of homeownership. Under this earlier method, the BLS treated the purchase of a home similarly to the way it treated the purchase of other consumer goods or services. In addition to changes in home prices, the pre-1983 homeownership component attempted to measure the change in expected financing costs resulting from the purchase of a home. The pre-1983 homeowner cost component also reflected changes in expenses incurred by all existing homeowners for property taxes, property insurance, and maintenance and repairs. According to many analysts, prior to the switch to the rental equivalence approach, the CPI-U overestimated increases in housing costs and the overall rate of price inflation.

The BLS adopted another revision in the shelter component in January 1995. This corrected a flaw in calculation procedures that overstated changes in owners' equivalent rent by about 0.6 percent a year.

Using the CPI-U as a price deflator

In addition to providing information on changes in shelter costs, the CPI-U is also used as a price deflator. For example, most of the tables on household income in this book depict current income (e.g., income without adjustment for price inflation) and constant-dollar income adjusted for inflation using one of two versions of the CPI-U time series. The official CPI-U time series is based on the old methodology of measuring changes in homeowner costs prior to 1983 and the rental equivalence approach for 1983 to the present. The BLS has also created an experimental series, the CPI-U-X1, that uses the rental equivalence approach for the period 1967 to the present and therefore provides a methodologically consistent series over time. The CPI-U and the CPI-U-X1 are identical after 1982.

Sources: 1. U.S. Bureau of Labor Statistics, "Consumer Price Indexes: Overview," <http://stats.bls.gov:80/cpiovrvw.htm>; "Consumer Price Indexes: How BLS Uses Rent Data in the Consumer Price Index," <http://stats.bls.gov:80/cpifact6.htm>; and "How the Consumer Price Index Measures Homeowners' Costs," <http://stats.bls.gov:80/cpifact1.htm>. 2. U.S. General Accounting Office, *Consumer Price Index: Cost-of-Living Concepts and the Housing and Medical Care Components*, GAO/GGD-96-166. 3. U.S. Bureau of the Census, *Money Income of Households, Families, and Persons in the United States: 1990*, Current Population Reports, P60-174, August 1991. 4. Michael Carliner, "Housing, the CPI, and the Deficit," *Housing Economics*, November 1995: 5–8.

Current Population Survey

U.S. Bureau of the Census

The Current Population Survey (CPS) is probably the best known and most widely used of all continuing federal household surveys. The Census Bureau conducts the survey every month, although this book uses much data from the March Supplement to the basic CPS, which collects additional demographic and economic information from surveyed households. The basic CPS and the March survey are described below.

Basic CPS

The primary purpose of the basic CPS is to collect labor force data on the civilian noninstitutional population. Field representatives ask questions concerning labor force participation about each member 15 years old and older in every sample household.

The CPS sample covers about 50,000 occupied housing units in all 50 states and the District of Columbia and is continuously updated to account for new residential construction. About 47,000 households are actually interviewed each month.

The survey's estimation procedure inflates weighted sample results to independent estimates of the civilian noninstitutional population of the United States by state, age, sex, race, and Hispanic/non-Hispanic categories. (Prior to 1984, there was no specific control of survey estimates for the Hispanic population.) Since the introduction of 1990 Census–based population controls in January 1994 (discussed below), these independent estimates have been based on the following:

- The 1990 Census of Population and Housing
- An adjustment for net undercoverage in the 1990 Census
- Statistics on births, deaths, immigration, and emigration
- Statistics on the size of the Armed Forces

Current Population Survey—March Supplement

In addition to the basic CPS questions, field representatives ask supplementary questions in March about marital status, living arrangements, mobility, and money income received the previous calendar year. To obtain more reliable data for the Hispanic-origin population, the March CPS sample is increased by about 2,500 eligible housing units that were interviewed the previous November and that contained at least one sample person of Hispanic origin. The March sample also includes persons in the Armed Forces living off post or with their families on post. In addition to the estimation procedures described above for the basic CPS, the March Supplement includes a further adjustment so that a husband and wife in a married-couple household receive the same weight.

Major recent changes in the CPS

A number of changes were made in CPS data collection and estimation procedures beginning with the January 1994 survey. These changes necessitate caution in comparing estimates from data collected in 1994 or later years with estimates from earlier years.

The major change beginning in 1994 was the use of a new questionnaire and computer-assisted interviewing. The questionnaire was redesigned to measure official labor force concepts more precisely, to expand the amount of data available, to implement several definitional changes, and to adapt to a computer-assisted interviewing environment. The March Supplement questions were also modified for adaptation to computer-assisted survey information collection (CASIC), although there were no changes in definitions and concepts. The March 1994 CPS was the first to use CASIC technology for its entire data collection process.

Another important change beginning with the January 1994 CPS was the switch from 1980 to 1990 Census–based population controls. These independent population controls are developed by using civilian noninstitutional population counts from the decennial census and projecting them forward to the current year using data on births, deaths, and net migration. In addition to the switch to 1990 Census–based population controls, for the first time in the history of the CPS, estimates of the net undercount in the decennial census were used in establishing the 1990 population benchmarks from which current estimates were derived.

These changes in population controls had relatively little impact on summary measures such as means, medians, and percentage distributions, but did have a significant impact on levels. Thus, estimates of levels for data collected in 1994 and later years will differ from those published for earlier years by more than what could be attributed to actual changes in the population. These differences could be disproportionately greater for certain subpopulation groups than for the total population.

During the period April 1994 through June 1995, the Census Bureau systematically introduced a new sample design for the CPS based on results from the 1990 Census. During this phase-in period, CPS estimates were be-ing made from two distinct sample designs: the old 1980 sample design and the new 1990 sample design. While most CPS estimates are unaffected by the transition from the 1980-based to 1990-based design, geographic estimates are subject to greater error and variability. Caution is particularly warranted when comparing estimates across years for metropolitan/nonmetropolitan categories.

Beginning with the January 1996 survey, the CPS sample was reduced by approximately 7,000 housing units for budgetary reasons. This sample reduction took place in seven states (Illinois, Massachusetts, Michigan, New Jersey, North Carolina, Ohio, and Pennsylvania), New York City, and the Los Angeles-Long Beach metropolitan area. The sample reduction affected the reliability of estimates at the national level and at the state and substate levels for those areas where the sample size was reduced. The reduction did not affect the reliability of estimates from those states not involved in the reduction.[4]

Finally, a revised edit and allocation procedure for race information was also introduced in January 1996. This new procedure assigns respondents reporting "Other (unspecified) race" in the race question to one of the four major race categories: White; Black; American Indian, Eskimo, and Aleut; and Asian or Pacific Islander. This new edit and allocation procedure was introduced in response to the rising proportion of the CPS population reporting their race as "Other."

Sources: 1. Steve W. Rawlings and Arlene F. Saluter, *Household and Family Characteristics: March 1994*, U.S. Bureau of the Census, Current Population Reports, P20-483, 1995. 2. U.S. Bureau of the Census, *Money Income in the United States: 1996 (With Separate Data on Valuation of Noncash Benefits)*, Current Population Reports, P60-197, 1997.

Current Population Survey/Housing Vacancy Survey

U.S. Bureau of the Census

Estimates from the Current Population Survey/Housing Vacancy Survey (CPS/HVS) are based on data obtained from two surveys conducted by the Census Bureau. Data concerning vacancy rates and tenure of occupied housing units are from the monthly sample of the CPS (the basic CPS, described above). Characteristics of occupied housing units for some tabulations are from the American Housing Survey (the AHS-N, described above).

Each month, about one-half of the vacant housing units from the basic CPS are interviewed for the HVS. In addition to producing quarterly estimates of the housing inventory and homeownership rates, the CPS/HVS also collects and reports data on vacancy rates by tenure and other housing unit characteristics, asking prices and rents for vacant-for-sale and vacant-for-rent units, and duration of vacancy.

The HVS estimation procedure for vacant units is similar to that used for occupied units. Weighted sample results are adjusted at the state level using 1990 Census vacant counts. A second adjustment inflates these results based on the CPS coverage of occupied units by geographic areas.

Quarterly data on vacancy rates and tenure of occupied units are averaged for three months. Data concerning the distribution of characteristics for occupied housing units, such as rooms in unit, structure type, and age of structure, are obtained primarily from the AHS-N sample. Distributions of characteristics of occupied housing units from the AHS-N estimates are applied to CPS current housing inventory independent estimates to obtain the characteristics of occupied housing units. The Survey of Construction (described later in this appendix) and the Consumer Price Index (described previously) also are used to improve estimates of the rent distribution.

Effects of recent changes in CPS and CPS/HVS on historical comparability

Historical comparability of estimates from the CPS/HVS is affected by changes in the CPS that were instituted beginning with January 1994 (see discussion under "Current Population Survey," previously). The new 1990-based weighting produces, on average, estimates of the total housing inventory that are about 0.1 percent lower than the 1980-based weighting. Generally, the vacancy rates are only minimally affected, while the homeownership rate is about one-half of a percentage point lower with the new weighting procedures. The shift to computer-assisted interviewing may affect vacancy rates and homeownership rates, but the Census Bureau is unable to determine the quantitative effects of this change on these indicators. Data users should exercise caution when comparing data for 1994 and later with earlier data.

There have also been several changes specific to the CPS/HVS that affect historical comparability. Starting with the first quarter 1980, several changes were implemented in the survey to improve the reliability of the data presented. These included adding a supplemental sample, refining the estimation procedures, and changing the

source of characteristics for occupied units from the Quarterly Housing Survey to the AHS. Beginning in the first quarter 1986, vacant seasonal mobile homes were included in the count of vacant seasonal units. This change resulted in a 12 percent increase in the number of vacant seasonal housing units. In the fourth quarter 1989, new edit procedures were implemented to allocate cases that would have been classified as "not reported" under previous procedures. In the first quarter 1990, year-round vacant mobile homes were included for the first time as part of the year-round vacant count of housing units. This change was made to make the composition of the housing unit inventory for the CPS/HVS similar to the decennial census and other surveys, which count all mobile homes as housing units whether occupied or vacant (available for occupancy on the site).

Sources: U.S. Bureau of the Census, "Housing Vacancy Survey: Description," <http://www.census.gov/ftp/pub/hhes/www/housing/hvstext.html>, and "Housing Vacancy Survey: Source and Accuracy of Estimates," <http://www.census.gov/ftp/pub/hhes/www/hvs.html>.

Existing Home Sales Survey
National Association of Realtors®

In the 1960s, the National Association of Realtors® (NAR) began collecting and disseminating statistics on existing single-family home sales and prices. Today, the Existing Home Sales Survey is used extensively as a source of monthly sales and price data for the nation, for the four census regions, and for quarterly data for metropolitan statistical areas. Quarterly data are also published on condominium/cooperative resales and prices and on total state resale activity.

Existing Home Sales Survey data is developed from home sales reported each month by more than 600 Boards/Associations of Realtors and multiple listing services. Participating Boards/Associations are located in every region of the country. While almost all of these Boards/Associations are located in, or adjacent to, metropolitan areas, comparisons with data from the American Housing Survey indicate that data from the Existing Home Sales Survey are representative of sales activity and prices that generally prevail in each region of the country. Weights based on the regional distribution of owner-occupied single-family housing and homeowner mobility are used to convert the reported data from each region into total existing single-family sales for each region.

Sources: 1. National Association of Realtors®, Existing Home Sales Survey Description. 2. John A. Tuccillo, Statement of the National Association of Realtors® Before the House Subcommittee on Policy Research and Insurance of the Committee on Banking, Finance and Urban Affairs, May 22, 1990.

Historical Statistics on Banking

Federal Deposit Insurance Corporation

Historical Statistics on Banking is a publication produced by the Federal Deposit Insurance Corporation (FDIC) that contains structure and financial data on FDIC-insured banks dating back to 1934. A similar publication, *Statistics on Banking*, is published annually and provides detailed data on bank industry condition and performance during a calendar year.

Historical Statistics on Banking contains data only on FDIC-insured commercial banks and savings institutions. The former category includes all commercial banks insured by FDIC through the Bank Insurance Fund (BIF). It also includes all commercial banks insured by the FDIC through the Savings Association Insurance Fund (SAIF) that are regulated by and submit financial data to one of the three federal commercial bank regulators (Board of Governors of the Federal Reserve System, Federal Deposit Insurance Corporation, or Office of the Comptroller of the Currency). FDIC-insured savings institutions include all institutions insured by either the BIF or the SAIF that operate under state or federal banking codes applicable to thrift institutions. Data on savings institutions that have been placed in Resolution Trust Corporation conservatorship are not aggregated with other savings institutions, since they do not operate as privately held entities, and their resolution costs do not accrue to the FDIC.

The structure and financial data sources used in the preparation of *Historical Statistics on Banking* are the following:

- *Annual Reports of the Federal Deposit Insurance Corporation, 1934–1996*
- *Statistics on Banking, 1981–1996*
- *Assets and Liabilities, Commercial and Mutual Savings Banks, 1934–1982*
- *Bank Operating Statistics, 1968–1982*
- *FDIC Research Information System (RIS), 1984–1996*

The primary sources of financial data are the Reports of Income and Condition, which are submitted by insured institutions to the federal commercial bank regulators, and the Thrift Financial Reports which are submitted by BIF-insured, FDIC-regulated savings banks to the Office of Thrift Supervision. Structure data are based on information contained in the FDIC financial institution structure database.

Reporting requirements and instructions have changed considerably over the period covered by *Historical Statistics on Banking*. Where possible, the FDIC has made adjustments to account for these differences and to make the historical data reflect, as closely as possible, current reporting requirements and instructions.

Source: Federal Deposit Insurance Corporation, *Historical Statistics on Banking: 1934–1996*, July 1997.

Home Mortgage Disclosure Act Data

Federal Financial Institutions Examination Council

The Home Mortgage Disclosure Act (HMDA) was enacted by Congress in 1975 and is implemented by the Federal Reserve Board's Regulation C. Prior to 1990, HMDA provided information on the geographic location of home loan originations and purchases of covered lending institutions. The scope of HMDA was expanded substantially in 1990 to require reporting of the disposition of applications for mortgage and home improvement loans in addition to data regarding loan originations and purchases. Covered lenders were also required to collect and report the race, sex, and income of applicants and borrowers. Finally, the 1990 changes required that lenders identify the type of purchaser for mortgage loans sold on the secondary market.

In 1996, 9,328 financial institutions reported approximately 14.8 million loans and applications. Data collected under HMDA include the disposition of loan applications; whether a loan is sold into the secondary market and if so, the type of buyer; the type of loan (home purchase, refinance, or home improvement) and type of mortgage insurance; type of property (single-family or multifamily); location of the property; and the race/ethnicity, gender, and income of the applicant. These data are used to help the public determine if lending institutions are meeting the housing credit needs of their communities, to help public officials target community development investment, and to help regulators identify possible discriminatory lending patterns and enforce fair lending laws.

For years prior to 1997, HMDA required depository and nondepository lending institutions with more than

$10 million in assets, and a home or branch office in a metropolitan statistical area, to report. Depository lending institutions are banks, savings associations, credit unions, and their subsidiaries; nondepository institutions are savings and loan service corporations, mortgage banking subsidiaries of bank holding companies, savings and loan holding companies, and independent mortgage companies. A depository institution that meets the tests for asset size and location, but did not have any first-lien home purchase loans (including refinancings) on one- to four-family dwellings in the preceding calendar year, is exempt from reporting.

Regardless of asset size, a nondepository mortgage lender must report if it originated 100 or more home purchase loans (including refinancings of such loans) in the preceding calendar year. On the other hand, nondepository institutions that meet the tests for location and asset size or number of home purchase loans are exempt from reporting if the home purchase loans originated in the preceding calendar year (including refinancings) came to less than 10 percent of the institution's total loan origination volume, measured in dollars.

Effective for calendar year 1997 HMDA data, the asset-size exemption for depository institutions was increased from $10 million to $28 million. Furthermore, the asset threshold will be adjusted each year based on changes in the Consumer Price Index, and the Federal Reserve Board will announce the revised asset threshold, if any, in December prior to the calendar year that it becomes effective. In December 1997, the Federal Reserve Board announced the new asset-size exemption of $29 million for depository institutions, effective for the calendar year 1998 data. The increase in the asset threshold does not apply to nondepository institutions subject to HMDA; the threshold for nondepository institutions remains at $10 million as in previous years.

Sources: Federal Financial Institutions Examination Council, "HMDA: History," <http://www.ffiec.gov/hmda/history.htm>; "HMDA: Introduction," <http://www.ffiec.gov/hmda/intro.htm>; and "Who Is Required to Report?" <http://www.ffiec.gov/hmda/reporter.htm>.

Low-Income Housing Tax Credit Database
U.S. Department of Housing and Urban Development

Under contract to the U.S. Department of Housing and Urban Development, Abt Associates collected data on virtually all Low-Income Housing Tax Credit (LIHTC) projects placed in service from 1992 through 1994 and on most LIHTC projects placed in service in 1990 and 1991. The LIHTC database, in its original form, contained records for 9,785 projects and 339,190 units placed in service between 1987 and 1994. Coverage for the 1992 to 1994 period is virtually complete, including projects from all LIHTC allocating agencies except for the city of Chicago. In late 1996, additional efforts were made to improve the coverage of the LIHTC database, resulting in the addition of 1,989 projects containing 67,056 units to the database.

The database contains a variety of information on LIHTC projects including total units, low-income units, project type (new construction, rehabilitation, existing), LIHTC credit percentage, year placed in service, nonprofit sponsorship, and use of tax-exempt bond or Farmers Home Administration Section 515 financing.

In addition, project street addresses were used to match LIHTC properties with their census tract as well as other geographic indicators such as metropolitan statistical area (MSA), where applicable. For those projects that were successfully geocoded, geographic indicators were used to develop information on project locations, for example, whether the property was located in an MSA or nonmetro area and, for projects in MSAs, whether the project was located in a central city of the MSA. HUD data files and listings were also used to identify projects located in areas that had been designated by HUD as "difficult development areas" in 1993. Tract-level census variables on income, housing units, and various population characteristics were also attached to each successfully geocoded project record.

Sources: 1. Abt Associates, Inc., *Development and Analysis of the National Low-Income Housing Tax Credit Database*, U.S. Department of Housing and Urban Development, Office of Policy Development and Research, July 1996. 2. U.S. Department of Housing and Urban Development, Office of Policy Development and Research, "Low-Income Housing Tax Credit Database," <http://www.huduser.org/>.

Monthly Interest Rate Survey
Federal Housing Finance Board

Commonly referred to as the Monthly Interest Rate Survey (MIRS), this data collection effort is formally called the Monthly Survey of Rates and Terms on Conventional One-Family Nonfarm Mortgage Loans. The MIRS asks a sample of mortgage lenders (including savings associations, mortgage companies, commercial banks, and mutual savings banks) to report the terms and conditions on all fully amortized conventional mortgage loans for the purchase of single-family, nonfarm homes that are closed in the last 5 working days of the month. Thus, the data excludes FHA-insured and VA-guaranteed mortgages, refinancing loans, balloon loans, multifamily loans, and mobile home loans. In June 1998, the MIRS data was based on 28,108 reported loans from 164 lenders. The total number of loans reported in 1996 was 133,458.

The survey provides national data on mortgage interest rates, mortgage terms, and house prices on a monthly basis. Data are provided by property type (new homes, previously occupied homes, and all homes), by loan type (fixed- or adjustable-rate), and by lender type (savings and loan associations, mortgage companies, commercial banks, and mutual savings banks). The MIRS is the only national survey that covers prices of both new and existing homes. In addition, the survey provides quarterly information on mortgage product shares and on conventional loans by major metropolitan area and by Federal Home Loan Bank district.

The sampling method for the MIRS draws sample lenders with equal probabilities of selection from a lender type/geographic stratum. The survey loan data are weighted to reflect shares of mortgage lending activity by lender type as reported in the latest release of the Federal Financial Institution Examination Council's Home Mortgage Disclosure Act data (see "Home Mortgage Disclosure Act Data" on page 501).

Data from the MIRS have many uses. Changes in house prices from the MIRS provide the basis for annual adjustments to the conforming loan limit, which is the maximum-size mortgage that may be purchased or guaranteed by Fannie Mae and Freddie Mac. High-cost-area mortgage limits for Federal Housing Administration–insured mortgages are, in turn, tied to the conforming loan limit. The Internal Revenue Service uses the data from MIRS to determine the safe-harbor limits for mortgages purchased with the proceeds of mortgage revenue bond issues. The MIRS is also used to derive an adjustable-rate mortgage (ARM) index, the National Average Contract Mortgage Rate for the Purchase of Previously Occupied Homes by Combined Lenders. Finally, the MIRS data are used by the housing industry and policymakers to track trends in the mortgage markets, including interest rates, down payments, terms to maturity, terms on ARMs, and initial fees and charges on mortgage loans.

Source: Federal Housing Finance Board, *Monthly Survey of Rates and Terms on Conventional, 1-Family,* *Nonfarm Mortgage Loans,* and *Federal Housing Finance Board News*, July 27, 1998.

National Delinquency Survey
Mortgage Bankers Association of America

The Mortgage Bankers Association of America's quarterly National Delinquency Survey has been conducted since 1953 and is the most comprehensive mortgage delinquency survey in the country. It currently covers about 23 million loans on one- to four-unit residential properties, nearly one-half of all residential mortgage loans outstanding in the United States. Loans surveyed are reported by more than 200 lenders, including mortgage bankers, commercial banks, thrifts, and life insurance companies.

Source: Mortgage Bankers Association of America, "Mortgage Delinquency Rate Up in First Quarter," press release, June 26, 1998.

National Housing Survey
Fannie Mae

This annual national telephone survey has been conducted for Fannie Mae since 1992 by the survey research firms of Peter D. Hart and Robert Teeter. The survey asks a variety of questions related to consumers' perceptions of the housing markets and housing finance system, attitudes toward homeownership, plans for home purchase, and perceived obstacles to becoming a homeowner.

The main sample, which included 1,509 adults in 1997, is drawn using a multistage cluster design. Responses are weighted to represent the distribution of the adult population in the contiguous United States by age, race, sex, size of household, education, occupation, and other demographic factors. Oversamples of specific segments of the population have been included in various years. The 1997 survey included an oversample of residents of the 110 largest cities who did not grow up in a large city and an oversample of former city residents who did not live in a large city at the time of the interview. In 1996, the survey included 354 renters with annual household incomes of less than $35,000. The 1995 survey included an oversample of almost 400 immigrants. In 1994, the survey included a sample of approximately 400 renters who reported themselves at least somewhat likely to purchase a home within 3 years.

Source: Fannie Mae, *Fannie Mae National Housing Survey*, various years.

Primary Mortgage Market Survey

Freddie Mac

Since April 1971, Freddie Mac has surveyed lenders across the nation weekly to determine the average rate of 30-year fixed-rate mortgages. The average rate for the 1-year adjustable-rate mortgage (ARM) was added to the survey in 1984, and the 15-year fixed-rate mortgage rate was included beginning in 1991. The average contract rate and average number of points are reported for each of the three loan products. The average margin for 1-year Treasury-indexed ARMs is also reported.

Currently, 125 lenders are surveyed each week and the mix of lender types—thrifts, commercial banks, and mortgage lending companies—is roughly proportional to the level of mortgage business that each type commands nationwide. The survey results are published extensively in the media and are used in several government agency reports and many other industry-related publications. For example, the Federal Reserve Board includes the 30-year rate on its list of Selected Interest Rates (Statistical Release H.15) as the measure of conventional mortgage rates.

Source: Freddie Mac, "About the Primary Mortgage Market Survey," <http://www.freddiemac.com/function/fm-news/fm-pmms/abtpmms.htm>.

Property Owners and Managers Survey

U.S. Bureau of the Census

The Property Owners and Managers Survey (POMS) is the first national survey of owners and managers of privately owned rental properties. The purpose of POMS is to gain a better understanding of who owns the nation's private rental stock and how they formulate their rental and maintenance policies.

POMS collected a variety of information related to owner characteristics, method of property acquisition and financing, maintenance and capital spending, management practices, tenant policy, governmental relations, and related topics. Two questionnaires were used: one for owners and managers of single-unit properties and one for owners and managers of multifamily (two units or more) properties. The U.S. Department of Housing and Urban Development and the Census Bureau developed these questionnaires after consulting with a panel of housing experts, a group of housing-related organizations, and focus groups of property owners and managers.

Approximately 16,300 housing units that were rented or vacant-for-rent in the 1993 American Housing Survey national sample (AHS-N) were included in the original POMS sample. More than 8,000 property owners, managers, or other agents of owners ultimately participated in POMS and were interviewed between November 1995 and June 1996. Because the sample for POMS was drawn from a list of all rental housing units and not from a list of property owners, results from POMS should be interpreted as reflecting the characteristics, policies, and practices of the "owner of the typical rental unit," and not the "typical owner."

Sources: 1. U.S. Bureau of the Census, "Property Owners and Managers Survey Overview," <http://www.census.gov/hhes/www/housing/poms/overview.html>. 2. U.S. Department of Housing and Urban Development, "Surveying the Owners and Managers of Rental Housing," *U.S. Housing Market Conditions*, November 1996.

Residential Finance Survey

U.S. Bureau of the Census

The Residential Finance Survey (RFS) has been conducted in connection with the census of population and housing since 1950. Unlike the decennial census, which collects information from every housing unit, the unit of tabulation in the RFS is the nonfarm, privately owned, residential property. If mortgaged, a property is defined as all the buildings and land covered by a single first mortgage. All other properties are defined by the owner.

For the latest RFS (conducted in 1991), the Census Bureau selected a sample of about 70,000 residential addresses from the 1990 Census address file. It then sent each owner a questionnaire. If their property had a mortgage, they were asked to identify their lenders. These lenders, in turn, received a form that asked them to provide detailed information about the mortgages on the properties.

The RFS collects a variety of information on owner-occupied and rental properties and their financial characteristics from the property owner. This information includes type of structure, when the structure was built, how acquisition of the property was financed, purchase price, current value of property, expenses on the property, and rental receipts for rental properties.

For mortgaged properties, lenders are asked a variety of detailed questions on the loan. Information collected from the lender includes the type of mortgage on the property, if the mortgage is insured and, if so, the type of insurance involved, loan term, current interest rate, amount of unpaid balance, the year the mortgage was originated or assumed, and the current holder and servicer of the loan.

Sources: 1. U.S. Bureau of the Census, "Residential Finance Survey: Description," <http://www.census.gov/hhes/housing/rftext.html>. 2. U.S. Bureau of the Census and U.S. Department of Housing and Urban Development, *1990 Census of Housing: Residential Finance*, 1990 CH-4-1, August 1994. 3. Fannie Mae Office of Housing Policy Research, *Proceedings: Roundtable Discussion on 1990 Census, Ongoing Survey Work, and Analysis Plans*, April 5, 1991.

Survey of Construction

U.S. Bureau of the Census

The Survey of Construction (SOC), conducted monthly by the Census Bureau, is used to produce estimates of new privately owned housing units started, under construction, completed, and for sale or sold. It also provides key information on the financial characteristics of new one-family houses and the physical characteristics of all new housing units. In addition, data from the SOC are used to create price indexes for new one-family houses sold and to estimate the value of new single-family construction put in place and the residential fixed investment component of Gross Domestic Product.[5]

Government agencies use these statistics to make policy decisions, formulate legislation, evaluate economic policy, and measure progress toward national housing goals. The private sector uses the information to estimate the demand for building materials, appliances, and other products consumed in new housing and to schedule production, distribution, and sales efforts. The housing finance sector uses the data to estimate the demand for construction and mortgage loans.

The SOC is composed of two separate but related survey efforts. The first, called the Survey of the Use of Permits (SUP), produces estimates of the rates at which housing units authorized by building permits are started, completed, placed for sale, or sold. When combined with estimates of permit issuance from the Building Permits Survey (BPS; see description elsewhere in this appendix), the SUP produces estimates of new housing construction and sales activity in permit-issuing places.

The second component of the SOC is the Nonpermit Survey (NP). The NP is designed to produce estimates of new housing production and sales activity in non-permit-issuing places. Estimates are combined from the SUP and NP to produce estimates of total new housing production and sales for all areas. Further description of the SUP and NP is provided in the next section, which explains how the Census Bureau produces estimates of housing starts.

Housing starts compilation

The housing starts compilation is a multistage process that develops estimates of the number of privately owned housing units that are started in 19,000 permit-issuing places and in non-permit-issuing areas. The start of construction of a privately owned housing unit is defined as when excavation begins for the footings or foundation of a residential building of which the housing unit is a part. Beginning with statistics for September 1992, estimates of housing starts also include units in residential structures totally rebuilt on an existing foundation.

The housing starts compilation begins with the division of each state into geographical areas called primary sampling units (PSUs). In the first stage of sampling, 169 PSUs are selected for the SOC. From these 169 selected PSUs, two separate sampling frames are constructed: one for the SUP consisting of permit-issuing places and one for the NP consisting of small land areas, called segments, that are not covered by building permit systems.

For the SUP, the next sampling stage involves the selection of 840 permit-issuing places from the total number of permit issuing places in the 169 selected PSUs. In the final stage of sampling for the SUP, a 1 in 40 sample of permits for one-to four-unit buildings is selected and all permits for buildings with five or more units are selected. For these selected permits, an inquiry is made of the owner or the builder to determine in which month and year the unit(s) covered by the permit was (were) started. In the case that the units authorized by permits in a particular month are not started by the end of the month, follow-ups are made in successive months to find out when the units were actually started.

Information from the interviews of owners and builders is used to calculate ratios (by type of structure) of the number of units started to the number of units covered by permits. Separate ratios are calculated for units started from permits of that month and of each preceding month. These ratios, or start rates, are then applied to the appropriate estimates of the number of units authorized by permits in the corresponding months from the BPS to provide preliminary estimates of the number of units started for each month of authorization in permit-issuing places.

Two additional adjustments are made to develop a final estimate of the total number of housing starts in permit-issuing places. First, an upward adjustment of 3.3 percent is made to the number of one-unit structures (single-family houses) started to account for those units started within permit-issuing places but without permit authorization. (A study spanning a 4-year period indicated that permits were obtained for all buildings with two housing units or more.) Second, upward imputations are made to account for those units started prior to permit authorization and for late reports.

To develop an estimate of the total number of housing units started in all areas, an estimate of starts in non-permit-issuing areas must be developed from the NP and added to the estimate of starts in permit-issuing places derived from the SUP. Of all segments in the selected 169 PSUs, approximately 70 are selected for intensive canvassing in the NP. During canvassing, Census field representatives drive all roads in the 70 segments to look for housing starts. Units identified as started in this monthly canvassing process are weighted appropriately to provide an estimate of total housing starts in areas not covered by building permit systems.

The estimate of starts in non-permit-issuing areas from the NP is added to the estimate of starts in permit-issuing places from the SUP to produce an estimate of total private housing units started in a given month.

Housing completions and under-construction compilation

The housing completions and under-construction compilation is basically the same as that used for housing starts. For each permit selected for the SUP, inquiries are made of the owners or builders of units that are under construction to determine if these units have been completed. For those units not completed, inquiries are made in successive months to determine when they are completed. Ratios are then calculated (by type of structure) of the number of units completed and under construction to the number of units covered by permits. Separate ratios are calculated for units authorized from permits of that month and each preceding month. These ratios are then applied to the appropriate estimates of the number of units authorized by permits in the corresponding months from the BPS. The ratios are applied to provide estimates of the total number of units completed and under construction for each month of authorization.

Having produced estimates of the number of units completed and under construction with permit authorization, an upward adjustment of 3.3 percent is made to the number of one-unit structures to account for those units built within permit-issuing areas without authorization. As with housing starts, upward imputations are also made for housing completions to account for late reports.

The total estimates of housing units completed and those under construction include estimates in areas where building permit systems do not exist. These estimates are derived from the NP. All buildings identified during canvassing of the 70 segments are followed up for completion information provided by the owners or builders or by site inspection and are weighted appropriately to produce an estimate of completions in all non-permit-issuing places.

Housing Sales Survey

The Census Bureau conducts the monthly Housing Sales Survey under contract to the U.S. Department of Housing and Urban Development. The monthly housing sales sample is a subset of the SOC sample and consists of those new one-family houses from the SUP and NP that the interviewer found to be either sold or for sale. Those few cases for which interviewers cannot obtain information about intention are also included in this monthly survey. Approximately 60 to 65 percent of these cases are found to be for sale. The remainder are removed from the survey. Monthly interviews continue with the owner or builder until the house is sold or withdrawn from the sales market.

The monthly sample for the Housing Sales Survey excludes contractor-built houses, owner-built houses, houses built to be rented, out-of-scope types (such as nonresidential buildings), and mobile homes (trailers). The number of houses for sale includes some houses that are not actively being marketed. This category includes model or sample houses and houses being used as temporary offices by builders. It also includes houses involved in business bankruptcy and liquidation procedures as well as estate settlements.

The Housing Sales Survey includes some units that were originally misclassified as multifamily units when they were in the Building Permits Survey. It also includes units that were not originally for sale, but for which builders' plans have changed, and units that were originally misclassified as contractor-built, owner-built, or built to be rented.

In general, houses are removed from the market by

being sold. However, a small, but not negligible, number of houses are removed from the sales market for other reasons and are classified as out of scope of the Housing Sales Survey. These removals include transfers from the sales to the rental market, decisions by the builder-owner to move into the house, abandonment of plans to build, and cancellation or expiration of permits.

During 1997, the Housing Sales Survey's average monthly sample size was 6,250 sample cases. Of these, an average of 900 were new entering the sample. The remaining cases were carried over from the previous month.

New houses are never considered for sale prior to issuance of a building permit in permit-issuing places or prior to start in nonpermit areas. Preliminary estimates of new houses sold in a given month include imputations for new houses sold prior to issuance of building permits and for late reporting of sales. No imputation is made for sales prior to start in nonpermit areas. Estimates of new houses for sale include adjustments for late reporting.

Failure to contact the respondent in the month of sale is responsible for most late reports of sales. The imputations used to adjust for late reporting simultaneously increases the number of new houses sold for the appropriate month and decreases the number of new houses for sale at the end of the same month. As late reports are received for houses sold, the preliminary monthly reports that reflect imputations are revised to show the estimates of houses sold and for sale based on more complete data.

Sources: 1. U.S. Bureau of the Census, *Housing Starts: January 1998*, Current Construction Reports, C20/98-1, March 1998. 2. U.S. Bureau of the Census and U.S. Department of Housing and Urban Development, *Housing Completions: January 1998*, Current Construction Reports, C22/98-1, March 1998. 3. U.S. Bureau of the Census and U.S. Department of Housing and Urban Development, *New One-Family Houses Sold: January 1998*, Current Construction Reports C25/98-1, March 1998. 4. U.S. Bureau of the Census, *Survey of Construction*, technical paper draft, October 26, 1990. 5. Personal communication with Steven Berman, U.S. Bureau of the Census, Manufacturing and Construction Division, May 20, 1997.

Survey of Consumer Finances

Board of Governors of the Federal Reserve System

The Survey of Consumer Finances (SCF) is a triennial survey sponsored by the Federal Reserve with the cooperation of the Department of the Treasury. It is designed to provide detailed information on U.S. families' balance sheets and their use of financial services, as well as on their pension rights, labor force participation, and demographic characteristics at the time of the interview. The survey also collects information on total family income, before taxes, for the calendar year preceding the survey.

To provide reliable information on assets that are broadly distributed in the population as well as assets that are highly concentrated in certain population groups, the SCF employs a dual-frame sample design that includes a standard geographically based random sample and a special oversample of relatively wealthy families. Weights are used to combine information from the two samples for estimates of statistics for the full population. For the 1992 survey, 3,906 families were interviewed, and for the 1995 survey, 4,299 were interviewed. The SCFs for 1992 and 1995 were conducted by the National Opinion Research Center at the University of Chicago between July and December of each survey year.

The underlying statistical methodology of the surveys has been largely unchanged since 1989, and the questionnaires have been modified only slightly. The modification was made mostly to reflect changes in the availability of financial services or in the financial behavior of families. Thus, the data since 1989 are comparable.

Source: Arthur B. Kennickell, Martha Starr-McCluer, and Annika E. Sunden, "Family Finances in the U.S.: Recent Evidence from the Survey of Consumer Finances," *Federal Reserve Bulletin*, January 1997.

Survey of Income and Program Participation

U.S. Bureau of the Census

The Survey of Income and Program Participation (SIPP) is a longitudinal panel survey designed to provide detailed information on the economic situation of the noninstitutionalized resident population of the United States. Data from SIPP are used to examine the distribution of income, wealth, and poverty and to gauge the effects of federal and state programs on the well-being of families and individuals.

There are three basic elements of the survey. The first is a control card that serves several important functions. The control card is used to record basic social and demographic characteristics for each person in the household at the time of the initial interview. Because households are interviewed a total of eight or nine times, the card is also used to record changes in characteristics such as age, educational attainment, and marital status, and to record the dates when persons enter or leave the household. During each interview, information on each source of income received and the name of each job or business is transcribed to the card so that this information can be used in the updating process in subsequent interviews.

The second major element of the SIPP is the core portion of the questionnaire. The core questions are repeated at each interview and cover labor force activity, the types and amounts of income received during the 4-month reference period, and participation status in various programs. Some of the important elements of labor force activity are recorded separately for each week of the period. Income amounts are recorded on a monthly basis with the exception of amounts of property income (interest, dividends, rent, etc.). Data for these types of income are recorded as totals for the 4-month period. The core also contains questions covering attendance in postsecondary schools, private health insurance coverage, public or subsidized rental housing, low-income energy assistance, and school breakfast and lunch participation.

The third major element is the various supplements or topical modules that are included during selected household visits. The topical modules cover areas that need not be examined every 4 months. Certain of these topical modules are considered to be so important that they are viewed as an integral part of the overall survey. Other topical modules have more specific and more limited purposes. A list of topical modules includes work history, health characteristics (including disability), assets and liabilities, pension plan coverage, housing characteristics, child care, child support agreements, support for nonhousehold members, program participation history, reasons for not working, calendar year income and benefits, taxes, and education and training.

The sample for the first SIPP panel in 1984 consisted of about 20,000 households selected to represent the noninstitutional population of the United States. SIPP panels have been introduced in February of each year since the initial 1984 panel. In 1996, the SIPP was expanded to 36,700 households and included an over-sample of low-income households.

Sources: 1. Howard A. Savage, *Who Can Afford to Buy a House in 1993?* Current Housing Reports H121/97-1, July 1997. 2. U.S. Bureau of the Census, "Overview of the SIPP," <http://www.census.gov/hhes/www/sippdesc.html>. 3. Daniel H. Weinberg, "Changing the Way the United States Measures Income and Poverty," paper presented at Census Bureau's 1996 Annual Research Conference, November 1996.

Survey of Market Absorption
U.S. Bureau of the Census

The Survey of Market Absorption (SOMA) is designed to provide data concerning the rate at which privately financed, unfurnished, nonsubsidized units in buildings with five or more units are rented or sold (i.e., absorbed). In addition, data on characteristics of the units, such as number of bedrooms and rent or price, are collected.

All statistics from SOMA are limited to apartments in newly constructed buildings with five units or more. Absorption rates are based on the first time an apartment offered for rent is rented after completion, or the first time a cooperative or condominium apartment is sold after completion. If apartments initially intended to be sold as cooperative or condominium units are offered by the builder or building owner for rent, they are counted as rental apartments. Units categorized as federally subsidized are those built under the following programs of the U.S. Department of Housing and Urban Development: Low-Income Housing Assistance (Section 8), Senior Citizens Housing Direct Loans (Section 202), and all units in buildings containing apartments in the Federal Housing Administration (FHA) rent supplement program. The data on privately financed units include privately owned housing subsidized by state and local governments. Units categorized as not in the scope of the survey include time-sharing units, continuing care retirement units, and turnkey units (privately built for and sold to local public housing authorities subsequent to completion).

The buildings selected for SOMA are those included in the Census Bureau's Survey of Construction (SOC; see description elsewhere in this appendix). Each quarter, a sample of buildings with five or more units from the SOC sample reported as completed during that quarter are chosen for SOMA. SOMA includes only buildings completed in permit-issuing places. Buildings completed in non-permit-issuing areas are excluded from consideration. Information on the proportion of units absorbed 3, 6, 9, and 12 months after completion is obtained for units in buildings selected in a given quarter in each of the next four quarters.

Beginning with data on completions in the fourth quarter of 1990 (which formed the base for absorptions in the first quarter of 1991), the estimation procedure for SOMA was modified. The modified estimation procedure was also applied to the data for the other three quarters of 1990 so that annual estimates could be derived using the same methodology for four quarters. No additional reestimation of past data has been performed and therefore caution must be used when comparing completions in 1990 and later with those in earlier years.

Source: U.S. Bureau of the Census and U.S. Department of Housing and Urban Development, *Market Absorption of Apartments: First Quarter 1998—Absorptions (Completions in Fourth Quarter 1997)*, Current Housing Reports H130/98-Q1, June 1998.

Survey of Mortgage Lending Activity

U.S. Department of Housing and Urban Development

The Survey of Mortgage Lending Activity (SMLA) was first conducted in 1970. Data are collected monthly from 11 major lender or mortgage investor groups: commercial banks, mutual savings banks, savings and loan associations, life insurance companies, private noninsured pension funds, mortgage companies, private mortgage-backed securities conduits, state and local retirement funds, federal credit agencies, federal mortgage pools, and state and local credit agencies.

The samples for commercial banks and mutual savings banks were recently redrawn and new benchmark expansion weighting factors were created. In some instances, the changed methodology resulted in substantial revisions to the 1996 data and a significant shift in the level of lending activity compared with historical data.

Organizations included in the SMLA report on their dollar volume of originations, purchases, sales and repayments of mortgage and construction loans and on outstanding loan balances for the month. SMLA also collects data on outstanding loan commitments and on new loan commitments made each month.

Reports produced from the SMLA contain information by lender type on the dollar volume of construction loans and long-term mortgages made on one- to four-family, multifamily, nonresidential, and farm properties. The one- to four-family loans are further broken out by type of loan (FHA-insured, VA-guaranteed, and conventional). Multifamily loans are broken out by FHA-insured and conventional loans.

The SMLA is widely used in the public and private sectors. Senior officials at HUD use SMLA data to formulate housing policies. The IRS uses the data in administering the mortgage revenue bond and mortgage credit certificate programs. Other applications include the following:

- The Federal Reserve Board uses the data to produce their quarterly estimates of mortgage debt outstanding and for conducting special housing studies.
- Freddie Mac uses the data to compute the weighted averages of regional conventional interest rates, fees, and points.
- Fannie Mae uses the data to compare the volume of its mortgage purchases with the volume of conventional mortgage originations and to forecast future mortgage originations.

Sources: 1. Personal communication with Robert Knight, U.S. Department of Housing and Urban Development, January 22, 1997. 2. U.S. Department of Housing and Urban Development, "Survey of Mortgage Lending Activity, Second Quarter 1997," press release, No. 97-289, January 16, 1998.

Survey of New Mobile Home Placements

U.S. Bureau of the Census

This survey is conducted by the Census Bureau under sponsorship of the U.S. Department of Housing and Urban Development. The methodology for collecting information on new mobile homes for 1974 through 1979 involved contacting a sample of mobile home dealers each month within 137 geographic areas or primary sampling units. The dealers were requested to provide data on the number of mobile homes received from manufacturers, the number placed on a site for residential use, and the number held in inventory.

The methodology used after 1979 involves a monthly sample from a list of new mobile homes shipped by manufacturers, as reported by the National Conference of States on Building Codes and Standards (NCSBCS). From lists of mobile home shipments provided by NCSBCS, the Census Bureau selects a random sample at an overall rate of 1 of every 40 units shipped. The dealer to whom the sampled unit was shipped is contacted by telephone and asked about the status of the selected unit. This is done each month until that unit is reported as placed.

In addition to providing information on the number of new mobile homes placed by type (e.g., single-wide or double-wide) and selected characteristics (e.g., number of bedrooms and square footage), the survey also collects information on sales prices and inventories on dealers' lots.

Sources: 1. U.S. Bureau of the Census, *Housing Starts: January 1998*, Current Construction Reports C20/98-1,

March 1998. 2. U.S. Bureau of the Census and U.S. Department of Housing and Urban Development, *Characteristics of New Housing: 1997*, Current Construction Reports C25/97-A, July 1998.

Survey of Real Estate Trends

Federal Deposit Insurance Corporation

The Survey of Real Estate Trends, conducted by the Federal Deposit Insurance Corporation (FDIC), is a quarterly survey of trends and conditions in the residential and commercial real estate markets. The survey asks examiners and asset managers about the general condition and direction of the residential real estate market, volume of home sales, changes in home prices, and volume of residential construction.

In October 1997, the survey consisted of 311 interviews of examiners and asset managers who were experienced in evaluating real estate loan portfolios or marketing real estate assets. The respondents at the FDIC represent senior experts from the Division of Supervision and from the Division of Resolutions and Receiverships. Senior real estate examiners from the Office of the Comptroller of the Currency, the Federal Reserve System, and the Office of Thrift Supervision also participate in the survey.

The number of respondents in the survey is down considerably from the 500-plus respondents when the survey was initiated in April 1991. This decline reflects recent agency downsizing and the fact that the survey included a large number of asset managers at the Resolution Trust Corporation, which was disbanded at year-end 1995.

Source: Federal Deposit Insurance Corporation, *Survey of Real Estate Trends: October 1997*.

Survey of Recent Home Buyers

Chicago Title and Trust Family of Title Insurers

This annual survey has been conducted since 1976 by the Chicago Title and Trust Family of Title Insurers. The survey collects information on the characteristics of a sample of all homebuyers and the houses they purchase, including first-time/repeat buyer status, marital status, age, household income, whether the purchased home is new or existing, unit type, purchase price, down payment, type of mortgage financing, and monthly mortgage payment. Phone interviews have been conducted by the same professional research company since the survey's inception in 1976. The current survey is based on a sample of homebuyers in the following metropolitan areas: Atlanta,

Boston, Chicago, Cleveland, Dallas/Fort Worth, Denver, Detroit, Houston, Los Angeles, Memphis, Miami, Minneapolis-St. Paul, New York, Orange County, CA, Orlando, FL, Philadelphia, Phoenix, San Francisco, Seattle-Tacoma, and Washington, DC. Miami and Houston were added to the survey in 1997.

Source: Chicago Title and Trust Family of Title Insurers, *Who's Buying Homes in America?* January 1996 and February 1998.

U.S. Department of Housing and Urban Development: Administrative and Research Databases on Households Assisted by HUD Low-Income Rental Programs

This section describes three of the administrative and research databases on assisted rental housing developed and maintained by the U.S. Department of Housing and Urban Development (HUD).

Multifamily Tenant Characteristics System (MTCS)

The MTCS is an automated database of households assisted by public housing and the tenant-based Section 8 certificate and voucher programs and other programs administered by HUD's Office of Public and Indian Housing. The database contains information about the demographic characteristics of each household, the level and sources of the household's income, and the address of the housing unit. The information is based on the form used by public housing authorities to calculate each household's rent and subsidy levels. As of February 1997, the MTCS contained 2.4 million household records, or about 85 percent of the possible total.

Tenant Rental Assistance Certification System (TRACS)

TRACS is similar to MTCS, but it contains information on households assisted in project-based Section 8 programs and other assisted projects administered by HUD's Office of Housing. Information in TRACS is based on forms completed by the private owner or manager of the project and submitted to HUD. As of June 1997, TRACS contained 1.6 million household records.

Housing Subsidy/American Housing Survey Data Base

This database is developed through case-by-case matching of administrative data on the addresses of assisted housing units and households to 1989, 1991, and 1993 American Housing Survey (AHS) data to determine which households in the AHS receive HUD rental assistance. By joining the AHS's detailed household, housing, and neighborhood data with HUD administrative records on receipt of housing assistance, the database provides a more accurate and complete picture of the characteristics and living conditions of HUD-assisted renters.

Two address-matching procedures were employed. To identify households in public housing and private assisted projects, HUD asked all public housing authorities and all private sponsors of subsidized multifamily rental projects to list the mailing addresses of all units in assisted projects under their management. The Census Bureau matched these assisted housing addresses with renters responding to the AHS. Public housing units were matched separately, and all other project-based subsidy programs were matched as a group.

Identification of voucher and certificate holders in the AHS was accomplished in a different manner. Field interviewers from the Census Bureau took lists of sampled AHS renter households to all identifiable local agencies who manage the certificate and voucher programs in the areas in which the AHS is conducted. The Census interviewers matched their AHS sampled renters against the local agency files of certificate and voucher holders.

Sources: 1. U.S. Department of Housing and Urban Development, Office of Policy Development and Research, *Rental Housing Assistance—The Crisis Continues*, April 1998. 2. Connie Casey, *Characteristics of HUD-Assisted Renters and Their Units in 1989*, U.S. Department of Housing and Urban Development, Office of Policy Development and Research, 1992. 3. Connie Casey, *Characteristics of HUD-Assisted Renters and Their Units in 1991*, U.S. Department of Housing and Urban Development, Office of Policy Development and Research, 1997. 4. Duane T. McGough, *Characteristics of HUD-Assisted Renters and Their Units in 1993*, U.S. Department of Housing and Urban Development, Office of Policy Development and Research, 1997.

Value of New Construction Put in Place

U.S. Bureau of the Census

Statistics on the value of new construction put in place result from direct measurement and indirect estimation of private residential, private nonresidential, and public construction. A series results from direct measurement when it is based on reports of the actual value of construction progress or construction expenditures obtained from a complete census or sample survey. All other series are developed by indirect estimation using related construction statistics.

This section focuses on the procedures used to estimate the value of private residential construction put in place. For a description of the procedures used for other types of construction, see the source referenced at the end of this section.

New, private one-unit housing

The construction cost of new one-unit houses started each month is estimated using data from the Census Bureau's Survey of Construction (SOC) (see "Survey of Construction" in this appendix). The estimated cost of all single units started is distributed into monthly value put in place by applying fixed patterns of monthly construction progress. These patterns, which vary both with the month in which construction starts and with the month of construction activity, are used to estimate how much of a unit's total construction cost is put in place in a given month.

Construction cost is estimated separately for units built to be sold or rented and units built by the owner or for the owner on contract. In both cases, the total cost is obtained by multiplying the number of units started by an average construction cost per unit. For units built to be sold or rented, the average construction cost is the average sales price at the time of start multiplied by the factor 0.7813. This factor eliminates an estimate of the cost of "nonconstruction" items such as raw land, marketing costs, closing costs, and movable appliances. The average construction cost for units built for the owner on contract is the average contract value at time of start increased by the factor 1.0190 to eliminate "nonconstruction" items and to add the value of land development not already accounted for.

New, private two-or-more-unit buildings

A subsample of new residential building projects with two units or more is selected from projects under construction from the Census Bureau's SOC. Once a project is selected, monthly construction progress reports are requested from the owner until the project is completed. About 2,100 projects under construction are in the survey each month. This includes newly selected projects as well as projects carried over from the previous months. Estimates of value put in place are obtained by weighting the reported value for each project and summing all projects.

Private residential improvements

Data for this series are obtained by the Census Bureau from household interviews in a representative sample of owner-occupied units and a mail survey of owners of a sample of rental or vacant properties (see "Consumer Expenditure Survey and Residential Improvements and Repairs Mail Survey" in this appendix). Prior to 1984, these data were collected as part of the Census Bureau's Quarterly Household Survey of Residential Alterations and Repairs. Beginning with January 1984 statistics, estimates of expenditures on owner-occupied properties have been based on data from the Consumer Expenditure Surveys (CES) conducted by the Census Bureau for the Bureau of Labor Statistics. (A comparison of the old and new series for 1984 appears in Current Construction Reports, C50-85-Q1, *Residential Alterations and Repairs*, October 1985.)

The CES was designed to provide the Bureau of Labor Statistics with a database for purposes relating to the Consumer Price Index. This survey was not designed to provide monthly estimates of residential improvements. As a result, these estimates have high variances and are not shown separately for monthly estimates.

Source: U.S. Bureau of the Census, *Value of New Construction Put in Place: May 1997*, Current Construction Reports C30/97-5, July 1997.

Notes

[1]Because of budget reductions, the BPS restricted data collection beginning in January 1996 to new privately owned residential construction. Prior to this time, the BPS collected data on the following items:

- New residential nonhousekeeping buildings (hotels, motels, and nonhousekeeping shelters)
- New nonresidential buildings (amusement, social, and recreational; churches and other religious; industrial; parking garages; service stations and repair garages; hospitals and institutional; offices, banks, and professional; public works and utilities; schools and other educational; stores and customer service; other miscellaneous buildings; and structures other than buildings)
- Additions, alterations, and conversions (residential, nonresidential, nonhousekeeping, and additions of residential garages and carports)
- Demolitions and razing of buildings (residential and nonresidential)

[2]This description focuses on the housing-unit-based portion of the census. The census also includes special enumeration procedures for collecting population characteristics from persons living in group quarters such as college dormitories, nursing homes, prisons, military barracks, and ships. The questionnaires (Individual Census Reports, Military Census Reports, and Shipboard Census Reports) include the 100-percent population questions but no housing questions.

In 1990, the Census Bureau also conducted a "Shelter and Street Night" (S-Night) special operation to count the population in four types of locations where homeless people are found. On the evening of March 20, 1990, and during the early morning hours of March 21, 1990, enumerators counted persons in emergency shelters for the homeless population, shelters with temporary lodging for runaway youths, shelters for abused women and their children, and open locations in streets or other places not intended for habitation.

[3]This description refers to the revised survey methods effective with first-quarter 1984 data. A description of the earlier methods appears in Current Construction Reports C50-84-A, issued in April 1985.

[4]For detailed information on the sample reduction, see the following report for the Department of Labor, Bureau of Labor Statistics, *Employment and Earnings*, vol. 43 no. 2, February 1996.

[5]In addition to providing this information on new housing production and new housing characteristics, the Surevy of Construction (SOC) also serves as the starting point for another important housing survey conducted by the Census Bureau, the Survey of Market Absorption (SOMA). Each quarter a sample of completed buildings with five or more housing units from the SOC is selected for the SOMA sample, which is then used to produce statistics on the rates at which new multifamily housing units are absorbed (that is, rented or sold) by the housing market. The SOMA is described in greater detail elsewhere in this appendix.

INDEX

Page references in italic type indicate figures and graphs.